CHILTON BOOK COMPANY
REPAIR MANUAL

ESCORT • LYNX
TEMPO • TOPAZ
1981-90

Covers all models of FORD Escort, Tempo • MERCURY Lynx, Topaz

President GARY R. INGERSOLL
Senior Vice President, Book Publishing and Research RONALD A. HOXTER
Publisher KERRY A. FREEMAN, S.A.E.
Editor-In-Chief DEAN F. MORGANTINI, S.A.E.
Senior Editor RICHARD J. RIVELE, S.A.E.
Editor LAWRENCE C. BRAUN

CHILTON BOOK COMPANY
Radnor, Pennsylvania
19089

CONTENTS

1 GENERAL INFORMATION and MAINTENANCE

- **1** How to use this book
- **1** Tools and Equipment
- **2** Safety
- **4** Vehicle Identification
- **5** Routine Maintenance
- **45** Trailer Towing

2 ENGINE PERFORMANCE and TUNE-UP

- **54** Tune-Up Procedures
- **55** Tune-Up Specifications
- **57** Firing Orders

3 ENGINE and ENGINE OVERHAUL

- **87** Engine Electrical System
- **107** Engine Service
- **182** Engine Troubleshooting
- **101** Engine Specifications
- **177** Exhaust System

4 EMISSION CONTROLS

- **189** Emission Controls System and Service
- **217** Vacuum Diagrams

5 FUEL SYSTEM

- **328** Carbureted Fuel System
- **334** Gasoline Fuel Injection System

6 CHASSIS ELECTRICAL

- **370** Heating and Air Conditioning
- **386** Instruments and Switches
- **395** Lighting
- **399** Circuit Protection

7 DRIVE TRAIN

409 Manual Transmission
438 Clutch
443 Automatic Transmission

8 SUSPENSION and STEERING

469 Front Suspension
480 Rear Suspension
487 Steering

9 BRAKES

509 Brake Systems
521 Front Disc Brakes
526 Rear Drum Brakes
533 Parking Brake

10 BODY

535 Exterior
557 Interior

11 MECHANIC'S DATA

579 Mechanic's Data
581 Glossary
587 Abbreviations

349 Chilton's Fuel Economy and Tune-Up Tips

541 Chilton's Body Repair Tips

SAFETY NOTICE

Proper service and repair procedures are vital to the safe, reliable operation of all motor vehicles, as well as the personal safety of those performing repairs. This book outlines procedures for servicing and repairing vehicles using safe, effective methods. The procedures contain many NOTES, CAUTIONS and WARNINGS which should be followed along with standard safety procedures to eliminate the possibility of personal injury or improper service which could damage the vehicle or compromise its safety.

It is important to note that repair procedures and techniques, tools and parts for servicing motor vehicles, as well as the skill and experience of the individual performing the work vary widley. It is not possible to anticipate all of the conceivable ways or conditions under which vehicles may be serviced, or to provide cautions as to all of the possible hazards that may result. Standard and accepted safety precautions and equipment should be used during cutting, grinding, chiseling, prying, or any other process that can cause material removal or projectiles

Some procedures require the use of tools specially designed for a specific purpose. Before substituting another tool or procedure, you must be completly satisfied that neither your personal safety, nor the performance of the the vehicle will be endangered.

Although the information in this guide is based on industry sources and is as complete as possible at the time of publication, the possibility exists that the manufacturer made later changes which could not be included here. While striving for total accuracy, Chilton Book Company cannot assume responsibility for any errors, changes, or omissions that may occur in the compilation of this data.

PART NUMBERS

Part numbers listed in this reference are not recommendations by Chilton for any product by brand name. They are references that can be used with interchange manuals and aftermarket supplier catalogs to locate each brand supplier's discrete part number.

SPECIAL TOOLS

Special tools are recommended by the vehicle manufacturer to perform their specific job. Use has been kept to a minimum, but where absolutely necessary, they are referred to in the text by the part number of the tool manufacturer. These tools can be purchased, under the appropriate part number, from Owatonna Tool Co., Owatonna, MN 55060, or an equivalent tool can be purchased locally from a tool supplier or parts outlet. Before substituting any tool for the one recommended, read the SAFETY NOTICE at the top of this page.

ACKNOWLEDGMENTS

Chilton Book Company expresses appreciation to Ford Motor Co., Ford Parts and Service Division. Service Technical Communications Department, Dearborn, MI for their generous assistance.

Copyright © 1990 by Chilton Book Company
All Rights Reserved
Published in Radnor, Pennsylvania 19089, by Chilton Book Company

Manufactured in the United States of America
   34567890   987654321

Chilton's Repair Manual: Escort, Lynx, Tempo, Topaz 1981–90
ISBN 0–8019–8059–7 pbk.
Library of Congress Caatalog Card No. 90–055427

General Information and Maintenance

HOW TO USE THIS BOOK

Chilton's Repair Manual for Escort, Lynx, Tempo and Topaz models is intended to teach you more about the inner workings of your car and save you money on its upkeep. The first two chapters will be used the most, since they contain maintenance and tune-up information and procedures. The following chapters concern themselves with the more complex systems. Operating systems from engine through brakes are covered to the extent that we feel the average do-it-yourselfer should get involved. We will tell you how to change your own brake pads and shoes, replace spark plugs, perform routine maintenance, and many more jobs that will save you money, give you personal satisfactions, and help you avoid problems.

A secondary purpose of this book is as a reference for owners who want to understand their can and/or their mechanics better. In this case, no tools at all are required.

Before removing any parts, read through the entire procedure. This will give you the overall view of what tools and supplies will be required.

The sections begin with a brief discussion of the system and what it involves, followed by adjustments, maintenance, removal and installation procedures, and repair or overhaul procedures. When repair is not considered feasible, we tell you how to remove the part and then how to install the new or rebuilt replacement. In this way, you at least save the labor costs. Backyard repair of such components as the alternator is just not practical.

Two basic mechanic's rules should be mentioned here. One, whenever the left side of your car or engine is referred to, it is meant to specify the driver's side. Conversely, the right side means the passenger's side. Secondly, most screws and bolts are removed by turning counterclockwise, and tightened by turning clockwise. Safety is always the most important rule. Constantly be aware of the dangers involved in working on an automobile and take the proper precautions. Use jackstands when working under a raised vehicle. Don't smoke or allow an exposed flame to came near the battery or any part of the fuel system. Always use the proper tool and use it correctly; bruised knuckles and skinned fingers aren't a mechanic's standard equipment. Always take your time and have patience. Once you have some experience, working on your car will become an enjoyable hobby.

TOOLS AND EQUIPMENT

Special tools are occasionally necessary to perform a specific job or are recommended to make a job easier. Their use has been kept to a minimum. When a special tool is indicated, it will be referred to by the manufacturer's part number, and where possible, an illustration of the tool will be provided so that an equivalent tool may be used.

The reason the use of special factory tools are kept to a minimum, is they are not readily available for the do-it-yourself mechanic. When it is possible to perform the job with more commonly available tools, it will be pointed out, but occasionally, a special tool was designed to perform a specific function and should be used. Before substituting another tool, you should be convinced that neither your safety nor the performance of the vehicle will be compromised.

Some special tools are available commercially from major tool manufacturers. Others for your car can be purchased from your dealer or from Owatonna Tool Co., Owatonna, Minnesota 55060. Some of the fuel injection equipment can be purchased from the Robert Bosch Corp. 2800 S. 25th Street, Broadview, Ill. 60153.

2 GENERAL INFORMATION AND MAINTENANCE

It would be impossible to catalog each and every tool that you may need to perform all the operations included in this book. It would also not be wise for the amateur to rush out and buy an expensive set of tools on the theory that he may need one of them at some time. The best approach is to proceed slowly, gathering together a good quality set of those tools that are used most frequently. Don't be misled by the low cost of bargain tools. It is far better to spend a little more for quality, name brand tools. Forged wrenches, 6- or 12-point sockets and fine tooth ratchets are by far preferable to their less expensive counterparts. As any good mechanic can tell you, there are few worse experiences than typing to work with bad tools. Your monetary savings will be far outweighed by frustration and mangled knuckles.

Begin accumulating those tools that are used most frequently; those associated with routine maintenance and tune-up. In addition to the normal assortment of screwdrivers and pliers, you should have the following tools for routine maintenance jobs.

1. SAE and metric wrenches, socket, and combination open end/box wrenches.
2. Jackstands, for support.
3. Oil filter wrench.
4. Oil filler spout or funnel.
5. Grease gun, for chassis lubrication.
6. Hydrometer, for checking the battery.
7. A low flat pan for draining oil.
8. Lots of rags for wiping up the inevitable mess.

In addition to the above items, there are several others that are not absolutely necessary, buy are handy to have around. These include oil drying compound, a transmission funnel, and the usual supply of lubricants, antifreeze and fluids, although these can be purchased as needed. This is a basic list for routine maintenance, but only your personal needs can accurately determine your list of tools.

The second list of tools is for tune-ups. While the tools involved here are slightly more sophisticated, they need not be outrageously expensive. There are several inexpensive tachometers on the market that are ever bit as good for the average mechanic as a $100.00 professional model. Just be sure that it goes to at least 1,200–1,500 rpm on the tach scale, and that it works on 4, 6, and 8 cylinder engines. A basic list of tune-up equipment could include:

1. Tachometer.
2. Spark plug wrench.
3. Timing light (preferably equipped with an inductive pickup).
4. A set of flat feeler gauges.
5. A set of round wire spark plug gauges.

In addition to these basic tools, there are several other tools and gauges you may find useful.
These include:

1. A compression gauge. The screw-in type is slower to use, buy eliminates the possibility of a faulty reading due to escaping pressure.
2. A manifold vacuum gauge.
3. A test light.
4. An induction meter. This is used for determining whether or not there is current in a wire. These are handy for use if a wire is broken somewhere in a wiring harness. As a final note, you will probably find a torque wrench necessary for all buy the most basic work. The beam type models are perfectly adequate, although the newer click type are more precise.

SERVICING YOUR CAR SAFELY

It is virtually impossible to anticipate all of the hazards involved with automotive maintenance and service but care and common sense will prevent most accidents.

The rules of safety for mechanics range from "don't smoke around gasoline," to "use the proper tool for the job." The trick to avoid injuries is to develop safe work habits and take every possible precaution.

Do's

• Do keep a fire extinguisher and first aid kit within easy reach.

• Do wear safety glasses or goggles when cutting, drilling, grinding or prying. If you wear glasses for the sake of vision, then they should be made of hardened glass that can serve also as safety glasses, or wear safety goggles over your regular glasses.

• Do shield your eyes whenever you work around the battery. Batteries contain sulphuric acid. In case of contact with the eyes or skin, flush the area with water or a mixture of water and baking soda and get medical attention immediately.

• Do use safety stands for any under-car service. Jacks are for raising vehicles; safety stands are for making sure the vehicle stays raised until you want it to come down. Whenever the vehicle is raised, block the wheels remaining on the ground and set the parking brake.

• Do use adequate ventilation when working

GENERAL INFORMATION AND MAINTENANCE 3

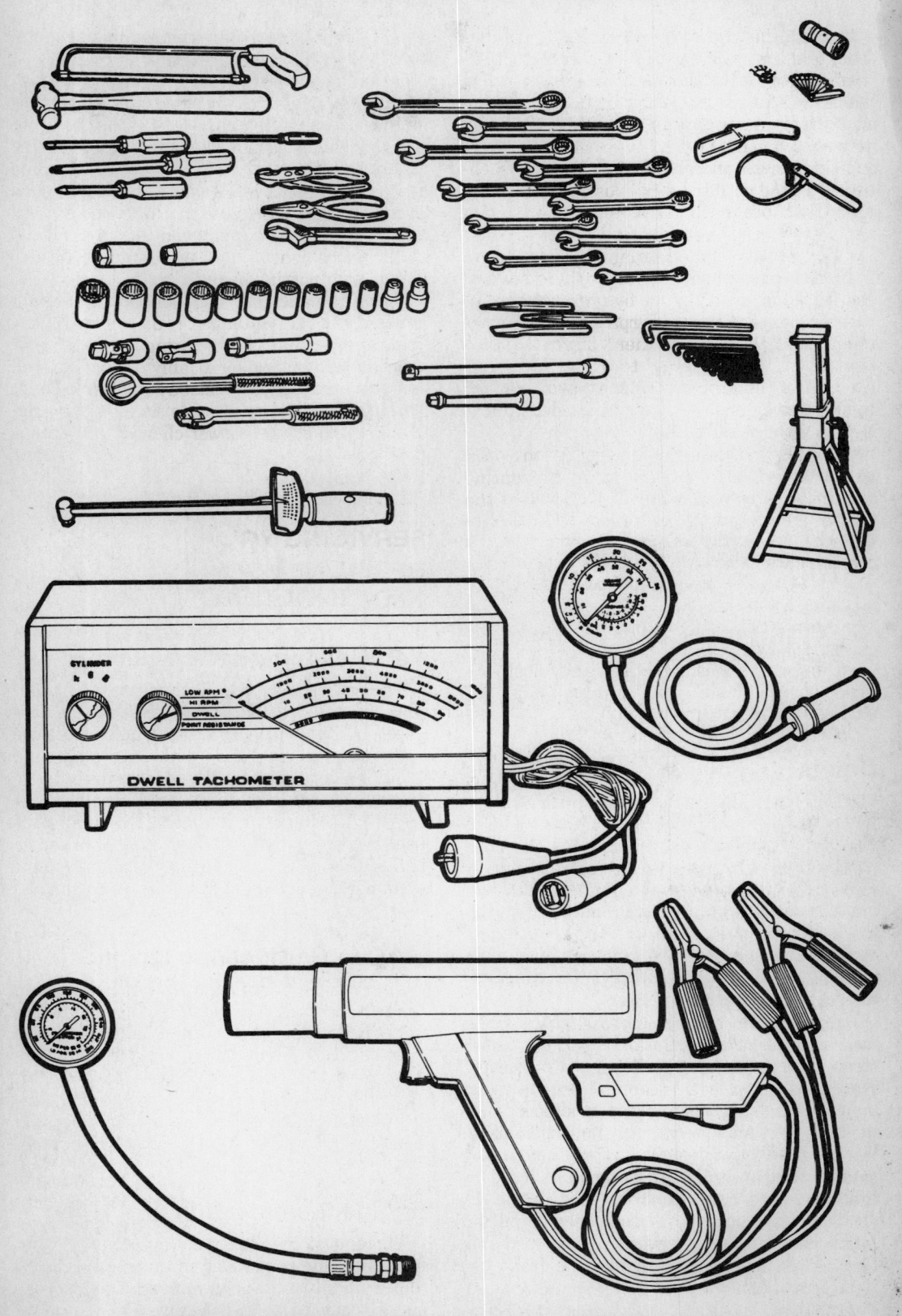

You need only a basic assortment of hand tools for maintenance and repair jobs

with any chemicals. Asbestos dust resulting from brake lining wear can cause cancer.
- Do disconnect the negative battery cable when working on the electrical system. The primary ignition system can contain up to 40,000 volts.
- Do follow manufacturer's directions whenever working with potentially hazardous materials. Both brake fluid and antifreeze are poisonous if taken internally.
- Do properly maintain your tools. Loose hammerheads, mushroomed punches and chisels, frayed or poorly grounded electrical cords, excessively worn screwdriver, spread wrenches (open end), cracked sockets can cause accidents.
- Do use the proper size and type of tool for the job being done.
- Do when possible, pull on a wrench handle rather than push on it, and adjust your stance to prevent a fall.
- Do be sure that adjustable wrenches are tightly adjusted on the nut or bolt and pulled so that the face is on the side of the fixed jaw.
- Do select a wrench or socket that fits the nut or bolt. The wrench or socket should sit straight, not cocked.
- Do strike squarely with a hammer to avoid glancing blows.
- Do set the parking brake and block the drive wheels if the work requires that the engine is running.

Don'ts

- Don't run an engine in a garage or anywhere else without proper ventilation—EVER! Carbon monoxide is poisonous. It is absorbed by the body 400 times faster than oxygen. It takes a long time to leave the human body and you can build up a deadly supply of it in you system by simply breathing in a little every day. You may not realize you are slowly poisoning yourself. Always use power vents, windows, fans or open the garage doors.
- Don't work around moving parts while wearing a necktie or other loose clothing. Short sleeves are much safer than long, loose sleeves. Hard-toed shoes with neoprene soles protect your toes and give a better grip on slippery surfaces. Jewelry such as watches, fancy belt buckles, beads or body adornment of any kind is not safe working around a car. Long hair should be hidden under a hat or cap.
- Don't use pockets for toolboxes. A fall or bump can drive a screwdriver deep into you body. Even a wiping cloth hanging from the back pocket can wrap around a spinning shaft or fan.
- Don't smoke when working around gasoline, cleaning solvent or other flammable material.
- Don't smoke when working around the battery. When the battery is being charged, it gives off explosive hydrogen gas.
- Don't use gasoline to wash your hands. There are excellent soaps available. Gasoline may contain lead, and lead can enter the body through a cut, accumulating in the body until you are very ill. Gasoline also removes all the natural oils from the skin so that bone dry hands will suck up oil and grease.
- Don't service the air conditioning system unless you are equipped with the necessary tools and training. The refrigerant, R-12, is extremely cold and when exposed to the air, will instantly freeze any surface it comes in contact with, including your eyes. Although the refrigerant is normally nontoxic, R-12 becomes a deadly poisonous gas in the presence of an open flame. One good whiff of the vapors from burning refrigerant can be fatal.

SERIAL NUMBER IDENTIFICATION

Vehicle Identification Number

The official vehicle identification (serial) number (used for title and registration purposes) is stamped on a metal tab fastened to the instrument panel and visible through the driver's side of the windshield from the outside. The vehicle identification (serial) number contains a 17 character number. The number is used for warranty identification of the vehicle and indicates: manufacturer, type of restraint system, line, series, body type, engine, model year, and consecutive unit number.

Vehicle Certification Label

The Vehicle Certification Label is found on the left door lock face panel or door pillar. The upper half of the label contains the name of the manufacturer, month and year of manufacture, gross weight rating, gross axle weight, and the certification statements pertinent. The certification also repeats the VIN number and gives the color code and the accessories found on the car.

Engine Identification

The engine code number representing what type of engine is installed in the vehicle can be found in the vehicle identification label. The eighth digit of the vehicle identification number is the engine I.D. code number.

GENERAL INFORMATION AND MAINTENANCE

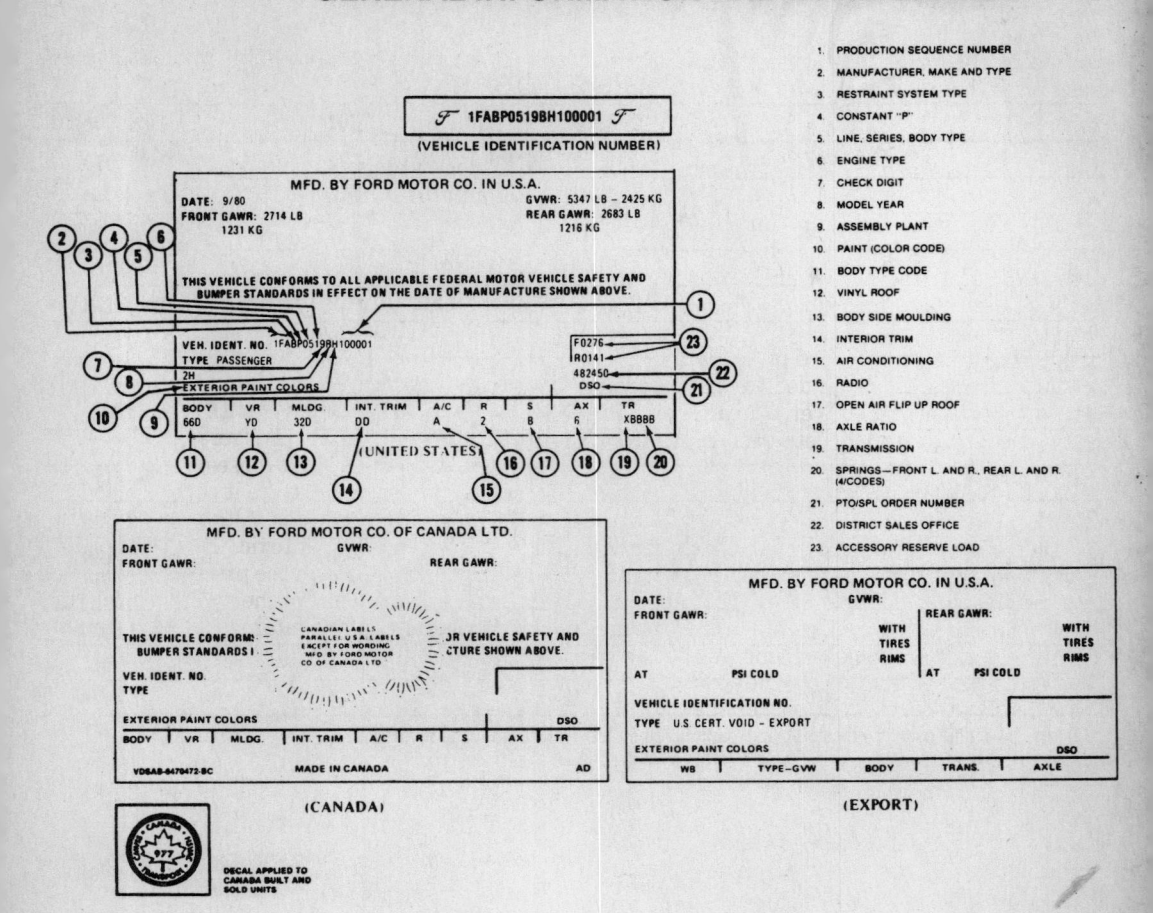

Vehicle Identification and Certification Plates

Transaxle Codes

The transmission code is located on the bottom edge of the Vehicle Certification Label.

Transfer Case

Beginning in 1987, some Tempo models have been equipped with All Wheel Drive. If your Tempo vehicle is equipped with the All Wheel Drive system, it will mean that there is a transfer case being used along with the transaxle that is installed in your vehicle. The transfer case I.D. number is usually stamped somewhere on the bottom or the side of the transaxle case.

ROUTINE MAINTENANCE

Major efforts have been undertaken by Ford to improve serviceability and provide reduced scheduled maintenance for our car. This is a built-in savings to you, the owner, in man hours and dollars.

Air Cleaner

The air cleaner element should be replaced every 30 months or 30,000 miles. More frequent changes are necessary if the car is operated in dust conditions.

Air Cleaner Element and Crankcase Emission Filter

REMOVAL AND INSTALLATION

1.6 Base and HO Engines

NOTE: *The crankcase emission filter should be changed each time you replace the air cleaner element.*

1. Remove the wing nut that retains the air cleaner assembly to the carburetor. Remove any support bracket bolts (engine to air cleaner). Disconnect the air duct tubing, vacuum lines and heat tubes connected to the air cleaner.

2. Remove the air cleaner assembly from the car.

6 GENERAL INFORMATION AND MAINTENANCE

ENGINE CODES

Code	Year	Liters	CID	Fuel System
H	1984–87	2.0	122	Diesel
J	1986–87	1.9	114	EFI
J	1988–90	1.9	114	EFI HO
R	1984–87	2.3 HSC	140	1 bbl
S	1985–86	2.3 HSC HO	140	1 bbl
S	1988	2.3 HSC	140	EFI
S	1989–90	2.3 HSO	140	EFI
X	1985–87	2.3 HSC	140	CFI
X	1988–90	2.3 HSC	140	EFI
1	1981	1.3	79	2 bbl
2	1981–85	1.6	98	2 bbl
4	1983–85	1.6 HO	98	2 bbl
5	1983–85	1.6	98	EFI
8	1984–85	1.6	98	EFI (Turbo)
9	1986–87	1.9	114	2 bbl
9	1988–90	1.9	114	EFI

NOTE: The engine code is indicated by the eighth digit of the vehicle identification number.

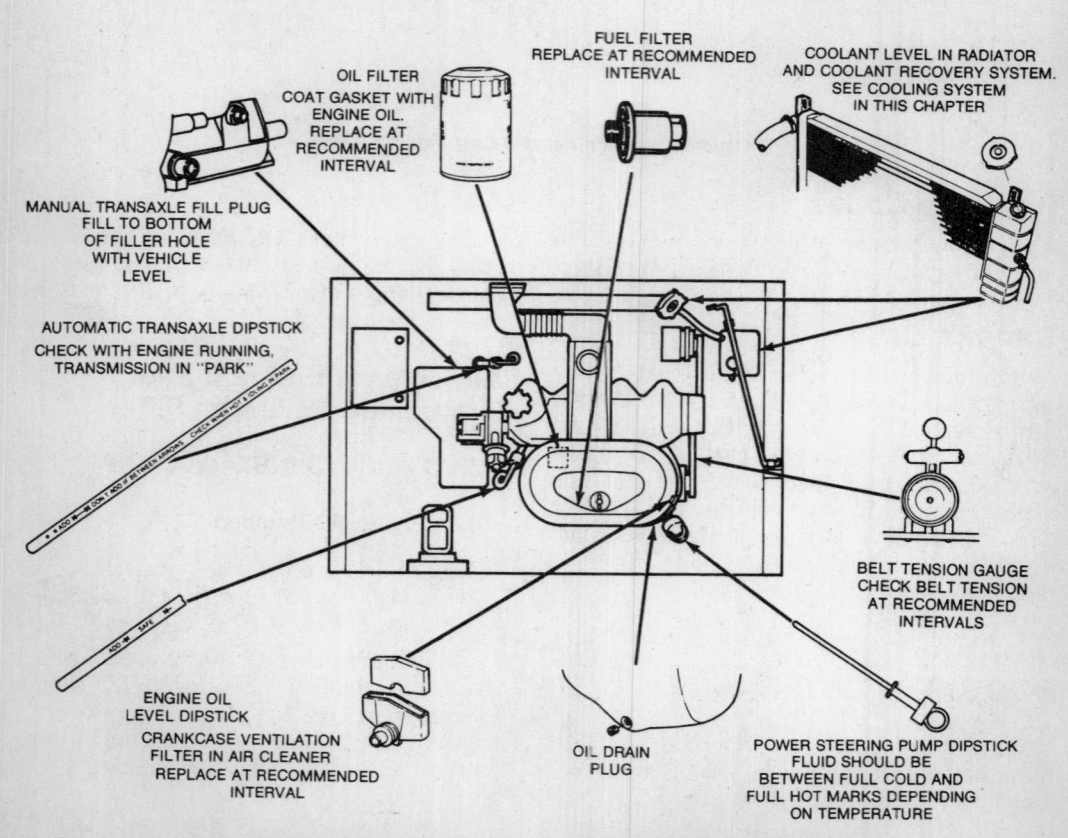

Lubrication and service points — 1.3L, 1.6L and 1.9L non-EFI engines

GENERAL INFORMATION AND MAINTENANCE

TRANSAXLE CODES

Code	Year	Type
4	1981–82	MTX 4 spd
9	1983–90	MTX 4 spd
D	1984–90	MTX 5 spd
B	1981–90	ATX Batavia
K	1988–90	ATX Mazda
O	1984–85	ATX Toyo Kogyo

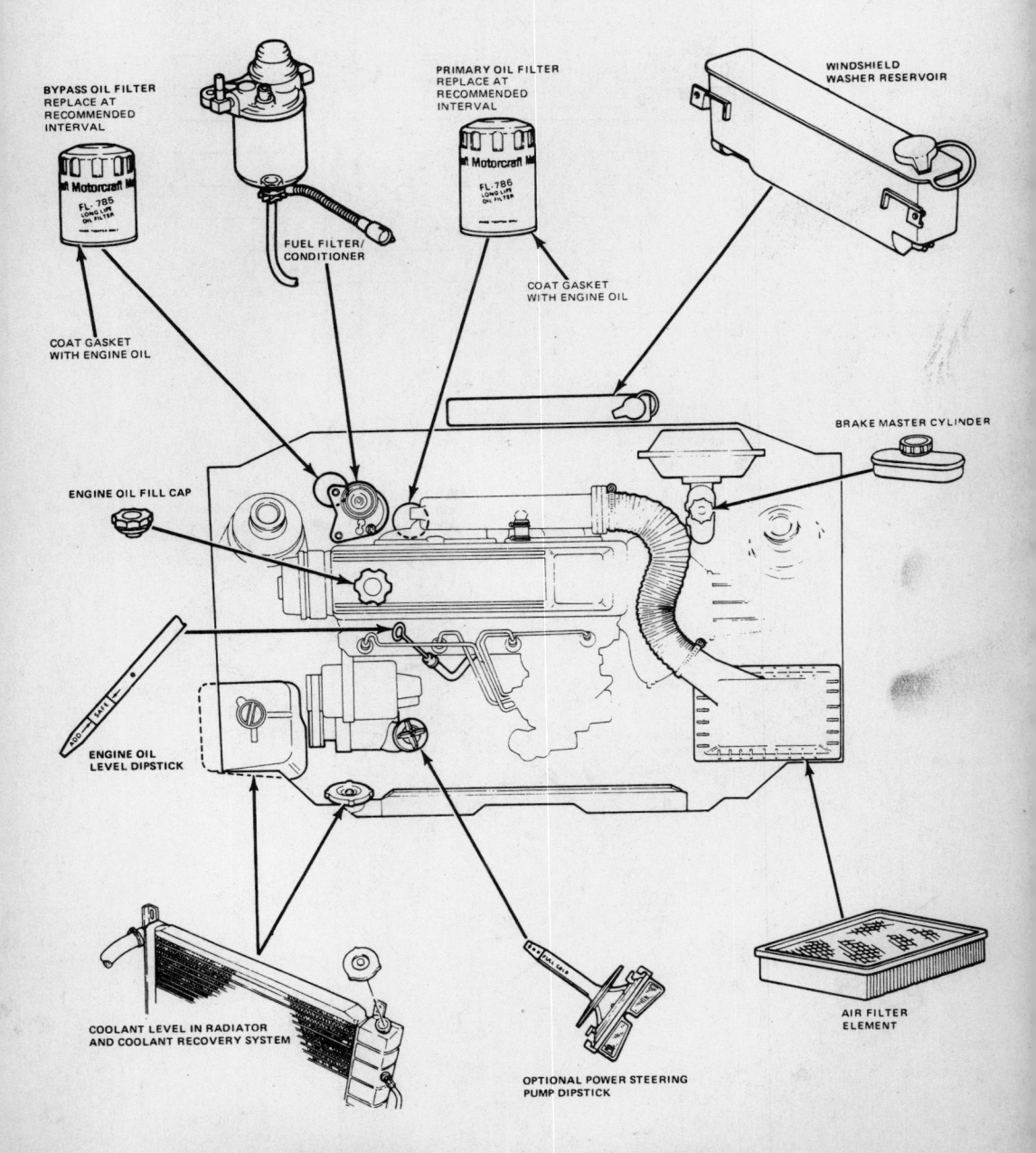

Lubrication and service points — 2.0L diesel engines

8 GENERAL INFORMATION AND MAINTENANCE

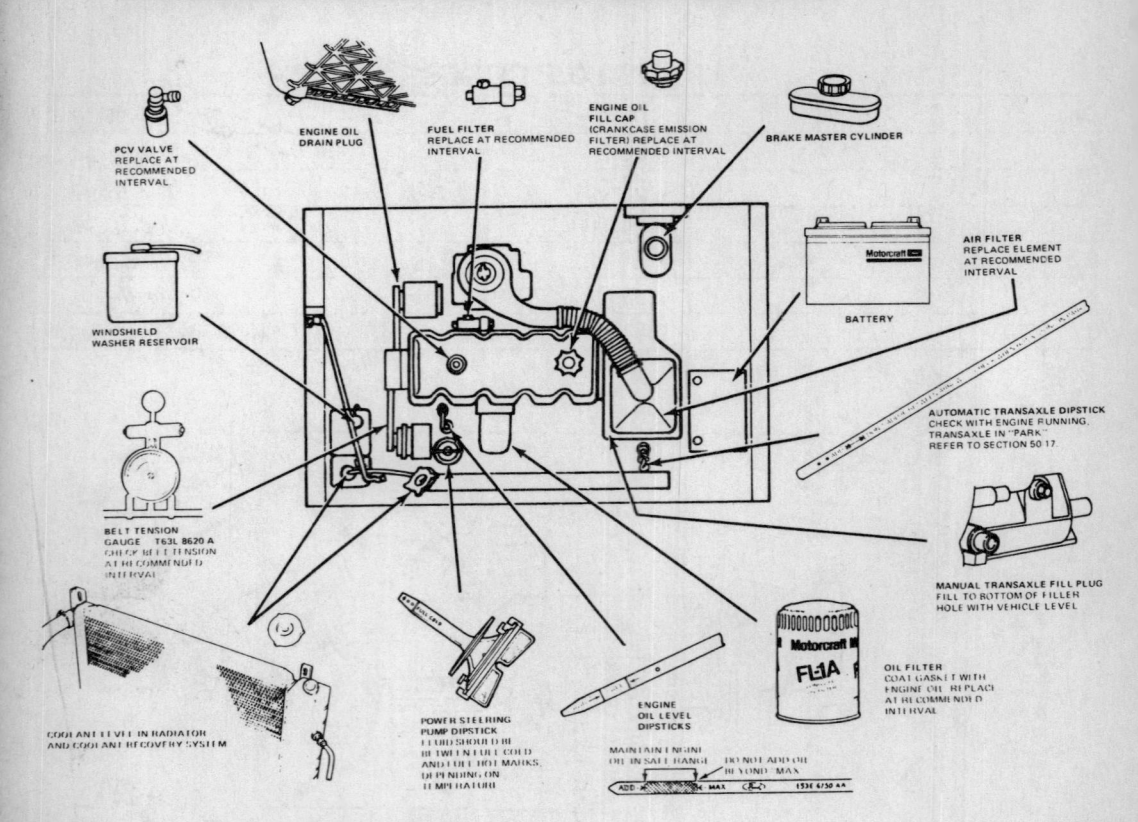

Lubrication and service points — 2.3L FSC engine

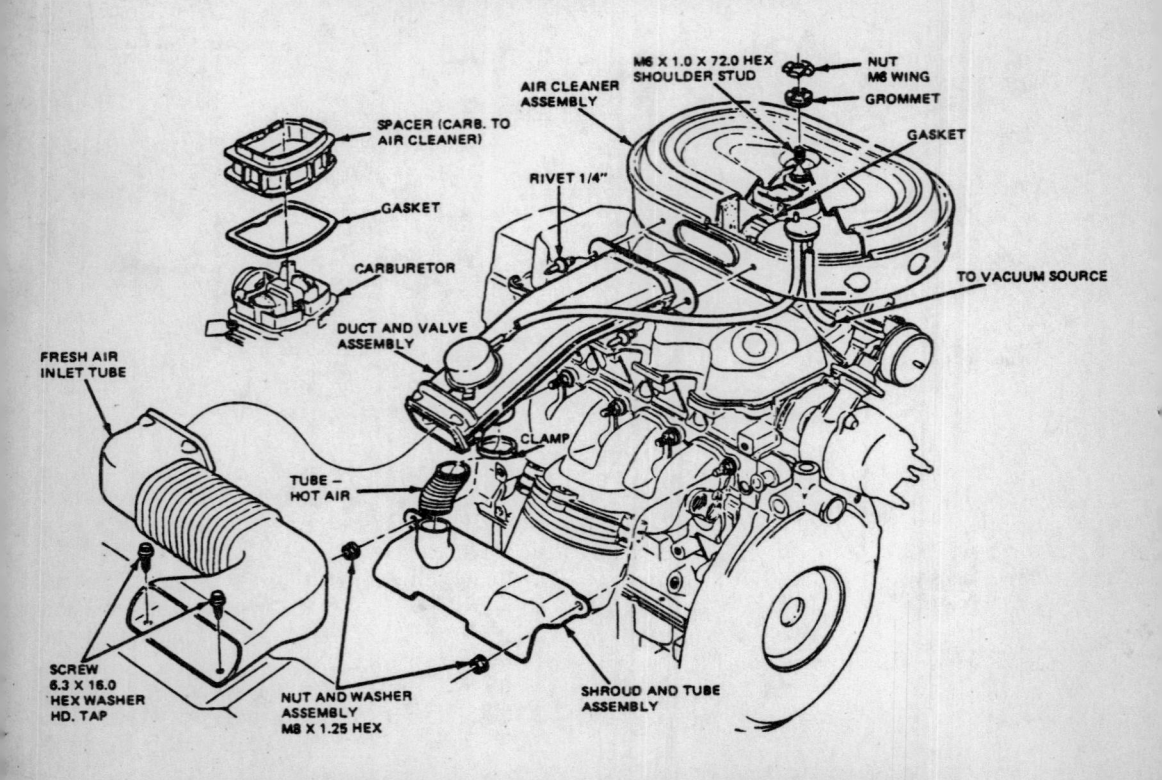

Air intake and cleaner system — 1.3L, 1.6L and 1.9L bade engine

GENERAL INFORMATION AND MAINTENANCE 9

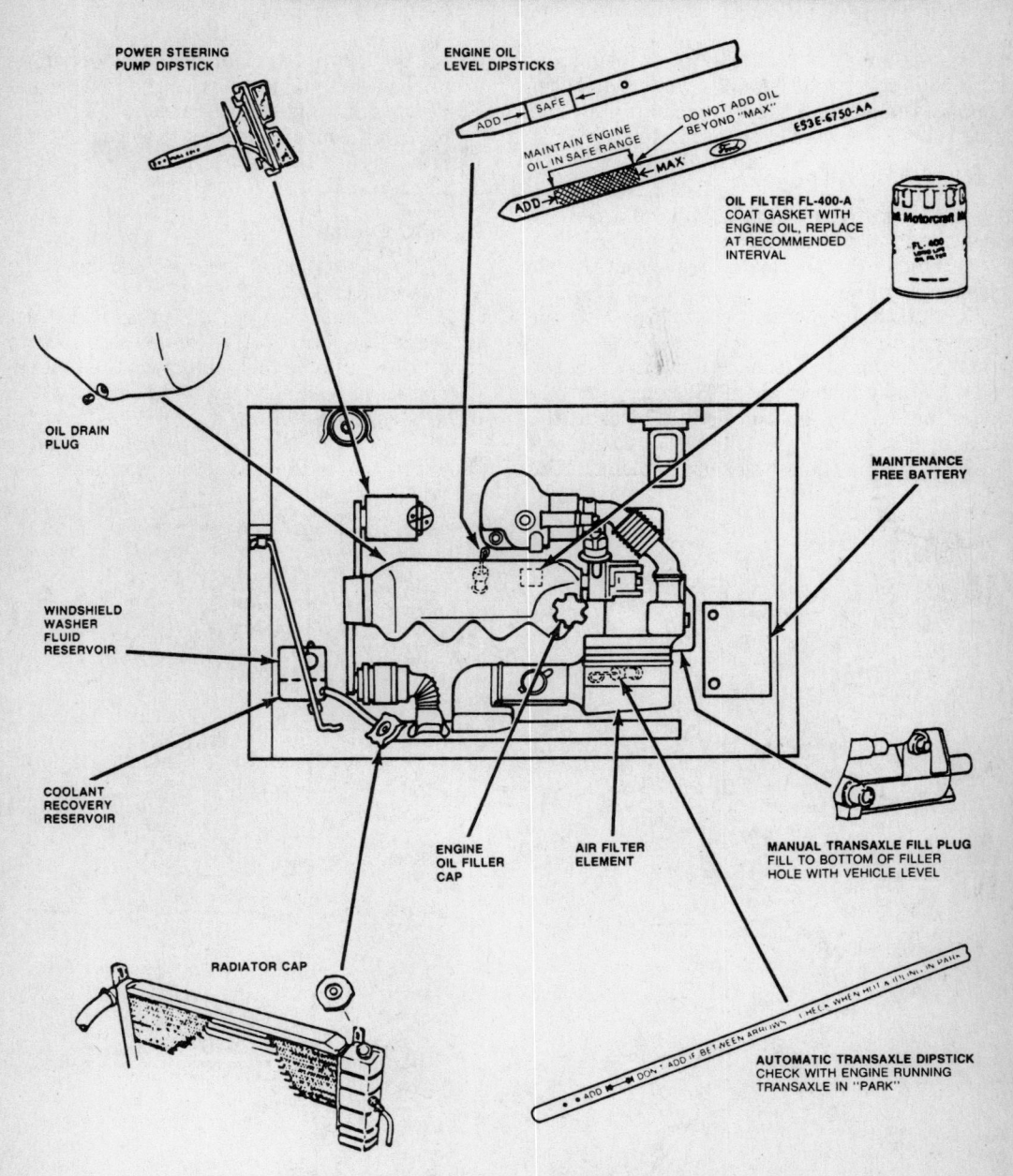

Lubrication and service points — 1.6L and 1.9L EFI engines

NOTE: *Removing the air cleaner as an assembly helps prevent dirt from falling into the carburetor.*

3. Remove the spring clips that hold the top of the air cleaner to the body. Remove the cover.

4. Remove the air cleaner element. Disconnect the spring clip that retains the emission filter to the air cleaner body, and remove the filter.

5. Clean the inside of the air cleaner body by wiping with a rag. Check the mounting gasket (gaskets, if the car is equipped with a spacer), replace any gasket(s) that show wear.

6. Install a new emission filter and a new air cleaner element.

7. Install the air cleaner element. Reconnect the spring clip that retains the emission filter to the air cleaner body, and install the filter.

8. Install the spring clips that hold the top of the air cleaner to the body. install the cover.

9. Install the air cleaner assembly from the car.

10. Install the wing nut that retains the air

10 GENERAL INFORMATION AND MAINTENANCE

cleaner assembly to the carburetor. install any support bracket bolts (engine to air cleaner). reconnect the air duct tubing, vacuum lines and heat tubes connected to the air cleaner.

1.6L and 1.9L EFI Engines

1. Unclip the air intake tube and remove the tube from the air cleaner tray.
2. Unclip the air cleaner tray from the air cleaner assembly.
3. Pull the cleaner tray out to expose the air cleaner element.
4. Pull the air cleaner element from the tray. Visually inspect the air cleaner tray and cover for signs of dust or leaking holes in the filter or past the seals.
5. Assemble the air cleaner element to the tray making sure the element is installed in its original position. Check to see that the seal is fully seated into the groove in the tray.
6. Clip the air intake tube to the air cleaner tray.

2.3 HSC Engine

1. Loosen the air cleaner outlet tube clamp and disconnect the tube.
2. Disconnect the hot air tube, PCV inlet tube and the zip tube. To disconnect the zip tube, use a suitable tool and insert the tool between the air cleaner tray and the top of the plastic adapter to release it.
3. Disconnect the cold weather modulator vacuum hose at the temperature sensor. Dis-

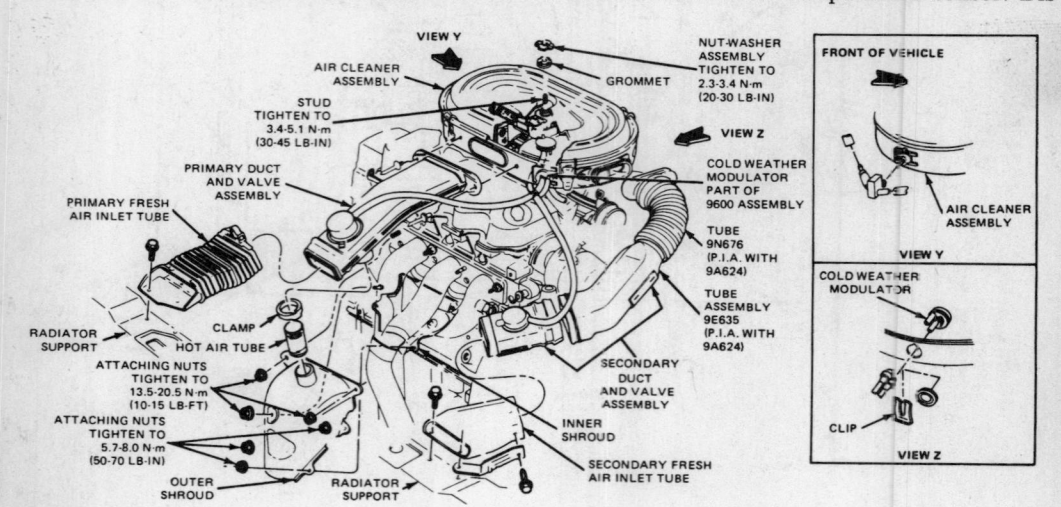

1.6L HO air intake system

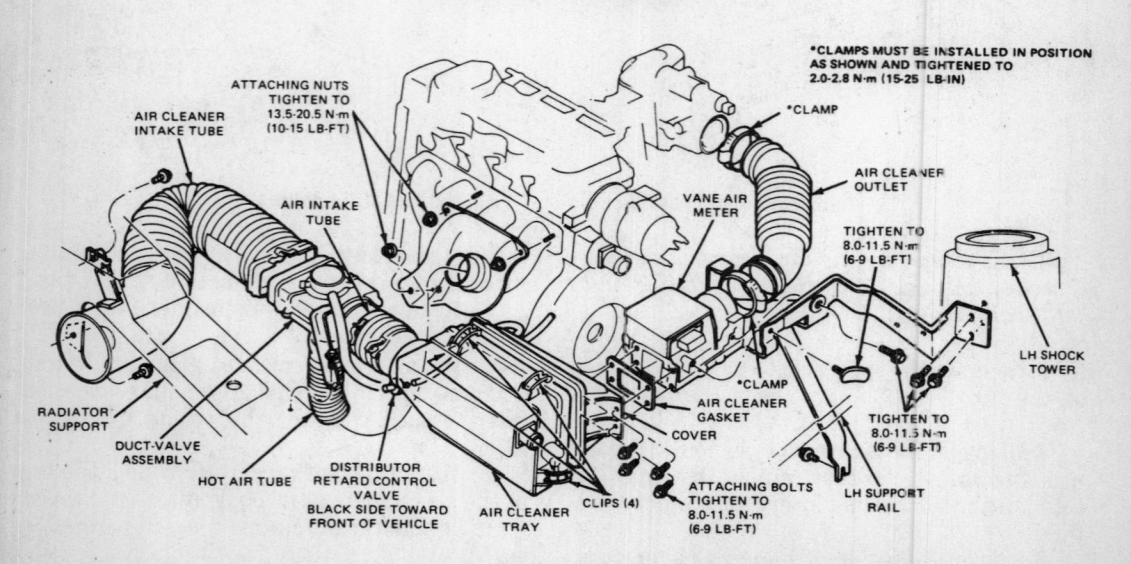

1.6L EFI air intake system

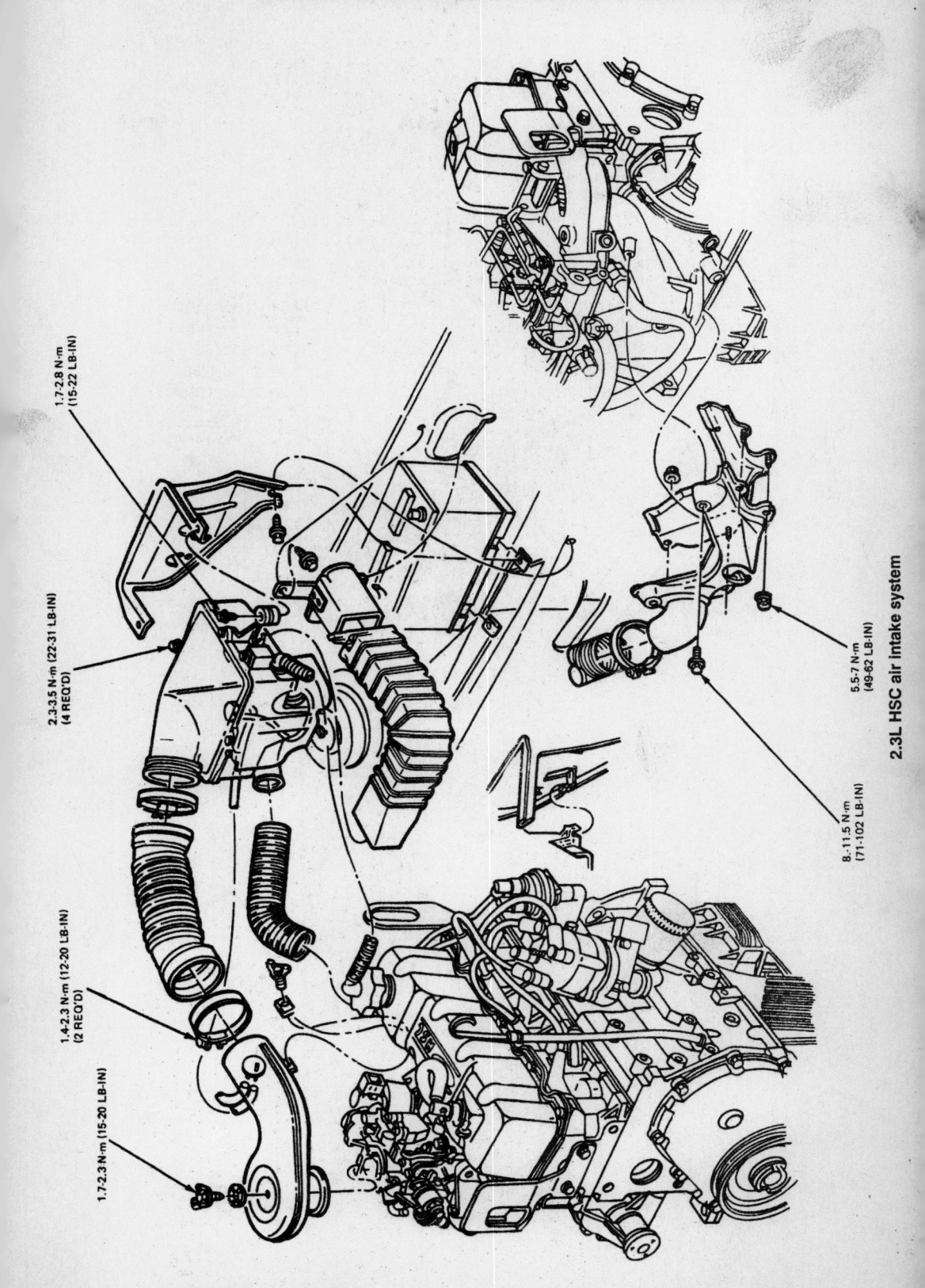

GENERAL INFORMATION AND MAINTENANCE

2.3L HSC air intake system

12 GENERAL INFORMATION AND MAINTENANCE

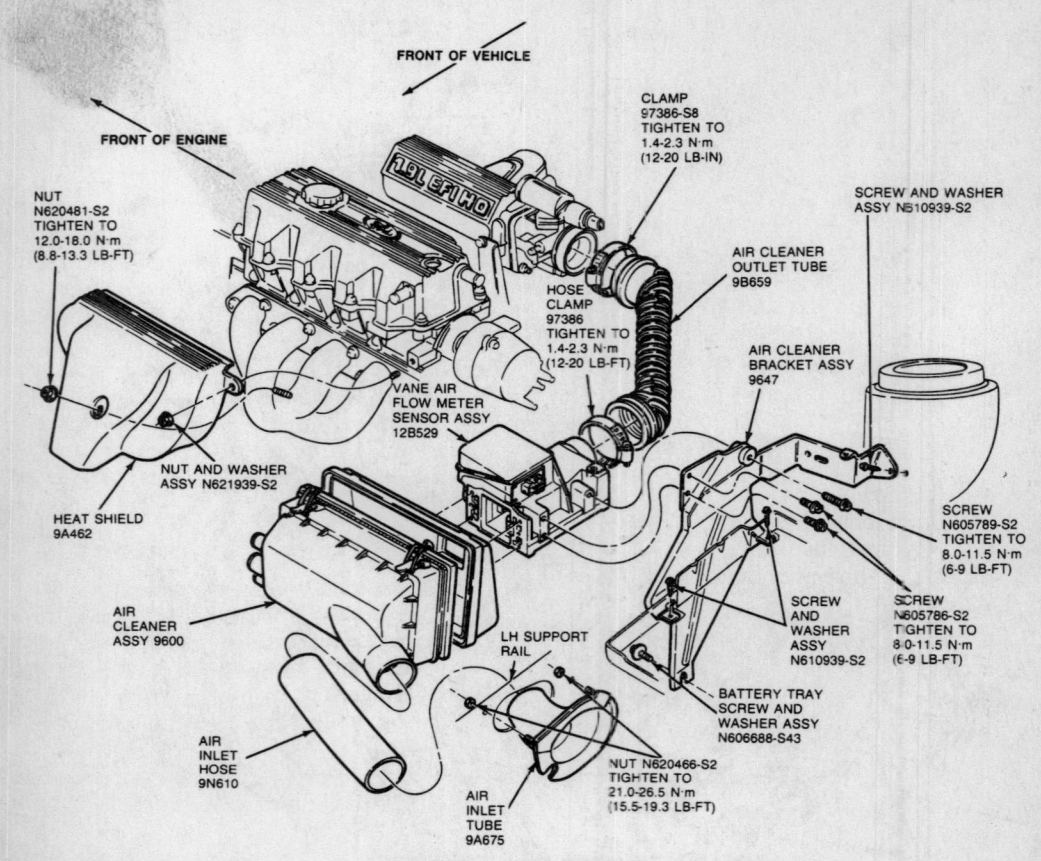

1.9L EFI air intake system

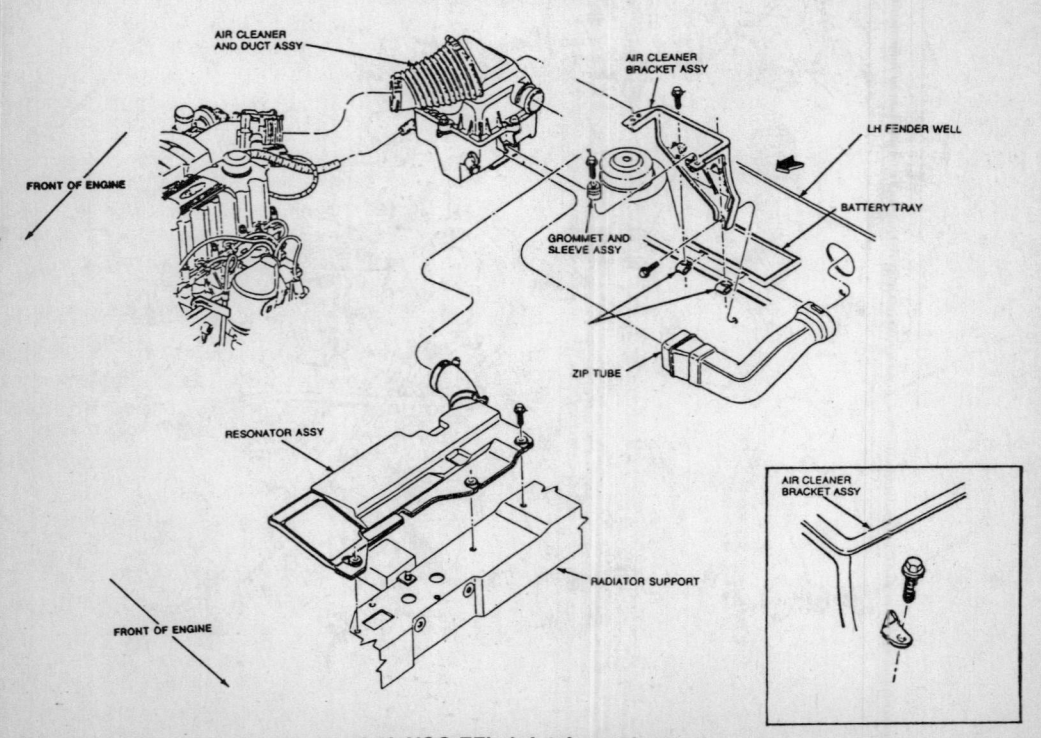

2.3L HSO EFI air intake system

GENERAL INFORMATION AND MAINTENANCE

connect the pulse air tube from the air cleaner tray.

4. Disconnect the vent hoses from the air cleaner cover. Loosen the resonator tuning tube clamp at the air cleaner cover.

5. Remove the air cleaner and cover retaining screws and the air cleaner assembly. Loosen the air cleaner outlet tube clamp and remove the tube from the cover.

6. Inspect the inside surfaces of the cover for traces of dirt leakage past the cleaner element as a result of damaged seals, incorrect element or inadequate tightness of the cover retaining screws.

7. Remove the air cleaner element and clean the inside surfaces of the cleaner tray and cover.

8. Install a new air cleaner element, install the cover and assembly. Tighten the retaining screws to 22–32 inch lbs.

9. Reconnect all vacuum and air duct hoses and lines.

Fuel Filter

The fuel filter should be replaced, immediately, upon evidence of dirt in the fuel system. Regular replacement of the fuel filter should be every 30,000 miles. If the engine seems to be suffering from fuel starvation, remove the filter and blow through it to see if it is clogged. If air won't pass through the filter easily, or if dirt is visible in the inlet passage, replace the filter.

NOTE: *A backup wrench is an open end wrench of the proper size used to hold a fuel filter or fitting in position while a fuel line is removed. A flared wrench is a special hex wrench with a narrow open end allowing the fuel line nut to be gripped tightly. A regular open end wrench may be substituted if used carefully so the fitting is not rounded.*

The fuel filter on the non-EFI models contains a screen to minimize the amount of contaminants entering the carburetor via the fuel system. The fuel filter on the non-EFI models is located in the carburetor.

The EFI model fuel filter provides extremely fine filtration to protect the small metering orifices of the injector nozzles. The filter is a one-piece construction which cannot be cleaned. If the filter becomes clogged or restricted, it should be replaced with a new filter. The filter is located downstream of the electric pump, mounted on the dash panel extension in the right rear corner of the engine compartment on the Escort and Lynx. And on the Tempo and Topaz the filter is mounted on the right fender apron.

REMOVAL AND INSTALLATION

Gasoline Engines

NOTE: *If the vehicle is equipped with a pressure relief valve, install an EFI/CFI fuel pressure gauge T80L–9974–B or equivalent and depressurize the fuel system. If the vehicle is not equipped with a pressure relief valve, the fuel filter connection should be covered with a shop rag or towel to prevent the fuel from spraying during the removal procedure. It is also possible to reduce the amount of pressure in the fuel system by locating the inertia switch (usually located in the luggage compartment) and disconnecting the electrical connection on the inertia switch. Next crank the engine for 15 seconds to reduce the system pressure.*

ESCORT, LYNX AND EXP w/CARBURETOR

1. Remove the air cleaner assembly.
2. Use a backup wrench on the fuel filter (located in the carburetor inlet) inlet hex nut. Loosen the fuel line nut with a flare wrench. Remove the fuel line from the filter.
3. Unscrew the filter from the carburetor.

To Install:

4. Apply a drop of Loctite® Hydraulic Sealant No. 069 to the external threads of the fuel filter.
5. Hand start the new filter into the carburetor, then use a wrench to tighten the fuel filter to 6.5–8 ft. lbs.
6. Apply a drop of engine oil to the fuel supply tube nut and flare, and hand start the nut into the filter inlet approximately two threads.
7. Use a backup wrench on the fuel filter to prevent the filter from rotating while tightening. Tighten the nut to 15–18 ft. lbs.
8. Start the engine and check for fuel leaks.
9. Install the air cleaner assembly.

ESCORT, LYNX AND EXP w/FUEL INJECTION

1. With the engine turned OFF, depressurize the fuel system on the EFI engines using special tool T80L–9974–A Fuel Pressure Gauge, or equivalent.
2. Remove the push connect fittings from both side of the fuel filter.

NOTE: *The fuel filter is located downstream of the electric fuel pump on the right rear corner of the engine compartment. Push connect fitting disconnection procedures are covered in Chapter 5 after Fuel Pumps.*

3. Remove the filter from the mounting bracket by loosening the retaining clamp enough to allow the filter to pass through.
4. Install the fuel filter in the bracket, en-

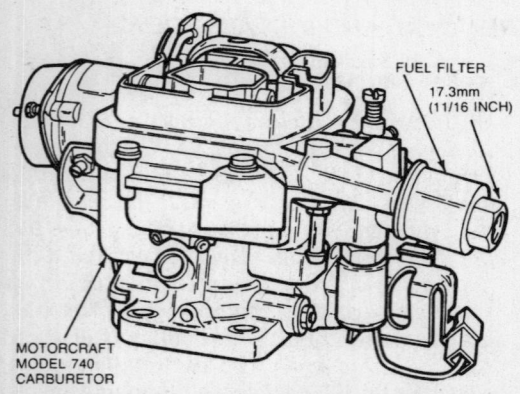

14 GENERAL INFORMATION AND MAINTENANCE

Fuel filter mounting Escort/Lynx/EXP with carburetor

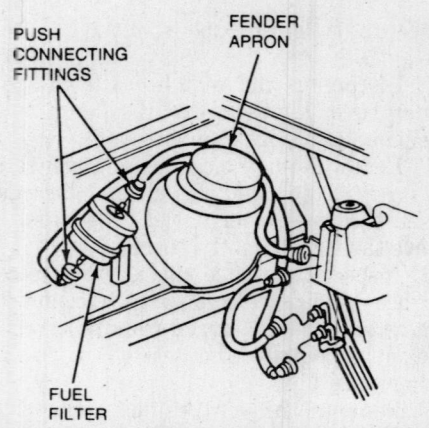

Fuel filter mounting Tempo/Topaz — CFI engines

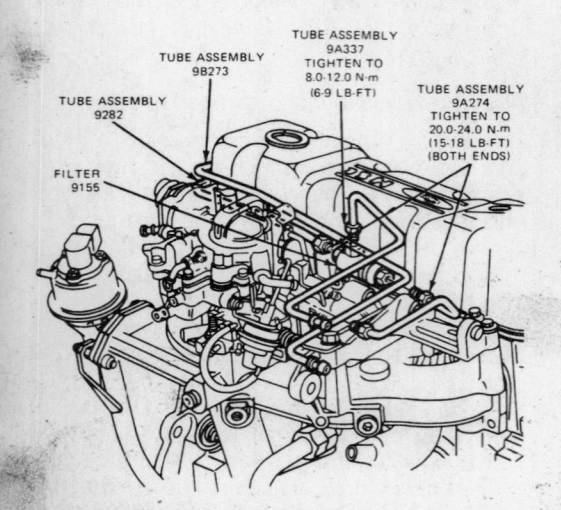

Fuel filter mounting Tempo/Topaz — Canada only

suring proper direction of the flow as noted earlier. Tighten the clamp to 15–25 inch lbs.

5. Install the push connect fittings at both ends of the filter.

6. Start the engine and check for fuel leaks.

TEMPO AND TOPAZ w/CARBURETOR CANADA ONLY

1. Remove the air cleaner bonnet assembly if necessary.

2. Using a backup wrench on the return line fitting on the top of the fuel filter, remove the fuel line with a flare nut wrench.

3. Using a backup wrench on the fuel filter inlet fitting, remove the fuel line from the fuel filter with a flare nut wrench.

4. Using a backup wrench on the fuel filter outlet fitting, loosen the fuel line and remove the fuel filter from the engine with a flare nut wrench.

To Install:

5. Apply engine oil the fuel line nuts and flared ends.

6. Position the fuel filter with flow arrow on the filter directed towards the fuel line to the carburetor.

7. Finger-tighten the fitting at the fuel filter outlet.

8. Finger-tighten the return line fitting into the top of the filter.

9. Finger-tighten the fitting at the fuel filter inlet.

10. Using a backup wrench on the fuel filter fittings, tighten the fuel lines in the following sequence:

    a. Tighten the return line nut to 6–9 ft. lbs.

    b. Tighten the nut on the fuel line at the filter outlet to 15–18 ft. lbs.

    c. Tighten the nut on the fuel line from the fuel pump to the fuel filter to 15–18 ft. lbs.

11. Inspect the fuel line routings and install the fuel line clips if loosened or removed during disassembly. Adjust the fuel lines if they are interfering with the carburetor, air pump, or fuel filter housing.

12. Start the engine and check for fuel leaks at all the fuel line connections, fuel pump, fuel filter and the carburetor while the engine is idling for two minutes. Retighten if necessary.

13. If removed, install the air filter bonnet assembly to the carburetor.

TEMPO AND TOPAZ w/FUEL INJECTION

NOTE: *If the vehicle is equipped with a pressure relief valve, install an EFI/CFI fuel pressure gauge T80L–9974–B or equivalent and depressurize the fuel system. If the vehicle is not equipped with a pressure relief valve, the fuel filter connection should be covered with a shop rag or towel to prevent the fuel from spraying during the removal procedure.*

1. Remove the air cleaner bonnet assembly for clearance if necessary.

2. Use a backup wrench on the return line

GENERAL INFORMATION AND MAINTENANCE

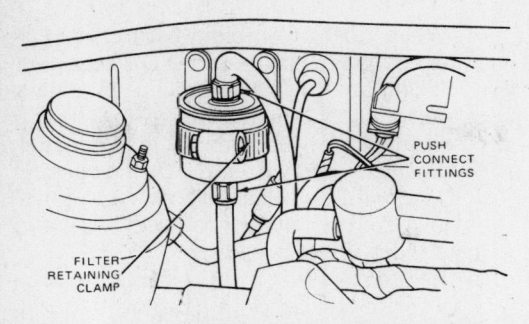

Fuel filter mounting Escort/Lynx/EXP with EFI engines

fitting on the top of the fuel filter. Remove the fuel line using a flare wrench.

3. Use a backup wrench on the fuel filter inlet fitting. Remove the fuel line using a flare wrench.

4. Use a backup wrench on the fuel filter outlet fitting. Remove the fuel line using a flare wrench. Remove the fuel filter.

NOTE: *The fuel filter on some models may be equipped with the push connect fittings instead of the typical flare nut set up. If so follow the instruction under the Push Connect Fittings, Removal and Installation.*

5. Position the fuel filter with the arrow on the filter pointing towards the fuel line to the carburetor.

6. Hand start all the fuel lines in their respective fittings.

7. Use a backup wrench and flare wrench to tighten all fuel lines. Tighten the return line first, the outlet line second and the inlet line last. Do not over tighten. Install the remaining parts in the reverse order of removal.

Diesel Engine

The fuel filter/conditioner must be serviced (water purged) at each engine oil change (7500 miles) interval. To purge water from the system:

1. Make sure the engine and ignition switch are off.
2. Place a suitable container under the fuel filter/conditioner water drain tube under the car.
3. Open the water drain valve at the bottom of the filter/conditioner element $2^{1}/_{2}$–3 turns.
4. Pump the prime pump at the top of the filter from 10 to 15 strokes, or until all of the water is purged from the filter, and clear diesel fuel is apparent.

NOTE: *If the water/fuel will not drain from the tube, open the drain valve one more turn or until the water/fuel starts to flow.*

5. Close the drain valve and tighten.
6. Start the engine and check for leaks.

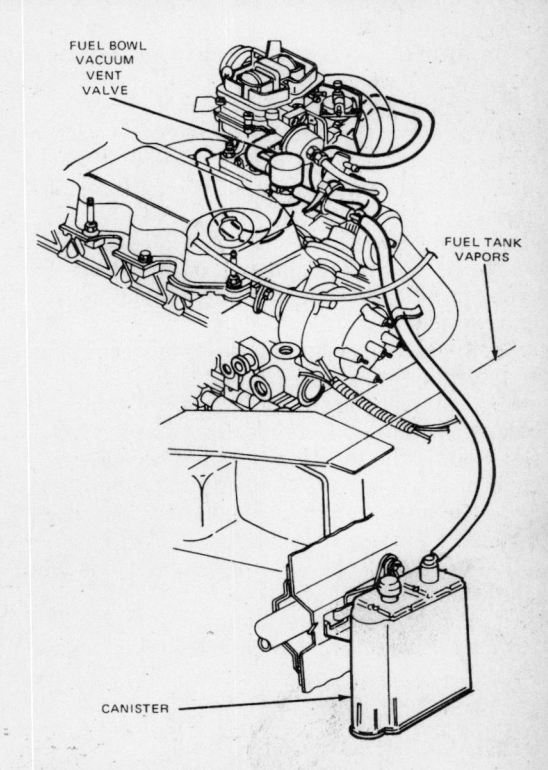

Evaporative canister — Escort/Lynx

NOTE: *Whenever the fuel filter is replaced, or system service performed, the filter must be air bleed as follows:*

a. Loosen the fuel filter air vent plug.
b. Pump the head of the filter in an up and down motion.
c. Continue to pump until the fuel flows from the air vent plug hole in a steady stream free of air bubbles.
d. Depress the head of the filter and close the air vent plug.
e. If the engine should run out of fuel during this operation or the system is opened allowing air to enter, bleed the air from the fuel filter first.
f. Pump the head of the filter repeatedly until it becomes hard to pump (approximately 15 times) to force air from the system.

To replace the filter/conditioner

1. Make sure that the engine and ignition are off.
2. Disconnect the module connector from the water level sensor located at the bottom of the filter element.
3. Use an appropriate filter strap wrench and turn the filter element counterclockwise to loosen from the top mounting bracket. Remove the element from the mount adapter.
4. Remove the water drain valve/sensor

16 GENERAL INFORMATION AND MAINTENANCE

probe from the bottom of the element. Wipe the probe with a clean dry cloth.

5. Unsnap the sensor probe pigtail from the bottom of the filter element and wipe with a clean dry rag.

6. Snap the probe onto the new filter element.

7. Lubricate the two O-rings on the water sensor probe with a light film of oil. Screw the probe into the bottom of the new filter element and tighten.

8. Clean the gasket mounting surface of the adapter mount.

9. Lubricate the sealing gasket of the filter element with oil. Screw the filter element onto the mount adapter. Hand tighten the element, then back off the filter to a point where the gasket is just touching the adapter. Retighten by hand and then an additional 1/2–5/8 turn.

10. Reconnect the water level sensor module connector.

11. Prime the fuel system by pumping the primer handle until pressure is felt when pumping.

12. Start the engine and check for fuel leaks.

Push Connect Fittings

Push connect fittings are designed with two different retaining clips. The fittings used with 5/16 in. (8mm) diameter tubing use a hairpin clip. The fittings used with 1/4 in. (6mm) and 1/2 in. (12.7mm) diameter tubing use a "duck bill" clip. Each type of fitting requires different procedures for service. Push connect fitting disassembly must be accomplished prior to fuel component removal (filter, pump, etc.) except for the fuel tank where removal is necessary for access to the push connects.

REMOVAL AND INSTALLATION

5/16 in. Fittings (Hairpin Clip)

1. Inspect internal portion of fitting for dirt accumulation. If more than a light coating of dust is present, clean the fitting before disassembly.

2. Remove hairpin type clip from fitting. This is done (using hands only) by spreading the two clip legs about 1/8 in. (3mm) each to disengage the body and pushing the legs into the fitting. Complete removal is accomplished by lightly pulling from the triangular end of the clip and working it clear of the tube and fitting.
NOTE: *Do not use any tools.*

3. Grasp the fitting and hose assembly and pull in an axial direction to remove the fitting from the steel tube. Adhesion between sealing surfaces may occur. A slight twist of the fitting may be required to break this adhesion and permit effortless removal.

4. When fitting is removed from the tube end, inspect clip to ensure it has not been damaged. If damaged, replace the clip. If undamaged, immediately reinstall clip, insert clip into any two adjacent openings with the triangular portion pointing away from the fitting opening. Install clip to fully engage the body (legs of hairpin clip locked on outside of body). Piloting with an index finger is necessary.

5. Before installing fitting on the tube, wipe tube end with a clean cloth. Inspect the inside of the fitting to ensure it is free of dirt and/or obstructions.

6. To reinstall the fitting onto the tube, align the fitting and tube axially and push the fitting onto the tube end. When the fitting is engaged, a definite click will be heard. Pull on fitting to ensure it is fully engaged.

1/2 in. and 1/4 in. Fittings (Duck Bill Clip)

The fitting consists of a body, spacers, O-rings and a duck bill retaining clip. The clip maintains the fitting to steel tube juncture. When disassembly is required for service, one of the two following methods are to be followed:

1/4 IN. FITTINGS

To disengage the tube from the fitting, align the slot on push connect disassembly Tool T82L–9500–AH or equivalent with either tab on the clip (90° from slots on side of fitting) and insert the tool. This disengages the duck bill from the tube. Holding the tool and the tube with one hand, pull fitting away from the tube.

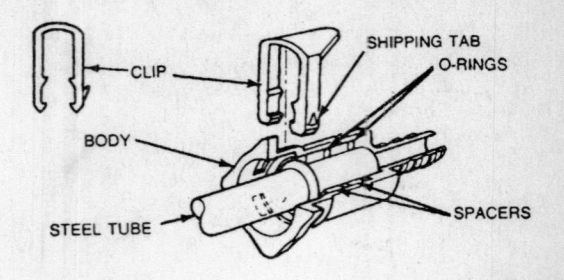

Typical hairpin clip

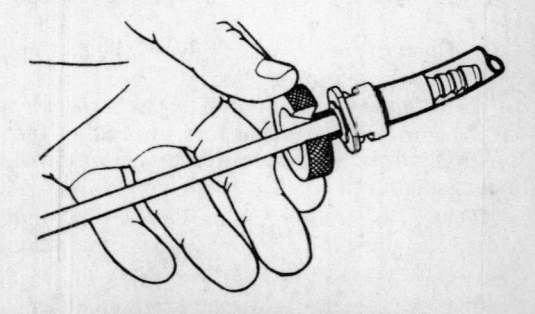

Removing push connect with the tool

GENERAL INFORMATION AND MAINTENANCE

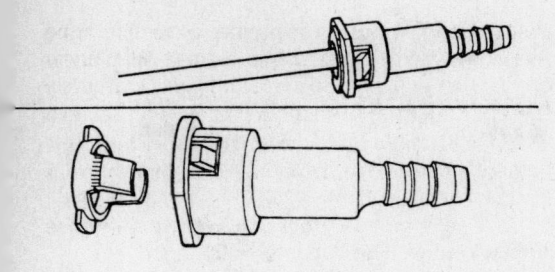

Duck bill clip

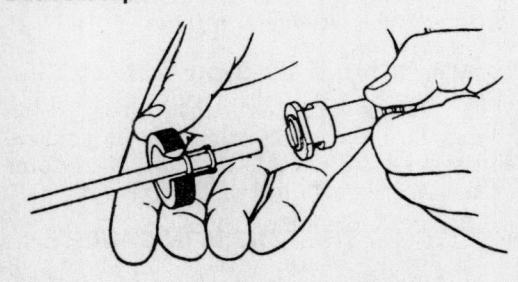

Pulling off the push connect fitting

NOTE: *Only moderate effort is required if the tube has been properly disengaged. Use hands only. After disassembly, inspect and clean the tube sealing surface. Also inspect the inside of the fitting for damage to the retaining clip. If the retaining clip appears to be damaged, replace it.*

Some fuel tubes have a secondary bead which aligns with the outer surface of the clip. These beads can make tool insertion difficult. If there is extreme difficulty, use the disassembly method following.

1/2 IN. FITTING AND ALTERNATE METHOD FOR 1/4 IN. FITTING

This method of disassembly disengages the retaining clip from the fitting body.

Use a pair of narrow pliers, (6 in. [153mm] locking pliers are ideal). The pliers must have a jaw width of 0.2 in. (5mm) or less.

Align the jaws of the pliers with the openings in the side of the fitting case and compress the portion of the retaining clip that engages the fitting case. This disengages the retaining clip from the case (often one side of the clip will disengage before the other. It is necessary to disengage the clip from both openings). Pull the fitting off the tube.

NOTE: *Only moderate effort is required if the retaining clip has been properly disengaged. Use hands only.*

The retaining clip will remain on the tube. Disengage the clip from the tube bead and remove. Replace the retaining clip if it appears to be damaged.

NOTE: *Slight ovality of the ring of the clip will usually occur. If there are no visible cracks and the ring will pinch back to its circular configuration, it is not damaged. If there is any doubt, replace the clip.*

Install the clip into the body by inserting one of the retaining clip serrated edges on the duck bill portion into one of the window openings. Push on the other side until the clip snaps into place. Slide fuel line back into the clip.

SPRING LOCK COUPLING

The spring lock coupling is a fuel line coupling held together by a garter spring inside a circular cage. When the coupling is connected together, the flared end of the female fitting slips behind the garter spring inside the cage of the male fitting. The garter spring and cage then prevent the flared end of the female fitting from pulling out of the cage.

Two O-rings are used to seal between the 2 halves of the coupling. These O-rings are made of special material and must be replaced with an O-ring made of the same material. To disconnect the coupling do the following:

1. Discharge the fuel from the fuel system.
2. Then fit Spring Lock Coupling Tool D87L–9280–A ($3/8$ in.), D87L–9280–B ($1/2$ in.) or equivalent to the coupling.
3. Fit the tool to the coupling so that the tool can enter the cage opening to release the garter spring.
4. Push on the tool into the cage opening to release the female fitting from the garter spring.
5. Pull the male and female fittings apart. Remove the tool from the disconnected spring lock coupling.
6. Be sure to check for missing or damaged garter spring. Remove the damaged spring with a small hooked wire and install a new spring. Remember to use only the special O-rings being used on that fitting.
7. Lubricate the O-rings with clean engine oil. Assemble the fitting by pushing with a slight twisting motion.
8. To ensure coupling engagement, pull on the fitting and visually check to be sure the garter spring is over the flared end of the female fitting.

PCV Valve

OPERATION AND INSPECTION

NOTE: *Most models do not use a PCV (positive crankcase ventilation) valve. Instead, an internal baffle and an orifice control the flow of crankcase gases. But there are some later model 2.3L engine that have a PCV valve incorporated into the emission system. (See*

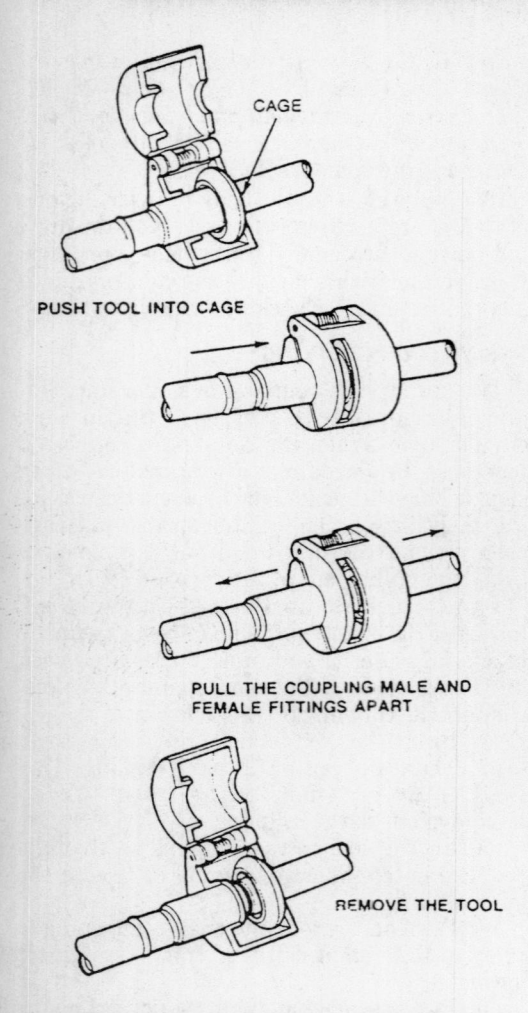

18 GENERAL INFORMATION AND MAINTENANCE

PUSH TOOL INTO CAGE

PULL THE COUPLING MALE AND FEMALE FITTINGS APART

REMOVE THE TOOL

Using the special tool to open the spring lock coupling

Chapter 4 for more details on emission controls).

The PCV valve is located on top of the valve cover or on the intake manifold. Its function is to purge the crankcase of harmful vapors through a system using engine vacuum to draw fresh air through the crankcase. It reburns crankcase vapors, rather than exhausting. Proper operation of the PCV valve depends on a sealed engine.

Engine operating conditions that would indicate a malfunctioning PCV system are rough idle, oil present in the air cleaner, oil leaks or excessive oil sludging.

The simplest check for the PCV valve is to remove it from its rubber grommet on top of the valve cover and shake it. If it rattles, it is functioning. If not, replace it. In any event, it should be replaced at the recommended interval whether it rattles or not. While you're at it, check the PCV hoses for breaks or restrictions. As necessary, the hoses should also be replaced.

REMOVAL AND INSTALLATION

1. Pull the valve, with the hose still attached to the valve, from the rubber grommet in the rocker cover.
2. Use a pair of pliers to release the hose clamp, remove the PCV valve from the hose.
3. Install the new valve into the hose, slide the clamp into position, and install the valve into the rubber grommet.

Evaporative Emission Canister

To prevent gasoline vapors from being vented into the atmosphere, an evaporative emission system captures the vapors and stores them in a charcoal filled canister.

SERVICING THE EMISSION CANISTER

Since the canister is purged of fumes when the engine is operating, no real maintenance is required. However, the canister should be visually inspected for cracks, loose connections, etc. Replacement is simply a matter of disconnecting the hoses, loosening the mount and replacing the canister.

Battery

Your car is equipped with a maintenance free battery which eliminates the need for periodic checking and adding fluid.

NOTE: *If you replace your battery with a non-maintenance free battery see the following section.*

FLUID LEVEL (EXCEPT MAINTENANCE FREE BATTERIES)

Check the battery electrolyte level at least once a month, or more often in hot weather or during periods of extended car operation. The

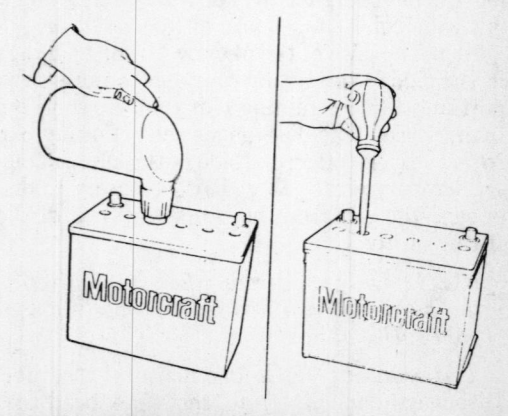

Adjusting the battery fluid level

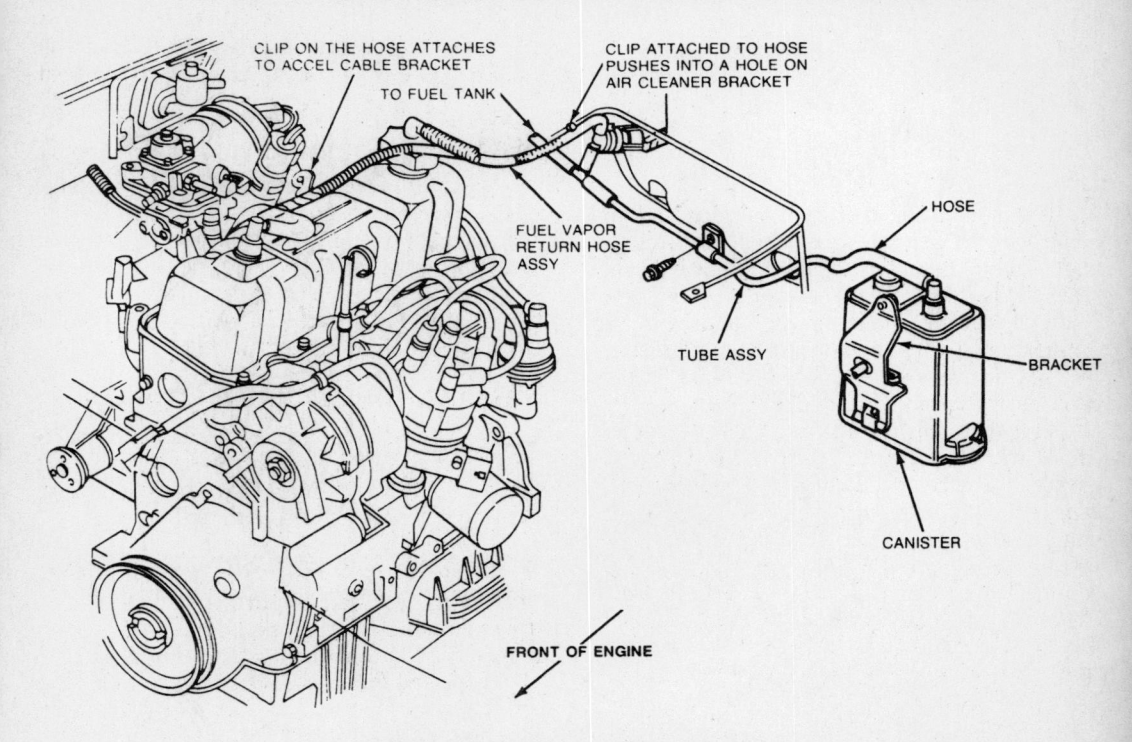

GENERAL INFORMATION AND MAINTENANCE

Evaporative canister — Tempo/Topaz

level can be checked through the case on translucent polypropylene battery cases; the cell caps must be removed on other models. The electrolyte level in each cell should be kept filled to the split ring inside, or the line marked on the outside of the case.

If the level is low, add only distilled water, or colorless, odorless drinking water, through the opening until the level is correct. Each cell is completely separate from the others, so each must be checked and filled individually.

If water is added in freezing weather, the car should be driven several miles to allow the water to mix with the electrolyte. Otherwise, the battery could freeze.

SPECIFIC GRAVITY

At least once a year, check the specific gravity of the battery. It should be between 1.20 and 1.26 at room temperature.

The specific gravity can be checked with the use of an hydrometer, an inexpensive instrument available from many sources, including auto parts stores. The hydrometer has a squeeze bulb at one end and a nozzle at the other. Battery electrolyte is sucked into the hydrometer until the float is lifted from its seat. The specific gravity is then read by noting the position of the float. Generally, if after charging, the specific gravity between any two cells varies more than 50 points (.050), the battery is bad and should be replaced.

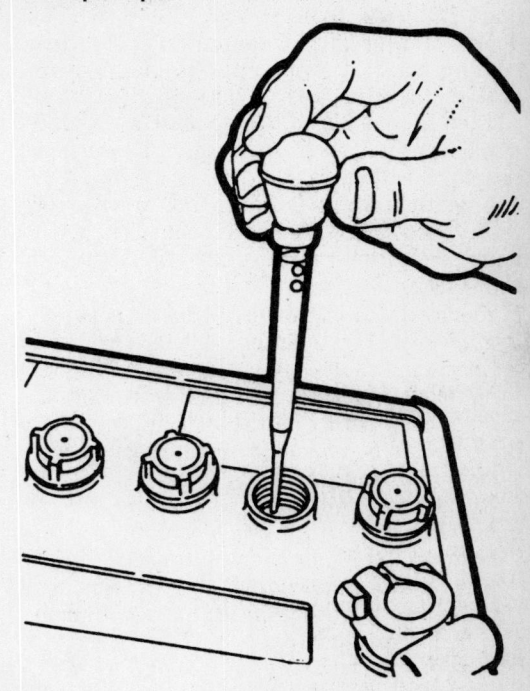

Checking the battery with a battery hydrometer

It is not possible to check the specific gravity in this manner on sealed maintenance free batteries. Instead, the indicator built into the top of the case (on some batteries) must be relied on to display any signs of battery deterioration.

GENERAL INFORMATION AND MAINTENANCE

If the indicator is dark, the battery can be assumed to be OK. If the indicator is light the specific gravity is low, and the battery should be charged or replaced.

CABLES AND CLAMPS

Once a year, the battery terminals and the cable clamps should be cleaned. Loosen the clamps and remove the cables, negative cable first. On batteries with posts on top, the use of a puller specially made for the purpose is recommended. These are inexpensive, and available in auto parts stores. Side terminal battery cables are secured with a bolt.

Clean the cable clamps and the battery terminal with a wire brush, until all corrosion, grease, etc. is removed and metal is shiny. It is especially important to clean the inside of the clamp thoroughly, since a small deposit of foreign material or oxidation there will prevent a sound electrical connection and inhibit either starting or charging. Special tools are available for cleaning these parts, one type of conventional batteries and another type for side terminal batteries.

Before installing the cable, loosen the battery hold down clamp or strap, remove the battery and check the battery tray. Clear it of any debris, and check it for soundness. Rust should be wire brushed away, and the metal given a coat of anti-rust paint. Replace the battery and tighten the hold down clamp or strap securely, but be careful not to over tighten, which will crack the battery case.

After the clamps and terminals are clean, reinstall the cables, negative cable last; do not hammer on the clamps to install. Tighten the clamps securely, but do not distort them. Give the clamps and terminals a thin external coat of grease after installation, to retard corrosion.

Check the cables at the same time that the terminals are cleaned. If the cable insulation is cracked or broken, or if the ends are frayed, the cable should be replace with a new cable of the same length and gauge.

NOTE: *Keep flame or sparks away from the battery; it gives off explosive hydrogen gas. Battery electrolyte contains sulphuric acid. If you should splash any on your skin or in your eyes, flush the affected areas with plenty of clear water; if it lands in your eyes, get medical help immediately.*

REPLACEMENT

When it becomes necessary to replace the battery, select a battery with a rating equal to or greater than the battery originally installed. Deterioration, embrittlement and just plain aging of the battery cables, starter motor, and associated wires makes the battery's job harder in successive years. The slow increase in electrical resistance over time makes it prudent to install a new battery with a greater capacity then the old. Details on battery removal and installation are covered in Chapter 3.

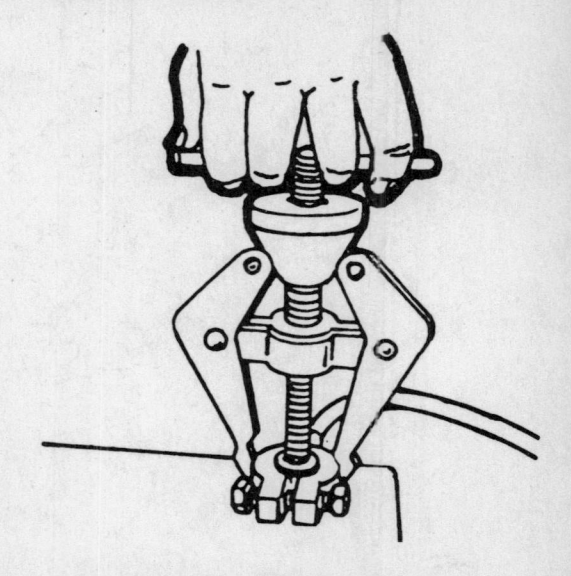

Use a puller to remove the battery cable

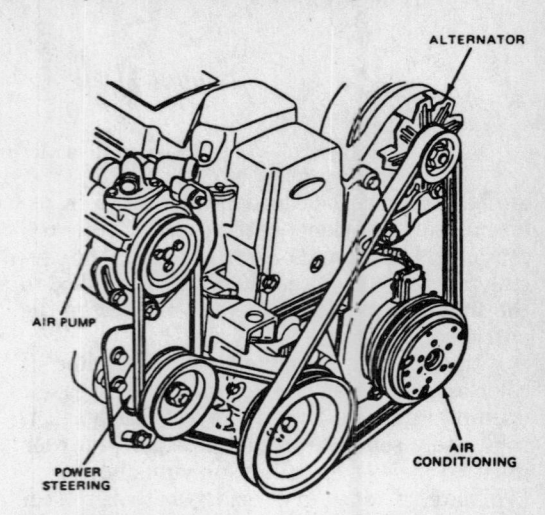

Drive belts, engine with air conditioning

Belts

NOTE: *Due to the compactness of the engine compartment, it may be necessary to disconnect some spark plug leads when adjusting or replacing drive belts. If a spark plug lead is disconnected it is necessary to coat the terminal of the lead with silicone grease (Part number D7AZ19A331A or the equivalent).*

Your car may be equipped with 4 rib, 5 rib, or a conventional $1/4$ in. (6mm) V-belt depending on accessories.

GENERAL INFORMATION AND MAINTENANCE

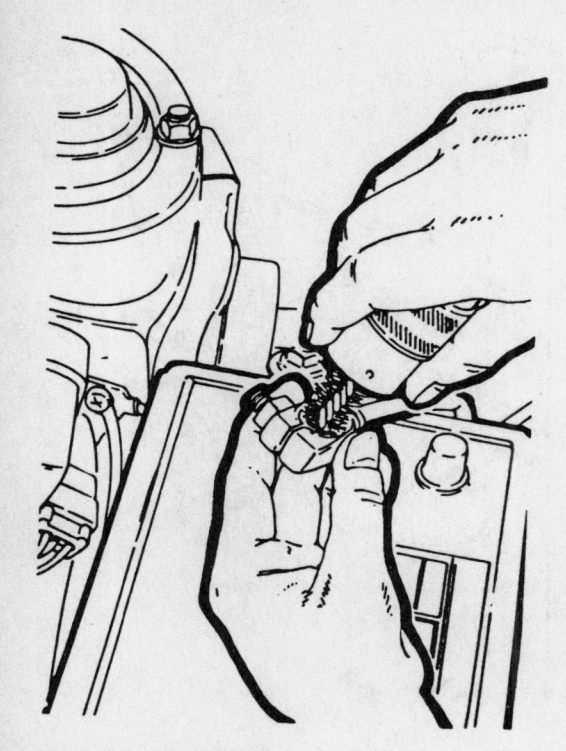

Clean the battery cable clamps with a wire brush

CAUTION: *On models equipped with power steering, the air pump belt tension cannot be adjusted until the power steering belt has been replaced and adjusted (or just adjusted if an old belt).*

INSPECTION

Inspect all drive belts for excessive wear, cracks, glazed condition and frayed or broken cords. Replace any drive belt showing the above condition(s).

NOTE: *If a drive belt continually gets cut, the crankshaft pulley might have a sharp projection on it. Have the pulley replaced if this condition exists.*

ADJUSTMENT

NOTE: *Proper adjustment requires the use of the tension gauge. Since most people don't have the necessary gauge, a deflection method of adjustment is given.*

1. Locate a point on the belt midway between the two pulleys driven.
2. The deflection of the belt should be:
• For all belts with a distance of 12 in. (305) between pulley: 1/8–1/4 in. (3–6mm).
• For all belts with a distance greater than 12 in. (305mm) between pulleys: 1/8–3/8 in. (3–6mm).
3. Correctly adjust the bolt deflection and

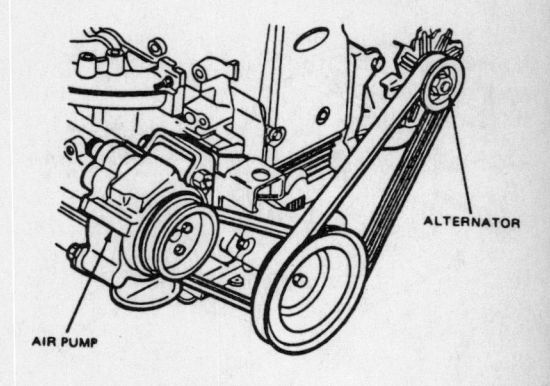

Drive belts, engine without air conditioning

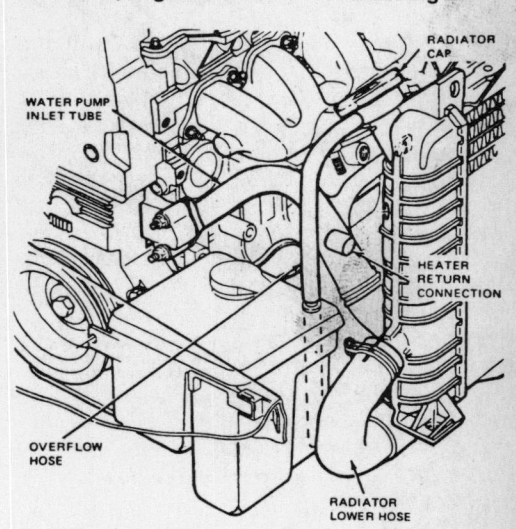

Hose locations

tighten all mounting bolts. Start the engine and allow it to reach the normal operating temperature. Shut the engine OFF and recheck belt deflection. Readjust if necessary.

1981–86 ALTERNATOR BELT ADJUSTMENT

Modified Bracket

Some later models are equipped with a modified alternator bracket (high mount alternator). The bracket incorporates a slot that will accommodate a tapered pry bar, such as a lug wrench, to give a place to apply leverage.

Insert the tire lug wrench into the slot opening. Pry on the alternator until the correct belt tension is reached.

While maintaining belt tension, first tighten the 3/8 in. adjusting bolt (24–30 ft. lbs.), then tighten the pivot bolt (45–65 ft. lbs.).

22 GENERAL INFORMATION AND MAINTENANCE

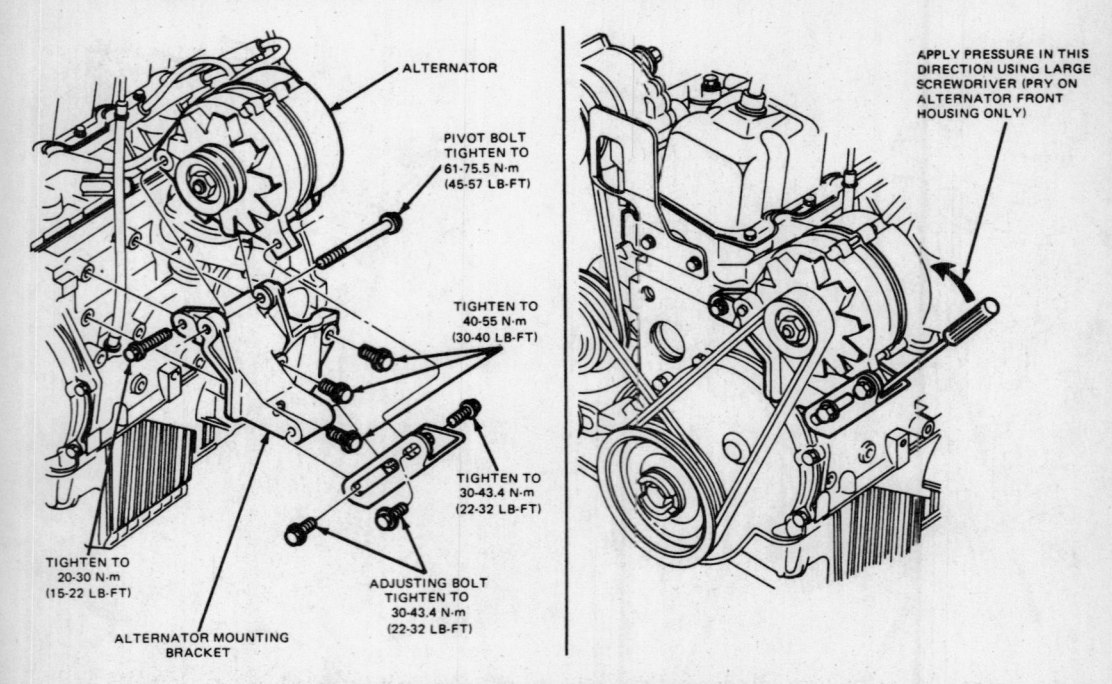

Belt tension adjustment — alternator etc.

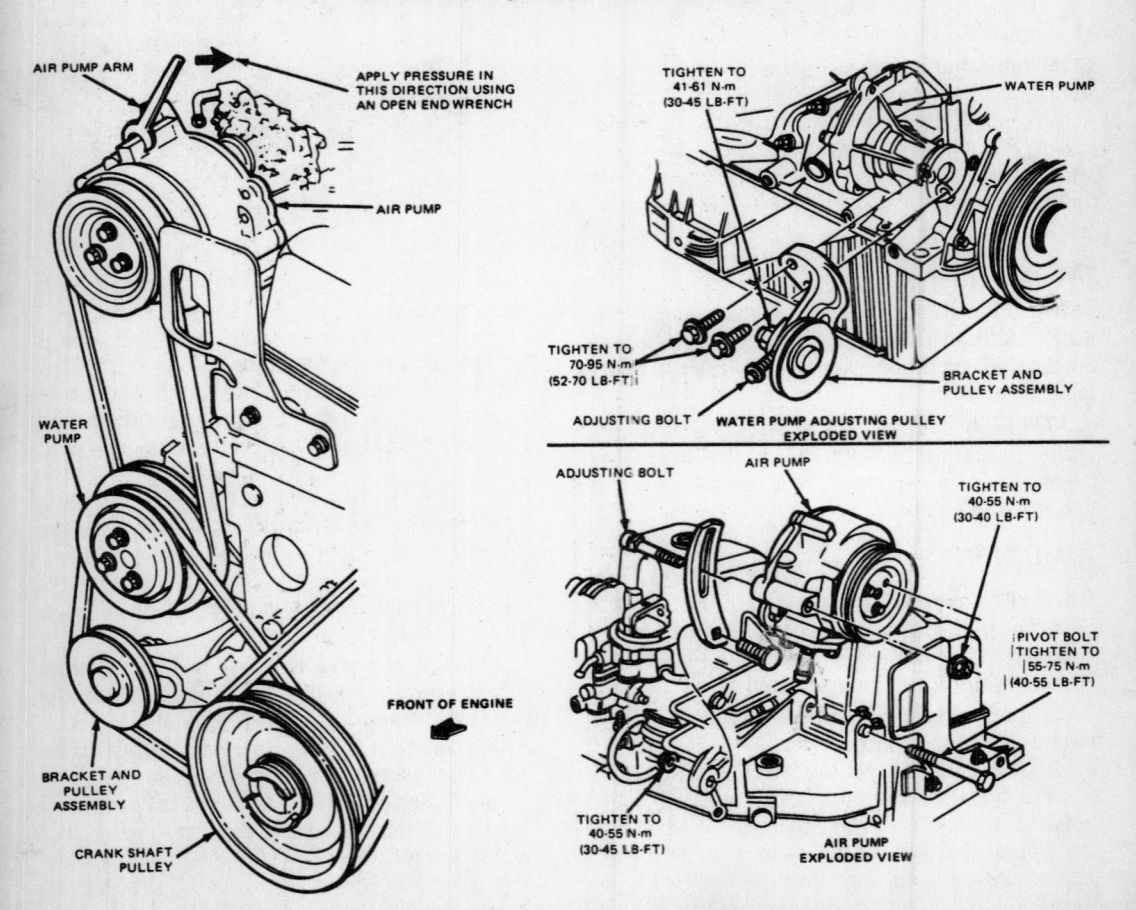

Belt tension adjustment — air pump, water pump

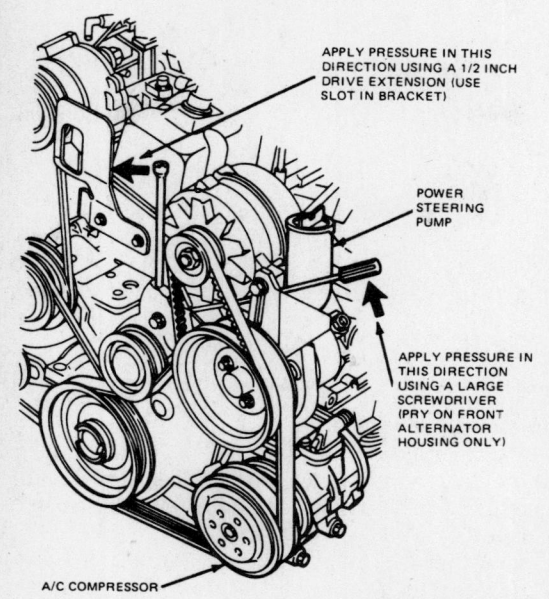

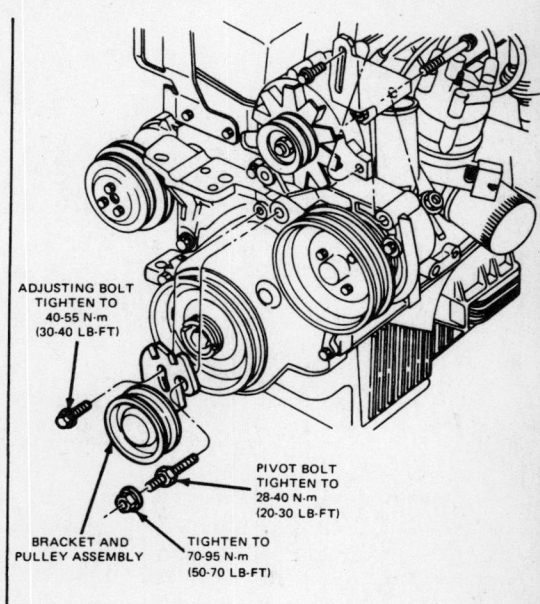

GENERAL INFORMATION AND MAINTENANCE

Belt tension adjustment — power steering etc.

1987–88 BELT ADJUSTMENT

All Except V-Ribbed Belts

1. Loosen the accessory adjustment and pivot belts.
2. On the 2.0L diesel engine, loosen the shake brace nut and bolt.
3. Using the proper pry tool, pry against the necessary accessory in order to gain the proper belt tension.
4. Tighten the adjustment bolts. Release the pressure on the pry bar. Tighten the pivot bolt.
5. Tighten the shake brace nut and bolt on the 2.0L diesel engine.
6. Check the belt tension and reset it if not up to specifications.

V-Ribbed Belts

2.0L ENGINE

1. Loosen the two idler pulley bracket bolts. Turn the adjusting bolt until the belt is adjusted to specifications.

NOTE: *Turning the wrench to the right tightens the belt adjustment and turning the wrench to the left loosens belt tension.*

2. Tighten the two idler pulley bracket bolts to specifications.
3. Check the belt tension and reset if not to specifications.

NOTE: *Belt tension on the 2.3L V-ribbed belt is maintained by an automatic tensioner and does not require adjustment. Movement of the automatic tensioner pulley is not a sign of a malfunctioning tensioner. The movement is required to maintain constant belt tension with cyclical engine and accessory loads. Use an 18 in. long 3/8 in. drive socket extension bar. Insert into the tension lift lug to remove and install the V-ribbed belt.*

1987–90 BELT ADJUSTMENT

V-Ribbed Belts

1.9L ENGINE

It is necessary to adjust the power steering belt prior to the air pump belt as follows:

1. From above the vehicle, loosen the pivot bolt and upper adjustment bolt.
2. From below the vehicle loosen the lower adjustment bolt and apply pressure with a 1/2 in. drive. Torque the lower bolts to 30–45 ft. lbs.
3. From above the vehicle, tighten the pivot bolt to 30–45 ft. lbs. and the upper adjustment bolts to 30–45 ft. lbs.
4. To adjust the alternator belt on the 1987–88 models, loosen the pivot bolt and upper adjustment bolt.
5. Using the proper pry tool, pry against the necessary accessory in order to gain the proper belt tension.
6. Tighten the pivot bolt to 15–22 ft. lbs. and the adjustment bolt to 24–34 ft. lbs. The alternator through bolts are torqued to 45–55 ft. lbs.
7. On the 1989–90 models adjust the alternator belt as follows:

   a. Install a 1/2 in. breaker bar or equivalent to the support bracket behind the alternator.

GENERAL INFORMATION AND MAINTENANCE

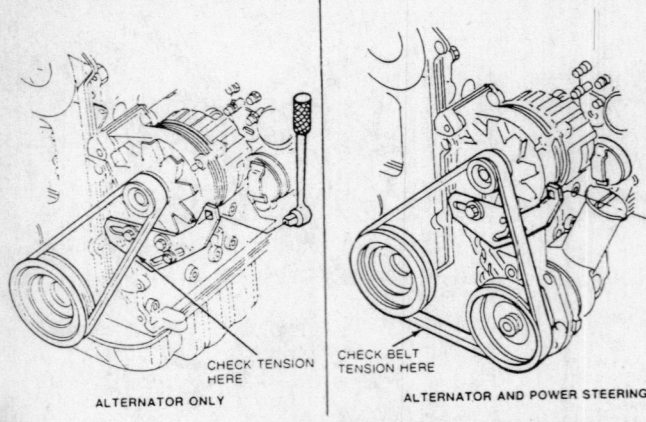

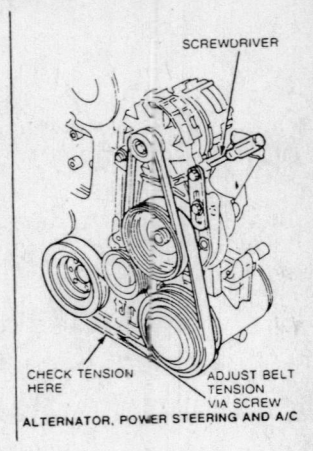

Drive belt set-ups for the 2.0L diesel engine

b. Apply tension to the belt using the breaker bar. Using a suitable belt tension gauge set the proper belt tension.

c. The tension should be 160 ± 20 lbs for a new belt and 130 ± 10 lbs. for a used belt.

d. Secure the alternator pivot bolt, leaving it loose enough to allow the alternator to move. While maintaining the proper belt tension, torque the alternator adjustment bolt to 30 ft. lbs. (40 Nm).

e. Remove the belt tension gauge and breaker bar and idle the engine for 5 minutes.

f. With the ignition switch in the **OFF** position, check the belt tension. If the tension is below 120 lbs., re-tension the belt with the tension gauge in place and tension being applied to the breaker bar so that the existing tension on the belt is not lost, slowly loosen the alternator adjustment bolt to allow belt tension to increase to used belt specifications and tighten the adjustment bolt.

g. Tighten the alternator pivot bolt to 50 ft. lbs. (68 Nm) and support bracket bolt to 35 ft. lbs. (47 Nm).

NOTE: *The power steering pump belt on the 1989–90 models is adjusted in the same manner as the alternator belt.*

Cogged V-Belts

1989–90 2.3L HSC ENGINE

When re-tensioning a loose belt, it is important that the belt is not allowed to relax and unseat while the belt is being re-tensioned.

1. Using a suitable adjustable 4 inch. C clamp or equivalent, apply tension to the belt. Place the bottom jaw of the pliers under the alternator adjustment boss and top jaw in the notch at the top of the alternator bracket.

2. Screw the **C** clamp in so as to squeeze the alternator and the bracket together.

3. Using a suitable belt tension gauge set the belt to the proper tension. Tension should be 160 lbs. for a new belt and 140 lbs. for a used belt.

4. Secure the alternator pivot bolt, leaving it loose enough to allow the alternator to move. While maintaining the proper belt tension, torque the alternator adjustment bolt to 26 ft. lbs. (35 Nm).

5. Remove the belt tension gauge and idle the engine for 5 minutes.

6. With the engine in the **OFF** position, check the belt tension. If the tension is below 120 lbs., re-tension the belt with the tension gauge in place and tension being applied to the C clamp so that the existing tension on the belt is not lost, slowly loosen the alternator adjustment bolt to allow belt tension to increase to used belt specifications and tighten the adjustment bolt.

7. Tighten the alternator pivot bolt to 52 ft. lbs. (70 Nm).

NOTE: *Belt tension on the 2.3L V-ribbed belt is maintained by an automatic tensioner and does not require adjustment. Movement of the automatic tensioner pulley is not a sign of a malfunctioning tensioner. The movement is required to maintain constant belt tension with cyclical engine and accessory loads. Use an 18 in. long $^{3}/_{8}$ in. drive socket extension bar. Insert into the tension lift lug to remove and install the V-ribbed belt.*

REPLACEMENT

1. Loosen the pivot bolt and/or the adjustment bolt.

2. Move the driven unit (power steering pump, air pump, etc.) toward or away from the engine to loosen the belt. Remove the belt.

3. Install the new bolt on the driven unit and either move toward or away from the engine to put tension on the belt.

4. Snug up the mounting and/or adjusting

GENERAL INFORMATION AND MAINTENANCE

HOW TO SPOT WORN V-BELTS

V-Belts are vital to efficient engine operation—they drive the fan, water pump and other accessories. They require little maintenance (occasional tightening) but they will not last forever. Slipping or failure of the V-belt will lead to overheating. If your V-belt looks like any of these, it should be replaced.

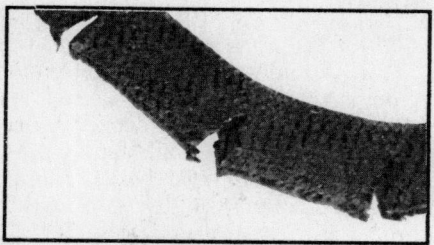

Cracking or weathering

This belt has deep cracks, which cause it to flex. Too much flexing leads to heat build-up and premature failure. These cracks can be caused by using the belt on a pulley that is too small. Notched belts are available for small diameter pulleys.

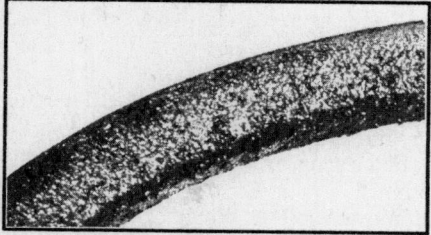

Softening (grease and oil)

Oil and grease on a belt can cause the belt's rubber compounds to soften and separate from the reinforcing cords that hold the belt together. The belt will first slip, then finally fail altogether.

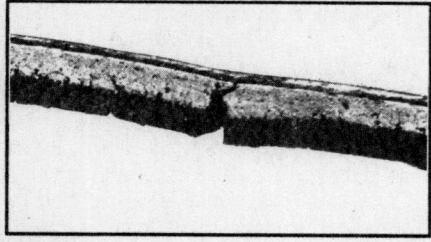

Glazing

Glazing is caused by a belt that is slipping. A slipping belt can cause a run-down battery, erratic power steering, overheating or poor accessory performance. The more the belt slips, the more glazing will be built up on the surface of the belt. The more the belt is glazed, the more it will slip. If the glazing is light, tighten the belt.

Worn cover

The cover of this belt is worn off and is peeling away. The reinforcing cords will begin to wear and the belt will shortly break. When the belt cover wears in spots or has a rough jagged appearance, check the pulley grooves for roughness.

Separation

This belt is on the verge of breaking and leaving you stranded. The layers of the belt are separating and the reinforcing cords are exposed. It's just a matter of time before it breaks completely.

GENERAL INFORMATION AND MAINTENANCE

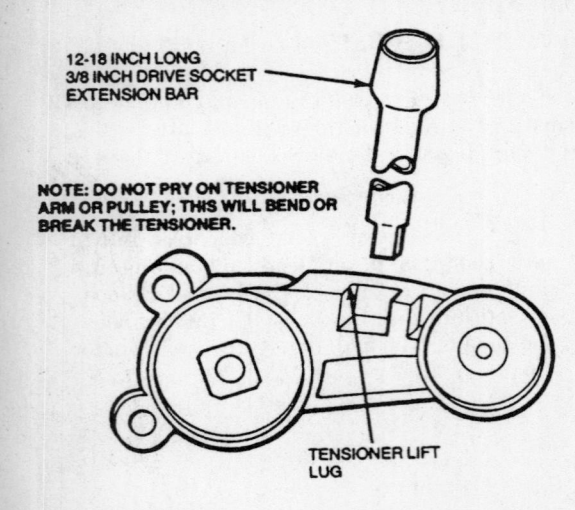

Typical belt tensioner — 2.3L engine

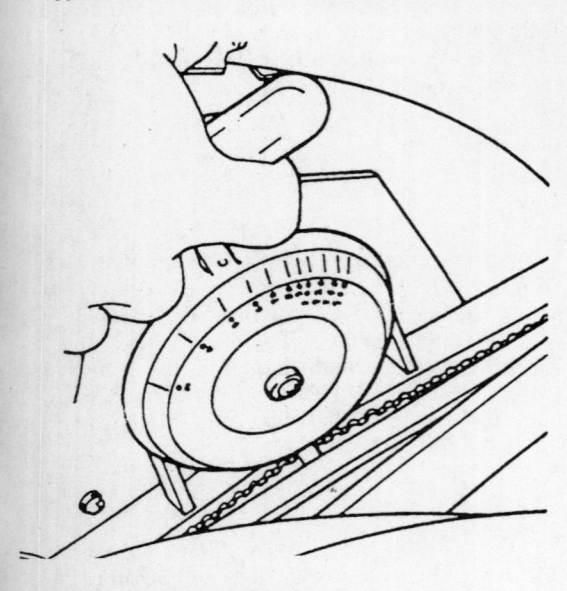

Typical belt tension tool

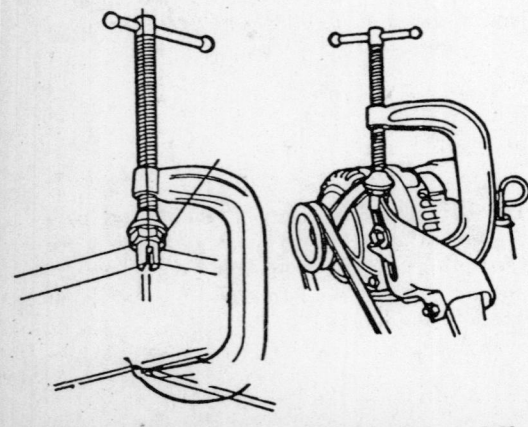

Using a C-clamp to adjust belt tension — 2.3L cogged V-belt

bolt to hold the driven unit, but do not completely tighten.

5. Use the procedure for the deflection method of belt adjustment.

CHILTON TIPS

1989 ESCORT

If your 1989 Escort is having problems with rattles, squeaks and squeals coming from the engine compartment, it may be caused by a loose accessory drive belt. New accessory drive belt specifications are now available.

Tighten the accessory drive belt to the new tightening specifications. Refer to the following procedure for service details.

Check to see if the accessory drive belt is loose. If it is loose, take the following action:

   a. Check the accessory drive belt for cracking and/or glazing. Determine if it should be replaced.

   b. Loosen the pivot bolt and/or the adjustment bolt.

   c. Install a 1/2 in. breaker bar or equivalent to the support bracket behind the alternator.

   d. Apply tension to the belt using the breaker bar. Using a suitable belt tension gauge set the proper belt tension.

   e. The tension should be 210 ± 10 lbs for a new belt with A/C and 180 ± 10 lbs fo a new belt without A/C. 160 ± 10 lbs. for a used belt with A/C and 130 ± 10 lbs old belt without A/C.

   f. Secure the alternator pivot bolt, leaving it loose enough to allow the alternator to move. While maintaining the proper belt tension, torque the alternator adjustment bolt to 30 ft. lbs. (40 Nm).

   g. Remove the belt tension gauge and breaker bar and idle the engine for 5 minutes.

   h. With the ignition switch in the **OFF** position, check the belt tension. If the tension is below 120 lbs., re-tension the belt with the tension gauge in place and tension being applied to the breaker bar so that the existing tension on the belt is not lost, slowly loosen the alternator adjustment bolt to allow belt tension to increase to used belt specifications and tighten the adjustment bolt.

   i. Tighten the alternator pivot bolt to 51 ft. lbs. (72 Nm), alternator attaching bolt to 51 ft. lbs. (72 Nm) and alternator brace arm to alternator 18 ft. lbs. (25 Nm).

Hoses

CAUTION: *The cooling fan motor is controlled by a temperature switch. The fan may come on when the engine is off. It will continue to run until the correct temperature is*

GENERAL INFORMATION AND MAINTENANCE

reached. Before working on or around the fan, disconnect the negative battery cable or the fan wiring connector.

HOSE REPLACEMENT

1. Open the hood and cover the fenders to protect them from scratches.
2. Disconnect the negative (ground) battery cable at the battery.
3. Place a suitable drain pan under the radiator and drain the cooling system. Place a small hose on the end of the radiator petcock, this will direct the coolant into the drain pan.
CAUTION: *When draining the coolant, keep in mind that cats and dogs are attracted by the ethylene glycol antifreeze, and are quite likely to drink any that is left in an uncovered container or in puddles on the ground. This will prove fatal in sufficient quantity. Always drain the coolant into a sealable container. Coolant should be reused unless it is contaminated or several years old.*
4. After the radiator has drained, position the drain pan under the lower hose. Loosen the lower hose clamps, disconnect the hose from the water pump inlet pipe and allow to drain. Disconnect the other end of the hose from the radiator and remove the hose.
5. Loosen the clamps retaining the upper hose, disconnect and remove the hose.
NOTE: *If only the upper hose is to be replaced, drain off enough coolant so the level is below the hose.*
6. If heater hoses need replacement, drain the coolant, loosen the clamps and remove the hose(s).
7. Installation of new hose(s) is in the reverse order of removal.
8. Be sure the petcock is closed. Fill the cooling system with the required protection mixture of water and permanent coolant/antifreeze. Connect the negative battery cable.
9. Run the engine until normal operating temperature is reached. Shut off the engine and check for coolant leaks. When the engine cools, recheck the coolant level in the radiator, or reservoir container.

Air Conditioning System

NOTE: *This book contains simple testing and charging procedures for your car's air conditioning system. More comprehensive testing, diagnosis and service procedures may be found in CHILTON'S GUIDE TO AIR CONDITIONING SERVICE AND REPAIR, book*

Air conditioning component layout

28 GENERAL INFORMATION AND MAINTENANCE

HOW TO SPOT BAD HOSES

Both the upper and lower radiator hoses are called upon to perform difficult jobs in an inhospitable environment. They are subject to nearly 18 psi at under hood temperatures often over 280°F., and must circulate nearly 7500 gallons of coolant an hour—3 good reasons to have good hoses.

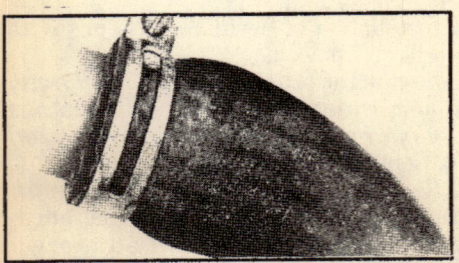

Swollen hose

A good test for any hose is to feel it for soft or spongy spots. Frequently these will appear as swollen areas of the hose. The most likely cause is oil soaking. This hose could burst at any time, when hot or under pressure.

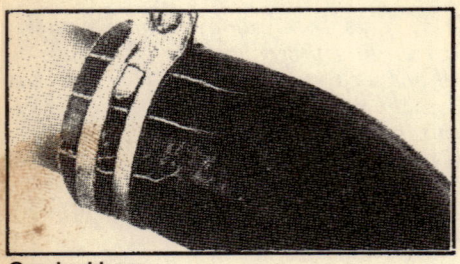

Cracked hose

Cracked hoses can usually be seen but feel the hoses to be sure they have not hardened; a prime cause of cracking. This hose has cracked down to the reinforcing cords and could split at any of the cracks.

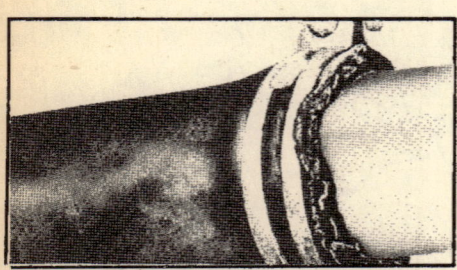

Frayed hose end (due to weak clamp)

Weakened clamps frequently are the cause of hose and cooling system failure. The connection between the pipe and hose has deteriorated enough to allow coolant to escape when the engine is hot.

Debris in cooling system

Debris, rust and scale in the cooling system can cause the inside of a hose to weaken. This can usually be felt on the outside of the hose as soft or thinner areas.

GENERAL INFORMATION AND MAINTENANCE

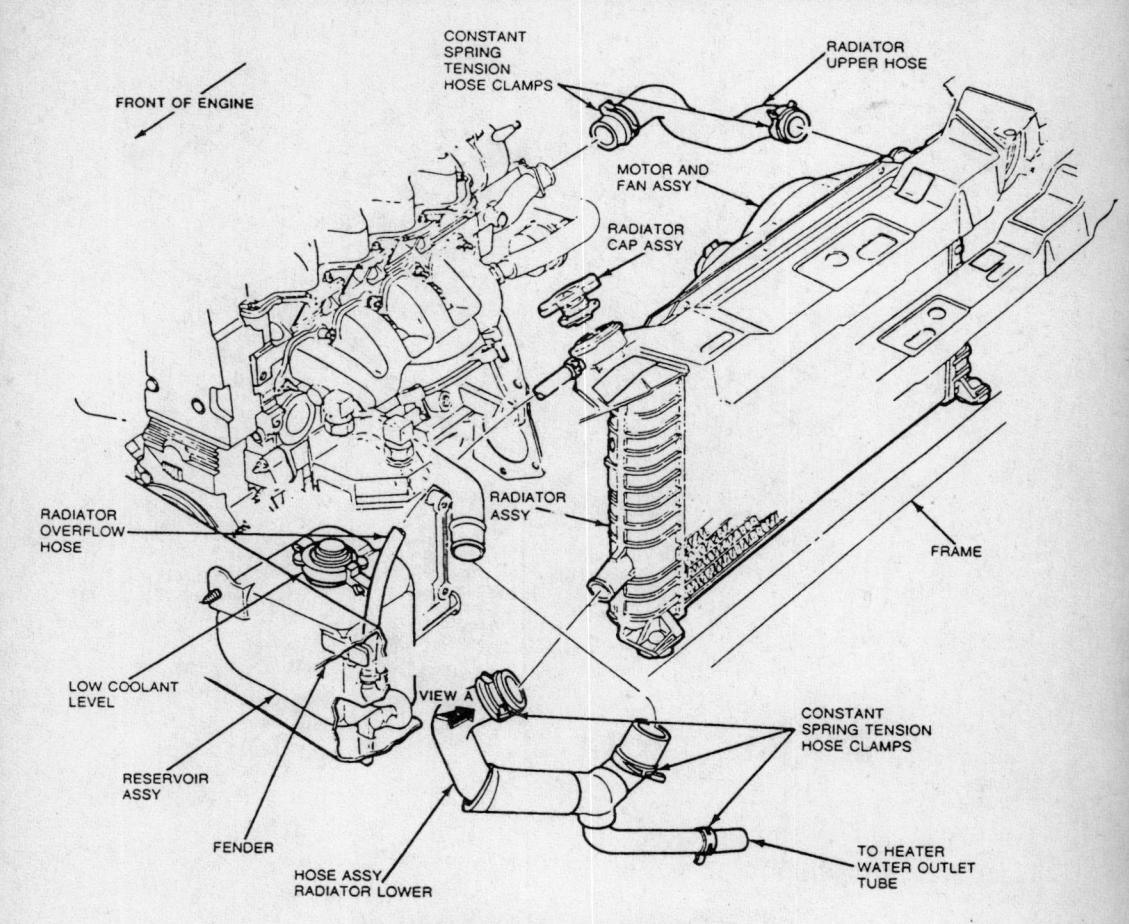

Exploded view of the 1.9L cooling system

part number 7580, available at your local retailer.

SAFETY PRECAUTIONS

There are two particular hazards associated with air conditioning systems and they both relate to the refrigerant gas.

First, the refrigerant gas is an extremely cold substance. When exposed to air, it will instantly freeze any surface it comes in contact with, including you eyes. The other hazard relates to fire. Although normally nontoxic, refrigerant gas becomes highly poisonous in the presence of an open flame. One good whiff of the vapor formed by burning refrigerant can be fatal. Keep all forms of fire (including cigarettes) well clear of the air conditioning system.

SAFETY INSPECTIONS

Checking For Oil Leaks

Refrigerant leaks show up as oily areas on the various components because the compressor oil is transported around the entire system along with the refrigerant. Look for only spots on all the hoses and lines, and especially on the hose and tubing connections. If there are oily deposits, the system may have a leak, and you should have it checked by a qualified repairman.

NOTE: *A small area of oil on the front of the compressor is normal and no cause for alarm.*

Keep The Condenser Clear

Periodically inspect the front of the condenser for bent fins or foreign material (dirt, bugs, leaves, etc.). If any cooling fins are bent, straighten them carefully with needle nosed pliers. You can remove any debris with a stiff bristle brush or hose.

Operate The Air Conditioning System Periodically

A lot of air conditioning problems can be avoided by simply running the air conditioner at least once a week, regardless of the season. Let the system run for at least 5 minutes a week (even in the winter), and you'll keep the

30   GENERAL INFORMATION AND MAINTENANCE

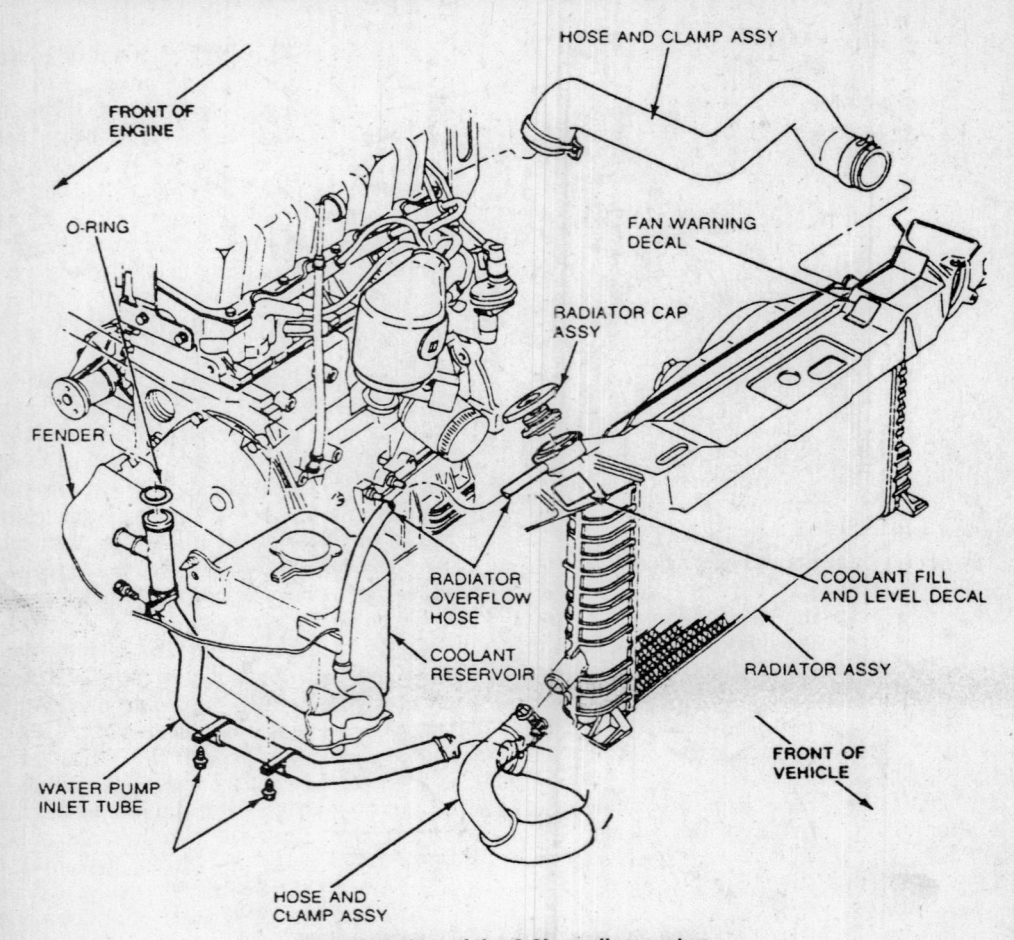

Exploded view of the 2.3L cooling system

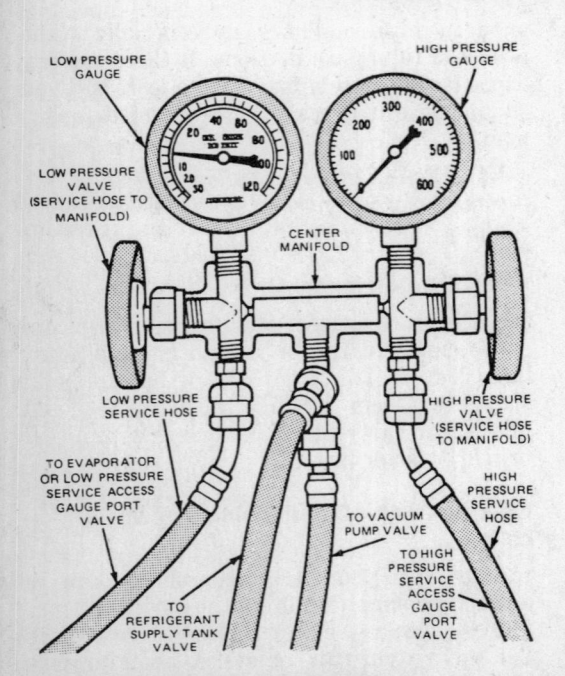

Air conditioning manifold gauge set

internal parts lubricated as well as preventing the hoses from hardening.

REFRIGERANT LEVEL CHECK

The only way to accurately check the refrigerant level to measure the system evaporator pressures with a manifold gauge set, although rapid on/off cycling of the compressor clutch indicates that the air conditioning system is low on refrigerant. The normal refrigerant capacity is 1981–87 41 oz. ± 1 oz. and for the 1988–90 models the capacity is 36 oz. ± 1 oz.

MANIFOLD TEST GAUGES

Most of the service work performed in air conditioning requires the use of a set of two gauges, one for the high (head) pressure side of the system, the other for the low (suction) side.

The low side gauge records both pressure and vacuum. Vacuum readings are calibrated from 0 to 30 in.Hg and the pressure graduations read from 0 to no less than 60 psi. The high side gauge measures pressure from 0 to at last 600 psi.

Both gauges are threaded into a manifold

GENERAL INFORMATION AND MAINTENANCE

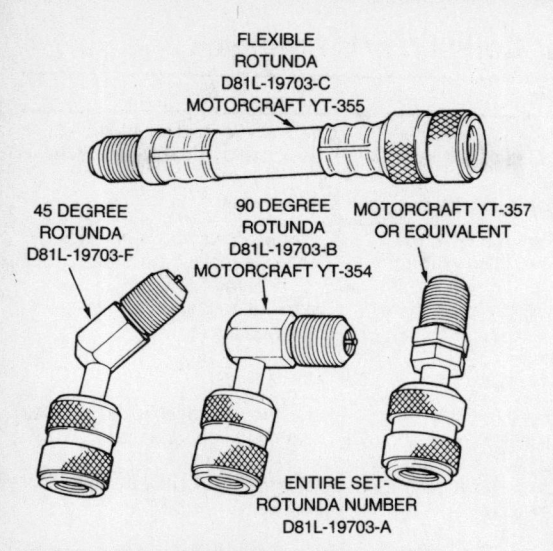

High pressure gauge port valve adapters

that contains two hand shut-off valves. Proper manipulation of these valves and the use of the attached test hoses allow the user to perform the following services:

1. Test high and low side pressures.
2. Remove air, moisture, and contaminated refrigerant.
3. Purge the system (of refrigerant).
4. Charge the system (with refrigerant).

The manifold valves are designed so that they have no direct effect on gauge readings, but serve only to provide for, or cut off, flow of refrigerant through the manifold. During all testing and hook-up operations, the valves are kept in a close position to avoid disturbing the refrigeration system. The valves are opened only to purge the system or refrigerant or to charge it.

MANIFOLD GAUGE SET ATTACHMENT

The following procedure is for the attachment of a manifold gauge set to the service gauge port valves. If charge station type of equipment is used, follow the equipment manufacturers instructions.

1. Turn both manifold gauge set valves fully clockwise to close the high and low pressure hoses at the gauge set refrigerant center outlet.

NOTE: *Rotunda high side adapter set D81L–19703–A or Motorcraft Tool YT–354 or 355 or equivalent is required to connect the manifold gauge set or a charging station to the high pressure service access gauge port valve.*

2. Remove the caps from the high and low pressure service gauge port valves.
3. If the manifold gauge set hoses do not have the valve depressing pins in them, install fitting adapters T71P–19703–S and R containing the pins on the manifold gauge hoses.
4. Connect the high and low pressure refrigerant hoses to their respective service ports, making sure they are hooked up correctly and fully seated. Tighten the fittings by hand and make sure they are not cross-threaded. Remember that an adapter is necessary to connect the manifold gauge hose to the high pressure fitting.

CHARGING THE SYSTEM

If the system has been completely purged of refrigerant, it must be evacuated before charging. A vacuum pump should be connected to the center hose of the manifold gauge set, both valves should be opened, and the vacuum pump operated until the low pressure gauge reads as close to 30 in.Hg as possible. If a part in the system has been replaced or excessive moisture is suspected, continue the vacuum pump operation for about 30 minutes.

Close the manifold gauge valves to the center hose, then disconnect the vacuum pump and connect the center hose to a charging cylinder, refrigerant drum or a small can refrigerant dispensing valve. Disconnect the wire harness from the clutch cycling pressure switch and install a jumper wire across the two terminals of the connector. Open the manifold gauge LOW side valve to allow refrigerant to enter the system, keeping the can(s) in an upright position to prevent liquid from entering the system.

When no more refrigerant is being drawn into the system, start the engine and move the function selector lever to the NORM A/C position and the blower switch to HI to draw the remaining refrigerant in. Continue to add refrigerant until the specified $3^{1}/_{2}$ lbs. is reached. Close the manifold gauge low pressure valve and the refrigerant supply valve. Remove the jumper wire from the clutch cycling pressure switch connector and reconnect the pressure switch. Disconnect the manifold gauge set and install the service port caps.

Charging From Small Containers

NOTE: *The refrigerant charge level of the air conditioning systems currently being used is critical to optimum performance. An undercharged or overcharged condition will adversely affect the air conditioning performance. Using small cans to charge these systems is not recommended because the charge level cannot be accurately controlled, a charging cylinder or a charging station is the only recommended method.*

When using a single can air conditioning charging kit, such as is available at local retailers, make the connection at the low pressure

GENERAL INFORMATION AND MAINTENANCE

Troubleshooting Basic Air Conditioning Problems

Problem	Cause	Solution
There's little or no air coming from the vents (and you're sure it's on)	• The A/C fuse is blown • Broken or loose wires or connections • The on/off switch is defective	• Check and/or replace fuse • Check and/or repair connections • Replace switch
The air coming from the vents is not cool enough	• Windows and air vent wings open • The compressor belt is slipping • Heater is on • Condenser is clogged with debris • Refrigerant has escaped through a leak in the system • Receiver/drier is plugged	• Close windows and vent wings • Tighten or replace compressor belt • Shut heater off • Clean the condenser • Check system • Service system
The air has an odor	• Vacuum system is disrupted • Odor producing substances on the evaporator case • Condensation has collected in the bottom of the evaporator housing	• Have the system checked/repaired • Clean the evaporator case • Clean the evaporator housing drains
System is noisy or vibrating	• Compressor belt or mountings loose • Air in the system	• Tighten or replace belt; tighten mounting bolts • Have the system serviced

Sight glass condition
  Constant bubbles, foam or oil streaks
  Clear sight glass, but no cold air
  Clear sight glass, but air is cold
  Clouded with milky fluid
	• Undercharged system
	
	• No refrigerant at all
	• System is OK
	• Receiver drier is leaking dessicant
		• Charge the system
		
		• Check and charge the system
		
		• Have system checked

Large difference in temperature of lines	• System undercharged	• Charge and leak test the system
Compressor noise	• Broken valves • Overcharged • Incorrect oil level • Piston slap • Broken rings • Drive belt pulley bolts are loose	• Replace the valve plate • Discharge, evacuate and install the correct charge • Isolate the compressor and check the oil level. Correct as necessary. • Replace the compressor • Replace the compressor • Tighten with the correct torque specification
Excessive vibration	• Incorrect belt tension • Clutch loose • Overcharged • Pulley is misaligned	• Adjust the belt tension • Tighten the clutch • Discharge, evacuate and install the correct charge • Align the pulley
Condensation dripping in the passenger compartment	• Drain hose plugged or improperly positioned • Insulation removed or improperly installed	• Clean the drain hose and check for proper installation • Replace the insulation on the expansion valve and hoses
Frozen evaporator coil	• Faulty thermostat • Thermostat capillary tube improperly installed • Thermostat not adjusted properly	• Replace the thermostat • Install the capillary tube correctly • Adjust the thermostat
Low side low—high side low	• System refrigerant is low • Expansion valve is restricted	• Evacuate, leak test and charge the system • Replace the expansion valve
Low side high—high side low	• Internal leak in the compressor—worn	• Remove the compressor cylinder head and inspect the compressor. Replace the valve plate assembly if necessary. If the compressor pistons, rings or

GENERAL INFORMATION AND MAINTENANCE

Troubleshooting Basic Air Conditioning Problems (cont.)

Problem	Cause	Solution
Low side high—high side low (cont.)		cylinders are excessively worn or scored replace the compressor
	• Cylinder head gasket is leaking	• Install a replacement cylinder head gasket
	• Expansion valve is defective	• Replace the expansion valve
	• Drive belt slipping	• Adjust the belt tension
Low side high—high side high	• Condenser fins obstructed	• Clean the condenser fins
	• Air in the system	• Evacuate, leak test and charge the system
	• Expansion valve is defective	• Replace the expansion valve
	• Loose or worn fan belts	• Adjust or replace the belts as necessary
Low side low—high side high	• Expansion valve is defective	• Replace the expansion valve
	• Restriction in the refrigerant hose	• Check the hose for kinks—replace if necessary
	• Restriction in the receiver/drier	• Replace the receiver/drier
	• Restriction in the condenser	• Replace the condenser
Low side and high side normal (inadequate cooling)	• Air in the system	• Evacuate, leak test and charge the system
	• Moisture in the system	• Evacuate, leak test and charge the system

service port, located on the accumulator/drier. This is very important as connecting the small can to the high pressure port will cause the can to explode. If a manifold gauge set is being used, the low pressure valve must be closed whenever another can is being connected to the center hose. Hold the cans upright to prevent liquid refrigerant from entering the system and possibly damaging the compressor.

1. A special refrigerant dispensing valve and valve retainer such as Motorcraft YT-280 or equivalent is required for connecting the small can to the air conditioning system. Use only a safety type refrigerant dispensing valve and follow the manufacturer's instructions when attaching the valve to the refrigerant container.

2. Connect the manifold gauge set to the system. Connect the hose (normally connected to the large refrigerant tank) to the special valve on the small can adapter. Make sure that the valve is closed (full clockwise position).

3. Once the can is connected, charge the system as outlined earlier. When the can is empty, close the valve and remove the empty can. Connect a new can, open the valve again and continue charging until the specified weight of R-12 refrigerant has entered the system.

NOTE: *Be sure to note the capacity of the refrigerant cans. If they contain less than 16 ounces of refrigerant, compensation for weight less than 16 ounces must be made for each can of refrigerant used. For example, when 8 ounces of refrigerant is needed such as with a $2^1/_2$ pound charge capacity and 14 ounce cans of refrigerant are used, all but 2 ounces of the third 14 ounce can of refrigerant should be installed in the system. Weigh the can to make sure the correct amount of refrigerant is installed.*

Windshield Wipers

BLADE AND ARM REPLACEMENT

1. Cycle the wiper arm and blade assembly and stop at a position on the windshield where removal can be accomplished without difficulty.

2. To remove the blade: Pull the wiper arm out and away from the windshield. Grasp the wiper blade assembly and pull away from the mounting pin of the wiper arm (Trico® type). Or pull back on the spring lock, where the arm is connected to the blade, and pull the wiper blade assembly from the wiper arm (Tridon® type).

3. To remove the wiper arm: Pull the bade and arm assembly away from the windshield. Move the slide latch (located at base of wiper arm) away from the arm mounting pivot shaft. The arm is now unlocked. Lift the arm up and away from the pivot shaft.

4. Installation is in the reverse order of removal.

34 GENERAL INFORMATION AND MAINTENANCE

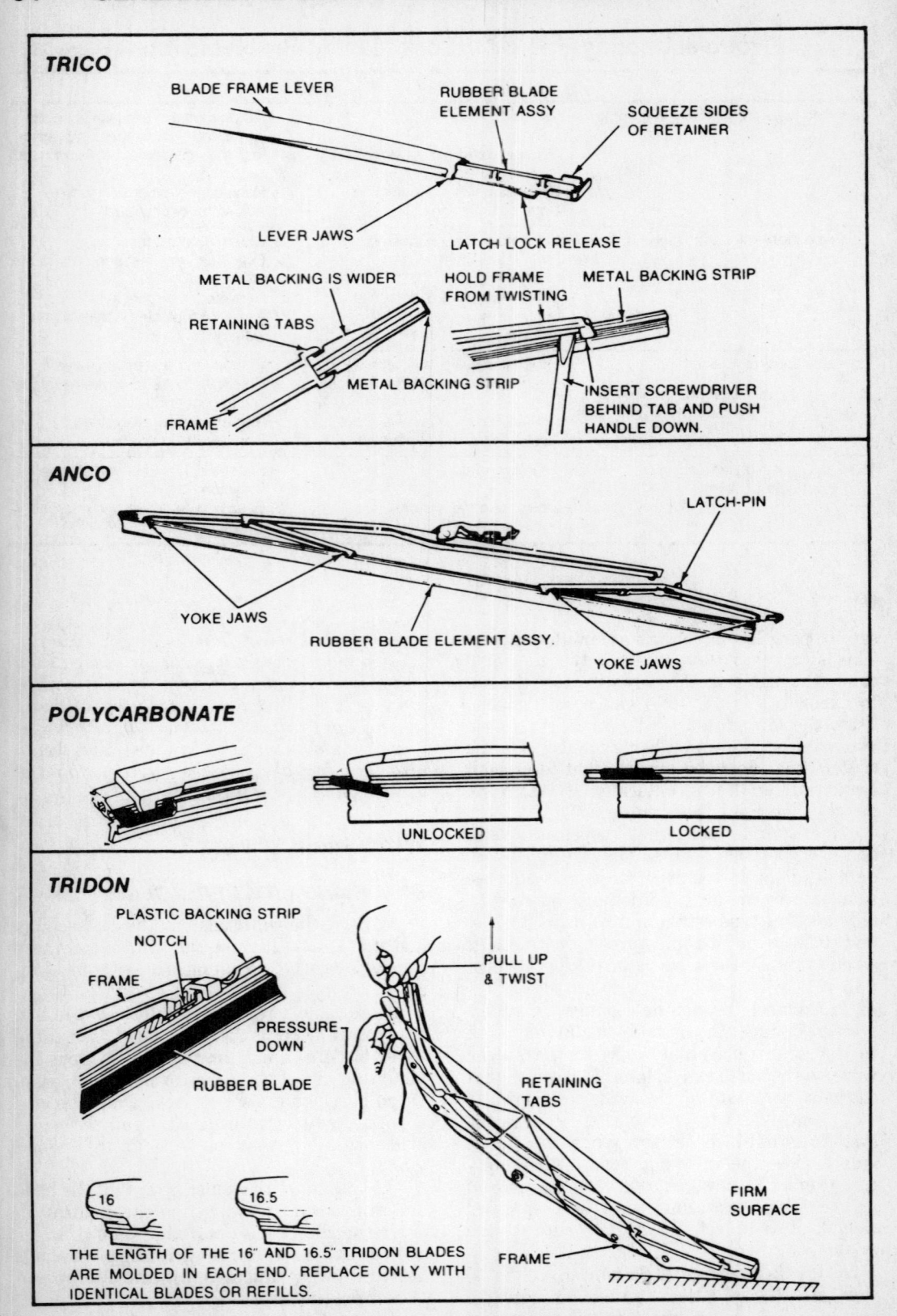

TRICO

ANCO

POLYCARBONATE

TRIDON

Wiper insert replacement

GENERAL INFORMATION AND MAINTENANCE

Tires and Wheels

TIRE ROTATION

NOTE: *Ford does not recommend tire rotation. They suggest that tires be replaced in pairs as needed without rotation.*

Tire wear can be equalized by switching the position of the tires about every 6,000 miles. Including a conventional spare in the rotation pattern can give up to 20% more tire life.

CAUTION: *Do not include the new Space-Saver® of temporary spare tires in the rotation pattern.*

There are certain exceptions to tire rotation, however. Studded snow tires should not be rotated, and radials should be kept on the same side of the car (maintain the same direction of rotation). The belts on radial tires get set in a pattern. If the direction of rotation is reversed, it can cause rough ride and vibration.

NOTE: *When radials or studded snows are taken off the car, mark them, so you can maintain the same direction of rotation.*

TIRE DESIGN

For maximum satisfaction, tires should be used in sets of five. Mixing or different types (radial, bias/belted, fiberglass belted) should be avoided. Conventional bias tires are constructed so that the cords run bead-to-bead at an angle. Alternate plies run at an opposite angle. This type of construction gives rigidity to both tread and sidewall. Bias/belted tires are similar in construction to conventional bias ply tires. Belts run at an angle and also at a 90° angle to the bead, as in the radial tire. Tread life is improved considerably over the conventional bias tire. The radial tire differs in construction, but instead of the carcass plies running at an angle of 90° to each other, they run at an angle of 90° to the bead. This gives the tread a great deal of rigidity and the sidewall a great deal of flexibility and accounts for the characteristic bulge associated with radial tires.

Remember that the tire sizes and wheel diameters should be selected to maintain ground clearance and tire load capacity equivalent to the minimum specified tire. Radial tires should always be used in sets of five, but in an emergency radial tires can be used with caution on the rear axle only. If this is done, both tires on the rear should be of radial design.

When buying new tires, give some thought to the following points, especially if you are considering a switch to larger tires or a different profile series;

1. All 4 tires must be of the same construction type. This rule should not be violated, radial, bias and bias belted tires should not be mixed.

2. The wheels should be the correct width for the tire. The tire dealers have charts of tire and rim compatibility. A mis-match will cause sloppy handling and rapid tire wear. The tread width should match the rim width (inside bead to inside bead) within an inch. For radial tires, the rim should be 80% or less of the tire (not tread) width.

3. The height (mounted diameter) of the new tires can change the speedometer accuracy, engine speed at a given road speed, fuel mileage, acceleration and ground clearance. Tire manufacturers furnish full measurement specifications.

4. The spare tire should be usable, at least for short distance and low speed operations, with new tires.

5. There should not be any body interference when loaded, on bumps or in turns.

TIRE INFLATION PRESSURE

Tire inflation is the most ignored item of auto maintenance. Gasoline mileage can drop as much as 0.8% for every 1 pound per square inch (psi) of under inflation.

Two items should be a permanent fixture in every glove compartment: a tire pressure gauge and a tread depth gauge. Check the tire air pressure (including the spare) regularly with a pocket type gauge. Kicking the tires won't tell you a thing, and the gauge on the service station air hose is notoriously inaccurate.

The tire pressures recommended for you car are usually found on a label attached to the door pillar or on the glove box inner cover or in the owner's manual. Ideally, inflation pressure should be checked when the tires are cool. When the air becomes heated it expands and the pressure increases. Every 10° rise (or drop) in temperature means a difference of 1 psi, which also explains why the tire appears to lose air on a very cold night. When it is impossible to check the ties cold, allow for pressure build-up due to heat. If the hot pressure exceeds the cold pressure by more than 15 psi, reduce you speed, lead or both. Otherwise internal heat is created in the tire. When the heat approaches the temperature at which the tire was cured, during manufacture, the tread can separate from the body.

CAUTION: *Never counteract excessive pressure build-up by bleeding off air pressure (letting some air out). This will only further raise the tire operating temperature.*

Before starting a long trip with lots of luggage, you can add about 2–4 psi to the tires to make them run cooler, but never exceed the maximum inflation pressure on the side of the tire.

36 GENERAL INFORMATION AND MAINTENANCE

TREAD DEPTH

All tires made since 1968 have 8 built-in tread wear indicator bars that show up as $1/2$ in. (12.7mm) wide smooth bands across the tire when $1/16$ in. (1.5mm) of tread remains. The appearance of tread wear indicators means that the tires should be replaced. In fact, many states have laws prohibiting the use of tires with less than $1/16$ in. (1.5mm) of tread remains. The appearance of tread wear indicators means that the tires should be replace. In fact, many states have laws prohibiting the use of tires with less than $1/16$ in. (1.5mm) tread.

You can check you own tread depth with an inexpensive gauge or by using a Lincoln head penny. Slip the Lincoln penny into several tread grooves. If you can see the top of Lincoln's head in 2 adjacent grooves, the tires have less than $1/16$ in. (1.5mm) tread left and should be replaced. You can measure snow ties in the same manner by using the tails side of the Lincoln penny. If you see the top of the Lincoln memorial, it's time to replace the snow tires.

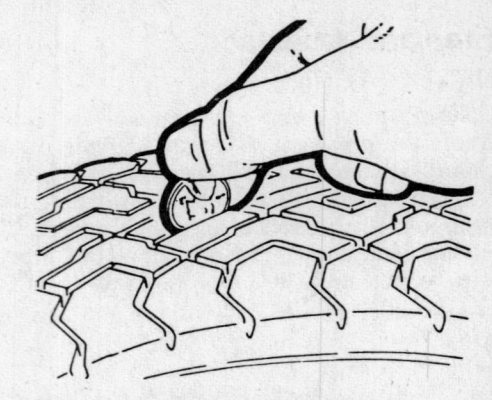

A penny used to determine tread depth

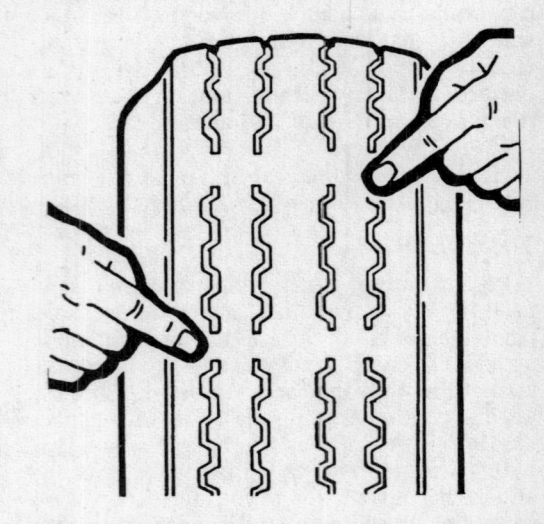

TIRE STORAGE

Store the tires at proper inflation pressures if they are mounted on wheels. All tires should be kept in a cool, dry place. If they are stored in the garage or basement, do not let them stand on a concrete floor; set them on strips of wood.

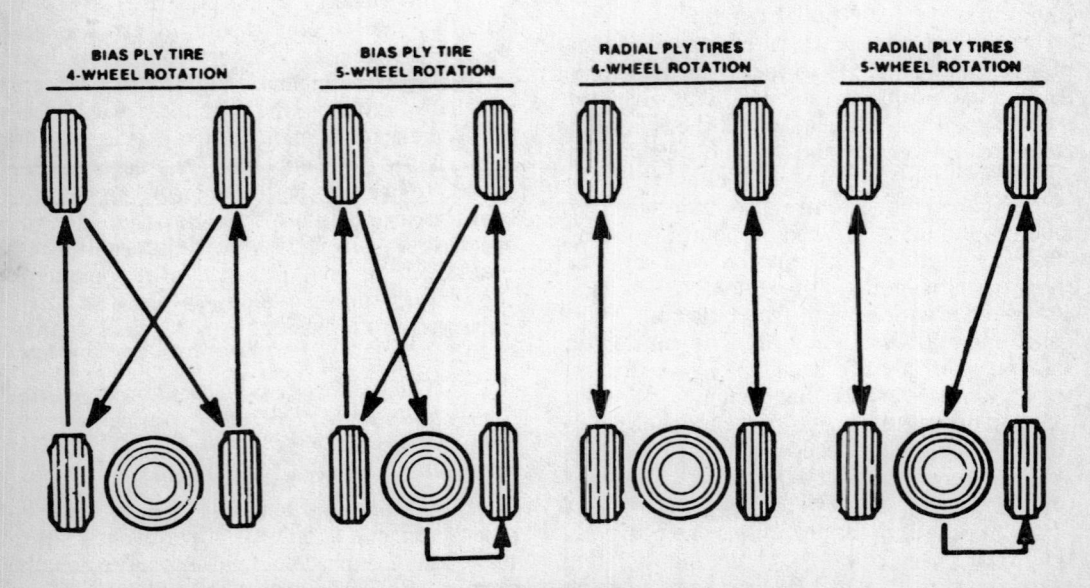

Replace a tire that shows the built-in "bump strip"

BIAS PLY TIRE 4-WHEEL ROTATION

BIAS PLY TIRE 5-WHEEL ROTATION

RADIAL PLY TIRES 4-WHEEL ROTATION

RADIAL PLY TIRES 5-WHEEL ROTATION

Tire rotation patterns

GENERAL INFORMATION AND MAINTENANCE

CARE OF SPECIAL WHEELS

To clean aluminum wheels, wheel covers and wheel ornamentation, use a mild soap and water solution and rinse thoroughly with clean water. Do not use steel woo, abrasive type cleaner or a strong detergents containing high alkaline or caustic agents to the protective coating and discoloration may be a result. Automatic car wash tire brushes may damage aluminum and styled road wheel protective coatings. Before using such a service, be sure abrasive type brushes are not being used.

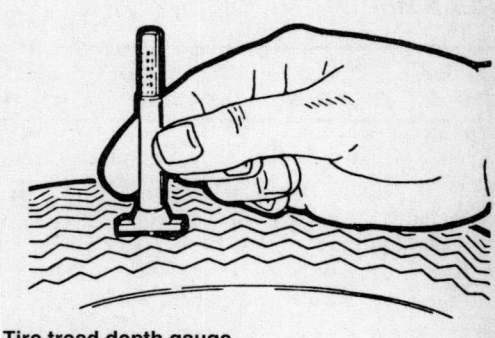

Tire tread depth gauge

Troubleshooting Basic Wheel Problems

Problem	Cause	Solution
The car's front end vibrates at high speed	• The wheels are out of balance • Wheels are out of alignment	• Have wheels balanced • Have wheel alignment checked/adjusted
Car pulls to either side	• Wheels are out of alignment • Unequal tire pressure • Different size tires or wheels	• Have wheel alignment checked/adjusted • Check/adjust tire pressure • Change tires or wheels to same size
The car's wheel(s) wobbles	• Loose wheel lug nuts • Wheels out of balance • Damaged wheel • Wheels are out of alignment • Worn or damaged ball joint • Excessive play in the steering linkage (usually due to worn parts) • Defective shock absorber	• Tighten wheel lug nuts • Have tires balanced • Raise car and spin the wheel. If the wheel is bent, it should be replaced • Have wheel alignment checked/adjusted • Check ball joints • Check steering linkage • Check shock absorbers
Tires wear unevenly or prematurely	• Incorrect wheel size • Wheels are out of balance • Wheels are out of alignment	• Check if wheel and tire size are compatible • Have wheels balanced • Have wheel alignment checked/adjusted

Troubleshooting Basic Tire Problems

Problem	Cause	Solution
The car's front end vibrates at high speeds and the steering wheel shakes	• Wheels out of balance • Front end needs aligning	• Have wheels balanced • Have front end alignment checked
The car pulls to one side while cruising	• Unequal tire pressure (car will usually pull to the low side) • Mismatched tires • Front end needs aligning	• Check/adjust tire pressure • Be sure tires are of the same type and size • Have front end alignment checked
Abnormal, excessive or uneven tire wear See "How to Read Tire Wear"	• Infrequent tire rotation • Improper tire pressure • Sudden stops/starts or high speed on curves	• Rotate tires more frequently to equalize wear • Check/adjust pressure • Correct driving habits
Tire squeals	• Improper tire pressure • Front end needs aligning	• Check/adjust tire pressure • Have front end alignment checked

GENERAL INFORMATION AND MAINTENANCE

Tire Size Comparison Chart

"Letter" sizes			Inch Sizes	Metric-inch Sizes		
"60 Series"	"70 Series"	"78 Series"	1965–77	"60 Series"	"70 Series"	"80 Series"
		Y78-12	5.50-12, 5.60-12 6.00-12	165/60-12	165/70-12	155-12
		W78-13 Y78-13	5.20-13 5.60-13 6.15-13	165/60-13 175/60-13 185/60-13	145/70-13 155/70-13 165/70-13	135-13 145-13 155-13, P155/80-13
A60-13 B60-13	A70-13 B70-13	A78-13 B78-13	6.40-13 6.70-13 6.90-13	195/60-13 205/60-13	175/70-13 185/70-13	165-13 175-13
C60-13 D60-13 E60-13	C70-13 D70-13 E70-13	C78-13 D78-13 E78-13	7.00-13 7.25-13 7.75-13	215/60-13	195/70-13	185-13 195-13
			5.20-14 5.60-14 5.90-14	165/60-14 175/60-14	145/70-14 155/70-14	135-14 145-14
A60-14	A70-14 B70-14 C70-14	A78-14 B78-14 C78-14	6.15-14 6.45-14 6.95-14	185/60-14 195/60-14 205/60-14	165/70-14 175/70-14 185/70-14	155-14 165-14 175-14
D60-14 E60-14 F60-14 G60-14 H60-14 J60-14 L60-14	D70-14 E70-14 F70-14 G70-14 H70-14 J70-14 L70-14	D78-14 E78-14 F78-14, F83-14 G77-14, G78-14 H78-14 J78-14	7.35-14 7.75-14 8.25-14 8.55-14 8.85-14 9.15-14	215/60-14 225/60-14 235/60-14 245/60-14 255/60-14 265/60-14	195/70-14 200/70-14 205/70-14 215/70-14 225/70-14 235/70-14	185-14 195-14 205-14 215-14 225-14
	A70-15	A78-15	5.60-15	185/60-15	165/70-15	155-15
B60-15 C60-15	B70-15 C70-15 D70-15	B78-15 C78-15 D78-15	6.35-15 6.85-15	195/60-15 205/60-15	175/70-15 185/70-15	165-15 175-15
E60-15 F60-15 G60-15 H60-15 J60-15	E70-15 F70-15 G70-15 H70-15 J70-15 K70-15	E78-15 F78-15 G78-15 H78-15 J78-15	7.35-15 7.75-15 8.15-15/8.25-15 8.45-15/8.55-15 8.85-15/8.90-15 9.00-15	215/60-15 225/60-15 235/60-15 245/60-15 255/60-15 265/60-15	195/70-15 205/70-15 215/70-15 225/70-15 235/70-15 245/70-15	185-15 195-15 205-15 215-15 225-15 230-15
L60-15	L70-15 M70-15	L78-15, L84-15 M78-15 N78-15	9.15-15			235-15 255-15

Note: Every size tire is not listed and many size comparisons are approximate, based on load ratings. Wider tires than those supplied new with the vehicle, should always be checked for clearance.

FLUIDS AND LUBRICANTS

Fuel And Engine Recommendations

Gasoline Engine

Unleaded gasoline having a Research Octane Number (RON) of 91, or an Antiknock Index of 87 is recommended for your car. Leaded gasoline will quickly interfere with the operation of the catalytic converter and just a few tankfuls of leaded gasoline will render the converter useless. This will cause the emission of much greater amounts of hydrocarbons and carbon

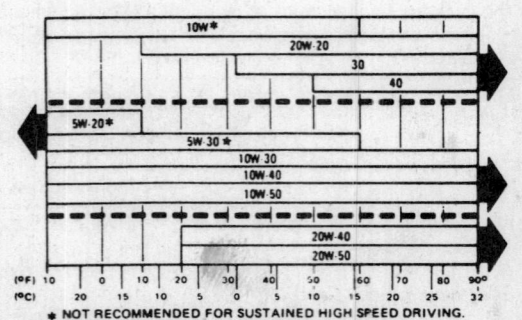

★ NOT RECOMMENDED FOR SUSTAINED HIGH SPEED DRIVING.
✱ 5W-30 RECOMMENDED WHEN TEMPERATURES ARE +10°F. (−12.2°C.) OR BELOW TO FACILITATE COLD CRANKING.

Engine oil viscosity recommendation — 1981–83

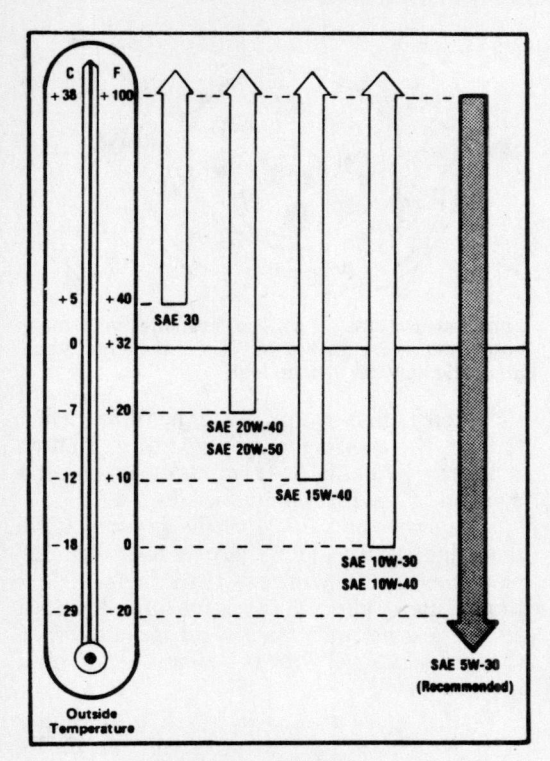

GENERAL INFORMATION AND MAINTENANCE

Engine oil viscosity recommendation — 1984 and later

monoxide from the exhaust system, void you warranty and cost a considerable amount of money for converter replacement.

Using a high quality unleaded gasoline will help maintain the driveability, fuel economy and emissions performance of your vehicle. A properly formulated gasoline will be comprised of well refined hydrocarbons and chemical additives and will perform the following.

- Minimize varnish, lacquer and other induction system deposits.
- Prevent gum formation or other deterioration.
- Protect the fuel tank and other fuel system components from corrosion or degradation.
- Provide the correct seasonally and geographically adjusted volatility. This will provide easy starting in the winter and avoid vapor lock in the summer. Avoid fuel system icing.

In addition, the fuel will be free of water debris and other impurities. Some driveability deterioration on multi-port electronically fuel injected vehicles can be traced to continuous use of certain gasolines which may have insufficient amounts of detergent additives to provide adequate deposit control protection.

Diesel Engine

The 2.0L diesel engine is designed to use number 2-D diesel fuel. Use of number 1-D diesel fuel in temperatures +20°F (–7°C) is acceptable, but not necessary.

Do not use number 1-D diesel fuel in temperatures above +20°F (–7°C) as damage to the engine may result. Also fuel economy will be reduced with the use of number 1-D diesel fuel.

The 2.0L diesel engines are equipped with an electric fuel heater to prevent cold fuel problems. For best results in cold weather use winterized number 2-D diesel fuel which is blended to minimize cold weather operation problems.

CAUTION: *DO NOT add gasoline, gasohol, alcohol or cetane improvers to the diesel fuel. Also, DO NOT use fluids such as ether (starting fluid) in the diesel air intake system. The use of these liquids or fluids will cause damage to the engine and/or fuel system.*

OIL RECOMMENDATIONS

Oil meeting API classification SG or SG/CC or SG/CD is recommended for use in your vehicle. Viscosity grades 10W-30 or 10W-40 are recommended on models before 1984 and 5W-30 on models 1984 and later. See the viscosity to temperature chart in this section.

NOTE: *If your vehicle is equipped with a diesel engine, be sure to check your owner's manual for the recommended oil viscosity to be used. There should be a diesel engine supplement included with your owner's manual.*

OIL LEVEL CHECK

It is a good idea to check the engine oil each time or at least every other time you fill your gas tank.

1. Be sure your car is on level ground. Shut off the engine and wait for a few minutes to allow the oil to drain back into the oil pan.
2. Remove the engine oil dipstick and wipe clean with a rag.
3. Reinsert the dipstick and push it down until it is fully seated in the tube.
4. Remove the stick and check the oil level shown. If the oil level is below the lower mark, add one quart.
5. If you wish, you may carefully fill the oil pan to the upper mark on the dipstick with less than a full quart. Do not, however, add a full quart when it would overfill the crankcase (level above the upper mark on the dipstick). The excess oil will generally be consumed at an excessive rate even if no damage to the engine seals occurs.

CHANGING OIL AND FILTER

The manufacturer recommends changing the engine oil and oil filter every 6 months or 7,500 miles. However, it is recommended that the engine oil and oil filter be changed every 3 months or 3,000 miles. The engine oil and oil

GENERAL INFORMATION AND MAINTENANCE

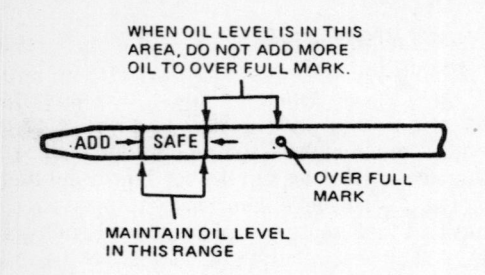

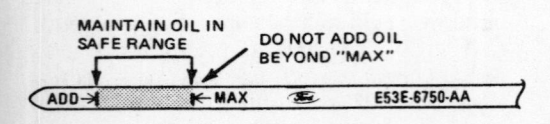

Engine oil level check recommendations

filter can be changed at 2000 or 2 month intervals if the driving conditions for your vehicle is done through severe dust and dirty conditions. Following these recommended intervals will help keep you car engine in good condition.

1. Make sure the engine is at normal operating temperature (this promotes complete draining of the old oil).

CAUTION: *The EPA warns that prolonged contact with used engine oil may cause a number of skin disorders, including cancer! You should make every effort to minimize your exposure to used engine oil. Protective gloves should be worn when changing the oil. Wash your hands and any other exposed skin areas as soon as possible after exposure to used engine oil. Soap and water, or waterless hand cleaner should be used.*

2. Apply the parking brake and block the wheels or raise and support the car evenly on jackstands.

3. Place a drain pan of about a gallon and a half capacity under the engine oil pan drain plug. Use the proper size wrench, loosen and remove the plug. Allow all the old oil to drain. Wipe the pan and the drain plug with a clean rag. Inspect the drain plug gasket, replace if necessary.

4. Reinstall and tighten the drain plug. DO NOT OVERTIGHTEN!

5. Move the drain pan under the engine oil filter. Use a strap wrench and loosen the oil filter (do not remove), allow the oil to drain. Unscrew the filter the rest of the way by hand. Use a rag, if necessary, to keep from burning your fingers. When the filter comes loose from the engine, turn the mounting base upward to avoid spilling the remaining oil.

6. Wipe the engine filter mount clean with a rag. Coat the rubber gasket on the new oil filter with clean engine oil, applying it with a finger. Carefully start the filter onto the

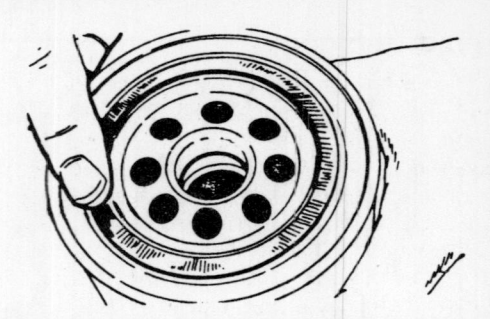

Lubricate the gasket on the new filter with clean engine oil. A dry gasket may not make a good seal and will allow the filter to leak

threaded engine mount. Turn the filter until it touches the engine mounting surface. Tighten the filter, by hand, $1/2$ turn more or as recommended by the filter manufacturer.

7. Lower the vehicle to the ground. Refill the crankcase with four quarts of engine oil. Replace the filler cap and start the engine. Allow the engine to idle and check for oil leaks. Shut off the engine, wait for several minutes, then check the oil level with the dipstick. Add oil if necessary.

NOTE: *Store the used oil in a container made for that purpose until you can find a service station or garage that accepts used oil for recycling.*

Manual Transaxle

FLUID RECOMMENDATIONS

If the oil is low, add Dexron®II automatic fluid. Manual transmission type GL is NOT to be used.

FLUID LEVEL CHECK

Each time the engine oil is changed, the fluid level of the transaxle should be checked. The car must be resting on level ground or supported on jackstands (front and back) evenly. To check the fluid, remove the filler plug, located on the upper front (driver's side) of the transaxle with a $9/16$ in. wrench or a $3/8$ inch extension and ratchet.

CAUTION: *The filler plug has a hex-head or it has a flat surface with a cut-in $3/8$ in. square box. Do not mistake any other bolts for the filler. Damage to the transaxle could occur if the wrong plug is removed.*

The oil level should be even with the edge of the filler hole or within $1/4$ in. (6mm) of the hole. If the oil is low, add Dexron®II automatic fluid. Manual transmission type GL is NOT to be used.

NOTE: *A rubber bulb syringe, such as a turkey baster, will be helpful in adding the Dexron®II fluid to the manual transaxle.*

GENERAL INFORMATION AND MAINTENANCE

DRAIN AND REFILL

Changing the fluid in a manual transaxle is not necessary under normal operating conditions. However, the fluid levels should by checked at normal intervals. The only two ways to drain the oil from the transaxle is by removing it and then turning the transaxle on its side to drain or by using a suction pump and a tube, then use the pump to suck the transaxle oil out. Then when refilling the transaxle, the oil level should be even with the edge of the filler hole or within 1/4 inch. (6mm) of the hole. Use Dexron®II automatic fluid. Manual transmission type GL is NOT to be used.

Automatic Transaxle

LEVEL CHECK

A dipstick is provided in the engine compartment to check the level of the automatic transaxle. Be sure the car is on level ground and that the car's engine and transmission have reached normal operating temperatures. Start the engine, put the parking brake on the transmission selector lever in the PARK position. Move the selector lever through all the positions and return to the PARK position. DO NOT TURN OFF THE ENGINE DURING THE FLUID LEVEL CHECK. Clean all dirt from the dipstick cap before removing the dipstick. Remove the dipstick and wipe clean. Reinsert the dipstick making sure it is fully seated. Pull the dipstick out of the tube and check the fluid level. The fluid level should be between the FULL and ADD marks.

If necessary, add enough fluid through the dipstick tube/filler to bring the level to the FULL mark on the dipstick. Use only Dexron®II fluid.

WARNING: *Do not overfill. Make sure the dipstick is fully seated.*

SAME OIL FILL AT 150°F (65.6°C)

OIL LEVEL AT 90°F (32.2°C)

TYPICAL FLUID LEVEL EXPANSION WITH RISE FROM ROOM TO OPERATING TEMPERATURE

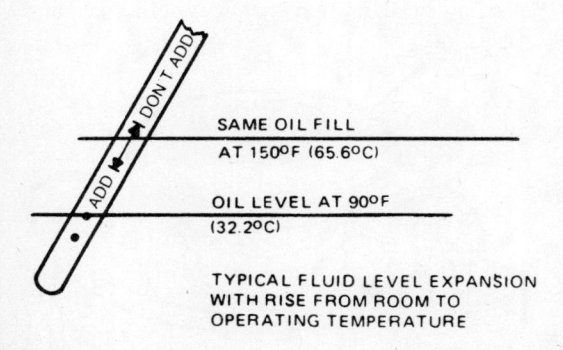

Dipstick markings showing typical fluid expansion from "room" to normal operating temperature

DRAIN AND REFILL

When your vehicle is equipped with an automatic transaxle and the region in which you live has severe cold weather, a multi-viscosity automatic transaxle fluid should be used. Ask your auto parts retailer about the availability of MV Automatic Transaxle Fluid.

If you operate you car in very dusty conditions, tow a trailer, have extended idling or low speed operation, it may be necessary to change the ATX fluid at regular intervals (20 months, 20,000 miles or more often). A description of the fluid change procedure may be found in Chapter 7.

Use of fluid other than specified could result in transaxle malfunctions and/or failure.

1. Raise the car and safely support it on jackstands.
2. Place a suitable drain pan underneath the transaxle oil pan. Loosen the oil pan mounting bolts and allow the fluid to drain until it reaches the level of the pan flange. Remove the attaching bolts, leaving one end attached so that the pan will tip and the rest of the fluid will drain.
3. Remove the oil pan. Thoroughly clean the pan. Remove the old gasket. Make sure that the gasket mounting surfaces are clean.
4. Remove the transmission filter screen retaining bolt. Remove the screen.
5. Install a new filter screen and O-ring. Place a new gasket on the pan and install the pan to the transmission.
6. Fill the transmission to the correct level. Remove the jackstands and lower the car to the ground.

Transfer Case

Changing the fluid in a transfer case is not necessary under normal operating conditions. The only way to drain the fluid from the transfer case is during the transfer case disassembly procedure. When reassembling the transfer case, add 1.5 oz. of EST–M2C118–A friction modifier for a complete refill of the transfer case and rear axle.

Differential

The differential is incorporated with the transaxle. The transmission fluid lubricates the differential so any checks or fluid changes can be done by following the procedures above, or in Chapter 7.

Cooling System

FLUID RECOMMENDATION

Whenever you add engine coolant use equal parts of water and Ford Premium Cooling

System Fluid E2FZ–19549–AA or equivalent (antifreeze) that meets ford specifications. Do not use alcohol or methanol antifreeze, or mix them with specified coolant.

NOTE: *These vehicles have aluminum radiators and require a unique corrosion inhibited coolant formulation to avoid damage. Use only permanent type coolant that meets Ford specifications such as, Ford Premium Cooling System Fluid E2FZ–19549–AA or equivalent (antifreeze). A coolant mixture of less than 40% (approximately 3.0 quarts) engine coolant concentrate may result in engine corrosion and over-heating.*

The factory installed solution of Ford cooling system fluid and water will protect your vehicle to –35°F (–37°C). Check the freezing protection rating of the coolant at least once a year, just before winter.

Maintain a protection rating consistent with the lowest temperature in which you operate your vehicle or at least –20°F (–29°C) to prevent engine damage as a result of freezing and to ensure proper engine operating temperature. Rust and corrosion inhibitors tend to deteriorate with time, changing the coolant every 3 years or 30,000 miles is recommended for proper protection of the cooling system.

NOTE: *The Ford Motor Company does not authorize the use of the recycled engine coolant nor do they sanction the use of any machines or devices that recycle engine coolant. Recycled engine coolant is not equivalent to the factory fill OEM coolant, the Ford premium cooling system fluid (E2FZ-19549-AA) or the Ford heavy duty low silicate cooling fluid (E6HZ-19549-A). The quality of the engine coolant degenerates with use. Recycling used engine coolant is very difficult to do without exposing the used coolant to additional foreign substances. Merely adding an additive to the coolant will not restore it. Always use new engine coolant that meets the Ford Motor coolant specifications for the engine being serviced.*

The disposal of all used engine coolant must always be done in accordance with all applicable Federal, State and Local laws and regulations.

FLUID LEVEL CHECK

The cooling system of your car contains, among other items, a radiator and a expansion tank. When the engine is running heat is generated. The rise in temperature causes the coolant, in the radiator, to expand and builds up internal pressure. When a certain pressure is reached, a pressure relief valve in the radiator filler cap (pressure cap) is lifted from its seat and allows coolant to flow through the radiator filler neck, down a hose, and into the expansion reservoir.

When the system temperature and pressure are reduced in the radiator, the water in the expansion reservoir is siphoned back into the radiator.

Check the level in the coolant recovery reservoir at least one month. With the cold engine the level must be maintained at or above the ADD mark. At normal operating temperatures, the coolant level should be at the FULL HOT mark. If the level is below the recommended level a 50/50 mixture of coolant (antifreeze) and water should be added to the reservoir. If the reservoir is empty, add the coolant to the radiator and then fill the reservoir to the required level.

CAUTION: *The cooling fan motor is controlled by a temperature switch. The fan may come on and run when the engine is off. It will continue to run until the correct temperature is reached. Take care not to get your fingers, etc. caught in the fan blades.*

Never remove the radiator cap under any circumstances when the engine is operating. Before removing the cap, switch off the engine and wait until it has cooled. Even then, use extreme care when removing the cap from a hot radiator. Wrap a thick cloth around the cap and turn it slowly to the first stop. Step back while the pressure is released from the cooling system. When you are sure all the pressure has been released, press down on the cap — still with a cloth — turn and remove it.

Check the coolant level in the radiator at least once a month, only when the engine is cool. Whenever coolant checks are made, check the condition of the radiator cap rubber seal. Make sure it is clean and free of any dirt particles. Rinse off with water if necessary. When replacing cap on radiator, also make sure that the radiator filler neck seat is clean. Check that overflow hose in the reservoir is not kinked and

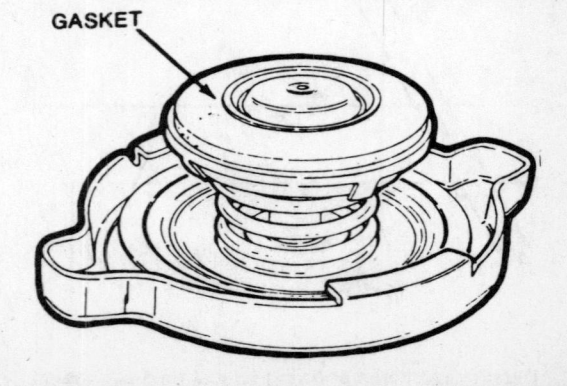

Check the radiator cap gasket for cuts or cracks

GENERAL INFORMATION AND MAINTENANCE

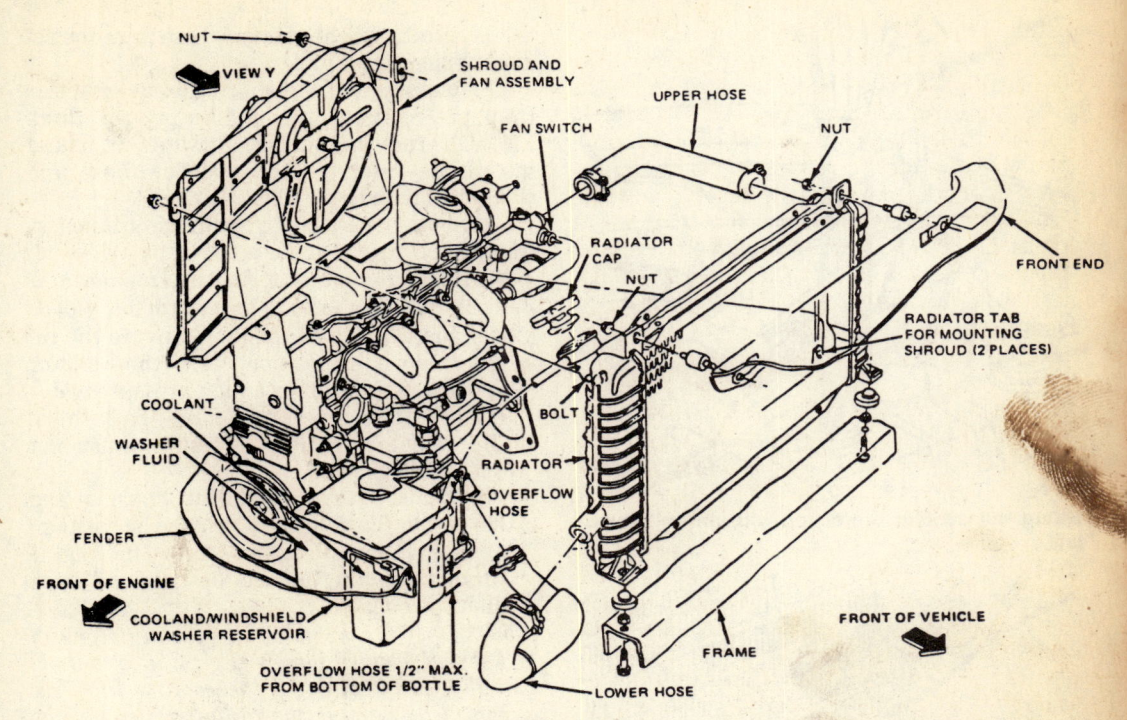

Cooling system

is inserted to within $1/2$ in. (13mm) of bottom of the bottle.

Anytime you add coolant to the radiator, use a 50/50 mixture of coolant and water. If you have to add coolant more than once a month, or if you have to add more than one quart at a time, have the cooling system checked for leaks.

DRAIN AND REFILL

To drain the coolant, connect an 18 in. (457mm) long, $3/8$ in. (9.5mm) inside diameter hose to the nipple on the drain valve located on the bottom of the radiator. With the engine cool, set the heater control to the maximum heat position, remove the radiator cap and open the drain valve or remove allen head plug ($3/16$ in.) allowing the coolant to drain into a container. When all of the coolant is drained, remove the $3/8$ in. hose and close the drain valve. There may be some coolant left in the engine block cavities, to drain the block, located the engine block coolant drain plug on the side of the engine block and drain the coolant out. Prior to reinstalling any coolant plugs or drain valves be sure to coat the threads with a suitable thread sealer or Teflon® tape.

CAUTION: *When draining the coolant, keep in mind that cats and dogs are attracted by the ethylene glycol antifreeze, and are quite likely to drink any that is left in an uncovered container or in puddles on the ground.*

This will prove fatal in sufficient quantity. Always drain the coolant into a sealable container. Coolant should be reused unless it is contaminated or several years old.

NOTE: *If there is any evidence of rust or scaling in the cooling system the system should be flushed thoroughly before refilling.*

Refill the coolant system as follows:

1. Install block drain plug, if removed and close the drain cock. With the engine in the **OFF** position, add 50 percent of system's capacity of specified coolant to the radiator. Then add water until the radiator is full.

NOTE: *Be sure to wait several minutes as the coolant level in the radiator drops, continue to slowly add coolant until the radiator remains full (approximately 10–15 minutes are required to fill the system). A coolant mixture of less than 30% (approximately 2.1 quarts) engine coolant concentrate may result in engine corrosion and over-heating.*

2. Reinstall the radiator cap to the pressure relief position by installing the cap to the fully installed position and then backing off to the first stop.

3. Start and idle the engine until the upper radiator hose is warm.

4. Immediately shut **OFF** the engine. Cautiously remove radiator cap and add water until the radiator is full. Reinstall radiator cap securely.

5. Add coolant to the ADD mark on the res-

GENERAL INFORMATION AND MAINTENANCE

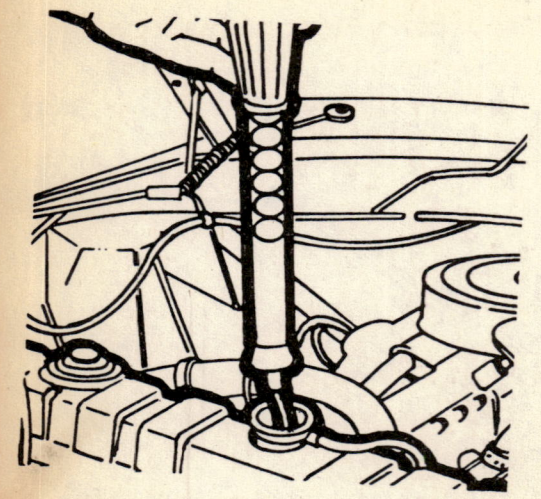

Testing the coolant protection with an antifreeze tester

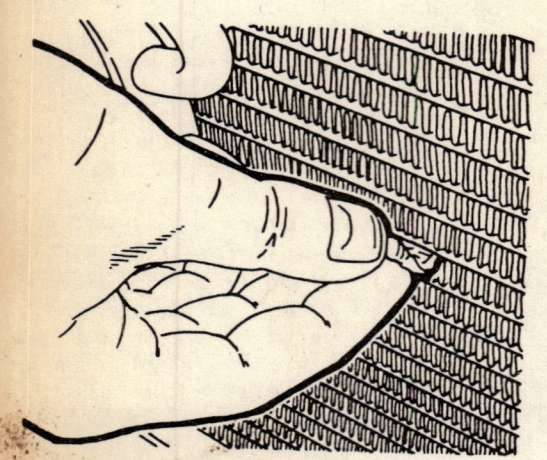

Clean the radiator fins of debris

ervoir, then fill to the **FULL HOT** mark with water.

6. Check system for leaks and return the heater temperature control to normal position.

FLUSHING AND CLEANING THE SYSTEM

1. Drain the radiator as outlined in this section. Then add water until the radiator is full.
2. Reinstall the radiator cap to the pressure relief position by installing the cap to the fully installed position and then backing off to the first stop.
3. Start and idle the engine until the upper radiator hose is warm.
4. Immediately shut off engine. Cautiously drain the water by opening the drain cock.
5. Repeat Steps 1–4 as many times as necessary until nearly clear water comes out of the radiator. Allow remaining water to drain and then close the petcock.

6. Disconnect the overflow hose from the radiator filler neck nipple.

7. Remove the coolant recovery reservoir from the fender apron and empty the fluid. Flush the reservoir with clean water, drain and install the reservoir and overflow hose and clamp to the radiator filler neck.

8. Refill the coolant system as outlined in this section.

NOTE: *If the radiator has been removed, it is possible to back flush the system as follows:*

a. Back flush the radiator, Ensure the radiator cap is in position. Turn the radiator upside down. Position a high pressure water in the bottom hose location and back flush. The radiator internal pressure must not exceed 20 psi.

b. Remove the thermostat housing and thermostat. Back flush the engine by positioning a high pressure hose into the engine through the thermostat location and back flush the engine.

NOTE: *If the radiator is showing signs of rust and wear, it may be a good idea to thoroughly clean and get the cooling fins free from debris, while the radiator is out of the vehicle. Then using a suitable high temperature rust proof engine paint, paint the radiator assembly.*

Brake Master Cylinder

FLUID RECOMMENDATION

The brake fluid to be used in these vehicles should be a only **DOT** 3 brake fluid meeting Ford specifications such as Ford Heavy Duty Brake Fluid.

LEVEL CHECK

The brake master cylinder is located under the hood, on the left side firewall. Before removing the master cylinder reservoir cap, make sure the vehicle is resting on level ground and clean all the dirt away from the top of the master cylinder. Pry the retaining clip off to the side. Remove the master cylinder cover.

If the level of the brake fluid is within $1/4$ in. (6mm) of the top it is OK. If the level is less than half the volume of the reservoir, check the brake system for leaks. Leaks in the brake system most commonly occur at the rear wheel cylinders. or at the front calipers. Leaks at brake lines or the master cylinder can also be the cause of the loss of brake fluid.

There is a rubber diaphragm at the top of the master cylinder cap. As the fluid level lowers due to normal brake shoe wear or leakage, the diaphragm takes up the space. This is to prevent the loss of brake fluid out the vented cap and to help stop contamination by dirt. After

GENERAL INFORMATION AND MAINTENANCE

filling the master cylinder to the proper level with brake fluid (Type DOT 3), but before replacing the cap, fold the rubber diaphragm up into the cap, then replace the cap on the reservoir and snap the retaining clip back in place.

On the later models, check the brake fluid by visually inspecting the fluid level through the translucent master cylinder reservoir. It should be between the **MIN** and the **MAX** level marks embossed on the side of the reservoir. If the level is found to be low, remove the reservoir cap and fill to the **MAX** level with DOT 3 brake fluid.

The level will decrease with accumulated mileage. This is a normal condition associated with a the wear of the disc brake linings. If the fluid is excessively low, it would be advisable to have the brake system checked.

NOTE: *To avoid the possibility of brake failure that could result in property damage or personal injury, do not allow the master cylinder to run dry. Never reuse brake fluid that has been drained from the hydraulic system or fluid that has been allowed to stand in an open container for an extended period of time.*

Manual Steering

No periodic lubrication is required. Lubrication is required only if the system is disassembled for service.

Power Steering Pump Reservoir

FLUID RECOMMENDATION

Use only power steering fluid that meets Ford Specifications such as Motorcraft Type **F** Automatic Transmission and Power Steering Fluid or an equivalent type **F** fluid which displays a Ford registration number (2P-followed by six numerals). Whenever the dipstick is inserted, always make sure it is properly seated and locked.

LEVEL CHECK

Run the engine until it reaches normal operating temperature. While the engine is idling, turn the steering wheel all the way to the right and then left several times. Shut **OFF** the engine. Open the hood and remove the power steering pump dipstick. Wipe the dipstick clean and reinstall into the pump reservoir. Withdraw the dipstick and note the fluid level shown. The level must show between the cold full mark and the hot full mark. Add fluid if necessary, buy do not overfill. Remove any excess fluid with a suction bulb or gun.

Windshield Washer Reservoir

LEVEL CHECK

You can fill the water tank with plain water in the summer time, but the pre-mixed solvents available help dissolve grime and dirt better and provide protection against freezing in the winter. Add fluid through the filler cover when the level drops below the line on the side of the reservoir case.

Chassis Greasing

Wheel Bearing

Front wheel bearings removal and installation on FWD cars, and rear axle bearings will be covered in Chapter 8 of this manual.

TRAILER TOWING

Towing a trailer puts additional load on your Ford FWD's engine, drivetrain, brakes, tires and suspension. For your safety and the care of your car, make sure the trailer towing equipment is properly matched to the trailer. All towing equipment should be safely attached to the vehicle and of the proper weight class.

The maximum trailer weight that your car is 1000 lbs. gross trailer axle weight with a minimum tongue load of 100 lbs. and must abide by the following qualifications:

• Any model equipped with a 2.85 manual transaxle final drive (green identification tag on the transaxle housing) should not be used to tow trailers of any size

• Auxiliary oil coolers are recommended for the power steering system and the automatic transaxle during long distance towing (greater than 50 miles, towing in hilly terrain or frequent towing).

• Vehicle speed no higher than 55 mph is recommended while towing a 1,000 lb. GVW trailer.

Trailer Hitches

Choose a proper hitch and ball and make sure its location is compatible with that of the trailer. Use a good weight carrying hitch that uniformly distributes the trailer tongue loads through the underbody structure for towing trailers up to 1,000 lb.

Under no circumstances should a single or multiclamp type hitch be installed on your Ford FWD, damage to the bumper would result. Nor should any hitch which attaches to the axle be used. Underbody mounted hitches are acceptable if installed properly. Never attach safety chains to the bumper.

46 GENERAL INFORMATION AND MAINTENANCE

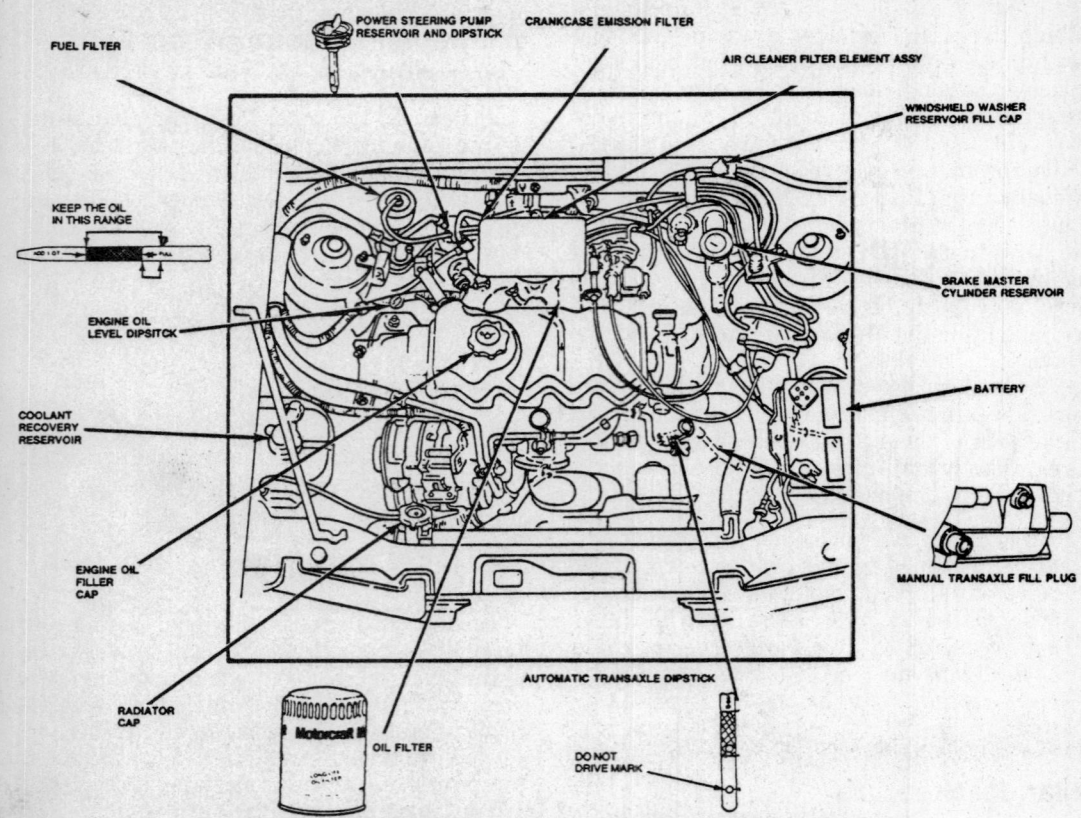

Engine lubrication service points — 1987–90 1.9L EFI engine

TOWING TIPS

Before starting on a trip, practice turning, stopping and backing up in an area away from other traffic (such as a deserted shopping center parking lot) to gain experience in handling the extra weight and length of the trailer. Take enough time to get the feel of the vehicle/trailer combination under a variety of situations.

Skillful backing requires practice. Back up slowly with an assistant acting as a guide and watching for obstructions. Use both rear view mirrors. Place your hand at the bottom of the steering wheel and move it in the direction you want the rear of the trailer to swing. Make small corrections, instead of exaggerated ones, as a slight movement of the steering wheel will result in a much larger movement of the rear of the trailer.

Allow considerable more room for stopping when a trailer is attached to the vehicle. If you have a manual brake controller, lead with the trailer brakes when approaching a stop. Trailer brakes are also handy for correcting side sway. Just touch them for a moment without using your vehicle brakes and the trailer should settle down and track straight again.

To assist in obtaining good handling with the car/trailer combination, it is important that the trailer tongue load be maintained at approximately 10–15% of the loaded trailer weight.

Check everything before starting out on the road, then stop after you've traveled about 50 miles and double-check the trailer hitch and electrical connections to make sure everything is still OK. Listen for sounds like chains dragging on the ground (indicating that a safety chain has come loose) and check your rear view mirrors frequently to make sure the trailer is still there and tracking properly. Check the trailer wheel lug nuts to make sure they're tight and never attempt to tow the trailer with a space saver spare installed on the car.

Remember that a car/trailer combination is more sensitive to cross winds and slow down when crossing bridges or wide open expanses in gusty wind conditions. Exceeding the speed limit while towing a trailer is not only illegal, it is foolhardy and invites disaster. A strong gust of wind can send a speeding car/trailer combination out of control.

Because the trailer wheels are closer than the towing vehicle wheels to the inside of a turn, drive slightly beyond the normal turning point when negotiating a sharp turn at a corner. Allow extra distance for passing other vehicles and downshift if necessary for better accelera-

GENERAL INFORMATION AND MAINTENANCE 47

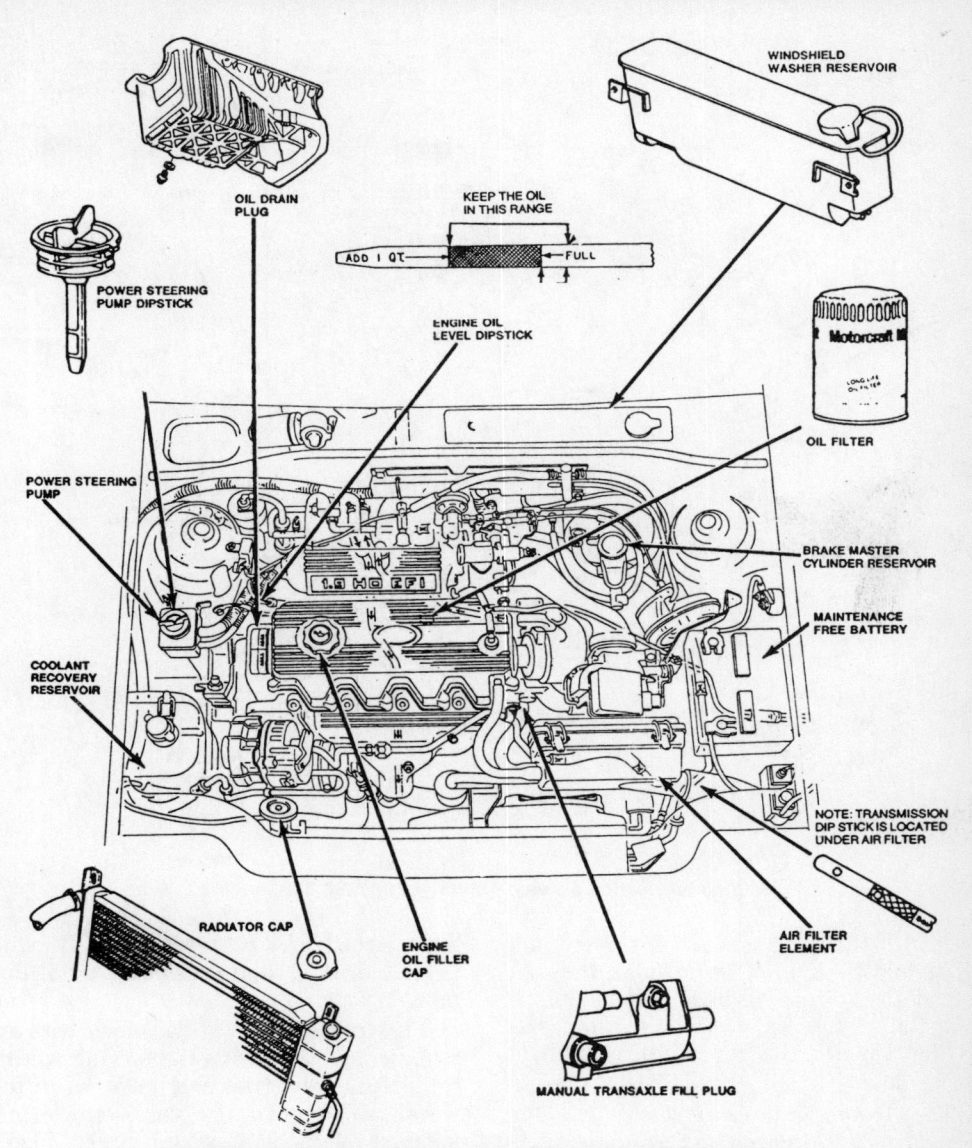

Engine lubrication service points — 1987-90 1.9L HO engine

tion. Allow at least the equivalent of one vehicle and trailer length combined for each 10 mph of road speed.

Finally, remember to check the height of the loaded car/trailer, allowing for luggage racks, antenna, etc. mounted on the roof and take note of low bridges or parking garage clearances.

PUSHING AND TOWING

Pushing

Push starting is not recommended on vehicles with a catalytic converter. Gas accumulation in the converter will cause damage to the system.

Towing

Whenever you are towing another vehicle, or being towed, make sure the chain or strap is sufficiently long and strong. Attach the chain securely at a point on the frame, shipping tie-down slots are provided on the front and rear of you car and should be used. Never attach a chain or strap to any steering or suspension part. Never try to start the vehicle when being towed, it might run into the back of the tow car. Do not allow too much slack in the tow line, the towed car could run over the line and damage to both cars could occur. If you car is being towed by a tow truck, the towing speed should be limited to 50 mph with the driving wheels off the ground. If it is necessary to tow

48 GENERAL INFORMATION AND MAINTENANCE

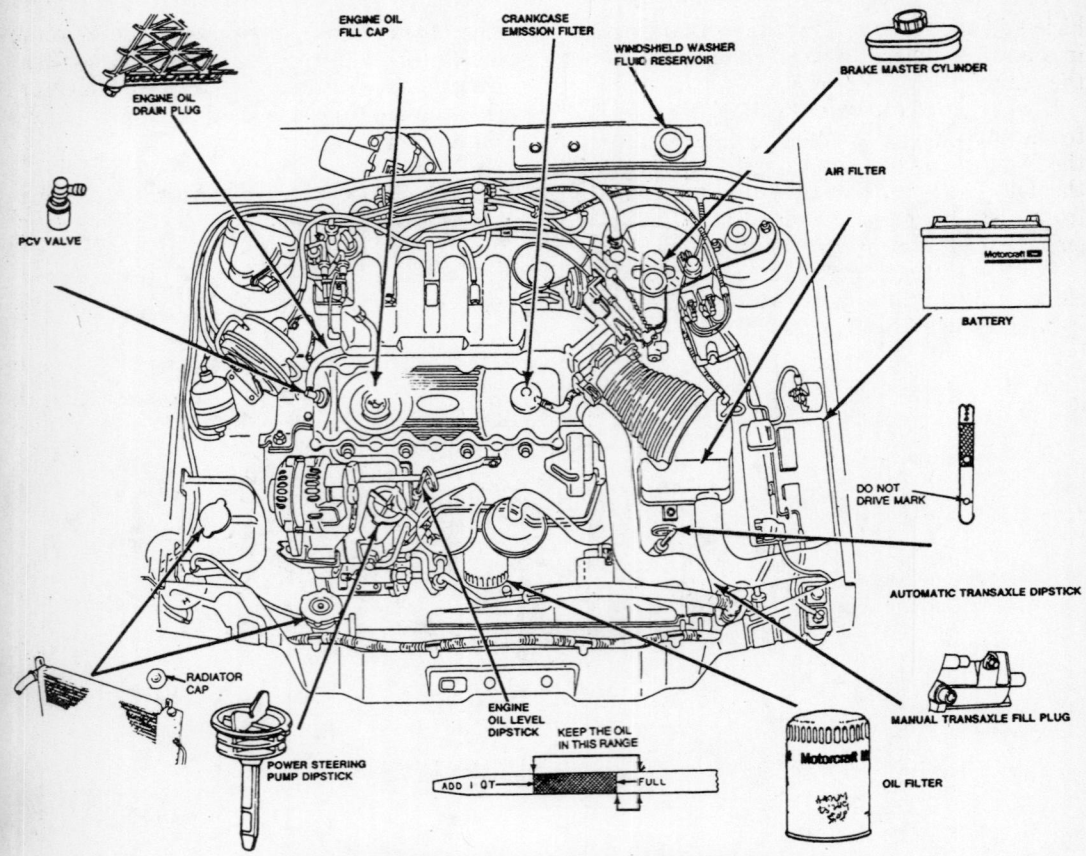

Engine lubrication service points — 1987–90 2.3L engine

the car with the drive wheels on the ground, speed should be limited to no more then 35 mph and the towing distance should not be greater than 50 miles. If towing distance is more than 50 miles the front of the car should be put on dollies.

NOTE: *If the car is being towed with the front (drive) wheels on the ground, never allow the steering lock to keep the wheels straight, damage to the steering could occur.*

Your vehicle may be towed by a wrecker from the front or rear as outlined in the following paragraphs. A 4 in. × 4 in. × 48 in. wood cross beam and T-hook chains are required for proper towing to prevent damage to your vehicle. This equipment is commonly found on commercial wreckers. For flat bed towing, T-hook chains are required to prevent damage to the driveline or suspension components.

NOTE: *J-hook chains should not be used under any circumstances or your vehicle may be damaged.*

As a general rule, vehicles should be towed with the driving (front) wheels off the ground. To tow your vehicle in this manner, release the parking brake and place the transaxle shift lever in the **NEUTRAL** position. Towing speed is limited to 50 mph on smooth roads and 35 mph on rough roads.

If it is necessary to tow a vehicle with an automatic transaxle with the driving wheels on the ground, the transaxle must be in proper working order. To tow your vehicle in this manner release the parking brake, place the shift lever in the **NEUTRAL** position and clamp the steering wheel in the straight ahead position with a steering wheel clamping device designed for towing service use. Do not exceed 35 mph and a distance of 50 miles or transaxle damage could result.

If it is necessary to tow a vehicle with a manual transaxle with the driving wheels on the ground, do not exceed 55 mph but the distance is not limited. When ever towing from the rear, chains must not be attached forward of rear suspension arms or directly to the rear suspension arms. This could result in vehicle damage.

If the ignition key is not available to unlock the steering column where applicable, place a dolly under the rear wheels and tow the vehicle with the front wheels raised. Do not use the ve-

GENERAL INFORMATION AND MAINTENANCE

hicle's steering column lock to secure the wheel in a straight ahead position when pulled from the rear.

If you cannot tow the vehicle by conforming to the above requirements, place a dolly under the front wheels and tow from the rear or place the dolly under the rear tires and tow from the front. Towing speed is limited to 50 mph on smooth roads and 35 mph on rough roads.

At times it may be desirable to tow your vehicle with all four wheels on the ground, such as behind an RV, another vehicle or truck. The design of your vehicle permits you to tow your vehicle with all four wheels on the ground with a automatic transaxle to 35 mph for 50 miles or with a manual transaxle at 55 mph with unlimited mileage.

NOTE: *On vehicles equipped with the All Wheel Drive (AWD) system, do not tow your vehicle IN the AWD mode. If the AWD does not disengage,, due to electrical or vacuum system failures, remove the driveshaft or use a dolly.*

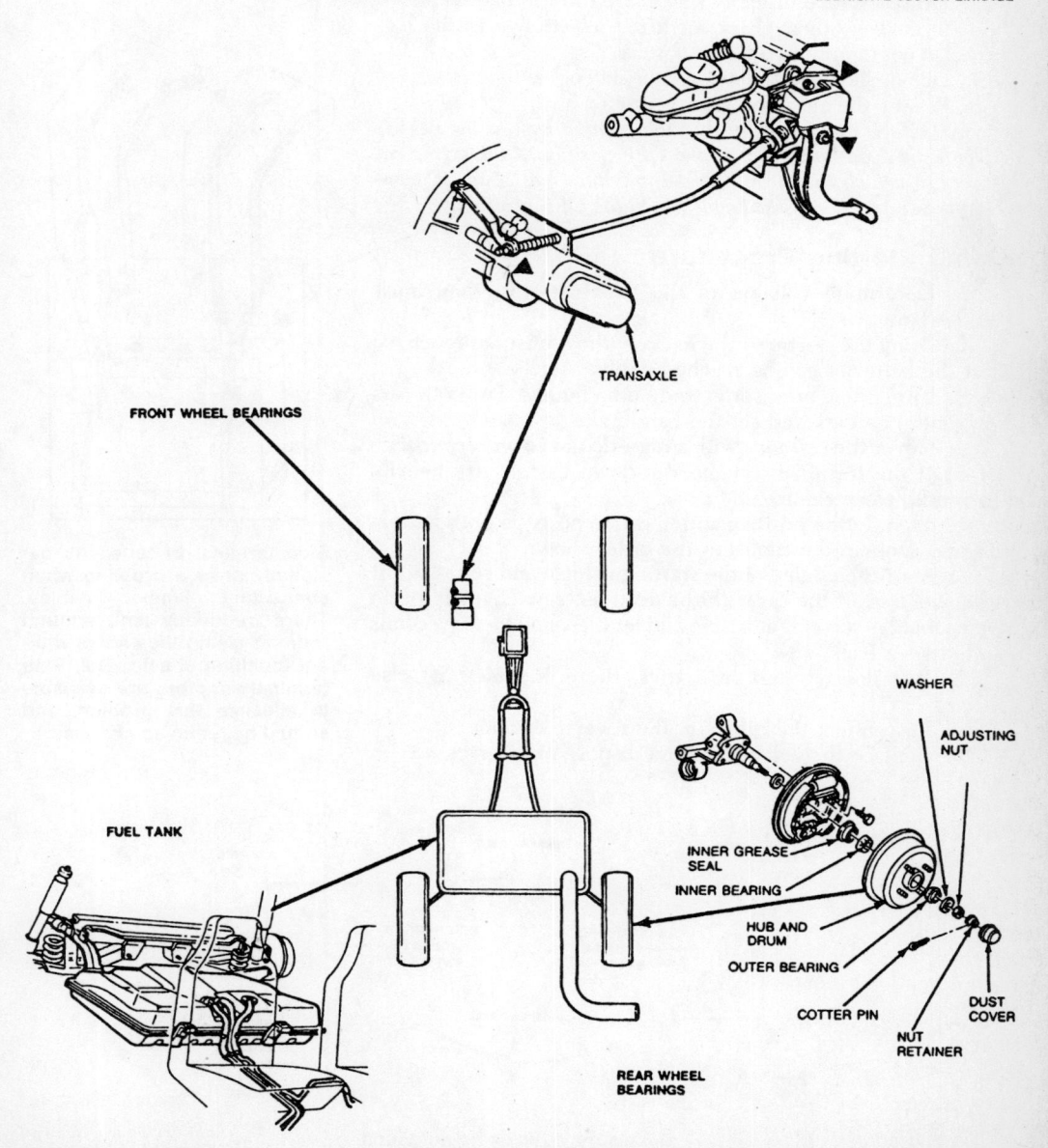

Chassis lubrication points

GENERAL INFORMATION AND MAINTENANCE

JUMP STARTING A DEAD BATTERY

The chemical reaction in a battery produces explosive hydrogen gas. This is the safe way to jump start a dead battery, reducing the chances of an accidental spark that could cause an explosion.

Jump Starting Precautions

1. Be sure both batteries are of the same voltage.
2. Be sure both batteries are of the same polarity (have the same grounded terminal).
3. Be sure the vehicles are not touching.
4. Be sure the vent cap holes are not obstructed.
5. Do not smoke or allow sparks around the battery.
6. In cold weather, check for frozen electrolyte in the battery. Do not jump start a frozen battery.
7. Do not allow electrolyte on your skin or clothing.
8. Be sure the electrolyte is not frozen.

CAUTION: *Make certain that the ignition key, in the vehicle with the dead battery, is in the OFF position. Connecting cables to vehicles with on-board computers will result in computer destruction if the key is not in the OFF position.*

Jump Starting Procedure

1. Determine voltages of the two batteries; they must be the same.
2. Bring the starting vehicle close (they must not touch) so that the batteries can be reached easily.
3. Turn off all accessories and both engines. Put both cars in Neutral or Park and set the handbrake.
4. Cover the cell caps with a rag—do not cover terminals.
5. If the terminals on the run-down battery are heavily corroded, clean them.
6. Identify the positive and negative posts on both batteries and connect the cables in the order shown.
7. Start the engine of the starting vehicle and run it at fast idle. Try to start the car with the dead battery. Crank it for no more than 10 seconds at a time and let it cool off for 20 seconds in between tries.
8. If it doesn't start in 3 tries, there is something else wrong.
9. Disconnect the cables in the reverse order.
10. Replace the cell covers and dispose of the rags.

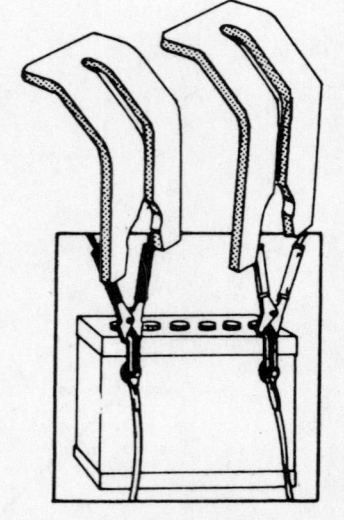

Side terminal batteries occasionally pose a problem when connecting jumper cables. There frequently isn't enough room to clamp the cables without touching sheet metal. Side terminal adaptors are available to alleviate this problem and should be removed after use.

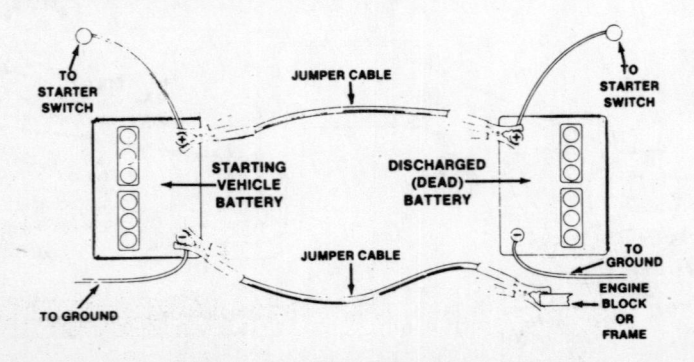

Make sure vehicles do not touch

This hook-up for negative ground cars only

GENERAL INFORMATION AND MAINTENANCE

JACKING

NOTE: *The service jack provided with the vehicle is only intended to be used in an emergency for changing a flat tire. Never use the service jack to hoist the vehicle for any other service. Refer to the Owner's manual when using the jack supplied with the vehicle.*

When using a floor jack, the front of the car may be raised by positioning the jack under the front body rail behind the suspension arm-to-body bracket. On the Tempo and Topaz, the rear of the car may be raised by positioning the jack forward of the rear suspension rod on the bracket. On the Escort and Lynx models, the rear may be raised by positioning the floor jack under either rear lower control arm.

NOTE: *Under no circumstances should the vehicle ever be lifted by the front or rear control arms, halfshafts or CV-joints. Severe damage to the vehicle could result. On vehicles equipped with All Wheel Drive (AWD), the vehicle must be in 2 wheel drive or rotation from the wheel being removed could be transferred to one or more of the other wheels, causing the vehicle to move or fall off the jack.*

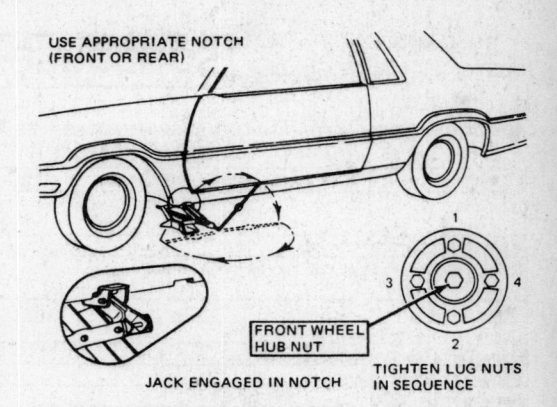

Jack locations, using the jack equipped with your vehicle

CUSTOMER MAINTENANCE — SCHEDULE A

Follow maintenance Schedule A if your driving habits **MAINLY** include one or more of the following conditions:
- Short trips of less than 10 miles (16 km) when outside temperatures remain below freezing.
- Towing a trailer, or using a car-top carrier.
- Operating in severe dust conditions.
- Operating during hot weather in stop-and-go "rush hour" traffic.
- Extensive idling, such as police, taxi or door-to-door delivery service.

PERFORM AT THE MONTHS OR DISTANCES SHOWN, WHICHEVER OCCURS FIRST																			
MILES (000)	3	6	9	12	15	18	21	24	27	30	33	36	39	42	45	48	51	54	57	60
KILOMETERS (000)	4.8	9.6	14.4	19.2	24	28.8	33.6	38.4	43.2	48	52.8	57.6	62.4	67.2	72	76.8	81.6	86.4	91.2	96
EMISSION CONTROL SERVICE																				
Change engine oil and oil filter (every 3 months) OR 3,000 miles whichever occurs first	X	X	X	X	X	X	X	X	X	X	X	X	X	X	X	X	X	X	X	X
Replace spark plugs										X										X
Inspect accessory drive belt(s)										X										X
Replace air cleaner filter (1)										X(1)										X(1)
Replace crankcase emission filter (1)										X(1)										X(1)
Replace engine coolant EVERY 36 months OR										X										X
Check engine coolant protection, hoses and clamps									ANNUALLY											
GENERAL MAINTENANCE																				
Inspect exhaust heat shields										X										X
Change automatic transaxle fluid										(2)										(2)
Inspect disc brake pads and rotors (front) (3)										X(3)										X(3)
Inspect brake linings and drums (rear) (3)										X(3)										X(3)
Inspect and repack rear wheel bearings										X										X
Rotate tires			X			X				X				X						

(1) If operating in severe dust, more frequent intervals may be required, consult your dealer.

(2) Change automatic transmission fluid if your driving habits frequently include one or more of the following conditions:
- Operation during hot weather (above 90°F, 32°C), carrying heavy loads in hilly terrain.
- Towing a trailer or using a car-top carrier.
- Police, taxi or door-to-door delivery service.

(3) If your driving includes continuous stop-and-go driving or driving in mountainous areas, more frequent intervals may be required.

Schedule A maintenance interval chart

GENERAL INFORMATION AND MAINTENANCE

CUSTOMER MAINTENANCE — SCHEDULE B

Follow maintenance Schedule B if, generally, you drive your vehicle on a daily basis for more than 10 miles (16 km) and NONE OF THE DRIVING CONDITIONS SHOWN IN SCHEDULE A APPLY TO YOUR DRIVING HABITS.

PERFORM AT THE MONTHS OR DISTANCES SHOWN, WHICHEVER OCCURS FIRST								
MILES (000)	7.5	15	22.5	30	37.5	45	52.5	60
KILOMETERS (000)	12	24	36	48	60	72	84	96
EMISSION CONTROL SERVICE								
Change engine oil and oil filter — **every 6 months** or 7500 miles, whichever occurs first	X	X	X	X	X	X	X	X
Replace spark plugs				X				X
Change crankcase filter (1)				X(1)				X(1)
Inspect accessory drive belt(s)				X				X
Replace air cleaner filter (1)				X(1)				X(1)
Replace engine coolant (every 36 months) OR				X				X
Check engine coolant protection, hoses and clamps				ANNUALLY				
GENERAL MAINTENANCE								
Check exhaust heat shields				X				X
Inspect disc brake pads and rotors (front) (2)				X(2)				X(2)
Inspect brake linings and drums (rear) (2)				X(2)				X(2)
Inspect and repack rear wheel bearings				X				X
Rotate tires	X		X		X		X	

Schedule B maintenance interval chart

CAPACITIES CHART—TEMPO/TOPAZ

Year	Engine L (cid)	Crankcase Includes Filter (qts.)	Transaxle (pts.) 4-sp	5-sp	Auto.	Drive Axle (pts.)	Fuel Tank (gal.)	Cooling System (qt.) w/AC	wo/AC
1984	2.0 (122)	7.2 ④	—	6.1	—	③	15.2	9.2	9.2
	2.3 (140)	4.5 ⑤	5.3	6.1	②	③	15.2	8.4	8.4
1985	2.0 (122)	7.2 ④	—	6.1	—	③	15.2	9.2	9.2
	2.3 (140)	4.5 ⑤	5.0	6.2	②	③	15.2	7.7	7.1
1986	2.0 (122)	7.2 ④	—	6.1	—	③	15.2	9.2	9.2
	2.3 (140)	4.5 ⑤	5.0	6.2	②	③	15.4	7.8 ①	8.3
1987	2.0 (122)	7.2 ④	—	6.1	—	③	15.2	9.2	9.2
	2.3 (140)	5.0	5.0	6.2	②	⑦	15.4 ⑥	7.8 ①	8.3
1988	2.3 (140)	5.0	5.0	6.2	②	⑦	15.4 ⑥	7.8 ①	8.3
1989	2.3 (140)	5.0	5.0	6.2	②	⑦	15.4 ⑥	7.8 ①	8.3
1990	2.3 (140)	5.0	5.0	6.2	②	⑦	15.4 ⑥	7.8 ①	8.3

① Man. Trans.: 7.3 qts.
② Total dry capacity-converter, cooler and sump drained 16.6 pts. for all models except the All Wheel Drive model with 20.2 pts. Partial fluid change (pan sump only), add 8 pts., start engine and check level. Add necessary fluid until correct level is reached.
③ Included in transmission capacity, but on All Wheel Drive models, add 1.5 oz. of EST-M2C118-A friction modifier for a complete refill of the transfer case and rear axle.
④ Capacity for complete system—pan capacity is 5.3 qts.
⑤ After filter replacement, add 4 qts. of oil and run engine. Shut engine off and check the oil level. Add 1/2 qt. if necessary.
⑥ 14.2 gallons on the All Wheel Drive models.
⑦ Included in transmission capacity. The rear axle on All Wheel Drive models is 1.3 pts. and add 1.5 oz. of EST-M2C118-A friction modifier for a complete refill of the transfer case and rear axle.

GENERAL INFORMATION AND MAINTENANCE

CAPACITIES CHART—ESCORT/LYNX

Year	Engine L (cid)	Crankcase Includes Filter (qts.)	Transaxle (pts.) 4-sp	5-sp	Auto.	Drive Axle (pts.)	Fuel Tank (gal.)	Cooling System (qt.) w/AC	wo/AC
1981	1.3 (79)	4.0	5.0	—	②	③	④	6.3	6.3
	1.6 (98)	4.0	5.0	—	②	③	④	6.4	6.3
1982	1.6 (98)	4.0	5.0	—	②	③	④	6.4	6.3
1983	1.6 (98)	4.0	5.0	6.1	②	③	④	6.4	6.3
1984	1.6 (98)	4.0	5.0	6.1	②	③	④	7.8	7.3
	2.0 (122)	7.2 ⑤	—	6.1	—	③	13	9.2	9.2
1985	1.6 (98)	4.0	5.0	6.2	②	③	④	7.1	6.6
	2.0 (122)	7.2 ⑤	—	6.1	—	③	13	9.2	9.2
1986	1.9 (114)	4.0	5.0	6.2	②	③	④	7.3 ①	7.9
	2.0 (122)	7.2 ⑤	—	6.1	—	③	13	9.2	9.2
1987	1.9 (114)	4.0	5.0	6.2	②	③	④	7.3 ①	7.9
	2.0 (122)	7.2 ⑤	—	6.1	—	③	13	9.2	9.2
1988	1.9 (114)	4.0	6.2	6.2	②	③	④	7.3 ①	8.3
1989	1.9 (114)	4.0	6.2	6.2	②	③	④	7.3 ①	8.3
1990	1.9 (114)	4.0	6.2	6.2	②	③	④	7.3 ①	8.3

① Man. Trans.: 6.8 qts.
② Total dry capacity-converter, cooler and sump drained.
   1981–82: 19.6 pts.
   1985–90: 16.6 pts.
   Partial fluid change (pan sump only), add 8 pts., start engine and check level. Add necessary fluid until correct level is reached.
③ Included in transmission capacity.
④ 1981–82: 10 gal. Auto. Trans.
            9 gal. Manual Trans.
            11.3 gal. Extended range
   1983–90: 10 gal. FE models
            13 gal. Standard
            13 gal. EXP/LN7
            11 gal. Escort (optional 1990)
⑤ Capacity for complete system—pan capacity is 5.3 qts.

Engine Performance and Tune-Up

TUNE-UP PROCEDURES

Spark Plugs

Spark plugs ignite the air and fuel mixture in the cylinder as the piston reaches the top of the compression stroke. The controlled explosion that results forces the piston down, turning the crankshaft and the rest of the drive train.

Ford recommends that spark plugs be changed every 30,000 miles (60,000 Calif.). Under severe driving conditions, those intervals should be halved. Severe driving conditions are:

1. Extended periods of idling or low speed operation, such as off-road or door-to-door delivery.
2. Driving short distances (less than 10 miles) when the average temperature is below 10°F (−12°C) for 60 days or more.
3. Excessive dust or blowing dirt conditions.

When you remove the spark plugs, check their condition. They are a good indicator of the condition of the engine. It is a good idea to remove the spark plugs at regular intervals, such as every 6,000 or so miles, just so you can keep an eye on the mechanical state of the engine.

A small deposit of light tan or gray material on a spark plug that has been used for any period of time is considered normal. Any other color, or abnormal amounts of deposit, indicate that there is something amiss in the engine.

The gap between the center electrode and the side or ground electrode can be expected to increase not more than 0.001 in. (0.025mm) every 1,000 miles under normal conditions. When, and if, a plug fouls and begins to misfire, you will have to investigate, correct the cause of the fouling and either clean or replace the plug.

There are several reasons why a spark plug will foul and you can learn which reason is at fault by just looking at the plug. A few of the most common reasons for plug fouling and a description of fouled plug appearance are shown in the Color section.

SPARK PLUG HEAT RANGE

Spark plug heat range is the ability of the plug to dissipate heat. The longer the insulator (or the farther it extends into the engine), the hotter the plug will operate; the shorter the insulator the cooler it will operate. A plug that absorbs little heat and remains too cool will quickly accumulate deposits of oil and carbon since it is not hot enough to burn them off. This leads to plug fouling and consequently to misfiring. A plug that absorbs too much heat will have no deposits, but, due to the excessive heat, the electrodes will burn away quickly and in some instances, preignition may result. Preignition takes place when plug tips get so hot that they glow sufficiently to ignite the fuel/air mixture before the actual spark occurs. This early ignition will usually cause a pinging during low speeds and heavy loads.

The general rule of thumb of choosing the correct heat range when picking a spark plug is: if most of your driving is long distance, high speed travel, use a cooler plug; if most of your driving is stop and go, use a hotter plug. Original equipment plugs are compromise plugs, but most people never have occasion to change their plugs from the factory recommended heat range.

SPARK PLUG REPLACEMENT

CAUTION: *Two different plug designs are used on early 1.6L engines. The designs are: gasket equipped and tapered seat (no gasket). All 1981 Escort/Lynx models, and 1982 EXP/ LN7 models built before 9/4/81 use gasket equipped plugs. All 1982 and later Escort/ Lynx and EXP/LN7 models built after 9/4/81 are equipped with tapered seat plugs. DO*

ENGINE PERFORMANCE AND TUNE-UP

GASOLINE ENGINE TUNE-UP SPECIFICATIONS

Year	Engine L (CID)	Spark Plug Type ④	Gap (in.)	Ignition Timing (deg.) Man. Trans.	Ignition Timing (deg.) Auto. Trans.	Idle Speed Man. Trans.	Idle Speed Auto. Trans.	Valve Clearance In.	Valve Clearance Exh.	Fuel Pump Pressure (psi)
1981	1.3 (79)	①	0.044	10B ①	10B ①	①	①	Hyd.	Hyd.	4–6
	1.6 (98)	AGSP-32 ④	0.044	10B ①	10B ①	①	①	Hyd.	Hyd.	4–6
1982	1.6 (98)	AWSF-32 ④	0.044	①	①	①	①	Hyd.	Hyd.	4–6
1983	1.6 (98)	AWSF-34 ②④	0.044	①	①	①	①	Hyd.	Hyd.	③
1984	1.6 (98)	AWSF-34 ②	0.044	①	①	①	①	Hyd.	Hyd.	③
	2.3 (140)	AWSF-62	0.044	10B ①	15B ①	①	①	Hyd.	Hyd.	5
1985	1.6 (98)	AWSF-34 ②	0.044	①	①	①	①	Hyd.	Hyd.	③
	2.3 (140)	AWSF-62	0.044	10B ①	15B ①	①	①	Hyd.	Hyd.	5
1986	1.9 (114)	AWSF-34C ⑤	0.044	10B ①	10B ①	①	①	Hyd.	Hyd.	③
	2.3 (140)	AWSF-44C ⑥	0.044	13B ①	10B ①	①	①	Hyd.	Hyd.	⑦
1987	1.9 (114)	AGSF-34C ⑤	0.044	10B ①	10B ①	①	①	Hyd.	Hyd.	③
	2.3 (140)	AWSF-52 ⑥	0.044	10B ①	10B ①	①	①	Hyd.	Hyd.	⑦
1988	1.9 (114)	AGSF-34C ⑤	0.044	10B ①	10B ①	①	①	Hyd.	Hyd.	③
	2.3 (140)	AWSF-42C ⑥	0.034	10B ①	10B ①	①	①	Hyd.	Hyd.	⑦
1989	1.9 (114)	AGSF-34C ⑤	0.044	10B ①	10B ①	①	①	Hyd.	Hyd.	③
	2.3 (140)	AWSF-42C ⑥	0.034	15B ①	10B ①	①	①	Hyd.	Hyd.	⑦
1990	1.9 (114)	AGSF-34C ⑤	0.044	10B ①	10B ①	①	①	Hyd.	Hyd.	③
	2.3 (140)	AWSF-42C ⑥	0.034	15B ①	10B ①	①	①	Hyd.	Hyd.	⑦

NOTE: The underhood specification sticker often reflects changes made in production. Stickers figures must be used if they disagree with those in the above chart.

① Calibration levels vary from model to model. Always refer to the underhood sticker for your car requirements.
② EFI Models: AWSF24
③ Carbureted system 4–6 psi, EFI system 35–45 psi
④ CAUTION: Two different plug designs are used on the 1.6L engines. The designs are: gasket equipped and tapered seat (no gasket). All 1981 Escort/Lynx models; and 1982 EXP/LN7 models built before 9/4/81 use gasket equipped plugs. All 1982 and later Escort/Lynx models; and EXP/LN7 models built after 9/4/81 are equipped with tapered seat plugs. DO NOT INTERCHANGE TYPES. Tighten gasket equipped plugs to 17–22 ft. lbs. Tapered seat plugs are tightened to 10–15 ft. lbs. DO NOT OVERTIGHTEN.
⑤ EFI Models: AWSF-24C
⑥ EFI Models: AWSF-32C
 Plug gap 1987 EFI—0.034
 Plug gap 1988–90 EFI/HSC—0.054
⑦ Carbureted system 5 psi, CFI system 15–16 psi.

DIESEL ENGINE TUNE-UP SPECIFICATIONS

Year	Engine L (cid)	Static Injection Timing	Compression Pressure (psi)	Injection Nozzle Opening Pressure (psi)	Idle Speed Man. Trans.	Idle Speed Auto. Trans.	Valve Clearance In.	Valve Clearance Exh.
1984–87	2.0 (122)	TDC	427 @ 200 rpm	1914	800–850	800–850	0.008–0.011	0.011–0.015

NOTE: The underhood specification sticker often reflects changes made in production. Stickers figures must be used if they disagree with those in the above chart.

ENGINE PERFORMANCE AND TUNE-UP

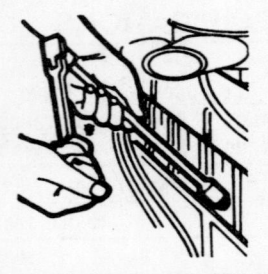

Remove the spark plugs with a ratchet and long extension

NOT INTERCHANGE TYPES. Tighten gasket equipped plugs to 17–22 ft. lbs. Tapered plugs are tightened to 10–15 ft. lbs. DO NOT OVER TIGHTEN.

A Set of spark plugs usually requires replacement every 30,000 miles, depending on your style of driving. In normal operation, plug gap increases about 0.001 in. (0.025mm) for every 1,000–2,500 miles. As the gap increases, the plug's voltage requirement also increases. It requires greater voltage to jump the wider gap and about two to three times as much voltage to fire a plug at higher speeds than at idle.

The spark plugs used in your car require a deep spark plug socket for removal and installation. A special designed pair of plug wire removal pliers is also a good tool to have. The special pliers have cupped jaws that grip the plug wire boot and make the job of twisting and pulling the wire from the plug easier.

REMOVAL AND INSTALLATION

NOTE: The original spark plug wires are marked for cylinder location. If replacement wires have been installed, be sure to tag them for proper location. It is a good idea to remove the wires one at a time, service the spark plug, reinstall the wire and move onto the next cylinder.

NOTE: For easy access for servicing the spark plugs, remove the air cleaner assembly and air intake tube.

1. Twist the spark plug boot and gently pull it and the wire from the spark plug. This is where the special plug wire pliers come in handy.

   CAUTION: *Never pull on the wire itself, damage to the inside conductor could occur!*

2. The plug wire boot has a cover which shields the plug cavity (in the head) against dirt. After removing the wire, blow out the cavity with air or clean it out with a small brush so dirt will not fall into the engine when the spark plug is removed.

3. Remove the spark plug with a plug socket. Turn the socket counterclockwise to remove the plug. Be sure to hold the socket straight on the plug to avoid breaking the insulator (a deep socket designed for spark plugs has a rubber cushion built-in to help prevent plug breakage).

4. Once the plug is out, compare it with the spark plug illustrations to determine the engine condition. This is crucial since spark plug readings are vital signs of engine condition and pending problems.

5. If the old plugs are to be reused, clean and re-gap them. If new spark plugs are to be installed, always check the gap. Use a round wire feeler gauge to check plug gap. The correct size gauge should pass through the electrode gap with a slight drag. If you're in doubt, try the next smaller and one size larger. The smaller gauge should go through easily and the larger should not go through at all. If adjustment is necessary use the bending tool on the end of the gauge. When adjusting the gap, always bend the side electrode. The center electrode is non-adjustable.

6. Squirt a drop of penetrating oil on the threads of the spark plug and install it. Don't oil the threads heavily. Turn the plug in clockwise by hand until it is snug.

7. When the plug is finger tight, tighten it to the proper torque 17–22 ft. lbs. DO NOT OVER TIGHTEN!

8. Install the plug wire and boot firmly over the spark plug after coating the inside of the boot and terminal with a thin coat of dielectric compound (Motorcraft D7AZ-19A331-A or the equivalent).

9. Proceed to the next spark plug.

CHECKING AND REPLACING SPARK PLUG CABLES

Your car is equipped with a electronic igni-

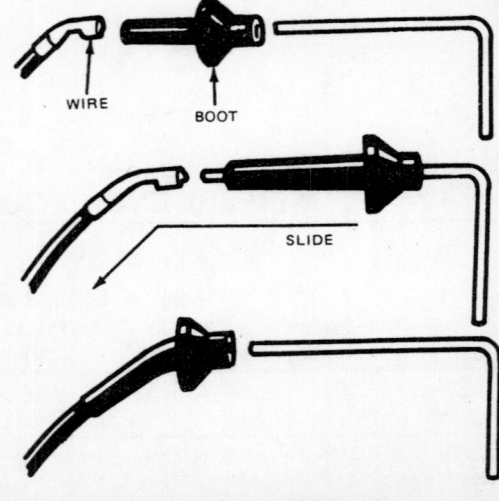

Use a bent tool to install new plug boots

ENGINE PERFORMANCE AND TUNE-UP 57

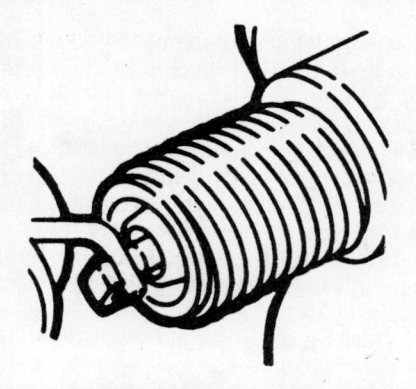

Check the spark plug gap with a wire feeler gauge

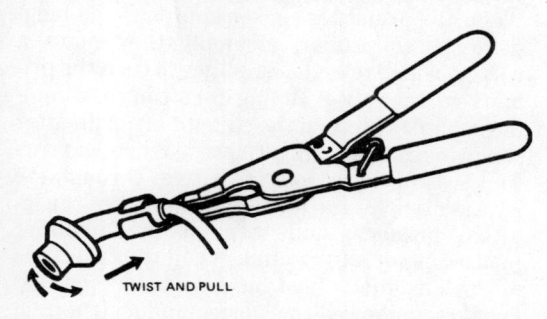

Special pliers used to remove the boots and wire from the spark plug

tion system which utilizes 8mm wires to conduct the hotter spark produced. The boots on these wires are designed to cover the spark plug cavities on the cylinder head.

Inspect the wires without removing them from the spark plugs, distributor cap or primary. Look for visible damage such as cuts, pinches, cracks or torn boots. Replace any wires that show damage. If the boot is damaged, it may be replaced by itself. It is not necessary to replace the complete wire just for the boot.

To replace the wire, grasp and twist the boot back and forth while pulling away from the spark plug. Use a special pliers if available.

NOTE: *Always coat the terminals of any wire removed or replaced with a thin layer of dielectric compound.*

When installing a wire be sure it is firmly mounted over or on the plug, distributor cap connector or primary terminal.

FIRING ORDER

If new wires have been installed (original wires are marked for cylinder location) and are not identified, or the wires have been removed from the distributor cap, the firing order is: 1-3-4-2 counterclockwise on 1.3L, 1.6L and 1.9L engines and clockwise on 2.3L HSC models.

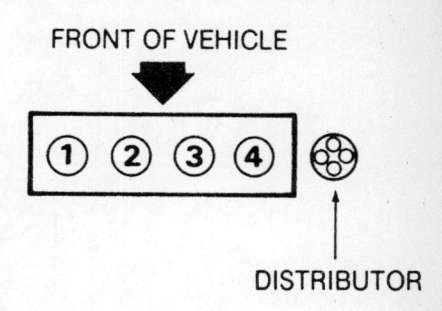

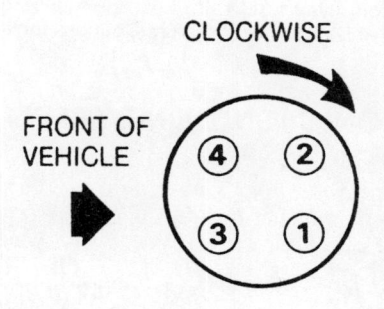

FIRING ORDER —1-3-4-2

1987–90 Escort, Lynx 1.9L Engine Firing Order; 1-3-4-2; Distributor Rotation; Clockwise

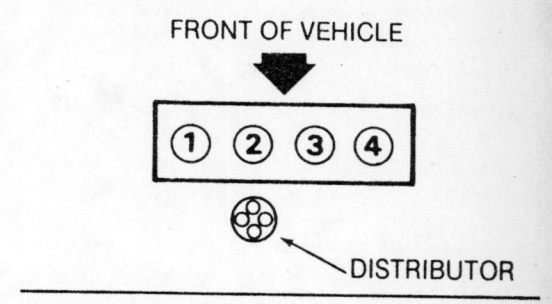

FIRING ORDER AND POSITION

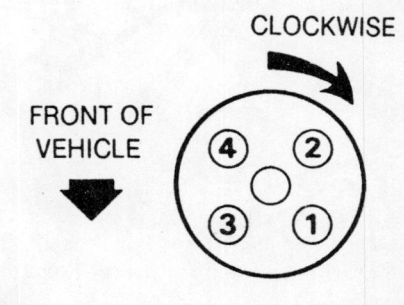

FIRING ORDER —1-3-4-2

Tempo, Topaz 2.3L Engine Firing Order; 1-3-4-2; Distributor Rotation; Clockwise

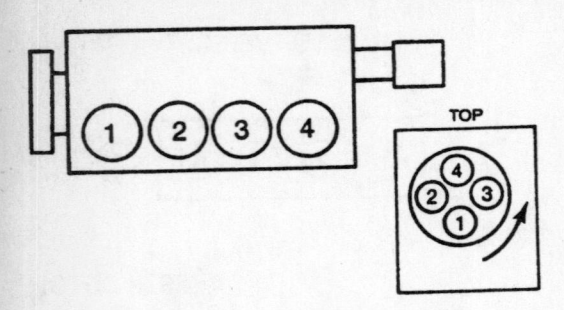

1981–86 Escort, Lynx 1.3L, 1.6L, 1.9L Engine Firing Order; 1–3–4–2 Distributor Rotation; Counterclockwise

ELECTRONIC IGNITION SYSTEM

NOTE: *This book contains simple testing procedures for your Ford's electronic ignition. More comprehensive testing on this system and other electronic control systems on your Ford can be found in CHILTON'S GUIDE TO ELECTRONIC ENGINE CONTROLS, book part number 7535 for 1978-85, #7768 for the 1984-88 years and #8024 for the 1988-90 years. All of these manuals are available at your local retailer.*

Your car uses an electronic ignition system. The purpose of using an electronic ignition system is: To eliminate the deterioration of spark quality which occur in the breaker point ignition system as the breaker points wore. To extend maintenance intervals. To provide a more intense and reliable spark at every firing impulse in order to ignite the leaner gas mixtures necessary to control emissions.

The breaker points, point actuating cam and the condenser have been eliminated in the solid state distributor. They are replace by an ignition module and a magnetic pulse-signal generator (pick-up).

The Dura Spark II is a pulse triggered, transistor controlled breakerless ignition system. With the ignition switch **ON**, the primary circuit is on and the ignition primary is energized. When the armature spokes approach the magnetic pick-up primary assembly, they induce a voltage which tells the amplifier to turn the primary current off. A timing circuit in the amplifier module will turn the current on again after the primary field has collapsed. When the current is on, it flows from the battery through the ignition switch, the primary windings of the ignition primary, and through the amplifier module circuits to ground. When the current is off, the magnetic field built up in the ignition primary is allowed to collapse, inducing a high voltage into the secondary windings of the primary. High voltage is produced each time the field is thus built up and collapsed.

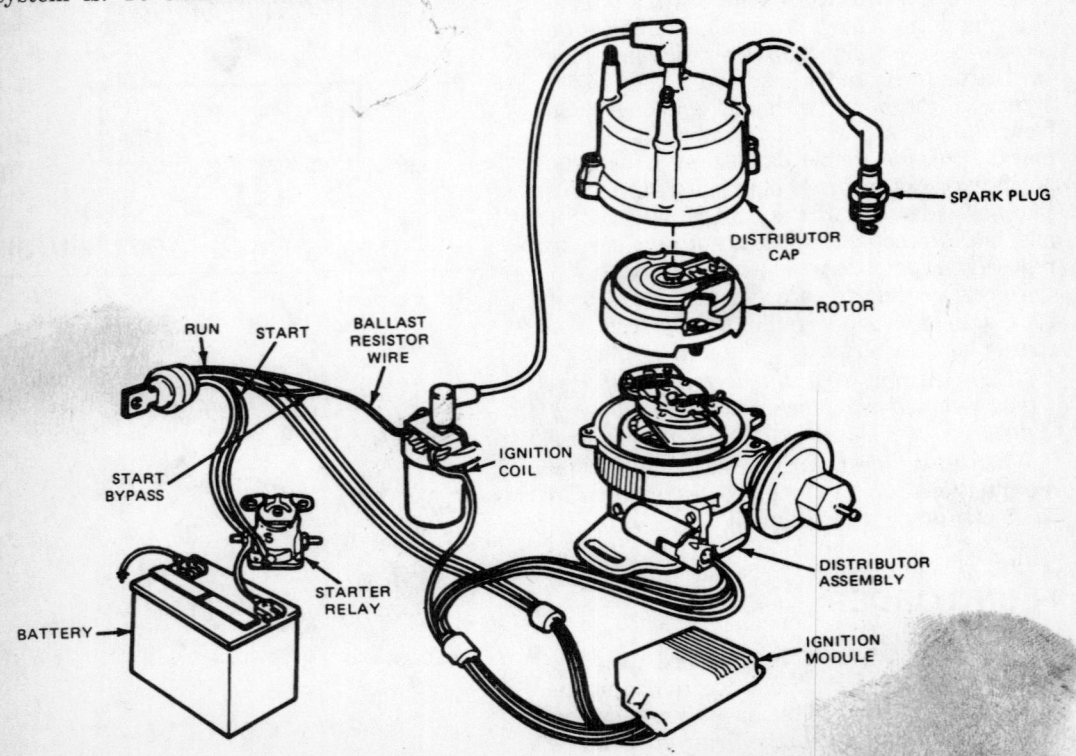

The Dura Spark ignition system

ENGINE PERFORMANCE AND TUNE-UP

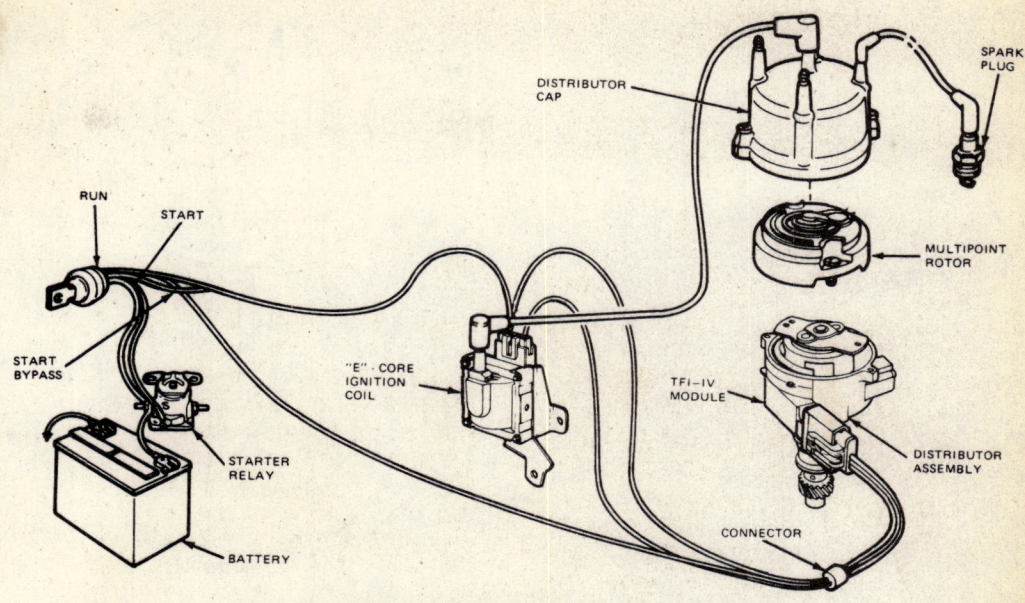

2.3L HSC TFI-IV on the Tempo/Topaz (early version)

The Thick Film Integrated IV Ignition System (TFI-IV) module is made of a thermo plastic and is mounted on the base of the distributor. This module supplies voltage to the profile ignition pick-up (PIP) sensor, which in turn sends the crankshaft position information to the TFI module.

The TFI module then sends this information to the electronic control module (computer), which determines the spark timing and sends an electronic signal to the TFI ignition module to turn off the primary and produce a spark to fire the spark plugs. The TFI-IV ignition system is used on the 1.6L, 1.9L and 2.3L engines. This ignition system also uses a universal distributor.

A Universal Distributor equipped with either a TFI-I or TFI-IV system is used on some models, depending on year, engine option, and model. Models equipped with TFI also use an **E** primary which replaces the oil filled design used with Dura-Spark.

The Universal Distributor equipped with TFI-IV uses a vane switch stator assembly

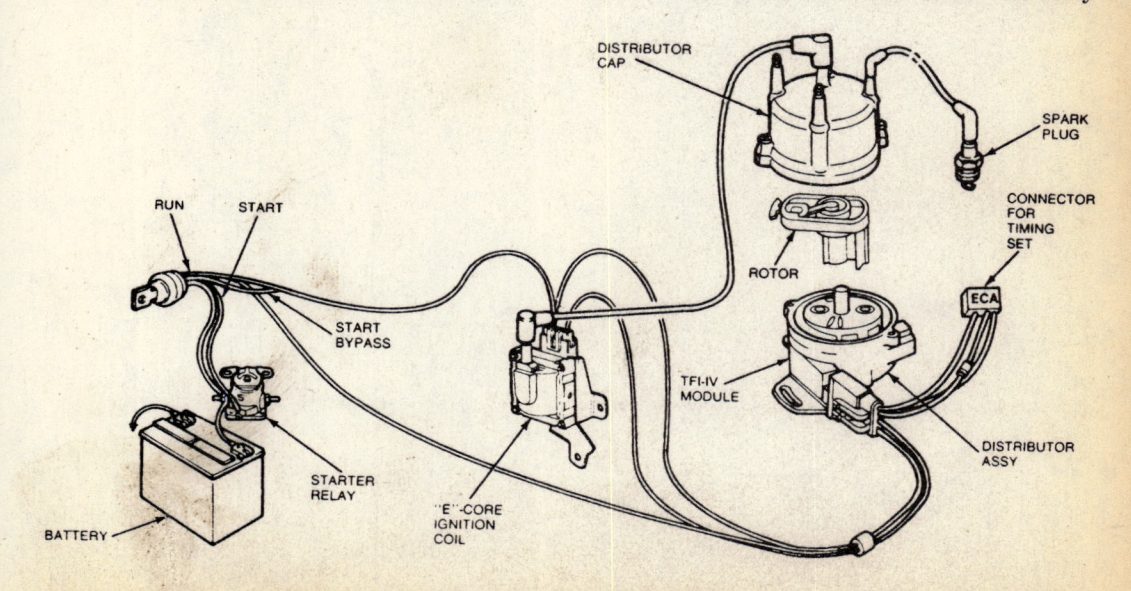

The TFI ignition system (later version)

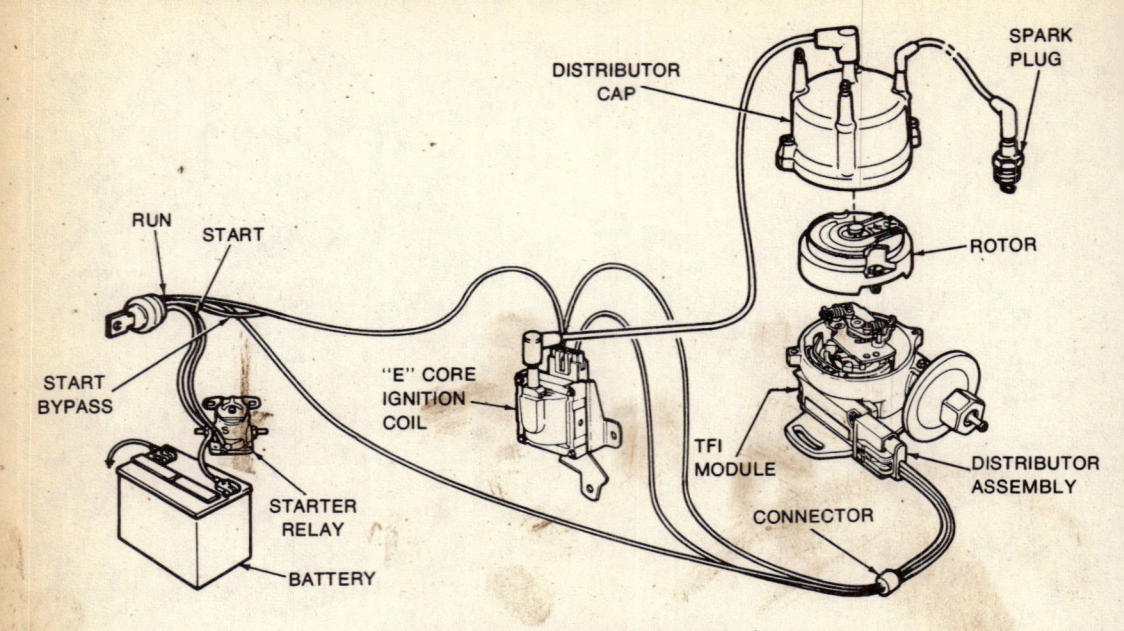

60 ENGINE PERFORMANCE AND TUNE-UP

The TFI ignition system (early version)

which replace the primary stator. The IV system incorporates provision for fixed octane adjustment and has no centrifugal or vacuum advance mechanisms. All necessary timing requirements are handled by the EEC-IV electronic engine control system. The TFI-IV system features a "Push Start" mode that will allow the vehicles equipped with manual transmissions to be push started. Do not attempt to push start a vehicle equipped with an automatic transmission.

NOTE: *Do not attempt to change the timing by the use of different octane rods without first having the proper authorization; federal emission requirements will be affected.*

The universal distributor operates by using a hall effect vane switch assembly, causing the ignition primary to be switched **OFF** and **ON** by the EEC-IV and the TFI-IV modules. The vane switch is an encapsulated package consisting of a Hall sensor on one side and a permanent magnet on the other side.

A rotary vane cup, made of ferrous metal, is used to trigger the signal **ON** and **OFF**. When the window of the vane cup is between the magnet and the Hall effect device, a magnetic

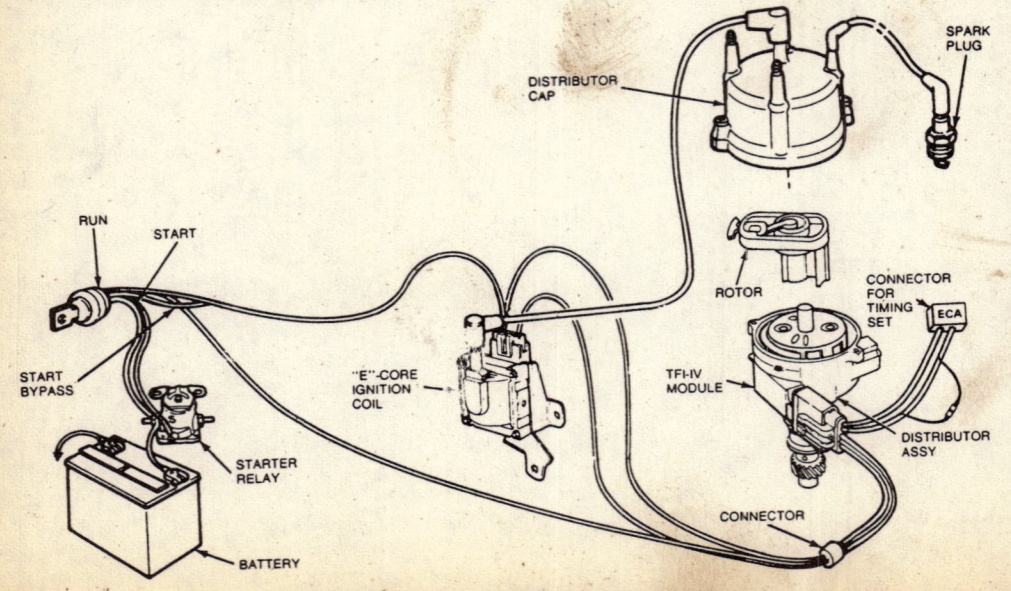

2.3L HSC TFI-IV on the Tempo/Topaz (later version)

ENGINE PERFORMANCE AND TUNE-UP

flux field id completed from the magnet through the Hall effect device and back to the magnet.

As the vane passes through the opening, the flux lines are shunted through the vane and back top the magnet. During this time, a voltage is produced as the vane passes through the opening. When the vane clears the opening, the window edge causes the signal to go to zero volts. The signal is then used by the EEC-IV system for crankshaft position sensing and the computation of the desired spark advance based on engine demand and calibration. The conditioned spark advance and voltage distribution is accomplished through a conventional rotor, cap and ignition wires.

Ignition Coil

PRIMARY RESISTANCE

1. Verify that the ignition switch is in the OFF position.
2. Remove the primary connector, clean and inspect for dirt or corrosion.
3. Measure the resistance between the positive and negative terminals of the primary with an ohmmeter. On TFI models, resistance should measure 0.3–1.0. On Dura-Spark models, the resistance should measure 0.8–1.6.
4. Replace the primary if resistance is not within specifications.

SECONDARY RESISTANCE

1. Follow Steps 1 and 2 of the Primary Resistance Test.
2. Measure resistance between the negative (BATT) and high tension lead terminal of the primary.
3. Resistance for Dura-Spark should be between 7,700–10,500. TFI should be between 8000–11,500.
4. Replace the primary if not within specifications.

Dura Spark II Troubleshooting

The following procedures can be used to determine whether the ignition system is working or not. If these procedures fail to locate and correct the problem, full troubleshooting procedures should be performed by a qualified service technician.

PRELIMINARY CHECKS

1. Check the battery's state of charge and connections.
2. Inspect all wires and connections for breaks, cuts, abrasions, or burn spots. Repair as necessary.
3. Unplug all connectors one at a time and inspect for corroded or burned contacts. Repair and plug connectors back together. DO NOT remove the dielectric compound in the connectors.
4. Check for loose or damaged spark plug or primary wires. Check for excessive resistance. If the boots or nipples are removed on 8mm ignition wires, reline the inside of each with silicone dielectric compound (Motorcraft WA 10).

Special Tools

To perform the following tests, two special tools are needed: the ignition test jumper shown in the illustration and a modified spark plug. Use the illustration to assemble the ignition test jumper. The test jumper must be used when performing the following tests. The modified spark plug is basically a spark plug with the side electrode removed. Ford makes a special tool called a Spark Tester for this purpose, which besides not having a side electrode is equipped with a spring clip so that it can be grounded to engine metal. It is recommended that the Spark Tester be used as there is less chance of being shocked.

NOTE: *After completing the following test (that involve using a straight pin) apply a small amount of silicone sealer to the pin holes in the wires.*

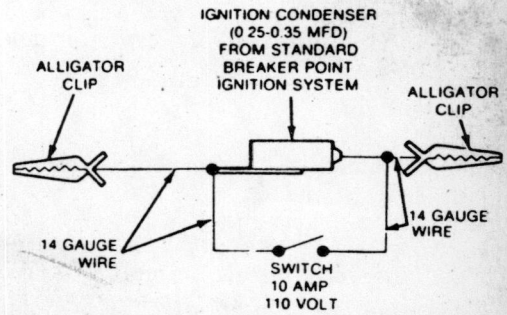

Test jumper switch used for troubleshooting the Ford electronic ignition system.

Run Mode Spark Test

NOTE: *The wire colors given here are the main color of the wires, not the dots or stripe marks.*

STEP 1

1. Remove the distributor cap and rotor from the distributor.
2. With the ignition off, turn the engine over by hand until one of the teeth on the distributor armature aligns with the magnet in the pick-up primary.
3. Remove the primary wire from the distributor cap. Install the modified spark plug (see Special Tools) in the primary wire terminal

62 ENGINE PERFORMANCE AND TUNE-UP

and using insulated pliers, hold the spark plug base against the engine block.

4. Turn the ignition to RUN (not START) and tap the distributor body with a screwdriver handle. There should be a spark at the modified spark plug or at the primary wire terminal.

5. If a good spark is evident, the primary circuit is OK, perform Start Mode Spark Test. If there is no spark, proceed to Step 2.

STEP 2

1. Unplug the module connector(s) which contains the green and black module leads.

2. In the harness side of the connector(s), connect the special test jumper (see special tools) between the leads which connect the green and black leads of the module pig tails. Use paper clips on connector socket holes to make contact. Do not allow clips to ground.

3. Turn the ignition switch to RUN (not START) and close the test jumper switch. Leave closed for about one second, then open. Repeat several times. There should be a spark each time the switch is opened.

4. If there is NO spark, the problem is probably in the primary circuit through the ignition switch, the primary, the green lead or the black lead, or the ground connection in the distributor. Perform Step 3. If there IS a spark, the primary circuit wiring and primary are probably OK. The problem is probably in the distributor pick-up, the module red wire, or the module. Perform Step 6.

STEP 3

1. Disconnect the test jumper lead from the black lead and connect it to a good ground. Turn the test jumper switch on and off several times as in Step 2.

2. If there is NO spark, the problem is probably in the green lead, the primary, or the primary feed circuit. Perform Step 5.

3. If there IS spark, the problem is probably

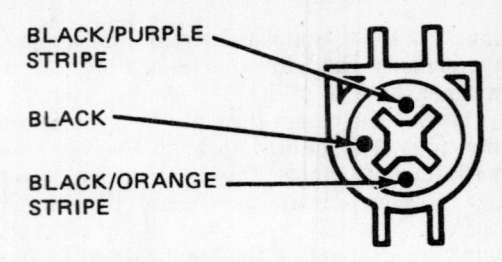

Dura Spark distributor connector color codes

in the black lead or the distributor ground connections. Perform Step 4.

STEP 4

1. Connect an ohmmeter between the black lead and ground. With the meter on its lowest scale, there should be NO measurable resistance in the circuit. If there is resistance, check the distributor ground connections and the black lead from the module. Repair as necessary, remove the ohmmeter, plug in all connections and repeat Step 1.

2. If there is NO resistance, the primary ground wiring is OK. Perform Step 6.

STEP 5

1. Disconnect the test jumper from the green lead and ground and connect it between the TACH-TEST terminal of the primary and a good ground on the engine.

2. With the ignition switch in the RUN position, turn the jumper switch on. Hold it on for about one second then turn it off as in Step 2. Repeat several times. There should be a spark each time the switch is turned off. If there is NO spark, the problem is probably in the primary circuit running through the ignition switch to the primary BAT terminal, or in the primary itself. Check primary resistance (test given later in this section), and check the primary for internal shorts or opens. Check the primary feed circuit for opens, shorts or high resistance. Repair as necessary, reconnect all

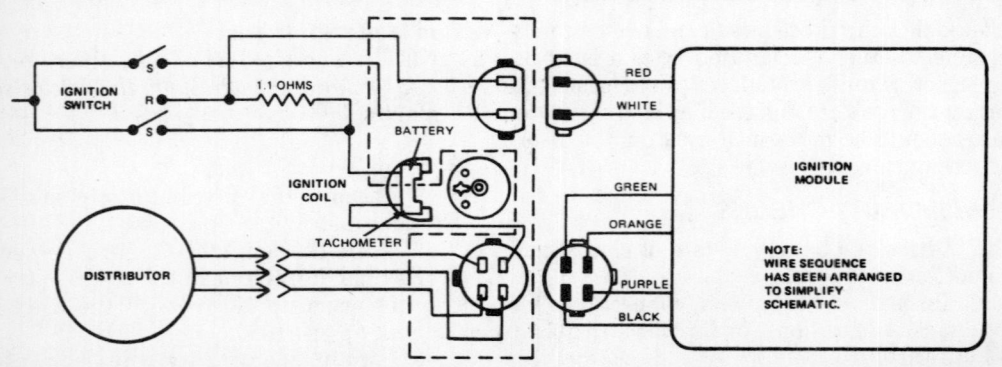

Color codes for Dura Spark module and harness

connectors and repeat Step 1. If there IS spark, the primary and its feed circuit are OK. The problem could be in the green lead between the primary and the module. Check for open or short, repair as necessary, reconnect all connectors and repeat Step 1.

STEP 6

To perform this step, a voltmeter which is not combined with a dwell meter is needed. The slight needle oscillations (0.5V) you'll be looking for may not be detectable on the combined voltmeter/dwell meter unit.

1. Connect a voltmeter between the orange and purple leads on the harness side of the module connectors.

CAUTION: *On catalytic converter equipped cars, disconnect the air supply line between the Thermactor by-pass valve and the manifold before cranking the engine with the ignition off. This will prevent damage to the catalytic converter. After testing, run the engine for at least 3 minutes before reconnecting the by-pass valve, to clear excess fuel from the exhaust system.*

2. Set the voltmeter on its lowest scale and crank the engine. The meter needle should oscillate slightly (about 0.5V). If the meter does not oscillate, check the circuit through the magnetic pick-up in the distributor for open shorts, shorts to ground and resistance. Resistance between the orange and purple leads should be 400–1,000, and between each lead and ground should be more than 70,000. Repair as necessary, reconnect all connectors and repeat Step 1.

3. If the meter oscillates, the problem is probably in the power feed to the module (red wire) or in the module itself. Proceed to Step 7.

STEP 7

1. Remove all meters and jumpers and plug in all connectors.

2. Turn the ignition switch to the RUN position and measure voltage between the battery positive terminal and engine ground. It should be 12 volts.

3. Next, measure voltage between the red lead of the module and engine ground. To make this measurement, it will be necessary to pierce the red wire with a straight pin and connect the voltmeter to the straight pin and to ground. DO NOT ALLOW THE STRAIGHT PIN TO GROUND ITSELF!

4. The two readings should be within one volts of each other. If not within one volt, the problem is in the power feed to the red lead. Check for shorts, open, or high resistance and correct as necessary. After repairs, repeat Step 1.

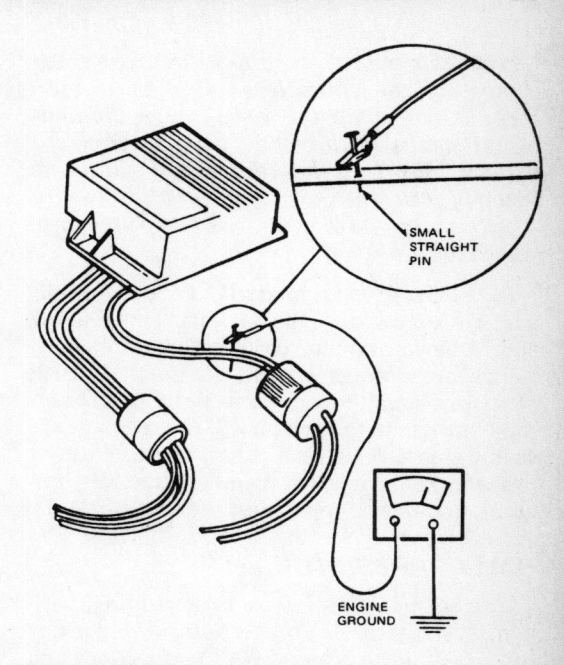

Inserting a straight pin to test a circuit

If the readings are within one volt, the problem is probably in the module. Replace with a good module and repeat Step 1. If this corrects the problem reconnect the old module and repeat Step 1. If the problem returns, replace the module.

Start Mode Spark Test

NOTE: *The wire colors given here are the main color of the wires, not the dots and stripe marks.*

1. Remove the primary wire from the distributor cap. Install the modified spark plug mentioned under Special Tools, above, in the primary wire and ground it to engine metal either by its spring clip (Spark Tester) or by holding the spark plug shell against the engine block with insulated pliers.

CAUTION: *See the Caution under Step 6 of Run Mode Spark Test.*

2. Have an assistant crank the engine using the ignition switch and check for spark. If there IS a good spark, the problem is most probably in the distributor cap, rotor, ignition cables or spark plugs. If there is NO spark, proceed to Step 3.

3. Measure the battery voltage. Next, measure the voltage at the white wire of the module while cranking the engine. To make this measurement, it will be necessary to pierce the white wire with a straight pin and connect the voltmeter to the straight pin and to ground.

NOTE: *DO NOT ALLOW THE STRAIGHT PIN TO GROUND ITSELF! The battery voltage and the voltage at the white wire should*

ENGINE PERFORMANCE AND TUNE-UP

be within one volt of each other. If the readings are not within one volt of each other, check and repair the feed through the ignition switch to the white wire. Recheck for spark (Step 1). If the readings are within one volt of each other, or if there is still NO spark after power feed to white wire is repaired, proceed to Step 4.

4. Measure the primary **BAT** terminal voltage while cranking the engine. The reading should be within one volt of battery voltage. If the readings are not within one volt of each other, check and repair the feed through the ignition switch to the primary. If the readings are within one volt of each other, the problem is probably in the ignition module. Substitute another module and repeat test for spark (Step 1).

BALLAST RESISTOR

The ballast resistor wire is usually red with light green stripes. To check it you must disconnect it at the primary **BAT** connections and at the connector at the end of the wiring harness. The connector at the end of the wiring harness is a rectangular connector with eight terminals. Connect an ohmmeter to each end of the wire and set it to the **High** scale. The resistance of the wire should be between 1.05 and 1.15. Any other reading merits replacement of the resistor wire with one of the correct service resistor wires.

TFI Troubleshooting

NOTE: *It is recommended that before performing this or any other test on your vehicle, you check with your local manufactures representative to make sure that if by doing these tests there may be a chance that you will violate your warranty, thus rendering you helpless to submit a claim on your vehicle if a problem should occur in the future.*

Refer to the comments, preliminary checks and special tool paragraphs of the proceeding Dura-Spark Troubleshooting section. In addition to preliminary checks mentioned, check to be sure the TFI module is securely attached to the distributor. The following test can be used for the TFI-1 and the TFI-IV system up to mid year of 1988. It is then that the open bowl distributor ignition system was introduced. This system involves a different test set-up and is more complex than the earlier version of the TFI ignition system. Testing for this system should be down by an authorized factory technician.

This book contains simple testing procedures for your Ford's electronic ignition. More comprehensive testing on this system and other electronic control systems on your Ford can be found in CHILTON'S GUIDE TO ELECTRONIC ENGINE CONTROLS, book part number 7535 for 1978–85, #7768 for the 1984–88 years and #8024 for the 1988–90 years. All of these manuals are available at your local retailer.

After completing the following test (that involve using a straight pin) apply a small amount of silicone sealer to the pin holes in the wires.

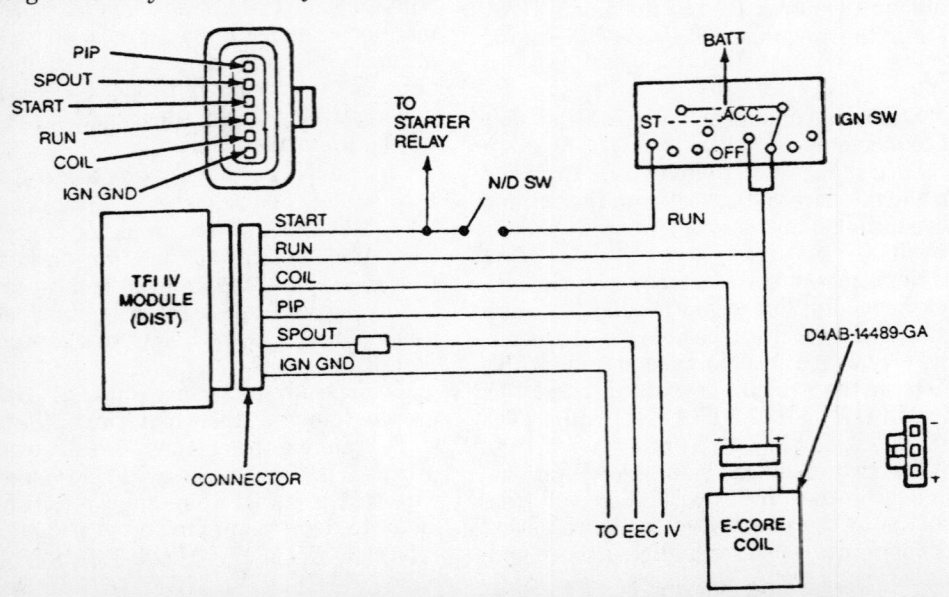

Typical thick film integrated ignition system with an open bowl distributor

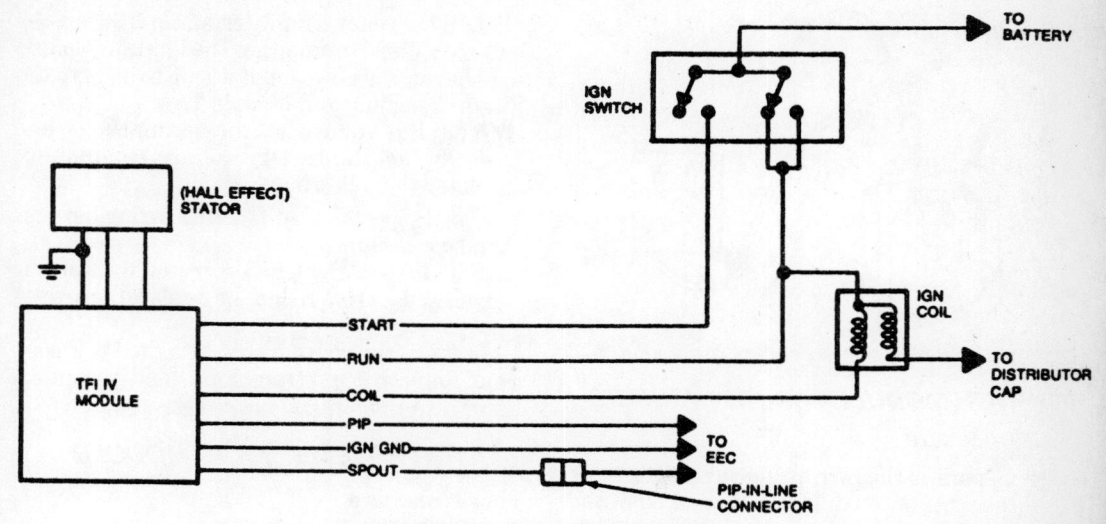

ENGINE PERFORMANCE AND TUNE-UP

Typical TFI-IV system electrical schematic

IGNITION COIL PRIMARY CIRCUIT SWITCHING

Test Procedure

1. Carefully insert a small straight pin or equivalent into the wire going to the negative terminal of the ignition primary. Place the pin approximately 1 inch from the TFI module connector.

NOTE: *Do not allow the straight pin to ground itself!*

2. Attach a 12 volt DC volt test light between the straight pin and the engine ground. Crank the engine.
3. If the test light flashes or the test light lights up but does not flash, do the following:

   a. Turn the ignition switch to the **OFF** position. Disconnect the ignition primary connector and inspect it for dirt, corrosion and damage.

   b. Using a suitable ohmmeter, measure the resistance from the positive terminal to the negative terminal of the ignition primary. If the ohmmeter reading is 0.3–1.0, the ignition primary is operating properly and it is good to go on to the Ignition Coil Secondary Resistance Test.

   c. If the resistance reading is less than 0.3 or greater than 1.0, replace the ignition primary.

4. Disconnect the test light and remove the straight pin.

IGNITION COIL SECONDARY RESISTANCE

Test Procedure

1. Disconnect the ignition primary connector and using a suitable ohmmeter, measure the resistance from the negative terminal to the high voltage terminal of the ignition primary.
2. If the ohmmeter reading is 6,500–11,500, the primary is operating properly and it is good to go onto the Wiring Harness Test.
3. If the ohmmeter reading is less than 6,500 or greater than 11,500, replace the ignition primary.
4. Reconnect the ignition primary connector.

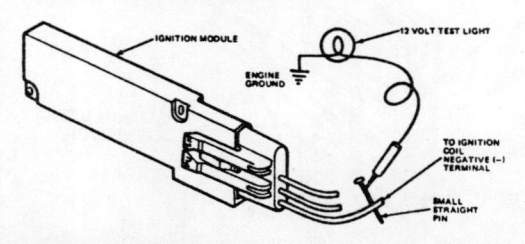

Making the ignition coil primary circuit switching test (TFI-1)

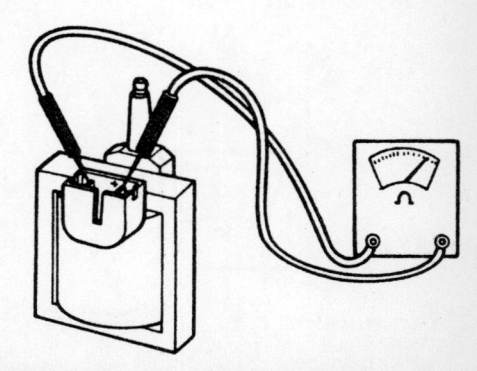

Testing the ignition coil primary resistance

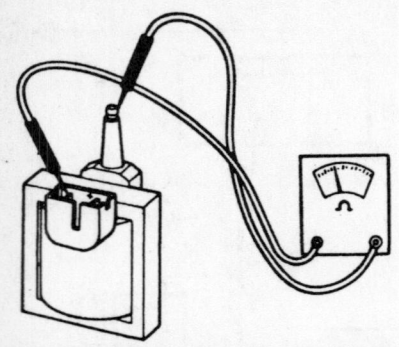

ENGINE PERFORMANCE AND TUNE-UP

Testing the ignition coil secondary resistance

IGNITION MODULE WIRING HARNESS

Test Procedure

1. Separate the wiring harness connector from the ignition module. Be sure to push the connector tabs to separate the connector from the harness. Inspect the harness for dirt, corrosion and damage.
2. Disconnect the wire at the **S** terminal of the starter relay. Attach the negative lead of a suitable volt/ohmmeter lead to the distributor base. Measure the battery voltage.
3. Insert a straight pin or equivalent into the ignition module connector and test each terminal on the connector with the positive terminal of the volt/ohmmeter as follows:
    a. Terminal number 1 (which will be terminal number 2 on the TFI-IV system) should be tested with the ignition switch in the **RUN** and **START** position. This terminal wire circuit is to the ignition primary negative terminal.
    b. Terminal number 2 (which will be terminal number 3 on the TFI-IV system) should be tested with the ignition switch in the **RUN** and **START** position. This terminal wire circuit is to the run circuit.
    c. Terminal number 3 (which will be terminal number 4 on the TFI-IV system) should be tested with the ignition switch in the **START** position. This terminal wire circuit is to the start circuit.

4. If the voltage at the terminals is 90% of the battery voltage (minimum) the ignition module wire harness is good and it is safe to go onto the Stator Assembly and Module Test.
5. If the voltage at the terminals is less than 90% of the battery voltage (minimum), check for the following:
    a. Inspect for faults in the wiring harness and connectors.
    b. Inspect the ignition switch for worn or damaged parts, repair or replace as necessary.
6. Turn the ignition switch to the **OFF** position. Remove the straight pin and reconnect the **S** terminal of the starter relay.

STATOR ASSEMBLY AND MODULE

Test Procedure

1. Remove the distributor from the engine and remove the TFI ignition module from the distributor.
2. Inspect the distributor ground screw, stator assembly wires and terminal.
3. Using a suitable ohmmeter, measure the resistance of the stator assembly.
4. If the ohmmeter reading is 650–1,300, the stator assembly is operating properly and the TFI ignition module should be replaced.
5. If the ohmmeter reading is less than 650 or greater than 1,300, the TFI ignition module is operating properly and the stator assembly should be replaced.
6. Install the TFI module onto the distributor. Install the distributor on the engine and make all necessary adjustments.

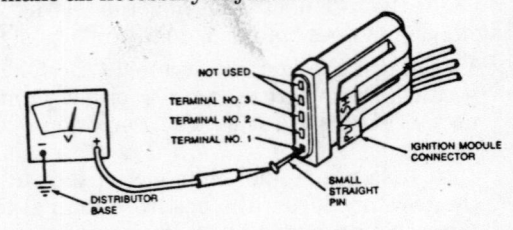

Testing the ignition module wiring harness (TFI-1)

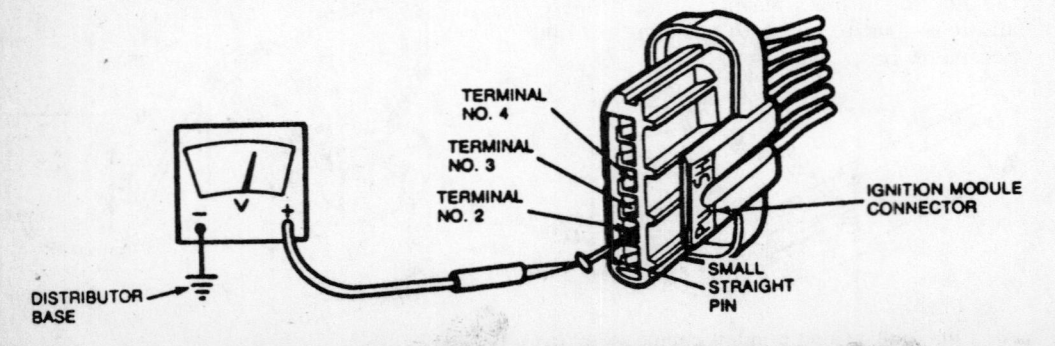

Testing the ignition module wiring harness (TFI-IV)

ENGINE PERFORMANCE AND TUNE-UP

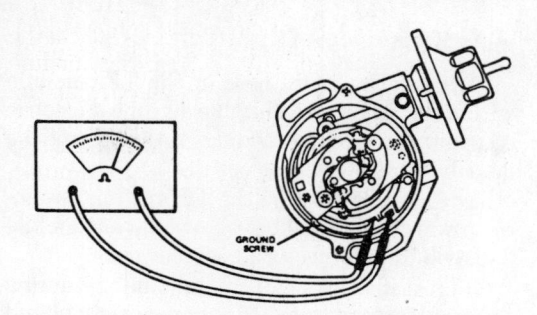

Testing the stator assembly with an ohmmeter

PRIMARY CIRCUIT CONTINUITY

Test Procedure

1. Separate the wiring harness connector from the TFI ignition module. Inspect for dirt, corrosion or damage. Be sure to push the connector tabs to separate the connector from the harness.
2. Attach the negative lead of a suitable volt/ohmmeter to the distributor base. Measure the battery voltage.
3. Attach a suitable volt/ohmmeter to a small straight pin or equivalent, which will be inserted into the TFI ignition module connector terminal number 1 (which will be terminal number 2 on the TFI-IV system).

NOTE: *Do not allow the straight pin to ground itself!*

4. Turn the ignition switch to the **RUN** position and measure the voltage at terminal number 1 (which will be terminal number 2 on the TFI-IV system) of the TFI module connector.
5. If the voltage is 90% of the battery voltage (minimum) refer to the Stator Assembly and Module Test.
6. If the voltage at the terminal is less than 90% of the battery voltage than proceed to the Ignition Coil Primary Voltage test.

IGNITION COIL PRIMARY VOLTAGE

Test Procedure

1. Attach the negative lead of a suitable volt/ohmmeter to the distributor base. Measure the voltage.
2. Turn the ignition switch to the **RUN** position and using the positive lead of the volt/ohmmeter measure the voltage at the negative side of the ignition primary.
3. If the voltage reading is 90% of the battery voltage (minimum), inspect the wiring harness between the ignition module and the primary negative terminal.
4. If the voltage reading is less than 90% of the battery voltage (minimum), inspect the wiring harness between the ignition module and the primary negative terminal and look for a short to ground. Then go onto the Ignition Coil Supply Voltage Test.
5. Turn the ignition switch to the **OFF** position and remove all the test equipment.

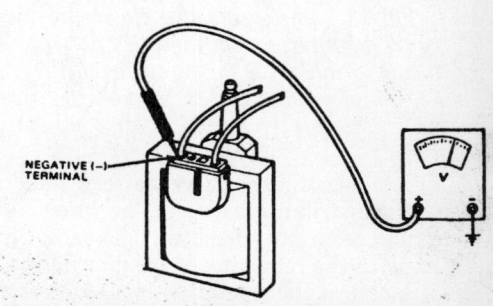

Making the ignition coil primary voltage test

IGNITION COIL SUPPLY VOLTAGE

Test Procedure

1. Attach the negative lead of a suitable volt/ohmmeter to the distributor base. Measure the voltage.
2. Turn the ignition switch to the **RUN** position and using the positive lead of the volt/ohmmeter measure the voltage at the positive side of the ignition primary.
3. If the voltage reading is 90% of the battery voltage (minimum), inspect the ignition primary connector for dirt, corrosion or other damage. If the primary connector is in good working condition, remove and replace the ignition primary.
4. If the voltage is less than 90% of the battery voltage, inspect the wiring between the ignition primary and the ignition switch. If the ignition switch is found to be a fault, replace it with a new one.
5. Turn the ignition switch to the **OFF** position and remove all the test equipment.

TFI MODULE

Removal

NOTE: *it may seem possible to remove the TFI module from the distributor without having to remove the distributor. But in reality there is not enough clearance allowed in*

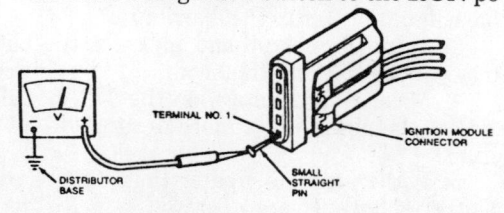

Testing the primary circuit continuity

ENGINE PERFORMANCE AND TUNE-UP

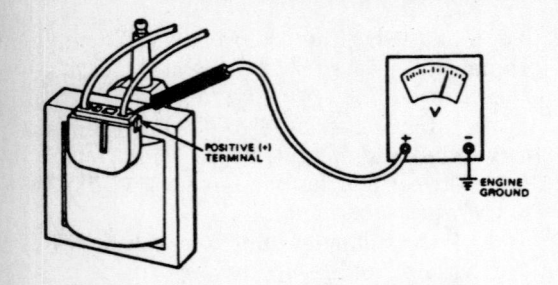

Making the ignition coil supply voltage test

order to remove the module without breaking any of its terminals. If the TFI module being removed is to be replaced with a new one, it is recommended that only a genuine factory replacement part be used. It has been discovered that in some cases the electronic circuitry in the aftermarket modules, is not always compatible with the circuitry of the on board computer installed in the vehicle, thus causing driveability problems and no-start conditions.

1. Disconnect the negative battery cables. Remove the distributor cap with the wires still in place and set it out of the way, so as not to interfere with the removing of the distributor.
2. Disconnect the primary wiring connector from the distributor.

NOTE: *Before removing the distributor cap, mark the position of the number one spark plug wire tower on the distributor base for future reference during installation.*

3. Remove the rotor by steadily pulling upward so as to remove it form the distributor shaft and armature. Remove the TFI harness connector.

NOTE: *Some engine may be equipped with a new security type hold down bolt which will require the use of special tool T82L-12270-A or equivalent (12 point socket) in order to remove these special hold down bolts.*

4. Remove the distributor hold down bolts and or clamps. Remove the distributor by lifting it straight out of the engine being careful not to disturb the intermediate shaft.
5. Place the distributor into a suitable vise. Remove the 2 module retaining screws.
6. Pull the right hand side of the TFI module down the distributor mounting flange and back up to disengage the module terminals from the connectors at the distributor base. The module may now be pulled toward the flange and away from the distributor.

NOTE: *Do not attempt to lift the module from the mounting surface prior to moving the entire module toward the distributor flange as the pins will break at the distributor and module connector.*

Installation

1. Coat the metal base of the TFI module with a thin layer of a suitable silicone dielectric compound. Place the module on the base of the distributor.
2. Carefully position the TFI module assembly toward the distributor bowl and engage the 3 distributor connector pins securely.
3. Install the 2 TFI module retaining screws starting with the upper right hand screw and torque them to 16–35 inch lbs.
4. Reinstall the distributor on the engine and torque the hold down bolts to 17–25 ft. lbs. Reinstall the distributor cap and wires.
5. Install the TFI wiring harness connector. Reset the initial timing and make all necessary adjustments.

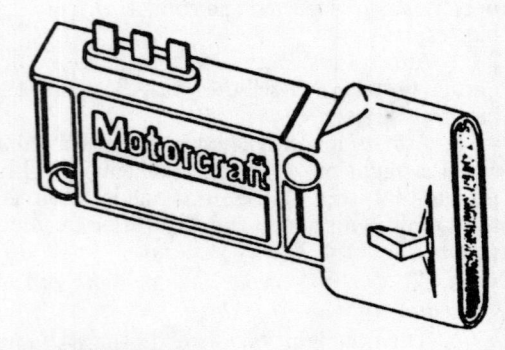

Typical TFI module

CHILTON TIPS

This following Chilton tip is for vehicles that exhibit conditions of rough idle or spark knock while the engine is cold or hot. Thus condition, could be linked to a stator problem and should be checked as follows:

Test 1

This procedure must be performed with the vehicle at or below the temperature where the symptoms occur.

1. With the key in the **OFF** position, disconnect the pin-in-line connector near the TFI module (Spout wire connector).
2. Attach the negative terminal of a suitable volt/ohmmeter to the distributor.
3. Start the engine and measure the battery voltage at 1200–1500 rpm.
4. Measure the voltage on the TFI module side of the pin-in-line connector at 1200–1500 rpm.
5. If the result is greater than 40% of the battery voltage, go onto Test 2.
6. If the result is less than 40% of the battery voltage, replace the stator assembly.

ENGINE PERFORMANCE AND TUNE-UP

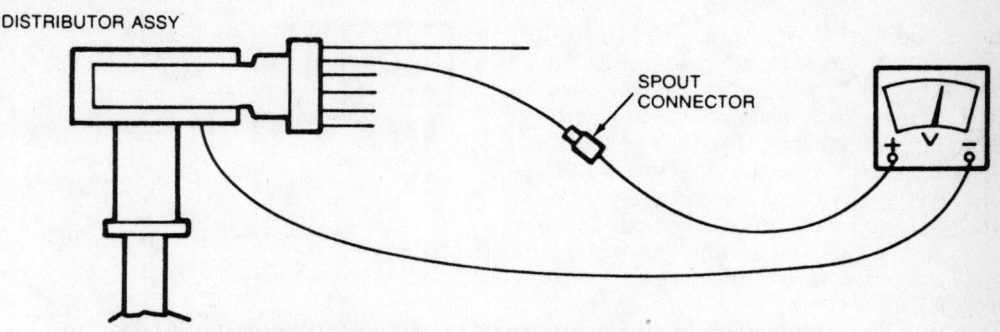

Making the test hook-up for inspecting the stator for drivability problems

Test 2

1. Warm the engine up until it reaches normal operating temperatures.
2. Using the same set-up procedure as in Test 1, measure the voltage on the TFI module side of the pin-in-line connector at approximately 1200 rpm and again at approximately 4000 rpm.

NOTE: *To avoid the risk of personal injury, close the hood for this test.*

3. Is the voltage at 4000 rpm less than 90% of the voltage at 1200 rpm?
4. If the voltage at 4000 rpm is less than 90% of the voltage at 1200 rpm, replace the stator assembly.
5. If the voltage at 4000 rpm is greater than 90% of the voltage at 1200 rpm, go onto Test 3.

Test 3

1. Warm the engine up until it reaches normal operating temperatures.
2. Using the same set-up procedure as in Test 1, measure the voltage on the TFI module side of the pin-in-line connector at 1200–1500 rpm.
3. If the voltage results obtained in Test 1 are less than 90% of the voltage obtained in this Test, replace the stator assembly.
4. If the voltage is greater than 90% the stator assembly is working properly.

All 1984 Models with the EEC E-Core Ignition Coil

There have been complaints of an engine stumble or stalls, noise in the radio and or and erratic clock operation. If the engines in these effected models, suffer from any one of these conditions, the problem is usually caused by an internal voltage arc in the E-core ignition primary. The arc is a result of an open or a high resistance secondary circuit. This condition generates a high frequency noise within the vehicle's electrical system and can be checked as follows:

1. Disconnect the negative battery cable. Place the ignition switch to the **OFF** position. Disconnect the E-core ignition primary priand secondary leads.
2. Using a suitable ohmmeter, measure the resistance between the primary (positive) terminal and the high voltage secondary terminal. If the resistance is greater than 7000–14,000, replace the ignition primary.
3. Reconnect the high voltage secondary lead and confirm that the protective boot is fully seated. Reconnect the coil primary lead and negative battery cable. Verify that the reported condition has been corrected.

Ignition Timing

1. Timing marks on 1.3/1.6/1.9L engines consist of a notch on the crankshaft pulley and a graduated scale molded into the camshaft drive belt cover. The number of degrees before or after TDC (top dead center) represented by each mark can be interpreted according to the decal affixed to the top of the belt cover (emissions decal).
2. Timing marks on 2.3 HSC engines are located on the flywheel edge (manual transaxle or flywheel face (automatic transaxle) and are visible through a slot in the transaxle case at the back of the engine. A cover plate retained by two screws must be removed to view the timing marks on manual cars. Each mark (small graduation) equals 2°. Early automatic cars have timing marks punched on the flywheel, the marks are 5° apart. The required degree mark should align with the timing slot pointer. Unless the emission decal specifies otherwise, timing for manual transaxle models is 10° BTDC and 15° BTDC for automatic transaxle models.
3. Turn the engine until No. 1 piston is at TDC on the compression stroke. Apply white paint or chalk to the rotating timing mark (notch on pulley or flywheel) after cleaning the metal surface.
4. Refer to the emissions decal for timing, engine rpm and vacuum hose (if equipped) status information. Disconnect and plug the distributor vacuum line(s) if equipped and re-

ENGINE PERFORMANCE AND TUNE-UP

quired. On models equipped with the EEC IV system engine, disconnect the ignition spout wire (circuit 36–yellow/light green dots or black) from the distributor connector or remove the shorting bar from the double spout wire connector if so equipped. On 1.6/1.9L engines equipped with a 2-bbl carburetor, disconnect the barometric pressure switch and connect a jumper wire across the ignition module black and yellow wire connector pins.

5. Attach a timing light and tachometer to the engine. Start the engine and allow to idle until normal operating temperature is reached.

6. Be sure the parking brake is applied and wheels blocked. Place the transmission in gear specified on emissions decal. Check idle rpm and adjust if necessary.

7. Aim the flashing timing light at the timing marks. If the proper marks are not aligned, loosen the distributor hold down bolt/nut slightly and rotate the distributor body until the marks are aligned. Tighten the hold down.

8. Recheck the ignition timing, readjust if necessary. Shut off the engine and reconnect vacuum hoses or spout connector. Start engine and readjust idle rpm is necessary.

TACHOMETER HOOKUP

Models equipped with a conventional type primary have an adapter on the top of the primary that provides a clip marked Tach Test. On models (TFI) equipped with an E type primary, the tach connection is made at the back of the

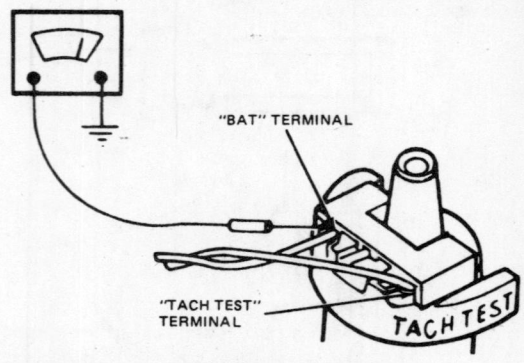

Hook up to test on coil "Bat" terminal

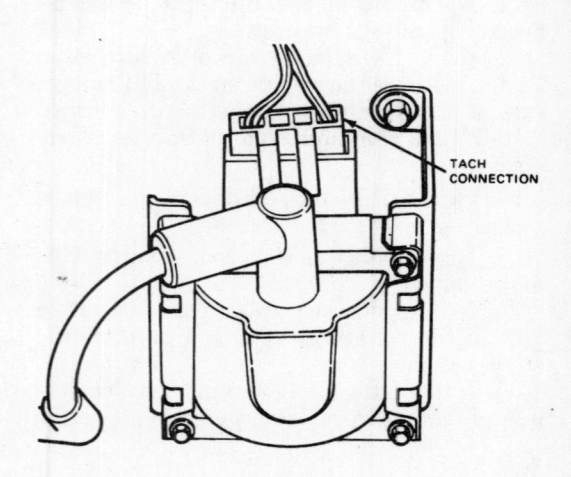

"E" coil tachometer connection

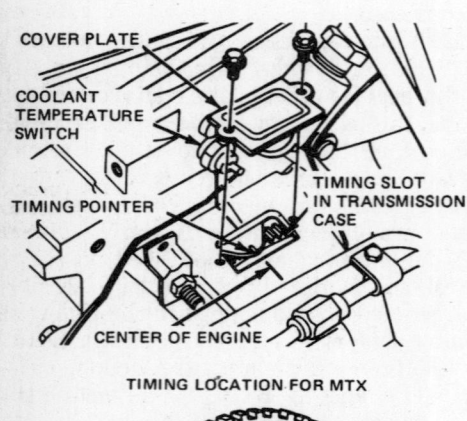

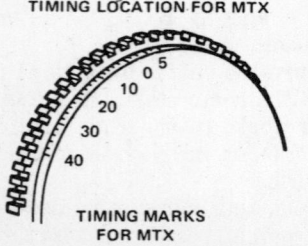

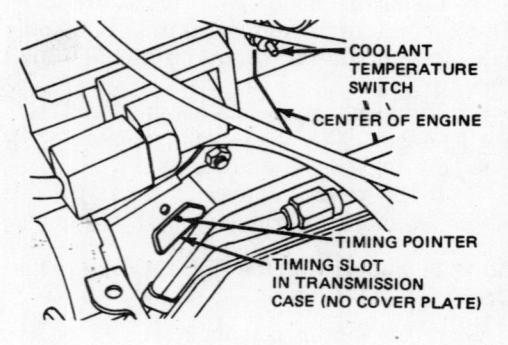

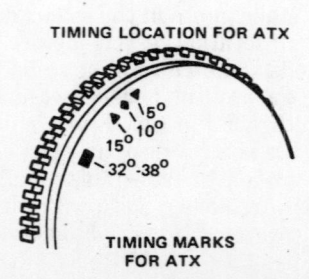

TIMING LOCATION FOR MTX

TIMING MARKS FOR MTX

TIMING LOCATION FOR ATX

TIMING MARKS FOR ATX

2.3L timing marks and identification

ENGINE PERFORMANCE AND TUNE-UP 71

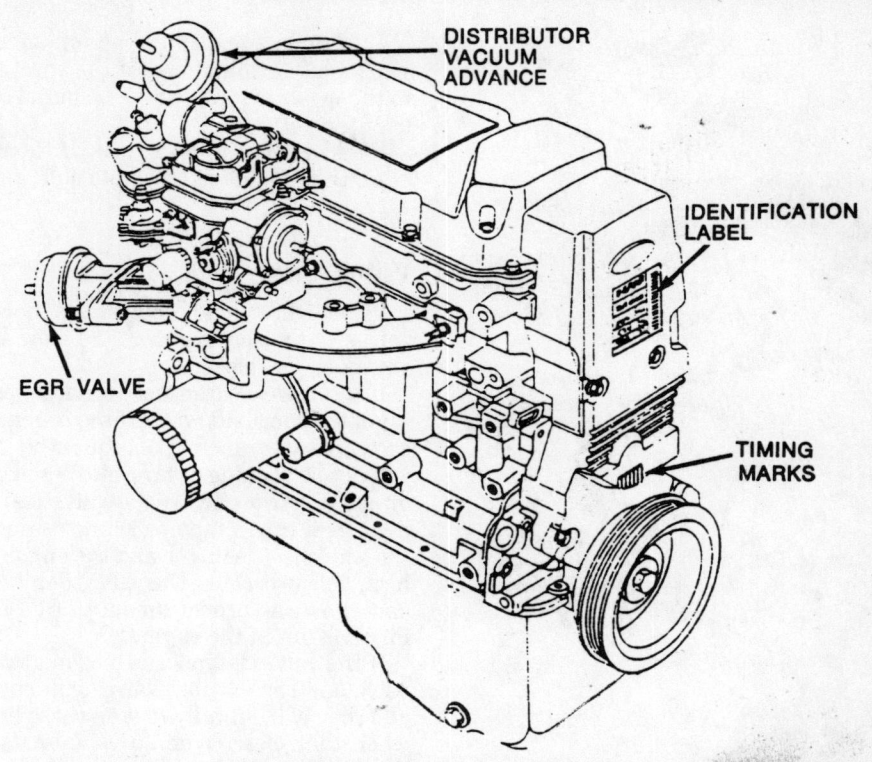

1.6L, 1.9L timing marks on the front cover

wire harness connector. A cutout is provided and the tachometer lead wire alligator clip can be connected to the dark green/yellow dotted wire of the electrical harness plug.

Distributor Cap and Rotor

1. The distributor cap is held on by two cap screws. Release them with a screwdriver and lift the cap straight up and off, with the wires attached. Inspect the cap for cracks, carbon tracks, or a worn center contact. Replace it if necessary, transferring the wires one at a time from the old cap to the new.

2. Remove the screw retaining the ignition rotor and remove the rotor. Replace it if its contacts are worn, burned, or pitted. Do not file the contact.

NOTE: *Always coat the cap and rotor contacts with dielectric compound.*

CONTINUITY TEST — PLUG WIRES

1. Remove the distributor cap with plug wires attached.

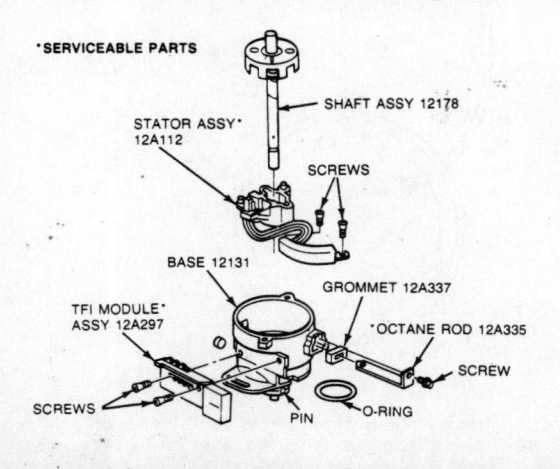

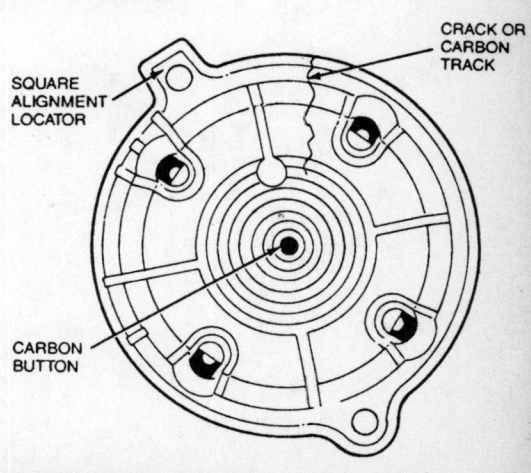

Semi-exploded view of the 1.6L, 1.9L EFI distributor

Inspecting the distributor cap for damage

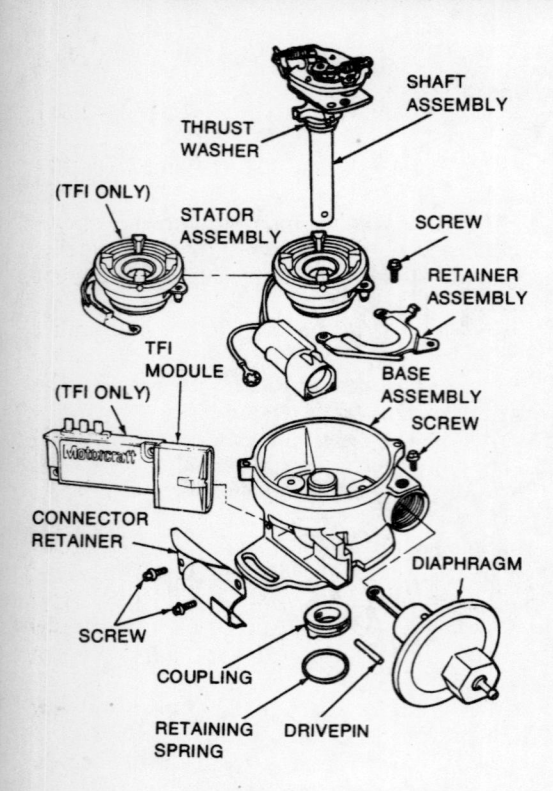

72 ENGINE PERFORMANCE AND TUNE-UP

2. Connect one end of an ohmmeter to the spark plug terminal end of the wire, the other to the inside corresponding terminal of the distributor cap.

3. Measure the resistance. If the reading is more than 5,000 per inch of cable, replace the wire.

Valve Lash

Valve adjustment determines how far the valves enter the cylinder and how long they stay open and closed.

If the valve clearance is too large, part of the lift of the camshaft will be used in removing the excessive clearance. Consequently, the valve will not be opening as far as it should. This condition has two effects: the valve train components will emit a tapping sound as they take up the excessive clearance and the engine will perform poorly because the valves don't open fully and allow the proper amount of gases to flow into and out of the engine.

If the valve clearance is too small, the intake valve and the exhaust valves will open too far and they will not fully seat on the cylinder head when they close. When a valve seats itself on the cylinder head, it does two things: it seals the combustion chamber so that none of the gases in the cylinder escape and it cools itself by transferring some of the heat it absorbs from

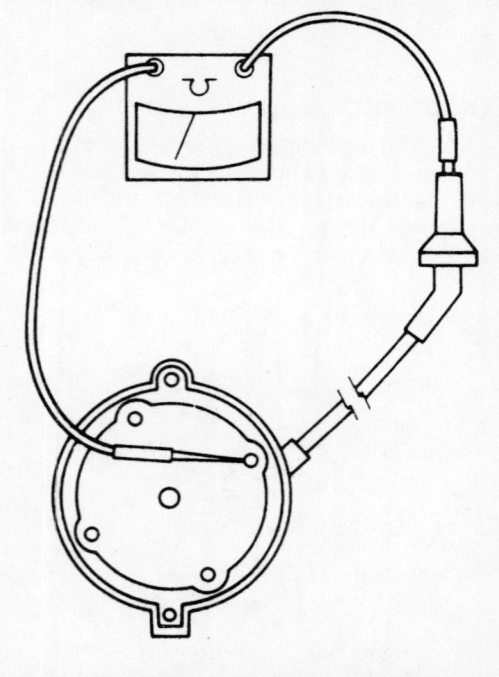

Semi-exploded view of the 1.6L, 1.9L non-EFI distributor

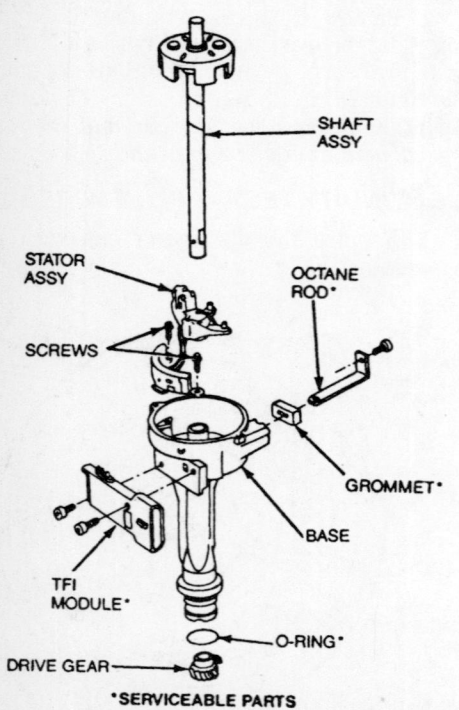

Exploded view of an open bowl distributor assembly

To check the spark plug wire resistance, measure from the cap terminal to the plug end of the wire with an ohmmeter. Resistance should be less than 5000 ohms per inch of the plug wire length

ENGINE PERFORMANCE AND TUNE-UP

the combustion in the cylinder to the cylinder head and to the engine's cooling system. If the valve clearance is too small, the engine will run poorly because of the gases escaping from the combustion chamber. The valves will also become overheated and will warp, since they cannot transfer heat unless they are touching the valve seat in the cylinder head.

VALVE LASH ADJUSTMENT

Gasoline Engines

The intake and exhaust valves are driven by the camshaft, working through hydraulic lash adjusters and stamped steel rocker arms. The lash adjusters eliminate the need for periodic valve lash adjustments.

Diesel Engine

1. Disconnect breather hose from the intake manifold and remove camshaft cover.
2. Rotate crankshaft until No. 1 piston is at TDC on the compression stroke.
3. Using a Go-No-Go feeler gauge, check the valve shim to cam lobe clearance for No. 1

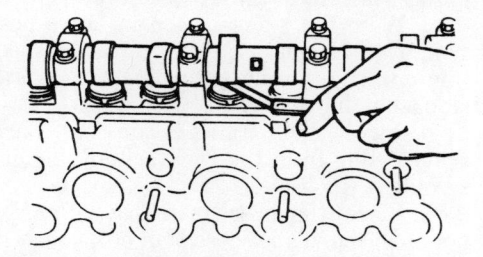

Checking the diesel engine valve clearance

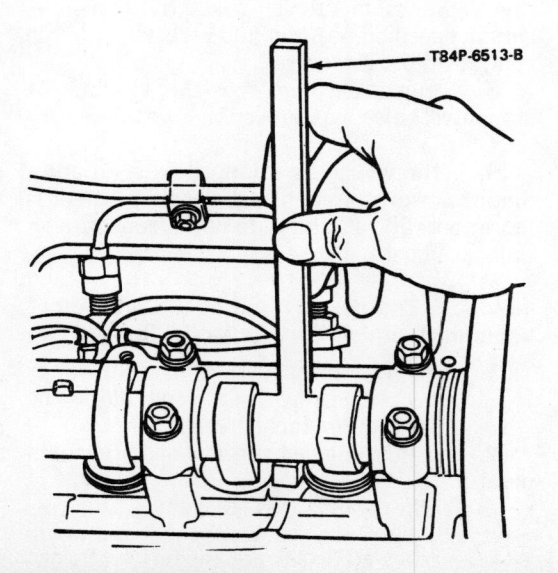

and No. 2 intake valves, and No. 1 and No. 3 exhaust valves.
 • Intake Valves: 0.20–0.30mm (0.008–0.011 in.).
 • Exhaust Valves: 0.30–0.40mm (0.011–0.015 in.).

4. Rotate crankshaft one complete revolution. Measure valve clearance for No. 3 and No. 4 intake valves, and No. 2 and No. 4 exhaust valves.
5. If a valve is out of specifications, adjust as follows:
 • Rotate crankshaft until the lobe of the valve to be adjusted is down.
 • Install cam follower retainer, T84P-6513-B.
 • Rotate crankshaft until the cam lobe is on the base circle.
 • Using O-ring pick tool T71P-19703-C or equivalent, pry the valve adjusting shim out of the cam follower.
 • Valve shims are available in thicknesses ranging from 0.13–0.18 in. (3.40mm to 4.60mm).
 • If the valve was too tight, install a new shim, of the appropriate size.
 • If the valve was too loose, install a new shim of the appropriate size.

NOTE: *Shim thickness is stamped on valve shim. Install new shim with numbers down, to avoid wearing the numbers off the shim. If numbers have been worn off, use a micrometer to measure shim thickness.*

6. Rotate crankshaft until cam lobe is down and remove cam follower retainer.
7. Recheck valve clearance.
8. Repeat Steps 4, 5 and 6 for each valve to be adjusted.

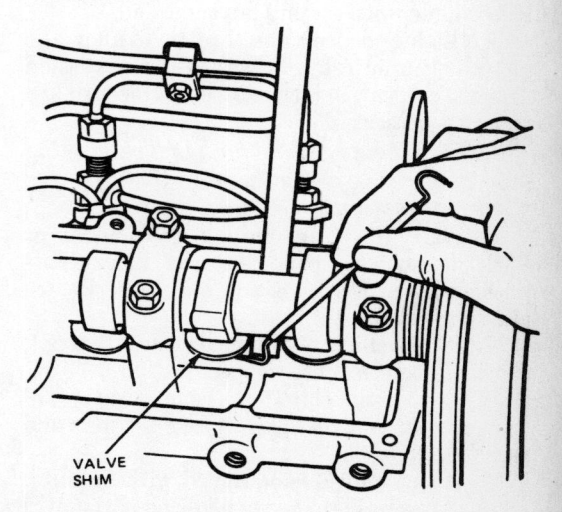

Cam follower retainer

Shim removal adjustment

ENGINE PERFORMANCE AND TUNE-UP

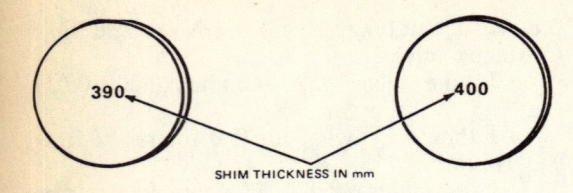

Valve shims

9. Make sure the camshaft cover gasket is fully seated in the camshaft cover and install valve cover. Tighten bolts to 5–7 ft. lbs.
10. Connect breather hose.

Idle Speed

NOTE: *A tachometer must be used while making any idle rpm adjustments. Refer to the preceding section for tach hook up instructions.*

Refer to emissions decal for idle speed and specific instructions. If the decal instructions differ from the following procedures, use the decal procedures. They reflect current production changes.

CURB IDLE

1.6L Engine w/740 Carburetor w/o Idle Speed Control

1. Place the transmission in Neutral or Park, set the parking brake and block the wheels. Connect tachometer.
2. Bring the engine to normal operating temperature.
3. Disconnect and plug the vacuum hose at the Thermactor air control valve bypass sections.
4. Place the fast idle adjustment screw on the second highest step of the fast idle cam. Run engine until cooling fan comes on.
5. Slightly depress the throttle to allow the fast idle cam to rotate. Place the transmission in specified gear, and check/adjust the curb idle rpm to specification.

NOTE: *Engine cooling fan must be running when checking curb idle rpm. (Use a jumper wire is necessary).*

6. Place the transmission in Neutral or Park. Rev the engine momentarily. Place transmission in specified position and recheck curb idle rpm. Readjust if requires.
7. If the vehicle is equipped with a dash pot, check/adjust clearance to specification.
8. Remove the plug from the hose at the Thermactor air control valve bypass sections and reconnect.
9. If the vehicle is equipped with an automatic transmission and curb idle adjustment is more than 50 rpm, an automatic transmission linkage adjustment may be necessary.

1.6L, 1.9L Engines w/740 & 5740 Carburetor Mechanical Vacuum Idle Speed Control (ISC)

1. Place the transmission in Neutral or Park, set the parking brake and block the wheels. Connect tachometer.
2. Bring the engine to normal operating temperature.
3. Disconnect and plug the vacuum hose at the Thermactor air control valve bypass section.
4. Place the fast idle adjustment screw on the second highest step of the fast idle cam. Run the engine until cooling fan comes on.
5. Slightly depress the throttle to allow fast idle cam to rotate. Place the transmission in Drive (fan on) and check curb idle rpm to specification.

NOTE: *Engine cooling fan must be running when checking curb idle rpm.*

6. If adjustment is required:
   a. Place the transmission in Park, deactivate the ISC by removing the vacuum hose at the ISC and plugging the hose.
   b. Turn ISC adjusting screw until ISC plunger is clear of the throttle lever.
   c. Place the transmission in Drive position, if rpm is not at the ISC retracted speed (fan on), adjust rpm by turning the throttle stop adjusting screw.
   d. Place the transmission in Park, remove plug from the ISC vacuum line and reconnect the ISC.
   e. Place transmission in Drive if rpm is not at the curb idle speed (fan on), adjust by turning the ISC adjustment screw.
7. Place transmission in Neutral or Park. Rev the engine momentarily. Place the transmission in specified position and recheck curb idle rpm. Readjust if required.
8. Remove the plug from the Thermactor air control valve bypass section hose and reconnect.
9. If the vehicle is equipped with an automatic transmission and curb idle adjustment is more than 50 rpm, an automatic transmission linkage adjustment may be necessary.

1.6L, 1.9L Engines w/740 & 5740 Carburetor Vacuum Operated Throttle Modulator (VOTM)

1. Place the transmission in Neutral or Park, set the parking brake and block the wheels. Connect the tachometer.
2. Bring the engine to normal operating temperature.
3. To check/adjust VOTM rpm:
• Place air conditioning heat selector in Heat position, blower switch on High.
• Disconnect the vacuum hose from VOTM

ENGINE PERFORMANCE AND TUNE-UP

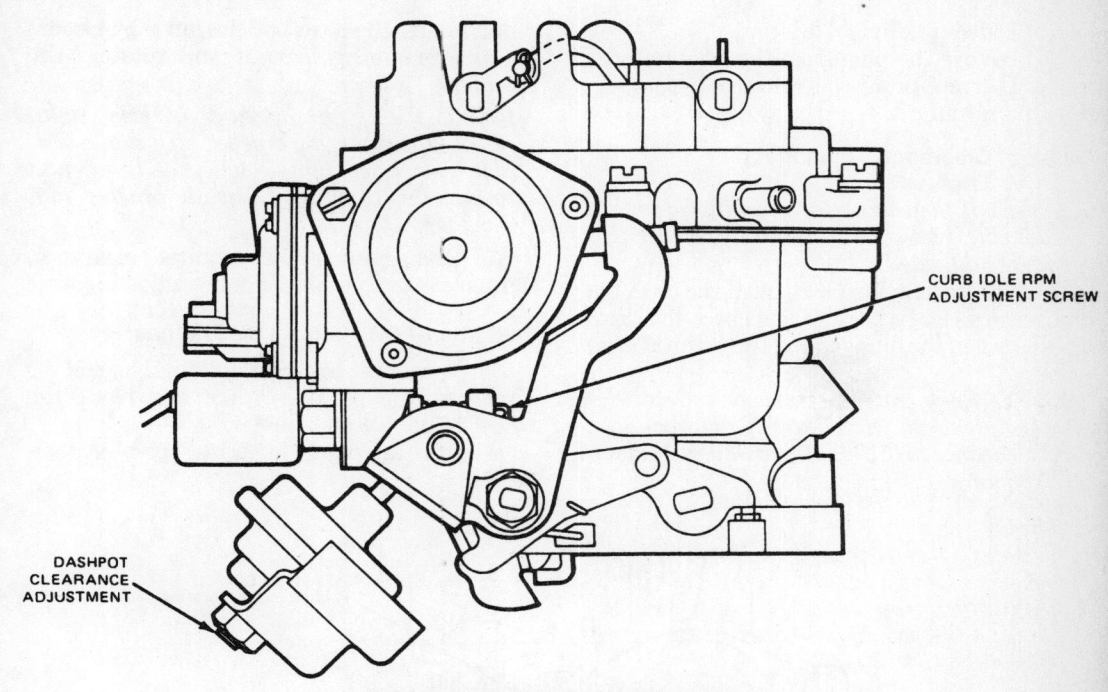

Location of curb idle adjusting screw

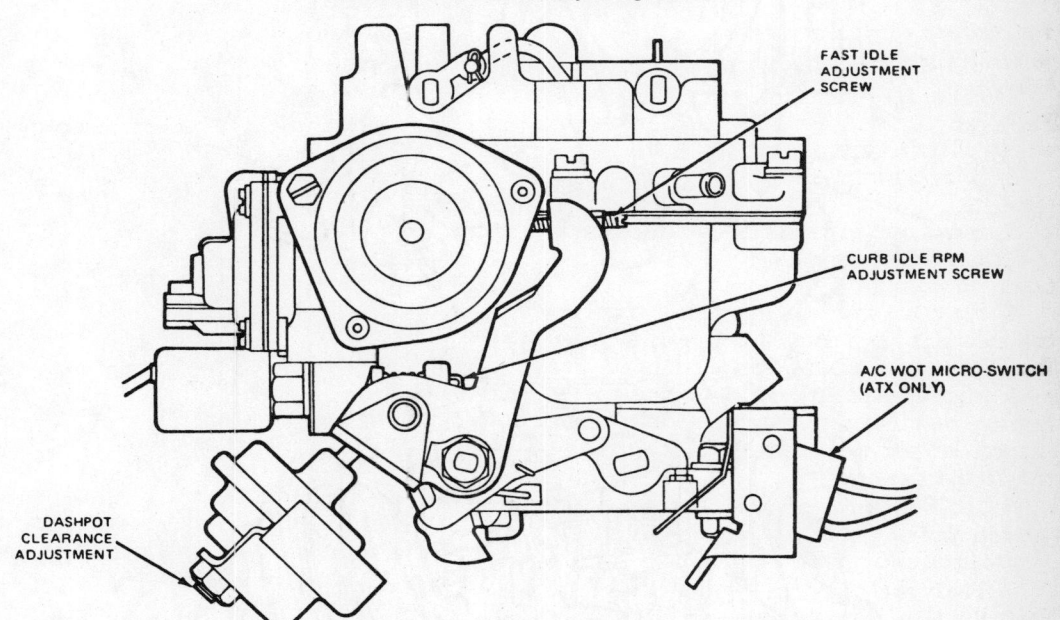

740 carburetor — fast idle and curb idle rpm adjustment

and plug, install a slave vacuum hose from the intake manifold vacuum to the VOTM.

4. Disconnect and plug the vacuum hose at the Thermactor air control valve bypass section.

5. Run the engine until the engine cooling fan comes on.

6. Place the transmission in specified gear, and check/adjust VOTM rpm to specification.

NOTE: *Engine cooling fan must be running when checking VOTM rpm. Adjust rpm by turning screw on VOTM.*

7. Remove the slave vacuum hose. Remove the plug from the VOTM vacuum hose and reconnect the hose to the VOTM.

8. Return the intake manifold vacuum

ENGINE PERFORMANCE AND TUNE-UP

supply source to original location.

9. Remove the plug from the vacuum hose at the Thermactor air control valve bypass section and reconnect.

Dashpot Clearance Adjustment
1.6, 1.9L Engines

NOTE: *If the carburetor is equipped with a dash pot, it must be adjusted if the curb idle speed is adjusted.*

1. With the engine OFF, push the dash pot plunger in as far as possible and check the clearance between the plunger and the throttle lever pad.

NOTE: *Refer to the emissions decal for proper dash pot clearance. If not available, set clearance to 0.138 in. ± 0.020 in. (3.5mm ± 0.5mm).*

2. Adjust the dash pot clearance by loosening the mounting locknut and rotating the dash pot.

CAUTION: *If the locknut is very tight, remove the mounting bracket, hold it in a suitable device, so that it will not bend, and loosen the locknut. Reinstall bracket and dash pot.*

3. After gaining the required clearance, tighten the locknut and recheck adjustment.

Fast Idle RPM — 1.6L, 1.9L Engines

1. Place the transmission in Neutral or Park, set the parking brake and block the wheels. Connect tachometer.

2. Bring the engine to normal operating temperature.

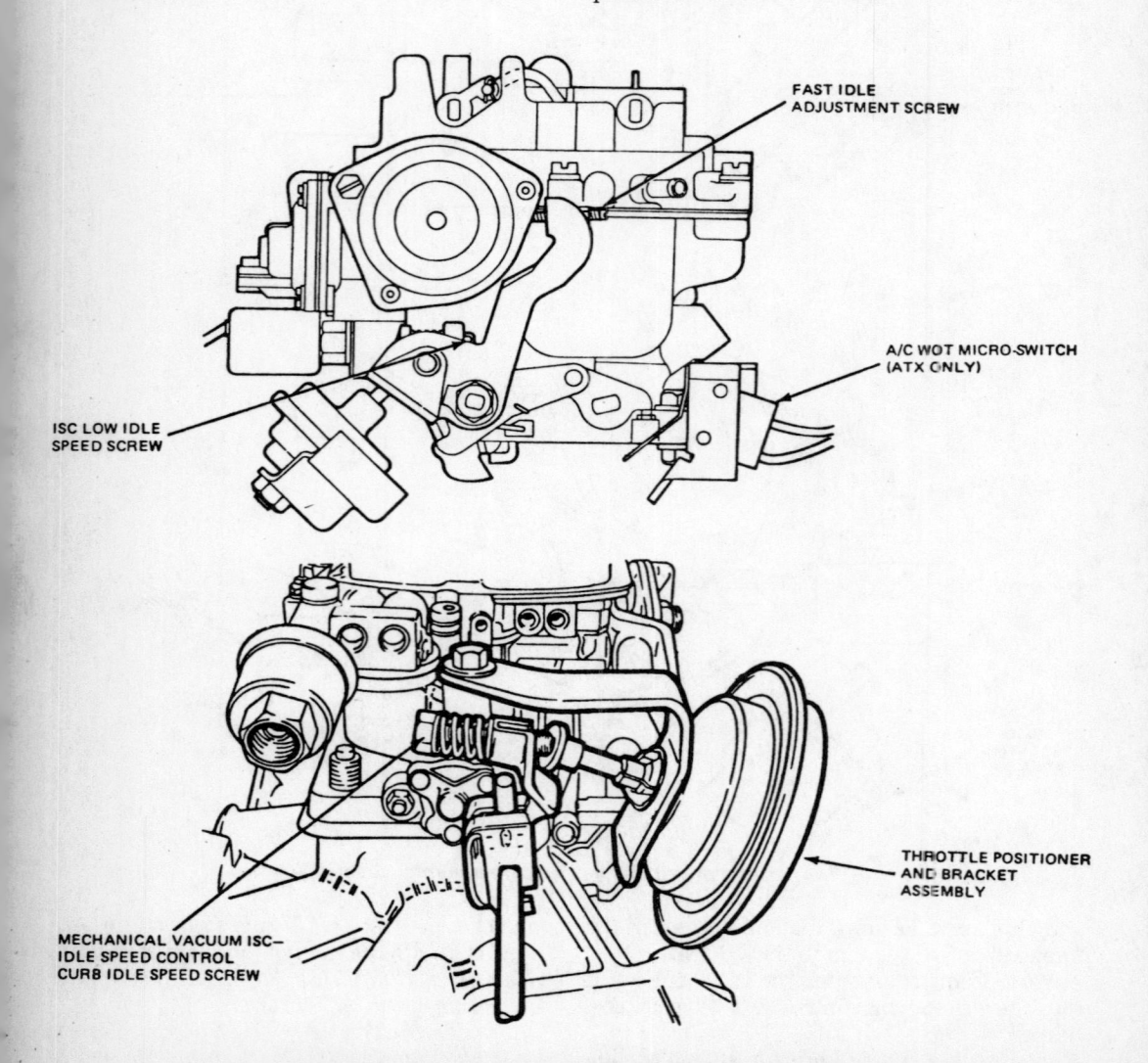

740 carburetor — mechanical idle speed control — curb idle

ENGINE PERFORMANCE AND TUNE-UP 77

VOTM RPM ADJUSTMENT SCREW

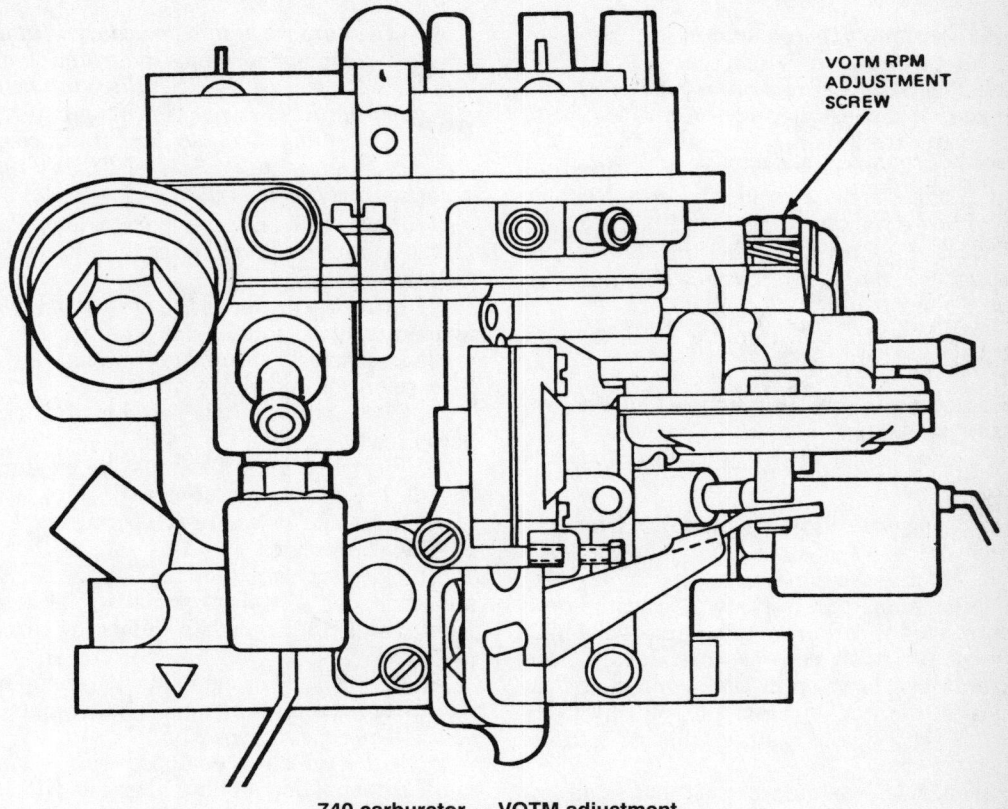

740 carburetor — VOTM adjustment

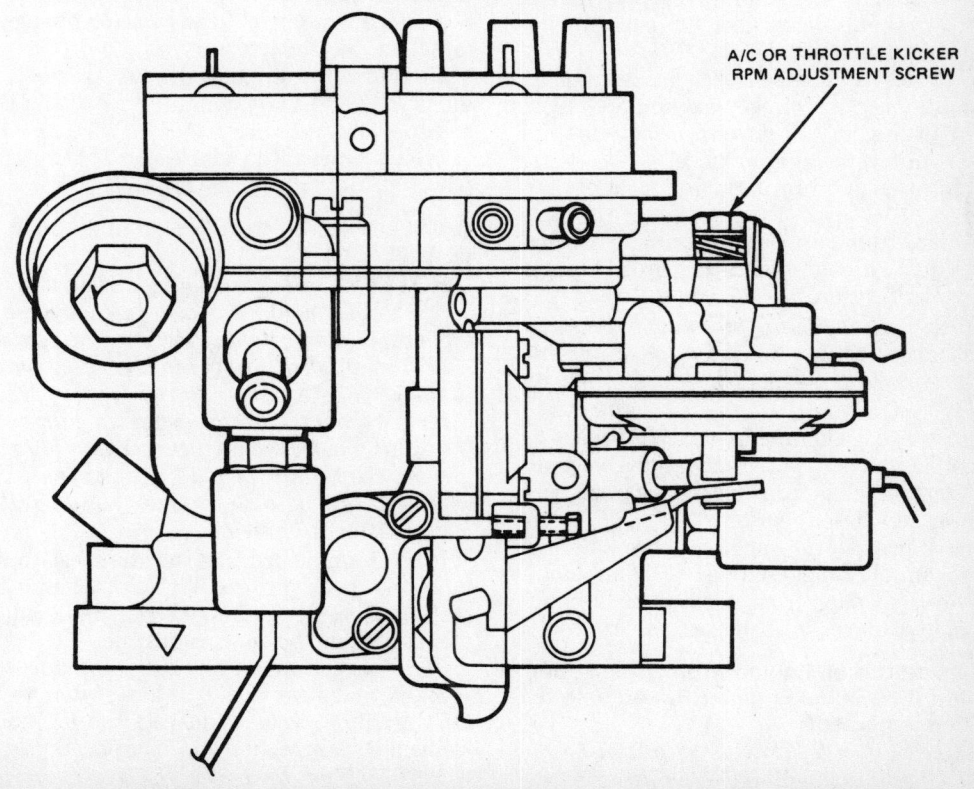

A/C OR THROTTLE KICKER RPM ADJUSTMENT SCREW

An adjustment is necessary, at times, if your car is equipped with air conditioning

ENGINE PERFORMANCE AND TUNE-UP

3. Disconnect the vacuum hose at the EGR and plug.

4. Place the fast idle adjustment screw on the second highest step of the fast idle cam. Run engine until cooling fan comes on.

5. Check/adjust fast idle rpm to specification. If adjustment is required, loosen locknut, adjust and retighten.

NOTE: *Engine cooling fan must be running when checking fast idle rpm. (Use a jumper wire is necessary).*

6. Remove the plug from the EGR hose and reconnect.

Air Conditioning/Throttle Kicker Adjustment 1.6L, 1.9L Engine

1. Place the transmission in Neutral or Park.

2. Bring engine to normal operating temperature.

3. Identify vacuum source to air bypass section of air supply control valve. If vacuum hose is connected to carburetor, disconnect and plug hose at air supply control valve. Install slave vacuum hose between intake manifold and air bypass connection on air supply control valve.

4. To check/adjust air conditioning or throttle kicker rpm:
- If vehicle is equipped with air conditioning, place selector to maximum cooling, blower switch on High. Disconnect air conditioning compressor clutch wire.
- If vehicle is equipped with kicker and no air conditioning, disconnect vacuum hose from kicker and plug, install slave vacuum hose from intake manifold vacuum to kicker.

5. Run engine until engine cooling fan comes on.

6. Place transmission in specified gear and check/adjust air conditioning or throttle kicker rpm to specification.

NOTE: *Engine cooling fan must be running when checking air conditioning or throttle kicker rpm. Adjust rpm by turning screw on kicker.*

7. If slave vacuum hose was installed to check/adjust kicker rpm, remove slave vacuum hose. Remove plug from kicker vacuum hose and reconnect hose to kicker.

8. Remove slave vacuum hose. Return intake manifold supply source to original condition. Remove plug from carburetor vacuum hose and reconnect to air bypass valve.

1984–86 1.6L, 1.9L Engine w/Electronic Fuel Injection (EFI) Initial Engine RPM Adjustment (ISC Disconnected)

NOTE: *Curb idle RPM is controlled by the EEC IV processor and the Idle Speed Control (ISC) device (part of the fuel charging assembly). The purpose of this procedure is to provide a means of verifying the initial engine RPM setting with the ISC disconnected. If engine idle RPM is not within specification after performing this procedure, it will be necessary to have 1.6L, 1.9L EFI EEC IV diagnostics performed.*

1. Place the transmission Neutral or Park, set the parking brake and block the wheels. Connect tachometer.

2. Bring the engine to the normal operating temperature and shut engine off.

3. Disconnect vacuum connector at the EGR solenoids and plug both lines.

4. Disconnect the idle speed control (ISC) power lead.

5. Electric cooling fan must be on during the idle speed setting procedure.

6. Start the engine and operate at 2,000 RPM for 60 seconds.

7. Place transmission in Neutral for MT and Drive for AT, check/adjust initial engine RPM within 120 seconds by adjusting throttle plate screw.

8. If idle adjustment is not completed within 120 second time limit, shut engine Off, restart and repeat Steps 6 and 7.

9. If the vehicle is equipped with an automatic transmission and initial engine RPM adjustment increases or decreases by more than 50 RPM, an automatic transmission linkage adjustment may be necessary.

10. Turn the engine Off and remove the plugs from the EGR vacuum lines at the EGR solenoid and reconnect.

11. Reconnect the idle speed control (ISC) power lead.

1987–90 1.9L CFI Engine With Idle Speed Control (ISC)

NOTE: *The idle speed and the idle speed mixture adjustments are controlled by the on board vehicle computerized engine controls. Also in order to adjust the idle speed on this model, it is necessary to remove the CFI assembly from the vehicle, so as to gain access to, and remove the tamper resistant plug covering the throttle stop adjusting screw. This procedure should be performed by an authorized factory technician.*

It is recommended that the idle speed control motor be checked to see if it is functioning correctly, before performing the curb idle adjustment. This can be done as follows:

1. Start the engine and run it for at least 30 seconds and turn the ignition switch to the **OFF** position. Visually inspect the ISC motor to see if it is retracting and repositioning.

NOTE: *If for any reason the battery has been disconnected or the vehicle has had to be*

ENGINE PERFORMANCE AND TUNE-UP

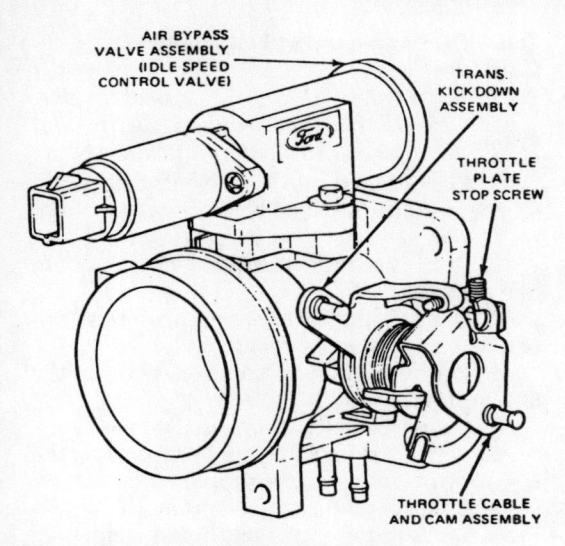

EFI — air intake throttle body assembly

jump started, this procedure may need to be performed.

2. Set the parking brake and block the wheels. Make all checks and or adjustments at normal operating temperature with all accessories off. Only a suitable tachometer is needed for this procedure. Before any adjustments are made, check for vacuum leaks and repair as necessary.

3. With the transmission in drive (automatic transmission) or neutral (manual transmission) and the engine is idled for 120 seconds, check to see that the idle speed is within specifications. The engine rpm should then increase by approximately 75 rpm, when the transmission is put in drive or neutral.

4. Lightly step on and off the accelerator pedal. The engine rpm should return to specification. If the rpm remains high, wait 120 seconds and repeat the sequence. Remember it may take the computerized system 120 seconds to **Learn** again.

NOTE: *The curb and fast idle speeds are controlled by the on board computer and the idle speed control device. If the control system is operating properly, these speeds are fixed and cannot be changed by traditional adjustment techniques.*

Adjustments are sometimes required to establish the correct operating limit which the ISC system can properly function. This adjustment, as outlined below, will normally have no direct effect on the actual idle speed and generally will not be required unless, the curb idle is higher than specified.

Mis-adjustment of the operating limit could restrict the operating range of the ISC system, so adjustment of this limit should never be made unless a specific casual factor exists. If the operating limit adjustment does not correct an out of specification curb idle speed correction, it will be necessary to take the vehicle to an authorized factory technician for further diagnostic evaluation.

ADJUSTMENT

1. With the engine off, remove the air cleaner assembly. Connect a jumper wire between the self-test input and the signal return pin on the self test connector.

2. Turn the ignition to the **ON** position, but do not start the engine. The idle speed control (ISC) plunger should retract within 10–15 seconds. If the plunger does not retract there is a malfunction within the on board diagnostic system and the vehicle should be taken to an authorized factory technician for further diagnostic evaluation.

3. Disconnect the ISC harness connector. Turn the ignition key off and remove the jumper wire.

4. Start the engine and check the idle rpm, if not within specification, use the following procedure:

   a. With the engine off, remove the CFI assembly from the vehicle.

   b. Remove the tamper resistant plug that covers the throttle stop adjusting screw.

   c. Remove the old throttle stop adjusting screw and install a new screw.

   d. Install the CFI assembly back on the intake manifold/engine.

5. Start the engine and let the idle stabilize. Adjust the throttle stop adjusting screw until the specified rpm is reached.

6. Shut the engine off and reconnect the vehicle harness to the ISC motor. Make sure the throttle plate is not binding in the bore or that the linkage is preventing the throttle plate from returning. Reinstall the air cleaner assembly.

7. Be sure to refer to the under hood emission/calibration sticker for the engine idle rpm specification.

1987–90 1.9L MPFI H.O. Engine

1. Apply the parking brake and block the wheels. Place the transmission in neutral and start the engine. Allow the engine to run until it reaches normal operating temperature. Turn off all accessories and shut the engine off.

2. Disconnect the idle speed control motor harness connector. Start the engine and run it at 2000 rpm for approximately 1 minute and return it to idle.

3. Disconnect the EGR vacuum connection at the EGR solenoid and plug both lines (if so equipped). Disconnect the idle speed control bypass air solenoid power lead (if so equipped).

4. With the transmission in drive (auto-

80 ENGINE PERFORMANCE AND TUNE-UP

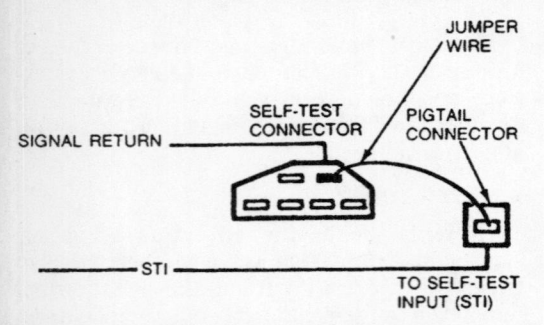

Using the jumper wire to retract the ISC plunger — 1.9L CFI engine

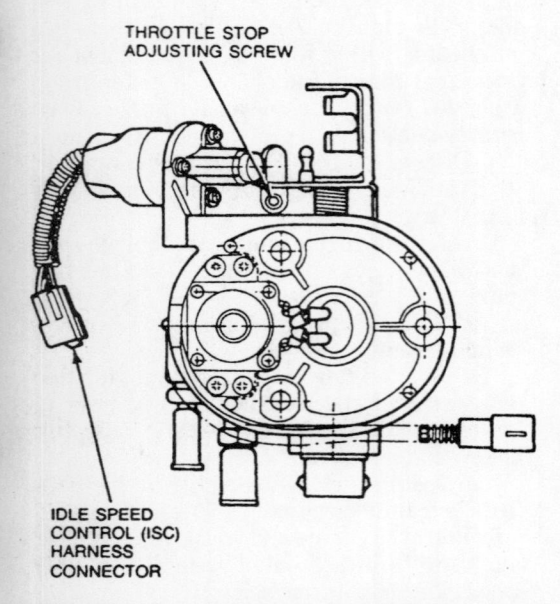

Location of the CFI throttle stop adjustment screw — 1.9L CFI engine

matic transmission) or neutral (manual transmission), check to see that the idle speed is 900–1000 rpm. If the idle speed is not within specifications, go on to the next Step.

5. Make sure that the cooling fan is off. Turn the throttle plate adjusting screw until the idle is within specifications. Adjustment must be made within 2 minutes after returning to idle.

6. If the idle speed adjustment was necessary, repeat Steps 2 through 5. Once the idle has been set to specifications, turn the ignition off. Reconnect the ISC connector. Make sure that the throttle plate is not binding in the bore or that the linkage is preventing the throttle plate from returning.

7. To make sure that the adjustment was good, run the engine at 2000 rpm for approximately 1 minute and return it to idle, Be sure to refer to the under hood emission/calibration sticker for the engine idle rpm specification.

2.3L HSC Engine w/1949 and 6149 FB
Curb Idle

NOTE: *A/C-On RPM is non-adjustable. TPS-Off RPM is not required. Verify that TPS plunger extends with ignition key On.*

1. Place the transaxle in Neutral or Park, set the parking brake and block the wheels. Connect tachometer.
2. Disconnect the throttle kicker vacuum line and plug.
3. Bring the engine to normal operating temperature. (Cooling fan should cycle).
4. Place the air conditioning selector in the Off position.
5. Place gear selector in specified position.
6. Activate the cooling fan by grounding the control wire with a jumper wire.
7. Check/adjust curb idle rpm. If adjustment is required, turn curb idle adjusting screw.
8. Place the transaxle in Neutral or Park. Rev the engine momentarily. Place the transaxle in specified position and recheck curb idle rpm. Readjust if required.
9. Reconnect the cooling fan wiring.
10. Turn the ignition key to the Off position.
11. Reconnect the vacuum line to the throttle kicker.
12. If the vehicle is equipped with an automatic transaxle and curb idle adjustment exceeds 50 rpm, an automatic transaxle linkage adjustment may be necessary.
13. Remove all test equipment and reinstall the air cleaner assembly.

2.3L HSC Engine w/1949 and 6149 FB
TPS Off RPM

NOTE: *This adjustment is not required as part of a normal engine idle RPM check/adjustment. Use if engine continues to run after ignition key is turned to OFF position.*

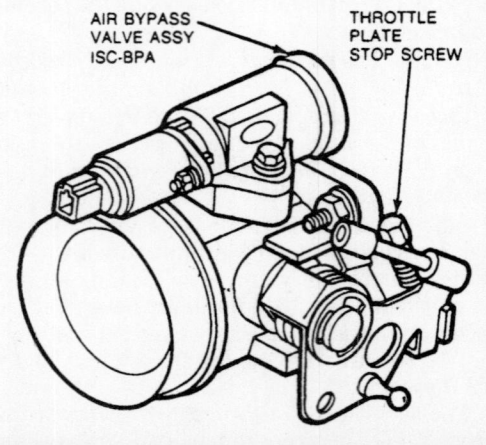

Location of the throttle stop adjusting screw — 1.9L MPFI engine

ENGINE PERFORMANCE AND TUNE-UP

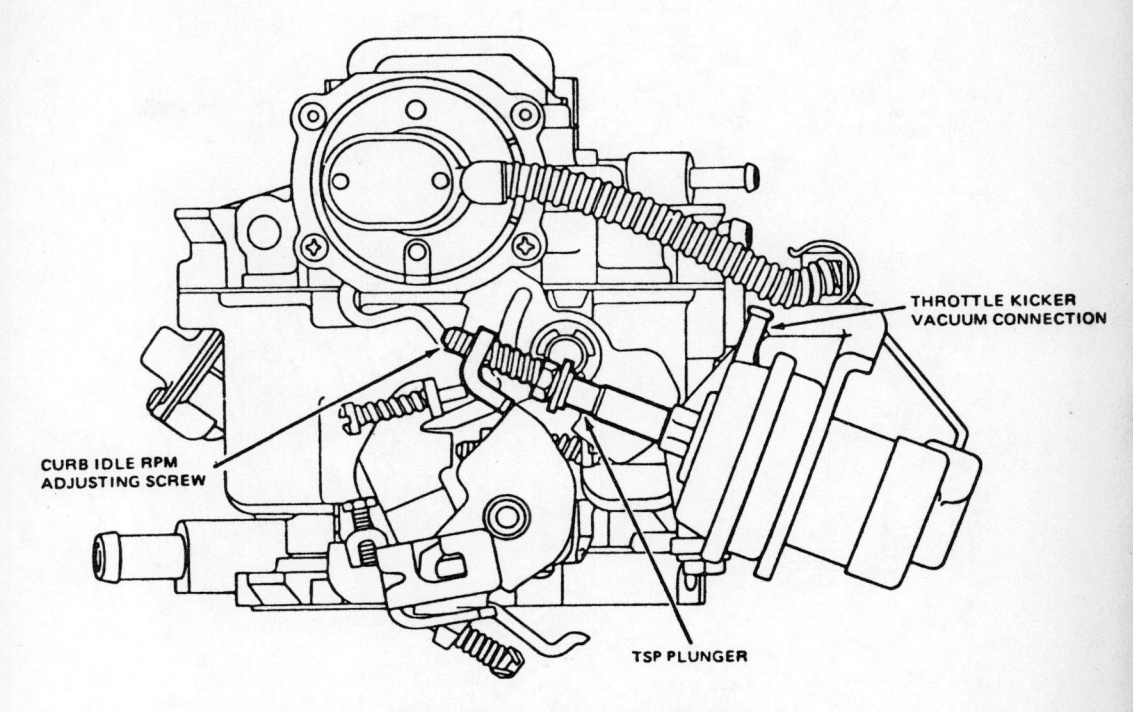

1949/6149FB — Curb idle adjustment

1. Place the transaxle in Neutral or Park, set the parking brake and block the wheels. Connect tachometer.
2. Bring the engine to normal operating temperature.
3. Disconnect the throttle kicker vacuum line and plug.
4. Place the air conditioning selector to Off position.
5. Disconnect the electrical lead to the TPS and verify that plunger collapses. Check/adjust engine RPM to specification (600 RPM).
6. Adjust the TPS Off RPM to specification.
7. Shut the engine off, reconnect TPS electrical lead and throttle kicker vacuum line.

2.3L HSC Engine w/1949 and 6149 FB Fast Idle RPM

1. Place the transaxle in Neutral or Park, set the parking brake and block the wheels.
2. Bring the engine to normal operating temperature with the carburetor set on second step of fast idle cam.
3. Return the throttle to normal idle position.
4. Place the air conditioning selector in the Off position.
5. Disconnect the vacuum hose at the EGR valve and plug.
6. Place the fast idle adjusting screw on the specific step of the fast idle cam.
7. Check/adjust the fast idle rpm to specification.
8. Rev the engine momentarily, allowing engine to return to idle and turn ignition key to Off position.
9. Remove the plug from the EGR vacuum hose and reconnect.

2.3L OHC Engine

1. Apply the parking brake and block the wheels. Place the transmission in neutral and start the engine. Allow the engine to run until it reaches normal operating temperature. Turn off all accessories and shut the engine off.
2. Disconnect the idle speed control air bypass valve connector. Start the engine and run it at 1500 rpm for approximately 20 seconds and return it to idle.
3. With the transmission in drive (automatic transmission) or neutral (manual transmission), check to see that the idle speed is 550–550 rpm. If the idle speed is not within specifications, go on to the next Step.
4. Make sure that the cooling fan is off. Turn the throttle plate adjusting screw until the idle is within specifications. Adjustment must be made within 2 minutes after returning to idle.
5. If the idle speed adjustment was necessary, repeat Steps 2 through 4. Once the idle has been set to specifications, turn the ignition

ENGINE PERFORMANCE AND TUNE-UP

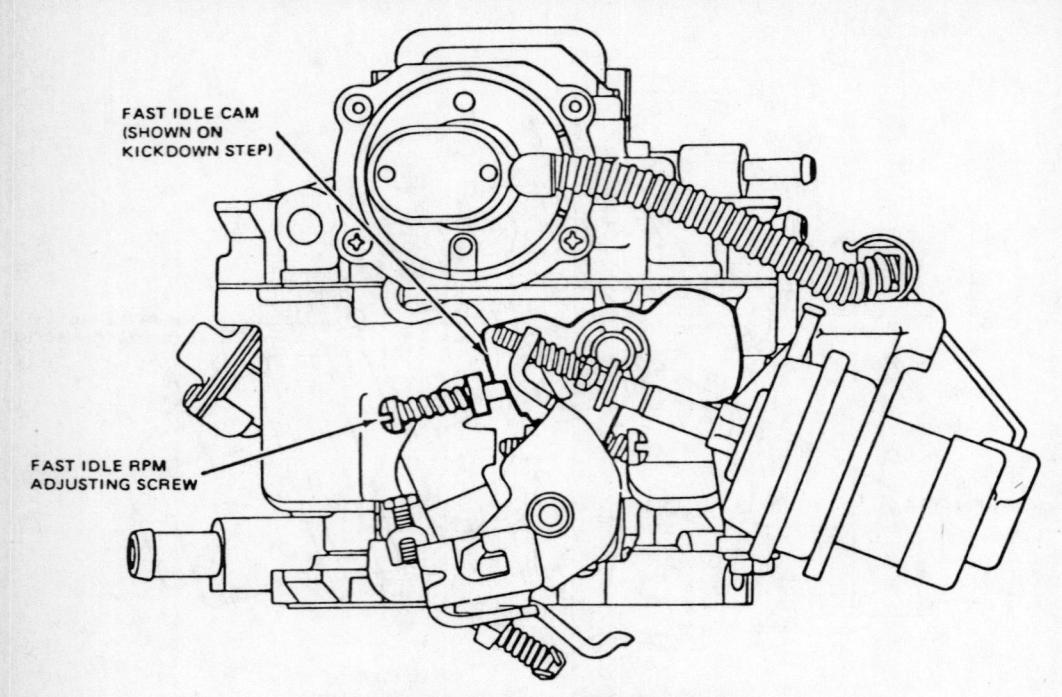

1949/6149FB — Fast idle adjustment

off. Reconnect the idle speed control air bypass valve assembly connector. Make sure that the throttle plate is not binding in the bore or that the linkage is preventing the throttle plate from returning.

7. To make sure that the adjustment was good, run the engine at 1500 rpm for approximately 20 seconds and return it to idle, Be sure to refer to the under hood emission/calibration sticker for the engine idle rpm specification.

2.3L HSC and 2.3L H.O. Engines

1. Apply the parking brake and block the wheels. Place the transmission in neutral and start the engine. Allow the engine to run until it reaches normal operating temperature. Turn off all accessories and shut the engine off.

2. Unplug the spout line connector and make sure the ignition timing is set to specifications. After checking the ignition timing, leave the in-line spout connector unplugged.

3. Turn the ignition switch off. Remove the PCV hose and install special orifice T86P-9600-A or an equivalent orifice with a 5mm (0.200 in.) diameter opening. Disconnect the idle speed control air bypass valve assembly connector.

4. Start the engine and run it at 2500 rpm for approximately 30 seconds and return it to idle.

5. With the transmission in drive (automatic transmission) or neutral (manual transmission), check to see that the idle speed is within specifications. If the idle speed is not within specifications, go on to the next Step.

6. Make sure that the cooling fan is off. Turn the throttle plate adjusting screw until the idle is within specifications. Adjustment must be made within 2 minutes after returning to idle.

7. Turn the engine off and reconnect the ignition timing in-line spout connector. Remove the orifice from the PCV line and reinstall the PCV line. Reconnect the idle speed control air bypass valve assembly connector.

8. Make sure that the throttle plate is not binding in the bore or that the linkage is preventing the throttle plate from returning.

9. To make sure that the adjustment was good, run the engine at 2500 rpm for approximately 30 seconds and return it to idle, Be sure to refer to the under hood emission/calibration sticker for the engine idle rpm specification.

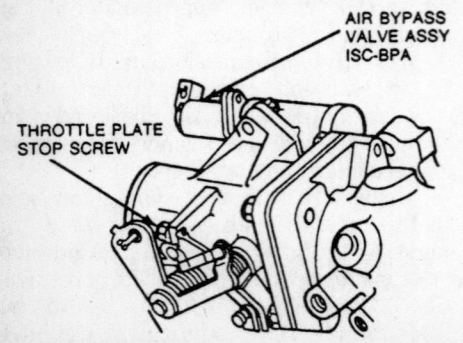

Location of the throttle plate adjusting screw — 2.3L OHC engine

ENGINE PERFORMANCE AND TUNE-UP

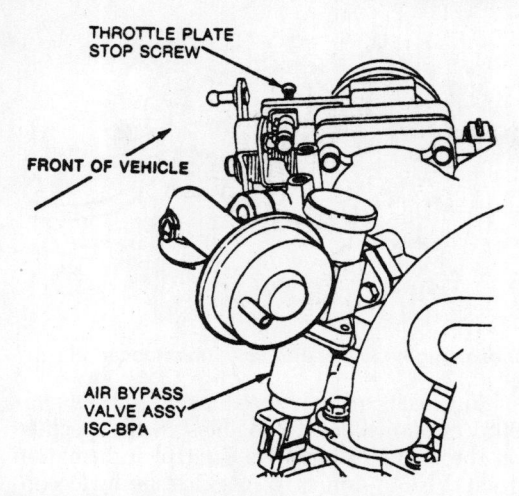

Location of the throttle plate adjusting screw — 2.3L HSC/H.O. engine

IDLE MIXTURE ADJUSTMENT

All Carbureted Models

There is no idle mixture adjustment possible on all the fuel injected models. There is an idle mixture procedure for the carbureted models, however, the carburetor must be removed in order to gain access to the tamper resistant plugs that cover the mixture screw. It should also be noted that a propane enrichment kit will be needed to perform this operation. The following procedure should be used in order to adjust the idle mixture.

1. Remove the carburetor from the engine and drain any remaining fuel from the fuel bowl.
2. On all engines except the 2.3L engine, drill a $3/32$ in. (2.4mm) hole through both the steel and the plastic tamper resistant plugs.
3. On the 2.3L engine, use a suitable hack saw and saw through the metal cup lengthwise and insert a suitable tool to twist the metal so as to expose the inner tamper resistant plug.
4. Install a screw extractor into the hole and remove the steel and or plastic plugs. Reinstall the carburetor assembly on the engine. Adjust the idle mixture speed as follows:

   a. Connect a tachometer and timing light to the engine. Make sure that the hot idle compensator is closed, if so equipped.

   b. Disconnect the fuel evaporative system purge hose at the air cleaner assembly and plug the fitting on the air cleaner.

   c. Disconnect the fresh air duct from the air cleaner and insert the hose off of the propane hose $3/4$ of the way into the air cleaner duct. Be sure to leave all vacuum lines attached to the air cleaner. The air cleaner can be positioned off to the side, but it must be intact and in place when making this adjustment.

   d. If the emission system is equipped with air injection, the air injection dump valves should be altered as follows; If the valve has 2 vacuum fittings, disconnect and plug the hoses. If there is only 1 vacuum fitting, disconnect and plug the hose and then run another vacuum hose from the fitting to manifold vacuum.

   e. On all engines but the 2.3L engine, equipped with automatic transmissions. Disconnect and plug the vacuum line at ISC motor. Connect a vacuum pump to the ISC and apply enough vacuum to retract the ISC plunger clear of the throttle linkage.

   f. On the 2.3L OHC 1-bbl engines, equipped with a feedback carburetor. Disconnect the electrical lead wire from the electric ported vacuum switch.

   g. On all models, check the curb idle and ignition timing. Make all necessary adjustments. Remove the PCV valve from the valve cover and allow it to draw fresh air. Run engine briefly at 2500 rpm.

   h. With the engine idling at operating temperature and the transmission in drive (automatic) or neutral (manual), slowly open the valve on the propane bottle and watch for the engine rpm to rise.

   NOTE: *The propane bottle must be held in a vertical (straight up and down) position during this adjustment.*

   i. When the engine rpm begins to drop off, note the maximum speed gained. If the gain is within the rpm gain range do not adjust.

   j. If the maximum speed gain was to high, turn the mixture screw counterclockwise (rich) slightly. If the maximum speed gain was to low, turn the mixture screw clockwise (lean) slightly.

   NOTE: *After turning the mixture screw, allow 15 seconds for idle to stabilize before turning the screw again.*

   k. Turn the mixture screw left or right while repeating the propane procedure until the rpm gained comes into the reset rpm specifications.

   l. Reconnect all disconnect hose and connections. Readjust the idle speed if necessary and remove all test equipment.

   • 1.6L 2bbl – RPM Gained: 0–60 – Reset RPM: 20.
   • 1.6L 2bbl HO (manual transaxle) – RPM Gained: 10–80 – Reset RPM: 40.
   • 1.6L 2bbl HO (automatic transaxle) – RPM Gained: 10–100 – Reset RPM: 30.
   • 1.6L 2bbl HO (automatic transaxle Calf.) – RPM Gained: 0–60 – Reset RPM: 20.

ENGINE PERFORMANCE AND TUNE-UP

- 1.9L 2bbl HO (manual transaxle) – RPM Gained: 10–80 – Reset RPM: 30–60.
- 1.9L 2bbl HO (automatic transaxle) – RPM Gained: 10–100 – Reset RPM: 20–40
- 1.9L 2bbl HO (automatic transaxle Cal.) – RPM Gained: 0–60 – Reset RPM: 10–30.
- 2.3L 1bbl OHC (manual transaxle) – RPM Gained: 60–100 – Reset RPM: 80.
- 2.3L 1bbl OHC (automatic transaxle Fed.) – RPM Gained: 150–200 – Reset RPM: 175.
- 2.3L 1bbl OHC (automatic transaxle Cal.) – RPM Gained: 160–240 – Reset RPM: 200.
- 1986–87 2.3L 1bbl OHC (manual transaxle) – RPM Gained: 60–100 – Reset RPM: 80.
- 1986–87 2.3L 1bbl OHC (automatic transaxle Fed.) – RPM Gained: 150–200 – Reset RPM: 175.
- 1986–87 2.3L 1bbl OHC (automatic transaxle Cal.) – RPM Gained: 160–240 – Reset RPM: 200.

THROTTLE POSITION SENSOR (TPS) ADJUSTMENT

There are 2 types of TPS sensors being used, one has slots so it can be adjusted and the other is a solid plate unit that is none adjustable. If the voltage reading on the non-adjustable type sensor is not 0.9–1.1 volts, and greater than 4 volts at wide open throttle, replace the sensor.

1. Connect a suitable digital volt/ohmmeter to terminal **A** (output terminal) and terminal **B** (ground) of the TPS.
2. Turn the ignition switch to the **ON** position and check the voltage reading at closed throttle. If the voltage reading is not 0.0–1.1 volts, loosen the TPS mounting screws and rotate the TPS until the correct voltage is obtained.
3. If the correct TPS voltage cannot be obtained, replace the TPS.
4. Slowly open the throttle and observe the digital volt/ohmmeter. The voltage should gradually increase to at least 4 volts at wide open throttle.

Diesel Engine

CURB IDLE

NOTE: *A special diesel engine tachometer is required for this procedure.*

1. Place the transmission in Neutral.
2. Bring the engine up to normal operating temperature. Stop engine.
3. Remove the timing hole cover. Clean the flywheel surface and install reflective tape.
4. Idle speed is measured with manual transmission in Neutral.

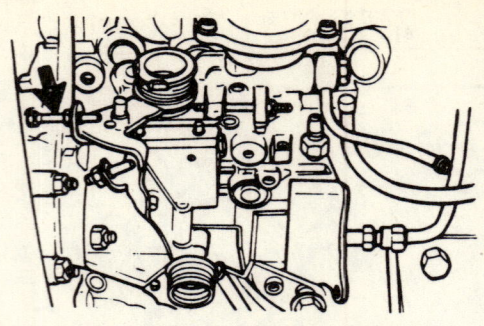

Diesel engine idle speed adjustment location

5. Check curb idle speed, using Rotunda 99-0001 or equivalent. Curb idle speed is specified on the vehicle Emissions Control Information decal (VECI). Adjust to specification by loosening the locknut on the idle speed bolt. Turn the idle speed adjusting bolt clockwise to increase, or counterclockwise to decrease engine idle speed. Tighten the locknut.
6. Place transmission in Neutral. Rev engine momentarily and recheck the curb idle RPM. Readjust if necessary.
7. Turn air conditioning On. Check the idle speed. Adjust to specification by loosening the nut on the air conditioning throttle kicker and rotating the screw.

CHILTON TIPS

This following Chilton Tips are specific problems and answers dealing with certain models and years.

1984 Tempo and Topaz

Some models may exhibit signs of poor acceleration at steady speeds when the engine is warm. This could be caused by an inoperative fuel control solenoid. There is a new replacement fuel control solenoid E43Z-9B998-A available which is designed to correct this condition. Check the condition of the fuel solenoid as follows:

1. Disconnect the electrical connector form the solenoid. Place a vacuum tee valve with a vacuum gauge into the vacuum ($5/32$ in.) hose between the solenoid and the carburetor.
2. Start the engine and let it run at idle speed. Read the vacuum gauge, the gauge should read between 1.0 and 1.5 in.Hg of vacuum. Now apply a 12 volt source to the fuel control solenoid.
3. The vacuum gauge should read between 4.0 and 5.5 in.Hg of vacuum. If the vacuum gauge readings do not agree with these specifications, replace the fuel control solenoid with the new replacement fuel control solenoid E43Z-9B998-A available at your local Ford Lincoln/Mercury dealer.

ENGINE PERFORMANCE AND TUNE-UP

Troubleshooting Engine Performance

Problem	Cause	Solution
Hard starting (engine cranks normally)	• Binding linkage, choke valve or choke piston	• Repair as necessary
	• Restricted choke vacuum diaphragm	• Clean passages
	• Improper fuel level	• Adjust float level
	• Dirty, worn or faulty needle valve and seat	• Repair as necessary
	• Float sticking	• Repair as necessary
	• Faulty fuel pump	• Replace fuel pump
	• Incorrect choke cover adjustment	• Adjust choke cover
	• Inadequate choke unloader adjustment	• Adjust choke unloader
	• Faulty ignition coil	• Test and replace as necessary
	• Improper spark plug gap	• Adjust gap
	• Incorrect ignition timing	• Adjust timing
	• Incorrect valve timing	• Check valve timing; repair as necessary
Rough idle or stalling	• Incorrect curb or fast idle speed	• Adjust curb or fast idle speed
	• Incorrect ignition timing	• Adjust timing to specification
	• Improper feedback system operation	• Refer to Chapter 4
	• Improper fast idle cam adjustment	• Adjust fast idle cam
	• Faulty EGR valve operation	• Test EGR system and replace as necessary
	• Faulty PCV valve air flow	• Test PCV valve and replace as necessary
	• Choke binding	• Locate and eliminate binding condition
	• Faulty TAC vacuum motor or valve	• Repair as necessary
	• Air leak into manifold vacuum	• Inspect manifold vacuum connections and repair as necessary
	• Improper fuel level	• Adjust fuel level
	• Faulty distributor rotor or cap	• Replace rotor or cap
	• Improperly seated valves	• Test cylinder compression, repair as necessary
	• Incorrect ignition wiring	• Inspect wiring and correct as necessary
	• Faulty ignition coil	• Test coil and replace as necessary
	• Restricted air vent or idle passages	• Clean passages
	• Restricted air cleaner	• Clean or replace air cleaner filler element
	• Faulty choke vacuum diaphragm	• Repair as necessary
Faulty low-speed operation	• Restricted idle transfer slots	• Clean transfer slots
	• Restricted idle air vents and passages	• Clean air vents and passages
	• Restricted air cleaner	• Clean or replace air cleaner filter element
	• Improper fuel level	• Adjust fuel level
	• Faulty spark plugs	• Clean or replace spark plugs
	• Dirty, corroded, or loose ignition secondary circuit wire connections	• Clean or tighten secondary circuit wire connections
	• Improper feedback system operation	• Refer to Chapter 4
	• Faulty ignition coil high voltage wire	• Replace ignition coil high voltage wire
	• Faulty distributor cap	• Replace cap
Faulty acceleration	• Improper accelerator pump stroke	• Adjust accelerator pump stroke
	• Incorrect ignition timing	• Adjust timing
	• Inoperative pump discharge check ball or needle	• Clean or replace as necessary
	• Worn or damaged pump diaphragm or piston	• Replace diaphragm or piston

ENGINE PERFORMANCE AND TUNE-UP

1984 Escort/EXP and Lynx

Some models may exhibit signs of a rough idle and or the engine stalling. This problem could be caused by the malfunctioning EGR valve position sensor that has been installed on the vehicle. The EGR valve position sensor (EVP) with the date codes prior to October 12, 1984 may cause this rough idle and stalling problem in some models, particularly the 1984 California vehicles equipped with the EEC-III system. These vehicles do not have the **KEEP ALIVE MEMORIES** to track the intermittent component concerns making the diagnosis more difficult.

When servicing the 1984 EEC-III equipped vehicles with this problem, check the EVP sensor. Replace the EVP sensor if the part is E43F-9G428-A2A with a date code prior to October 12, 1984. The date code is listed below the part number on the sensor. Normal diagnostic procedures will usually detect the above conditions on all EEC-IV applications. Be sure that the replacement EVP sensor has a date code of October 12, 1984 or later. The EVP sensors with part number E43F-9G428-A1A/A1B are not effected and all date codes are acceptable for service.

When trying to figure out the date number on the EVP sensor, use the following example as a guide, date number 4C7B:

1. The 4 stand for the year 1984.
2. The C stands for the month, the months are lined up in the following manner:
 - A – January.
 - B – February.
 - C – March, ETC.
3. The 7 stands for the day of the month.
4. The B stands for the shift that produced the sensor. A–1st, B–2nd and C, 3rd shift.
5. So by using the example it states that sensor was built on March 7, 1984 by the second shift.

1984 Escort/EXP and Lynx with 1.6L Engine and Automatic Transmission

Some of these models may exhibit conditions of stalling and or no-start during cold engine operation, This can be corrected by installing a new purge control valve in the evaporative emission control system and removing the cold weather modulator.

1. Remove and discard the tee connector (D9AE–9E645–AB) from the existing evaporative emission control harness (E4EE–9C987–BA).
2. Install purge control valve E3TZ-9B-963–A in the evaporative emission control harness where the tee connector used to be located.

   a. Position the new purge control valve in such a way that the round portion (top of the cap) is right side up with the $3/8$ in. and the $1/4$ in. nipple pointing towards the battery.

   b. Route the $1/4$ in. hose under the $3/8$ in. hose from the carburetor Bowl Vent Valve and attach it to the $1/4$ in. nipple on the purge control valve. Attach a piece of $5/32$ in. bulk hose 13 in. long to the end of the $3/16$ in. open port of the purge control valve and secure with a suitable wire strap.

   c. Attach a 3-way tee connector to the open end of the 13 in. hose.

3. Disconnect the vacuum connector, (the vacuum line from the air control valve) and insert into the open port of the 3-way tee connector. Attach a piece of rubber tubing from the air control valve to the remaining open port of the 3-way tee connector.
4. Remove the air cleaner cover by unfastening the retaining clips to the cleaner tray and set it a side. Disconnect the vacuum harness assembly from the cold weather modulator.
5. Remove and discard the cold weather modulator (D8BE–9E862–AA Yellow) from the air cleaner tray. Obtain and install a non-functional cold weather modulator (E4FZ–9E862–A orange and black or equivalent), in place of the component removed.
6. Reconnect the vacuum harness that was removed in Step 4.

Engine and Engine Overhaul

ENGINE ELECTRICAL

Understanding the Engine Electrical System

The engine electrical system can be broken down into three separate and distinct systems: (1) the starting system, (2) the charging system, and (3) the ignition system.

BATTERY AND STARTING SYSTEM

Basic Operating Principles

The battery is the first link in the chain of mechanisms which work together to provide cranking of the automobile engine. In most modern cars, the battery is a lead/acid electrochemical device consisting of six two-volt (2 V) subsections connected in series so the unit is capable of producing approximately 12 V of electrical pressure. Each subsection, or cell, consists of a series of positive and negative plates held a short distance apart in a solution of sulfuric acid and water. The two types of plates are of dissimilar metals. This causes a chemical reaction to be set up, and it is this reaction which produces current flow from the battery when its positive and negative terminals are connected to an electrical appliance such as a lamp or motor. The continued transfer of electrons would eventually convert the sulfuric acid in the electrolyte to water, and make the two plates identical in chemical composition. As electrical energy is removed from the battery, its voltage output tends to drop. Thus, measuring battery voltage and battery electrolyte composition are two ways of checking the ability of the unit to supply power. During the starting of the engine, electrical energy is removed from the battery. However, if the charging circuit is in good condition and the operating conditions are normal, the power removed from the battery will be replaced by the generator (or alternator) which will force electrons back through the battery, reversing the normal flow, and restoring the battery to its original chemical state.

The battery and starting motor are linked by very heavy electrical cables designed to minimize resistance to the flow of current. Generally, the major power supply cable that leaves the battery goes directly to the starter, while other electrical system needs are supplied by a smaller cable. During starter operation, power flows from the battery to the starter and is grounded through the car's frame and the battery's negative ground strap.

The starting motor is a specially designed, direct current electric motor capable of producing a very great amount of power for its size. One thing that allows the motor to produce a great deal of power is its tremendous rotating speed. It drives the engine through a tiny pinion gear (attached to the starter's armature), which drives the very large flywheel ring gear at a greatly reduced speed. Another factor allowing it to produce so much power is that only intermittent operation is required of it. This, little allowance for air circulation is required, and the windings can be built into a very small space.

The starter solenoid is a magnetic device which employs the small current supplied by the starting switch circuit of the ignition switch. This magnetic action moves a plunger which mechanically engages the starter and electrically closes the heavy switch which connects it to the battery. The starting switch circuit consists of the starting switch contained within the ignition switch, a transmission neutral safety switch or clutch pedal switch, and the wiring necessary to connect these in series with the starter solenoid or relay.

A pinion, which is a small gear, is mounted to a one-way drive clutch. This clutch is splined to

88 ENGINE AND ENGINE OVERHAUL

the starter armature shaft. When the ignition switch is moved to the **START** position, the solenoid plunger slides the pinion toward the flywheel ring gear via a collar and spring. If the teeth on the pinion and flywheel match properly, the pinion will engage the flywheel immediately. If the gear teeth butt one another, the spring will be compressed and will force the gears to mesh as soon as the starter turns far enough to allow them to do so. As the solenoid plunger reaches the end of its travel, it closes the contacts that connect the battery and starter and then the engine is cranked.

As soon as the engine starts, the flywheel ring gear begins turning fast enough to drive the pinion at an extremely high rate of speed. At this point, the one-way clutch begins allowing the pinion to spin faster than the starter shaft so that the starter will not operate at excessive speed. When the ignition switch is released from the starter position, the solenoid is de-energized, and a spring contained within the solenoid assembly pulls the gear out of mesh and interrupts the current flow to the starter.

Some starter employ a separate relay, mounted away from the starter, to switch the motor and solenoid current on and off. The relay thus replaces the solenoid electrical switch, buy does not eliminate the need for a solenoid mounted on the starter used to mechanically engage the starter drive gears. The relay is used to reduce the amount of current the starting switch must carry.

THE CHARGING SYSTEM

Basic Operating Principles

The automobile charging system provides electrical power for operation of the vehicle's ignition and starting systems and all the electrical accessories. The battery services as an electrical surge or storage tank, storing (in chemical form) the energy originally produced by the engine driven generator. The system also provides a means of regulating generator output to

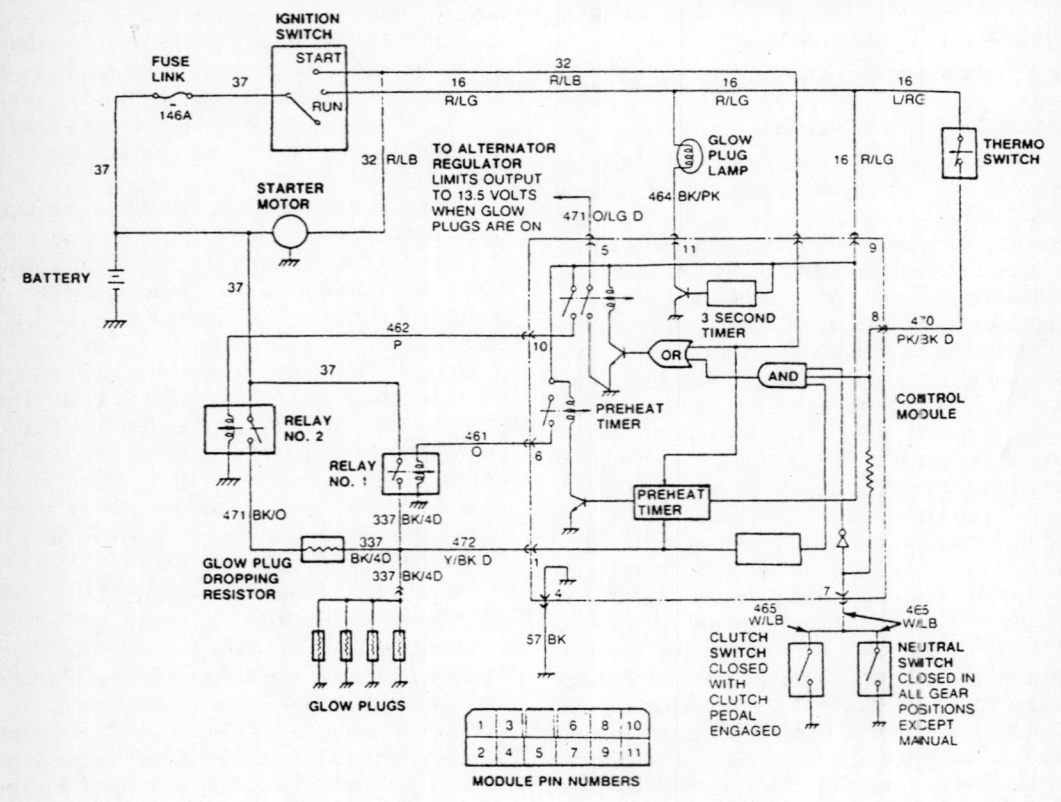

Typical starter system wiring schematic - diesel engines

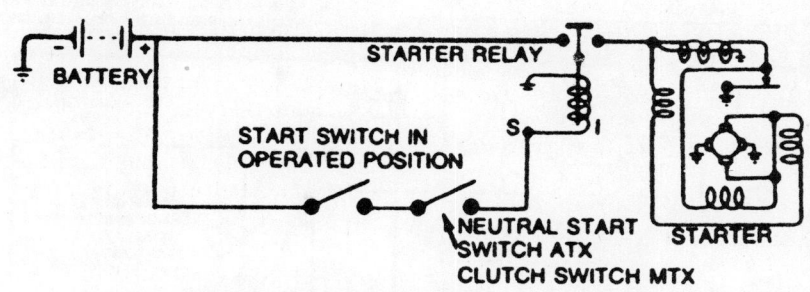

ENGINE AND ENGINE OVERHAUL

Typical starter system wiring schematic - gas engines

protect the battery from being overcharged and to avoid excessive voltage to the accessories.

The storage battery is a chemical device incorporating parallel lead plates in a tank containing a sulfuric acid/water solution. Adjacent plates are slightly dissimilar, and the chemical reaction of the two dissimilar plates produces electrical energy when the battery is connected to a load such as the starter motor. The chemical reaction is reversible, so that when the generator is producing a voltage (electrical pressure) greater than that produced by the battery, electricity is forced into the battery, and the battery is returned to its fully charged state.

The vehicle's generator is driven mechanically, through V belts, by the engine crankshaft. It consists of two coils of fine wire, one stationary (the stator), and one movable (the rotor). The rotor may also be known as the armature, and consists of fine wire wrapped around an iron core which is mounted on a shaft. The electricity which flows through the two coils of wire (provided initially by the battery in some cases) creates an intense magnetic field around both rotor and stator, and the interaction between the two fields creates voltage, allowing the generator to power the accessories and charge the battery.

There are two types of generators: the earlier is the direct current (DC) type. The current produced by the DC generator is generated in the armature and carried off the spinning armature by stationary brushes contacting the commutator. The commutator is a series of smooth metal contact plates on the end of the armature. The commutator is a series of smooth metal contact plates on the end of the armature. The commutator plates, which are separated from one another by a very short gap, are connected to the armature circuits so that current will flow in one directions only in the wires carrying the generator output. The generator stator consists of two stationary coils of wire which draw some of the output current of the generator to form a powerful magnetic field and create the interaction of fields which generates the voltage. The generator field is wired in series with the regulator.

Newer automobiles use alternating current generators or alternators, because they are more efficient, can be rotated at higher speeds, and have fewer brush problems. In an alternator, the field rotates while all the current produced passes only through the stator winding. The brushes bear against continuous slip rings rather than a commutator. This causes the current produced to periodically reverse the direction of its flow. Diodes (electrical one-way switches) block the flow of current from traveling in the wrong direction. A series of diodes is wired together to permit the alternating flow of the stator to be converted to a pulsating, but unidirectional flow at the alternator output. The alternator's field is wired in series with the voltage regulator.

The regulator consists of several circuits. Each circuit has a core, or magnetic coil of wire, which operates a switch. Each switch is connected to ground through one or more resistors. The coil of wire responds directly to system voltage. When the voltage reaches the required level, the magnetic field created by the winding of wire closes the switch and inserts a resistance into the generator field circuit, thus reducing the output. The contacts of the switch cycle open and close many times each second to precisely control voltage.

While alternators are self-limiting as far as maximum current is concerned, DC generators employ a current regulating circuit which responds directly to the total amount of current flowing through the generator circuit rather than to the output voltage. The current regulator is similar to the voltage regulator except that all system current must flow through the energizing coil on its way to the various accessories.

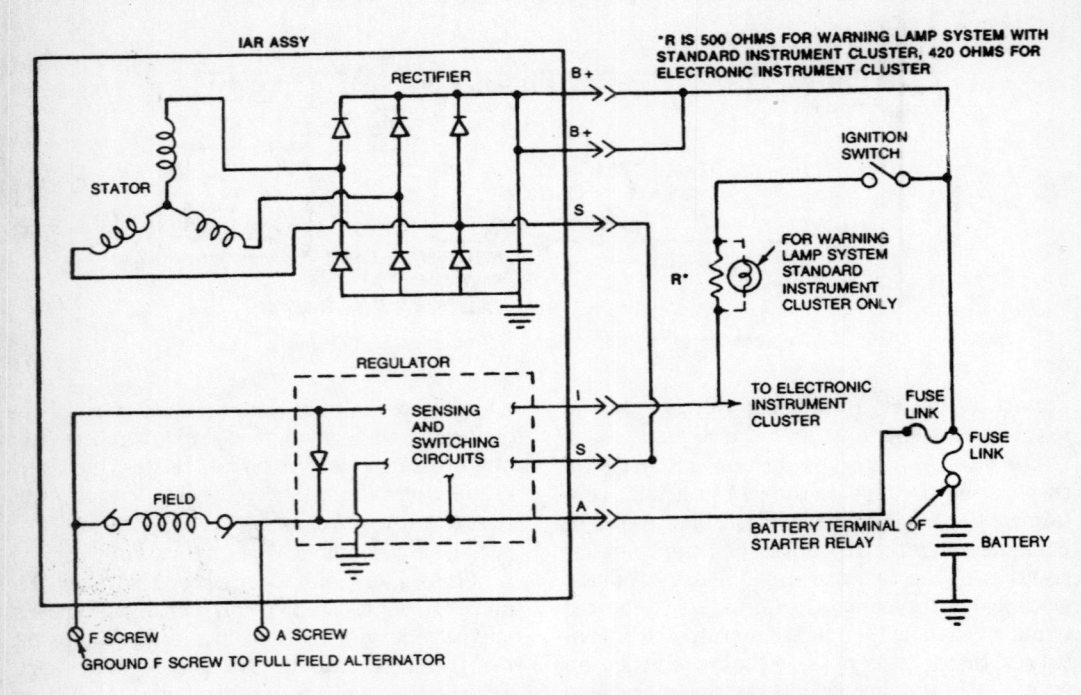

Typical alternator schematic - External fan and internal regulator type

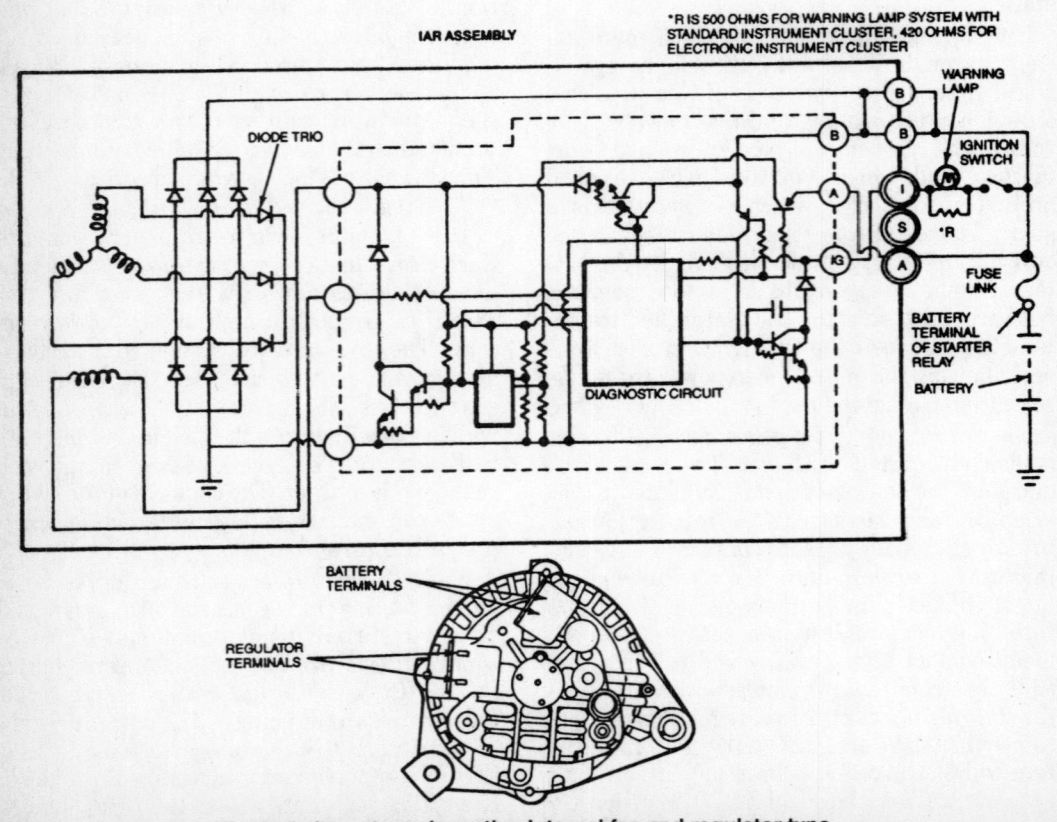

Typical alternator schematic - Internal fan and regulator type

ENGINE AND ENGINE OVERHAUL

Distributor

REMOVAL AND INSTALLATION

1.3L, 1.6L and 1.9L Engines

The camshaft driven distributor is located at the top left end of the cylinder head. It is retained by two holddown bolts at the base of the distributor shaft housing.

1. Turn engine to No. 1 piston at TDC of the compression stroke. Disconnect negative battery cable. Disconnect the vacuum hose(s) from the advance unit. Disconnect the wiring harness at the distributor.
2. Remove the capscrews and remove the distributor cap.
3. Scribe a mark on the distributor body, showing the position of the ignition rotor. Scribe another mark on the distributor body and cylinder head, showing the position of the body in relation to the head. These marks can be used for reference when installing the distributor, as long as the engine remains undisturbed.
4. Remove the two distributor holddown bolts. Pull the distributor out of the head.

NOTE: *Some engine may be equipped with a new security type hold down bolt which will require the use of special tool T82L–12270–A or equivalent (12 point socket) in order to remove these special hold down bolts.*

To install:

5. To install the distributor with the engine undisturbed, place the distributor in the cylinder head, seating the offset tang of the drive coupling into the groove on the end of the camshaft.
6. Install the two distributor holddown screws and tighten them so that the distributor can just barely be moved. Install the rotor (if removed), the distributor cap and all wiring, then set the ignition timing.
7. If the crankshaft was rotated while the distributor was removed, the engine must be brought to TDC (Top Dead Center) on the compression stroke of the No. 1 cylinder.
8. Remove the No. 1 spark plug. Place your finger over the hole and rotate the crankshaft slowly (use a wrench on the crankshaft pulley bolt) in the direction of normal engine rotation, until engine compression is felt.

NOTE: *Turn the engine only in the direction of normal rotation. Backward rotation will cause the cam belt to slip or lose teeth, altering engine timing.*

9. When engine compression is felt at the spark plug hole, indicating that the piston is approaching TDC, continue to turn the crankshaft until the timing mark on the pulley is aligned with the **0** mark (timing mark) on the engine front cover. Turn the distributor shaft until the ignition rotor is at the No. 1 firing position. Install the distributor into the cylinder head, by repeating Steps 5 and 6 of this procedure.

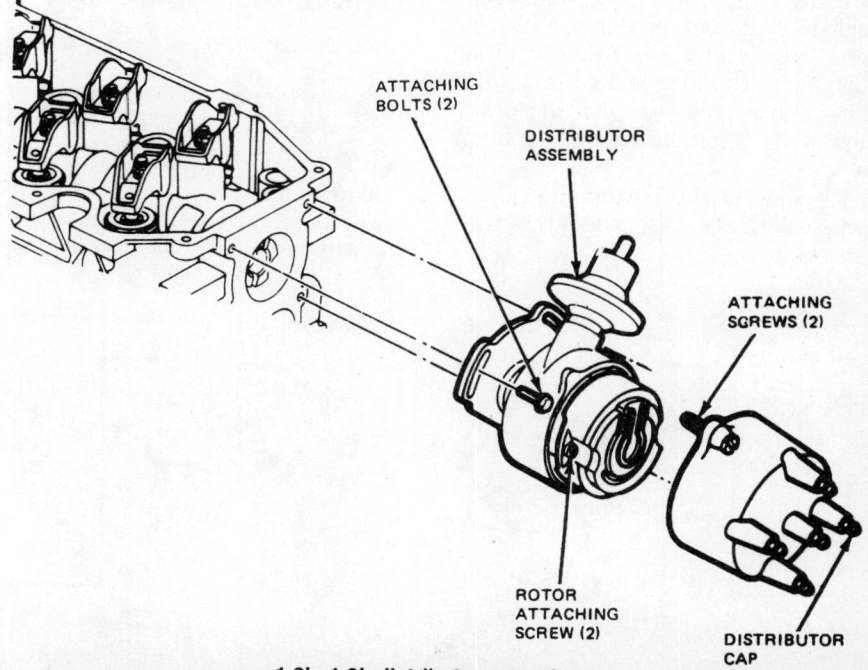

1.6L, 1.9L distributor mounting

ENGINE AND ENGINE OVERHAUL

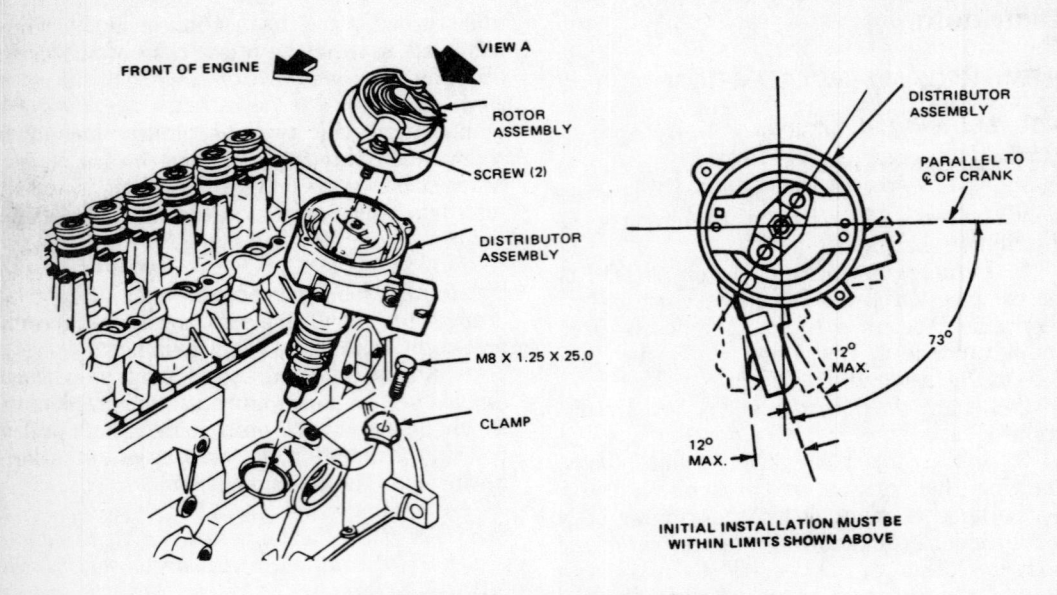

Distributor installation, 2.3L HSC engine

2.3L HSC Engine

The TFI-IV distributor is mounted on the side of the engine block. Some engines may be equipped with a security type distributor hold down bolt which requires a special wrench for removal. The TFI-IV distributor incorporates a Hall Effect advance switch stator assembly and an integrally mounted thick-film module. When the Hall Effect device is turned on and a pulse is produced, the EEC-IV electronics computes crankshaft position and engine demand to calibrate spark advance. Initial ignition timing adjustment/checking is necessary when the distributor has been removed. Repairs to the distributor are accomplished by distributor replacement.

1. Turn engine to No. 1 piston at TDC of the compression stroke. Disconnect the negative battery cable.

2. Disconnect the wiring harness at the distributor. Mark No. 1 spark plug wire cap terminal location on the distributor base. Remove the coil wire from the cap.

3. Remove he distributor cap with plug wires attached and position out of the way. Remove the rotor.

4. Remove the distributor base hold down bolt and clamp. Slowly remove the distributor from the engine. Be careful not to disturb the intermediate driveshaft.

NOTE: *Some engine may be equipped with a new security type hold down bolt which will require the use of special tool T82L-12270-A or equivalent (12 point socket) in order to remove these special hold down bolts.*

To install:

5. To install the distributor with the engine undisturbed, align the locating boss on the

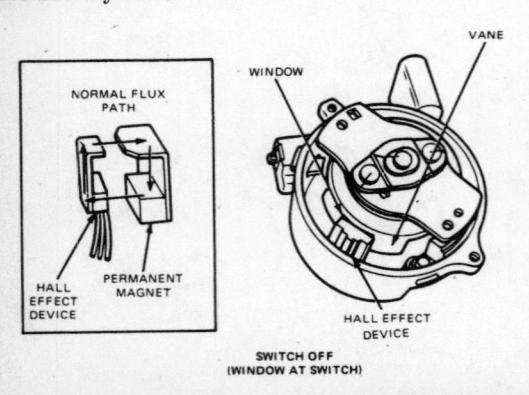

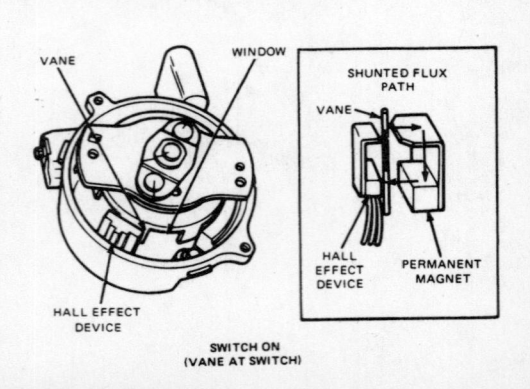

2.3L HSC-Hall effect distributor operation

rotor with the hole on the armature. Fully seat the rotor onto the distributor shaft.

6. Rotate the distributor shaft so that the blade on the rotor is pointing toward the mark on the distributor base made earlier during the removal procedure.

7. While installing the distributor continue to rotate the rotor slightly so the leading edge of the vane is centered in the vane switch stator assembly.

8. Rotate the distributor in the block to align the leading edge of the and vane switch stator assembly. Verify that the rotor is pointing at the No.1 mark on the distributor base.

9. If the vane and vane switch stator assembly cannot be aligned by rotating the distributor in the cylinder block, remove the distributor just enough to disengage the distributor gear from the camshaft gear. Rotate the rotor enough to engage the distributor gear on another tooth of the camshaft gear.

10. Install the two distributor holddown screws and tighten them so that the distributor can just barely be moved. Install the rotor (if removed), the distributor cap and all wiring, then set the ignition timing.

11. If the crankshaft was rotated while the distributor was removed, the engine must be brought to TDC (Top Dead Center) on the compression stroke of the No. 1 cylinder.

12. Remove the No. 1 spark plug. Place your finger over the hole and rotate the crankshaft slowly (use a wrench on the crankshaft pulley bolt) in the direction of normal engine rotation, until engine compression is felt.

NOTE: *Turn the engine only in the direction of normal rotation. Backward rotation will cause the cam belt to slip or lose teeth, altering engine timing.*

13. When engine compression is felt at the spark plug hole, indicating that the piston is approaching TDC, continue to turn the crankshaft until the timing mark on the pulley is aligned with the **0** mark (timing mark) on the engine front cover. Turn the distributor shaft until the ignition rotor is at the No. 1 firing position. Install the distributor into the cylinder head, by repeating Steps 5 and 6 of this procedure.

Alternator

ALTERNATOR PRECAUTIONS

To prevent damage to the alternator and regulator, the following precautionary measures must be taken when working with the electrical system.

1. Never reverse battery connections. Always check the battery polarity visually. This is to be done before any connections are made to ensure that all of the connections correspond to the battery ground polarity of the car.

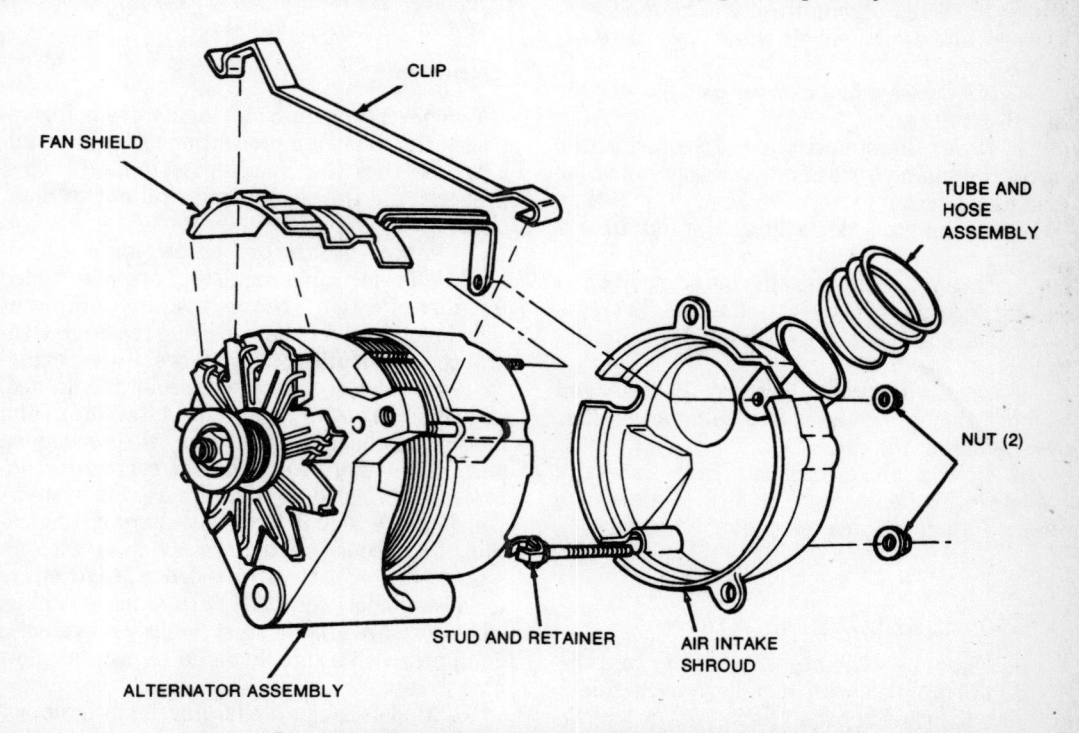

On air-conditioned cars, cool air shrouding is added

94 ENGINE AND ENGINE OVERHAUL

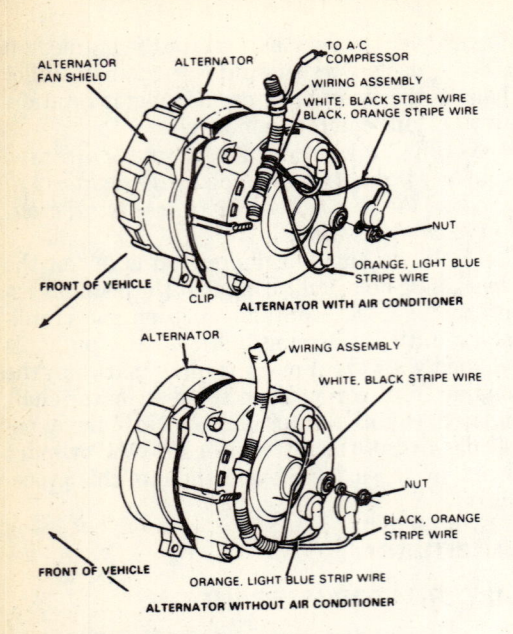

Harness connections for alternators

2. Booster batteries must be connected properly. Make sure the positive cable of the booster battery is connected to the positive terminal of the battery which is getting the boost. Engines must be shut off before cables are connected.

3. Disconnect the battery cables before using a fast charger; the charger has a tendency to force current through the diodes in the opposite directions for which they were designed.

4. Never use a fast charger as a booster for starting the car.

5. Never disconnect the voltage regulator while the engine is running, unless as noted for testing purposes.

6. Do not ground the alternator output terminal.

7. Do not operate the alternator on an open circuit with the field energized.

8. Do not attempt to polarize the alternator.

9. Disconnect the battery cables and remove the alternator before using an electric arc welder on the car.

10. Protect the alternator from excessive moisture. If the engine is to be steam cleaned, cover or remove the alternator.

REMOVAL AND INSTALLATION

1. Disconnect the negative battery cable.
2. If equipped with a pulley cover shield, remove the shield at this time.
3. Loosen the alternator pivot bolt. Remove the adjustment bracket to alternator bolt (and nut, if equipped). Pivot the alternator to gain slack in the drive belt and remove the belt.
4. Disconnect and label (for correct installation) the alternator wiring.

NOTE: *Some models use a push-on wiring connector on the field and stator connections. Pull or push straight when removing or installing, or damage to the connectors may occur.*

5. Remove the pivot bolt and the alternator.

To install:

6. Position the alternator assembly onto the vehicle. Install the alternator pivot and adjuster arm bolts, but do not tighten them at this time.

7. Install the alternator drive belt. Adjust the drive belt tension so that there is approximately $1/4$–$1/2$ in. (6–13mm) deflection on the longest span between the pulleys.

8. Reconnect the alternator wiring. Install the pulley shield, if equipped and connect the negative battery cable.

Regulator

NOTE: *Three different types of regulators are used, depending on models, engine, alternator output and type of dash mounted charging indicator used (light or ammeter). The regulators are 100 percent solid state and are calibrated and preset by the manufacturer. No readjustment is required or possible on these regulators.*

SERVICE

Whenever system components are being replaced the following precautions should be followed so that the charging system will work properly and the components will not be damaged.

1. Always use the proper alternator.
2. The electronic regulators are color coded for identification. Never install a different coded regulator for the one being replaced. General coding identification follows, if the regulator removed does not have the color mentioned, identify the output of the alternator and method of charging indication, then consult a parts department to obtain the correct regulator. A black coded regulator is used in systems which use a signal lamp for charging indication. Gray coded regulators are used with an ammeter gauge. Neutral coded regulators are used on models equipped with a diesel engine. The special regulator must be used on vehicles equipped with a diesel engine to prevent glow plug failure.
3. Models using a charging lamp indicator are equipped with a 500 resistor on the back of the instrument panel.

ENGINE AND ENGINE OVERHAUL

REMOVAL AND INSTALLATION

1. Disconnect the negative battery cable.
2. Unplug the wiring harness from the regulator.
3. Remove the regulator mounting bolts.
4. Install in the reverse order.

Fuse Link

The fuse link is a short length of insulated wire contained in the alternator wiring harness, between the alternator and the starter relay. The fuse link is several wire gauge sizes smaller than the other wires in the harness. If a booster battery is connected incorrectly in the car battery or if some component of the charging system is shorted to ground, the fuse link melts and protects the alternator. The fuse link is attached to the starter relay. The insulation on the wire reads: Fuse Link. A melted fuse link can usually be identified by cracked or bubbled insulation. If it is difficult to determine if the fuse link is melted, connect a test light to both ends of the wire. If the fuse link is not melted, the test light will light showing that an open circuit does not exist in the wire.

REPLACEMENT

NOTE: *Also refer to the end of this chapter for procedures.*

1. Disconnect the negative battery cable.
2. Disconnect the eyelet end of the link from the starter relay.
3. Cut the other end of the link from the wiring harness at the splice.
4. Connect the eyelet end of the new fuse link to the starter relay.

NOTE: *Use only an original equipment type fuse link. Do not replace with standard wire.*

5. Splice the open end of the new fuse link into the wiring harness.
6. Solder the splice with rosin core solder and wrap the splice in electrical tape. This splice must be soldered.
7. Connect the negative battery cable.

Battery

REMOVAL AND INSTALLATION

NOTE: *The diesel equipped models have the battery located in the luggage compartment.*

1. Loosen the battery cable bolts and spread the ends of the battery cable terminals.
2. Disconnect the negative battery cable first.
3. Disconnect the positive battery cable.
4. Remove the battery holddown.
5. Wearing heavy gloves, clean the cable terminals and battery with an acid neutralizing solution and terminal cleaning brush. Remove the battery from under the hood. Be careful not to tip the battery and spill acid on yourself or the car during removal.

To install:

6. Wearing heavy gloves, place the battery in its holder under the hood. Use care not to spill the acid.
7. Install the battery holddown.
8. Install the positive battery cable first.
9. Install the negative battery cable.
10. Apply a light coating of grease to the cable ends.

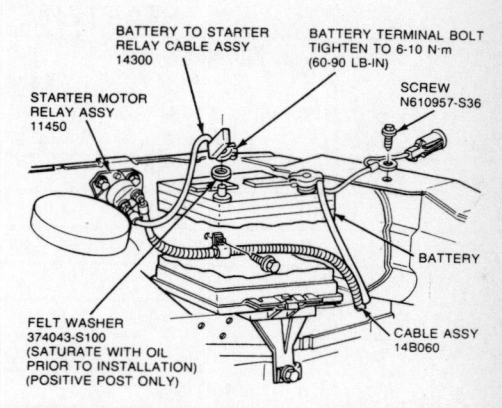

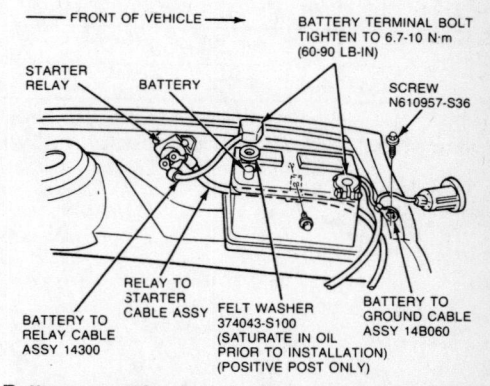

Battery mounting location-2.3L HSC engine

Battery mounting location-1.6L and 1.9L engines

Starter

REMOVAL AND INSTALLATION

Gasoline Engines

1. Disconnect the negative battery cable.
2. Raise and safely support the front of the vehicle on jackstands. Disconnect the starter cable from the starter motor.
3. On models that are equipped with a manual transaxle, remove the three nuts that attach the roll restrictor brace to the starter

ENGINE AND ENGINE OVERHAUL

STARTER SPECIFICATIONS

Year	Engine L (cid)	Current Draw Normal Load (Amps)	Lock Test Volts	Lock Test Torque (ft. lb.)	No-Load Current Draw (Amps)	Engine Cranking Speed (rpm)	Brush Length (in.)	Brush Spring Tension (oz.)
1981	1.3 (79)	150–250	5	9.5	80	190–260	0.45	80
	1.6 (98)	150–250	5	9.5	80	190–260	0.45	80
1982	1.6 (98)	150–250	5	9.5	80	190–260	0.45	80
1983	1.6 (98)	150–250	5	9.5	80	190–260	0.45	80
1984	1.6 (98)	150–250	5	9.5	80	190–260	0.45	80
	2.0 (122)	375	—	—	190	250–350	0.485	—
	2.3 (140)	150–250	5	9.5	80	190–260	0.45	80
1985	1.6 (98)	150–250	5	9.5	80	190–260	0.45	80
	2.0 (122)	375	—	—	190	250–350	0.485	—
	2.3 (140)	150–250	5	9.5	80	190–260	0.45	80
1986	1.9 (114)	150–250	5	9.5	80	190–260	0.45	80
	2.0 (122)	375	—	—	190	250–350	0.485	—
	2.3 (140)	150–250	5	9.5	80	190–260	0.45	80
1987	1.9 (114)	150–250	5	9.5	80	190–260	0.45	80
	2.0 (122)	375	—	—	190	250–350	0.485	—
	2.3 (140)	150–250	5	9.5	80	190–260	0.45	80
1988	1.9 (114)	150–250	5	9.5	80	190–260	0.45	80
	2.3 (140)	150–250	5	9.5	80	190–260	0.45	80
1989	1.9 (114)	150–250	5	9.5	80	190–260	0.45	80
	2.3 (140)	150–250	5	9.5	80	190–260	0.45	80
1990	1.9 (114)	150–250	5	9.5	80	190–260	0.45	80
	2.3 (140)	150–250	5	9.5	80	190–260	0.45	80

NOTE: Maximum commutator runout is 0.005 in. (0.12mm). Maximum starting circuit voltage drop (battery positive terminal to starter terminal) at normal operating temperature is 0.5 volt.

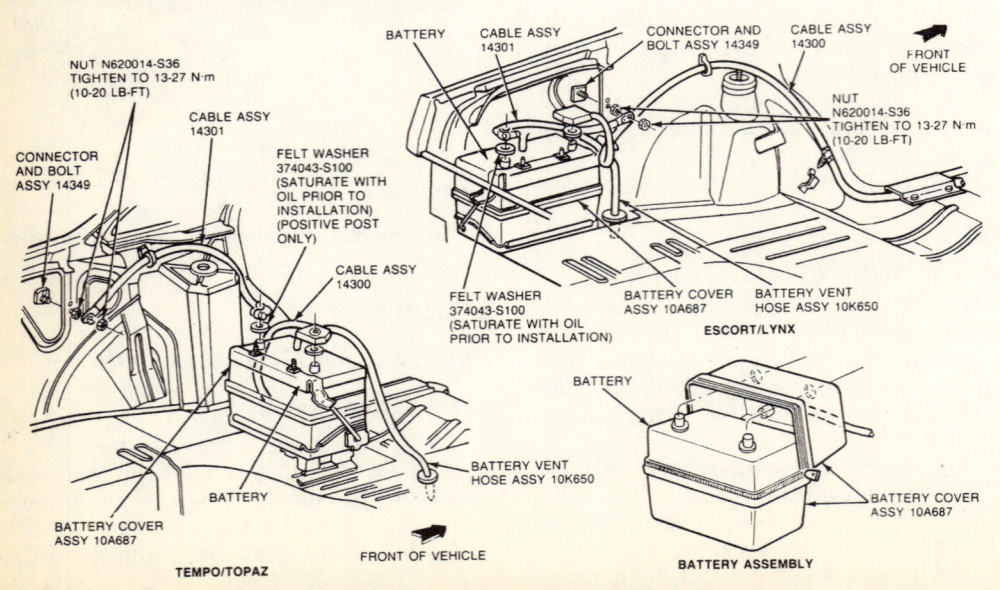

Battery mounting location-2.0L diesel engine

mounting studs at the transaxle. Remove the brace. On models that are equipped with an automatic transaxle, remove the nose bracket mounted on the starter studs.

4. Remove the two bolts attaching the rear starter support bracket, remove the retaining nut from the rear of the starter motor and remove the support bracket.

5. On models equipped with a manual transaxle, remove the three starter mounting studs and the starter motor. On models equipped with a automatic transaxle, remove the two starter mounting studs and the starter motor.

To install:

7. Position the starter to the transaxle housing. Install the attaching studs or bolts. Torque the studs or bolts to 30–40 ft. lbs. (41–54 Nm).

8. On vehicles equipped with a roll restrictor brace, install the brace on the starter mounting studs at the transmission housing. On the Tempo/Topaz models, install the cable support on the top of the brace. Attach the 3 retaining bolts.

9. Position the starter rear support bracket to the starter. Attach the 2 attaching bolts. Connect the starter cable at the starter terminal.

10. Lower the vehicle and connect the negative battery cable.

OVERHAUL

Brush Replacement

1. Remove the top cover by taking out the retaining screw. Loosen and remove the two through bolts. Remove the starter drive end housing and the starter drive plunger lever return spring.

2. Remove the starter drive plunger lever pivot pin and lever, and remove the armature.

3. Remove the brush end plate.

4. Remove the ground brush retaining screws from the frame and remove the brushes.

5. Cut the insulated brush leads from the field coils, as close to the field connection point as possible.

6. Clean and inspect the starter motor.

7. Replace the brash end plate if the insulator between the field brush holder and the end plate is cracked or broken.

8. Position the new insulated field brushes lead on the field coil connections. Position and crimp the clip provided with the brushes to hold the brush lead to the connection. Solder the lead, clip, and connection together using rosin core solder. Use a 300W soldering iron.

9. Install the ground brush leads to the frame with the retaining screws.

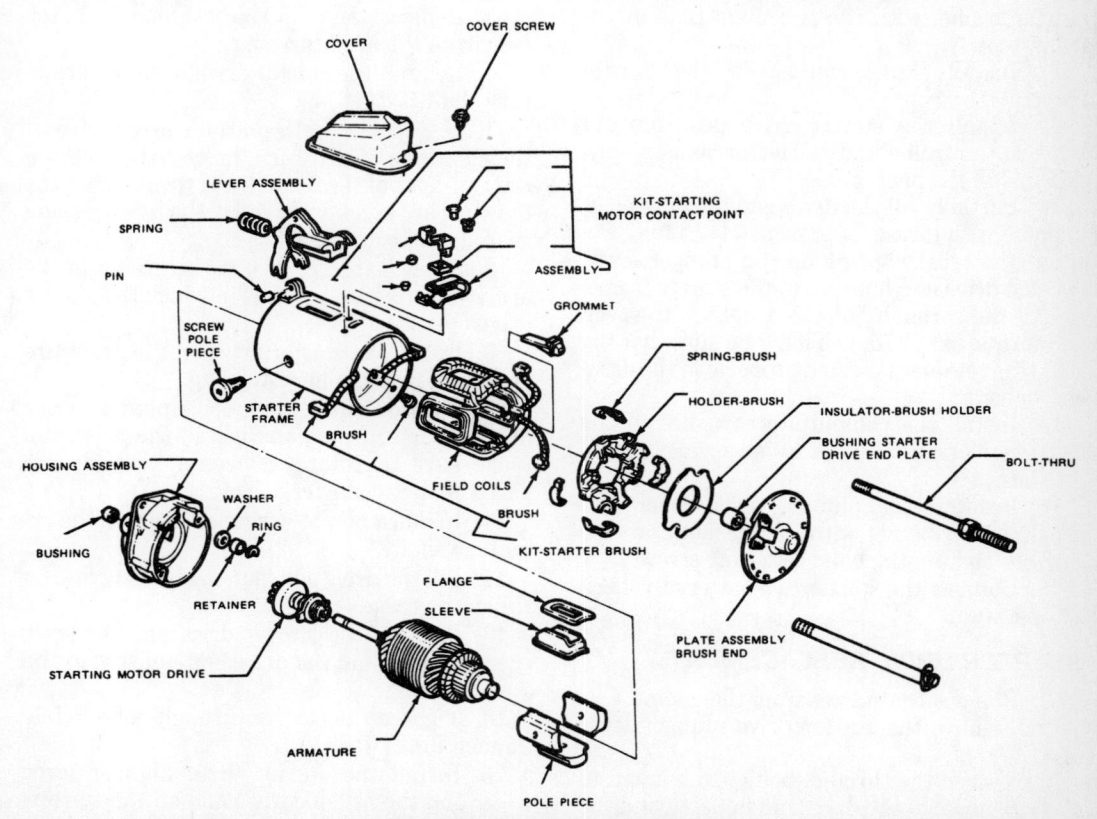

Exploded view of a starter motor

ENGINE AND ENGINE OVERHAUL

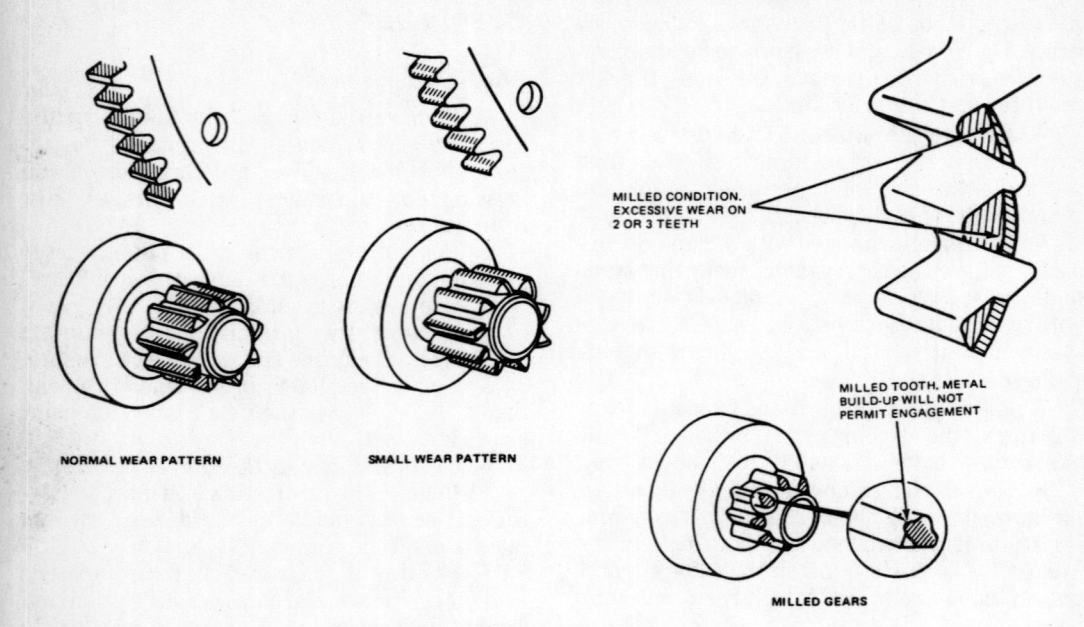

Starter drive gear wear pattern

10. Clean the commutator with special commutator paper.
11. Position the brush end plate to the starter frame, with the end plate boss in the frame slot.
12. Install the armature in the starter frame.
13. Install the starter drive gear plunger lever to the frame and starter drive assembly, and install the pivot pin.
14. Partially fill the drive end housing bearing bore with grease (approximately 1/4 full). Position the return spring on the plunger lever, and the drive end housing to the starter frame. Install the through-bolts and tighten to specified torque (55 to 75 inch lbs.). Be sure that the stop ring retainer is seated properly in the drive end housing.
15. Install the commutator brushes in the brush holders. Center the brush springs on the brushes.
16. Position the plunger lever cover and brush cover band, with its gasket, on the starter. Tighten the band retaining screw.
17. Connect the starter to a battery to check its operation.

STARTER DRIVE REPLACEMENT

1. Remove the starter from the engine.
2. Remove the starter drive plunger lever cover.
3. Loosen the through-bolts just enough to allow removal of the drive end housing and the starter drive plunger lever return spring.
4. Remove the pivot pin which attaches the starter drive plunger lever to the starter frame and remove the lever.
5. Remove the stop ring retainer and stop ring from the armature shaft.
6. Remove the starter drive from the armature shaft.
7. Inspect the teeth on the starter drive. If they are excessively worn, inspect the teeth on the ring gear of the flywheel. If the teeth on the flywheel are excessively worn, the flywheel ring gear should be replaced.
8. Apply a thin coat of white grease to the armature shaft, in the area in which the starter drive operates.
9. Install the starter drive on the armature shaft and install a new stopring.
10. Position the starter drive plunger lever on the starter frame and install the pivot pin. Make sure the plunger lever is properly engaged with the starter drive.
11. Install a new stop ring retainer on the armature shaft.
12. Fill the drive end housing bearing fore 1/4 full with grease.
13. Position the starter drive plunger lever return spring and the drive end housing to the starter frame.
14. Tighten the starter through-bolts to 55–75 inch lbs.
15. Install the starter drive plunger lever cover and the brush cover band on the starter.
16. Install the starter.

ENGINE AND ENGINE OVERHAUL

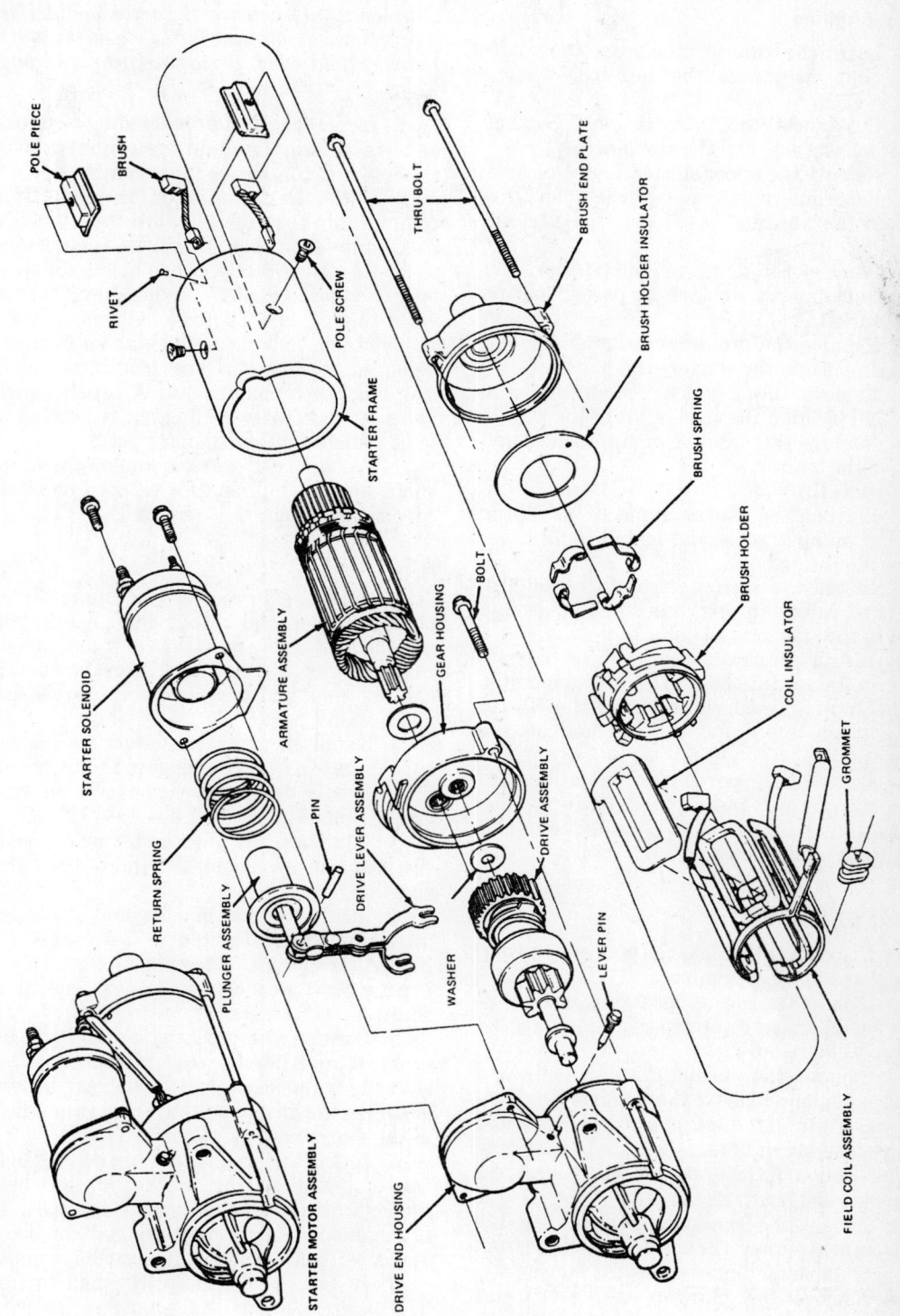

Exploded view of the diesel engine starter motor

ENGINE AND ENGINE OVERHAUL

Diesel Engines

1. Locate the battery in the luggage compartment and disconnect the negative battery cable.
2. Disconnect the cable assembly at the fender apron relay and the starter relay.
3. Remove the upper starter mounting bolt.
4. Raise and support the vehicle safely. Disconnect the vacuum hose from the vacuum pump.
5. Remove the 3 starter support bracket screws and bracket. Remove the power steering hose bracket.
6. Remove the ground wire assembly and cable support on the starter stud bolts.
7. Remove the 2 starter mounting stud bolts and position the starter out of the way.
8. Remove the vacuum pump bracket and remove the starter.

To install:

9. Position the starter in place. Install the vacuum pump bracket and install the 2 lower stator mounting bolt.
10. Install the starter support bracket. Install the cable support bracket and ground cable to the starter stud bolts.
11. Install the power steering hose bracket. Connect the vacuum hose to the vacuum pump.
12. Lower the vehicle. Connect the starter cable to the relay and the solenoid on the fender apron.
13. Install the upper starter mounting stud and bolt. Connect the negative battery cable. Check the starter operation. Torque the starter mounting stud bolts to 29–41 ft. lbs. (39–56 Nm).

DISASSEMBLY

1. Disconnect the field coil connection from the solenoid motor terminal.
2. Remove the solenoid attaching screws, solenoid and plunger return spring. Rotate the solenoid 90° to remove it.
3. Remove the starter through bolts and brush end plate. Remove the brush springs and brushes from the plastic brush holder and remove the brush holder. Be sure to take note of the location of the brush holder with respect to the ground brush terminals.
4. Remove the frame assembly. Remove the armature assembly. Remove the screw from the gear housing. Remove the gear housing.
5. Remove the plunger and lever pivot screw. Remove the plunger and lever assembly.
6. Remove the gear, output shaft and drive assembly.

Cleaning and Inspection

NOTE: *Do not wash the starter drive because the solvent will wash out all of its lubricants, thus causing the drive to slip. Use a brush or compressed air to clean the starter drive, field coils, armature, gear and housing.*

1. Inspect the armature winding for broken or burned insulation and open connections at the commutator. Check for grounds.
2. Check the commutator for runout. If the commutator is rough or more than 0.005 in. (0.127mm) out-of-round, service as necessary.
3. Check the plastic brush holder for cracks or broken pads. Replace the brushes if they are worn to 0.25 in. (6.35mm) in length. Inspect the field coils and plastic bobbins for burned or damaged conditions. Check continuity of the coil and brush connections. A brush replacement kit is available. All other assemblies are to be replaced rather than serviced.
4. Examine the gears, spline on the output shaft, and drive pinion for chipped or broken conditions. Replaced as required.

ASSEMBLY

1. Apply a thin coat of long life multi purpose grease on the output shaft spline. Slide the drive assembly onto the shaft and install a new stop ring, retainer and thrust washer. Install the shaft and drive assembly into the drive end housing.
2. Install the plunger and lever assembly ensuring the lever notches engage the flange ears of the starter drive. Attach the lever pin screw and tighten it top 7–11 ft. lbs. (9–15 Nm).
3. Lubricate the gear and washer. Install the gear and washer on the end of the output shaft.
4. Install the gear housing and attach with mounting screw. Tighten to 5–7 ft. lbs. (7–9 Nm). After lubricating the pinion, install the armature with washer on the gear end of the shaft.
5. Position the grommet around the field lead and press into the starter frame notch. Install the frame assembly to the gear housing, ensuring the grommet positioned in the notch in the gear housing.
6. Install the brush holder on the end of the frame, lining up the notches in the brush holder with the ground brush terminals. The brush holder is symmetrical and can be installed with either notch and brush terminal.
7. Install the brush springs and brushes. The positive brush leads must be placed in their respective slots to prevent grounding the starter assembly.
8. Install the brush end plate (be sure the end plate insulator is positioned properly in the end plate). Install the through bolts and tighten to 5–7 ft. lbs (7–9 Nm).

ENGINE AND ENGINE OVERHAUL

GENERAL ENGINE SPECIFICATIONS

Year	Engine L (cid)	Fuel System Type	SAE net Horsepower @ rpm	SAE net Torque ft. lbs. @ rpm	Bore × Stroke (in.)	Comp. Ratio	Oil Press. (psi.) @ 2000 rpm
1981	1.3 (79)	2V	NA	NA	3.15 × 2.40	NA	40
	1.6 (98)	2V	65 @ 5200	85 @ 3000	3.15 × 3.13	8.8:1	45–50
1982	1.6 (98)	2V	70 @ 4600	89 @ 3000	3.15 × 3.13	8.8:1	35–65
1983	1.6 (98)	2V	70 @ 4600	89 @ 3000	3.15 × 3.13	8.8:1	35–65
1984	1.6 (98)	2V	70 @ 4600	88 @ 2600	3.15 × 3.13	9.0:1	35–65
	1.6 (98) ④	2V	80 @ 5400	88 @ 3000	3.15 × 3.13	9.0:1	35–65
	1.6 (98) ⑤	EFI	120 @ 5200	120 @ 3400	3.15 × 3.13	8.0:1	35–65
	2.0 (122)	Diesel	52 @ 4000	82 @ 2400	3.39 × 3.39	22.7:1	55–60
	2.3 (140)	1V	84 @ 4600	118 @ 2600	3.70 × 3.30	9.0:1	55–70
1985	1.6 (98)	2V	70 @ 4600	88 @ 2600	3.15 × 3.13	9.0:1	35–65
	1.6 (98) ④	2V	80 @ 5400	88 @ 3000	3.15 × 3.13	9.0:1	35–65
	1.6 (98)	EFI	84 @ 5200	90 @ 2800	3.15 × 3.13	9.0:1	35–65
	1.6 (98) ⑤	EFI	120 @ 5200	120 @ 3400	3.15 × 3.13	8.0:1	35–65
	2.0 (122)	Diesel	52 @ 4000	82 @ 2400	3.39 × 3.39	22.7:1	55–60
	2.3 (140)	CFI ①	86 @ 4000	124 @ 2800	3.70 × 3.30	9.0:1	55–70
	2.3 (140) ②	CFI	100 @ 4600	125 @ 3200	3.70 × 3.30	9.0:1	55–70
1986	1.9 (114)	2V	86 @ 4800	100 @ 3000	3.23 × 3.46	9.0:1	35–65
	1.9 (114) ③	EFI	108 @ 5200	114 @ 4000	3.23 × 3.46	9.0:1	35–65
	2.0 (122)	Diesel	52 @ 4000	82 @ 2400	3.39 × 3.39	22.7:1	55–60
	2.3 (140)	CFI ①	86 @ 4000	124 @ 2800	3.70 × 3.30	9.0:1	55–70
	2.3 (140)	CFI ②	100 @ 4600	125 @ 3200	3.70 × 3.30	9.0:1	55–70
1987	1.9 (114)	2V	90 @ 4600	106 @ 3400	3.23 × 3.46	9.0:1	35–65
	1.9 (114)	EFI	115 @ 5200	120 @ 4400	3.23 × 3.46	9.0:1	35–65
	2.0 (122)	Diesel	52 @ 4000	82 @ 2400	3.39 × 3.39	22.7:1	55–60
	2.3 (140)	MPI ⑥	90 @ 3800	130 @ 2800	3.78 × 3.30	9.5:1	55–70
	2.3 (140)	MPI ⑦	150 @ 4600	200 @ 3000	3.78 × 3.30	8.0:1	55–70
	2.3 (140)	MPI ⑧	190 @ 4600	240 @ 3400	3.78 × 3.30	8.0:1	55–70
	2.3 (140)	CFI ⑨	88 @ 4000	124 @ 4800	3.68 × 3.30	9.0:1	55–70
1988	1.9 (114)	EFI	90 @ 4600	106 @ 3400	3.23 × 3.46	9.0:1	35–65
	2.3 (140)	MPI ⑥	90 @ 3800	130 @ 2800	3.78 × 3.30	9.5:1	55–70
	2.3 (140)	MPI ⑦	150 @ 4600	200 @ 3000	3.78 × 3.30	8.0:1	55–70
	2.3 (140)	MPI ⑧	190 @ 4600	240 @ 3400	3.78 × 3.30	8.0:1	55–70
	2.3 (140)	MPI ⑩	86 @ 3800	124 @ 3200	3.68 × 3.30	9.0:1	55–70
	2.3 (140)	MPI ⑪	94 @ 4000	126 @ 3200	3.68 × 3.30	9.0:1	55–70
1989	1.9 (114)	CFI	90 @ 4600	106 @ 3400	3.23 × 3.46	9.0:1	35–65
	1.9 (114)	MPI	110 @ 5200	115 @ 4200	3.23 × 3.46	9.0:1	35–65
	2.3 (140)	EFI	88 @ 4000	132 @ 2600	3.78 × 3.30	9.5:1	55–70
	2.3 (140)	MPI ⑩	98 @ 4400	124 @ 2200	3.68 × 3.30	9.0:1	55–70
	2.3 (140)	MPI ⑪	100 @ 4000	130 @ 3200	3.68 × 3.30	9.0:1	55–70

GENERAL ENGINE SPECIFICATIONS (cont.)

Year	Engine L (cid)	Fuel System Type	SAE net Horsepower @ rpm	SAE net Torque ft. lbs. @ rpm	Bore × Stroke (in.)	Comp. Ratio	Oil Press. (psi.) @ 2000 rpm
1990	1.9 (114)	CFI	90 @ 4600	106 @ 3400	3.23 × 3.46	9.0:1	35–65
	1.9 (114)	MPI	110 @ 5400	115 @ 4200	3.23 × 3.46	9.0:1	35–65
	2.3 (140)	EFI	88 @ 4000	132 @ 2600	3.78 × 3.30	9.5:1	55–70
	2.3 (140)	MPI ⑩	98 @ 4400	124 @ 2200	3.68 × 3.30	9.0:1	55–70
	2.3 (140)	MPI ⑪	100 @ 4400	130 @ 3200	3.68 × 3.30	9.0:1	55–70

EFI—Electronic Fuel Injection
CFI—Central Fuel Injection
MPI—Multi-Point Fuel Injection
① 1V carburetor, Canada only
② Sport option
③ Escort GT, Lynx XR3, EXP Sport Coupe
④ HO—High Output
⑤ Turbo Charged
⑥ MPFI—OHC Turbo Charged
⑦ MPFI—OHC Automatic transmission
⑧ MPFI—OHC Manual transmission
⑨ HSC—High Swirl Combustion
⑩ MPFI—High Swirl Combustion
⑪ MPFI—High Swirl Output Engine

TORQUE SPECIFICATIONS

Year	Engine L (cid)	Cyl. Head	Conn. Rod	Main Bearing	Crankshaft Damper	Flywheel	Manifold Intake	Manifold Exhaust
1981	1.3 (79)	①	19–25	67–80	74–90	59–69	12–15 ②	15–20
	1.6 (98)	①	19–25	67–80	74–90	59–69	12–15 ②	15–20
1982	1.6 (98)	①	19–25	67–80	74–90	59–69	12–15 ②	15–20
1983	1.6 (98)	①	19–25	67–80	74–90	59–69	3.7–7.4 ②	15–20
1984	1.6 (98)	①	19–25	67–80	74–90	59–69	3.7–7.4 ②	15–20
	2.0 (122)	①	48–51	61–65	115–123	130–137	12–16	16–19
	2.3 (140)	③	21–26	51–66	140–170	54–64	15–23	④
1985	1.6 (98)	①	19–25	67–80	74–90	59–69	1.5–7.4 ②	15–20
	2.0 (122)	①	48–51	61–65	115–123	130–137	12–16	16–19
	2.3 (140)	③	21–26	51–66	140–170	54–64	15–23	④
1986	1.9 (114)	①	19–25	67–80	74–90	59–69	1.5–7.4 ②	15–20
	2.0 (122)	①	48–51	61–65	115–123	130–137	12–16	16–19
	2.3 (140)	③	21–26	51–66	140–170	54–64	15–23	④
1987	1.9 (114)	①	19–25	67–80	74–90	54–64	1.5–7.4 ②	15–20
	2.0 (122)	①	48–51	61–65	115–123	130–137	12–16	16–19
	2.3 (140)	③	21–26	51–66	140–170	54–64	15–23	④
1988	1.9 (114)	①	19–25	67–80	74–90	54–64	1.5–7.4 ②	15–20
	2.3 (140)	③	21–26	51–66	140–170	54–64	15–23	④
1989	1.9 (114)	①	26–30	67–80	81–96	54–64	1.5–7.4 ②	15–20
	2.3 (140)	③	21–26	51–66	140–170	54–64	15–23	④
1990	1.9 (114)	①	26–30	67–80	81–96	54–64	1.5–7.4 ②	15–20
	2.3 (140)	③	21–26	51–66	140–170	54–64	15–23	④

① See head removal procedure for instructions
② Manifold stud nuts 12–15 ft. lbs.
③ Tighten in two stages: 52–59 ft. lbs., then 70–76 ft. lbs.
④ Tighten in two stages: 5–7 ft. lbs., then 20–30 ft. lbs.

ENGINE AND ENGINE OVERHAUL

VALVE SPECIFICATIONS

Year	Engine L (cid)	Seat Angle (deg.)	Face Angle (deg.)	Spring Test Pressure (lbs. @ in.)	Spring Installed Height (in.)	Stem-to-Guide Clearance (in.) Intake	Stem-to-Guide Clearance (in.) Exhaust	Stem Diameter (in.) Intake	Stem Diameter (in.) Exhaust
1981	1.3 (79)	45	45.5	180 @ 1.09	1.46	0.0008–0.0027	0.0015–0.0032	0.3160	0.3150
	1.6 (98)	45	45.5	180 @ 1.09	1.46	0.0008–0.0027	0.0015–0.0032	0.3160	0.3150
1982	1.6 (98)	45	45.5	180 @ 1.09	1.46	0.0010	0.0021	0.3200	0.3100
1983	1.6 (98)	45	45.5	200 @ 1.09 ①	1.48 ②	0.0008–0.0027	0.0018–0.0037	0.3160	0.3150
1984	1.6 (98)	45	45.5	200 @ 1.09 ①	1.48 ②	0.0008–0.0027	0.0018–0.0037	0.3160	0.3150
	2.0 (122)	45	45	NA	1.776	0.0016–0.0029	0.0018–0.0031	0.3138	0.3138
	2.3 (140)	45	45.5	182 @ 1.10	1.49	0.0018	0.0023	0.3415	0.3411
1985	1.6 (98)	45	45.5	200 @ 1.09 ①	1.48 ②	0.0008–0.0027	0.0018–0.0037	0.3160	0.3150
	2.0 (122)	45	45	NA	1.776	0.0016–0.0029	0.0018–0.0031	0.3138	0.3138
	2.3 (140)	45	45.5	182 @ 1.10	1.49	0.0018	0.0023	0.3415	0.3411
1986	1.9 (114)	45	45.5	200 @ 1.09	1.46	0.0008–0.0027	0.0018–0.0037	0.3167–0.3159	0.3156–0.3149
	2.0 (122)	45	45	NA	1.776	0.0016–0.0029	0.0018–0.0031	0.3138–0.3144	0.3138–0.3142
	2.3 (140)	45	45.5	182 @ 1.10	1.49	0.0018	0.0023	0.3415	0.3411
1987	1.9 (114)	45	45.6	200 @ 1.09 ③	1.46	0.0008–0.0027	0.0018–0.0037	0.3167–0.3159	0.3156–0.3149
	2.0 (122)	45	45	NA	1.776	0.0016–0.0029	0.0018–0.0031	0.3138–0.3144	0.3138–0.3142
	2.3 (140)	45	45.5	185 @ 1.11	1.49	0.0018	0.0023	0.3415–0.3422	0.3411–0.3418
1988	1.9 (114)	45	45.6	200 @ 1.09 ③	1.46	0.0008–0.0027	0.0018–0.0037	0.3167–0.3159	0.3156–0.3149
	2.3 (140)	45	45	185 @ 1.11	1.49	0.0018	0.0023	0.3415–0.3422	0.3411–0.3418
1989	1.9 (114)	45	45	200 @ 1.09 ③	1.46	0.0008–0.0027	0.0018–0.0037	0.3167–0.3159	0.3156–0.3149
	2.3 (140)	45	45	185 @ 1.11	1.49	0.0018	0.0023	0.3415–0.3422	0.3411–0.3418
1990	1.9 (114)	45	45	200 @ 1.09 ③	1.46	0.0008–0.0027	0.0018–0.0037	0.3167–0.3159	0.3156–0.3149
	2.3 (140)	45	45	185 @ 1.11	1.49	0.0018	0.0023	0.3415–0.3422	0.3411–0.3418

① H.O. and E.F.I. Engines: 206 @ 1.09
② H.O. and E.F.I. Engines: 1.450–1.480
③ H.O. and E.F.I. Engines: 216 @ 1.016

ENGINE AND ENGINE OVERHAUL

CRANKSHAFT AND CONNECTING ROD SPECIFICATIONS
(All specifications in inches)

Years	Engine L (cid)	Crankshaft Main Bearing Journal Dia.	Main Bearing Oil Clearance	Shaft End Play	Thrust on No.	Connecting Rod Journal Dia.	Oil Clearance	Side Clearance
1981	1.3 (79)	2.2826–2.2834	0.0008–0.0015	0.0040–0.0080	3	1.8850–1.8860	0.0002–0.0003	0.0040–0.0110
	1.6 (98)	2.2826–2.2834	0.0008–0.0015	0.0040–0.0080	3	1.8850–1.8860	0.0002–0.0003	0.0004–0.0110
1982	1.6 (98)	2.2826–2.2834	0.0008–0.0015	0.0040–0.0080	3	1.8850–1.8860	0.0002–0.0003	0.0040–0.0110
1983	1.6 (98)	2.2826–2.2834	0.0008–0.0015	0.0040–0.0080	3	1.8850–1.8860	0.0002–0.0003	0.0040–0.0110
1984	1.6 (98)	2.2826–2.2834	0.0008–0.0015	0.0040–0.0080	3	1.8850–1.8860	0.0002–0.0003	0.0040–0.0110
	2.0 (122)	2.3598–2.3605	0.0012–0.0020	0.0016–0.0011	3	2.0055–2.0061	0.0010–0.0022	0.0043–0.0103
	2.3 (140)	2.2489–2.2490	0.0008–0.0015	0.0040–0.0080	3	2.1232–2.1240	0.0008–0.0015	0.0035–0.0105
1985	1.6 (98)	2.2826–2.2834	0.0008–0.0015	0.0040–0.0080	3	1.8850–1.8860	0.0002–0.0003	0.0040–0.0110
	2.0 (122)	2.3598–2.3605	0.0012–0.0020	0.0016–0.0111	3	2.0055–2.0061	0.0010–0.0022	0.0043–0.0103
	2.3 (140)	2.2489–2.2490	0.0008–0.0015	0.0040–0.0080	3	2.1232–2.1240	0.0008–0.0015	0.0035–0.0105
1986	1.9 (114)	2.2827–2.2835	0.0008–0.0015	0.0040–0.0080	3	1.8854–1.8862	0.0008–0.0015	0.0040–0.0110
	2.0 (122)	2.3598–2.3605	0.0012–0.0020	0.0016–0.0111	3	2.0055–2.0061	0.0010–0.0022	0.0043–0.0103
	2.3 (140)	2.2489–2.2490	0.0008–0.0015	0.0040–0.0080	3	2.1232–2.1240	0.0008–0.0015	0.0035–0.0105
1987	1.9 (114)	2.2827–2.2835	0.0008–0.0015	0.0040–0.0080	3	1.8854–1.8862	0.0008–0.0015	0.0040–0.0110
	2.0 (122)	2.3598–2.3605	0.0012–0.0020	0.0016–0.0111	3	2.0055–2.0061	0.0010–0.0022	0.0043–0.0103
	2.3 (140)	2.2489–2.2490	0.0008–0.0015	0.0040–0.0080	3	2.1232–2.1240	0.0008–0.0015	0.0035–0.0105
1988	1.9 (114)	2.2827–2.2835	0.0008–0.0015	0.0040–0.0080	3	1.7279–1.7287	0.0008–0.0015	0.0040–0.0110
	2.3 (140)	2.2489–2.2490	0.0008–0.0015	0.0040–0.0080	3	2.1232–2.1240	0.0008–0.0015	0.0035–0.0105
1989	1.9 (114)	2.2827–2.2835	0.0008–0.0015	0.0040–0.0080	3	1.7279–1.7287	0.0008–0.0015	0.0040–0.0110
	2.3 (140)	2.2489–2.2490	0.0008–0.0015	0.0040–0.0080	3	2.1232–2.1240	0.0008–0.0015	0.0035–0.0105
1990	1.9 (114)	2.2827–2.2835	0.0008–0.0015	0.0040–0.0080	3	1.7279–1.7287	0.0008–0.0015	0.0040–0.0110
	2.3 (140)	2.2489–2.2490	0.0008–0.0015	0.0040–0.0080	3	2.1232–2.1240	0.0008–0.0015	0.0035–0.0105

ENGINE AND ENGINE OVERHAUL

PISTON AND RING SPECIFICATIONS
(All specifications in inches)

Year	Engine L (cid)	Ring Gap #1 Compr.	Ring Gap #2 Compr.	Ring Gap Oil Control	Ring Side Clearance #1 Compr.	Ring Side Clearance #2 Compr.	Ring Side Clearance Oil Control	Piston Clearance
1981	1.3 (79)	0.0120–0.0200	0.0120–0.0200	0.0160–0.0550	0.001–0.003	0.002–0.003	Snug	0.0008–0.0016
	1.6 (98)	0.0120–0.0200	0.0120–0.0200	0.0160–0.0550	0.001–0.003	0.002–0.003	Snug	0.0008–0.0016
1982	1.6 (98)	0.0120–0.0200	0.0120–0.0200	0.0160–0.0550	0.001–0.003	0.002–0.003	Snug	0.0012–0.0020
1983	1.6 (98)	0.0120–0.0200	0.0120–0.0200	0.0160–0.0550	0.001–0.003	0.002–0.003	Snug	0.0018–0.0026
1984	1.6 (98)	0.0120–0.0200	0.0120–0.0200	0.0160–0.0550	0.001–0.003	0.002–0.003	Snug	0.0018–0.0026
	2.0 (122)	0.0079–0.0157	0.0079–0.0157	0.0079–0.0157	0.0020–0.0035	0.0016–0.0031	Snug	0.0013–0.0020
	2.3 (140)	0.0080–0.0160	0.0080–0.0160	0.0150–0.0550	0.002–0.004	0.002–0.004	Snug	0.0013–0.0021
1985	1.6 (98)	0.0120–0.0200	0.0120–0.0200	0.0160–0.0550	0.001–0.003	0.002–0.003	Snug	0.0018–0.0026
	2.0 (122)	0.0079–0.0157	0.0079–0.0157	0.0079–0.0157	0.0020–0.0035	0.0016–0.0031	Snug	0.0013–0.0020
	2.3 (140)	0.0080–0.0160	0.0080–0.0160	0.0150–0.0550	0.002–0.004	0.002–0.004	Snug	0.0013–0.0021
1986	1.9 (114)	0.0100–0.0200	0.0100–0.0200	0.0160–0.0550	0.0015–0.0032	0.0015–0.0035	Snug	0.0016–0.0024
	2.0 (122)	0.0079–0.0157	0.0079–0.0157	0.0079–0.0157	0.0020–0.0035	0.0016–0.0031	Snug	0.0013–0.0020
	2.3 (140)	0.0080–0.0160	0.0080–0.0160	0.0150–0.0550	0.002–0.004	0.002–0.004	Snug	0.0012–0.0022
1987	1.9 (114)	0.0100–0.0200	0.0100–0.0200	0.0160–0.0550	0.0015–0.0032	0.0015–0.0035	Snug	0.0016–0.0024
	2.0 (122)	0.0079–0.0157	0.0079–0.0157	0.0079–0.0157	0.0020–0.0035	0.0016–0.0031	Snug	0.0013–0.0020
	2.3 (140)	0.0080–0.0160	0.0080–0.0160	0.0150–0.0550	0.002–0.004	0.002–0.004	Snug	0.0012–0.0022
1988	1.9 (114)	0.0100–0.0200	0.0100–0.0200	0.0160–0.0550	0.0015–0.0032	0.0015–0.0035	Snug	0.0016–0.0024
	2.3 (140)	0.0080–0.0160	0.0080–0.0160	0.0150–0.0550	0.002–0.004	0.002–0.004	Snug	0.0012–0.0022
1989	1.9 (114)	0.0100–0.0200	0.0100–0.0200	0.0160–0.0550	0.0015–0.0032	0.0015–0.0035	Snug	0.0016–0.0024
	2.3 (140)	0.0080–0.0160	0.0080–0.0160	0.0150–0.0550	0.002–0.004	0.002–0.004	Snug	0.0012–0.0022
1990	1.9 (114)	0.0100–0.0200	0.0100–0.0200	0.0160–0.0550	0.0015–0.0032	0.0015–0.0035	Snug	0.0016–0.0024
	2.3 (140)	0.0080–0.0160	0.0080–0.0160	0.0150–0.0550	0.002–0.004	0.002–0.004	Snug	0.0012–0.0022

ENGINE AND ENGINE OVERHAUL

CAMSHAFT SPECIFICATIONS
(All specifications in inches)

Year	Engine L (cid)	Journal Diameter 1	2	3	4	5	Bearing Clearance	Valve Lift Int.	Exh.	End Play
1981	1.3 (79)	1.761–1.762	1.771–1.772	1.781–1.782	1.791–1.792	1.801–1.802	0.0008–0.0028	0.377 ①	0.377 ①	0.0018–0.0060
	1.6 (98)	1.761–1.762	1.771–1.772	1.781–1.782	1.791–1.792	1.801–1.802	0.0008–0.0028	0.377 ①	0.377 ①	0.0018–0.0060
1982	1.6 (98)	1.761–1.762	1.771–1.772	1.781–1.782	1.791–1.792	1.801–1.802	0.0008–0.0028	0.377 ①	0.377 ①	0.0018–0.0060
1983	1.6 (98)	1.761–1.762	1.771–1.772	1.781–1.782	1.791–1.792	1.801–1.802	0.0008–0.0028	0.377 ①	0.377 ①	0.0018–0.0060
1984	1.6 (98)	1.761–1.762	1.771–1.772	1.781–1.782	1.791–1.792	1.801–1.802	0.0008–0.0028	0.377 ①	0.377 ①	0.0018–0.0060
	2.0 (122)	—	—	1.2582–1.2589	—	—	0.0010–0.0026	NA	NA	0.0059–0.0080
	2.3 (140)	NA	NA	NA	NA	NA	0.0010–0.0030	0.392 ②	0.377 ②	0.0090
1985	1.6 (98)	1.761–1.762	1.771–1.772	1.781–1.782	1.791–1.792	1.801–1.802	0.0008–0.0028	0.377 ①	0.377 ①	0.0018–0.0060
	2.0 (122)	—	—	1.2582–1.2589	—	—	0.0010–0.0026	NA	NA	0.0059–0.0080
	2.3 (140)	NA	NA	NA	NA	NA	0.0010–0.0030	0.392 ②	0.377 ②	0.0090
1986	1.9 (114)	—	—	1.8007–1.8017	—	—	0.0013–0.0033	0.468 ①	0.468 ①	0.0018–0.0060
	2.0 (122)	—	—	1.2582–1.2589	—	—	0.0010–0.0026	NA	NA	0.0059–0.0080
	2.3 (140)	NA	NA	NA	NA	NA	0.0010–0.0030	0.392 ②	0.377 ②	0.0090
1987	1.9 (114)	—	—	1.8007–1.8017	—	—	0.0013–0.0033	0.468 ①	0.468 ①	0.0060–0.0018
	2.0 (122)	—	—	1.2582–1.2589	—	—	0.0010–0.0026	NA	NA	0.0059–0.0080
	2.3 (140) ③	—	—	1.7713–1.7720	—	—	0.0010–0.0030	0.392 ②	0.377 ②	0.0090
	2.3 (140) ④	—	—	2.0006–2.0008	—	—	0.0010–0.0030	0.392 ②	0.377 ②	0.0090
1988	1.9 (114)	—	—	1.8007–1.8017	—	—	0.0013–0.0033	0.468 ①	0.468 ①	0.0060–0.0018
	2.3 (140) ③	—	—	1.7713–1.7720	—	—	0.0010–0.0030	0.392 ②	0.377 ②	0.0090
	2.3 (140) ④	—	—	2.0006–2.0008	—	—	0.0010–0.0030	0.392 ②	0.377 ②	0.0090
1989	1.9 (114)	—	—	1.8007–1.8017	—	—	0.0013–0.0033	0.468 ①	0.468 ①	0.0060–0.0018
	2.3 (140) ③	—	—	1.7713–1.7720	—	—	0.0010–0.0030	0.392 ②	0.377 ②	0.0090
	2.3 (140) ④	NA	NA	NA	NA	NA	0.0010–0.0030	0.392 ②	0.377 ②	0.0090

ENGINE AND ENGINE OVERHAUL 107

CAMSHAFT SPECIFICATIONS (cont.)
(All measurements in inches)

Year	Engine Displacement (Liters)	Journal Diameter 1	2	3	4	5	Lobe Lift Intake	Exhaust		Camshaft End Play
1990	1.9 (114)	—	—	1.8007–1.8017	—	—	0.0013–0.0033	0.468 ①	0.468 ①	0.0060–0.0018
	2.3 (140) ③	—	—	1.7713–1.7720	—	—	0.0010–0.0030	0.392 ②	0.377 ②	0.0090
	2.3 (140) ④	NA	NA	NA	NA	NA	0.0010–0.0030	0.392 ②	0.377 ②	0.0090

NA—Not available
① HO and EFI: 0.396 in.
② HO: 0.413 in.
③ 2.3L Overhead cam engine
④ 2.3L High Swirl Combustion engine

NOTE: *The brush and plate has threaded holes in the protruding ear which must be oriented properly so that the starter to vacuum pump support bracket can be installed.*

9. Install the return spring on the solenoid plunger and install the solenoid. Attach the 2 solenoid attaching screws and tighten them to 5–7 ft. lbs. (7–9 Nm). Apply sealing compound to the junction of the solenoid case flange, gear and drive end housing.

10. Attach the motor field terminal **M** of the solenoid and tighten the nut to 20–30 inch lbs. (2.5–3.4 Nm). Check the starter no-load current draw.

ENGINE MECHANICAL

Engine Overhaul

Most engine overhaul procedures are fairly standard. In addition to specific parts replacement procedures and complete specifications for each individual engine, this chapter is also a guide to acceptable rebuilding procedures. Examples of standard rebuilding practice are shown and should be used along with specific details concerning your particular engine.

Competent and accurate machine shop services will insure maximum performance, reliability and engine life. In most instances, it is more profitable for the do-it-yourself mechanic to remove, clean and inspect the component, buy the necessary parts and deliver these to a shop for actual machine work.

On the other hand, much of the rebuilding work (crankshaft, block, bearings, piston rods, and other components) is well within the scope of the do-it-yourself mechanic.

TOOLS

The tools required for an engine overhaul or parts replacement will depend on the depth of your involvement. With few exceptions, they will be the tools found in any mechanic's tool kit (see Chapter 1). More in-depth work will require some or all of the following:
- a dial indicator (reading in thousandths) mounted on a universal base
- micrometers and telescope gauges
- jaw and screw-type pullers
- scraper
- valve spring compressor
- ring groove cleaner
- piston ring expander and compressor
- ridge reamer
- cylinder hone or glaze breaker
- Plastigage®
- engine stand

The use of most of these tools is illustrated in this chapter. Many can be rented for a one-time use from a local parts jobber or tool supply house specializing in automotive work. Occasionally, the use of special tools is called for. See the information on Special Tools and Safety Notice in the front of this book before substituting another tool.

INSPECTION TECHNIQUES

Procedures and specifications are given in this chapter for inspecting, cleaning and assessing the wear limits of most major components. Other procedures such as Magnaflux® and Zyglo® can be used to locate material flaws and stress cracks. Magnaflux® is a magnetic process applicable only to ferrous materials. The Zyglo® process coats the material with a fluorescent dye penetrate and can be used on any material Check for suspected surface cracks can be more readily made using spot check dye. The dye is

ENGINE AND ENGINE OVERHAUL

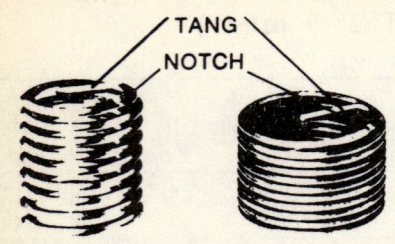

Standard thread repair insert (left) and spark plug thread insert (right)

sprayed onto the suspected area, wiped off and the area sprayed with a developer. Cracks will show up brightly.

OVERHAUL NOTES

Aluminum has become extremely popular for use in engines, due to its low weight. Observe the following precautions when handling aluminum parts:
- Never hot tank aluminum parts; the caustic hot-tank solution will eat the aluminum.
- Remove all aluminum parts (identification tag, etc.) from engine parts prior to the tanking.
- Always coat threads lightly with engine oil or anti-seize compounds before installation, to prevent seizure.
- Never over torque bolts or spark plugs, especially in aluminum threads.

When assembling the engine, any parts that will be in frictional contact must be prelubed to provide lubrication at initial start-up. Any product specifically formulated for this purpose can be used, but engine oil is not recommended as a prelube.

When semi-permanent (locked, but removable) installation of bolts or nuts is desired, threads should be cleaned and coated with Loctite® or other similar, commercial non-hardening sealant.

REPAIRING DAMAGED THREADS

Several methods of repairing damaged threads are available. Heli-Coil® (shown here), Keenserts® and Microdot® are among the most widely used. All involve basically the same principle (drilling out stripped threads, tapping the hole and installing a prewound insert), making welding, plugging and oversize fasteners unnecessary.

Two types of thread repair inserts are usually supplied: a standard type for most Inch Coarse, Inch Fine, Metric Course and Metric Fine thread sizes and a spark lug type to fit most spark plug port sizes. Consult the individual manufacturer's catalog to determine exact applications. Typical thread repair kits will contain a selection of prewound threaded inserts, a tap (corresponding to the outside diameter

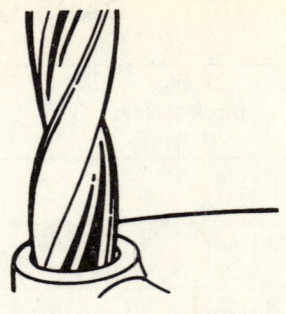

Drill out the damaged threads with specified drill. Drill completely through the hole or to the bottom of a blind hold

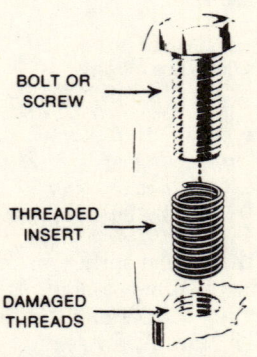

Damaged bolt holes can be repaired with thread repair inserts

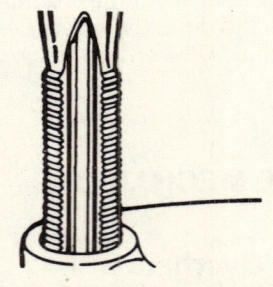

With the tap supplied, tap the hole to receive the thread insert. Keep the tap well oiled and back it out frequently to avoid clogging the threads

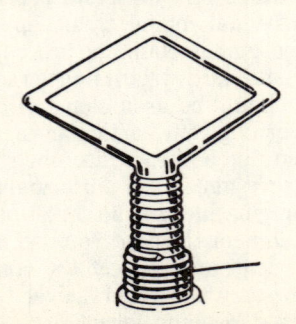

Screw the threaded insert onto the installation tool until the tang engages the slot. Screw the insert into the tapped hole until it is $1/4$–$1/2$ turn below the top surface. After installation break off the tang with a hammer and punch

threads of the insert) and an installation tool. Spark plug inserts usually differ because they require a tap equipped with pilot threads and a combined reamer/tap section. Most manufacturers also supply blister packed thread repair inserts separately in addition to a master kit containing a variety of taps and inserts plus installation tools.

Before effecting a repair to a threaded hole, remove any snapped, broken or damaged bolts or studs. Penetrating oil can be used to free frozen threads. The offending item can be removed with locking pliers or with a screw or stud extractor. After the hole is clear, the thread can be repaired.

CHECKING ENGINE COMPRESSION

Gasoline Engines

A noticeable lack of engine power, excessive oil consumption and/or poor fuel mileage measured over an extended period are all indicators of internal engine war. Worn piston rings, scored or worn cylinder bores, blown head gaskets, sticking or burnt valves and worn valve seats are all possible culprits here. A check of each cylinder's compression will help you locate the problems.

As mentioned in the Tools and Equipment section of Chapter 1, a screw-in type compression gauge is more accurate that the type you simply hold against the spark plug hole, although it takes slightly longer to use. It's worth it to obtain a more accurate reading. Follow the procedures below.

1. Warm up the engine to normal operating temperature.
2. Remove all spark plugs.
3. Disconnect the high tension lead from the ignition coil.
4. Disconnect all fuel injector electrical connections.
5. Screw the compression gauge into the No. 1 spark plug hole until the fitting is snug.

NOTE: *Be careful not to crossthread the plug hole. On aluminum cylinder heads use extra care, as the threads in these heads are easily ruined.*

6. Have an assistant depress the accelerator pedal fully. Then, while you read the compression gauge, ask the assistant to crank the engine two or three times in short bursts using the ignition switch.
7. Read the compression gauge at the end of each series of cranks, and record the highest of these readings. Repeat this procedure for each of the engine's cylinders. Maximum compression should be 175–185 psi. A cylinder's compression pressure is usually acceptable if it is not less than 80% of maximum. The difference between each cylinder should be no more than 12–14 psi.

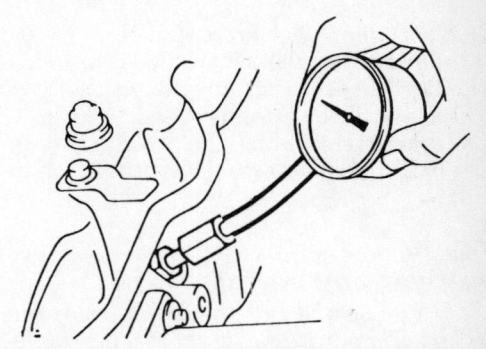

The screw-in type compression gauge is more accurate

8. If a cylinder is unusually low, pour a tablespoon of clean engine oil into the cylinder through the spark plug hole and repeat the compression test. If the compression comes up after adding the oil, it appears that the cylinder's piston rings or bore are damaged or worn. If the pressure remains low, the valves may not be seating properly (a valve job is needed), or the head gasket may be blown near that cylinder. If compression in any two adjacent cylinders is low, and if the addition of oil doesn't help the compression, there is leakage past the head gasket. Oil and coolant water in the combustion chamber can result from this problem. There may be evidence of water droplets on the engine dipstick when a head gasket has blown.

Diesel Engines

Checking cylinder compression on diesel engines is basically the same procedure as on gasoline engines except for the following:

1. A special compression gauge adaptor suitable for diesel engines (because these engines have much greater compression pressures) must be used.
2. Remove the injector tubes and remove the injectors from each cylinder.

NOTE: *Don't forget to remove the washer underneath each injector. Otherwise, it may get*

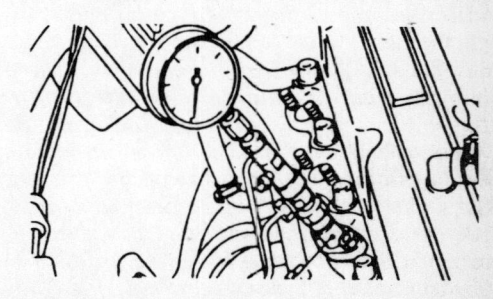

Diesel engines require a special compression gauge adaptor

ENGINE AND ENGINE OVERHAUL

lost when the engine is cranked.

3. When fitting the compression gauge adaptor to the cylinder head, make sure the bleeder of the gauge (if equipped) is closed.

4. When reinstalling the injector assemblies, install new washers underneath each injector.

Engine

REMOVAL AND INSTALLATION

NOTE: *A special engine support bar is necessary. The bar is used to support the engine/transaxle while disconnecting the various engine mounts Ford Part No. T81P-6000-A. A suitable support can be made using angle iron, a heavy J-hook and some strong chain.*

When performing engine removal and installation procedures on the 1.9L engine, check and record the distance between the crankshaft damper and the frame rail, and the distance between the transaxle and frame rail. Check the manual transaxle at the transaxle case. Check the automatic transaxle at the oil pump housing. This check should be done before the engine is removed and after the engine is installed. If necessary, loosen the motor mount-to-engine bolts to shift the engine to obtain the proper engine/transaxle to frame rail clearance. Proper clearances are necessary to ensure the half shaft alignment. The crankshaft damper-to-frame rail clearance should be 0.62 in. (16.0mm) + 0.15 in. (4.0mm). The transaxle to frame rail clearance should be 0.98 in. (25.0mm) + 0.19 in.(5.0mm).

1.3L, 1.6L, 1.9L Engine — Engine w/Transaxle

NOTE: *The following procedure is for engine and transaxle removal and installation as an assembly. Procedure for removing the engine only is in following section.*

1. Mark the location of the hinges and remove the hood.

2. Remove the air cleaner, hot air tube and alternator fresh air intake tube.

3. Disconnect the battery cables, remove the battery and tray.

4. Drain the radiator, engine oil and transaxle fluid.

CAUTION: *When draining the coolant, keep in mind that cats and dogs are attracted by the ethylene glycol antifreeze, and are quite likely to drink any that is left in an uncovered container or in puddles on the ground. This will prove fatal in sufficient quantity. Always drain the coolant into a sealable container. Coolant should be reused unless it is contaminated or several years old.*

WARNING: *The EPA warns that prolonged contact with used engine oil may cause a number of skin disorders, including cancer! You should make every effort to minimize your exposure to used engine oil. Protective gloves should be worn when changing the oil. Wash your hands and any other exposed skin areas as soon as possible after exposure to used engine oil. Soap and water, or waterless hand cleaner should be used.*

5. Remove the coil the mounting bracket and the coil wire harness.

6. If the vehicle is equipped with air conditioning, remove the compressor from the engine with the refrigerant hoses still attached. Position compressor to the side.

CAUTION: *Never loosen air conditioning refrigerant lines, as the escaping refrigerant is a deadly poison and can freeze exposed skin instantly.*

7. Disconnect the upper and lower radiator hose.

8. Disconnect the heater hoses from the engine.

9. If equipped with an automatic transaxle disconnect and plug the cooler lines at the rubber coupler.

10. Disconnect the electric fan.

11. Remove the fan motor, shroud assembly and the radiator.

12. If equipped with power steering, remove the filler tube.

13. Disconnect the following electrical connections:
   a. Main wiring harness
   b. Neutral safety switch (automatic only)
   c. Choke cap wire
   d. Starter cable
   e. Alternator wiring

14. Disconnect the fuel supply and return lines. Relieve fuel pressure on injected models before disconnecting fuel lines.

15. Disconnect the (3) altitude compensator lines if so equipped. Mark each line as you remove it. for easy installation.

16. Disconnect the vacuum lines from the "tree" on the firewall.

17. Disconnect the power brake booster vacuum line.

18. Disconnect the cruise control is so equipped.

19. Disconnect all carburetor linkage.

20. Disconnect all engine vacuum lines. Mark each line as you remove it, for easy installation.

21. Disconnect the clutch cable if so equipped.

22. Remove the Thermactor pump bracket bolt.

23. Install engine support T81P-6000-A or equivalent. Using a short piece of chain, attach it to the engine using the 10 mm bolt holes at the transaxle, the exhaust manifold side of the

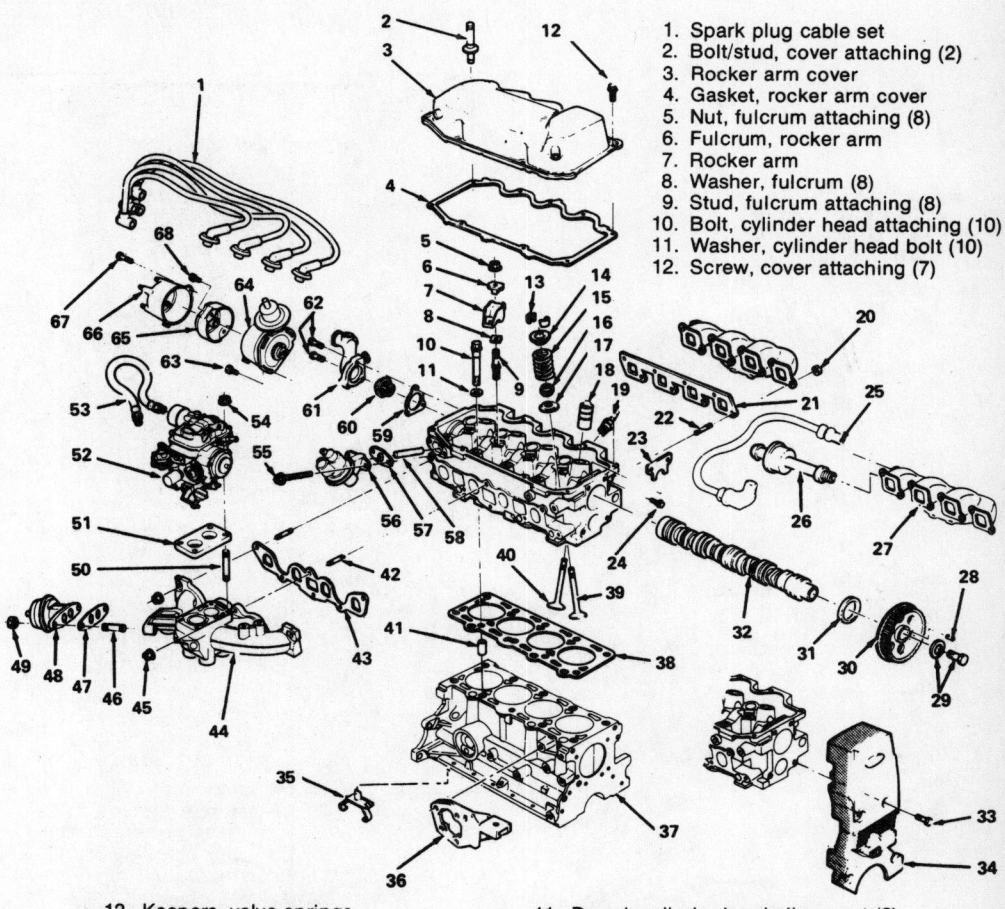

ENGINE AND ENGINE OVERHAUL

1. Spark plug cable set
2. Bolt/stud, cover attaching (2)
3. Rocker arm cover
4. Gasket, rocker arm cover
5. Nut, fulcrum attaching (8)
6. Fulcrum, rocker arm
7. Rocker arm
8. Washer, fulcrum (8)
9. Stud, fulcrum attaching (8)
10. Bolt, cylinder head attaching (10)
11. Washer, cylinder head bolt (10)
12. Screw, cover attaching (7)
13. Keepers, valve springs
14. Retainer, valve spring
15. Valve spring
16. Seal, valve stem
17. Washer, valve spring
18. Valve lifter
19. Spark plug
20. Nut, manifold attaching (8)
21. Gasket, exhaust manifold
22. Stud, manifold attaching (8)
23. Plate, camshaft thrust
24. Bolt, thrust plate attaching (2)
25. EGR tube
26. Check valve, air injection
27. Exhaust manifold
28. Shaft key, cam sprocket
29. Bolt/washer sprocket attaching (1)
30. Camshaft sprocket
31. Seal, camshaft
32. Camshaft
33. Bolts (2) & nuts (2), cover attaching (2)
34. Timing belt cover
35. Crankcase ventilation baffle
36. Engine mount
37. Cylinder block
38. Gasket, cylinder head
39. Exhaust valve
40. Intake valve
41. Dowel, cylinder head alignment (2)
42. Stud, manifold attaching (6)
43. Gasket, intake manifold
44. Intake manifold
45. Nut, manifold attaching (6)
46. Stud, valve attaching (2)
47. Gasket, EGR valve
48. EGR valve
49. Nut, valve attaching (2)
50. Stud, carburetor attaching (4)
51. Gasket, carburetor mounting
52. Carburetor
53. Fuel line
54. Nut, carburetor attaching (4)
55. Bolt, pump attaching (2)
56. Fuel pump
57. Gasket, fuel pump
58. Push rod, fuel pump
59. Gasket, housing
60. Thermostat
61. Thermostat housing
62. Bolt, housing attaching (2)
63. Bolt, distributor attaching (3)
64. Distributor
65. Rotor
66. Distributor cap
67. Screwn cap attaching (2).
68. Screw, rotor attaching (2)

Exploded view of upper part of the 1.6L, 1.9L engines

112　ENGINE AND ENGINE OVERHAUL

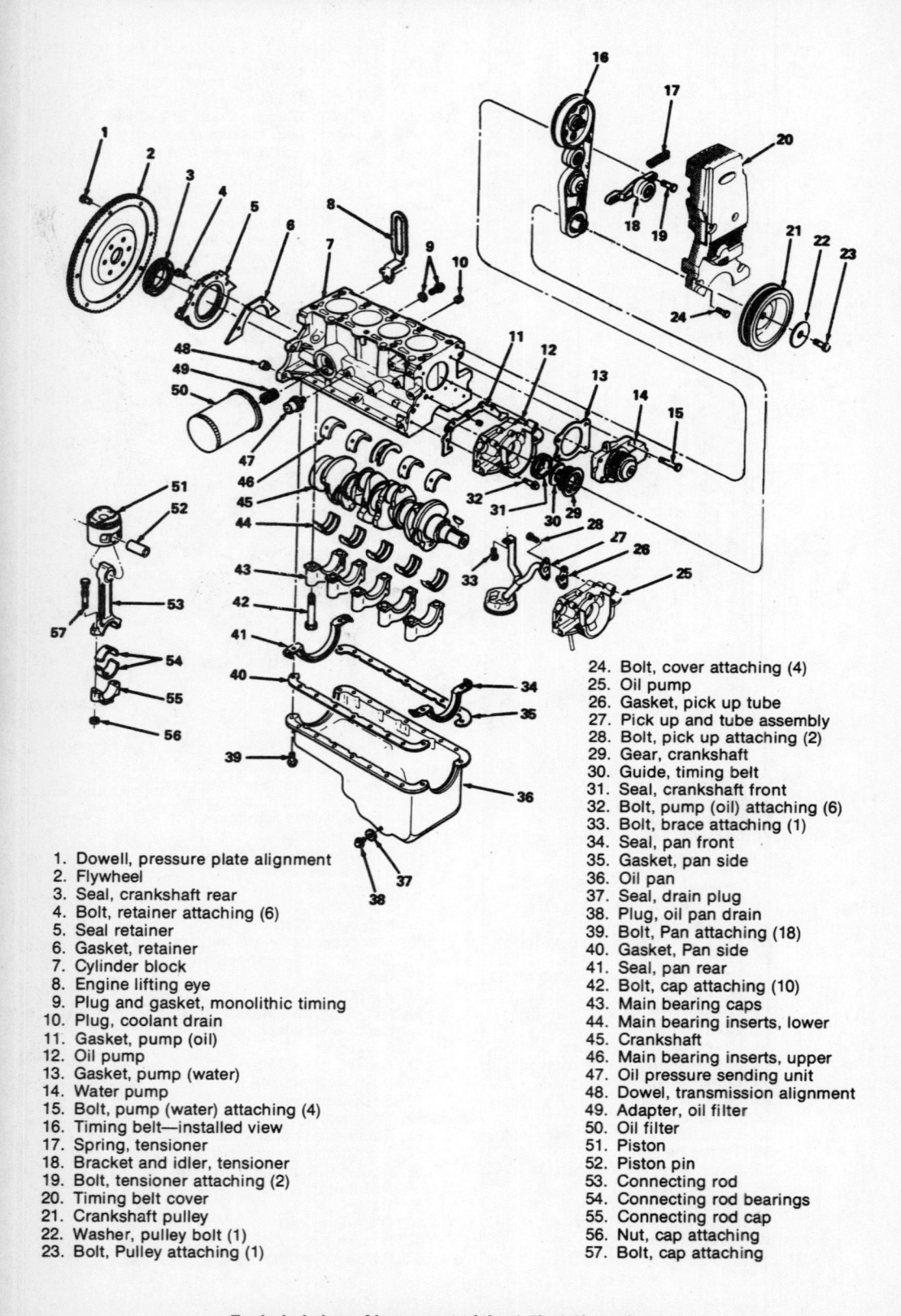

1. Dowell, pressure plate alignment
2. Flywheel
3. Seal, crankshaft rear
4. Bolt, retainer attaching (6)
5. Seal retainer
6. Gasket, retainer
7. Cylinder block
8. Engine lifting eye
9. Plug and gasket, monolithic timing
10. Plug, coolant drain
11. Gasket, pump (oil)
12. Oil pump
13. Gasket, pump (water)
14. Water pump
15. Bolt, pump (water) attaching (4)
16. Timing belt—installed view
17. Spring, tensioner
18. Bracket and idler, tensioner
19. Bolt, tensioner attaching (2)
20. Timing belt cover
21. Crankshaft pulley
22. Washer, pulley bolt (1)
23. Bolt, Pulley attaching (1)
24. Bolt, cover attaching (4)
25. Oil pump
26. Gasket, pick up tube
27. Pick up and tube assembly
28. Bolt, pick up attaching (2)
29. Gear, crankshaft
30. Guide, timing belt
31. Seal, crankshaft front
32. Bolt, pump (oil) attaching (6)
33. Bolt, brace attaching (1)
34. Seal, pan front
35. Gasket, pan side
36. Oil pan
37. Seal, drain plug
38. Plug, oil pan drain
39. Bolt, Pan attaching (18)
40. Gasket, Pan side
41. Seal, pan rear
42. Bolt, cap attaching (10)
43. Main bearing caps
44. Main bearing inserts, lower
45. Crankshaft
46. Main bearing inserts, upper
47. Oil pressure sending unit
48. Dowel, transmission alignment
49. Adapter, oil filter
50. Oil filter
51. Piston
52. Piston pin
53. Connecting rod
54. Connecting rod bearings
55. Connecting rod cap
56. Nut, cap attaching
57. Bolt, cap attaching

Exploded view of lower part of the 1.6L, 1.9L engines

ENGINE AND ENGINE OVERHAUL

head, and the Thermactor bracket hole. Tighten the J-bolt. Place a piece of tape around the J-bolt threads where the bolt passes through the bottom of the support bar. This will act as a reference later.

24. Jack up the vehicle and support it with jackstands.
25. Remove the splash shields.
26. If equipped with a manual transaxle, remove the roll restrictor at the engine and body.
27. Remove the stabilizer bar.
28. Remove the lower control arm through-bolts at the body brackets.
29. Disconnect the left tie rod at the steering knuckle.
30. Disconnect the secondary air tube (catalyst) at the check valve.
31. Disconnect the exhaust system at the exhaust manifold and tail pipe.
32. Remove the right halfshaft from the transaxle. Some fluid will leak out when the shaft is removed.
33. Remove the left side halfshaft.
34. Install shipping plugs T81P–1177–B or equivalent in the differential seals.
35. Disconnect the speedometer cable.
36. If equipped with an automatic transaxle, disconnect the shift selector cable. On manual transaxles, disconnect the shift control rod.

NOTE: *Mark the position of the shift control before disconnecting it.*

37. If equipped with power steering, disconnect the pump return line at the pump, and the pressure line at the intermediate fitting.
38. Remove the left front motor mount attaching bracket and remove the mount with its through-bolt. Remove the left rear motor mount stud nut. Carefully reach into the engine compartment and loosen the engine support bar J-bolt until the left rear motor mount stud clears the mounting bracket. Remove the left rear mount to transaxle attaching bracket.
39. Lower the vehicle, then tighten the support bar J-bolt until the piece of tape installed earlier contacts the bottom of the support bar. Attach a lifting sling to the engine, disconnect the right engine mount and lift the engine from the vehicle.

To Install:
40. Attach a lowering sling to the engine, Reconnect the right engine mount and lower the engine into the vehicle.
41. Install the left front motor mount attaching bracket and install the mount with its through-bolt. Install the left rear motor mount stud nut. Reach into the engine compartment and tighten the engine support bar J-bolt until the left rear motor mount stud clears the mount-

ing bracket. Install the left rear mount to transaxle attaching bracket.
42. If equipped with power steering, reconnect the pump return line at the pump, and the pressure line at the intermediate fitting.
43. If equipped with an automatic transaxle, reconnect the shift selector cable. On manual transaxles, reconnect the shift control rod.
44. Reconnect the speedometer cable.
45. Remove the shipping plugs T81P–1177–B or equivalent in the differential seals.
46. Install the left side halfshaft.
47. Install the right halfshaft to the transaxle.
48. Reconnect the exhaust system at the exhaust manifold and tail pipe.
49. Reconnect the secondary air tube (catalyst) at the check valve.
50. Reconnect the left tie rod at the steering knuckle.
51. Install the lower control arm through-bolts at the body brackets.
52. Install the stabilizer bar.
53. If equipped with a manual transaxle, install the roll restrictor at the engine and body.
54. Install the splash shields.
55. Jack up the vehicle and support it with jackstands.
56. Remove the engine support T81P–6000–A or equivalent.
57. Install the Thermactor pump bracket bolt.
58. Reconnect the clutch cable if so equipped.
59. Reconnect all engine vacuum lines. Mark each line as you Install it, for easy installation.
60. Reconnect all carburetor linkage.
61. Reconnect the cruise control is so equipped.
62. Reconnect the power brake booster vacuum line.
63. Reconnect the vacuum lines to the "tree" on the firewall.
64. Reconnect the (3) altitude compensator lines if so equipped. Mark each line as you Install it. for easy installation.
65. Reconnect the fuel supply and return lines. Relieve fuel pressure on injected models before reconnecting fuel lines.
66. Reconnect the following electrical connections:
    a. Main wiring harness
    b. Neutral safety switch (automatic only)
    c. Choke cap wire
    d. Starter cable
    e. Alternator wiring
67. If equipped with power steering, install the filler tube.
68. Install the fan motor, shroud assembly and the radiator.

69. Reconnect the electric fan.
70. If equipped with an automatic transaxle reconnect and plug the cooler lines at the rubber coupler.
71. Reconnect the heater hoses to the engine.
72. Reconnect the upper and lower radiator hose.
73. If the vehicle is equipped with air conditioning, install the compressor to the engine.
74. Install the coil the mounting bracket and the coil wire harness.
75. Refill the radiator, engine oil and transaxle fluid.
76. Reconnect the battery cables, install the battery and tray.
77. Install the air cleaner, hot air tube and alternator fresh air intake tube.
78. Install the hood.

1.3L, 1.6L and 1.9L Engine — Engine Alone

NOTE: *The following procedure is for engine only removal and installation.*

1. Mark the position of the hinges on the hood underside and remove the hood.
2. Remove the air cleaner assembly. Remove the air feed duct and the heat tube. Remove the air duct to the alternator.
3. Disconnect the battery cables from the battery. Remove the battery. If equipped with air conditioning, remove compressor with line still connected and position out of the way.

CAUTION: *Never loosen refrigerant lines, as the escaping refrigerant is a deadly poison and can freeze exposed skin instantly.*

4. Drain the cooling system. Remove the drive belts from the alternator and Thermactor pump. Disconnect the Thermactor air supply hose. Disconnect the wiring harness at the alternator. Remove alternator and Thermactor.

CAUTION: *When draining the coolant, keep in mind that cats and dogs are attracted by the ethylene glycol antifreeze, and are quite likely to drink any that is left in an uncovered container or in puddles on the ground. This will prove fatal in sufficient quantity. Always drain the coolant into a sealable container. Coolant should be reused unless it is contaminated or several years old.*

5. Disconnect and remove the upper and lower radiator hoses. If equipped with an automatic transaxle, disconnect and plug the fluid cooler lines at the radiator.
6. Disconnect the heater hoses from the engine. Unplug the electric cooling fan wiring harness. Remove the fan and radiator shroud as an assembly.
7. Remove the radiator. Label and disconnect all vacuum lines, including power brake booster, from the engine. Label and disconnect all linkage, including kickdown linkage if automatic, and wiring harness connectors from the engine.
8. If equipped with fuel injection, discharge the system pressure. Remove supply and return fuel lines to the fuel pump. Plug the line from the gas tank.
9. Raise and safely support the car on jackstands. Remove the clamp from the heater supply and return tubes. remove the tubes.
10. Disconnect the battery cable from the starter motor. Remove the brace or bracket from the back of the starter and remove the starter.
11. Disconnect the exhaust system from the exhaust manifold. Drain the engine oil.

CAUTION: *The EPA warns that prolonged contact with used engine oil may cause a number of skin disorders, including cancer! You should make every effort to minimize your exposure to used engine oil. Protective gloves should be worn when changing the oil. Wash your hands and any other exposed skin areas as soon as possible after exposure to used engine oil. Soap and water, or waterless hand cleaner should be used.*

12. Remove the brace in front of the bell housing (flywheel or converter) inspection cover. Remove the inspection cover.
13. Remove the crankshaft pulley. If equipped with a manual transaxle, remove the timing belt cover lower attaching bolts.
14. If equipped with an automatic transaxle, remove the torque converter to flywheel mounting nuts.
15. Remove the lower engine to transaxle attaching bolts.
16. Loosen the hose clamps on the bypass hose and remove the hose from the intake manifold.
17. Remove the bolt and nut attaching the right front mount insulator to the engine bracket.
18. Lower the car from the jackstands.
19. Attach an engine lifting sling to the engine. Connect a chain hoist to the lifting sling and remove all slack. Remove the through bolt from the right front engine mount and remove the insulator.
20. If the car is equipped with a manual transaxle, remove the timing belt cover upper mounting bolts and remove the cover.
21. Remove the right front insulator attaching bracket from the engine.
22. Position a floor jack under the transaxle. Raise the jack just enough to take the weight of the transaxle.
23. Remove the upper bolts connecting the engine and transaxle.
24. Slowly raise the engine and separate

ENGINE AND ENGINE OVERHAUL

from the transaxle. Be sure the torque converter stays on the transxaxle. Remove the engine from the car. On models equipped with manual transaxles, the engine must be separated from the input shaft of the transaxle before raising.

To install:

25. Slowly lower the engine and connect it to the transaxle.
26. Install the upper bolts connecting the engine and transaxle.
27. Lower the jack under the transaxle.
28. Install the right front insulator attaching bracket to the engine.
29. If the car is equipped with a manual transaxle, install the timing belt cover upper mounting bolts and install the cover.
30. Remove the engine sling from the engine. Install the through bolt to the right front engine mount and install the insulator.
31. Raise the car and support on jackstands.
32. Install the bolt and nut attaching the right front mount insulator to the engine bracket.
33. Install the bypass hose to the intake manifold and tighten the clamps.
34. Install the lower engine to transaxle attaching bolts.
35. If equipped with an automatic transaxle, install the torque converter to the flywheel.
36. Install the crankshaft pulley. If equipped with a manual transaxle, install the timing belt cover lower attaching bolts.
37. Install the brace in front of the bell housing (flywheel or converter) inspection cover. Install the inspection cover.
38. Reconnect the exhaust system to the exhaust manifold. Refill the engine oil.
39. Reconnect the battery cable to the starter motor. Install the brace or bracket to the back of the starter and install the starter.
40. Lower the car from the jackstands. Install the clamp to the heater supply and return tubes.
41. If equipped with fuel injection, install the supply and return fuel lines to the fuel pump.
42. Install the radiator. Reconnect all vacuum lines, including power brake booster, to the engine. Reconnect all linkage, including kickdown linkage if automatic, and wiring harness connectors to the engine.
43. Reconnect the heater hoses to the engine. Unplug the electric cooling fan wiring harness. Install the fan and radiator shroud as an assembly.
44. Reconnect the upper and lower radiator hoses. If equipped with an automatic transaxle, reconnect the fluid cooler lines at the radiator.
45. Refill the cooling system. Install alternator and Thermactor. Install the drive belts to the alternator and Thermactor pump. Reconnect the Thermactor air supply hose. Reconnect the wiring harness at the alternator.
46. Install the battery. Reconnect the battery cables to the battery. If equipped with air conditioning, install the compressor.
47. Install the air cleaner assembly. Install the air feed duct and the heat tube. Install the air duct to the alternator.
48. Install the hood.

2.0 Diesel Engine

NOTE: *Suitable jackstands or hoisting equipment are necessary to remove the engine and transaxle assembly. The assembly is removed from underneath the vehicle.*

CAUTION: *The air conditioning system contains refrigerant (R-12) under high pressure. Use extreme care when discharging the system. If the tools and know-how are not on hand, have the system discharged prior to the start of engine removal.*

These procedures cover the removal and installation of the 2.0L Diesel engine and transaxle as an assembly.

1. Mark the position of the hood hinges and remove the hood.
2. Remove the negative ground cable from the battery that is located in luggage compartment.
3. Remove the air cleaner assembly.
4. Position a drain pan under the lower radiator hose. Remove the hose and drain the engine coolant.

CAUTION: *When draining the coolant, keep in mind that cats and dogs are attracted by the ethylene glycol antifreeze, and are quite likely to drink any that is left in an uncovered container or in puddles on the ground. This will prove fatal in sufficient quantity. Always drain the coolant into a sealable container. Coolant should be reused unless it is contaminated or several years old.*

5. Remove the upper radiator hose from the engine.
6. Disconnect the cooling fan at the electrical connector.
7. Remove the radiator shroud and cooling fan as an assembly. Remove the radiator.
8. Remove the starter cable from the starter.
9. Discharge air conditioning system (see opening CAUTION) if so equipped. Remove the pressure and suction lines from the air conditioning compressor.
10. Identify and disconnect all vacuum lines as necessary.
11. Disconnect the engine harness connec-

ENGINE AND ENGINE OVERHAUL

tors (two) at the dash panel. Disconnect the glow plug relay connectors at the dash panel.

NOTE: *Connectors are located under the plastic shield on the dash panel. Remove and save plastic retainer pins. Disconnect the alternator wiring connector on the right fender apron.*

12. Disconnect the clutch cable from the shift lever on transaxle.
13. Disconnect the injection pump throttle linkage.
14. Disconnect the fuel supply and return hoses on the engine.
15. Disconnect the power steering pressure and return lines at the power steering pump, if so equipped. Remove the power steering lines bracket at the cylinder head.
16. Install Engine Support Tool D79P–8000–A or equivalent to existing engine lifting eye.
17. Raise vehicle and safely support on jackstands.
18. Remove the bolt attaching the exhaust pipe bracket to the oil pan.
19. Remove the two exhaust pipes to exhaust manifold attaching nuts.
20. Pull the exhaust system out of rubber insulating grommets and set aside.
21. Remove the speedometer cable from the transaxle.
22. Position an drain pan under the heater hoses. Remove one heater hose form the water pump inlet tube. Remove the other heater hose from the oil cooler.
23. Remove the bolts attaching the control arms to the body. Remove the stabilizer bar bracket retaining bolts and remove the brackets.
24. Halfshaft assemblies must be removed from the transaxle at this time.
25. On MT models, remove the shift stabilizer bar-to-transaxle attaching bolts. Remove the shift mechanism to shift shaft attaching nut and bolt at the transaxle.
26. Remove the LH rear insulator mount bracket from body bracket by removing the two nuts.
27. Remove the LH front insulator to transaxle mounting bolts.
28. Lower vehicle (see CAUTION below). Install lifting equipment to the two existing lifting eyes on engine.

CAUTION: *Do not allow front wheels to touch floor!*

29. Remove Engine Support Tool D79L–8000–A or equivalent.
30. Remove RH insulator intermediate bracket to engine bracket bolts, intermediate bracket to insulator attaching nuts and the nut on the bottom of the double ended stud attaching the intermediate bracket to engine bracket.
31. Carefully lower the engine and the transaxle assembly to the floor.
32. Raise the vehicle and safely support.
33. Position the engine and transaxle assembly directly below the engine compartment.
34. Slowly lower the vehicle over the engine and transaxle assembly.

CAUTION: *Do not allow the front wheels to touch the floor.*

35. Install the lifting equipment to both existing engine lifting eyes on engine.
36. Raise the engine and transaxle assembly up through engine compartment and position accordingly.
37. Install RH insulator intermediate attaching nuts and intermediate bracket to engine bracket bolts. Install nut on bottom of double ended stud attaching intermediate bracket to engine bracket. Tighten to 75–100 ft. lbs.
38. Install Engine Support Tool D79L–8000–A or equivalent to the engine lifting eye.
39. Remove the lifting equipment.
40. Raise vehicle.
41. Position a suitable floor or transaxle jack under engine. Raise the engine and transaxle assembly into mounted position.
42. Install insulator to bracket nut and tighten to 75–100 ft. lbs.
43. Tighten the LH rear insulator bracket to body bracket nuts to 75–100 ft. lbs.
44. Install the lower radiator hose and install retaining bracket and bolt.
45. Install the shift stabilizer bar to transaxle attaching bolt. Tighten to 23–35 ft. lbs.
46. Install the shift mechanism to input shift shaft (on transaxle) bolt and nut. Tighten to 7–10 ft. lbs.
47. Install the lower radiator hose to the radiator.
48. Install the speedometer cable to the transaxle.
49. Connect the heater hoses to the water pump and oil cooler.
50. Position the exhaust system up and into insulating rubber grommets located at the rear of the vehicle.
51. Install the exhaust pipe to exhaust manifold bolts.
52. Install the exhaust pipe bracket to the oil pan bolt.
53. Place the stabilizer bar and control arm assembly into position. Install control arm to body attaching bolts. Install the stabilizer bar brackets and tighten all fasteners.
54. Halfshaft assemblies must be installed at this time.
55. Lower the vehicle.
56. Remove the Engine Support Tool D79L–6000–A or equivalent.

ENGINE AND ENGINE OVERHAUL

57. Connect the alternator wiring at RH fender apron.
58. Connect the engine harness to main harness and glow plug relays at dash panel.

NOTE: *Reinstall plastic shield.*

59. Connect the vacuum lines.
60. Install the air conditioning discharge and suction lines to air conditioning compressor, if so equipped. Do not charge system at this time.
61. Connect the fuel supply and return lines to the injection pump.
62. Connect the injection pump throttle cable.
63. Install the power steering pressure and return lines. Install bracket.
64. Connect the clutch cable to shift lever on transaxle.
65. Connect the battery cable to starter.
66. Install the radiator shroud and coolant fan assembly. Tighten attaching bolts.
67. Connect the coolant fan electrical connector.
68. Install the upper radiator hose to engine.
69. Fill and bleed the cooling system.
70. Install the negative ground battery cable to battery.
71. Install the air cleaner assembly.
72. Install the hood.
73. Charge air conditioning system, if so equipped. System can be charged at a later time if outside source is used.
74. Check and refill all fluid levels, (power steering, engine, MT).
75. Start the vehicle. Check for leaks.

2.3L HSC Engine

NOTE: *The following procedure is for engine and transaxle removal and installation as an assembly.*

CAUTION: *The engine and transaxle assembly are removed together as a unit from underneath the car. Provision must be made to safely raise and support the car for power train removal and installation.*

The air conditioning system (if equipped) must be discharged prior to engine removal. The refrigerant is contained under high pressure and is very dangerous when released. The system should be discharged by a knowledgeable person using the proper equipment.

1. Mark the position of the lines on the underside of the hood and remove the hood.
2. Disconnect the battery cables from the battery, negative cable first. Remove the air cleaner assembly.
3. Remove the radiator cap and disconnect the lower radiator hose from the radiator to drain the cooling system.

CAUTION: *When draining the coolant, keep in mind that cats and dogs are attracted by the ethylene glycol antifreeze, and are quite likely to drink any that is left in an uncovered container or in puddles on the ground. This will prove fatal in sufficient quantity. Always drain the coolant into a sealable container. Coolant should be reused unless it is contaminated or several years old.*

4. Remove the upper and lower radiator hoses. On models equipped with an automatic transaxle, disconnect and plug the oil cooler lines from the rubber connectors at the radiator.
5. Disconnect and remove the coil from the cylinder head. Disconnect the cooling fan wiring harness. Remove the radiator shroud and electric fan as an assembly.
6. Be sure the air conditioning system is properly and safely discharged. Remove the hoses from the compressor. Label and disconnect all electrical harness connections, linkage and vacuum lines from the engine.
7. On automatic transaxle models disconnect the TV (throttle valve) linkage at the transaxle. On manual transaxle models disconnect the clutch cable from the lever at the transaxle.
8. Disconnect the fuel supply and return lines. Plug the fuel line from the gas tank. Disconnect the Thermactor pump discharge hose at the pump.
9. Disconnect the power steering lines at the pump. Remove the hose support bracket from the cylinder head.
10. Install an engine support sling (Ford Tool T79L-6000-A, or equivalent), see the 1.3L, 1.6L and 1.9L engines removal and installation engine/transaxle assembly section for details.
11. Raise and safely support the car on jackstands.
12. Remove the starter cable from the starter motor terminal. Drain the engine oil and the transaxle lubricant.

CAUTION: *The EPA warns that prolonged contact with used engine oil may cause a number of skin disorders, including cancer! You should make every effort to minimize your exposure to used engine oil. Protective gloves should be worn when changing the oil. Wash your hands and any other exposed skin areas as soon as possible after exposure to used engine oil. Soap and water, or waterless hand cleaner should be used.*

13. Disconnect the hose from the catalytic converter. Remove the bolts retaining the exhaust pipe bracket to the oil pan.
14. Remove the exhaust pipe to exhaust manifold mounting nuts. Remove the pipes from the mounting bracket insulators and position out of the way.

ENGINE AND ENGINE OVERHAUL

15. Disconnect the speedometer cable from the transaxle. Remove the heater hoses from the water pump inlet and intake manifold connector.
16. Remove the water intake tube bracket from the engine block. Remove the two clamp attaching bolts from the bottom of the oil pan. Remove the water pump inlet tube.
17. Remove the bolts attaching the control arms to the body. Remove the stabilizer bar bracket retaining bolts and remove the brackets.
18. Remove the half shafts (drive axles) from the transaxle. Plug transaxle with shipping plugs or equivalent.
19. On models equipped with a manual transaxle, remove the roll restrictor nuts from the transaxle and pull the roll restrictor from mounting bracket.
20. On models equipped with a manual transaxle, remove the shift stabilizer bar to transaxle attaching bolts. Remove the shift mechanism to shift shaft attaching nut and bolt at the transaxle.
21. On models equipped with an automatic transaxle, disconnect the shift cable clip from the transaxle lever. Remove the manual shift linkage bracket bolts from the transaxle and remove the bracket.
22. Remove the left rear No. 4 insulator mount bracket from the body by removing the retaining nuts.
23. Remove the left front No. 1 insulator to transaxle mounting bolts.
24. Lower the car and support with stands so that the front wheels are just above the ground. Do not allow the wheels to touch the ground.
25. Connect an engine sling to the lifting brackets provided. Connect a hoist to the sling and apply slight tension. Remove and support sling (Step 10).
26. Remove the right hand insulator intermediate bracket to engine bracket bolts, intermediate bracket to insulator attaching nuts and the nut on the bottom of the double ended stud which attaches the intermediate bracket and engine bracket. Remove the bracket.
27. Lower the engine and transaxle assembly to the ground.
28. Raise and support the car at a height suitable from assembly to be removed.

To install:

29. Raise the engine and transaxle assembly and lower it into the vehicle.
30. Install the right hand insulator intermediate bracket to engine bracket bolts, intermediate bracket to insulator attaching nuts and the nut on the bottom of the double ended stud which attaches the intermediate bracket and engine bracket. Install the bracket.
31. Connect an engine sling to the lowering brackets provided. Connect a hoist to the sling and apply slight tension. Install and support sling.
32. Raise the car and support with stands so that the front wheels are just above the ground. Do not allow the wheels to touch the ground.
33. Install the left front No. 1 insulator to transaxle mounting bolts.
34. Install the left rear No. 4 insulator mount bracket to the body by removing the retaining nuts.
35. On models equipped with an automatic transaxle, reconnect the shift cable clip to the transaxle lever. Install the manual shift linkage bracket bolts to the transaxle and install the bracket.
36. On models equipped with a manual transaxle, install the shift stabilizer bar to transaxle attaching bolts. Install the shift mechanism to shift shaft attaching nut and bolt at the transaxle.
37. On models equipped with a manual transaxle, install the roll restrictor nuts to the transaxle and pull the roll restrictor to mounting bracket.
38. Remove the shipping plugs and install the half shafts (drive axles) to the transaxle.
39. Install the bolts attaching the control arms to the body. Install the stabilizer bar bracket retaining bolts and install the brackets.
40. Install the water intake tube bracket to the engine block. Install the two clamp attaching bolts to the bottom of the oil pan. Install the water pump inlet tube.
41. Reconnect the speedometer cable to the transaxle. Install the heater hoses to the water pump inlet and intake manifold connector.
42. Install the exhaust pipe to exhaust manifold mounting nuts. Install the pipes to the mounting bracket insulators.
43. Reconnect the hose to the catalytic converter. Install the bolts retaining the exhaust pipe bracket to the oil pan.
44. Install the starter cable to the starter motor terminal. Refill the engine oil and the transaxle lubricant.
45. Lower the car from the jackstands.
46. Remove the engine support sling.
47. Reconnect the power steering lines at the pump. Install the hose support bracket to the cylinder head.
48. Reconnect the fuel supply and return lines. Reconnect the Thermactor pump discharge hose at the pump.
49. On automatic transaxle models reconnect the TV (throttle valve) linkage at the tran-

ENGINE AND ENGINE OVERHAUL

saxle. On manual transaxle models reconnect the clutch cable to the lever at the transaxle.

50. Install the hoses to the compressor. Reconnect all electrical harness connections, linkage and vacuum lines to the engine. Be sure the air conditioning system is properly and safely recharged.

51. Reconnect and install the coil to the cylinder head. Reconnect the cooling fan wiring harness. Install the radiator shroud and electric fan as an assembly.

52. Install the upper and lower radiator hoses. On models equipped with an automatic transaxle, reconnect and plug the oil cooler lines to the rubber connectors at the radiator.

53. Reconnect the lower radiator hose to the radiator. Refill the cooling system.

54. Reconnect the battery cables to the battery. Install the air cleaner assembly.

55. Install the hood.

Engine Mounts

REMOVAL AND INSTALLATION

All Gasoline Engines

RIGHT ENGINE INSULATOR (No. 3A)

1. Disconnect the negative battery cable. Place a floor jack and a block of wood under the engine oil pan. Raise the engine approximately $1/2$ in. or enough to take the load off of the insulator.

2. Remove the lower support bracket attaching nut, bottom of the double ended stud. Remove the insulator-to-support bracket attaching nuts. Do not remove the nut on top of the double ended stud.

3. Remove the insulator support bracket from the vehicle. Remove the insulator attaching nuts through the right hand front wheel opening.

4. Remove the insulator attaching bolts through the engine compartment. Work the insulator out of the body and remove it from the vehicle.

To install:

5. Work insulator into the body opening.

6. Position the insulator and install the attaching nuts and bolts. Tighten the nuts to 75–100 ft. lbs. (100–135 Nm) and tighten the bolts to 37–55 ft. lbs. (50–75 Nm).

7. Install insulator support casting on top of the insulator and engine support bracket. Make sure the double-edged stud is through the hole in the engine bracket.

8. Tighten the insulator support casting-to-insulator attaching nuts to 55–75 ft. lbs. (75–100 Nm). Install and tighten lower support bracket nut to 60–90 ft. lbs. (80–120 Nm).

9. Install the insulator casting-to-engine bracket bolt and tighten to 60–90 ft. lbs. (80–120 Nm).

10. Lower engine. Connect negative battery cable.

LEFT REAR ENGINE INSULATOR (No. 4)

1. Disconnect the negative battery cable. Raise the vehicle and support safely. Place a transaxle jack and a block of wood under the transaxle.

2. Raise the transaxle approximately $1/2$ in. or enough to take the load off of the insulator.

3. Remove the insulator attaching nuts from the support bracket. Remove the 2 through bolts and remove the insulator from the transaxle.

To install:

4. Install the insulator over the left rear transaxle housing and support bracket studs.

5. Install the 2 insulator through bolts and tighten to 30–45 ft. lbs. (41–61 Nm).

6. Install 2 insulator-to-support bracket attaching nuts. Tighten to 80–100 ft. lbs. (108–136 Nm).

7. Lower vehicle and remove floor jack. Connect negative battery cable.

NOTE: *To remove the left rear support bracket, remove the left rear engine insulator No. 4. Then remove the support bracket attaching bolts. When installing the support bracket, torque the attaching bolts to 45–65 ft. lbs. (61–88 Nm).*

LEFT FRONT ENGINE INSULATOR (No. 1)

1. Disconnect the negative battery cable. Raise and the vehicle and support safely. Place a transaxle jack and a block of wood under the transaxle. Raise the transaxle approximately $1/2$ in. or enough to take the load off of the insulator.

2. Remove the insulator-to-support bracket attaching nut. Remove the insulators and transaxle attaching bolts and remove the insulator from the vehicle.

3. Complete the installation of the insulator by reversing the removal procedure. Torque the insulator to transaxle attaching bolts to 25–37 ft. lbs. (35–50 Nm). Torque the insulator-to-support bracket nut to 80–100 ft. lbs. (108–136 Nm).

Diesel Engine Only

FRONT ENGINE MOUNT

1. Disconnect the negative battery cable.

2. Support engine and transaxle using a floor jack and a wood block. Raise engine approximately $1/2$ in. (12.7mm) to unload engine mount.

ENGINE AND ENGINE OVERHAUL

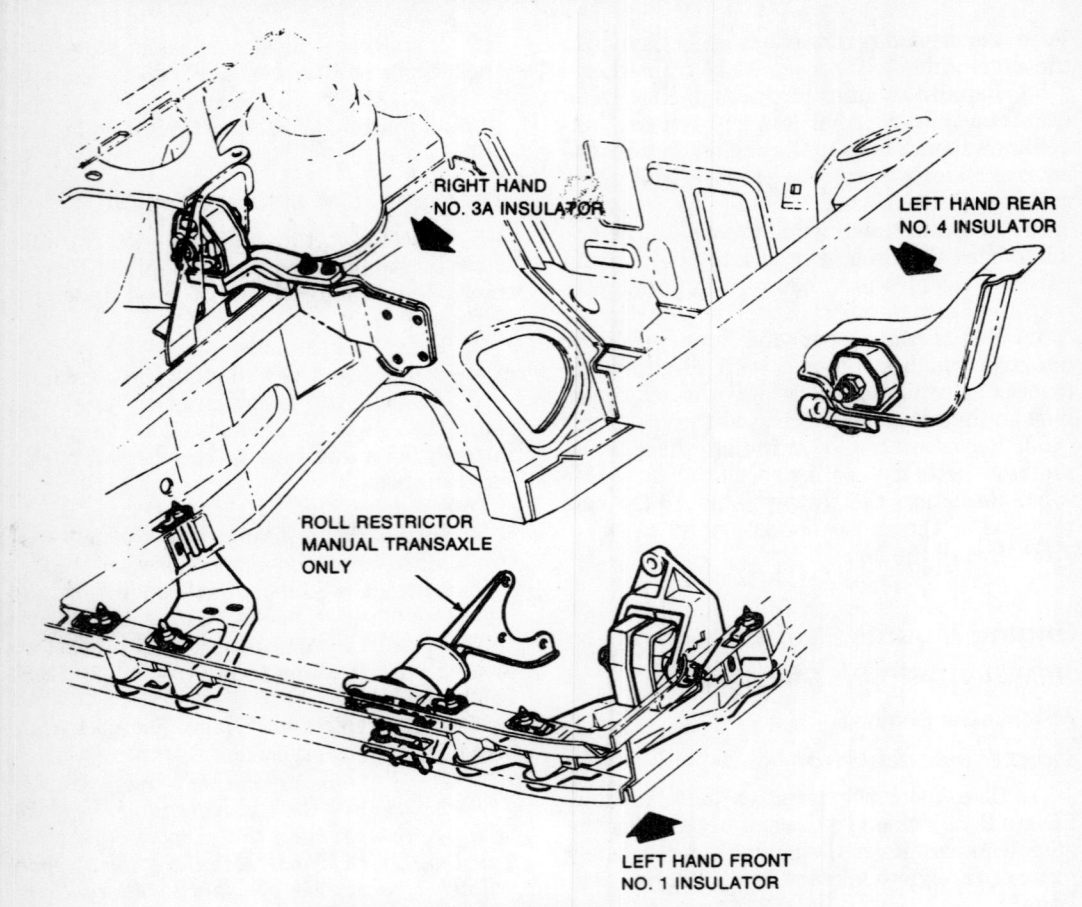

Typical 1.6L, 1.9L engine and transaxle mounting

3. Remove nut B from engine mount. Nut B is removed from underneath the vehicle.
4. Remove top bolts from engine mount.
5. Lower engine assembly 1–2 in. (25–50mm) for clearance.
6. From inside right hand front wheel well, remove 2 nuts attaching engine mount to fender apron.
7. Remove 2 bolts attaching engine mount to right hand front rail.
8. Slide engine mount toward engine until studs clear fender apron. Remove mount.

To install:

9. Position engine mount on right hand front side members and loosely install 2 attaching bolts.
10. From inside right hand wheel well, install 2 attaching nuts and tighten to 75–100 ft. lbs. (100–135 Nm). Tighten 2 mount bolts on right front rail to 37–55 ft. lbs. (50–75 Nm).
11. Raise engine until engine bracket contacts engine mount.
12. Install nut B and top bolts. Tighten to 60–90 ft. lbs. (80–120 Nm).
13. Remove floor jack and wood block.
14. Connect negative battery cable.

FRONT TRANSAXLE MOUNT

1. Disconnect the negative battery cable.
2. Support transaxle with a floor jack and wood block.
3. Remove 3 bolts attaching mount to transaxle. Raise engine approximately $1/2$ in. (12.7mm) to unload mount.
3. Remove nut attaching mount to left hand stabilizer bar bracket and remove mount.

To install:

4. Position mount on stabilizer bar bracket and install 3 bolts attaching mount to transaxle and tighten to 25–37 ft. lbs. (35–50 Nm).
5. Install attaching nut to stabilizer bar bracket and tighten to 80–100 ft. lbs. (108–136 Nm).
6. Remove floor jack and wood block and connect battery ground cable.

REAR TRANSAXLE MOUNT

1. Disconnect the negative battery cable.
2. Support with a floor jack and wood block.

ENGINE AND ENGINE OVERHAUL 121

Raise engine approximately 1/2 in. (12.7mm) to unload mount.

3. Remove 2 nuts attaching mount to bracket.

4. Remove 2 bolts attaching mount to transaxle and remove mount.

To install:

5. Position mount on transaxle and install 2 attaching bolts. Tighten bolts to 30–45 ft. lbs. (41–61 Nm).

6. Install 2 nuts attaching engine mount to bracket and tighten to 80–100 ft. lbs. (108–136 Nm).

7. Remove floor jack and wood block and connect battery ground cable.

Rocker Arms

REMOVAL AND INSTALLATION

Gasoline Engines

1. Open and secure the hood. Disconnect the negative battery cable. Remove the air cleaner nuts and disconnect the duct work and valve assembly from the fresh air inlet tube.

2. Disconnect hot air tube from the hot air shroud, if so equipped. Disconnect the vacuum source tube from the temperature sensor, if so equipped.

3. Remove the air cleaner assembly and place it on a suitable work bench.

4. Disconnect and label all hoses and wires connected to or crossing the valve cover. Loosen and remove all of the rocker arm cover retaining bolts and nuts. Loosen the PCV oil separator to allow the hoses to clear the rocker cover, if so equipped. Remove the cover.

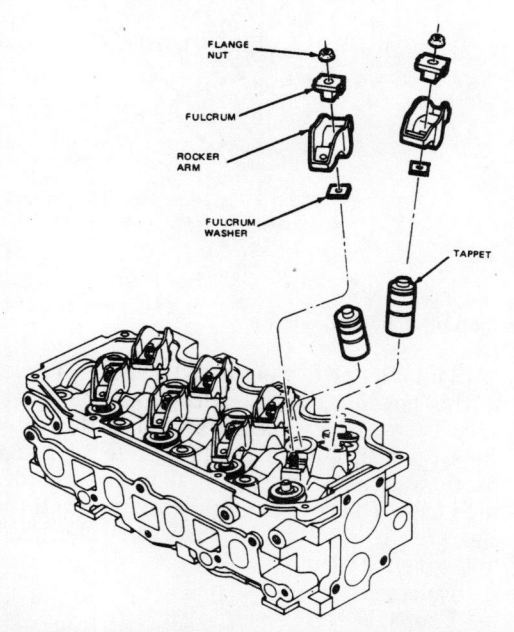

5. On 1.6 & 1.9L engines, remove the rocker arm nuts and discard. On 2.3L HSC engines, remove the rocker bolts and fulcrums. Remove the rocker arms. Keep all parts in order; they must be returned to their original positions.

To install:

6. Coat the valve tips and the rocker arm contact areas with Lubriplate® or the equivalent.

7. Rotate the engine until the lifter is on the base circle of the cam (valve closed).

NOTE: *On 1.3L, 1.6L and 1.9L engines, turn the engine only in the direction of normal rotation. Backward rotation will cause the camshaft belt to slip or lose teeth, altering valve timing and causing serious engine damage.*

6. Install the rocker arm and new hex flange nuts or fulcrum and bolt. Be sure the lifter is on the base circle of the cam for each rocker arm as it is installed. Be sure that each fulcrum is seated in the rocker arm pedestal slot. Install the attaching nuts and torque them to 15–22 ft. lbs.

7. Clean the valve cover mating surfaces. Apply a bead of sealer to the cover flange and install the cover. Install all disconnected hoses and wires.

TAPPET CLEARANCE

The 1.3L, 1.6 and 1.9L engines are cam in head engines with hydraulic tappets.

Valve stem to valve rocker arm clearance should be within specifications with the tappet completely collapsed. Repeated valve reconditioning operations (valve and/or valve seat refacing) will decrease the clearance to the point that if not compensated for, the tappet will

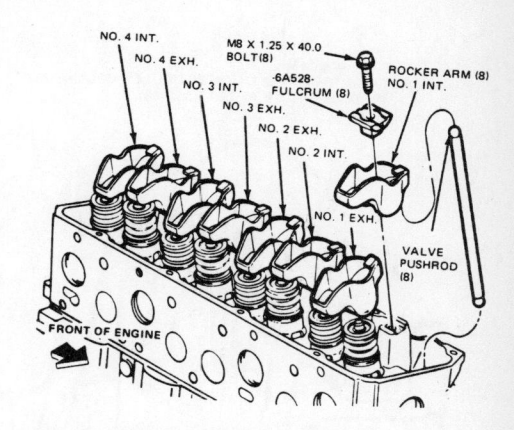

Valve train components-2.3L HSC

Exploded view of the upper valve train-1.6L, 1.9L engines

122 ENGINE AND ENGINE OVERHAUL

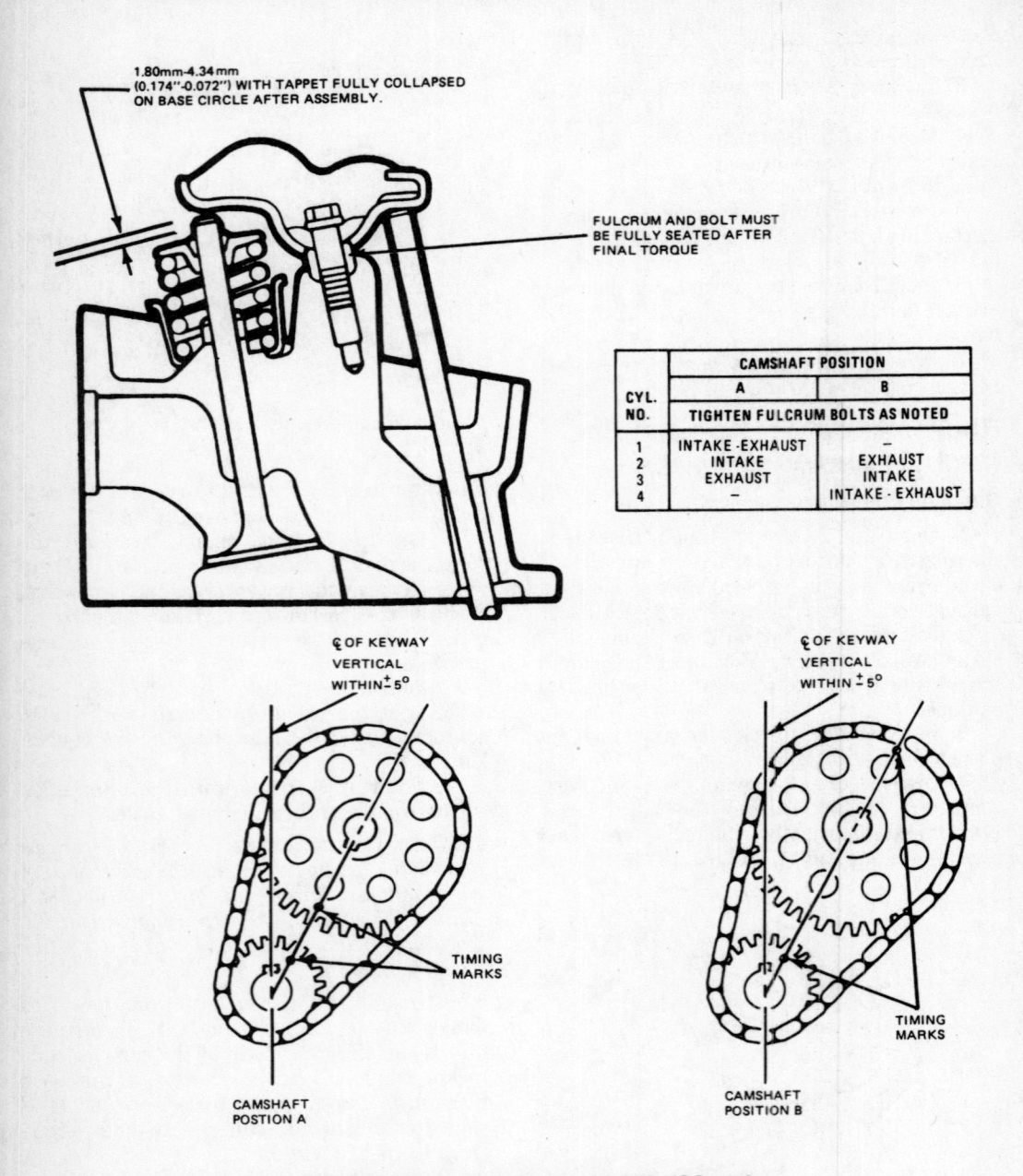

1.80mm-4.34 mm (0.174"-0.072") WITH TAPPET FULLY COLLAPSED ON BASE CIRCLE AFTER ASSEMBLY.

FULCRUM AND BOLT MUST BE FULLY SEATED AFTER FINAL TORQUE

CYL. NO.	CAMSHAFT POSITION A	CAMSHAFT POSITION B
	TIGHTEN FULCRUM BOLTS AS NOTED	
1	INTAKE-EXHAUST	—
2	INTAKE	EXHAUST
3	EXHAUST	INTAKE
4	—	INTAKE-EXHAUST

₵ OF KEYWAY VERTICAL WITHIN ±5°

₵ OF KEYWAY VERTICAL WITHIN ±5°

TIMING MARKS

TIMING MARKS

CAMSHAFT POSITION A

CAMSHAFT POSITION B

Checking the collapsed tappet gap on 2.3L HSC engine

cease to function and the valve will be held open.

To determine the rocker arm-to-tappet clearance, make the following check:

1. Connect an auxiliary starter switch in the starting circuit. Crank the engine with the ignition switch Off until No. 1 piston is on TDC after the compression stroke.
2. With the crankshaft in the position designated in Steps 3 and 4, position the hydraulic lifter compressor tool on the rocker arm. Slowly apply pressure to bleed down the tappet until it is completely bottomed. Hold the tappet in this position and check the available clearance between the rocker arm and the valve stem tip with a feeler gauge. The feeler gauge width must not exceed 3/8 in. (9.5mm), in order to fit between the rails on the rocker arm. If the clearance is less than specifications, check the following for wear:
   - Fulcrum
   - Tappet
   - Cam lobe
   - Valve tip

ENGINE AND ENGINE OVERHAUL

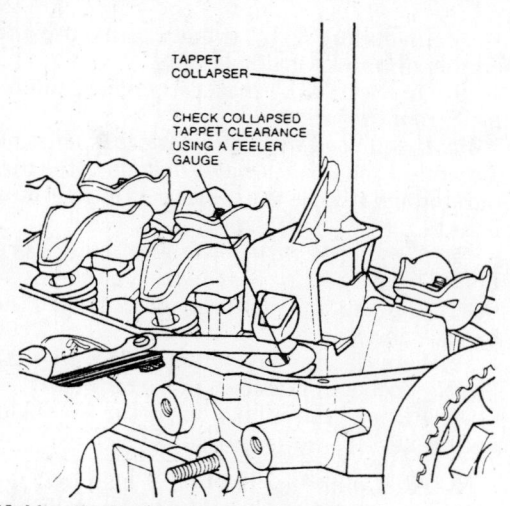

Making the tappet clearance check

3. With the No. 1 piston on TDC at the end of the compression stroke (Position No. 1), check the following valves:
- No. 1 Intake No. 1 Exhaust.
- No. 2 Intake.

4. Rotate the crankshaft to Position No. 2 and check the following valves:
- No. 3 Intake No. 3 Exhaust.

5. Rotate the crankshaft another 180° from Position No. 2 back to TDC and check the following valves:
- No. 4 Intake No. 4 Exhaust.
- No. 2 Exhaust.

6. Collapsed tappet clearance should be as follows:
- 1981–86 Carb/EFI: 0.59–0.194 in. (1.50–4.93mm).
- 1987–89 Carb/CFI: 0.47–0.138 in. (1.2–1.5mm).
- 1987–89 EFI/EFI: 0.59–0.138 in. (1.2–1.5mm).
- 1990 EFI w/Roller tappet: Minimum – 0.0 in. (0.0mm); Normal – 0.09 in. (2.2mm); Maximum – 0.18 in. (4.5mm).
- 1990 EFI w/Flat tappet: Minimum – 0.03 in. (0.7mm); Normal – 0.12 in. (2.9mm); Maximum – 0.21 in. (5.2mm).
- 1990 EFI HO w/Roller tappet: Minimum – 0.02 in. (0.5mm); Normal – 0.11 in. (2.7mm); Maximum – 0.20 in. (4.9mm).
- 1990 EFI HO w/Flat tappet: Minimum – 0.05 in. (1.2mm); Normal – 0.14 in. (3.4mm); Maximum – 0.22 in. (5.6mm).

NOTE: *For 2.3L HSC engine refer to illustration provided for procedure. Rotate the camshaft to position A. Check the intake and exhaust valves on the compression stroke under camshaft position A. The tappet gap should be 0.072–0.174 in. Rotate the camshaft to position B and check the remaining tappets.*

Thermostat

REMOVAL AND INSTALLATION

1. Disconnect the negative battery cable. Drain the radiator until the coolant level is below the thermostat.

CAUTION: *When draining the coolant, keep in mind that cats and dogs are attracted by the ethylene glycol antifreeze, and are quite likely to drink any that is left in an uncovered container or in puddles on the ground. This will prove fatal in sufficient quantity. Always drain the coolant into a sealable container. Coolant should be reused unless it is contaminated or several years old.*

2. Disconnect the wire connector at the thermostat housing thermo-switch.

3. Loosen the top radiator hose clamp. Remove the thermostat housing mounting bolts and lift up the housing.

4. Remove the thermostat by turning counterclockwise.

5. Clean the thermostat housing and engine gasket mounting surfaces. Install new mounting gasket and fully insert the thermostat to compress the mounting gasket. Turn the thermostat clockwise to secure in housing.

6. Position the housing onto the engine. Install the mounting bolts and torque to 6–8 ft. lbs. on 1.3, 1.6 & 1.9L engines and 15–22 ft. lbs. on 2.3L HSC engines.

7. The rest of the installation is in the reverse order of removal.

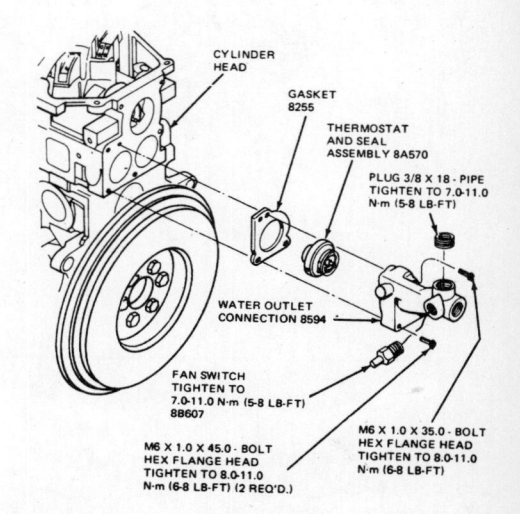

Typical thermostat installation

124 ENGINE AND ENGINE OVERHAUL

Intake Manifold

REMOVAL AND INSTALLATION

Gasoline Engine — Except Fuel Injection

1. Disconnect the negative battery terminal.
2. Remove the air cleaner housing.
3. Partially drain the cooling system and disconnect the heater hose from under the intake manifold.

CAUTION: *When draining the coolant, keep in mind that cats and dogs are attracted by the ethylene glycol antifreeze, and are quite likely to drink any that is left in an uncovered container or in puddles on the ground. This will prove fatal in sufficient quantity. Always drain the coolant into a sealable container. Coolant should be reused unless it is contaminated or several years old.*

4. Disconnect and label all vacuum and electrical connections.
5. Disconnect the fuel line and carburetor linkage.
6. Disconnect the EGR vacuum hose and supply tube.
7. On Escort & Lynx models, jack up the vehicle and support it with jackstands.
8. On Escort & Lynx models, remove the bottom (3) intake manifold nuts.
9. On Escort & Lynx models, remove the vehicle from the jackstands.
10. If equipped with automatic transmission disconnect the throttle valve linkage at the carburetor and remove the cable bracket attaching bolts.
11. If equipped with power steering (Escort/Lynx), remove the Thermactor pump drive belt, the pump, the mounting bracket, and the by-pass hose.
12. Remove the fuel pump (Escort/Lynx). See the fuel pump removal procedure.
13. Remove the intake bolts, the manifold, and gasket.

NOTE: *Do not lay the intake manifold flat as the gasket surfaces may be damaged.*

To install:

14. Install the intake manifold, and gasket.
15. Install the fuel pump (Escort/Lynx).
16. If equipped with power steering (Escort/Lynx), install the Thermactor pump drive belt, the pump, the mounting bracket, and the by-pass hose.
17. If equipped with automatic transmission reconnect the throttle valve linkage at the car-

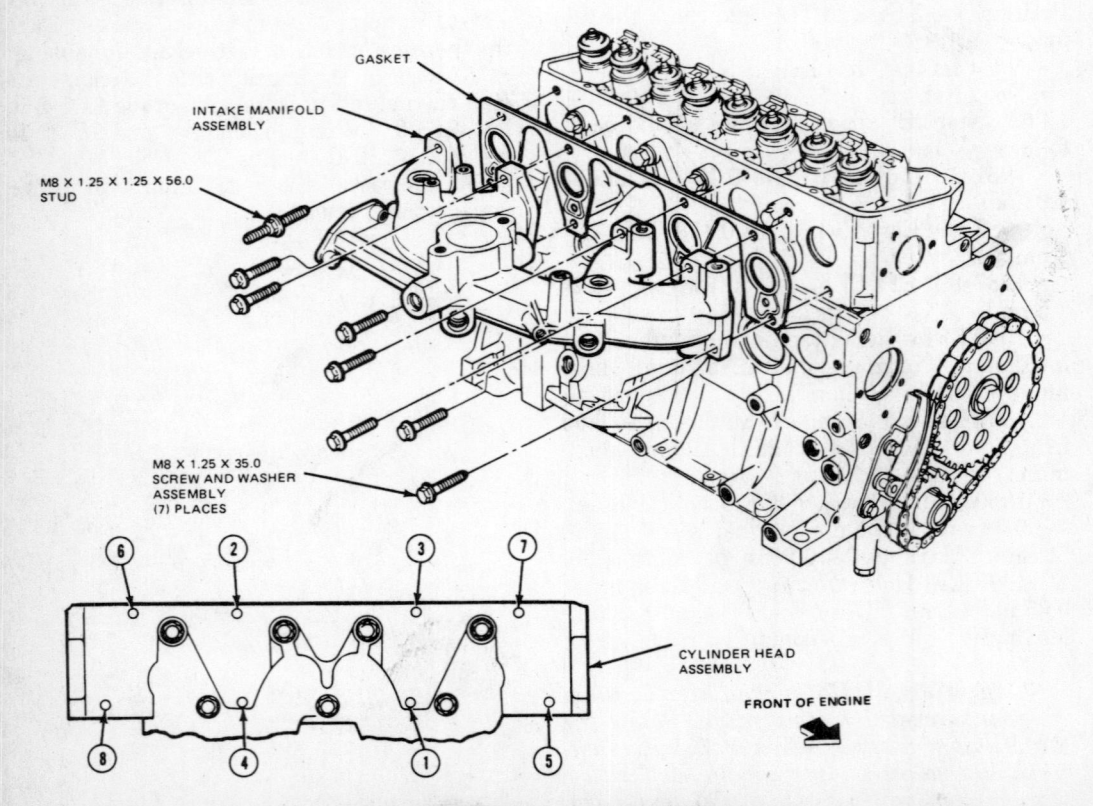

Intake manifold installation-2.3L HSC engine

ENGINE AND ENGINE OVERHAUL 125

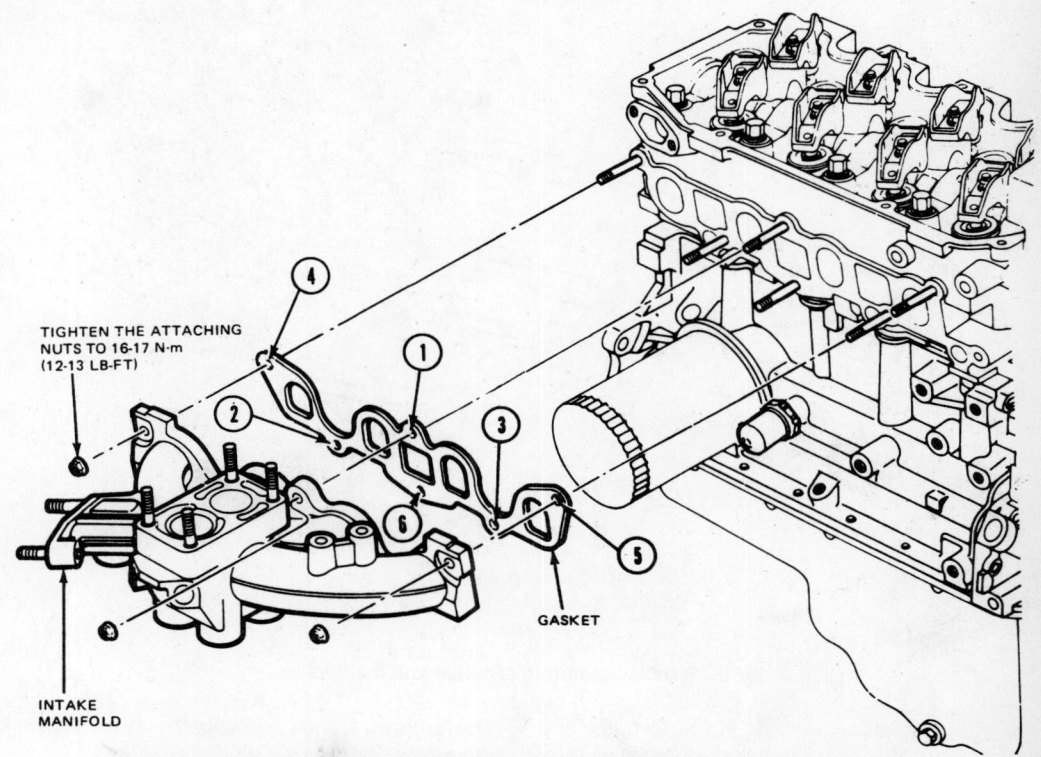

Install the intake manifold and tighten the retaining bolts in the sequence shown 1.6L, 1.9L carbureted engines

buretor and install the cable bracket attaching bolts.

18. On Escort & Lynx models, jack up the vehicle and support it with jackstands.
19. On Escort & Lynx models, install the bottom (3) intake manifold nuts.
20. On Escort & Lynx models, remove the vehicle from the jackstands.
21. Reconnect the EGR vacuum hose and supply tube.
22. Reconnect the fuel line and carburetor linkage.
23. Reconnect all vacuum and electrical connections.
24. Reconnect the heater hose to under the intake manifold and refill the cooling system.
25. Install the air cleaner housing.
26. Reconnect the negative battery terminal.

Gasoline Engine w/EFI/CFI Fuel Injection

1. Raise and secure the hood properly. Disconnect the negative battery cable.
2. Partially drain the cooling system and disconnect the heater hoses at the fitting locations on the side of the intake manifold.

   CAUTION: *When draining the coolant, keep in mind that cats and dogs are attracted by the ethylene glycol antifreeze, and are quite likely to drink any that is left in an uncovered container or in puddles on the ground. This will prove fatal in sufficient quantity. Always drain the coolant into a sealable container. Coolant should be reused unless it is contaminated or several years old.*

3. Remove the air cleaner assembly. Disconnect and tag all necessary vacuum lines and wiring connections that are in the way of removal of the intake manifold. Disconnect the EGR supply tube.
4. Raise and safely support the vehicle.
5. Remove the PVS hose connectors, label the connectors and set them aside.
6. Remove the bottom 4 intake manifold nuts. Lower the vehicle.
7. Disconnect the fuel lines at the throttle body using fuel line disconnect tool D87L-9280-A or B or equivalent.
8. Disconnect the accelerator cable and if equipped the speed control cable.
9. Disconnect the throttle valve linkage at the throttle body and remove the cable bracket attaching bolts.
10. Remove the 3 remaining intake manifold nuts, intake manifold and gasket. It may be necessary to use intake manifold torque wrench adapter tool T81P-9425-A or equivalent on the

ENGINE AND ENGINE OVERHAUL

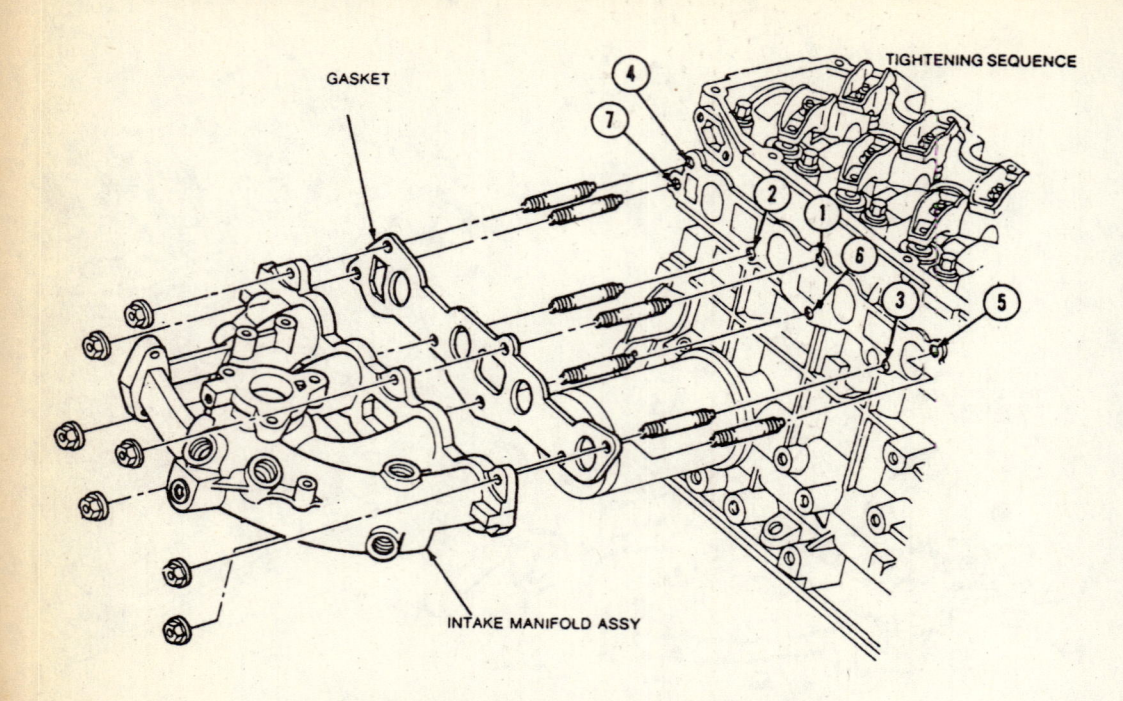

EFI/CFI intake manifold removal and installation

center No.1 position nut. Be sure not to lay the intake manifold flat as the gasket surfaces may be damaged.

To install:

11. Ensure the mating surfaces on the intake manifold and the cylinder head are clean and free of gasket material.

12. Install the intake manifold gasket. Position the intake manifold on the engine and install the attaching nuts. Install No.1 first, then No.6, then number 2 and 3 together, and then numbers 4, 5 and 7 together. Torque the nuts to 12–25 ft. lbs. It may be necessary to use intake manifold torque wrench adapter tool T81P–9425–A or equivalent on the center No.1 position nut.

13. Connect the throttle valve linkage and install the cable bracket attaching bolts, if removed.

14. Connect the accelerator cable and if removed the speed control cable.

15. Connect the fuel lines at the fuel charging assembly.

16. Raise and support the vehicle safely. Connect the heater hoses to the fitting located on the side of the intake manifold. Lower the vehicle.

17. Reconnect the EGR supply tube. Reconnect the all disconnected vacuum lines and electrical connectors.

18. Install the air cleaner assembly. Refill the coolant system with the proper coolant. Reconnect the negative battery cable and start the engine. Check for coolant and fuel leaks, repair as necessary.

Gasoline Engine w/EFI HO Fuel Injection

NOTE: The air intake manifold is a 2 piece aluminum casting consisting of an upper intake and lower intake manifold. If the upper and lower sub-assemblies are to be serviced and/or removed, with the fuel charging assembly mounted to the engine, perform the following steps.

1. Open hood and install protective covers.
2. Make sure that ignition key is in **OFF** position.
3. Drain the cooling system.

CAUTION: *When draining the coolant, keep in mind that cats and dogs are attracted by the ethylene glycol antifreeze, and are quite likely to drink any that is left in an uncovered container or in puddles on the ground. This will prove fatal in sufficient quantity. Always drain the coolant into a sealable container. Coolant should be reused unless it is contaminated or several years old.*

4. Disconnect the negative battery cable and set aside.
5. Remove fuel cap to relieve fuel tank pressure.
6. Release pressure from the fuel system at the fuel pressure relief valve on the fuel injector manifold assembly. To gain access to the fuel pressure relief valve, the valve cap must first be removed.

ENGINE AND ENGINE OVERHAUL

7. Disconnect the push connect fuel supply line. With a suitable prying tool inserted under the hairpin clip tab, "pop" the clip free from the push connect tube fitting and disconnect the push connect tube fitting and disconnect the tube. Save the hairpin clip for use in reassembly.

8. Identify and disconnect the fuel return lines and vacuum connections. Have a shop towel on hand to absorb any excess fuel.

9. Disconnect the injector wiring harness by disconnecting the ECT sensor in the heater supply tube under lower intake manifold and the electronic engine control harness.

10. Disconnect air bypass connector from EEC harness.

NOTE: *Not all assemblies may be serviceable while on the engine. In some cases, removal of the fuel charging assembly may facilitate service of the various sub-assemblies. Remove the fuel charging assembly as required and proceed with the following steps:*

11. Disconnect the engine air cleaner outlet tube from the air intake throttle body.

12. Unplug the throttle position sensor from the wiring harness.

13. Unplug the air bypass valve connector.

14. Remove the upper manifold retaining bolts.

15. Remove upper manifold assembly and set it aside.

16. Remove and discard the gasket from the lower manifold assembly.

NOTE: *If scraping is necessary, be careful not to damage the gasket surfaces of the upper and lower manifold assemblies, or allow material to drop into lower manifold.*

To install:

17. Ensure that the gasket surfaces of the upper and lower intake manifolds are clean.

18. Place a new service gasket on the lower manifold assembly and mount the upper intake manifold to the lower, securing it with the retaining bolts. Torque the bolts to 15-22 ft. lbs.

19. Ensure the wiring harness is properly installed.

20. Connect electrical connectors to air bypass valve and throttle position sensor and the vacuum hose to the fuel pressure regulator.

21. Connect the engine air cleaner outlet tube to the throttle body intake securing it with a hose clamp tighten to 15-25 inch lbs.

22. Connect negative battery cable.

Diesel Engine

1. Disconnect the air inlet duct from the intake manifold and install the protective cap in the intake manifold (part or Protective Cap Set T84P-9395-A or equivalent).

2. Disconnect the glow plug resistor electrical connector.

3. Disconnect the breather hose.

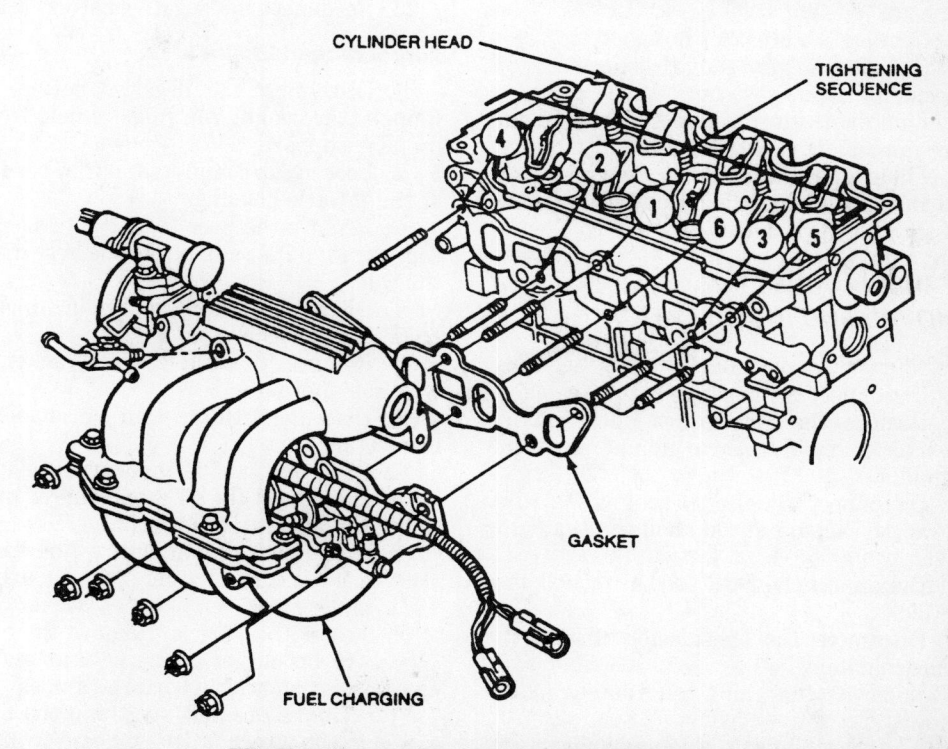

EFI HO intake manifold removal and installation

ENGINE AND ENGINE OVERHAUL

4. Drain the cooling system.
CAUTION: *When draining the coolant, keep in mind that cats and dogs are attracted by the ethylene glycol antifreeze, and are quite likely to drink any that is left in an uncovered container or in puddles on the ground. This will prove fatal in sufficient quantity. Always drain the coolant into a sealable container. Coolant should be reused unless it is contaminated or several years old.*
5. Disconnect the upper radiator hose at the thermostat housing.
6. Disconnect the tow coolant hoses at the thermostat housing.
7. Disconnect the connectors to the temperature sensors in the thermostat housing.
8. Remove the bolts attaching the intake manifold to the cylinder head and remove the intake manifold.
9. Clean the intake manifold and cylinder head gasket mating surfaces.
10. Install the intake manifold, using a new gasket, and tighten the bolts to 12–16 ft. lbs.
11. Connect the temperature sensor connectors.
12. Connect the lower coolant hose to the thermostat housing and tighten the hose clamp.
13. Connect the upper coolant tube, using a new gasket and tighten bolts to 5–7 ft. lbs.
14. Connect the upper radiator hose to the thermostat housing.
15. Connect the breather hose.
16. Connect the glow plug resistor electrical connector.
17. Remove the protective cap and install the air inlet duct.
18. Fill and bleed the cooling system.
19. Run the engine and check for intake air leaks and coolant leaks.

Exhaust Manifold

REMOVAL AND INSTALLATION

Gasoline Engine

1. Disconnect the negative battery cable.
2. Remove the air cleaner duct and air cleaner assembly in order to gain access to the manifold.
3. Disconnect the electric cooling fan wire. Remove the radiator shroud bolts and radiator shroud.
4. Disconnect the EGR tube at the exhaust manifold.
5. Disconnect the Thermactor tube art the exhaust manifold.
6. Remove the air conditioning hose bracket.
7. Remove the exhaust manifold heat stove. Remove the exhaust manifold retaining nuts.
8. Raise and support the vehicle safely. Remove the anti roll brace.
9. Disconnect the water tube brackets.
10. Disconnect the water tube brackets.
11. Disconnect the exhaust pipe at the catalyst.
12. Remove the exhaust manifold.

To install:
13. Ensure the mating surfaces on the exhaust manifold and the cylinder head are clean and free of gasket material.
14. Install the exhaust manifold.
15. Reconnect the exhaust pipe at the catalyst.
16. Reconnect the water tube brackets.
17. Reconnect the water tube brackets.
18. Install the anti roll brace. Lower the vehicle.
19. Install the exhaust manifold heat stove. Install the exhaust manifold retaining nuts. Torque them to specifications (15–20 ft. Lbs.)
20. Install the air conditioning hose bracket.
21. Reconnect the Thermactor tube art the exhaust manifold.
22. Reconnect the EGR tube at the exhaust manifold.
23. Reconnect the electric cooling fan wire. Install the radiator shroud and radiator shroud bolts.
24. Install the air cleaner duct and air cleaner assembly.
25. Reconnect the negative battery cable.

Turbocharged Engines

1. Disconnect the negative battery cable. Remove the cooling fan finger shield from the radiator support.
2. Loosen the compressor outlet hose clamp at the throttle housing.
3. Remove the hose from the turbocharger compressor outlet and rotate the hose up out of the way.
4. Disconnect the compressor inlet hose from the turbocharger.
5. Remove the alternator bracket along with the alternator.
6. Disconnect the oxygen sensor electrical connector.
7. Raise and safely support the vehicle.
8. Disconnect the oil supply line at the coolant outlet and at the turbocharger.
9. Disconnect the oil return line from the bottom of the turbocharger center housing and the cylinder block.
10. Lower the vehicle. Remove the exhaust pipe-to-turbocharger attaching nuts and move the exhaust pipe away from the studs.
11. Remove the bolt attaching the exhaust shield to the water outlet connector.
12. Remove the nuts attaching the exhaust

ENGINE AND ENGINE OVERHAUL 129

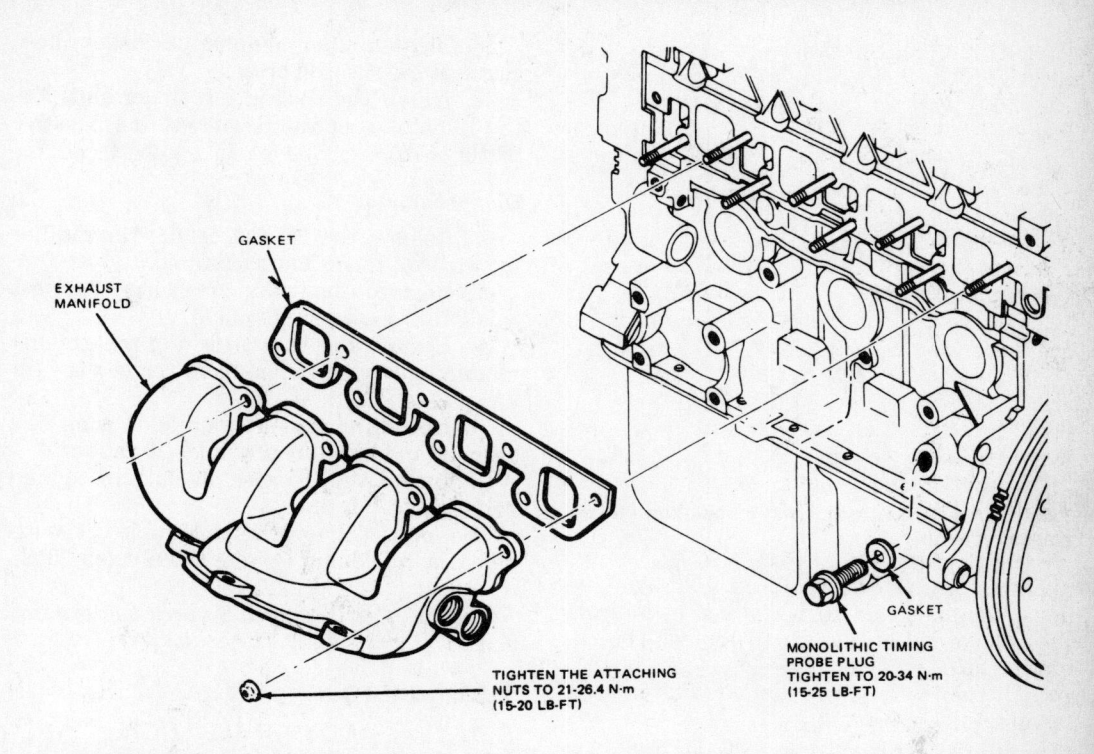

Install the exhaust manifold and tighten the retaining bolts in the sequence shown—1.6L, 1.9L engines

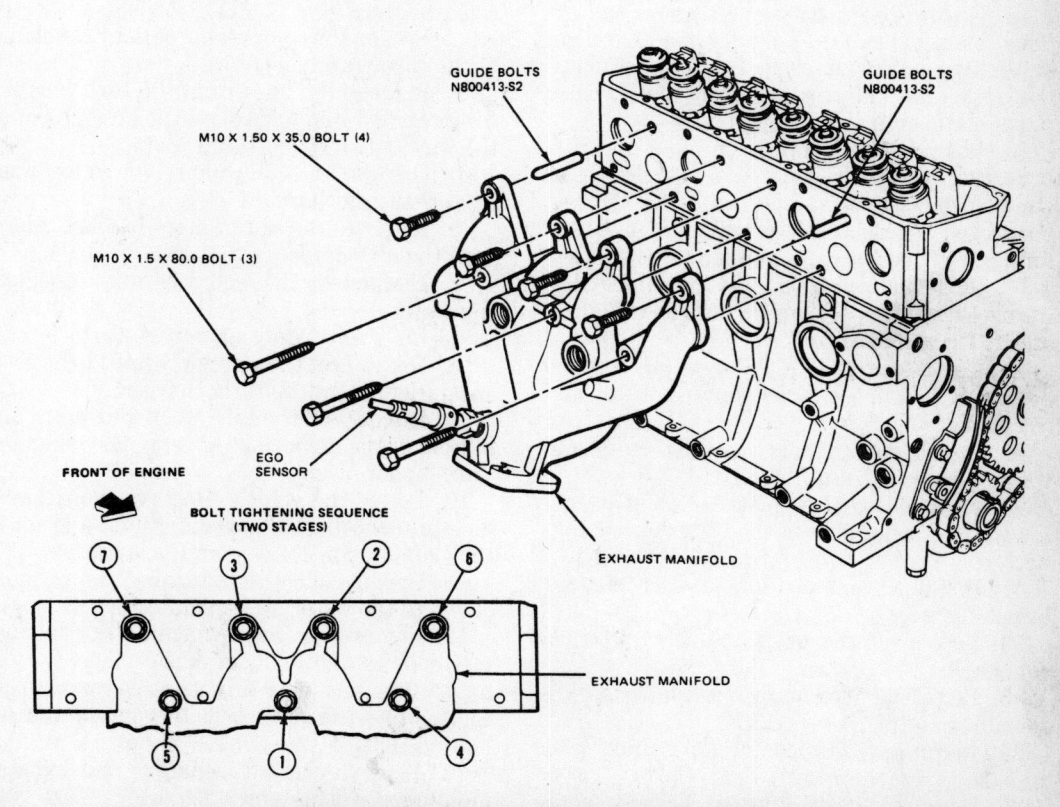

Exhaust manifold installation—2.3L HSC engine

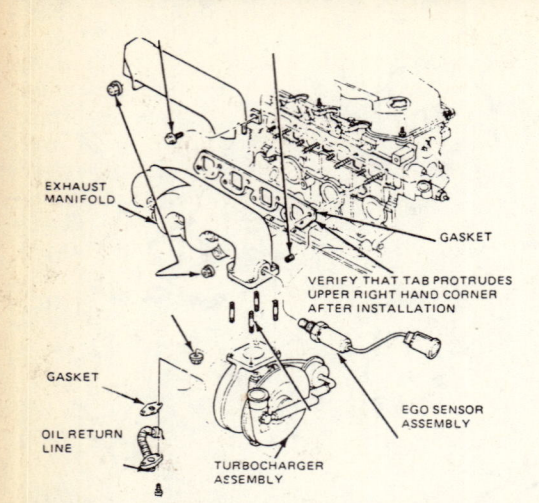

ENGINE AND ENGINE OVERHAUL

Exhaust manifold removal and installation - turbocharged engine

manifold to the cylinder head. Slide the exhaust manifold and turbocharger away from the cylinder head enough to remove the exhaust shield.

13. Remove the turbocharger and exhaust manifolds as an assembly.
14. If the exhaust manifold is being replaced, remove the exhaust oxygen sensor.

To install:
15. Ensure the mating surfaces on the exhaust manifold and the cylinder head are clean and free of gasket material. The exhaust manifold gasket has a top and a bottom to it, be sure to install it correctly.
16. Position the exhaust manifold and turbocharger assembly onto the cylinder head studs. The exhaust manifold studs for the turbocharged engine are different than the studs for a non-turbocharger engine.
17. Raise and safely support the vehicle. Reconnect the oil supply line at the coolant outlet and at the turbocharger.
18. Reconnect the oil return line to the bottom of the turbocharger center housing and the cylinder block.
19. Install the exhaust manifold nuts and torque them to 16–19 ft. lbs.
20. Lower the vehicle. Install the bolt attaching the exhaust shield to the water outlet connector.
21. Install the exhaust pipe-to-turbocharger attaching nuts.
22. Reconnect the oxygen sensor electrical connector.
23. Install the alternator bracket along with the alternator.
24. Reconnect the compressor inlet hose from the turbocharger.
25. Install the hose to the turbocharger compressor outlet.
26. Tighten the compressor outlet hose clamp at the throttle housing.
27. Install the cooling fan finger shield to the radiator support. Reconnect the negative battery cable.

Diesel Engine

1. Remove the nuts attaching the muffler inlet pipe to the exhaust manifold.
2. Remove the bolts attaching the heat shield to the exhaust manifold.
3. Remove the nuts attaching the exhaust manifold to cylinder head and remove the exhaust manifold.
4. Install the exhaust manifold, using new gaskets, and tighten nuts to 16–20 ft. lbs.
5. Install the exhaust shield and tighten bolts to 12–16 ft. lbs.
6. Connect the muffler inlet pipe to the exhaust manifold and tighten the nuts to 25–35 ft. lbs.
7. Run the engine and check for exhaust leaks.

Turbocharger

REMOVAL AND INSTALLATION

1. Disconnect the negative battery cable. Remove the cooling fan finger shield from the radiator support.
2. Loosen the compressor outlet hose clamp at the throttle housing.
3. Remove the hose from the turbocharger compressor outlet and rotate the hose up out of the way.
4. Disconnect the compressor inlet hose from the turbocharger.
5. Remove the alternator bracket along with the alternator.
6. Disconnect the oxygen sensor electrical connector.
7. Raise and safely support the vehicle.
8. Disconnect the oil supply line at the coolant outlet and at the turbocharger.
9. Disconnect the oil return line from the bottom of the turbocharger center housing and the cylinder block.
10. Lower the vehicle. Remove the exhaust pipe-to-turbocharger attaching nuts and move the exhaust pipe away from the studs.
11. Remove the bolt attaching the exhaust shield to the water outlet connector.
12. Remove the nuts attaching the exhaust manifold to the cylinder head. Slide the exhaust manifold and turbocharger away from the cylinder head enough to remove the exhaust shield.
13. Remove the turbocharger and exhaust manifolds as an assembly.
14. Remove the 4 turbocharger retaining

ENGINE AND ENGINE OVERHAUL

bolts and remove the turbocharger assembly. If the exhaust manifold is being replaced, remove the exhaust oxygen sensor.

To install:

15. Install the 4 turbocharger retaining bolts and torque them to 16–19 ft. lbs. Ensure the mating surfaces on the exhaust manifold and the cylinder head are clean and free of gasket material. The exhaust manifold gasket has a top and a bottom to it, be sure to install it correctly.
16. Position the exhaust manifold and turbocharger assembly onto the cylinder head studs. The exhaust manifold studs for the turbocharged engine are different than the studs for a non-turbocharger engine.
17. Raise and safely support the vehicle. Reconnect the oil supply line at the coolant outlet and at the turbocharger.
18. Reconnect the oil return line to the bottom of the turbocharger center housing and the cylinder block.
19. Install the exhaust manifold nuts and torque them to 16–19 ft. lbs.
20. Lower the vehicle. Install the bolt attaching the exhaust shield to the water outlet connector.
21. Install the exhaust pipe-to-turbocharger attaching nuts.
22. Reconnect the oxygen sensor electrical connector.
23. Install the alternator bracket along with the alternator.
24. Reconnect the compressor inlet hose from the turbocharger.
25. Install the hose to the turbocharger compressor outlet.
26. Tighten the compressor outlet hose clamp at the throttle housing.
27. Install the cooling fan finger shield to the radiator support. Reconnect the negative battery cable.

NOTE: *After installing the turbocharger, or after an oil and filter change, disconnect the coil wire to the distributor and crank the engine with the starter motor until the oil pressure light on the dash goes out. Oil pressure must be up before starting the engine. Also always make sure that you use Turbo approved motor oil when changing the oil in your turbocharged vehicle. Failure to use such an oil can cause premature bearing failure in your turbocharger assembly.*

Air Conditioning Compressor

NOTE: *When removing the air conditioning compressor from your vehicle, it will be necessary to discharge and evacuate the refrigerant from the air conditioning system and also it will be necessary to replace the suction accumulator/drier due to contamination once the refrigerant system is opened up. This is a procedure that should be performed by an authorized technician due to the dangers involved with handling R-12 refrigerant. When ever working around R-12 refrigerant, it is recommended that gloves and goggles be worn at all times.*

REMOVAL AND INSTALLATION

ESCORT/EXP AND LYNX/LN7

1981–83

1. Discharge the system following the recommended service procedures in Chapter 1. Observe all safety precautions.
2. Disconnect the alternator wire at the multiple connector.
3. Remove the carburetor air cleaner and the air intake and tube assembly from the radiator support.
4. Disconnect the alternator air tube from the air inlet on the radiator support.
5. Remove the alternator from the engine.
6. Disconnect the compressor clutch wires at the field coil connector on the compressor.
7. Disconnect the discharge hose and the suction hose from the compressor manifolds. Cap the refrigerant lines and compressor manifolds to prevent the entrance of dirt and moisture.
8. Raise the vehicle and remove two bolts attaching the front legs of the compressor to the mounting bracket.
9. Remove two screws attaching the heater water return tube to the underside of the engine supports.
10. Remove two bolts attaching the compressor bracket assembly to the compressor bracket.
11. Lower the vehicle and remove one bolt attaching the top of the compressor to the mounting bracket.
12. Tilt the top of the compressor toward the radiator to disengage the top mounting tab from the compressor bracket. Then, lift the compressor from the engine compartment, rear head first.
13. If the compressor is to be replaced, remove the clutch and field coil assembly and the compressor bracket assembly from the compressor.

To install:

14. Place the compressor into position.
15. Install the one bolt attaching the top of the compressor to the mounting bracket.
16. Raise and safely support the vehicle.
17. Install the two bolts attaching the compressor bracket assembly to the compressor bracket.

132 ENGINE AND ENGINE OVERHAUL

18. Install the two screws attaching the heater water return tube to the underside of the engine supports.
19. Install the two bolts attaching the front legs of the compressor to the mounting bracket.
20. Reconnect the discharge hose and the suction hose from the compressor manifolds.
21. Reconnect the compressor clutch wires at the field coil connector on the compressor.
22. Install the alternator to the engine.
23. Reconnect the alternator air tube to the air inlet on the radiator support.
24. Install the carburetor air cleaner and the air intake and tube assembly to the radiator support.
25. Reconnect the alternator wire at the multiple connector.
26. Installation is the reverse of the removal procedure. Leak test, evacuate and charge the system.

NOTE: *If the compressor is to be replaced, drain the oil from the removed compressor into a calibrated measuring container. Record the amount of oil (fluid ounces) drained from the old compressor, discard the oil. Check the system for proper operation.*

1984–90

1. Disconnect the alternator wires at the multiple connector and remove the alternator from the engine.
2. Discharge the air conditioning system and disconnect the compressor clutch wires at the field coil connector on the compressor.
3. On the EFI and HO engines, remove the discharge and suction hoses at the compressor manifolds.

NOTE: *The suction hose of the CFI engines has a tube "O" fitting and must be removed with the aid of a back-up wrench. On the EFI engines the suction hose has a spring lock coupling and a spring lock coupling tool or equivalent must be used.*

4. On the 1.6L Turbo and 2.0L Diesel engines, remove the discharge hose from the manifold tube with a $1/2$ in. lock coupling tool (#T81P-19623-G2 or equivalent). Use a $5/8$ in. spring lock coupling tool (#T83P-19632-C or equivalent) to remove the suction hose.
5. Remove the four retaining bolts attaching the compressor to the compressor bracket and remove the compressor from the engine compartment.
6. Installation is the reverse of the removal procedure. Leak test, evacuate and charge the system.

NOTE: *If the compressor is to be replaced, drain the oil from the removed compressor into a calibrated measuring container. Record the amount of oil (fluid ounces) drained from the old compressor, discard the oil. Check the system for proper operation.*

Tempo/Topaz

1. Discharge the system following the recommended service procedures in Chapter 1. Observe all safety precautions.
2. Disconnect the compressor clutch wires at the field coil connector on the compressor.
3. Disconnect the discharge hose and the suction hose from the compressor manifolds. Cap the refrigerant lines and compressor manifolds to prevent the entrance of dirt and moisture.
4. Separate the discharge refrigerant line at the spring lock coupling above the compressor with Tool T81P-19623-G or equivalent and remove the lower end of the discharge line.
5. On the 2.3L EFI engine, remove the suc-

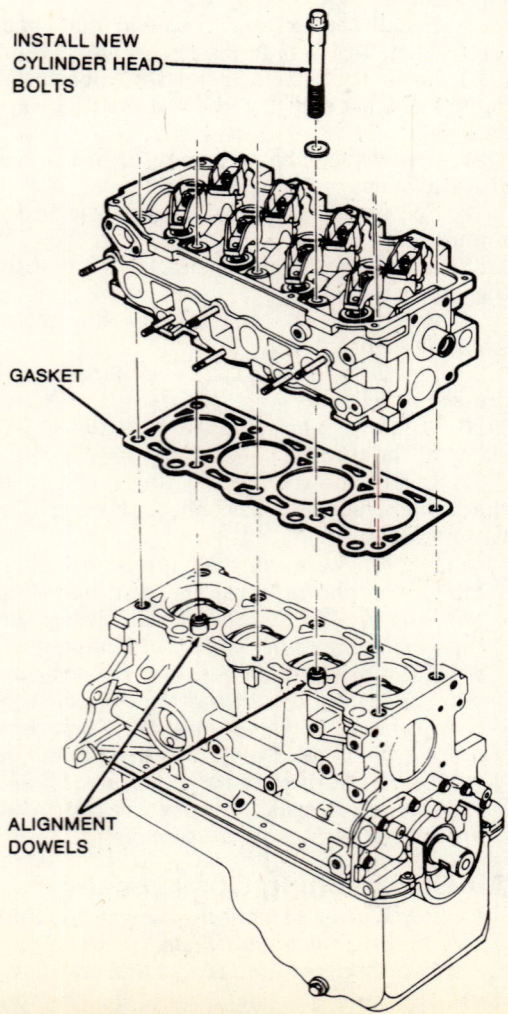

1.9L cylinder head installation

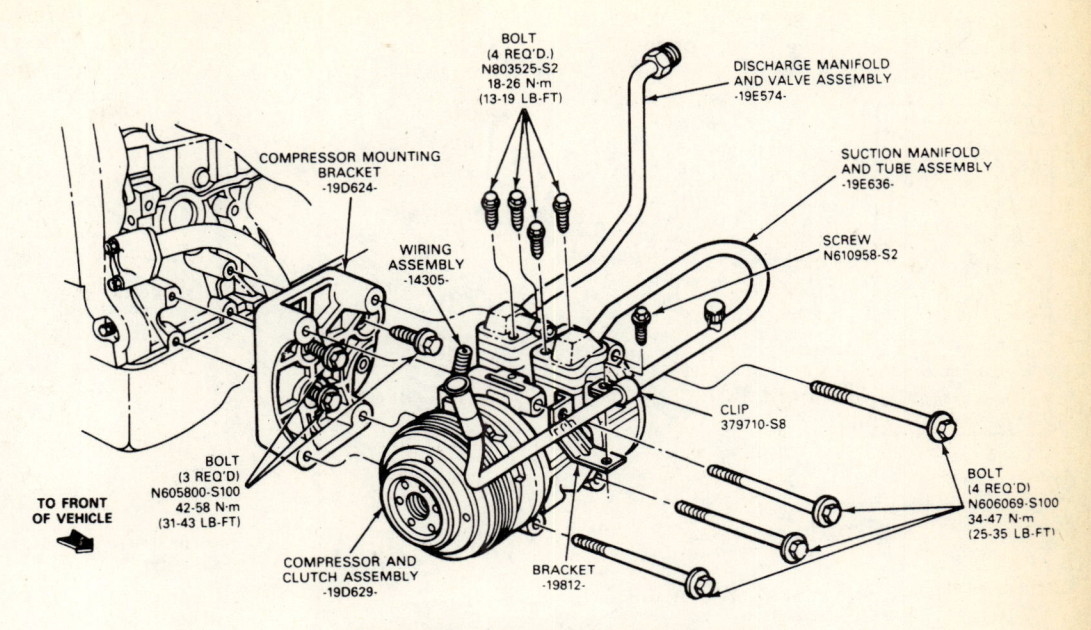

ENGINE AND ENGINE OVERHAUL

Escort/Lynx compressor mounting-typical

tion line from the suction manifold using a back-up wrench on each fitting.

6. Loosen the two idler attaching screws and release the compressor belt tension.

7. Raise the vehicle and remove the four bolts attaching the front legs of the compressor to the mounting bracket.

8. Remove two screws attaching the heater water return tube to the underside of the engine supports.

9. Move the compressor to the left and remove the compressor from the underside of the vehicle.

10. If the compressor is to be replaced, remove the clutch and field coil assembly from the compressor.

To install:

11. Place the compressor into position. Install the 2 screws attaching the heater water return tube to the underside of the engine supports.

12. Install the 4 bolts attaching the front legs of the compressor to the mounting bracket. Lower the vehicle.

13. Install the compressor belt and tighten the 2 idler attaching screws.

14. On the 2.3L EFI engine, install the suction line to the suction manifold using a back-up wrench on each fitting. Use a new O-rings lubricated with clean refrigerant oil.

15. Reconnect the discharge refrigerant line at the spring lock coupling above the compressor on the lower end of the discharge line. Use new O-rings lubricated with clean refrigerant oil.

16. Reconnect the discharge hose and the suction hose to the compressor manifolds.

17. Reconnect the compressor clutch wires at the field coil connector on the compressor.

18. Leak test, evacuate and charge the system.

NOTE: *If the compressor is to be replaced, drain the oil from the removed compressor into a calibrated measuring container. Record the amount of oil (fluid ounces) drained from the old compressor, discard the oil. Check the system for proper operation.*

Radiator

REMOVAL AND INSTALLATION

1. Remove the negative battery cable.

2. Drain coolant from cooling system. Retain coolant in a suitable container for reuse.

CAUTION: *When draining the coolant, keep in mind that cats and dogs are attracted by the ethylene glycol antifreeze, and are quite likely to drink any that is left in an uncovered container or in puddles on the ground. This will prove fatal in sufficient quantity. Always drain the coolant into a sealable container. Coolant should be reused unless it is contaminated or several years old.*

3. On the Escort, remove air intake tube from radiator support.

4. Remove upper hose from radiator.

5. Remove 2 fasteners retaining upper end

134 ENGINE AND ENGINE OVERHAUL

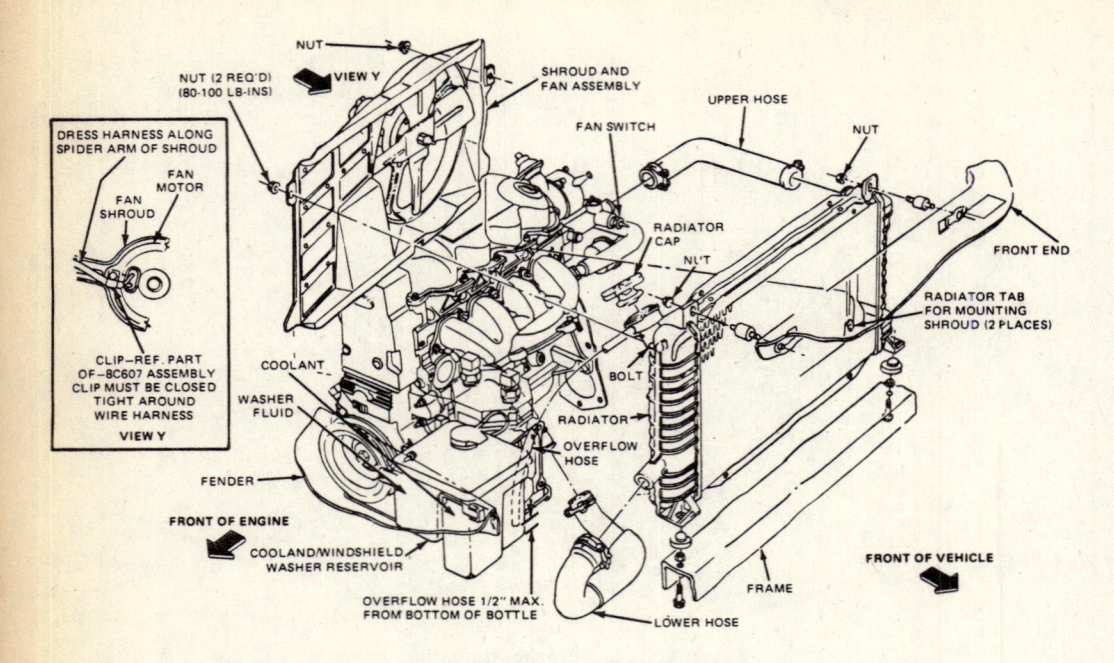

Typical engine cooling system components

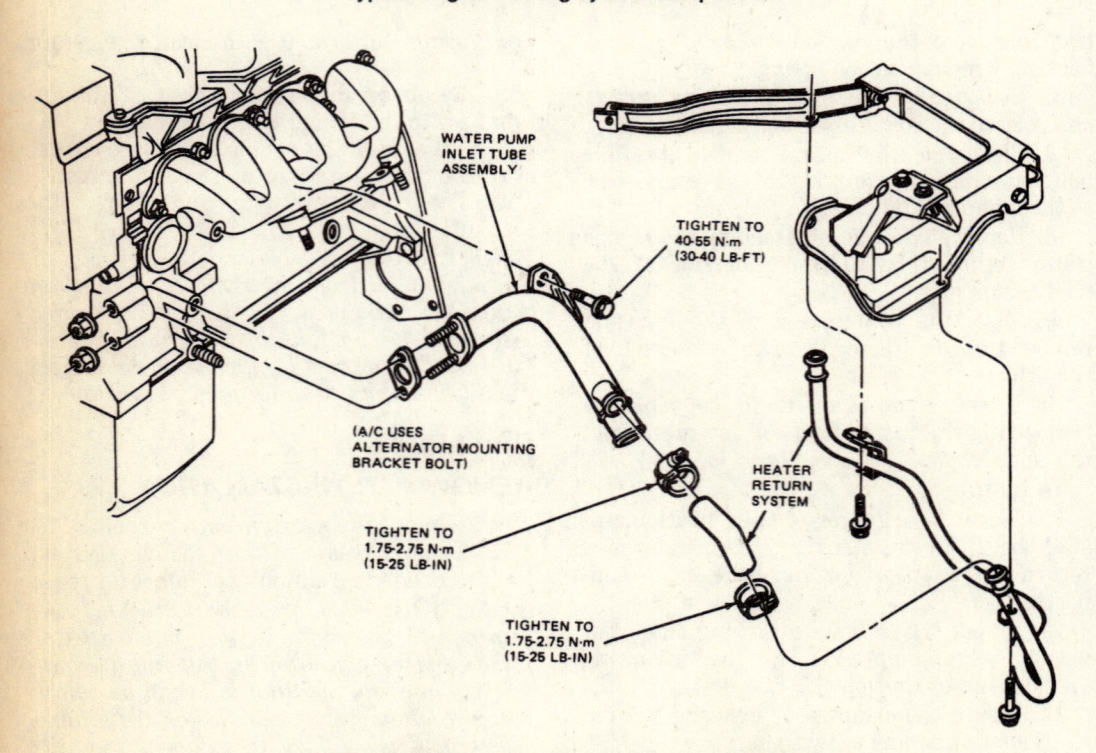

Typical water inlet system, car shown non-air conditioned

ENGINE AND ENGINE OVERHAUL 135

of fan shroud to radiator, and sight shield.
NOTE: *If equipped with air conditioning, remove nut and screw retaining upper end of fan shroud to radiator at cross support, and nut and screw at inlet end of tank.*

6. Disconnect electric cooling fan motor wires and air conditioning discharge line, if so equipped, from shroud and remove fan shroud from vehicle.
7. Loosen hose clamp and disconnect radiator lower hose from radiator.
8. Disconnect overflow hose from radiator filler neck.
9. If vehicle is equipped with an automatic transaxle, disconnect oil cooler hoses at transaxle using a quick-disconnect tool. Cap oil tubes and plug oil cooler hoses.
10. Remove 2 nuts retaining top of radiator to radiator support. If stud loosens, ensure it is tightened before radiator is installed. Tilt the top of radiator rearward to allow clearance with upper mounting stud and lift radiator from vehicle. Ensure mounts do not stick to radiator lower mounting brackets.

To install:
11. Ensure that lower radiator mounts are installed over the bolts on the radiator support.
12. Position radiator to radiator support making sure that radiator lower brackets are positioned properly on lower mounts.
13. Position top of radiator to mounting studs on radiator support and install 2 retaining nuts. Tighten to 5–7 ft. lbs. (7–9.5 Nm).
14. Connect radiator lower hose to engine water pump inlet tube. Install constant tension hose clamp between alignment marks on the hose.
15. Check to ensure radiator lower hose is properly positioned on outlet tank and install constant tension hose clamp. The stripe on lower hose should be indexed with rib on tank outlet.
16. Connect oil cooler hoses to automatic transaxle oil cooler lines, if so equipped. Use an appropriate oil resistant sealer.
17. Position fan shroud to radiator lower mounting bosses. On vehicles with air conditioning, insert lower edge of shroud into clip at lower center of radiator. Install 2 nuts and bolts retaining upper end of fan shroud to radiator. Tighten nuts on Tempo/Topaz to 35–41 inch lbs. (3.9–4.6 Nm). On Escort, tighten nut to 23–33 inch lbs. (2.6–3.7 Nm). Do not over tighten.
18. Connect electric cooling fan motor wires to wire harness.
19. Connect upper hose to radiator inlet tank fitting and install constant tension hose clamp.
20. Connect overflow hose to nipple just below radiator filler neck.
21. Install air intake tube or sight shield.
22. Connect negative battery cable.
23. Refill cooling system. Start engine and allow to come to normal operating temperature. Check for leaks. Confirm operation of electric cooling fan.

Air Conditioning Condenser

NOTE: *When removing the air conditioning condenser from your vehicle, it will be necessary to discharge and evacuate the refrigerant from the air conditioning system and also it will be necessary to replace the suction accumulator/drier due to contamination once the refrigerant system is opened to the atmosphere. This is a procedure that should be performed by an authorized technician due to the dangers involved with handling R-12 refrigerant. When ever working around R-12 refrigerant, it is recommended that gloves and goggles be worn at all times. If a condenser leak is suspected, the condenser must be leak tested before it is removed from the vehicle.*

REMOVAL AND INSTALLATION

Escort/EXP and Lynx/LN7

1. Discharge the system following the recommended service procedures in Chapter 1. Observe all safety precautions.
2. Disconnect the negative battery cable. Drain the engine coolant from the cooling system.

CAUTION: *When draining the coolant, keep in mind that cats and dogs are attracted by the ethylene glycol antifreeze, and are quite likely to drink any that is left in an uncovered container or in puddles on the ground. This will prove fatal in sufficient quantity. Always drain the coolant into a sealable container. Coolant should be reused unless it is contaminated or several years old.*

3. Remove the carburetor air intake tube and alternator air tube from the radiator support, if so equipped. Remove the ignition coil from the engine, if necessary.
4. Remove 1 screw and 1 nut retaining the fan shroud to the radiator.
5. Disconnect the fan motor wires and remove the fan shroud.
6. Disconnect the upper radiator hose from the radiator. Disconnect the lower radiator hose from the engine water tube.
7. Disconnect and cap the transmission oil cooler lines from the oil tubes on the transmission, if so equipped.
8. Remove the 2 nuts attaching the radiator

ENGINE AND ENGINE OVERHAUL

to the radiator support. Remove the radiator and lower hose as an assembly.

9. Disconnect the liquid line and compressor discharge line from the condenser. If the lines are equipped with spring locks, it will be necessary to use a spring lock coupler removal tool or equivalent.

10. Remove the condenser upper bracket attaching screws and remove the condenser from the vehicle.

To install:

11. Position the condenser on the lower mounts. Move the top of the condenser forward and push the condenser into the radiator opening. Install the upper mounting brackets.

12. Use special new O-rings (#E1ZZ-19B596-A or E35Y-19D690-A) lubricated with clean refrigerant oil, connect the liquid line and the compressor discharge line to condenser.

13. Position the radiator to the radiator support. Be sure that the bottom of the radiator is engaged with the lower studs of the radiator support.

14. Install the 2 nuts to attach the top of the radiator to the radiator support.

15. Connect the lower radiator hose to the engine water tube. Connect the oil cooler hoses to the transmission oil cooler lines.

16. Position the fan shroud to the radiator. Install the 1 retaining nut and 1 attaching screw.

17. Connect the radiator fan motor wires. Connect the upper radiator hose.

18. Install the ignition coil to the engine.

Refill the cooling system and reconnect the negative battery cable.

19. Leak test, evacuate and charge the refrigerant system.

Water Pump

REMOVAL AND INSTALLATION

1.3L, 1.6L and 1.9L Engine

1. Disconnect the negative battery cable. Drain the cooling system.

CAUTION: *When draining the coolant, keep in mind that cats and dogs are attracted by the ethylene glycol antifreeze, and are quite likely to drink any that is left in an uncovered container or in puddles on the ground. This will prove fatal in sufficient quantity. Always drain the coolant into a sealable container. Coolant should be reused unless it is contaminated or several years old.*

2. Remove the alternator drive belt. If equipped with air conditioning or power steering, remove the drive belts.

3. Use a wrench on the crankshaft pulley to rotate the engine so No. 1 piston is on TDC of the compression stroke.

CAUTION: *Turn the engine only in the direction of normal rotation. Backward rotation will cause the camshaft belt to slip or lose teeth.*

4. Remove the cam belt cover.

5. Loosen the bolt tensioner attaching bolts, then secure the tensioner over as far as possible.

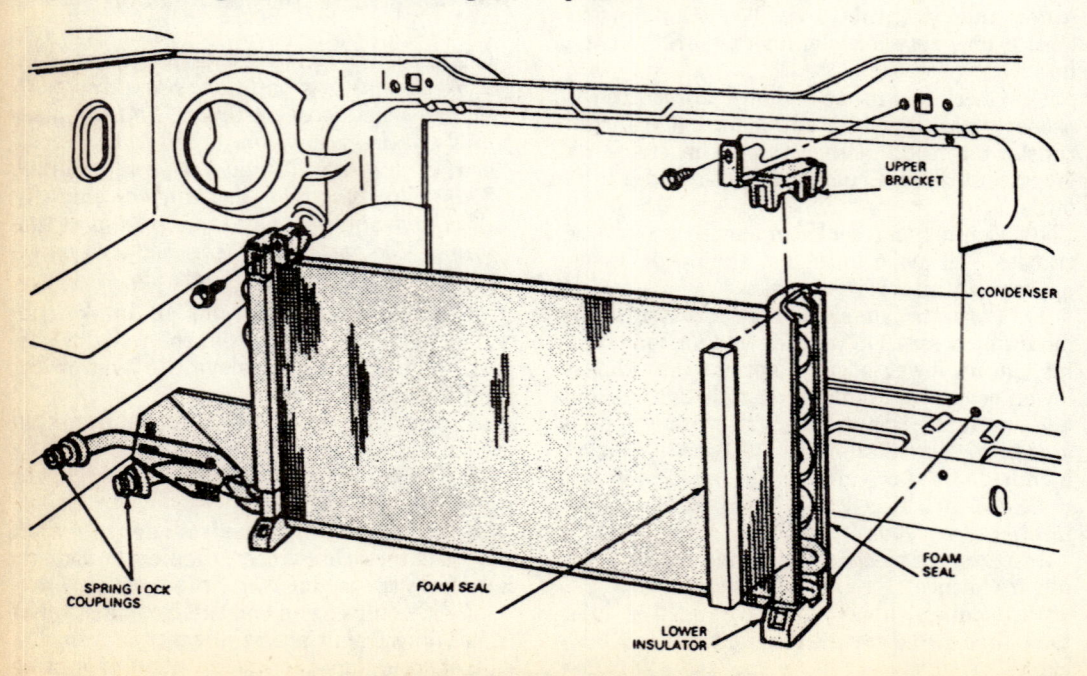

A/C condenser removal and installation

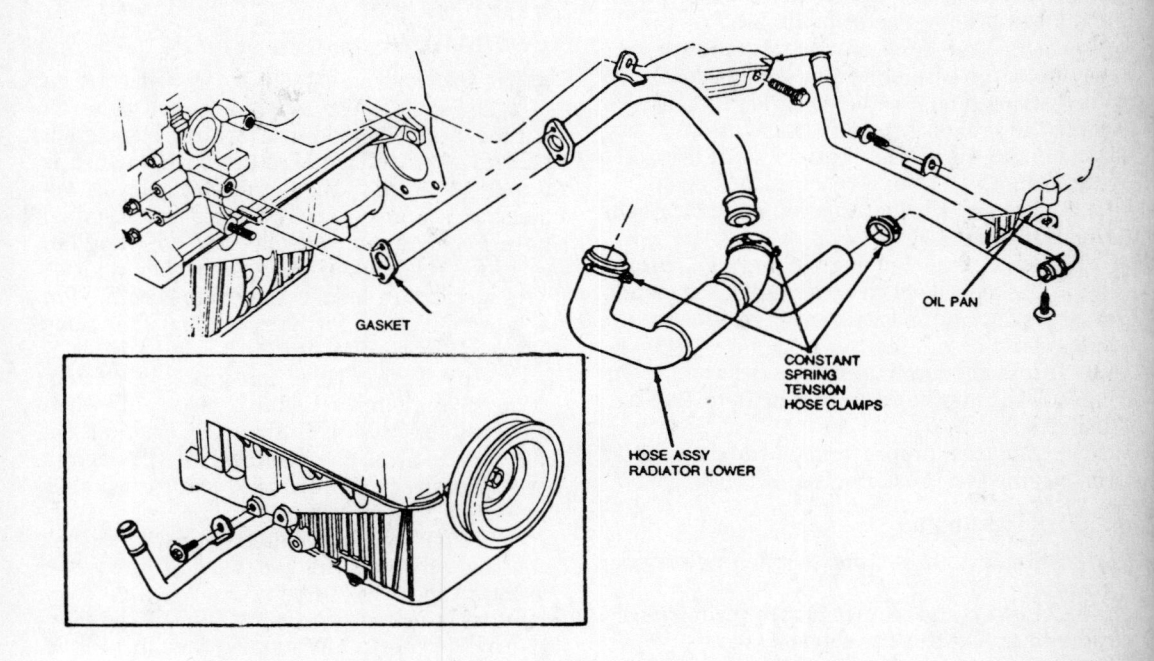

ENGINE AND ENGINE OVERHAUL   137

Water pump inlet tubes and fasteners - 1.9L engine

6. Pull the bolt from the camshaft, tensioner, and water pump sprocket. Do not remove it from, or allow it to change its position on, the crankshaft sprocket.

NOTE: *Do not rotate the engine with the camshaft belt removed.*

7. Remove the camshaft sprocket.
8. Remove the rear timing cover stud. Remove the heater return tube hose connection at the water pump inlet tube.
9. Remove the water pump inlet tube fasteners and the inlet tube and gasket.
10. Remove the water pump to the cylinder block bolts and remove the water pump and its gasket.

To install:
11. To install, make sure the mating surfaces on the pump and the block are clean.
12. Using a new gasket and sealer, install the water pump and tighten the bolts to 5–7 ft. lbs. on models through 1982, 1983–88 – 30–40 ft. lbs. and 1989–90 6–9 ft. lbs. Make sure the pump impeller turns freely.
13. Install the water pump inlet tube and the inlet tube gasket and fasteners.
14. Install the rear timing cover stud. Install the heater return tube hose connection at the water pump inlet tube.
15. Install the camshaft sprocket.
16. Install the bolt from the camshaft, tensioner, and water pump sprocket.

NOTE: *Do not rotate the engine with the camshaft belt removed.*
17. Tighten the bolt tensioner attaching bolts, then secure the tensioner over as far as possible.
18. Install the cam belt cover.
19. Install the alternator drive belt. If equipped with air conditioning or power steering, install the drive belts.
20. Refill the cooling system and reconnect the negative battery cable.

NOTE: *Always use new gaskets and sealer. Install the camshaft sprocket over the cam key. See below the procedure. Install new timing belt and adjust tension. See Timing Belt Removal and Installation for procedure.*

2.3L HSC Engine

1. Disconnect the negative battery cable. Drain the cooling system.

CAUTION: *When draining the coolant, keep in mind that cats and dogs are attracted by the ethylene glycol antifreeze, and are quite likely to drink any that is left in an uncovered container or in puddles on the ground. This will prove fatal in sufficient quantity. Always drain the coolant into a sealable container. Coolant should be reused unless it is contaminated or several years old.*

2. Loosen the Thermactor pump mounting and remove the drive belt. Disconnect and

ENGINE AND ENGINE OVERHAUL

remove the hose clamp below the pump. Remove the Thermactor pump bracket mounting bolts and remove the Thermactor and bracket as an assembly, if so equipped.

3. Loosen the water pump drive belt idler pulley and remove the drive belt.

4. Disconnect the heater hose from the water pump.

5. Remove the water pump mounting bolts and the pump.

6. Clean the engine mounting surface. Apply gasket cement to both sides of the mounting gasket and position the gasket on the engine.

7. Install the pump in reverse order of removal. Torque the mounting bolts to 15–22 ft. lbs.

8. Add the proper coolant mixture, start the engine and check for leaks.

2.0L Diesel Engine

1. Remove the front timing belt upper cover.

2. Loosen and remove the front timing belt, refer to timing belt in-vehicle services.

3. Drain the cooling system.

CAUTION: *When draining the coolant, keep in mind that cats and dogs are attracted by the ethylene glycol antifreeze, and are quite likely to drink any that is left in an uncovered container or in puddles on the ground. This will prove fatal in sufficient quantity. Always drain the coolant into a sealable container. Coolant should be reused unless it is contaminated or several years old.*

4. Raise the vehicle and support safely on jackstands.

5. Disconnect the lower radiator hose and heater hose from the water pump.

6. Disconnect the coolant tube from the thermostat housing and discard gasket.

7. Remove the three bolts attaching the water pump to the crankcase. Remove the water pump. Discard gasket.

To install:

8. Clean the water pump and crankshaft gasket mating surfaces.

9. Install the water pump, using a new gasket. Tighten bolts to 23–34 ft. lbs.

10. Connect the coolant tube from the thermostat housing to the water pump using a new gasket. Tighten bolts to 5–7 ft. lbs.

11. Connect the heater hose and lower radiator hose to the water pump.

12. Lower vehicle.

13. Fill and bleed the cooling system.

14. Install and adjust the front timing belt.

15. Run the engine and check for coolant leaks.

16. Install the front timing belt upper cover.

Electric Fan

OPERATION

The electro-drive cooling fan system consists of a fan and electric motor attached to a fan shroud located behind the radiator. The system utilizes a coolant temperature switch which is usually mounted in the thermostat housing. Vehicles that are equipped with air conditioning, have a cooling fan controller and a cooling fan relay for the cooling fan system. On vehicles with a standard heater, the engine cooling fan is powered through the cooling fan relay (Tempo/Topaz only).

On the Tempo/Topaz models, the electro-drive cooling fan is wired to operate only when the ignition switch is in the RUN position. On all other models, the cooling fan will operate whenever the cooling fan temperature switch is closed.

A thermal switch mounted in the thermostat housing activates the fan when the coolant reaches a specified temperature. When the temperature is approximately 210°F (85°C) the thermal switch closes thus starting the fan.

The electric fan also operates when the air conditioner (if equipped) is turned on. When the temperature drops to between 185–193°F (85–90°C) the thermal switch opens and the fan shuts off.

CAUTION: *Since the fan is governed by temperature the engine does not have to be* **ON** *for the fan to operate. If any underhood operations must be performed on a warm engine, disconnect the wiring harness to the fan.*

Various Relays

TEMPO AND TOPAZ

Cooling Fan Controller—located behind the left side of the instrument panel or

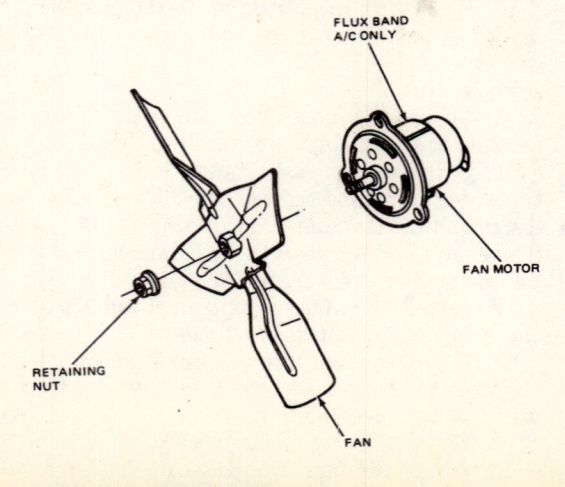

Cooling fan and electric motor

ENGINE AND ENGINE OVERHAUL 139

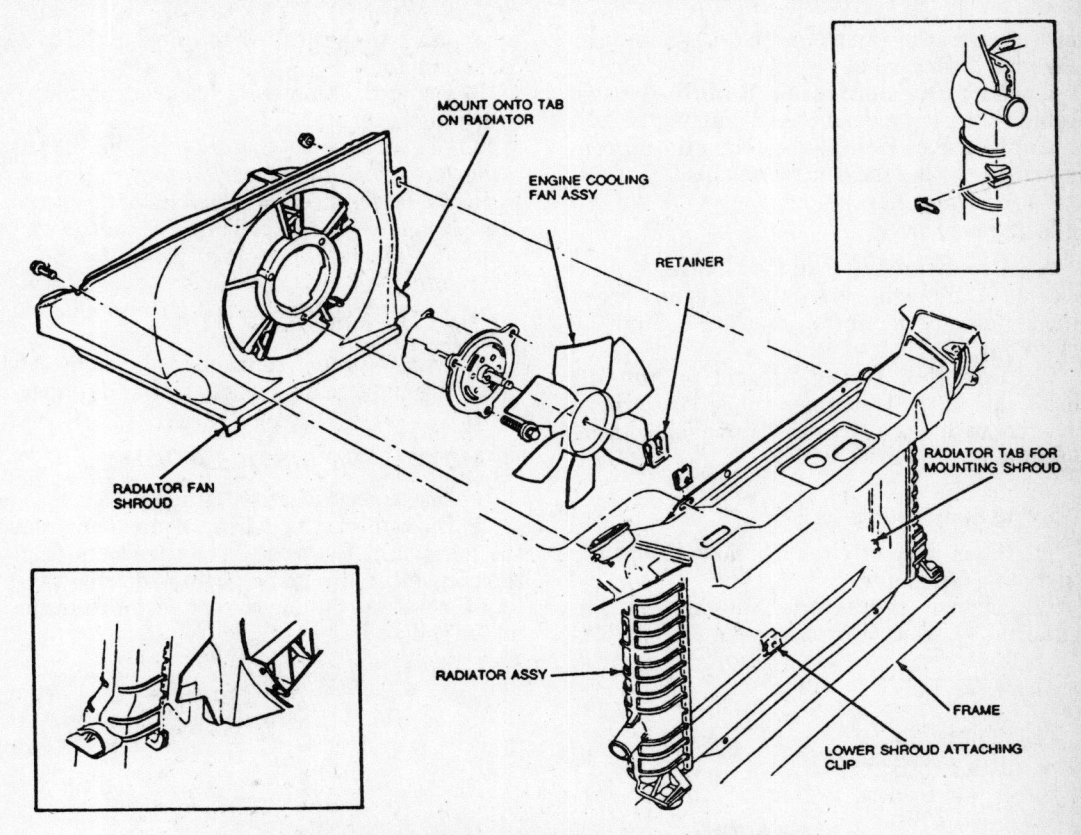

Electric fan removal and installation - Tempo/Topaz

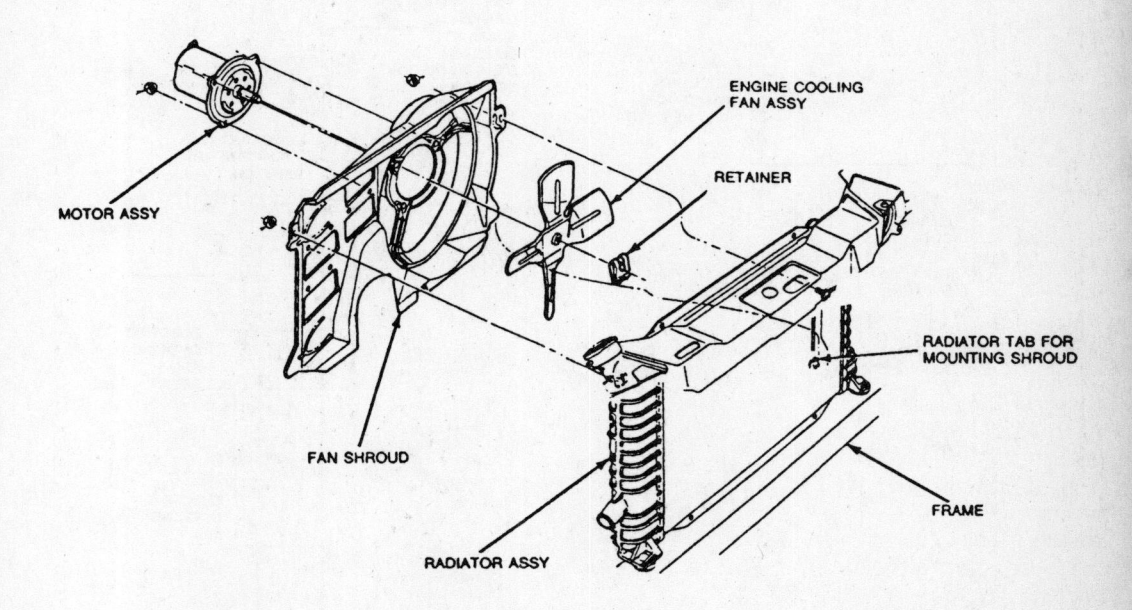

Electric fan removal and installation - Escort/EXP/Lynx

ENGINE AND ENGINE OVERHAUL

mounted on the right hand cowl panel under the instrument panel.

Cooling Fan Controller Module – located behind the right side of the instrument panel.

Cooling Fan Relay – located in the air conditioning cooling fan control module.

ESCORT AND LYNX

Air Conditioning Fan Controller – located on the right side of the dash, forward of the evaporator mounting bracket, behind the glove box.

Cooling Fan Relay – located on the left hand side of the instrument panel or could be incorporated in the air conditioning fan controller unit.

Cooling Fan Testing

1. Check fuse or circuit breaker for power to cooling fan motor.
2. Remove connector(s) at cooling fan motor(s). Connect jumper wire and apply battery voltage to the positive terminal of the cooling fan motor.
3. Using an ohmmeter, check for continuity in cooling fan motor.

NOTE: *Remove the cooling fan connector at the fan motor before performing continuity checks. Perform continuity check of the motor windings only. The cooling fan control circuit is connected electrically to the ECM through the cooling fan relay center. Ohmmeter battery voltage must NOT be applied to the ECM.*

4. Ensure proper continuity of cooling fan motor ground circuit at chassis ground connector.

REMOVAL AND INSTALLATION

1. Disconnect negative battery cable.
2. Disconnect the wiring connector from the fan motor. Disconnect the wire loom from the clip on the shroud by pushing down on the lock fingers and pulling the connector from the motor end.

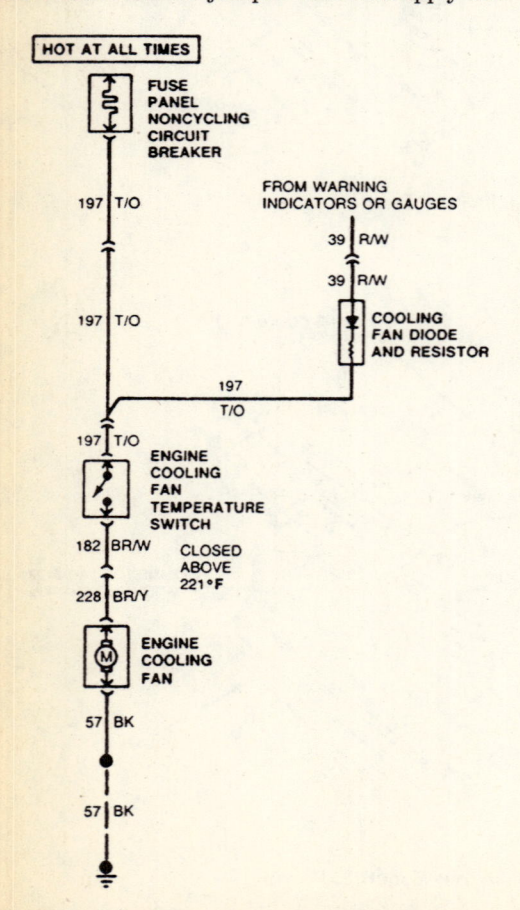

Electrical schematic of the electric cooling fan Escort without A/C

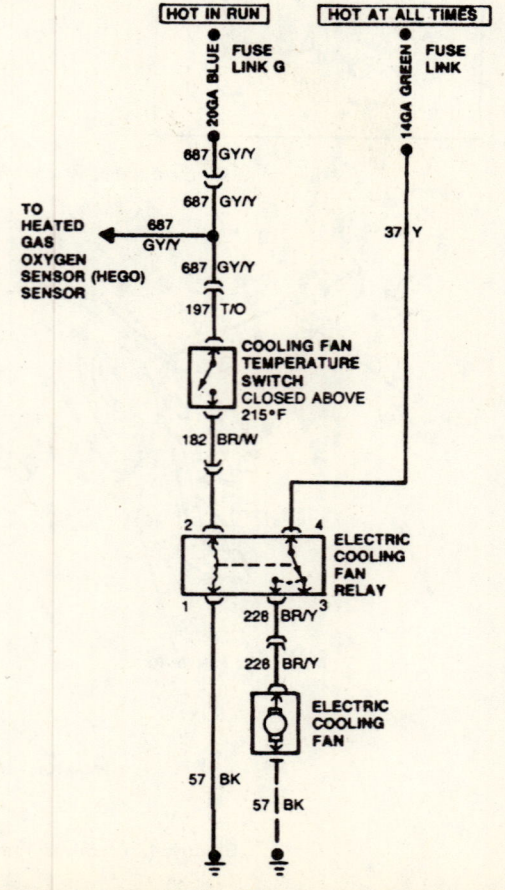

Electrical schematic of the electric cooling fan Tempo/Topaz without A/C

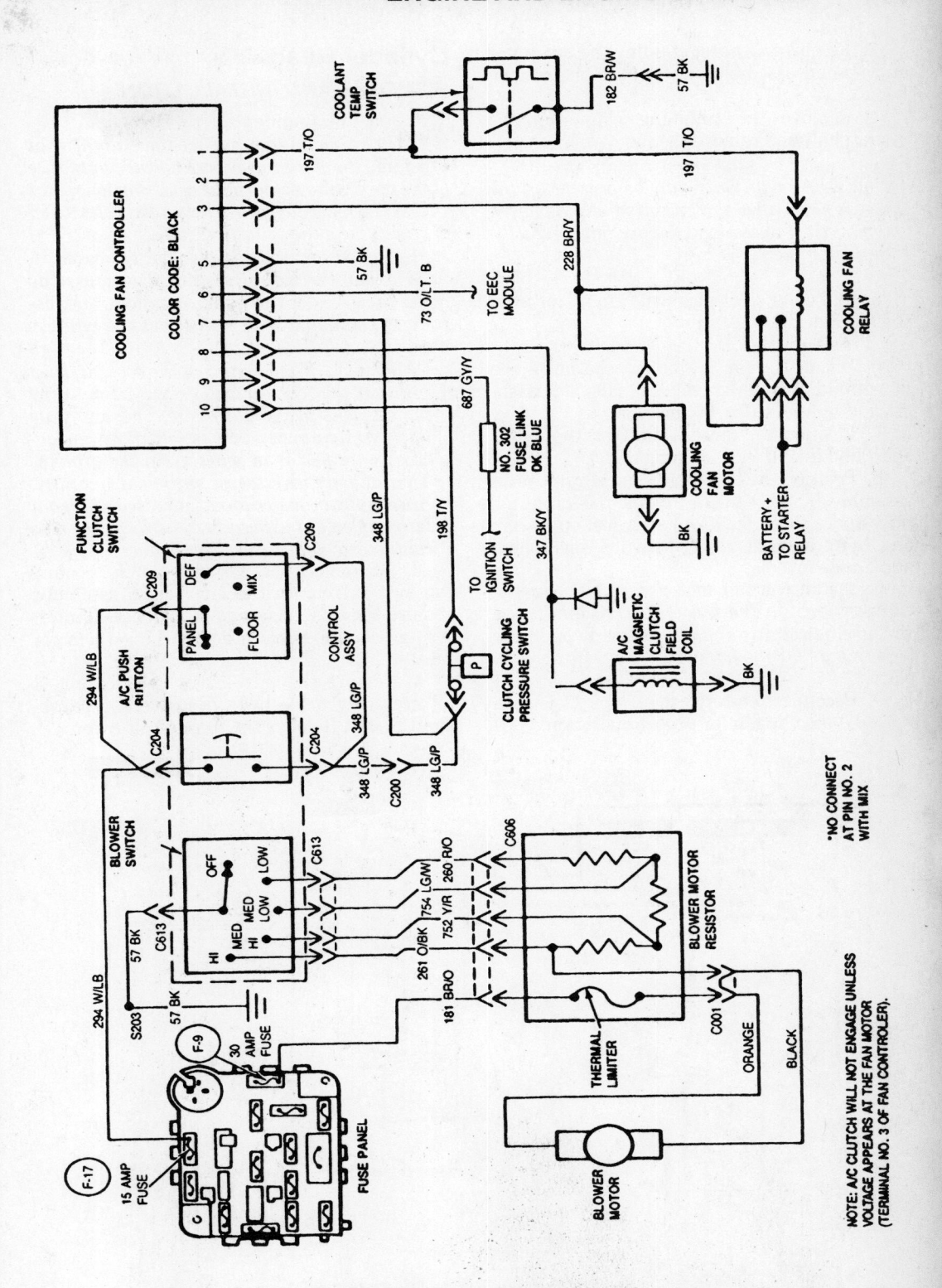

ENGINE AND ENGINE OVERHAUL

Electrical schematic of the electric cooling fan Escort with A/C

ENGINE AND ENGINE OVERHAUL

3. Remove the nuts retaining the fan motor and shroud assembly and remove the component.
4. Remove the retaining clip from the motor shaft and remove the fan.

NOTE: *A metal burr may be present on the motor shaft after the retaining clip has been removed. If necessary, remove burr to facilitate fan removal.*

5. Unbolt and withdraw the fan motor from the shroud.

To install:

6. Install the fan motor in position in the fan shroud. Install the retaining nuts and washers and tighten to 44–66 inch lbs.
7. Position the fan assembly on the motor shaft and install the retaining clip.
8. Position the fan, motor and shroud as an assembly in the vehicle. Install the retaining nuts and tighten to 35–45 inch lbs. on Escort and Lynx models; 23–33 inch lbs. on Tempo and Topaz models.
9. Install the fan motor wire loom in the clip provided on the fan shroud. Connect the wiring connector to the fan motor. Be sure the lock fingers on the connector snap firmly into place.
10. Reconnect battery cable.
11. Check the fan for proper operation.

Cylinder Head

REMOVAL AND INSTALLATION

1.3L and 1.6L Engines

NOTE: *The engine must be overnight cold before removing the cylinder head, to reduce the possibility of warpage or distortion.*

CAUTION: *Always use new head bolts when reinstalling the cylinder head.*

1. Disconnect the negative battery cable.
2. Drain the cooling system, disconnect the heater hose under the intake manifold, and disconnect the radiator upper hose at the cylinder head.

CAUTION: *When draining the coolant, keep in mind that cats and dogs are attracted by the ethylene glycol antifreeze, and are quite likely to drink any that is left in an uncovered container or in puddles on the ground. This will prove fatal in sufficient quantity. Always drain the coolant into a sealable container. Coolant should be reused unless it is contaminated or several years old.*

3. Disconnect the wiring from the cooling fan switch, remove the air cleaner assembly, remove the PCV hose, and disconnect all interfering vacuum hoses after marking them for reassembly.
4. Remove the valve cover and disconnect all accessory drive belts. Remove the crankshaft pulley. Remove the timing belt cover.

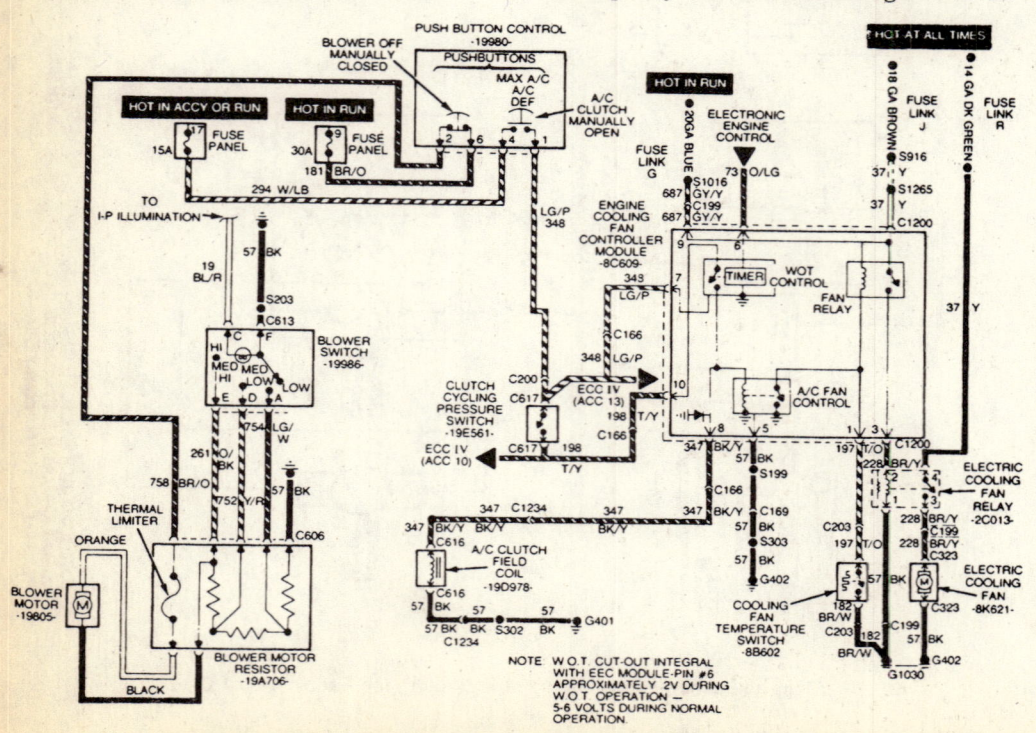

Electrical schematic of the electric cooling fan Tempo/Topaz with A/C

ENGINE AND ENGINE OVERHAUL

5. Set the No.1 cylinder to top dead center compression stroke. See distributor removal and installation procedure for details.
6. Remove the distributor cap and spark plug wires as an assembly.
7. Loosen both belt tensioner attaching bolts using special Ford tool T81P-6254-A or the equivalent. Secure the belt tensioner as far left as possible. Remove the timing belt and discard.

NOTE: *Once the tension on the timing belt has been released, the belt cannot be used again.*

8. Disconnect the tube at the EGR valve, then remove the PVS hose connectors using tool T81P-8564-A or equivalent. Label the connectors and set aside.
9. Disconnect the choke wire, the fuel supply and return lines, the accelerator cable and speed control cable (if equipped). Disconnect the altitude compensator, if equipped, from the dash panel and place on the heater/air conditioner air intake.

NOTE: *Use caution not to damage the compensator.*

10. Disconnect and remove the alternator.
11. If equipped with power steering, remove the Thermactor pump drive belt, the pump and its bracket. If equipped with a turbocharger, refer to the previous section for removal procedure. Refer to the Fuel Injection section for pressure discharge and removal instructions.
12. Raise the vehicle and disconnect the exhaust pipe from the manifold.
13. Lower the vehicle and remove the cylinder head bolts and washers. Discard the bolts, they cannot be used again.
14. Remove the cylinder head with the manifolds attached. Remove and discard the head gasket. Do not place the cylinder head with combustion chambers down or damage to the spark plugs or gasket surfaces may result.

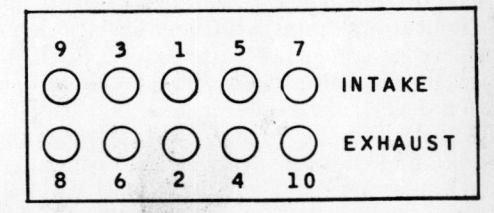

To install:

15. To install, clean all gasket material from both the block face and the cylinder head, then rotate the crankshaft so that the No.1 piston is 90° BTDC. In this position, the crankshaft pulley keyway is at 9 o'clock.
16. Turn the camshaft so its keyway is at 6 o'clock. When installing the timing belt, turn

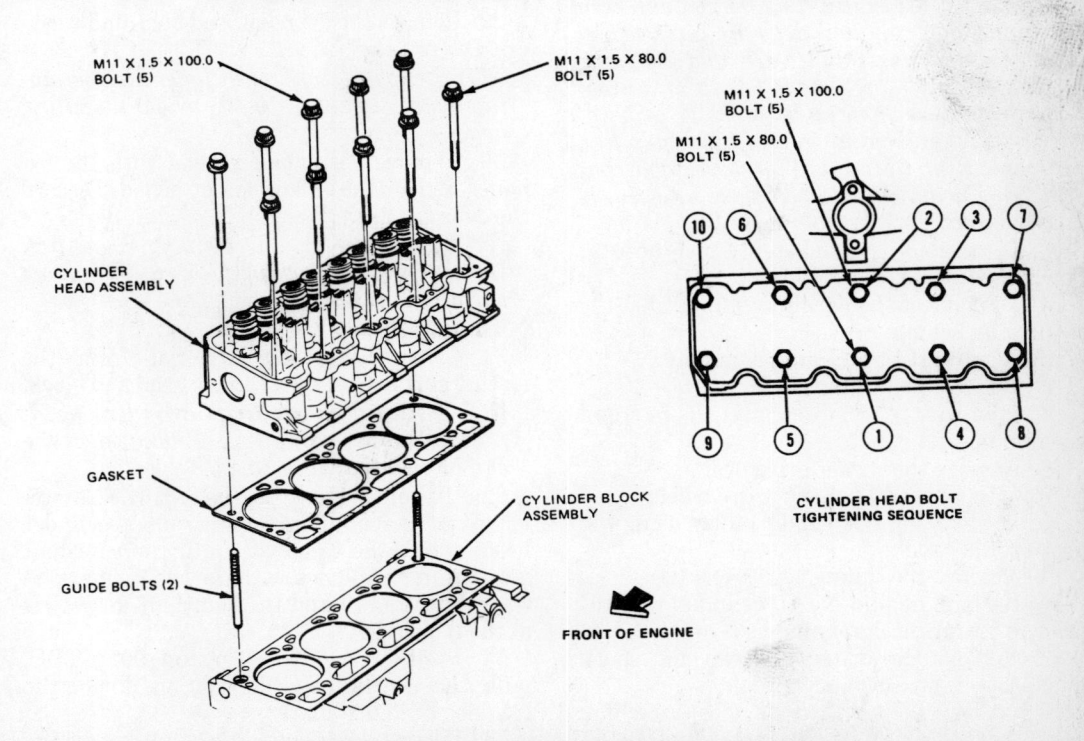

Tightening sequence for the 1.6L, 1.9L cylinder head

Torque sequence, cylinder head installation-2.3L HSC

ENGINE AND ENGINE OVERHAUL

the crankshaft keyway back to 12 o'clock but do not turn the camshaft from its 6 o'clock position. The crankshaft is turned 90° BTDC to prevent the valves from hitting the pistons when the cylinder head is installed.

17. Position the cylinder head gasket on the block and install the cylinder head using new bolts and washers. Tighten the bolts to 44 ft. lbs. in the sequence shown, then back off 2 turns and retighten to 44 ft. lbs. After tightening, turn the bolts an additional 90° in the same sequence. Complete the bolt tightening by turning an additional 90° in the same sequence.

18. Remaining installation is the reverse of removal. See Timing Belt Removal and Installation for timing belt installation procedures. Fill the cooling system only with Ford Cooling System Fluid, Prestone® II or the equivalent. Using the wrong type of coolant can damage the engine.

1.9L Engine

NOTE: *The engine must be cold before removing the cylinder head, to reduce the possibility of warpage or distortion.*

1. Disconnect the negative battery cable. Properly relieve the fuel system pressure.
2. Drain the cooling system and disconnect the heater hose at the fitting located under the intake manifold.

CAUTION: *When draining the coolant, keep in mind that cats and dogs are attracted by the ethylene glycol antifreeze, and are quite likely to drink any that is left in an uncovered container or in puddles on the ground. This will prove fatal in sufficient quantity. Always drain the coolant into a sealable container. Coolant should be reused unless it is contaminated or several years old.*

3. Disconnect the radiator upper hose at the cylinder head.
4. Disconnect the wiring terminal from the cooling fan switch.
5. Remove the air cleaner assembly.
6. Remove the PCV hose.
7. Identify, tag and disconnect the required vacuum hoses.
8. Remove the rocker arm cover.
9. Disconnect all accessory drive belts.
10. Remove the crankshaft pulley using the proper puller tool.
11. Remove the timing belt cover.
12. Set the engine No. 1 cylinder to TDC prior to removing the timing belt.
13. Remove the distributor cap and spark plug wires as an assembly.
14. Loosen both belt tensioner attaching bolts using torque wrench adapter tool T81P-6254-A or equivalent.
15. Secure the belt tensioner as far left as possible.
16. Remove the timing belt.
17. Disconnect the EGR tube at the EGR valve.
18. Disconnect the PVS hose connectors, as required, using tool T81P-8564-A or equivalent. Label the connectors and set aside.
19. Disconnect the choke cap wire.
20. Disconnect the fuel supply and return lines at the metal connectors, located on the right side of the engine, set rubber lines aside.
21. Disconnect the accelerator cable and, if equipped, the speed control cable.
22. Disconnect the altitude compensator, if equipped from the dash panel and place on the heater/air conditioner air intake.

NOTE: *Caution should be taken not to damage the altitude compensator.*

23. Disconnect the alternator air intake tube, if equipped, and the alternator wiring harness.
24. Remove the alternator and its mounting bracket.
25. If equipped with power steering, remove the Thermactor pump drive belt, the pump and the pump mounting bracket.
26. Raise and safely support the vehicle.
27. Disconnect the exhaust system at the exhaust pipe.
28. Lower the vehicle.
29. Remove the cylinder head bolts and washers. Discard the bolts.

NOTE: *Do not reuse the cylinder head retaining bolts. Use new bolts when installing head.*

30. Remove the cylinder head with the exhaust and intake manifolds attached. Discard the cylinder head gasket.

NOTE: *Do not lay the cylinder head flat. Damage to the spark plug or gasket contact surfaces may result.*

To install:

31. Clean all gasket material from the mating surfaces on the cylinder head and block.

NOTE: *Before installing cylinder head, check piston squish height. Procedure at the end of installation section.*

32. If the camshaft has been turned or removed or if installing a replacement cylinder head, rotate the camshaft until the camshaft gear pointer is aligned with the timing mark on the cylinder head and the camshaft keyway is at the 6 o'clock.
33. Position the No. 1 piston 90° BTDC, pulley keyway at 9 o'clock position, during the cylinder head installation.
34. Position the cylinder head gasket on the cylinder block.

ENGINE AND ENGINE OVERHAUL

35. Install the cylinder head and install new bolts and washers in the following order:
   a. Apply a light coat of engine oil to the threads of the new cylinder head bolts and install the new bolts into the head.
   b. Torque the cylinder head bolts in sequence to 44 ft. lbs. (60 Nm).
   c. Loosen the cylinder head bolts approximately 2 turns and then torque again to 44 ft. lbs. (60 Nm) using the same torque sequence.
   d. After setting the torque again, turn the head bolts 90° in sequence and to complete the head bolt installation, turn the head bolts an additional 90° in the same torque sequence.
   NOTE: *The cylinder head attaching bolts cannot be tightened to the specified torque more than once and must therefore be replaced when installing a cylinder head.*
36. Raise and safely support the vehicle.
37. Connect the exhaust system at the exhaust pipe.
38. Lower the vehicle.
39. Install the Thermactor pump mounting bracket, pump and drive belt, if removed.
40. Install the alternator mounting bracket and the alternator. Connect the alternator wiring harness and alternator air intake tube.
41. Connect the altitude compensator, if equipped.
42. Connect the accelerator cable and, if equipped, the speed control cable.
43. Connect the fuel supply and return lines at the metal connector, located on the right side of the engine.
44. Connect the choke cap wire. Connect the EGR tube to the EGR valve.
45. Rotate the crankshaft to bring No. 1 piston to TDC on its compression stroke. The crankshaft keyway should then be at the 12 o'clock position. The distributor rotor should be pointing toward the No. 1 spark plug firing position. Install the timing belt, the timing belt cover and the crankshaft pulley.
46. Install the distributor cap and spark plug wires.
47. Apply a thin bead of sealer to the valve cover flange.
48. Tighten the attaching bolts to 6–8 ft. lbs.
49. Connect the required vacuum hoses.
50. Connect the wiring terminal to the cooling fan switch.
51. Connect the radiator upper hose at the cylinder head.
52. Connect the heater hose to the fitting located below the intake manifold.
53. Fill the cooling system to the proper level and connect the negative battery cable.
54. Start the engine and check for leaks.

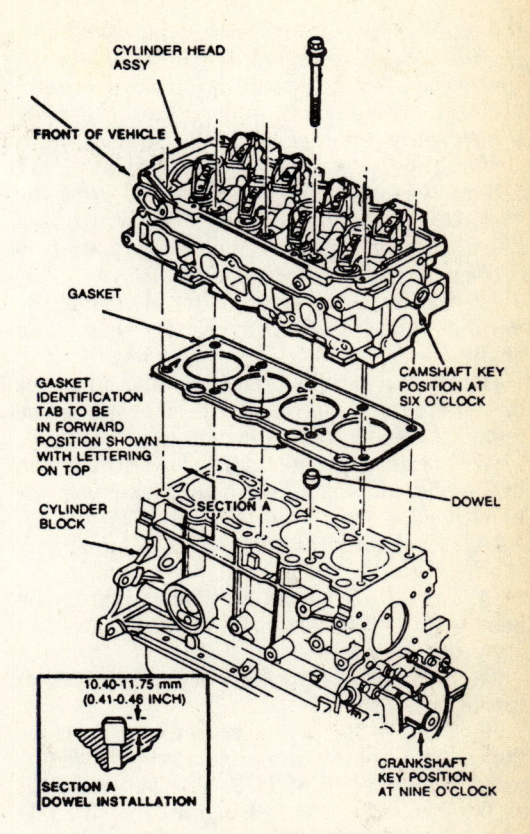

Installing the cylinder head on the 1.9L engine

55. After engine has reached operating temperature, check and, if necessary, add coolant.
56. Adjust the ignition timing.
57. Install the PVS hose, if equipped.
58. Install the air cleaner assembly.

PISTON SQUISH HEIGHT

Before final installation of the cylinder head to the engine, piston "squish height" must be checked. Squish height is the clearance of the piston dome to the cylinder head dome at piston TDC. No rework of the head gasket surfaces (slabbing) or use of replacement parts

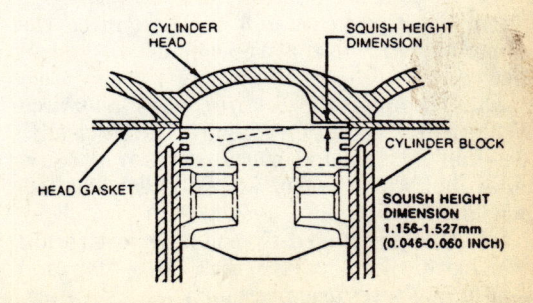

Making the piston squish height measurement - 1.9L EFI engine

ENGINE AND ENGINE OVERHAUL

(crankshaft, piston and connecting rod) causing the assembled squish height to be over or under the tolerance specification is permitted.

NOTE: *If no parts other than the head gasket are replaced, the piston squish height should be within specification. If parts other than the head gasket or replaced, check the squish height. If the squish height is out of specification, replace the parts again and recheck the piston squish height.*

1. Clean all gasket material from the mating surfaces on the cylinder head and engine block.
2. Place a small amount of soft lead solder or shot of an appropriate thickness on the piston spherical areas shown.
3. Rotate the crankshaft to lower the piston in the bore and install the head gasket and cylinder head.

NOTE: *A compressed (used) head gasket is preferred.*

4. Install used head bolts and tighten the head bolts to 30–44 ft. lbs. (40–60 Nm) following proper sequence.
5. Rotate the crankshaft to move the piston through its TDC position.
6. Remove the cylinder head and measure the thickness of the compressed solder to determine squish height at TDC. The solder should be 0.039–0.070 in. (1.0–1.77mm) for EFI HO engine and 0.046–0.060 in. (1.156–1.527mm) for EFI engine.

1981–86 2.3L HSC Engine

1. Disconnect the negative battery cable. Drain the cooling system by disconnecting the lower radiator hose.

CAUTION: *When draining the coolant, keep in mind that cats and dogs are attracted by the ethylene glycol antifreeze, and are quite likely to drink any that is left in an uncovered container or in puddles on the ground. This will prove fatal in sufficient quantity. Always drain the coolant into a sealable container. Coolant should be reused unless it is contaminated or several years old.*

2. Disconnect the heater hose at the fitting under the intake manifold. Disconnect the upper radiator hose at the cylinder head connector.
3. Disconnect the electric cooling fan switch at the plastic connector. Remove the air cleaner assembly. Label and disconnect any vacuum lines that will interfere with cylinder head removal.
4. Disconnect all drive belts. Remove rocker arm cover. Remove the distributor cap and spark plug wires as an assembly.
5. Disconnect the EGR tube at EGR valve. Disconnect the choke wire from the choke.

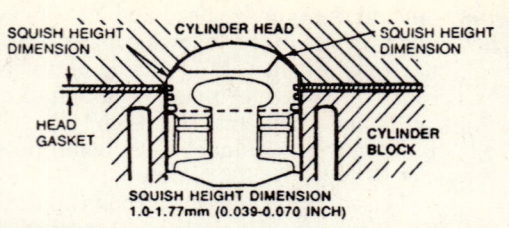

Making the piston squish height measurement - 1.9L EFI-HO engine

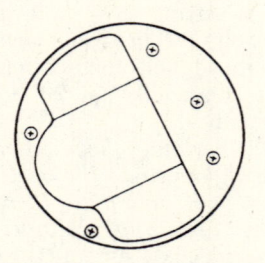

Lead solder location marks for piston squish height measurement

6. Disconnect the fuel supply and return lines at the rubber connector. Disconnect the accelerator cable and speed control cable, if equipped. Loosen the bolts retaining the Thermactor pump pulley.
7. Raise and safely support the front of the car. Disconnect the exhaust pipe from the exhaust manifold. Lower car.
8. Loosen the rocker arm bolts until the arms can pivot for pushrod removal. Remove the pushrods. Keep the pushrods in order for installation in original position.
9. Remove the cylinder head bolts. Remove the cylinder head, gasket, Thermactor pump, intake and exhaust manifolds as an assembly. Do not lay the cylinder head down flat before removing the spark plugs. Take care not to damage the gasket surface.

To install:

10. Clean all gasket material from the head and block surfaces.
11. Position a new head gasket on the block surface. Do not use a sealer, unless directions with gasket specify.
12. To help with head installation alignment, purchase two head bolts and cut off the heads. Install the modified bolts at opposite corners of the block to act as guides.
13. Position the cylinder head over the guide bolts and lower onto the engine block.
14. Install head bolts, remove the guides and replace with regular bolts.
15. Tighten the heads bolts to 53–59 ft. lbs. in two stages in the sequence shown.
16. The rest of the cylinder head installation is in the reverse order of removal.

ENGINE AND ENGINE OVERHAUL 147

1987–90 2.3L Engine

1. Disconnect the negative battery cable. Drain the cooling system.
CAUTION: *When draining the coolant, keep in mind that cats and dogs are attracted by the ethylene glycol antifreeze, and are quite likely to drink any that is left in an uncovered container or in puddles on the ground. This will prove fatal in sufficient quantity. Always drain the coolant into a sealable container. Coolant should be reused unless it is contaminated or several years old.*
2. Remove the air cleaner assembly. Properly relieve the fuel system pressure.
3. Disconnect the heater hose at the fitting located under the intake manifold. Disconnect the upper radiator hose at the cylinder head.
4. Disconnect distributor cap and spark plug wire and remove as an assembly.
5. Remove spark plugs, if necessary.
6. Disconnect and tag required vacuum hoses.
7. Remove dipstick. Disconnect the choke cap wire.
8. Remove rocker cover retaining bolts and remove cover. Disconnect the EGR tube at the EGR valve.
9. Disconnect the fuel supply and return lines at the rubber connections. Disconnect the accelerator cable and speed control cable, if equipped.
10. Loosen the Thermactor pump belt pulley. Raise and support the vehicle safely.
11. Disconnect the exhaust system at the exhaust pipe, hose and tube. Lower the vehicle.
12. Remove Thermactor pump. Remove the cylinder head bolts. Remove cylinder head and gasket with exhaust and intake manifolds attached.

To install:
NOTE: *Do not lay the cylinder head flat. Damage to spark plugs or gasket surfaces may result.*
13. Clean all gasket material from the mating surface of the cylinder head and block. Position the cylinder head gasket on the cylinder block, using a suitable sealer to retain the gasket.
14. Before installing the cylinder head, thread 2 cylinder head alignment studs, using exhaust manifold alignment studs T84P-6065-A or equivalent, through the head bolt holes in the gasket and into the block at opposite corners of the block.
15. Install the cylinder head and cylinder head bolts. Run down several head bolts until snug and remove the 2 guide bolts. Replace them with the remaining head bolts. Torque the cylinder head bolts to 52–59 ft. lbs. (70–80 Nm) and re-torque the bolts to 70–76 ft. lbs. (95–103 Nm) following the proper sequence.
16. Raise and safely support the vehicle. Connect the exhaust system at the exhaust pipe and hose to metal tube.
17. Lower the vehicle and install the Thermactor pump and drive belt. Connect the accelerator cable and, if equipped, speed control cable.
18. Connect the fuel supply and return lines. Connect the choke cap wire.
19. Connect the EGR tube at the EGR valve. Install the distributor cap and spark plug wires as an assembly. Install the spark plugs, if removed.
20. Connect all accessory drive belts. Install the rocker arm cover.
21. Connect the required vacuum hoses. Install the air cleaner assembly. Connect the electric cooling fan switch at the connector.
22. Connect the upper radiator hose at the intake manifold. Fill the cooling system. Connect the negative battery cable.
23. Start the engine and check for leaks. After the engine has reached normal operating temperature, check and add coolant as necessary.

Diesel Engine

1. Disconnect the battery ground cable from the battery, which is located in the luggage compartment.
2. Drain the cooling system.
CAUTION: *When draining the coolant, keep in mind that cats and dogs are attracted by the ethylene glycol antifreeze, and are quite likely to drink any that is left in an uncovered container or in puddles on the ground. This will prove fatal in sufficient quantity. Always drain the coolant into a sealable con-*

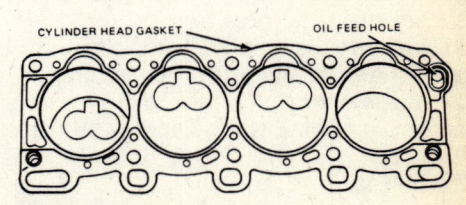

Head gasket installation

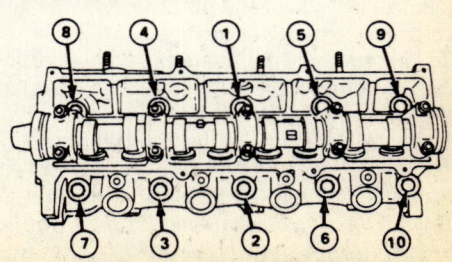

Torque sequence, cylinder head installation

ENGINE AND ENGINE OVERHAUL

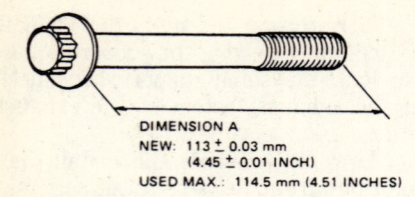

Head bolt dimension
DIMENSION A
NEW: 113 ± 0.03 mm
(4.45 ± 0.01 INCH)
USED MAX.: 114.5 mm (4.51 INCHES)

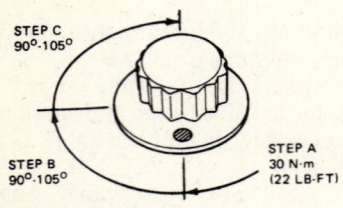

Head bolt tightening steps
STEP A: 30 N·m (22 LB-FT)
STEP B: 90°-105°
STEP C: 90°-105°

tainer. Coolant should be reused unless it is contaminated or several years old.

3. Remove the camshaft cover, front and rear timing bolt covers, and front and rear timing belts.

4. Raise the vehicle and safely support on jackstands.

5. Disconnect the muffler inlet pipe at the exhaust manifold. Lower the vehicle.

6. Disconnect the air inlet duct at the air cleaner and intake manifold. Install a protective cover.

7. Disconnect the electrical connectors and vacuum hoses to the temperature sensors located in the thermostat housing.

8. Disconnect the upper and lower coolant hoses, and the upper radiator hose at the thermostat housing.

9. Disconnect and remove the injection lines at the injection pump and nozzles. Cap all lines and fittings with Cap Protective Set T84P-9395-A or equivalent.

10. Disconnect the glow plug harness from the main engine harness.

11. Remove the cylinder head bolts in the sequence shown. Remove the cylinder head.

12. Remove the glow plugs. Then, remove prechamber cups from the cylinder head using a brass drift.

To install:

13. Clean the prechamber cups, prechambers in the cylinder head and the cylinder head and crankcase gasket mating surfaces.

14. Install the prechambers in the cylinder heads, making sure the locating pins are aligned with the slots provided.

15. Install the glow plugs and tighten to 11-15 ft. lbs. Connect glow plug harness to the glow plugs. Tighten the nuts to 5-7 ft. lbs.

CAUTION: *Carefully blow out the head bolt threads in the crankcase with compressed air. Failure to thoroughly clean the thread bores can result in incorrect cylinder head torque or possible cracking of the crankcase.*

16. Position a new cylinder head gasket on the crankcase making sure the cylinder head oil feed hold is not blocked.

17. Measure each cylinder head bolt dimension A. If the measurement is more than 114.5mm (4.51 in.), replace the head bolt.

CAUTION: *Rotate the camshaft in the cylinder head until the cam lobes for No. 1 cylinder are at the base circle (both valves closed). Then, rotate the crankshaft clockwise until No. 1 piston is halfway up in the cylinder bore toward TDC. This is to prevent contact between the pistons and valves.*

18. Install the cylinder head on the crankcase.

NOTE: *Before installing the cylinder head bolts, paint a white reference dot on each one, and apply a light coat of engine oil on the bolt threads.*

19. Tighten cylinder head bolts as follows:
   a. Tighten bolts to 22 ft. lbs. in the sequence shown.
   b. Using the painted reference marks, tighten each bolt in sequence, another 90°-105°.
   c. Repeat Step b turning the bolts another 90°-105°.

20. Connect the glow plug harness to main engine harness.

21. Remove the protective caps and install injection lines to the injection pump and nozzles. Tighten capnuts to 18-22 ft. lbs.

22. Air bleed the system.

23. Connect the upper (with a new gasket) and lower coolant hoses, and the upper radiator hose to the thermostat housing. Tighten upper coolant hose bolts to 5-7 ft. lbs.

24. Connect the electrical connectors and the vacuum hoses to the temperature sensors in the thermostat housing.

25. Remove the protective cover and install the air inlet duct to the intake manifold and air cleaner.

26. Raise vehicle and support on jackstands. Connect the muffler inlet pipe to the exhaust manifold. Tighten nuts to 25-35 ft. lbs.

27. Lower the vehicle.

28. Install and adjust the front timing belt.

29. Install and adjust the rear timing belt.

30. Install the front upper timing belt cover and rear timing belt cover. Tighten the bolts to 5-7 ft. lbs.

31. Check and adjust the valves as outlined. Install the valve cover and tighten the bolts to 5-7 ft. lbs.

32. Fill and bleed the cooling system.

33. Check and adjust the injection pump timing.

ENGINE AND ENGINE OVERHAUL 149

34. Connect battery ground cable to battery. Run engine and check for oil, fuel and coolant leaks.

OVERHAUL

1. Remove the cylinder head form the car engine (see Cylinder Head Removal and Installation). Place the head on a workbench and remove any manifolds that are still connected. Remove all rocker arm retaining parts and the rocker arms, if still installed or the camshaft (see Camshaft Removal).

2. Turn the cylinder head over so that the mounting surface is facing up and support evenly on wooden blocks.

CAUTION: *If an aluminum cylinder head, exercise care when cleaning.*

3. Use a scraper and remove all of the gasket material stuck to the head mounting surface. Mount a wire carbon removal brush in an electric drill and clean away the carbon on the valves and head combustion chambers.

CAUTION: *When scraping or carbonizing the cylinder head take care not to damage or nick the gasket mounting surface.*

4. Number the valve heads with a permanent felt-tip marker for cylinder location.

RESURFACING

If the cylinder head is warped resurfacing by a machine shop is required. Place a straight-edge across the gasket surface of the head. Using feeler gauges, determine the clearance at the center and along the length between the head and straightedge. Measure clearance at the center and along the lengths of both diagonals. If warpage exceeds 0.003 in. (0.076mm) in a 6 in. (152mm) span, or 0.006 in. (0.15mm) over the total length the cylinder head must be resurfaced.

Valves and Springs

REMOVAL AND INSTALLATION

1. Block the head on its side, or install a pair of head-holding brackets made especially for valve removal.

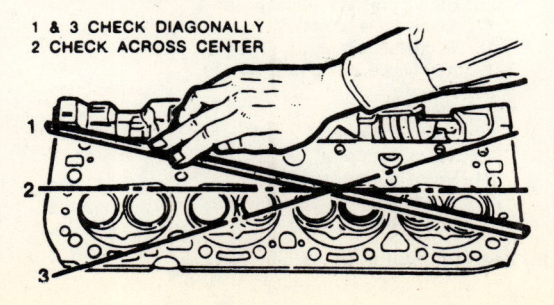

Check the cylinder head for warpage

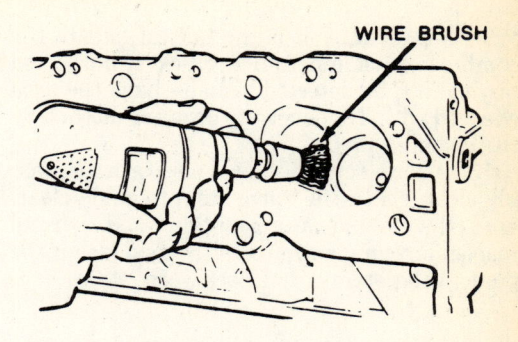

Remove the carbon from cylinder head with a wire brush and electric drill

2. Use a socket slightly larger than the valve stem and keepers, place the socket over the valve stem and gently hit the socket with a plastic hammer to break loose any varnish buildup.

3. Remove the valve keepers, retainer, spring shield and valve spring using a valve spring compressor (the locking C-clamp type is the easiest kind to use).

4. Put the parts in a separate container numbered for the cylinder being worked on. Do not mix them with other parts removed.

5. Remove and discard the valve stem oil seal, a new seal will be used at assembly time.

6. Remove the valve from the cylinder head and place, in order, through numbered holes punched in a stiff piece of cardboard or wooden valve holding stick.

NOTE: *The exhaust valve stems, on some engines, are equipped with small metal caps. Take care not to lose the caps. Make sure to reinstall them at assembly time. Replace any caps that are worn.*

7. Use an electric drill and rotary wire brush to clean the intake and exhaust valve ports, combustion chamber and valve seats. In some cases, the carbon will need to be chipped away. Use a blunt pointed drift for carbon chipping, be careful around the valve seat areas.

8. Use a wire valve guide cleaning brush and safe solvent to clean the valve guides.

9. Clean the valves with a revolving wire brush. Heavy carbon deposits may be removed with the blunt drift.

NOTE: *When using a wire brush to clean carbon on the valve ports, valves etc., be sure that the deposits are actually removed, rather than burnished.*

10. Wash and clean all valve spring, keepers, retaining caps etc., in safe solvent.

11. Clean the head with a brush and some safe solvent and wipe dry.

12. Check the head for cracks. Cracks in the cylinder head usually start around an exhaust

150 ENGINE AND ENGINE OVERHAUL

valve seat because it is the hottest part of the combustion chamber. If a crack is suspected buy cannot be detected visually have the area checked with dye penetrate or other method by the machine shop.

13. After all cylinder head parts are reasonably clean check the valve stem-to-guide clearance. If a dial indicator is not on hand, a visual inspection can give you a fairly good idea if the guide, valve stem or both are worn.

14. Insert the valve into the guide until slightly away from the valve seat. Wiggle the valve sideways. A small amount of wobble is normal, excessive wobble means a worn guide or valve stem. If a dial indicator is on hand, mount the indicator so that the stem of the valve is at 90° to the valve stem, as close to the valve guide as possible. Move the valve off the seat, and measure the valve guide-to-stem clearance by rocking the stem back and forth to ac-

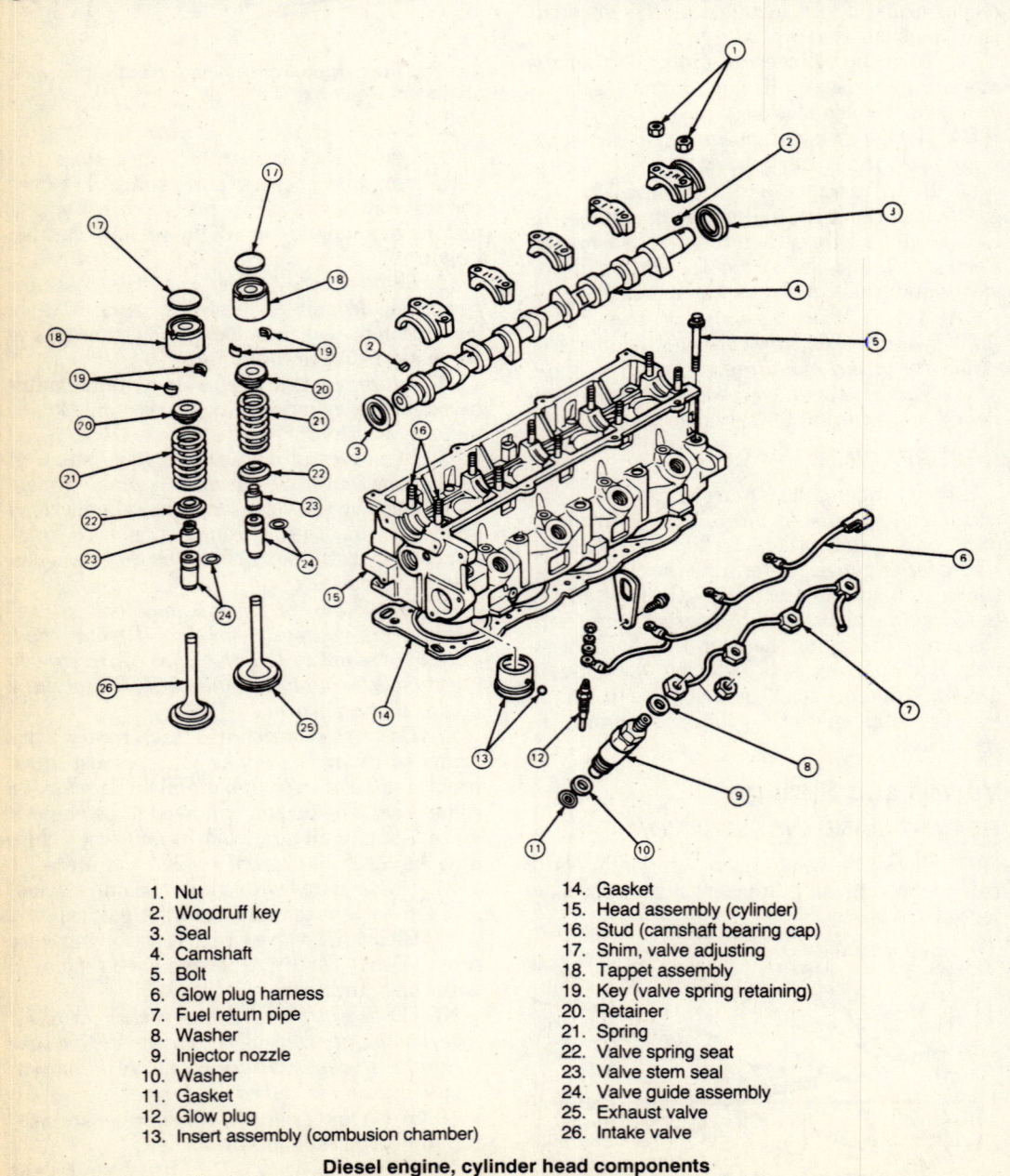

1. Nut
2. Woodruff key
3. Seal
4. Camshaft
5. Bolt
6. Glow plug harness
7. Fuel return pipe
8. Washer
9. Injector nozzle
10. Washer
11. Gasket
12. Glow plug
13. Insert assembly (combusion chamber)
14. Gasket
15. Head assembly (cylinder)
16. Stud (camshaft bearing cap)
17. Shim, valve adjusting
18. Tappet assembly
19. Key (valve spring retaining)
20. Retainer
21. Spring
22. Valve spring seat
23. Valve stem seal
24. Valve guide assembly
25. Exhaust valve
26. Intake valve

Diesel engine, cylinder head components

ENGINE AND ENGINE OVERHAUL

tuate the dial indicator. Measure the valve stem using a micrometer and compare to specifications to determine whether stem or guide wear is causing excessive clearance.

15. The valve guide, if worn, must be repaired before the valve seats can be resurfaced. Ford supplies valves with oversize stems to fit valve guides that are reamed to oversize for repair. The machine shop will be able to handle the guide reaming for you. In some cases, if the guide is not too badly worn, knurling may be all that is required.

16. Reface, or have the valves and valve seats refaced. The valve seats should be a true 45° angle. Remove only enough material to clean up any pits or grooves. Be sure the valve seat is not too wide or narrow. Use a 60° grinding wheel to remove material from the bottom of the seat for raising and a 30° grinding wheel to remove material from the top of the seat to narrow.

17. After the valves are refaced by machine, hand lap them to the valve seat. Clean the grinding compound off and check the position of face-to-seat contact. Contact should be close to the center of the valve face. If contact is close to the top edge of the valve narrow the seat; if too close to the bottom edge, raise the seat.

18. Valves should be refaced to a true angle of 44°. Remove only enough metal to clean up the valve face or to correct runout. If the edge of the valve head, after machining, is $\frac{1}{32}$ in. (0.8mm) or less replace the valve. The tip of the valve stem should also be dressed on the valve grinding machine, however, do not remove more than 0.010 in. (0.25mm).

19. After all valve and valve seats have been machined, check the remaining valve train parts (springs, retainers, keepers, etc.) for wear. Check the valve springs for straightness and tension.

20. Reassemble the head in the reverse order of disassembly using new valve guide seals and lubricating the valve stems. Check the valve

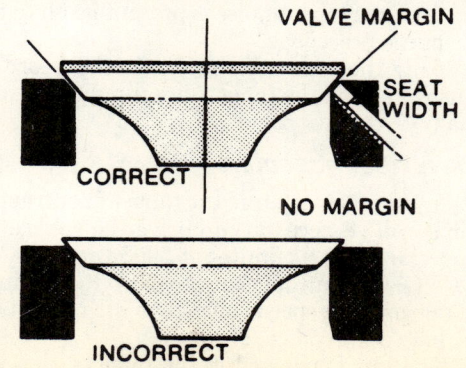

Valve seat width and centering

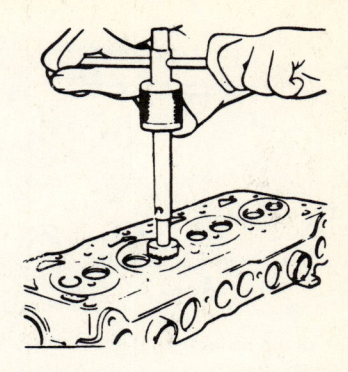

Reaming the valve seat with a hand reamer

spring installed height, shim or replace as necessary.

Valve Lifters

REMOVAL AND INSTALLATION

1.6L and 1.9L Engines

1. Disconnect the negative battery cable.
2. Remove air cleaner assembly. Remove valve cover and gasket.
3. Remove rocker arms, lifter guides, lifter retainers and lifters.

NOTE: *Always return lifters to the original bores unless they are being replaced.*

To install:

4. Lubricate each lifter bore with heavy SG engine oil.
5. If equipped with flat bottom lifters, install with oil hole in plunger upward. If equipped with roller lifters, install with plunger upward and position guide flats of lifters to be parallel with centerline of camshaft. Color orientation dots on lifters should be opposite the oil feed holes in cylinder head.
6. For roller lifters only, install lifter guide plates over tappet guide flats with notch toward exhaust side. For flat lifters, no guide plate is required.
7. Lubricate lifter plunger cap and valve tip with heavy SG engine oil.
8. Install lifter guide plate retainers into rocker arm fulcrum slots, in both intake and exhaust side. Notch to be with exhaust valve lifter.
9. Install 4 rocker arms in lifter position No's 3, 6, 7 and 8.
10. Lubricate rocker arm surface that will contact fulcrum surface with heavy SG engine oil.
11. Install 4 fulcrums. Fulcrums must be fully seated in slots of cylinder head.
12. Install 4 bolts. Tighten to 17–22 ft. lbs. (23–30 Nm).
13. Rotate the engine until the camshaft sprocket keyway is in the 6 o'clock position.

ENGINE AND ENGINE OVERHAUL

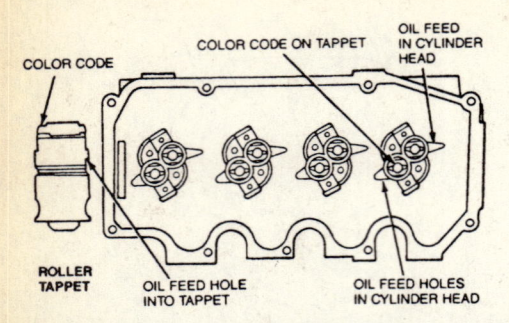

Installation of the roller tappet assemblies 1.6L and 1.9L engines

14. Repeat steps 9–12 in lifter position No's 1, 2, 4 and 5.
15. Install valve cover and gasket. Install air cleaner assembly.
16. Connect negative battery cable.

NOTE: *If equipped with a roller tappet camshaft, install cup plug using sealer ESE–M46127–A or equivalent. Use sparingly, excess sealer may cause the oil holes in the camshaft to clog.*

2.3L Engine

1. Disconnect the negative battery cable. Remove the cylinder head and related parts.
2. Using a magnet, remove the lifters. Identify, tag and place the lifters in a rack so they can be installed in the original positions.
3. If the lifters are stuck in their bores by excessive varnish or gum, it may be necessary to use a hydraulic lifter puller tool to remove the lifters. Rotate the lifters back and forth to loosen any gum and varnish which may have formed. Keep the assemblies intact until they are to be cleaned.

To install:

4. Install new or cleaned hydraulic lifters through the pushrod openings with a magnet.
5. Install the cylinder head and related parts.
6. Connect negative battery cable.

CHILTON TIPS

This following Chilton tip is for 1987–88 EXP/Lynx and 1987–91 Escort vehicles equipped with roller tappets may exhibit conditions of a loud tapping noise inside the engine compartment that may be caused by mechanical failure of the roller tappets or there is air trapped inside the roller tappets. The air that is trapped inside the roller tappets will not allow enough oil to enter the tappets which causes the tapping noise.

Use the following procedure to determine if the tappet has air trapped inside or if tappet replacement is required.

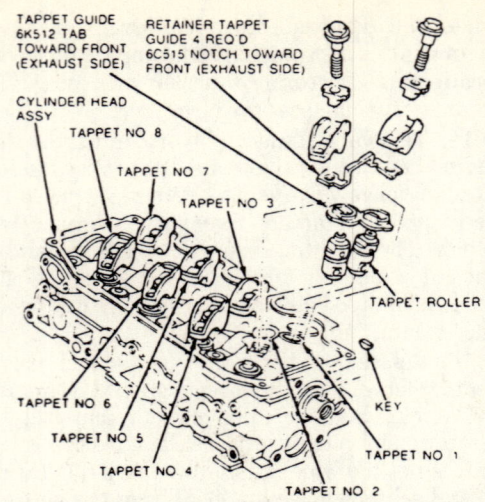

Tappet numerical identification 1.6L and 1.9L engines

NOTE: *A tappet noise for up to 3 seconds after initial engine start-up is normal and requires no corrective action.*

Tappet Inspection & Correction Procedure

1. Check the engine code tag, which is usually located on the timing belt cover, for one of the following codes:
   a. 7G460, 7G461 and 7G473.
   b. 8G460, 8G461 and 8G473.
   c. 9G460, 9G461 and 9G473.
   d. 0G480, 0G481, 0G482 and 0G483.

These codes indicate that the engine does use roller tappets.

2. Make sure that the coolant overflow bottle is filled to the full mark.
3. Start the engine and bring it up to normal operating temperature, by running it at idle for approximately 10 minutes or until the temperature gauge is in the normal range.
4. Run the engine at 1500 to 2000 rpm. Listen for the tappet noise, which is a constant loud tapping sound that can be heard at normal operating temperature, at this rpm.
5. If the tappet noise is present go on to the air purge procedure.
6. If the tappet noise cannot be heard at this rpm, then the tappets are functioning normally.

AIR PURGE PROCEDURE

1. In order to purge the tappet of entrapped air it will be necessary to drive the vehicle for approximately 8 minutes at 3000 rpm.
2. Select an appropriate gear to maintain 3000 rpm at a speed consistent with local traffic laws and road conditions.
3. If air is trapped in the tappets, this will remove it.

ENGINE AND ENGINE OVERHAUL

4. If the tappet noise is no longer present, discontinue this procedure and return your vehicle back to normal driving conditions.

5. If the tappet noise is still present, find which tappet is spongy and remove just that tappet.

6. If any roller tappet is replaced, align the paint dot (blue or orange) on the top of the tappet retainer clip with the oil feed hole in the cylinder head bore. The intake tappets should have the paint dot facing toward the distributor end and the exhaust tappets paint dot will face the timing belt end.

CHECKING VALVE SPRINGS

Place the valve spring on a flat surface next to a carpenters square. Measure the height of the spring, and rotate the spring against the edge of the square to measure distortion. If the spring height varies (by comparison) by more than $1/16$ in. (1.6mm) or if the distortion exceeds $1/16$ in. (1.6mm), replace the spring.

Have the valve springs tested for spring pressure at the installed and compressed (installed height minus valve lift) height using a valve spring tester. Springs should be within one pound, plus or minus each other. Replace spring as necessary.

VALVE SPRING INSTALLED HEIGHT

After installing the valve spring, measure the distance between the spring mounting pad and the lower edge of the spring retainer. Compare the measurement to specifications. If the installed height is incorrect, add shim washers between the spring mounting pad and the spring. Use only washers designed for valve springs, available at most parts houses.

VALVE STEM OIL SEALS

Most engines are equipped with a positive valve stem seal using a Teflon® insert. Teflon® seals are available for other engines buy usually require valve guide machining, consult

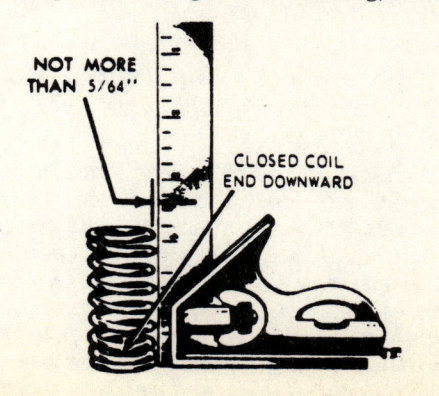

Check the valve spring free length and squareness

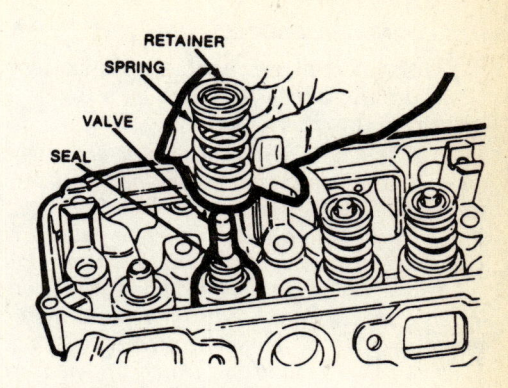

Install valve stem oil seals

your automotive machine shop for advice on having positive valve stem oil seals installed.

When installing valve stem oil seals, ensure that a small amount of oil is able to pass the seal to lubricate the valve stems and guide walls; otherwise, excessive wear will occur.

VALVE SEATS

If a valve seat is damaged or burnt and cannot be serviced by refacing, it may be possible to have the seat machined and an insert installed. Consult the automotive machine shop for their advice.

NOTE: *The aluminum heads on V6 engines are equipped with inserts.*

VALVE GUIDES

Worn valve guides can, in most cases, be reamed to accept a valve with an oversized stem. Valve guides that are not excessively worn or distorted may, in some cases, be knurled rather than reamed. However, if the valve stem is worn reaming for an oversized valve stem is the answer since a new valve would be required.

Knurling is a process in which metal is displaced and raised, thereby reducing clearance. Knurling also produces excellent oil control. The possibility of knurling instead of reaming the valve guides should be discussed with a machinist.

Oil Pan

REMOVAL AND INSTALLATION

Gasoline Engines

The oil pan can be removed with the engine in the car. No suspension or chassis components need be removed. However, on Tempo/Topaz model, the transaxle case must be mounted to the engine.

ENGINE AND ENGINE OVERHAUL

1.3L, 1.6L AND 1.9L ENGINES

1. Disconnect negative cable at the battery.
2. Raise the vehicle and support safely.
3. Drain the crankcase.

CAUTION: *The EPA warns that prolonged contact with used engine oil may cause a number of skin disorders, including cancer! You should make every effort to minimize your exposure to used engine oil. Protective gloves should be worn when changing the oil. Wash your hands and any other exposed skin areas as soon as possible after exposure to used engine oil. Soap and water, or waterless hand cleaner should be used.*

4. Disconnect cable at the starter.
5. Remove knee-brace located at the front of the starter.
6. Remove starter attaching bolts and starter.
7. Remove knee-braces at the transaxle.
8. Disconnect the exhaust inlet pipe at the manifold and converter. Remove pipe.
9. Remove oil pan retaining bolts and oil pan.
10. Remove oil pan gasket and discard.

To install:

11. Clean the oil pan gasket surface and the mating surface on the cylinder block. Wipe the oil pan rail with a solvent-soaked cloth to remove oil traces.
12. Remove the clean the oil pump pick up tube and screen assembly. Install tube and screen assembly using a new gasket.
13. Apply a bead of suitable silicone rubber sealer at the corner of the oil pan front and rear seals and at the seating point of the oil pump to the block retainer joint.
14. Install the gasket in oil pan ensuring press fit tabs are fully engaged in oil pan gasket channel.
15. Install the oil pan attaching bolts. Tighten the bolts lightly until the 2 oil pan-to-transmission bolts can be installed.

NOTE: *If the oil pan is installed on the engine outside of the vehicle, a transaxle case or equivalent, fixture must be bolted to the*

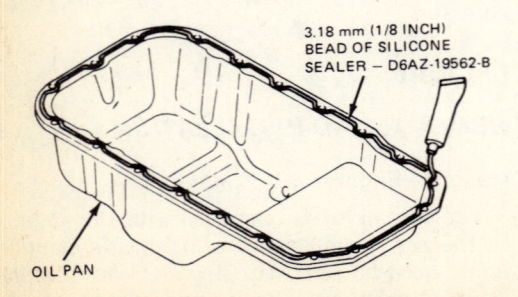

Applying sealant to the oil pan-2.0L diesel engine

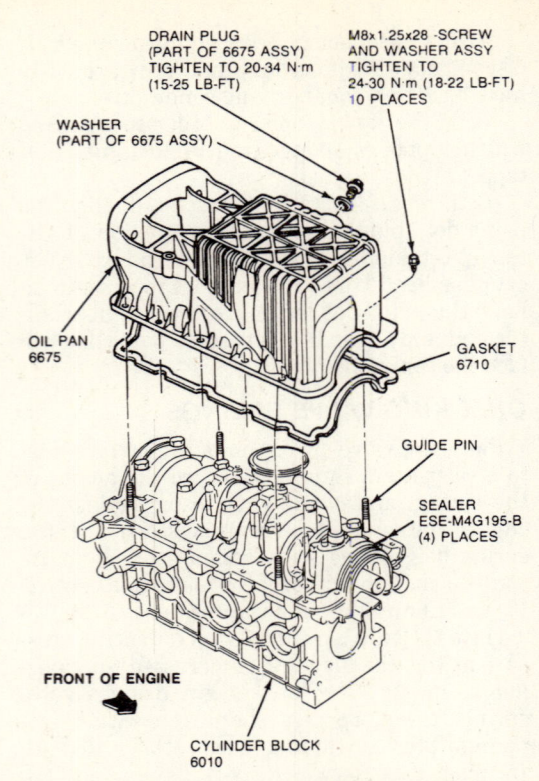

Oil Pan installation-1.6L and 1.9L engines

block to line the oil pan up, flush with the rear face of the block.

16. Tighten the 2 pan-to-transmission bolts to 30–40 ft. lbs. (40–54 Nm).
17. Tighten the oil pan flange-to-cylinder block bolts to 15–22 ft. lbs. (20–30 Nm).
18. Install the transaxle inspection plate.
19. Install the starter, knee brace at the starter and connect the starter cable.
20. Install the exhaust inlet pipe. Lower the vehicle and fill the crankcase.
21. Connect negative battery cable.
23. Start the engine and check for oil leaks.

2.0L ENGINE

1. Disconnect the negative battery cable.
2. Raise and safely support the vehicle.
3. Drain engine oil.

CAUTION: *The EPA warns that prolonged contact with used engine oil may cause a number of skin disorders, including cancer! You should make every effort to minimize your exposure to used engine oil. Protective gloves should be worn when changing the oil. Wash your hands and any other exposed skin areas as soon as possible after exposure to used engine oil. Soap and water, or waterless hand cleaner should be used.*

ENGINE AND ENGINE OVERHAUL 155

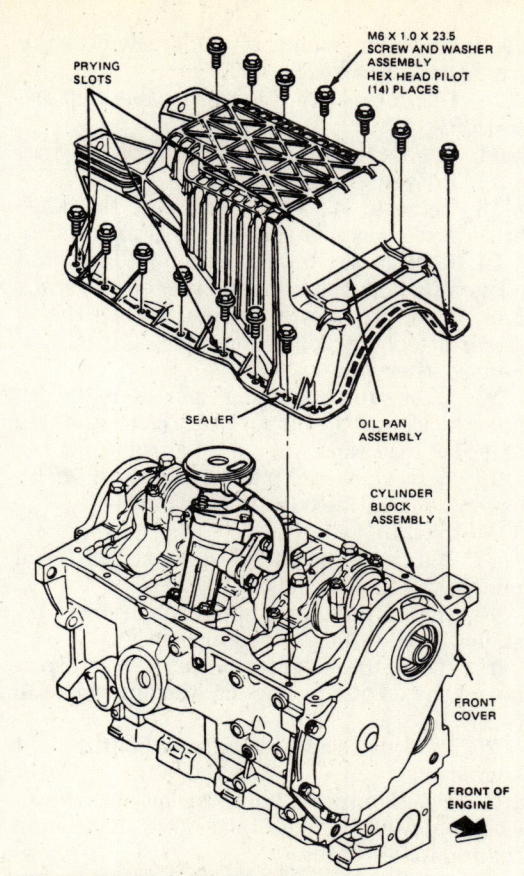

Oil pan installation-2.3L HSC engine

4. Remove bolts attaching oil pan to crankcase, and remove pan.
5. Clean oil pan and crankcase gasket mating surfaces.

To install:

6. Apply a 1/8 in. (3.18mm) bead of silicone sealer or equivalent, to oil pan-to-crankcase mating surface.
7. Install oil pan. Tighten bolts to 5–7 ft. lbs. (7–10 Nm).
8. Lower vehicle.
9. Fill crankcase with specified quantity and quality of engine oil.
10. Connect negative battery cable.
11. Run engine and check for oil leaks.

2.3L ENGINE

1. Disconnect the negative battery cable. Raise the vehicle and support safely.
2. Drain the crankcase and drain the cooling system by removing the lower radiator hose.

CAUTION: *The EPA warns that prolonged contact with used engine oil may cause a number of skin disorders, including cancer! You should make every effort to minimize your exposure to used engine oil. Protective gloves should be worn when changing the oil. Wash your hands and any other exposed skin areas as soon as possible after exposure to used engine oil. Soap and water, or waterless hand cleaner should be used. When draining the coolant, keep in mind that cats and dogs are attracted by the ethylene glycol antifreeze, and are quite likely to drink any that is left in an uncovered container or in puddles on the ground. This will prove fatal in sufficient quantity. Always drain the coolant into a sealable container. Coolant should be reused unless it is contaminated or several years old.*

3. Remove the roll restrictor on manual transaxle equipped vehicles.
4. Disconnect the starter cable.
5. Remove the starter.
6. Disconnect the exhaust pipe from oil pan.
7. Remove the engine coolant tube from the lower radiator hose, water pump and at the tabs on the oil pan. Position air conditioner line off to the side. Remove the retaining bolts and remove the oil pan.

To install:

8. Clean both mating surfaces of oil pan and cylinder block making certain that all traces of RTV sealant are removed. Ensure that the block rails, front cover and rear cover retainer are also clean.
9. Remove and clean oil pump pick-up tube and screen assembly. After cleaning, install tube and screen assembly.
10. Apply RTV E8AZ–19562–A Sealer or equivalent, in oil pan groove. Completely fill oil pan groove with sealer. Sealer bead should be 0.200 in. (5mm) wide and 0.080–0.150 in. (2.0–3.8mm) high (above oil pan surface) in all areas except the half-rounds. The half-rounds should have a bead 0.200 in. (5mm) wide and 0.150–0.200 in. (3.8–5.1mm) high, above the oil pan surface.

NOTE: *Applying RTV in excess of the specified amount will not improve the sealing of the oil pan, and could cause the oil pickup screen to become clogged with sealer. Use adequate ventilation when applying sealer.*

11. Install oil pan to cylinder block within 5 minutes to prevent skinning over. RTV needs to cure completely before coming in contact with any engine oil, about 1 hour at ambient temperature between 65–75°F.
12. Install oil pan bolts lightly until the 2 oil pan-to-transmission bolts can be installed.

NOTE: *If oil pan is installed on engine outside of vehicle, a transaxle case or equivalent, fixture must be bolted to the block to line the oil pan up, flush with the rear face of block.*

ENGINE AND ENGINE OVERHAUL

13. Install 2 oil pan-to-transaxle bolts. Tighten to 30–39 ft. lbs. (40–54 Nm) to align oil pan with transaxle. Loosen bolts $1/2$ turn.

14. Tighten all oil pan flange bolts to 15–22 ft. lbs. (20–30 Nm).

15. Tighten 2 oil pan-to-transmission bolts to 30–39 ft. lbs. (40–54 Nm).

16. If required, rework exhaust bracket to fit to oil pan.

17. Replace water inlet tube O-ring and install tube.

18. Install roll restrictor.

19. Lower vehicle.

20. Install engine oil and coolant.

21. Connect negative battery cable.

22. Start engine and check for coolant and oil leaks.

Oil Pump

REMOVAL AND INSTALLATION

1.3L, 1.6L AND 1.9L Engines

1. Disconnect the negative cable at the battery.

2. Loosen the alternator bolt on the alternator adjusting arm. Lower the alternator to remove the accessory drive belt from the crankshaft pulley.

3. Remove the timing belt cover.

NOTE: *Set No. 1 cylinder at TDC prior to timing belt removal.*

4. Loosen both belt tensioner attaching bolts using Tool T8AP-6254-A or equivalent on the left bolt. Using a pry bar or other suitable tool pry the tensioner away from the belt. While holding the tensioner away from the belt, tighten one of the tensioner attaching bolts.

5. Disengage the timing belt from the camshaft sprocket, water pump sprocket and crankshaft sprocket.

6. Raise the vehicle and safely support on jackstands. Drain the crankcase.

CAUTION: *The EPA warns that prolonged contact with used engine oil may cause a number of skin disorders, including cancer! You should make every effort to minimize your exposure to used engine oil. Protective gloves should be worn when changing the oil. Wash your hands and any other exposed skin areas as soon as possible after exposure to used engine oil. Soap and water, or waterless hand cleaner should be used.*

7. Using a crankshaft Pulley Wrench T81P-6312-A and Crankshaft Bolt Wrench YA-826 or equivalent, remove the crankshaft pulley attaching bolt.

8. Remove the timing belt.

9. Remove the crankshaft drive plate assembly. Remove the crankshaft pulley. Remove the crankshaft sprocket.

10. Disconnect the starter cable at the starter.

11. Remove the knee brace from the engine.

12. Remove the starter.

13. Remove the rear section of the knee brace and inspection plate at the transmission.

14. Remove the oil pan retaining bolts and oil pan. Remove the front and rear oil pan seals. Remove the oil pan side gaskets. Remove the oil pump attaching bolts, oil pump and gasket. Remove the oil pump seal.

15. Make sure the mating surfaces on the cylinder block and the oil pump are clean and free of gasket material.

16. Remove the oil pick-up tube and screen assembly from the pump for cleaning.

To install:

17. Lubricate the outside diameter of the oil pump seal with engine oil.

18. Install the oil pump seal using Seal Installer T81P-6700-A or equivalent.

19. Install the pick-up tube and screen assembly on the oil pump. Tighten attaching bolts to 6–9 ft. lbs.

20. Lubricate the oil pump seal lip with light engine oil.

21. Position the oil pump gasket over the locating dowels. Install attaching bolts and tighten to 5–7 ft. lbs.

22. Apply a bead of Silicone Sealer approximately 3.0mm wide at the corner of the front and rear oil pan seals, and at the seating point of the oil pump to the block retainer joint.

23. Install the front oil pan seal by pressing firmly into the slot cut into the bottom of the pump.

24. Install the rear oil seal by pressing firmly into the slot cut into rear retainer assembly.

NOTE: *Install the seal before the sealer has cured (within 10 minutes of application).*

25. Apply adhesive sealer evenly to oil pan flange and to the oil pan side of the gasket. Allow the adhesive to dry past the wet stage and then install the gaskets on the oil pan. Position the oil pan on the cylinder block.

26. Install oil pan attaching bolts. Tighten bolts in the proper sequence to 6–8 ft. lbs.

27. Position the transmission inspection plate and the rear section of the knee brace on the transmission. Install the two attaching bolts and tighten to specification.

28. Install the starter.

29. Install the knee brace.

30. Connect the starter cable.

31. Install the crankshaft gear. Install crankshaft pulley. Install crankshaft drive plate assembly. Install timing belt over the crankshaft pulley.

ENGINE AND ENGINE OVERHAUL 157

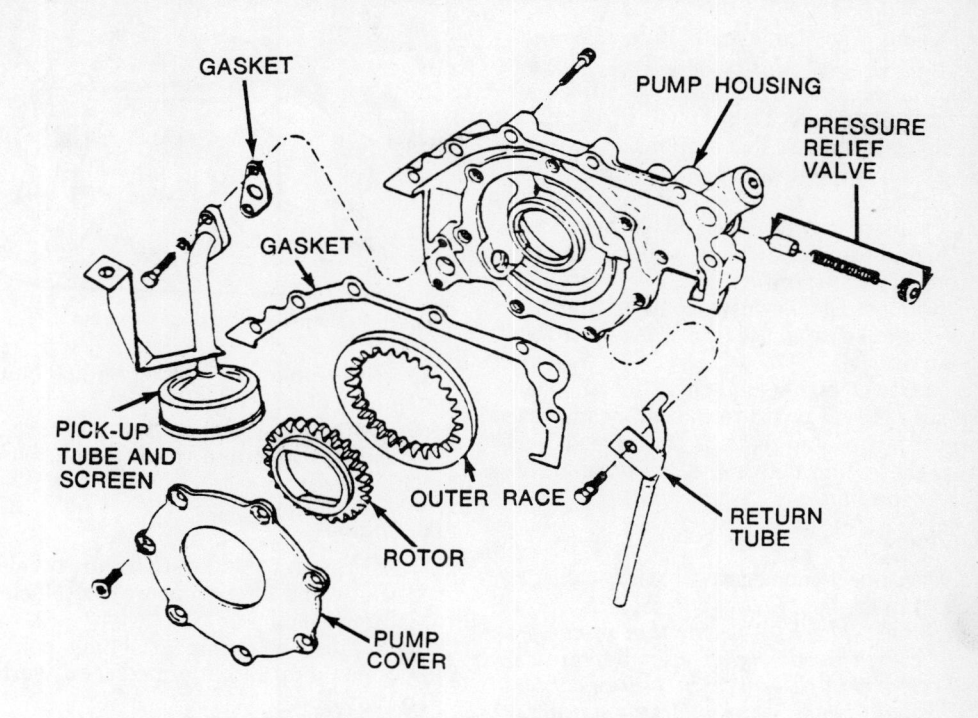

Exploded view of the oil pump-1.6L and 1.9L engines

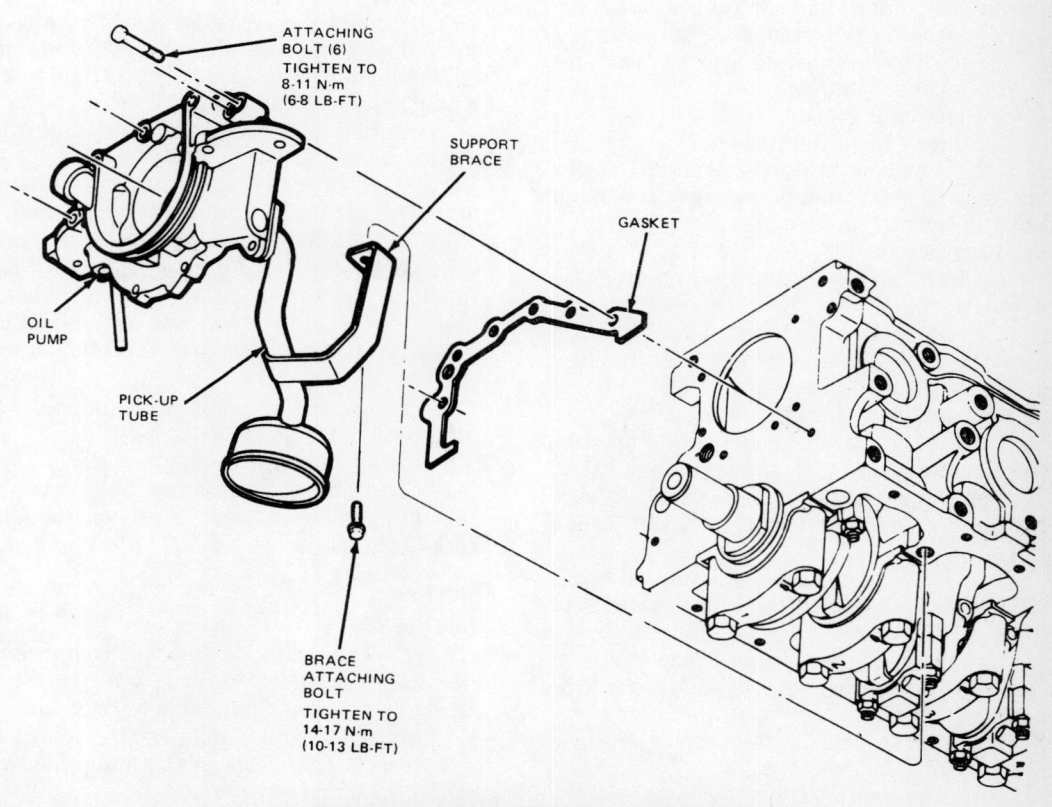

Oil pump installation-1.6L and 1.9L engines

ENGINE AND ENGINE OVERHAUL

32. Using the Crankshaft Pulley Wrench T81P-6312-A and Crankshaft Bolt Wrench YA-826 or equivalent, install the crankshaft pulley attaching bolt. Tighten bolt to specification. (Refer to Timing Belt section).
33. Lower the vehicle.
34. Install the engine front timing cover.
35. Position the accessory drive belts over the alternator and crankshaft pulleys. Tighten the drive belts to specification.
36. Connect the negative cable at the battery. Fill crankcase to the proper level with the specified oil.
37. Start the engine and check for oil leaks. Make sure the oil pressure indicator lamp has gone out. If the lamp remains On, immediately shut off the engine, determine the case and correct the condition.

2.0L Engine

1. Disconnect the negative battery cable.
2. Drain engine oil.

CAUTION: *The EPA warns that prolonged contact with used engine oil may cause a number of skin disorders, including cancer! You should make every effort to minimize your exposure to used engine oil. Protective gloves should be worn when changing the oil. Wash your hands and any other exposed skin areas as soon as possible after exposure to used engine oil. Soap and water, or waterless hand cleaner should be used.*

3. Remove oil pan.
4. Remove front timing belt.
5. Remove bolts attaching oil pump to crankcase and remove pump. Remove crankshaft front oil seal.

To install:

6. Clean oil pump and crankcase gasket mating surfaces.
7. Apply a 1/8 in. (3.18mm) bead of silicone sealer or equivalent, on oil pump-to-crankcase mating surface.
8. Install new O-ring.
9. Install oil pump, ensuring that oil pump inner gear engages with splines on crankshaft. Tighten 10mm bolts to 23-34 ft. lbs. (32-47 Nm) and 8mm bolts to 12-16 ft. lbs. (16-23 Nm).
10. Install a new crankshaft front oil seal.
11. Clean oil pan-to-crankcase mating surfaces.
12. Apply a 1/8 in. (3.18mm) bead of silicone sealer or equivalent, to oil pan-to-crankcase mating surface.
13. Install oil pan. Tighten bolts to 5-7 ft. lbs. (7-10 Nm).
14. Install and adjust, as necessary, crankshaft sprocket, front timing belt tensioner and front timing belt.

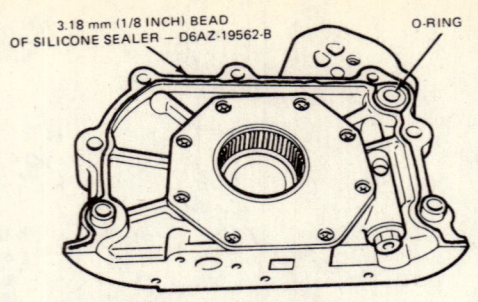

Oil pump assembly-2.0L diesel engine

15. Fill crankcase with specified quantity and quality of oil.
16. Connect negative battery cable.
17. Start engine and check for oil, fuel and coolant leaks.

2.3L Engine

1. Disconnect the negative battery cable.
2. Raise and safely support the vehicle.
3. Remove oil pan.
4. Remove oil pump attaching bolts and remove oil pump and intermediate driveshaft.

To install:

5. Prime oil pump by filling inlet port with engine oil. Rotate pump shaft until oil flows from outlet port.
6. If screen and cover assembly have been removed, replace gasket. Clean screen and reinstall screen and cover assembly and tighten attaching bolts and nut.
7. Position intermediate driveshaft into distributor socket.
8. Insert intermediate driveshaft into oil pump. Install pump and shaft as an assembly.

NOTE: *Do not attempt to force the pump into position if it will not seat. The shaft hex may be mis-aligned with the distributor shaft. To align, remove the oil pump and rotate the intermediate driveshaft into a new position.*

9. Tighten the oil pump attaching bolts to 15-23 ft. lbs. (20-30 Nm).
10. Install oil pan with new gasket.
11. Connect negative battery cable.
12. Fill the crankcase. Start engine and check for leaks.

Checking

ALL ENGINES

NOTE: *The oil pump internal components are not serviceable. If any component is out of specification, the pump must be replaced.*

1. Remove the oil pump from the vehicle.
2. Inspect the inside of the pump housing for damage or excessive wear.
3. Check the mating surface for wear. Minor scuff marks are normal, but if the cover,

ENGINE AND ENGINE OVERHAUL

gears or housing are excessively worn, scored or grooved, replace the pump.

4. Inspect the rotor for nicks, burrs or score marks. Remove minor imperfections with an oil stone.

5. Measure the inner-to-outer rotor tip clearance. On 1.6L and 1.9L engines, the clearance should be 0.002–0.007 in. (0.05–0.18mm). On 2.3L engine, the clearance must not exceed 0.012 in. (0.30mm) with a feeler gauge inserted $1/2$ in. minimum with the rotors removed from the pump housing.

6. With the rotor assembly installed in the housing, place a straight edge across the rotor assembly and housing. Measure the rotor end-play or clearance, between the inner and outer rotors. On 1.6L and 1.9L engine, this clearance should be 0.0005–0.0035 in. (0.013–0.0089mm). On 2.3L engine, the clearance is 0.004 in. (0.101mm).

7. Check the relief valve spring tension. If the spring is worn or damaged, replace the pump. Check the relief valve piston for freedom of movement in the bore.

Timing Belt

CHECKING ENGINE TIMING

1.3L, 1.6 & 1.9L Engines

Should the camshaft drive belt jump timing by a tooth or two, the engine could still run, although very poorly. To visually check for correct timing, remove the No.1 spark plug and place your thumb over the hole. Use a wrench on the crankshaft pulley bolt to rotate the engine to TDC of the compression stroke for No. 1 cylinder.

CAUTION: *Turn the crankshaft only in the direction of normal rotation. Backward rotation will cause the belt to slip or lose teeth, altering engine timing.*

As the No. 1 piston rises on the compression stroke, your thumb will be pushed out by compression pressure. At the same time, the timing notch on the crankshaft pulley will be approaching the **0**, or **TDC**, mark on the timing degree scale molded into the camshaft belt cover. Continue to turn the crankshaft until the pulley mark and **0** mark are aligned, indicating that No. 1 cylinder is at TDC.

Remove the alternator drive belt, and the power steering pump and air conditioning compressor drive belts, if so equipped. Remove the camshaft belt cover.

The camshaft sprocket has a mark next to one of the holes. The cylinder head is similarly marked. These marks should be aligned, dot-to-dot, indicating that camshaft timing is correct.

NOTE: *As a further check, the distributor cap can be removed. The ignition rotor should be pointing toward the No. 1 spark plug tower in the cap.*

If the marks are aligned, the engine timing is correct. If not, the belt must be removed from the cam sprocket and the camshaft turned until its marks are aligned (crankshaft still at TDC).

CAUTION: *Never attempt to rotate the engine by means of the camshaft sprocket. The 2:1 ratio between the camshaft and crankshaft sprockets will place a severe strain on the belt, stretching or tearing it.*

Timing Belt Front Cover

REMOVAL AND INSTALLATION

1.3L, 1.6L and 1.9L Engines

1. Disconnect the negative battery cable. Remove all the drive belts.

2. Remove the alternator, if necessary, to allow enough room to reach the top cover retaining bolts. Position the air conditioner compressor out of the way, if equipped to allow enough room to reach the bottom cover retainer bolts.

3. Remove the top 2 timing cover retaining nuts. Raise and safely support the vehicle.

4. Working from underneath the vehicle, remove the bottom 2 timing cover retaining cover screws. Lower the vehicle and remove the timing belt cover.

5. Complete the installation of the timing belt cover by reversing the removal procedure.

FRONT COVER OIL SEAL REPLACEMENT

1.3L, 1.6L and 1.9L Engines

1. Disconnect the negative battery cable.
2. Remove the accessory drive belts.
3. Remove the timing belt cover.
4. Remove the timing belt.

NOTE: *With the timing belt removed and pistons at TDC, do not rotate the engine. If the camshaft must be rotated, align the crankshaft pulley to 90° BTDC.*

5. Remove the crankshaft damper.
6. Remove the crankshaft sprocket.
7. Remove the crankshaft front seal.

To install:

8. Coat the new seal with clean engine oil.
9. Install the crankshaft front seal using a suitable seal installer tool.
10. Install the crankshaft sprocket.
11. Install the crankshaft damper.
12. Install the timing belt. Observe proper installation procedure.
13. Install the timing belt cover.
14. Install the accessory drive belts. Adjust the drive belt tension.

ENGINE AND ENGINE OVERHAUL

15. Connect negative battery cable.

Timing Belt and Tensioner
ADJUSTMENT

The timing belt tensioner is spring-loaded, on the 1.9L engine. The spring automatically maintains the proper tension and periodic belt tension adjustments are not necessary.

REMOVAL AND INSTALLATION
1.3L, 1.6L and 1.9L Engines

NOTE: *With the timing belt removed and pistons at TDC, do not rotate the camshaft for fear of bending the valves. If the camshaft must be rotated, align the crankshaft pulley 90° BTDC. When actually installing the belt, the crankshaft pulley must be at TDC.*

1. Disconnect the negative battery cable.
2. Remove the timing belt cover.
3. Align the timing mark on the camshaft sprocket with the timing mark on the cylinder head.
4. Install the timing belt cover and confirm that the timing mark on the crankshaft pulley aligns with the **TDC** on the front cover.
5. Remove the timing belt cover.
6. Loosen both timing belt tensioner attaching bolts.
7. Pry the belt tensioner away from the belt as far as possible and tighten 1 of the tensioner attaching bolts.
8. Remove crankshaft pulley (damper) and remove the timing belt.

NOTE: *With the timing belt removed and pistons at TDC, do not rotate the engine. If the camshaft must be rotated, align the crankshaft pulley to 90° BTDC.*

To install:

NOTE: *Prior to installing the timing belt, make certain that the timing pointers on the sprockets are aligned with the timing marks on the cylinder head and oil pump.*

9. After the timing sprockets are properly aligned, install the timing belt over the sprockets in a counterclockwise direction starting at the crankshaft. Keep the belt span from the crankshaft to the camshaft tight as the belt is installed over the remaining sprocket.
10. Loosen belt tensioner attaching bolts and allow the tensioner to snap against the belt.
11. Tighten 1 of the tensioner attaching bolts.
12. Install the crankshaft pulley, drive plate and pulley attaching bolt. Hold the crankshaft pulley stationary and tighten the pulley attaching bolt to 74–90 ft. lbs. (100–121 Nm).
13. To seat the belt on the sprocket teeth, complete the following:
    a. Connect cable to the battery negative terminal.
    b. Crank engine for 30 seconds.
    c. Disconnect cable from the battery negative terminal.
    d. Turn camshaft, as necessary, to align the timing pointer on the cam sprocket with the timing mark on the cylinder head.
    e. Position the timing belt cover on the engine and check to see that the timing mark on the crankshaft aligns with the TDC pointer on the cover. If the timing marks do not align, remove the belt, align the timing marks and return to Step 11.
14. Loosen the belt tensioner attaching bolt tightened in Step 13.
15. Hold the crankshaft stationary and position a suitable torque wrench onto the camshaft sprocket bolt.
16. Turn the camshaft sprocket counterclockwise. Tighten the belt tensioner attaching bolt when the torque wrench reads as follows:
    a. New belt – 27–32 ft. lbs.
    b. Used belt (30 days or more in service) – 10 ft. lbs.

NOTE: *The engine must be at room temperature. Do not set belt tension on a hot engine.*

17. Install timing belt cover.
18. Install accessory drive belts and adjust the belt tension.
19. Connect negative battery cable.

Timing Chain Front Cover
REMOVAL AND INSTALLATION
2.3L Engine

1. Remove the engine and transaxle from the vehicle as an assembly and position in a suitable holding fixture. Remove the dipstick.
2. Remove accessory drive pulley, if equipped, Remove the crankshaft pulley attaching bolt and washer and remove pulley.
3. Remove front cover attaching bolts from front cover. Pry the top of the front cover away from the block.
4. Clean any gasket material from the surfaces.
5. Check timing chain and sprockets for excessive wear. If the timing chain and sprockets are worn, replace with new.
6. Check timing chain tensioner blade for wear depth. If the wear depth exceeds specification, replace tensioner.
7. Turn engine over until the timing marks are aligned. Remove camshaft sprocket attaching bolt and washer. Slide both sprockets and timing chain forward and remove as an assembly.

ENGINE AND ENGINE OVERHAUL 161

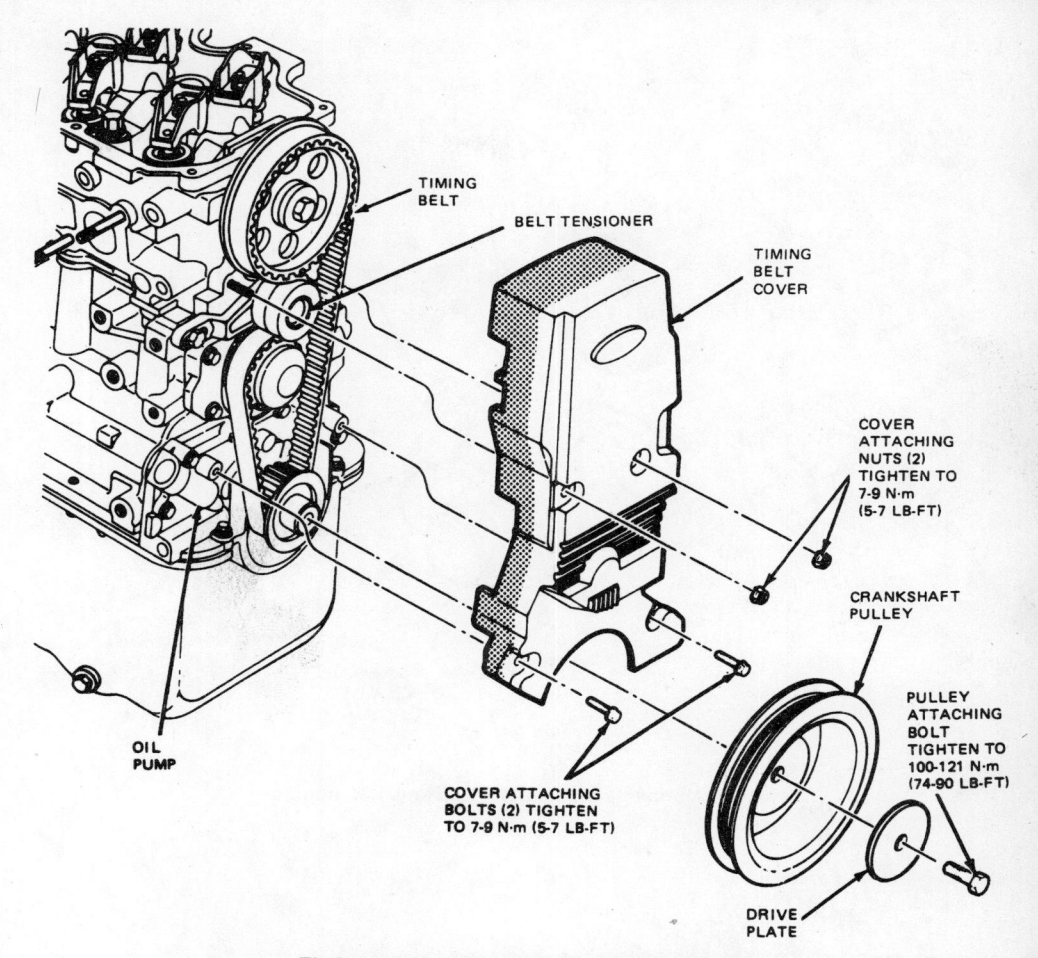

Timing cover and parts—1.6L and 1.9L engines

8. Check timing chain vibration damper for excessive wear and replace if necessary. The damper is located inside the front cover.
9. Remove the oil pan.

NOTE: *Oil pan removal is recommended to ensure proper sealing to front cover.*

To install:
10. Clean and inspect all parts before installation. Clean the oil pan, cylinder block and front cover of gasket material and dirt.
11. Slide both sprockets and timing chain onto the camshaft and crankshaft with timing marks aligned. Install camshaft bolt and washer and tighten 41–56 ft. lbs. (55–75 Nm). Oil timing chain, sprockets and tensioner after installation with clean engine oil.
12. Apply oil resistant sealer to a new front cover gasket and position gasket into front cover.
13. Remove the front cover oil seal and position the front cover on the engine.
14. Position front cover alignment tool T84P-6019-C or equivalent, onto the end of the crankshaft, ensuring the crank key is aligned with the keyway in the tool. Bolt the front cover to the engine and torque bolts to 6–9 ft. lbs. (8–12 Nm). Remove the front cover alignment tool.
15. If the front cover oil seal is damaged or worn, replace with new. Lubricate the hub of the crankshaft pulley with polyethylene grease to prevent damage to the seal during installation and initial engine start. Install crankshaft pulley.
16. Install the oil pan.
17. Install the accessory drive pulley, if equipped.
18. Install crankshaft pulley attaching bolt and washer. Tighten to 140–170 ft. lbs. (190–230 Nm).
19. Remove engine from work stand and install in vehicle.

162 ENGINE AND ENGINE OVERHAUL

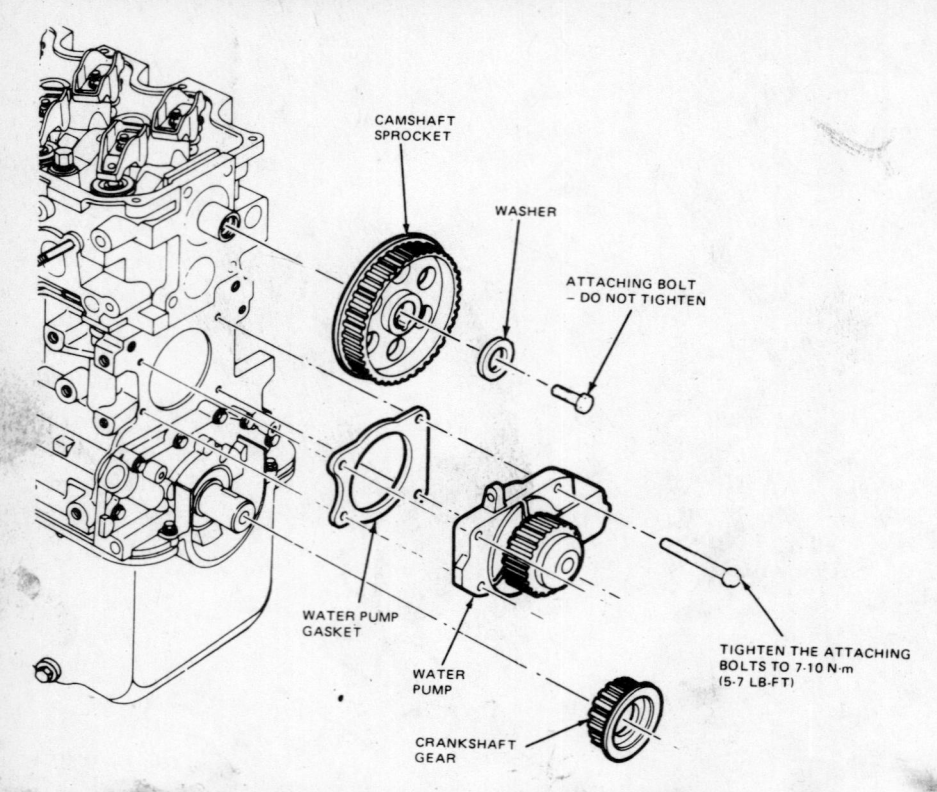

Timing components installation-1.6L and 1.9L engines

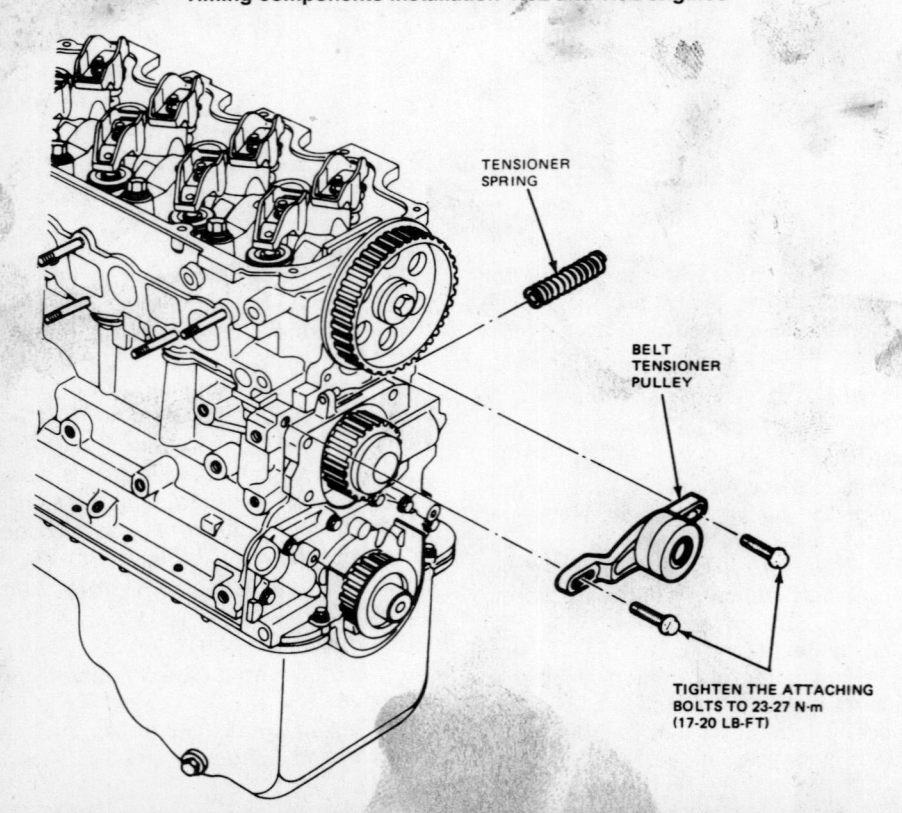

Tensioner and spring installation-1.6L and 1.9L engines

ENGINE AND ENGINE OVERHAUL 163

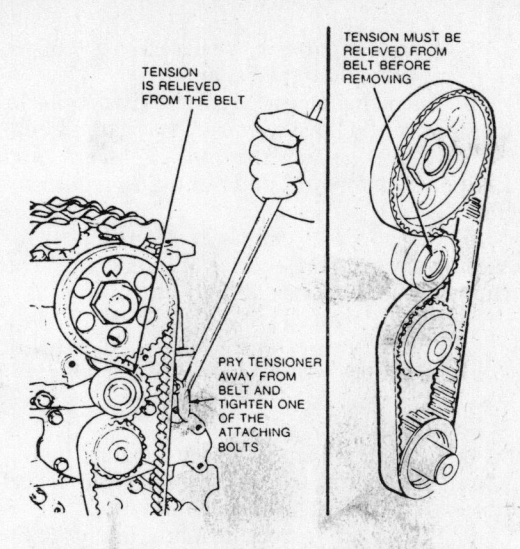

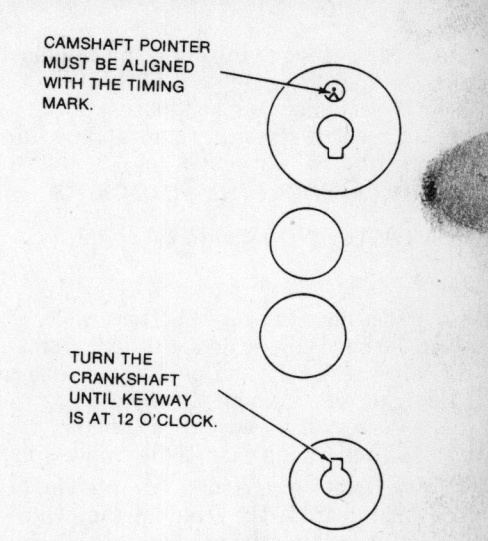

Relieving the belt tension on the 1.9L engine

Camshaft and crankshaft alignment-1.6L and 1.9L engines

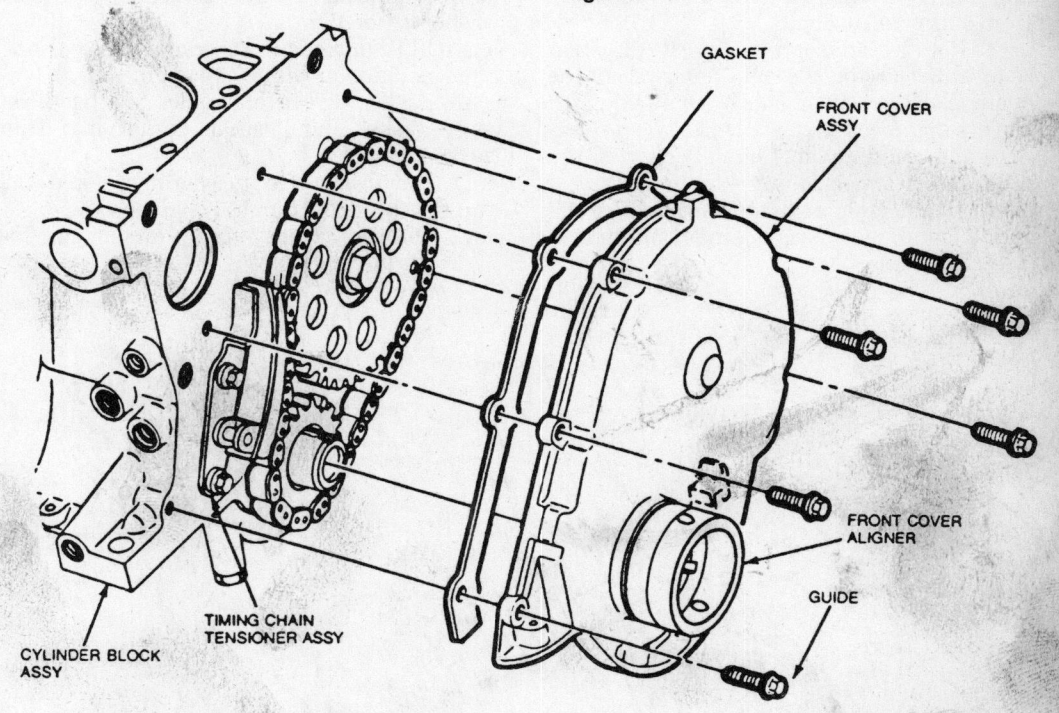

Timing chain cover removal and installation - 2.3L engine

Front Cover Oil Seal

REPLACEMENT

2.3L Engine

NOTE: *The removal and installation of the front cover oil seal on these engines can only be accomplished with the engine removed from the vehicle.*

1. Remove the engine from the vehicle and position in a suitable holding fixture.
2. Remove bolt and washer at crankshaft pulley.
3. Remove the crankshaft pulley.
4. Remove the front cover oil seal.
5. Coat a new seal with grease. Install and drive the seal until it is fully seated. Check the seal after installation to be sure the spring is properly positioned in the seal.
6. Install crankshaft pulley, attaching bolt

ENGINE AND ENGINE OVERHAUL

and washer. Torque the crankshaft pulley bolt to 140–170 ft. lbs. (190–230 Nm).

7. To complete the installation of the front cover oil seal, reverse the removal procedure.

Timing Chain and Sprockets

REMOVAL AND INSTALLATION

2.3L Engine

1. Disconnect negative battery cable.
2. Remove engine and transaxle from vehicle as an assembly and position in a suitable holding fixture. Remove the dipstick.
3. Remove front cover from engine.
4. Check timing chain deflection as follows:

   a. Rotate crankshaft counterclockwise, as viewed from the front of the engine, to take up slack on the left hand side of chain.

   b. Make a reference mark on the block at approximately mid-point of chain. Measure from this point to chain.

   c. Rotate crankshaft in opposite direction to take up slack on the right hand side of the chain. Force left hand side of chain out with fingers and measure distance between reference point and chain. The deflection is the difference between the 2 measurements.

   d. If deflection measurement exceeds 0.5 in. (12.7mm), replace timing chain and sprockets. If wear on tensioner face exceeds 0.06 in. (1.5mm), replace tensioner.

5. Turn engine over until the timing marks are aligned. Remove camshaft sprocket attaching bolt and washer. Slide both sprockets and timing chain forward and remove as an assembly.

6. Check timing chain vibration damper for excessive wear and replace if necessary. The damper is located inside the front cover.

7. Remove the oil pan.

NOTE: *Oil pan removal is recommended to ensure proper sealing to front cover upon installation.*

To install:

8. Clean and inspect all parts before installation. Clean the oil pan, cylinder block and front cover of gasket material and dirt.

9. Slide both sprockets and timing chain onto the camshaft and crankshaft with timing marks aligned. Install camshaft bolt and washer and tighten 41–56 ft. lbs. (55–75 Nm). Oil timing chain, sprockets and tensioner after installation with clean engine oil.

10. Apply oil resistant sealer to a new front cover gasket and position gasket into front cover.

11. Remove the front cover oil seal and position the front cover on the engine.

12. Position front cover alignment tool

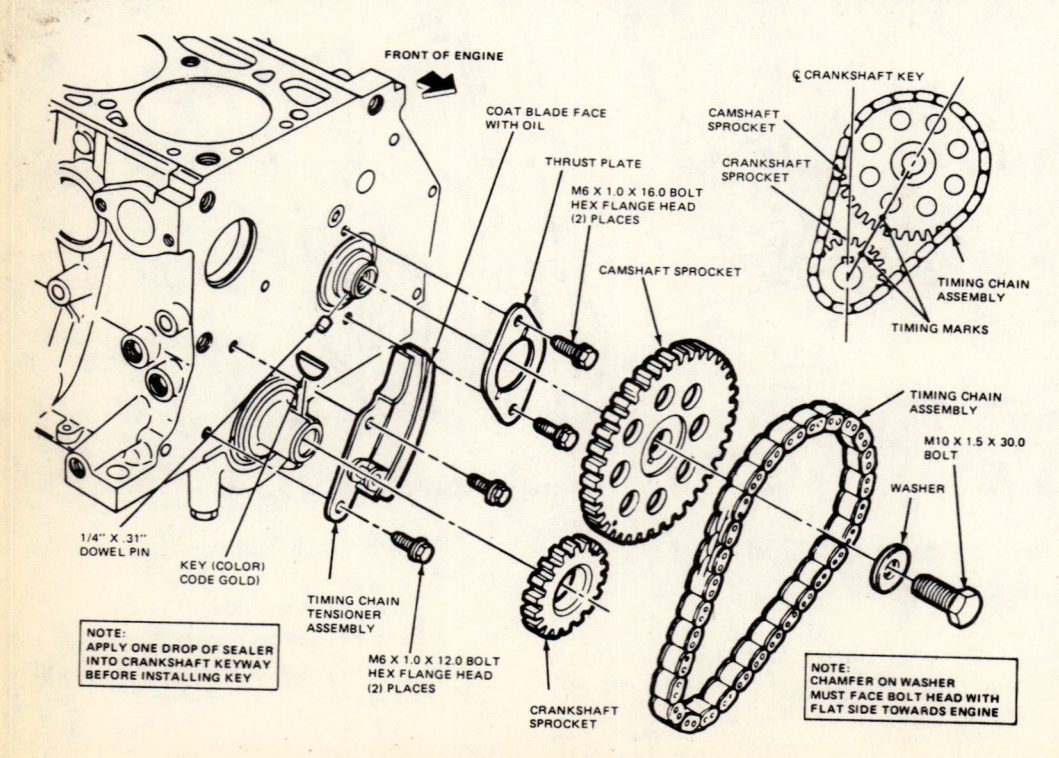

Timing gear components and alignment, 2.3L engine

ENGINE AND ENGINE OVERHAUL

T84P–6019–C or equivalent, onto the end of the crankshaft, ensuring the crank key is aligned with the keyway in the tool. Bolt the front cover to the engine and torque bolts to 6–9 ft. lbs. (8–12 Nm). Remove the front cover alignment tool.

13. If the front cover oil seal is damaged or worn, replace with new. Lubricate the hub of the crankshaft pulley with polyethylene grease to prevent damage to the seal during installation and initial engine start. Install crankshaft pulley.

14. Install the oil pan.

15. Install the accessory drive pulley, if equipped.

16. Install crankshaft pulley attaching bolt and washer. Tighten to 140–170 ft. lbs. (190–230 Nm).

17. Remove engine from work stand and install in vehicle.

18. Connect negative battery cable.

Timing Sprockets

REMOVAL AND INSTALLATION

All Models

1. Disconnect the negative battery cable.
2. Remove the timing belt cover and timing belt.

NOTE: *With the timing belt removed and pistons at TDC, do not rotate the engine. If the camshaft must be rotated, align the crankshaft pulley to 90° BTDC.*

3. Remove the camshaft sprocket attaching bolt and washer and camshaft sprocket.
4. Remove the crankshaft sprocket attaching bolt and washer and crankshaft sprocket.
5. Install the camshaft sprocket and attaching bolt and washer. Tighten to 71–84 ft. lbs. (95–115 Nm) on all engines except the 2.3L engine, 41–56 ft. lbs. (55–75 Nm) on the 2.3L engine.
6. Install the crankshaft sprocket.
7. Complete the installation of the timing sprockets by reversing the removal procedure. Observe proper installation of timing belt.

2.0L Diesel Engine

IN CAR SERVICE

NOTE: *This procedure is for Removal and Installation of the front timing belt for in-vehicle service of the water pump, camshaft, or cylinder head. The timing belt cannot be replaced with the engine installed in the vehicle.*

1. Remove the front timing belt upper cover and the flywheel timing mark cover.
2. Rotate engine clockwise until the timing marks on the flywheel and the front camshaft sprocket are aligned with their pointers.
3. Loosen tensioner pulley lockbolt and slide the timing belt off the water pump and camshaft sprockets.
4. The water pump and/or camshaft can now be serviced.

FRONT BELT ADJUSTMENTS

1. Remove the flywheel timing mark cover.
2. Remove the front timing belt upper cover.
3. Remove the belt tension spring from the storage pocket in the front cover.
4. Install the tensioner spring in the belt tensioner lever and over the stud mounted on the front of the crankcase.
5. Loosen the tensioner pulley lockbolt.
6. Rotate the crankshaft pulley two revolutions clockwise until the flywheel TDC timing mark aligns with the pointer on the rear cover plate.
7. Check the front camshaft sprocket to see that it is aligned with its timing mark.
8. Tighten the tensioner lockbolt to 23–34 ft. lbs.
9. Check the belt tension using Rotunda Belt Tension Gauge model 21–0028 or equivalent. Belt tension should be 33–44 lbs.
10. Remove the tensioner spring and install it in the storage pocket in the front cover.
11. Install the front cover and tighten the attaching bolts to 5–7 ft. lbs.
12. Install the flywheel timing mark cover.

REAR BELT ADJUSTMENTS

1. Remove the flywheel timing mark cover.
2. Remove the rear timing belt cover.
3. Loosen the tensioner pulley locknut.
4. Rotate the crankshaft two revolutions until the flywheel TDC timing mark aligns with the pointer on the rear cover plate.
5. Check that the camshaft sprocket and injection pump sprocket are aligned with their timing marks.
6. Tighten tensioner locknut to 15–20 ft. lbs.
7. Check belt tension using Rotunda Belt Tension Gauge model 21–0028 or equivalent. Belt tension should be 22–33 lbs.
8. Install the rear timing belt cover. Tighten the 6mm bolts to 5–7 ft. lbs. and the 8mm bolt to 12–16 ft. lbs.
9. Install the flywheel timing mark cover.

REAR BELT REMOVAL AND INSTALLATION

1. Remove the rear timing belt cover.
2. Remove the flywheel timing mark cover from clutch housing.

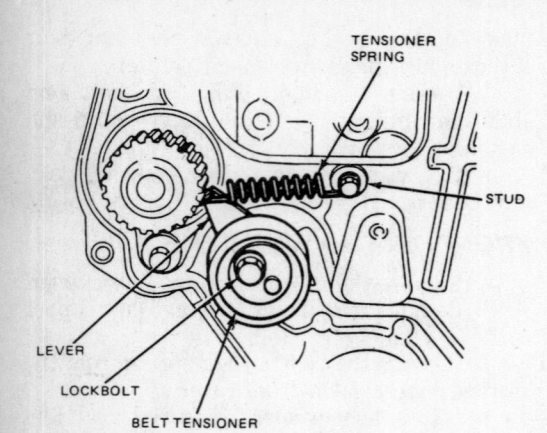

166 ENGINE AND ENGINE OVERHAUL

Front timing belt tensioner-diesel engine

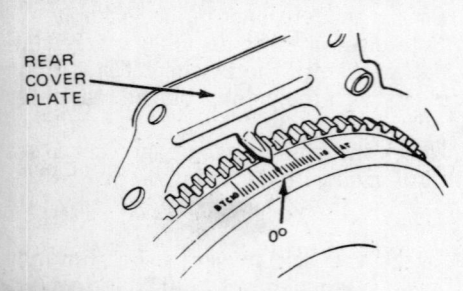

Flywheel timing marks-diesel engine

3. Rotate the crankshaft until the flywheel timing mark is at TDC on No. 1 cylinder.
4. Check that the injection pump and camshaft sprocket timing marks are aligned.
5. Loosen the tensioner locknut. With a screwdriver, or equivalent tool, inserted in the slot provided, rotate the tensioner clockwise to relieve belt tension. Tighten locknut snug.
6. Remove the timing belt.
7. Install the belt.
8. Loosen the tensioner locknut and adjust timing belt as outlined in previous section.
9. Install rear timing belt cover and tighten belts to 5–7 ft. lbs.

FRONT BELT REMOVAL AND INSTALLATION

NOTE: *The engine must be removed from the vehicle to replace the front timing belt.*

1. With engine removed from the vehicle and installed on an engine stand, remove front timing belt upper cover.
2. Install a Flywheel Holding Tool T84P–6375–A or equivalent.
3. Remove the six bolts attaching the crankshaft pulley to the crankshaft sprocket.
4. Install a crankshaft pulley Remover T58P–6316–D or equivalent using Adapter T74P–6700–B or equivalent, and remove crankshaft pulley.
5. Remove the front timing belt lower cover.
6. Loosen the tensioning pulley and remove timing belt.
7. Align the camshaft sprocket with the timing mark.

NOTE: *Check the crankshaft sprocket to see that the timing marks are aligned.*

8. Remove the tensioner spring from the pocket in the front timing belt upper cover and install it in the slot in the tensioner lever and over the stud in the crankcase.
9. Push the tensioner lever toward the water pump as far as it will travel and tighten lockbolt snug.
10. Install timing belt.
11. Adjust the timing belt tension as outlined in previous section.
12. Install the front timing belt lower cover and tighten bolts to 5–7 ft. lbs.
13. Install the crankshaft pulley and tighten bolts to 17–24 ft. lbs.
14. Install the front timing belt upper cover and tighten bolts to 5–7 ft. lbs.

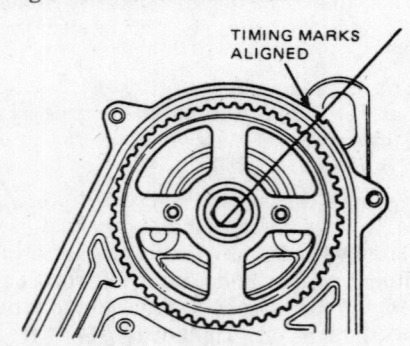

Camshaft timing mark-diesel engine

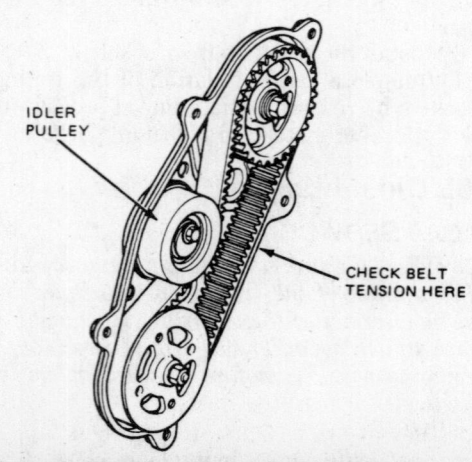

Timing belt tensioner, rear-diesel engine

ENGINE AND ENGINE OVERHAUL 167

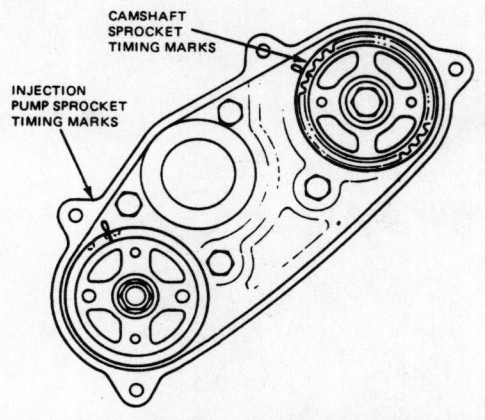

Camshaft and injector pump timing marks-diesel engine

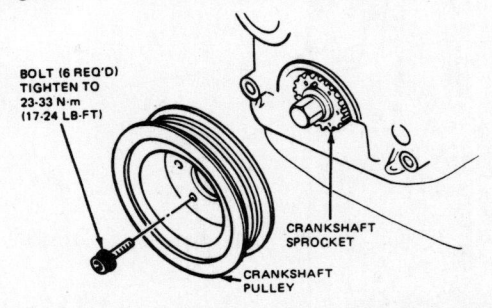

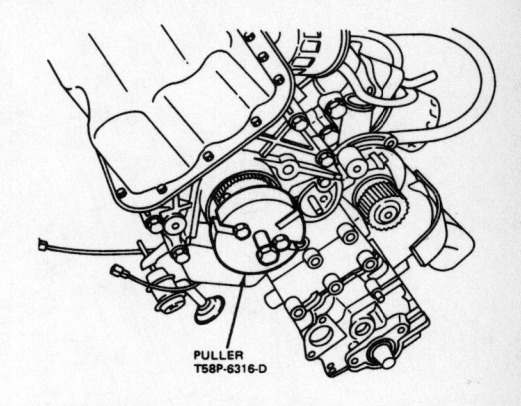

Crankshaft pulley removal-diesel engine

Crankshaft sprocket and pulley removal-diesel engine

Camshaft

REMOVAL AND INSTALLATION

1.3L and 1.6L Engines

The camshaft can be removed with the engine in the car.

1. Remove the fuel pump and plunger. Set the engine to TDC on the compression stroke of No. 1 cylinder. Remove the negative battery cable.
2. Remove the alternator drive belt. Remove the power steering and air conditioning compressor drive belts, if equipped.
3. Remove the camshaft belt cover.
4. Remove the distributor.
5. Remove the rocker arms.
6. Remove the hydraulic valve lash adjusters. Keep the parts in order, as they must be returned to their original positions.
7. Remove and discard the timing belt.
8. Remove the camshaft sprocket and key.
9. Remove the camshaft thrust plate.
10. Remove the ignition coil and coil bracket.
11. Remove the camshaft through the back of the head towards the transaxle.

To install:

12. Before installing the camshaft, coat the bearing journals, cam lobe surfaces, seal and thrust plate groove with engine oil. Install the camshaft through the rear of the cylinder head. Rotate the camshaft during installation.
13. Install the camshaft thrust plate and tighten the two attaching bolts to 7–11 ft. lbs.
14. Install the cam sprocket and key.
15. Install a new timing belt. See timing belt removal and installation procedure.
16. Install remaining parts in the reverse order of removal. When installing rocker arms, use new hex flange nuts.

1.9L Engine

1. Disconnect the negative battery cable.
2. Properly relieve the fuel system pressure. Remove the air cleaner and PCV hose.
3. Remove the accessory drive belts and crankshaft pulley.
4. Remove the timing belt cover and valve cover.
5. Set the engine No. 1 cylinder at TDC prior to removing timing belt.

NOTE: *Make sure the crankshaft is positioned at TDC and do not turn the crankshaft until the timing belt is installed.*

6. Remove rocker arms and lifters as follows:
   a. Remove hex flange bolts.
   b. Remove fulcrums.

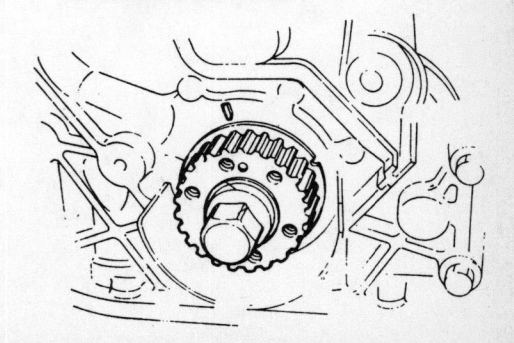

Loosening tensioner pulley-diesel engine

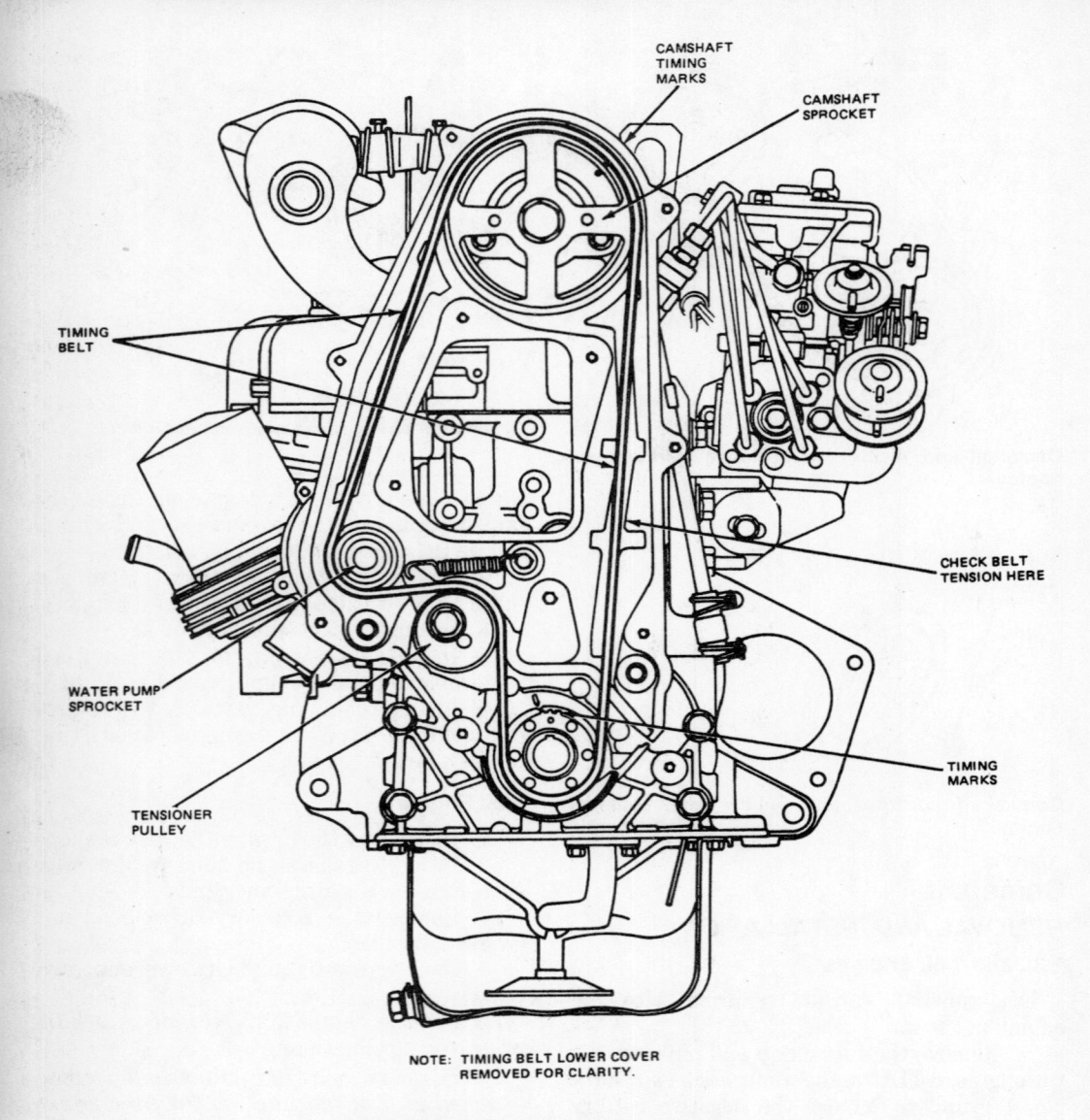

168 ENGINE AND ENGINE OVERHAUL

NOTE: TIMING BELT LOWER COVER REMOVED FOR CLARITY.

Front timing belt installation, diesel engine

Camshaft distributor drive -1.6L and 1.9L engines

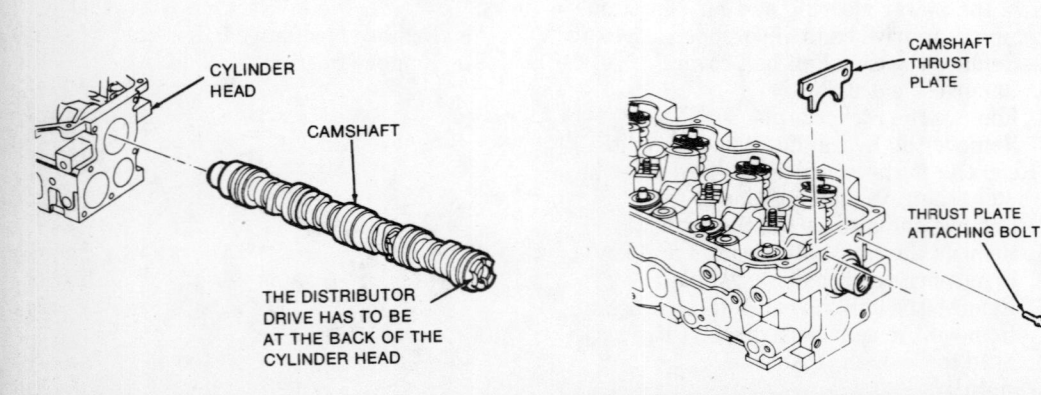

Camshaft thrust plate removal-1.6L and 1.9L engines

ENGINE AND ENGINE OVERHAUL

    c. Remove rocker arms.
    d. Remove fulcrum washer.
    e. Remove tappets.
7. Remove the distributor assembly.
8. Loosen both timing belt tensioner attaching bolts using torque wrench adapter or equivalent.
9. Remove timing belt.
10. Remove the camshaft sprocket and key.
11. Remove the camshaft thrust plate.
12. Remove the ignition coil and coil bracket.
13. Remove the camshaft through the back of the head toward the transaxle.
14. Replace camshaft seal.

To install:
15. Thoroughly coat the camshaft bearing journals, cam lobe surfaces and thrust plate groove with a suitable lubricant.
16. Install camshaft through the rear of the cylinder head. Rotate camshaft during installation.
17. Install the camshaft thrust plate. Tighten attaching bolts to 7–11 ft. lbs. (10–15 Nm).
18. Align and install the cam sprocket over the cam key. Install attaching washer and bolt. While holding camshaft stationary, tighten the bolt to 37–46 ft. lbs. (50–62.5 Nm).
19. Install the timing belt.
20. Install the timing belt cover.
21. Install the rocker arm assembly as follows:

NOTE: *Replace used hex flange nuts with new ones. Lubricate all the parts with a heavy engine oil before installation.*

    a. Install the lifters.
    b. Install the fulcrum washers.
    c. Install the rocker arms.
    d. Install the fulcrums.
    e. Install new rocker arm stud hex flange bolts. Tighten to 17–22 ft. lbs. (23–30 Nm).
22. Install the distributor assembly.
23. Install new valve cover gasket.

NOTE: *Make sure the surfaces on the cylinder head and valve cover are clean and free of sealant material.*

24. Install the rocker arm cover attaching bolts and studs. Tighten bolts and studs to 6–8 ft. lbs. (8–11.5 Nm).
25. Install PCV hose and the air cleaner assembly.
26. Connect negative battery cable.
27. Start engine and set the ignition timing.

2.3L Engine
1. Drain the cooling system, fuel system and crankcase.

CAUTION: *When draining the coolant, keep in mind that cats and dogs are attracted by the ethylene glycol antifreeze, and are quite likely to drink any that is left in an uncovered container or in puddles on the ground. This will prove fatal in sufficient quantity. Always drain the coolant into a sealable container. Coolant should be reused unless it is contaminated or several years old. The EPA warns that prolonged contact with used engine oil may cause a number of skin disorders, including cancer! You should make every effort to minimize your exposure to used engine oil. Protective gloves should be worn when changing the oil. Wash your hands and any other exposed skin areas as soon as possible after exposure to used engine oil. Soap and water, or waterless hand cleaner should be used.*

2. Remove the engine from the vehicle and position in a suitable holding fixture. Remove the engine oil dipstick.
3. Remove necessary drive belts and pulleys.
4. Remove cylinder head. Remove the distributor.
5. Using a magnet, remove the hydraulic tappets and label them so that they can be installed in their original positions. If the tappets are stuck in the bores by excessive varnish, etc., use a suitable claw-type puller to remove the tappets.
6. Loosen and remove the drive belt, fan and pulley and crankshaft pulley.
7. Remove the oil pan.
8. Remove the cylinder front cover and gasket.
9. Check the camshaft endplay as follows:
    a. Push the camshaft toward the rear of the engine and install a dial indicator tool, so that the indicator point is on the camshaft sprocket attaching screw.
    b. Zero the dial indicator. Position a small pry bar or equivalent, between the camshaft sprocket or gear and block.
    c. Pull the camshaft forward and release it. Compare the dial indicator reading with the camshaft endplay specification of 0.009 in.
    d. If the camshaft endplay is over the amount specified, replace the thrust plate.
10. Remove fuel pump, gasket and fuel pump pushrod, if so equipped.
11. Remove the timing chain, sprockets and timing chain tensioner.
12. Remove camshaft thrust plate. Carefully remove the camshaft by pulling it toward the front of the engine. Use caution to avoid damaging bearings, journals and lobes.

To install:
13. Clean and inspect all parts before installation.
14. Lubricate camshaft lobes and journals

170 ENGINE AND ENGINE OVERHAUL

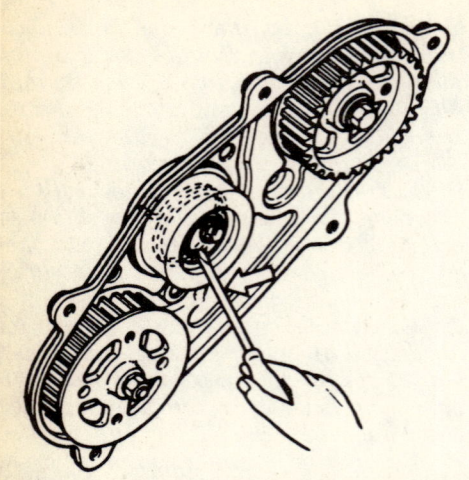

Front timing case cover installation-2.3L HSC engine

with heavy engine oil. Carefully slide the camshaft through the bearings in the cylinder block.

15. Install the thrust plate. Tighten attaching bolts to 6–9 ft. lbs (8–12 Nm).
16. Install the timing chain, sprockets and timing chain tensioner. Check timing chain deflection.
17. Install the cylinder front cover and crankshaft pulley.
18. Clean the oil pump inlet tube screen, oil pan and cylinder block gasket surfaces. Prime oil pump by filling the inlet opening with oil and rotate the pump shaft until oil emerges from the outlet tube. Install oil pump, oil pump inlet tube screen and oil pan.
19. Install the accessory drive belts and pulleys.
20. Lubricate the tappets and tappets bores with heavy engine oil. Install tappets into their original bores.
21. Install cylinder head.
22. Install fuel pump, new gasket and fuel pump push rod, if so equipped. Tighten bolts to 15–21 ft. lbs. (20–28 Nm).
23. Position No. 1 piston at TDC after the compression stroke. Position distributor in the block with the rotor at the No. 1 firing position. Install distributor retaining clamp.
24. Connect engine temperature sending unit wire. Connect coil primary wire. Install distributor cap. Connect spark plug wires and the coil high tension lead.
25. Install engine in vehicle.
26. Fill the cooling system and crankcase to the proper levels.
27. Connect negative battery cable.
28. Start the engine. Check and adjust ignition timing. Connect distributor vacuum line to distributor. Check for leaks. Adjust engine idle speed.

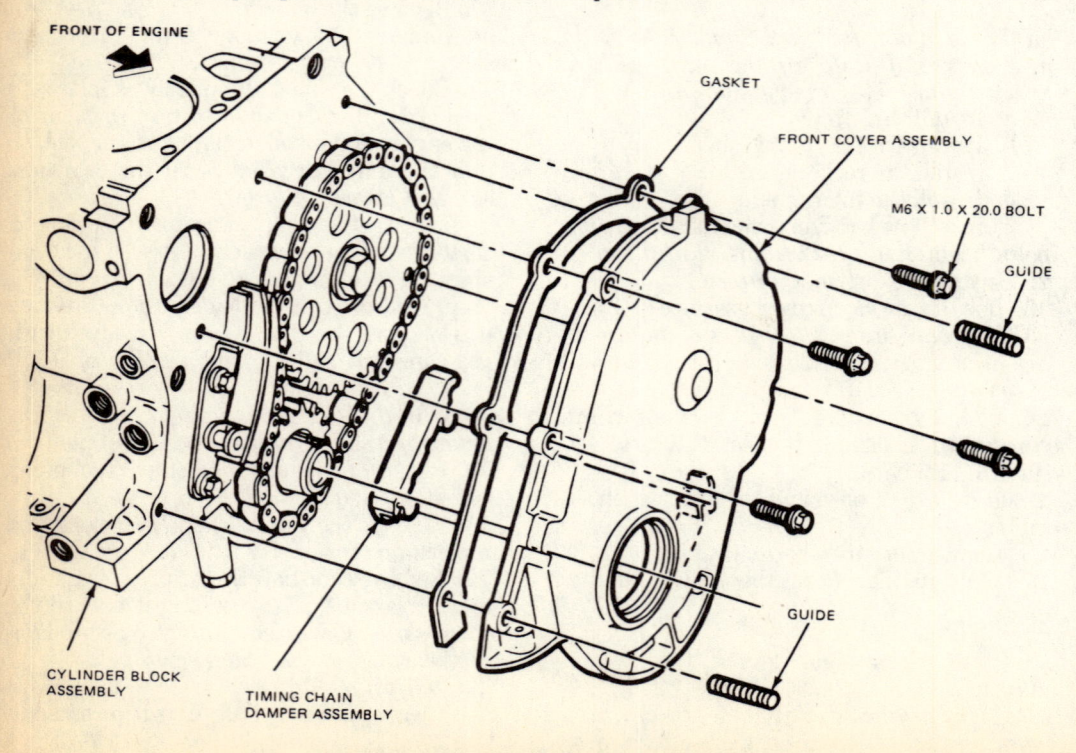

2.3L HSC Engine timing cover components

ENGINE AND ENGINE OVERHAUL

CHECKING CAMSHAFT

Degrease the camshaft using safe solvent, clean all oil grooves. Visually inspect the cam lobes and bearing journals for excessive wear. If a lobe is questionable, check all lobes and journals with a micrometer.

Measure the lobes from nose to base and again at 90°. The lift is determined by subtracting the second measurement from the first. If all exhaust lobes and all intake lobes are not identical, the camshaft must be reground or replaced. Measure the bearing journals and compare to specifications. If a journal is worn there is a good chance that the cam bearings are worn too, requiring replacement.

If the lobes and journals appear intact, place the front and rear cam journals in V-blocks and rest a dial indicator on the center journal. Rotate the camshaft to check for straightness, if deviation exceeds 0.001 in. (0.025mm), replace the camshaft.

Pistons and Connection Rods

REMOVAL AND INSTALLATION

NOTE: *Although, in most cases, the pistons and connecting rods can be removed from the engine (after the cylinder head and oil pan are removed) while the engine is still in the car, it is far easier to remove the engine from the car. If removing pistons with the engine still installed, disconnect the radiator hoses, automatic transmission cooler lines and radiator shroud. Unbolt front mounts before jacking up the engine. Block the engine in position with wooden blocks between the mounts.*

1. Remove the engine from the car. Remove cylinder head(s), oil pan and front cover (if necessary).
2. Because the top piston ring does not travel to the very top of the cylinder bore, a ridge is built up between the end of the travel and the top of the cylinder. Pushing the piston and connecting rod assembly past the ridge is difficult and may cause damage to the piston. If new rings are installed and the ridge has not been removed, ring breakage and piston damage can occur when the ridge is encountered at engine speed.
3. Turn the crankshaft to position the piston at the bottom of the cylinder bore. Cover the top of the piston with a rag. Install a ridge reamer in the bore and follow the manufacturer's instructions to remove the ridge. Use caution. Avoid cutting too deeply or into the ring travel area. Remove the rag and cuttings from the top of the piston. Remove the ridge from all cylinders.

Use lengths of vacuum hose or rubber tubing to protect the crankshaft journals and cylinder walls during installation

4. Check the edges of the connecting rod and bearing cap for numbers or matchmarks, if none are present mark the rod and cap numerically and in sequence from front to back of engine. The numbers or marks not only tell from which cylinder the piston came from buy also ensures that the rod caps are installed in the correct matching position.
5. Turn the crankshaft until the connecting rod is at the bottom of travel. Remove the two attaching nuts and the bearing cap. Take two pieces of rubber tubing and cover the rod bolts to prevent crank or cylinder scoring. Use a wooden hammer handle to help push the piston and rod up and out of the cylinder. Reinstall the rod cap in proper position. Remove all pis-

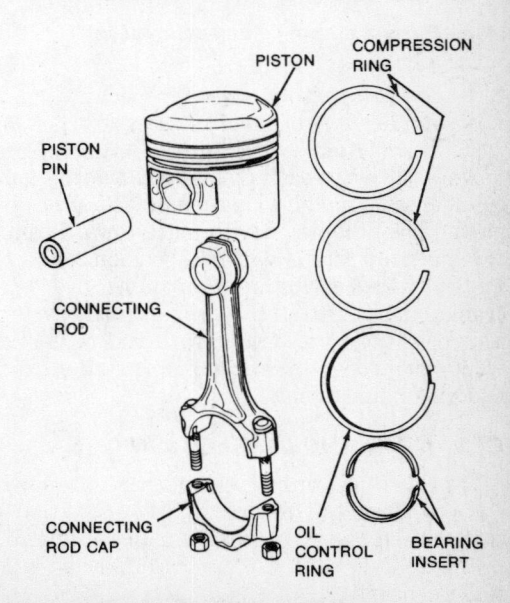

Piston and connecting rod assembly

ENGINE AND ENGINE OVERHAUL

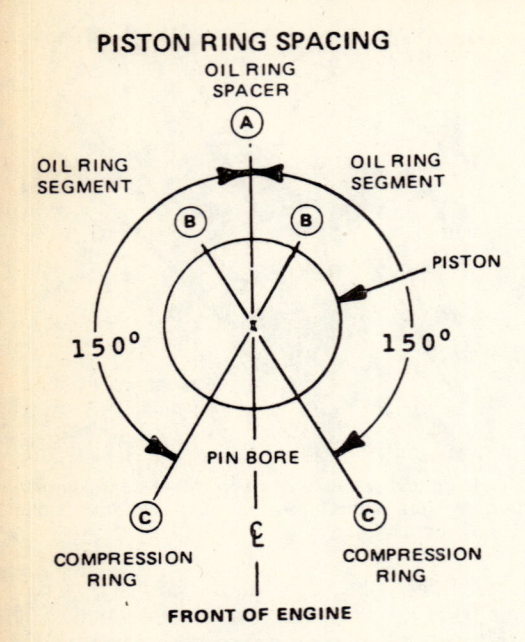

Recommended piston ring spacing. Refer to the ring manufacturer's instruction sheet before installing new piston rings

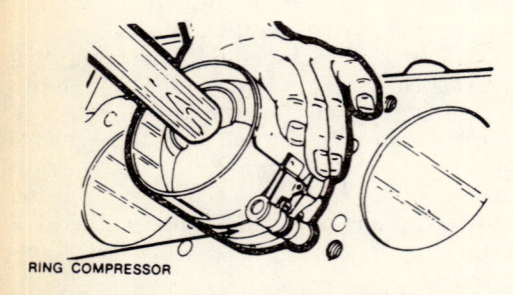

Install the piston using a ring compressor

tons and connecting rods. Inspect cylinder walls and de-glaze or hone as necessary.

6. Installation is the reverse order of removal. Lubricate each piston, rod bearing and cylinder wall. Install a ring compressor over the piston, position piston with mark toward front of engine and carefully install. Position connecting rod with bearing insert installed over the crank journal. Install the rod cap with bearing in proper position. Secure with rod nuts and torque to proper specifications. Install all rod and piston assemblies.

CLEANING AND INSPECTION

1. Use a piston ring expander and remove the rings from the piston.
2. Clean the ring grooves using an appropriate cleaning tool, exercise care to avoid cutting too deeply.
3. Clean all varnish and carbon from the piston with a safe solvent. Do not use a wire brush or caustic solution on the pistons.
4. Inspect the pistons for scuffing, scoring, cracks, pitting or excessive ring groove wear. If wear is evident, the piston must be replaced.
5. Have the piston and connecting rod assembly checked by a machine shop for correct alignment, piston pin wear and piston diameter. If the piston has collapsed it will have to be replace or knurled to restore original diameter. Connecting rod bushing replacement, piston pin fitting and piston changing can be handled by the machine shop.

CYLINDER BORE

Check the cylinder bore for wear using a telescope gauge and a micrometer, measure the cylinder bore diameter perpendicular to the piston pin at a point $2^{1}/_{2}$ in. (63.5mm) below the top of the engine block. Measure the piston skirt perpendicular to the piston pin. The difference between the two measurements is the piston clearance. If the clearance is within specifications, finish honing or glaze breaking is all that is required. If clearance is excessive a slightly oversize piston may be required. If greatly oversize, the engine will have to be bored and 0.010 in. (0.25mm) or larger oversized pistons installed.

FITTING AND POSITIONING PISTON RINGS

1. Take the new piston rings and compress them, one at a time into the cylinder that they will be used in. Press the ring about 1 in. (25mm) below the top of the cylinder block using an inverted piston.
2. Use a feeler gauge and measure the distance between the ends of the ring. This is called measuring the ring end gap. Compare the reading to the one called for in the specifications table. File the ends of the ring with a fine file to obtain necessary clearance.

NOTE: *If inadequate ring end gap is utilized, ring breakage will result.*

3. Inspect the ring grooves on the piston for excessive wear or taper. If necessary have the grooves recut for use with a standard ring and spacer. The machine shop can handle the job for you.
4. Check the ring grooves by rolling the new piston ring around the groove to check for burrs or carbon deposits. If any are found, remove with a fine file. Hold the ring in the groove and measure side clearance with a feeler gauge. If clearance is excessive, spacer(s) will have to be added.

NOTE: *Always add spacers above the piston ring.*

5. Install the ring on the piston, lower oil ring first. Use a ring installing tool on the com-

ENGINE AND ENGINE OVERHAUL

pression rings. Consult the instruction sheet that comes with the rings to be sure they are installed with the correct side up. A mark on the ring usually faces upward.

6. When installing oil rings, first, install the expanding ring in the groove. Hold the ends of the ring butted together (they must not overlap) and install the bottom rail (scraper) with the end about 1 in. (25mm) away from the butted end of the control ring. Install the top rail about 1 in. (25mm) away from the butted end of the control but on the opposite side from the lower rail.

7. Install the two compression rings.

8. Consult the illustration for ring positioning, arrange the rings as shown, install a ring compressor and insert the piston and rod assembly into the engine.

Rear Main Bearing Oil Seal

REMOVAL AND INSTALLATION

Gasoline Engines

1. Remove the transaxle.
2. Remove the rear cover plate, and flywheel.
3. Using a suitable tool, punch two holes in the metal surface of the seal between the lip and block.
4. Screw in the threaded end of a small slide hammer and remove the seal.

To install:

5. Inspect the crankshaft seal area for any damage which may cause the seal to leak. If there is damage evident, service or replace the crankshaft as necessary.
6. Clean the seal mounting surfaces. Coat the crankshaft and seal with engine oil.
7. Place the crankshaft rear seal pilot tool T88P–6701–B or equivalent into the crankshaft rear seal replacer tool T88P–6701–B1 or equivalent. Lubricate the pilot and seal replacer with oil. Slide the rear seal over the pilot onto the replacer tool. Be sure that the seal is

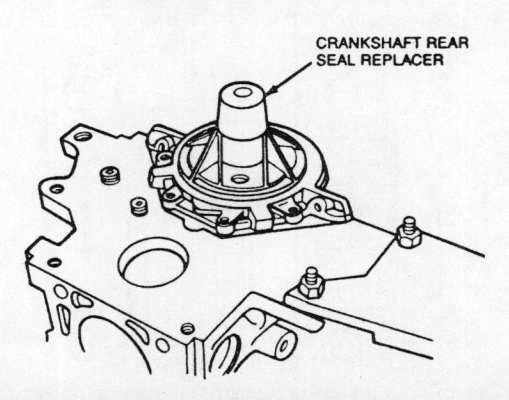

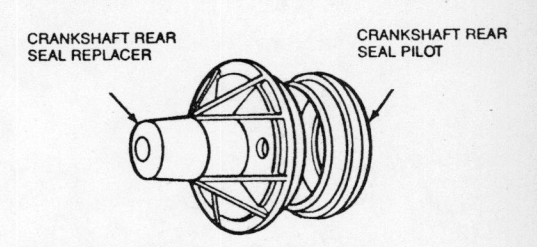

Typical Rear crankshaft seal installer

on correctly and that the edges are not rolled over.

NOTE: *When installing the seal on the 2.3L engine, use seal installer T81P–6701–A or equivalent. Apply a Anaerobic Sealer ESEM4G-A2 or B2 on the seal retainer side facing the engine block. after removing the old seal.*

8. Remove the crankshaft pilot tool from the rear seal installer tool. Place the seal and replacer tool over the crankshaft and install the seal.
9. Install the flywheel. Torque the attaching bolts to 54–64 ft. lbs. (73–87 Nm).
10. Install the rear cover plate. Install the transaxle.

Diesel Engine

1. Disconnect the negative battery cable, located in the luggage compartment.
2. Remove the transaxle and clutch assemblies.
3. Install a suitable flywheel holding tool and remove the flywheel retaining bolts. Remove the flywheel
4. Remove the rear main seal.

To install:

5. Inspect the crankshaft seal area for any damage which may cause the seal to leak. If there is damage evident, service or replace the crankshaft as necessary.

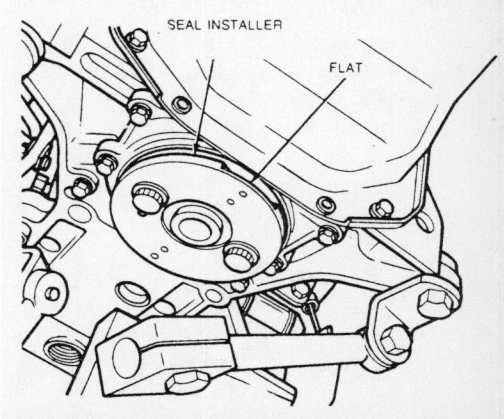

Installing the rear crankshaft seal

Installing the rear crankshaft seal – 2.0L diesel engine

174 ENGINE AND ENGINE OVERHAUL

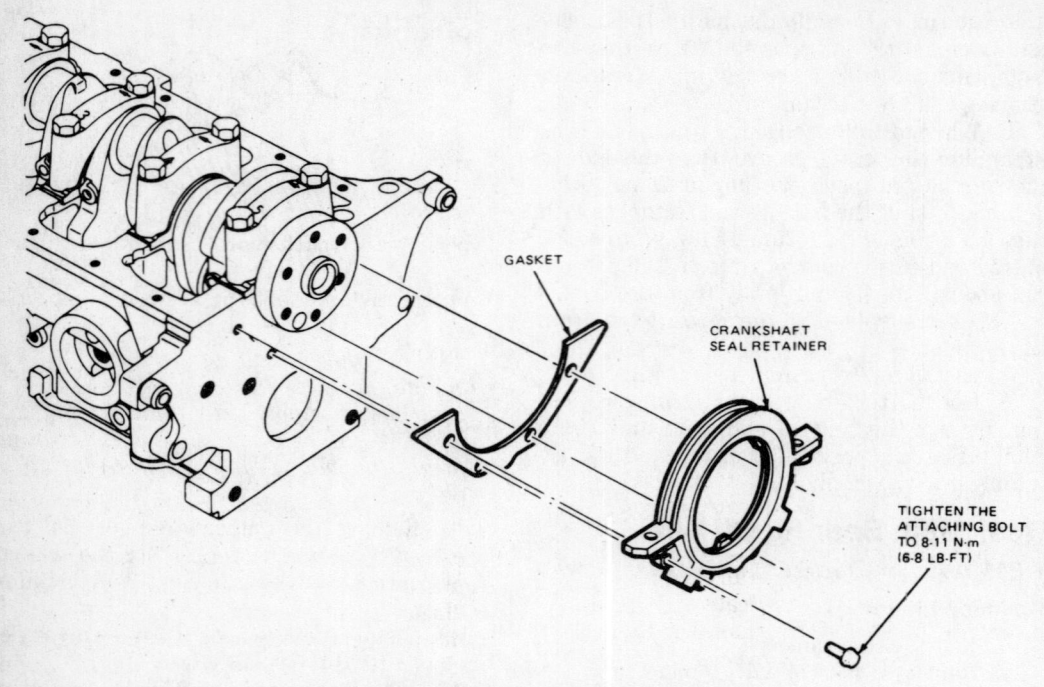

Typical rear main bearing oil seal installation

6. Clean the seal mounting surfaces. Coat the crankshaft and seal with engine oil.

7. Using a suitable seal installer, install the new rear main seal.

NOTE: *The flat edge of the seal installer must be parallel to the oil pan or damage to the seal retainer and/or oil pan may result.*

8. Install the flywheel and using a suitable flywheel holding tool, torque the flywheel retaining bolts to 131–137 ft. lbs. (180–190 Nm).

9. Install the clutch and transaxle assemblies. Reconnect the negative battery. Start the engine and check for oil leaks.

Crankshaft and Bearings

REMOVAL AND INSTALLATION

1. Rod bearings can be installed when the pistons have been removed for servicing (rings etc.) or, in most cases, while the engine is still in the car. Bearing replacement, however, is far easier with the engine out of the car and disassembled.

2. For in car service, remove the oil pan, spark plugs and front cover if necessary. Turn the engine until the connecting rod to be serviced is at the bottom of travel. Remove the bearing cap, place two pieces of rubber hose over the rod cap bolts and push the piston and rod assembly up the cylinder bore until enough room is gained for bearing insert removal. Take care not to push the rod assembly up too far or the top ring will engage the cylinder ridge or come out of the cylinder and require head removal for installation.

3. Clean the rod journal, the connecting rod end and the bearing cap after removing the old bearing inserts. Install the new inserts in the rod and bearing cap, lubricate them with oil. Po-

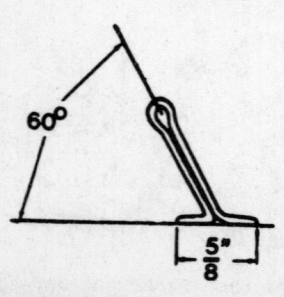

Home made roll-out pin

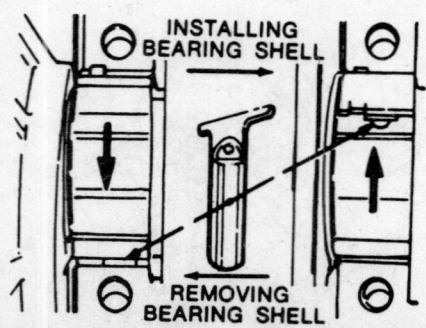

Remove or install the upper main bearing insert using a roll-out pin

ENGINE AND ENGINE OVERHAUL

sition the rod over the crankshaft journal and install the rod cap. Make sure the cap and rod numbers match, torque the rod nuts to specifications.

4. Main bearings may be replaced while the engine is still in the car by rolling them out and in.

5. Special roll out pins are available from automotive parts houses or can be fabricated from a cotter pin. The roll out pin fits in the oil hole of the main bearing journal. When the crankshaft is rotated opposite the directions of the bearing lock tab, the pin engages the end of the bearing and rolls out the insert.

6. Remove main bearing cap and roll out upper bearing insert. Remove insert from main bearing cap. Clean the inside of the bearing cap and crankshaft journal.

7. Lubricate and roll upper insert into position, make sure the lock tab is anchored and the insert is not cocked. Install the lower bearing insert into the cap, lubricate and install on the engine. Make sure the main bearing cap is installed facing in the correct direction and torque to specifications.

8. With the engine out of the car, remove the intake manifold, cylinder heads, front cover, timing gears and/or chain, oil pan, oil pump and flywheel.

9. Remove the piston and rod assemblies. Remove the main bearing caps after marking them for position and direction.

10. Remove the crankshaft, bearing inserts and rear main oil seal. Clean the engine block and cap bearing saddles. Clean the crankshaft and inspect for wear. Check the bearing journals with a micrometer for out-of-round condition and to determine wheat size rod and main bearing inserts to install.

11. Install the main bearing upper inserts and rear main oil seal half into the engine block.

12. Lubricate the bearing inserts and the

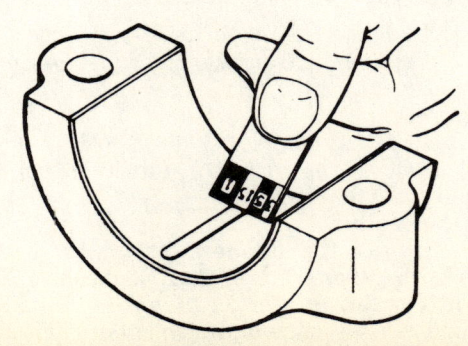

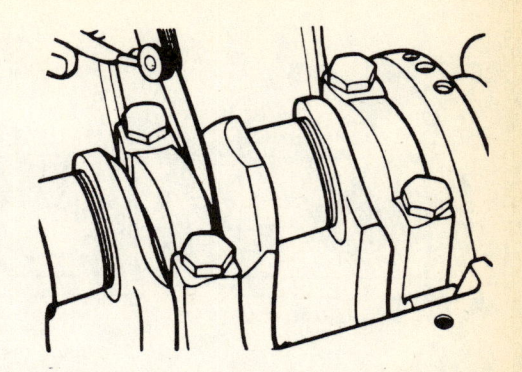

Check the crankshaft end-play with a feeler gauge

crankshaft journals. Slowly and carefully lower the crankshaft into position.

13. Install the bearing inserts and rear main seal into the bearing caps, install the caps working from the middle out. Torque cap bolts to specifications in stages, rotate the crankshaft after each torque state. Note the illustration for thrust bearing alignment.

14. Remove bearing caps, one at a time and check the oil clearance with Plastigage®. Reinstall if clearance is within specifications. Check the crankshaft endplay, if within specifications install connecting rod and piston assemblies with new rod bearing inserts. Check connecting rod bearing oil clearance and side play, if correct assemble the rest of the engine.

BEARING OIL CLEARANCE

Remove cap from the bearing to be checked. Using a clean, dry rag, thoroughly clean all oil from crankshaft journal and bearing insert.

NOTE: *Plastigage® is soluble in oil, therefore, oil on the journal or bearing could result in erroneous readings.*

Place a pieced of Plastigage® along the full width of the bearing insert, reinstall cap, and torque to specifications.

NOTE: *Specifications are given in the engine specifications earlier in this chapter.*

Remove bearing cap, and determine bearing clearance by comparing width of Plastigage® to the scale on Plastigage® envelope. Journal

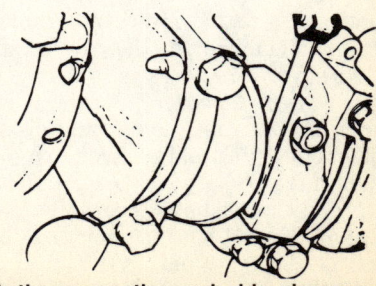

Measure the Plastigage® to determine bearing clearance

Check the connecting rod side clearance with a feeler gauge

ENGINE AND ENGINE OVERHAUL

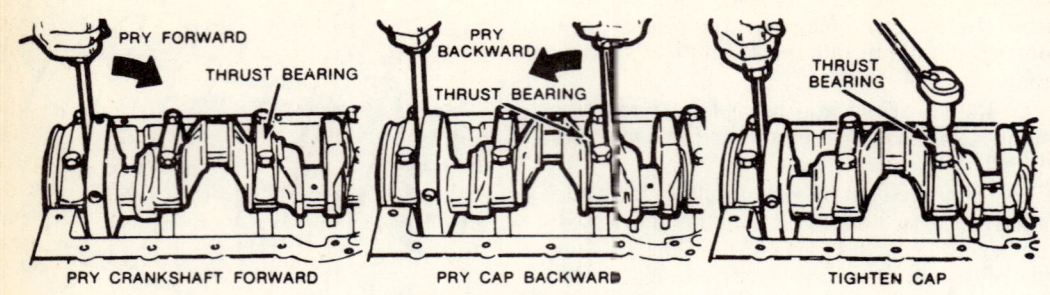

Aligning the thrust bearing

taper is determined by comparing width of the bearing insert, reinstall cap, and torque to specifications.

NOTE: *Do not rotate crankshaft with Plastigage® installed. If bearing insert and journal appear intact, and are within tolerances, no further main bearing service is required. If bearing or journal appear defective, cause of failure should be determined before replacement.*

CRANKSHAFT ENDPLAY/CONNECTING ROD SIDE PLAY

Place a pry bar between a main bearing cap and crankshaft casting taking care not to damage any journals. Pry backward and forward, measure the distance between the thrust bearing and crankshaft with a feeler gauge. Compare reading with specifications. If too great a clearance is determined, a main bearing with a larger thrust surface or crank machining may be required. Check with an automotive machine shop for their advice.

Connecting rod clearance between the rod and crank throw casting can be checked with a feeler gauge. Pry the rod carefully on one side as far as possible and measure the distance on the other side of the rod.

CRANKSHAFT REPAIRS

If a journal is damaged on the crankshaft, repair is possible by having the crankshaft machined to a standard undersize.

In most cases, however, since the engine must be removed from the car and disassembled, some thought should be given to replacing the damaged crankshaft with a reground shaft kit. A reground crankshaft kit contains the necessary main and rod bearings for installation. The shaft has been ground and polished to undersize specifications and will usually hold up well if installed correctly.

Completing the Rebuilding Process

Complete the rebuilding process as follows:

1. Fill the oil pump with oil, to prevent cavitating (sucking air) on initial engine start up. Install the oil pump and the pickup tube on the engine. Coat the oil pan gasket as necessary, and install the gasket and the oil pan. Mount the flywheel and the crankshaft vibration damper or pulley on the crankshaft.

NOTE: *Always use new bolts when install the flywheel. Inspect the clutch shaft pilot bushing in the crankshaft. If the bushing is excessively worn, remove it with an expanding puller and a slide hammer, and tap a new bushing into place.*

2. Position the engine, cylinder head side up. Lubricate the lifters, and install them into their bores. Install the cylinder head, and torque it as specified. Insert the pushrods (where applicable), and install the rocker shaft(s) (if so equipped) or position the rocker.

3. Install the intake and exhaust manifolds, the carburetor(s), the distributor and spark plugs. Mount all accessories and install the engine in the car. Fill the radiator with coolant, and the crankcase with high quality engine oil.

Flywheel and Ring Gear

REMOVAL AND INSTALLATION

1. Disconnect the negative battery cable.
2. Remove the transaxle and clutch assemblies. Remove the rear cover plate, if so equipped.
3. Install a suitable flywheel holding tool and remove the flywheel retaining bolts. Remove the flywheel.

To install:

4. Inspect the flywheel for cracks, heat checks or other damage that would make it unfit for further service. On the vehicles equipped with manual transmissions, check the machine surface of the flywheel to see if it is scored or worn. On the diesel equipped vehi-

cles if it is necessary to remove more than 0.45 in. (1.143mm) of stock from the original thickness of the flywheel, replace the flywheel with a new one.

5. Install the flywheel and using a suitable flywheel holding tool, torque the flywheel retaining bolts to 54–64 ft. lbs. (73–87 Nm) for gasoline engines and 131–137 ft. lbs. (180–190 Nm) on diesel engines.

6. Install the clutch and transaxle assemblies. Rear cover plate, if so equipped.

7. Reconnect the negative battery. Start the engine and check for proper starter gear to flywheel meshing.

RING GEAR REPLACEMENT

Manual Transaxle Only

1. Remove the flywheel from the vehicle.
2. Heat the ring gear with a suitable blow torch on the engine side of the ring gear and knock it off of the flywheel. Do not hit the flywheel when removing the ring gear.

To install:

3. Inspect the ring gear for worn, chipped or cracked teeth. If the teeth are damaged, change the ring gear and check the corresponding starter drive gear for damage and repair or replace as necessary.
4. Heat the new ring gear evenly until the ring gear expands enough to slip onto the flywheel.
5. Be sure that the gear is seated properly against the shoulder.
6. Do not heat any portion of the gear to a temperature higher than 500°F (260°C). If this limit is exceeded, the temper will be removed from the ring gear teeth, which in turn will cause premature ring gear failure.

EXHAUST SYSTEM

The converter contains 2 separate ceramic honeycombs coated with different catalytic material. The front catalyst is coated with a rhodium/platinum catalyst designed to control oxides of nitrogen (NOx), unburned hydrocarbons (HC) and carbon monoxide (CO). This is therefore called a three way catalytic converter (TWC). The rear catalyst is coated with platinum/palladium and is called a conventional oxidation catalyst (COC).

The TWC converter operates on the exhaust gases as they arrive from the engine. As the gases flow from the TWC to the COC converter, they mix with the air in the secondary air system into the mixing chamber between the two ceramic honeycombs. This air is required for optimum operating conditions for the oxidation of the HC and CO on the COC converter. Air is diverted upstream of the TWC during cold start to provide faster catalyst light off and better HC/CO control.

The converter system used on the 1.9L CFI engines, contains one ceramic honeycomb coated with a different material. The catalyst is coated with a rhodium/platinum catalyst designed to control oxides of nitrogen (NOx), unburned hydrocarbons (HC) and carbon monoxide (CO). This is therefore called a three way catalytic converter (TWC).

The other engines being used, use a single pipe type exhaust system. This production exhaust system differs from the service replacement system in the number of basic pieces.

The factory-installed exhaust system uses a one-piece muffler system. The converter assembly is a bolt on catalyst installed at the rear of the flex joint and between the inlet pipe and muffler.

A slip joint is used between the converter and muffler on the underbody converter systems and the muffler is secured with a U-bolt. The exhaust system is usually serviced in four pieces. The rear section of the muffler inlet pipe (intermediate muffler inlet) is furnished separate from the muffler.

Inspect inlet pipes, outlet pipes and mufflers for cracked joints, broken welds and corrosion damage that would result in a leaking exhaust system. It is normal for a certain amount of moisture and staining to be present around the muffler seams. The presence of soot, light surface rust or moisture does not indicate a faulty muffler. Inspect the clamps, brackets and insulators for cracks and stripped or badly corroded bolt threads. When flat joints are loosened and/or disconnected to replace a shield pipe or muffler, replace the bolts and flange nuts if there is reasonable doubt that its service life is limited.

The exhaust system, including brush shields, must be free of leaks, binding, grounding and excessive vibrations. These conditions are usually caused by loose or broken flange bolts, shields, brackets or pipes. If any of these conditions exist, check the exhaust system components and alignment. Align or replace as necessary. Brush shields are positioned on the underside of the catalytic converter and should be free from bends which would bring any part of the shield in contact with the catalytic converter or muffler. The shield should also be clear of any combustible material such as dried grass or leaves.

NOTE: *The operating temperature of the exhaust system is very high. Never attempt to service any part of the system until it has cooled. Be especially careful when working around the catalytic converter. The tempera-*

178 ENGINE AND ENGINE OVERHAUL

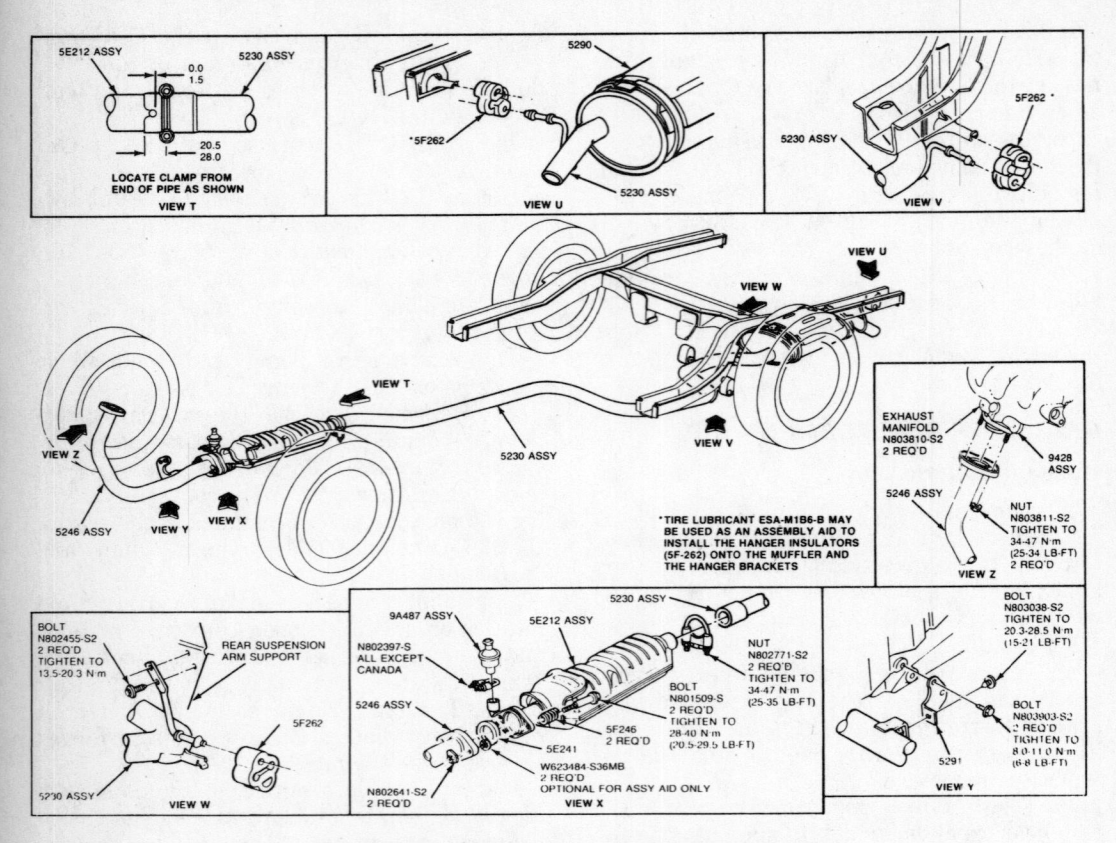

Exhaust system-1.6L and 1.9L engines without EFI

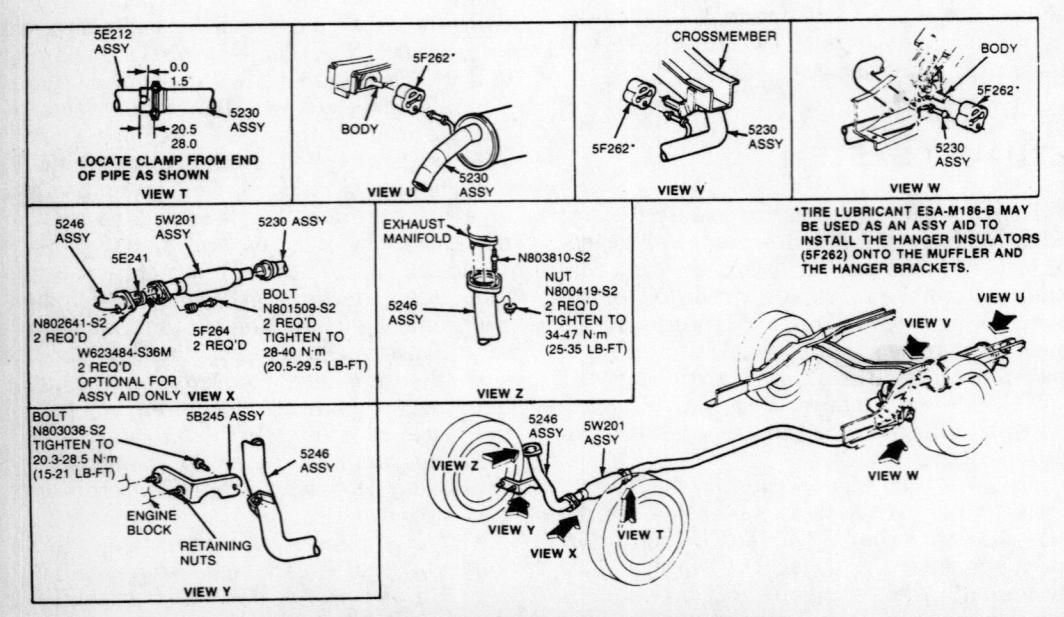

Exhaust system 2.0L diesel engine-Tempo/Topaz

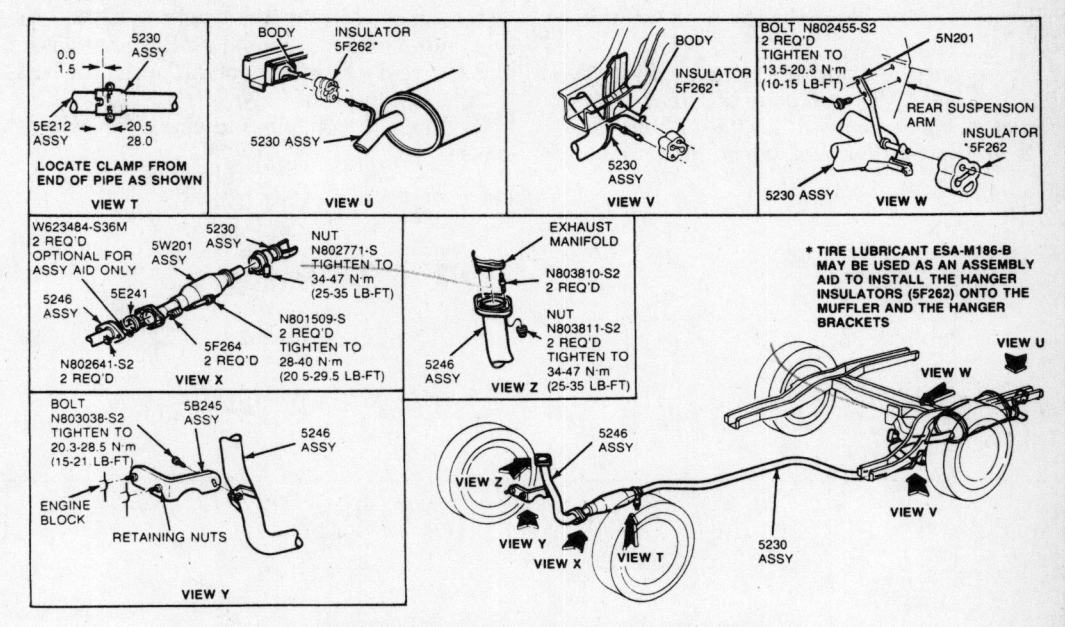

ENGINE AND ENGINE OVERHAUL

Exhaust system 2.0L diesel engine-Escort/Lynx

ture of the converter rise to high level after only a few minutes of operating temperature.

Muffler and Outlet Pipe Assembly

REMOVAL AND INSTALLATION

1. Raise the vehicle and support on jackstands.
2. Remove the U-bolt assembly and the rubber insulators from the hanger brackets and remove the muffler assembly. Slide the muffler assembly toward the rear of the car to disconnect it from the converter.
3. Replace parts as needed.

To install:

4. Position the muffler assembly under the car and slide it forward onto the converter outlet pipe. Check that the slot in the muffler and the tab on the converter are fully engaged.
5. Install the rubber insulators on the hanger assemblies. Install the U-bolt and tighten
6. Check the system for leaks. Lower the vehicle.

Catalytic Converter and/or Pipe Assembly

REMOVAL AND INSTALLATION

1. Raise the vehicle and support on jackstands.
2. Remove the front catalytic converter flange fasteners, loosen the rear U-bolt connection and disconnect the air hoses.

3. Separate the catalytic converter inlet and outlet connections. Remove the converter.

To install:

4. Install the converter to the muffler.
5. Install the converter and muffler assembly to the inlet pipe/flex joint. Connect the air hoses and position the U-bolt.
6. Align the exhaust system into position and, starting at the front of the system, tighten all the nuts and bolts.
7. Check the system for leaks. Lower the vehicle.

Close Couple Catalyst

REMOVAL AND INSTALLATION

1.9L CFI Engine

1. Raise and support the vehicle safely.
2. Remove the 2 spring loaded bolts and nuts from the flex joints.
3. Separate the muffler and inlet pipe assembly from the flex joints.
4. Loosen the steady rest-to-inlet bolt, do not remove this bolt.
5. Remove the 2 steady rest-to-oil pan bolts.
6. Remove the 2 nuts from the manifold studs.
7. Remove the close couple catalyst.

To install:

8. Install the close couple catalyst inlet pipe flange onto the manifold studs and loosely start the 2 manifold nuts.
9. Secure the steady rest bracket to oil pan.

180 ENGINE AND ENGINE OVERHAUL

Tighten to specifications with the 2 retaining bolts.

10. Torque the 2 nuts at the manifold to 25–35 ft. lbs. (34–47 Nm). Torque the steady rests-to-inlet pipe bolt to 6–8 ft. lbs. (8–11 Nm).

11. If the muffler and inlet pipe assembly were removed from the vehicle, install the system to hangers. Install new flex joint gasket and secure the flex joint bolts. Torque the bolts to 20–29 ft. lbs. (28–40 Nm).

12. Start the engine and check for exhaust leaks.

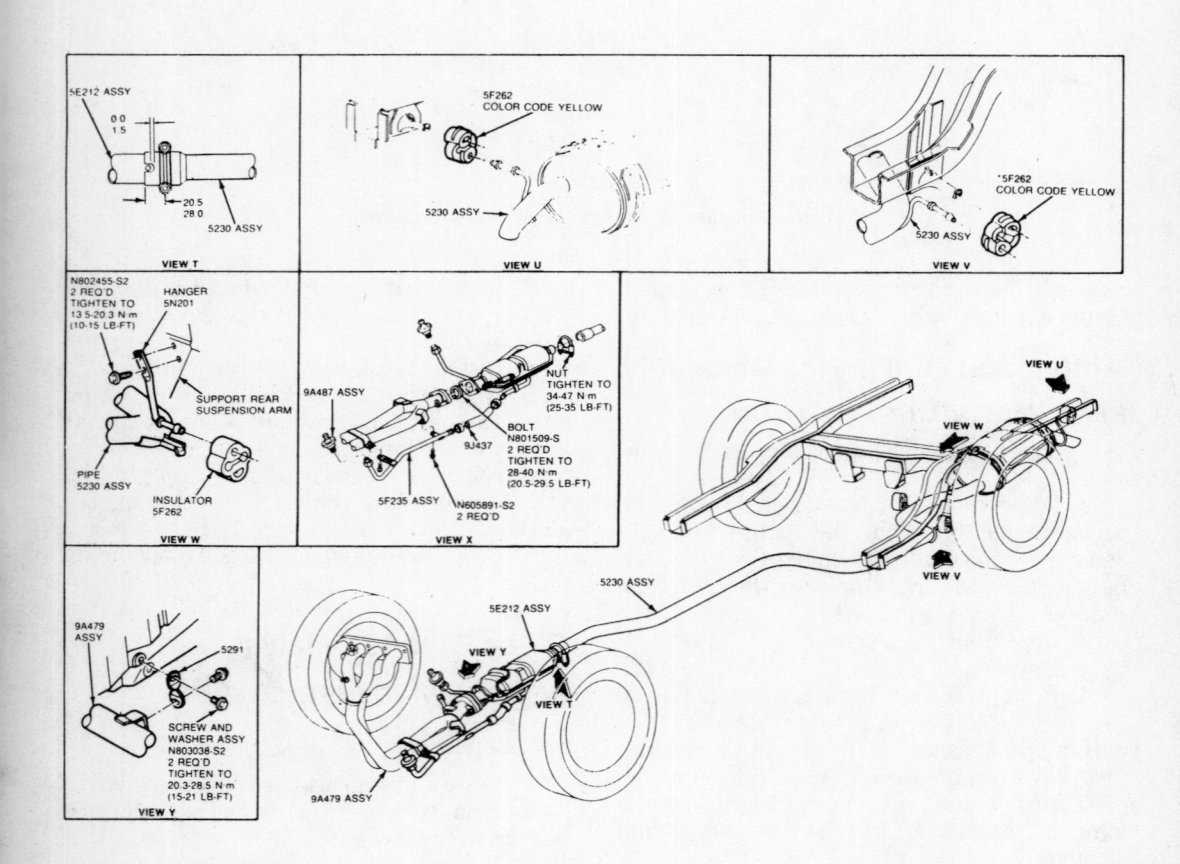

Exhaust system-1.6L and 1.9L engines with EFI

ENGINE AND ENGINE OVERHAUL

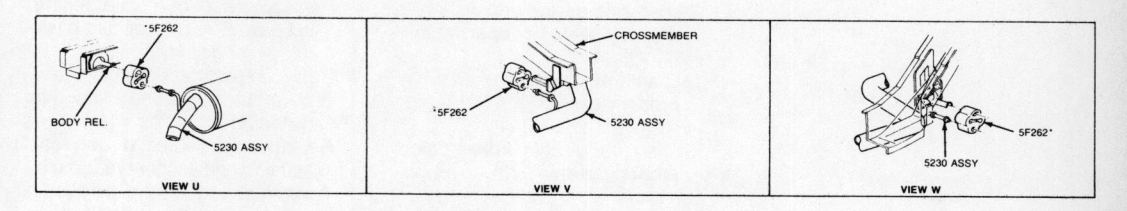

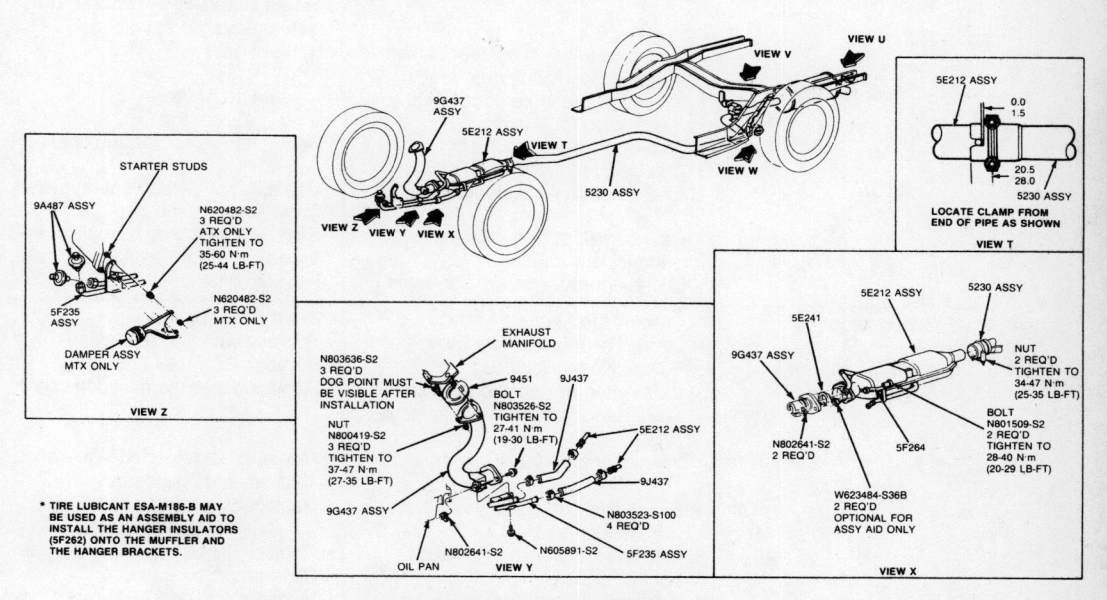

Exhaust system 2.3L HSC engine

ENGINE AND ENGINE OVERHAUL

Troubleshooting Engine Mechanical Problems

Problem	Cause	Solution
External oil leaks	• Fuel pump gasket broken or improperly seated	• Replace gasket
	• Cylinder head cover RTV sealant broken or improperly seated	• Replace sealant; inspect cylinder head cover sealant flange and cylinder head sealant surface for distortion and cracks
	• Oil filler cap leaking or missing	• Replace cap
	• Oil filter gasket broken or improperly seated	• Replace oil filter
	• Oil pan side gasket broken, improperly seated or opening in RTV sealant	• Replace gasket or repair opening in sealant; inspect oil pan gasket flange for distortion
	• Oil pan front oil seal broken or improperly seated	• Replace seal; inspect timing case cover and oil pan seal flange for distortion
	• Oil pan rear oil seal broken or improperly seated	• Replace seal; inspect oil pan rear oil seal flange; inspect rear main bearing cap for cracks, plugged oil return channels, or distortion in seal groove
	• Timing case cover oil seal broken or improperly seated	• Replace seal
	• Excess oil pressure because of restricted PCV valve	• Replace PCV valve
	• Oil pan drain plug loose or has stripped threads	• Repair as necessary and tighten
	• Rear oil gallery plug loose	• Use appropriate sealant on gallery plug and tighten
	• Rear camshaft plug loose or improperly seated	• Seat camshaft plug or replace and seal, as necessary
	• Distributor base gasket damaged	• Replace gasket
Excessive oil consumption	• Oil level too high	• Drain oil to specified level
	• Oil with wrong viscosity being used	• Replace with specified oil
	• PCV valve stuck closed	• Replace PCV valve
	• Valve stem oil deflectors (or seals) are damaged, missing, or incorrect type	• Replace valve stem oil deflectors
	• Valve stems or valve guides worn	• Measure stem-to-guide clearance and repair as necessary
	• Poorly fitted or missing valve cover baffles	• Replace valve cover
	• Piston rings broken or missing	• Replace broken or missing rings
	• Scuffed piston	• Replace piston
	• Incorrect piston ring gap	• Measure ring gap, repair as necessary
	• Piston rings sticking or excessively loose in grooves	• Measure ring side clearance, repair as necessary
	• Compression rings installed upside down	• Repair as necessary
	• Cylinder walls worn, scored, or glazed	• Repair as necessary
	• Piston ring gaps not properly staggered	• Repair as necessary
	• Excessive main or connecting rod bearing clearance	• Measure bearing clearance, repair as necessary
No oil pressure	• Low oil level	• Add oil to correct level
	• Oil pressure gauge, warning lamp or sending unit inaccurate	• Replace oil pressure gauge or warning lamp
	• Oil pump malfunction	• Replace oil pump
	• Oil pressure relief valve sticking	• Remove and inspect oil pressure relief valve assembly
	• Oil passages on pressure side of pump obstructed	• Inspect oil passages for obstruction

ENGINE AND ENGINE OVERHAUL

Troubleshooting Engine Mechanical Problems (cont.)

Problem	Cause	Solution
No oil pressure (cont.)	• Oil pickup screen or tube obstructed • Loose oil inlet tube	• Inspect oil pickup for obstruction • Tighten or seal inlet tube
Low oil pressure	• Low oil level • Inaccurate gauge, warning lamp or sending unit • Oil excessively thin because of dilution, poor quality, or improper grade • Excessive oil temperature • Oil pressure relief spring weak or sticking • Oil inlet tube and screen assembly has restriction or air leak • Excessive oil pump clearance • Excessive main, rod, or camshaft bearing clearance	• Add oil to correct level • Replace oil pressure gauge or warning lamp • Drain and refill crankcase with recommended oil • Correct cause of overheating engine • Remove and inspect oil pressure relief valve assembly • Remove and inspect oil inlet tube and screen assembly. (Fill inlet tube with lacquer thinner to locate leaks.) • Measure clearances • Measure bearing clearances, repair as necessary
High oil pressure	• Improper oil viscosity • Oil pressure gauge or sending unit inaccurate • Oil pressure relief valve sticking closed	• Drain and refill crankcase with correct viscosity oil • Replace oil pressure gauge • Remove and inspect oil pressure relief valve assembly
Main bearing noise	• Insufficient oil supply • Main bearing clearance excessive • Bearing insert missing • Crankshaft end play excessive • Improperly tightened main bearing cap bolts • Loose flywheel or drive plate • Loose or damaged vibration damper	• Inspect for low oil level and low oil pressure • Measure main bearing clearance, repair as necessary • Replace missing insert • Measure end play, repair as necessary • Tighten bolts with specified torque • Tighten flywheel or drive plate attaching bolts • Repair as necessary
Connecting rod bearing noise	• Insufficient oil supply • Carbon build-up on piston • Bearing clearance excessive or bearing missing • Crankshaft connecting rod journal out-of-round • Misaligned connecting rod or cap • Connecting rod bolts tightened improperly	• Inspect for low oil level and low oil pressure • Remove carbon from piston crown • Measure clearance, repair as necessary • Measure journal dimensions, repair or replace as necessary • Repair as necessary • Tighten bolts with specified torque
Piston noise	• Piston-to-cylinder wall clearance excessive (scuffed piston) • Cylinder walls excessively tapered or out-of-round • Piston ring broken • Loose or seized piston pin • Connecting rods misaligned • Piston ring side clearance excessively loose or tight • Carbon build-up on piston is excessive	• Measure clearance and examine piston • Measure cylinder wall dimensions, rebore cylinder • Replace all rings on piston • Measure piston-to-pin clearance, repair as necessary • Measure rod alignment, straighten or replace • Measure ring side clearance, repair as necessary • Remove carbon from piston

ENGINE AND ENGINE OVERHAUL

Troubleshooting Engine Mechanical Problems (cont.)

Problem	Cause	Solution
Valve actuating component noise	• Insufficient oil supply	• Check for: (a) Low oil level (b) Low oil pressure (c) Plugged push rods (d) Wrong hydraulic tappets (e) Restricted oil gallery (f) Excessive tappet to bore clearance
	• Push rods worn or bent • Rocker arms or pivots worn	• Replace worn or bent push rods • Replace worn rocker arms or pivots
	• Foreign objects or chips in hydraulic tappets • Excessive tappet leak-down • Tappet face worn	• Clean tappets • Replace valve tappet • Replace tappet; inspect corresponding cam lobe for wear
	• Broken or cocked valve springs	• Properly seat cocked springs; replace broken springs
	• Stem-to-guide clearance excessive	• Measure stem-to-guide clearance, repair as required
	• Valve bent • Loose rocker arms • Valve seat runout excessive • Missing valve lock • Push rod rubbing or contacting cylinder head • Excessive engine oil (four-cylinder engine)	• Replace valve • Tighten bolts with specified torque • Regrind valve seat/valves • Install valve lock • Remove cylinder head and remove obstruction in head • Correct oil level

Troubleshooting Basic Charging System Problems

Problem	Cause	Solution
Noisy alternator	• Loose mountings • Loose drive pulley • Worn bearings • Brush noise • Internal circuits shorted (High pitched whine)	• Tighten mounting bolts • Tighten pulley • Replace alternator • Replace alternator • Replace alternator
Squeal when starting engine or accelerating	• Glazed or loose belt	• Replace or adjust belt
Indicator light remains on or ammeter indicates discharge (engine running)	• Broken fan belt • Broken or disconnected wires • Internal alternator problems • Defective voltage regulator	• Install belt • Repair or connect wiring • Replace alternator • Replace voltage regulator
Car light bulbs continually burn out—battery needs water continually	• Alternator/regulator overcharging	• Replace voltage regulator/alternator
Car lights flare on acceleration	• Battery low • Internal alternator/regulator problems	• Charge or replace battery • Replace alternator/regulator
Low voltage output (alternator light flickers continually or ammeter needle wanders)	• Loose or worn belt • Dirty or corroded connections • Internal alternator/regulator problems	• Replace or adjust belt • Clean or replace connections • Replace alternator or regulator

ENGINE AND ENGINE OVERHAUL

Troubleshooting the Cooling System

Problem	Cause	Solution
High temperature gauge indication—overheating	• Coolant level low • Fan belt loose • Radiator hose(s) collapsed • Radiator airflow blocked • Faulty radiator cap • Ignition timing incorrect • Idle speed low • Air trapped in cooling system • Heavy traffic driving • Incorrect cooling system component(s) installed • Faulty thermostat • Water pump shaft broken or impeller loose • Radiator tubes clogged • Cooling system clogged • Casting flash in cooling passages • Brakes dragging • Excessive engine friction • Antifreeze concentration over 68% • Missing air seals • Faulty gauge or sending unit • Loss of coolant flow caused by leakage or foaming • Viscous fan drive failed	• Replenish coolant • Adjust fan belt tension • Replace hose(s) • Remove restriction (bug screen, fog lamps, etc.) • Replace radiator cap • Adjust ignition timing • Adjust idle speed • Purge air • Operate at fast idle in neutral intermittently to cool engine • Install proper component(s) • Replace thermostat • Replace water pump • Flush radiator • Flush system • Repair or replace as necessary. Flash may be visible by removing cooling system components or removing core plugs. • Repair brakes • Repair engine • Lower antifreeze concentration percentage • Replace air seals • Repair or replace faulty component • Repair or replace leaking component, replace coolant • Replace unit
Low temperature indication—undercooling	• Thermostat stuck open • Faulty gauge or sending unit	• Replace thermostat • Repair or replace faulty component
Coolant loss—boilover	• Overfilled cooling system • Quick shutdown after hard (hot) run • Air in system resulting in occasional "burping" of coolant • Insufficient antifreeze allowing coolant boiling point to be too low • Antifreeze deteriorated because of age or contamination • Leaks due to loose hose clamps, loose nuts, bolts, drain plugs, faulty hoses, or defective radiator • Faulty head gasket • Cracked head, manifold, or block • Faulty radiator cap	• Reduce coolant level to proper specification • Allow engine to run at fast idle prior to shutdown • Purge system • Add antifreeze to raise boiling point • Replace coolant • Pressure test system to locate source of leak(s) then repair as necessary • Replace head gasket • Replace as necessary • Replace cap
Coolant entry into crankcase or cylinder(s)	• Faulty head gasket • Crack in head, manifold or block	• Replace head gasket • Replace as necessary
Coolant recovery system inoperative	• Coolant level low • Leak in system • Pressure cap not tight or seal missing, or leaking • Pressure cap defective • Overflow tube clogged or leaking • Recovery bottle vent restricted	• Replenish coolant to FULL mark • Pressure test to isolate leak and repair as necessary • Repair as necessary • Replace cap • Repair as necessary • Remove restriction

ENGINE AND ENGINE OVERHAUL

Troubleshooting Basic Starting System Problems

Problem	Cause	Solution
Starter motor rotates engine slowly	• Battery charge low or battery defective • Defective circuit between battery and starter motor • Low load current • High load current	• Charge or replace battery • Clean and tighten, or replace cables • Bench-test starter motor. Inspect for worn brushes and weak brush springs. • Bench-test starter motor. Check engine for friction, drag or coolant in cylinders. Check ring gear-to-pinion gear clearance.
Starter motor will not rotate engine	• Battery charge low or battery defective • Faulty solenoid • Damage drive pinion gear or ring gear • Starter motor engagement weak • Starter motor rotates slowly with high load current • Engine seized	• Charge or replace battery • Check solenoid ground. Repair or replace as necessary. • Replace damaged gear(s) • Bench-test starter motor • Inspect drive yoke pull-down and point gap, check for worn end bushings, check ring gear clearance • Repair engine
Starter motor drive will not engage (solenoid known to be good)	• Defective contact point assembly • Inadequate contact point assembly ground • Defective hold-in coil	• Repair or replace contact point assembly • Repair connection at ground screw • Replace field winding assembly
Starter motor drive will not disengage	• Starter motor loose on flywheel housing • Worn drive end busing • Damaged ring gear teeth • Drive yoke return spring broken or missing	• Tighten mounting bolts • Replace bushing • Replace ring gear or driveplate • Replace spring
Starter motor drive disengages prematurely	• Weak drive assembly thrust spring • Hold-in coil defective	• Replace drive mechanism • Replace field winding assembly
Low load current	• Worn brushes • Weak brush springs	• Replace brushes • Replace springs

Troubleshooting the Serpentine Drive Belt

Problem	Cause	Solution
Tension sheeting fabric failure (woven fabric on outside circumference of belt has cracked or separated from body of belt)	• Grooved or backside idler pulley diameters are less than minimum recommended • Tension sheeting contacting (rubbing) stationary object • Excessive heat causing woven fabric to age • Tension sheeting splice has fractured	• Replace pulley(s) not conforming to specification • Correct rubbing condition • Replace belt • Replace belt
Noise (objectional squeal, squeak, or rumble is heard or felt while drive belt is in operation)	• Belt slippage • Bearing noise • Belt misalignment • Belt-to-pulley mismatch • Driven component inducing vibration • System resonant frequency inducing vibration	• Adjust belt • Locate and repair • Align belt/pulley(s) • Install correct belt • Locate defective driven component and repair • Vary belt tension within specifications. Replace belt.
Rib chunking (one or more ribs has separated from belt body)	• Foreign objects imbedded in pulley grooves • Installation damage • Drive loads in excess of design specifications • Insufficient internal belt adhesion	• Remove foreign objects from pulley grooves • Replace belt • Adjust belt tension • Replace belt
Rib or belt wear (belt ribs contact bottom of pulley grooves)	• Pulley(s) misaligned • Mismatch of belt and pulley groove widths • Abrasive environment • Rusted pulley(s) • Sharp or jagged pulley groove tips • Rubber deteriorated	• Align pulley(s) • Replace belt • Replace belt • Clean rust from pulley(s) • Replace pulley • Replace belt
Longitudinal belt cracking (cracks between two ribs)	• Belt has mistracked from pulley groove • Pulley groove tip has worn away rubber-to-tensile member	• Replace belt • Replace belt
Belt slips	• Belt slipping because of insufficient tension • Belt or pulley subjected to substance (belt dressing, oil, ethylene glycol) that has reduced friction • Driven component bearing failure • Belt glazed and hardened from heat and excessive slippage	• Adjust tension • Replace belt and clean pulleys • Replace faulty component bearing • Replace belt
"Groove jumping" (belt does not maintain correct position on pulley, or turns over and/or runs off pulleys)	• Insufficient belt tension • Pulley(s) not within design tolerance • Foreign object(s) in grooves • Excessive belt speed • Pulley misalignment • Belt-to-pulley profile mismatched • Belt cordline is distorted	• Adjust belt tension • Replace pulley(s) • Remove foreign objects from grooves • Avoid excessive engine acceleration • Align pulley(s) • Install correct belt • Replace belt
Belt broken (Note: identify and correct problem before replacement belt is installed)	• Excessive tension • Tensile members damaged during belt installation • Belt turnover • Severe pulley misalignment • Bracket, pulley, or bearing failure	• Replace belt and adjust tension to specification • Replace belt • Replace belt • Align pulley(s) • Replace defective component and belt

Troubleshooting the Serpentine Drive Belt (cont.)

Problem	Cause	Solution
Cord edge failure (tensile member exposed at edges of belt or separated from belt body)	• Excessive tension • Drive pulley misalignment • Belt contacting stationary object • Pulley irregularities • Improper pulley construction • Insufficient adhesion between tensile member and rubber matrix	• Adjust belt tension • Align pulley • Correct as necessary • Replace pulley • Replace pulley • Replace belt and adjust tension to specifications
Sporadic rib cracking (multiple cracks in belt ribs at random intervals)	• Ribbed pulley(s) diameter less than minimum specification • Backside bend flat pulley(s) diameter less than minimum • Excessive heat condition causing rubber to harden • Excessive belt thickness • Belt overcured • Excessive tension	• Replace pulley(s) • Replace pulley(s) • Correct heat condition as necessary • Replace belt • Replace belt • Adjust belt tension

Emission Controls

EMISSION CONTROLS

There are three basic sources of automotive pollution in the modern internal combustion engine. They are the crankcase with its accompanying blow-by vapors, the fuel system with its evaporation of unburned gasoline and the combustion chambers with their resulting exhaust emissions. Pollution arising from the incomplete combustion of fuel generally falls into three categories: hydrocarbons (HC), carbon monoxide (CO) and oxides of nitrogen (NOx).

Engines are equipped with an air pump system, positive crankcase ventilation, exhaust gas recirculation, electronic ignition, catalytic converter, thermostatically controlled air cleaner, and an evaporative emissions system. Electronic engine controls are used on various engines, depending on model and year.

The belt driven air pump injects clean air either into the exhaust manifold, or downstream into the catalytic converter, depending on engine conditions. The oxygen contained in the injected air supports continued combustion of the hot carbon monoxide (CO) and hydrocarbon (HC) gases, reducing their release into the atmosphere.

No external PCV valve is necessary on the Escort and Lynx PCV system. Instead, an internal baffle and an orifice control flow of crankcase gases.

The back pressure modulated EGR valve is mounted next to the carburetor on the intake manifold. Vacuum applied to the EGR diaphragm raises the pintle valve from its seat, allowing hot exhaust gases to be drawn into the intake manifold with the intake charge. The exhaust gases reduce peak combustion temperature; lower temperatures reduce the formation of oxides of nitrogen (NOx).

The dual brick catalytic converter is mounted in the exhaust system, ahead of the muffler. Catalytic converters use noble metals (platinum and palladium) and great heat — 1,200°F (650°C) to catalytically oxidize HC and CO gases into H_2O and CO_2. The Thermactor system is used as a fresh air (and therefore, oxygen) supply.

The thermostatically controlled air cleaner housing is able to draw fresh air from two sources: cool air from outside the car (behind the grille), or warm air obtained from a heat stove encircling the exhaust manifold. A warm air supply is desirable during cold engine operation. Because it promotes better atomization of the air/fuel mixture, while cool air promotes better combustion in a hot engine.

Instead of venting gasoline vapors from the carburetor float bowl into the atmosphere, an evaporative emission system captures the vapors and stores them in a charcoal filled canister, located ahead of the left front wheel arch. When the engine is running, a purge control solenoid allows fresh air to be drawn through the canister. The fresh air and vapors are then routed to the carburetor, to be mixed with the intake charge.

CRANKCASE EMISSION CONTROL SYSTEM

Positive Crankcase Ventilation System

OPERATION

A small amount of the fuel/air mixture in each cylinder escapes from the combustion chamber around the piston rings and enters the engine's crankcase, above the oil level. Since this material has been cooled by the lubricating oil and metal parts well below burning temperature, it is only partially burned and constitutes a large source of pollution. The PCV system allows outside air to be drawn in to

EMISSION CONTROLS

the crankcase and to sweep this material back into the intake passages of the engine to be reburned before it either dirties the oil or escaped to the outside air. An internal baffle and an orifice control the flow of crankcase gases.

The venting system used on the 1.6L engine does not depend on a flow of scavenging air, as do all other engines. This system evacuates crankcase vapors that are drawn into the intake manifold in metered amounts according to the manifold depression and the fixed orifice as they become available. If availability is low, air may be drawn in along with the vapors. If the availability is high, some vapors will be delivered to the intake manifold and any amount over that will go into the air cleaner. The fixed orifice is the critical point of this system.

System Services

1. If the valve rattles when shaken, reconnect it. If it does not rattle, replace it.
2. With the engine idling, disconnect the hose from the air cleaner and check for vacuum at the hose. If vacuum exist the system is functioning normally.
3. If vacuum does not exist, the system is plugged or the evaporative valve is leaking.
4. Disconnect the evaporative hose, cap the tee and recheck the system. If the vacuum exist, the PCV system is functioning. Check the evaporative emission system.
5. If vacuum still does not exist at the PCV, check for vacuum back through the system (filler cap, PCV valve, hoses, the oil separator on the 2.3L engine and the rocker cover bolt torque). Service the defective components as required.

FUEL EVAPORATIVE EMISSION CONTROLS

Evaporative Emission Controls

OPERATION

Changes in atmospheric temperature cause fuel tanks to breathe, that is, the air within the tank expands and contracts with outside temperature changes. As the temperature rises, air escapes through the tank vent tube or the vent in the tank cap. The air which escapes contains gasoline vapors. In a similar manner, the gasoline which fills the carburetor float bowl expands when the engine is stopped. Engine heat causes this expansion. The vapors escape through the carburetor and air cleaner.

The Evaporative Emission Control System provides a sealed fuel system with the capability to store and condense fuel vapors. The system has three parts: a fill control vent system; a vapor vent and storage system; and a pressure and vacuum relief system (special fill cap).

The fill control vent system is a modification to the fuel tank. It uses an air space within the tank which is 10–12% of the tank's volume. The air space is sufficient to provide for the thermal expansion of the fuel. The space also serves as part of the in-tank vapor vent system.

The in-tank vent system consists of the air space previously described and a vapor separator assembly. The separator assembly is mounted on the top of the fuel tank and is secured by a cam lockring, similar to the one which secures the fuel sending unit. Foam material fills the vapor separator assembly. The foam material separates raw fuel and vapors, thus retarding the entrance of fuel into the vapor line.

The sealed filler cap has a pressure vacuum relief valve. Under normal operating conditions, the filler cap operates as a check valve, allowing air to enter the tank to replace the fuel consumed. At the same time, it prevents vapors from escaping through the cap. In case of excessive pressure within the tank, the filler cap valve opens to relieve the pressure.

Because the filler cap is sealed, fuel vapors have but one place through which they may escape — the vapor separator assembly at the top of the fuel tank. The vapors pass through the foam material and continue through a single vapor line which leads to a canister in the engine compartment. The canister is filled with activated charcoal.

Another vapor line runs from the top of the carburetor float chamber to the charcoal canister.

As the fuel vapors (hydrocarbons) enter the charcoal canister, they are absorbed by the charcoal. The air is dispelled through the open bottom of the charcoal canister, leaving the hydrocarbons trapped within the charcoal. When the engine is started, vacuum causes fresh air to be drawn into the canister from its open bottom. The fresh air passes through the charcoal picking up the hydrocarbons which are trapped there and feeding them into the carburetor for burning with the fuel mixture.

Canister Purge Solenoid

OPERATION

The canister purge solenoid is part of the evaporative emission control system. This solenoid is used in conjunction with the electronic engine control system. The solenoid valve controls the flow of vapors from the carbon canister to the intake manifold during various

EMISSION CONTROLS 191

POSITIVE CRANKCASE SYSTEM DIAGNOSIS

Condition	Possible Cause	Correction
PCV valve does not click when shaken	Shuttle valve plugged with combustion chamber blow-by products	Replace PCV valve
No air flow through PCV valve hose to carburetor	Hose or carburetor base plugged with combustion blow-by products	Clean or replace hose, Remove carburetor and clean PCV system passages.
Rough engine idle	Inoperative PCV valve, clogged PCV system or filter	Replace valve, open PCV system and replace filter
Excessive sludge in engine oil	Inoperative PCV valve, clogged PCV system or filters	Replace valve and filter, open PCV system

engine mode operations. It also controls carbon canister purging. The valve is normally closed and is opened by a signal from the electronic control assembly.

System Service

1. With the valve de-energized, apply 5 in.Hg of vacuum to the vacuum source part of the valve.

2. The valve should not pass air, if it does, replace it.

3. While applying 9–14 volts (DC current) to the valve, the valve should open and air should pass through.

4. If the valve does not allow air to pass through, replace it.

Canister Purge Valve

OPERATION

The canister purge valve is part of the evaporative control system. The valve is inline with the carbon canister and control the flow of vapor from the carbon canister to the engine.

System Service

1. Application of vacuum to Port B only, should indicate no air flow as the valve should be closed. If air flow exists, replace the valve.

2. After applying and maintaining 16 in. Hg of vacuum to port A, apply vacuum to port B. Air should not pass, if it does pass, replace the valve.

3. Never apply vacuum to port C, doing so may damage the internal diaphragm and destroy the function of the valve.

Carbon Canister

OPERATION

The fuel vapors from the fuel tank and the carburetor bowl are stored in the carbon canister until the vehicle is operated, at which time the vapors will purge from the canister into the engine for combustion. Some vehicles are equipped with duel carbon canisters, both of which have the same function as vehicles equipped with a single carbon canister.

Carburetor Fuel Bowl Solenoid Vent Valve

OPERATION

This component is part of the evaporative emission control system. The valve is located in the fuel bowl vent line and is normally opened. The vent solenoid valve closes off the fuel bowl vent line when the engine is running and re-

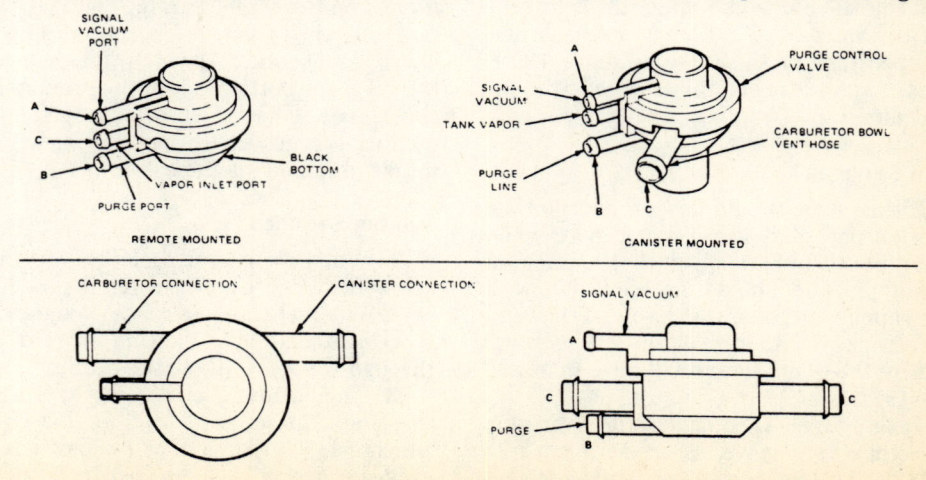

Typical canister purge valves

EMISSION CONTROLS

turns to the normally open condition when the ignition switch is turned off. To test the valve apply 9–14 volts (DC current) to the valve. The valve should close, allowing no air to pass through. If the valve does not close, replace it.

NOTE: *If a lean fuel mixture is suspected as the cause of a driveability problem, inspect the fuel bowl vent solenoid valve for proper closing during engine operation. If the valve leaks or does not close, the carburetor will provide a leaner air fuel mixture ratio to the engine.*

Fuel Bowl Thermal Vent Valve

OPERATION

The thermal vent valve is a temperature actuated ON/Off valve. It is inserted in the carburetor to the canister vent line and is closed when the engine compartment is cold. This prevents fuel tank vapors from being vented through the carburetor fuel bowl. The thermal vent valve forces these vapors into the carbon canister.

Vacuum And Vacuum Thermostatic Bowl Vent Valve

OPERATION

The vacuum bowl vent valve and the vacuum thermostatic bowl vent valve are vacuum and vacuum/temperature actuated ON/OFF valves. These two valves are similar in appearance and are used in the evaporative emission control system to control vapor flow from the carburetor bowl to the carbon canister. With either valve the flow path from the bowl to canister is closed by manifold vacuum when the engine is running. The thermostatic valve also closes the bowl to canister flow path when the temperature of the valve is 90°F (32°C) or less. When the temperature of the valve is above 120°F (49°C), the valve is open, unless closed by manifold vacuum.

System Services

1. Either valve should flow air between the carburetor port and the canister port when there is no vacuum applied to the vacuum signal nipple and should not flow air with vacuum applied to the signal nipple. If the vehicle is equipped with a vacuum thermostatic vent valve the temperature will have to exceed 120°F (49°C).
2. If the vehicle is equipped with a vacuum thermostatic vent valve, at temperature of a 90°F (32°C) or less, the valve should not flow air or be very restrictive to air flow.

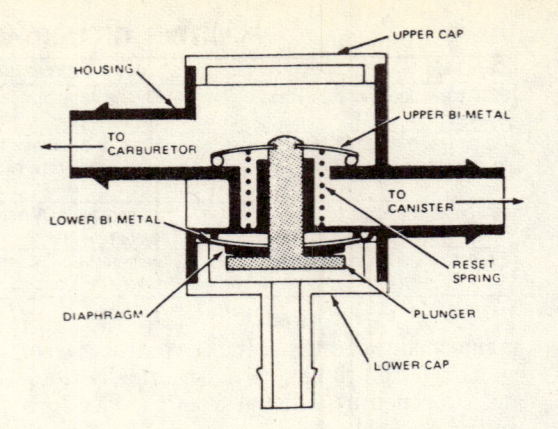

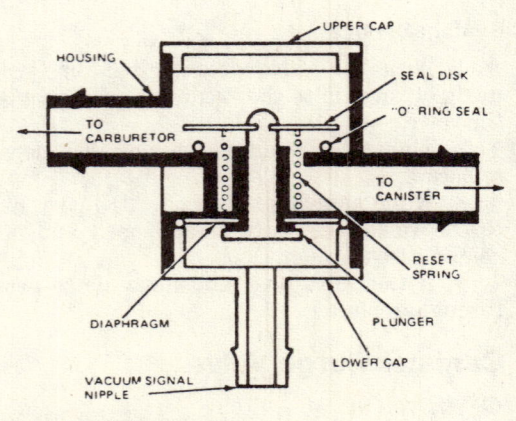

Typical bowl vent valves

Fuel Evaporative Heater/Spacer Assembly

OPERATION

This component is a twelve volt grid type heater that heats the air/fuel mixture below the carburetor for better for better fuel evaporation when the engine is cold. The fuel evaporation heater consists of a spacer, upper and lower gaskets and a 12 volt grid type heater attached to the bottom side of the primary bore of the spacer. The offset design of the heater mounting bracket positions the heater in the intake manifold inlet opening.

System Services

1. When the engine coolant temperature is below 128°F (53°C), the switch is closed.
2. When the heater relay is energized, the relay contacts close allowing current to flow through the relay and to the heater.
3. The heater operates for approximately the first 3 minutes of cold engine operation which aids in a leaner choke calibration for improved emissions without cold drive-away problems.

EMISSION CONTROLS

4. At ambient temperatures of less than 40°F (4°C), the leaner choke calibrations reduce loading and spark plug fouling.

5. The heater grid is functioning if radiant heat can be detected when the heater grid is energized.

NOTE: *Do not probe the heater grid while the grid is in the heat mode, as it is possible to cause a direct short in the circuit. The heater is designed to operate at a constant temperature of approximately 320–383°F (160–195°C), and could result in burns if touched.*

Fuel Evaporative Heater Switch
OPERATION

This switch is mounted upside down on the rear of the engine, on the bottom of the intake manifold. The function of the switch is to control the relay and the heater element in the early fuel evaporative emission system, based on engine temperature. The normally closed switch will activate the relay and the heater at low engine temperature and will open at the specified calibration of the temperature switch. This will open the control relay, which in turn will shut off the early fuel evaporation heater after the engine has warmed up.

Fuel/Vacuum Separator
OPERATION

The fuel/vacuum separator is used in vacuum systems in order to prevent fuel travel to a vacuum operated device. This component requires positive orientation to insure that any fuel collected will drain back to the carburetor. If the separator becomes clogged or cracked, it must be replaced.

Fuel Pressure Regulator
OPERATION

This component is used on vehicles equipped with fuel injection. The fuel pressure regulator is usually attached to the fuel supply manifold assembly, which is upstream of the fuel injectors. Its function is to regulate fuel pressure that is supplied to the fuel injectors. The regulator is a diaphragm operated relief valve in which one side of the diaphragm senses fuel pressure and the other side is subjected to intake manifold pressure for multi-point fuel injection and fresh air for single point fuel injection. The nominal fuel pressure is established by a spring preload applied to the diaphragm. One side of the diaphragm is exposed to the manifold pressure which maintains a constant pressure drop across the injectors. Excess fuel that is consumed by the engine passes through the regulator and returns to the fuel tank.

EXHAUST EMISSION CONTROL SYSTEM

Thermostatically Controlled Air Cleaner
OPERATION

The air cleaner assembly intake duct is attached to a cold air intake as well as a heat shroud that surrounds the exhaust manifold. Air flow from these two sources is controlled by a door in the intake duct operated by a vacuum motor. The vacuum motor is controlled by a thermal sensor and a vacuum control system.

The thermal sensor is attached to the air valve actuating lever, along with the vacuum motor lever, both of which control the position of the air valve to supply either heated air from the exhaust manifold or cooler air from the engine compartment.

During the warm-up period, when the under-the-hood temperatures are low, the thermal sensor doesn't exert enough tension on the air valve actuating lever to close (heat off) the air valve. Thus, the carburetor receives heated air from around the exhaust manifold.

As the temperature of the air entering the air cleaner approaches approximately 110°F (43°C), the thermal sensor begins to push on the air valve actuating lever and overcome the spring tension which holds the air valve in the open (heat on) position. The air valve begins to move to the closed (heat off position, allowing only under-the-hood air to enter the air cleaner.

The air valve in the air cleaner will also open, regardless of the air temperature, during heavy acceleration to obtain maximum airflow through the air cleaner. The extreme decrease in intake manifold vacuum during heavy acceleration permits the vacuum motor to override the thermostatic control. This opens the system to both heated air and air from the engine compartment.

HEATED AIR INTAKE TEST

1. With the engine completely cold, look inside the cold air duct and make sure that the valve plate is fully in the up position (closing the cold air duct).

2. Start the engine and bring it to operating temperature.

3. Stop the engine and look inside the cold air duct again. The valve plate should be down, allowing an opening from the cold air duct into the air cleaner.

4. If the unit appears to be malfunctioning, remove it and examine it to make sure that the springs are not broken or disconnected, and re-

EMISSION CONTROLS

place the thermostat if all other parts appear intact and properly connected.

Air Cleaner Cold Weather Modulator

OPERATION

A cold weather modulator is used on some vehicles, in addition to the air cleaner temperature control sensor, to control inlet air temperature. This component traps vacuum in the system, so that the door will not shut to cold air when the vacuum drops during acceleration. The cold weather modulator only works when the outside air is cold.

Air Cleaner Temperature Sensor

OPERATION

The air cleaner temperature sensor is installed in the air cleaner assembly. This sensor is subjected to temperature changes within the air cleaner assembly. At given increase in temperature, the sensor bleeds off vacuum, which permits the vacuum motor to open the duct door and allow fresh air in while shutting off full heat. At a temperature of less than 75°F (24°C), the sensor will allow vacuum to close the duct door to fresh air. The sensor will bleed off vacuum in order to allow the duct door to open and let in fresh air if the temperature is above 75°F (24°C) (brown sensor) 90°F (32°C) (pink sensor or clear sensor) and 105°F (41°C) (blue, yellow or green sensor).

Air Silencer

OPERATION

The air silencer is a combination silencer and filter for air supply pumps that are not equipped with an impeller type centrifugal air filter fan or for pulse air systems. The air silencer is mounted inside the engine compartment and connected to the air supply pump or pulse air valve inlet by means of a flexible hose. The air silencer is performing properly if when inspected, the component is not plugged and no leaks exist.

Air Cleaner Vacuum Motor

OPERATION

The air cleaner vacuum motor operates the door within the duct, which allows either cold or warm air to enter the engine, depending on the air temperature inside the air cleaner housing. As vacuum is applied to the vacuum motor the door stem should pull up and stay up as long as vacuum is applied to the vacuum motor.

Exhaust Gas Recirculation (EGR)

OPERATION

The Exhaust Gas Recirculation System is designed to introduce small amounts of exhaust gas into the combustion cycle. Re-introducing the exhaust gas helps reduce the generation of nitrous oxides (NOx). The amount of exhaust gases re-introduced and the timing of the cycle

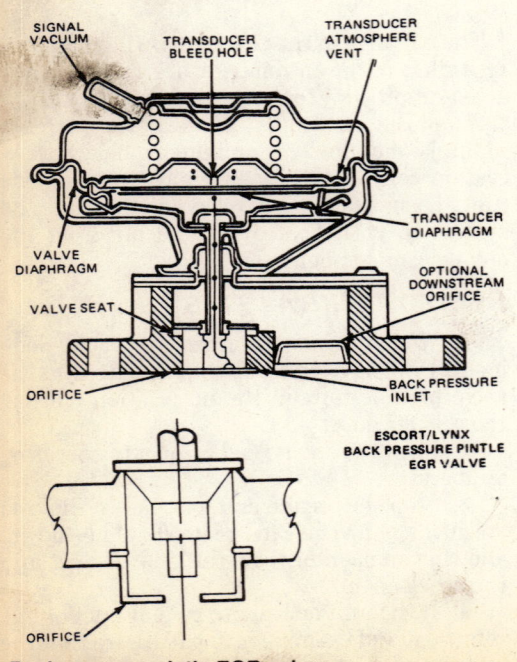

Backpressure pintle EGR valve

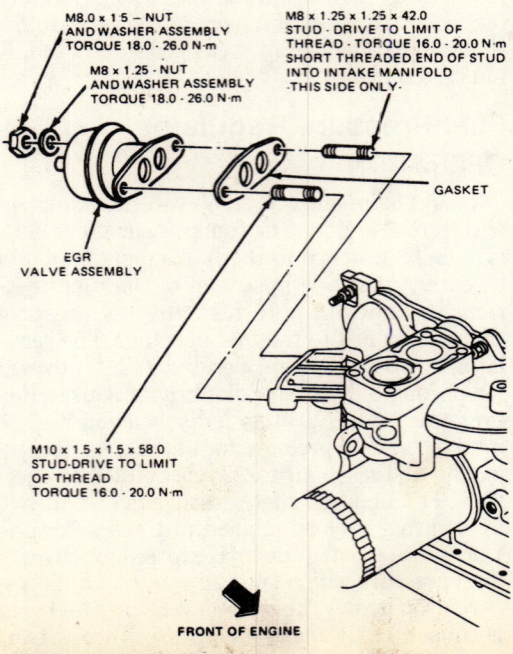

EGR valve installation

EMISSION CONTROLS

Troubleshooting the EGR System

Condition	Possible Source	Resolution
• Rough Idle and/or Stalling	• EGR valve receiving vacuum at idle, vacuum hoses misrouted	• Check EGR valve vacuum hose routing. Correct as required. Check vacuum supply at idle with engine at operating temperature.
	• EGR valve not closing fully or stuck open	• Remove EGR valve to inspect for proper closing and seating of valve components. Clean or replace valve as required.
	• EGR valve gasket blown, or valve attachment loose.	• Check EGR valve attaching bolts for tightness. Inspect gasket. Tighten valve or replace gasket as required.
	• EGR valve air bleeds plugged	• Check to see if valve holds vacuum with engine off. If so, replace valve.
• Rough running, surge, hesitation and general poor performance at part throttle when engine is cold	• EGR valve receiving vacuum. Vacuum hoses misrouted.	• Check EGR valve vacuum hose routing. Correct as required.
	• EGR valve not closing fully or stuck open	• Remove EGR valve to inspect for proper closing and seating of valve components. Clean or replace valve as required.
	• EGR valve gasket blown, or valve attachment loose.	• Check EGR valve attaching bolts for tightness. Inspect gasket. Tighten valve or replace gasket as required.
	• EGR valve air bleeds plugged (back pressure-type valve only)	• Check to see if valve holds vacuum with engine off. If so, replace valve.
• Rough running, surge, hesitation, and general poor performance at part-throttle when engine is hot or cold.	Excessive EGR due to: • EGR valve stuck wide open	• Remove EGR valve to inspect for proper freedom of movement of valve components. Clean or replace as required.
• Engine stalls on deceleration	• EGR valve sticking open or not closing fully	• Remove EGR valve to inspect for proper closing and seating of valve components. Clean or replace as required.
• Part-throttle engine detonation	Insufficient EGR due to: • EGR valve stuck closed	• Check EGR valve for freedom of operation by pressing and releasing valve diaphragm to stroke the valve mechanism. Clean or replace valve if not operating smoothly.
	• Leaky valve diaphragm not actuating valve	• Check valve by applying vacuum. (Back pressure-type valves only—block tailpipe with drive socket of outside diameter approximately $1/16"$ less than inside diameter of tailpipe. DO NOT BLOCK FULLY. Idle engine while applying vacuum to valve. DO NOT RUN ENGINE FASTER THAN IDLE OR FOR PROLONGED PERIODS OF TIME. BE SURE TO REMOVE SOCKET FROM TAILPIPE AT END OF THIS TEST. IF THESE PRECAUTIONS ARE NOT OBSERVED, ENGINE AND/OR EXHAUST SYSTEM DAMAGE COULD OCCUR.) If valve leaks vacuum, replace it.
	• Vacuum restricted to EGR valve	• Check vacuum hoses, fittings, routing, and supply for blockage.

EMISSION CONTROLS

Troubleshooting the EGR System (cont.)

Condition	Possible Source	Resolution
• Part-throttle engine detonation (cont'd).	• EGR disconnected	• Check connections and reconnect as required.
	• Load control valve venting	• Check for proper functioning. Vacuum should be present at load control valve vacuum port to EGR valve. Replace if damaged.
	• EGR passages blocked.	• Check EGR passages for restrictions and blockage.
	• Insufficient exhaust back pressure (back pressure EGR valve only)	• Check for exhaust leaks ahead of muffler/catalyst or for blown-out muffler/catalyst. Also check for blockage to EGR valve. Service or replace all damaged components.
	• Vacuum hose leaking (cracked, split, broken, loose connections)	• Check all vacuum hoses for breaks and all connections for proper fit. Service or replace as required.
(NOTE: Detonation can also be due to carburetor or ignition malfunction.)		
• Abnormally low power at wide open throttle.	• Load control valve not venting	• Check for proper functioning. Vacuum should not be present at vacuum port to EGR valve at wide-open throttle or heavy load. If vacuum is present, replace damaged valve.
• Engine starts but stalls immediately thereafter when cold	• EGR valve receiving vacuum, vacuum hoses misrouted • EGR valve not closing fully	• Check EGR valve hose routing. Correct as required. • Remove EGR valve to inspect for proper closing and seating of valve components. Clean or replace as required.
(NOTE: Stalling can also be due to carburetor malfunction.)		
• Engine hard to start, or no start condition	• EGR valve receiving vacuum. Vacuum hoses misrouted • EGR valve stuck open	• Check EGR valve hose routing. Correct as required. • Remove EGR valve to inspect for proper closing and seating of valve components. Clean or replace as required.
• Poor Fuel Economy	EGR related if: • Caused by detonation or other symptom of restricted or no EGR flow	• See Resolution for part-throttle engine detonation condition.

varies as to engine speed, altitude, engine vacuum and exhaust system.

EGR MAINTENANCE REMINDER SYSTEM

Some Escort/Lynx models are equipped with an EGR Maintenance Reminder System that consists of a mileage sensor module, an instrument panel warning light and associated wiring harness. The system provides a visual warning to indicate EGR service at 30,000 miles. The mileage sensor module is a blue plastic box mounted on the dash panel in the passenger's compartment forward of the glove box. The warning lamp is snapped into a pre-punched hole in the instrument cluster finish panel, left of the steering column. After performing the required service, the warning light is reset by installing a new sensor module.

Exhaust Heat Control Valve

OPERATION

The function of the exhaust heat control valve is to divert hot exhaust gas from the exhaust manifold to the intake manifold riser pad. Heat is transferred from exhaust gas to the riser pad, which in turn heats the incoming air/fuel charge. There are 2 types of exhaust heat control valves being used. They are vacuum operated type and a bimetal type.

EMISSION CONTROLS

System Services

BIMETAL TYPE

1. Inspect the valve assembly for any obvious defects. Replace the valve as required.
2. Check the valve thermostatic spring operation by manually rotating the valve shaft. The valve must be free and return to the closed position when cold.
3. If the valve does not function as indicated, replace the defective component as necessary.

VACUUM TYPE

1. Inspect the valve assembly for any obvious defects. Replace the valve as required.
2. Apply 10–15 in. Hg of vacuum to the vacuum motor, using a held hand vacuum pump. Trap the vacuum for approximately 1 minute.
3. The valve must close and not leak more than 2 in. Hg of vacuum and must also open when the vacuum is released.
4. If the valve does not function as indicated, replace the defective component as necessary.

Backpressure Variable Transducer EGR Valve

OPERATION

This system combines a ported EGR valve with a backpressure variable transducer in order to control nitrous oxides. The amount of exhaust gas reintroduced and the timing of the cycle varies by engine calibration and is controlled by various factors such as engine speed, altitude, engine vacuum, exhaust system backpressure, coolant temperature and throttle angle. The typical system consists of 3 components, a vacuum regulator, a EGR valve and a flow control orifice. The regulator modulates the vacuum signal to the EGR valve using 2 backpressure inputs. One input is standard vehicle backpressure and the other is backpressure downstream of the flow control orifice.

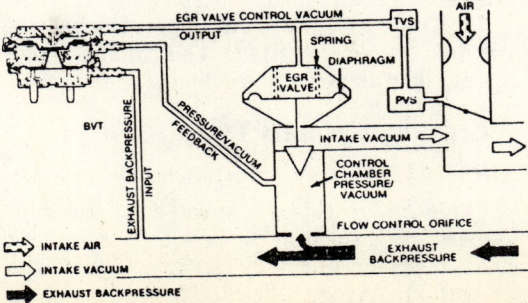

Diaphragm of the backpressure variable transducer

The control chamber pick-up is in the EGR tube and the flow control orifice is integral with upstream EGR tube connector.

System Services

1. Individually, apply a minimum of 5 in. Hg of vacuum to the 3 ports of the valve.
2. Ports B and C should hold vacuum. Port E should not hold vacuum.
3. If the above results are not achieved, replace the valve.

Integral Backpressure Transducer EGR Valve

OPERATION

The integral backpressure transducer EGR valve combines inputs of backpressure and EGR port vacuum to one unit. The valve requires both inputs in order to function properly. The valve will not operate on vacuum alone. There are 2 types of integral backpressure valves, poppet type and tapered pintle type.

System Service

1. Check to be sure that the vacuum lines are properly routed, all connections are secure and that the lines are not crimped or broken.
2. Disconnect and plug the vacuum line to the EGR valve. Connect a vacuum pump to the EGR valve. Start the engine and let it ride.
3. Apply vacuum to the valve. About 6 in. Hg of vacuum should bleed off and the valve should not operate. If the vacuum holds and the valve stays open, replace the valve.
4. There should be no vacuum to the valve or valve operation when the engine is cold. If vacuum is present check the TVS or PVS. Replace the defective component as required.
5. There should be no vacuum to the valve at 4000 rpm for the 1.6L engine and 3000 rpm for the 2.3L engine and kickdown rpm for all other engines with a normally warm engine. If not recheck back through the vacuum line from the EGR to the vacuum source. Check and replace the defective component as required.

Ported EGR Valve

OPERATION

The ported EGR valve is operated by a vacuum signal from the carburetor EGR port signal which actuates the valve diaphragm. As the vacuum signal increases to overcome the power spring, the valve opens allowing the EGR to function. The amount of EGR flow is dependent on the tappers pintle or the poppet position which is a direct result of the vacuum signal.

EMISSION CONTROLS

System Service

1. Check to be sure that the vacuum lines are properly routed, all connections are secure and that the lines are not crimped or broken.
2. There should be no vacuum to the valve or valve operation when the engine is cold. If vacuum is present check the TVS or PVS. Replace the defective component as required.
3. There should be no vacuum to the valve or valve operation when the engine is warm at curb idle.
4. There should be no vacuum to the valve at 4000 rpm for the 1.6L engine and 3000 rpm for the 2.3L engine and kickdown rpm for all other engines with a normally warm engine. If not recheck back through the vacuum line from the EGR to the vacuum source. Check and replace the defective component as required.
5. With the engine at idle, apply 8 in. Hg of vacuum to the valve. The valve stem should move opening the valve and the engine idle should roughen.
6. If the valve stem moves but the engine idle does not roughen, remove the valve and clean the inlet and outlet ports of the valve with a wire brush.
7. With the engine running at idle, trap approximately 4 in. Hg of vacuum and hold it. About 1 in. Hg of vacuum should bleed off in approximately 30 seconds. If the valve does not perform properly, replace the valve.
8. If the valve is suspected of leaking, insert a blocking gasket between the valve and the mounting base and retighten the valve.
9. If the engine idle improves, replace the valve and remove the blocking gasket.

ELECTRONIC EGR VALVE

OPERATION

An electronic EGR valve is required in the EEC systems where EGR air flow is controlled according to computer demands, by means of an EGR valve position sensor attaches to the EGR valve. The valve is operated by a vacuum signal from the dual EGR solenoid valves of the electronic vacuum regulator which actuates the valve diaphragm. As supply vacuum overcomes the spring load, the diaphragm is activated which lifts the pintle of its seat allowing exhaust gas to recirculate. The amount of the recirculation is proportional to the pintle position. The EVP sensor mounted on top of the EGR valve, sends a electrical signal regarding its position to the electronic control assembly.

System Service

1. Check to be sure that the vacuum lines are properly routed, all connections are secure and that the lines are not crimped or broken.

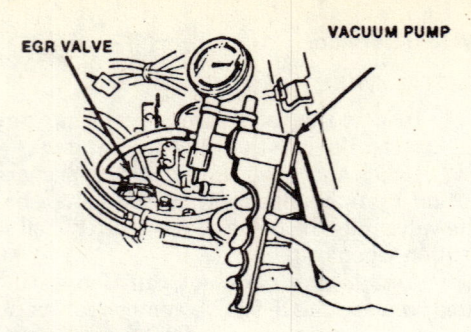

Testing the EGR valve

2. Connect a suitable vacuum pump to the EGR valve and apply 5–6 in. Hg of vacuum to the valve.
3. Trap the vacuum and hold it. The vacuum should not drop more than 1 in. Hg of vacuum in approximately 30 seconds.
4. If the above conditions were not met, service or replace the valve, O-ring or EVP assembly as required.

EGR SOLENOID VACUUM VALVE ASSEMBLY

DITHERING TYPE

The dual EGR solenoid valve assembly consists of 2 dithering solenoid valves. One valve is a vacuum valve, which supplies vacuum to the sonic EGR valve when energized. The second valve is a vent valve, which vents the EGR valve to the atmosphere when de-energized. Both components receive variable duty cycle signals from the ECU according to EGR requirements. A restrictor is incorporated in the vacuum valve inlet port in order to reduce its flow, compared to that of the vent valve, so that in case the vacuum valve sticks open, the vent valve will be capable of venting the vacuum flow immediately without affecting the devices being controlled.

System Service

1. The electrical resistance of each solenoid should be 32–64. If the solenoid resistance is not as indicated, replace the solenoid.
2. The vent valve should flow air when the solenoid is de-energized. The control valve should flow air when the solenoid is energized.

Normally Closed Type

OPERATED

The normally closed solenoid valve assembly consists of 2 vacuum ports with atmospheric vent. The valve assembly can be equipped with or without a control bleed. The outlet port of the valve is opened to the atmospheric vent and closed to the inlet port when the system is de-

EMISSION CONTROLS 199

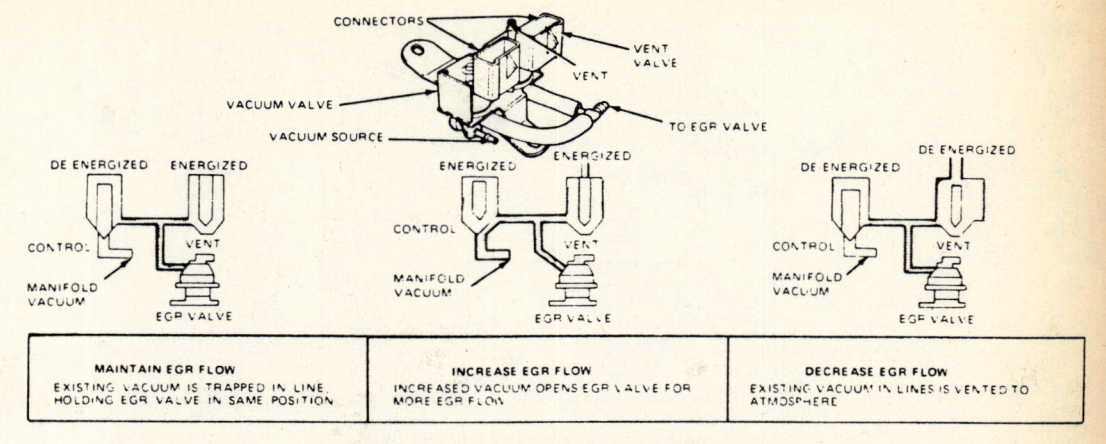

Dithering type EGR solenoid valve assembly

energized. When energized, the outlet port is opened to the inlet port and closed to the atmospheric vent. If equipped, the control bleed valve is provided to prevent contamination from entering the solenoid valve assembly from the intake manifold. This solenoid valve assembly is used on the throttle kicker, air dump, air diverter and exhaust heat control system.

Combination EGR Solenoid Vacuum Valve Assembly

OPERATION

These normally open and normally closed solenoid valves operate independently and each controls different devices. However the valves are mounted on the same mounting bracket. Type one valves are used for the Thermactor air dump and the Thermactor diverter. Type two valves, the one port normally open and the two port normally closed solenoid valve assembly, is used for choke pull down and the air conditioning throttle kicker.

EGR Venturi Vacuum Amplifier

OPERATION

The exhaust gas recirculation venturi vacuum amplifier uses weak venturi vacuum to control a manifold vacuum signal to operate the exhaust gas recirculation valve. It contains a check valve that opens whenever the venturi vacuum signal is equal to or greater than manifold vacuum.

System Service

1. Warm the engine to operating temperature. Set the curb idle. Check for adequate manifold vacuum.
2. Connect a vacuum gauge to the hose at the EGR port O. The gauge may read as much as 2 in. Hg of vacuum.
3. Disconnect the venturi hose at the carburetor, increase the engine speed to 2000 rpm (3000 rpm for the 2.3L engine and 4000 rpm for the 1.6L engine). Vacuum reading should not change.
4. Maintain high engine speed and connect the venturi hose. The gauge should register at least 4 in. Hg of vacuum.
5. Return the engine to idle. The gauge should return to its initial reading.
6. If the above conditions do not occur, replace the venturi vacuum amplifier.

Remote Transducer Backpressure EGR Valve

OPERATION

The component combines a ported vacuum operated EGR valve with a remote transducer in order to provide a backpressure EGR system identical to the integral back pressure EGR valve. The remote system is used on vehicle equipped with the 2.0L and 2.3L engines. This system utilizes the external entry ported valve with modifications for various orifice diameters and a pressure tap to provide a backpressure signal to the transducer.

Thermactor Air Pump System

OPERATION

A typical air injection system consists of an air supply pump and centrifugal filter, an air bypass valve, check valve, air manifold and air hoses.

Simply, the air pump injects air into the engine which reduces the hydrocarbon and carbon monoxide content of exhaust gases by continuing the combustion of the unburned gases after they leave the combustion chamber. Fresh air mixed with the hot exhaust gases promotes further oxidation of both the hydrocar-

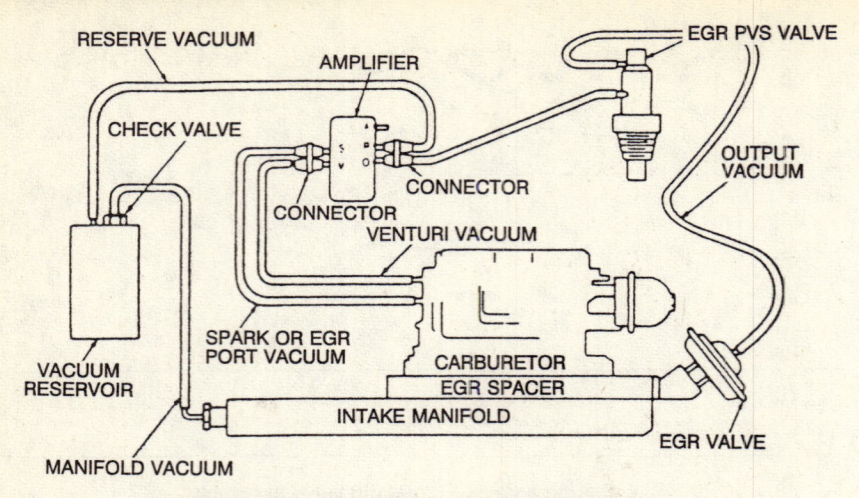

EMISSION CONTROLS

Typical EGR system using a venturi vacuum amplifier

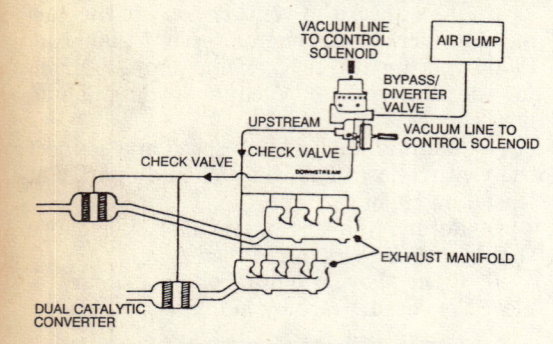

Typical Thermactor air injection system

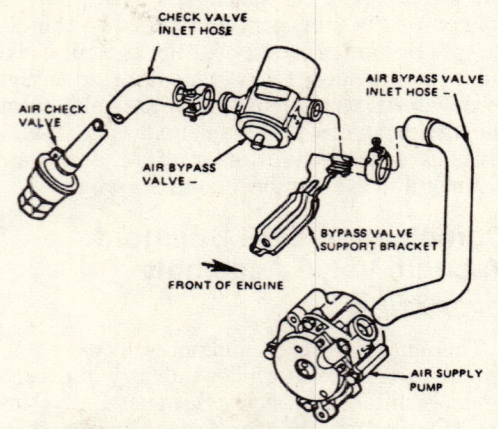

Typical Thermactor air injection system

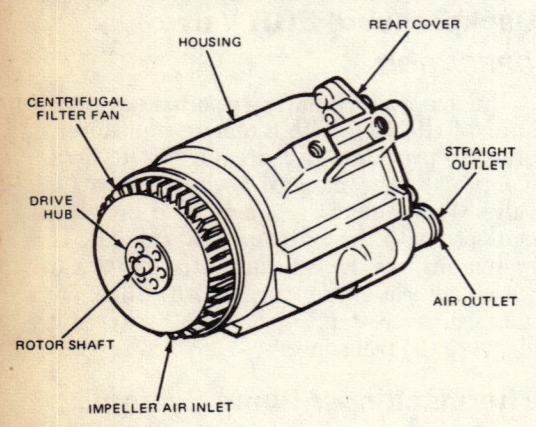

Air supply pump

bons and carbon monoxide, thereby reducing their concentration and converting some of them into harmless carbon dioxide and water.

Air for the system is cleaned by means of a centrifugal filter fan mounted on the air pump driveshaft.

To prevent excessive pressure, the air pump is equipped with a pressure relief valve.

The air pump has sealed bearings which are lubricated for the lift of the unit, and preset rotor vane ad bearing clearances, which do not require any periodic adjustments.

The air supply from the pump is controlled by the air by-pass valve, sometimes a dump valve. During deceleration, the air by-pass valve opens, momentarily diverting the air supply into the atmosphere, thus preventing backfires within the exhaust system.

A check valve is incorporated in the air inlet side of the air manifold. It purpose is to prevent the exhaust gases from backing up into the system. The valve is especially important in the event of drive belt failure and during deceleration, when the air by-pass valve is dumping the air supply. The air manifold channel the air from the pump into the exhaust thus completing the cycle of the Thermactor system.

Air Bypass Valves
OPERATION

There are 2 types of air bypass valves, normally closed valves and normally opened valves. Both types are available in remote

EMISSION CONTROLS

(inline) versions or pump mounted (installed directly on the air pump) versions. These bypass valves are part of the Thermactor system. Normally closed vales supply air to the exhaust system using medium and high applied vacuum signals during normal engine operating modes and short idles with some accelerations. With low or no vacuum applied, the pump air is dumped through the silencer ports of the valve. Normally open air bypass valves are available with or without vacuum vents. Normally open valves using a vacuum vent provide a timed air dump during decelerations and also dump when a vacuum pressure difference is maintained between the signal port and the vent port. The signal port must have 3 in. Hg or more of vacuum than the vent port to hold the dump. This mode is required in order to protect the catalyst from overheating. Normally open air bypass valves without a vacuum vent, provide a timed dump of air for 1.0 or 2.8 seconds when a sudden high vacuum of about 20 in. Hg is applied to the signal port. This prevents backfire during deceleration.

Air Check Valve/Pulse Air Valve

OPERATION

The air check valve is a one way valve that allows the Thermactor air to pass into the exhaust system while preventing exhaust gases from passing in the opposite direction. The pulse air valve replaces the air pump in some Thermactor systems. It draws air into the exhaust system on vacuum exhaust pulses and blocks the backflow of high pressure exhaust pulses. The fresh air completes the oxidation of exhaust gas components.

Anti-Backfire (Gulp) Valve

OPERATIONS

The anti-backfire (gulp) valve is located downstream from the air bypass valve. Its function is to divert a portion of the Thermactor air to the intake manifold when it is triggered by intake manifold vacuum signals on deceleration.

System Services

1. Disconnect the air supply hose from the air pump side of the anti-backfire valve.
2. Look inside the valve through the disconnect port and observe the valve pintle.
3. Accelerate the engine to about 3000 rpm. Release the throttle, the pintle should be open and then close.
4. If the valve does not perform as indicated, replace the defective part.

NOTE: *If your vehicle backfires while decelerating, a good and quick way to tell if this valve is working or if the problem is in the Thermactor system, is to remove the belt from the air pump and test drive the vehicle. If the backfire is gone, then your problem lies with the Thermactor system. If the backfire still remains, go over the basic first and then maybe a possible exhaust valve problem.*

Air Supply Pump

OPERATION

The air supply is a belt driven, positive engagement vane type pump, that supplies air for the Thermactor system. The pump is available in 2 sizes: 11 cubic inch and 19 cubic inch, depending on the particular vehicle application. The 11 cubic inch pump receives air through a remote filter that is attached to the air inlet

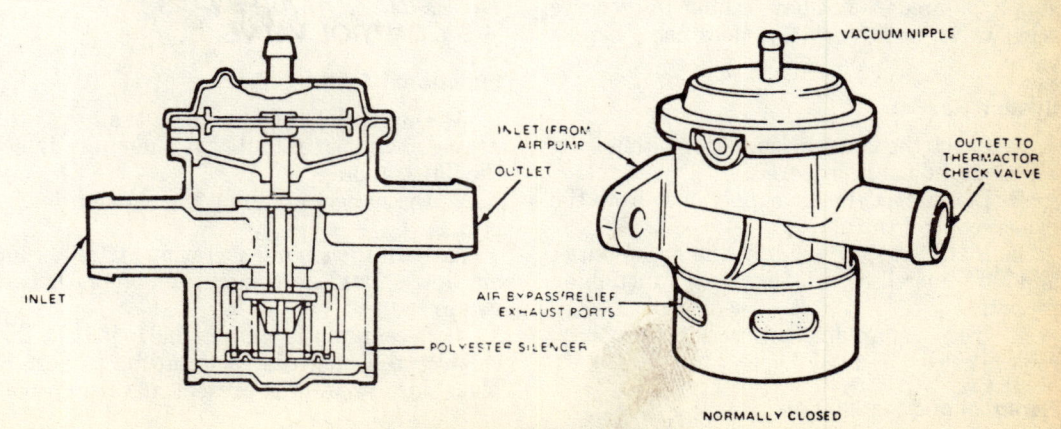

Normally closed air bypass valve

202 EMISSION CONTROLS

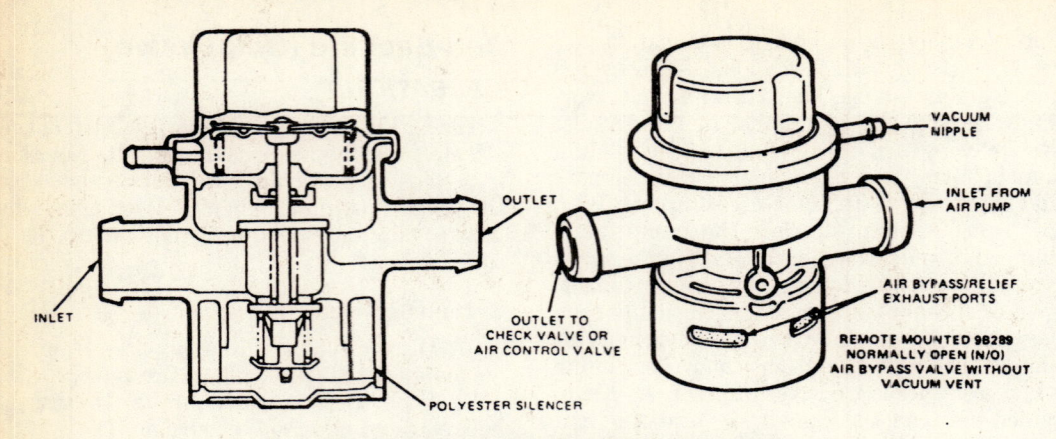

Normally open air bypass valve without vacuum vent

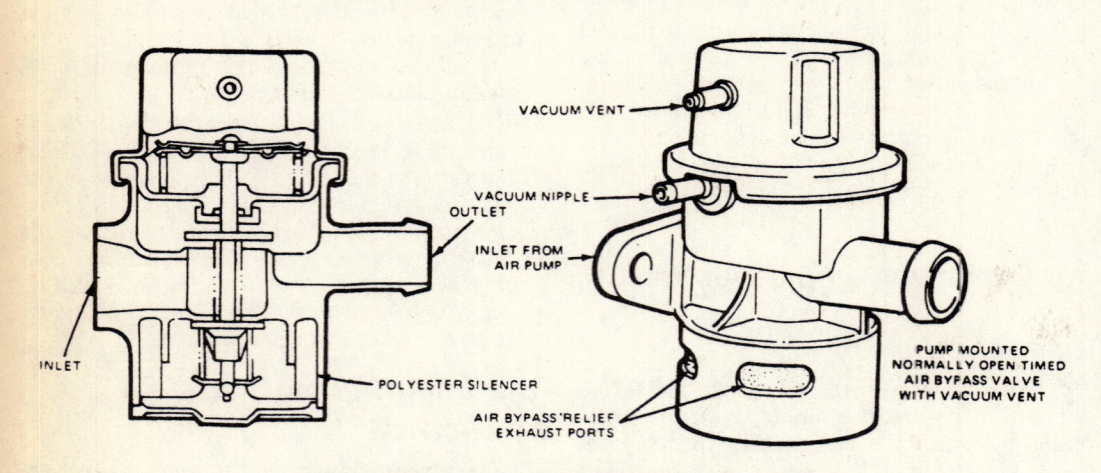

Normally open air bypass valve with vacuum vent

nipple or through an impeller type centrifugal air filter fan. The 19 cubic inch pump uses an impeller type centrifugal air filter fan which separates dirt, dust and other contaminants from the intake air, using centrifugal force. The air supply pump does not have a built in pressure relief valve, but the system does use a bypass valve.

System Service

1. Check the belt tension. If not within specifications, adjust it properly.
2. Disconnect the air supply hose from the bypass control valve.
3. If the air flow is felt at the pump outlet and flow increases, the pump is functioning properly.
4. If the pump does not perform properly, replace as required.

Removal and Installation

1. Loosen the pivot mounting and adjustment bolt. Relax the drive belt tension and remove the belt. Disconnect the air hoses.
2. Remove the adjuster and pivot nuts and bolts. Remove the air pump.
3. Installation is in the reverse order of removal. Adjust the belt to its proper tension.

COMBINATION AIR BYPASS AIR CONTROL VALVE

Functional Test

1. Disconnect the two hoses that go to the engine or converter (outlet **A** and outlet **B**, see the illustration).
2. Disconnect and plug the vacuum line at port **D**.
3. With the engine operating at 1,500 rpm, air flow should be coming out of the bypass vents.
4. Reconnect the vacuum line to port **D**. Disconnect and plug the vacuum line to port **S**. Make sure vacuum is present at vacuum port **D**.
5. Operate the engine at 1,500 rpm, air flow should be detected at outlet B. No air flow should be at outlet **A**.

EMISSION CONTROLS

Troubleshooting the Thermactor System

Condition	Possible Source	Resolution
• Excessive Belt Noise	• Loose belt	• Tighten to specification CAUTION: *Do not use a pry bar to move the air pump.*
	• Seized pump	• Replace pump.
	• Loose pulley	• Replace pulley and/or pump if damaged. Tighten bolts to specification 130–180 in. lbs.
	• Loose or broken mounting brackets or bolts	• Replace parts as required and tighten bolts to specification.
• Excessive Mechanical Clicking	• Over-tightened mounting bolt	• Tighten to 25 ft. lbs.
	• Excessive flash on the air pump adjusting arm boss.	• Remove flash from the boss.
	• Distorted adjusting arm.	• Replace adjusting arm.
• Excessive Thermactor System Noise (Putt-Putt, Whirling or Hissing)	• Leak in hose	• Locate source of leak using soap solution, and replace hoses as necessary.
	• Loose, pinched or kinked hose	• Reassemble, straighten, or replace hose and clamps as required.
	• Hose touching other engine parts	• Adjust hose to prevent contact with other engine parts.
	• Bypass valve inoperative	• Test the valve.
	• Check valve inoperative	• Test the valve.
	• Pump mounting fasteners loose	• Tighten fasteners to specification.
	• Restricted or bent pump outlet fitting	• Inspect fitting, and remove any flash blocking the air passage way. Replace bent fittings.
	• Air dumping through bypass valve (at idle only)	• On many vehicles, the thermactor system has been designed to dump air at idle to prevent overheating the catalyst. This condition is normal. Determine that the noise persists at higher speeds before proceeding further.
• Excessive Pump Noise (Chirps, Squeaks and Ticks)	• Insufficient break-in or worn or damaged pump	• Check the thermactor system for wear or damage and make any necessary corrections.

6. Use a hand vacuum pump and apply 8–10 in.Hg to port S. With the engine operating at 1,500 rpm, air flow should be noted coming out of outlet **A**.

7. Replace the combination valve if any of the tests indicate a problem.

CHECK VALVE

The check valve is a one way valve. Pressure at the inlet allows air to flow past a viton disc. Vacuum at the outlet causes the reed to open, effecting one-way air flow in reed type valves. Air is prevented from passing through the valve if pressure at the outlet side of the valve is positive.

Functional Test

1. Disconnect the air supply at the pump side of the valve.
2. Blow through the check valve, toward the manifold, then attempt to suck back through the valve. Air should pass in the direction of the exhaust manifold only. Replace the valve if air flows both ways.

Dual Thermactor Air Control Solenoid Valve

OPERATIONS

This component consists of 2 normally closed solenoid vacuum valves, one controlling the Thermactor air bypass valve and the other controlling the Thermactor diverter valve. Both valves are vented when de-energized, sourced by the intake manifold vacuum reservoir and controlled by the EEC system. The function of each valve can be determined by externally energizing it with vacuum sourced and output gauge. The resistance of each solenoid should be between 51–108 when checked at the coil terminals. If the resistance is not as indicated, the solenoid should be replaced.

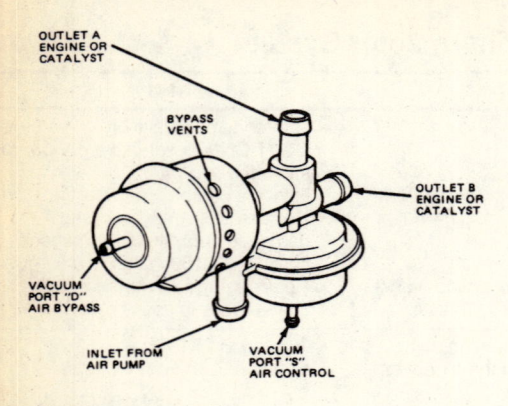

204 EMISSION CONTROLS

Combination valve

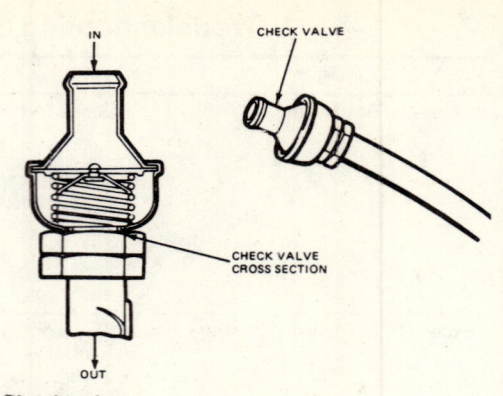

Check valve

Thermactor Idle Vacuum Valve

OPERATIONS

This component vents the vacuum signal to the atmosphere when the preset manifold vacuum or pressure is exceeded. It is used to divert Thermactor air flow during extended idle conditions in order to limit exhaust temperature and to cut out the EGR in the heavy boost mode for turbocharged vehicles.

Pulse Air System

OPERATIONS

Some engines are equipped with an air injection system called Pulse Air or Thermactor II. This system does not use an air pump. The system uses natural pulses present in the exhaust system to pull air into the exhaust manifold and catalyst through pulse air vanes. The pulse air valve is connected to the exhaust manifold and catalyst with a long tube and to the air cleaner silencer with a hose.

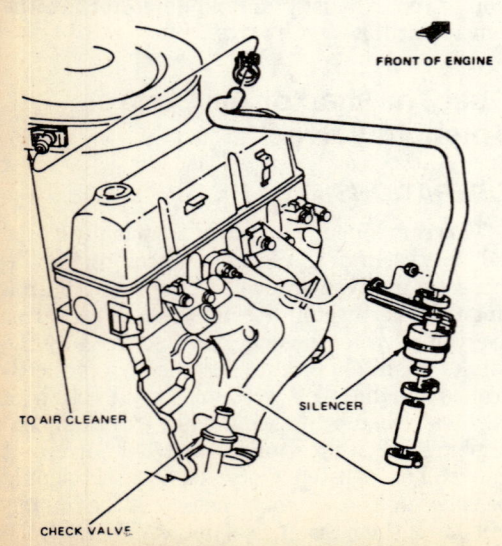

Typical Thermactor II pulse air injection system

Air Supply Control Valves

OPERATION

Vehicles that are equipped with a Thermactor air system use an air supply control valve. This valve directs air pump output to the exhaust manifold or down to the catalyst system, depending upon the particular engine that is used in the vehicle.

System Service

1. Check to be sure that air flow is being supplied to the valve inlet. Do this by disconnecting the air supply hose at the inlet valve with the engine running at 1500 rpm. Reconnect the hose.
2. Disconnect the air supply hoses at the outlet tubes A and B of the valve. Remove the vacuum line from the vacuum nipple.
3. Accelerator the engine to 1500 rpm. Air flow should be felt and heard at outlet B with little or no air flow at outlet A.
4. Accelerate the engine to 1500 rpm, connect a direct vacuum line from any manifold vacuum source to the air control valve vacuum

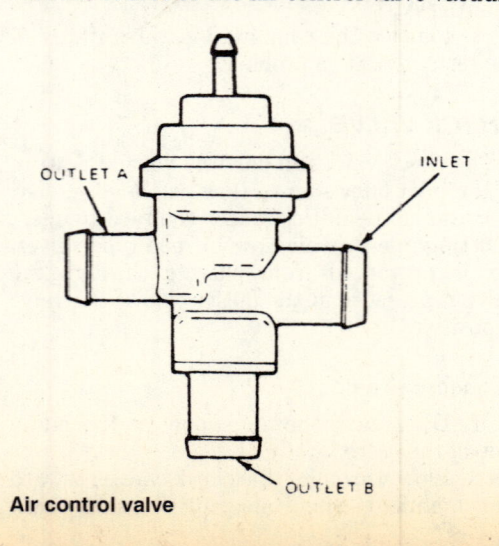

Air control valve

EMISSION CONTROLS 205

PULSE AIR SYSTEM TROUBLE DIAGNOSIS CHART

Condition	Cause	Correction
Excessive Mechanical Clicking	a) Tighten to 34 N·m (25 lb-ft).	a) Overtightened mounting bolt
	b) Same as loose belt.	b) Overtightened drive belt
	c) Remove flash from the boss.	c) Excessive flash on the air pump adjusting arm boss
	rd) Replace adjusting arm.	d) Distorted adjusting gum.
Excessive Thermactor System Noise (Putt-Putt, Whirling or Hissing)	a) Locate source of leak using soap solution, and replace hoses as necessary.	a) Leak in hose
	b) Reassemble, straighten, or replace hose and clamps as required.	b) Loose, pinched or kinked hose
	c) Adjust hose to prevent contact with other engine parts.	c) Hose touching other engine parts
	d) Test the valve.	d) Bypass valve inoperative
	e) Test the valve.	e) Check valve inoperative
	f) Tighten fasteners to specification.	f) Pump or pulley mounting fasteners loose
	g) Inspect fitting, and remove any flash blocking the air passage way. Replace bent fittings.	g) Restricted or bent pump outlet fitting
Excessive Thermactor System Noise (Putt-Putt, Whirling or Hissing)	h) On many vehicles, the thermactor system has been designed to dump air at idle to prevent overheating the catalyst. This condition is normal. Determine that the noise persists at higher speeds before proceeding.	h) Air dumping through bypass valve (at idle only)
Excessive Pump Noise (Chirps, Squeaks and Ticks)	a) Check the thermactor system for wear of damage and make necessary corrections. If pump is not damaged and has less than 804.5 Km (500 miles) in service, do NOT replace pump. A 804.5 Km (500 mile) break-in is required.	a) Insufficient break-in or worn or damaged pump

nipple. Air flow should be felt and heard at outlet A with little or no air flow from outlet B.

5. If the valve is the bleed type, less air will flow from outlet A or B, the main discharge will change when vacuum is applied to the vacuum nipple.

6. Reconnect the hoses and lines. If the valve does not performs indicated, replace the valve.

FORD EEC IV ENGINE CONTROL SYSTEM

General Information

The Ford Electronic Engine Control (EEC) IV system is the fifth generation of engine control systems used on Ford passenger cars and light trucks. EEC IV is similar to previous Ford engine control systems in that the heart of the system is a microcomputer called an Electronic Control Assembly (ECA). The ECA receives data (system inputs) from sensors, switches, relays and other electronic components and issues command signals (system outputs) to various devices in order to control engine operation under a variety of loads and ambient conditions. The ECA is calibrated according to the powertrain, axle ratio and gross vehicle weight (GVW) to optimize fuel economy and driveability while minimizing harmful emissions.

The ECA in the EEC IV system is similar in appearance to earlier control units, except that the calibration module is located within the ECA assembly instead of being attached to the outside as on earlier systems. The harness connectors are edge-card type contacts which provide a more positive connection and allow probing with volt/ohmmeter leads from the rear while connected to simplify diagnosis and testing. The ECA is usually mounted in the passenger compartment, under the front section of the center console, but the location will vary on different models. The ECA could also be located under the right (passenger) seat, or behind the right front (passenger) kick panel, for example.

The EEC IV engine control system is used in conjunction with either a throttle body (CFI) injection, multi-port (EFI) injection, or feedback carburetor (FBC) fuel delivery system depending on the year, model and powertrain. Although the individual system components vary, the electronic control system operation is basically the same. The major difference is the number and type of output devices being controlled by the ECA.

The EEC IV system electronically controls the fuel injectors or carburetor feedback and mixture control solenoids to maintain a 14.7:1 air/fuel ratio under all driving conditions. This 14.7:1 air/fuel mixture allows the three-way catalytic converter to operate at peak efficiency while getting the most performance and economy from the engine. Ignition spark timing, deceleration fuel cut-off, EGR function (on or off), curb and fast idle speed, evaporative emissions purge, A/C cut-off during wide open throttle, cold engine start and enrichment, electric fuel pump and self-test engine diagnostics are also controlled by the ECA to maintain consistent driveability across a wide range of operating conditions, temperatures and altitudes. The EEC IV system is self-adjusting for operation at high altitude elevations (over 4,000 ft. above sea level) and can actually compensate for engine component wear (a worn timing chain, for example).

The EEC IV engine control system is divided into three major subsystems:

- **Fuel Delivery Subsystem** – which includes the fuel tank and lines, fuel pump and fuel injection or feedback carburetor components. On fuel injected models, this includes the fuel supply manifold, fuel pressure regulator, injectors and fuel filter. On models with feedback carburetors, it includes the carburetor metering circuits, choke assembly and the carburetor body itself.
- **Air Induction Subsystem** – which includes the air cleaner and ducts, intake manifold, carburetor or fuel injection throttle body, throttle air bypass valve, vane airflow meter, turbocharger (if equipped) and related vacuum hoses and air ducts.
- **Electronic Control Subsystem** – which consists of the ECA and its various engine sensors (such as the oxygen sensor and coolant temperature sensor, etc.), along with the wiring harness, relays, fuses, battery and self-diagnostic system. On feedback carburetor models, it would include the throttle position sensor and mixture control solenoid. On fuel injected models, it would include the throttle position switch and the wire harness to the fuel injectors, but not the fuel injectors themselves. On turbocharged models, it would include the same multi-port fuel injection components, along with such items like over boost pressure switches that are peculiar to turbocharged engines.

EEC IV SYSTEM OPERATION

Crank Mode

The crank mode is entered after initial engine starting, or after engine stall when key is in START. A special operation program is used in the crank mode to aid engine starting. After engine start, one of the run modes is entered and normal engine operation is performed. If the engine stumbles during a run mode, the underspeed mode is entered to help it recover from the stumble and prevent stalling. When cranking the engine, the fuel control is in the open loop mode (no feedback to the ECA) of operation and the ECA sets engine timing at 10–15° BTDC (for the correct timing specification, refer to the Engine Emissions Decal under the hood.

On fuel injected (EFI) models, the injectors fire either in a simultaneous, double-fire manner (fires twice every crankshaft revolution), or once per engine revolution in the normal engine firing order, to provide the base crank air/fuel control. The throttle air bypass valve solenoid is set to open the bypass valve to provide the fast idle/no-touch start.

On models with a feedback carburetor, the air/fuel ratio is controlled through the feedback solenoid. The EGR cut-off solenoid is not energized, so EGR valve if Off.

NOTE: *On some engines, the vapor canister purge solenoid is teed with the Thermactor Air Divert (TAD) solenoid, so when Thermactor air is upstream, the canister purge if off.*

At start-up, the throttle position sensor (TPS) keeps the ECA informed on the position of the throttle plate. When the throttle is kicked after start-up, the ECA will bring the engine down from fast idle by changing the signal to the throttle air bypass valve.

Underspeed Mode

Operation in the underspeed mode (under 500 rpm) is similar to that previously described for the crank mode. The system switches from the underspeed mode to the normal run mode when the required rpm is reached. The underspeed mode is used to provide a good pulse width to the injectors and ignores any signal from the vane meter. During this mode, the vane meter used on fuel injection models flutters and the signal generated would vary with the flutter. Therefore, the vane meter signal is ignored by the ECA in the underspeed mode.

EMISSION CONTROLS

Closed Throttle Mode (Idle or Deceleration)

In the closed throttle mode, the air/fuel ratio is trimmed by either varying the pulse width of the output from the ECA to the injectors, or by varying the duty cycle of the feedback solenoid on carbureted models, to obtain the desired mixture. To calculate what this output signal should be, the ECA evaluates inputs from the ECT sensor, the vane meter, the TPS, the EGO sensor, the PIP sensor and the A/C clutch. These sensors inform the ECA of the various conditions that must be evaluated in order for the ECA to determine the correct air/fuel ratio for the closed-throttle condition present. Therefore, with the input from the EGO sensor, the system is maintained in closed-loop operation at idle. If the EGO sensor fails to switch rich/lean, the ECA programming assumes the EGO sensor has cooled off, and the system goes to open-loop fuel control. Under a deceleration condition, the TPS signal indicates closed throttle and the ECA shut-off fuel for improved fuel economy and emissions. The injectors are turned back on, as required, to prevent engine stalling.

NOTE: *The point at which the injectors are turned back on will occur at different rpm's, depending on calibration factors and engine temperature, although the injectors are turned back on if the throttle is opened.*

Ignition timing is also determined by ECA using these same inputs. The ECA has a series of tables programmed into the assembly at the factory. These tables provide the ECA with a reference of desired ignition timing for the various operating conditions reflected by the sensor inputs. The throttle air bypass valve position is determined by the ECA as a function of RPM, ECT, A/C On or Off, throttle mode and time since start-up inputs. The signal from the TPS to the ECA indicates that the throttle plate is closed, and the ECA de-energizes the EGR shut-off solenoid to close the EGR valve.

Part Throttle Mode (Cruise)

The air/fuel mixture ratio and ignition timing are calculated in the same manner as previously described for the closed throttle mode. The fuel control system remains in closed-loop during part throttle operation, as long as the EGO sensor is operational. In part throttle operation, the throttle air bypass valve is positioned to provide an electronic dashpot function in the event the throttle is closed. Again, as in the closed throttle mode, the ECA makes this determination based on the inputs from the applicable sensors. The TPS provides the throttle plate position signal to the ECA. With the throttle plate being in a partial open position, the ECA energizes the EGR shut-off solenoid to open the EGR valve.

Wide Open Throttle Mode (WOT)

Control of the air/fuel ratio in WOT mode is the same as in part, or closed throttle situations, except that fuel control switches to open-loop, and the fuel injector pulse width is increased to provide additional fuel enrichment. This pulse width increase is applied as a result of the WOT signal from the TPS to the ECA. This signal from the TPS also causes the ECA to remove the energizing signal from the EGR shut-off solenoid (if present). More spark advance is added in WOT for improved performance.

Cold or Hot Engine Operation

This modified operation changes the normal engine operation output signals, as required, to adjust for uncommon engine operating conditions. These include cold or excessively hot engine.

Limited Operation Strategy (LOS)

In this operation, the ECA provides the necessary output signals to allow the vehicle to "limp home" when an electronic malfunction occurs. The EGR valve is shut-off, the air bypass valve goes to a fixed voltage, timing is locked at the fixed timing (depends on calibration, refer to Engine Emissions Decal on the vehicle), and the injector pulse width is constant.

Central Fuel Injection (CFI) System

The Ford Central Fuel Injection (CFI) System is a single point, pulse time modulated injection system. Fuel is metered into the air intake stream according to engine demands by one or two solenoid injection valves, mounted in a throttle body on the intake manifold. Fuel is supplied from the fuel tank by a high-pressure electric fuel pump (either by itself or in addition to a low-pressure pump) on all except 2.3L HSC engines, which use a single low-pressure pump. The fuel is filtered, and sent to the air throttle body where a regulator keeps the fuel delivery pressure at a constant 39 psi (269 kPa) on high-pressure systems, or 14.5 psi (100kPa) on low-pressure systems. One or two injector nozzles are mounted vertically above the throttle plates and connected in parallel with the fuel pressure regulator. Excess fuel supplied by the pump but not needed by the engine is returned to the fuel tank by a steel fuel return line.

NOTE: *1984–85 CFI models use a pintle-type fuel injector, while 1986–90 models with a single injector use a new design that incorporates a ball and seat to meter the fuel. Although both injectors are solenoid-operated, they are physically different and not interchangeable.*

CFI FUEL DELIVERY SYSTEM

Fuel Charging Assembly

The fuel charging assembly controls air/fuel ratio. It consists of a typical carburetor throttle body. It has two bores without venturi's. The throttle shaft and valves control engine air flow based on driver demand. The throttle body attaches to the intake manifold mounting pad.

A throttle position sensor is attached to the throttle shaft. It includes a potentiometer (or rheostat) that electrically senses throttle opening A throttle kicker solenoid fastens opposite the throttle position sensor. During air conditioning operation, the solenoid extends to slightly increase engine idle speed.

Cold engine speed is controlled by an automatic kick-down vacuum motor. There is also an all-electric, bimetal coil spring which controls cold idle speed. The bimetal electric coil operates like a conventional carburetor choke coil, but the electronic fuel injection system uses no choke. Fuel enrichment for cold starts is controlled by the computer and injectors.

Fuel Pressure Regulator

The fuel pressure regulator controls critical injector fuel pressure. The regulator receives fuel from the electric fuel pump and then adjusts the fuel pressure for uniform fuel injection. The regulator sets fuel pressure at 39 psi on high pressure systems, or 14.5 psi on low pressure systems.

Fuel Manifold

The fuel manifold (or fuel rail) evenly distributes fuel to each injector. Its main purpose is to equalize the fuel flow. One end of the fuel rail contains a relief valve for testing fuel pressure during engine operation.

Fuel Injectors

The fuel injectors are electromechanical devices. The electrical solenoid operates a pintle or ball metering valve which always travels the same distance from closed to open to closed. Injection is controlled by varying the length of time the valve is open.

The computer, based on voltage inputs from the crank position sensor, operates each injector solenoid two times per engine revolution. When the injector metering valve unseats, fuel is sprayed in a fine mist into the intake manifold. The computer varies fuel enrichment based on voltage inputs from the exhaust gas oxygen sensor, barometric pressure sensor, manifold absolute pressure sensor, etc., by calculating how long to hold the injectors open. The longer the injectors remain open, the richer the mixture. This injector ON time is called pulse duration.

Fuel Pump

The fuel delivery system uses either a high or low-pressure inline or in-tank electric fuel pump, with some models equipped with both. It is a recirculating system that delivers fuel to a pressure regulating valve in the throttle body and returns excess fuel from the throttle body regulator back to the fuel tank. The electrical system uses two types of control relays, one controlled by a vacuum switch and the other controlled by the electronic control assembly (ECA) to provide power to the fuel pump under various operating conditions.

CAUTION: *Fuel supply lines on vehicles equipped with a high pressure fuel system will remain pressurized for long periods of time after engine shutdown. The fuel pressure must be relieved before servicing the fuel system.*

An inertia switch is used as a safety device in the fuel system. The inertia switch is located in the trunk, near the left rear wheel well. It is designed to open the fuel pump power circuit in the event of a collision. The switch is reset by pushing each of 2 buttons on the switch simultaneously (some models use switches with only 1 reset button). The inertia switch should not be reset until the fuel system has been inspected for damage or leaks.

With the ignition switch OFF, the vacuum switch controlled relay is closed and the EEC controlled relay is open. Then the ignition switch is first turned to ignition ON position, the vacuum switch controlled relay remains closed and the EEC controlled relay also closes. This provides power to the fuel pump to pre-pressurize the fuel system. If the ignition switch is not turned to the CRANK position, the EEC module will open its relay after approximately two seconds and shut off power to the pump. Then the ignition switch is turned to the CRANK position, both the vacuum switch controlled relay and the EEC controlled relay are closed. This provides full battery power to the pump. When the engine starts, manifold vacuum increases and causes the vacuum switch to close and the vacuum controlled relay to open. This provides reduced normal operating voltage to the fuel pump through the resistor which by-passes the vacuum controlled relay. Under heavy engine load conditions, manifold vacuum will reduce, causing the vacuum

EMISSION CONTROLS

switch to open. This causes the vacuum controlled relay to close, thus providing the return of full battery power to the pump. The EEC module senses engine speed and shuts off the pump by opening the EEC controlled relay when the engine stops.

ELECTRONIC CONTROL SYSTEM

Electronic Control Assembly (ECA)

The Electronic Control Assembly (ECA) is located under the instrument panel or passenger's seat and is usually covered by a kick panel. A multi-pin connector links the ECA with all system components. The processor provides a continuous reference voltage to the B/MAP, EVP and TPS sensors. EEC IV systems use a 5 volt reference signal. On early models, the calibration assembly is contained in a black plastic housing which plugs into the top of the processor assembly, while later model ECA's have the calibration module mounted internally. The calibration module contains the memory and programming information used by the processor to determine optimum operating conditions. Different calibration information is used in different vehicle applications, such as California or Federal models. For this reason, careful identification of the engine, year, model and type of electronic control system is essential to insure correct component replacement.

CFI ENGINE SENSORS

Air Charge Temperature Sensor (ACT)

The ACT is threaded into the intake manifold air runner. It is located next to the throttle body on 4-cylinder engines, and behind the distributor on V6 engines. The ACT monitors air/fuel charge temperature and sends an appropriate signal to the ECA. This information is used to correct fuel enrichment for variations in intake air density due to temperature changes.

Barometric & Manifold Absolute Pressure Sensors (B/MAP)

The MAP sensor used on V6 engines is separate from the barometric sensor and is located on the left finder panel in the engine compartment. The barometric sensor signals the ECA of changes in atmospheric pressure and density to regulate calculated air flow into the engine. The MAP sensor monitors and load, speed and atmospheric pressure changes.

EGR Valve Position Sensor (EVP)

This sensor, mounted on EGR valve, signals the computer of EGR opening so that it may subtract EGR flow from total air flow into the manifold. In this way, EGR flow is excluded from air flow information used to determine mixture requirements.

Engine Coolant Temperature Sensor (ECT)

The ECT is threaded into the intake manifold water jacket directly above the water pump by-pass hose. The ECT monitors coolant temperature and signals the ECA, which then uses these signals for mixture enrichment (during cool operation), ignition timing and EGR operation. The resistance value of the ECT increases with temperature, causing a voltage signal drop as the engine warms up.

Exhaust Gas Oxygen Sensor (EGO)

An exhaust gas oxygen sensor, mounted in the exhaust manifold, is used on all engines. The V6 engines use two sensors, one in each exhaust manifold. The EGO monitors oxygen content of exhaust gases and sends a constantly changing voltage signal to the ECA. The ECA analyzes this signal and adjusts the air/fuel mixture to obtain the optimum (stoichiometric) ratio for combustion and three-way catalyst performance.

Knock Sensor (KS)

This sensor is attached to the intake manifold in front of the ACT sensor. The KS detects engine vibrations caused by pre-ignition (or detonation) and provides signals to the ECA, which then retards the ignition timing to eliminate detonation in the affected cylinder(s).

Thick Film Integrated Module Sensor (TFI)

The TFI module sensor plugs into the distributor just below the distributor cap and replaces the CP sensor for some engines. Its function is to provide the ECA with ignition timing information, similar to what the CP sensor provides. On manual transmission models, the TFI module allows the vehicle to be push-started if necessary.

Throttle Position Sensor (TPS)

The rotary-type TPS is mounted on the side of the throttle body, directly connected to the throttle shaft. The TPS senses throttle movement and position and transmits an appropriate electrical signal to the ECA. These signals are used by the ECA to adjust the air/fuel mixture, spark timing and EGR operation according to engine load at idle, part throttle, or full throttle. There are two types of throttle position sensors used, rotary and linear. The linear TPS is used on feedback carburetors and is adjustable. The rotary TPS has two versions, one adjustable and one non-adjustable; the differ-

EMISSION CONTROLS

ence being elongated mounting holes that allow the rotary sensor to be turned slightly to adjust the output voltage. The rotary TPS with round mounting holes are not adjustable.

Multi-port (EFI) Fuel Injection Systems

The EFI fuel subsystems include a high pressure inline electric fuel pump, a low-pressure tank-mounted fuel pump, fuel charging manifold, pressure regulator, fuel filter and both solid and flexible fuel lines. The fuel charging manifold includes four electronically controlled fuel injectors, each mounted directly above an intake port in the lower intake manifold. On the 4 cylinder EFI system, all injectors are energized simultaneously and spray once every crankshaft revolution, delivering a predetermined quantity of fuel into the intake air stream.

The fuel pressure regulator maintains a constant pressure drop across the injector nozzles. The regulator is referenced to intake manifold vacuum and is connected parallel to the fuel injectors and positioned on the far end of the fuel rail. Any excess fuel supplied by the pump passes through the regulator and is returned to the fuel tank via a return line.

NOTE: *The pressure regulator reduces fuel pressure to 39–40 psi under normal operating conditions. At idle or high manifold vacuum condition, fuel pressure is reduced to about 30 psi.*

The fuel pressure regulator is a diaphragm operated relief valve in which one side of the diaphragm senses fuel pressure and the other side senses manifold vacuum. Normal fuel pressure is established by a spring preload applied to the diaphragm. Control of the fuel system is maintained through the EEC power relay and the EEC IV control unit, although electrical power is routed through the fuel pump relay and an inertia switch. The fuel pump relay is normally located on a bracket somewhere above the Electronic Control Assembly (ECA) and the Inertia Switch is located in the trunk. The inline fuel pump is usually mounted on a bracket at the fuel tank, or on a frame rail. Tank-mounted pumps can be either high or low-pressure, depending on the model.

The inertia switch opens the power circuit to the fuel pump in the event of a collision. Once tripped, the switch must be reset manually by pushing the reset button on the assembly. Check that the inertia switch is reset before diagnosing power supply problems to the fuel pump circuit.

Fuel Injectors

The fuel injectors used with the EFI system are electromechanical (solenoid) type designed to meter and atomize fuel delivered to the intake ports of the engine. The injectors are mounted in the lower intake manifold and positioned so that their spray nozzles direct the fuel charge in front of the intake valves. The injector body consists of a solenoid actuated pintle and needle valve assembly. The control unit sends an electrical impulse that activates the solenoid, causing the pintle to move inward off the seat and allow the fuel to flow. The amount of fuel delivered is controlled by the length of time the injector is energized (pulse width), since the fuel flow orifice is fixed and the fuel pressure drop across the injector tip is constant. Correct atomization is achieved by contouring the pintle at the point where the fuel enters the pintle chamber.

NOTE: *Exercise care when handling fuel injectors during service. Be careful not to lose the pintle cap and replace O-rings to assure a tight seal. Never apply direct battery voltage to test a fuel injector.*

The injectors receive high pressure fuel from the fuel manifold (fuel rail) assembly. The complete assembly includes a single, preformed tube with four injector connectors, mounting flange for the pressure regulator, mounting attachments to locate the manifold and provide the fuel injector retainers and a Schrader® quick-disconnect fitting used to perform fuel pressure tests.

The fuel manifold is normally removed with fuel injectors and pressure regulator attached. Fuel injector electrical connectors are plastic and have locking tabs that must be released when disconnecting when disconnecting the wiring harness.

AIR SUBSYSTEM

The air subsystem components include the air cleaner assembly, air flow (vane) meter, throttle air bypass valve and air ducts that connect the air system to the throttle body assembly. The throttle body regulates the air flow to the engine through a single butterfly-type throttle plate controlled by conventional accelerator linkage. The throttle body has an idle adjustment screw (throttle air bypass valve) to set the throttle plate position, a PCV fresh air source upstream of the throttle plate, individual vacuum taps for PCV and control signals and a throttle position sensor that provides a voltage signal for the EEC IV control unit.

The hot air intake system uses a thermostatic flap valve assembly whose components and operation are similar to previous hot

EMISSION CONTROLS

air intake systems. Intake air volume and temperature are measured by the vane meter assembly which is mounted between the air cleaner and throttle body. The vane meter consists two separate devices; the van air flow sensor (VAF) uses a counterbalanced L-shaped flap valve mounted on a pivot pin and connected to a variable resistor (potentiometer). The control unit measures the amount of deflection of the flap vane by measuring the voltage signal from the potentiometer mounted on top of the meter body; larger air volume moves the vane further and produces a higher voltage signal. The vane air temperature (VAT) sensor is mounted in the middle of the air stream just before the flap valve. Since the mass (weight) of a specific volume of air varies with pressure and temperature, the control unit uses the voltage signal from the air temperature sensor to compensate for these variables and provide a more exact measurement of actual air mass that is necessary to calculate the fuel required to obtain the optimum air/fuel ratio under a wide range of operating conditions. On the EEC IV system, the VAT sensor affects spark timing as a function of air temperature.

NOTE: *Make sure all air intake connections are tight before testing. Air leaking into the engine through a loose bellows connection can result in abnormal engine operation or idle speed and affect the air/fuel mixture ratio.*

Throttle Air Bypass Valve

The throttle air bypass valve is an electromechanical (solenoid) device whose operation is controlled by the EEC IV control unit. A variable air metering valve controls both cold and warm idle air flow in response to commands from the control unit. The valve operates by by-passing a regulated amount of air around the throttle plate; the higher the voltage signal from the control unit, the more air is bypassed through the valve. In this manner, additional air can be added to the fuel mixture without moving the throttle plate. At curb idle, the valve provides smooth idle for various engine coolant temperatures, compensates for A/C load and compensates for transaxle load and no-load conditions. The valve also provides fast idle for start-up, replacing the fast idle cam, throttle kicker and anti-dieseling solenoid common to previous models.

There are no curb idle or fast idle adjustments. As in curb idle operation, the fast idle speed is proportional to engine coolant temperature. Fast idle kick-down will occur when the throttle is kicked. A time-out feature in the ECA will also automatically kick-down fast idle to curb idle after a time period of approximately 15–25 seconds; after coolant has reached approximately 71°C (160°F). The signal duty cycle from the ECA to the valve will be at 100% (maximum current) during the crank to provide maximum air flow to allow no touch starting at any time (engine cold or hot).

CHILTON TIPS

1983-88 Escort/Lynx and 1988 Tempo/Topaz

After replacing the throttle air bypass valve, a rough idle situation may occur. This rough idle condition may be caused by a revision made to the valve's wiring harness.

Vehicles built before the 1989 model year had a diode in the air-bypass valve wiring harness. The new replacement valves have a 3D marking on the plastic portion of the solenoid, above the connector cap. They have a diode in air by-pass valve.

On the air by-pass valves used on vehicles built before the 1989 model year, the positive and negative leads are not important to the operation of the valve. However, the polarity on the new replacement air by-pass valve is important because if the wiring harness is reversed the air by-pass valve will not work.

To correct this condition, reverse the wires in the air by-pass valve connector and retest the valve.

ELECTRONIC ENGINE CONTROL SUBSYSTEM

The electronic engine control subsystem consists of the ECA and various sensors and actuators. The ECA reads inputs from engine sensors, then outputs a voltage signal to various components (actuators) to control engine functions. The period of time that the injectors are energized (on-time or "pulse width") determines the amount of fuel delivered to each cylinder. The longer the pulse width, the richer the fuel mixture.

NOTE: *The operating reference voltage (Vref) between the ECA and its sensors and actuators is five volts. This allows these components to work during the crank operation even though the battery voltage drops.*

In order for the ECA to properly control engine operation, it must first receive current status reports on various operating conditions. The control unit constantly monitors crankshaft position, throttle plate position, engine coolant temperature, exhaust gas oxygen level, air intake volume and temperature, A/C (On/Off), spark knock and barometric pressure.

Universal Distributor

The primary function of the TFI-IV ignition system universal distributor is to direct the high secondary voltage to the spark plugs. In addition, the universal distributor supplies crankshaft position and frequency information to the ECA using a profile ignition pick-up (PIP) sensor in place of the magnetic pick-up or the crankshaft position sensor used on other models. This distributor does not have any mechanical or vacuum advance. The universal distributor assembly is adjustable for resetting base timing, if required, by disconnecting the spout connector.

NOTE: *The PIP replaces the crankshaft position sensor found on other EEC IV models.*

The PIP sensor has an armature with four windows and four metal tabs that rotates past the stator assembly (Hall effect switch). When a metal tab enters the stator assembly, a positive signal (approximately 10 volts) is sent to the ECA, indicating the 10° BTDC crankshaft position.

The ECA calculates the precise time to energize the spark output signal to the TFI module. When the TFI module receives the spark output signal, it shuts off the coil primary current and the collapsing field energizes the secondary output.

NOTE: *Misadjustment of the base timing affects the spark advance in the same manner as a conventional solid-state ignition system.*

Thick Film Ignition (TFI-IV) Module

The TFI-IV ignition module has six connector pins at the engine wiring harness that supply the following signals:
- Ignition switch in RUN position
- Engine cranking
- Tachometer
- PIP (crankshaft position to ECA)
- Spark advance (from ECA)
- Internal ground from the ECA to the distributor

The TFI-IV module supplies the spark to the distributor through the ignition coil and calculates the duration. It receives its control signal from the ECA (spark output).

Throttle Position Sensor (TPS)

The TPS is mounted on the throttle body. This sensor provides the ECA with a signal that indicates the opening angle of the throttle plate. The sensor output signal uses the 5 volt reference voltage (Vref) previously described. From this input, the ECA controls:

1. Operating modes, which are wide-open throttle (WOT), part throttle (PT) and closed throttle (CT).
2. Fuel enrichment at WOT.
3. Additional spark advance at WOT.
4. EGR cut off during WOT, deceleration and idle.
5. A/C cut off during WOT (30 seconds maximum).
6. Cold start kick-down.
7. Fuel cut off during deceleration.
8. WOT dechoke during crank mode (starting).

On the EEC IV system, the TPS signal to the ECA only changes the spark timing during the WOT mode. As the throttle plate rotates, the TPS varies its voltage output. As the throttle plate moves from a closed throttle position to a WOT Position, the voltage output of the TPS will change from a low voltage (approximately 1.0 volt) to a high voltage (approximately 4.75 volts). The TPS used is not adjustable and must be replaced if it is out of specification. The EEC IV programming compensates for differences between sensors.

Engine Coolant Temperature (ECT) Sensor

The ECT sensor is located either in the heater supply tube at the rear of the engine, or in the lower intake manifold. The ECT is a thermistor (changes resistance as temperature changes). The sensor detects the temperature of engine coolant and provides a corresponding signal to the ECA. From this signal, the ECA will modify the air/fuel ratio (mixture), idle speed, spark advance, EGR and Canister purge control. When the engine coolant is cold, the ECT signal causes the ECA to provide enrichment to the air/fuel ratio for good cold drive away as engine coolant warms up, the voltage will drop.

Exhaust Gas Oxygen (EGO) Sensor

The EGO sensor on the EEC IV system is a little different from others used and is mounted in its own mounting boss, located between the two downstream tubes in the header near the exhaust system. On turbocharged models, the EGO sensor is mounted in the turbocharger exhaust elbow. The EGO sensor works between zero and one volt output, depending on the presence (lean) or absence (rich) of oxygen in the exhaust gas. A voltage reading greater than 0.6 volts indicates a rich air/fuel ratio, while a reading of less than 0.4 volts indicates a lean ratio.

CAUTION: *Never apply voltage to the EGO sensor because it could destroy the sensor's calibration. This includes the use of an ohmmeter. Before connecting and using a voltmeter, make sure it has a high-input impedance (at least 10M) and is set on the proper resistance range. Any attempt to use a powered voltmeter to measure the EGO voltage output directly will damage or destroy the sensor.*

Operation of the sensor is the same as previous models. One difference that should be noted is that the rubber protective cap used on top of the sensor on the earlier models has been replaced with a metal cap. In addition, later model sensors incorporate a heating element to bring the sensor up to operating temperature more quickly and keep it there during extended idle periods to prevent the sensor from cooling off and placing the system into open loop operation.

Vane Meter

The vane meter is actually two sensors in one assembly — a vane air flow (VAF) sensor and vane air temperature (VAT) sensor. This meter measures air flow to the engine and the temperature of the air stream. The vane meter is located either behind or under the air cleaner.

Air flow through the body moves a vane mounted on a pivot pin. The more air flowing through the meter, the further the vane rotates about the pivot pin. The air vane pivot pin is connected to a variable resistor (potentiometer) on top of the assembly. The vane meter uses the 5 volt reference voltage. The output of the potentiometer to the ECA varies between zero and Vref (5 volts), depending on the volume of air flowing through the sensor. A higher volume of air will produce a higher voltage output.

The volume of air measured through the meter has to be converted into an air mass value. The mass (weight) of a specific volume of air varies with pressure and temperature. To compensate for these variables, a temperature sensor in front of the vane measures incoming air temperature. The ECA uses the air temperature and a programmed pressure value to convert the VAF signal into a mass air flow value. This value is used to calculate the fuel flow necessary for the optimum air/fuel ratio. The VAT also affects spark timing as a function of air temperature.

A/C Compressor Clutch (ACC) Signal

Anytime battery voltage is applied to the A/C clutch, the same signal is also applied to the ECA. The ECA then maintains the engine idle speed with the throttle air bypass valve control solenoid (fuel injection), or throttle kicker (carburetor), to compensate for the added load created by the A/C clutch operation. Shutting down the A/C clutch will have a reverse effect. The ECA will maintain the engine idle speed at 850–950 rpm.

Knock Sensor (KS)

The knock sensor is used to detect detonation. In situations of excessive knock the ECA receives a signal from this sensor and retards the spark accordingly. The operation of the knock sensor during boost on turbocharged models improves the engine's durability. It is mounted in the lower intake manifold at the rear of the engine.

Barometric (BAP) Sensor

The barometric sensor is used to compensate for altitude variations. From this signal, the ECA modifies the air/fuel ratio, spark timing, idle speed, and EGR flow. The barometric sensor is a design that produces a frequency based on atmospheric pressure (altitude). The barometric sensor is mounted on the right-hand fender apron.

EGR Shut-Off Solenoid

The electrical signal to the EGR shut-off solenoid is controlled by the ECA. The signal is either ON or OFF. It is OFF during cold start, closed throttle or WOT. It is ON at all other times.

The solenoid is the same as the EGR control solenoid used on previous EEC systems. It is usually mounted on the LH side of the dash panel in the engine compartment, or on the RH shock tower in the engine compartment. The solenoid is normally closed, and the control vacuum from the solenoid is applied to the EGR valve.

NOTE: *The canister purge valve is controlled by vacuum from the EGR solenoid. The purge valve is a standard-type valve and operates the same as in previous systems.*

COMPONENT TESTS

Before beginning any EEC IV component testing, always check the ignition and fuel systems to make sure there is fuel and spark. Check the distributor cap, rotor and internal components for damage, corrosion or signs of excessive wear.

• Remove air cleaner assembly and inspect all vacuum and pressure hoses for proper connection to fittings. Check for damaged or pinched hoses.

• Inspect all sub-system wiring harnesses for proper connections to the EGR solenoid valves, injectors, sensors, etc.

• Check for loose or detached connectors and broken or detached wires. Check that all terminals are seated firmly and are not corroded. Look for partially broken or grayed wires or any shorting between wires.

• Inspect sensors for physical damage. Inspect vehicle electrical system. Check battery for full charge and cable connections for tightness.

• Inspect the relay connector and make sure the ECA power relay is securely attached and making a good ground connection.

214 EMISSION CONTROLS

• Twist the oil filler cap on turbocharged engines to make sure it is tight. A loose oil filler cap will cause turbocharged engines to run rough at idle.

Solenoid and Sensor Resistance Tests

All CFI components must be disconnected form the circuit before testing resistance with a suitable ohmmeter. Replace any component whose measure resistance does not agree with the specifications chart. Shorting the wiring harness across a solenoid valve can burn out the circuitry in the ECA that controls the solenoid valve actuator. Exercise caution when testing solenoid valves to avoid accidental damage to ECA.

EEC IV SYSTEM TESTING

NOTE: *It is recommended that before performing this or any other test on your vehicle, you check with your local manufactures representative to make sure that if by doing these tests there may be a chance that you will violate your warranty, thus rendering you helpless to submit a claim on your vehicle if a problem should occur in the future.*

This book contains simple testing procedures for your Ford's electronic engine controls. More comprehensive testing on this system and other electronic control systems on your Ford can be found in CHILTON'S GUIDE TO ELECTRONIC ENGINE CONTROLS, book part number No. 7535 for 1978–85, No. 7768 for the 1984–88 years and No. 8024 for the 1988–90 years. All of these manuals are available at your local retailer.

As in any service procedure, a routine inspection of the EEC IV system for loose connections, broken wires or obvious damage is the best way to start. Perform the system Quick Test outlined below before going any further. Check all vacuum connections and secondary ignition wiring before assuming that the problem lies with the EEC IV system. A self-diagnosis capability is built into the EEC IV system to aid in troubleshooting. The primary tool necessary to read the trouble codes stored in the system is an analog voltmeter or special Self Test Automatic Readout (STAR) tester (Motorcraft No. 007–0M004, or equivalent). While the self-test is not conclusive by itself, when activated it checks the EEC IV system by testing its memory integrity and processing capability. The self-test also verifies that all sensors and actuators are connected and working properly.

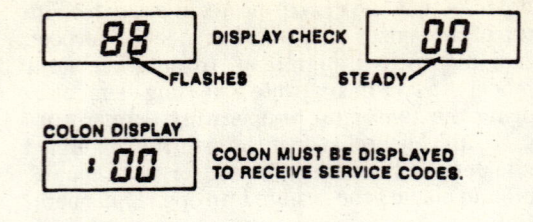

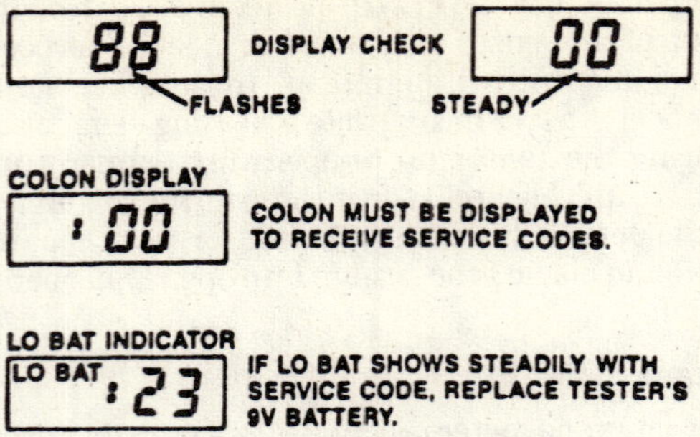

When a service code is displayed on an analog voltmeter, each code number is represented by pulses or sweeps of the meter needle. A code 3, for example, will be read as three needle pulses followed by a 6 second delay. If a two digit code is stored, there will be a two second delay between the pulses for each digit of the number. Code 23, for example, will be displayed as two needle pulses, a two second pause, then three more pulses followed by a four second pause. All testing is complete when the codes have

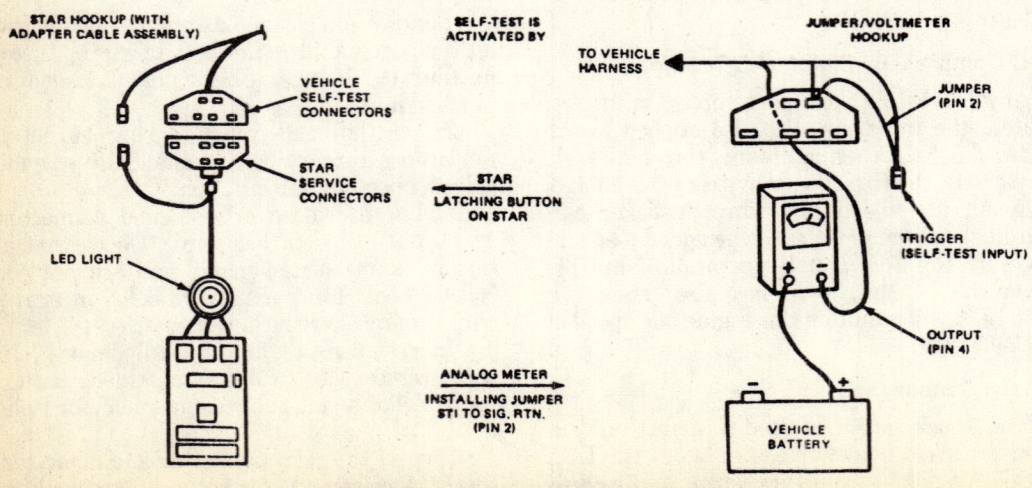

Self-test output code format - Star Tester

Making the self test equipment hook-ups

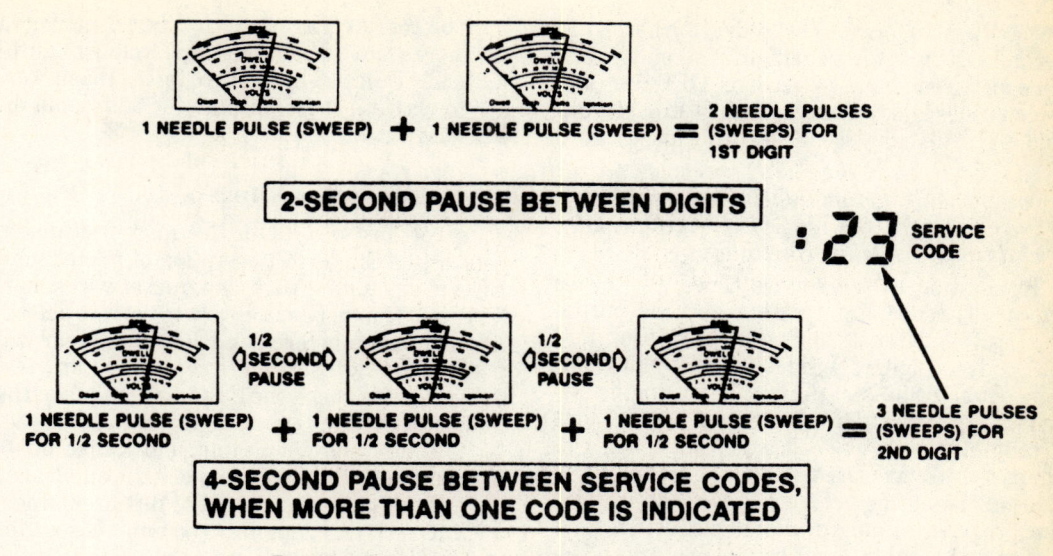

EMISSION CONTROLS 215

1 NEEDLE PULSE (SWEEP) + **1 NEEDLE PULSE (SWEEP)** = **2 NEEDLE PULSES (SWEEPS) FOR 1ST DIGIT**

2-SECOND PAUSE BETWEEN DIGITS

:23 SERVICE CODE

1 NEEDLE PULSE (SWEEP) FOR 1/2 SECOND + 1/2 SECOND PAUSE + **1 NEEDLE PULSE (SWEEP) FOR 1/2 SECOND** + 1/2 SECOND PAUSE + **1 NEEDLE PULSE (SWEEP) FOR 1/2 SECOND** = **3 NEEDLE PULSES (SWEEPS) FOR 2ND DIGIT**

4-SECOND PAUSE BETWEEN SERVICE CODES, WHEN MORE THAN ONE CODE IS INDICATED

Reading the service code on the analog voltmeter

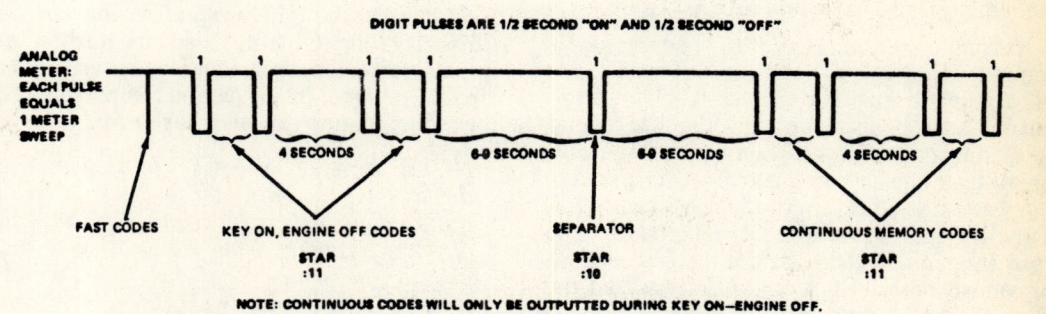

DIGIT PULSES ARE 1/2 SECOND "ON" AND 1/2 SECOND "OFF"

ANALOG METER: EACH PULSE EQUALS 1 METER SWEEP

FAST CODES | KEY ON, ENGINE OFF CODES (4 SECONDS) | SEPARATOR (6-9 SECONDS) | (6-9 SECONDS) | CONTINUOUS MEMORY CODES (4 SECONDS)

STAR :11 | STAR :10 | STAR :11

NOTE: CONTINUOUS CODES WILL ONLY BE OUTPUTTED DURING KEY ON—ENGINE OFF.

Self-test output code format with the ignition key on and the engine off

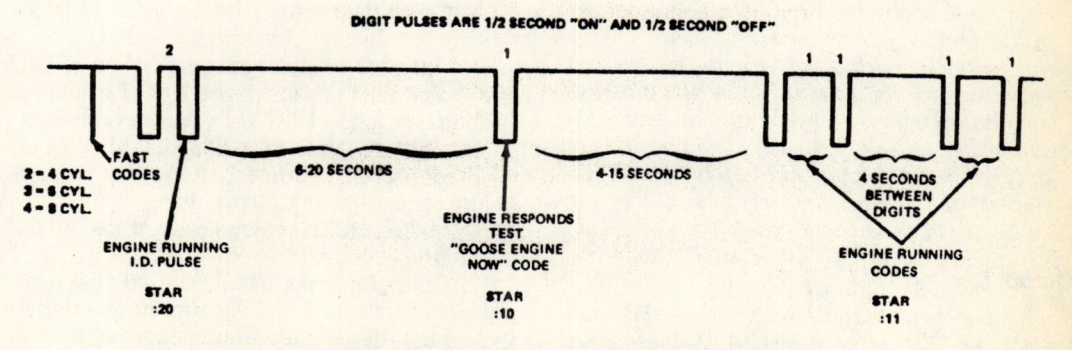

DIGIT PULSES ARE 1/2 SECOND "ON" AND 1/2 SECOND "OFF"

2 = 4 CYL
3 = 6 CYL
4 = 8 CYL

FAST CODES | ENGINE RUNNING I.D. PULSE (6-20 SECONDS) | ENGINE RESPONDS TEST "GOOSE ENGINE NOW" CODE (4-15 SECONDS) | 4 SECONDS BETWEEN DIGITS | ENGINE RUNNING CODES

STAR :20 | STAR :10 | STAR :11

Self-test output code format with the engine running

EMISSION CONTROLS

been repeated once. The pulse format is $1/2$ second ON-time for each digit, 2 seconds OFF-time between digits, 4 seconds OFF-time between codes and 6–10 seconds OFF-time before and after the half-second separator pulse.

NOTE: *If using the STAR tester, or equivalent, consult the manufacturers instructions included with the unit for correct hook-up and trouble code interpretation.*

In addition to the service codes, two other types of coded information are outputted during the self-test; engine identification and fast codes. Engine ID codes are one digit numbers equal to one-half the number of engine cylinders (e.g. 4 cylinder is code 2, etc.). Fast codes are simply the service codes transmitted at 100 times the normal rate in a short burst of information. Some meters may detect these codes and register a slight meter deflection just before the trouble codes are flashed. Both the ID and fast codes serve no purpose in the field and this meter deflection should be ignored.

Activating Self-Test Mode on EEC IV

Turn the ignition key OFF, then connect a jumper wire from the self-test input (STI) to pin 2 (signal return) on the self-test connector. Set the analog voltmeter on a DC voltage range to read from 0–15 volts, then connect the voltmeter from the battery positive (+) terminal to pin 4 self-test output in the self-test connector. Turn the ignition switch ON (engine off) and read the trouble codes on the meter needle as previously described. A code 11 means that the EEC IV system is operating properly and no faults are detected by the computer.

NOTE: *This test will only detect "hard" failures that are present when the self-test is activated. For intermittent problems, remove the voltmeter clip from the self-test trigger terminal and wiggle the wiring harness. With the voltmeter still attached to the self-test output, watch for a needle deflection that signals an intermittent condition has occurred. The meter will deflect each time the fault is induced and a trouble code will be stored. Reconnect the self-test trigger terminal to the voltmeter to retrieve the code.*

Output Cycling Test

This test is performed with the key ON and the engine OFF after the self-test codes have been sent and recorded. Without disconnecting the voltmeter or turning the key OFF, momentarily depress the accelerator pedal to the floor and then release it. All auxiliary EEC IV codes (including the self-test) will be activated and can be read on the voltmeter as before. Another pedal depression will turn them off. This cycle may be repeated as necessary, but if activated for more than 10 minutes, the cycle will automatically cancel. This feature forces the processor to activate these outputs for additional diagnosis.

EEV IV System Quick Test

Correct test results for the quick test are dependent on the correct operation of related non-EEC components, such as ignition wires, battery, etc. It may be necessary to correct defects in these areas before the EEC IV system will pass the quick test. Before connecting any test equipment to check the EEC system, make the following checks:

1. Check the air cleaner and intake ducts for leaks or restrictions. Replace the air cleaner if excessive amounts of dust or dirt are found.

2. Check all engine vacuum hoses for proper routing according to the vacuum schematic on the underhood sticker. Check for proper connections and repair any broken, cracked or pinched hoses or fittings.

3. Check the EEC system wiring harness connectors for tight fit, loose or detached terminals, corrosion, broken or frayed wires, short circuits to metal in the engine compartment or melted insulation exposing bare wire.

NOTE: *It may be necessary to disconnect or disassemble the connector to check for terminal damage or corrosion and perform some of the inspections. Note the location of each pin in the connector before disassembly. When doing continuity checks to make sure there are no breaks in the wire, shake or wiggle the harness and connector during testing to check for looseness or intermittent contact.*

4. Check the control module, sensors and actuators for obvious physical damage.

5. Turn off all electrical loads when testing and make sure the doors are closed whenever readings are made. DO NOT disconnect any electrical connector with key ON. Turn the key off to disconnect or reconnect the wiring harness to any sensor or the control unit.

6. Make sure the engine coolant and oil are at the proper level.

7. Check for leaks around the exhaust manifold, oxygen sensor and vacuum hoses connections with the engine idling at normal operating temperature.

8. Only after all the above checks have been performed should the voltmeter be connected to read the trouble codes. If not, the self-diagnosis system may indicate a failed component when all that is wrong is a loose or broken connection.

EMISSION CONTROLS

EEC IV TROUBLE CODES (2.3L)

Code	Diagnosis
11	Normal operation (no codes stored)
12	Incorrect high idle rpm value
13	Incorrect curb idle rpm value
14	Erratic Profile Ignition Pickup (PIP) signal
15	Read Only Memory (ROM) failure
21	Incorrect engine coolant temperature (ECT) sensor signal
22	Incorrect barometric pressure (BAP) sensor signal
23	Incorrect throttle position sensor (TPS) signal
24	Incorrect vane air temperature (VAT) sensor signal
26	Incorrect vane air flow (VAF) sensor signal
41	System always lean
42	System always rich
51	Engine coolant temperature (ECT) sensor signal too high
53	Throttle position sensor (TPS) signal too high
54	Vane air temperature (VAT) sensor signal too high
56	Vane air flow (VAF) sensor signal too high
61	Engine coolant temperature (ECT) signal too low
63	Throttle position sensor (TPS) signal too low
64	Vane air temperature (VAT) signal too low
66	Vane air flow (VAF) sensor signal too low
67	A/C compressor clutch ON
73	No vane air temperature (VAT) signal change when engine speed is increased
76	No vane air flow (VAF) signal change when engine speed is increased
77	Engine speed not increased to check VAT and VAF signal change

NOTE: Incorrect sensor signals could be out of range or not being received by the control unit. Perform wiring harness and sensor checks to determine the cause, or check for additional codes to indicate high or low reading

CHILTON TIPS

1987–89 Escort/Lynx

A no start or stall condition may be caused by the inertia switch (fuel pump shut-off switch) that has been activated. The switch is located in the luggage compartment and is intended to shut off the fuel supply in the event of a collision. However, the switch may be activated by a jolt, such as slamming the left rear door or hitting a large bump or pothole.

It will be necessary to reset the switch by pushing the reset button in order to get the vehicle started. It may also be necessary to relocate the inertia switch to an area that is less sensitive to bumps and jolts. There is a new Inertia switch kit that includes the bracket necessary to relocate the inertia switch. The kit part number No. E7FZ–9B364–A is available at your local authorized dealer.

VACUUM DIAGRAMS

The following pages are vacuum diagrams, some of the decals were not available at the time of publication.

EMISSION CONTROLS

MODEL YEAR: 1982   **CALIBRATION: 1—3S—R0**   **ENGINE: 1.6L**

A/C

Non A/C

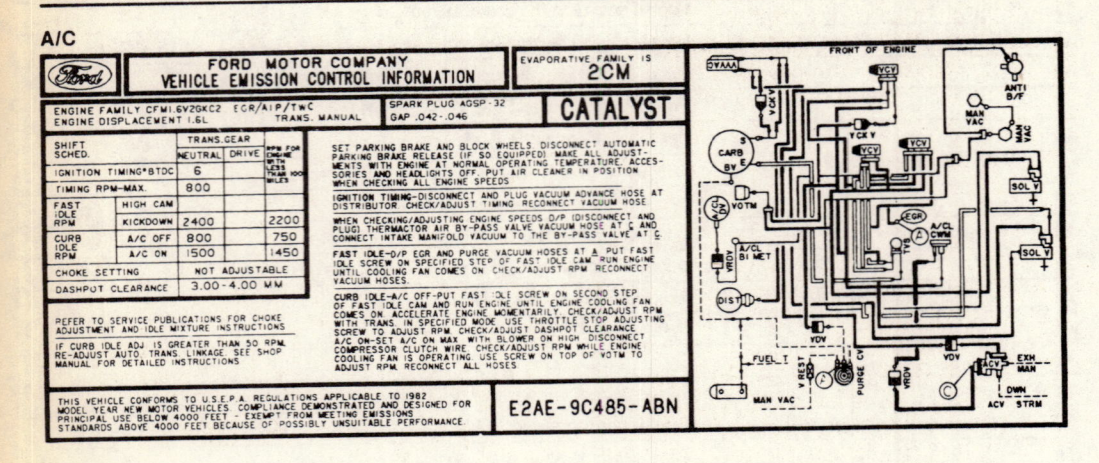

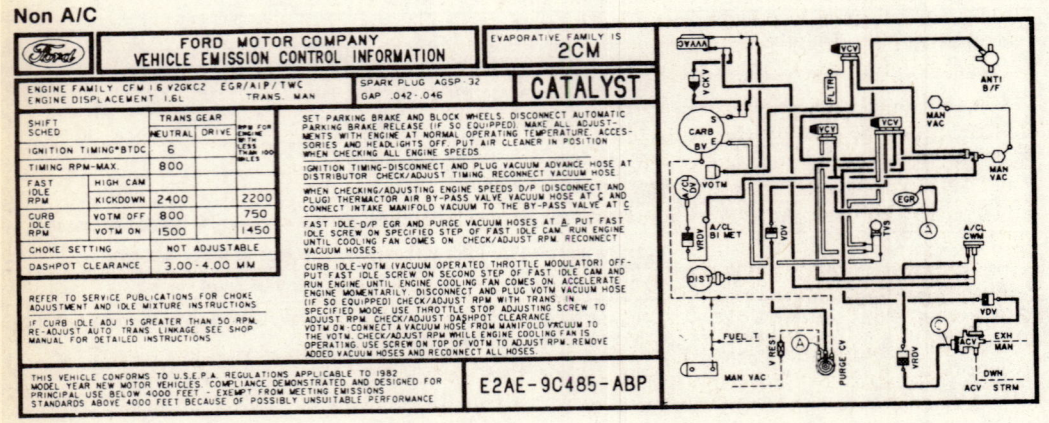

MODEL YEAR: 1982   **CALIBRATION: 2—3C—R11**   **ENGINE: 1.6L**

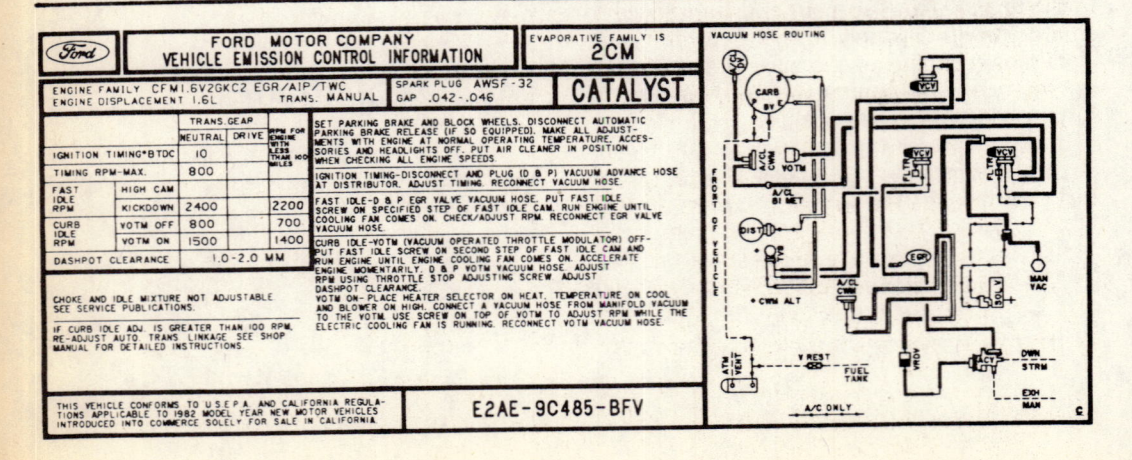

EMISSION CONTROLS 219

MODEL YEAR: 1982 **CALIBRATION: 1—3S—R11** **ENGINE: 1.6L**

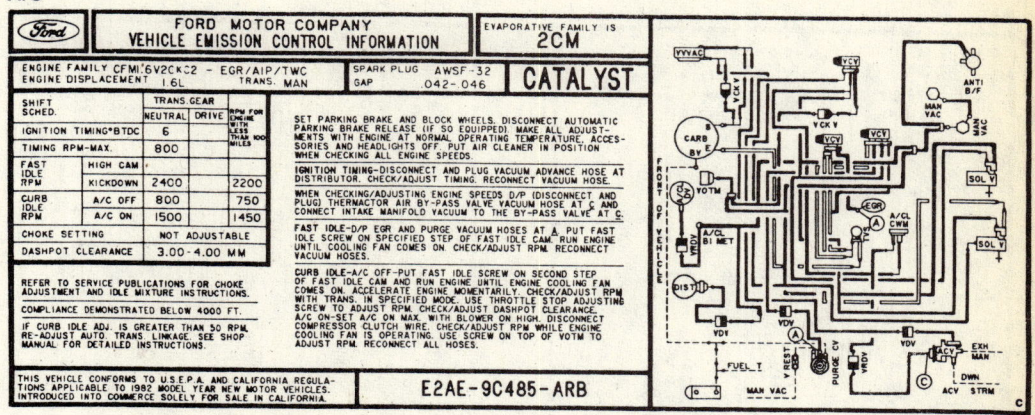

A/C

FORD MOTOR COMPANY — VEHICLE EMISSION CONTROL INFORMATION

EVAPORATIVE FAMILY IS **2CM**

ENGINE FAMILY CFMI.6V2CKC2 - EGR/AIP/TWC
ENGINE DISPLACEMENT 1.6L   TRANS. MAN
SPARK PLUG AWSF-32   GAP .042-.046   **CATALYST**

SHIFT SCHED.	TRANS. GEAR		RPM FOR ENGINE WITH LESS THAN 100 MILES
	NEUTRAL	DRIVE	
IGNITION TIMING°BTDC	6		
TIMING RPM-MAX.	800		
FAST IDLE RPM	HIGH CAM		
	KICKDOWN	2400	2200
CURB IDLE RPM	A/C OFF	800	750
	A/C ON	1500	1450
CHOKE SETTING	NOT ADJUSTABLE		
DASHPOT CLEARANCE	3.00-4.00 MM		

REFER TO SERVICE PUBLICATIONS FOR CHOKE ADJUSTMENT AND IDLE MIXTURE INSTRUCTIONS.
COMPLIANCE DEMONSTRATED BELOW 4000 FT.
IF CURB IDLE ADJ. IS GREATER THAN 50 RPM, RE-ADJUST AUTO. TRANS. LINKAGE. SEE SHOP MANUAL FOR DETAILED INSTRUCTIONS.
THIS VEHICLE CONFORMS TO U.S.E.P.A. AND CALIFORNIA REGULATIONS APPLICABLE TO 1982 MODEL YEAR NEW MOTOR VEHICLES INTRODUCED INTO COMMERCE SOLELY FOR SALE IN CALIFORNIA.

SET PARKING BRAKE AND BLOCK WHEELS. DISCONNECT AUTOMATIC PARKING BRAKE RELEASE (IF SO EQUIPPED). MAKE ALL ADJUSTMENTS WITH ENGINE AT NORMAL OPERATING TEMPERATURE, ACCESSORIES AND HEADLIGHTS OFF. PUT AIR CLEANER IN POSITION WHEN CHECKING ALL ENGINE SPEEDS.
IGNITION TIMING-DISCONNECT AND PLUG VACUUM ADVANCE HOSE AT DISTRIBUTOR. CHECK/ADJUST TIMING. RECONNECT VACUUM HOSE.
WHEN CHECKING/ADJUSTING ENGINE SPEEDS D/P (DISCONNECT AND PLUG) THERMACTOR AIR BY-PASS VALVE VACUUM HOSE AT C AND CONNECT INTAKE MANIFOLD VACUUM TO THE BY-PASS VALVE AT C.
FAST IDLE-D/P EGR AND PURGE VACUUM HOSES AT A. PUT FAST IDLE SCREW ON SPECIFIED STEP OF FAST IDLE CAM. RUN ENGINE UNTIL COOLING FAN COMES ON. CHECK/ADJUST RPM. RECONNECT VACUUM HOSES.
CURB IDLE-A/C OFF-PUT FAST IDLE SCREW ON SECOND STEP OF FAST IDLE CAM. RUN ENGINE UNTIL COOLING FAN COMES ON. ACCELERATE ENGINE MOMENTARILY. CHECK/ADJUST RPM WITH TRANS. IN SPECIFIED MODE. USE THROTTLE STOP ADJUSTING SCREW TO ADJUST RPM. CHECK/ADJUST DASHPOT CLEARANCE. A/C-ON-SET A/C ON MAX. WITH BLOWER ON HIGH. DISCONNECT COMPRESSOR CLUTCH WIRE. CHECK/ADJUST RPM WHILE ENGINE COOLING FAN IS OPERATING. USE SCREW ON TOP OF VOTM TO ADJUST RPM. RECONNECT ALL HOSES.

E2AE-9C485-ARB

Non A/C

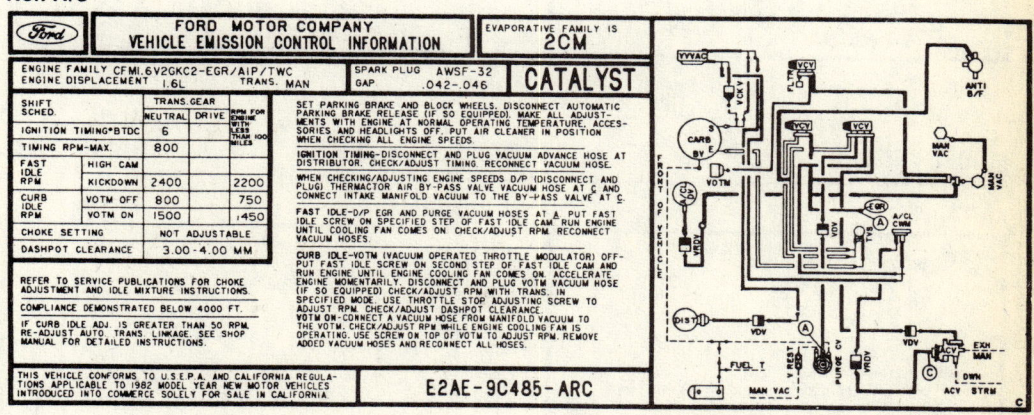

FORD MOTOR COMPANY — VEHICLE EMISSION CONTROL INFORMATION

EVAPORATIVE FAMILY IS **2CM**

ENGINE FAMILY CFMI.6V2CKC2-EGR/AIP/TWC
ENGINE DISPLACEMENT 1.6L   TRANS. MAN
SPARK PLUG AWSF-32   GAP .042-.046   **CATALYST**

SHIFT SCHED.	TRANS. GEAR		RPM FOR ENGINE WITH LESS THAN 100 MILES
	NEUTRAL	DRIVE	
IGNITION TIMING°BTDC	6		
TIMING RPM-MAX.	800		
FAST IDLE RPM	HIGH CAM		
	KICKDOWN	2400	2200
CURB IDLE RPM	VOTM OFF	800	750
	VOTM ON	1500	1450
CHOKE SETTING	NOT ADJUSTABLE		
DASHPOT CLEARANCE	3.00-4.00 MM		

REFER TO SERVICE PUBLICATIONS FOR CHOKE ADJUSTMENT AND IDLE MIXTURE INSTRUCTIONS.
COMPLIANCE DEMONSTRATED BELOW 4000 FT.
IF CURB IDLE ADJ. IS GREATER THAN 50 RPM, RE-ADJUST AUTO. TRANS. LINKAGE. SEE SHOP MANUAL FOR DETAILED INSTRUCTIONS.
THIS VEHICLE CONFORMS TO U.S.E.P.A. AND CALIFORNIA REGULATIONS APPLICABLE TO 1982 MODEL YEAR NEW MOTOR VEHICLES INTRODUCED INTO COMMERCE SOLELY FOR SALE IN CALIFORNIA.

SET PARKING BRAKE AND BLOCK WHEELS. DISCONNECT AUTOMATIC PARKING BRAKE RELEASE (IF SO EQUIPPED). MAKE ALL ADJUSTMENTS WITH ENGINE AT NORMAL OPERATING TEMPERATURE, ACCESSORIES AND HEADLIGHTS OFF. PUT AIR CLEANER IN POSITION WHEN CHECKING ALL ENGINE SPEEDS.
IGNITION TIMING-DISCONNECT AND PLUG VACUUM ADVANCE HOSE AT DISTRIBUTOR. CHECK/ADJUST TIMING. RECONNECT VACUUM HOSE.
WHEN CHECKING/ADJUSTING ENGINE SPEEDS D/P (DISCONNECT AND PLUG) THERMACTOR AIR BY-PASS VALVE VACUUM HOSE AT C AND CONNECT INTAKE MANIFOLD VACUUM TO THE BY-PASS VALVE AT C.
FAST IDLE SCREW ON SPECIFIED STEP OF FAST IDLE CAM. RUN ENGINE UNTIL COOLING FAN COMES ON. CHECK/ADJUST RPM. RECONNECT VACUUM HOSES.
CURB IDLE-VOTM (VACUUM OPERATED THROTTLE MODULATOR) OFF-PUT FAST IDLE SCREW ON SECOND STEP OF FAST IDLE CAM AND RUN ENGINE UNTIL ENGINE COOLING FAN COMES ON. ACCELERATE ENGINE MOMENTARILY. DISCONNECT AND PLUG VOTM VACUUM HOSE (IF SO EQUIPPED) CHECK/ADJUST RPM WITH TRANS. IN SPECIFIED MODE. USE THROTTLE STOP ADJUSTING SCREW TO ADJUST RPM. CHECK/ADJUST DASHPOT CLEARANCE.
VOTM ON-CONNECT A VACUUM HOSE FROM MANIFOLD VACUUM TO THE VOTM. CHECK/ADJUST RPM WHILE ENGINE COOLING FAN IS OPERATING. USE SCREW ON TOP OF VOTM TO ADJUST RPM. REMOVE ADDED VACUUM HOSES AND RECONNECT ALL HOSES.

E2AE-9C485-ARC

MODEL YEAR: 1982 **CALIBRATION: 2—3D—R0** **ENGINE: 1.6L**

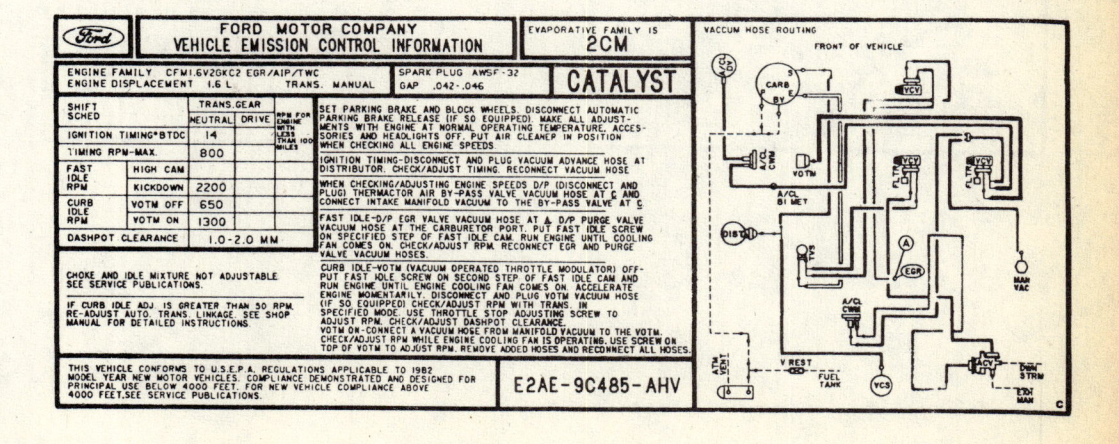

FORD MOTOR COMPANY — VEHICLE EMISSION CONTROL INFORMATION

EVAPORATIVE FAMILY IS **2CM**

ENGINE FAMILY CFMI.6V2GKC2 EGR/AIP/TWC
ENGINE DISPLACEMENT 1.6 L   TRANS. MANUAL
SPARK PLUG AWSF-32   GAP .042-.046   **CATALYST**

SHIFT SCHED.	TRANS. GEAR		RPM FOR ENGINE WITH LESS THAN 100 MILES
	NEUTRAL	DRIVE	
IGNITION TIMING°BTDC	14		
TIMING RPM-MAX.	800		
FAST IDLE RPM	HIGH CAM		
	KICKDOWN	2200	
CURB IDLE RPM	VOTM OFF	650	
	VOTM ON	1300	
DASHPOT CLEARANCE	1.0-2.0 MM		

CHOKE AND IDLE MIXTURE NOT ADJUSTABLE. SEE SERVICE PUBLICATIONS.
IF CURB IDLE ADJ. IS GREATER THAN 50 RPM, RE-ADJUST AUTO. TRANS. LINKAGE. SEE SHOP MANUAL FOR DETAILED INSTRUCTIONS.
THIS VEHICLE CONFORMS TO U.S.E.P.A. REGULATIONS APPLICABLE TO 1982 MODEL YEAR NEW MOTOR VEHICLES. COMPLIANCE DEMONSTRATED AND DESIGNED FOR PRINCIPAL USE BELOW 4000 FEET. FOR NEW VEHICLE COMPLIANCE ABOVE 4000 FEET, SEE SERVICE PUBLICATIONS.

SET PARKING BRAKE AND BLOCK WHEELS. DISCONNECT AUTOMATIC PARKING BRAKE RELEASE (IF SO EQUIPPED). MAKE ALL ADJUSTMENTS WITH ENGINE AT NORMAL OPERATING TEMPERATURE, ACCESSORIES AND HEADLIGHTS OFF. PUT AIR CLEANER IN POSITION WHEN CHECKING ALL ENGINE SPEEDS.
IGNITION TIMING-DISCONNECT AND PLUG VACUUM ADVANCE HOSE AT DISTRIBUTOR. CHECK/ADJUST TIMING. RECONNECT VACUUM HOSE.
WHEN CHECKING/ADJUSTING ENGINE SPEEDS D/P (DISCONNECT AND PLUG) THERMACTOR AIR BY-PASS VALVE VACUUM HOSE AT C AND CONNECT INTAKE MANIFOLD VACUUM TO THE BY-PASS VALVE AT C.
FAST IDLE-D/P EGR VALVE VACUUM HOSE AT A. & D/P PURGE VALVE VACUUM HOSE AT THE CARBURETOR PORT. PUT FAST IDLE SCREW ON SPECIFIED STEP OF FAST IDLE CAM. RUN ENGINE UNTIL COOLING FAN COMES ON. CHECK/ADJUST RPM. RECONNECT EGR AND PURGE VALVE VACUUM HOSES.
CURB IDLE-VOTM (VACUUM OPERATED THROTTLE MODULATOR) OFF-PUT FAST IDLE SCREW ON SECOND STEP OF FAST IDLE CAM AND RUN ENGINE UNTIL ENGINE COOLING FAN COMES ON. ACCELERATE ENGINE MOMENTARILY. DISCONNECT AND PLUG VOTM VACUUM HOSE (IF SO EQUIPPED) CHECK/ADJUST RPM WITH TRANS. IN SPECIFIED MODE. USE THROTTLE STOP ADJUSTING SCREW TO ADJUST RPM. CHECK/ADJUST DASHPOT CLEARANCE.
VOTM ON-CONNECT A VACUUM HOSE FROM MANIFOLD VACUUM TO THE VOTM. CHECK/ADJUST RPM WHILE ENGINE COOLING FAN IS OPERATING. USE SCREW ON TOP OF VOTM TO ADJUST RPM. REMOVE ADDED HOSES AND RECONNECT ALL HOSES.

E2AE-9C485-AHV

EMISSION CONTROLS

MODEL YEAR: 1982 **CALIBRATION: 1—3Y—R10** **ENGINE: 1.6L**

A/C

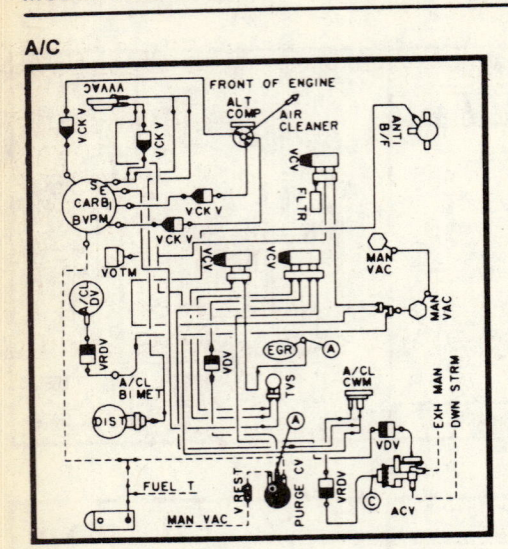

Non A/C

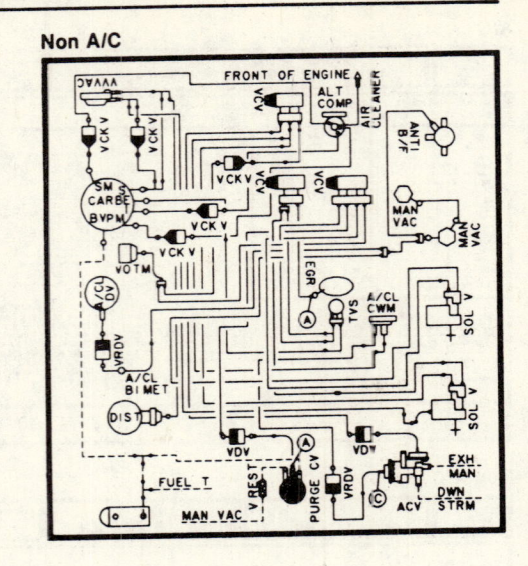

MODEL YEAR: 1982 **CALIBRATION: 1—4E—R0** **ENGINE: 1.6L**

A/C

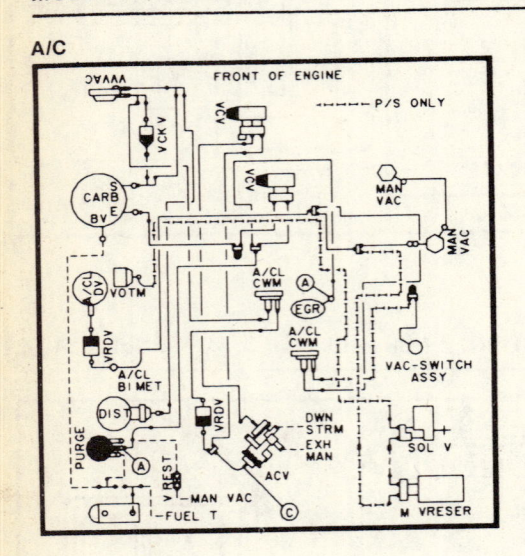

Non A/C

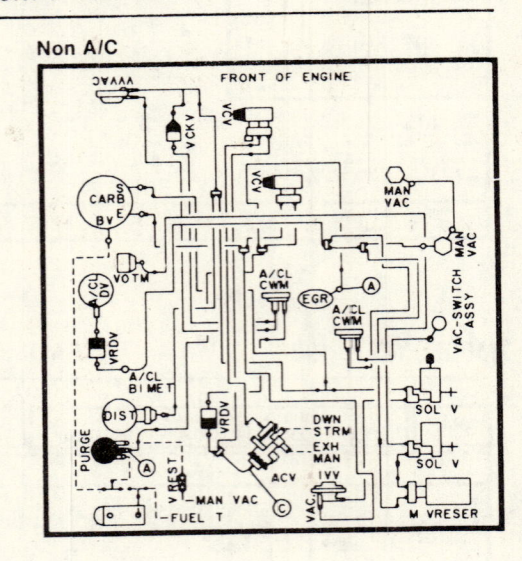

EMISSION CONTROLS

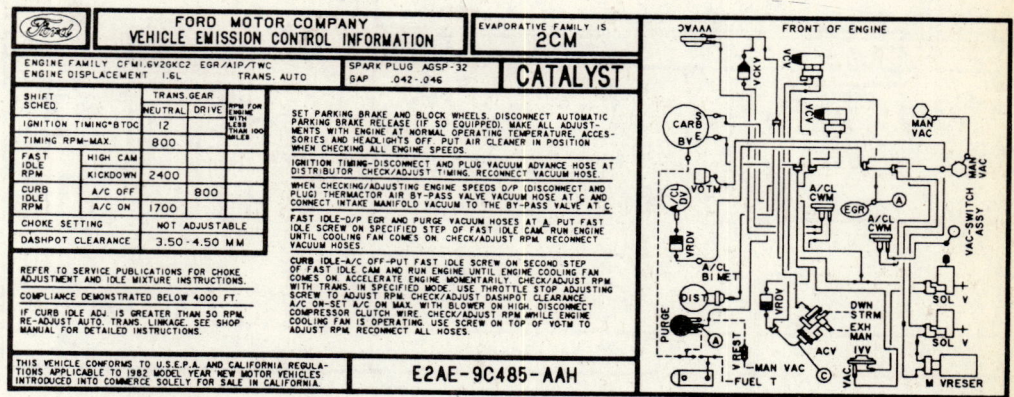

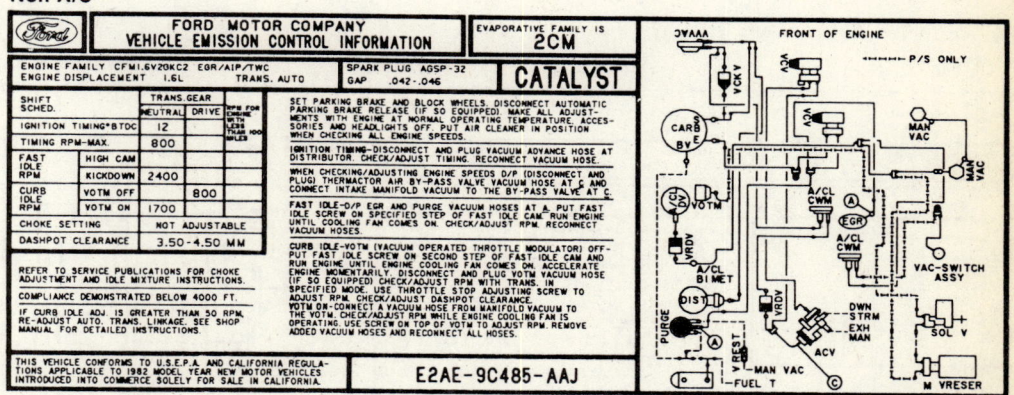

MODEL YEAR: 1982 **CALIBRATION: 1—4S—R0** **ENGINE: 1.6L**

A/C

Non A/C

MODEL YEAR: 1982 **CALIBRATION: 1—4S—R10** **ENGINE: 1.6L**

A/C

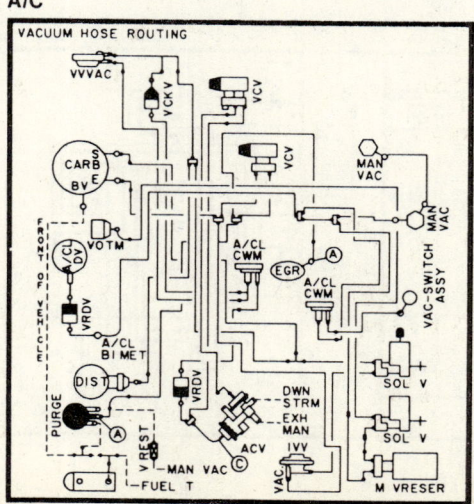

Non A/C

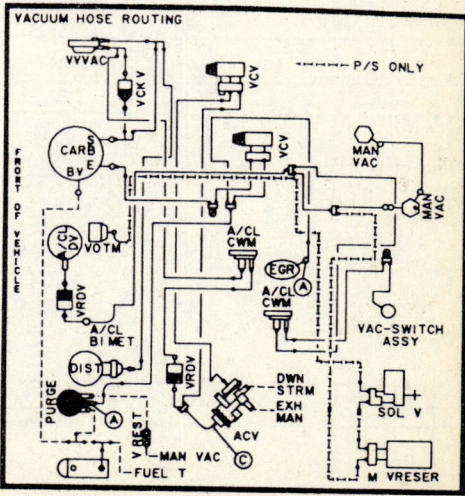

EMISSION CONTROLS

MODEL YEAR: 1982   **CALIBRATION: 2—3B—R10**   **ENGINE: 1.6L**

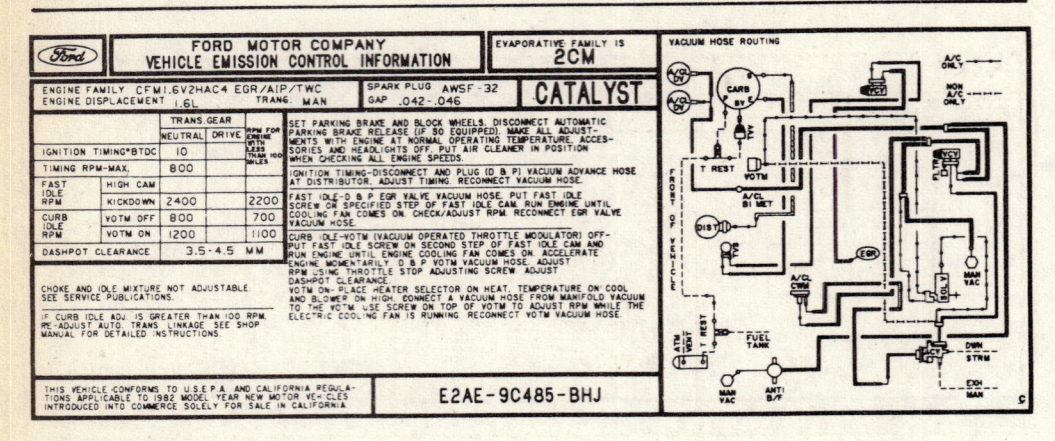

MODEL YEAR: 1982   **CALIBRATION: 2—3C—R0**   **ENGINE: 1.6L**

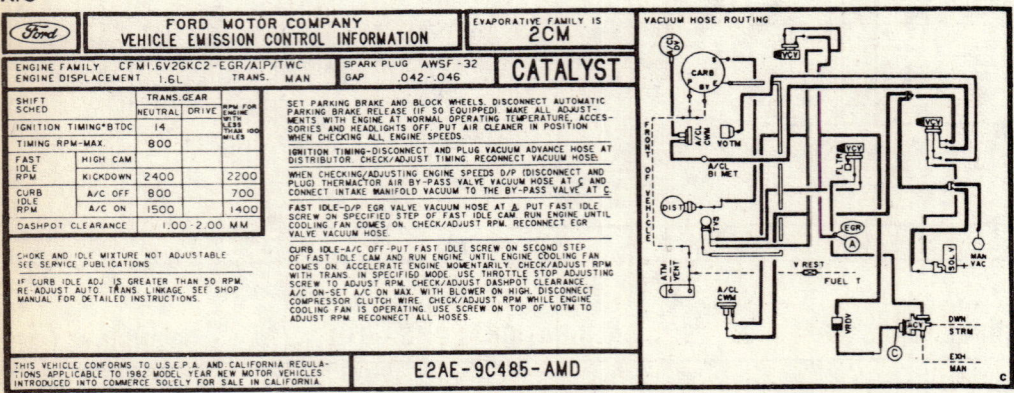

A/C

Non A/C

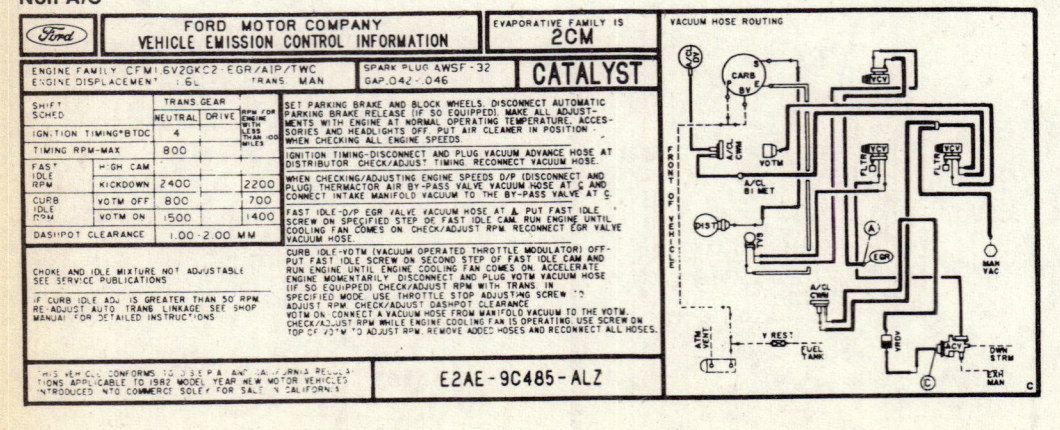

EMISSION CONTROLS 223

MODEL YEAR: 1982 **CALIBRATION: 2—3G—R1** **ENGINE: 1.6L**

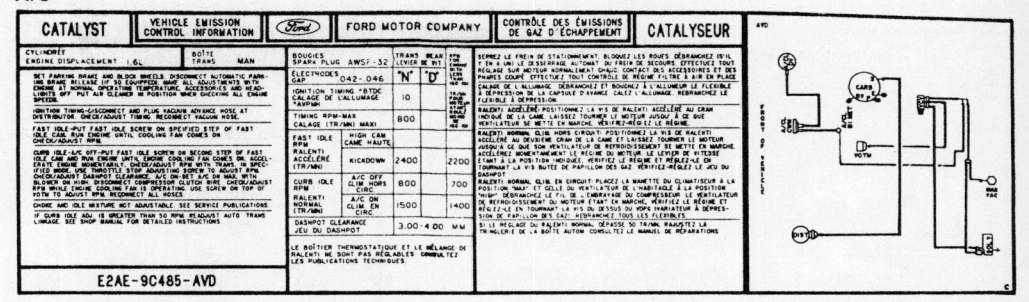

A/C

E2AE-9C485-AVD

Non A/C

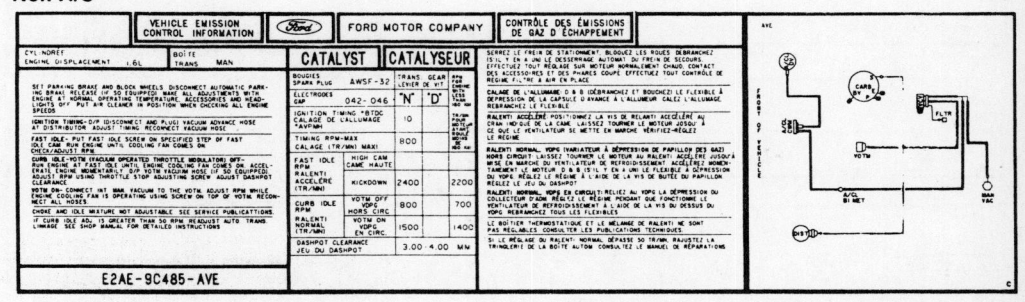

E2AE-9C485-AVE

MODEL YEAR: 1982 **CALIBRATION: 2—3D—R16** **ENGINE: 1.6L**

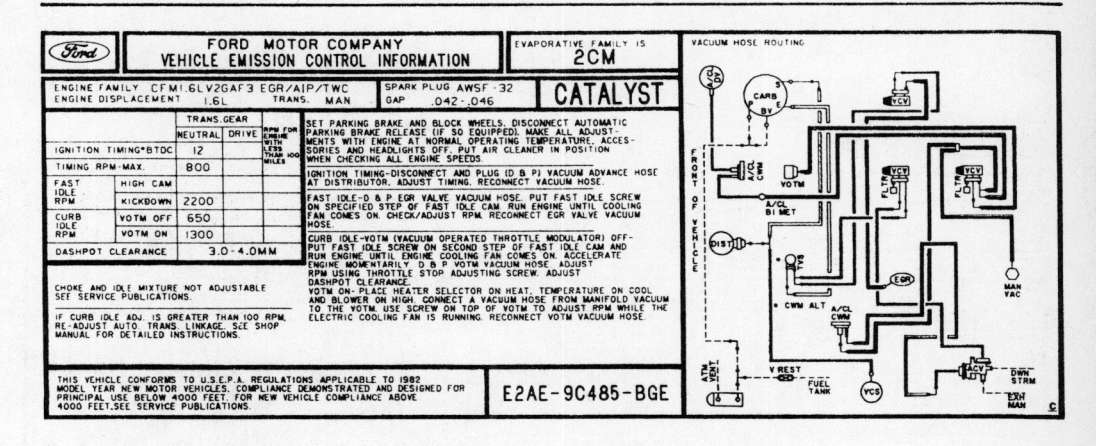

E2AE-9C485-BGE

EMISSION CONTROLS

MODEL YEAR: 1982 **CALIBRATION: 2—3E—R0** **ENGINE: 1.6L**

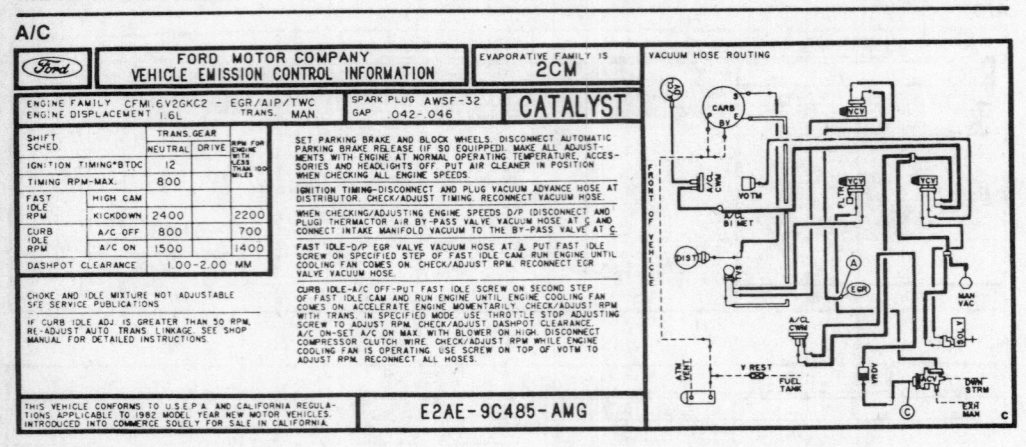

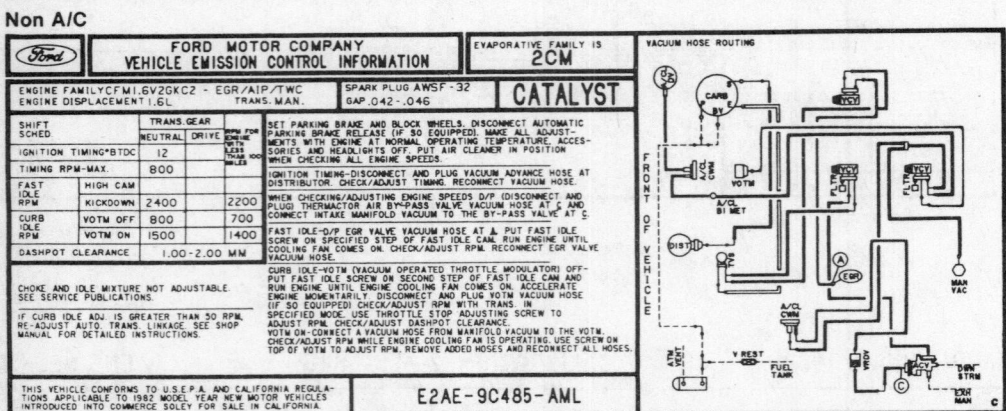

A/C

FORD MOTOR COMPANY
VEHICLE EMISSION CONTROL INFORMATION

EVAPORATIVE FAMILY IS **2CM**

ENGINE FAMILY CFMI.6V2GKC2 — EGR/AIP/TWC
ENGINE DISPLACEMENT 1.6L TRANS. MAN.
SPARK PLUG AWSF-32 GAP .042-.046 **CATALYST**

SHIFT SCHED.	TRANS. GEAR		RPM FOR ENGINE WITH LESS THAN 100 MILES
	NEUTRAL	DRIVE	
IGNITION TIMING °BTDC	12		
TIMING RPM-MAX.	800		
FAST IDLE RPM	HIGH CAM		
	KICKDOWN 2400	2200	
CURB IDLE RPM	A/C OFF 800	700	
	A/C ON 1500	1400	
DASHPOT CLEARANCE	1.00-2.00 MM		

SET PARKING BRAKE AND BLOCK WHEELS. DISCONNECT AUTOMATIC PARKING BRAKE RELEASE (IF SO EQUIPPED). MAKE ALL ADJUSTMENTS WITH ENGINE AT NORMAL OPERATING TEMPERATURE, ACCESSORIES AND HEADLIGHTS OFF. PUT AIR CLEANER IN POSITION WHEN CHECKING ALL ENGINE SPEEDS.

IGNITION TIMING-DISCONNECT AND PLUG VACUUM ADVANCE HOSE AT DISTRIBUTOR. CHECK/ADJUST TIMING. RECONNECT VACUUM HOSE.

WHEN CHECKING/ADJUSTING ENGINE SPEEDS D/P (DISCONNECT AND PLUG) THERMACTOR AIR BY-PASS VALVE VACUUM HOSE AT C AND CONNECT INTAKE MANIFOLD VACUUM TO THE BY-PASS VALVE AT C.

FAST IDLE-D/P EGR VALVE VACUUM HOSE AT A, PUT FAST IDLE SCREW ON SPECIFIED STEP OF FAST IDLE CAM. RUN ENGINE UNTIL COOLING FAN COMES ON. CHECK/ADJUST RPM. RECONNECT EGR VALVE VACUUM HOSE.

CURB IDLE-A/C OFF-PUT FAST IDLE SCREW ON SECOND STEP OF FAST IDLE CAM AND RUN ENGINE UNTIL ENGINE COOLING FAN COMES ON. ACCELERATE ENGINE MOMENTARILY. CHECK/ADJUST RPM WITH TRANS. IN SPECIFIED MODE. USE THROTTLE STOP ADJUSTING SCREW ON TOP OF VOTM. CHECK/ADJUST RPM. A/C ON-SET A/C ON MAX. WITH BLOWER ON HIGH. DISCONNECT COMPRESSOR CLUTCH WIRE. CHECK/ADJUST RPM WHILE ENGINE COOLING FAN IS OPERATING. USE SCREW ON TOP OF VOTM TO ADJUST RPM. RECONNECT ALL HOSES.

CHOKE AND IDLE MIXTURE NOT ADJUSTABLE. SEE SERVICE PUBLICATIONS.

IF CURB IDLE ADJ. IS GREATER THAN 50 RPM, RE-ADJUST AUTO. TRANS. LINKAGE, SEE SHOP MANUAL FOR DETAILED INSTRUCTIONS.

THIS VEHICLE CONFORMS TO U.S.E.P.A. AND CALIFORNIA REGULATIONS APPLICABLE TO 1982 MODEL YEAR NEW MOTOR VEHICLES INTRODUCED INTO COMMERCE SOLELY FOR SALE IN CALIFORNIA.

E2AE-9C485-AMG

Non A/C

FORD MOTOR COMPANY
VEHICLE EMISSION CONTROL INFORMATION

EVAPORATIVE FAMILY IS **2CM**

ENGINE FAMILY CFMI.6V2GKC2 — EGR/AIP/TWC
ENGINE DISPLACEMENT 1.6L TRANS. MAN.
SPARK PLUG AWSF-32 GAP .042-.046 **CATALYST**

SHIFT SCHED.	TRANS. GEAR		RPM FOR ENGINE WITH LESS THAN 100 MILES
	NEUTRAL	DRIVE	
IGNITION TIMING °BTDC	12		
TIMING RPM-MAX.	800		
FAST IDLE RPM	HIGH CAM		
	KICKDOWN 2400	2200	
CURB IDLE RPM	VOTM OFF 800	700	
	VOTM ON 1500	1400	
DASHPOT CLEARANCE	1.00-2.00 MM		

SET PARKING BRAKE AND BLOCK WHEELS. DISCONNECT AUTOMATIC PARKING BRAKE RELEASE (IF SO EQUIPPED). MAKE ALL ADJUSTMENTS WITH ENGINE AT NORMAL OPERATING TEMPERATURE, ACCESSORIES AND HEADLIGHTS OFF. PUT AIR CLEANER IN POSITION WHEN CHECKING ALL ENGINE SPEEDS.

IGNITION TIMING-DISCONNECT AND PLUG VACUUM ADVANCE HOSE AT DISTRIBUTOR. CHECK/ADJUST TIMING. RECONNECT VACUUM HOSE.

WHEN CHECKING/ADJUSTING ENGINE SPEEDS D/P (DISCONNECT AND PLUG) THERMACTOR AIR BY-PASS VALVE VACUUM HOSE AT C AND CONNECT INTAKE MANIFOLD VACUUM TO THE BY-PASS VALVE AT C.

FAST IDLE-D/P EGR VALVE VACUUM HOSE AT A, PUT FAST IDLE SCREW ON SPECIFIED STEP OF FAST IDLE CAM. RUN ENGINE UNTIL COOLING FAN COMES ON. CHECK/ADJUST RPM. RECONNECT EGR VALVE VACUUM HOSE.

CURB IDLE-VOTM (VACUUM OPERATED THROTTLE MODULATOR) OFF-PUT FAST IDLE SCREW ON SECOND STEP OF FAST IDLE CAM AND RUN ENGINE UNTIL ENGINE COOLING FAN COMES ON. ACCELERATE ENGINE MOMENTARILY. DISCONNECT AND PLUG VOTM VACUUM HOSE (IF SO EQUIPPED). CHECK/ADJUST RPM WITH TRANS. IN SPECIFIED MODE. USE THROTTLE STOP ADJUSTING SCREW TO ADJUST RPM. CHECK/ADJUST DASHPOT CLEARANCE. VOTM ON-CONNECT A VACUUM HOSE FROM MANIFOLD VACUUM TO THE VOTM. CHECK/ADJUST RPM WHILE ENGINE COOLING FAN IS OPERATING. USE SCREW ON TOP OF VOTM TO ADJUST RPM. REMOVE ADDED HOSES AND RECONNECT ALL HOSES.

CHOKE AND IDLE MIXTURE NOT ADJUSTABLE. SEE SERVICE PUBLICATIONS.

IF CURB IDLE ADJ. IS GREATER THAN 50 RPM, RE-ADJUST AUTO. TRANS. LINKAGE, SEE SHOP MANUAL FOR DETAILED INSTRUCTIONS.

THIS VEHICLE CONFORMS TO U.S.E.P.A. AND CALIFORNIA REGULATIONS APPLICABLE TO 1982 MODEL YEAR NEW MOTOR VEHICLES INTRODUCED INTO COMMERCE SOLEY FOR SALE IN CALIFORNIA.

E2AE-9C485-AML

MODEL YEAR: 1982 **CALIBRATION: 2—3D—R1** **ENGINE: 1.6L**

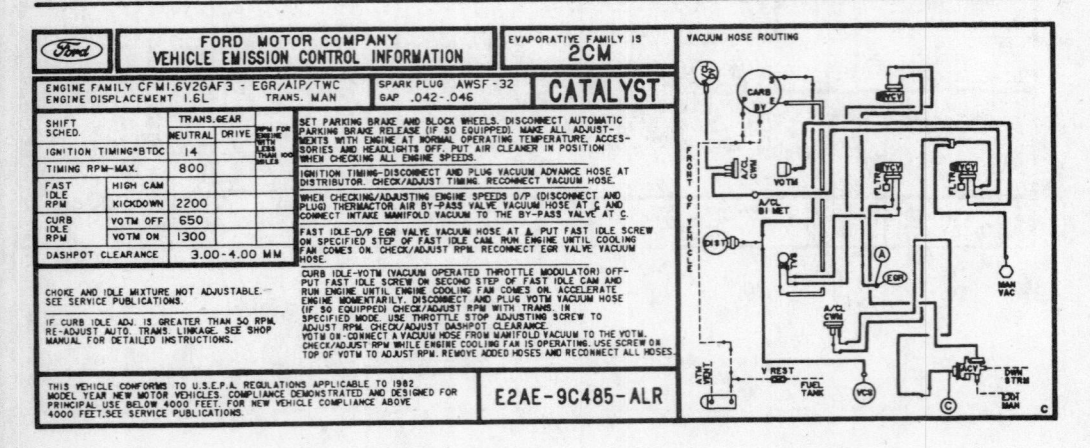

FORD MOTOR COMPANY
VEHICLE EMISSION CONTROL INFORMATION

EVAPORATIVE FAMILY IS **2CM**

ENGINE FAMILY CFMI.6V2GAF3 — EGR/AIP/TWC
ENGINE DISPLACEMENT 1.6L TRANS. MAN.
SPARK PLUG AWSF-32 GAP .042-.046 **CATALYST**

SHIFT SCHED.	TRANS. GEAR		RPM FOR ENGINE WITH LESS THAN 100 MILES
	NEUTRAL	DRIVE	
IGNITION TIMING °BTDC	14		
TIMING RPM-MAX.	800		
FAST IDLE RPM	HIGH CAM		
	KICKDOWN 2200		
CURB IDLE RPM	VOTM OFF 650		
	VOTM ON 1300		
DASHPOT CLEARANCE	3.00-4.00 MM		

SET PARKING BRAKE AND BLOCK WHEELS. DISCONNECT AUTOMATIC PARKING BRAKE RELEASE (IF SO EQUIPPED). MAKE ALL ADJUSTMENTS WITH ENGINE AT NORMAL OPERATING TEMPERATURE, ACCESSORIES AND HEADLIGHTS OFF. PUT AIR CLEANER IN POSITION WHEN CHECKING ALL ENGINE SPEEDS.

IGNITION TIMING-DISCONNECT AND PLUG VACUUM ADVANCE HOSE AT DISTRIBUTOR. CHECK/ADJUST TIMING. RECONNECT VACUUM HOSE.

WHEN CHECKING/ADJUSTING ENGINE SPEEDS D/P (DISCONNECT AND PLUG) THERMACTOR AIR BY-PASS VALVE VACUUM HOSE AT C AND CONNECT INTAKE MANIFOLD VACUUM TO THE BY-PASS VALVE AT C.

FAST IDLE-D/P EGR VALVE VACUUM HOSE AT A, PUT FAST IDLE SCREW ON SPECIFIED STEP OF FAST IDLE CAM. RUN ENGINE UNTIL COOLING FAN COMES ON. CHECK/ADJUST RPM. RECONNECT EGR VALVE VACUUM HOSE.

CURB IDLE-VOTM (VACUUM OPERATED THROTTLE MODULATOR)-PUT FAST IDLE SCREW ON SECOND STEP OF FAST IDLE CAM AND RUN ENGINE UNTIL ENGINE COOLING FAN COMES ON. ACCELERATE ENGINE MOMENTARILY. DISCONNECT AND PLUG VOTM VACUUM HOSE (IF SO EQUIPPED). CHECK/ADJUST RPM WITH TRANS. IN SPECIFIED MODE. USE THROTTLE STOP ADJUSTING SCREW TO ADJUST RPM. CHECK/ADJUST DASHPOT CLEARANCE. VOTM ON-CONNECT A VACUUM HOSE FROM MANIFOLD VACUUM TO THE VOTM. CHECK/ADJUST RPM WHILE ENGINE COOLING FAN IS OPERATING. USE SCREW ON TOP OF VOTM TO ADJUST RPM. REMOVE ADDED HOSES AND RECONNECT ALL HOSES.

THIS VEHICLE CONFORMS TO U.S.E.P.A. REGULATIONS APPLICABLE TO 1982 MODEL YEAR NEW MOTOR VEHICLES. COMPLIANCE DEMONSTRATED AND DESIGNED FOR PRINCIPAL USE BELOW 4000 FEET. FOR NEW VEHICLE COMPLIANCE ABOVE 4000 FEET, SEE SERVICE PUBLICATIONS.

E2AE-9C485-ALR

EMISSION CONTROLS 225

MODEL YEAR: 1982   **CALIBRATION: 2—3X—R0**   **ENGINE: 1.6L**

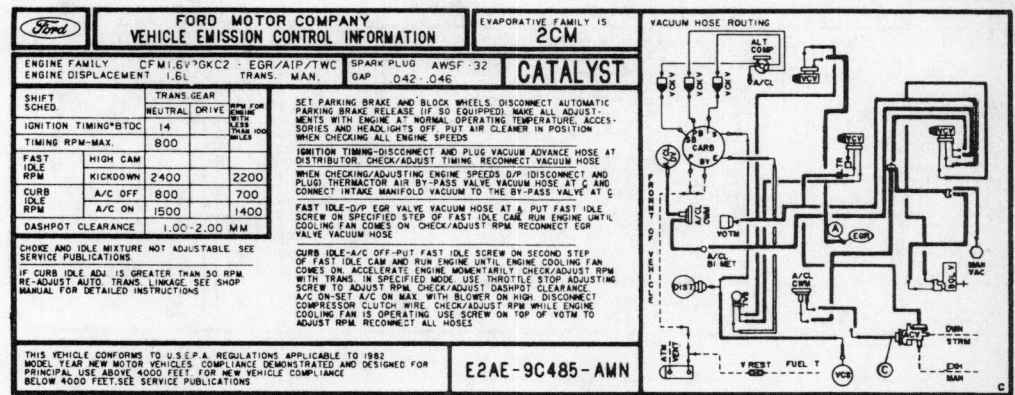

A/C

FORD MOTOR COMPANY — VEHICLE EMISSION CONTROL INFORMATION

EVAPORATIVE FAMILY IS **2CM**

ENGINE FAMILY: CFMI.6V2GKC2 — EGR/AIP/TWC
ENGINE DISPLACEMENT: 1.6L   TRANS. MAN.
SPARK PLUG: AWSF-32   GAP: .042–.046   **CATALYST**

SHIFT SCHED.	TRANS. GEAR		RPM FOR ENGINE WITH LESS THAN 100 MILES
	NEUTRAL	DRIVE	
IGNITION TIMING°BTDC	14		
TIMING RPM-MAX.	800		
FAST IDLE RPM	HIGH CAM KICKDOWN	2400	2200
CURB IDLE RPM	A/C OFF	800	700
	A/C ON	1500	1400
DASHPOT CLEARANCE	1.00–2.00 MM		

CHOKE AND IDLE MIXTURE NOT ADJUSTABLE. SEE SERVICE PUBLICATIONS.

IF CURB IDLE ADJ IS GREATER THAN 50 RPM RE-ADJUST AUTO. TRANS. LINKAGE. SEE SHOP MANUAL FOR DETAILED INSTRUCTIONS.

SET PARKING BRAKE AND BLOCK WHEELS. DISCONNECT AUTOMATIC PARKING BRAKE RELEASE (IF SO EQUIPPED). MAKE ALL ADJUSTMENTS WITH ENGINE AT NORMAL OPERATING TEMPERATURE, ACCESSORIES AND HEADLIGHTS OFF. PUT AIR CLEANER IN POSITION WHEN CHECKING ALL ENGINE SPEEDS.

IGNITION TIMING-DISCONNECT AND PLUG VACUUM ADVANCE HOSE AT DISTRIBUTOR. CHECK/ADJUST TIMING. RECONNECT VACUUM HOSE.

WHEN CHECKING/ADJUSTING ENGINE SPEEDS D/P (DISCONNECT AND PLUG) THERMACTOR AIR BY-PASS VALVE VACUUM HOSE AT C AND CONNECT INTAKE MANIFOLD VACUUM TO THE BY-PASS VALVE AT C.

FAST IDLE-D/P EGR VALVE VACUUM HOSE, PUT FAST IDLE SCREW ON SPECIFIED STEP OF FAST IDLE CAM. RUN ENGINE UNTIL COOLING FAN COMES ON. CHECK/ADJUST RPM. RECONNECT EGR VALVE VACUUM HOSE.

CURB IDLE-A/C OFF-PUT FAST IDLE SCREW ON SECOND STEP OF FAST IDLE CAM AND RUN ENGINE UNTIL COOLING FAN COMES ON. ACCELERATE ENGINE MOMENTARILY. CHECK/ADJUST RPM WITH TRANS. IN SPECIFIED MODE. USE THROTTLE STOP ADJUSTING SCREW. CHECK/ADJUST DASHPOT CLEARANCE. A/C ON-SET A/C ON MAX WITH BLOWER ON HIGH. DISCONNECT COMPRESSOR CLUTCH WIRE. CHECK/ADJUST RPM WHILE ENGINE COOLING FAN IS OPERATING. USE SCREW ON TOP OF VOTM TO ADJUST RPM. RECONNECT ALL HOSES.

THIS VEHICLE CONFORMS TO U.S.EPA REGULATIONS APPLICABLE TO 1982 MODEL YEAR NEW MOTOR VEHICLES. COMPLIANCE DEMONSTRATED AND DESIGNED FOR PRINCIPAL USE ABOVE 4000 FEET. FOR NEW VEHICLE COMPLIANCE BELOW 4000 FEET, SEE SERVICE PUBLICATIONS.

E2AE-9C485-AMN

Non A/C

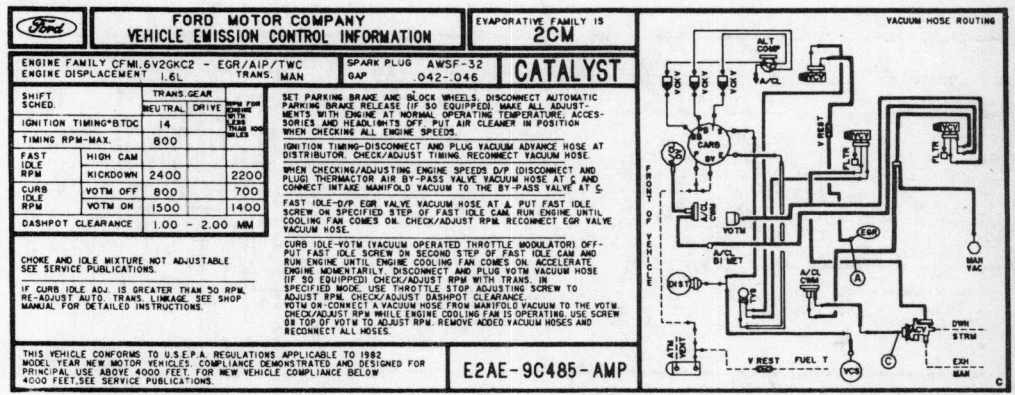

FORD MOTOR COMPANY — VEHICLE EMISSION CONTROL INFORMATION

EVAPORATIVE FAMILY IS **2CM**

ENGINE FAMILY: CFMI.6V2GKC2 — EGR/AIP/TWC
ENGINE DISPLACEMENT: 1.6L   TRANS. MAN
SPARK PLUG: AWSF-32   GAP: .042–.046   **CATALYST**

SHIFT SCHED.	TRANS. GEAR		
	NEUTRAL	DRIVE	
IGNITION TIMING°BTDC	14		
TIMING RPM-MAX.	800		
FAST IDLE RPM	HIGH CAM KICKDOWN	2400	2200
CURB IDLE RPM	VOTM OFF	800	700
	VOTM ON	1500	1400
DASHPOT CLEARANCE	1.00–2.00 MM		

CHOKE AND IDLE MIXTURE NOT ADJUSTABLE. SEE SERVICE PUBLICATIONS.

IF CURB IDLE ADJ IS GREATER THAN 50 RPM RE-ADJUST AUTO. TRANS. LINKAGE. SEE SHOP MANUAL FOR DETAILED INSTRUCTIONS.

SET PARKING BRAKE AND BLOCK WHEELS. DISCONNECT AUTOMATIC PARKING BRAKE RELEASE (IF SO EQUIPPED). MAKE ALL ADJUSTMENTS WITH ENGINE AT NORMAL OPERATING TEMPERATURE, ACCESSORIES AND HEADLIGHTS OFF. PUT AIR CLEANER IN POSITION WHEN CHECKING ALL ENGINE SPEEDS.

IGNITION TIMING-DISCONNECT AND PLUG VACUUM ADVANCE HOSE AT DISTRIBUTOR. CHECK/ADJUST TIMING. RECONNECT VACUUM HOSE.

WHEN CHECKING/ADJUSTING ENGINE SPEEDS D/P (DISCONNECT AND PLUG) THERMACTOR AIR BY-PASS VALVE VACUUM HOSE AT C AND CONNECT INTAKE MANIFOLD VACUUM TO THE BY-PASS VALVE AT C.

FAST IDLE-D/P EGR VALVE VACUUM HOSE, PUT FAST IDLE SCREW ON SPECIFIED STEP OF FAST IDLE CAM. RUN ENGINE UNTIL COOLING FAN COMES ON. CHECK/ADJUST RPM. RECONNECT EGR VALVE VACUUM HOSE.

CURB IDLE-VOTM (VACUUM OPERATED THROTTLE MODULATOR) OFF-PUT FAST IDLE SCREW ON SECOND STEP OF FAST IDLE CAM AND RUN ENGINE UNTIL ENGINE COOLING FAN COMES ON. ACCELERATE ENGINE MOMENTARILY. DISCONNECT AND PLUG VOTM VACUUM HOSE (IF SO EQUIPPED) CHECK/ADJUST RPM WITH TRANS. IN SPECIFIED MODE. USE THROTTLE STOP ADJUSTING SCREW TO CHECK/ADJUST DASHPOT CLEARANCE.
VOTM ON-CONNECT A VACUUM HOSE FROM MANIFOLD VACUUM TO THE VOTM. CHECK/ADJUST RPM WHILE ENGINE COOLING FAN IS OPERATING. USE SCREW ON TOP OF VOTM TO ADJUST RPM. REMOVE ADDED VACUUM HOSES AND RECONNECT ALL HOSES.

THIS VEHICLE CONFORMS TO U.S.EPA REGULATIONS APPLICABLE TO 1982 MODEL YEAR NEW MOTOR VEHICLES. COMPLIANCE DEMONSTRATED AND DESIGNED FOR PRINCIPAL USE ABOVE 4000 FEET. FOR NEW VEHICLE COMPLIANCE BELOW 4000 FEET, SEE SERVICE PUBLICATIONS.

E2AE-9C485-AMP

MODEL YEAR: 1982   **CALIBRATION: 2—4B—R10**   **ENGINE: 1.6L**

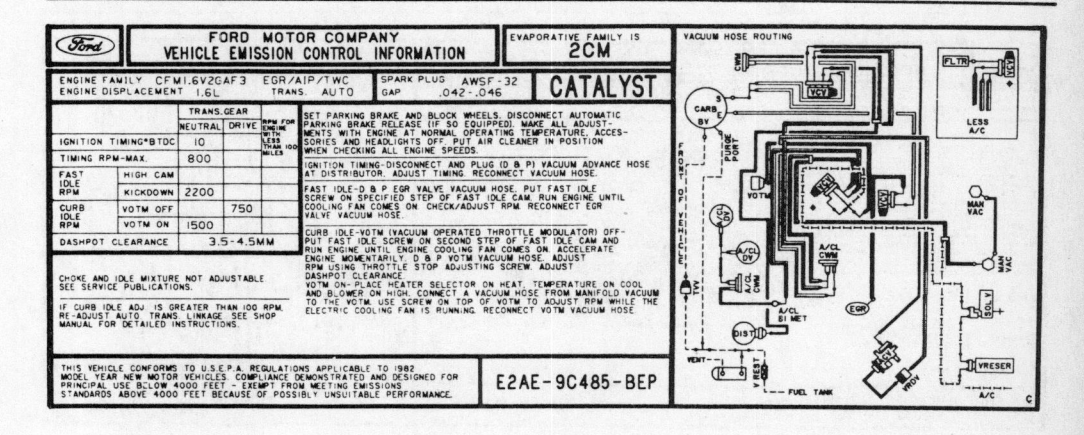

FORD MOTOR COMPANY — VEHICLE EMISSION CONTROL INFORMATION

EVAPORATIVE FAMILY IS **2CM**

ENGINE FAMILY: CFMI.6V2GAF3 — EGR/AIP/TWC
ENGINE DISPLACEMENT: 1.6L   TRANS. AUTO
SPARK PLUG: AWSF-32   GAP: .042–.046   **CATALYST**

	TRANS. GEAR		
	NEUTRAL	DRIVE	
IGNITION TIMING°BTDC	10		
TIMING RPM-MAX.	800		
FAST IDLE RPM	HIGH CAM KICKDOWN	2200	
CURB IDLE RPM	VOTM OFF		750
	VOTM ON	1500	
DASHPOT CLEARANCE	3.5–4.5MM		

CHOKE AND IDLE MIXTURE NOT ADJUSTABLE. SEE SERVICE PUBLICATIONS.

IF CURB IDLE ADJ IS GREATER THAN 100 RPM, RE-ADJUST AUTO. TRANS. LINKAGE. SEE SHOP MANUAL FOR DETAILED INSTRUCTIONS.

SET PARKING BRAKE AND BLOCK WHEELS. DISCONNECT AUTOMATIC PARKING BRAKE RELEASE (IF SO EQUIPPED). MAKE ALL ADJUSTMENTS WITH ENGINE AT NORMAL OPERATING TEMPERATURE, ACCESSORIES AND HEADLIGHTS OFF. PUT AIR CLEANER IN POSITION WHEN CHECKING ALL ENGINE SPEEDS.

IGNITION TIMING-DISCONNECT AND PLUG (D & P) VACUUM ADVANCE HOSE AT DISTRIBUTOR. ADJUST TIMING. RECONNECT VACUUM HOSE.

FAST IDLE-D & P EGR VALVE VACUUM HOSE. PUT FAST IDLE SCREW ON SPECIFIED STEP OF FAST IDLE CAM. RUN ENGINE UNTIL COOLING FAN COMES ON. CHECK/ADJUST RPM. RECONNECT EGR VALVE VACUUM HOSE.

CURB IDLE-VOTM (VACUUM OPERATED THROTTLE MODULATOR) OFF-PUT FAST IDLE SCREW ON SECOND STEP OF FAST IDLE CAM AND RUN ENGINE UNTIL ENGINE COOLING FAN COMES ON. ACCELERATE ENGINE MOMENTARILY, D & P VOTM VACUUM HOSE. ADJUST RPM USING THROTTLE STOP ADJUSTING SCREW. ADJUST DASHPOT CLEARANCE.
VOTM ON- PLACE HEATER SELECTOR ON HEAT, TEMPERATURE ON COOL AND BLOWER ON HIGH. CONNECT A VACUUM HOSE FROM MANIFOLD VACUUM TO THE VOTM. USE SCREW ON TOP OF VOTM TO ADJUST RPM WHILE THE ELECTRIC COOLING FAN IS RUNNING. RECONNECT VOTM VACUUM HOSE.

THIS VEHICLE CONFORMS TO U.S.EPA REGULATIONS APPLICABLE TO 1982 MODEL YEAR NEW MOTOR VEHICLES. COMPLIANCE DEMONSTRATED AND DESIGNED FOR PRINCIPAL USE BELOW 4000 FEET — EXEMPT FROM MEETING EMISSIONS STANDARDS ABOVE 4000 FEET BECAUSE OF POSSIBLY UNSUITABLE PERFORMANCE.

E2AE-9C485-BEP

EMISSION CONTROLS

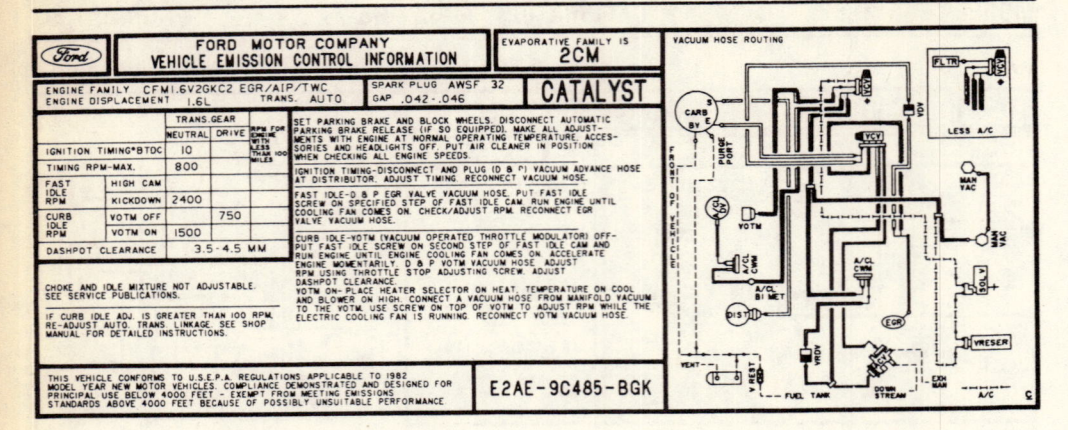

MODEL YEAR: 1982 **CALIBRATION: 2—4C—R0** **ENGINE: 1.6L**

MODEL YEAR: 1982 **CALIBRATION: 2—4C—R14** **ENGINE: 1.6L**

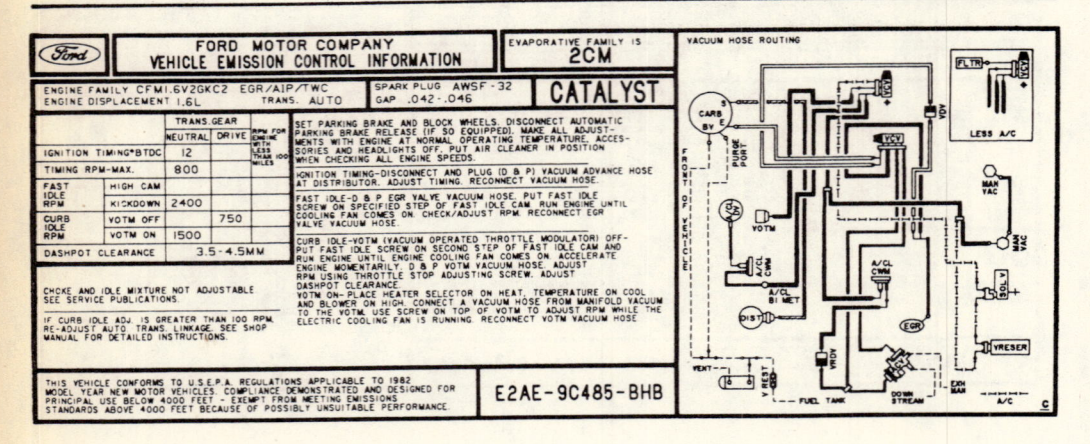

MODEL YEAR: 1982 **CALIBRATION: 2—4Q—R10** **ENGINE: 1.6L**

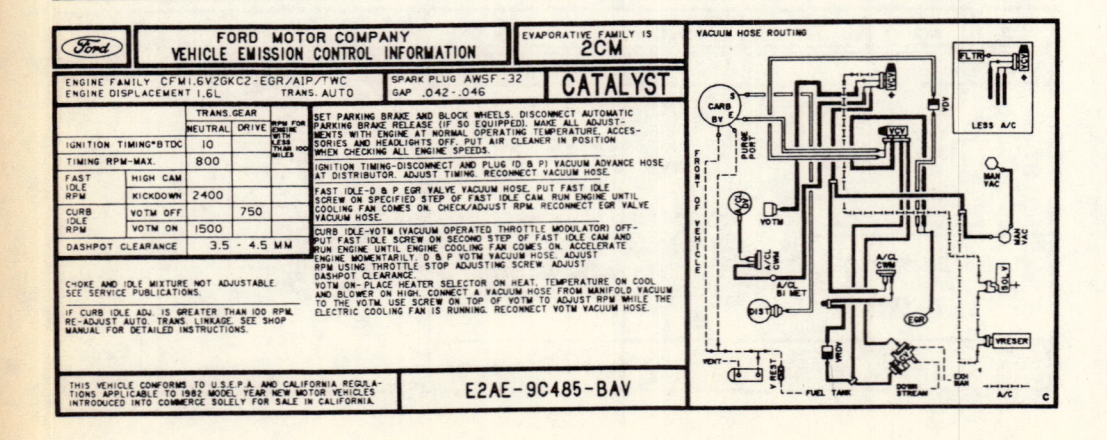

EMISSION CONTROLS

MODEL YEAR: 1982 **CALIBRATION: 2—4Q—R0** **ENGINE: 1.6L**

A/C

FORD MOTOR COMPANY — VEHICLE EMISSION CONTROL INFORMATION

EVAPORATIVE FAMILY IS **2CM**

ENGINE FAMILY: CFM1.6V2GKC2-EGR/AIP/TWC
ENGINE DISPLACEMENT: 1.6L, TRANS. AUTO
SPARK PLUG: AWSF-32, GAP .042-.046 — **CATALYST**

SHIFT SCHED	TRANS. GEAR		RPM FOR ENGINE WITH LESS THAN 100 MILES
	NEUTRAL	DRIVE	
IGNITION TIMING °BTDC	8		
TIMING RPM-MAX.	800		
FAST IDLE RPM	HIGH CAM		
	KICKDOWN	2400	
CURB IDLE RPM	A/C OFF		750
	A/C ON	1500	
DASHPOT CLEARANCE	3.50-4.50 MM		

SET PARKING BRAKE AND BLOCK WHEELS. DISCONNECT AUTOMATIC PARKING BRAKE RELEASE (IF SO EQUIPPED). MAKE ALL ADJUSTMENTS WITH ENGINE AT NORMAL OPERATING TEMPERATURE, ACCESSORIES AND HEADLIGHTS OFF. PUT AIR CLEANER IN POSITION WHEN CHECKING ALL ENGINE SPEEDS.
IGNITION TIMING-DISCONNECT AND PLUG VACUUM ADVANCE HOSE AT DISTRIBUTOR. CHECK/ADJUST TIMING. RECONNECT VACUUM HOSE.
WHEN CHECKING/ADJUSTING ENGINE SPEEDS D/P (DISCONNECT AND PLUG) THERMACTOR AIR BY-PASS VALVE VACUUM HOSE AT C AND CONNECT INTAKE MANIFOLD VACUUM TO THE BY-PASS VALVE AT C.
FAST IDLE-D/P EGR VALVE VACUUM HOSE AT A PUT FAST IDLE SCREW ON SPECIFIED STEP OF FAST IDLE CAM. RUN ENGINE UNTIL COOLING FAN COMES ON. CHECK/ADJUST RPM. RECONNECT EGR VALVE VACUUM HOSE.
CURB IDLE-A/C OFF-PUT FAST IDLE SCREW ON SECOND STEP OF FAST IDLE CAM AND RUN ENGINE UNTIL ENGINE COOLING FAN COMES ON. ACCELERATE ENGINE MOMENTARILY. CHECK/ADJUST RPM WITH TRANS. IN SPECIFIED MODE. USE THROTTLE STOP ADJUSTING SCREW TO ADJUST RPM. CHECK/ADJUST DASHPOT CLEARANCE. A/C ON-SET A/C ON MAX. WITH BLOWER ON HIGH. DISCONNECT COMPRESSOR CLUTCH WIRE. CHECK/ADJUST RPM WHILE ENGINE COOLING FAN IS OPERATING. USE SCREW ON TOP OF VOTM TO ADJUST RPM. RECONNECT ALL HOSES.

CHOKE AND IDLE MIXTURE NOT ADJUSTABLE. SEE SERVICE PUBLICATIONS.
IF CURB IDLE ADJ. IS GREATER THAN 50 RPM, RE-ADJUST AUTO. TRANS. LINKAGE SEE SHOP MANUAL FOR DETAILED INSTRUCTIONS.

THIS VEHICLE CONFORMS TO U.S.E.P.A. AND CALIFORNIA REGULATIONS APPLICABLE TO 1982 MODEL YEAR NEW MOTOR VEHICLES INTRODUCED INTO COMMERCE SOLELY FOR SALE IN CALIFORNIA.

E2AE-9C485-ANZ

VACUUM HOSE ROUTING — LESS BOTH A/C & P/S

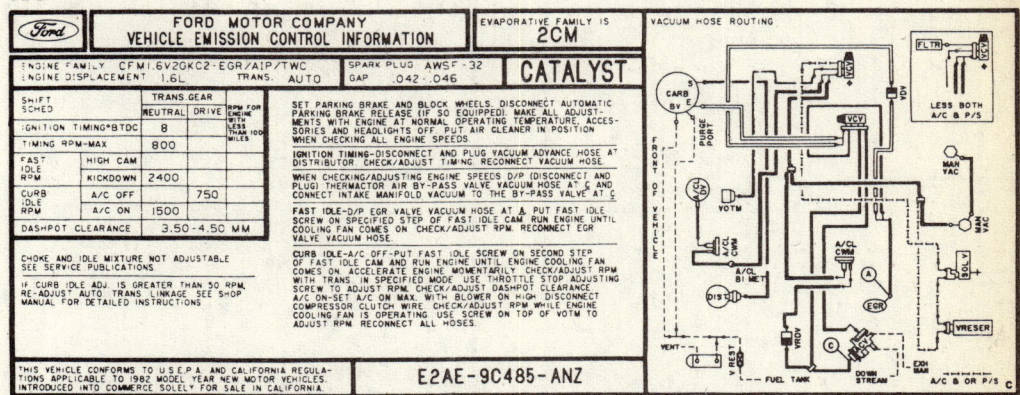

Non A/C

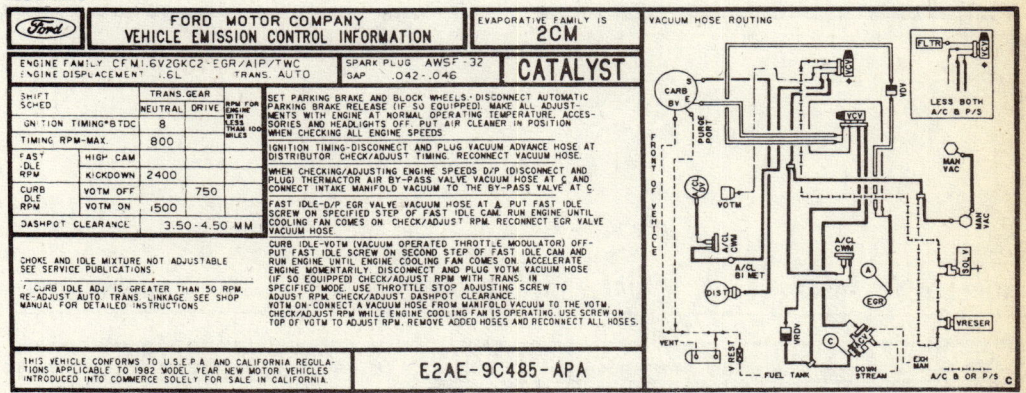

FORD MOTOR COMPANY — VEHICLE EMISSION CONTROL INFORMATION

EVAPORATIVE FAMILY IS **2CM**

ENGINE FAMILY: CFM1.6V2GKC2-EGR/AIP/TWC
ENGINE DISPLACEMENT: 1.6L, TRANS. AUTO
SPARK PLUG: AWSF-32, GAP .042-.046 — **CATALYST**

SHIFT SCHED	TRANS. GEAR		RPM FOR ENGINE WITH LESS THAN 100 MILES
	NEUTRAL	DRIVE	
IGNITION TIMING °BTDC	8		
TIMING RPM-MAX.	800		
FAST IDLE RPM	HIGH CAM		
	KICKDOWN	2400	
CURB IDLE RPM	VOTM OFF		750
	VOTM ON	1500	
DASHPOT CLEARANCE	3.50-4.50 MM		

SET PARKING BRAKE AND BLOCK WHEELS. DISCONNECT AUTOMATIC PARKING BRAKE RELEASE (IF SO EQUIPPED). MAKE ALL ADJUSTMENTS WITH ENGINE AT NORMAL OPERATING TEMPERATURE, ACCESSORIES AND HEADLIGHTS OFF. PUT AIR CLEANER IN POSITION WHEN CHECKING ALL ENGINE SPEEDS.
IGNITION TIMING-DISCONNECT AND PLUG VACUUM ADVANCE HOSE AT DISTRIBUTOR. CHECK/ADJUST TIMING. RECONNECT VACUUM HOSE.
WHEN CHECKING/ADJUSTING ENGINE SPEEDS D/P (DISCONNECT AND PLUG) THERMACTOR AIR BY-PASS VALVE VACUUM HOSE AT C AND CONNECT INTAKE MANIFOLD VACUUM TO THE BY-PASS VALVE AT C.
FAST IDLE-D/P EGR VALVE VACUUM HOSE AT A PUT FAST IDLE SCREW ON SPECIFIED STEP OF FAST IDLE CAM. RUN ENGINE UNTIL COOLING FAN COMES ON. CHECK/ADJUST RPM. RECONNECT EGR VALVE VACUUM HOSE.
CURB IDLE-VOTM (VACUUM OPERATED THROTTLE MODULATOR) OFF-PUT FAST IDLE SCREW ON SECOND STEP OF FAST IDLE CAM AND RUN ENGINE UNTIL ENGINE COOLING FAN COMES ON. ACCELERATE ENGINE MOMENTARILY. DISCONNECT AND PLUG VOTM VACUUM HOSE (IF SO EQUIPPED) CHECK/ADJUST RPM WITH TRANS. IN SPECIFIED MODE. USE THROTTLE STOP ADJUSTING SCREW TO ADJUST RPM. CHECK/ADJUST DASHPOT CLEARANCE. VOTM ON-CONNECT A VACUUM HOSE FROM MANIFOLD VACUUM TO THE VOTM. CHECK/ADJUST RPM WHILE ENGINE COOLING FAN IS OPERATING. USE SCREW ON TOP OF VOTM TO ADJUST RPM. REMOVE ADDED HOSES AND RECONNECT ALL HOSES.

CHOKE AND IDLE MIXTURE NOT ADJUSTABLE. SEE SERVICE PUBLICATIONS.
IF CURB IDLE ADJ. IS GREATER THAN 50 RPM, RE-ADJUST AUTO. TRANS. LINKAGE SEE SHOP MANUAL FOR DETAILED INSTRUCTIONS.

THIS VEHICLE CONFORMS TO U.S.E.P.A. AND CALIFORNIA REGULATIONS APPLICABLE TO 1982 MODEL YEAR NEW MOTOR VEHICLES INTRODUCED INTO COMMERCE SOLELY FOR SALE IN CALIFORNIA.

E2AE-9C485-APA

VACUUM HOSE ROUTING — LESS BOTH A/C & P/S

MODEL YEAR: 1982 **CALIBRATION: 2—4Q—R11** **ENGINE: 1.6L**

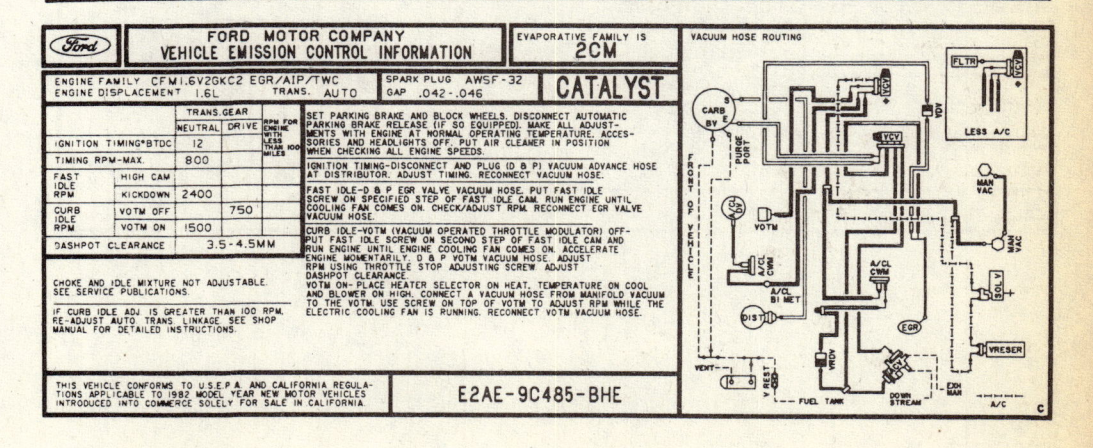

FORD MOTOR COMPANY — VEHICLE EMISSION CONTROL INFORMATION

EVAPORATIVE FAMILY IS **2CM**

ENGINE FAMILY: CFM1.6V2GKC2-EGR/AIP/TWC
ENGINE DISPLACEMENT: 1.6L, TRANS. AUTO
SPARK PLUG: AWSF-32, GAP .042-.046 — **CATALYST**

SHIFT SCHED	TRANS. GEAR		RPM FOR ENGINE WITH LESS THAN 100 MILES
	NEUTRAL	DRIVE	
IGNITION TIMING °BTDC	12		
TIMING RPM-MAX.	800		
FAST IDLE RPM	HIGH CAM		
	KICKDOWN	2400	
CURB IDLE RPM	VOTM OFF		750
	VOTM ON	1500	
DASHPOT CLEARANCE	3.5-4.5MM		

SET PARKING BRAKE AND BLOCK WHEELS. DISCONNECT AUTOMATIC PARKING BRAKE RELEASE (IF SO EQUIPPED). MAKE ALL ADJUSTMENTS WITH ENGINE AT NORMAL OPERATING TEMPERATURE, ACCESSORIES AND HEADLIGHTS OFF. PUT AIR CLEANER IN POSITION WHEN CHECKING ALL ENGINE SPEEDS.
IGNITION TIMING-DISCONNECT AND PLUG (D & P) VACUUM ADVANCE HOSE AT DISTRIBUTOR. ADJUST TIMING. RECONNECT VACUUM HOSE.
FAST IDLE-D & P EGR VALVE VACUUM HOSE. PUT FAST IDLE SCREW ON SPECIFIED STEP OF FAST IDLE CAM. RUN ENGINE UNTIL COOLING FAN COMES ON. CHECK/ADJUST RPM. RECONNECT EGR VALVE VACUUM HOSE.
CURB IDLE-VOTM (VACUUM OPERATED THROTTLE MODULATOR) OFF-PUT FAST IDLE SCREW ON SECOND STEP OF FAST IDLE CAM AND RUN ENGINE UNTIL ENGINE COOLING FAN COMES ON. ACCELERATE ENGINE MOMENTARILY. D & P VOTM VACUUM HOSE. ADJUST RPM USING THROTTLE STOP ADJUSTING SCREW. ADJUST DASHPOT CLEARANCE.
VOTM ON- PLACE HEATER SELECTOR ON HEAT, TEMPERATURE ON COOL AND BLOWER ON HIGH. CONNECT A VACUUM HOSE FROM MANIFOLD VACUUM TO THE VOTM. USE SCREW ON TOP OF VOTM TO ADJUST RPM WHILE THE ELECTRIC COOLING FAN IS RUNNING. RECONNECT VOTM VACUUM HOSE.

CHOKE AND IDLE MIXTURE NOT ADJUSTABLE. SEE SERVICE PUBLICATIONS.
IF CURB IDLE ADJ. IS GREATER THAN 100 RPM, RE-ADJUST AUTO. TRANS. LINKAGE SEE SHOP MANUAL FOR DETAILED INSTRUCTIONS.

THIS VEHICLE CONFORMS TO U.S.E.P.A. AND CALIFORNIA REGULATIONS APPLICABLE TO 1982 MODEL YEAR NEW MOTOR VEHICLES INTRODUCED INTO COMMERCE SOLELY FOR SALE IN CALIFORNIA.

E2AE-9C485-BHE

VACUUM HOSE ROUTING — LESS A/C

EMISSION CONTROLS

MODEL YEAR: 1982   **ENGINE: 1.6L**

MODEL YEAR: 1982   **CALIBRATION: 2—4Q—R13**   **ENGINE: 1.6L**

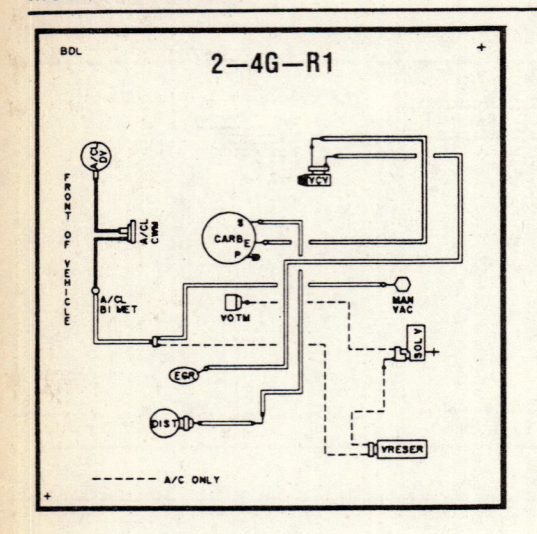

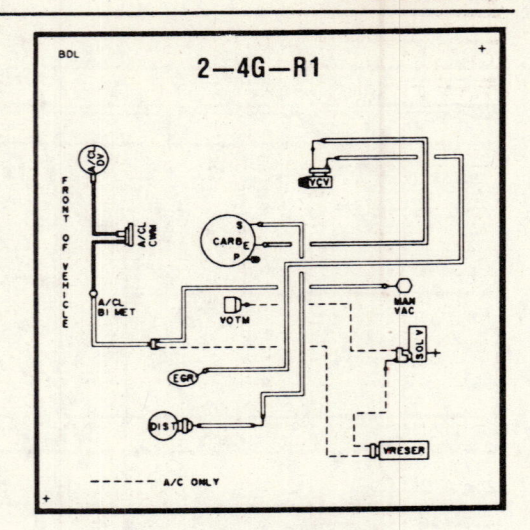

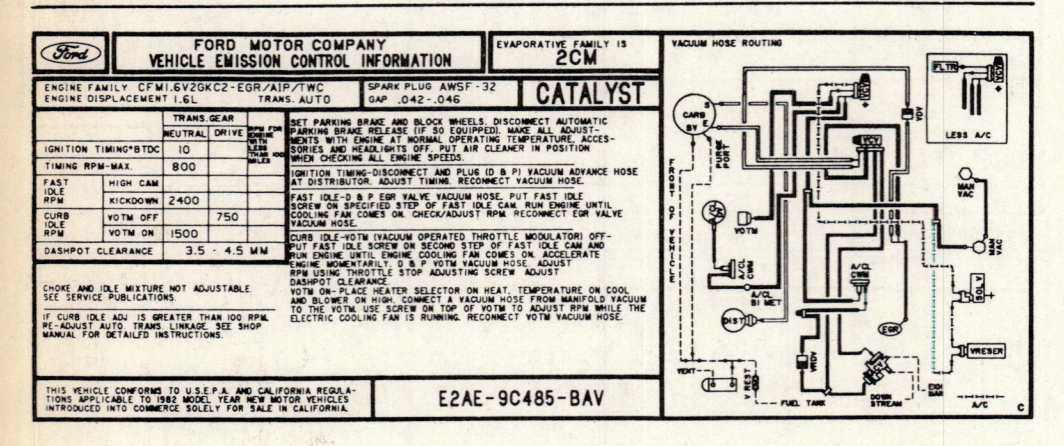

EMISSION CONTROLS 229

MODEL YEAR: 1982 **CALIBRATION: 2—4T—R10** **ENGINE: 1.6L**

Ford Motor Company — Vehicle Emission Control Information
Evaporative Family is 2CM

Engine Family	CFM1.6V2GACO EGR/AIP/TWC
Engine Displacement	1.6L, Trans. AUTO
Spark Plug	AWSF-32, Gap .042-.046

CATALYST

Trans. Gear	Neutral	Drive	RPM for engine with less than 100 miles
Ignition Timing° BTDC	10		
Timing RPM-Max.	800		
Fast Idle RPM — High Cam Kickdown	2200		
Curb Idle RPM — VOTM OFF		750	
VOTM ON	1500		
Dashpot Clearance	3.5-4.5 MM		

SET PARKING BRAKE AND BLOCK WHEELS. DISCONNECT AUTOMATIC PARKING BRAKE RELEASE (IF SO EQUIPPED). MAKE ALL ADJUSTMENTS WITH ENGINE AT NORMAL OPERATING TEMPERATURE, ACCESSORIES AND HEADLIGHTS OFF. PUT AIR CLEANER IN POSITION WHEN CHECKING ALL ENGINE SPEEDS.

IGNITION TIMING—DISCONNECT AND PLUG (D & P) VACUUM ADVANCE HOSE AT DISTRIBUTOR. ADJUST TIMING. RECONNECT VACUUM HOSE.

FAST IDLE—D & P EGR VALVE VACUUM HOSE. PUT FAST IDLE SCREW ON SPECIFIED STEP OF FAST IDLE CAM. RUN ENGINE UNTIL COOLING FAN COMES ON. CHECK/ADJUST RPM. RECONNECT EGR VALVE VACUUM HOSE.

CURB IDLE-VOTM (VACUUM OPERATED THROTTLE MODULATOR) OFF—PUT FAST IDLE SCREW ON SECOND STEP OF FAST IDLE CAM AND RUN ENGINE UNTIL ENGINE COOLING FAN COMES ON. ACCELERATE ENGINE MOMENTARILY. D & P VOTM VACUUM HOSE. ADJUST RPM USING THROTTLE STOP ADJUSTING SCREW. ADJUST DASHPOT CLEARANCE.

VOTM ON-PLACE HEATER SELECTOR ON HEAT, TEMPERATURE ON COOL AND BLOWER ON HIGH. CONNECT A VACUUM HOSE FROM MANIFOLD VACUUM TO THE VOTM. USE SCREW ON TOP OF VOTM TO ADJUST RPM WHILE THE ELECTRIC COOLING FAN IS RUNNING. RECONNECT VOTM VACUUM HOSE.

CHOKE AND IDLE MIXTURE NOT ADJUSTABLE. SEE SERVICE PUBLICATIONS.

IF CURB IDLE ADJ. IS GREATER THAN 100 RPM, RE-ADJUST AUTO. TRANS. LINKAGE. SEE SHOP MANUAL FOR DETAILED INSTRUCTIONS.

THIS VEHICLE CONFORMS TO U.S.E.P.A. AND CALIFORNIA REGULATIONS APPLICABLE TO 1982 MODEL YEAR NEW MOTOR VEHICLES INTRODUCED INTO COMMERCE SOLELY FOR SALE IN CALIFORNIA.

E2AE-9C485-BJL

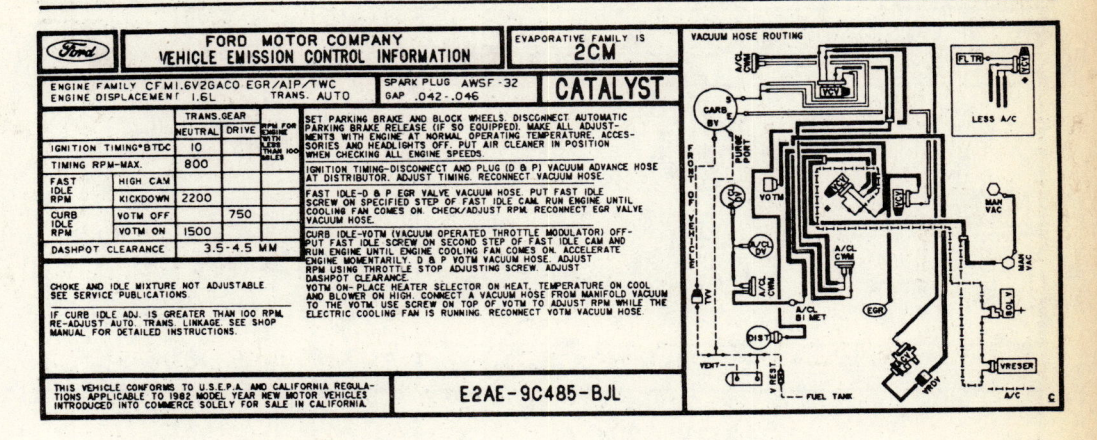

MODEL YEAR: 1982 **CALIBRATION: 2—4X—R0** **ENGINE: 1.6L**

Ford Motor Company — Vehicle Emission Control Information
Evaporative Family is 2CM

Engine Family	CFM1.6V2GKC2 EGR/AIP/TWC
Engine Displacement	1.6L, Trans. AUTO
Spark Plug	AWSF-32, Gap .042-.046

CATALYST

Trans. Gear	Neutral	Drive	
Ignition Timing° BTDC	10		
Timing RPM-Max.	800		
Fast Idle RPM — High Cam Kickdown	2400		
Curb Idle RPM — VOTM OFF		750	
VOTM ON	1500		
Dashpot Clearance	3.5-4.5 MM		

SET PARKING BRAKE AND BLOCK WHEELS. DISCONNECT AUTOMATIC PARKING BRAKE RELEASE (IF SO EQUIPPED). MAKE ALL ADJUSTMENTS WITH ENGINE AT NORMAL OPERATING TEMPERATURE, ACCESSORIES AND HEADLIGHTS OFF. PUT AIR CLEANER IN POSITION WHEN CHECKING ALL ENGINE SPEEDS.

IGNITION TIMING—DISCONNECT AND PLUG (D & P) VACUUM ADVANCE HOSE AT DISTRIBUTOR. ADJUST TIMING. RECONNECT VACUUM HOSE.

FAST IDLE—D & P EGR VALVE VACUUM HOSE. PUT FAST IDLE SCREW ON SPECIFIED STEP OF FAST IDLE CAM. RUN ENGINE UNTIL COOLING FAN COMES ON. CHECK/ADJUST RPM. RECONNECT EGR VALVE VACUUM HOSE.

CURB IDLE-VOTM (VACUUM OPERATED THROTTLE MODULATOR) OFF—PUT FAST IDLE SCREW ON SECOND STEP OF FAST IDLE CAM AND RUN ENGINE UNTIL ENGINE COOLING FAN COMES ON. ACCELERATE ENGINE MOMENTARILY. D & P VOTM VACUUM HOSE. ADJUST RPM USING THROTTLE STOP ADJUSTING SCREW. ADJUST DASHPOT CLEARANCE.

VOTM ON-PLACE HEATER SELECTOR ON HEAT, TEMPERATURE ON COOL AND BLOWER ON HIGH. CONNECT A VACUUM HOSE FROM MANIFOLD VACUUM TO THE VOTM. USE SCREW ON TOP OF VOTM TO ADJUST RPM WHILE THE ELECTRIC COOLING FAN IS RUNNING. RECONNECT VOTM VACUUM HOSE.

CHOKE AND IDLE MIXTURE NOT ADJUSTABLE. SEE SERVICE PUBLICATIONS.

IF CURB IDLE ADJ. IS GREATER THAN 100 RPM, RE-ADJUST AUTO. TRANS. LINKAGE. SEE SHOP MANUAL FOR DETAILED INSTRUCTIONS.

THIS VEHICLE CONFORMS TO U.S.E.P.A. REGULATIONS APPLICABLE TO 1982 MODEL YEAR NEW MOTOR VEHICLES. COMPLIANCE DEMONSTRATED AND DESIGNED FOR PRINCIPAL USE ABOVE 4000 FEET. FOR NEW VEHICLE COMPLIANCE BELOW 4000 FEET, SEE SERVICE PUBLICATIONS.

E2AE-9C485-BDN

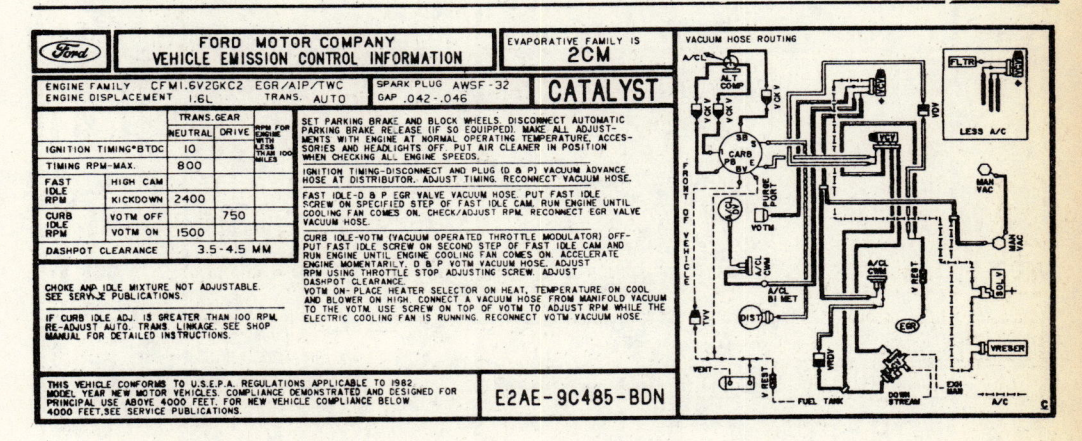

MODEL YEAR: 1982 **CALIBRATION: 2—4X—R11** **ENGINE: 1.6L**

Ford Motor Company — Vehicle Emission Control Information
Evaporative Family is 2CM

Engine Family	CFM1.6V2GKC2 EGR/AIP/TWC
Engine Displacement	1.6L, Trans. AUTO
Spark Plug	AWSF-32, Gap .042-.046

CATALYST

Trans. Gear	Neutral	Drive	
Ignition Timing° BTDC	12		
Timing RPM-Max.	800		
Fast Idle RPM — High Cam Kickdown	2400		
Curb Idle RPM — VOTM OFF		750	
VOTM ON	1500		
Dashpot Clearance	3.5-4.5MM		

SET PARKING BRAKE AND BLOCK WHEELS. DISCONNECT AUTOMATIC PARKING BRAKE RELEASE (IF SO EQUIPPED). MAKE ALL ADJUSTMENTS WITH ENGINE AT NORMAL OPERATING TEMPERATURE, ACCESSORIES AND HEADLIGHTS OFF. PUT AIR CLEANER IN POSITION WHEN CHECKING ALL ENGINE SPEEDS.

IGNITION TIMING—DISCONNECT AND PLUG (D & P) VACUUM ADVANCE HOSE AT DISTRIBUTOR. ADJUST TIMING. RECONNECT VACUUM HOSE.

FAST IDLE—D & P EGR VALVE VACUUM HOSE. PUT FAST IDLE SCREW ON SPECIFIED STEP OF FAST IDLE CAM. RUN ENGINE UNTIL COOLING FAN COMES ON. CHECK/ADJUST RPM. RECONNECT EGR VALVE VACUUM HOSE.

CURB IDLE-VOTM (VACUUM OPERATED THROTTLE MODULATOR) OFF—PUT FAST IDLE SCREW ON SECOND STEP OF FAST IDLE CAM AND RUN ENGINE UNTIL ENGINE COOLING FAN COMES ON. ACCELERATE ENGINE MOMENTARILY. D & P VOTM VACUUM HOSE. ADJUST RPM USING THROTTLE STOP ADJUSTING SCREW. ADJUST DASHPOT CLEARANCE.

VOTM ON-PLACE HEATER SELECTOR ON HEAT, TEMPERATURE ON COOL AND BLOWER ON HIGH. CONNECT A VACUUM HOSE FROM MANIFOLD VACUUM TO THE VOTM. USE SCREW ON TOP OF VOTM TO ADJUST RPM WHILE THE ELECTRIC COOLING FAN IS RUNNING. RECONNECT VOTM VACUUM HOSE.

CHOKE AND IDLE MIXTURE NOT ADJUSTABLE. SEE SERVICE PUBLICATIONS.

IF CURB IDLE ADJ. IS GREATER THAN 100 RPM, RE-ADJUST AUTO. TRANS. LINKAGE. SEE SHOP MANUAL FOR DETAILED INSTRUCTIONS.

THIS VEHICLE CONFORMS TO U.S.E.P.A. REGULATIONS APPLICABLE TO 1982 MODEL YEAR NEW MOTOR VEHICLES. COMPLIANCE DEMONSTRATED AND DESIGNED FOR PRINCIPAL USE ABOVE 4000 FEET. FOR NEW VEHICLE COMPLIANCE BELOW 4000 FEET, SEE SERVICE PUBLICATIONS.

E2AE-9C485-BHD

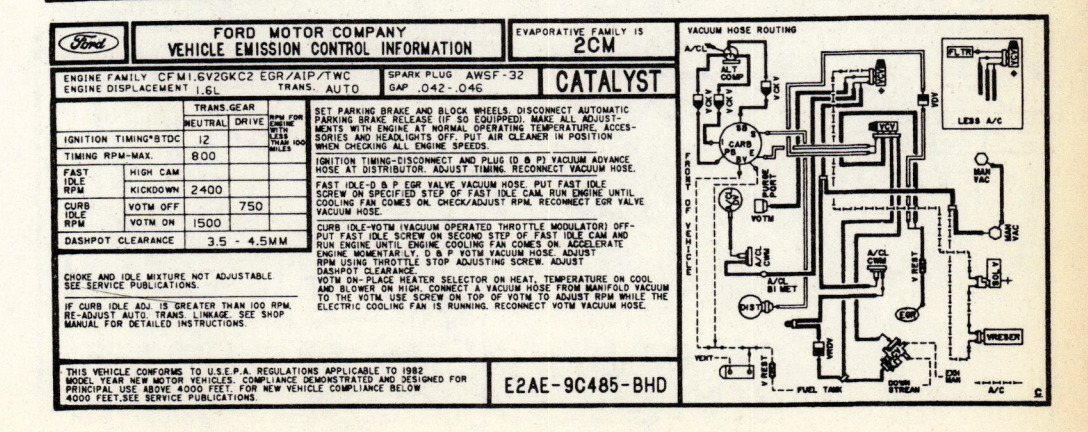

230 EMISSION CONTROLS

MODEL YEAR: 1982   **CALIBRATION: 2—4Y—R10**   **ENGINE: 1.6L**

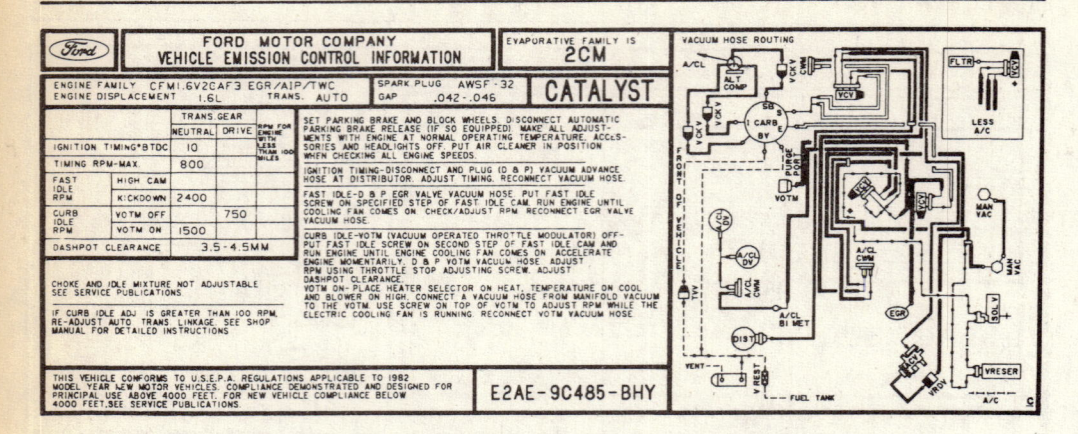

CALIBRATION: 4—03A—R00

MODEL YEAR: 1984   **ENGINE: 1.6L**

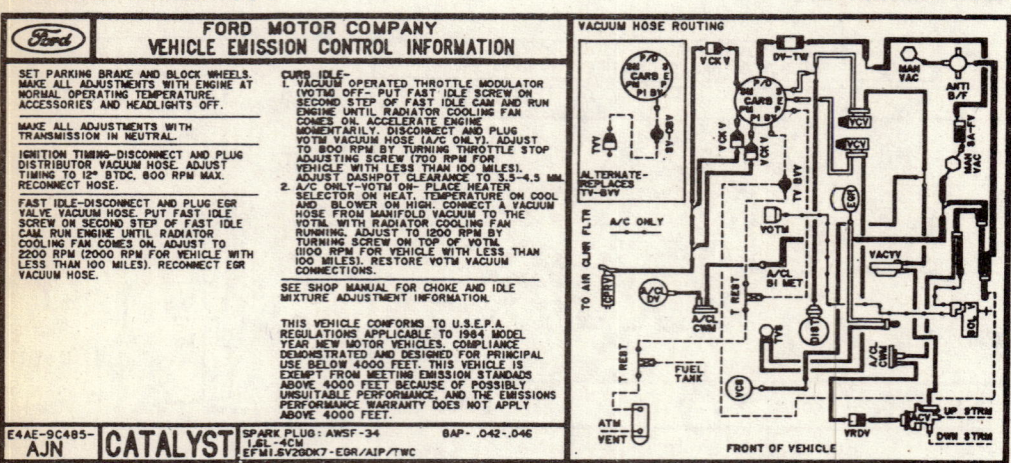

CALIBRATION: 4—03A—R10

MODEL YEAR: 1984   **ENGINE: 1.6L**

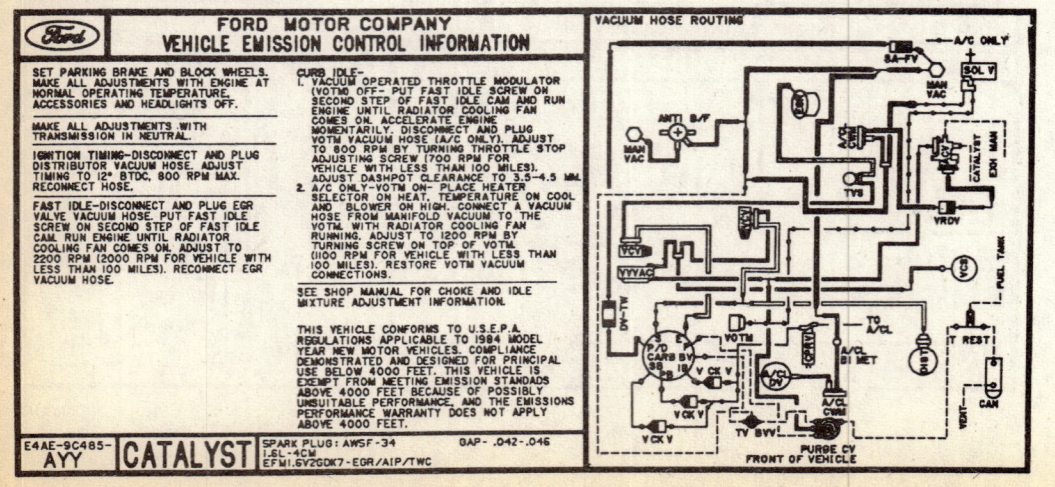

EMISSION CONTROLS 231

CALIBRATION: 4—03F—R00

MODEL YEAR: 1984   **ENGINE: 1.6L**

FORD MOTOR COMPANY — VEHICLE EMISSION CONTROL INFORMATION

SET PARKING BRAKE AND BLOCK WHEELS. MAKE ALL ADJUSTMENTS WITH ENGINE AT NORMAL OPERATING TEMPERATURE, ACCESSORIES AND HEADLIGHTS OFF.

MAKE ALL ADJUSTMENTS WITH TRANSMISSION IN NEUTRAL.

IGNITION TIMING-DISCONNECT AND PLUG DISTRIBUTOR VACUUM HOSE. ADJUST TIMING TO 8° BTDC, 800 RPM MAX. RECONNECT HOSE.

FAST IDLE-DISCONNECT AND PLUG EGR VALVE VACUUM HOSE. PUT FAST IDLE SCREW ON SECOND STEP OF FAST IDLE CAM. RUN ENGINE UNTIL RADIATOR COOLING FAN COMES ON. ADJUST TO 2200 RPM. RECONNECT EGR VACUUM HOSE.

CURB IDLE-PUT FAST IDLE SCREW ON SECOND STEP OF FAST IDLE CAM AND RUN ENGINE UNTIL RADIATOR COOLING FAN COMES ON. ACCELERATE ENGINE MOMENTARILY. ADJUST TO 720 RPM BY TURNING THROTTLE STOP ADJUSTING SCREW. ADJUST DASHPOT CLEARANCE TO 1.5-2.5 MM.

SEE SHOP MANUAL FOR CHOKE AND IDLE MIXTURE ADJUSTMENT INFORMATION.

THIS VEHICLE CONFORMS TO U.S.E.P.A. REGULATIONS APPLICABLE TO 1984 MODEL YEAR NEW MOTOR VEHICLES. COMPLIANCE DEMONSTRATED AND DESIGNED FOR PRINCIPAL USE BELOW 4000 FEET. THIS VEHICLE IS EXEMPT FROM MEETING EMISSION STANDARDS ABOVE 4000 FEET BECAUSE OF POSSIBLY UNSUITABLE PERFORMANCE, AND THE EMISSIONS PERFORMANCE WARRANTY DOES NOT APPLY ABOVE 4000 FEET.

E4AE-9C485-AJK   CATALYST   SPARK PLUG: AWSF-34   1.6 L -4CM   GAP- .042-.046   EFM1.6V2GOK7 - EGR/AIP/TWC

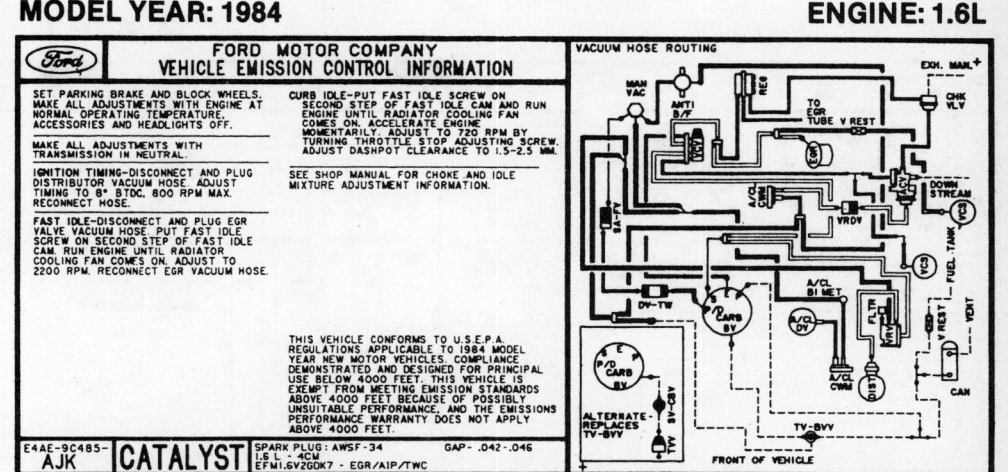

CALIBRATION: 4—03G—R00

MODEL YEAR: 1984   **ENGINE: 1.6L**

VEHICLE EMISSION CONTROL INFORMATION — FORD MOTOR COMPANY

CATALYST / CATALYSEUR

SET PARKING BRAKE AND BLOCK WHEELS. MAKE ALL ADJUSTMENTS WITH ENGINE AT NORMAL OPERATING TEMPERATURE, ACCESSORIES AND HEADLIGHTS OFF.

MAKE ALL ADJUSTMENTS WITH TRANSMISSION IN NEUTRAL.

IGNITION TIMING-DISCONNECT AND PLUG DISTRIBUTOR VACUUM HOSE. ADJUST TIMING TO 14° BTDC, 800 RPM MAX. RECONNECT HOSE.

FAST IDLE-D & P EGR VALVE VACUUM HOSE. PUT FAST IDLE SCREW ON SECOND STEP OF FAST IDLE CAM. RUN ENGINE UNTIL RADIATOR COOLING FAN COMES ON. ADJUST TO 2200 RPM (2000 RPM FOR VEHICLE WITH LESS THAN 160 KM). RECONNECT EGR VACUUM HOSE.

CURB IDLE-1. VACUUM OPERATED THROTTLE MODULATOR (VOTM) OFF. PUT FAST IDLE SCREW ON SECOND STEP OF FAST IDLE CAM AND RUN ENGINE UNTIL RADIATOR COOLING FAN COMES ON. ACCELERATE ENGINE MOMENTARILY. D/P VOTM VACUUM HOSE. (A/C ONLY), ADJUST TO 750 RPM BY TURNING THROTTLE STOP ADJUSTING SCREW (650 RPM FOR VEHICLE WITH LESS THAN 160 KM). ADJUST DASHPOT CLEARANCE TO 3.0-4.0 MM.

2.A/C ONLY-VOTM ON- PLACE HEATER SELECTOR ON HEAT. TEMPERATURE ON COOL AND BLOWER ON HIGH. CONNECT A VACUUM HOSE FROM MANIFOLD VACUUM TO THE VOTM WITH RADIATOR COOLING FAN RUNNING. ADJUST TO 1200 RPM BY TURNING SCREW ON TOP ON VOTM (1100 RPM FOR VEHICLE WITH LESS THAN 160 KM). RESTORE VOTM VACUUM CONNECTIONS.

SEE SHOP MANUAL FOR IDLE MIXTURE ADJUSTMENT INFORMATION.

E4AE-9C485-AJR   1.6L   SPARK PLUG/BOUGIES AWSF-34   GAP/ÉLECTRODES .042-.046

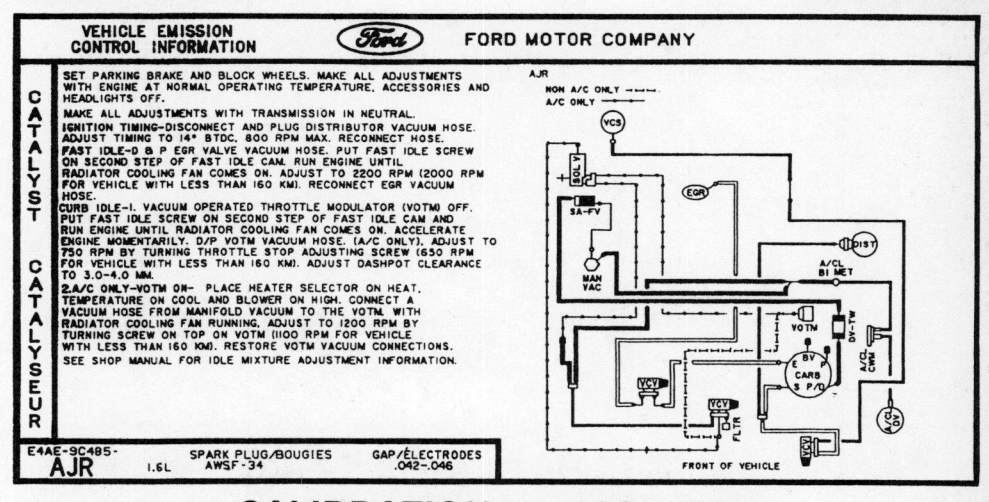

CALIBRATION: 4—03G—R10

MODEL YEAR: 1984   **ENGINE: 1.6L**

VEHICLE EMISSION CONTROL INFORMATION — FORD MOTOR COMPANY

CATALYST / CATALYSEUR

SET PARKING BRAKE AND BLOCK WHEELS. MAKE ALL ADJUSTMENTS WITH ENGINE AT NORMAL OPERATING TEMPERATURE, ACCESSORIES AND HEADLIGHTS OFF.

MAKE ALL ADJUSTMENTS WITH TRANSMISSION IN NEUTRAL.

IGNITION TIMING-DISCONNECT AND PLUG DISTRIBUTOR VACUUM HOSE. ADJUST TIMING TO 14° BTDC, 800 RPM MAX. RECONNECT HOSE.

FAST IDLE-D & P EGR VALVE VACUUM HOSE. PUT FAST IDLE SCREW ON SECOND STEP OF FAST IDLE CAM. RUN ENGINE UNTIL RADIATOR COOLING FAN COMES ON. ADJUST TO 2200 RPM (2200 RPM FOR VEHICLE WITH LESS THAN 160 KM). RECONNECT EGR VACUUM HOSE.

CURB IDLE-1. VACUUM OPERATED THROTTLE MODULATOR (VOTM) OFF. PUT FAST IDLE SCREW ON SECOND STEP OF FAST IDLE CAM AND RUN ENGINE UNTIL RADIATOR COOLING FAN COMES ON. ACCELERATE ENGINE MOMENTARILY. D/P VOTM VACUUM HOSE. (A/C ONLY), ADJUST TO 750 RPM BY TURNING THROTTLE STOP ADJUSTING SCREW (650 RPM FOR VEHICLE WITH LESS THAN 160 KM). ADJUST DASHPOT CLEARANCE TO 3.0 - 4.0.

2.A/C ONLY-VOTM ON- PLACE HEATER SELECTOR ON HEAT. TEMPERATURE ON COOL AND BLOWER ON HIGH. CONNECT A VACUUM HOSE FROM MANIFOLD VACUUM TO THE VOTM WITH RADIATOR COOLING FAN RUNNING. ADJUST TO 1200 RPM BY TURNING SCREW ON TOP ON VOTM (1100 RPM FOR VEHICLE WITH LESS THAN 160 KM). RESTORE VOTM VACUUM CONNECTIONS.

SEE SHOP MANUAL FOR IDLE MIXTURE ADJUSTMENT INFORMATION.

E4AE-9C485-AYN   1.6L   SPARK PLUG/BOUGIES AWSF-34   GAP/ÉLECTRODES .042-.046

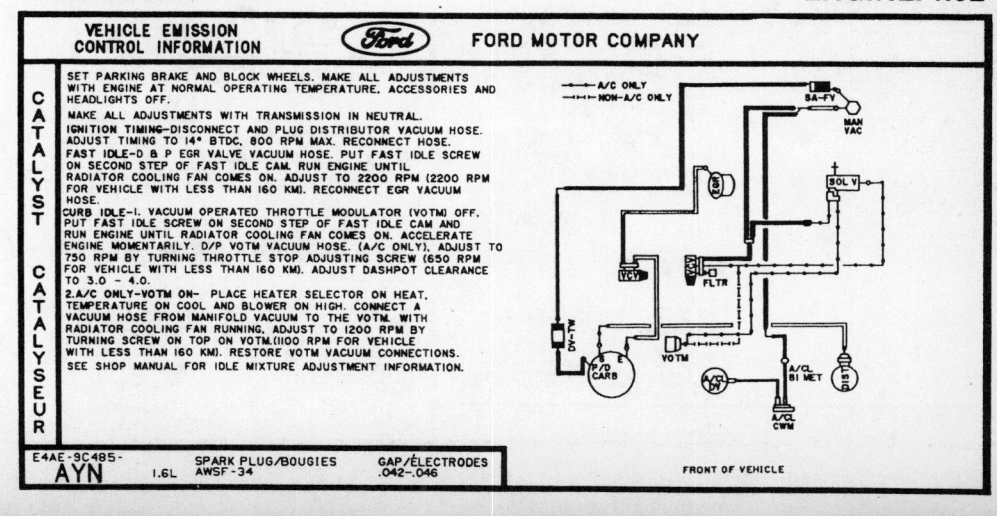

EMISSION CONTROLS

CALIBRATION: 4—03H—R00

MODEL YEAR: 1984   **ENGINE: 1.6L**

VEHICLE EMISSION CONTROL INFORMATION — Ford — FORD MOTOR COMPANY

CATALYST / CATALYSEUR

SET PARKING BRAKE AND BLOCK WHEELS. MAKE ALL ADJUSTMENTS WITH ENGINE AT NORMAL OPERATING TEMPERATURE, ACCESSORIES AND HEADLIGHTS OFF.

MAKE ALL ADJUSTMENTS WITH TRANSMISSION IN NEUTRAL.

IGNITION TIMING-DISCONNECT AND PLUG DISTRIBUTOR VACUUM HOSE. ADJUST TIMING TO 12° BTDC, 800 RPM MAX. RECONNECT HOSE.

FAST IDLE-D & P EGR VALVE VACUUM HOSE. PUT FAST IDLE SCREW ON SECOND STEP OF FAST IDLE CAM. RUN ENGINE UNTIL RADIATOR COOLING FAN COMES ON. ADJUST TO 2400 RPM (2200 RPM FOR VEHICLE WITH LESS THAN 160 KM). RECONNECT EGR VACUUM HOSE.

CURB IDLE-1. VACUUM OPERATED THROTTLE MODULATOR (VOTM) OFF. PUT FAST IDLE SCREW ON SECOND STEP OF FAST IDLE CAM AND RUN ENGINE UNTIL RADIATOR COOLING FAN COMES ON. ACCELERATE ENGINE MOMENTARILY. D/P VOTM VACUUM HOSE. (A/C ONLY). ADJUST TO 800 RPM BY TURNING THROTTLE STOP ADJUSTING SCREW (700 RPM FOR VEHICLE WITH LESS THAN 160 KM). ADJUST DASHPOT CLEARANCE TO 3.5-4.5 MM.

2. A/C ONLY-VOTM ON- PLACE HEATER SELECTOR ON HEAT. TEMPERATURE ON COOL AND BLOWER ON HIGH. CONNECT A VACUUM HOSE FROM MANIFOLD VACUUM TO THE VOTM. WITH RADIATOR COOLING FAN RUNNING, ADJUST TO 1200 RPM BY TURNING SCREW ON TOP ON VOTM.(1100 RPM FOR VEHICLE WITH LESS THAN 160 KM). RESTORE VOTM VACUUM CONNECTIONS. SEE SHOP MANUAL FOR IDLE MIXTURE ADJUSTMENT INFORMATION.

E4AE-9C485-AJS   1.6L   SPARK PLUG/BOUGIES AWSF-34   GAP/ÉLECTRODES .042-.046

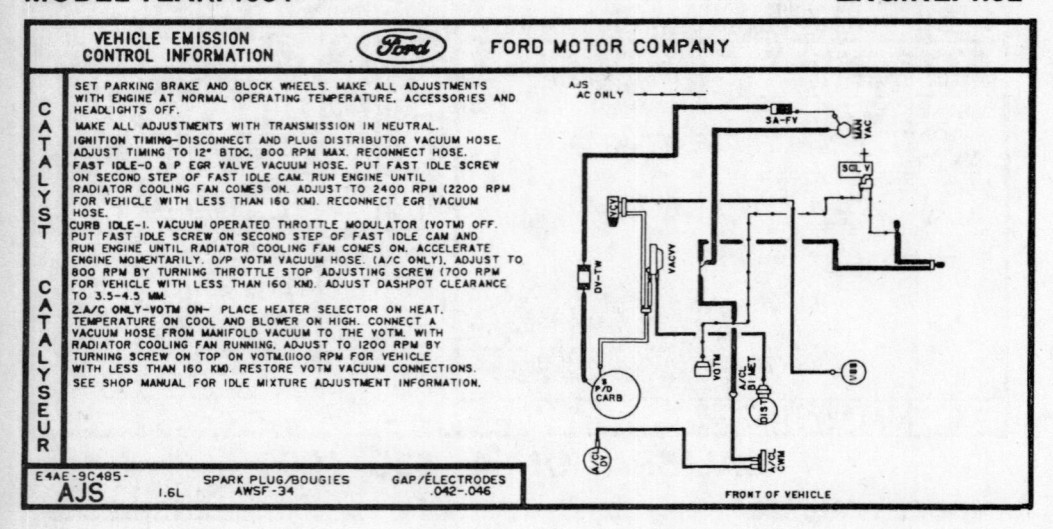

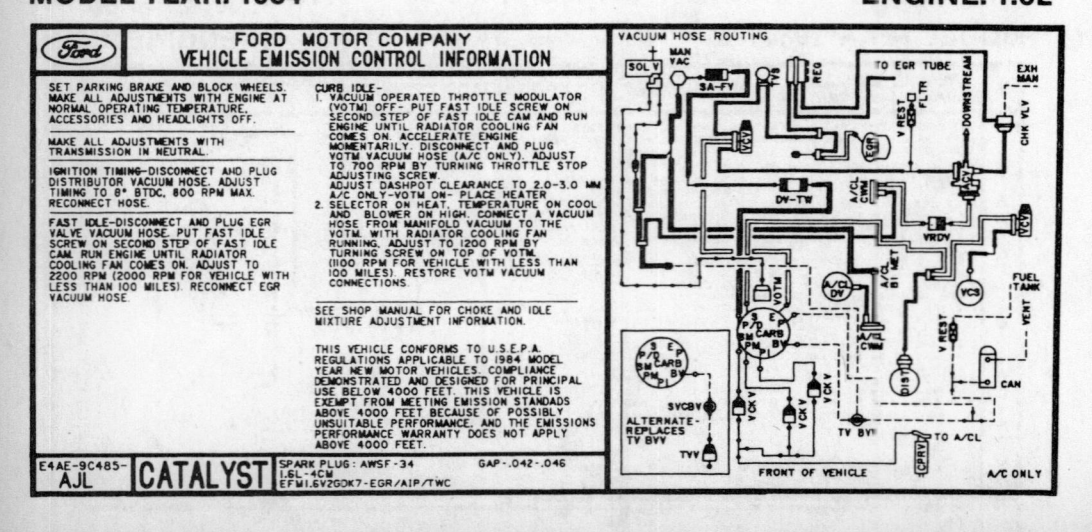

CALIBRATION: 4—03K—R00

MODEL YEAR: 1984   **ENGINE: 1.6L**

FORD MOTOR COMPANY — VEHICLE EMISSION CONTROL INFORMATION

SET PARKING BRAKE AND BLOCK WHEELS. MAKE ALL ADJUSTMENTS WITH ENGINE AT NORMAL OPERATING TEMPERATURE, ACCESSORIES AND HEADLIGHTS OFF.

MAKE ALL ADJUSTMENTS WITH TRANSMISSION IN NEUTRAL.

IGNITION TIMING-DISCONNECT AND PLUG DISTRIBUTOR VACUUM HOSE. ADJUST TIMING TO 8° BTDC, 800 RPM MAX. RECONNECT HOSE.

FAST IDLE-DISCONNECT AND PLUG EGR VALVE VACUUM HOSE. PUT FAST IDLE SCREW ON SECOND STEP OF FAST IDLE CAM. RUN ENGINE UNTIL RADIATOR COOLING FAN COMES ON. ADJUST TO 2200 RPM (2000 RPM FOR VEHICLE WITH LESS THAN 100 MILES). RECONNECT EGR VACUUM HOSE.

CURB IDLE-
1. VACUUM OPERATED THROTTLE MODULATOR (VOTM) OFF- PUT FAST IDLE SCREW ON SECOND STEP OF FAST IDLE CAM AND RUN ENGINE UNTIL RADIATOR COOLING FAN COMES ON. ACCELERATE ENGINE MOMENTARILY. DISCONNECT AND PLUG VOTM VACUUM HOSE (A/C ONLY). ADJUST TO 700 RPM BY TURNING THROTTLE STOP ADJUSTING SCREW. ADJUST DASHPOT CLEARANCE TO 2.0-3.0 MM. A/C ONLY-VOTM ON - PLACE HEATER
2. SELECTOR ON HEAT, TEMPERATURE ON COOL AND BLOWER ON HIGH. CONNECT A VACUUM HOSE FROM MANIFOLD VACUUM TO THE VOTM. WITH RADIATOR COOLING FAN RUNNING, ADJUST TO 1200 RPM BY TURNING SCREW ON TOP OF VOTM. (1100 RPM FOR VEHICLE WITH LESS THAN 100 MILES). RESTORE VOTM VACUUM CONNECTIONS.

SEE SHOP MANUAL FOR CHOKE AND IDLE MIXTURE ADJUSTMENT INFORMATION.

THIS VEHICLE CONFORMS TO U.S.E.P.A. REGULATIONS APPLICABLE TO 1984 MODEL YEAR NEW MOTOR VEHICLES. COMPLIANCE DEMONSTRATED AND DESIGNED FOR PRINCIPAL USE BELOW 4000 FEET. THIS VEHICLE IS EXEMPT FROM MEETING EMISSION STANDARDS ABOVE 4000 FEET BECAUSE OF POSSIBLY UNSUITABLE PERFORMANCE. AND THE EMISSIONS PERFORMANCE WARRANTY DOES NOT APPLY ABOVE 4000 FEET.

E4AE-9C485-AJL   CATALYST   SPARK PLUG: AWSF-34   1.6L-4CM   GAP-.042-.046   EFM1.6V2GOK7-EGR/AIP/TWC

EMISSION CONTROLS

CALIBRATION: 4—03K—R10

MODEL YEAR: 1984 **ENGINE: 1.6L**

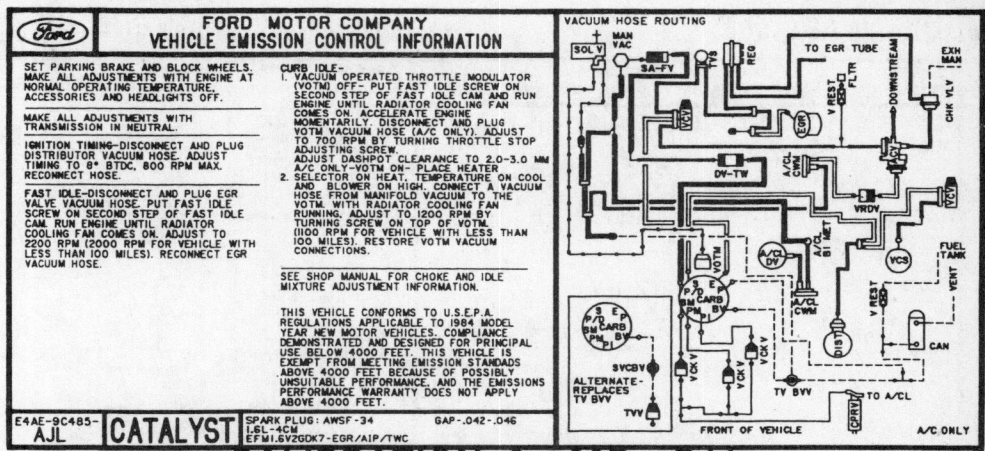

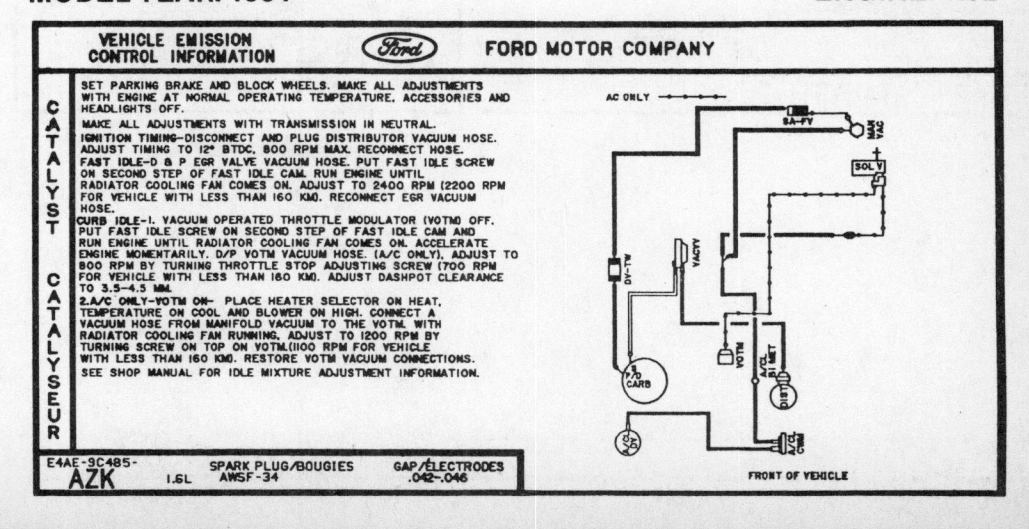

FORD MOTOR COMPANY — VEHICLE EMISSION CONTROL INFORMATION

SET PARKING BRAKE AND BLOCK WHEELS. MAKE ALL ADJUSTMENTS WITH ENGINE AT NORMAL OPERATING TEMPERATURE, ACCESSORIES AND HEADLIGHTS OFF.

MAKE ALL ADJUSTMENTS WITH TRANSMISSION IN NEUTRAL.

IGNITION TIMING–DISCONNECT AND PLUG DISTRIBUTOR VACUUM HOSE. ADJUST TIMING TO 8° BTDC, 800 RPM MAX. RECONNECT HOSE.

FAST IDLE–DISCONNECT AND PLUG EGR VALVE VACUUM HOSE. PUT FAST IDLE SCREW ON SECOND STEP OF FAST IDLE CAM. RUN ENGINE UNTIL RADIATOR COOLING FAN COMES ON. ADJUST TO 2200 RPM (2000 RPM FOR VEHICLE WITH LESS THAN 100 MILES). RECONNECT EGR VACUUM HOSE.

CURB IDLE–
1. VACUUM OPERATED THROTTLE MODULATOR (VOTM) OFF– PUT FAST IDLE SCREW ON SECOND STEP OF FAST IDLE CAM AND RUN ENGINE UNTIL RADIATOR COOLING FAN COMES ON. ACCELERATE ENGINE MOMENTARILY. DISCONNECT AND PLUG VOTM VACUUM HOSE (A/C ONLY). ADJUST TO 700 RPM BY TURNING THROTTLE STOP ADJUSTING SCREW. ADJUST DASHPOT CLEARANCE TO 2.0–3.0 MM (A/C ONLY–VOTM ON– PLACE HEATER
2. SELECTOR ON HEAT, TEMPERATURE ON COOL AND BLOWER ON HIGH. CONNECT A VACUUM HOSE FROM MANIFOLD VACUUM TO THE VOTM. WITH RADIATOR COOLING FAN RUNNING, ADJUST TO 1200 RPM BY TURNING SCREW ON TOP OF VOTM. (1100 RPM FOR VEHICLE WITH LESS THAN 100 MILES). RESTORE VOTM VACUUM CONNECTIONS.

SEE SHOP MANUAL FOR CHOKE AND IDLE MIXTURE ADJUSTMENT INFORMATION.

THIS VEHICLE CONFORMS TO U.S.E.P.A. REGULATIONS APPLICABLE TO 1984 MODEL YEAR NEW MOTOR VEHICLES. COMPLIANCE DEMONSTRATED AND DESIGNED FOR PRINCIPAL USE BELOW 4000 FEET. THIS VEHICLE IS EXEMPT FROM MEETING EMISSION STANDADS ABOVE 4000 FEET BECAUSE OF POSSIBLY UNSUITABLE PERFORMANCE, AND THE EMISSIONS PERFORMANCE WARRANTY DOES NOT APPLY ABOVE 4000 FEET.

E4AE-9C485-AJL   CATALYST   SPARK PLUG: AWSF-34   1.6L-4CM   EFMI.6V2GDK7-EGR/AIP/TWC   GAP-.042-.046

CALIBRATION: 2—03B—R11

MODEL YEAR: 1983 **ENGINE: 1.6L**

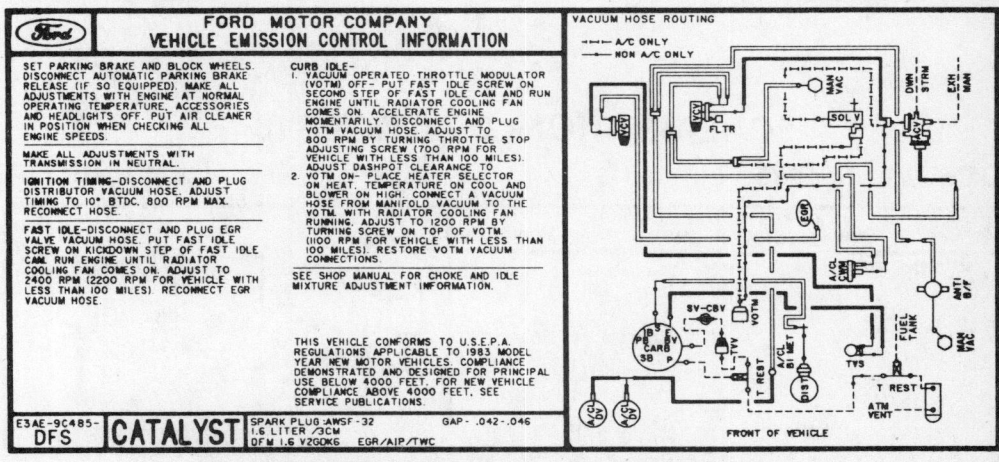

FORD MOTOR COMPANY — VEHICLE EMISSION CONTROL INFORMATION

SET PARKING BRAKE AND BLOCK WHEELS. DISCONNECT AUTOMATIC PARKING BRAKE RELEASE (IF SO EQUIPPED). MAKE ALL ADJUSTMENTS WITH ENGINE AT NORMAL OPERATING TEMPERATURE, ACCESSORIES AND HEADLIGHTS OFF. PUT AIR CLEANER IN POSITION WHEN CHECKING ALL ENGINE SPEEDS.

MAKE ALL ADJUSTMENTS WITH TRANSMISSION IN NEUTRAL.

IGNITION TIMING–DISCONNECT AND PLUG DISTRIBUTOR VACUUM HOSE. ADJUST TIMING TO 10° BTDC, 800 RPM MAX. RECONNECT HOSE.

FAST IDLE–DISCONNECT AND PLUG EGR VALVE VACUUM HOSE. PUT FAST IDLE SCREW ON KICKDOWN STEP OF FAST IDLE CAM. RUN ENGINE UNTIL RADIATOR COOLING FAN COMES ON. ADJUST TO 2400 RPM (2200 RPM FOR VEHICLE WITH LESS THAN 100 MILES). RECONNECT EGR VACUUM HOSE.

CURB IDLE–
1. VACUUM OPERATED THROTTLE MODULATOR (VOTM) OFF– PUT FAST IDLE SCREW ON SECOND STEP OF FAST IDLE CAM AND RUN ENGINE UNTIL RADIATOR COOLING FAN COMES ON. ACCELERATE ENGINE MOMENTARILY. DISCONNECT AND PLUG VOTM VACUUM HOSE. ADJUST TO 800 RPM BY TURNING THROTTLE STOP ADJUSTING SCREW. (700 RPM FOR VEHICLE WITH LESS THAN 100 MILES). ADJUST DASHPOT CLEARANCE TO
2. VOTM ON– PLACE HEATER SELECTOR ON HEAT, TEMPERATURE ON COOL AND BLOWER ON HIGH. CONNECT A VACUUM HOSE FROM MANIFOLD VACUUM TO THE VOTM. WITH RADIATOR COOLING FAN RUNNING, ADJUST TO 1200 RPM BY TURNING SCREW ON TOP OF VOTM. (1100 RPM FOR VEHICLE WITH LESS THAN 100 MILES). RESTORE VOTM VACUUM CONNECTIONS.

SEE SHOP MANUAL FOR CHOKE AND IDLE MIXTURE ADJUSTMENT INFORMATION.

THIS VEHICLE CONFORMS TO U.S.E.P.A. REGULATIONS APPLICABLE TO 1983 MODEL YEAR NEW MOTOR VEHICLES. COMPLIANCE DEMONSTRATED AND DESIGNED FOR PRINCIPAL USE BELOW 4000 FEET. FOR NEW VEHICLE COMPLIANCE ABOVE 4000 FEET, SEE SERVICE PUBLICATIONS.

E3AE-9C485-DFS   CATALYST   SPARK PLUG AWSF-32   1.6 LITER /3CM   OFM 1.6 V2GOKG   EGR/AIP/TWC   GAP-.042-.046

CALIBRATION: 4—03H—R00
(Alternate)

MODEL YEAR: 1984 **ENGINE: 1.6L**

VEHICLE EMISSION CONTROL INFORMATION — FORD MOTOR COMPANY

SET PARKING BRAKE AND BLOCK WHEELS. MAKE ALL ADJUSTMENTS WITH ENGINE AT NORMAL OPERATING TEMPERATURE, ACCESSORIES AND HEADLIGHTS OFF.

MAKE ALL ADJUSTMENTS WITH TRANSMISSION IN NEUTRAL.

IGNITION TIMING–DISCONNECT AND PLUG DISTRIBUTOR VACUUM HOSE. ADJUST TIMING TO 12° BTDC, 800 RPM MAX. RECONNECT HOSE.

FAST IDLE–D & P EGR VALVE VACUUM HOSE. PUT FAST IDLE SCREW ON SECOND STEP OF FAST IDLE CAM. RUN ENGINE UNTIL RADIATOR COOLING FAN COMES ON. ADJUST TO 2400 RPM (2200 RPM FOR VEHICLE WITH LESS THAN 160 KM). RECONNECT EGR VACUUM HOSE.

CURB IDLE–1. VACUUM OPERATED THROTTLE MODULATOR (VOTM) OFF. PUT FAST IDLE SCREW ON SECOND STEP OF FAST IDLE CAM AND RUN ENGINE UNTIL RADIATOR COOLING FAN COMES ON. ACCELERATE ENGINE MOMENTARILY. D/P VOTM VACUUM HOSE. (A/C ONLY). ADJUST TO 800 RPM BY TURNING THROTTLE STOP ADJUSTING SCREW (700 RPM FOR VEHICLE WITH LESS THAN 160 KM). ADJUST DASHPOT CLEARANCE TO 3.5–4.5 MM.

2. A/C ONLY–VOTM ON– PLACE HEATER SELECTOR ON HEAT, TEMPERATURE ON COOL AND BLOWER ON HIGH. CONNECT A VACUUM HOSE FROM MANIFOLD VACUUM TO THE VOTM. WITH RADIATOR COOLING FAN RUNNING, ADJUST TO 1200 RPM BY TURNING SCREW ON TOP ON VOTM.(1100 RPM FOR VEHICLE WITH LESS THAN 160 KM). RESTORE VOTM VACUUM CONNECTIONS.

SEE SHOP MANUAL FOR IDLE MIXTURE ADJUSTMENT INFORMATION.

CATALYST / CATALYSEUR

E4AE-9C485-AZK   1.6L   SPARK PLUG/BOUGIES AWSF-34   GAP/ELECTRODES .042-.046

EMISSION CONTROLS

CALIBRATION: 2—03B—R17

MODEL YEAR: 1983 **ENGINE: 1.6L**

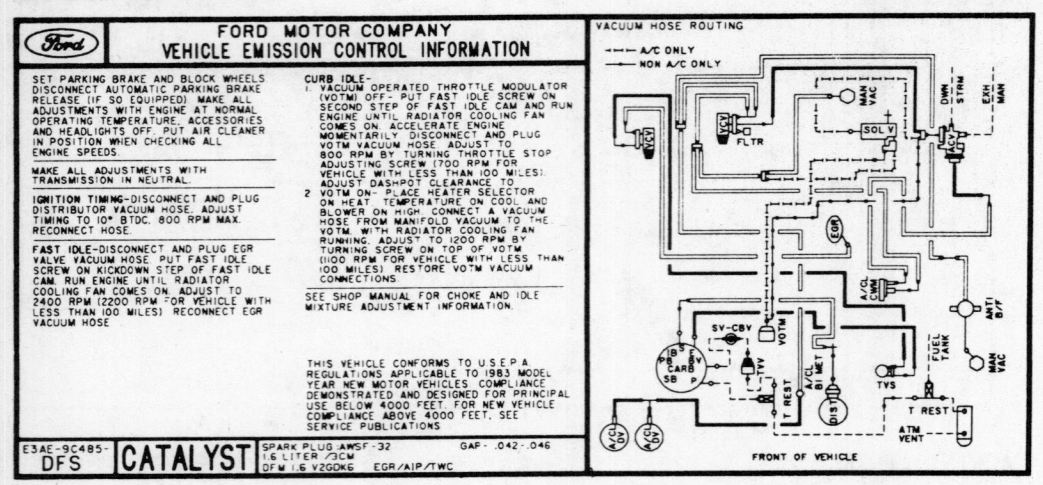

CALIBRATION: 2—03B—R18

MODEL YEAR: 1983 **ENGINE: 1.6L**

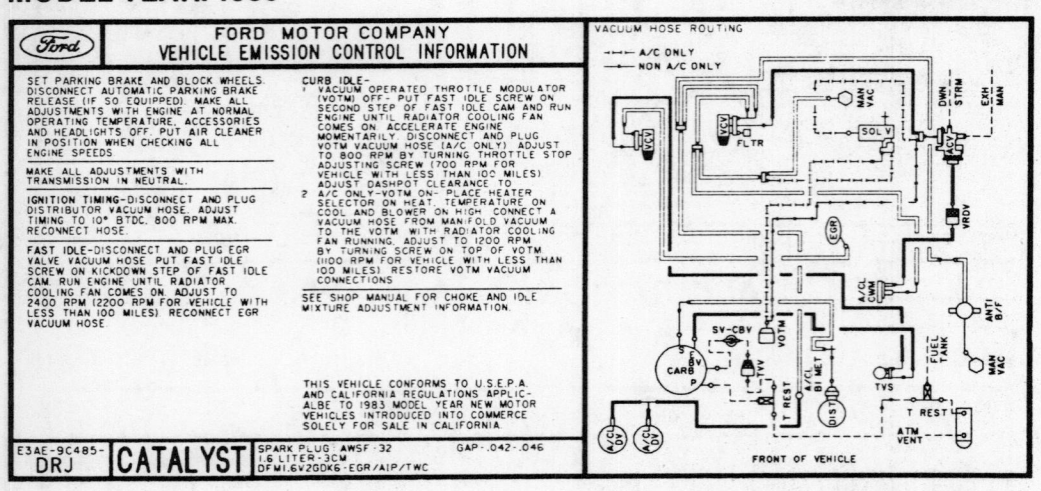

EMISSION CONTROLS 235

CALIBRATION: 2—03B—R20

MODEL YEAR: 1983   **ENGINE: 1.6L**

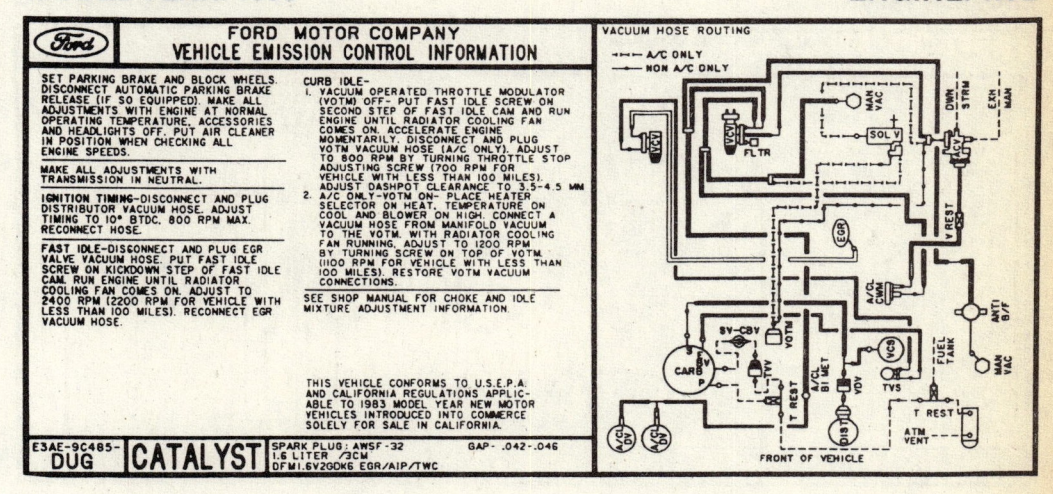

CALIBRATION: 2—03Y—R11

MODEL YEAR: 1983   **ENGINE: 1.6L**

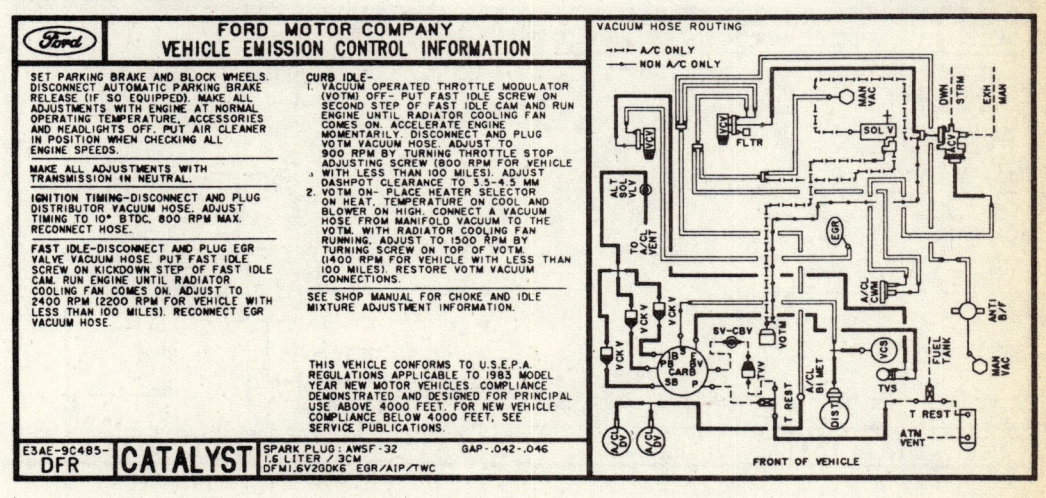

EMISSION CONTROLS

CALIBRATION: 3—03A—R01

MODEL YEAR: 1983 **ENGINE: 1.6L**

FORD MOTOR COMPANY
VEHICLE EMISSION CONTROL INFORMATION

THIS VEHICLE IS EQUIPPED WITH ELECTRONIC FUEL INJECTION. IDLE MIXTURE, COLD ENGINE IDLE SPEED AND COLD ENGINE FUEL ENRICHMENT NOT ADJUSTABLE.

SET PARKING BRAKE AND BLOCK WHEELS. MAKE ALL ADJUSTMENTS WITH ENGINE AT NORMAL OPERATING TEMPERATURE, ACCESSORIES AND HEADLIGHTS OFF. PUT AIR CLEANER IN PLACE WHEN CHECKING ENGINE SPEEDS.

IGNITION TIMING-
(1) DISCONNECT THE SINGLE WIRE WHITE CONNECTOR NEAR THE DISTRIBUTOR.
(2) RE-START PREVIOUSLY WARMED-UP ENGINE.
(3) ADJUST IGNITION TIMING TO 10° BTDC.
(4) TURN OFF ENGINE AND RESTORE ELECTRICAL CONNECTION.

THROTTLE PLATE ADJUSTMENT -
(1) DISCONNECT AND PLUG VACUUM HOSES AT "A". ELECTRICALLY DISCONNECT IDLE SPEED CONTROL (ISC).
(2) RUN ENGINE AT IDLE UNTIL ENGINE COOLING FAN COMES ON.
(3) RUN ENGINE AT 2000 RPM FOR 60 SECONDS MINIMUM.
(4) RETURN TO IDLE AND TURN THROTTLE PLATE ADJUSTING SCREW UNTIL IDLE SPEED IS 800 RPM WITH TRANS IN NEUTRAL (650 RPM FOR VEHICLES WITH LESS THAN 100 MILES) ADJUSTMENT MUST BE MADE WITHIN 120 SECONDS OF RETURN TO IDLE. TURN OFF ENGINE, RESTART AND REPEAT STEP 3 AND 4 IF 120 SECONDS ARE EXCEEDED.
(5) RESTORE VACUUM AND ELECTRICAL CONNECTIONS.

THIS VEHICLE CONFORMS TO U.S.E.P.A. REGULATIONS APPLICABLE TO 1983 MODEL YEAR NEW MOTOR VEHICLES. COMPLIANCE DEMONSTRATED AND DESIGNED FOR PRINCIPAL USE BELOW 4000 FEET. FOR NEW VEHICLE COMPLIANCE ABOVE 4000 FEET, SEE SERVICE PUBLICATIONS.

E3AE-9C485-DRR CATALYST SPARK PLUG: AWSF-24 GAP-.042-.046
1.6L - 3HM
DFM1.6V5HMF3-EGS/EGR/AIV/TWC/FI

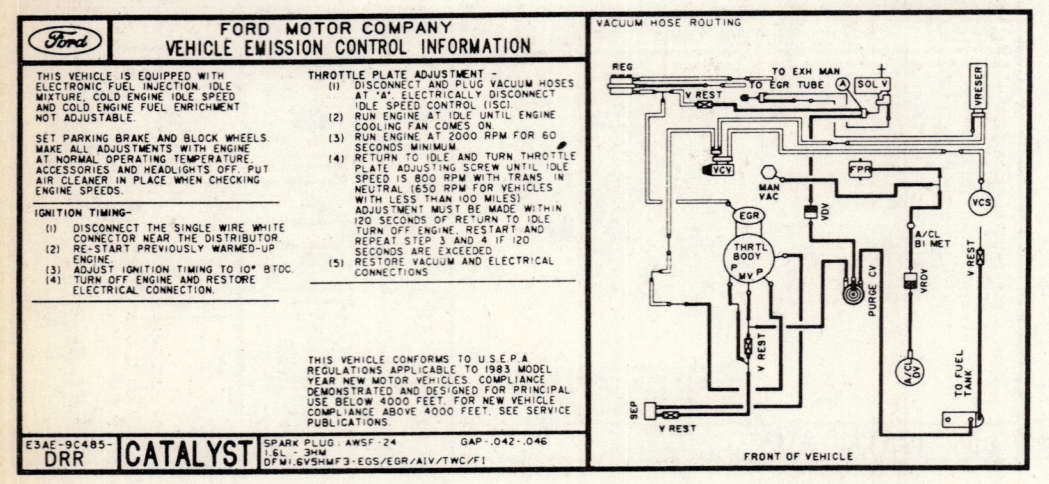

CALIBRATION: 3—03A—R05

MODEL YEAR: 1983 **ENGINE: 1.6L**

FORD MOTOR COMPANY
VEHICLE EMISSION CONTROL INFORMATION

THIS VEHICLE IS EQUIPPED WITH ELECTRONIC FUEL INJECTION. IDLE MIXTURE, COLD ENGINE IDLE SPEED AND COLD ENGINE FUEL ENRICHMENT NOT ADJUSTABLE.

SET PARKING BRAKE AND BLOCK WHEELS. MAKE ALL ADJUSTMENTS WITH ENGINE AT NORMAL OPERATING TEMPERATURE, ACCESSORIES AND HEADLIGHTS OFF. PUT AIR CLEANER IN PLACE WHEN CHECKING ENGINE SPEEDS.

IGNITION TIMING-
(1) DISCONNECT THE SINGLE WIRE WHITE CONNECTOR NEAR THE DISTRIBUTOR.
(2) RE-START PREVIOUSLY WARMED-UP ENGINE.
(3) ADJUST IGNITION TIMING TO 10° BTDC.
(4) TURN OFF ENGINE AND RESTORE ELECTRICAL CONNECTION.

THROTTLE PLATE ADJUSTMENT -
(1) DISCONNECT AND PLUG VACUUM HOSES AT "A". ELECTRICALLY DISCONNECT IDLE SPEED CONTROL (ISC).
(2) RUN ENGINE AT IDLE UNTIL ENGINE COOLING FAN COMES ON.
(3) RUN ENGINE AT 2000 RPM FOR 60 SECONDS MINIMUM.
(4) RETURN TO IDLE AND TURN THROTTLE PLATE ADJUSTING SCREW UNTIL IDLE SPEED IS 800 RPM WITH TRANS IN NEUTRAL (650 RPM FOR VEHICLES WITH LESS THAN 100 MILES). ADJUSTMENT MUST BE MADE WITHIN 120 SECONDS OF RETURN TO IDLE. TURN OFF ENGINE, RESTART AND REPEAT STEP 3 AND 4 IF 120 SECONDS ARE EXCEEDED.
(5) RESTORE VACUUM AND ELECTRICAL CONNECTIONS.

THIS VEHICLE CONFORMS TO U.S.E.P.A. AND CALIFORNIA REGULATIONS APPLICABLE TO 1983 MODEL YEAR NEW MOTOR VEHICLES INTRODUCED INTO COMMERCE SOLELY FOR SALE IN CALIFORNIA.

E3AE-9C485-DRS CATALYST SPARK PLUG: AWSF-24 GAP-.042-.046
1.6L - 3HM
DFM1.6V5HMF3-EGS/EGR/AIV/TWC/FI

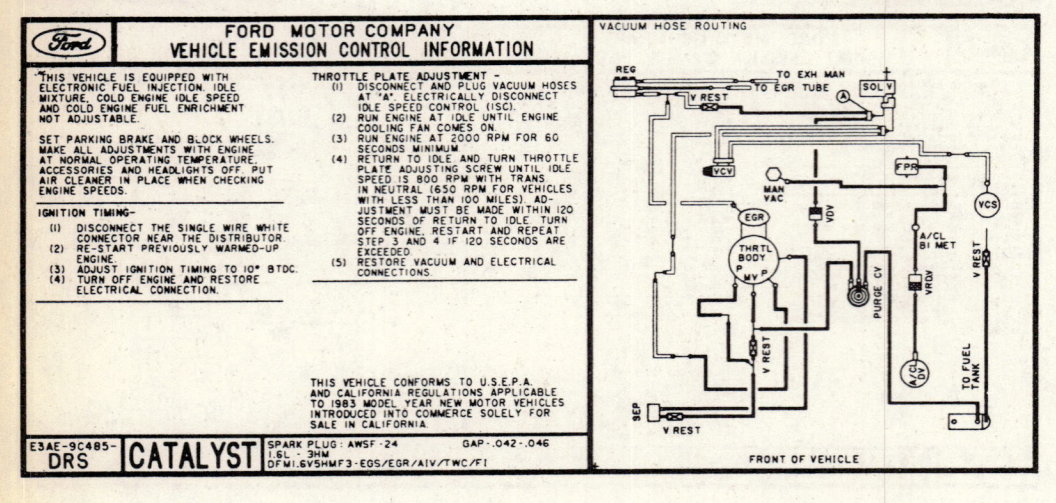

EMISSION CONTROLS

CALIBRATION: 3—03A—R12

MODEL YEAR: 1983 **ENGINE: 1.6L**

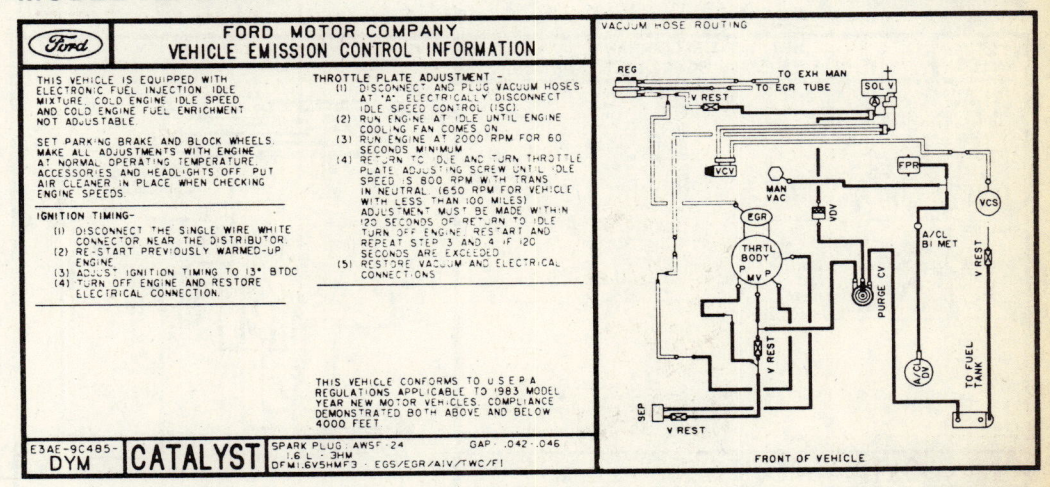

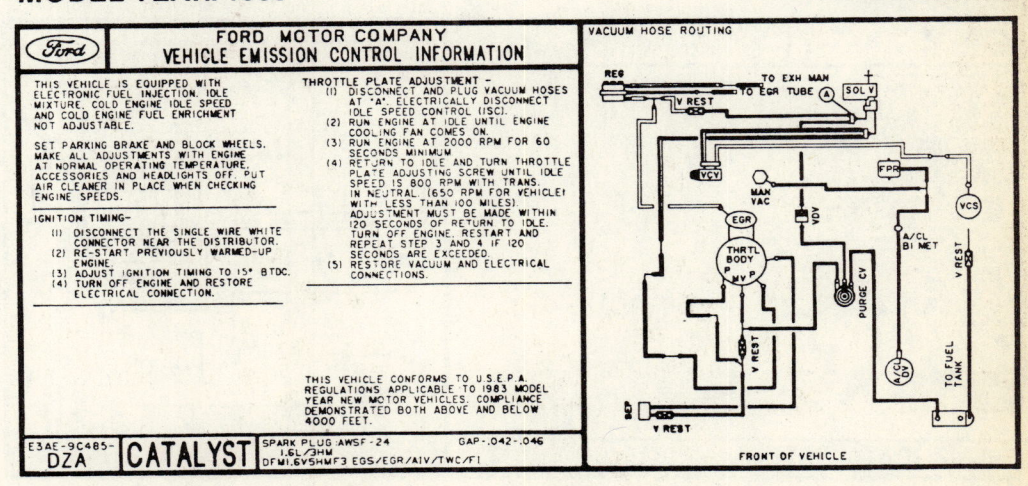

FORD MOTOR COMPANY
VEHICLE EMISSION CONTROL INFORMATION

THIS VEHICLE IS EQUIPPED WITH ELECTRONIC FUEL INJECTION. IDLE MIXTURE, COLD ENGINE IDLE SPEED AND COLD ENGINE FUEL ENRICHMENT NOT ADJUSTABLE.

SET PARKING BRAKE AND BLOCK WHEELS. MAKE ALL ADJUSTMENTS WITH ENGINE AT NORMAL OPERATING TEMPERATURE, ACCESSORIES AND HEADLIGHTS OFF. PUT AIR CLEANER IN PLACE WHEN CHECKING ENGINE SPEEDS.

IGNITION TIMING-
(1) DISCONNECT THE SINGLE WIRE WHITE CONNECTOR NEAR THE DISTRIBUTOR.
(2) RE-START PREVIOUSLY WARMED-UP ENGINE.
(3) ADJUST IGNITION TIMING TO 13° BTDC.
(4) TURN OFF ENGINE AND RESTORE ELECTRICAL CONNECTION.

THROTTLE PLATE ADJUSTMENT -
(1) DISCONNECT AND PLUG VACUUM HOSES AT "A". ELECTRICALLY DISCONNECT IDLE SPEED CONTROL (ISC).
(2) RUN ENGINE AT IDLE UNTIL ENGINE COOLING FAN COMES ON.
(3) RUN ENGINE AT 2000 RPM FOR 60 SECONDS MINIMUM.
(4) RETURN TO IDLE AND TURN THROTTLE PLATE ADJUSTING SCREW UNTIL IDLE SPEED IS 800 RPM WITH TRANS IN NEUTRAL. (650 RPM FOR VEHICLE WITH LESS THAN 100 MILES). ADJUSTMENT MUST BE MADE WITHIN 120 SECONDS OF RETURN TO IDLE. TURN OFF ENGINE, RESTART AND REPEAT STEP 3 AND 4 IF 120 SECONDS ARE EXCEEDED.
(5) RESTORE VACUUM AND ELECTRICAL CONNECTIONS.

THIS VEHICLE CONFORMS TO U.S.E.P.A. REGULATIONS APPLICABLE TO 1983 MODEL YEAR NEW MOTOR VEHICLES. COMPLIANCE DEMONSTRATED BOTH ABOVE AND BELOW 4000 FEET.

E3AE-9C485-DYM CATALYST SPARK PLUG: AWSF-24 GAP: .042-.046
1.6L - 3HM DFMI.6V5HMF3 EGS/EGR/AIV/TWC/FI

VACUUM HOSE ROUTING — FRONT OF VEHICLE

CALIBRATION: 3—03A—R13
(Models Before May '83)

MODEL YEAR: 1983 **ENGINE: 1.6L**

FORD MOTOR COMPANY
VEHICLE EMISSION CONTROL INFORMATION

THIS VEHICLE IS EQUIPPED WITH ELECTRONIC FUEL INJECTION. IDLE MIXTURE, COLD ENGINE IDLE SPEED AND COLD ENGINE FUEL ENRICHMENT NOT ADJUSTABLE.

SET PARKING BRAKE AND BLOCK WHEELS. MAKE ALL ADJUSTMENTS WITH ENGINE AT NORMAL OPERATING TEMPERATURE, ACCESSORIES AND HEADLIGHTS OFF. PUT AIR CLEANER IN PLACE WHEN CHECKING ENGINE SPEEDS.

IGNITION TIMING-
(1) DISCONNECT THE SINGLE WIRE WHITE CONNECTOR NEAR THE DISTRIBUTOR.
(2) RESTART PREVIOUSLY WARMED-UP ENGINE.
(3) ADJUST IGNITION TIMING TO 15° BTDC.
(4) TURN OFF ENGINE AND RESTORE ELECTRICAL CONNECTION.

THROTTLE PLATE ADJUSTMENT -
(1) DISCONNECT AND PLUG VACUUM HOSES AT "A". ELECTRICALLY DISCONNECT IDLE SPEED CONTROL (ISC).
(2) RUN ENGINE AT IDLE UNTIL ENGINE COOLING FAN COMES ON.
(3) RUN ENGINE AT 2000 RPM FOR 60 SECONDS MINIMUM.
(4) RETURN TO IDLE AND TURN THROTTLE PLATE ADJUSTING SCREW UNTIL IDLE SPEED IS 800 RPM WITH TRANS IN NEUTRAL. (650 RPM FOR VEHICLE WITH LESS THAN 100 MILES). ADJUSTMENT MUST BE MADE WITHIN 120 SECONDS OF RETURN TO IDLE. TURN OFF ENGINE, RESTART AND REPEAT STEP 3 AND 4 IF 120 SECONDS ARE EXCEEDED.
(5) RESTORE VACUUM AND ELECTRICAL CONNECTIONS.

THIS VEHICLE CONFORMS TO U.S.E.P.A. REGULATIONS APPLICABLE TO 1983 MODEL YEAR NEW MOTOR VEHICLES. COMPLIANCE DEMONSTRATED BOTH ABOVE AND BELOW 4000 FEET.

E3AE-9C485-DZA CATALYST SPARK PLUG: AWSF-24 GAP: .042-.046
1.6L-3HM DFMI.6V5HMF3 EGS/EGR/AIV/TWC/FI

VACUUM HOSE ROUTING — FRONT OF VEHICLE

EMISSION CONTROLS

CALIBRATION: 3—03A—R13
(Models After April '83)

MODEL YEAR: 1983 **ENGINE: 1.6L**

FORD MOTOR COMPANY
VEHICLE EMISSION CONTROL INFORMATION

THIS VEHICLE IS EQUIPPED WITH ELECTRONIC FUEL INJECTION. IDLE MIXTURE, COLD ENGINE IDLE SPEED AND COLD ENGINE FUEL ENRICHMENT NOT ADJUSTABLE.

SET PARKING BRAKE AND BLOCK WHEELS. MAKE ALL ADJUSTMENTS WITH ENGINE AT NORMAL OPERATING TEMPERATURE. ACCESSORIES AND HEADLIGHTS OFF. PUT AIR CLEANER IN PLACE WHEN CHECKING ENGINE SPEEDS.

IGNITION TIMING—
(1) DISCONNECT THE SINGLE WIRE WHITE CONNECTOR NEAR THE DISTRIBUTOR.
(2) RE-START PREVIOUSLY WARMED-UP ENGINE.
(3) ADJUST IGNITION TIMING TO 15° BTDC.
(4) TURN OFF ENGINE AND RESTORE ELECTRICAL CONNECTION.

THROTTLE PLATE ADJUSTMENT —
(1) DISCONNECT AND PLUG VACUUM HOSES AT "A". ELECTRICALLY DISCONNECT IDLE SPEED CONTROL (ISC).
(2) RUN ENGINE AT IDLE UNTIL ENGINE COOLING FAN COMES ON.
(3) RUN ENGINE AT 2000 RPM FOR 60 SECONDS MINIMUM.
(4) RETURN TO IDLE AND TURN THROTTLE PLATE ADJUSTING SCREW UNTIL IDLE SPEED IS 800 RPM WITH TRANS IN NEUTRAL. (650 RPM FOR VEHICLE WITH LESS THAN 100 MILES). ADJUSTMENT MUST BE MADE WITHIN 120 SECONDS OF RETURN TO IDLE. TURN OFF ENGINE. RESTART AND REPEAT STEP 3 AND 4 IF 120 SECONDS ARE EXCEEDED.
(5) RESTORE VACUUM AND ELECTRICAL CONNECTIONS.

THIS VEHICLE CONFORMS TO U.S.E.P.A. REGULATIONS APPLICABLE TO 1983 MODEL YEAR NEW MOTOR VEHICLES. COMPLIANCE DEMONSTRATED BOTH ABOVE AND BELOW 4000 FEET.

E3AE-9C485-EAJ   CATALYST   SPARK PLUG: AWSF-24 1.6 L-3M   GAP .042-.046
DFM 1.6V5HMF3-EGR/EGS/AIV/TWC/FI

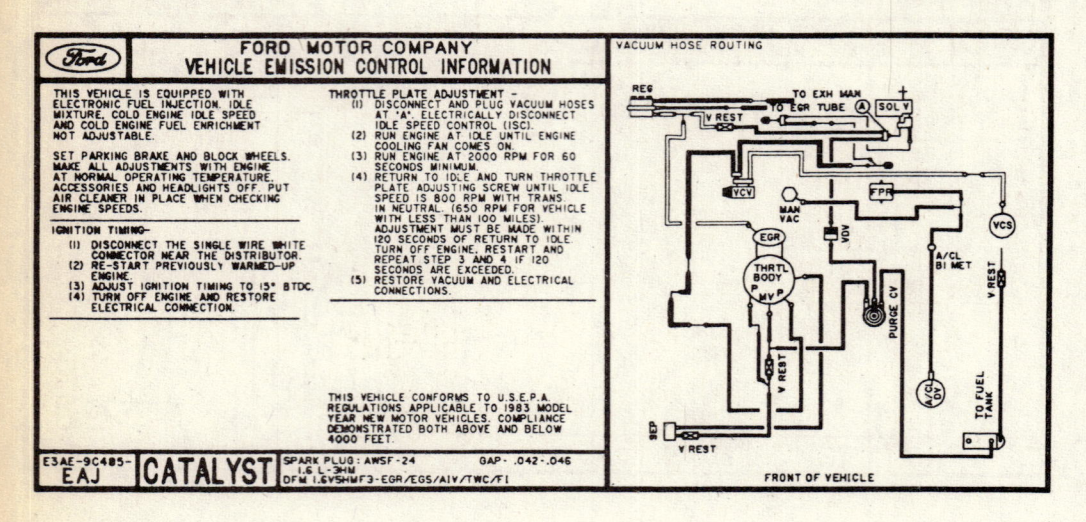

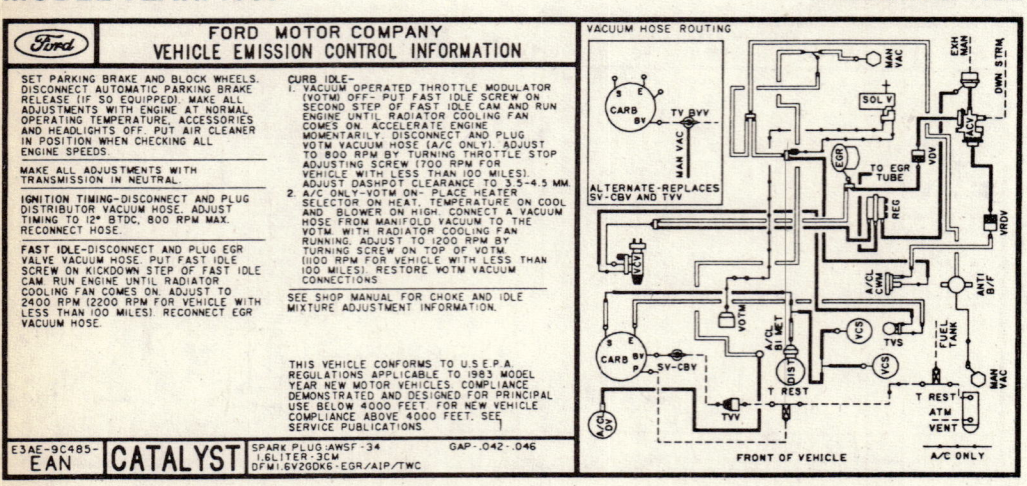

CALIBRATION: 3—03B—R10

MODEL YEAR: 1983 **ENGINE: 1.6L**

FORD MOTOR COMPANY
VEHICLE EMISSION CONTROL INFORMATION

SET PARKING BRAKE AND BLOCK WHEELS. DISCONNECT AUTOMATIC PARKING BRAKE RELEASE (IF SO EQUIPPED). MAKE ALL ADJUSTMENTS WITH ENGINE AT NORMAL OPERATING TEMPERATURE, ACCESSORIES AND HEADLIGHTS OFF. PUT AIR CLEANER IN POSITION WHEN CHECKING ALL ENGINE SPEEDS.

MAKE ALL ADJUSTMENTS WITH TRANSMISSION IN NEUTRAL.

IGNITION TIMING-DISCONNECT AND PLUG DISTRIBUTOR VACUUM HOSE. ADJUST TIMING TO 12° BTDC, 800 RPM MAX. RECONNECT HOSE.

FAST IDLE-DISCONNECT AND PLUG EGR VALVE VACUUM HOSE. PUT FAST IDLE SCREW ON KICKDOWN STEP OF FAST IDLE CAM. RUN ENGINE UNTIL RADIATOR COOLING FAN COMES ON. ADJUST TO 2400 RPM (2200 RPM FOR VEHICLE WITH LESS THAN 100 MILES). RECONNECT EGR VACUUM HOSE.

CURB IDLE-
1. VACUUM OPERATED THROTTLE MODULATOR (VOTM) OFF- PUT FAST IDLE SCREW ON SECOND STEP OF FAST IDLE CAM AND RUN ENGINE UNTIL RADIATOR COOLING FAN COMES ON. ACCELERATE ENGINE MOMENTARILY. DISCONNECT AND PLUG VOTM VACUUM HOSE (A/C ONLY). ADJUST TO 800 RPM BY TURNING THROTTLE STOP ADJUSTING SCREW (700 RPM FOR VEHICLE WITH LESS THAN 100 MILES). ADJUST DASHPOT CLEARANCE TO 3.5-4.5 MM.
2. A/C ONLY-VOTM ON- PLACE HEATER SELECTOR ON HEAT, TEMPERATURE ON COOL AND BLOWER ON HIGH. CONNECT A VACUUM HOSE FROM MANIFOLD VACUUM TO THE VOTM. WITH RADIATOR COOLING FAN RUNNING, ADJUST TO 1200 RPM BY TURNING SCREW ON TOP OF VOTM. (1100 RPM FOR VEHICLE WITH LESS THAN 100 MILES) RESTORE VOTM VACUUM CONNECTIONS.

SEE SHOP MANUAL FOR CHOKE AND IDLE MIXTURE ADJUSTMENT INFORMATION.

THIS VEHICLE CONFORMS TO U.S.E.P.A. REGULATIONS APPLICABLE TO 1983 MODEL YEAR NEW MOTOR VEHICLES. COMPLIANCE DEMONSTRATED AND DESIGNED FOR PRINCIPAL USE BELOW 4000 FEET. FOR NEW VEHICLE COMPLIANCE ABOVE 4000 FEET, SEE SERVICE PUBLICATIONS.

E3AE-9C485-EAN   CATALYST   SPARK PLUG: AWSF-34 1.6 LITER-3CM   GAP .042-.046
DFM 1.6V2GDK6-EGR/AIP/TWC

EMISSION CONTROLS

CALIBRATION: 3—03B—R11

MODEL YEAR: 1983   **ENGINE: 1.6L**

FORD MOTOR COMPANY — VEHICLE EMISSION CONTROL INFORMATION

SET PARKING BRAKE AND BLOCK WHEELS. DISCONNECT AUTOMATIC PARKING BRAKE RELEASE (IF SO EQUIPPED). MAKE ALL ADJUSTMENTS WITH ENGINE AT NORMAL OPERATING TEMPERATURE, ACCESSORIES AND HEADLIGHTS OFF. PUT AIR CLEANER IN POSITION WHEN CHECKING ALL ENGINE SPEEDS.

MAKE ALL ADJUSTMENTS WITH TRANSMISSION IN NEUTRAL.

IGNITION TIMING—DISCONNECT AND PLUG DISTRIBUTOR VACUUM HOSE. ADJUST TIMING TO 12° BTDC, 800 RPM MAX. RECONNECT HOSE.

FAST IDLE—DISCONNECT AND PLUG EGR VALVE VACUUM HOSE. PUT FAST IDLE SCREW ON KICKDOWN STEP OF FAST IDLE CAM. RUN ENGINE UNTIL RADIATOR COOLING FAN COMES ON. ADJUST TO 2400 RPM (2200 RPM FOR VEHICLE WITH LESS THAN 100 MILES). RECONNECT EGR VACUUM HOSE.

CURB IDLE-
1. VACUUM OPERATED THROTTLE MODULATOR (VOTM) OFF— PUT FAST IDLE SCREW ON SECOND STEP OF FAST IDLE CAM AND RUN ENGINE UNTIL RADIATOR COOLING FAN COMES ON. ACCELERATE ENGINE MOMENTARILY. DISCONNECT AND PLUG VOTM VACUUM HOSE (A/C ONLY). ADJUST TO 800 RPM BY TURNING THROTTLE STOP ADJUSTING SCREW (700 RPM FOR VEHICLE WITH LESS THAN 100 MILES). ADJUST DASHPOT CLEARANCE TO 3-4.5 MM.
2. A/C ONLY—VOTM ON— PLACE HEATER SELECTOR ON HEAT, TEMPERATURE ON COOL AND BLOWER ON HIGH. CONNECT A VACUUM HOSE FROM MANIFOLD VACUUM TO THE VOTM. WITH RADIATOR COOLING FAN RUNNING, ADJUST TO 1200 RPM BY TURNING SCREW ON TOP OF VOTM (1100 RPM FOR VEHICLE WITH LESS THAN 100 MILES). RESTORE VOTM VACUUM CONNECTIONS.

SEE SHOP MANUAL FOR CHOKE AND IDLE MIXTURE ADJUSTMENT INFORMATION.

THIS VEHICLE CONFORMS TO U.S.E.P.A. REGULATIONS APPLICABLE TO 1983 MODEL YEAR NEW MOTOR VEHICLES. COMPLIANCE DEMONSTRATED AND DESIGNED FOR PRINCIPAL USE BELOW 4000 FEET. FOR NEW VEHICLE COMPLIANCE ABOVE 4000 FEET, SEE SERVICE PUBLICATIONS.

E3AE-9C485-ECB   **CATALYST**   SPARK PLUG: AWSF-34   GAP: .042-.046
1.6 L / 3CM
DFMI.6V2GDK6 — EGR/AIP/TWC

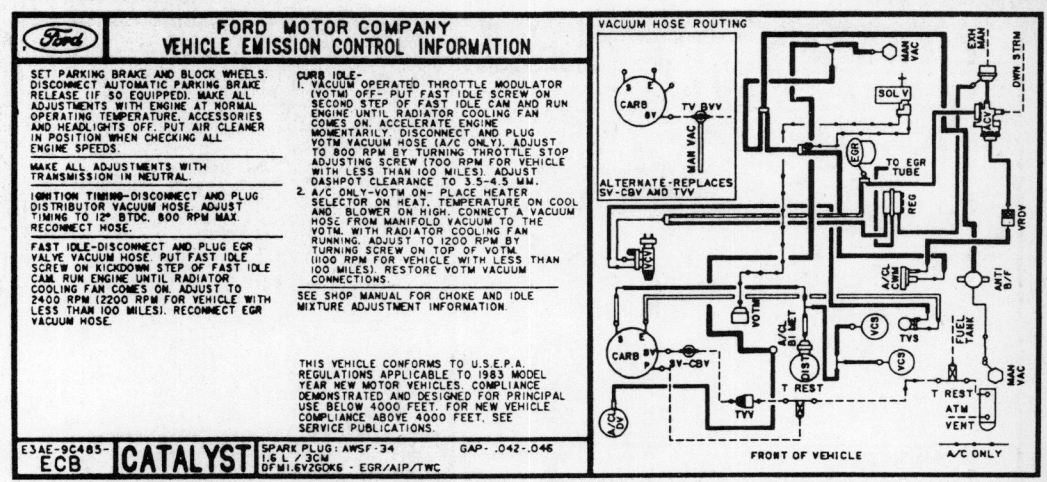

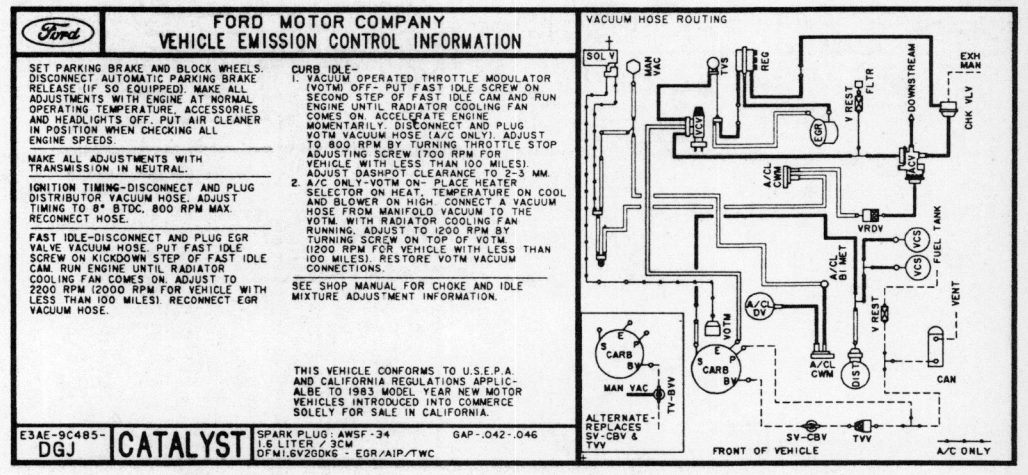

CALIBRATION: 3—03C—R00

MODEL YEAR: 1983   **ENGINE: 1.6L**

FORD MOTOR COMPANY — VEHICLE EMISSION CONTROL INFORMATION

SET PARKING BRAKE AND BLOCK WHEELS. DISCONNECT AUTOMATIC PARKING BRAKE RELEASE (IF SO EQUIPPED). MAKE ALL ADJUSTMENTS WITH ENGINE AT NORMAL OPERATING TEMPERATURE, ACCESSORIES AND HEADLIGHTS OFF. PUT AIR CLEANER IN POSITION WHEN CHECKING ALL ENGINE SPEEDS.

MAKE ALL ADJUSTMENTS WITH TRANSMISSION IN NEUTRAL.

IGNITION TIMING—DISCONNECT AND PLUG DISTRIBUTOR VACUUM HOSE. ADJUST TIMING TO 8° BTDC, 800 RPM MAX. RECONNECT HOSE.

FAST IDLE—DISCONNECT AND PLUG EGR VALVE VACUUM HOSE. PUT FAST IDLE SCREW ON KICKDOWN STEP OF FAST IDLE CAM. RUN ENGINE UNTIL RADIATOR COOLING FAN COMES ON. ADJUST TO 2200 RPM (2000 RPM FOR VEHICLE WITH LESS THAN 100 MILES). RECONNECT EGR VACUUM HOSE.

CURB IDLE-
1. VACUUM OPERATED THROTTLE MODULATOR (VOTM) OFF— PUT FAST IDLE SCREW ON SECOND STEP OF FAST IDLE CAM AND RUN ENGINE UNTIL RADIATOR COOLING FAN COMES ON. ACCELERATE ENGINE MOMENTARILY. DISCONNECT AND PLUG VOTM VACUUM HOSE (A/C ONLY). ADJUST TO 800 RPM BY TURNING THROTTLE STOP ADJUSTING SCREW (700 RPM FOR VEHICLE WITH LESS THAN 100 MILES). ADJUST DASHPOT CLEARANCE TO 2-3 MM.
2. A/C ONLY—VOTM ON— PLACE HEATER SELECTOR ON HEAT, TEMPERATURE ON COOL AND BLOWER ON HIGH. CONNECT A VACUUM HOSE FROM MANIFOLD VACUUM TO THE VOTM. WITH RADIATOR COOLING FAN RUNNING, ADJUST TO 1200 RPM BY TURNING SCREW ON TOP OF VOTM (1200 RPM FOR VEHICLE WITH LESS THAN 100 MILES). RESTORE VOTM VACUUM CONNECTIONS.

SEE SHOP MANUAL FOR CHOKE AND IDLE MIXTURE ADJUSTMENT INFORMATION.

THIS VEHICLE CONFORMS TO U.S.E.P.A. AND CALIFORNIA REGULATIONS APPLICABLE TO 1983 MODEL YEAR NEW MOTOR VEHICLES INTRODUCED INTO COMMERCE SOLELY FOR SALE IN CALIFORNIA.

E3AE-9C485-DGJ   **CATALYST**   SPARK PLUG: AWSF-34   GAP: .042-.046
1.6 LITER / 3CM
DFMI.6V2GDK6 — EGR/AIP/TWC

EMISSION CONTROLS

CALIBRATION: 3—03C—R09

MODEL YEAR: 1983 **ENGINE: 1.6L**

FORD MOTOR COMPANY — VEHICLE EMISSION CONTROL INFORMATION

SET PARKING BRAKE AND BLOCK WHEELS. DISCONNECT AUTOMATIC PARKING BRAKE RELEASE (IF SO EQUIPPED). MAKE ALL ADJUSTMENTS WITH ENGINE AT NORMAL OPERATING TEMPERATURE, ACCESSORIES AND HEADLIGHTS OFF. PUT AIR CLEANER IN POSITION WHEN CHECKING ALL ENGINE SPEEDS.

MAKE ALL ADJUSTMENTS WITH TRANSMISSION IN NEUTRAL.

IGNITION TIMING—DISCONNECT AND PLUG DISTRIBUTOR VACUUM HOSE. ADJUST TIMING TO 8° BTDC, 800 RPM MAX. RECONNECT HOSE.

FAST IDLE—DISCONNECT AND PLUG EGR VALVE VACUUM HOSE. PUT FAST IDLE SCREW ON KICKDOWN STEP OF FAST IDLE CAM. RUN ENGINE UNTIL RADIATOR COOLING FAN COMES ON. ADJUST TO 2200 RPM (2000 RPM FOR VEHICLE WITH LESS THAN 100 MILES). RECONNECT EGR VACUUM HOSE.

CURB IDLE—
1. VACUUM OPERATED THROTTLE MODULATOR (VOTM) OFF- PUT FAST IDLE SCREW ON SECOND STEP OF FAST IDLE CAM AND RUN ENGINE UNTIL RADIATOR COOLING FAN COMES ON. ACCELERATE ENGINE MOMENTARILY. DISCONNECT AND PLUG VOTM VACUUM HOSE (A/C ONLY). ADJUST TO 800 RPM BY TURNING THROTTLE STOP ADJUSTING SCREW (700 RPM FOR VEHICLE WITH LESS THAN 100 MILES). ADJUST DASHPOT CLEARANCE TO 2-3 MM.
2. A/C ONLY-VOTM ON- PLACE HEATER SELECTOR ON HEAT, TEMPERATURE ON COOL AND BLOWER ON HIGH. CONNECT A VACUUM HOSE FROM MANIFOLD VACUUM TO THE VOTM. WITH RADIATOR COOLING FAN RUNNING, ADJUST TO 1200 RPM BY TURNING SCREW ON TOP OF VOTM. (1100 RPM FOR VEHICLE WITH LESS THAN 100 MILES). RESTORE VOTM VACUUM CONNECTIONS.

SEE SHOP MANUAL FOR CHOKE AND IDLE MIXTURE ADJUSTMENT INFORMATION.

THIS VEHICLE CONFORMS TO U.S.E.P.A. AND CALIFORNIA REGULATIONS APPLICABLE TO 1983 MODEL YEAR NEW MOTOR VEHICLES INTRODUCED INTO COMMERCE SOLELY FOR SALE IN CALIFORNIA.

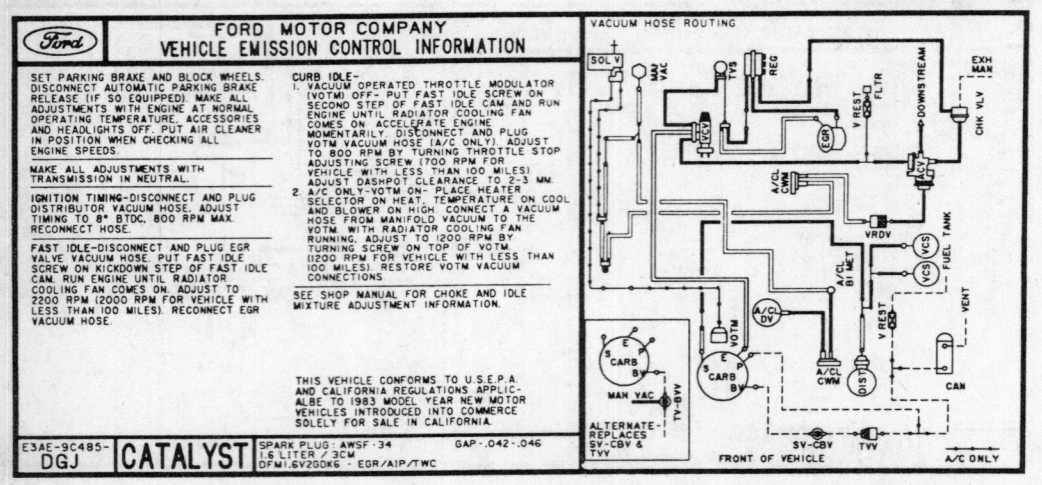

E3AE-9C485-DGJ CATALYST SPARK PLUG: AWSF-34 1.6 LITER/3CM DFMI.6V2GOK6 - EGR/AIP/TWC GAP .042-.046

CALIBRATION: 3—03C—R14

MODEL YEAR: 1983 **ENGINE: 1.6L**

FORD MOTOR COMPANY — VEHICLE EMISSION CONTROL INFORMATION

SET PARKING BRAKE AND BLOCK WHEELS. DISCONNECT AUTOMATIC PARKING BRAKE RELEASE (IF SO EQUIPPED). MAKE ALL ADJUSTMENTS WITH ENGINE AT NORMAL OPERATING TEMPERATURE, ACCESSORIES AND HEADLIGHTS OFF. PUT AIR CLEANER IN POSITION WHEN CHECKING ALL ENGINE SPEEDS.

MAKE ALL ADJUSTMENTS WITH TRANSMISSION IN NEUTRAL.

IGNITION TIMING—DISCONNECT AND PLUG DISTRIBUTOR VACUUM HOSE. ADJUST TIMING TO 8° BTDC, 800 RPM MAX. RECONNECT HOSE.

FAST IDLE—DISCONNECT AND PLUG EGR VALVE VACUUM HOSE. PUT FAST IDLE SCREW ON KICKDOWN STEP OF FAST IDLE CAM. RUN ENGINE UNTIL RADIATOR COOLING FAN COMES ON. ADJUST TO 2200 RPM (2000 RPM FOR VEHICLE WITH LESS THAN 100 MILES). RECONNECT EGR VACUUM HOSE.

CURB IDLE—
1. VACUUM OPERATED THROTTLE MODULATOR (VOTM) OFF- PUT FAST IDLE SCREW ON SECOND STEP OF FAST IDLE CAM AND RUN ENGINE UNTIL RADIATOR COOLING FAN COMES ON. ACCELERATE ENGINE MOMENTARILY. DISCONNECT AND PLUG VOTM VACUUM HOSE (A/C ONLY). ADJUST TO 800 RPM BY TURNING THROTTLE STOP ADJUSTING SCREW (700 RPM FOR VEHICLE WITH LESS THAN 100 MILES). ADJUST DASHPOT CLEARANCE TO 2.0-3.0 MM.
2. A/C ONLY-VOTM ON- PLACE HEATER SELECTOR ON HEAT, TEMPERATURE ON COOL AND BLOWER ON HIGH. CONNECT A VACUUM HOSE FROM MANIFOLD VACUUM TO THE VOTM. WITH RADIATOR COOLING FAN RUNNING, ADJUST TO 1200 RPM BY TURNING SCREW ON TOP OF VOTM. (1100 RPM FOR VEHICLE WITH LESS THAN 100 MILES). RESTORE VOTM VACUUM CONNECTIONS.

SEE SHOP MANUAL FOR CHOKE AND IDLE MIXTURE ADJUSTMENT INFORMATION.

THIS VEHICLE CONFORMS TO U.S.E.P.A. REGULATIONS APPLICABLE TO 1983 MODEL YEAR NEW MOTOR VEHICLES. COMPLIANCE DEMONSTRATED AND DESIGNED FOR PRINCIPAL USE BELOW 4000 FEET. FOR NEW VEHICLE COMPLIANCE ABOVE 4000 FEET, SEE SERVICE PUBLICATIONS.

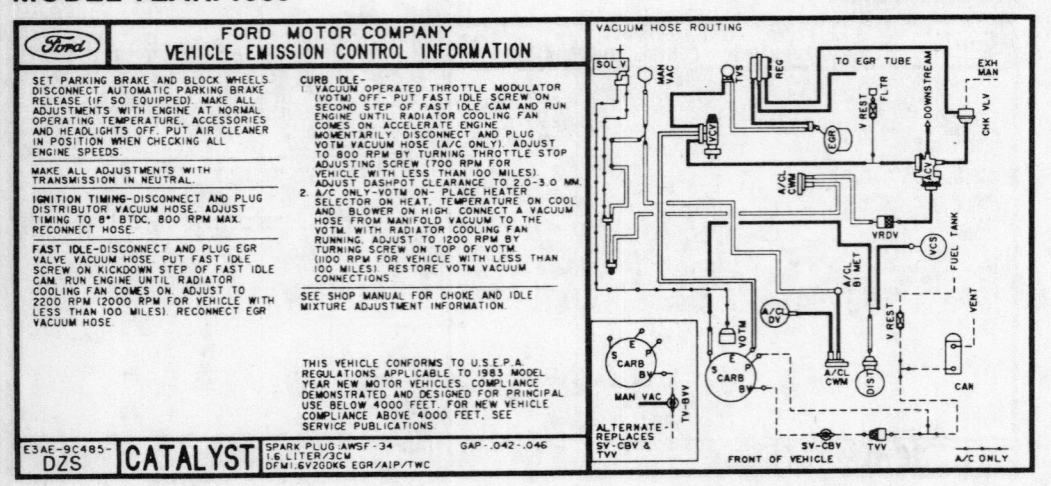

E3AE-9C485-DZS CATALYST SPARK PLUG: AWSF-34 1.6 LITER/3CM DFMI.6V2GOK6 EGR/AIP/TWC GAP .042-.046

EMISSION CONTROLS 241

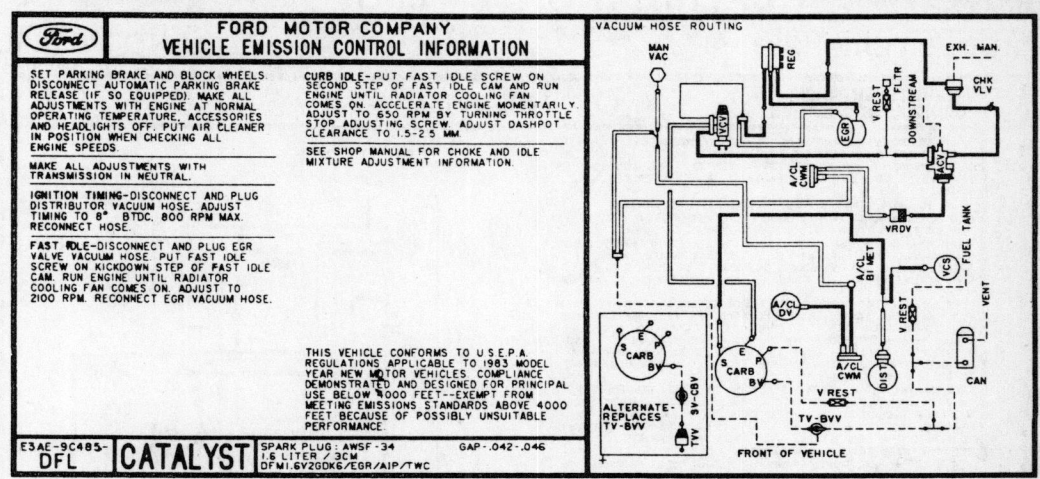

CALIBRATION: 3—03D—R01

MODEL YEAR: 1983   **ENGINE: 1.6L**

CALIBRATION: 3—03D—R01

MODEL YEAR: 1983   **ENGINE: 1.6L**

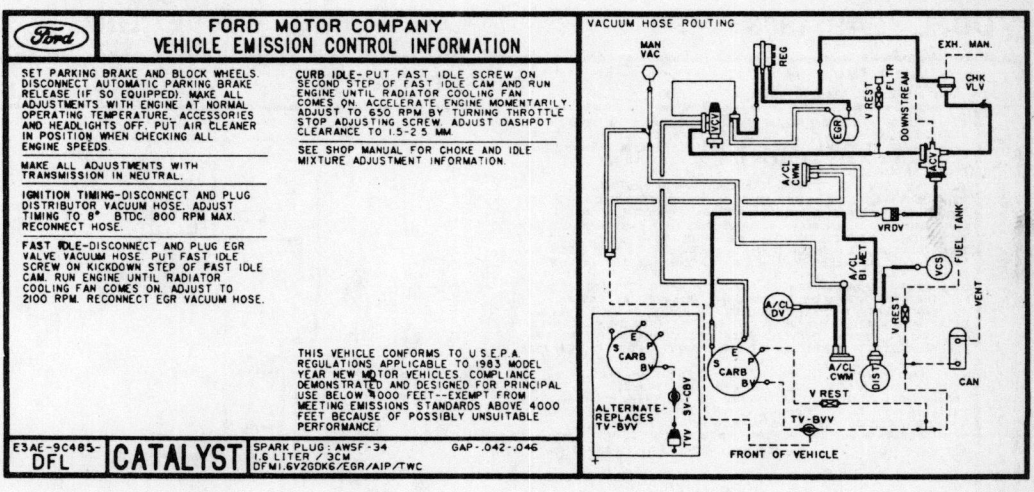

EMISSION CONTROLS

CALIBRATION: 3—03G—R11

MODEL YEAR: 1983 **ENGINE: 1.6L**

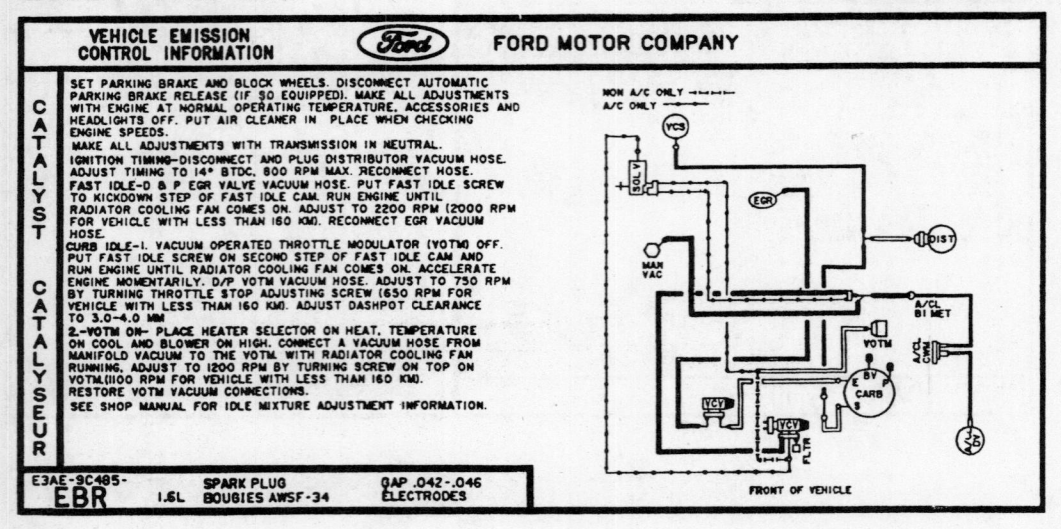

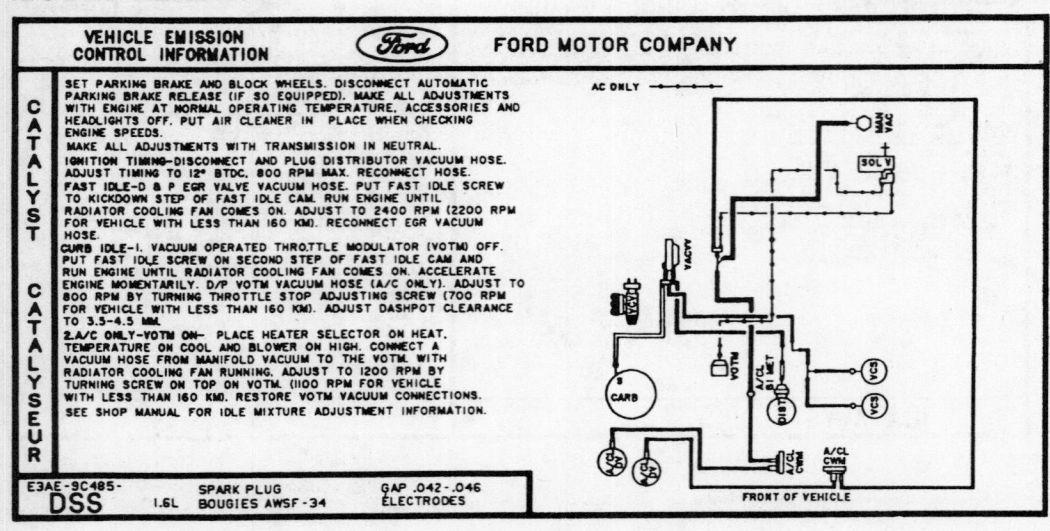

VEHICLE EMISSION CONTROL INFORMATION — Ford — FORD MOTOR COMPANY

CATALYST / CATALYSEUR

SET PARKING BRAKE AND BLOCK WHEELS. DISCONNECT AUTOMATIC PARKING BRAKE RELEASE (IF SO EQUIPPED). MAKE ALL ADJUSTMENTS WITH ENGINE AT NORMAL OPERATING TEMPERATURE, ACCESSORIES AND HEADLIGHTS OFF. PUT AIR CLEANER IN PLACE WHEN CHECKING ENGINE SPEEDS.
MAKE ALL ADJUSTMENTS WITH TRANSMISSION IN NEUTRAL.
IGNITION TIMING-DISCONNECT AND PLUG DISTRIBUTOR VACUUM HOSE. ADJUST TIMING TO 14° BTDC, 800 RPM MAX. RECONNECT HOSE.
FAST IDLE-D & P EGR VALVE VACUUM HOSE. PUT FAST IDLE SCREW TO KICKDOWN STEP OF FAST IDLE CAM. RUN ENGINE UNTIL RADIATOR COOLING FAN COMES ON. ADJUST TO 2200 RPM (2000 RPM FOR VEHICLE WITH LESS THAN 160 KM). RECONNECT EGR VACUUM HOSE.
CURB IDLE-1. VACUUM OPERATED THROTTLE MODULATOR (VOTM) OFF. PUT FAST IDLE SCREW ON SECOND STEP OF FAST IDLE CAM AND RUN ENGINE UNTIL RADIATOR COOLING FAN COMES ON. ACCELERATE ENGINE MOMENTARILY. D/P VOTM VACUUM HOSE. ADJUST TO 750 RPM BY TURNING THROTTLE STOP ADJUSTING SCREW (650 RPM FOR VEHICLE WITH LESS THAN 160 KM). ADJUST DASHPOT CLEARANCE TO 3.0-4.0 MM.
2-VOTM ON- PLACE HEATER SELECTOR ON HEAT, TEMPERATURE ON COOL AND BLOWER ON HIGH. CONNECT A VACUUM HOSE FROM MANIFOLD VACUUM TO THE VOTM WITH RADIATOR COOLING FAN RUNNING, ADJUST TO 1200 RPM BY TURNING SCREW ON TOP ON VOTM.(1100 RPM FOR VEHICLE WITH LESS THAN 160 KM).
RESTORE VOTM VACUUM CONNECTIONS.
SEE SHOP MANUAL FOR IDLE MIXTURE ADJUSTMENT INFORMATION.

E3AE-9C485-**EBR**   SPARK PLUG 1.6L BOUGIES AWSF-34   GAP .042-.046 ELECTRODES

CALIBRATION: 3—03H—R01

MODEL YEAR: 1983 **ENGINE: 1.6L**

VEHICLE EMISSION CONTROL INFORMATION — Ford — FORD MOTOR COMPANY

CATALYST / CATALYSEUR

SET PARKING BRAKE AND BLOCK WHEELS. DISCONNECT AUTOMATIC PARKING BRAKE RELEASE (IF SO EQUIPPED). MAKE ALL ADJUSTMENTS WITH ENGINE AT NORMAL OPERATING TEMPERATURE, ACCESSORIES AND HEADLIGHTS OFF. PUT AIR CLEANER IN PLACE WHEN CHECKING ENGINE SPEEDS.
MAKE ALL ADJUSTMENTS WITH TRANSMISSION IN NEUTRAL.
IGNITION TIMING-DISCONNECT AND PLUG DISTRIBUTOR VACUUM HOSE. ADJUST TIMING TO 12° BTDC, 800 RPM MAX. RECONNECT HOSE.
FAST IDLE-D & P EGR VALVE VACUUM HOSE. PUT FAST IDLE SCREW TO KICKDOWN STEP OF FAST IDLE CAM. RUN ENGINE UNTIL RADIATOR COOLING FAN COMES ON. ADJUST TO 2400 RPM (2200 RPM FOR VEHICLE WITH LESS THAN 160 KM). RECONNECT EGR VACUUM HOSE.
CURB IDLE-1. VACUUM OPERATED THROTTLE MODULATOR (VOTM) OFF. PUT FAST IDLE SCREW ON SECOND STEP OF FAST IDLE CAM AND RUN ENGINE UNTIL RADIATOR COOLING FAN COMES ON. ACCELERATE ENGINE MOMENTARILY. D/P VOTM VACUUM HOSE (A/C ONLY). ADJUST TO 800 RPM BY TURNING THROTTLE STOP ADJUSTING SCREW (700 RPM FOR VEHICLE WITH LESS THAN 160 KM). ADJUST DASHPOT CLEARANCE TO 3.5-4.5 MM.
2.A/C ONLY-VOTM ON- PLACE HEATER SELECTOR ON HEAT, TEMPERATURE ON COOL AND BLOWER ON HIGH. CONNECT A VACUUM HOSE FROM MANIFOLD VACUUM TO THE VOTM. WITH RADIATOR COOLING FAN RUNNING, ADJUST TO 1200 RPM BY TURNING SCREW ON TOP ON VOTM. (1100 RPM FOR VEHICLE WITH LESS THAN 160 KM). RESTORE VOTM VACUUM CONNECTIONS.
SEE SHOP MANUAL FOR IDLE MIXTURE ADJUSTMENT INFORMATION.

E3AE-9C485-**DSS**   SPARK PLUG 1.6L BOUGIES AWSF-34   GAP .042-.046 ELECTRODES

EMISSION CONTROLS 243

CALIBRATION: 3—03H—R02
(Models Before May '83)

MODEL YEAR: 1983 **ENGINE: 1.6L**

```
VEHICLE EMISSION                 Ford    FORD MOTOR COMPANY
CONTROL INFORMATION
```

CATALYST / CATALYSEUR

SET PARKING BRAKE AND BLOCK WHEELS. DISCONNECT AUTOMATIC PARKING BRAKE RELEASE (IF SO EQUIPPED). MAKE ALL ADJUSTMENTS WITH ENGINE AT NORMAL OPERATING TEMPERATURE. ACCESSORIES AND HEADLIGHTS OFF. PUT AIR CLEANER IN POSITION WHEN CHECKING ALL ENGINE SPEEDS.

IGNITION TIMING - DISCONNECT AND PLUG VACUUM ADVANCE HOSE AT DISTRIBUTOR. WITH TRANS IN PARK ADJUST TIMING TO 8° BTDC 800 RPM MAX. RECONNECT HOSE.

FAST IDLE - DISCONNECT AND PLUG VACUUM HOSES AT THE EGR VALVE AND AT THE PURGE CV. PUT FAST IDLE SCREW ON HIGHEST STEP OF FAST IDLE CAM AND ADJUST TO 2200 RPM WITH TRANS IN PARK. RECONNECT HOSES.

CURB IDLE - WITH A/C - TRANSMISSION IN DRIVE.
1. VOTM (VACUUM OPERATED THROTTLE MODULATOR) ON - DISCONNECT AND PLUG VOTM VACUUM HOSE. INSTALL SLAVE VACUUM HOSE FROM MANIFOLD VACUUM TO THE VOTM. ADJUST IDLE TO 650 RPM BY TURNING SADDLE BRACKET ADJUSTING SCREW. REMOVE SLAVE VACUUM HOSE.
2. VOTM OFF - ADJUST IDLE TO 550 RPM BY TURNING SOLENOID ADJUSTING SCREW.
3. THROTTLE SOLENOID POSITIONER (TSP) OFF - ELECTRICALLY DISCONNECT TSP AND ADJUST IDLE TO 450 RPM BY TURNING THROTTLE STOP SCREW. RECONNECT VOTM AND TSP.

CURB IDLE - NON A/C - TRANSMISSION IN DRIVE.
1. ADJUST IDLE TO 550 RPM BY TURNING SADDLE BRACKET ADJUSTING SCREW.
2. THROTTLE SOLENOID POSITIONER (TSP) OFF - ELECTRICALLY DISCONNECT TSP AND ADJUST IDLE TO 450 RPM BY TURNING THROTTLE STOP SCREW. RECONNECT TSP.

IF EQUIPPED WITH AUTO O.D. TRANS AND CURB IDLE ADJ IS GREATER THAN 50 RPM RE-ADJUST AUTO TRANS LINKAGE. SEE SHOP MANUAL FOR DETAILED INSTRUCTIONS.

CHOKE AND IDLE MIXTURE NOT ADJUSTABLE.

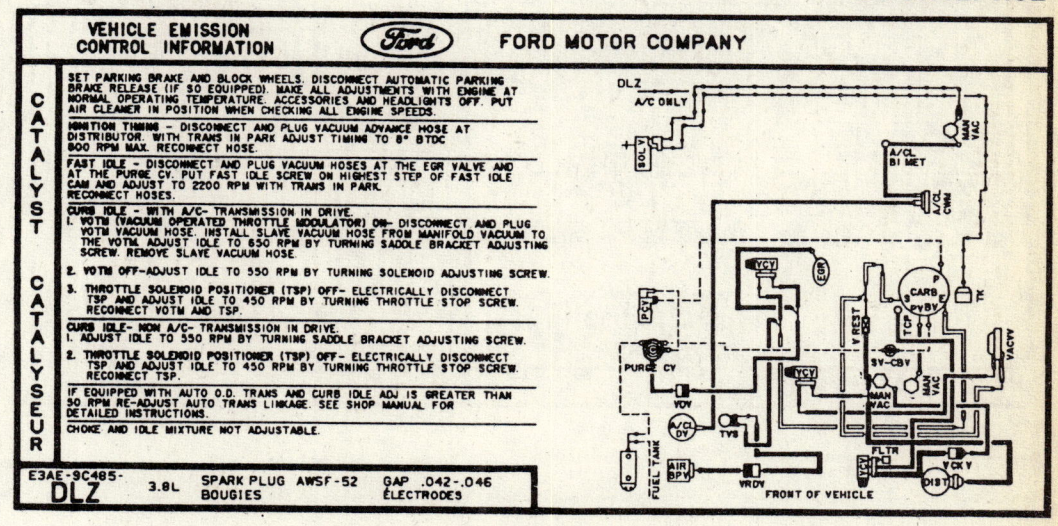

E3AE-9C485-**DLZ** 3.8L SPARK PLUG AWSF-52 GAP .042-.046
BOUGIES ÉLECTRODES

CALIBRATION: 3—03H—R02
(Models After April '83)

MODEL YEAR: 1983 **ENGINE: 1.6L**

```
VEHICLE EMISSION                 Ford    FORD MOTOR COMPANY
CONTROL INFORMATION
```

CATALYST / CATALYSEUR

SET PARKING BRAKE AND BLOCK WHEELS. DISCONNECT AUTOMATIC PARKING BRAKE RELEASE (IF SO EQUIPPED). MAKE ALL ADJUSTMENTS WITH ENGINE AT NORMAL OPERATING TEMPERATURE. ACCESSORIES AND HEADLIGHTS OFF. PUT AIR CLEANER IN PLACE WHEN CHECKING ENGINE SPEEDS.

MAKE ALL ADJUSTMENTS WITH TRANSMISSION IN NEUTRAL.

IGNITION TIMING-DISCONNECT AND PLUG DISTRIBUTOR VACUUM HOSE. ADJUST TIMING TO 12° BTDC, 800 RPM MAX. RECONNECT HOSE.

FAST IDLE-D & P EGR VALVE VACUUM HOSE. PUT FAST IDLE SCREW TO KICKDOWN STEP OF FAST IDLE CAM. RUN ENGINE UNTIL RADIATOR COOLING FAN COMES ON ADJUST TO 2400 RPM (2200 RPM FOR VEHICLE WITH LESS THAN 160 KM). RECONNECT EGR VACUUM HOSE.

CURB IDLE-1 VACUUM OPERATED THROTTLE MODULATOR (VOTM) OFF. PUT FAST IDLE SCREW ON SECOND STEP OF FAST IDLE CAM AND RUN ENGINE UNTIL RADIATOR COOLING FAN COMES ON. ACCELERATE ENGINE MOMENTARILY. D/P VOTM VACUUM HOSE (A/C ONLY). ADJUST TO 800 RPM BY TURNING THROTTLE STOP ADJUSTING SCREW (700 RPM FOR VEHICLE WITH LESS THAN 160 KM). ADJUST DASHPOT CLEARANCE TO 3.5-4.5 MM.

2. A/C ONLY-VOTM ON - PLACE HEATER SELECTOR ON HEAT, TEMPERATURE ON COOL AND BLOWER ON HIGH. CONNECT A VACUUM HOSE FROM MANIFOLD VACUUM TO THE VOTM. WITH RADIATOR COOLING FAN RUNNING, ADJUST TO 1200 RPM BY TURNING SCREW ON TOP ON VOTM (1100 RPM FOR VEHICLE WITH LESS THAN 160 KM). RESTORE VOTM VACUUM CONNECTIONS.

SEE SHOP MANUAL FOR IDLE MIXTURE ADJUSTMENT INFORMATION.

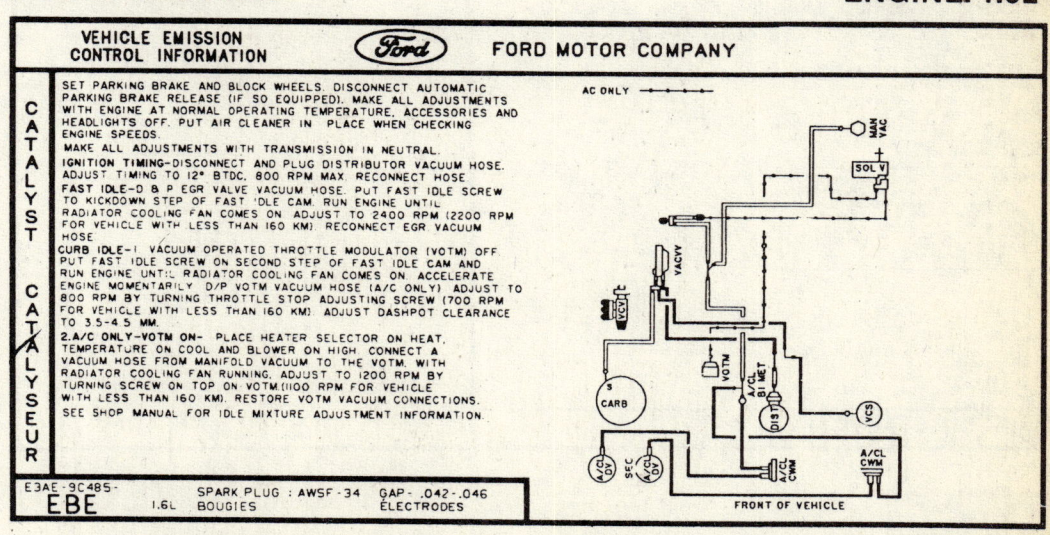

E3AE-9C485-**EBE** SPARK PLUG : AWSF-34 GAP .042-.046
1.6L BOUGIES ÉLECTRODES

EMISSION CONTROLS

CALIBRATION: 3—03Y—R10

MODEL YEAR: 1983　　　　　　　　　　　　　　**ENGINE: 1.6L**

FORD MOTOR COMPANY — VEHICLE EMISSION CONTROL INFORMATION

SET PARKING BRAKE AND BLOCK WHEELS. DISCONNECT AUTOMATIC PARKING BRAKE RELEASE (IF SO EQUIPPED). MAKE ALL ADJUSTMENTS WITH ENGINE AT NORMAL OPERATING TEMPERATURE, ACCESSORIES AND HEADLIGHTS OFF. PUT AIR CLEANER IN POSITION WHEN CHECKING ALL ENGINE SPEEDS.

MAKE ALL ADJUSTMENTS WITH TRANSMISSION IN NEUTRAL.

IGNITION TIMING—DISCONNECT AND PLUG DISTRIBUTOR VACUUM HOSE. ADJUST TIMING TO 12° BTDC. 800 RPM MAX. RECONNECT HOSE.

FAST IDLE—DISCONNECT AND PLUG EGR VALVE VACUUM HOSE. PUT FAST IDLE SCREW ON KICKDOWN STEP OF FAST IDLE CAM. RUN ENGINE UNTIL RADIATOR COOLING FAN COMES ON. ADJUST TO 2400 RPM (2200 RPM FOR VEHICLE WITH LESS THAN 100 MILES). RECONNECT EGR VACUUM HOSE.

CURB IDLE—
1. VACUUM OPERATED THROTTLE MODULATOR (VOTM) OFF - PUT FAST IDLE SCREW ON SECOND STEP OF FAST IDLE CAM AND RUN ENGINE UNTIL RADIATOR COOLING FAN COMES ON. ACCELERATE ENGINE MOMENTARILY. DISCONNECT AND PLUG VOTM VACUUM HOSE (A/C ONLY). ADJUST TO 900 RPM BY TURNING THROTTLE STOP ADJUSTING SCREW (800 RPM FOR VEHICLE WITH LESS THAN 100 MILES). ADJUST DASHPOT CLEARANCE TO
2. A/C ONLY—VOTM ON— PLACE HEATER SELECTOR ON HEAT, TEMPERATURE ON COOL AND BLOWER ON HIGH. CONNECT A VACUUM HOSE FROM MANIFOLD VACUUM TO THE VOTM WITH RADIATOR COOLING FAN RUNNING. ADJUST TO 1200 RPM BY TURNING SCREW ON TOP OF VOTM. (1100 RPM FOR VEHICLE WITH LESS THAN 100 MILES). RESTORE VOTM VACUUM CONNECTIONS.

SEE SHOP MANUAL FOR CHOKE AND IDLE MIXTURE ADJUSTMENT INFORMATION.

THIS VEHICLE CONFORMS TO U.S.E.P.A. REGULATIONS APPLICABLE TO 1983 MODEL YEAR NEW MOTOR VEHICLES. COMPLIANCE DEMONSTRATED AND DESIGNED FOR PRINCIPAL USE ABOVE 4000 FEET. FOR NEW VEHICLE COMPLIANCE BELOW 4000 FEET, SEE SERVICE PUBLICATIONS.

E3AE-9C485-EBA　CATALYST　SPARK PLUG AWSF-34　GAP .042-.046
1.6LITER/3CM
DFM1.6Y2GDK6 - EGR/AIP/TWC

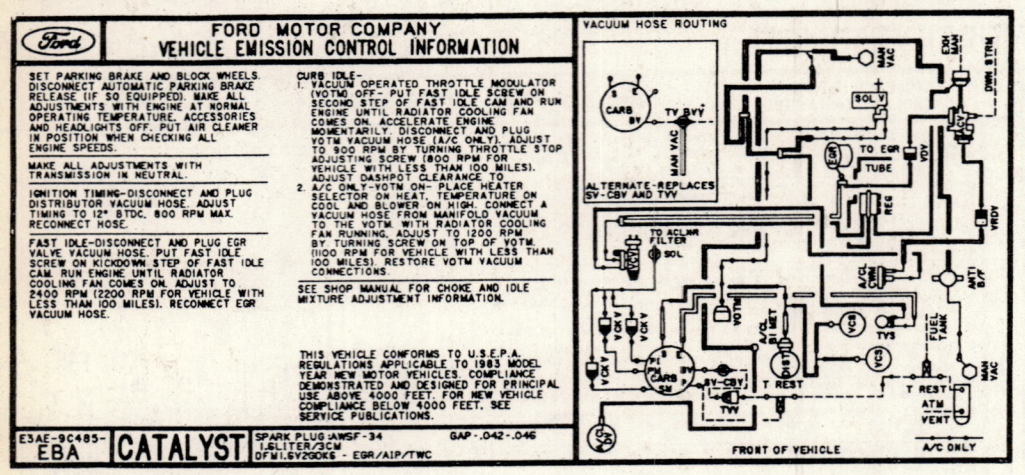

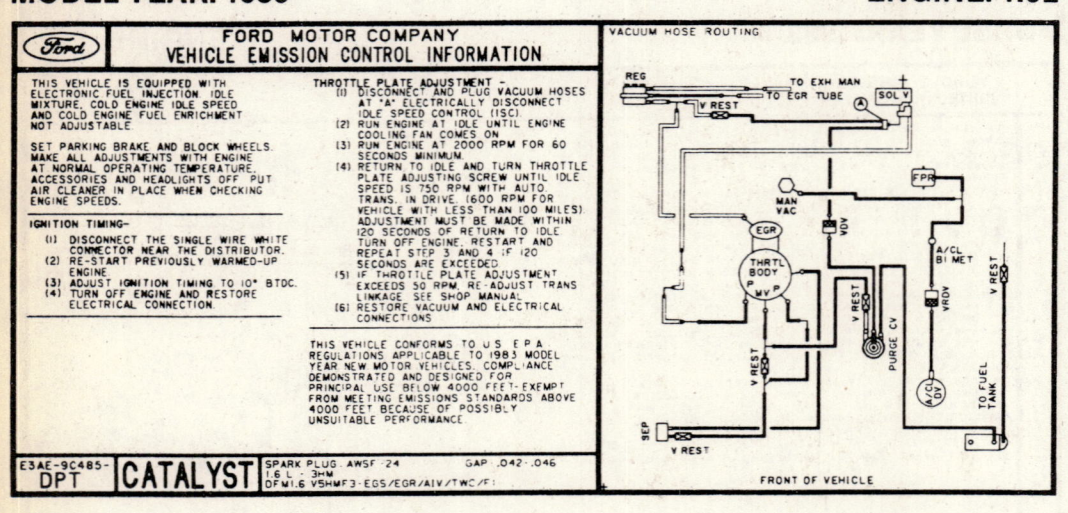

CALIBRATION: 3—04A—R01

MODEL YEAR: 1983　　　　　　　　　　　　　　**ENGINE: 1.6L**

FORD MOTOR COMPANY — VEHICLE EMISSION CONTROL INFORMATION

THIS VEHICLE IS EQUIPPED WITH ELECTRONIC FUEL INJECTION. IDLE MIXTURE, COLD ENGINE IDLE SPEED AND COLD ENGINE FUEL ENRICHMENT NOT ADJUSTABLE.

SET PARKING BRAKE AND BLOCK WHEELS. MAKE ALL ADJUSTMENTS WITH ENGINE AT NORMAL OPERATING TEMPERATURE, ACCESSORIES AND HEADLIGHTS OFF. PUT AIR CLEANER IN PLACE WHEN CHECKING ENGINE SPEEDS.

IGNITION TIMING
(1) DISCONNECT THE SINGLE WIRE WHITE CONNECTOR NEAR THE DISTRIBUTOR.
(2) RE-START PREVIOUSLY WARMED-UP ENGINE.
(3) ADJUST IGNITION TIMING TO 10° BTDC.
(4) TURN OFF ENGINE AND RESTORE ELECTRICAL CONNECTION.

THROTTLE PLATE ADJUSTMENT —
(1) DISCONNECT AND PLUG VACUUM HOSES AT "A" ELECTRICALLY DISCONNECT IDLE SPEED CONTROL (ISC).
(2) RUN ENGINE AT IDLE UNTIL ENGINE COOLING FAN COMES ON.
(3) RUN ENGINE AT 2000 RPM FOR 60 SECONDS MINIMUM.
(4) RETURN TO IDLE AND TURN THROTTLE PLATE ADJUSTING SCREW UNTIL IDLE SPEED IS 750 RPM WITH AUTO. TRANS. IN DRIVE. (600 RPM FOR VEHICLE WITH LESS THAN 100 MILES). ADJUSTMENT MUST BE MADE WITHIN 120 SECONDS OR RETURN TO IDLE. TURN OFF ENGINE. RESTART AND REPEAT STEP 3 AND 4 IF 120 SECONDS ARE EXCEEDED.
(5) IF THROTTLE PLATE ADJUSTMENT EXCEEDS 50 RPM, RE-ADJUST TRANS LINKAGE SEE SHOP MANUAL.
(6) RESTORE VACUUM AND ELECTRICAL CONNECTIONS.

THIS VEHICLE CONFORMS TO U.S E.P.A REGULATIONS APPLICABLE TO 1983 MODEL YEAR NEW MOTOR VEHICLES. COMPLIANCE DEMONSTRATED AND DESIGNED FOR PRINCIPAL USE BELOW 4000 FEET-EXEMPT FROM MEETING EMISSIONS STANDARDS ABOVE 4000 FEET BECAUSE OF POSSIBLY UNSUITABLE PERFORMANCE.

E3AE-9C485-DPT　CATALYST　SPARK PLUG AWSF-24　GAP .042-.046
1.6 L - 3HM
DFM1.6 V5HMF3-EGS/EGR/AIV/TWC/FI

EMISSION CONTROLS

CALIBRATION: 3—04A—R10

MODEL YEAR: 1983　　　　　　　　　　　　　　　　　**ENGINE: 1.6L**

FORD MOTOR COMPANY
VEHICLE EMISSION CONTROL INFORMATION

THIS VEHICLE IS EQUIPPED WITH ELECTRONIC FUEL INJECTION. IDLE MIXTURE, COLD ENGINE IDLE SPEED AND COLD ENGINE FUEL ENRICHMENT NOT ADJUSTABLE.

SET PARKING BRAKE AND BLOCK WHEELS. MAKE ALL ADJUSTMENTS WITH ENGINE AT NORMAL OPERATING TEMPERATURE, ACCESSORIES AND HEADLIGHTS OFF. PUT AIR CLEANER IN PLACE WHEN CHECKING ENGINE SPEEDS.

IGNITION TIMING— TURN OFF ENGINE
(1) DISCONNECT THE SINGLE WIRE BLACK CONNECTOR NEAR THE DISTRIBUTOR.
(2) RE-START PREVIOUSLY WARMED-UP ENGINE
(3) ADJUST IGNITION TIMING TO 15° BTDC.
(4) TURN OFF ENGINE AND RESTORE ELECTRICAL CONNECTION.

THROTTLE PLATE ADJUSTMENT —
(1) DISCONNECT AND PLUG VACUUM HOSES AT "A". ELECTRICALLY DISCONNECT IDLE SPEED CONTROL (ISC).
(2) RUN ENGINE AT IDLE UNTIL ENGINE COOLING FAN COMES ON.
(3) RUN ENGINE AT 2000 RPM FOR 60 SECONDS MINIMUM
(4) RETURN TO IDLE AND TURN THROTTLE PLATE ADJUSTING SCREW UNTIL IDLE SPEED IS 750 RPM WITH AUTO TRANS. IN DRIVE. (600 RPM FOR VEHICLE WITH LESS THAN 100 MILES) ADJUSTMENT MUST BE MADE WITHIN 120 SECONDS OF RETURN TO IDLE. TURN OFF ENGINE. RESTART AND REPEAT STEP 3 AND 4 IF 120 SECONDS ARE EXCEEDED
(5) IF THROTTLE PLATE ADJUSTMENT EXCEEDS 50 RPM RE-ADJUST TRANS LINKAGE. SEE SHOP MANUAL.
(6) RESTORE VACUUM AND ELECTRICAL CONNECTIONS

THIS VEHICLE CONFORMS TO U.S.E.P.A. REGULATIONS APPLICABLE TO 1983 MODEL YEAR NEW MOTOR VEHICLES. COMPLIANCE DEMONSTRATED AND DESIGNED FOR PRINCIPAL USE BELOW 4000 FEET--EXEMPT FROM MEETING EMISSIONS STANDARDS ABOVE 4000 FEET BECAUSE OF POSSIBLY UNSUITABLE PERFORMANCE

E3AE-9C485-ECJ　CATALYST　SPARK PLUG: AWSF 24　GAP .042 .046
1.6 L / 3HM
DFM1.6V5HMF3 EGS/EGR/AIV/TWC/FI

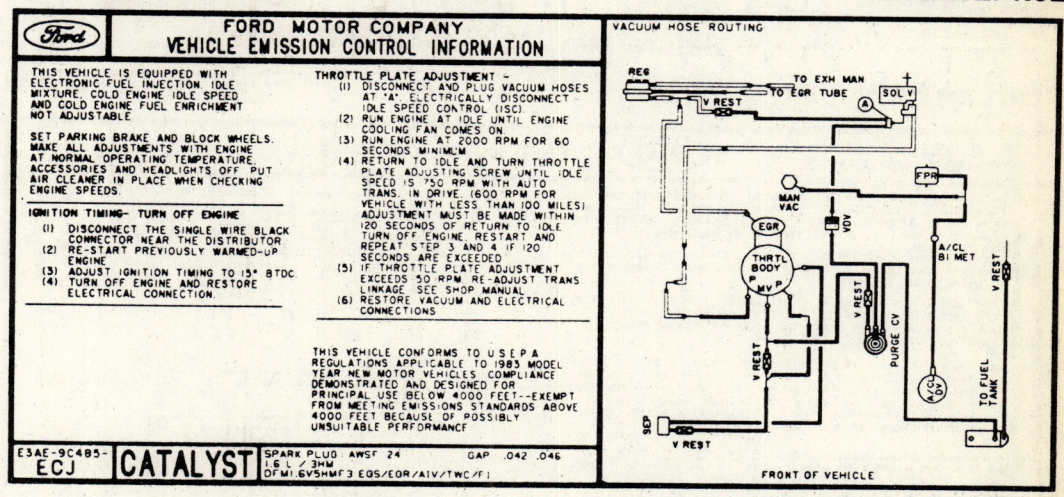

CALIBRATION: 3—04C—R00

MODEL YEAR: 1983　　　　　　　　　　　　　　　　　**ENGINE: 1.6L**

FORD MOTOR COMPANY
VEHICLE EMISSION CONTROL INFORMATION

SET PARKING BRAKE AND BLOCK WHEELS. DISCONNECT AUTOMATIC PARKING BRAKE RELEASE (IF SO EQUIPPED). MAKE ALL ADJUSTMENTS WITH ENGINE AT NORMAL OPERATING TEMPERATURE, ACCESSORIES AND HEADLIGHTS OFF. PUT AIR CLEANER IN POSITION WHEN CHECKING ALL ENGINE SPEEDS.

IGNITION TIMING- DISCONNECT AND PLUG DISTRIBUTOR VACUUM HOSE. WITH TRANS. IN DRIVE, ADJUST TIMING TO 10° BTDC. 800 RPM MAX. RECONNECT HOSE.

FAST IDLE- DISCONNECT AND PLUG EGR VALVE VACUUM HOSE. PUT FAST IDLE SCREW ON KICKDOWN STEP OF FAST IDLE CAM. RUN ENGINE UNTIL RADIATOR COOLING FAN COMES ON. ADJUST TO 2400 RPM WITH TRANS. IN NEUTRAL. RECONNECT EGR HOSE.

CURB IDLE- PUT FAST IDLE SCREW ON SECOND STEP OF FAST IDLE CAM. RUN ENGINE UNTIL RADIATOR COOLING FAN COMES ON. ACCELERATE ENGINE MOMENTARILY. PUT TRANSMISSION IN DRIVE.

WITHOUT IDLE SPEED CONTROL (ISC)- ADJUST TO 750 RPM BY TURNING THROTTLE STOP ADJUSTING SCREW. ADJUST DASHPOT CLEARANCE TO 3.5-4.5 MM.

WITH ISC- TURN ISC ADJUSTING SCREW UNTIL ISC PLUNGER IS CLEAR OF THE THROTTLE LEVER. ADJUST RPM TO 720 BY TURNING THROTTLE STOP ADJUSTING SCREW. THEN TURN ISC ADJUSTING SCREW UNTIL 750 RPM IS REACHED.

IF IDLE RPM ADJUSTMENT IS GREATER THAN 50 RPM, RE-ADJUST AUTO. TRANS. LINKAGE. SEE SHOP MANUAL.

SEE SHOP MANUAL FOR CHOKE AND IDLE MIXTURE ADJUSTMENT INFORMATION.

THIS VEHICLE CONFORMS TO U.S.E.P.A. REGULATIONS APPLICABLE TO 1983 MODEL YEAR NEW MOTOR VEHICLES. COMPLIANCE DEMONSTRATED AND DESIGNED FOR PRINCIPAL USE BELOW 4000 FEET--EXEMPT FROM MEETING EMISSIONS STANDARDS ABOVE 4000 FEET BECAUSE OF POSSIBLY UNSUITABLE PERFORMANCE.

E3AE-9C485-DJV　CATALYST　SPARK PLUG: AWSF-34　GAP .042-.046
1.6 LITER/3CM
DFM1.6V2G0K6-EGR/AIP/TWC

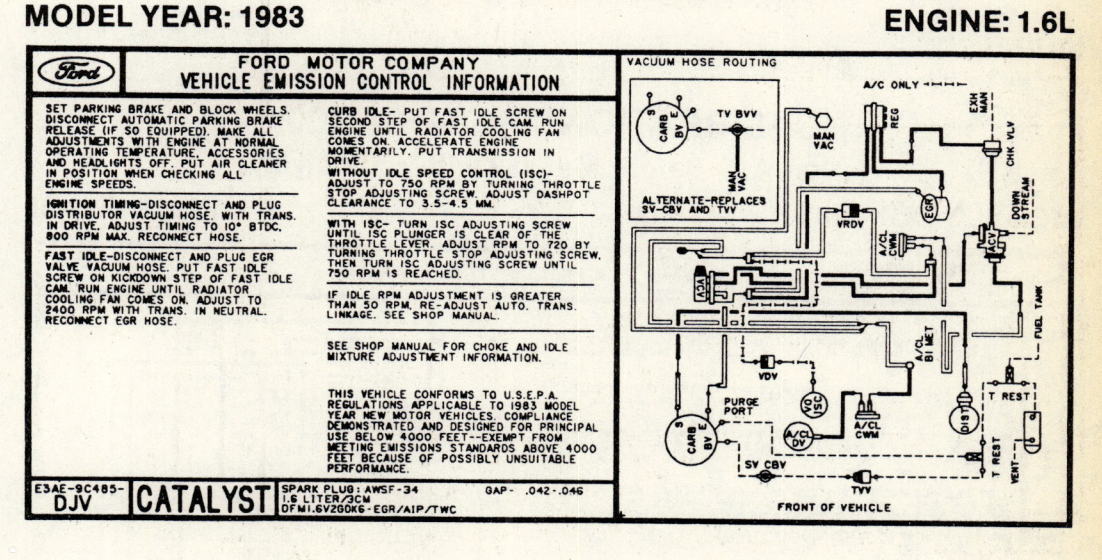

EMISSION CONTROLS

CALIBRATION: 3—04H—R00
(Non A/C Before May '83 Without a Catalyst)

MODEL YEAR: 1983 **ENGINE: 1.6L**

VEHICLE EMISSION CONTROL INFORMATION — Ford Motor Company

CATALYST / CATALYSEUR

SET PARKING BRAKE AND BLOCK WHEELS. DISCONNECT AUTOMATIC PARKING BRAKE RELEASE (IF SO EQUIPPED). MAKE ALL ADJUSTMENTS WITH ENGINE AT NORMAL OPERATING TEMPERATURE, ACCESSORIES AND HEADLIGHTS OFF. PUT AIR CLEANER IN PLACE WHEN CHECKING ENGINE SPEEDS.

IGNITION TIMING—DISCONNECT AND PLUG DISTRIBUTOR VACUUM HOSE. ADJUST TIMING TO 14° BTDC, 800 RPM MAX. WITH TRANSMISSION IN "D". RECONNECT HOSE.

FAST IDLE—D & P EGR VALVE VACUUM HOSE. PUT FAST IDLE SCREW TO KICKDOWN STEP OF FAST IDLE CAM. RUN ENGINE UNTIL RADIATOR COOLING FAN COMES ON. ADJUST TO 2400 RPM WITH TRANS. IN "N". RECONNECT EGR VACUUM HOSE.

CURB IDLE—1. VACUUM OPERATED THROTTLE MODULATOR (VOTM) OFF. PUT FAST IDLE SCREW ON SECOND STEP OF FAST IDLE CAM AND RUN ENGINE UNTIL RADIATOR COOLING FAN COMES ON. ACCELERATE ENGINE MOMENTARILY. D/P VOTM VACUUM HOSE. ADJUST TO 750 RPM BY TURNING THROTTLE STOP ADJUSTING SCREW, TRANS IN "D". ADJUST DASHPOT CLEARANCE TO 3.5-4.5 MM.

2. VOTM ON— PLACE HEATER SELECTOR ON HEAT. TEMPERATURE ON COOL AND BLOWER ON HIGH. CONNECT A VACUUM HOSE FROM MANIFOLD VACUUM TO THE VOTM WITH RADIATOR COOLING FAN RUNNING. ADJUST TO 1300 RPM BY TURNING SCREW ON TOP ON VOTM. TRANS. IN "D". RESTORE VOTM VACUUM CONNECTIONS.

SEE SHOP MANUAL FOR IDLE MIXTURE ADJUSTMENT INFORMATION.

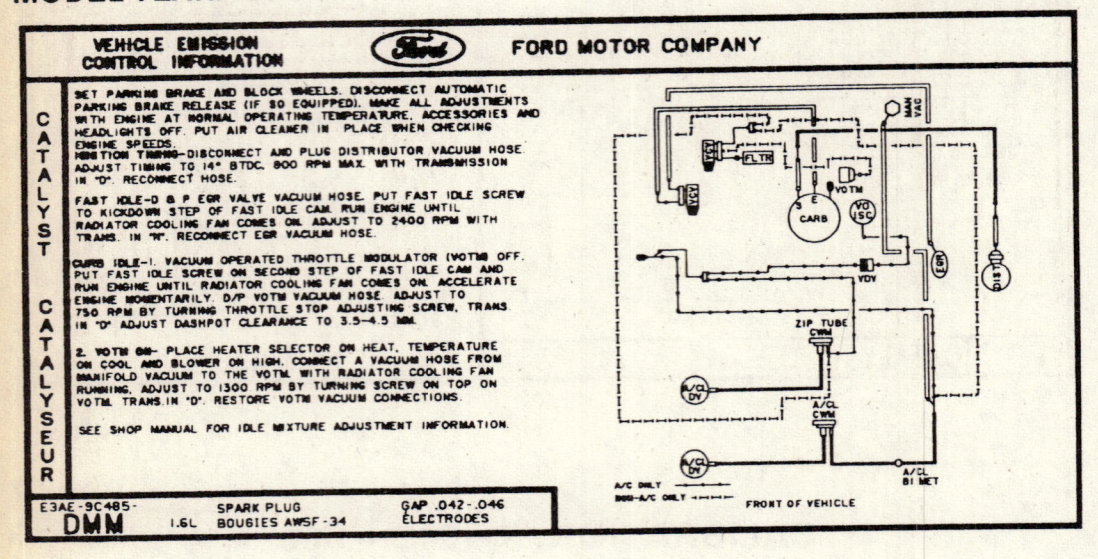

E3AE-9C485-DMM   SPARK PLUG 1.6L BOUGIES AWSF-34   GAP .042-.046 ÉLECTRODES

CALIBRATION: 3—04H—R00
(Non A/C Before May '83 with a Catalyst)

MODEL YEAR: 1983 **ENGINE: 1.6L**

VEHICLE EMISSION CONTROL INFORMATION — Ford Motor Company

CATALYST / CATALYSEUR

SET PARKING BRAKE AND BLOCK WHEELS. DISCONNECT AUTOMATIC PARKING BRAKE RELEASE (IF SO EQUIPPED). MAKE ALL ADJUSTMENTS WITH ENGINE AT NORMAL OPERATING TEMPERATURE, ACCESSORIES AND HEADLIGHTS OFF. PUT AIR CLEANER IN PLACE WHEN CHECKING ENGINE SPEEDS.

IGNITION TIMING—DISCONNECT AND PLUG DISTRIBUTOR VACUUM HOSE. WITH TRANS IN "D", ADJUST TIMING TO 14° BTDC, 800 RPM MAX. RECONNECT HOSE.

FAST IDLE—D & P EGR VALVE VACUUM HOSE. PUT FAST IDLE SCREW ON KICKDOWN STEP OF FAST IDLE CAM. RUN ENGINE UNTIL RADIATOR COOLING FAN COMES ON. ADJUST TO 2400 RPM WITH TRANS. IN NEUTRAL. RECONNECT EGR HOSE.

CURB IDLE—PUT FAST IDLE SCREW ON SECOND STEP OF FAST IDLE CAM. RUN ENGINE UNTIL RADIATOR COOLING FAN COMES ON. ACCELERATE ENGINE MOMENTARILY. PUT TRANSMISSION IN DRIVE.

WITHOUT IDLE SPEED CONTROL (ISC) — ADJUST TO 750 RPM BY TURNING THROTTLE STOP ADJUSTING SCREW. ADJUST DASHPOT CLEARANCE TO 3.5-4.5 MM.

WITH ISC — TURN ISC ADJUSTING SCREW UNTIL ISC PLUNGER IS CLEAR OF THE THROTTLE LEVER. ADJUST RPM TO 720 BY TURNING THROTTLE STOP ADJUSTING SCREW, THEN TURN ISC ADJUSTING SCREW UNTIL 750 RPM IS REACHED.

IF CURB IDLE ADJUSTMENT IS GREATER THAN 50 RPM, RE-ADJUST AUTO. TRANS. LINKAGE. SEE SHOP MANUAL.

SEE SHOP MANUAL FOR CHOKE AND IDLE MIXTURE ADJUSTMENT INFORMATION.

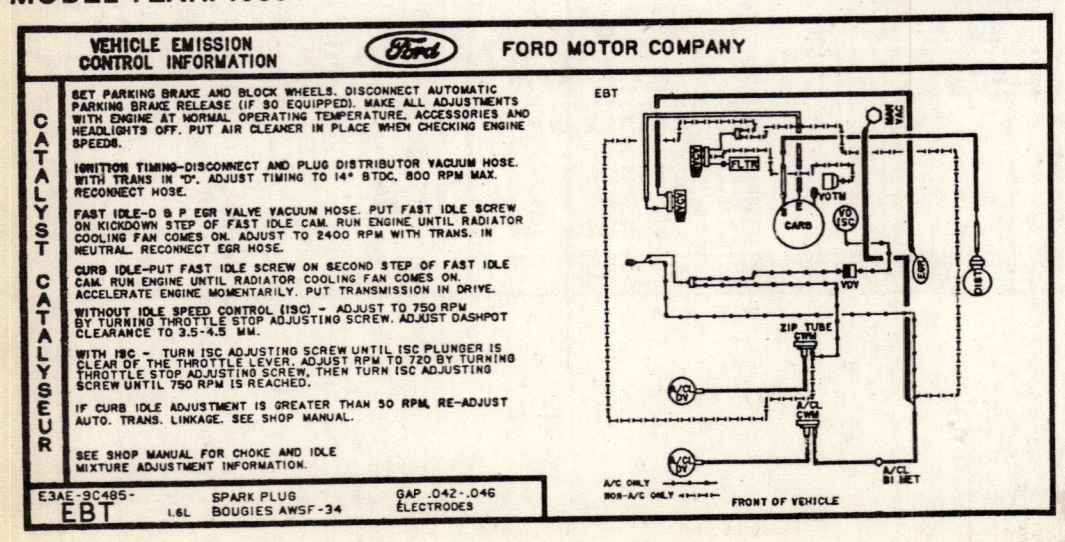

E3AE-9C485-EBT   SPARK PLUG 1.6L BOUGIES AWSF-34   GAP .042-.046 ÉLECTRODES

EMISSION CONTROLS

CALIBRATION: 3—04H—R00
(A/C Before May '83 Without a Catalyst)

MODEL YEAR: 1983 **ENGINE: 1.6L**

```
VEHICLE EMISSION                    FORD MOTOR COMPANY
CONTROL INFORMATION

SET PARKING BRAKE AND BLOCK WHEELS. DISCONNECT AUTOMATIC
PARKING BRAKE RELEASE (IF SO EQUIPPED). MAKE ALL ADJUSTMENTS
WITH ENGINE AT NORMAL OPERATING TEMPERATURE, ACCESSORIES AND
HEADLIGHTS OFF. PUT AIR CLEANER IN PLACE WHEN CHECKING ENGINE
SPEEDS.

IGNITION TIMING-DISCONNECT AND PLUG DISTRIBUTOR VACUUM HOSE.
WITH TRANS IN "D". ADJUST TIMING TO 14° BTDC. 800 RPM MAX
RECONNECT HOSE.

FAST IDLE-D & P EGR VALVE VACUUM HOSE. PUT FAST IDLE SCREW
ON KICKDOWN STEP OF FAST IDLE CAM. RUN ENGINE UNTIL RADIATOR
COOLING FAN COMES ON. ADJUST TO 2400 RPM WITH TRANS. IN
NEUTRAL. RECONNECT EGR HOSE.

CURB IDLE-PUT FAST IDLE SCREW ON SECOND STEP OF FAST IDLE
CAM. RUN ENGINE UNTIL RADIATOR COOLING FAN COMES ON.
ACCELERATE ENGINE MOMENTARILY. PUT TRANSMISSION IN DRIVE.

WITHOUT IDLE SPEED CONTROL (ISC) - ADJUST TO 750 RPM
BY TURNING THROTTLE STOP ADJUSTING SCREW. ADJUST DASHPOT
CLEARANCE TO 3.5-4.5 MM.

WITH ISC - TURN ISC ADJUSTING SCREW UNTIL ISC PLUNGER IS
CLEAR OF THE THROTTLE LEVER. ADJUST RPM TO 720 BY TURNING
THROTTLE STOP ADJUSTING SCREW, THEN TURN ISC ADJUSTING
SCREW UNTIL 750 RPM IS REACHED.

IF CURB IDLE ADJUSTMENT IS GREATER THAN 50 RPM. RE-ADJUST
AUTO. TRANS. LINKAGE. SEE SHOP MANUAL.

SEE SHOP MANUAL FOR CHOKE AND IDLE
MIXTURE ADJUSTMENT INFORMATION.

E3AE-9C485-    SPARK PLUG      GAP .042-.046
    DMN    1.6L  BOUGIES AWSF-34  ELECTRODES
```

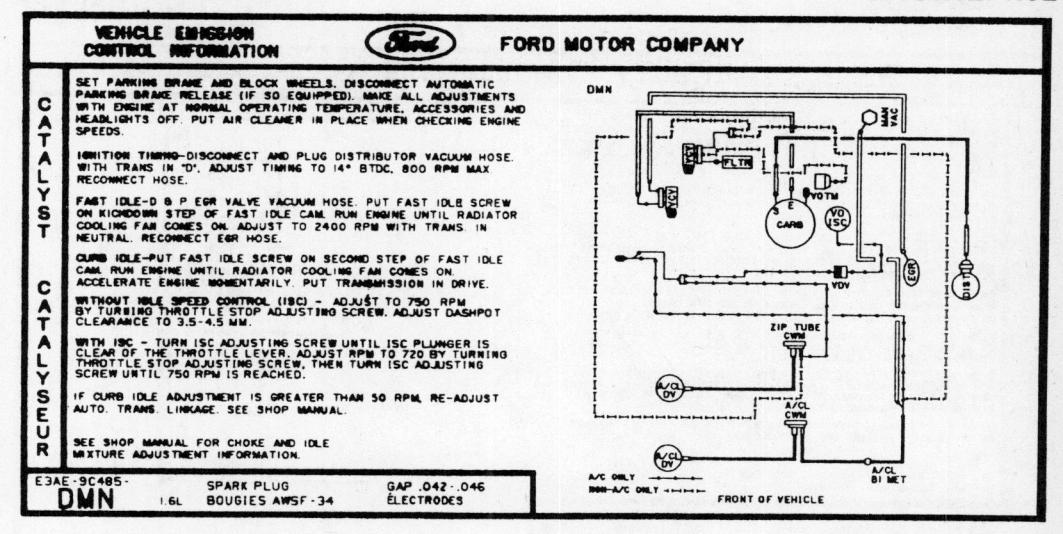

CALIBRATION: 3—04H—R00
(A/C Before May '83 with a Catalyst)

MODEL YEAR: 1983 **ENGINE: 1.6L**

```
VEHICLE EMISSION                    FORD MOTOR COMPANY
CONTROL INFORMATION

SET PARKING BRAKE AND BLOCK WHEELS. DISCONNECT AUTOMATIC
PARKING BRAKE RELEASE (IF SO EQUIPPED). MAKE ALL ADJUSTMENTS
WITH ENGINE AT NORMAL OPERATING TEMPERATURE, ACCESSORIES AND
HEADLIGHTS OFF. PUT AIR CLEANER IN PLACE WHEN CHECKING
ENGINE SPEEDS.
IGNITION TIMING-DISCONNECT AND PLUG DISTRIBUTOR VACUUM HOSE.
ADJUST TIMING TO 14° BTDC, 800 RPM MAX. WITH TRANSMISSION
IN "D". RECONNECT HOSE.

FAST IDLE-D & P EGR VALVE VACUUM HOSE. PUT FAST IDLE SCREW
TO KICKDOWN STEP OF FAST IDLE CAM. RUN ENGINE UNTIL
RADIATOR COOLING FAN COMES ON. ADJUST TO 2400 RPM WITH
TRANS. IN "N". RECONNECT EGR VACUUM HOSE.

CURB IDLE-1. VACUUM OPERATED THROTTLE MODULATOR (VOTM) OFF.
PUT FAST IDLE SCREW ON SECOND STEP OF FAST IDLE CAM AND
RUN ENGINE UNTIL RADIATOR COOLING FAN COMES ON. ACCELERATE
ENGINE MOMENTARILY. D/P VOTM VACUUM HOSE (A/C ONLY). ADJUST
TO 750 RPM BY TURNING THROTTLE STOP ADJUSTING SCREW, TRANS.
IN "D". ALSO ADJUST DASHPOT CLEARANCE TO 3.5-4.5 MM.

2. VOTM ON- PLACE HEATER SELECTOR ON HEAT. TEMPERATURE
ON COOL AND BLOWER ON HIGH. CONNECT A VACUUM HOSE FROM
MANIFOLD VACUUM TO THE VOTM. WITH RADIATOR COOLING FAN
RUNNING, ADJUST TO 1300 RPM BY TURNING SCREW ON TOP ON
VOTM. WITH TRANS. IN "D". RESTORE VOTM VACUUM CONNECTIONS.

SEE SHOP MANUAL FOR IDLE MIXTURE ADJUSTMENT INFORMATION.

E3AE-9C485-    SPARK PLUG      GAP .042-.046
    EBS    1.6L  BOUGIES AWSF-34  ELECTRODES
```

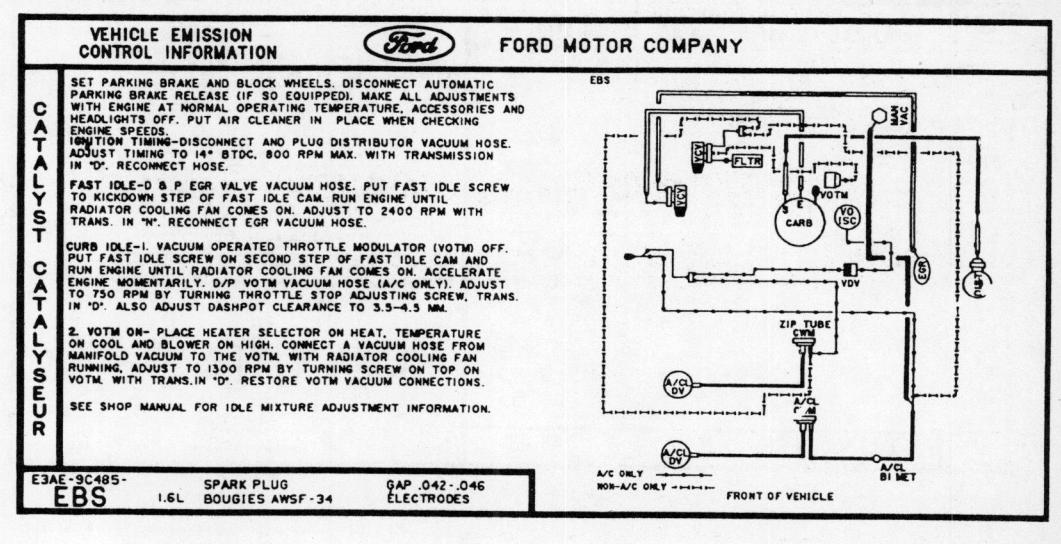

EMISSION CONTROLS

CALIBRATION: 3—04H—R00
(A/C or Non A/C with a Catalyst)

MODEL YEAR: 1983 **ENGINE: 1.6L**

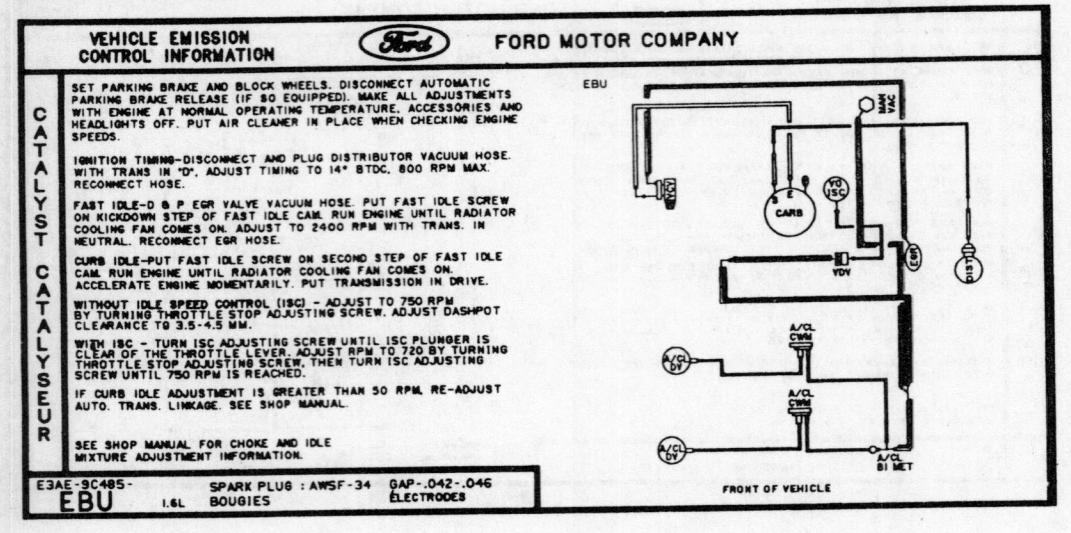

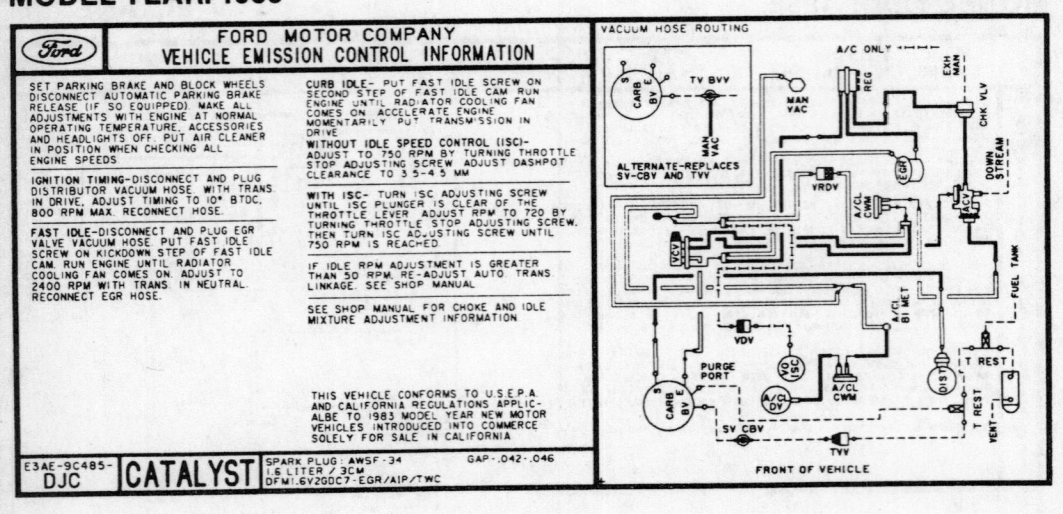

CALIBRATION: 3—04Q—R00

MODEL YEAR: 1983 **ENGINE: 1.6L**

EMISSION CONTROLS 249

CALIBRATION: 3—04Q—R12
(Models Before May '83)

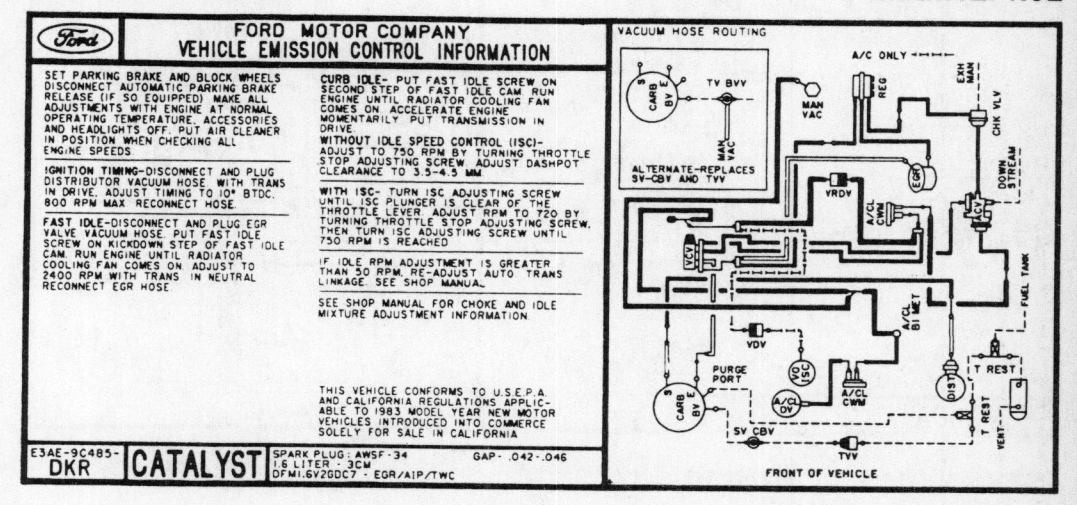

MODEL YEAR: 1983 **ENGINE: 1.6L**

CALIBRATION: 3—04Q—R12
(Models After April '83)

MODEL YEAR: 1983 **ENGINE: 1.6L**

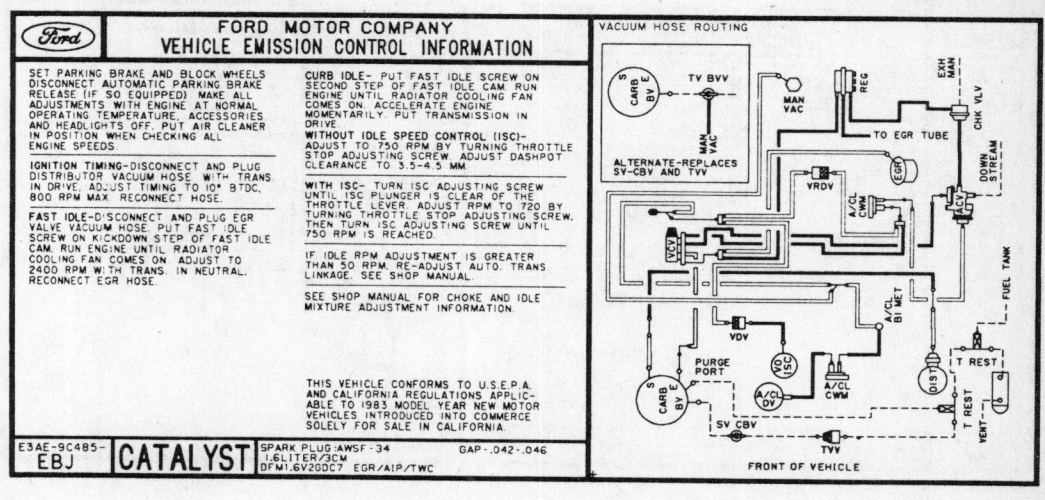

EMISSION CONTROLS

CALIBRATION: 3—04T—R00

MODEL YEAR: 1983 **ENGINE: 1.6L**

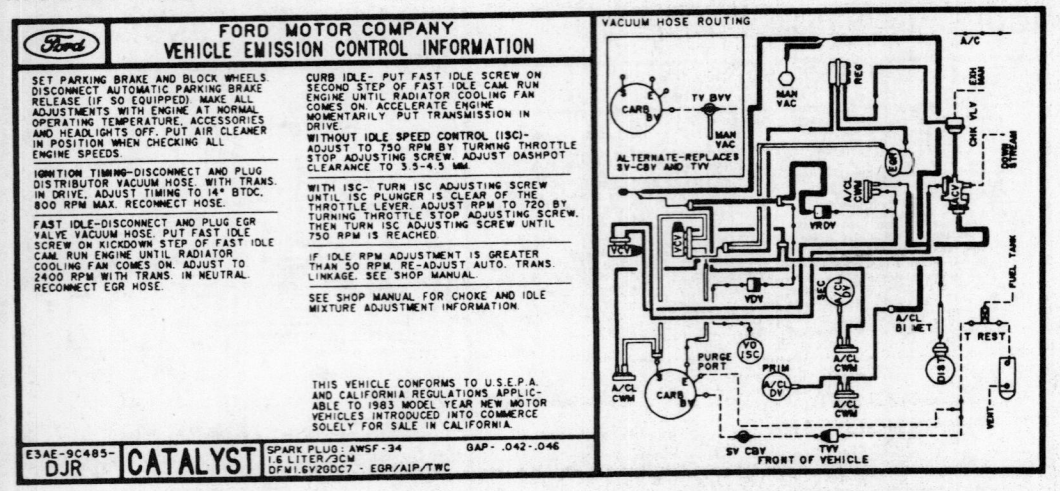

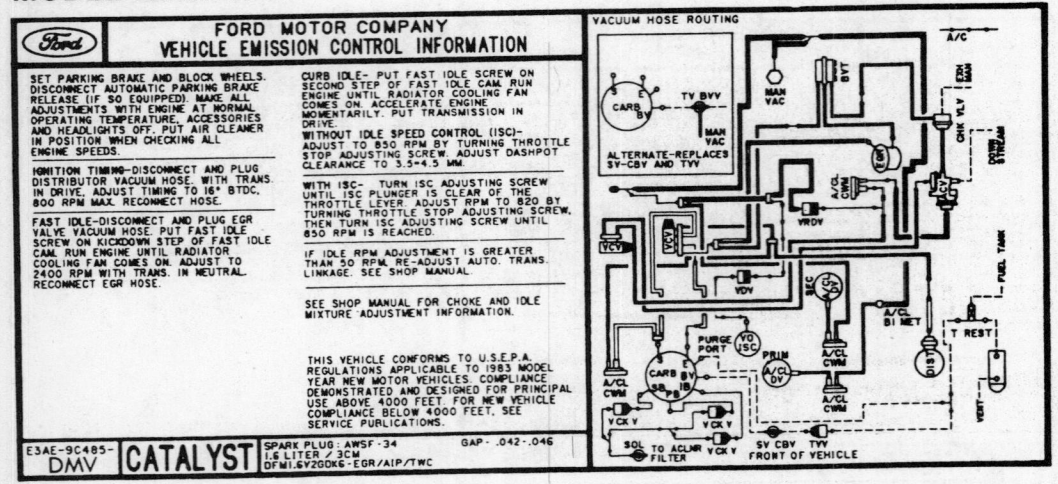

CALIBRATION: 3—04Y—R00
(Models Before May '83)

MODEL YEAR: 1983 **ENGINE: 1.6L**

EMISSION CONTROLS

CALIBRATION: 3—04Y—R00
(Models After April '83)

MODEL YEAR: 1983 **ENGINE: 1.6L**

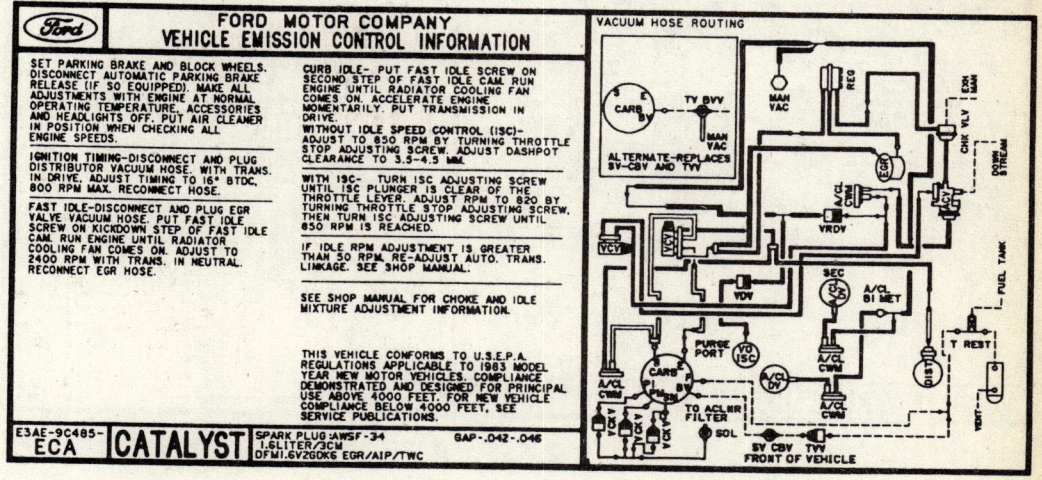

CALIBRATION: 4—03P—R00

MODEL YEAR: 1984 **ENGINE: 1.6L**

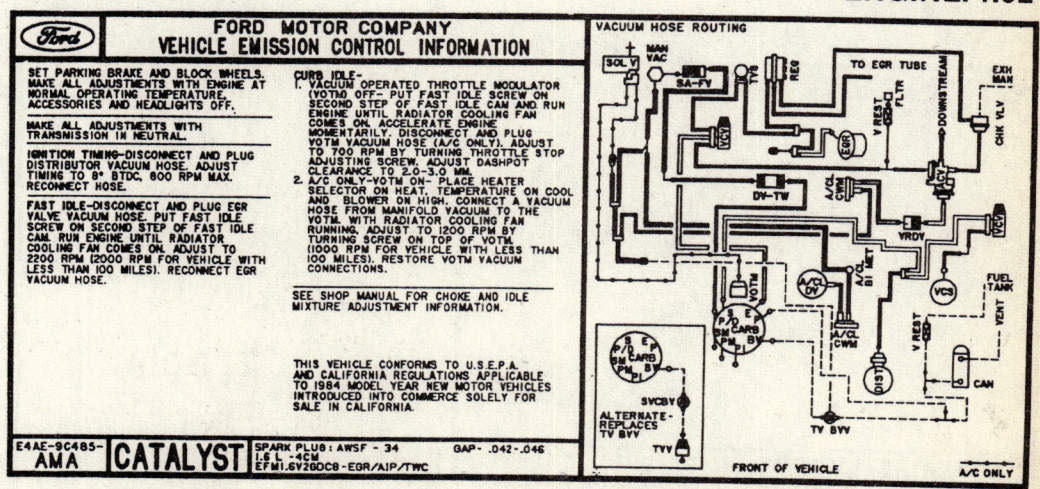

EMISSION CONTROLS

CALIBRATION: 4—03P—R10

MODEL YEAR: 1984 **ENGINE: 1.6L**

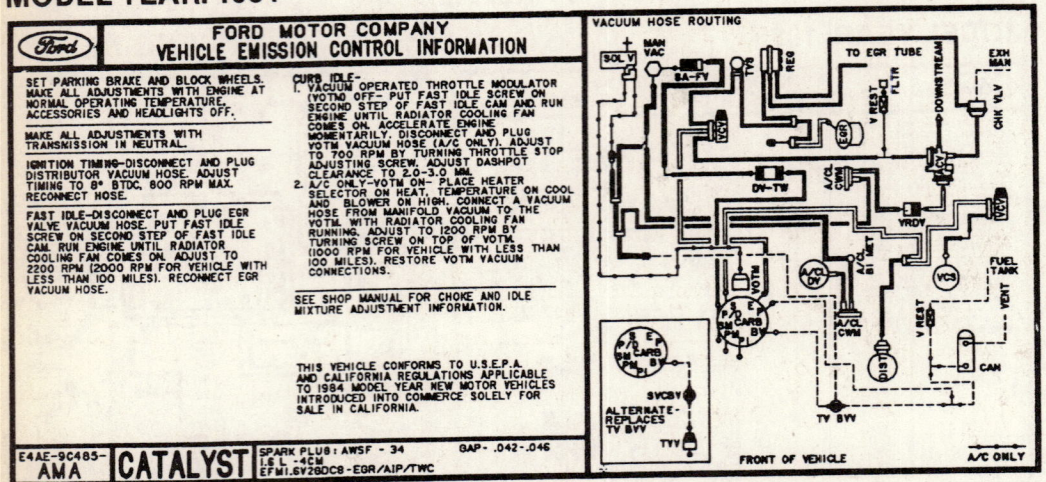

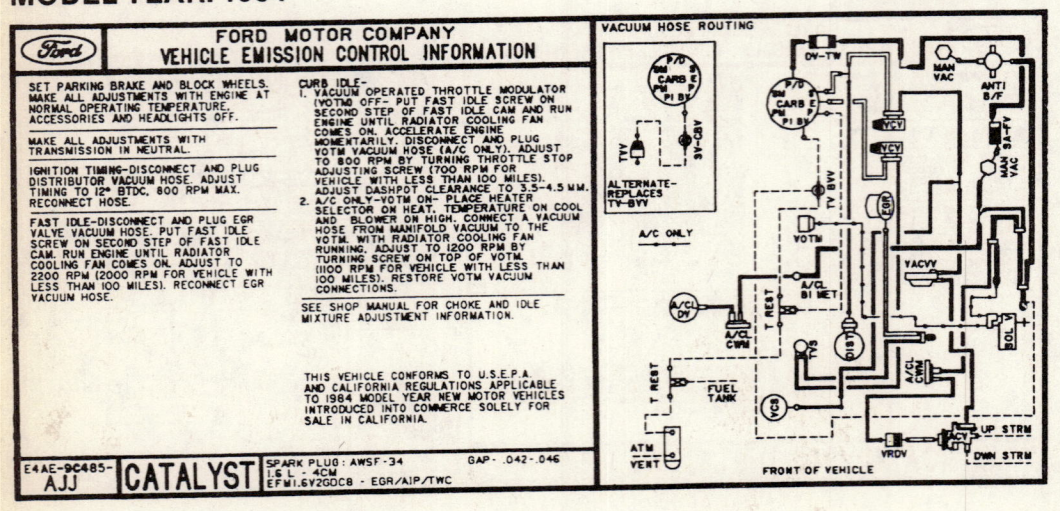

CALIBRATION: 4—03S—R00

MODEL YEAR: 1984 **ENGINE: 1.6L**

EMISSION CONTROLS 253

CALIBRATION: 4—03S—R10

MODEL YEAR: 1984 **ENGINE: 1.6L**

FORD MOTOR COMPANY
VEHICLE EMISSION CONTROL INFORMATION

SET PARKING BRAKE AND BLOCK WHEELS. MAKE ALL ADJUSTMENTS WITH ENGINE AT NORMAL OPERATING TEMPERATURE, ACCESSORIES AND HEADLIGHTS OFF.

MAKE ALL ADJUSTMENTS WITH TRANSMISSION IN NEUTRAL.

IGNITION TIMING-DISCONNECT AND PLUG DISTRIBUTOR VACUUM HOSE. ADJUST TIMING TO 12° BTDC, 800 RPM MAX. RECONNECT HOSE.

FAST IDLE-DISCONNECT AND PLUG EGR VALVE VACUUM HOSE. PUT FAST IDLE SCREW ON SECOND STEP OF FAST IDLE CAM. RUN ENGINE UNTIL RADIATOR COOLING FAN COMES ON. ADJUST TO 2200 RPM (2000 RPM FOR VEHICLE WITH LESS THAN 100 MILES). RECONNECT EGR VACUUM HOSE.

CURB IDLE—
1. VACUUM OPERATED THROTTLE MODULATOR (VOTM) OFF- PUT FAST IDLE SCREW ON SECOND STEP OF FAST IDLE CAM AND RUN ENGINE UNTIL RADIATOR COOLING FAN COMES ON. ACCELERATE ENGINE MOMENTARILY. DISCONNECT AND PLUG VOTM VACUUM HOSE (A/C ONLY). ADJUST TO 800 RPM BY TURNING THROTTLE STOP ADJUSTING SCREW (700 RPM FOR VEHICLE WITH LESS THAN 100 MILES). ADJUST DASHPOT CLEARANCE TO 3.5-4.5 MM.
2. A/C ONLY-VOTM ON- PLACE HEATER SELECTOR ON HEAT, TEMPERATURE ON COOL AND BLOWER ON HIGH. CONNECT A VACUUM HOSE FROM MANIFOLD VACUUM TO THE VOTM. WITH RADIATOR COOLING FAN RUNNING, ADJUST TO 1200 RPM BY TURNING SCREW ON TOP OF VOTM (1100 RPM FOR VEHICLE WITH LESS THAN 100 MILES). RESTORE VOTM VACUUM CONNECTIONS.

SEE SHOP MANUAL FOR CHOKE AND IDLE MIXTURE ADJUSTMENT INFORMATION.

THIS VEHICLE CONFORMS TO U.S.E.P.A. AND CALIFORNIA REGULATIONS APPLICABLE TO 1984 MODEL YEAR NEW MOTOR VEHICLES INTRODUCED INTO COMMERCE SOLELY FOR SALE IN CALIFORNIA.

E4AE-9C485-AYV CATALYST SPARK PLUG: AWSF-34 GAP .042-.046 1.6L-4CM EFM1.6V2GDC8-EGR/AIP/TWC

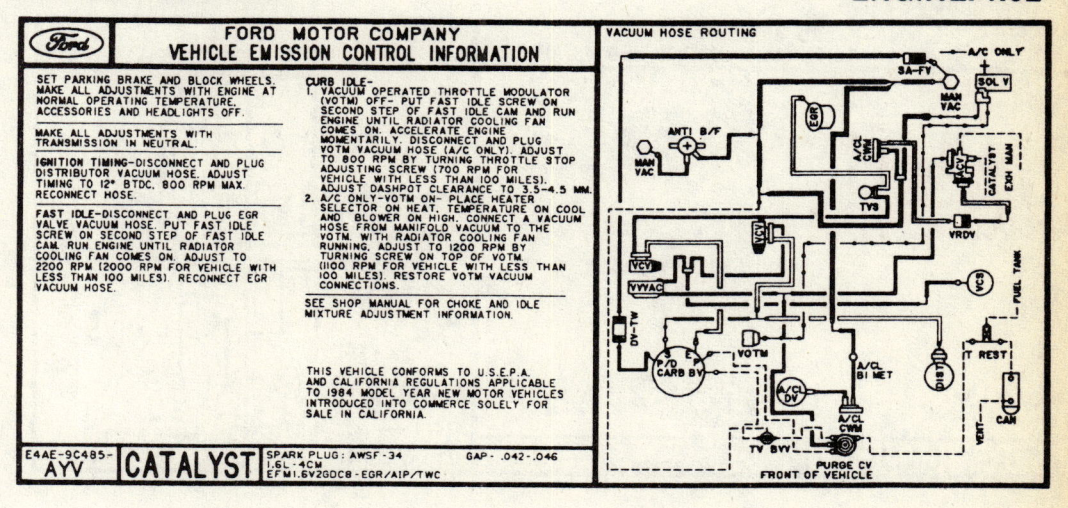

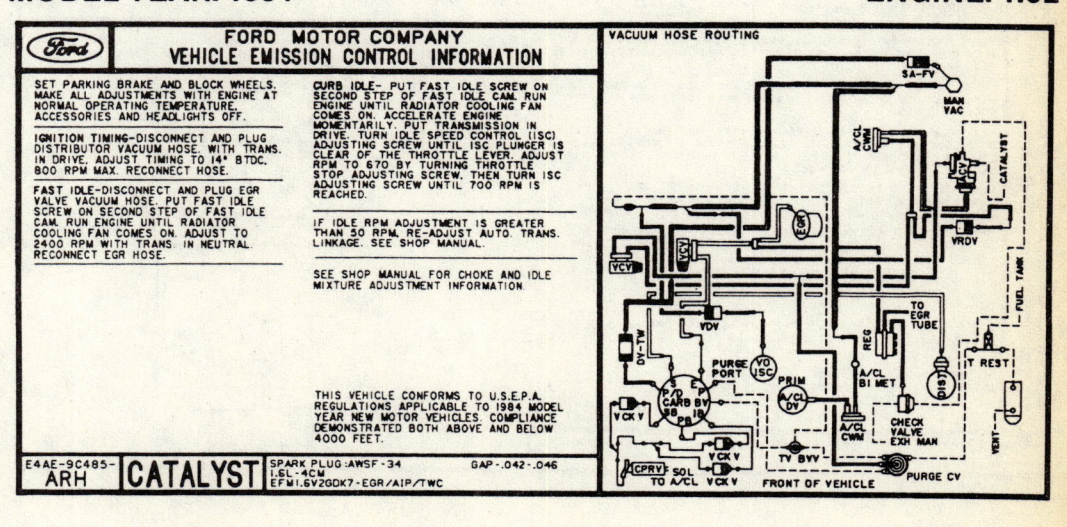

CALIBRATION: 4—04A—R14

MODEL YEAR: 1984 **ENGINE: 1.6L**

FORD MOTOR COMPANY
VEHICLE EMISSION CONTROL INFORMATION

SET PARKING BRAKE AND BLOCK WHEELS. MAKE ALL ADJUSTMENTS WITH ENGINE AT NORMAL OPERATING TEMPERATURE, ACCESSORIES AND HEADLIGHTS OFF.

IGNITION TIMING-DISCONNECT AND PLUG DISTRIBUTOR VACUUM HOSE. WITH TRANS. IN DRIVE, ADJUST TIMING TO 14° BTDC, 800 RPM MAX. RECONNECT HOSE.

FAST IDLE-DISCONNECT AND PLUG EGR VALVE VACUUM HOSE. PUT FAST IDLE SCREW ON SECOND STEP OF FAST IDLE CAM. RUN ENGINE UNTIL RADIATOR COOLING FAN COMES ON. ADJUST TO 2400 RPM WITH TRANS. IN NEUTRAL. RECONNECT EGR HOSE.

CURB IDLE- PUT FAST IDLE SCREW ON SECOND STEP OF FAST IDLE CAM. RUN ENGINE UNTIL RADIATOR COOLING FAN COMES ON. ACCELERATE ENGINE MOMENTARILY. PUT TRANSMISSION IN DRIVE. TURN IDLE SPEED CONTROL (ISC) ADJUSTING SCREW UNTIL ISC PLUNGER IS CLEAR OF THE THROTTLE LEVER. ADJUST RPM TO 670 BY TURNING THROTTLE STOP ADJUSTING SCREW. THEN TURN ISC ADJUSTING SCREW UNTIL 700 RPM IS REACHED.

IF IDLE RPM ADJUSTMENT IS GREATER THAN 50 RPM RE-ADJUST AUTO. TRANS. LINKAGE. SEE SHOP MANUAL.

SEE SHOP MANUAL FOR CHOKE AND IDLE MIXTURE ADJUSTMENT INFORMATION.

THIS VEHICLE CONFORMS TO U.S.E.P.A. REGULATIONS APPLICABLE TO 1984 MODEL YEAR NEW MOTOR VEHICLES. COMPLIANCE DEMONSTRATED BOTH ABOVE AND BELOW 4000 FEET.

E4AE-9C485-ARH CATALYST SPARK PLUG: AWSF-34 GAP .042-.046 1.6L-4CM EFM1.6V2GDK7-EGR/AIP/TWC

EMISSION CONTROLS

CALIBRATION: 4—04A—R16

MODEL YEAR: 1984   **ENGINE: 1.6L**

FORD MOTOR COMPANY
VEHICLE EMISSION CONTROL INFORMATION

SET PARKING BRAKE AND BLOCK WHEELS. MAKE ALL ADJUSTMENTS WITH ENGINE AT NORMAL OPERATING TEMPERATURE. ACCESSORIES AND HEADLIGHTS OFF.

IGNITION TIMING-DISCONNECT AND PLUG DISTRIBUTOR VACUUM HOSE. WITH TRANS. IN DRIVE, ADJUST TIMING TO 14° BTDC, 800 RPM MAX. RECONNECT HOSE.

FAST IDLE-DISCONNECT AND PLUG EGR VALVE VACUUM HOSE. PUT FAST IDLE SCREW ON SECOND STEP OF FAST IDLE CAM. RUN ENGINE UNTIL RADIATOR COOLING FAN COMES ON. ADJUST TO 2400 RPM WITH TRANS. IN NEUTRAL. RECONNECT EGR HOSE.

CURB IDLE- PUT FAST IDLE SCREW ON SECOND STEP OF FAST IDLE CAM. RUN ENGINE UNTIL RADIATOR COOLING FAN COMES ON. ACCELERATE ENGINE MOMENTARILY. PUT TRANSMISSION IN DRIVE. TURN IDLE SPEED CONTROL (ISC) ADJUSTING SCREW UNTIL ISC PLUNGER IS CLEAR OF THE THROTTLE LEVER. ADJUST RPM TO 670 BY TURNING THROTTLE STOP ADJUSTING SCREW. THEN TURN ISC ADJUSTING SCREW UNTIL 700 RPM IS REACHED.

IF IDLE RPM ADJUSTMENT IS GREATER THAN 50 RPM, RE-ADJUST AUTO. TRANS. LINKAGE. SEE SHOP MANUAL.

SEE SHOP MANUAL FOR CHOKE AND IDLE MIXTURE ADJUSTMENT INFORMATION.

THIS VEHICLE CONFORMS TO U.S.E.P.A. REGULATIONS APPLICABLE TO 1984 MODEL YEAR NEW MOTOR VEHICLES. COMPLIANCE DEMONSTRATED BOTH ABOVE AND BELOW 4000 FEET.

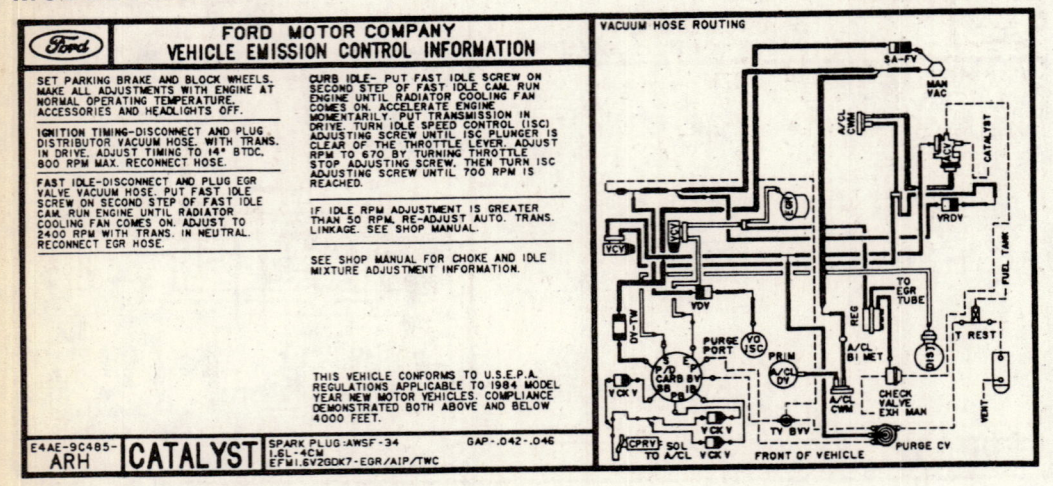

E4AE-9C485- **ARH**   **CATALYST**   SPARK PLUG: AWSF-34   GAP: .042-.046
1.6L-4CYL
EFMI.6V2GDK7-EGR/AIP/TWC

CALIBRATION: 4—04H—R00

MODEL YEAR: 1984   **ENGINE: 1.6L**

VEHICLE EMISSION CONTROL INFORMATION — FORD MOTOR COMPANY

CATALYST / CATALYSEUR

SET PARKING BRAKE AND BLOCK WHEELS. MAKE ALL ADJUSTMENTS WITH ENGINE AT NORMAL OPERATING TEMPERATURE, ACCESSORIES AND HEADLIGHTS OFF.

IGNITION TIMING-DISCONNECT AND PLUG DISTRIBUTOR VACUUM HOSE. WITH TRANS IN "D", ADJUST TIMING TO 14° BTDC, 800 RPM MAX. RECONNECT HOSE.

FAST IDLE-D & P EGR VALVE VACUUM HOSE. PUT FAST IDLE SCREW ON SECOND STEP OF FAST IDLE CAM. RUN ENGINE UNTIL RADIATOR COOLING FAN COMES ON. ADJUST TO 2400 RPM WITH TRANS. IN NEUTRAL. RECONNECT EGR HOSE.

CURB IDLE-PUT FAST IDLE SCREW ON SECOND STEP OF FAST IDLE CAM. RUN ENGINE UNTIL RADIATOR COOLING FAN COMES ON. ACCELERATE ENGINE MOMENTARILY. PUT TRANSMISSION IN DRIVE.

WITHOUT IDLE SPEED CONTROL (ISC) - ADJUST TO 750 RPM BY TURNING THROTTLE STOP ADJUSTING SCREW.

WITH ISC - TURN ISC ADJUSTING SCREW UNTIL ISC PLUNGER IS CLEAR OF THE THROTTLE LEVER. ADJUST RPM TO 720 BY TURNING THROTTLE STOP ADJUSTING SCREW, THEN TURN ISC ADJUSTING SCREW UNTIL 750 RPM IS REACHED.

IF CURB IDLE ADJUSTMENT IS GREATER THAN 50 RPM, RE-ADJUST AUTO. TRANS. LINKAGE. SEE SHOP MANUAL.

SEE SHOP MANUAL FOR CHOKE AND IDLE MIXTURE ADJUSTMENT INFORMATION.

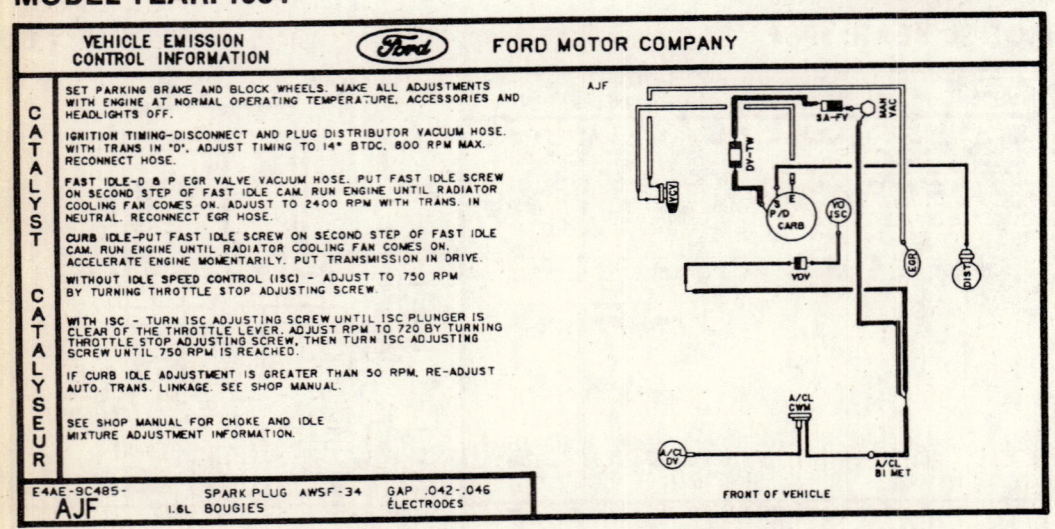

E4AE-9C485- **AJF**   SPARK PLUG AWSF-34   GAP .042-.046
1.6L BOUGIES   ÉLECTRODES

EMISSION CONTROLS 255

CALIBRATION: 4—04S—R12

MODEL YEAR: 1984 **ENGINE: 1.6L**

FORD MOTOR COMPANY
VEHICLE EMISSION CONTROL INFORMATION

SET PARKING BRAKE AND BLOCK WHEELS. MAKE ALL ADJUSTMENTS WITH ENGINE AT NORMAL OPERATING TEMPERATURE, ACCESSORIES AND HEADLIGHTS OFF.

IGNITION TIMING-DISCONNECT AND PLUG DISTRIBUTOR VACUUM HOSE. WITH TRANS. IN DRIVE, ADJUST TIMING TO 14° BTDC, 800 RPM MAX. RECONNECT HOSE.

FAST IDLE-DISCONNECT AND PLUG EGR VALVE VACUUM HOSE. PUT FAST IDLE SCREW ON SECOND STEP OF FAST IDLE CAM. RUN ENGINE UNTIL RADIATOR COOLING FAN COMES ON. ADJUST TO 2400 RPM WITH TRANS. IN NEUTRAL. RECONNECT EGR HOSE.

CURB IDLE- PUT FAST IDLE SCREW ON SECOND STEP OF FAST IDLE CAM. RUN ENGINE UNTIL RADIATOR COOLING FAN COMES ON. ACCELERATE ENGINE MOMENTARILY. PUT TRANSMISSION IN DRIVE. TURN IDLE SPEED CONTROL (ISC) ADJUSTING SCREW UNTIL ISC PLUNGER IS CLEAR OF THE THROTTLE LEVER. ADJUST RPM TO 670 BY TURNING THROTTLE STOP ADJUSTING SCREW. THEN TURN ISC ADJUSTING SCREW UNTIL 700 RPM IS REACHED.

IF IDLE RPM ADJUSTMENT IS GREATER THAN 50 RPM, RE-ADJUST AUTO. TRANS. LINKAGE. SEE SHOP MANUAL.

SEE SHOP MANUAL FOR CHOKE AND IDLE MIXTURE ADJUSTMENT INFORMATION.

THIS VEHICLE CONFORMS TO U.S.E.P.A. AND CALIFORNIA REGULATIONS APPLICABLE TO 1984 MODEL YEAR NEW MOTOR VEHICLES INTRODUCED INTO COMMERCE SOLELY FOR SALE IN CALIFORNIA.

E4AE-9C485-ARJ   CATALYST   SPARK PLUG: AWSF-34   1.6L-4CM   GAP-.042-.046   EFM1.6V2GDC8-EGR/AIP/TWC

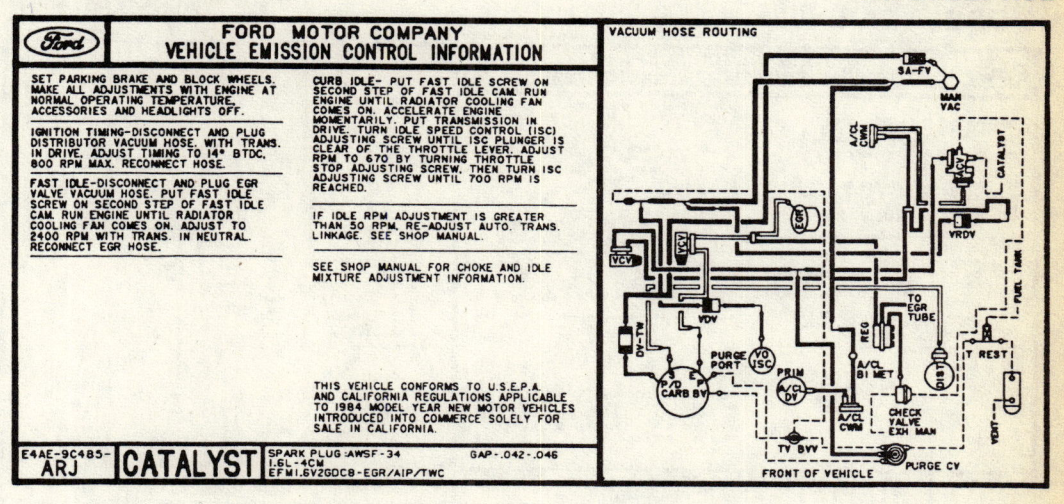

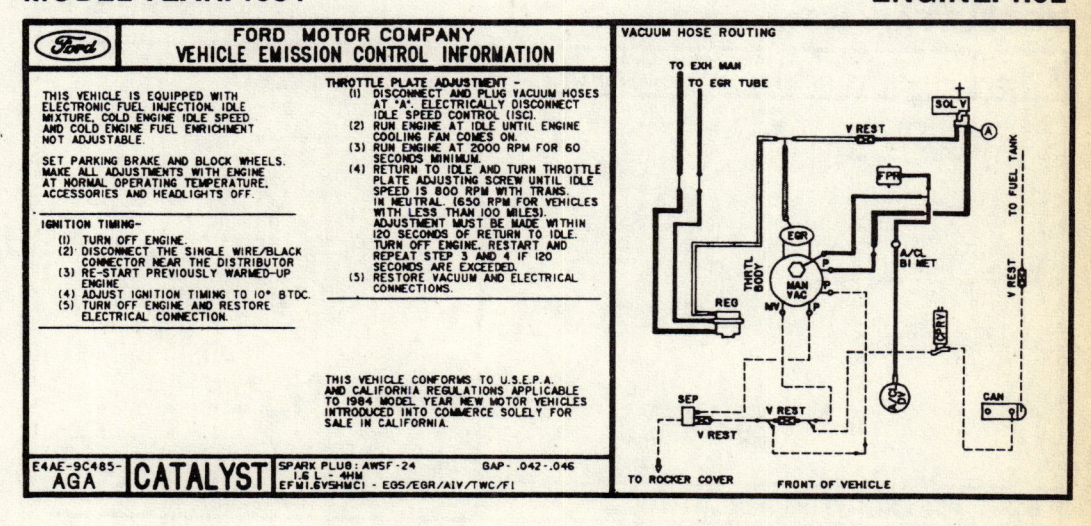

CALIBRATION: 4—27A—R00

MODEL YEAR: 1984 **ENGINE: 1.6L**

FORD MOTOR COMPANY
VEHICLE EMISSION CONTROL INFORMATION

THIS VEHICLE IS EQUIPPED WITH ELECTRONIC FUEL INJECTION. IDLE MIXTURE, COLD ENGINE IDLE SPEED AND COLD ENGINE FUEL ENRICHMENT NOT ADJUSTABLE.

SET PARKING BRAKE AND BLOCK WHEELS. MAKE ALL ADJUSTMENTS WITH ENGINE AT NORMAL OPERATING TEMPERATURE, ACCESSORIES AND HEADLIGHTS OFF.

IGNITION TIMING:
(1) TURN OFF ENGINE.
(2) DISCONNECT THE SINGLE WIRE/BLACK CONNECTOR NEAR THE DISTRIBUTOR
(3) RE-START PREVIOUSLY WARMED-UP ENGINE
(4) ADJUST IGNITION TIMING TO 10° BTDC.
(5) TURN OFF ENGINE AND RESTORE ELECTRICAL CONNECTION.

THROTTLE PLATE ADJUSTMENT –
(1) DISCONNECT AND PLUG VACUUM HOSES AT "A". ELECTRICALLY DISCONNECT IDLE SPEED CONTROL (ISC).
(2) RUN ENGINE AT IDLE UNTIL ENGINE COOLING FAN COMES ON.
(3) RUN ENGINE AT 2000 RPM FOR 60 SECONDS MINIMUM.
(4) RETURN TO IDLE AND TURN THROTTLE PLATE ADJUSTING SCREW UNTIL IDLE SPEED IS 800 RPM WITH TRANS. IN NEUTRAL. (650 RPM FOR VEHICLES WITH LESS THAN 100 MILES). ADJUSTMENT MUST BE MADE WITHIN 120 SECONDS OF RETURN TO IDLE. TURN OFF ENGINE. RESTART AND REPEAT STEP 3 AND 4 IF 120 SECONDS ARE EXCEEDED.
(5) RESTORE VACUUM AND ELECTRICAL CONNECTIONS.

THIS VEHICLE CONFORMS TO U.S.E.P.A. AND CALIFORNIA REGULATIONS APPLICABLE TO 1984 MODEL YEAR NEW MOTOR VEHICLES INTRODUCED INTO COMMERCE SOLELY FOR SALE IN CALIFORNIA.

E4AE-9C485-AGA   CATALYST   SPARK PLUG: AWSF-24   1.6L-4HM   GAP-.042-.046   EFM1.6V5HMC1-EGS/EGR/AIV/TWC/FI

EMISSION CONTROLS

CALIBRATION: 4—27A—R02

MODEL YEAR: 1984 **ENGINE: 1.6L**

FORD MOTOR COMPANY
VEHICLE EMISSION CONTROL INFORMATION

THIS VEHICLE IS EQUIPPED WITH ELECTRONIC FUEL INJECTION. IDLE MIXTURE, COLD ENGINE IDLE SPEED AND COLD ENGINE FUEL ENRICHMENT NOT ADJUSTABLE.

SET PARKING BRAKE AND BLOCK WHEELS. MAKE ALL ADJUSTMENTS WITH ENGINE AT NORMAL OPERATING TEMPERATURE, ACCESSORIES AND HEADLIGHTS OFF.

IGNITION TIMING—
1. TURN OFF ENGINE.
2. DISCONNECT THE SINGLE WIRE/BLACK CONNECTOR NEAR THE DISTRIBUTOR
3. RE-START PREVIOUSLY WARMED-UP ENGINE
4. ADJUST IGNITION TIMING TO 10° BTDC
5. TURN OFF ENGINE AND RESTORE ELECTRICAL CONNECTION.

THROTTLE PLATE ADJUSTMENT —
1. DISCONNECT AND PLUG VACUUM HOSES AT "A". ELECTRICALLY DISCONNECT IDLE SPEED CONTROL (ISC).
2. RUN ENGINE AT IDLE UNTIL ENGINE COOLING FAN COMES ON.
3. RUN ENGINE AT 2000 RPM FOR 60 SECONDS MINIMUM.
4. RETURN TO IDLE AND TURN THROTTLE PLATE ADJUSTING SCREW UNTIL IDLE SPEED IS 800 RPM WITH TRANS. IN NEUTRAL. (650 RPM FOR VEHICLES WITH LESS THAN 100 MILES). ADJUSTMENT MUST BE MADE WITHIN 120 SECONDS OF RETURN TO IDLE. TURN OFF ENGINE, RESTART AND REPEAT STEP 3 AND 4 IF 120 SECONDS ARE EXCEEDED.
5. RESTORE VACUUM AND ELECTRICAL CONNECTIONS.

THIS VEHICLE CONFORMS TO U.S.E.P.A. AND CALIFORNIA REGULATIONS APPLICABLE TO 1984 MODEL YEAR NEW MOTOR VEHICLES INTRODUCED INTO COMMERCE SOLELY FOR SALE IN CALIFORNIA.

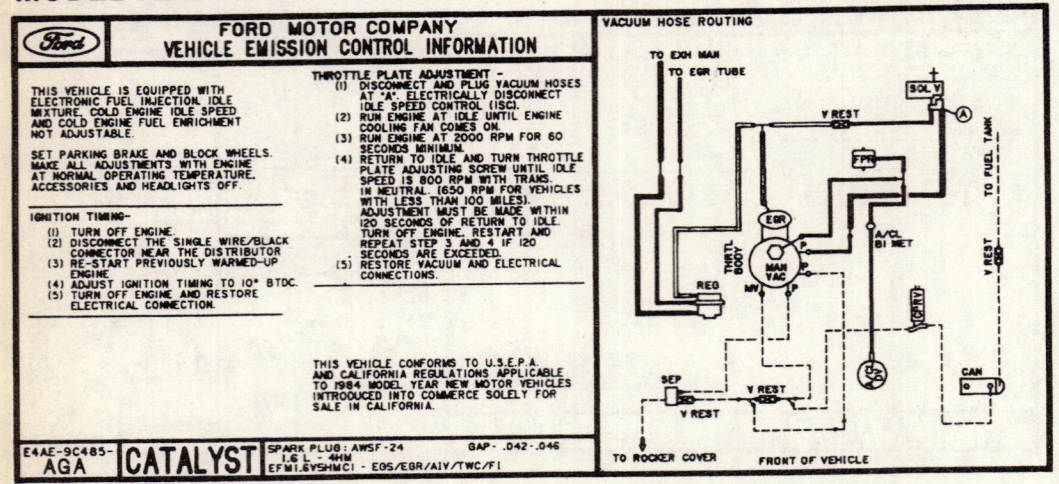

E4AE-9C485-AGA CATALYST SPARK PLUG: AWSF-24 GAP: .042-.046
1.6L - 4HM
EFMI.6V5HMCI - EGS/EGR/AIV/TWC/FI

CALIBRATION: 4—27T—R00

MODEL YEAR: 1984 **ENGINE: 1.6L**

FORD MOTOR COMPANY
VEHICLE EMISSION CONTROL INFORMATION

THIS VEHICLE IS EQUIPPED WITH ELECTRONIC FUEL INJECTION. IDLE MIXTURE, COLD ENGINE IDLE SPEED AND COLD ENGINE FUEL ENRICHMENT NOT ADJUSTABLE.

SET PARKING BRAKE AND BLOCK WHEELS. MAKE ALL ADJUSTMENTS WITH ENGINE AT NORMAL OPERATING TEMPERATURE, ACCESSORIES AND HEADLIGHTS OFF.

IGNITION TIMING—
1. TURN OFF ENGINE.
2. DISCONNECT THE SINGLE WIRE/BLACK CONNECTOR NEAR THE DISTRIBUTOR
3. RE-START PREVIOUSLY WARMED-UP ENGINE
4. ADJUST IGNITION TIMING TO 10° BTDC
5. TURN OFF ENGINE AND RESTORE ELECTRICAL CONNECTION.

THROTTLE PLATE ADJUSTMENT —
1. DISCONNECT AND PLUG VACUUM HOSES AT "A". ELECTRICALLY DISCONNECT IDLE SPEED CONTROL (ISC).
2. RUN ENGINE AT IDLE UNTIL ENGINE COOLING FAN COMES ON.
3. RUN ENGINE AT 2000 RPM FOR 60 SECONDS MINIMUM.
4. RETURN TO IDLE AND TURN THROTTLE PLATE ADJUSTING SCREW UNTIL IDLE SPEED IS 800 RPM WITH TRANS. IN NEUTRAL. (650 RPM FOR VEHICLE WITH LESS THAN 100 MILES) ADJUSTMENT MUST BE MADE WITHIN 120 SECONDS OF RETURN TO IDLE. TURN OFF ENGINE, RESTART AND REPEAT STEP 3 AND 4 IF 120 SECONDS ARE EXCEEDED.
5. RESTORE VACUUM AND ELECTRICAL CONNECTIONS.

THIS VEHICLE CONFORMS TO U.S.E.P.A. REGULATIONS APPLICABLE TO 1984 MODEL YEAR NEW MOTOR VEHICLES. COMPLIANCE DEMONSTRATED BOTH ABOVE AND BELOW 4000 FEET.

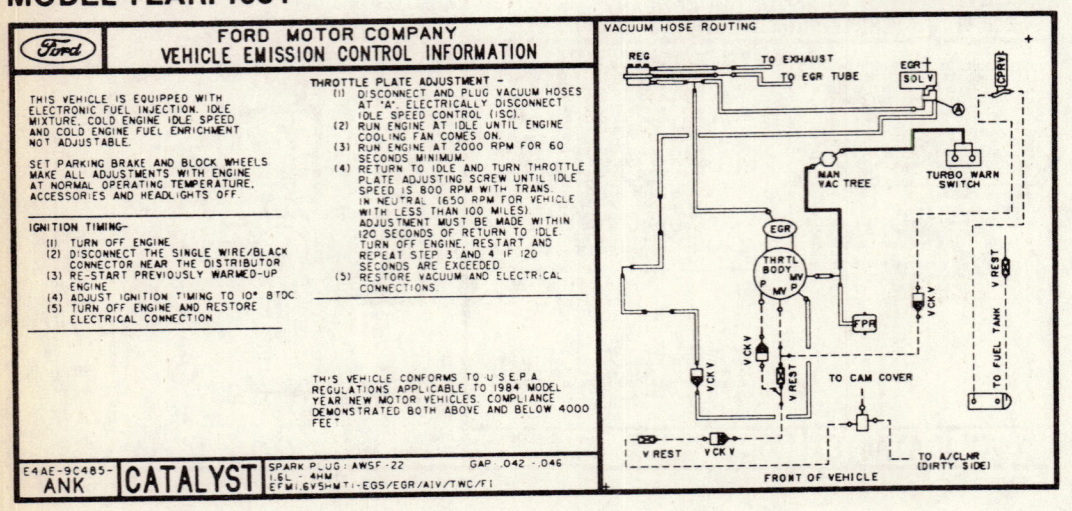

E4AE-9C485-ANK CATALYST SPARK PLUG: AWSF-22 GAP .042-.046
1.6L - 4HM
EFMI.6V5HMTI-EGS/EGR/AIV/TWC/FI

EMISSION CONTROLS

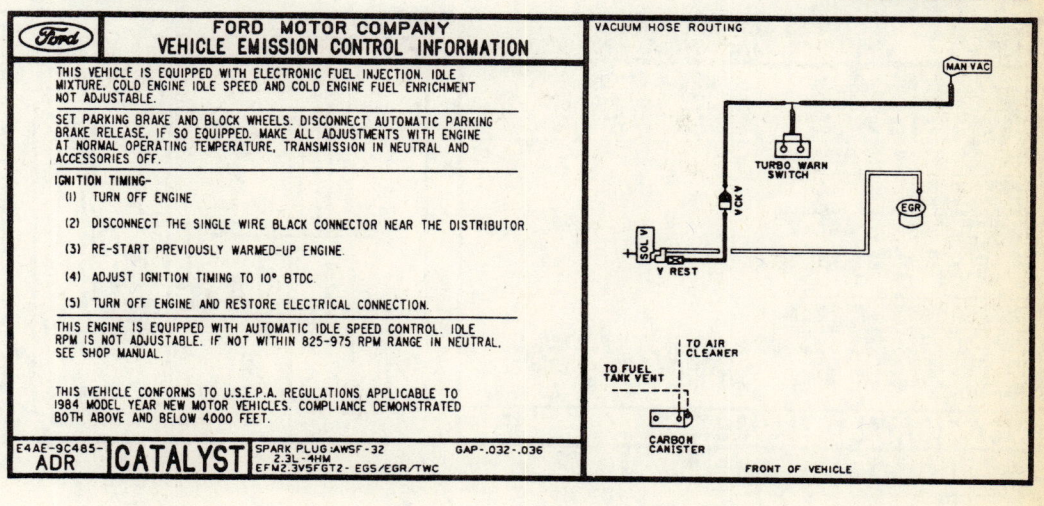

CALIBRATION: 4—28A—R00

MODEL YEAR: 1984 **ENGINE: 1.6L**

FORD MOTOR COMPANY — VEHICLE EMISSION CONTROL INFORMATION

THIS VEHICLE IS EQUIPPED WITH ELECTRONIC FUEL INJECTION. IDLE MIXTURE, COLD ENGINE IDLE SPEED AND COLD ENGINE FUEL ENRICHMENT NOT ADJUSTABLE.

SET PARKING BRAKE AND BLOCK WHEELS. MAKE ALL ADJUSTMENTS WITH ENGINE AT NORMAL OPERATING TEMPERATURE. ACCESSORIES AND HEADLIGHTS OFF.

IGNITION TIMING—
(1) TURN OFF ENGINE.
(2) DISCONNECT THE SINGLE WIRE/BLACK CONNECTOR NEAR THE DISTRIBUTOR
(3) RE-START PREVIOUSLY WARMED-UP ENGINE
(4) ADJUST IGNITION TIMING TO 10° BTDC.
(5) TURN OFF ENGINE AND RESTORE ELECTRICAL CONNECTION.

THROTTLE PLATE ADJUSTMENT —
(1) DISCONNECT AND PLUG VACUUM HOSES AT "A". ELECTRICALLY DISCONNECT IDLE SPEED CONTROL (ISC).
(2) RUN ENGINE AT IDLE UNTIL ENGINE COOLING FAN COMES ON.
(3) RUN ENGINE AT 2000 RPM FOR 60 SECONDS MINIMUM.
(4) RETURN TO IDLE AND TURN THROTTLE PLATE ADJUSTING SCREW UNTIL IDLE SPEED IS 750 RPM WITH AUTO. TRANS. IN DRIVE. (600 RPM FOR VEHICLE WITH LESS THAN 100 MILES). ADJUSTMENT MUST BE MADE WITHIN 120 SECONDS OF RETURN TO IDLE. TURN OFF ENGINE, RESTART AND REPEAT STEP 3 AND 4 IF 120 SECONDS ARE EXCEEDED.
(5) IF THROTTLE PLATE RE-ADJUST TRANS. LINKAGE. SEE SHOP MANUAL. RESTORE VACUUM AND ELECTRICAL CONNECTIONS.

THIS VEHICLE CONFORMS TO U.S.E.P.A. REGULATIONS APPLICABLE TO 1984 MODEL YEAR NEW MOTOR VEHICLES. COMPLIANCE DEMONSTRATED BOTH ABOVE AND BELOW 4000 FEET.

E4AE-9C485 **AFM** CATALYST
SPARK PLUG: AWSF-24   GAP: .042-.046
1.6L-4HM
EFM1.6V5HMF8-EGS/EGR/AIV/TWC/FI

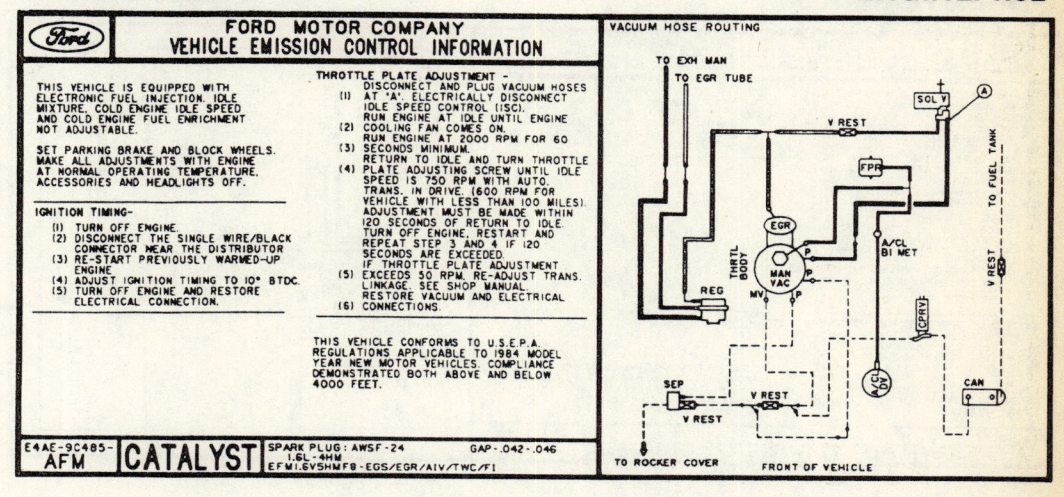

CALIBRATION: 3—05E—R12

MODEL YEAR: 1984 **ENGINE: 2.3L**

FORD MOTOR COMPANY — VEHICLE EMISSION CONTROL INFORMATION

THIS VEHICLE IS EQUIPPED WITH ELECTRONIC FUEL INJECTION. IDLE MIXTURE, COLD ENGINE IDLE SPEED AND COLD ENGINE FUEL ENRICHMENT NOT ADJUSTABLE.

SET PARKING BRAKE AND BLOCK WHEELS. DISCONNECT AUTOMATIC PARKING BRAKE RELEASE, IF SO EQUIPPED. MAKE ALL ADJUSTMENTS WITH ENGINE AT NORMAL OPERATING TEMPERATURE, TRANSMISSION IN NEUTRAL AND ACCESSORIES OFF.

IGNITION TIMING—
(1) TURN OFF ENGINE
(2) DISCONNECT THE SINGLE WIRE BLACK CONNECTOR NEAR THE DISTRIBUTOR
(3) RE-START PREVIOUSLY WARMED-UP ENGINE
(4) ADJUST IGNITION TIMING TO 10° BTDC
(5) TURN OFF ENGINE AND RESTORE ELECTRICAL CONNECTION.

THIS ENGINE IS EQUIPPED WITH AUTOMATIC IDLE SPEED CONTROL. IDLE RPM IS NOT ADJUSTABLE. IF NOT WITHIN 825-975 RPM RANGE IN NEUTRAL, SEE SHOP MANUAL.

THIS VEHICLE CONFORMS TO U.S.E.P.A. REGULATIONS APPLICABLE TO 1984 MODEL YEAR NEW MOTOR VEHICLES. COMPLIANCE DEMONSTRATED BOTH ABOVE AND BELOW 4000 FEET.

E4AE-9C485 **ADR** CATALYST
SPARK PLUG: AWSF-32   GAP: .032-.036
2.3L-4HM
EFM2.3V5FGT2-EGS/EGR/TWC

EMISSION CONTROLS

CALIBRATION: 4—05A—R00

MODEL YEAR: 1984   **ENGINE: 2.3L**

FORD MOTOR COMPANY
VEHICLE EMISSION CONTROL INFORMATION

THIS VEHICLE IS EQUIPPED WITH EEC IV ENGINE CONTROLS AND A FEEDBACK CARBURETOR.

SET PARKING BRAKE AND BLOCK WHEELS. MAKE ALL ADJUSTMENTS WITH ENGINE AT NORMAL OPERATING TEMPERATURE, ACCESSORIES OFF AND THE TRANSMISSION IN NEUTRAL.

IGNITION TIMING—
(1) TURN OFF ENGINE.
(2) DISCONNECT THE SINGLE WIRE/BLACK CONNECTOR NEAR THE DISTRIBUTOR.
(3) RE-START PREVIOUSLY WARMED-UP ENGINE.
(4) ADJUST IGNITION TIMING TO 10° BTDC.
(5) TURN OFF ENGINE AND RESTORE ELECTRICAL CONNECTION.

FAST IDLE - DISCONNECT AND PLUG EGR VACUUM HOSE AND ELECTRICALLY DISCONNECT THE PURGE SOLENOID. START ENGINE AND PUT FAST IDLE SCREW ON THE KICKDOWN STEP OF THE FAST IDLE CAM. ADJUST THE FAST IDLE TO 2000 RPM (1800 FOR VEHICLE WITH LESS THAN 100 MILES). RECONNECT EGR VACUUM HOSE AND THE PURGE SOLENOID.

THIS ENGINE IS EQUIPPED WITH AUTOMATIC IDLE SPEED CONTROL. IDLE RPM IS NOT ADJUSTABLE. IF NOT WITHIN 775-925 RPM FOR MANUAL TRANS. (IN NEUTRAL), OR 675-825 RPM FOR AUTO TRANS. (IN DRIVE), WITH ALL ACCESSORIES OFF, SEE SHOP MANUAL.

THIS VEHICLE CONFORMS TO U.S.E.P.A. REGULATIONS APPLICABLE TO 1984 MODEL YEAR NEW MOTOR VEHICLES. COMPLIANCE DEMONSTRATED AND DESIGNED FOR PRINCIPLE USE BELOW 4000 FEET. THIS VEHICLE IS EXEMPT FROM MEETING EMISSION STANDARDS ABOVE 4000 FEET BECAUSE OF POSSIBLY UNSUITABLE PERFORMANCE. AND THE EMISSIONS PERFORMANCE WARRANTY DOES NOT APPLY ABOVE 4000 FEET.

E4AE-9C485-AHR   CATALYST   SPARK PLUG: AWSF-44   GAP - .042-.046
2.3L-4GQ
EFM2.3VIHPK2-EGR/EGS/AIP/TWC

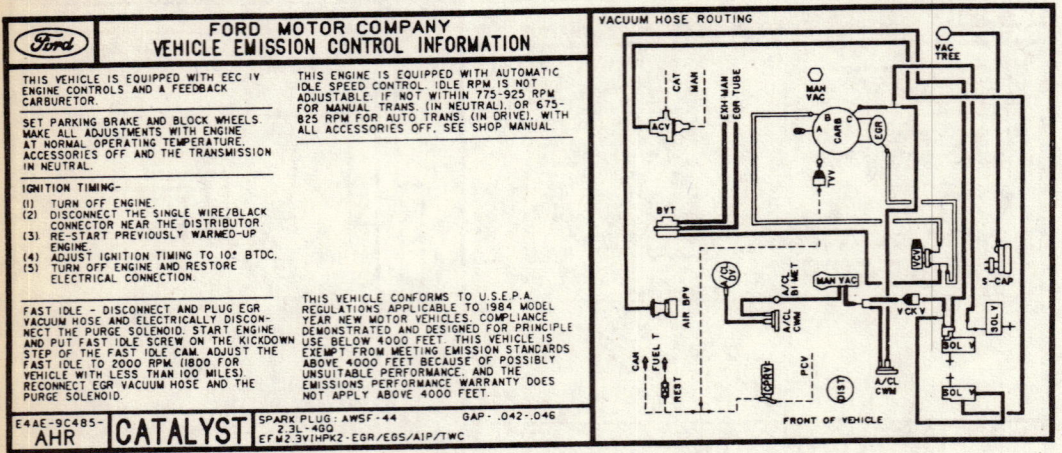

CALIBRATION: 4—05B—R00

MODEL YEAR: 1984   **ENGINE: 2.3L**

FORD MOTOR COMPANY
VEHICLE EMISSION CONTROL INFORMATION

THIS VEHICLE IS EQUIPPED WITH EEC IV ENGINE CONTROLS AND A FEEDBACK CARBURETOR.

SET PARKING BRAKE AND BLOCK WHEELS. MAKE ALL ADJUSTMENTS WITH ENGINE AT NORMAL OPERATING TEMPERATURE, ACCESSORIES OFF AND THE TRANSMISSION IN NEUTRAL.

IGNITION TIMING—
(1) TURN OFF ENGINE.
(2) DISCONNECT THE SINGLE WIRE/BLACK CONNECTOR NEAR THE DISTRIBUTOR.
(3) RE-START PREVIOUSLY WARMED-UP ENGINE.
(4) ADJUST IGNITION TIMING TO 10° BTDC.
(5) TURN OFF ENGINE AND RESTORE ELECTRICAL CONNECTION.

FAST IDLE - DISCONNECT AND PLUG EGR VACUUM HOSE AND ELECTRICALLY DISCONNECT THE PURGE SOLENOID. START ENGINE AND PUT FAST IDLE SCREW ON THE KICKDOWN STEP OF THE FAST IDLE CAM. ADJUST THE FAST IDLE TO 2000 RPM (1800 FOR VEHICLE WITH LESS THAN 100 MILES). RECONNECT EGR VACUUM HOSE AND THE PURGE SOLENOID.

THIS ENGINE IS EQUIPPED WITH AUTOMATIC IDLE SPEED CONTROL. IDLE RPM IS NOT ADJUSTABLE. IF NOT WITHIN 775-925 RPM FOR MANUAL TRANS. (IN NEUTRAL), OR 675-825 RPM FOR AUTO TRANS. (IN DRIVE), WITH ALL ACCESSORIES OFF, SEE SHOP MANUAL.

THIS VEHICLE CONFORMS TO U.S.E.P.A. REGULATIONS APPLICABLE TO 1984 MODEL YEAR NEW MOTOR VEHICLES. COMPLIANCE DEMONSTRATED BOTH ABOVE AND BELOW 4000 FEET.

E4AE-9C485-AGT   CATALYST   SPARK PLUG: AWSF-44   GAP - .042-.046
2.3L-4GQ
EFM2.3VIHPK2-EGR/EGS/AIP/TWC

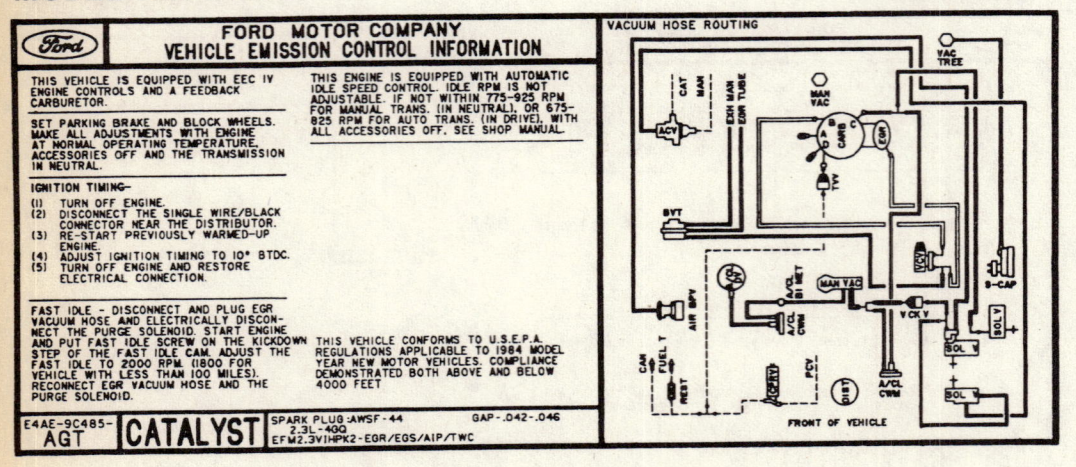

EMISSION CONTROLS 259

CALIBRATION: 4—05H—R00

MODEL YEAR: 1984 **ENGINE: 2.3L**

```
VEHICLE EMISSION
CONTROL INFORMATION           Ford    FORD MOTOR COMPANY

C  SET PARKING BRAKE AND BLOCK WHEELS. DISCONNECT AUTOMATIC
A  PARKING BRAKE RELEASE (IF SO EQUIPPED). MAKE ALL ADJUSTMENTS
T  WITH ENGINE AT NORMAL OPERATING TEMPERATURE. ACCESSORIES AND
A  HEADLIGHTS OFF. PUT AIR CLEANER IN POSITION WHEN CHECKING ALL
L  ENGINE SPEEDS.
Y
S  IGNITION TIMING-DISCONNECT AND PLUG DISTRIBUTOR VACUUM HOSE.
T  WITH TRANS IN NEUTRAL, ADJUST TIMING TO 12° BTDC, 700 RPM
   MAX. RECONNECT HOSE.
C
A  FAST IDLE-DISCONNECT AND PLUG PURGE VALVE VACUUM HOSE.
T  PUT FAST IDLE SCREW ON KICKDOWN STEP OF FAST IDLE CAM
A  AND ADJUST TO 2000 RPM WITH TRANS. IN NEUTRAL. (1750 RPM
L  FOR VEHICLE WITH LESS THAN 160 KM).
Y
S  CURB IDLE-DISCONNECT ELECTRIC COOLING FAN (IF SO EQUIPPED).
E  ADJUST TO 850 RPM BY TURNING THE HEX HEAD ROD AT REAR OF
U  THROTTLE SOLENOID POSITIONER WITH ALL VACUUM HOSES
R  CONNECTED AND TRANS. IN NEUTRAL (750 RPM FOR VEHICLES WITH
   LESS THAN 160 KM).

   PLACE TRANS. IN NEUTRAL AND REV ENGINE MOMENTARILY.
   CHECK/READJUST IDLE WITH TRANS. IN SPECIFIED POSITION.
   RECONNECT ELECTRIC FAN.

   IF IDLE ADJUSTMENT IS MADE, CHECK/ADJUST BOWL VENT SETTING.
   SEE SHOP MANUAL.

   SEE SHOP MANUAL FOR CHOKE AND IDLE MIXTURE ADJUSTMENT INFO.

E4AE-9C485-      SPARK PLUG         GAP .042-.046
   AGY     2.3L  BOUGIES AWSF-44    ÉLECTRODES
```

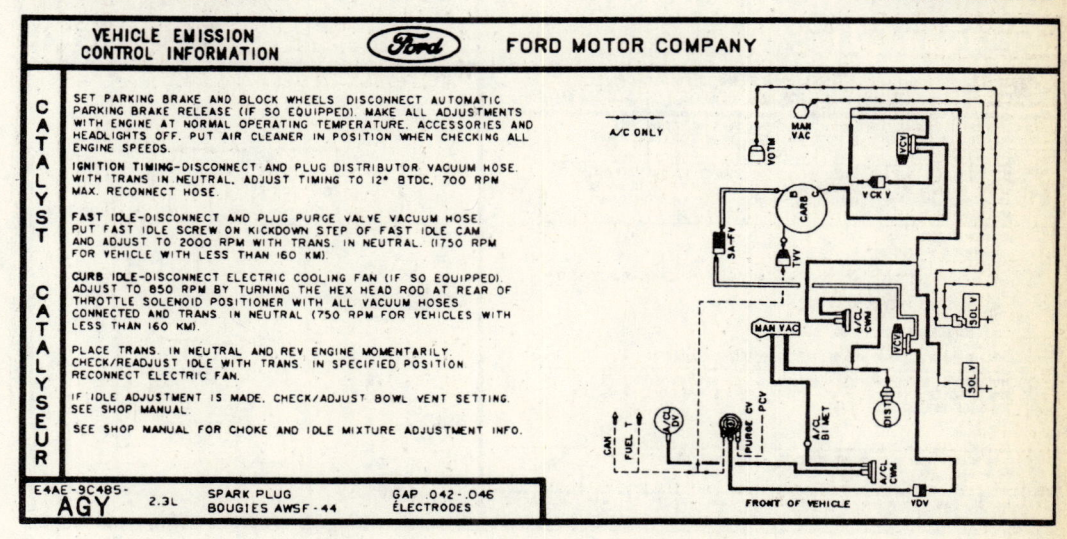

CALIBRATION: 4—05H—R10

MODEL YEAR: 1984 **ENGINE: 2.3L**

```
VEHICLE EMISSION
CONTROL INFORMATION           Ford    FORD MOTOR COMPANY

C  SET PARKING BRAKE AND BLOCK WHEELS. DISCONNECT AUTOMATIC
A  PARKING BRAKE RELEASE (IF SO EQUIPPED). MAKE ALL ADJUSTMENTS
T  WITH ENGINE AT NORMAL OPERATING TEMPERATURE. ACCESSORIES AND
A  HEADLIGHTS OFF. PUT AIR CLEANER IN POSITION WHEN CHECKING ALL
L  ENGINE SPEEDS.
Y
S  IGNITION TIMING-DISCONNECT AND PLUG DISTRIBUTOR VACUUM HOSE.
T  WITH TRANS IN NEUTRAL, ADJUST TIMING TO 12° BTDC, 700 RPM
   MAX. RECONNECT HOSE.
C
A  FAST IDLE-DISCONNECT AND PLUG PURGE VALVE VACUUM HOSE.
T  PUT FAST IDLE SCREW ON KICKDOWN STEP OF FAST
A  IDLE CAM AND ADJUST TO 2000 RPM WITH TRANS. IN NEUTRAL.
L  (1750 RPM FOR VEHICLE WITH LESS THAN 160 KM).
Y
S  CURB IDLE-DISCONNECT ELECTRIC COOLING FAN (IF SO EQUIPPED).
E  ADJUST TO 850 RPM BY TURNING THE HEX HEAD ROD AT REAR OF
U  THROTTLE SOLENOID POSITIONER WITH ALL VACUUM HOSES
R  CONNECTED AND TRANS. IN NEUTRAL (750 RPM FOR VEHICLES WITH
   LESS THAN 160 KM).

   PLACE TRANS. IN NEUTRAL AND REV ENGINE MOMENTARILY.
   CHECK/READJUST IDLE WITH TRANS. IN SPECIFIED POSITION.
   RECONNECT ELECTRIC FAN.

   IF IDLE ADJUSTMENT IS MADE, CHECK/ADJUST BOWL VENT SETTING.
   SEE SHOP MANUAL.

   SEE SHOP MANUAL FOR CHOKE AND IDLE MIXTURE ADJUSTMENT INFO.

E4AE-9C485-AMB   SPARK PLUG         GAP .042-.046
   AMB    2.3L   BOUGIES AWSF-44    ÉLECTRODES
```

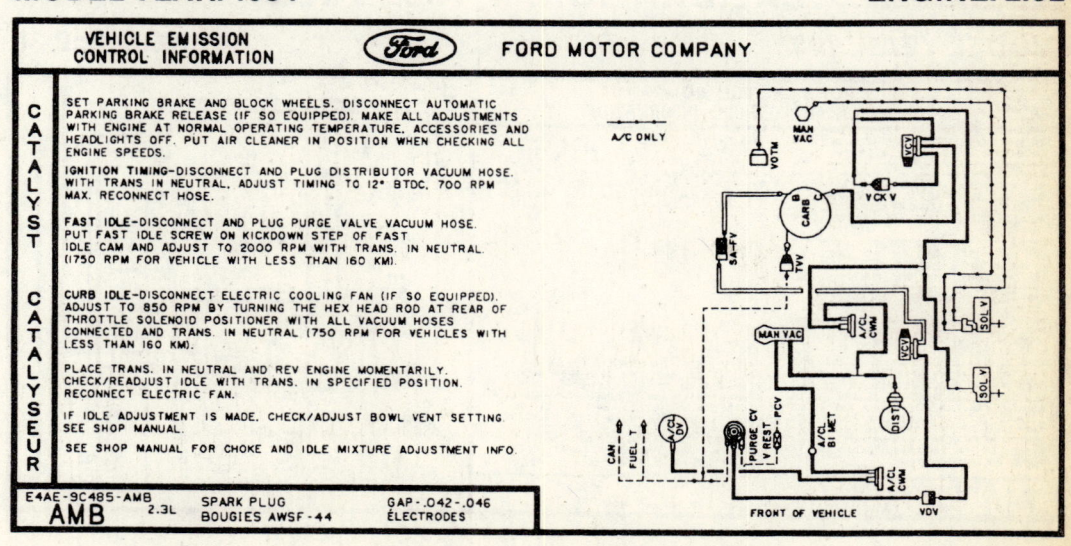

EMISSION CONTROLS

CALIBRATION: 4—05S—R00

MODEL YEAR: 1984　　　　　　　　　　　**ENGINE: 2.3L**

FORD MOTOR COMPANY
VEHICLE EMISSION CONTROL INFORMATION

THIS VEHICLE IS EQUIPPED WITH ELECTRONIC FUEL INJECTION. IDLE MIXTURE, COLD ENGINE IDLE SPEED AND COLD ENGINE FUEL ENRICHMENT NOT ADJUSTABLE.

SET PARKING BRAKE AND BLOCK WHEELS. DISCONNECT AUTOMATIC PARKING BRAKE RELEASE, IF SO EQUIPPED. MAKE ALL ADJUSTMENTS WITH ENGINE AT NORMAL OPERATING TEMPERATURE, TRANSMISSION IN NEUTRAL AND ACCESSORIES OFF.

IGNITION TIMING—
(1) TURN OFF ENGINE
(2) DISCONNECT THE SINGLE WIRE BLACK CONNECTOR NEAR THE DISTRIBUTOR.
(3) RE-START PREVIOUSLY WARMED-UP ENGINE.
(4) ADJUST IGNITION TIMING TO 10° BTDC.
(5) TURN OFF ENGINE AND RESTORE ELECTRICAL CONNECTION.

THIS ENGINE IS EQUIPPED WITH AUTOMATIC IDLE SPEED CONTROL. IDLE RPM IS NOT ADJUSTABLE. IF NOT WITHIN 825-975 RPM RANGE IN NEUTRAL, SEE SHOP MANUAL.

THIS VEHICLE CONFORMS TO U.S.E.P.A. REGULATIONS APPLICABLE TO 1984 MODEL YEAR NEW MOTOR VEHICLES. COMPLIANCE DEMONSTRATED BOTH ABOVE AND BELOW 4000 FEET.

E4AE-9C485-ALV　CATALYST　SPARK PLUG: AWSF-32　GAP: .032-.036
2.3L — 4HM
EFM2.3V5FGT2 — EGS/EGR/TWC

VACUUM HOSE ROUTING

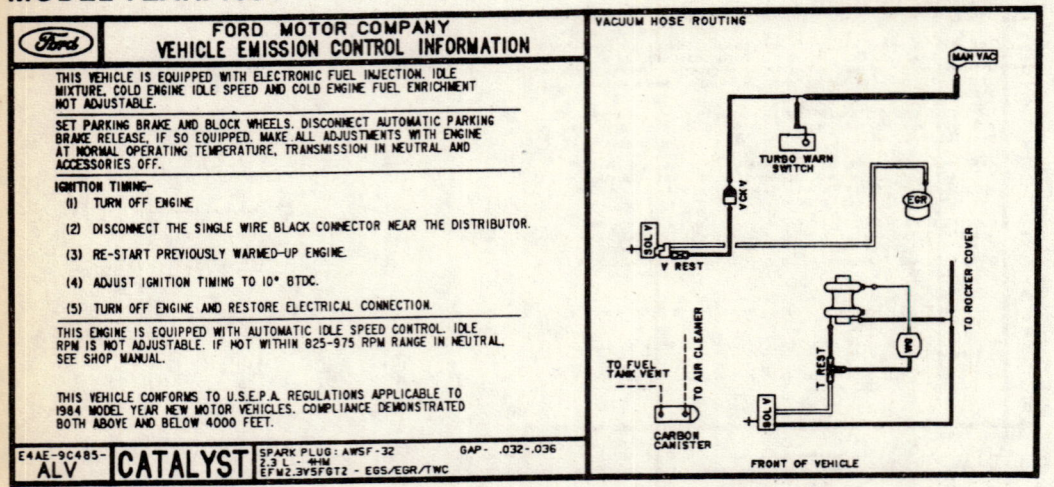

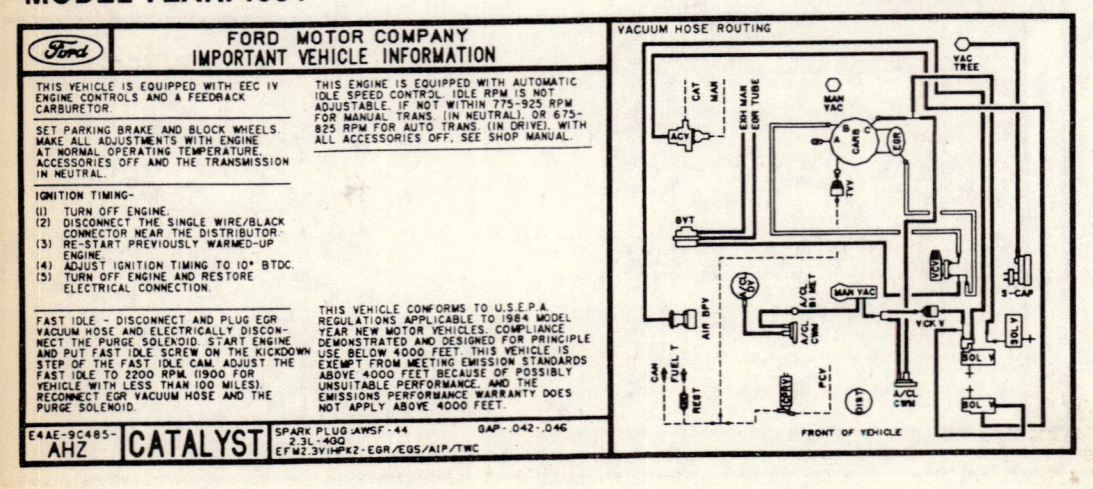

CALIBRATION: 4—06A—R10

MODEL YEAR: 1984　　　　　　　　　　　**ENGINE: 2.3L**

FORD MOTOR COMPANY
IMPORTANT VEHICLE INFORMATION

THIS VEHICLE IS EQUIPPED WITH EEC IV ENGINE CONTROLS AND A FEEDBACK CARBURETOR.

SET PARKING BRAKE AND BLOCK WHEELS. MAKE ALL ADJUSTMENTS WITH ENGINE AT NORMAL OPERATING TEMPERATURE, ACCESSORIES OFF AND THE TRANSMISSION IN NEUTRAL.

IGNITION TIMING—
(1) TURN OFF ENGINE.
(2) DISCONNECT THE SINGLE WIRE/BLACK CONNECTOR NEAR THE DISTRIBUTOR.
(3) RE-START PREVIOUSLY WARMED-UP ENGINE.
(4) ADJUST IGNITION TIMING TO 10° BTDC.
(5) TURN OFF ENGINE AND RESTORE ELECTRICAL CONNECTION.

FAST IDLE - DISCONNECT AND PLUG EGR VACUUM HOSE AND ELECTRICALLY DISCONNECT THE PURGE SOLENOID. START ENGINE AND PUT FAST IDLE SCREW ON THE KICKDOWN STEP OF THE FAST IDLE CAM. ADJUST THE FAST IDLE TO 2200 RPM. (1900 FOR VEHICLE WITH LESS THAN 100 MILES). RECONNECT EGR VACUUM HOSE AND THE PURGE SOLENOID.

THIS ENGINE IS EQUIPPED WITH AUTOMATIC IDLE SPEED CONTROL. IDLE RPM IS NOT ADJUSTABLE. IF NOT WITHIN 775-925 RPM FOR MANUAL TRANS (IN NEUTRAL), OR 675-825 RPM FOR AUTO TRANS (IN DRIVE), WITH ALL ACCESSORIES OFF, SEE SHOP MANUAL.

THIS VEHICLE CONFORMS TO U.S.E.P.A. REGULATIONS APPLICABLE TO 1984 MODEL YEAR NEW MOTOR VEHICLES. COMPLIANCE DEMONSTRATED AND DESIGNED FOR PRINCIPLE USE BELOW 4000 FEET. THIS VEHICLE IS EXEMPT FROM MEETING EMISSION STANDARDS ABOVE 4000 FEET BECAUSE OF POSSIBLY UNSUITABLE PERFORMANCE, AND THE EMISSIONS WARRANTY DOES NOT APPLY ABOVE 4000 FEET.

E4AE-9C485-AHZ　CATALYST　SPARK PLUG: AWSF-44　GAP: .042-.046
2.3L — 4GQ
EFM2.3V1HPK2 — EGR/EGS/AIP/TWC

VACUUM HOSE ROUTING

EMISSION CONTROLS 261

CALIBRATION: 4—06E—R00

MODEL YEAR: 1984   **ENGINE: 2.3L**

FORD MOTOR COMPANY — VEHICLE EMISSION CONTROL INFORMATION

THIS VEHICLE IS EQUIPPED WITH ELECTRONIC FUEL INJECTION. IDLE MIXTURE, COLD ENGINE IDLE SPEED AND COLD ENGINE FUEL ENRICHMENT NOT ADJUSTABLE.

SET PARKING BRAKE AND BLOCK WHEELS. DISCONNECT AUTOMATIC PARKING BRAKE RELEASE, IF SO EQUIPPED. MAKE ALL ADJUSTMENTS WITH ENGINE AT NORMAL OPERATING TEMPERATURE, TRANSMISSION IN NEUTRAL AND ACCESSORIES OFF.

IGNITION TIMING-
(1) TURN OFF ENGINE
(2) DISCONNECT THE SINGLE WIRE BLACK CONNECTOR NEAR THE DISTRIBUTOR
(3) RE-START PREVIOUSLY WARMED-UP ENGINE.
(4) ADJUST IGNITION TIMING TO 10° BTDC.
(5) TURN OFF ENGINE AND RESTORE ELECTRICAL CONNECTION.

THIS ENGINE IS EQUIPPED WITH AUTOMATIC IDLE SPEED CONTROL. IDLE RPM IS NOT ADJUSTABLE. IF NOT WITHIN 825-975 RPM RANGE IN NEUTRAL, SEE SHOP MANUAL.

THIS VEHICLE CONFORMS TO U.S.E.P.A. REGULATIONS APPLICABLE TO 1984 MODEL YEAR NEW MOTOR VEHICLES. COMPLIANCE DEMONSTRATED BOTH ABOVE AND BELOW 4000 FEET.

E4AE-9C485-ADR   CATALYST   SPARK PLUG: AWSF-32   2.3L-4HM   EFM2.3V5FGT2 - EGS/EGR/TWC   GAP .032-.036

VACUUM HOSE ROUTING — MAN VAC, TURBO WARN SWITCH, V CK V, EGR, SOL A, V REST, TO FUEL TANK VENT, TO AIR CLEANER, CARBON CANISTER, FRONT OF VEHICLE

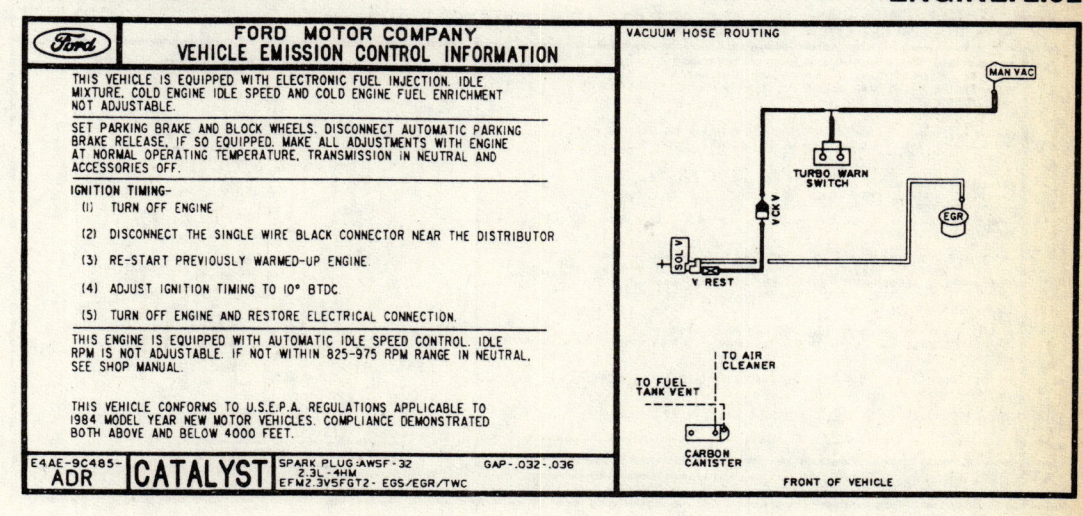

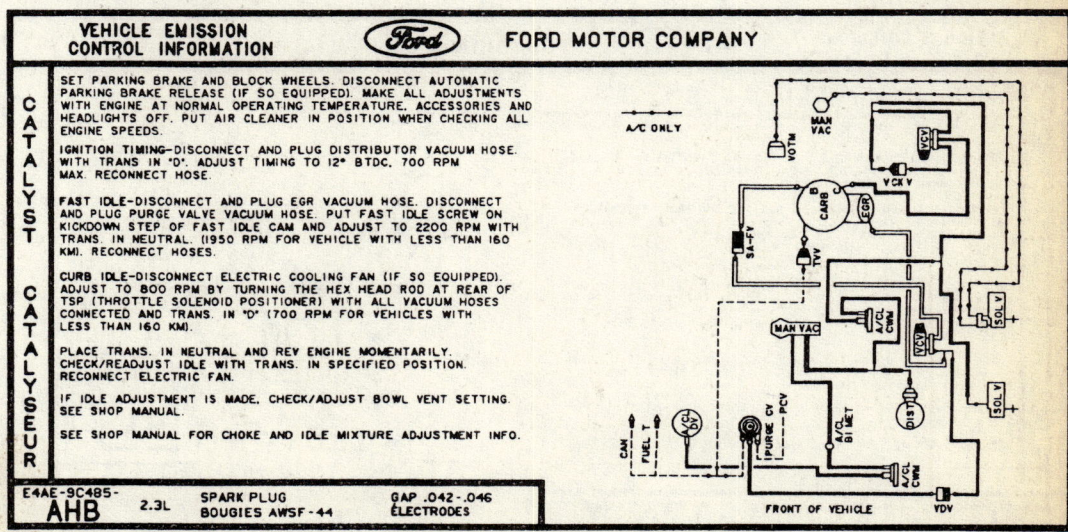

CALIBRATION: 4—06H—R00

MODEL YEAR: 1984   **ENGINE: 2.3L**

VEHICLE EMISSION CONTROL INFORMATION — FORD MOTOR COMPANY

SET PARKING BRAKE AND BLOCK WHEELS. DISCONNECT AUTOMATIC PARKING BRAKE RELEASE (IF SO EQUIPPED). MAKE ALL ADJUSTMENTS WITH ENGINE AT NORMAL OPERATING TEMPERATURE, ACCESSORIES AND HEADLIGHTS OFF. PUT AIR CLEANER IN POSITION WHEN CHECKING ALL ENGINE SPEEDS.

IGNITION TIMING-DISCONNECT AND PLUG DISTRIBUTOR VACUUM HOSE. WITH TRANS IN "D". ADJUST TIMING TO 12° BTDC, 700 RPM MAX. RECONNECT HOSE.

FAST IDLE-DISCONNECT AND PLUG EGR VACUUM HOSE. DISCONNECT AND PLUG PURGE VALVE VACUUM HOSE. PUT FAST IDLE SCREW ON KICKDOWN STEP OF FAST IDLE CAM AND ADJUST TO 2200 RPM WITH TRANS. IN NEUTRAL. (1950 RPM FOR VEHICLE WITH LESS THAN 160 KM). RECONNECT HOSES.

CURB IDLE-DISCONNECT ELECTRIC COOLING FAN (IF SO EQUIPPED). ADJUST TO 800 RPM BY TURNING THE HEX HEAD ROD AT REAR OF TSP (THROTTLE SOLENOID POSITIONER) WITH ALL VACUUM HOSES CONNECTED AND TRANS. IN "D" (700 RPM FOR VEHICLES WITH LESS THAN 160 KM).

PLACE TRANS. IN NEUTRAL AND REV ENGINE MOMENTARILY. CHECK/READJUST IDLE WITH TRANS. IN SPECIFIED POSITION. RECONNECT ELECTRIC FAN.

IF IDLE ADJUSTMENT IS MADE, CHECK/ADJUST BOWL VENT SETTING. SEE SHOP MANUAL.

SEE SHOP MANUAL FOR CHOKE AND IDLE MIXTURE ADJUSTMENT INFO.

CATALYST / CATALYSEUR   E4AE-9C485-AHB   2.3L   SPARK PLUG / BOUGIES AWSF-44   GAP .042-.046 ÉLECTRODES

A/C ONLY, VOTM, MAN VAC, VCKY, CARB, EGR, VCK V, SA-FV, TVV, A/CL CWM, MAN VAC, VCV, SOL V, PURGE CV, PCV, A/CL BI MET, DIST, SOL V, CAM, FUEL T, CV, CV, A/CL CWM, VDV, FRONT OF VEHICLE

262 EMISSION CONTROLS

CALIBRATION: 4—06H—R10

MODEL YEAR: 1984 **ENGINE: 2.3L**

VEHICLE EMISSION CONTROL INFORMATION — FORD MOTOR COMPANY

CATALYST / CATALYSEUR

SET PARKING BRAKE AND BLOCK WHEELS. DISCONNECT AUTOMATIC PARKING BRAKE RELEASE (IF SO EQUIPPED). MAKE ALL ADJUSTMENTS WITH ENGINE AT NORMAL OPERATING TEMPERATURE, ACCESSORIES AND HEADLIGHTS OFF. PUT AIR CLEANER IN POSITION WHEN CHECKING ALL ENGINE SPEEDS.

IGNITION TIMING-DISCONNECT AND PLUG DISTRIBUTOR VACUUM HOSE. WITH TRANS IN "D". ADJUST TIMING TO 12° BTDC, 700 RPM MAX. RECONNECT HOSE.

FAST IDLE-DISCONNECT AND PLUG EGR VACUUM HOSE. DISCONNECT AND PLUG PURGE VALVE VACUUM HOSE. PUT FAST IDLE SCREW ON KICKDOWN STEP OF FAST IDLE CAM AND ADJUST TO 2200 RPM WITH TRANS. IN NEUTRAL. (1950 RPM FOR VEHICLE WITH LESS THAN 160 KM). RECONNECT HOSES.

CURB IDLE-DISCONNECT ELECTRIC COOLING FAN (IF SO EQUIPPED). ADJUST TO 800 RPM BY TURNING THE HEX HEAD ROD AT REAR OF TSP (THROTTLE SOLENOID POSITIONER) WITH ALL VACUUM HOSES CONNECTED AND TRANS. IN "D" (700 RPM FOR VEHICLES WITH LESS THAN 160 KM).

PLACE TRANS. IN NEUTRAL AND REV ENGINE MOMENTARILY. CHECK/READJUST IDLE WITH TRANS. IN SPECIFIED POSITION. RECONNECT ELECTRIC FAN.

IF IDLE ADJUSTMENT IS MADE, CHECK/ADJUST BOWL VENT SETTING. SEE SHOP MANUAL.

SEE SHOP MANUAL FOR CHOKE AND IDLE MIXTURE ADJUSTMENT INFO.

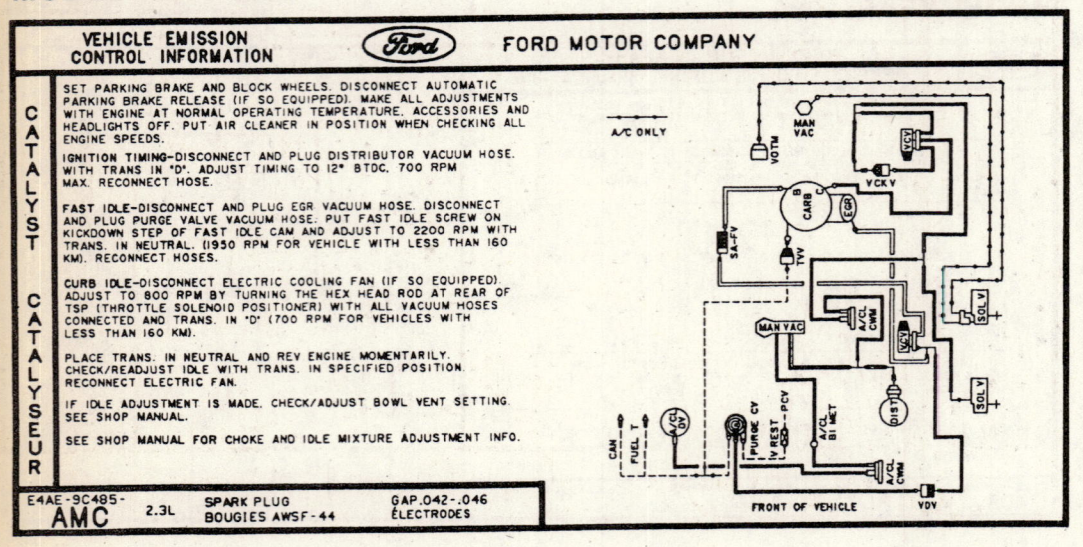

E4AE-9C485- AMC 2.3L SPARK PLUG BOUGIES AWSF-44 GAP .042-.046 ÉLECTRODES

CALIBRATION: 4—06H—R11

MODEL YEAR: 1984 **ENGINE: 2.3L**

VEHICLE EMISSION CONTROL INFORMATION — FORD MOTOR COMPANY

CATALYST / CATALYSEUR

SET PARKING BRAKE AND BLOCK WHEELS. DISCONNECT AUTOMATIC PARKING BRAKE RELEASE (IF SO EQUIPPED). MAKE ALL ADJUSTMENTS WITH ENGINE AT NORMAL OPERATING TEMPERATURE, ACCESSORIES AND HEADLIGHTS OFF. PUT AIR CLEANER IN POSITION WHEN CHECKING ALL ENGINE SPEEDS.

IGNITION TIMING-DISCONNECT AND PLUG DISTRIBUTOR VACUUM HOSE. WITH TRANS IN "D". ADJUST TIMING TO 12° BTDC, 700 RPM MAX. RECONNECT HOSE.

FAST IDLE-DISCONNECT AND PLUG EGR VACUUM HOSE. DISCONNECT AND PLUG PURGE VALVE VACUUM HOSE. PUT FAST IDLE SCREW ON KICKDOWN STEP OF FAST IDLE CAM AND ADJUST TO 2200 RPM WITH TRANS. IN NEUTRAL. (1950 RPM FOR VEHICLE WITH LESS THAN 160 KM). RECONNECT HOSES.

CURB IDLE-DISCONNECT ELECTRIC COOLING FAN (IF SO EQUIPPED). ADJUST TO 800 RPM BY TURNING THE HEX HEAD ROD AT REAR OF TSP (THROTTLE SOLENOID POSITIONER) WITH ALL VACUUM HOSES CONNECTED AND TRANS. IN "D" (700 RPM FOR VEHICLES WITH LESS THAN 160 KM).

PLACE TRANS. IN NEUTRAL AND REV ENGINE MOMENTARILY. CHECK/READJUST IDLE WITH TRANS. IN SPECIFIED POSITION. RECONNECT ELECTRIC FAN.

IF IDLE ADJUSTMENT IS MADE, CHECK/ADJUST BOWL VENT SETTING. SEE SHOP MANUAL.

SEE SHOP MANUAL FOR CHOKE AND IDLE MIXTURE ADJUSTMENT INFO.

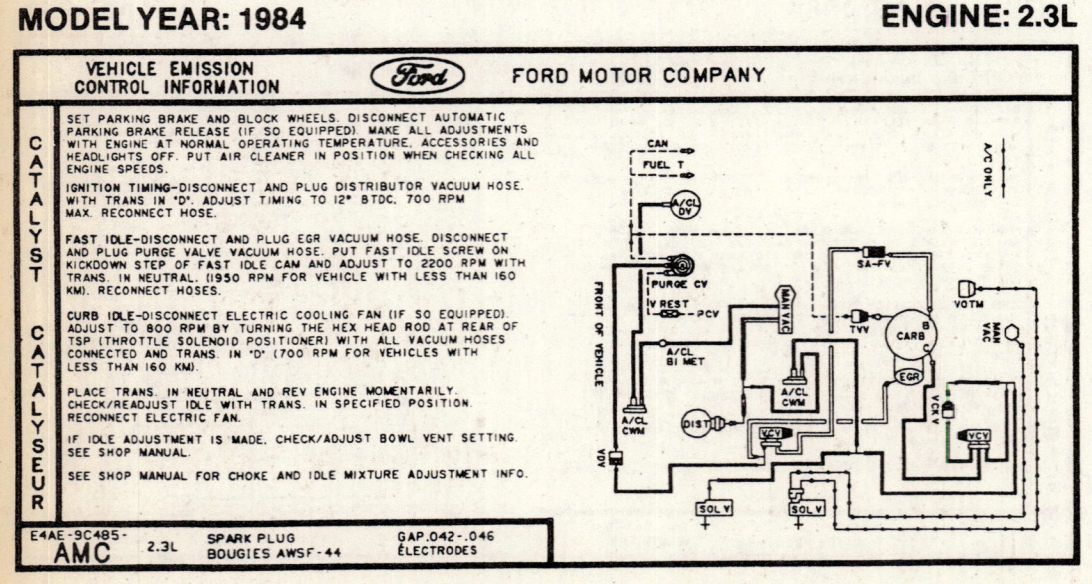

E4AE-9C485- AMC 2.3L SPARK PLUG BOUGIES AWSF-44 GAP .042-.046 ÉLECTRODES

EMISSION CONTROLS 263

CALIBRATION: 4—06N—R00

MODEL YEAR: 1984 **ENGINE: 2.3L**

FORD MOTOR COMPANY
VEHICLE EMISSION CONTROL INFORMATION

THIS VEHICLE IS EQUIPPED WITH EEC 'IV ENGINE CONTROLS AND A FEEDBACK CARBURETOR.

SET PARKING BRAKE AND BLOCK WHEELS. MAKE ALL ADJUSTMENTS WITH ENGINE AT NORMAL OPERATING TEMPERATURE, ACCESSORIES OFF AND THE TRANSMISSION IN NEUTRAL.

IGNITION TIMING-
(1) TURN OFF ENGINE.
(2) DISCONNECT THE SINGLE WIRE/BLACK CONNECTOR NEAR THE DISTRIBUTOR
(3) RE-START PREVIOUSLY WARMED-UP ENGINE
(4) ADJUST IGNITION TIMING TO 10° BTDC
(5) TURN OFF ENGINE AND RESTORE ELECTRICAL CONNECTION

FAST IDLE - DISCONNECT AND PLUG EGR VACUUM HOSE AND ELECTRICALLY DISCONNECT THE PURGE SOLENOID. START ENGINE AND PUT FAST IDLE SCREW ON THE KICKDOWN STEP OF THE FAST IDLE CAM. ADJUST THE FAST IDLE TO 2200 RPM. (1900 FOR VEHICLE WITH LESS THAN 100 MILES). RECONNECT EGR VACUUM HOSE AND THE PURGE SOLENOID.

THIS ENGINE IS EQUIPPED WITH AUTOMATIC IDLE SPEED CONTROL. IDLE RPM IS NOT ADJUSTABLE. IF NOT WITHIN 775-925 RPM FOR MANUAL TRANS (IN NEUTRAL), OR 675-825 RPM FOR AUTO TRANS (IN DRIVE), WITH ALL ACCESSORIES OFF, SEE SHOP MANUAL.

THIS VEHICLE CONFORMS TO U.S.E.P.A. AND CALIFORNIA REGULATIONS APPLICABLE TO 1984 MODEL YEAR NEW MOTOR VEHICLES INTRODUCED INTO COMMERCE SOLELY FOR SALE IN CALIFORNIA.

E4AE-9C485-AHA CATALYST SPARK PLUG: AWSF-44 2.3L-4G0 GAP .042-.046
EFM2.3V1HPC3-EGR/EGS/AIP/TWC

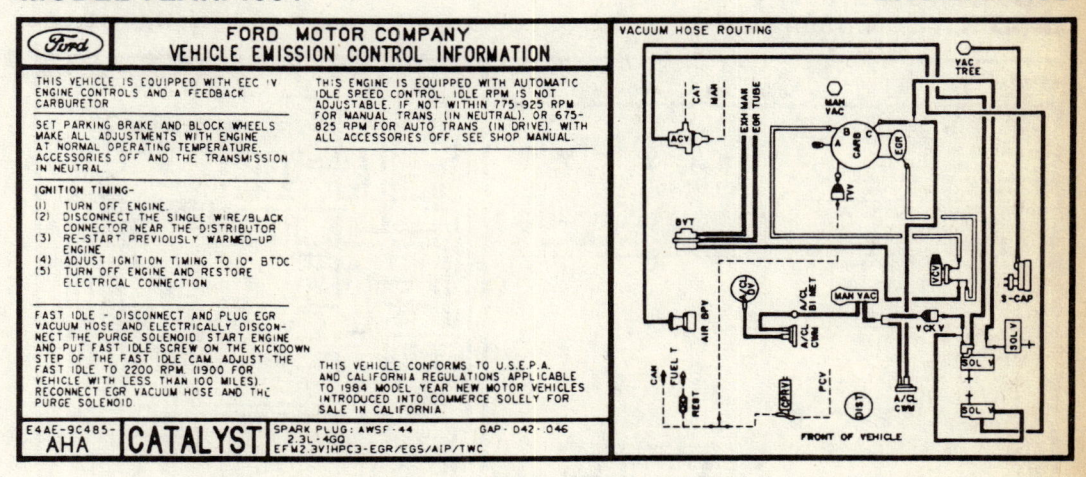

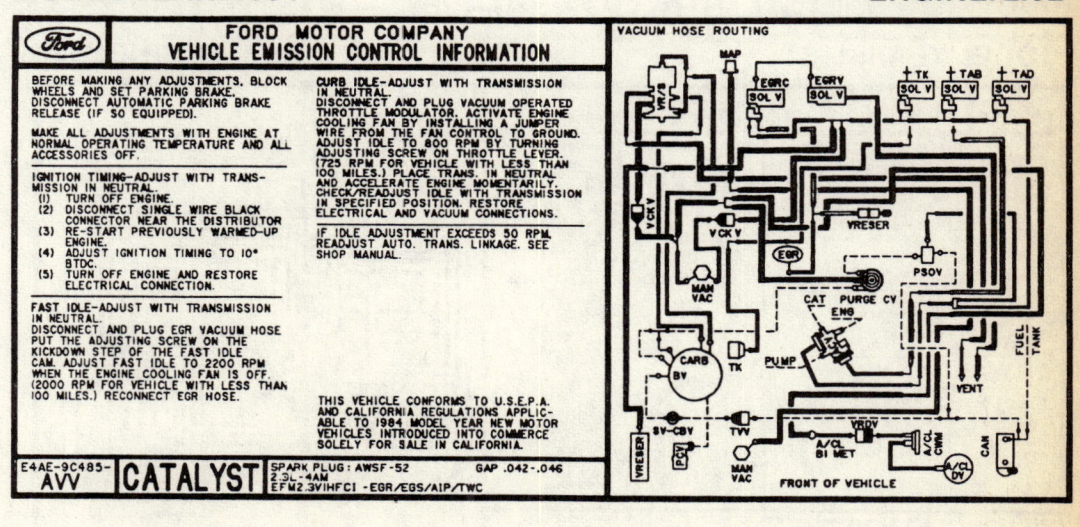

CALIBRATION: 4—25A—R10

MODEL YEAR: 1984 **ENGINE: 2.3L**

FORD MOTOR COMPANY
VEHICLE EMISSION CONTROL INFORMATION

BEFORE MAKING ANY ADJUSTMENTS, BLOCK WHEELS AND SET PARKING BRAKE. DISCONNECT AUTOMATIC PARKING BRAKE RELEASE (IF SO EQUIPPED).

MAKE ALL ADJUSTMENTS WITH ENGINE AT NORMAL OPERATING TEMPERATURE AND ALL ACCESSORIES OFF.

IGNITION TIMING-ADJUST WITH TRANSMISSION IN NEUTRAL.
(1) TURN OFF ENGINE.
(2) DISCONNECT SINGLE WIRE BLACK CONNECTOR NEAR THE DISTRIBUTOR
(3) RE-START PREVIOUSLY WARMED-UP ENGINE.
(4) ADJUST IGNITION TIMING TO 10° BTDC.
(5) TURN OFF ENGINE AND RESTORE ELECTRICAL CONNECTION.

FAST IDLE-ADJUST WITH TRANSMISSION IN NEUTRAL.
DISCONNECT AND PLUG EGR VACUUM HOSE. PUT THE ADJUSTING SCREW ON THE KICKDOWN STEP OF THE FAST IDLE CAM. ADJUST FAST IDLE TO 2200 RPM WHEN THE ENGINE COOLING FAN IS OFF. (2000 RPM FOR VEHICLE WITH LESS THAN 100 MILES.) RECONNECT EGR HOSE.

CURB IDLE-ADJUST WITH TRANSMISSION IN NEUTRAL.
DISCONNECT AND PLUG VACUUM OPERATED THROTTLE MODULATOR. ACTIVATE ENGINE COOLING FAN BY INSTALLING A JUMPER WIRE FROM THE FAN CONTROL TO GROUND. ADJUST IDLE TO 800 RPM BY TURNING ADJUSTING SCREW ON THROTTLE LEVER. (725 RPM FOR VEHICLE WITH LESS THAN 100 MILES.) PLACE TRANS. IN NEUTRAL AND ACCELERATE ENGINE MOMENTARILY. CHECK/READJUST IDLE WITH TRANSMISSION IN SPECIFIED POSITION. RESTORE ELECTRICAL AND VACUUM CONNECTIONS.

IF IDLE ADJUSTMENT EXCEEDS 50 RPM, READJUST AUTO. TRANS. LINKAGE. SEE SHOP MANUAL.

THIS VEHICLE CONFORMS TO U.S.E.P.A. AND CALIFORNIA REGULATIONS APPLICABLE TO 1984 MODEL YEAR NEW MOTOR VEHICLES INTRODUCED INTO COMMERCE SOLELY FOR SALE IN CALIFORNIA.

E4AE-9C485-AVV CATALYST SPARK PLUG: AWSF-52 2.3L-4AM GAP .042-.046
EFM2.3V1HFC1-EGR/EGS/AIP/TWC

EMISSION CONTROLS

CALIBRATION: 4—25D—R12

MODEL YEAR: 1984 **ENGINE: 2.3L**

FORD MOTOR COMPANY
VEHICLE EMISSION CONTROL INFORMATION

BEFORE MAKING ANY ADJUSTMENTS, BLOCK WHEELS AND SET PARKING BRAKE, DISCONNECT AUTOMATIC PARKING BRAKE RELEASE (IF SO EQUIPPED).

MAKE ALL ADJUSTMENTS WITH ENGINE AT NORMAL OPERATING TEMPERATURE AND ALL ACCESSORIES OFF.

IGNITION TIMING—ADJUST WITH TRANSMISSION IN NEUTRAL.
(1) TURN OFF ENGINE.
(2) DISCONNECT SINGLE WIRE BLACK CONNECTOR NEAR THE DISTRIBUTOR.
(3) RE-START PREVIOUSLY WARMED-UP ENGINE.
(4) ADJUST IGNITION TIMING TO 15° BTDC.
(5) TURN OFF ENGINE AND RESTORE ELECTRICAL CONNECTION.

FAST IDLE—ADJUST WITH TRANSMISSION IN NEUTRAL.
DISCONNECT AND PLUG EGR VACUUM HOSE. PUT THE ADJUSTING SCREW ON THE KICKDOWN STEP OF THE FAST IDLE CAM. ADJUST FAST IDLE TO 1900 RPM WHEN THE ENGINE COOLING FAN IS OFF. (1700 RPM FOR VEHICLE WITH LESS THAN 100 MILES.) RECONNECT EGR HOSE.

CURB IDLE—ADJUST WITH TRANSMISSION IN NEUTRAL.
DISCONNECT AND PLUG VACUUM OPERATED THROTTLE MODULATOR. ACTIVATE ENGINE COOLING FAN BY INSTALLING A JUMPER WIRE FROM THE FAN CONTROL TO GROUND. ADJUST IDLE TO 800 RPM BY TURNING ADJUSTING SCREW ON THROTTLE LEVER. (725 RPM FOR VEHICLE WITH LESS THAN 100 MILES.) PLACE TRANS. IN NEUTRAL AND ACCELERATE ENGINE MOMENTARILY. CHECK/READJUST IDLE WITH TRANSMISSION IN SPECIFIED POSITION. RESTORE ELECTRICAL AND VACUUM CONNECTIONS.

THIS VEHICLE CONFORMS TO U.S.E.P.A. REGULATIONS APPLICABLE TO 1984 MODEL YEAR NEW MOTOR VEHICLES. COMPLIANCE DEMONSTRATED BOTH ABOVE AND BELOW 4000 FEET.

E4AE-9C485-AVG   CATALYST   SPARK PLUG: AWSF-52   GAP: .042–.046
2.3L-4AM
EFM2.3VIHFKO-EGR/EGS/AIP/TWC

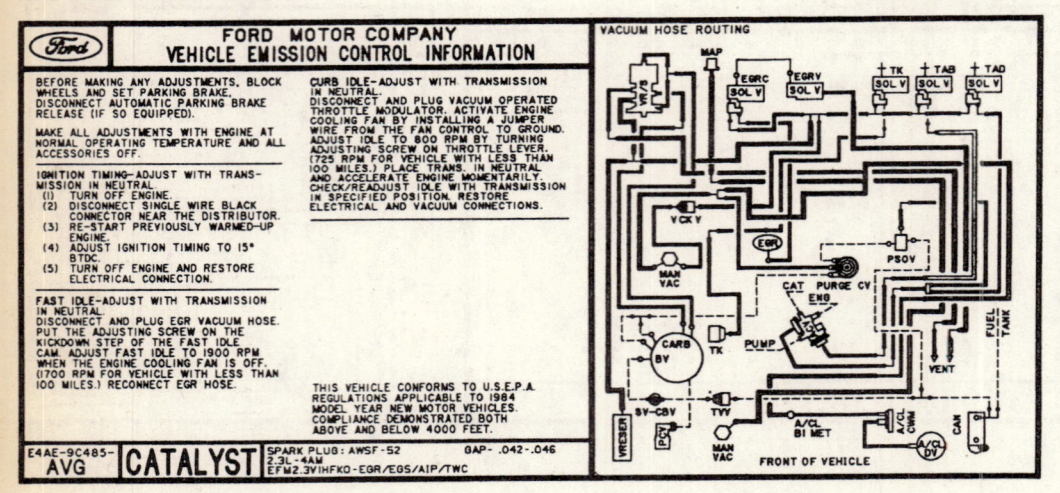

CALIBRATION: 4—25D—R13

MODEL YEAR: 1984 **ENGINE: 2.3L**

FORD MOTOR COMPANY
VEHICLE EMISSION CONTROL INFORMATION

BEFORE MAKING ANY ADJUSTMENTS, BLOCK WHEELS AND SET PARKING BRAKE, DISCONNECT AUTOMATIC PARKING BRAKE RELEASE (IF SO EQUIPPED).

MAKE ALL ADJUSTMENTS WITH ENGINE AT NORMAL OPERATING TEMPERATURE AND ALL ACCESSORIES OFF.

IGNITION TIMING—ADJUST WITH TRANSMISSION IN NEUTRAL.
(1) TURN OFF ENGINE.
(2) DISCONNECT SINGLE WIRE BLACK CONNECTOR NEAR THE DISTRIBUTOR.
(3) RE-START PREVIOUSLY WARMED-UP ENGINE.
(4) ADJUST IGNITION TIMING TO 15° BTDC.
(5) TURN OFF ENGINE AND RESTORE ELECTRICAL CONNECTION.

FAST IDLE—ADJUST WITH TRANSMISSION IN NEUTRAL.
DISCONNECT AND PLUG EGR VACUUM HOSE. PUT THE ADJUSTING SCREW ON THE KICKDOWN STEP OF THE FAST IDLE CAM. ADJUST FAST IDLE TO 1900 RPM WHEN THE ENGINE COOLING FAN IS OFF. (1700 RPM FOR VEHICLE WITH LESS THAN 100 MILES.) RECONNECT EGR HOSE.

CURB IDLE—ADJUST WITH TRANSMISSION IN NEUTRAL.
DISCONNECT AND PLUG VACUUM OPERATED THROTTLE MODULATOR. ACTIVATE ENGINE COOLING FAN BY INSTALLING A JUMPER WIRE FROM THE FAN CONTROL TO GROUND. ADJUST IDLE TO 800 RPM BY TURNING ADJUSTING SCREW ON THROTTLE LEVER. (725 RPM FOR VEHICLE WITH LESS THAN 100 MILES.) PLACE TRANS. IN NEUTRAL AND ACCELERATE ENGINE MOMENTARILY. CHECK/READJUST IDLE WITH TRANSMISSION IN SPECIFIED POSITION. RESTORE ELECTRICAL AND VACUUM CONNECTIONS.

THIS VEHICLE CONFORMS TO U.S.E.P.A. AND CALIFORNIA REGULATIONS APPLICABLE TO 1984 MODEL YEAR NEW MOTOR VEHICLES INTRODUCED INTO COMMERCE SOLELY FOR SALE IN CALIFORNIA.

E4AE-9C485-AVH   CATALYST   SPARK PLUG: AWSF-52   GAP: .042–.046
2.3L-4AM
EFM2.3VIHFCI-EGR/EGS/AIP/TWC

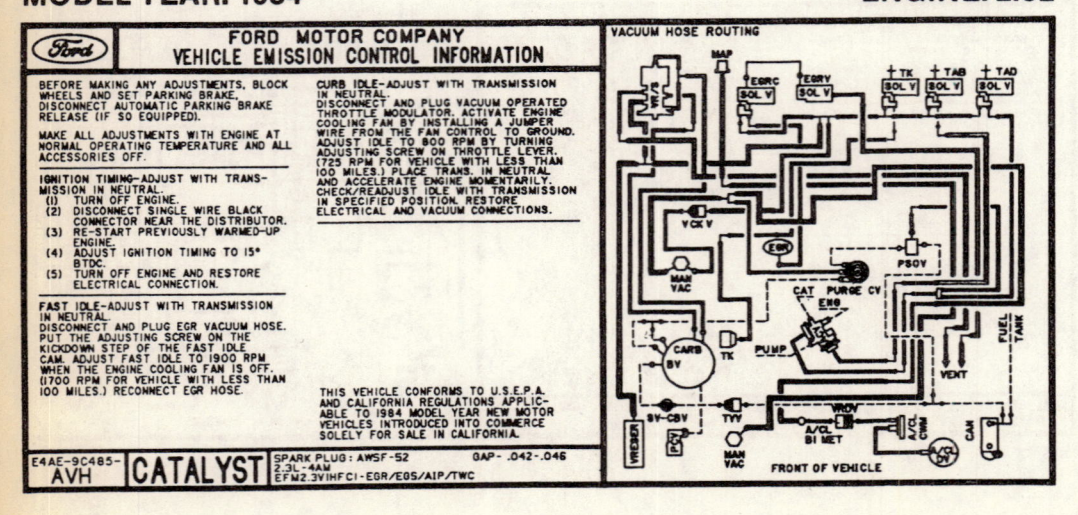

EMISSION CONTROLS 265

CALIBRATION: 4—25E—R01

MODEL YEAR: 1984 **ENGINE: 2.3L**

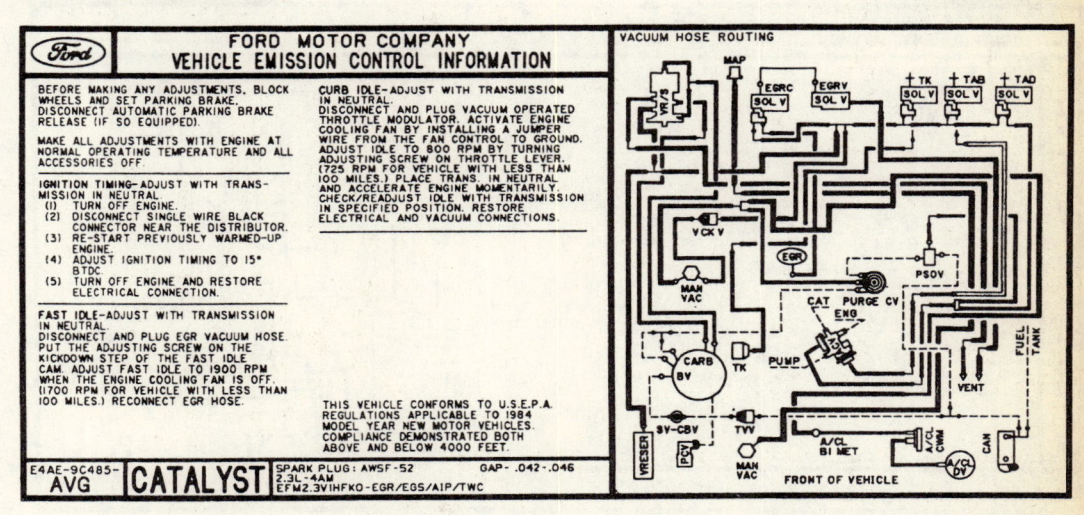

CALIBRATION: 4—25F—R00

MODEL YEAR: 1984 **ENGINE: 2.3L**

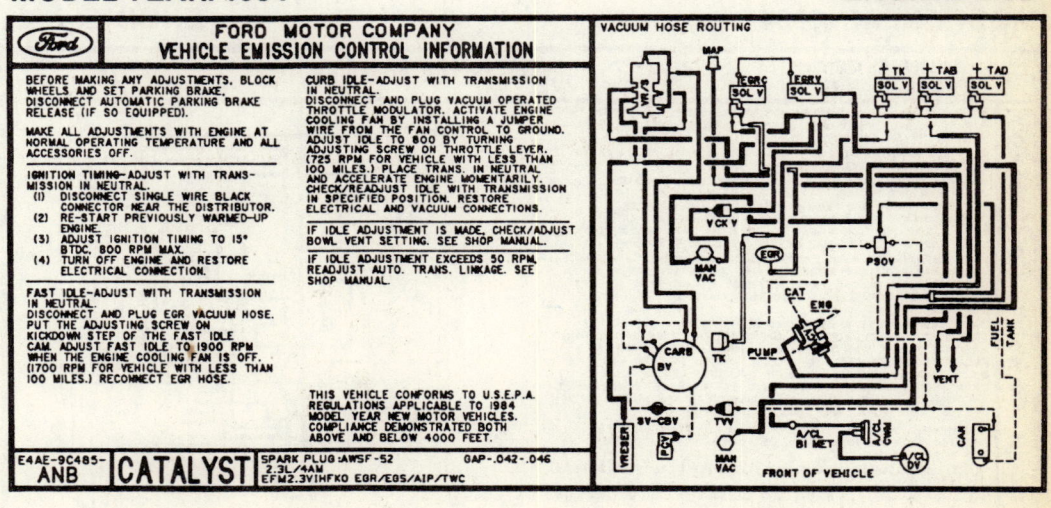

EMISSION CONTROLS

CALIBRATION: 4—25G—R11

MODEL YEAR: 1984   **ENGINE: 2.3L**

VEHICLE EMISSION CONTROL INFORMATION — Ford — FORD MOTOR COMPANY

BEFORE MAKING ANY ADJUSTMENTS, BLOCK WHEELS AND SET PARKING BRAKE. DISCONNECT AUTOMATIC PARKING BRAKE RELEASE (IF SO EQUIPPED).
MAKE ALL ADJUSTMENTS WITH ENGINE AT NORMAL OPERATING TEMPERATURE AND ALL ACCESSORIES OFF.
IGNITION TIMING- ADJUST WITH TRANSMISSION IN NEUTRAL.
 (1) DISCONNECT AND PLUG DISTRIBUTOR VACUUM HOSE.
 (2) RE-START PREVIOUSLY WARMED-UP ENGINE.
 (3) ADJUST IGNITION TIMING TO 10° BTDC. (800 RPM MAX)
 (4) TURN OFF ENGINE AND RESTORE VACUUM CONNECTION.
FAST IDLE-ADJUST WITH TRANSMISSION IN NEUTRAL. DISCONNECT AND PLUG EGR VACUUM HOSE. PUT THE ADJUSTING SCREW ON KICKDOWN STEP OF THE FAST IDLE CAM. ADJUST FAST IDLE TO 2200 RPM WHEN THE ENGINE COOLING FAN IS OFF. RECONNECT EGR HOSE.
CURB IDLE- ADJUST WITH TRANSMISSION IN "N".
DISCONNECT AND PLUG VACUUM OPERATED THROTTLE MODULATOR. ACTIVATE ENGINE COOLING FAN BY INSTALLING A JUMPER WIRE FROM THE FAN CONTROL TO GROUND. ADJUST IDLE TO 800 RPM BY TURNING ADJUSTING SCREW ON THROTTLE LEVER. PLACE TRANSMISSION IN NEUTRAL AND ACCELERATE ENGINE MOMENTARILY. CHECK/READJUST IDLE WITH TRANSMISSION IN SPECIFIED POSITION. RESTORE ELECTRICAL AND VACUUM CONNECTIONS.
IF IDLE ADJUSTMENT IS MADE, CHECK/ADJUST BOWL VENT SETTING SEE SHOP MANUAL.

SEE SHOP MANUAL FOR CHOKE AND IDLE MIXTURE ADJUSTMENT INFO.

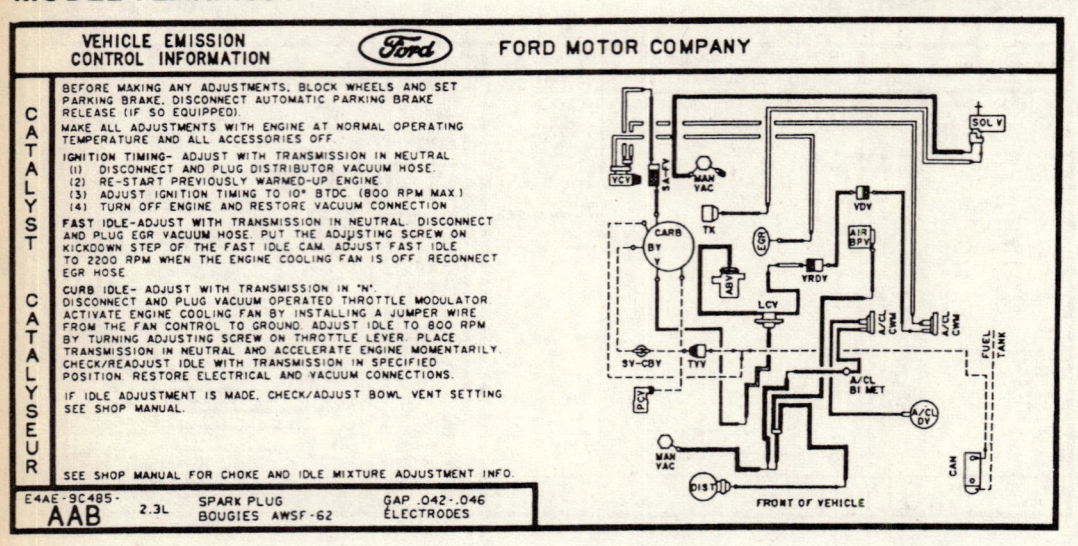

E4AE-9C485- **AAB**   2.3L   SPARK PLUG BOUGIES AWSF-62   GAP .042-.046 ÉLECTRODES

CALIBRATION: 4—25G—R13

MODEL YEAR: 1984   **ENGINE: 2.3L**

VEHICLE EMISSION CONTROL INFORMATION — Ford — FORD MOTOR COMPANY

BEFORE MAKING ANY ADJUSTMENTS, BLOCK WHEELS AND SET PARKING BRAKE. DISCONNECT AUTOMATIC PARKING BRAKE RELEASE (IF SO EQUIPPED).
MAKE ALL ADJUSTMENTS WITH ENGINE AT NORMAL OPERATING TEMPERATURE AND ALL ACCESSORIES OFF.
IGNITION TIMING- ADJUST WITH TRANSMISSION IN NEUTRAL.
 (1) TURN OFF ENGINE.
 (2) DISCONNECT AND PLUG DISTRIBUTOR VACUUM HOSE.
 (3) RE-START PREVIOUSLY WARMED-UP ENGINE.
 (4) ADJUST IGNITION TIMING TO 10° BTDC, 800 RPM MAX.
 (5) TURN OFF ENGINE AND RESTORE VACUUM CONNECTION.
FAST IDLE-ADJUST WITH TRANSMISSION IN NEUTRAL. DISCONNECT AND PLUG EGR VACUUM HOSE. PUT THE ADJUSTING SCREW ON KICKDOWN STEP OF THE FAST IDLE CAM. ADJUST FAST IDLE TO 2200 RPM WHEN THE ENGINE COOLING FAN IS OFF. RECONNECT EGR HOSE.
CURB IDLE- ADJUST WITH TRANSMISSION IN "N".
DISCONNECT AND PLUG VACUUM OPERATED THROTTLE MODULATOR. ACTIVATE ENGINE COOLING FAN BY INSTALLING A JUMPER WIRE FROM THE FAN CONTROL TO GROUND. ADJUST IDLE TO 800 RPM BY TURNING ADJUSTING SCREW ON THROTTLE LEVER. PLACE TRANSMISSION IN NEUTRAL AND ACCELERATE ENGINE MOMENTARILY. CHECK/READJUST IDLE WITH TRANSMISSION IN SPECIFIED POSITION. RESTORE ELECTRICAL AND VACUUM CONNECTIONS.
IF EQUIPPED WITH AUTO. O.D. TRANS. & CURB IDLE ADJ. IS GREATER THAN 150 RPM RE-ADJUST AUTO. TRANS. LINKAGE. SEE SHOP MANUAL.
IF IDLE ADJUSTMENT IS MADE, CHECK/ADJUST BOWL VENT SETTING. SEE SHOP MANUAL FOR CHOKE AND IDLE MIXTURE ADJUSTMENT INFO.

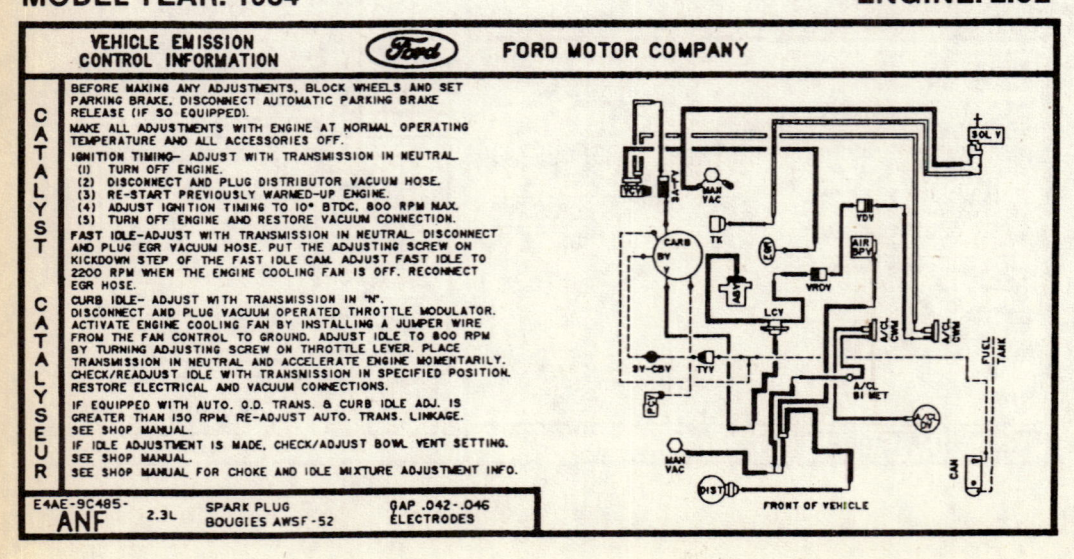

E4AE-9C485- **ANF**   2.3L   SPARK PLUG BOUGIES AWSF-52   GAP .042-.046 ÉLECTRODES

EMISSION CONTROLS

CALIBRATION: 4—26D—R16

MODEL YEAR: 1984   **ENGINE: 2.3L**

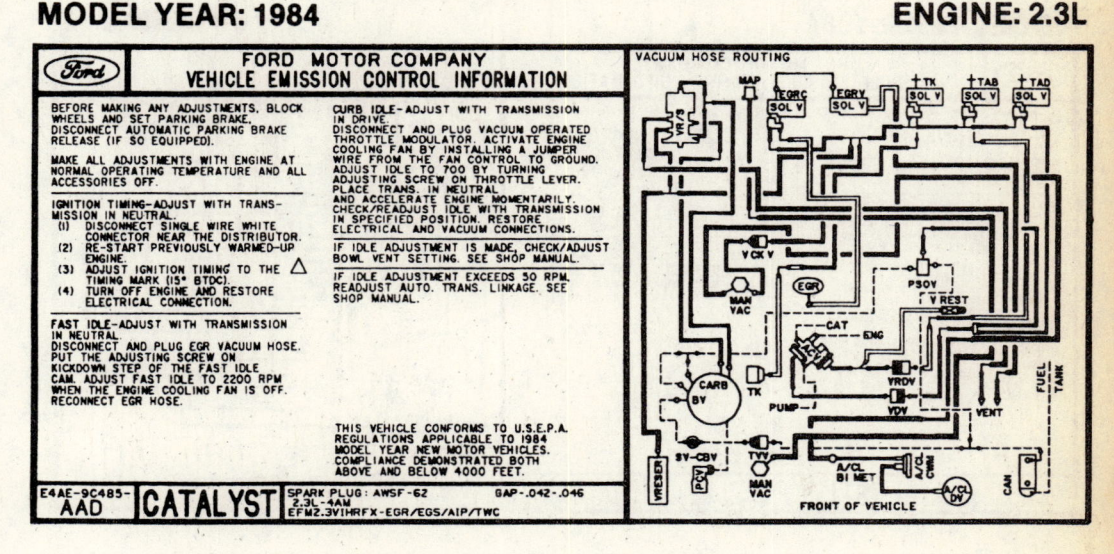

CALIBRATION: 4—26D—R18

MODEL YEAR: 1984   **ENGINE: 2.3L**

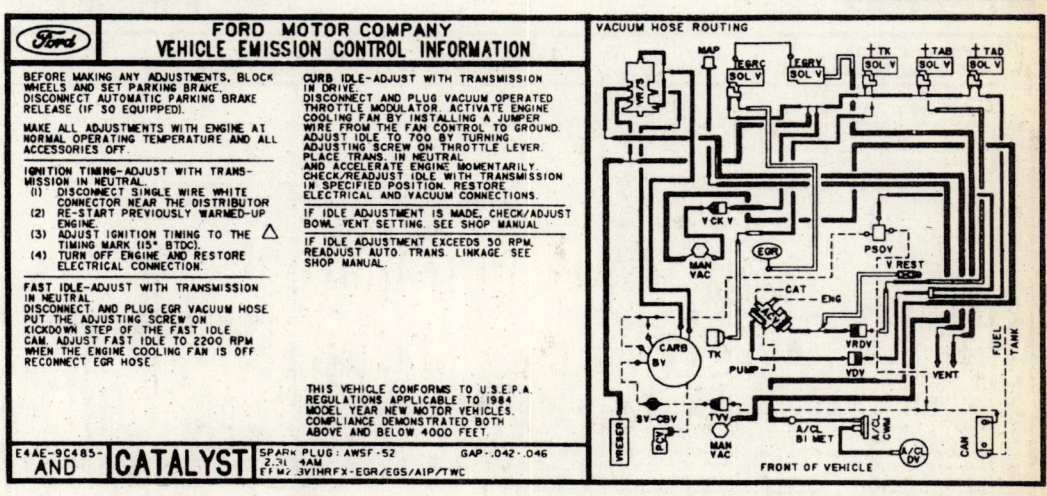

EMISSION CONTROLS

CALIBRATION: 4—26E—R00

MODEL YEAR: 1984 **ENGINE: 2.3L**

FORD MOTOR COMPANY
VEHICLE EMISSION CONTROL INFORMATION

BEFORE MAKING ANY ADJUSTMENTS, BLOCK WHEELS AND SET PARKING BRAKE. DISCONNECT AUTOMATIC PARKING BRAKE RELEASE (IF SO EQUIPPED).

MAKE ALL ADJUSTMENTS WITH ENGINE AT NORMAL OPERATING TEMPERATURE AND ALL ACCESSORIES OFF.

IGNITION TIMING-ADJUST WITH TRANSMISSION IN NEUTRAL.
(1) DISCONNECT SINGLE WIRE WHITE CONNECTOR NEAR THE DISTRIBUTOR
(2) RE-START PREVIOUSLY WARMED-UP ENGINE.
(3) ADJUST IGNITION TIMING TO THE △ TIMING MARK (15° BTDC).
(4) TURN OFF ENGINE AND RESTORE ELECTRICAL CONNECTION.

FAST IDLE-ADJUST WITH TRANSMISSION IN NEUTRAL
DISCONNECT AND PLUG EGR VACUUM HOSE. PUT THE ADJUSTING SCREW ON KICKDOWN STEP OF THE FAST IDLE CAM. ADJUST FAST IDLE TO 2200 RPM WHEN THE ENGINE COOLING FAN IS OFF RECONNECT EGR HOSE.

CURB IDLE-ADJUST WITH TRANSMISSION IN DRIVE.
DISCONNECT AND PLUG VACUUM OPERATED THROTTLE MODULATOR. ACTIVATE ENGINE COOLING FAN BY INSTALLING A JUMPER WIRE FROM THE FAN CONTROL TO GROUND. ADJUST IDLE TO 700 BY TURNING ADJUSTING SCREW ON THROTTLE LEVER. PLACE TRANS. IN NEUTRAL AND ACCELERATE ENGINE MOMENTARILY. CHECK/READJUST IDLE WITH TRANSMISSION IN SPECIFIED POSITION. RESTORE ELECTRICAL AND VACUUM CONNECTIONS.

IF IDLE ADJUSTMENT IS MADE, CHECK/ADJUST BOWL VENT SETTING. SEE SHOP MANUAL.

IF IDLE ADJUSTMENT EXCEEDS 50 RPM, READJUST AUTO. TRANS. LINKAGE SEE SHOP MANUAL.

THIS VEHICLE CONFORMS TO U.S.E.P.A. REGULATIONS APPLICABLE TO 1984 MODEL YEAR NEW MOTOR VEHICLES. COMPLIANCE DEMONSTRATED BOTH ABOVE AND BELOW 4000 FEET

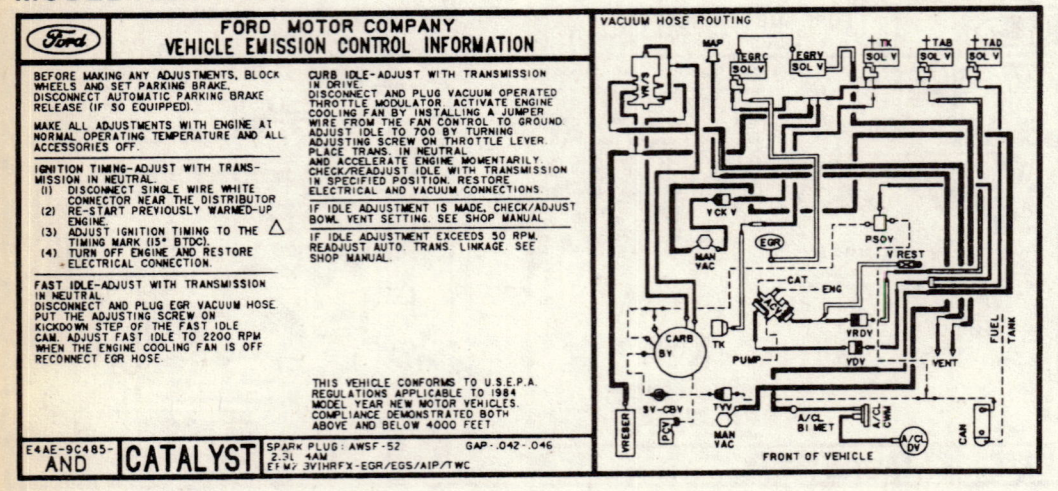

E4AE-9C485-AND CATALYST SPARK PLUG: AWSF-52 2.3L 4AM GAP .042-.046
EFM/ 3V1HRFX-EGR/EGS/AIP/TWC

CALIBRATION: 4—26G—R11

MODEL YEAR: 1984 **ENGINE: 2.3L**

VEHICLE EMISSION CONTROL INFORMATION — FORD MOTOR COMPANY

CATALYST / CATALYSEUR

BEFORE MAKING ANY ADJUSTMENTS, BLOCK WHEELS AND SET PARKING BRAKE. DISCONNECT AUTOMATIC PARKING BRAKE RELEASE (IF SO EQUIPPED).
MAKE ALL ADJUSTMENTS WITH ENGINE AT NORMAL OPERATING TEMPERATURE AND ALL ACCESSORIES OFF.
IGNITION TIMING- ADJUST WITH TRANSMISSION IN NEUTRAL.
(1) DISCONNECT AND PLUG DISTRIBUTOR VACUUM HOSE.
(2) RE-START PREVIOUSLY WARMED-UP ENGINE.
(3) ADJUST IGNITION TIMING TO THE △ TIMING MARK (10° BTDC). 800 RPM MAX.
(4) TURN OFF ENGINE AND RESTORE VACUUM CONNECTION.
FAST IDLE-ADJUST WITH TRANSMISSION IN NEUTRAL. DISCONNECT AND PLUG EGR VACUUM HOSE. PUT THE ADJUSTING SCREW ON KICKDOWN STEP OF THE FAST IDLE CAM. ADJUST FAST IDLE TO 2200 RPM WHEN THE ENGINE COOLING FAN IS OFF (2100 RPM FOR VEHICLE WITH LESS THAN 160 KM). RECONNECT EGR HOSE.
CURB IDLE- ADJUST WITH TRANSMISSION IN "D".
DISCONNECT AND PLUG VACUUM OPERATED THROTTLE MODULATOR. ACTIVATE ENGINE COOLING FAN BY INSTALLING A JUMPER WIRE FROM THE FAN CONTROL TO GROUND. ADJUST IDLE TO 730 RPM BY TURNING ADJUSTING SCREW ON THROTTLE LEVER (655 RPM FOR VEHICLE WITH LESS THAN 160 KM). PLACE TRANSMISSION IN NEUTRAL AND ACCELERATE ENGINE MOMENTARILY. CHECK/READJUST IDLE WITH TRANSMISSION IN SPECIFIED POSITION. RESTORE ELECTRICAL AND VACUUM CONNECTIONS.
IF EQUIPPED WITH AUTO. O.D. TRANS. & CURB IDLE ADJ. IS GREATER THAN 150 RPM, RE-ADJUST AUTO. TRANS. LINKAGE. SEE SHOP MANUAL.
IF IDLE ADJUSTMENT IS MADE, CHECK/ADJUST BOWL VENT SETTING. SEE SHOP MANUAL.
SEE SHOP MANUAL FOR CHOKE AND IDLE MIXTURE ADJUSTMENT INFO.

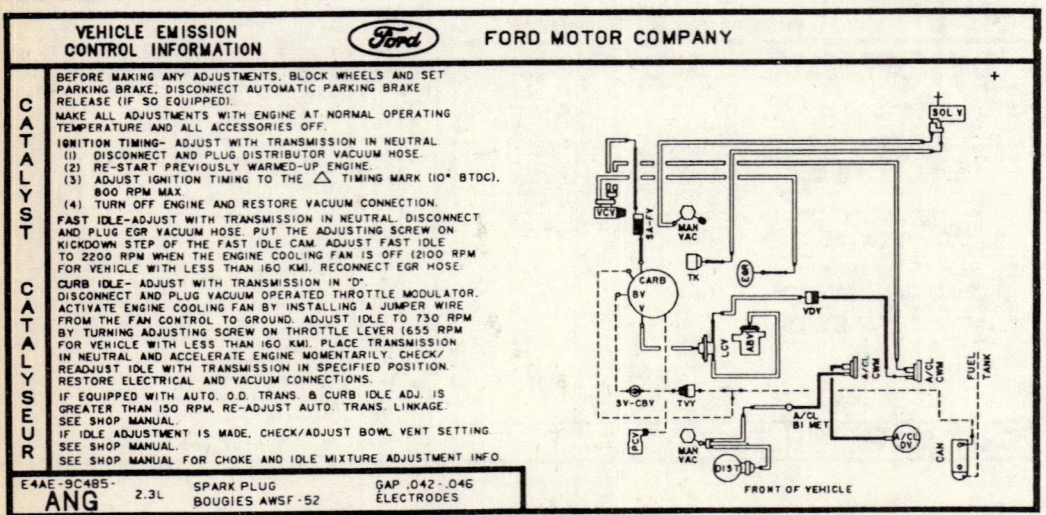

E4AE-9C485-ANG 2.3L SPARK PLUG / BOUGIES AWSF-52 GAP .042-.046 ELECTRODES

CALIBRATION: 4—26J—R28

MODEL YEAR: 1984 **ENGINE: 2.3L**

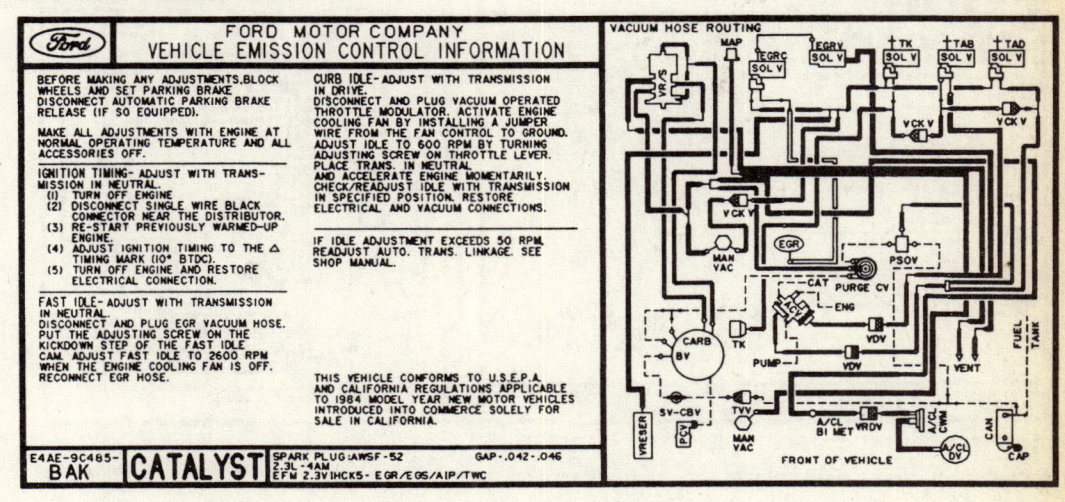

CALIBRATION: 4—26K—R22

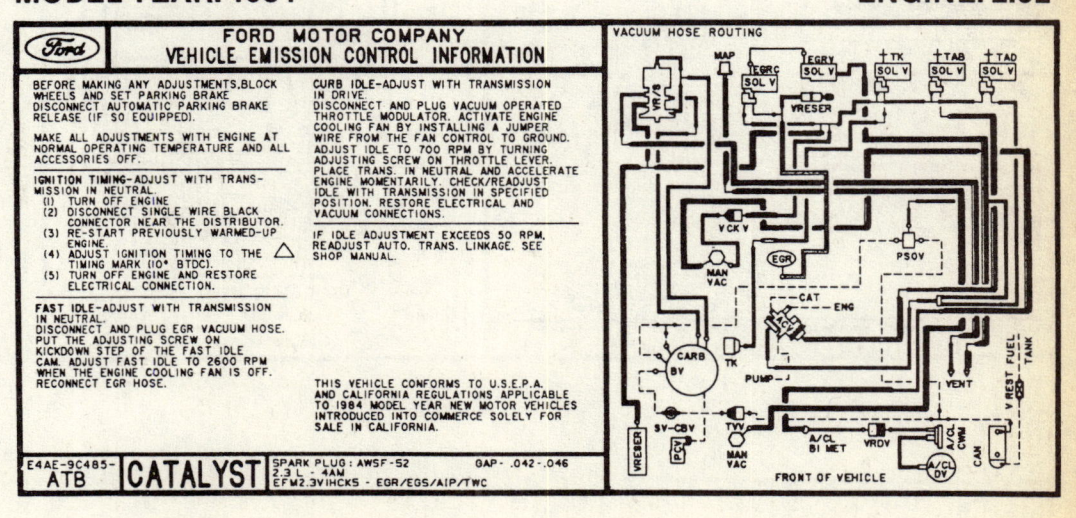

MODEL YEAR: 1984 **ENGINE: 2.3L**

EMISSION CONTROLS

CALIBRATION: 4—26K—R24

MODEL YEAR: 1984 **ENGINE: 2.3L**

FORD MOTOR COMPANY
VEHICLE EMISSION CONTROL INFORMATION

BEFORE MAKING ANY ADJUSTMENTS, BLOCK WHEELS AND SET PARKING BRAKE. DISCONNECT AUTOMATIC PARKING BRAKE RELEASE (IF SO EQUIPPED).

MAKE ALL ADJUSTMENTS WITH ENGINE AT NORMAL OPERATING TEMPERATURE AND ALL ACCESSORIES OFF.

IGNITION TIMING - ADJUST WITH TRANSMISSION IN NEUTRAL.
(1) TURN OFF ENGINE
(2) DISCONNECT SINGLE WIRE BLACK CONNECTOR NEAR THE DISTRIBUTOR.
(3) RE-START PREVIOUSLY WARMED-UP ENGINE.
(4) ADJUST IGNITION TIMING TO THE △ TIMING MARK (10° BTDC).
(5) TURN OFF ENGINE AND RESTORE ELECTRICAL CONNECTION.

FAST IDLE - ADJUST WITH TRANSMISSION IN NEUTRAL.
DISCONNECT AND PLUG EGR VACUUM HOSE. PUT THE ADJUSTING SCREW ON THE KICKDOWN STEP OF THE FAST IDLE CAM. ADJUST FAST IDLE TO 2600 RPM WHEN THE ENGINE COOLING FAN IS OFF. RECONNECT EGR HOSE.

CURB IDLE - ADJUST WITH TRANSMISSION IN DRIVE.
DISCONNECT AND PLUG VACUUM OPERATED THROTTLE MODULATOR. ACTIVATE ENGINE COOLING FAN BY INSTALLING A JUMPER WIRE FROM THE FAN CONTROL TO GROUND. ADJUST IDLE TO 700 RPM BY TURNING ADJUSTING SCREW ON THROTTLE LEVER. PLACE TRANS. IN NEUTRAL AND ACCELERATE ENGINE MOMENTARILY. CHECK/READJUST IDLE WITH TRANSMISSION IN SPECIFIED POSITION. RESTORE ELECTRICAL AND VACUUM CONNECTIONS.

IF IDLE ADJUSTMENT EXCEEDS 50 RPM, READJUST AUTO. TRANS. LINKAGE. SEE SHOP MANUAL.

THIS VEHICLE CONFORMS TO U.S.E.P.A. AND CALIFORNIA REGULATIONS APPLICABLE TO 1984 MODEL YEAR NEW MOTOR VEHICLES INTRODUCED INTO COMMERCE SOLELY FOR SALE IN CALIFORNIA.

E4AE-9C485-BAM **CATALYST** SPARK PLUG: AWSF-52 GAP: .042-.046
2.3L - 4AM
EFM2.3V1HCX5 - EGR/EGS/AIP/TWC

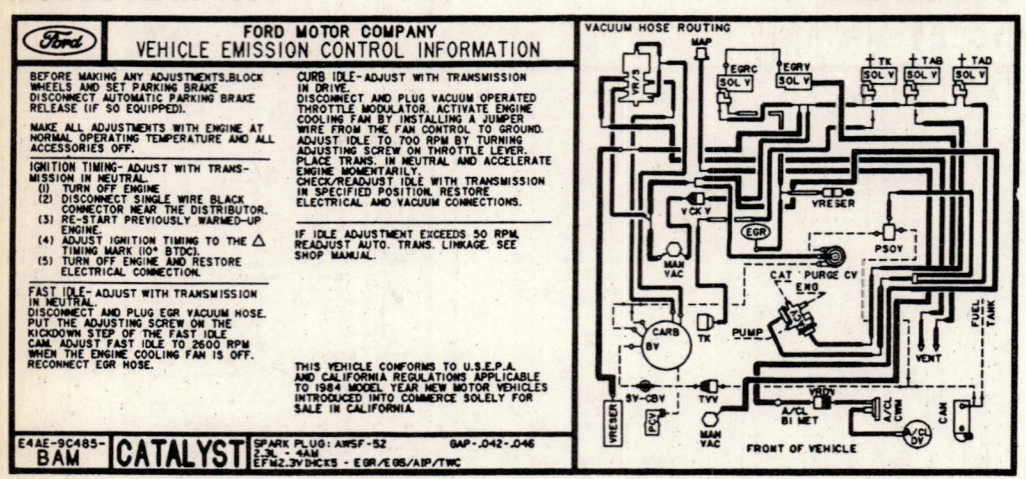

CALIBRATION: 4—26S—R13

MODEL YEAR: 1984 **ENGINE: 2.3L**

FORD MOTOR COMPANY
VEHICLE EMISSION CONTROL INFORMATION

BEFORE MAKING ANY ADJUSTMENTS, BLOCK WHEELS AND SET PARKING BRAKE. DISCONNECT AUTOMATIC PARKING BRAKE RELEASE (IF SO EQUIPPED).

MAKE ALL ADJUSTMENTS WITH ENGINE AT NORMAL OPERATING TEMPERATURE AND ALL ACCESSORIES OFF.

IGNITION TIMING - ADJUST WITH TRANSMISSION IN NEUTRAL.
(1) DISCONNECT SINGLE WIRE WHITE CONNECTOR NEAR THE DISTRIBUTOR.
(2) RE-START PREVIOUSLY WARMED-UP ENGINE.
(3) ADJUST IGNITION TIMING TO THE △ TIMING MARK (15° BTDC).
(4) TURN OFF ENGINE AND RESTORE ELECTRICAL CONNECTION.

FAST IDLE - ADJUST WITH TRANSMISSION IN NEUTRAL.
DISCONNECT AND PLUG EGR VACUUM HOSE. PUT THE ADJUSTING SCREW ON KICKDOWN STEP OF THE FAST IDLE CAM. ADJUST FAST IDLE TO 2200 RPM WHEN THE ENGINE COOLING FAN IS OFF. RECONNECT EGR HOSE.

CURB IDLE - ADJUST WITH TRANSMISSION IN DRIVE.
DISCONNECT AND PLUG VACUUM OPERATED THROTTLE MODULATOR. ACTIVATE ENGINE COOLING FAN BY INSTALLING A JUMPER WIRE FROM THE FAN CONTROL TO GROUND. ADJUST IDLE TO 700 RPM BY TURNING ADJUSTING SCREW ON THROTTLE LEVER. PLACE TRANS. IN NEUTRAL AND ACCELERATE ENGINE MOMENTARILY. CHECK/READJUST IDLE WITH TRANSMISSION IN SPECIFIED POSITION. RESTORE ELECTRICAL AND VACUUM CONNECTIONS.

IF IDLE ADJUSTMENT IS MADE, CHECK/ADJUST BOWL VENT SETTING. SEE SHOP MANUAL.

IF IDLE ADJUSTMENT EXCEEDS 50 RPM, READJUST AUTO. TRANS. LINKAGE. SEE SHOP MANUAL.

THIS VEHICLE CONFORMS TO U.S.E.P.A. AND CALIFORNIA REGULATIONS APPLICABLE TO 1984 MODEL YEAR NEW MOTOR VEHICLES INTRODUCED INTO COMMERCE SOLELY FOR SALE IN CALIFORNIA.

E4AE-9C485-ANE **CATALYST** SPARK PLUG: AWSF-52 GAP: .042-.046
2.3L/4AM
EFM2.3V1HECX-EGR/EGS/AIP/TWC

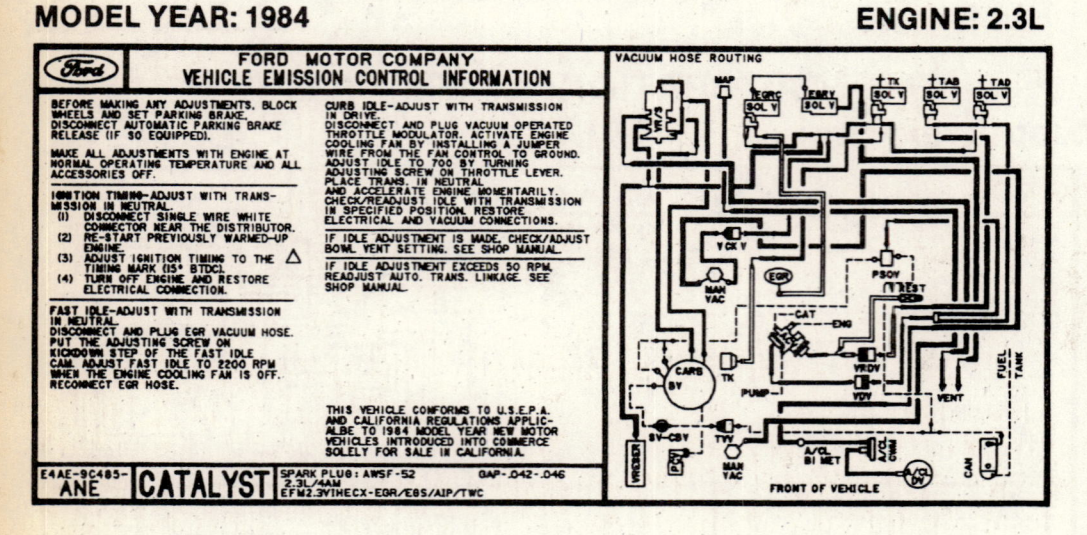

EMISSION CONTROLS 271

CALIBRATION: 4—03A—R10

MODEL YEAR: 1985 **ENGINE: 1.6L**

FORD MOTOR COMPANY
VEHICLE EMISSION CONTROL INFORMATION

SET PARKING BRAKE AND BLOCK WHEELS. MAKE ALL ADJUSTMENTS WITH ENGINE AT NORMAL OPERATING TEMPERATURE, ACCESSORIES AND HEADLIGHTS OFF.

MAKE ALL ADJUSTMENTS WITH TRANSMISSION IN NEUTRAL.

IGNITION TIMING- DISCONNECT AND PLUG DISTRIBUTOR VACUUM HOSE. ADJUST TIMING TO 12° BTDC. 800 RPM MAX. RECONNECT HOSE.

FAST IDLE- DISCONNECT AND PLUG EGR VALVE VACUUM HOSE. PUT FAST IDLE SCREW ON SECOND STEP OF FAST IDLE CAM. RUN ENGINE UNTIL RADIATOR COOLING FAN COMES ON. ADJUST TO 2200 RPM (2000 RPM FOR VEHICLE WITH LESS THAN 100 MILES). RECONNECT EGR VACUUM HOSE.

CURB IDLE-
1. VACUUM OPERATED THROTTLE MODULATOR (VOTM) OFF- PUT FAST IDLE SCREW ON SECOND STEP OF FAST IDLE CAM AND RUN ENGINE UNTIL RADIATOR COOLING FAN COMES ON. ACCELERATE ENGINE MOMENTARILY. DISCONNECT AND PLUG VOTM VACUUM HOSE (A/C ONLY). ADJUST TO 800 RPM BY TURNING THROTTLE STOP ADJUSTING SCREW (700 RPM FOR VEHICLE WITH LESS THAN 100 MILES). ADJUST DASHPOT CLEARANCE TO 3.5-4.5 MM.

2. A/C ONLY-VOTM ON- PLACE HEATER SELECTOR ON HEAT, TEMPERATURE ON COOL AND BLOWER ON HIGH. CONNECT A VACUUM HOSE FROM MANIFOLD VACUUM TO THE VOTM WITH RADIATOR COOLING FAN RUNNING. ADJUST TO 1200 RPM BY TURNING SCREW ON TOP OF VOTM (1100 RPM FOR VEHICLE WITH LESS THAN 100 MILES). RECONNECT VOTM VACUUM HOSE.

SEE SHOP MANUAL FOR CHOKE AND IDLE MIXTURE ADJUSTMENT INFORMATION.

THIS VEHICLE CONFORMS TO U.S. EPA REGULATIONS APPLICABLE TO 1985 MODEL YEAR NEW MOTOR VEHICLES.

E5AE-9C485-CEB CATALYST SPARK PLUG: AWSF-34C 1.6L-5CM GAP: .042-.046
EFMI.6V2GDK8-EGR/AIP/TWC

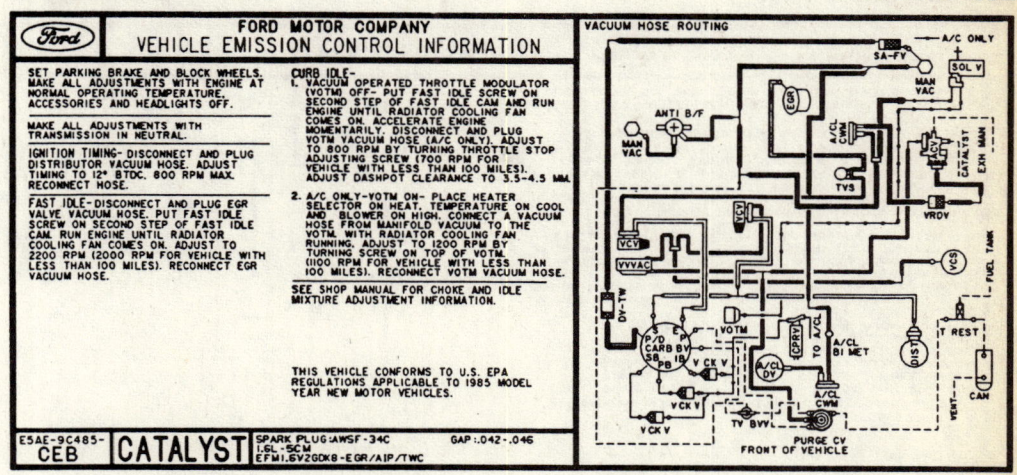

CALIBRATION: 4—03F—R00

MODEL YEAR: 1985 **ENGINE: 1.6L**

FORD MOTOR COMPANY
VEHICLE EMISSION CONTROL INFORMATION

SET PARKING BRAKE AND BLOCK WHEELS. MAKE ALL ADJUSTMENTS WITH ENGINE AT NORMAL OPERATING TEMPERATURE, ACCESSORIES AND HEADLIGHTS OFF.

MAKE ALL ADJUSTMENTS WITH TRANSMISSION IN NEUTRAL.

IGNITION TIMING- DISCONNECT AND PLUG DISTRIBUTOR VACUUM HOSE. ADJUST TIMING TO 8° BTDC. 800 RPM MAX. RECONNECT HOSE.

FAST IDLE- DISCONNECT AND PLUG EGR VALVE VACUUM HOSE. PUT FAST IDLE SCREW ON SECOND STEP OF FAST IDLE CAM. RUN ENGINE UNTIL RADIATOR COOLING FAN COMES ON. ADJUST TO 2200 RPM. RECONNECT EGR VACUUM HOSE.

CURB IDLE- PUT FAST IDLE SCREW ON SECOND STEP OF FAST IDLE CAM AND RUN ENGINE UNTIL RADIATOR COOLING FAN COMES ON. ACCELERATE ENGINE MOMENTARILY. ADJUST TO 720 RPM BY TURNING THROTTLE STOP ADJUSTING SCREW. ADJUST DASHPOT CLEARANCE TO 1.5-2.5 MM

SEE SHOP MANUAL FOR CHOKE AND IDLE MIXTURE ADJUSTMENT INFORMATION.

THIS VEHICLE CONFORMS TO U.S. EPA REGULATIONS APPLICABLE TO 1985 MODEL YEAR NEW MOTOR VEHICLES. COMPLIANCE DEMONSTRATED AND DESIGNED FOR PRINCIPAL USE BELOW 4000 FEET. THIS VEHICLE IS EXEMPT FROM MEETING EMISSION STANDARDS ABOVE 4000 FEET BECAUSE OF POSSIBLY UNSUITABLE PERFORMANCE AND THE EMISSIONS PERFORMANCE WARRANTY DOES NOT APPLY ABOVE 4000 FEET.

E5AE-9C485-CEC CATALYST SPARK PLUG: AWSF-34C 1.6L-5CM GAP: .042-.046
FFMI.6V2GDK8-EGR/AIP/TWC

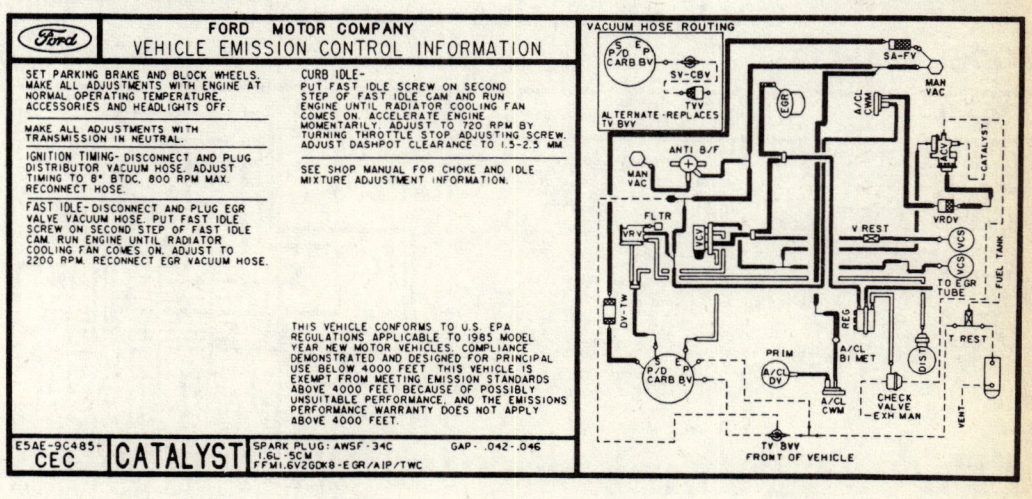

EMISSION CONTROLS

CALIBRATION: 4—03H—R00

MODEL YEAR: 1985 **ENGINE: 1.6L**

VEHICLE EMISSION CONTROL INFORMATION — Ford — FORD MOTOR COMPANY

CATALYST / CATALYST / CATALYSEUR

SET PARKING BRAKE AND BLOCK WHEELS. MAKE ALL ADJUSTMENTS WITH ENGINE AT NORMAL OPERATING TEMPERATURE, ACCESSORIES AND HEADLIGHTS OFF.

MAKE ALL ADJUSTMENTS WITH TRANSMISSION IN NEUTRAL.

IGNITION TIMING-DISCONNECT AND PLUG DISTRIBUTOR VACUUM HOSE. ADJUST TIMING TO 12° BTDC, 800 RPM MAX. RECONNECT HOSE.

FAST IDLE-D & P EGR VALVE VACUUM HOSE. PUT FAST IDLE SCREW ON SECOND STEP OF FAST IDLE CAM. RUN ENGINE UNTIL RADIATOR COOLING FAN COMES ON. ADJUST TO 2400 RPM (2200 RPM FOR VEHICLE WITH LESS THAN 160 KM). RECONNECT EGR VACUUM HOSE.

CURB IDLE-1. VACUUM OPERATED THROTTLE MODULATOR (VOTM) OFF. PUT FAST IDLE SCREW ON SECOND STEP OF FAST IDLE CAM AND RUN ENGINE UNTIL RADIATOR COOLING FAN COMES ON. ACCELERATE ENGINE MOMENTARILY. D/P VOTM VACUUM HOSE. (A/C ONLY). ADJUST TO 800 RPM BY TURNING THROTTLE STOP ADJUSTING SCREW (700 RPM FOR VEHICLE WITH LESS THAN 160 KM). ADJUST DASHPOT CLEARANCE TO 3.5-4.5 MM.

2. A/C ONLY-VOTM ON— PLACE HEATER SELECTOR ON HEAT, TEMPERATURE ON COOL AND BLOWER ON HIGH. CONNECT A VACUUM HOSE FROM MANIFOLD VACUUM TO THE VOTM. WITH RADIATOR COOLING FAN RUNNING, ADJUST TO 1200 RPM BY TURNING SCREW ON TOP ON VOTM.(1100 RPM FOR VEHICLE WITH LESS THAN 160 KM). RESTORE VOTM VACUUM CONNECTIONS.

SEE SHOP MANUAL FOR IDLE MIXTURE ADJUSTMENT INFORMATION.

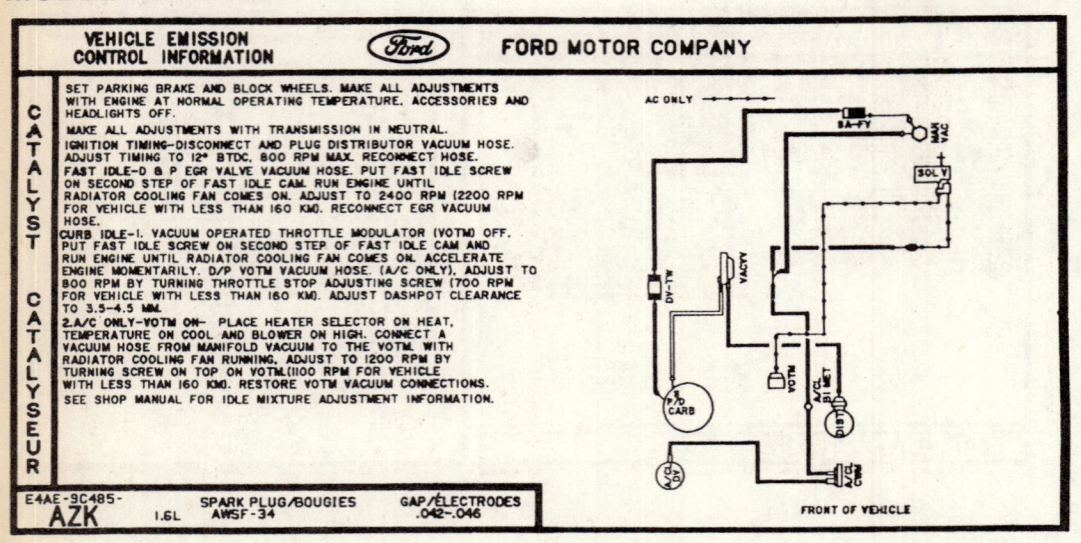

E4AE-9C485- AZK   1.6L   SPARK PLUG/BOUGIES AWSF-34   GAP/ELECTRODES .042-.046

AC ONLY — FRONT OF VEHICLE

CALIBRATION: 4—03K—R10

MODEL YEAR: 1985 **ENGINE: 1.6L**

FORD MOTOR COMPANY — VEHICLE EMISSION CONTROL INFORMATION

SET PARKING BRAKE AND BLOCK WHEELS. MAKE ALL ADJUSTMENTS WITH ENGINE AT NORMAL OPERATING TEMPERATURE, ACCESSORIES AND HEADLIGHTS OFF.

MAKE ALL ADJUSTMENTS WITH TRANSMISSION IN NEUTRAL.

IGNITION TIMING- DISCONNECT AND PLUG DISTRIBUTOR VACUUM HOSE. ADJUST TIMING TO 8° BTDC, 800 RPM MAX. RECONNECT HOSE.

FAST IDLE-DISCONNECT AND PLUG EGR VALVE VACUUM HOSE. PUT FAST IDLE SCREW ON SECOND STEP OF FAST IDLE CAM. RUN ENGINE UNTIL RADIATOR COOLING FAN COMES ON. ADJUST TO 2200 RPM (2000 RPM FOR VEHICLE WITH LESS THAN 100 MILES). RECONNECT EGR VACUUM HOSE.

CURB IDLE-
1. VACUUM OPERATED THROTTLE MODULATOR (VOTM) OFF- PUT FAST IDLE SCREW ON SECOND STEP OF FAST IDLE CAM AND RUN ENGINE UNTIL RADIATOR COOLING FAN COMES ON. ACCELERATE ENGINE MOMENTARILY. DISCONNECT AND PLUG VOTM VACUUM HOSE (A/C ONLY). ADJUST TO 700 RPM BY TURNING THROTTLE STOP ADJUSTING SCREW.
ADJUST DASHPOT CLEARANCE TO 2.0-3.0 MM.

2. A/C ONLY-VOTM ON- PLACE HEATER SELECTOR ON HEAT, TEMPERATURE ON COOL AND BLOWER ON HIGH. CONNECT A VACUUM HOSE FROM MANIFOLD VACUUM TO THE VOTM WITH RADIATOR COOLING FAN RUNNING. ADJUST TO 1200 RPM BY TURNING SCREW ON TOP OF VOTM. RECONNECT VOTM VACUUM HOSE.

SEE SHOP MANUAL FOR CHOKE AND IDLE MIXTURE ADJUSTMENT INFORMATION.

THIS VEHICLE CONFORMS TO U.S. EPA REGULATIONS APPLICABLE TO 1985 MODEL YEAR NEW MOTOR VEHICLES.

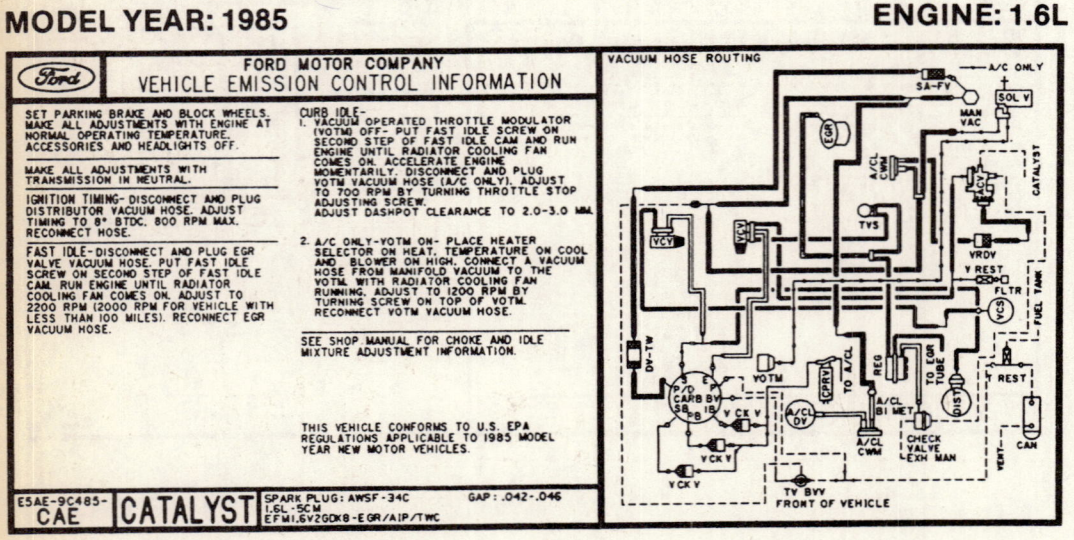

E5AE-9C485- CAE   CATALYST   SPARK PLUG: AWSF-34C 1.6L-5CM EFMI,6V2GOX8-EGR/AIP/TWC   GAP: .042-.046

VACUUM HOSE ROUTING — FRONT OF VEHICLE

EMISSION CONTROLS

CALIBRATION: 4—03P—R10

MODEL YEAR: 1985 **ENGINE: 1.6L**

FORD MOTOR COMPANY
VEHICLE EMISSION CONTROL INFORMATION

SET PARKING BRAKE AND BLOCK WHEELS. MAKE ALL ADJUSTMENTS WITH ENGINE AT NORMAL OPERATING TEMPERATURE. ACCESSORIES AND HEADLIGHTS OFF.

MAKE ALL ADJUSTMENTS WITH TRANSMISSION IN NEUTRAL.

IGNITION TIMING-DISCONNECT AND PLUG DISTRIBUTOR VACUUM HOSE. ADJUST TIMING TO 8° BTDC, 800 RPM MAX. RECONNECT HOSE.

FAST IDLE-DISCONNECT AND PLUG EGR VALVE VACUUM HOSE. PUT FAST IDLE SCREW ON SECOND STEP OF FAST IDLE CAM. RUN ENGINE UNTIL RADIATOR COOLING FAN COMES ON. ADJUST TO 2200 RPM (2000 RPM FOR VEHICLE WITH LESS THAN 100 MILES). RECONNECT EGR VACUUM HOSE.

CURB IDLE-
1. VACUUM OPERATED THROTTLE MODULATOR (VOTM) OFF— PUT FAST IDLE SCREW ON SECOND STEP OF FAST IDLE CAM AND RUN ENGINE UNTIL RADIATOR COOLING FAN COMES ON. ACCELERATE ENGINE MOMENTARILY. DISCONNECT AND PLUG VOTM VACUUM HOSE (A/C ONLY). ADJUST TO 700 RPM BY TURNING THROTTLE STOP ADJUSTING SCREW. ADJUST DASHPOT CLEARANCE TO 2.0 - 3.0 MM.

2. A/C ONLY-VOTM ON - PLACE HEATER SELECTOR ON HEAT, TEMPERATURE ON COOL AND BLOWER ON HIGH. CONNECT A VACUUM HOSE FROM MANIFOLD VACUUM TO THE VOTM. WITH RADIATOR COOLING FAN RUNNING, ADJUST TO 1200 RPM BY TURNING SCREW ON TOP OF VOTM. RECONNECT VOTM VACUUM HOSE.

SEE SHOP MANUAL FOR CHOKE AND IDLE MIXTURE ADJUSTMENT INFORMATION.

THIS VEHICLE CONFORMS TO U.S. EPA AND CALIFORNIA REGULATIONS APPLICABLE TO 1985 MODEL YEAR NEW MOTOR VEHICLES INTRODUCED INTO COMMERCE SOLELY FOR SALE IN CALIFORNIA.

E5AE-9C485-CAB CATALYST SPARK PLUG:AWSF-34C 1.6L-5CM GAP:.042-.046 FFM1.6V2G0C9-EGR/AIP/TWC

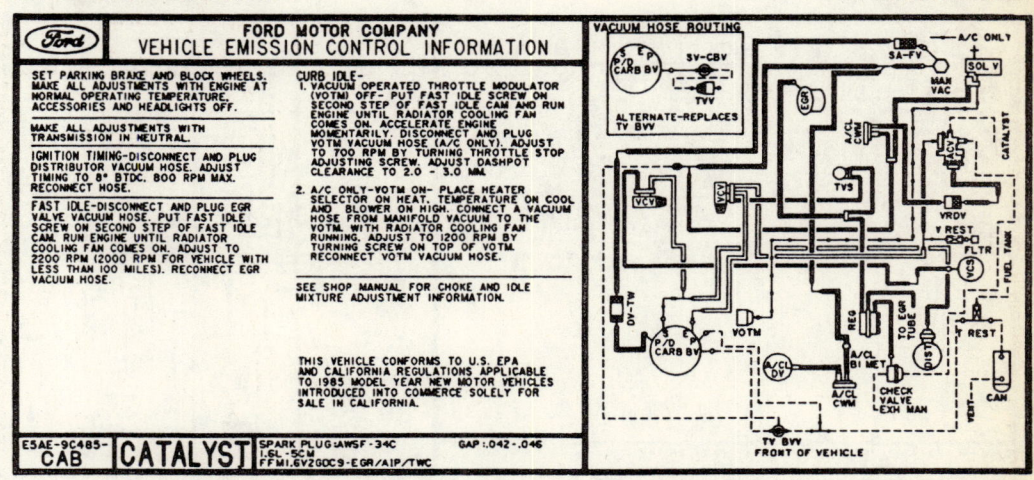

CALIBRATION: 4—03S—R10

MODEL YEAR: 1985 **ENGINE: 1.6L**

FORD MOTOR COMPANY
VEHICLE EMISSION CONTROL INFORMATION

SET PARKING BRAKE AND BLOCK WHEELS. MAKE ALL ADJUSTMENTS WITH ENGINE AT NORMAL OPERATING TEMPERATURE. ACCESSORIES AND HEADLIGHTS OFF.

MAKE ALL ADJUSTMENTS WITH TRANSMISSION IN NEUTRAL.

IGNITION TIMING-DISCONNECT AND PLUG DISTRIBUTOR VACUUM HOSE. ADJUST TIMING TO 12° BTDC, 800 RPM MAX. RECONNECT HOSE.

FAST IDLE-DISCONNECT AND PLUG EGR VALVE VACUUM HOSE. PUT FAST IDLE SCREW ON SECOND STEP OF FAST IDLE CAM. RUN ENGINE UNTIL RADIATOR COOLING FAN COMES ON. ADJUST TO 2200 RPM (2000 RPM FOR VEHICLE WITH LESS THAN 100 MILES). RECONNECT EGR VACUUM HOSE.

CURB IDLE-
1. VACUUM OPERATED THROTTLE MODULATOR (VOTM) OFF— PUT FAST IDLE SCREW ON SECOND STEP OF FAST IDLE CAM AND RUN ENGINE UNTIL RADIATOR COOLING FAN COMES ON. ACCELERATE ENGINE MOMENTARILY. DISCONNECT AND PLUG VOTM VACUUM HOSE (A/C ONLY). ADJUST TO 800 RPM (700 RPM FOR VEHICLE WITH LESS THAN 100 MILES) BY TURNING THROTTLE STOP ADJUSTING SCREW. ADJUST DASHPOT CLEARANCE TO 2.0-3.0 MM.

2. A/C ONLY-VOTM ON- PLACE HEATER SELECTOR ON HEAT, TEMPERATURE ON COOL AND BLOWER ON HIGH. CONNECT A VACUUM HOSE FROM MANIFOLD VACUUM TO THE VOTM. WITH RADIATOR COOLING FAN RUNNING, ADJUST TO 1200 RPM BY TURNING SCREW ON TOP OF VOTM (1100 RPM FOR VEHICLE WITH LESS THAN 100 MILES). RECONNECT VOTM VACUUM HOSE.

SEE SHOP MANUAL FOR CHOKE AND IDLE MIXTURE ADJUSTMENT INFORMATION.

THIS VEHICLE CONFORMS TO U.S. EPA AND CALIFORNIA REGULATIONS APPLICABLE TO 1985 MODEL YEAR NEW MOTOR VEHICLES INTRODUCED INTO COMMERCE SOLELY FOR SALE IN CALIFORNIA.

E5AE-9C485-CAD CATALYST SPARK PLUG:AWSF-34C 1.6L-5CM GAP:.042-.046 FFM1.6V2G0C9-EGR/AIP/TWC

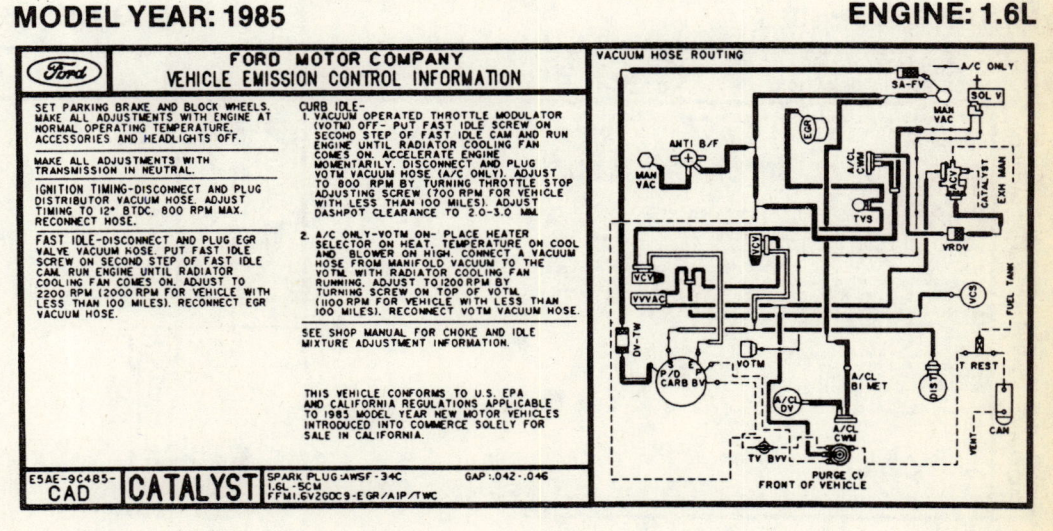

EMISSION CONTROLS

CALIBRATION: 4—04A—R16

MODEL YEAR: 1985 **ENGINE: 1.6L**

FORD MOTOR COMPANY
VEHICLE EMISSION CONTROL INFORMATION

SET PARKING BRAKE AND BLOCK WHEELS. MAKE ALL ADJUSTMENTS WITH ENGINE AT NORMAL OPERATING TEMPERATURE. ACCESSORIES AND HEADLIGHTS OFF.

IGNITION TIMING- DISCONNECT AND PLUG DISTRIBUTOR VACUUM HOSE. WITH TRANS. IN DRIVE, ADJUST TIMING TO 14° BTDC. 800 RPM MAX. RECONNECT HOSE.

FAST IDLE- DISCONNECT AND PLUG EGR VALVE VACUUM HOSE. PUT FAST IDLE SCREW ON SECOND STEP OF FAST IDLE CAM. RUN ENGINE UNTIL RADIATOR COOLING FAN COMES ON. ADJUST TO 2400 RPM WITH TRANS. IN NEUTRAL. RECONNECT EGR HOSE.

CURB IDLE- PUT FAST IDLE SCREW ON SECOND STEP OF FAST IDLE CAM. RUN ENGINE UNTIL RADIATOR COOLING FAN COMES ON. ACCELERATE ENGINE MOMENTARILY. PUT TRANSMISSION IN DRIVE. TURN IDLE SPEED CONTROL (ISC) ADJUSTING SCREW UNTIL ISC PLUNGER IS CLEAR OF THE THROTTLE LEVER. ADJUST RPM TO 670 BY TURNING THROTTLE STOP ADJUSTING SCREW. THEN TURN ISC ADJUSTING SCREW UNTIL 700 RPM IS REACHED.

IF IDLE RPM ADJUSTMENT IS GREATER THAN 50 RPM, RE-ADJUST AUTO. TRANS. LINKAGE. SEE SHOP MANUAL.

SEE SHOP MANUAL FOR CHOKE AND IDLE MIXTURE ADJUSTMENT INFORMATION.

THIS VEHICLE CONFORMS TO U.S. EPA REGULATIONS APPLICABLE TO 1985 MODEL YEAR NEW MOTOR VEHICLES.

E5AE-9C485-CED CATALYST SPARK PLUG: AWSF-34C GAP: .042-.046
1.6L-5CM
FFM1.6V2GDK8-EGR/AIP/TWC

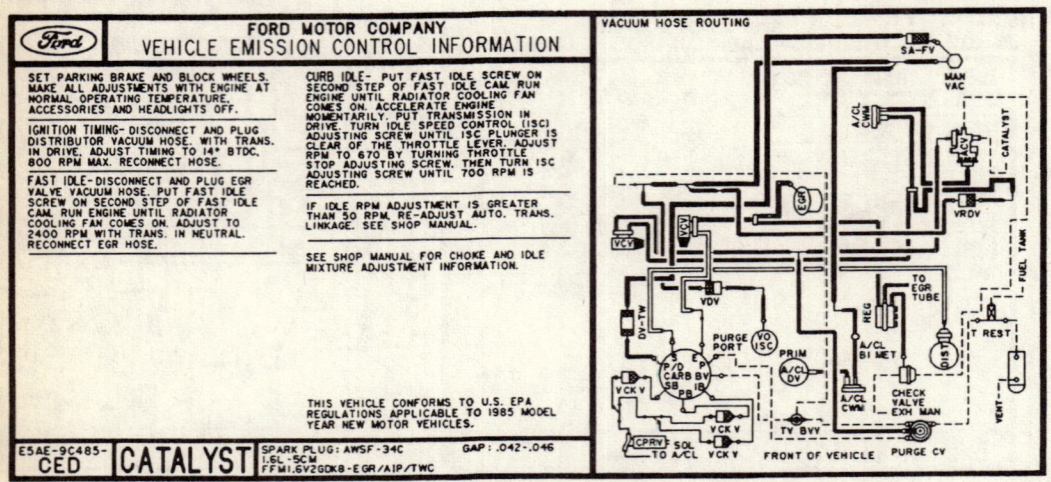

CALIBRATION: 4—04H—R00

MODEL YEAR: 1985 **ENGINE: 1.6L**

VEHICLE EMISSION CONTROL INFORMATION — FORD MOTOR COMPANY

CATALYST / CATALYSEUR

SET PARKING BRAKE AND BLOCK WHEELS. MAKE ALL ADJUSTMENTS WITH ENGINE AT NORMAL OPERATING TEMPERATURE, ACCESSORIES AND HEADLIGHTS OFF.

IGNITION TIMING-DISCONNECT AND PLUG DISTRIBUTOR VACUUM HOSE. WITH TRANS IN "D". ADJUST TIMING TO 14° BTDC. 800 RPM MAX. RECONNECT HOSE.

FAST IDLE-D & P EGR VALVE VACUUM HOSE. PUT FAST IDLE SCREW ON SECOND STEP OF FAST IDLE CAM. RUN ENGINE UNTIL RADIATOR COOLING FAN COMES ON. ADJUST TO 2400 RPM WITH TRANS. IN NEUTRAL. RECONNECT EGR HOSE.

CURB IDLE-PUT FAST IDLE SCREW ON SECOND STEP OF FAST IDLE CAM. RUN ENGINE UNTIL RADIATOR COOLING FAN COMES ON. ACCELERATE ENGINE MOMENTARILY. PUT TRANSMISSION IN DRIVE.

WITHOUT IDLE SPEED CONTROL (ISC) - ADJUST TO 750 RPM BY TURNING THROTTLE STOP ADJUSTING SCREW

WITH ISC - TURN ISC ADJUSTING SCREW UNTIL ISC PLUNGER IS CLEAR OF THE THROTTLE LEVER. ADJUST RPM TO 720 BY TURNING THROTTLE STOP ADJUSTING SCREW, THEN TURN ISC ADJUSTING SCREW UNTIL 750 RPM IS REACHED.

IF CURB IDLE ADJUSTMENT IS GREATER THAN 50 RPM, RE-ADJUST AUTO. TRANS. LINKAGE. SEE SHOP MANUAL.

SEE SHOP MANUAL FOR CHOKE AND IDLE MIXTURE ADJUSTMENT INFORMATION.

E4AE-9C485-AJF SPARK PLUG AWSF-34 GAP .042-.046
1.6L BOUGIES ÉLECTRODES

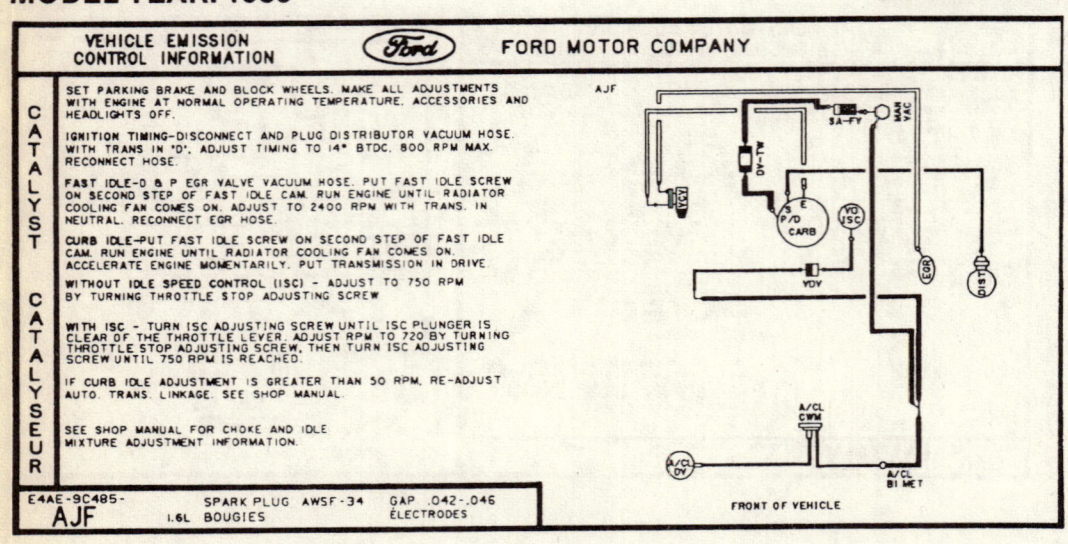

EMISSION CONTROLS

CALIBRATION: 4—04S—R12

MODEL YEAR: 1985 **ENGINE: 1.6L**

FORD MOTOR COMPANY
VEHICLE EMISSION CONTROL INFORMATION

SET PARKING BRAKE AND BLOCK WHEELS. MAKE ALL ADJUSTMENTS WITH ENGINE AT NORMAL OPERATING TEMPERATURE, ACCESSORIES AND HEADLIGHTS OFF.

IGNITION TIMING- DISCONNECT AND PLUG DISTRIBUTOR VACUUM HOSE. WITH TRANS. IN DRIVE, ADJUST TIMING TO 14° BTDC. 800 RPM MAX. RECONNECT HOSE.

FAST IDLE- DISCONNECT AND PLUG EGR VALVE VACUUM HOSE. PUT FAST IDLE SCREW ON SECOND STEP OF FAST IDLE CAM. RUN ENGINE UNTIL RADIATOR COOLING FAN COMES ON. ADJUST TO 2400 RPM WITH TRANS. IN NEUTRAL. RECONNECT EGR HOSE.

CURB IDLE- PUT FAST IDLE SCREW ON SECOND STEP OF FAST IDLE CAM RUN ENGINE UNTIL RADIATOR COOLING FAN COMES ON. ACCELERATE ENGINE MOMENTARILY. PUT TRANSMISSION IN DRIVE. TURN IDLE SPEED CONTROL (ISC) ADJUSTING SCREW UNTIL ISC PLUNGER IS CLEAR OF THE THROTTLE LEVER. ADJUST RPM TO 670 BY TURNING THROTTLE STOP ADJUSTING SCREW. THEN TURN ISC ADJUSTING SCREW UNTIL 700 RPM IS REACHED.

IF IDLE RPM ADJUSTMENT IS GREATER THAN 50 RPM RE-ADJUST AUTO. TRANS. LINKAGE. SEE SHOP MANUAL.

SEE SHOP MANUAL FOR CHOKE AND IDLE MIXTURE ADJUSTMENT INFORMATION.

THIS VEHICLE CONFORMS TO U.S. EPA AND CALIFORNIA REGULATIONS APPLICABLE TO 1985 MODEL YEAR NEW MOTOR VEHICLES.

E5AE-9C485-CAC CATALYST SPARK PLUG: AWSF-34C GAP: .042-.046
1.6L-5CM
FFM1.6V2GDC9-EGR/AIP/TWC

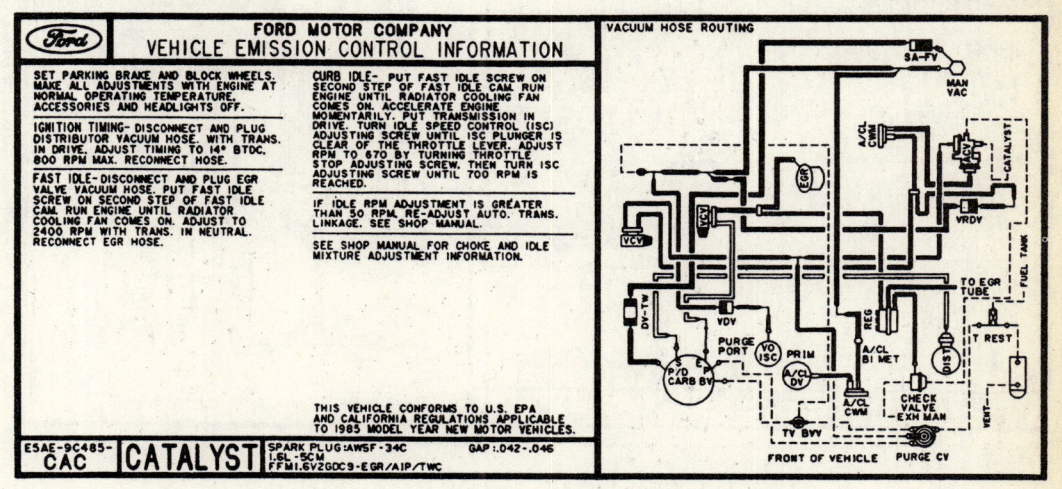

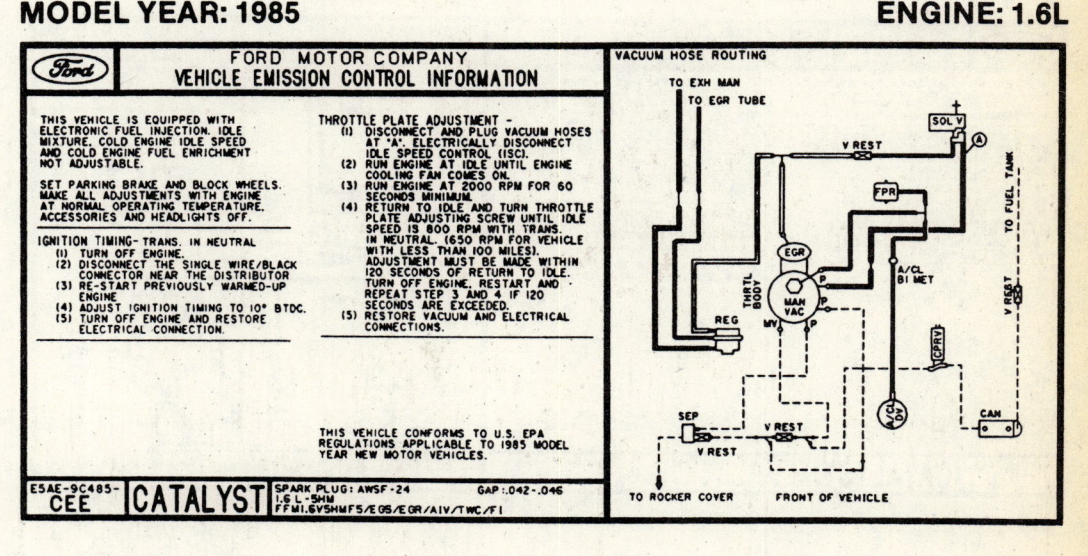

CALIBRATION: 4—27A—R02

MODEL YEAR: 1985 **ENGINE: 1.6L**

FORD MOTOR COMPANY
VEHICLE EMISSION CONTROL INFORMATION

THIS VEHICLE IS EQUIPPED WITH ELECTRONIC FUEL INJECTION. IDLE MIXTURE, COLD ENGINE IDLE SPEED AND COLD ENGINE FUEL ENRICHMENT NOT ADJUSTABLE.

SET PARKING BRAKE AND BLOCK WHEELS. MAKE ALL ADJUSTMENTS WITH ENGINE AT NORMAL OPERATING TEMPERATURE, ACCESSORIES AND HEADLIGHTS OFF.

IGNITION TIMING- TRANS. IN NEUTRAL
(1) TURN OFF ENGINE.
(2) DISCONNECT THE SINGLE WIRE/BLACK CONNECTOR NEAR THE DISTRIBUTOR
(3) RE-START PREVIOUSLY WARMED-UP ENGINE
(4) ADJUST IGNITION TIMING TO 10° BTDC.
(5) TURN OFF ENGINE AND RESTORE ELECTRICAL CONNECTION.

THROTTLE PLATE ADJUSTMENT -
(1) DISCONNECT AND PLUG VACUUM HOSES AT "A". ELECTRICALLY DISCONNECT IDLE SPEED CONTROL (ISC)
(2) RUN ENGINE AT IDLE UNTIL ENGINE COOLING FAN COMES ON.
(3) RUN ENGINE AT 2000 RPM FOR 60 SECONDS MINIMUM
(4) RETURN TO IDLE AND TURN THROTTLE PLATE ADJUSTING SCREW UNTIL IDLE SPEED IS 800 RPM WITH TRANS. IN NEUTRAL. (650 RPM FOR VEHICLE WITH LESS THAN 100 MILES). ADJUSTMENT MUST BE MADE WITHIN 120 SECONDS OF RETURN TO IDLE. TURN OFF ENGINE. RESTART AND REPEAT STEP 3 AND 4 IF 120 SECONDS ARE EXCEEDED.
(5) RESTORE VACUUM AND ELECTRICAL CONNECTIONS.

THIS VEHICLE CONFORMS TO U.S. EPA REGULATIONS APPLICABLE TO 1985 MODEL YEAR NEW MOTOR VEHICLES.

E5AE-9C485-CEE CATALYST SPARK PLUG: AWSF-24 GAP: .042-.046
1.6L-5HM
FFM1.6V5HMF5/EGS/EGR/AIV/TWC/FI

EMISSION CONTROLS

CALIBRATION: 4—28A—R00

MODEL YEAR: 1985 **ENGINE: 1.6L**

FORD MOTOR COMPANY
VEHICLE EMISSION CONTROL INFORMATION

THIS VEHICLE IS EQUIPPED WITH ELECTRONIC FUEL INJECTION. IDLE MIXTURE, COLD ENGINE IDLE SPEED AND COLD ENGINE FUEL ENRICHMENT NOT ADJUSTABLE.

SET PARKING BRAKE AND BLOCK WHEELS. MAKE ALL ADJUSTMENTS WITH ENGINE AT NORMAL OPERATING TEMPERATURE, ACCESSORIES AND HEADLIGHTS OFF.

IGNITION TIMING- TRANS. IN NEUTRAL
(1) TURN OFF ENGINE.
(2) DISCONNECT THE SINGLE WIRE/BLACK CONNECTOR NEAR THE DISTRIBUTOR
(3) RE-START PREVIOUSLY WARMED-UP ENGINE.
(4) ADJUST IGNITION TIMING TO 10° BTDC.
(5) TURN OFF ENGINE AND RESTORE ELECTRICAL CONNECTION.

THROTTLE PLATE ADJUSTMENT -
(1) DISCONNECT AND PLUG VACUUM HOSES AT "A". ELECTRICALLY DISCONNECT IDLE SPEED CONTROL (ISC).
(2) RUN ENGINE AT IDLE UNTIL ENGINE COOLING FAN COMES ON.
(3) RUN ENGINE AT 2000 RPM FOR 60 SECONDS MINIMUM.
(4) RETURN TO IDLE AND TURN THROTTLE PLATE ADJUSTING SCREW UNTIL IDLE SPEED IS 750 RPM WITH AUTO. TRANS. IN DRIVE. (600 RPM FOR VEHICLE WITH LESS THAN 100 MILES). ADJUSTMENT MUST BE MADE WITHIN 120 SECONDS OF RETURN TO IDLE. TURN OFF ENGINE. RESTART AND REPEAT STEP 3 AND 4 IF 120 SECONDS ARE EXCEEDED.
(5) IF THROTTLE PLATE ADJUSTMENT EXCEEDS 50 RPM, RE-ADJUST TRANS. LINKAGE. SEE SHOP MANUAL.
(6) RESTORE VACUUM AND ELECTRICAL CONNECTIONS.

THIS VEHICLE CONFORMS TO U.S. EPA REGULATIONS APPLICABLE TO 1985 MODEL YEAR NEW MOTOR VEHICLES.

E5AE-9C485-CEG   CATALYST   SPARK PLUG: AWSF-24   GAP: .042-.046
1.6L-5HM
FFM1.6V5HMF5-EGS/EGR/AIV/TWC/FI

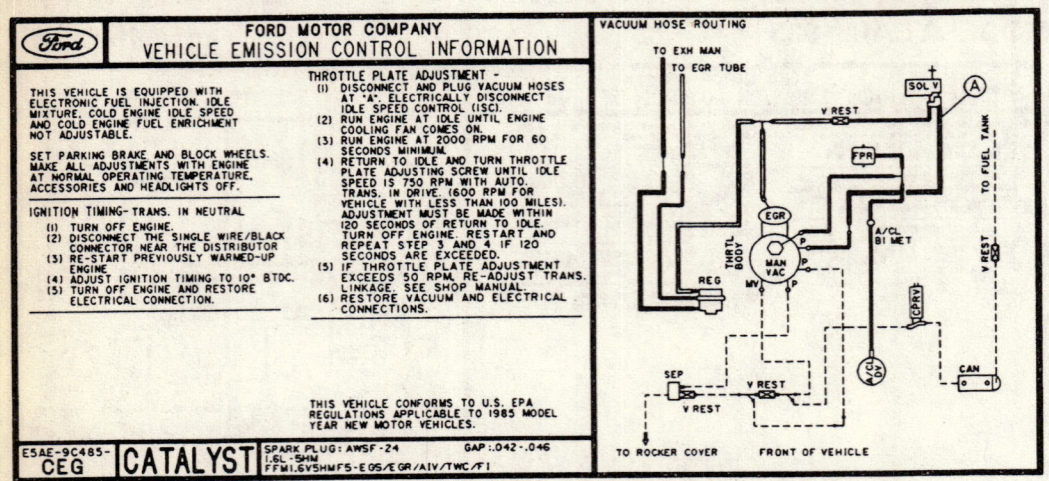

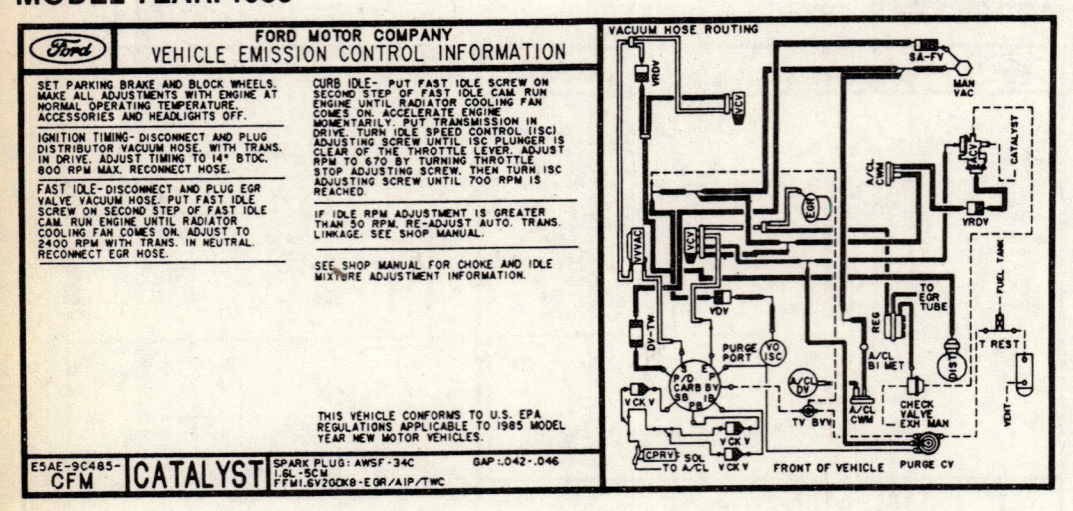

CALIBRATION: 5—04A—R12

MODEL YEAR: 1985 **ENGINE: 1.6L**

FORD MOTOR COMPANY
VEHICLE EMISSION CONTROL INFORMATION

SET PARKING BRAKE AND BLOCK WHEELS. MAKE ALL ADJUSTMENTS WITH ENGINE AT NORMAL OPERATING TEMPERATURE, ACCESSORIES AND HEADLIGHTS OFF.

IGNITION TIMING- DISCONNECT AND PLUG DISTRIBUTOR VACUUM HOSE. WITH TRANS. IN DRIVE. ADJUST TIMING TO 14° BTDC. 800 RPM MAX. RECONNECT HOSE.

FAST IDLE- DISCONNECT AND PLUG EGR VALVE VACUUM HOSE. PUT FAST IDLE SCREW ON SECOND STEP OF FAST IDLE CAM. RUN ENGINE UNTIL RADIATOR COOLING FAN COMES ON. ADJUST TO 2400 RPM WITH TRANS. IN NEUTRAL. RECONNECT EGR HOSE.

CURB IDLE- PUT FAST IDLE SCREW ON SECOND STEP OF FAST IDLE CAM. RUN ENGINE UNTIL RADIATOR COOLING FAN COMES ON. ACCELERATE ENGINE MOMENTARILY. PUT TRANSMISSION IN DRIVE. TURN IDLE SPEED CONTROL (ISC) ADJUSTING SCREW UNTIL ISC PLUNGER IS CLEAR OF THE THROTTLE LEVER. ADJUST RPM TO 670 BY TURNING THROTTLE STOP ADJUSTING SCREW. THEN TURN ISC ADJUSTING SCREW UNTIL 700 RPM IS REACHED.

IF IDLE RPM ADJUSTMENT IS GREATER THAN 50 RPM, RE-ADJUST AUTO. TRANS. LINKAGE. SEE SHOP MANUAL.

SEE SHOP MANUAL FOR CHOKE AND IDLE MIXTURE ADJUSTMENT INFORMATION.

THIS VEHICLE CONFORMS TO U.S. EPA REGULATIONS APPLICABLE TO 1985 MODEL YEAR NEW MOTOR VEHICLES.

E5AE-9C485-CFM   CATALYST   SPARK PLUG: AWSF-34C   GAP: .042-.046
1.6L-5CM
FFM1.6V2GCK8-EGR/AIP/TWC

EMISSION CONTROLS 277

CALIBRATION: 5—27T—R00

MODEL YEAR: 1984 **ENGINE: 1.6L**

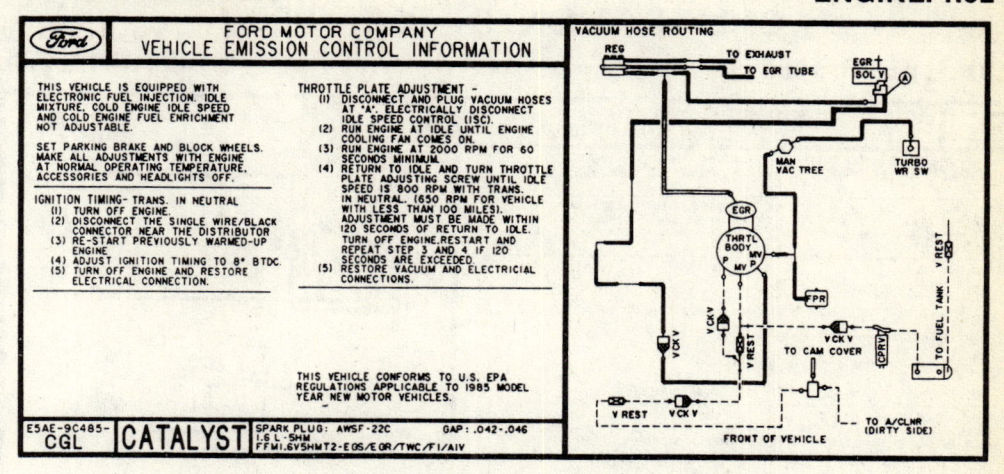

FORD MOTOR COMPANY
VEHICLE EMISSION CONTROL INFORMATION

THIS VEHICLE IS EQUIPPED WITH ELECTRONIC FUEL INJECTION. IDLE MIXTURE, COLD ENGINE IDLE SPEED AND COLD ENGINE FUEL ENRICHMENT NOT ADJUSTABLE.

SET PARKING BRAKE AND BLOCK WHEELS. MAKE ALL ADJUSTMENTS WITH ENGINE AT NORMAL OPERATING TEMPERATURE, ACCESSORIES AND HEADLIGHTS OFF.

IGNITION TIMING- TRANS. IN NEUTRAL
(1) TURN OFF ENGINE.
(2) DISCONNECT THE SINGLE WIRE/BLACK CONNECTOR NEAR THE DISTRIBUTOR.
(3) RE-START PREVIOUSLY WARMED-UP ENGINE
(4) ADJUST IGNITION TIMING TO 8° BTDC.
(5) TURN OFF ENGINE AND RESTORE ELECTRICAL CONNECTION.

THROTTLE PLATE ADJUSTMENT -
(1) DISCONNECT AND PLUG VACUUM HOSES AT "A". ELECTRICALLY DISCONNECT IDLE SPEED CONTROL (ISC).
(2) RUN ENGINE AT IDLE UNTIL ENGINE COOLING FAN COMES ON.
(3) RUN ENGINE AT 2000 RPM FOR 60 SECONDS MINIMUM.
(4) RETURN TO IDLE AND TURN THROTTLE PLATE ADJUSTING SCREW UNTIL IDLE SPEED IS 800 RPM FOR VEHICLE IN NEUTRAL. (650 RPM FOR VEHICLE WITH LESS THAN 100 MILES). ADJUSTMENT MUST BE MADE WITHIN 120 SECONDS OF RETURN TO IDLE. TURN OFF ENGINE, RESTART AND REPEAT STEP 3 AND 4 IF 120 SECONDS ARE EXCEEDED.
(5) RESTORE VACUUM AND ELECTRICAL CONNECTIONS.

THIS VEHICLE CONFORMS TO U.S. EPA REGULATIONS APPLICABLE TO 1985 MODEL YEAR NEW MOTOR VEHICLES.

E5AE-9C485- **CGL** | **CATALYST** | SPARK PLUG: AWSF-22C GAP: .042-.046 1.6 L-5HM FFM1.6V5HMT2-EOS/EGR/TWC/FI/AIV

CALIBRATION: 5—05A—R00

MODEL YEAR: 1985 **ENGINE: 2.3L**

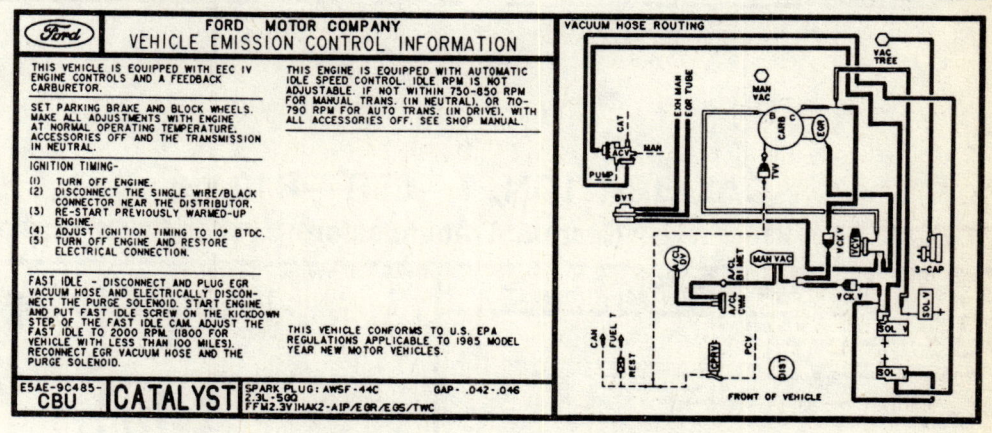

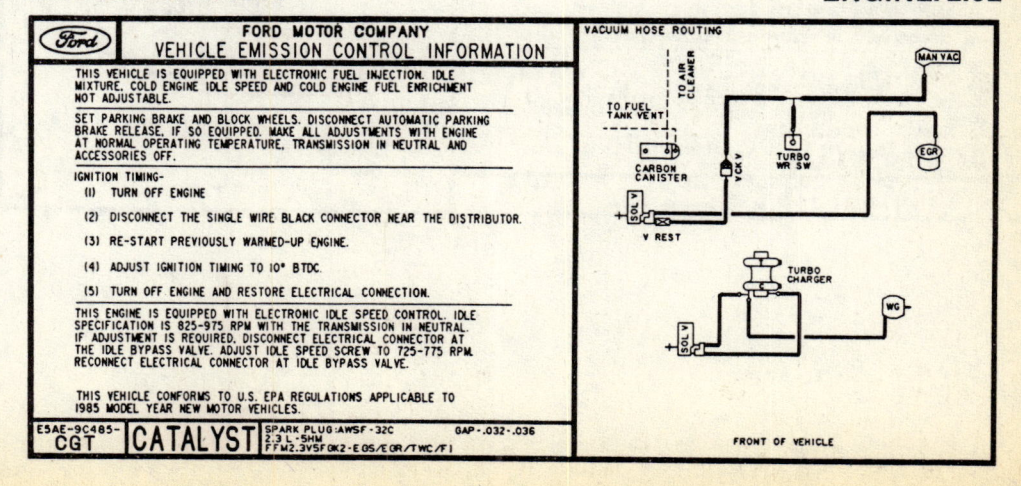

FORD MOTOR COMPANY
VEHICLE EMISSION CONTROL INFORMATION

THIS VEHICLE IS EQUIPPED WITH EEC IV ENGINE CONTROLS AND A FEEDBACK CARBURETOR.

SET PARKING BRAKE AND BLOCK WHEELS. MAKE ALL ADJUSTMENTS WITH ENGINE AT NORMAL OPERATING TEMPERATURE, ACCESSORIES OFF AND THE TRANSMISSION IN NEUTRAL.

IGNITION TIMING-
(1) TURN OFF ENGINE.
(2) DISCONNECT THE SINGLE WIRE/BLACK CONNECTOR NEAR THE DISTRIBUTOR.
(3) RE-START PREVIOUSLY WARMED-UP ENGINE.
(4) ADJUST IGNITION TIMING TO 10° BTDC.
(5) TURN OFF ENGINE AND RESTORE ELECTRICAL CONNECTION.

FAST IDLE - DISCONNECT AND PLUG EGR VACUUM HOSE AND ELECTRICALLY DISCONNECT THE PURGE SOLENOID. START ENGINE AND PUT FAST IDLE SCREW ON THE KICKDOWN STEP OF THE FAST IDLE CAM. ADJUST THE FAST IDLE TO 2000 RPM. (1800 FOR VEHICLE WITH LESS THAN 100 MILES). RECONNECT EGR VACUUM HOSE AND THE PURGE SOLENOID.

THIS ENGINE IS EQUIPPED WITH AUTOMATIC IDLE SPEED CONTROL. IDLE RPM IS NOT ADJUSTABLE. IF NOT WITHIN 750-850 RPM FOR MANUAL TRANS. (IN NEUTRAL), OR 710-790 RPM FOR AUTO TRANS. (IN DRIVE), WITH ALL ACCESSORIES OFF, SEE SHOP MANUAL.

THIS VEHICLE CONFORMS TO U.S. EPA REGULATIONS APPLICABLE TO 1985 MODEL YEAR NEW MOTOR VEHICLES.

E5AE-9C485- **CBU** | **CATALYST** | SPARK PLUG: AWSF-44C GAP: .042-.046 2.3L-5OO FFM2.3V1HAK2-AIP/EGR/EOS/TWC

CALIBRATION: 5—05D—R00

MODEL YEAR: 1985 **ENGINE: 2.3L**

FORD MOTOR COMPANY
VEHICLE EMISSION CONTROL INFORMATION

THIS VEHICLE IS EQUIPPED WITH ELECTRONIC FUEL INJECTION. IDLE MIXTURE, COLD ENGINE IDLE SPEED AND COLD ENGINE FUEL ENRICHMENT NOT ADJUSTABLE.

SET PARKING BRAKE AND BLOCK WHEELS. DISCONNECT AUTOMATIC PARKING BRAKE RELEASE, IF SO EQUIPPED. MAKE ALL ADJUSTMENTS WITH ENGINE AT NORMAL OPERATING TEMPERATURE, TRANSMISSION IN NEUTRAL AND ACCESSORIES OFF.

IGNITION TIMING-
(1) TURN OFF ENGINE
(2) DISCONNECT THE SINGLE WIRE BLACK CONNECTOR NEAR THE DISTRIBUTOR.
(3) RE-START PREVIOUSLY WARMED-UP ENGINE.
(4) ADJUST IGNITION TIMING TO 10° BTDC.
(5) TURN OFF ENGINE AND RESTORE ELECTRICAL CONNECTION.

THIS ENGINE IS EQUIPPED WITH ELECTRONIC IDLE SPEED CONTROL. IDLE SPECIFICATION IS 825-975 RPM WITH THE TRANSMISSION IN NEUTRAL. IF ADJUSTMENT IS REQUIRED, DISCONNECT ELECTRICAL CONNECTOR AT THE IDLE BYPASS VALVE. ADJUST IDLE SPEED SCREW TO 725-775 RPM. RECONNECT ELECTRICAL CONNECTOR AT IDLE BYPASS VALVE.

THIS VEHICLE CONFORMS TO U.S. EPA REGULATIONS APPLICABLE TO 1985 MODEL YEAR NEW MOTOR VEHICLES.

E5AE-9C485- **CGT** | **CATALYST** | SPARK PLUG: AWSF-32C GAP: .032-.036 2.3 L-5HM FFM2.3V5FOK2-EOS/EGR/TWC/FI

EMISSION CONTROLS

CALIBRATION: 5—05E—R00

MODEL YEAR: 1985 **ENGINE: 2.3L**

FORD MOTOR COMPANY
VEHICLE EMISSION CONTROL INFORMATION

THIS VEHICLE IS EQUIPPED WITH ELECTRONIC FUEL INJECTION. IDLE MIXTURE, COLD ENGINE IDLE SPEED AND COLD ENGINE FUEL ENRICHMENT NOT ADJUSTABLE.

SET PARKING BRAKE AND BLOCK WHEELS. DISCONNECT AUTOMATIC PARKING BRAKE RELEASE, IF SO EQUIPPED. MAKE ALL ADJUSTMENTS WITH ENGINE AT NORMAL OPERATING TEMPERATURE, TRANSMISSION IN NEUTRAL AND ACCESSORIES OFF.

IGNITION TIMING-
(1) TURN OFF ENGINE
(2) DISCONNECT THE SINGLE WIRE BLACK CONNECTOR NEAR THE DISTRIBUTOR.
(3) RE-START PREVIOUSLY WARMED-UP ENGINE.
(4) ADJUST IGNITION TIMING TO 10° BTDC.
(5) TURN OFF ENGINE AND RESTORE ELECTRICAL CONNECTION.

THIS ENGINE IS EQUIPPED WITH ELECTRONIC IDLE SPEED CONTROL. IDLE SPECIFICATION IS 825-975 RPM FOR MANUAL TRANSMISSION OR 925-1075 RPM FOR AUTOMATIC TRANSMISSION WITH THE TRANSMISSION IN NEUTRAL. IF ADJUSTMENT IS REQUIRED, DISCONNECT ELECTRICAL CONNECTOR AT THE IDLE BYPASS VALVE. ADJUST IDLE SPEED SCREW TO 725-775 RPM. RECONNECT ELECTRICAL CONNECTOR AT IDLE BYPASS VALVE.

THIS VEHICLE CONFORMS TO U.S. EPA REGULATIONS APPLICABLE TO 1985 MODEL YEAR NEW MOTOR VEHICLES.

E5AE-9C485-CGY CATALYST SPARK PLUG: AWSF-32C GAP: .032-.036
2.3L-5HM
FFM2.3V5FGK2-EOS/EGR/TWC

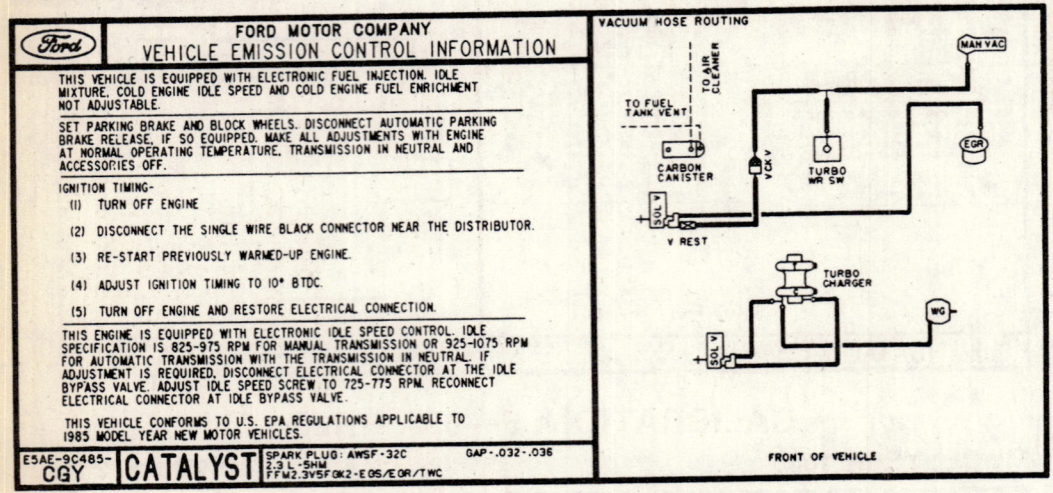

CALIBRATION: 5—05R—R10

MODEL YEAR: 1985 (Manual Transmission) **ENGINE: 2.3L**

FORD MOTOR COMPANY
VEHICLE EMISSION CONTROL INFORMATION

THIS VEHICLE IS EQUIPPED WITH ELECTRONIC FUEL INJECTION. IDLE MIXTURE, COLD ENGINE IDLE SPEED AND COLD ENGINE FUEL ENRICHMENT NOT ADJUSTABLE.

SET PARKING BRAKE AND BLOCK WHEELS. DISCONNECT AUTOMATIC PARKING BRAKE RELEASE, IF SO EQUIPPED. MAKE ALL ADJUSTMENTS WITH ENGINE AT NORMAL OPERATING TEMPERATURE, TRANSMISSION IN NEUTRAL AND ACCESSORIES OFF.

IGNITION TIMING-
(1) TURN OFF ENGINE
(2) DISCONNECT THE SINGLE WIRE BLACK CONNECTOR NEAR THE DISTRIBUTOR.
(3) RE-START PREVIOUSLY WARMED-UP ENGINE.
(4) ADJUST IGNITION TIMING TO 13° BTDC.
(5) TURN OFF ENGINE AND RESTORE ELECTRICAL CONNECTION.

THIS ENGINE IS EQUIPPED WITH ELECTRONIC IDLE SPEED CONTROL. IDLE SPECIFICATION IS 825-975 RPM FOR MANUAL TRANSMISSION OR 925-1075 RPM FOR AUTOMATIC TRANSMISSION WITH THE TRANSMISSION IN NEUTRAL. IF ADJUSTMENT IS REQUIRED. DISCONNECT ELECTRICAL CONNECTOR AT THE IDLE BYPASS VALVE. ADJUST IDLE SPEED SCREW TO 725-775 RPM. RECONNECT ELECTRICAL CONNECTOR AT IDLE BYPASS VALVE.

THIS VEHICLE CONFORMS TO U.S. EPA REGULATIONS APPLICABLE TO 1985 MODEL YEAR NEW MOTOR VEHICLES.

E5RD-9C485-XAS CATALYST SPARK PLUG: AWSF-32C GAP: .032-.036
2.3L-5HM
FFM2.3V5FGK2-EOS/EGR/TWC

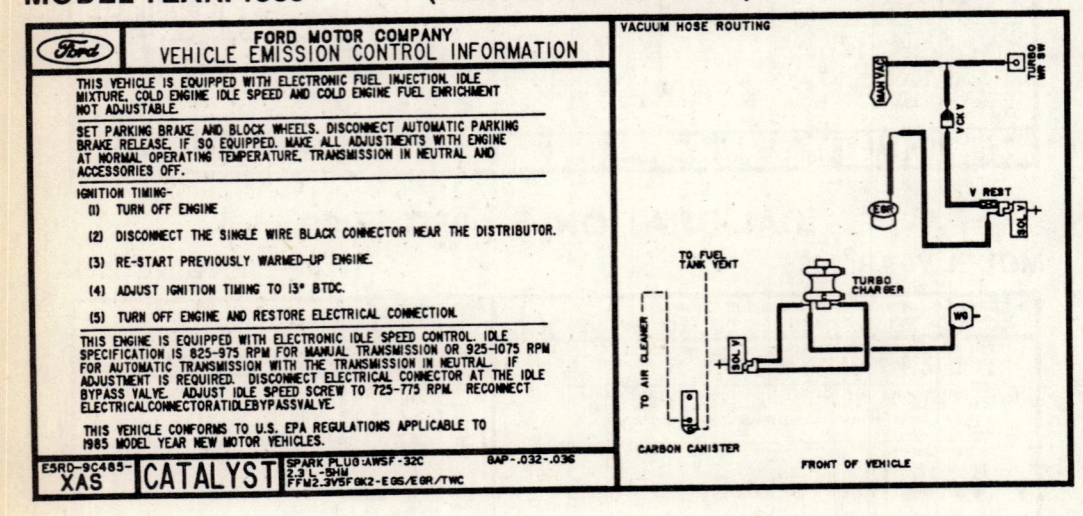

EMISSION CONTROLS

CALIBRATION: 5—06A—R00

MODEL YEAR: 1985 **ENGINE: 2.3L**

FORD MOTOR COMPANY
VEHICLE EMISSION CONTROL INFORMATION

THIS VEHICLE IS EQUIPPED WITH EEC IV ENGINE CONTROLS AND A FEEDBACK CARBURETOR.

SET PARKING BRAKE AND BLOCK WHEELS. MAKE ALL ADJUSTMENTS WITH ENGINE AT NORMAL OPERATING TEMPERATURE, ACCESSORIES OFF AND THE TRANSMISSION IN NEUTRAL.

IGNITION TIMING:
(1) TURN OFF ENGINE.
(2) DISCONNECT THE SINGLE WIRE/BLACK CONNECTOR NEAR THE DISTRIBUTOR.
(3) RE-START PREVIOUSLY WARMED-UP ENGINE.
(4) ADJUST IGNITION TIMING TO 10° BTDC.
(5) TURN OFF ENGINE AND RESTORE ELECTRICAL CONNECTION.

FAST IDLE-DISCONNECT AND PLUG EGR VACUUM HOSE AND ELECTRICALLY DISCONNECT THE PURGE SOLENOID. START ENGINE AND PUT FAST IDLE SCREW ON THE KICKDOWN STEP OF THE FAST IDLE CAM. ADJUST THE FAST IDLE TO 2200 RPM (1900 FOR VEHICLE WITH LESS THAN 100 MILES). RECONNECT EGR VACUUM HOSE AND THE PURGE SOLENOID.

THIS ENGINE IS EQUIPPED WITH AUTOMATIC IDLE SPEED CONTROL. IDLE RPM IS NOT ADJUSTABLE. IF NOT WITHIN 750-850 RPM FOR MANUAL TRANS. (IN NEUTRAL), OR 710-790 RPM FOR AUTO TRANS. (IN DRIVE), WITH ALL ACCESSORIES OFF, SEE SHOP MANUAL.

THIS VEHICLE CONFORMS TO U.S. EPA REGULATIONS APPLICABLE TO 1985 MODEL YEAR NEW MOTOR VEHICLES.

E5AE-9C485-CBY CATALYST SPARK PLUG: AWSF-44C GAP: .042-.046
2.3L-5GQ
FFM2.3V1HAK2-AIP/EGR/EGS/TWC

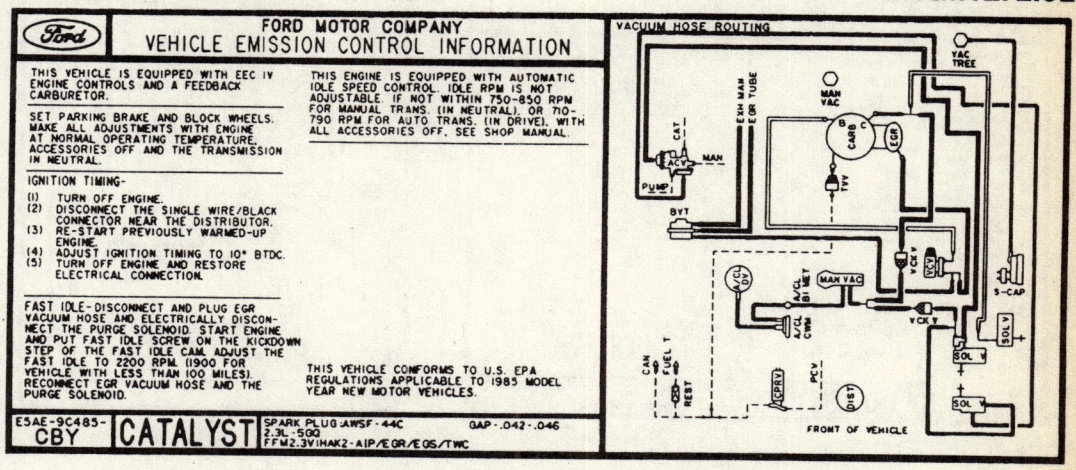

CALIBRATION: 5—06E—R00

MODEL YEAR: 1985 **ENGINE: 2.3L**

FORD MOTOR COMPANY
VEHICLE EMISSION CONTROL INFORMATION

THIS VEHICLE IS EQUIPPED WITH ELECTRONIC FUEL INJECTION. IDLE MIXTURE, COLD ENGINE IDLE SPEED AND COLD ENGINE FUEL ENRICHMENT NOT ADJUSTABLE.

SET PARKING BRAKE AND BLOCK WHEELS. DISCONNECT AUTOMATIC PARKING BRAKE RELEASE, IF SO EQUIPPED. MAKE ALL ADJUSTMENTS WITH ENGINE AT NORMAL OPERATING TEMPERATURE, TRANSMISSION IN NEUTRAL AND ACCESSORIES OFF.

IGNITION TIMING-
(1) TURN OFF ENGINE
(2) DISCONNECT THE SINGLE WIRE BLACK CONNECTOR NEAR THE DISTRIBUTOR.
(3) RE-START PREVIOUSLY WARMED-UP ENGINE.
(4) ADJUST IGNITION TIMING TO 10° BTDC.
(5) TURN OFF ENGINE AND RESTORE ELECTRICAL CONNECTION.

THIS ENGINE IS EQUIPPED WITH ELECTRONIC IDLE SPEED CONTROL. IDLE SPECIFICATION IS 825-975 RPM FOR MANUAL TRANSMISSION OR 925-1075 RPM FOR AUTOMATIC TRANSMISSION WITH THE TRANSMISSION IN NEUTRAL. IF ADJUSTMENT IS REQUIRED, DISCONNECT ELECTRICAL CONNECTOR AT THE IDLE BYPASS VALVE. ADJUST IDLE SPEED SCREW TO 725-775 RPM. RECONNECT ELECTRICAL CONNECTOR AT IDLE BYPASS VALVE.

THIS VEHICLE CONFORMS TO U.S. EPA REGULATIONS APPLICABLE TO 1985 MODEL YEAR NEW MOTOR VEHICLES.

E5AE-9C485-CGY CATALYST SPARK PLUG: AWSF-32C GAP: .032-.036
2.3L-5HM
FFM2.3V5FQK2-EGS/EGR/TWC

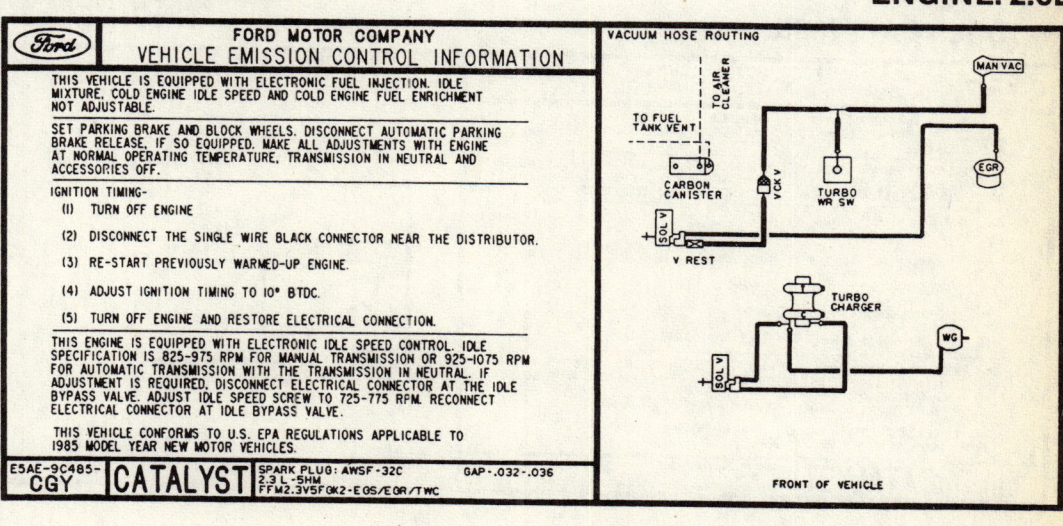

EMISSION CONTROLS

CALIBRATION: 5—06N—R00

MODEL YEAR: 1985 **ENGINE: 2.3L**

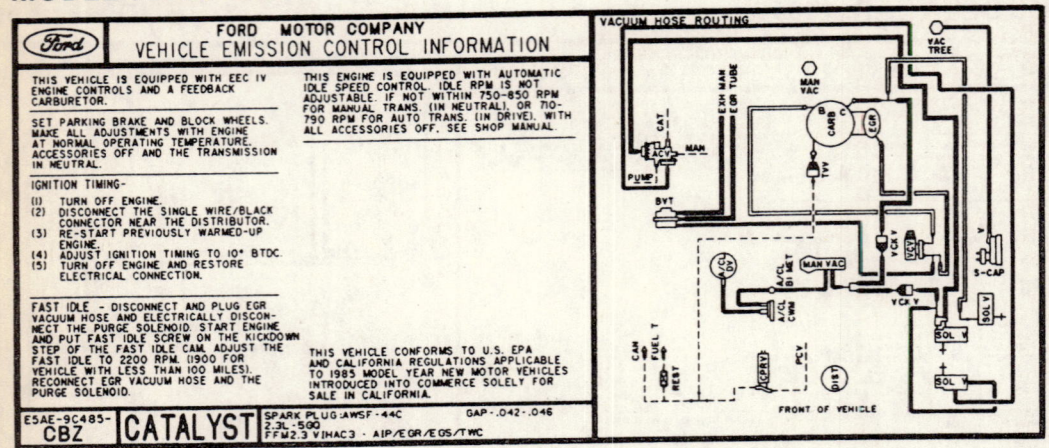

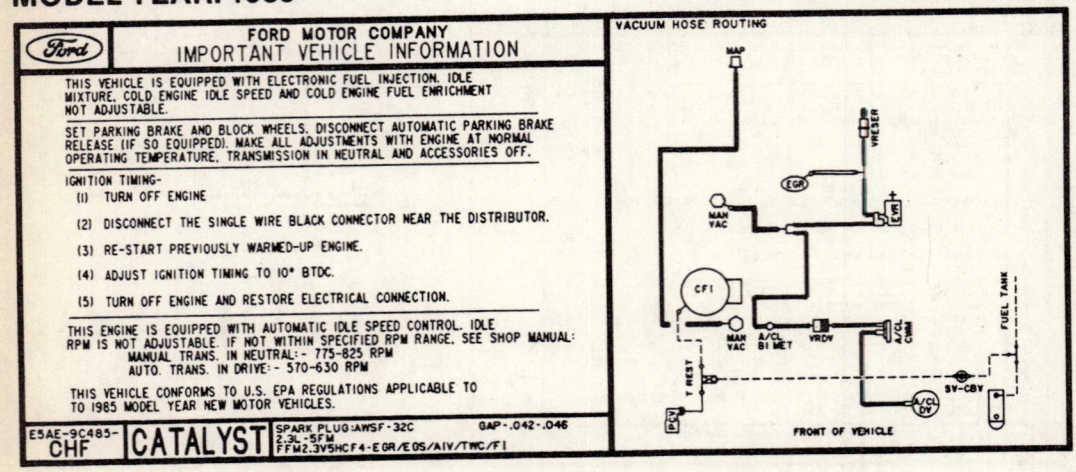

FORD MOTOR COMPANY
VEHICLE EMISSION CONTROL INFORMATION

THIS VEHICLE IS EQUIPPED WITH EEC IV ENGINE CONTROLS AND A FEEDBACK CARBURETOR.

SET PARKING BRAKE AND BLOCK WHEELS. MAKE ALL ADJUSTMENTS WITH ENGINE AT NORMAL OPERATING TEMPERATURE, ACCESSORIES OFF AND THE TRANSMISSION IN NEUTRAL.

IGNITION TIMING-
(1) TURN OFF ENGINE.
(2) DISCONNECT THE SINGLE WIRE/BLACK CONNECTOR NEAR THE DISTRIBUTOR.
(3) RE-START PREVIOUSLY WARMED-UP ENGINE.
(4) ADJUST IGNITION TIMING TO 10° BTDC.
(5) TURN OFF ENGINE AND RESTORE ELECTRICAL CONNECTION.

FAST IDLE - DISCONNECT AND PLUG EGR VACUUM HOSE AND ELECTRICALLY DISCONNECT THE PURGE SOLENOID. START ENGINE AND PUT FAST IDLE SCREW ON THE KICKDOWN STEP OF THE FAST IDLE CAM. ADJUST THE FAST IDLE TO 2200 RPM. (1900 FOR VEHICLE WITH LESS THAN 100 MILES). RECONNECT EGR VACUUM HOSE AND THE PURGE SOLENOID.

THIS ENGINE IS EQUIPPED WITH AUTOMATIC IDLE SPEED CONTROL. IDLE RPM IS NOT ADJUSTABLE. IF NOT WITHIN 750-850 RPM FOR MANUAL TRANS. (IN NEUTRAL), OR 710-790 RPM FOR AUTO TRANS. (IN DRIVE), WITH ALL ACCESSORIES OFF, SEE SHOP MANUAL.

THIS VEHICLE CONFORMS TO U.S. EPA AND CALIFORNIA REGULATIONS APPLICABLE TO 1985 MODEL YEAR NEW MOTOR VEHICLES INTRODUCED INTO COMMERCE SOLELY FOR SALE IN CALIFORNIA.

E5AE-9C485-CBZ CATALYST SPARK PLUG: AWSF-44C GAP: .042-.046
2.3L-5G0
FFM2.3VIHAC3 - AIP/EGR/EGS/TWC

CALIBRATION: 5—25C—R01

MODEL YEAR: 1985 **ENGINE: 2.3L**

FORD MOTOR COMPANY
IMPORTANT VEHICLE INFORMATION

THIS VEHICLE IS EQUIPPED WITH ELECTRONIC FUEL INJECTION. IDLE MIXTURE, COLD ENGINE IDLE SPEED AND COLD ENGINE FUEL ENRICHMENT NOT ADJUSTABLE.

SET PARKING BRAKE AND BLOCK WHEELS. DISCONNECT AUTOMATIC PARKING BRAKE RELEASE (IF SO EQUIPPED). MAKE ALL ADJUSTMENTS WITH ENGINE AT NORMAL OPERATING TEMPERATURE, TRANSMISSION IN NEUTRAL AND ACCESSORIES OFF.

IGNITION TIMING-
(1) TURN OFF ENGINE
(2) DISCONNECT THE SINGLE WIRE BLACK CONNECTOR NEAR THE DISTRIBUTOR.
(3) RE-START PREVIOUSLY WARMED-UP ENGINE.
(4) ADJUST IGNITION TIMING TO 10° BTDC.
(5) TURN OFF ENGINE AND RESTORE ELECTRICAL CONNECTION.

THIS ENGINE IS EQUIPPED WITH AUTOMATIC IDLE SPEED CONTROL. IDLE RPM IS NOT ADJUSTABLE. IF NOT WITHIN SPECIFIED RPM RANGE, SEE SHOP MANUAL:
MANUAL TRANS. IN NEUTRAL:- 775-825 RPM
AUTO. TRANS. IN DRIVE:- 570-630 RPM

THIS VEHICLE CONFORMS TO U.S. EPA REGULATIONS APPLICABLE TO 1985 MODEL YEAR NEW MOTOR VEHICLES.

E5AE-9C485-CHF CATALYST SPARK PLUG: AWSF-32C GAP: .042-.046
2.3L-5FM
FFM2.3V5HCF4-EGR/EOS/AIV/TWC/FI

EMISSION CONTROLS

CALIBRATION: 5—25F—R00

MODEL YEAR: 1985 **ENGINE: 2.3L**

FORD MOTOR COMPANY
IMPORTANT VEHICLE INFORMATION

THIS VEHICLE IS EQUIPPED WITH ELECTRONIC FUEL INJECTION. IDLE MIXTURE, COLD ENGINE IDLE SPEED AND COLD ENGINE FUEL ENRICHMENT NOT ADJUSTABLE.

SET PARKING BRAKE AND BLOCK WHEELS. DISCONNECT AUTOMATIC PARKING BRAKE RELEASE (IF SO EQUIPPED). MAKE ALL ADJUSTMENTS WITH ENGINE AT NORMAL OPERATING TEMPERATURE, TRANSMISSION IN NEUTRAL AND ACCESSORIES OFF.

IGNITION TIMING-
(1) TURN OFF ENGINE
(2) DISCONNECT THE SINGLE WIRE BLACK CONNECTOR NEAR THE DISTRIBUTOR.
(3) RE-START PREVIOUSLY WARMED-UP ENGINE.
(4) ADJUST IGNITION TIMING TO 10° BTDC.
(5) TURN OFF ENGINE AND RESTORE ELECTRICAL CONNECTION.

THIS ENGINE IS EQUIPPED WITH AUTOMATIC IDLE SPEED CONTROL. IDLE RPM IS NOT ADJUSTABLE. IF NOT WITHIN SPECIFIED RPM RANGE, SEE SHOP MANUAL.
MANUAL TRANS. IN NEUTRAL:- 725-775 RPM
AUTO. TRANS. IN DRIVE:- 570-630 RPM

THIS VEHICLE CONFORMS TO U.S. EPA REGULATIONS APPLICABLE TO 1985 MODEL YEAR NEW MOTOR VEHICLES.

E5AE-9C485-CEV CATALYST SPARK PLUG: AWSF-52C GAP-.042-.046
2.3L-5FM
FFM2.3V5HCF4-EGR/EGS/AIP/TWC

VACUUM HOSE ROUTING

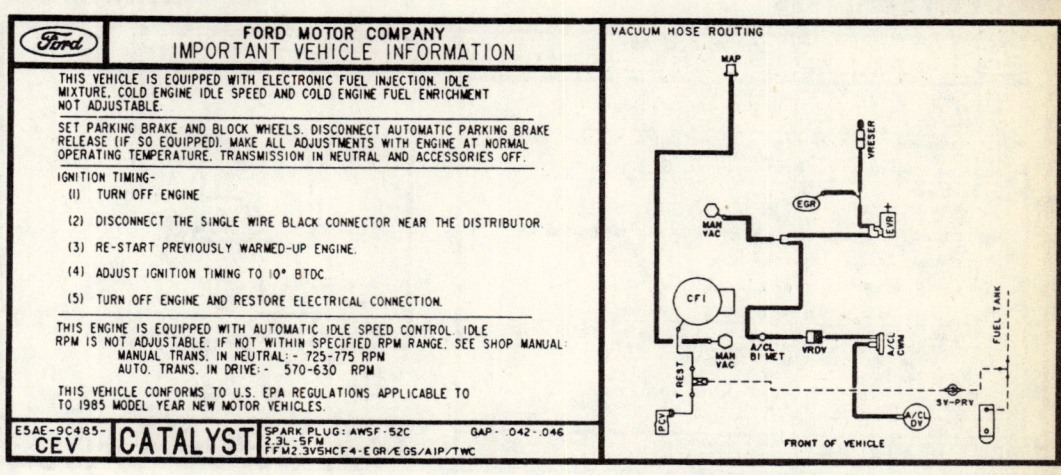

CALIBRATION: 5—25G—R00

MODEL YEAR: 1985 **ENGINE: 2.3L**

VEHICLE EMISSION CONTROL INFORMATION **FORD MOTOR COMPANY**

BEFORE MAKING ANY ADJUSTMENTS, BLOCK WHEELS AND SET PARKING BRAKE. DISCONNECT AUTOMATIC PARKING BRAKE RELEASE (IF SO EQUIPPED).
MAKE ALL ADJUSTMENTS WITH ENGINE AT NORMAL OPERATING TEMPERATURE AND ALL ACCESSORIES OFF.
IGNITION TIMING- ADJUST WITH TRANSMISSION IN NEUTRAL.
(1) TURN OFF ENGINE.
(2) DISCONNECT AND PLUG DISTRIBUTOR VACUUM HOSE.
(3) RE-START PREVIOUSLY WARMED-UP ENGINE.
(4) ADJUST IGNITION TIMING TO 10° BTDC, 800 RPM MAX.
(5) TURN OFF ENGINE AND RESTORE VACUUM CONNECTION.
FAST IDLE- ADJUST WITH TRANSMISSION IN NEUTRAL. DISCONNECT AND PLUG EGR VACUUM HOSE. PUT THE ADJUSTING SCREW ON KICKDOWN STEP OF THE FAST IDLE CAM. ADJUST FAST IDLE TO 2200 RPM WHEN THE ENGINE COOLING FAN IS OFF. RECONNECT EGR HOSE.
CURB IDLE- ADJUST WITH TRANSMISSION IN "N".
DISCONNECT AND PLUG VACUUM OPERATED THROTTLE MODULATOR. ACTIVATE ENGINE COOLING FAN BY INSTALLING A JUMPER WIRE FROM THE FAN CONTROL TO GROUND. ADJUST IDLE TO 800 RPM BY TURNING ADJUSTING SCREW ON THROTTLE LEVER. PLACE TRANSMISSION IN NEUTRAL AND ACCELERATE ENGINE MOMENTARILY. CHECK/READJUST IDLE WITH TRANSMISSION IN SPECIFIED POSITION. RESTORE ELECTRICAL AND VACUUM CONNECTIONS.

IF EQUIPPED WITH AUTO. O.D. TRANS. & CURB IDLE ADJ. IS GREATER THAN 150 RPM, RE-ADJUST AUTO. TRANS. LINKAGE.
SEE SHOP MANUAL.
SEE SHOP MANUAL FOR CHOKE AND IDLE MIXTURE ADJUSTMENT INFO.

E5AE-9C485-CHH 2.3L SPARK PLUG/BOUGIES AWSF-52 GAP/ÉLECTRODES .042-.046

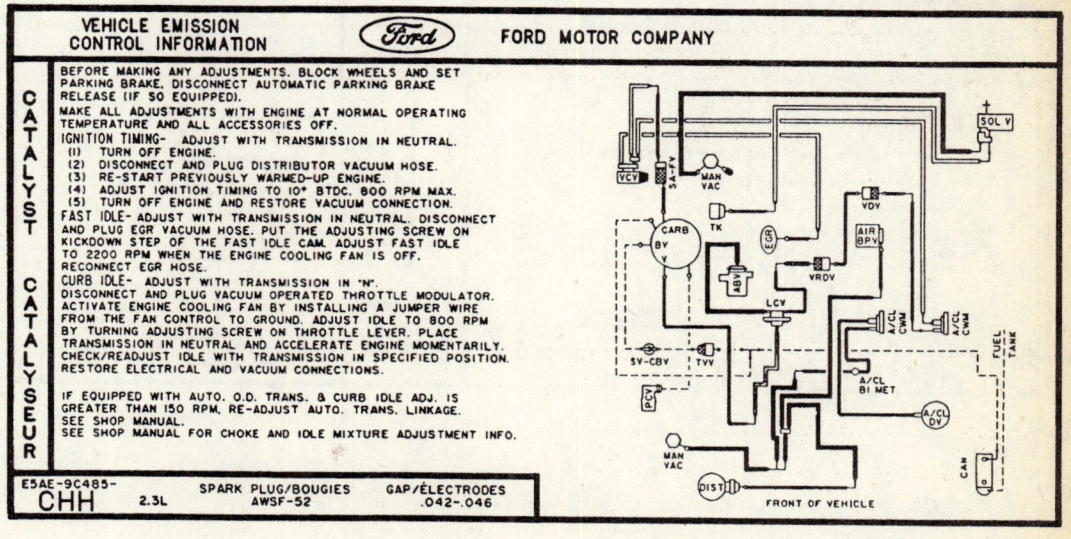

CATALYST / CATALYSEUR

EMISSION CONTROLS

CALIBRATION: 5—25P—R00

MODEL YEAR: 1985 **ENGINE: 2.3L**

FORD MOTOR COMPANY
VEHICLE EMISSION CONTROL INFORMATION

THIS VEHICLE IS EQUIPPED WITH ELECTRONIC FUEL INJECTION. IDLE MIXTURE, COLD ENGINE IDLE SPEED AND COLD ENGINE FUEL ENRICHMENT NOT ADJUSTABLE.

SET PARKING BRAKE AND BLOCK WHEELS. DISCONNECT AUTOMATIC PARKING BRAKE RELEASE (IF SO EQUIPPED). MAKE ALL ADJUSTMENTS WITH ENGINE AT NORMAL OPERATING TEMPERATURE, TRANSMISSION IN NEUTRAL AND ACCESSORIES OFF.

IGNITION TIMING-
(1) TURN OFF ENGINE
(2) DISCONNECT THE SINGLE WIRE BLACK CONNECTOR NEAR THE DISTRIBUTOR.
(3) RE-START PREVIOUSLY WARMED-UP ENGINE.
(4) ADJUST IGNITION TIMING TO 10° BTDC.
(5) TURN OFF ENGINE AND RESTORE ELECTRICAL CONNECTION.

THIS ENGINE IS EQUIPPED WITH AUTOMATIC IDLE SPEED CONTROL. IDLE RPM IS NOT ADJUSTABLE. IF NOT WITHIN SPECIFIED RPM RANGE, SEE SHOP MANUAL:
MANUAL TRANS. IN NEUTRAL:- 775-825 RPM
AUTO. TRANS. IN DRIVE:- 570-630 RPM

THIS VEHICLE CONFORMS TO U.S. EPA AND CALIFORNIA REGULATIONS APPLICABLE TO 1985 MODEL YEAR NEW MOTOR VEHICLES. INTRODUCED INTO COMMERCE SOLELY FOR SALE IN CALIFORNIA.

E5AE-9C485-CHE CATALYST SPARK PLUG: AWSF-32C GAP .042-.046
2.3L-5FM
FFM2.3V5HCH6-EGR/EGS/A1V/TWC/FI

VACUUM HOSE ROUTING

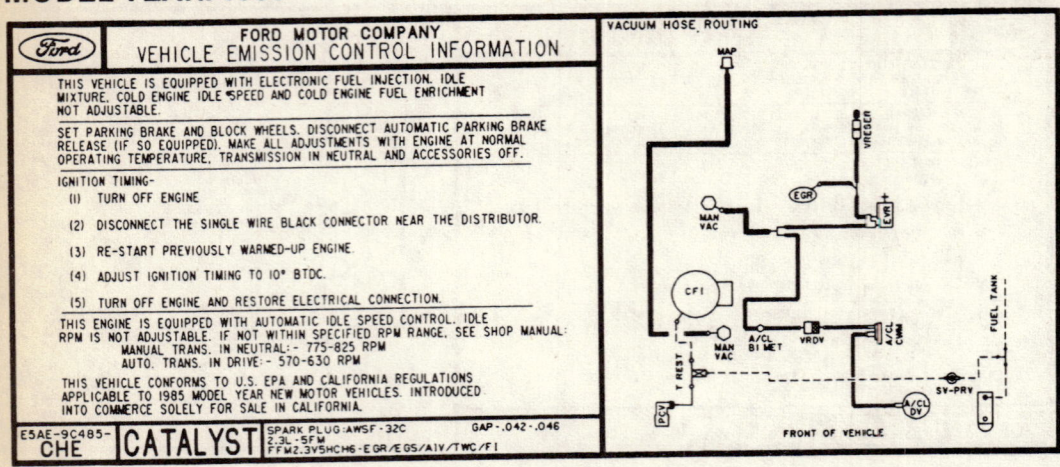

CALIBRATION: 5—25Q—R00

MODEL YEAR: 1985 **ENGINE: 2.3L**

FORD MOTOR COMPANY
VEHICLE EMISSION CONTROL INFORMATION

THIS VEHICLE IS EQUIPPED WITH ELECTRONIC FUEL INJECTION. IDLE MIXTURE, COLD ENGINE IDLE SPEED AND COLD ENGINE FUEL ENRICHMENT NOT ADJUSTABLE.

SET PARKING BRAKE AND BLOCK WHEELS. DISCONNECT AUTOMATIC PARKING BRAKE RELEASE (IF SO EQUIPPED). MAKE ALL ADJUSTMENTS WITH ENGINE AT NORMAL OPERATING TEMPERATURE, TRANSMISSION IN NEUTRAL AND ACCESSORIES OFF.

IGNITION TIMING-
(1) TURN OFF ENGINE
(2) DISCONNECT THE SINGLE WIRE BLACK CONNECTOR NEAR THE DISTRIBUTOR.
(3) RE-START PREVIOUSLY WARMED-UP ENGINE.
(4) ADJUST IGNITION TIMING TO 10° BTDC.
(5) TURN OFF ENGINE AND RESTORE ELECTRICAL CONNECTION.

THIS ENGINE IS EQUIPPED WITH AUTOMATIC IDLE SPEED CONTROL. IDLE RPM IS NOT ADJUSTABLE. IF NOT WITHIN SPECIFIED RPM RANGE, SEE SHOP MANUAL:
MANUAL TRANS. IN NEUTRAL:- 725-775 RPM
AUTO. TRANS. IN DRIVE:- 570-630 RPM

THIS VEHICLE CONFORMS TO U.S. EPA AND CALIFORNIA REGULATIONS APPLICABLE TO 1985 MODEL YEAR NEW MOTOR VEHICLES. INTRODUCED INTO COMMERCE SOLELY FOR SALE IN CALIFORNIA.

E5AE-9C485-CEY CATALYST SPARK PLUG: AWSF-52C GAP .042-.046
2.3L-5FM
FFM2.3V5HCH6-EGR/EGS/AIP/TWC

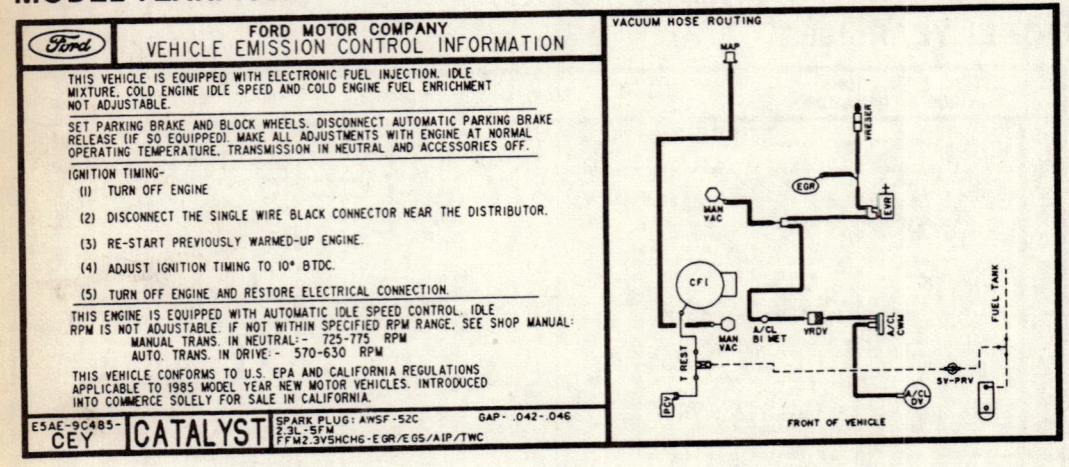

VACUUM HOSE ROUTING

EMISSION CONTROLS 283

CALIBRATION: 5—26E—R00

MODEL YEAR: 1985   **ENGINE: 2.3L**

FORD MOTOR COMPANY
IMPORTANT VEHICLE INFORMATION

THIS VEHICLE IS EQUIPPED WITH ELECTRONIC FUEL INJECTION. IDLE MIXTURE, COLD ENGINE IDLE SPEED AND COLD ENGINE FUEL ENRICHMENT NOT ADJUSTABLE.

SET PARKING BRAKE AND BLOCK WHEELS. DISCONNECT AUTOMATIC PARKING BRAKE RELEASE (IF SO EQUIPPED). MAKE ALL ADJUSTMENTS WITH ENGINE AT NORMAL OPERATING TEMPERATURE, TRANSMISSION IN NEUTRAL AND ACCESSORIES OFF.

IGNITION TIMING—
(1) TURN OFF ENGINE
(2) DISCONNECT THE SINGLE WIRE BLACK CONNECTOR NEAR THE DISTRIBUTOR.
(3) RE-START PREVIOUSLY WARMED-UP ENGINE.
(4) ADJUST IGNITION TIMING TO 10° BTDC.
(5) TURN OFF ENGINE AND RESTORE ELECTRICAL CONNECTION.

THIS ENGINE IS EQUIPPED WITH AUTOMATIC IDLE SPEED CONTROL. IDLE RPM IS NOT ADJUSTABLE. IF NOT WITHIN SPECIFIED RPM RANGE, SEE SHOP MANUAL:
    MANUAL TRANS. IN NEUTRAL:- 725-775 RPM
    AUTO. TRANS. IN DRIVE:- 570-630 RPM

THIS VEHICLE CONFORMS TO U.S. EPA REGULATIONS APPLICABLE TO 1985 MODEL YEAR NEW MOTOR VEHICLES.

E5AE-9C485-CEV   **CATALYST**   SPARK PLUG: AWSF-52C   GAP- .042-.046
2.3L-5FM
FFM2.3V5HCF4-EGR/EOS/AIP/TWC

VACUUM HOSE ROUTING

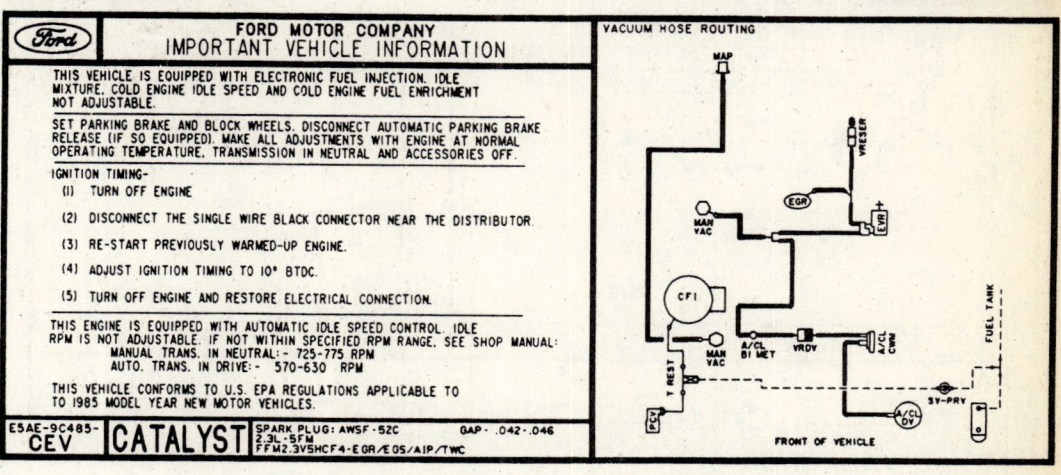

CALIBRATION: 5—26G—R00

MODEL YEAR: 1985   **ENGINE: 2.3L**

VEHICLE EMISSION CONTROL INFORMATION   **Ford**   **FORD MOTOR COMPANY**

BEFORE MAKING ANY ADJUSTMENTS, BLOCK WHEELS AND SET PARKING BRAKE. DISCONNECT AUTOMATIC PARKING BRAKE RELEASE (IF SO EQUIPPED).
MAKE ALL ADJUSTMENTS WITH ENGINE AT NORMAL OPERATING TEMPERATURE AND ALL ACCESSORIES OFF.
IGNITION TIMING— ADJUST WITH TRANSMISSION IN NEUTRAL.
(1) TURN OFF ENGINE.
(2) DISCONNECT AND PLUG DISTRIBUTOR VACUUM HOSE.
(3) RE-START PREVIOUSLY WARMED-UP ENGINE.
(4) ADJUST IGNITION TIMING TO THE △ TIMING MARK (10° BTDC). 800 RPM MAX.
(5) TURN OFF ENGINE AND RESTORE VACUUM CONNECTION.
FAST IDLE- ADJUST WITH TRANSMISSION IN NEUTRAL. DISCONNECT AND PLUG EGR VACUUM HOSE. PUT THE ADJUSTING SCREW ON KICKDOWN STEP OF THE FAST IDLE CAM. ADJUST FAST IDLE TO 2200 RPM WHEN THE ENGINE COOLING FAN IS OFF (2100 RPM FOR VEHICLE WITH LESS THAN 160 KM). RECONNECT EGR HOSE.
CURB IDLE- ADJUST WITH TRANSMISSION IN "D".
DISCONNECT AND PLUG VACUUM OPERATED THROTTLE MODULATOR. ACTIVATE ENGINE COOLING FAN BY INSTALLING A JUMPER WIRE FROM THE FAN CONTROL TO GROUND. ADJUST IDLE TO 730 RPM BY TURNING ADJUSTING SCREW ON THROTTLE LEVER (655 RPM FOR VEHICLE WITH LESS THAN 160 KM). PLACE TRANSMISSION IN NEUTRAL AND ACCELERATE ENGINE MOMENTARILY. CHECK/READJUST IDLE WITH TRANSMISSION IN SPECIFIED POSITION. RESTORE ELECTRICAL AND VACUUM CONNECTIONS.
IF EQUIPPED WITH AUTO. O.D. TRANS. & CURB IDLE ADJ. IS GREATER THAN 150 RPM, RE-ADJUST AUTO. TRANS. LINKAGE.
SEE SHOP MANUAL.
SEE SHOP MANUAL FOR CHOKE AND IDLE MIXTURE ADJUSTMENT INFO.

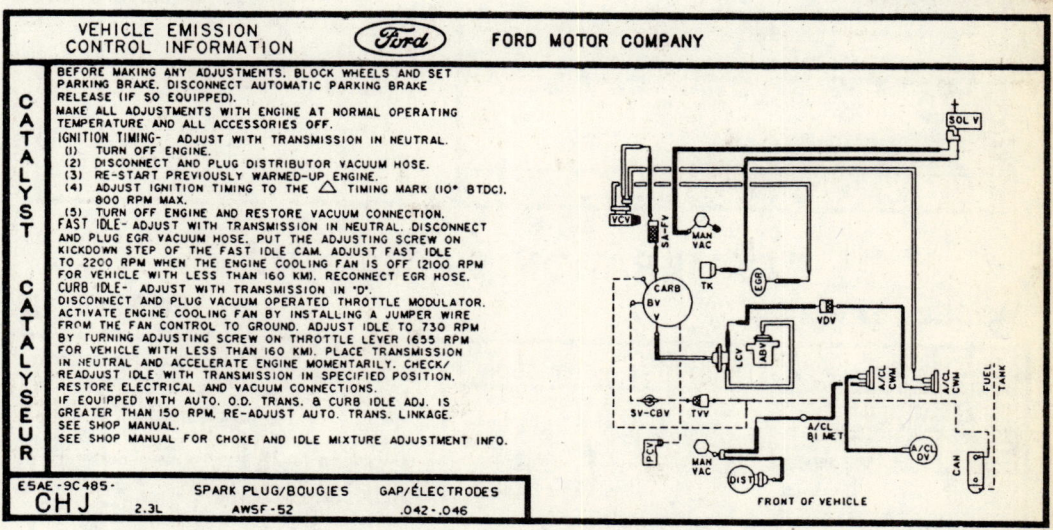

E5AE-9C485-CHJ   **CATALYST / CATALYSEUR**   2.3L   SPARK PLUG/BOUGIES AWSF-52   GAP/ÉLECTRODES .042-.046

EMISSION CONTROLS

CALIBRATION: 5—26J—R01

MODEL YEAR: 1985 **ENGINE: 2.3L**

FORD MOTOR COMPANY — IMPORTANT VEHICLE INFORMATION

THIS VEHICLE IS EQUIPPED WITH ELECTRONIC FUEL INJECTION. IDLE MIXTURE, COLD ENGINE IDLE SPEED AND COLD ENGINE FUEL ENRICHMENT NOT ADJUSTABLE.

SET PARKING BRAKE AND BLOCK WHEELS. DISCONNECT AUTOMATIC PARKING BRAKE RELEASE (IF SO EQUIPPED). MAKE ALL ADJUSTMENTS WITH ENGINE AT NORMAL OPERATING TEMPERATURE, TRANSMISSION IN NEUTRAL AND ACCESSORIES OFF.

IGNITION TIMING-
(1) TURN OFF ENGINE
(2) DISCONNECT THE SINGLE WIRE BLACK CONNECTOR NEAR THE DISTRIBUTOR.
(3) RE-START PREVIOUSLY WARMED-UP ENGINE.
(4) ADJUST IGNITION TIMING TO 10° BTDC.
(5) TURN OFF ENGINE AND RESTORE ELECTRICAL CONNECTION.

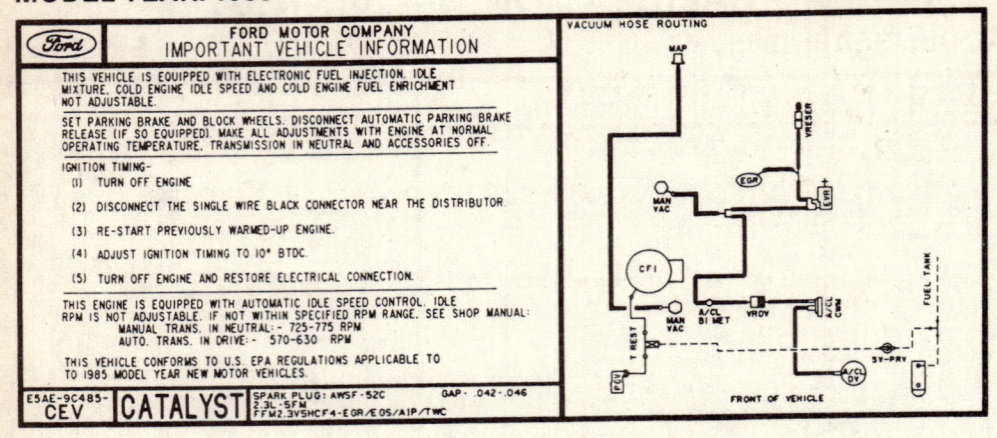

THIS ENGINE IS EQUIPPED WITH AUTOMATIC IDLE SPEED CONTROL. IDLE RPM IS NOT ADJUSTABLE. IF NOT WITHIN SPECIFIED RPM RANGE, SEE SHOP MANUAL:
MANUAL TRANS. IN NEUTRAL: - 725-775 RPM
AUTO. TRANS. IN DRIVE: - 570-630 RPM

THIS VEHICLE CONFORMS TO U.S. EPA REGULATIONS APPLICABLE TO 1985 MODEL YEAR NEW MOTOR VEHICLES.

E5AE-9C485-CEV CATALYST SPARK PLUG: AWSF-52C GAP: .042-.046
2.3L-5FM FFM2.3V5HCF4-EGR/EOS/AIP/TWC

VACUUM HOSE ROUTING

CALIBRATION: 5—26R—R01

MODEL YEAR: 1985 **ENGINE: 2.3L**

FORD MOTOR COMPANY — VEHICLE EMISSION CONTROL INFORMATION

THIS VEHICLE IS EQUIPPED WITH ELECTRONIC FUEL INJECTION. IDLE MIXTURE, COLD ENGINE IDLE SPEED AND COLD ENGINE FUEL ENRICHMENT NOT ADJUSTABLE.

SET PARKING BRAKE AND BLOCK WHEELS. DISCONNECT AUTOMATIC PARKING BRAKE RELEASE (IF SO EQUIPPED). MAKE ALL ADJUSTMENTS WITH ENGINE AT NORMAL OPERATING TEMPERATURE, TRANSMISSION IN NEUTRAL AND ACCESSORIES OFF.

IGNITION TIMING-
(1) TURN OFF ENGINE
(2) DISCONNECT THE SINGLE WIRE BLACK CONNECTOR NEAR THE DISTRIBUTOR.
(3) RE-START PREVIOUSLY WARMED-UP ENGINE.
(4) ADJUST IGNITION TIMING TO 10° BTDC.
(5) TURN OFF ENGINE AND RESTORE ELECTRICAL CONNECTION.

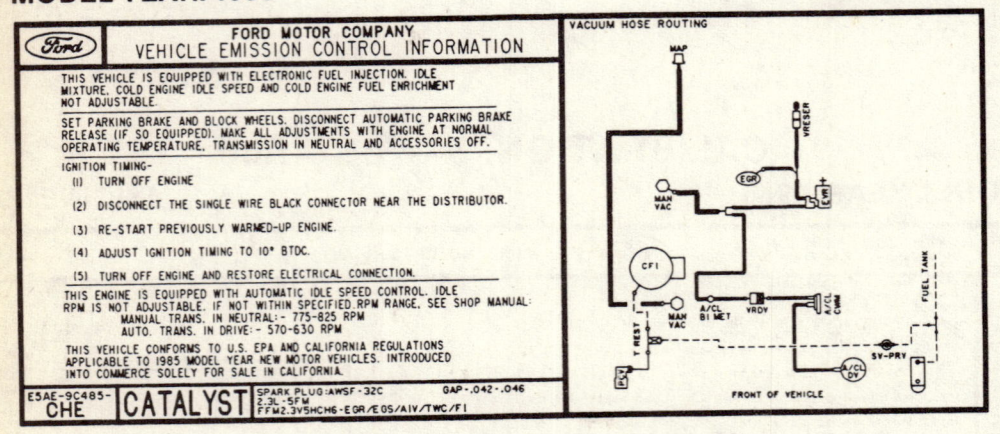

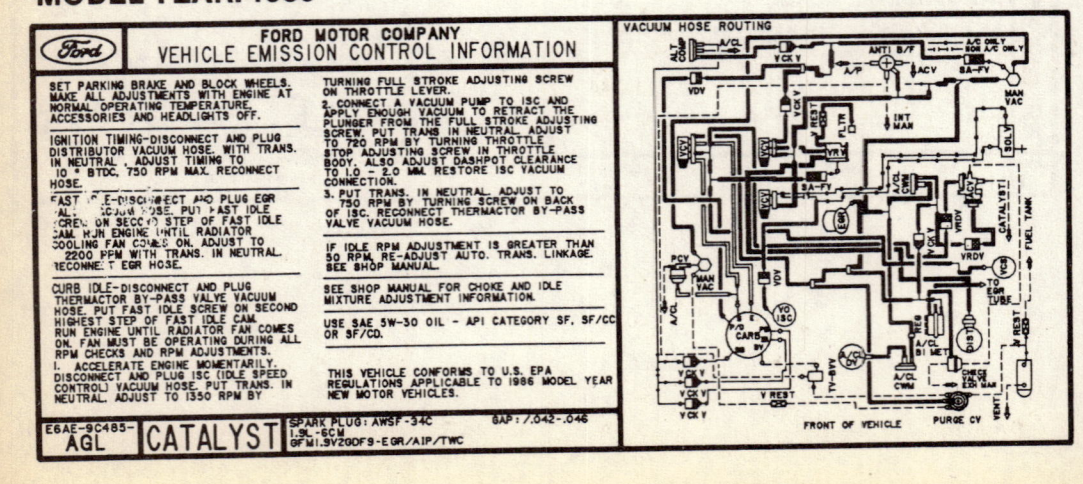

THIS ENGINE IS EQUIPPED WITH AUTOMATIC IDLE SPEED CONTROL. IDLE RPM IS NOT ADJUSTABLE. IF NOT WITHIN SPECIFIED RPM RANGE, SEE SHOP MANUAL:
MANUAL TRANS. IN NEUTRAL: - 775-825 RPM
AUTO. TRANS. IN DRIVE: - 570-630 RPM

THIS VEHICLE CONFORMS TO U.S. EPA AND CALIFORNIA REGULATIONS APPLICABLE TO 1985 MODEL YEAR NEW MOTOR VEHICLES. INTRODUCED INTO COMMERCE SOLELY FOR SALE IN CALIFORNIA.

E5AE-9C485-CHE CATALYST SPARK PLUG: AWSF-32C GAP: .042-.046
2.3L-5FM FFM2.3V5HCH6-EGR/EOS/AIV/TWC/FI

VACUUM HOSE ROUTING

CALIBRATION: 6—07A—R12

MODEL YEAR: 1986 **ENGINE: 1.9L**

FORD MOTOR COMPANY — VEHICLE EMISSION CONTROL INFORMATION

SET PARKING BRAKE AND BLOCK WHEELS. MAKE ALL ADJUSTMENTS WITH ENGINE AT NORMAL OPERATING TEMPERATURE. ACCESSORIES AND HEADLIGHTS OFF.

IGNITION TIMING-DISCONNECT AND PLUG DISTRIBUTOR VACUUM HOSE. WITH TRANS. IN NEUTRAL, ADJUST TIMING TO 10° BTDC, 750 RPM MAX. RECONNECT HOSE.

FAST IDLE-DISCONNECT AND PLUG EGR VALVE VACUUM HOSE. PUT FAST IDLE SCREW ON SECOND STEP OF FAST IDLE CAM. RUN ENGINE UNTIL RADIATOR COOLING FAN COMES ON. ADJUST TO 2200 RPM WITH TRANS. IN NEUTRAL. RECONNECT EGR HOSE.

CURB IDLE-DISCONNECT AND PLUG THERMACTOR BY-PASS VALVE VACUUM HOSE. PUT FAST IDLE SCREW ON SECOND HIGHEST STEP OF FAST IDLE CAM. RUN ENGINE UNTIL RADIATOR FAN COMES ON. FAN MUST BE OPERATING DURING ALL RPM CHECKS AND RPM ADJUSTMENTS.
1. ACCELERATE ENGINE MOMENTARILY. DISCONNECT AND PLUG ISC (IDLE SPEED CONTROL) VACUUM HOSE. IN NEUTRAL, ADJUST TO 1350 RPM BY TURNING FULL STROKE ADJUSTING SCREW ON THROTTLE LEVER.
2. CONNECT A VACUUM PUMP TO ISC AND APPLY ENOUGH VACUUM TO RETRACT THE PLUNGER FROM THE FULL STROKE ADJUSTING SCREW. PUT TRANS. IN NEUTRAL. ADJUST TO 720 RPM BY TURNING THROTTLE STOP ADJUSTING SCREW IN THROTTLE BODY. ALSO ADJUST DASHPOT CLEARANCE TO 1.0 - 2.0 MM. RESTORE ISC VACUUM CONNECTION.
3. PUT TRANS. IN NEUTRAL. ADJUST TO 750 RPM BY TURNING SCREW ON BACK OF ISC. RECONNECT THERMACTOR BY-PASS VALVE VACUUM HOSE.

IF IDLE RPM ADJUSTMENT IS GREATER THAN 50 RPM, RE-ADJUST AUTO. TRANS. LINKAGE. SEE SHOP MANUAL.

SEE SHOP MANUAL FOR CHOKE AND IDLE MIXTURE ADJUSTMENT INFORMATION.

USE SAE 5W-30 OIL - API CATEGORY SF, SF/CC OR SF/CD.

THIS VEHICLE CONFORMS TO U.S. EPA REGULATIONS APPLICABLE TO 1986 MODEL YEAR NEW MOTOR VEHICLES.

E6AE-9C485-AGL CATALYST SPARK PLUG: AWSF-34C GAP: .042-.046
1.9L-6CM GFM1.9V2GOF9-EGR/AIP/TWC

VACUUM HOSE ROUTING

EMISSION CONTROLS

CALIBRATION: 6—07E—R00

MODEL YEAR: 1986 **ENGINE: 1.9L**

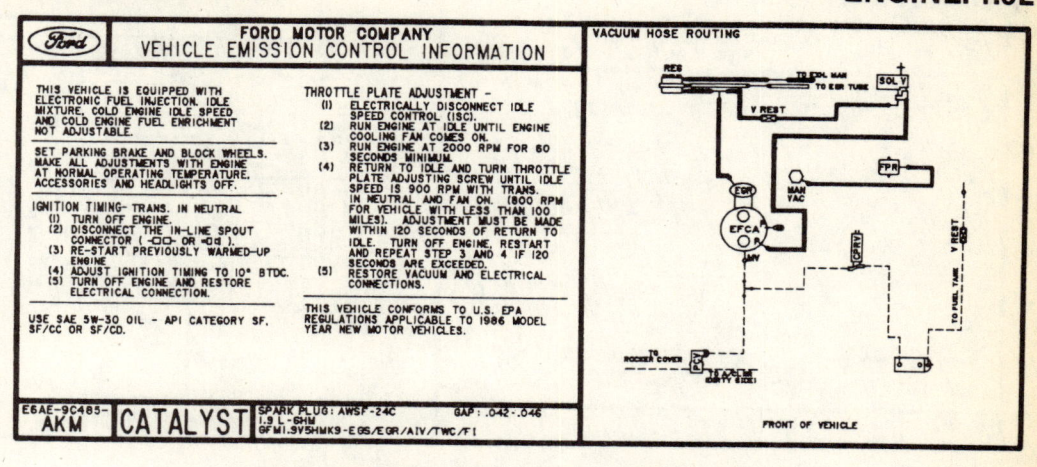

CALIBRATION: 6—07F—R13

MODEL YEAR: 1986 **ENGINE: 1.9L**

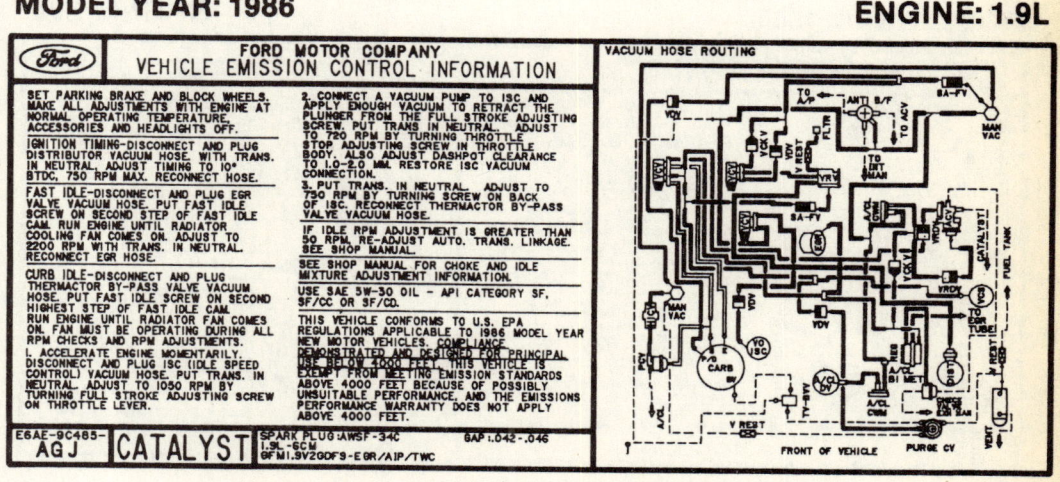

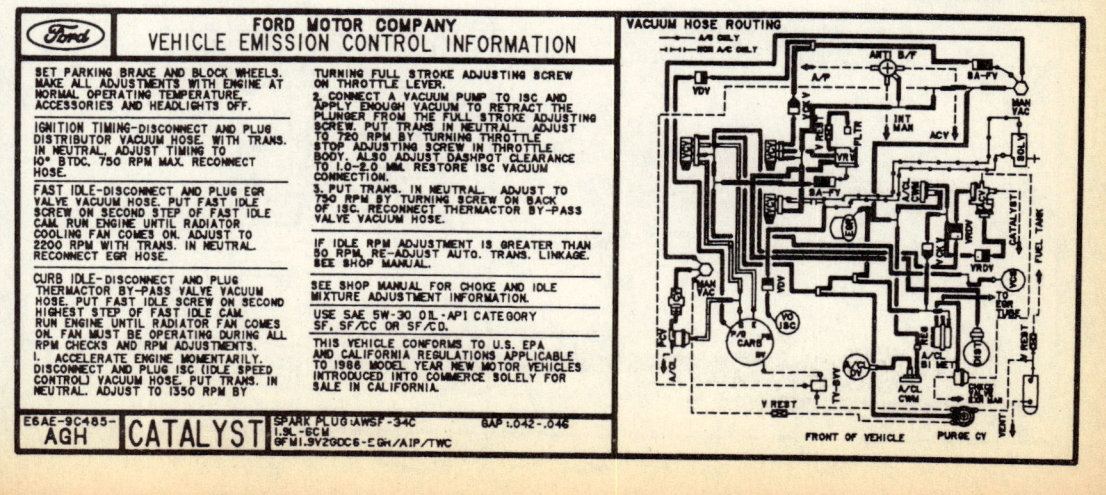

CALIBRATION: 6—07S—R12

MODEL YEAR: 1986 **ENGINE: 1.9L**

EMISSION CONTROLS

CALIBRATION: 6—07S—R13

MODEL YEAR: 1986 **ENGINE: 1.9L**

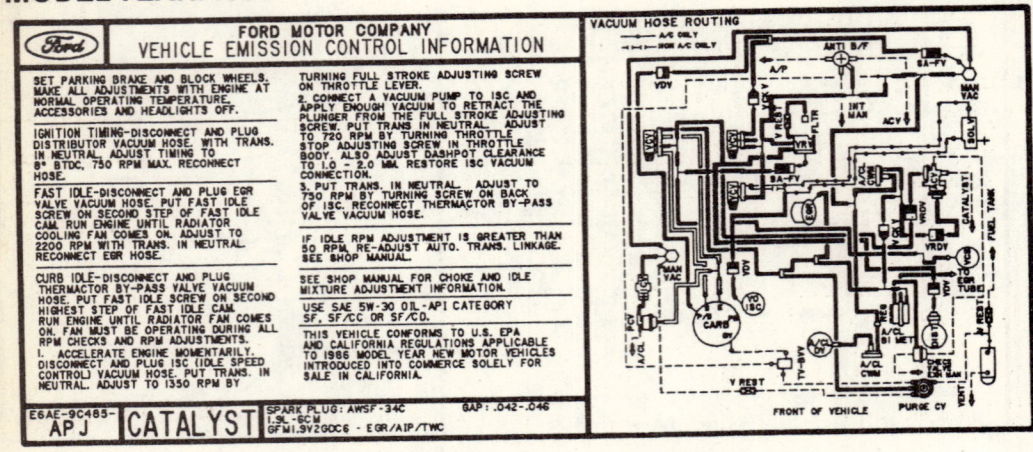

CALIBRATION: 6—08A—R17

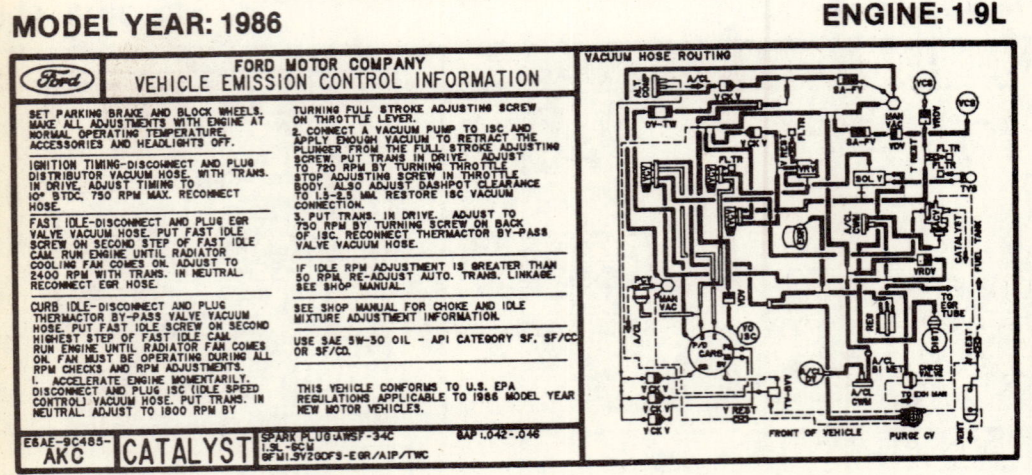

MODEL YEAR: 1986 **ENGINE: 1.9L**

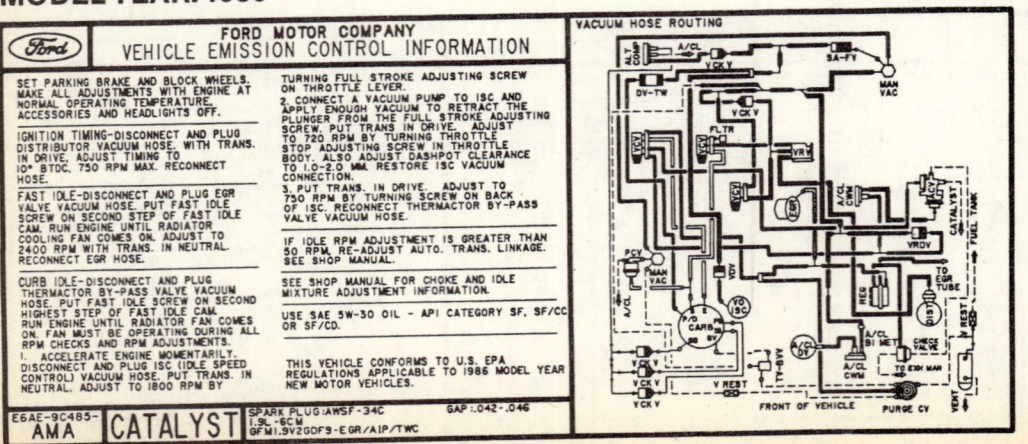

CALIBRATION: 6—08A—R25

MODEL YEAR: 1986 **ENGINE: 1.9L**

EMISSION CONTROLS

CALIBRATION: 6—08A—R28

MODEL YEAR: 1986 **ENGINE: 1.9L**

FORD MOTOR COMPANY — VEHICLE EMISSION CONTROL INFORMATION

THIS VEHICLE IS EQUIPPED WITH ELECTRONIC FUEL INJECTION. IDLE MIXTURE, COLD ENGINE IDLE SPEED AND COLD ENGINE FUEL ENRICHMENT NOT ADJUSTABLE.

SET PARKING BRAKE AND BLOCK WHEELS. DISCONNECT AUTOMATIC PARKING BRAKE RELEASE (IF SO EQUIPPED). MAKE ALL ADJUSTMENTS WITH ENGINE AT NORMAL OPERATING TEMPERATURE, TRANSMISSION IN NEUTRAL AND ACCESSORIES OFF.

IGNITION TIMING-
(1) TURN OFF ENGINE
(2) DISCONNECT THE IN-LINE SPOUT CONNECTOR (-☐☐- OR -◁◁-).
(3) RE-START PREVIOUSLY WARMED-UP ENGINE.
(4) ADJUST IGNITION TIMING TO 10° BTDC OR △.
(5) TURN OFF ENGINE AND RESTORE ELECTRICAL CONNECTION.

THIS ENGINE IS EQUIPPED WITH AUTOMATIC IDLE SPEED CONTROL. IDLE RPM IS NOT ADJUSTABLE. IF NOT WITHIN SPECIFIED RPM RANGE, SEE SHOP MANUAL:
 MANUAL TRANS. IN NEUTRAL:-750-850 RPM
 AUTO. TRANS. IN DRIVE:-650-750 RPM

USE SAE 5W-30 OIL - API CATEGORY SF, SF/CC OR SF/CD.

THIS VEHICLE CONFORMS TO U.S. EPA REGULATIONS APPLICABLE TO 1986 MODEL YEAR NEW MOTOR VEHICLES.

E6AE-9C485-AML CATALYST SPARK PLUG: AWSF-32C GAP .042-.046
2.5L-6FM
GFM2.5V5HCF6-EGR/EOS/AIV/TWC/FI

VACUUM HOSE ROUTING

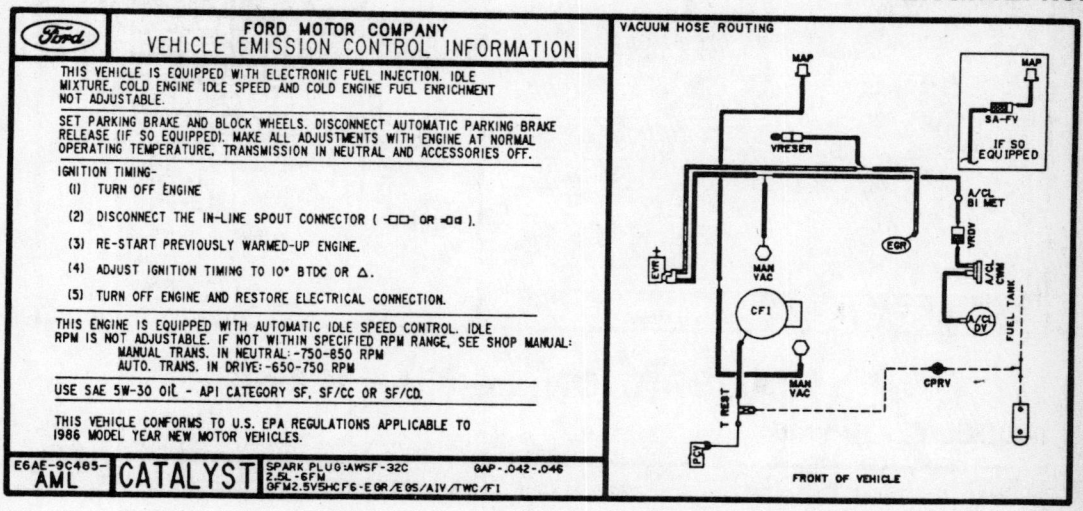

CALIBRATION: 6—08E—R00

MODEL YEAR: 1986 **ENGINE: 1.9L**

FORD MOTOR COMPANY — VEHICLE EMISSION CONTROL INFORMATION

THIS VEHICLE IS EQUIPPED WITH ELECTRONIC FUEL INJECTION. IDLE MIXTURE, COLD ENGINE IDLE SPEED AND COLD ENGINE FUEL ENRICHMENT NOT ADJUSTABLE.

SET PARKING BRAKE AND BLOCK WHEELS. MAKE ALL ADJUSTMENTS WITH ENGINE AT NORMAL OPERATING TEMPERATURE, ACCESSORIES AND HEADLIGHTS OFF.

IGNITION TIMING- TRANS. IN NEUTRAL
(1) TURN OFF ENGINE.
(2) DISCONNECT THE IN-LINE SPOUT CONNECTOR (-☐☐- OR -◁◁-).
(3) RE-START PREVIOUSLY WARMED-UP ENGINE
(4) ADJUST IGNITION TIMING TO 10° BTDC.
(5) TURN OFF ENGINE AND RESTORE ELECTRICAL CONNECTION.

THROTTLE PLATE ADJUSTMENT -
(1) ELECTRICALLY DISCONNECT IDLE SPEED CONTROL (ISC).
(2) RUN ENGINE AT IDLE UNTIL ENGINE COOLING FAN COMES ON.
(3) RUN ENGINE AT 2000 RPM FOR 60 SECONDS MINIMUM.
(4) RETURN TO IDLE AND TURN THROTTLE PLATE ADJUSTING SCREW UNTIL IDLE SPEED IS 800 RPM WITH AUTO. TRANS. IN DRIVE AND FAN ON. (700 RPM FOR VEHICLE WITH LESS THAN 100 MILES). ADJUSTMENT MUST BE MADE WITHIN 120 SECONDS OF RETURN TO IDLE. TURN OFF ENGINE, RESTART AND REPEAT STEP 3 AND 4 IF 120 SECONDS ARE EXCEEDED.
(5) IF THROTTLE PLATE ADJUSTMENT EXCEEDS 50 RPM, RE-ADJUST TRANS. LINKAGE. SEE SHOP MANUAL.
(6) RESTORE VACUUM AND ELECTRICAL CONNECTIONS.

USE SAE 5W-30 OIL - API CATEGORY SF, SF/CC OR SF/CD.

THIS VEHICLE CONFORMS TO U.S. EPA REGULATIONS APPLICABLE TO 1986 MODEL YEAR NEW MOTOR VEHICLES.

E6AE-9C485-AKR CATALYST SPARK PLUG: AWSF-24C GAP .042-.046
1.9L-6HM
GFM1.9V5HMK9-EGS/EOR/AIV/TWC/FI

VACUUM HOSE ROUTING

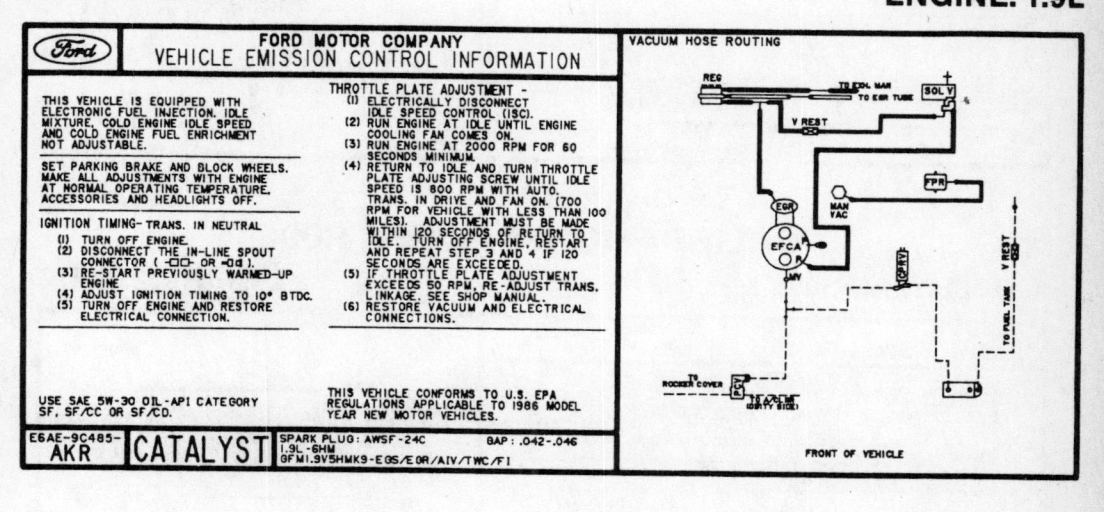

EMISSION CONTROLS

CALIBRATION: 6—08S—R21

MODEL YEAR: 1986 **ENGINE: 1.9L**

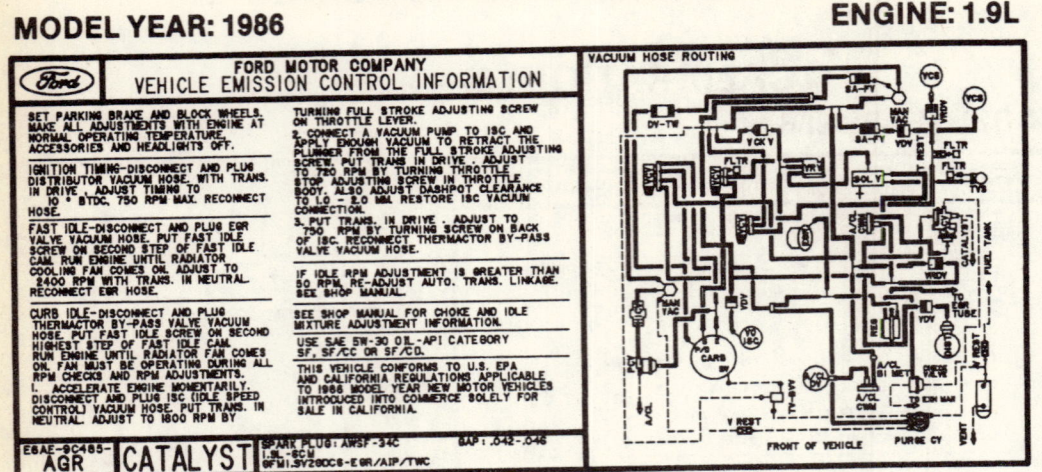

CALIBRATION: 5—05A—R00

MODEL YEAR: 1986 **ENGINE: 2.3L**

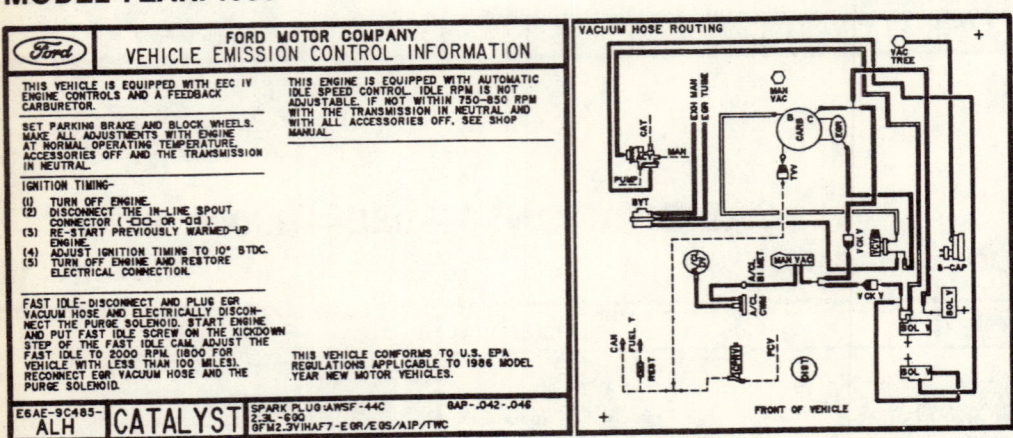

CALIBRATION: 5—05E—R00

MODEL YEAR: 1986 **ENGINE: 2.3L T/C**

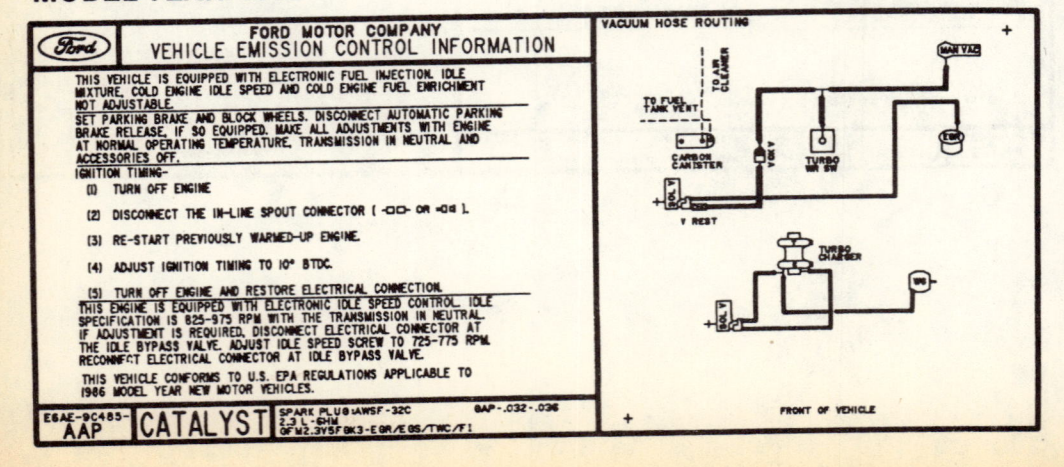

EMISSION CONTROLS 289

CALIBRATION: 5—05R—R10

MODEL YEAR: 1986 **ENGINE: 2.3L T/C**

FORD MOTOR COMPANY
VEHICLE EMISSION CONTROL INFORMATION

THIS VEHICLE IS EQUIPPED WITH ELECTRONIC FUEL INJECTION. IDLE MIXTURE, COLD ENGINE IDLE SPEED AND COLD ENGINE FUEL ENRICHMENT NOT ADJUSTABLE.

SET PARKING BRAKE AND BLOCK WHEELS. DISCONNECT AUTOMATIC PARKING BRAKE RELEASE, IF SO EQUIPPED. MAKE ALL ADJUSTMENTS WITH ENGINE AT NORMAL OPERATING TEMPERATURE, TRANSMISSION IN NEUTRAL AND ACCESSORIES OFF.

IGNITION TIMING—
(1) TURN OFF ENGINE
(2) DISCONNECT THE SINGLE WIRE CONNECTOR NEAR THE DISTRIBUTOR.
(3) RE-START PREVIOUSLY WARMED-UP ENGINE.
(4) ADJUST IGNITION TIMING TO 13° BTDC FOR MANUAL TRANSMISSION.
    10° BTDC FOR AUTOMATIC TRANSMISSION.
(5) TURN OFF ENGINE AND RESTORE ELECTRICAL CONNECTION.

THIS ENGINE IS EQUIPPED WITH ELECTRONIC IDLE SPEED CONTROL. IDLE SPECIFICATION IS 825-975 RPM FOR MANUAL TRANSMISSION OR 925-1075 RPM FOR AUTOMATIC TRANSMISSION WITH THE TRANSMISSION IN NEUTRAL. IF ADJUSTMENT IS REQUIRED, DISCONNECT ELECTRICAL CONNECTOR AT THE IDLE BYPASS VALVE. ADJUST IDLE SPEED SCREW TO 725-775 RPM. RECONNECT ELECTRICAL CONNECTOR AT IDLE BYPASS VALVE.

THIS VEHICLE CONFORMS TO U.S. EPA AND CALIFORNIA REGULATIONS APPLICABLE TO 1986 MODEL YEAR NEW MOTOR VEHICLES INTRODUCED INTO COMMERCE SOLELY FOR SALE IN CALIFORNIA.

E6RD-9C485-XCE CATALYST SPARK PLUG: AWSF-32C GAP -.032-.036
2.3L-SHM
0FMZ.3V5FGK3-E0S/EGR/TWC/FI

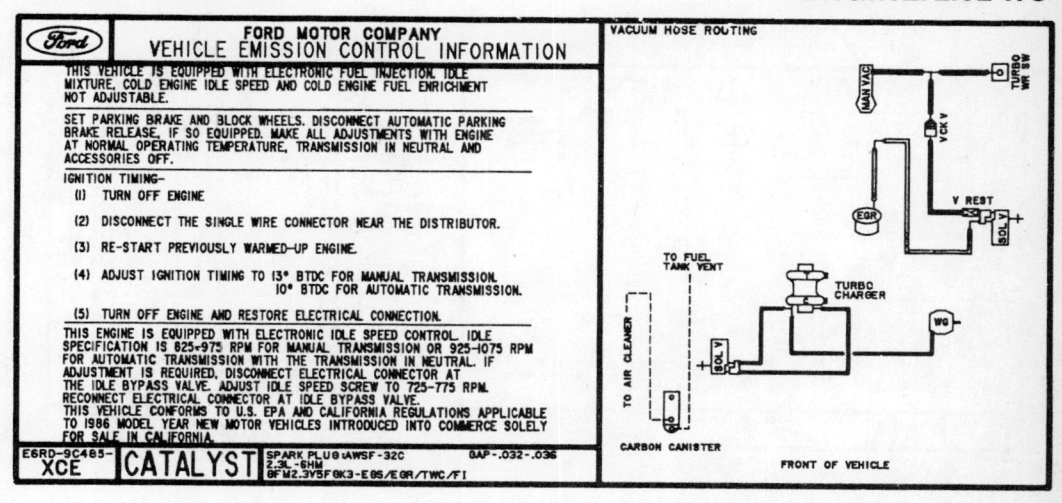

CALIBRATION: 5—05S—R01

MODEL YEAR: 1986 **ENGINE: 2.3L T/C**

FORD MOTOR COMPANY
VEHICLE EMISSION CONTROL INFORMATION

THIS VEHICLE IS EQUIPPED WITH ELECTRONIC FUEL INJECTION. IDLE MIXTURE, COLD ENGINE IDLE SPEED AND COLD ENGINE FUEL ENRICHMENT NOT ADJUSTABLE.

SET PARKING BRAKE AND BLOCK WHEELS. DISCONNECT AUTOMATIC PARKING BRAKE RELEASE, IF SO EQUIPPED. MAKE ALL ADJUSTMENTS WITH ENGINE AT NORMAL OPERATING TEMPERATURE, TRANSMISSION IN NEUTRAL AND ACCESSORIES OFF.

IGNITION TIMING—
(1) TURN OFF ENGINE
(2) DISCONNECT THE IN-LINE SPOUT CONNECTOR (-OO- OR -O-⊲).
(3) RE-START PREVIOUSLY WARMED-UP ENGINE.
(4) ADJUST IGNITION TIMING TO 10° BTDC.
(5) TURN OFF ENGINE AND RESTORE ELECTRICAL CONNECTION.

THIS ENGINE IS EQUIPPED WITH ELECTRONIC IDLE SPEED CONTROL. IDLE SPECIFICATION IS 825-975 RPM WITH THE TRANSMISSION IN NEUTRAL. IF ADJUSTMENT IS REQUIRED, DISCONNECT ELECTRICAL CONNECTOR AT THE IDLE BYPASS VALVE. ADJUST IDLE SPEED SCREW TO 725-775 RPM. RECONNECT ELECTRICAL CONNECTOR AT IDLE BYPASS VALVE.

THIS VEHICLE CONFORMS TO U.S. EPA REGULATIONS APPLICABLE TO 1986 MODEL YEAR NEW MOTOR VEHICLES.

E6AE-9C485-AFM CATALYST SPARK PLUG: AWSF-32C GAP -.032-.036
2.3L-SHM
0FMZ.3V5FGK3-E0S/EGR/TWC/FI

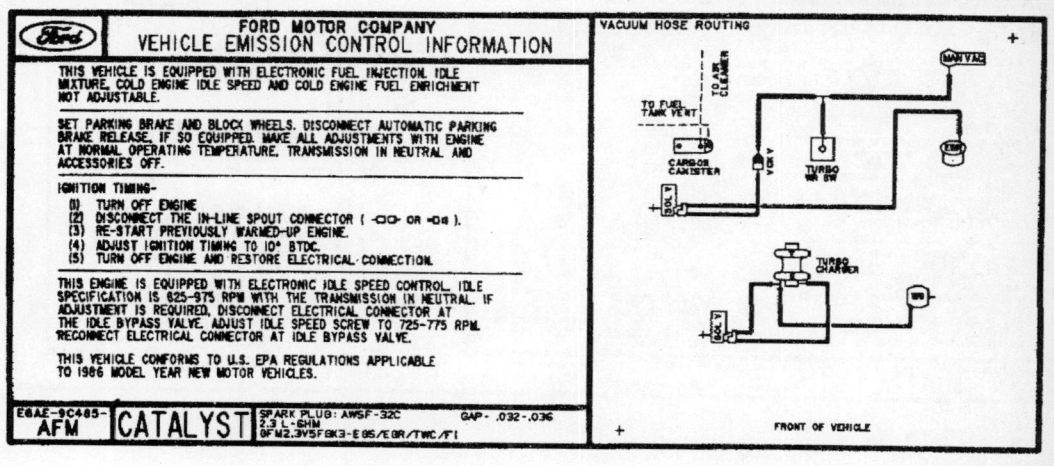

EMISSION CONTROLS

CALIBRATION: 5—06A—R00

MODEL YEAR: 1986 **ENGINE: 2.3L**

FORD MOTOR COMPANY — VEHICLE EMISSION CONTROL INFORMATION

THIS VEHICLE IS EQUIPPED WITH EEC IV ENGINE CONTROLS AND A FEEDBACK CARBURETOR.

SET PARKING BRAKE AND BLOCK WHEELS. MAKE ALL ADJUSTMENTS WITH ENGINE AT NORMAL OPERATING TEMPERATURE, ACCESSORIES OFF AND THE TRANSMISSION IN NEUTRAL.

IGNITION TIMING-
(1) TURN OFF ENGINE.
(2) DISCONNECT THE IN-LINE SPOUT CONNECTOR (-◯◯- OR -◯◯).
(3) RE-START PREVIOUSLY WARMED-UP ENGINE.
(4) ADJUST IGNITION TIMING TO 10° BTDC.
(5) TURN OFF ENGINE AND RESTORE ELECTRICAL CONNECTION.

FAST IDLE- DISCONNECT AND PLUG EGR VACUUM HOSE AND ELECTRICALLY DISCONNECT THE PURGE SOLENOID. START ENGINE AND PUT FAST IDLE SCREW ON THE KICKDOWN STEP OF THE FAST IDLE CAM. ADJUST THE FAST IDLE TO 2200 RPM. (1900 FOR VEHICLE WITH LESS THAN 100 MILES). RECONNECT EGR VACUUM HOSE AND THE PURGE SOLENOID.

THIS ENGINE IS EQUIPPED WITH AUTOMATIC IDLE SPEED CONTROL. IDLE RPM IS NOT ADJUSTABLE. IF NOT WITHIN 710-790 RPM FOR AUTO TRANS. (IN DRIVE), WITH ALL ACCESSORIES OFF, SEE SHOP MANUAL.

THIS VEHICLE CONFORMS TO U.S. EPA REGULATIONS APPLICABLE TO 1986 MODEL YEAR NEW MOTOR VEHICLES.

E6AE-9C485- AAL CATALYST SPARK PLUG :AWSF-44C GAP-.042-.046 2.3L -6CYL OFM2.3VIHAF2-EGR/EGS/AIP/TWC

VACUUM HOSE ROUTING — FRONT OF VEHICLE

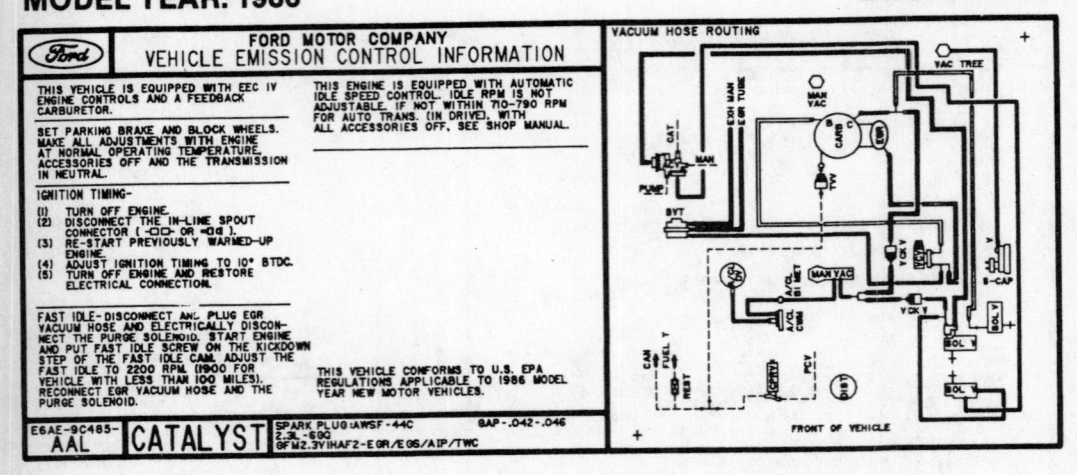

CALIBRATION: 5—06N—R00

MODEL YEAR: 1986 **ENGINE: 2.3L**

FORD MOTOR COMPANY — VEHICLE EMISSION CONTROL INFORMATION

THIS VEHICLE IS EQUIPPED WITH EEC IV ENGINE CONTROLS AND A FEEDBACK CARBURETOR.

SET PARKING BRAKE AND BLOCK WHEELS. MAKE ALL ADJUSTMENTS WITH ENGINE AT NORMAL OPERATING TEMPERATURE, ACCESSORIES OFF AND THE TRANSMISSION IN NEUTRAL.

IGNITION TIMING-
(1) TURN OFF ENGINE.
(2) DISCONNECT THE IN-LINE SPOUT CONNECTOR (-◯◯- OR -◯◯).
(3) RE-START PREVIOUSLY WARMED-UP ENGINE.
(4) ADJUST IGNITION TIMING TO 10° BTDC.
(5) TURN OFF ENGINE AND RESTORE ELECTRICAL CONNECTION.

FAST IDLE - DISCONNECT AND PLUG EGR VACUUM HOSE AND ELECTRICALLY DISCONNECT THE PURGE SOLENOID. START ENGINE AND PUT FAST IDLE SCREW ON THE KICKDOWN STEP OF THE FAST IDLE CAM. ADJUST THE FAST IDLE TO 2200 RPM. (1900 FOR VEHICLE WITH LESS THAN 100 MILES). RECONNECT EGR VACUUM HOSE AND THE PURGE SOLENOID.

THIS ENGINE IS EQUIPPED WITH AUTOMATIC IDLE SPEED CONTROL. IDLE RPM IS NOT ADJUSTABLE. IF NOT WITHIN 710-790 RPM FOR AUTO TRANS. (IN DRIVE), WITH ALL ACCESSORIES OFF, SEE SHOP MANUAL.

THIS VEHICLE CONFORMS TO U.S. EPA AND CALIFORNIA REGULATIONS APPLICABLE TO 1986 MODEL YEAR NEW MOTOR VEHICLES INTRODUCED INTO COMMERCE SOLELY FOR SALE IN CALIFORNIA.

E6AE-9C485- AAN CATALYST SPARK PLUG :AWSF-44C GAP-.042-.046 2.3L -6CYL OFM2.3VIHAC4-EGR/EGS/AIP/TWC

VACUUM HOSE ROUTING — FRONT OF VEHICLE

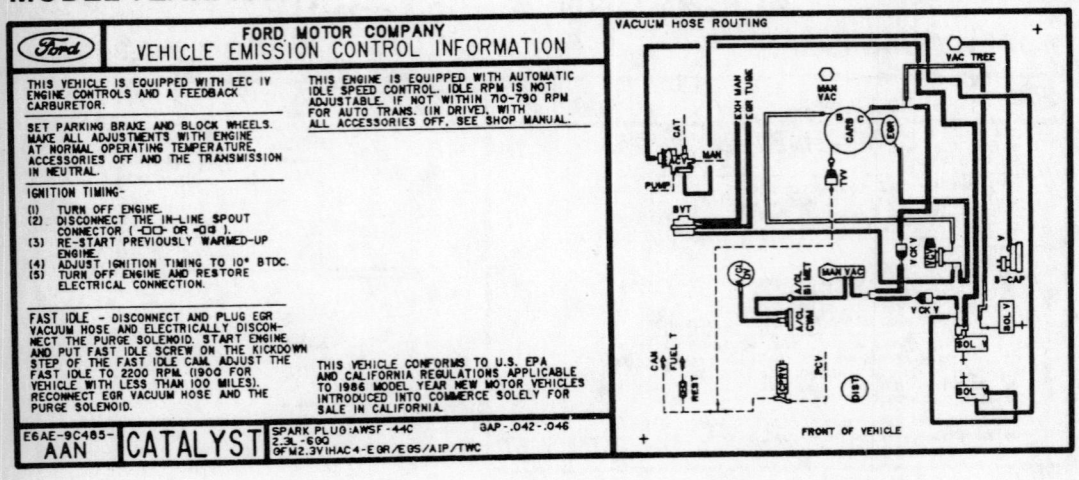

EMISSION CONTROLS

CALIBRATION: 5—25C—R01

MODEL YEAR: 1986　　　　　　　　　　　　　　　**ENGINE: 2.3L**

FORD MOTOR COMPANY
VEHICLE EMISSION CONTROL INFORMATION

THIS VEHICLE IS EQUIPPED WITH ELECTRONIC FUEL INJECTION. IDLE MIXTURE, COLD ENGINE IDLE SPEED AND COLD ENGINE FUEL ENRICHMENT NOT ADJUSTABLE.

SET PARKING BRAKE AND BLOCK WHEELS. DISCONNECT AUTOMATIC PARKING BRAKE RELEASE (IF SO EQUIPPED). MAKE ALL ADJUSTMENTS WITH ENGINE AT NORMAL OPERATING TEMPERATURE, TRANSMISSION IN NEUTRAL AND ACCESSORIES OFF.

IGNITION TIMING—
(1) TURN OFF ENGINE
(2) DISCONNECT THE IN-LINE SPOUT CONNECTOR (-⊂⊃- OR -⊂◁).
(3) RE-START PREVIOUSLY WARMED-UP ENGINE.
(4) ADJUST IGNITION TIMING TO 10° BTDC OR △.
(5) TURN OFF ENGINE AND RESTORE ELECTRICAL CONNECTION.

THIS ENGINE IS EQUIPPED WITH AUTOMATIC IDLE SPEED CONTROL. IDLE RPM IS NOT ADJUSTABLE. IF NOT WITHIN SPECIFIED RPM RANGE, SEE SHOP MANUAL:
　　MANUAL TRANS. IN NEUTRAL: -775-825 RPM

USE SAE 5W-30 OIL - API CATEGORY SF, SF/CC OR SF/CD.

THIS VEHICLE CONFORMS TO U.S. EPA REGULATIONS APPLICABLE TO 1986 MODEL YEAR NEW MOTOR VEHICLES.

E6AE-9C485-AJR　CATALYST　SPARK PLUG AWSF-32C　GAP-.042-.046
　　　　　　　　　　　　　2.3L-6FM
　　　　　　　　　　　　　6FM2.5V5HCF6-EGR/EGS/AIV/TWC/FI

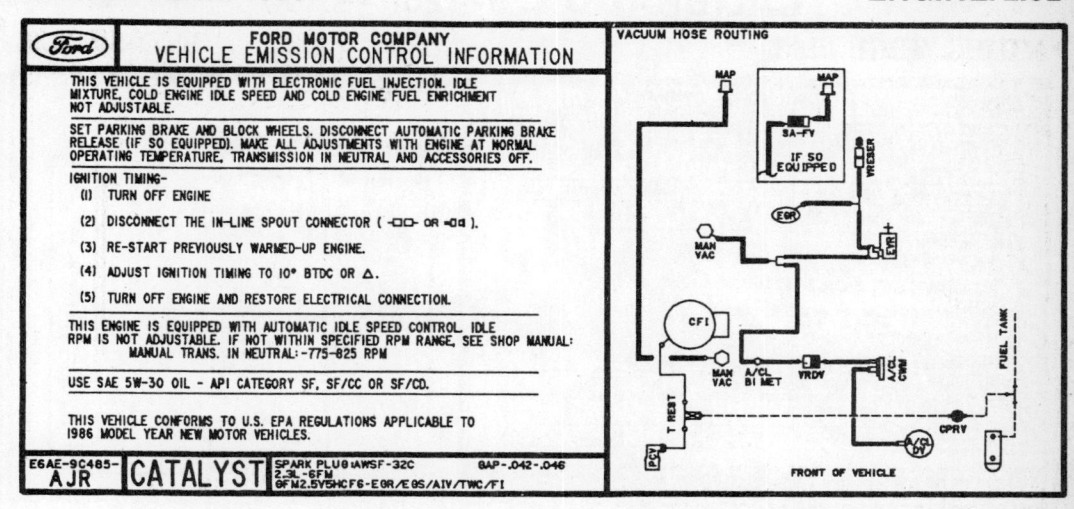

CALIBRATION: 5—25F—R10
(Tempo/Topaz)

MODEL YEAR: 1986　　　　　　　　　　　　　　　**ENGINE: 2.3L**

FORD MOTOR COMPANY
VEHICLE EMISSION CONTROL INFORMATION

THIS VEHICLE IS EQUIPPED WITH ELECTRONIC FUEL INJECTION. IDLE MIXTURE, COLD ENGINE IDLE SPEED AND COLD ENGINE FUEL ENRICHMENT NOT ADJUSTABLE.

SET PARKING BRAKE AND BLOCK WHEELS. DISCONNECT AUTOMATIC PARKING BRAKE RELEASE (IF SO EQUIPPED). MAKE ALL ADJUSTMENTS WITH ENGINE AT NORMAL OPERATING TEMPERATURE, TRANSMISSION IN NEUTRAL AND ACCESSORIES OFF.

IGNITION TIMING—
(1) TURN OFF ENGINE
(2) DISCONNECT THE IN-LINE SPOUT CONNECTOR (-⊂⊃- OR -⊂◁).
(3) RE-START PREVIOUSLY WARMED-UP ENGINE.
(4) ADJUST IGNITION TIMING TO 10° BTDC OR △.
(5) TURN OFF ENGINE AND RESTORE ELECTRICAL CONNECTION.

THIS ENGINE IS EQUIPPED WITH AUTOMATIC IDLE SPEED CONTROL. IDLE RPM IS NOT ADJUSTABLE. IF NOT WITHIN SPECIFIED RPM RANGE, SEE SHOP MANUAL:
　　MANUAL TRANS. IN NEUTRAL: -725-775 RPM
　　AUTO. TRANS. IN DRIVE: -625-675 RPM

USE SAE 5W-30 OIL - API CATEGORY SF, SF/CC OR SF/CD.

THIS VEHICLE CONFORMS TO U.S. EPA REGULATIONS APPLICABLE TO 1986 MODEL YEAR NEW MOTOR VEHICLES.

E6AE-9C485-AJT　CATALYST　SPARK PLUG AWSF-52　GAP-.042-.046
　　　　　　　　　　　　　2.3L-6FM
　　　　　　　　　　　　　6FM2.5V5HCF6-EGR/EGS/AIV/TWC/FI

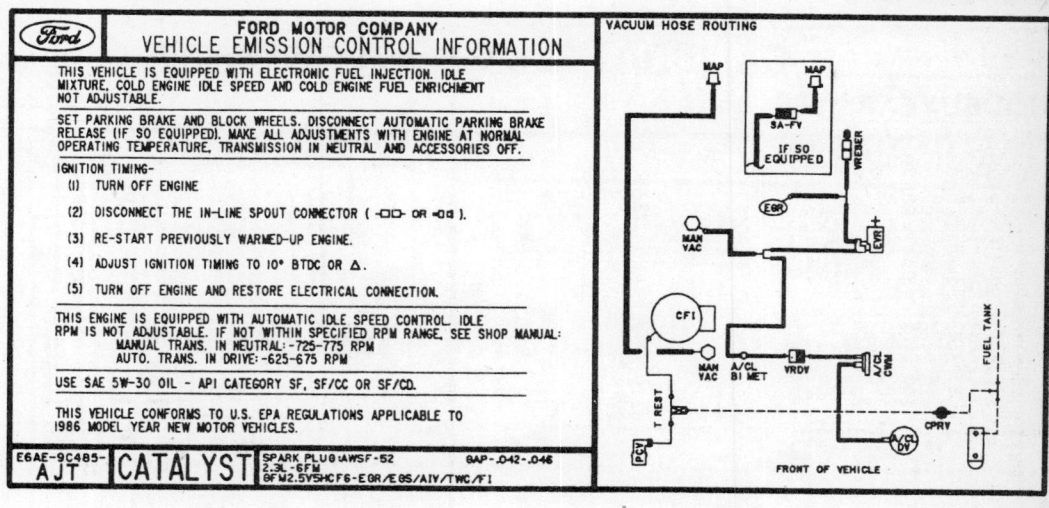

EMISSION CONTROLS

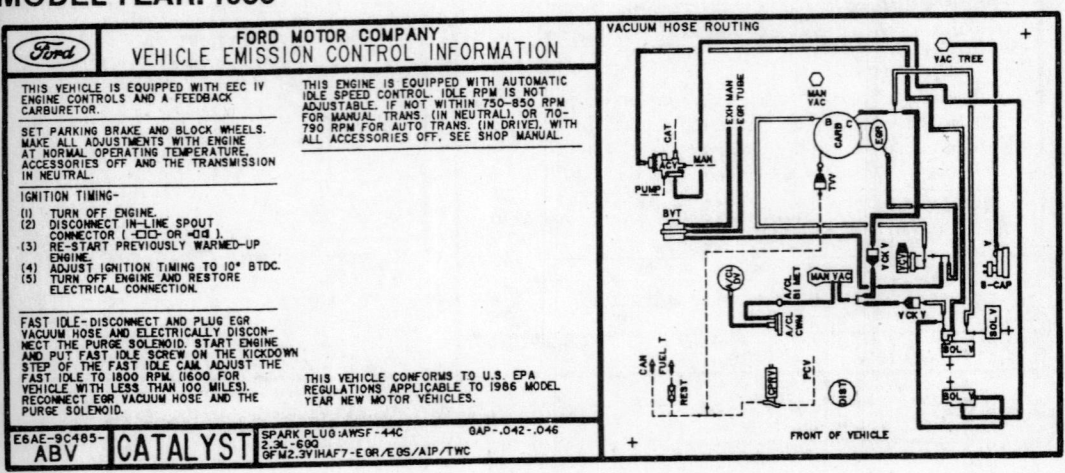

CALIBRATION: 5—25P—R00

MODEL YEAR: 1986 **ENGINE: 2.3L**

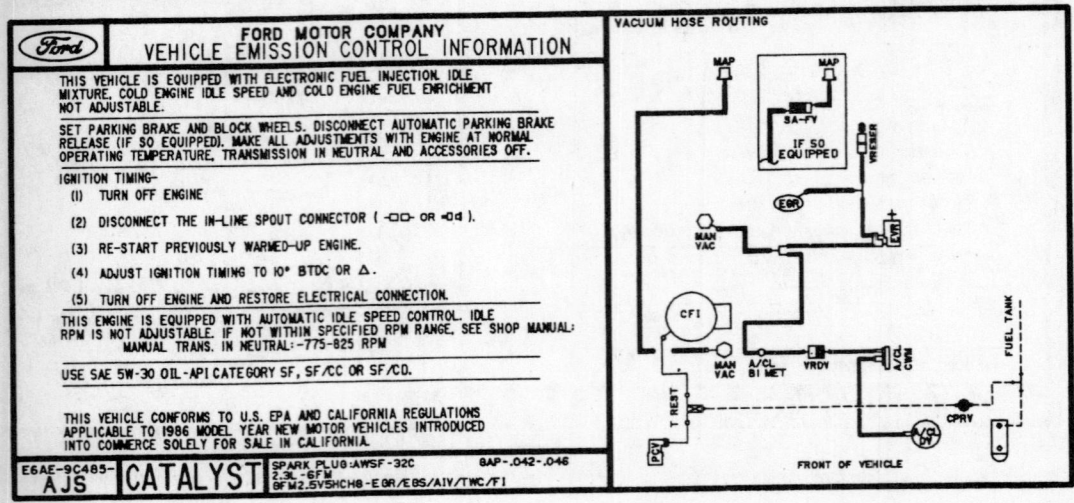

FORD MOTOR COMPANY — VEHICLE EMISSION CONTROL INFORMATION

THIS VEHICLE IS EQUIPPED WITH ELECTRONIC FUEL INJECTION. IDLE MIXTURE, COLD ENGINE IDLE SPEED AND COLD ENGINE FUEL ENRICHMENT NOT ADJUSTABLE.

SET PARKING BRAKE AND BLOCK WHEELS. DISCONNECT AUTOMATIC PARKING BRAKE RELEASE (IF SO EQUIPPED). MAKE ALL ADJUSTMENTS WITH ENGINE AT NORMAL OPERATING TEMPERATURE, TRANSMISSION IN NEUTRAL AND ACCESSORIES OFF.

IGNITION TIMING-
(1) TURN OFF ENGINE
(2) DISCONNECT THE IN-LINE SPOUT CONNECTOR (-☐☐- OR -◁◁).
(3) RE-START PREVIOUSLY WARMED-UP ENGINE.
(4) ADJUST IGNITION TIMING TO 10° BTDC OR Δ.
(5) TURN OFF ENGINE AND RESTORE ELECTRICAL CONNECTION.

THIS ENGINE IS EQUIPPED WITH AUTOMATIC IDLE SPEED CONTROL. IDLE RPM IS NOT ADJUSTABLE. IF NOT WITHIN SPECIFIED RPM RANGE, SEE SHOP MANUAL: MANUAL TRANS. IN NEUTRAL: ~775-825 RPM

USE SAE 5W-30 OIL-API CATEGORY SF, SF/CC OR SF/CD.

THIS VEHICLE CONFORMS TO U.S. EPA AND CALIFORNIA REGULATIONS APPLICABLE TO 1986 MODEL YEAR NEW MOTOR VEHICLES INTRODUCED INTO COMMERCE SOLELY FOR SALE IN CALIFORNIA.

E6AE-9C485-AJS CATALYST SPARK PLUG: AWSF-32C GAP-.042-.046
2.3L-6FM
9FM2.5V5HCH8-EGR/EGS/AIV/TWC/FI

CALIBRATION: 6—05A—R11

MODEL YEAR: 1986 **ENGINE: 2.3L**

FORD MOTOR COMPANY — VEHICLE EMISSION CONTROL INFORMATION

THIS VEHICLE IS EQUIPPED WITH EEC IV ENGINE CONTROLS AND A FEEDBACK CARBURETOR.

SET PARKING BRAKE AND BLOCK WHEELS. MAKE ALL ADJUSTMENTS WITH ENGINE AT NORMAL OPERATING TEMPERATURE, ACCESSORIES OFF AND THE TRANSMISSION IN NEUTRAL.

IGNITION TIMING-
(1) TURN OFF ENGINE.
(2) DISCONNECT IN-LINE SPOUT CONNECTOR (-☐☐- OR -◁◁).
(3) RE-START PREVIOUSLY WARMED-UP ENGINE.
(4) ADJUST IGNITION TIMING TO 10° BTDC.
(5) TURN OFF ENGINE AND RESTORE ELECTRICAL CONNECTION.

FAST IDLE- DISCONNECT AND PLUG EGR VACUUM HOSE AND ELECTRICALLY DISCONNECT THE PURGE SOLENOID. START ENGINE AND PUT FAST IDLE SCREW ON THE KICKDOWN STEP OF THE FAST IDLE CAM. ADJUST THE FAST IDLE TO 1800 RPM (1600 FOR VEHICLE WITH LESS THAN 100 MILES). RECONNECT EGR VACUUM HOSE AND THE PURGE SOLENOID.

THIS ENGINE IS EQUIPPED WITH AUTOMATIC IDLE SPEED CONTROL. IDLE RPM IS NOT ADJUSTABLE. IF NOT WITHIN 750-850 RPM FOR MANUAL TRANS. (IN NEUTRAL), OR 710-790 RPM FOR AUTO TRANS. (IN DRIVE), WITH ALL ACCESSORIES OFF, SEE SHOP MANUAL.

THIS VEHICLE CONFORMS TO U.S. EPA REGULATIONS APPLICABLE TO 1986 MODEL YEAR NEW MOTOR VEHICLES.

E6AE-9C485-ABV CATALYST SPARK PLUG: AWSF-44C GAP-.042-.046
2.3L-6DQ
9FM2.3V1HAF7-EGR/EGS/AIP/TWC

EMISSION CONTROLS

CALIBRATION: 5—25Q—R10

MODEL YEAR: 1986 **ENGINE: 2.3L**

Ford Motor Company — Vehicle Emission Control Information

THIS VEHICLE IS EQUIPPED WITH ELECTRONIC FUEL INJECTION. IDLE MIXTURE, COLD ENGINE IDLE SPEED AND COLD ENGINE FUEL ENRICHMENT NOT ADJUSTABLE.

SET PARKING BRAKE AND BLOCK WHEELS. DISCONNECT AUTOMATIC PARKING BRAKE RELEASE (IF SO EQUIPPED). MAKE ALL ADJUSTMENTS WITH ENGINE AT NORMAL OPERATING TEMPERATURE, TRANSMISSION IN NEUTRAL AND ACCESSORIES OFF.

IGNITION TIMING-
(1) TURN OFF ENGINE
(2) DISCONNECT THE IN-LINE SPOUT CONNECTOR (-☐☐- OR -◁▷-).
(3) RE-START PREVIOUSLY WARMED-UP ENGINE.
(4) ADJUST IGNITION TIMING TO 10° BTDC OR Δ.
(5) TURN OFF ENGINE AND RESTORE ELECTRICAL CONNECTION.

THIS ENGINE IS EQUIPPED WITH AUTOMATIC IDLE SPEED CONTROL. IDLE RPM IS NOT ADJUSTABLE. IF NOT WITHIN SPECIFIED RPM RANGE, SEE SHOP MANUAL:
MANUAL TRANS. IN NEUTRAL: -725-775 RPM
AUTO. TRANS. IN DRIVE: -625-675 RPM
USE SAE 5W-30 OIL - API CATEGORY SF, SF/CC OR SF/CD.

THIS VEHICLE CONFORMS TO U.S. EPA AND CALIFORNIA REGULATIONS APPLICABLE TO 1986 MODEL YEAR NEW MOTOR VEHICLES INTRODUCED INTO COMMERCE SOLELY FOR SALE IN CALIFORNIA.

E6AE-9C485-AJV   CATALYST
SPARK PLUG: AWSF-52   GAP - .042-.046
2.3L-6FM
6FM2.5V5HCH8-EGR/EGS/AIV/TWC/FI

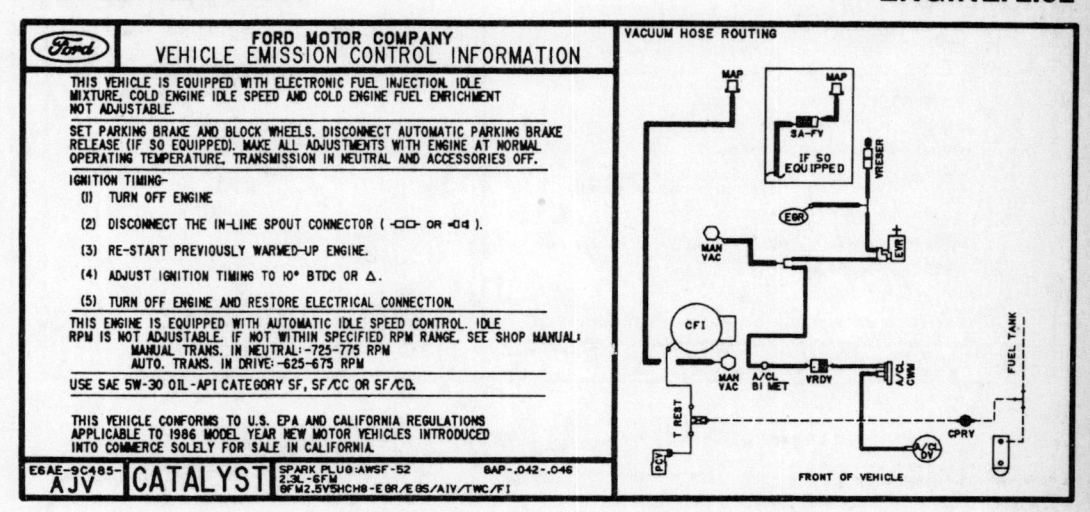

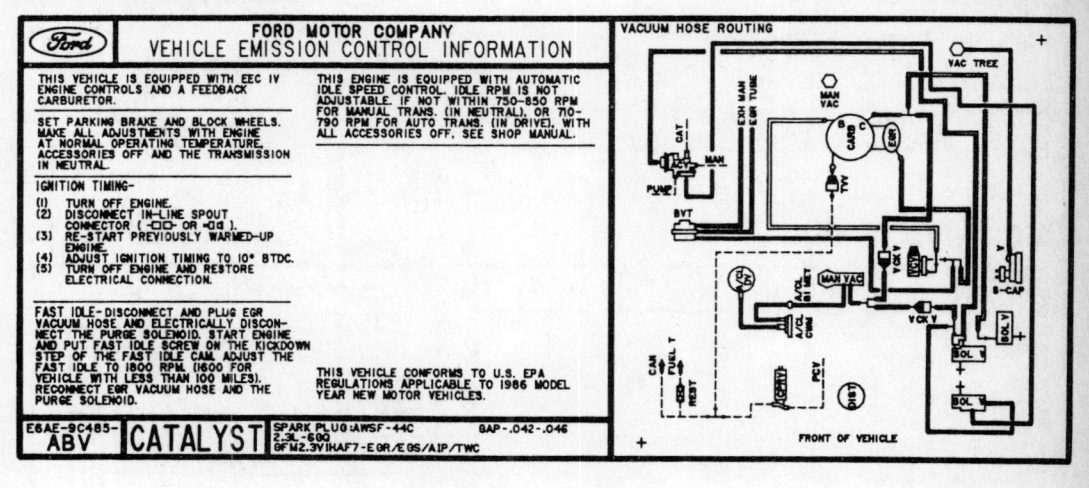

CALIBRATION: 6—05A—R12

MODEL YEAR: 1986 **ENGINE: 2.3L**

Ford Motor Company — Vehicle Emission Control Information

THIS VEHICLE IS EQUIPPED WITH EEC IV ENGINE CONTROLS AND A FEEDBACK CARBURETOR.

SET PARKING BRAKE AND BLOCK WHEELS. MAKE ALL ADJUSTMENTS WITH ENGINE AT NORMAL OPERATING TEMPERATURE, ACCESSORIES OFF AND THE TRANSMISSION IN NEUTRAL.

IGNITION TIMING-
(1) TURN OFF ENGINE.
(2) DISCONNECT IN-LINE SPOUT CONNECTOR (-☐☐- OR -◁▷-).
(3) RE-START PREVIOUSLY WARMED-UP ENGINE.
(4) ADJUST IGNITION TIMING TO 10° BTDC.
(5) TURN OFF ENGINE AND RESTORE ELECTRICAL CONNECTION.

FAST IDLE - DISCONNECT AND PLUG EGR VACUUM HOSE AND ELECTRICALLY DISCONNECT THE PURGE SOLENOID. START ENGINE AND PUT FAST IDLE SCREW ON THE KICKDOWN STEP OF THE FAST IDLE CAM. ADJUST THE FAST IDLE TO 1800 RPM (1600 FOR VEHICLE WITH LESS THAN 100 MILES). RECONNECT EGR VACUUM HOSE AND THE PURGE SOLENOID.

THIS ENGINE IS EQUIPPED WITH AUTOMATIC IDLE SPEED CONTROL. IDLE RPM IS NOT ADJUSTABLE. IF NOT WITHIN 750-850 RPM FOR MANUAL TRANS. (IN NEUTRAL), OR 710-790 RPM FOR AUTO TRANS. (IN DRIVE), WITH ALL ACCESSORIES OFF, SEE SHOP MANUAL.

THIS VEHICLE CONFORMS TO U.S. EPA REGULATIONS APPLICABLE TO 1986 MODEL YEAR NEW MOTOR VEHICLES.

E6AE-9C485-ABV   CATALYST
SPARK PLUG: AWSF-44C   GAP - .042-.046
2.3L-6SQ
6FM2.3V1HAF7-EGR/EGS/AIP/TWC

EMISSION CONTROLS

CALIBRATION: 6—05R—R00

MODEL YEAR: 1986 **ENGINE: 2.3L T/C**

FORD MOTOR COMPANY — VEHICLE EMISSION CONTROL INFORMATION

THIS VEHICLE IS EQUIPPED WITH ELECTRONIC FUEL INJECTION. IDLE MIXTURE, COLD ENGINE IDLE SPEED AND COLD ENGINE FUEL ENRICHMENT NOT ADJUSTABLE.

SET PARKING BRAKE AND BLOCK WHEELS. DISCONNECT AUTOMATIC PARKING BRAKE RELEASE, IF SO EQUIPPED. MAKE ALL ADJUSTMENTS WITH ENGINE AT NORMAL OPERATING TEMPERATURE, TRANSMISSION IN NEUTRAL AND ACCESSORIES OFF.

IGNITION TIMING:
(1) TURN OFF ENGINE.
(2) DISCONNECT THE SINGLE WIRE CONNECTOR NEAR THE DISTRIBUTOR.
(3) RE-START PREVIOUSLY WARMED-UP ENGINE.
(4) ADJUST IGNITION TIMING TO 13° BTDC FOR MANUAL TRANSMISSION, 10° BTDC FOR AUTOMATIC TRANSMISSION.
(5) TURN OFF ENGINE AND RESTORE ELECTRICAL CONNECTION.

THIS ENGINE IS EQUIPPED WITH ELECTRONIC IDLE SPEED CONTROL. IDLE SPECIFICATION IS 825-975 RPM FOR MANUAL TRANSMISSION OR 925-1075 RPM FOR AUTOMATIC TRANSMISSION WITH THE TRANSMISSION IN NEUTRAL. IF ADJUSTMENT IS REQUIRED, DISCONNECT ELECTRICAL CONNECTOR AT THE IDLE BYPASS VALVE. ADJUST IDLE SPEED SCREW TO 725-775 RPM. RECONNECT ELECTRICAL CONNECTOR AT IDLE BYPASS VALVE.

THIS VEHICLE CONFORMS TO U.S. EPA AND CALIFORNIA REGULATIONS APPLICABLE TO 1986 MODEL YEAR NEW MOTOR VEHICLES INTRODUCED INTO COMMERCE SOLELY FOR SALE IN CALIFORNIA.

E6RD-9C485- **XCE** **CATALYST**   SPARK PLUG: AWSF-32C GAP: .032-.036
2.3L-6HU
GFM2.3V5FOK3-EOS/EGR/TWC/FI

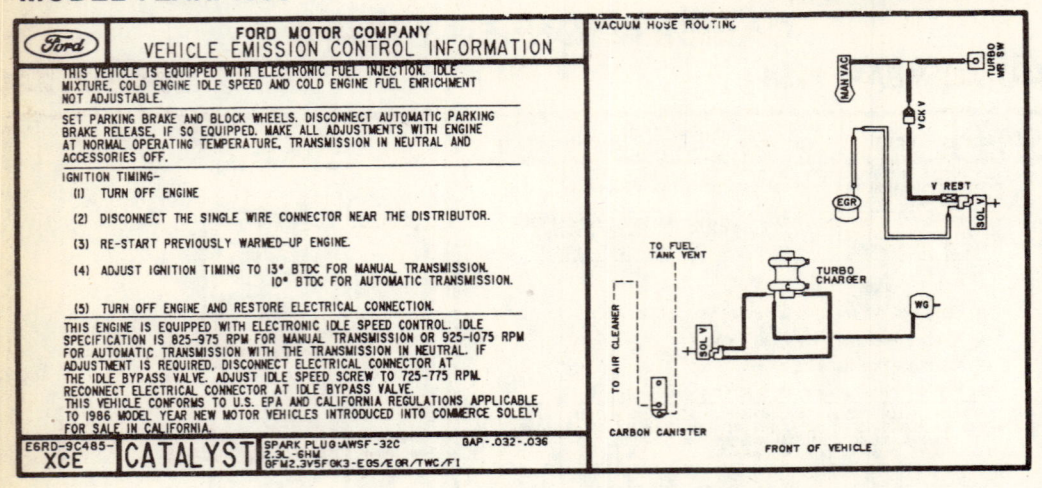

CALIBRATION: 6—06A—R10

MODEL YEAR: 1986 **ENGINE: 2.3L**

FORD MOTOR COMPANY — VEHICLE EMISSION CONTROL INFORMATION

THIS VEHICLE IS EQUIPPED WITH EEC IV ENGINE CONTROLS AND A FEEDBACK CARBURETOR.

SET PARKING BRAKE AND BLOCK WHEELS. MAKE ALL ADJUSTMENTS WITH ENGINE AT NORMAL OPERATING TEMPERATURE, ACCESSORIES OFF AND THE TRANSMISSION IN NEUTRAL.

IGNITION TIMING:
(1) TURN OFF ENGINE.
(2) DISCONNECT IN-LINE SPOUT CONNECTOR.
(3) RE-START PREVIOUSLY WARMED-UP ENGINE.
(4) ADJUST IGNITION TIMING TO 10° BTDC.
(5) TURN OFF ENGINE AND RESTORE ELECTRICAL CONNECTION.

FAST IDLE- DISCONNECT AND PLUG EGR VACUUM HOSE AND ELECTRICALLY DISCONNECT THE PURGE SOLENOID. START ENGINE AND PUT FAST IDLE SCREW ON THE KICKDOWN STEP OF THE FAST IDLE CAM. ADJUST THE FAST IDLE TO 2200 RPM. (1900 FOR VEHICLE WITH LESS THAN 100 MILES). RECONNECT EGR VACUUM HOSE AND THE PURGE SOLENOID.

THIS ENGINE IS EQUIPPED WITH AUTOMATIC IDLE SPEED CONTROL. IDLE RPM IS NOT ADJUSTABLE. IF NOT WITHIN 750-850 RPM FOR MANUAL TRANS. (IN NEUTRAL), OR 710-790 RPM FOR AUTO TRANS (IN DRIVE), WITH ALL ACCESSORIES OFF, SEE SHOP MANUAL.

THIS VEHICLE CONFORMS TO U.S. EPA REGULATIONS APPLICABLE TO 1986 MODEL YEAR NEW MOTOR VEHICLES.

E6AE-9C485- **ACC** **CATALYST**   SPARK PLUG: AWSF-44C GAP: .042-.046
2.3L-6GQ
GFM2.3V1HAF7-EGR/EOS/AIP/TWC

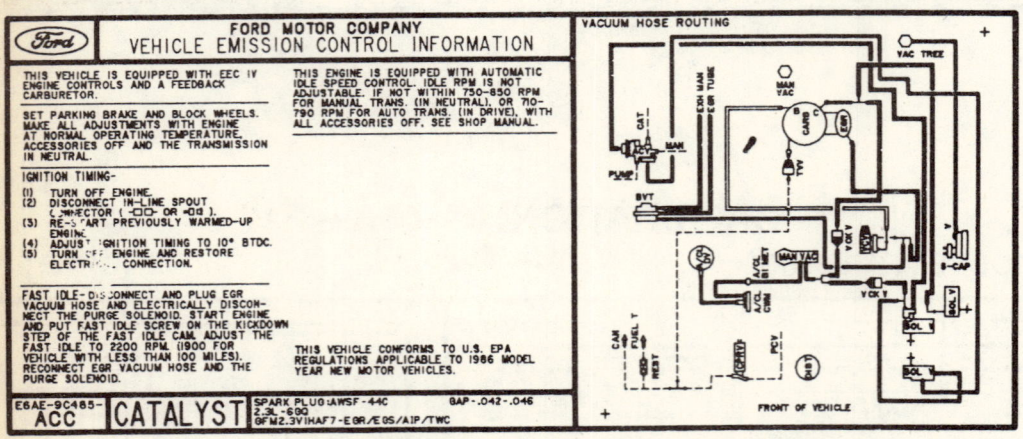

CALIBRATION: 6—06A—R11

MODEL YEAR: 1986 **ENGINE: 2.3L**

FORD MOTOR COMPANY — VEHICLE EMISSION CONTROL INFORMATION

THIS VEHICLE IS EQUIPPED WITH EEC IV ENGINE CONTROLS AND A FEEDBACK CARBURETOR.

SET PARKING BRAKE AND BLOCK WHEELS. MAKE ALL ADJUSTMENTS WITH ENGINE AT NORMAL OPERATING TEMPERATURE, ACCESSORIES OFF AND THE TRANSMISSION IN NEUTRAL.

IGNITION TIMING:
(1) TURN OFF ENGINE.
(2) DISCONNECT IN-LINE SPOUT CONNECTOR.
(3) RE-START PREVIOUSLY WARMED-UP ENGINE.
(4) ADJUST IGNITION TIMING TO 10° BTDC.
(5) TURN OFF ENGINE AND RESTORE ELECTRICAL CONNECTION.

FAST IDLE- DISCONNECT AND PLUG EGR VACUUM HOSE AND ELECTRICALLY DISCONNECT THE PURGE SOLENOID. START ENGINE AND PUT FAST IDLE SCREW ON THE KICKDOWN STEP OF THE FAST IDLE CAM. ADJUST THE FAST IDLE TO 2200 RPM. (1900 FOR VEHICLE WITH LESS THAN 100 MILES). RECONNECT EGR VACUUM HOSE AND THE PURGE SOLENOID.

THIS ENGINE IS EQUIPPED WITH AUTOMATIC IDLE SPEED CONTROL. IDLE RPM IS NOT ADJUSTABLE. IF NOT WITHIN 750-850 RPM FOR MANUAL TRANS. (IN NEUTRAL), OR 710-790 RPM FOR AUTO TRANS (IN DRIVE), WITH ALL ACCESSORIES OFF, SEE SHOP MANUAL.

THIS VEHICLE CONFORMS TO U.S. EPA REGULATIONS APPLICABLE TO 1986 MODEL YEAR NEW MOTOR VEHICLES.

E6AE-9C485- **ACC** **CATALYST**   SPARK PLUG: AWSF-44C GAP: .042-.046
2.3L-6GQ
GFM2.3V1HAF7-EGR/EOS/AIP/TWC

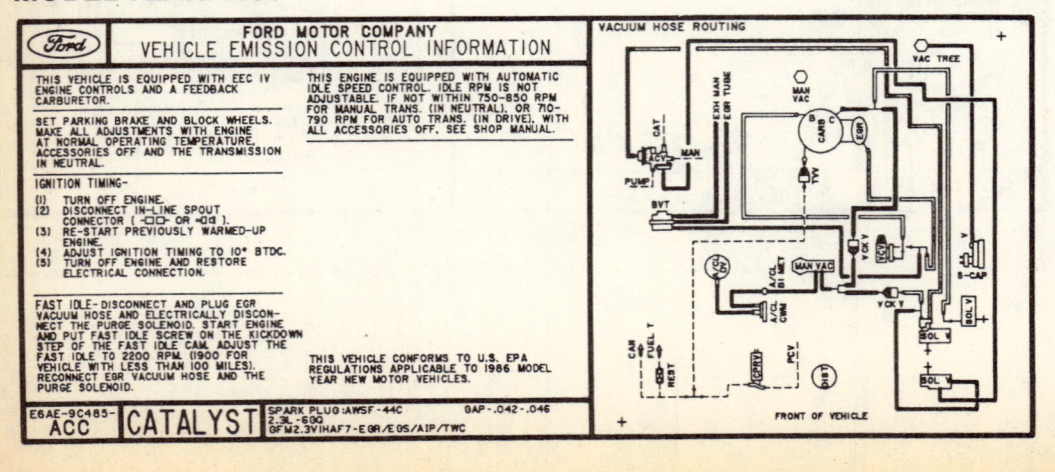

EMISSION CONTROLS 295

CALIBRATION: 6—25F—R10
(Tempo/Topaz)

MODEL YEAR: 1986 **ENGINE: 2.3L**

```
FORD MOTOR COMPANY
VEHICLE EMISSION CONTROL INFORMATION

THIS VEHICLE IS EQUIPPED WITH ELECTRONIC FUEL INJECTION. IDLE
MIXTURE, COLD ENGINE IDLE SPEED AND COLD ENGINE FUEL ENRICHMENT
NOT ADJUSTABLE.
SET PARKING BRAKE AND BLOCK WHEELS. DISCONNECT AUTOMATIC PARKING BRAKE
RELEASE (IF SO EQUIPPED). MAKE ALL ADJUSTMENTS WITH ENGINE AT NORMAL
OPERATING TEMPERATURE, TRANSMISSION IN NEUTRAL AND ACCESSORIES OFF.
IGNITION TIMING-
  (1) TURN OFF ENGINE
  (2) DISCONNECT THE IN-LINE SPOUT CONNECTOR ( -⊂⊃- OR -◁◁ ).
  (3) RE-START PREVIOUSLY WARMED-UP ENGINE.
  (4) ADJUST IGNITION TIMING TO 10° BTDC OR △.
  (5) TURN OFF ENGINE AND RESTORE ELECTRICAL CONNECTION.
THIS ENGINE IS EQUIPPED WITH AUTOMATIC IDLE SPEED CONTROL. IDLE
RPM IS NOT ADJUSTABLE. IF NOT WITHIN SPECIFIED RPM RANGE, SEE SHOP MANUAL:
       MANUAL TRANS. IN NEUTRAL: -775-825 RPM
       AUTO. TRANS. IN DRIVE: -625-675 RPM
USE SAE 5W-30 OIL - API CATEGORY SF, SF/CC OR SF/CD.
THIS VEHICLE CONFORMS TO U.S. EPA REGULATIONS APPLICABLE TO
1986 MODEL YEAR NEW MOTOR VEHICLES.

E6AE-9C485-  CATALYST   SPARK PLUG: AWSF-52      GAP- .042-.046
   AJZ                  2.3L-6FM
                        6FM2.5V5HCF6-EGR/EOS/AIV/TWC/FI
```

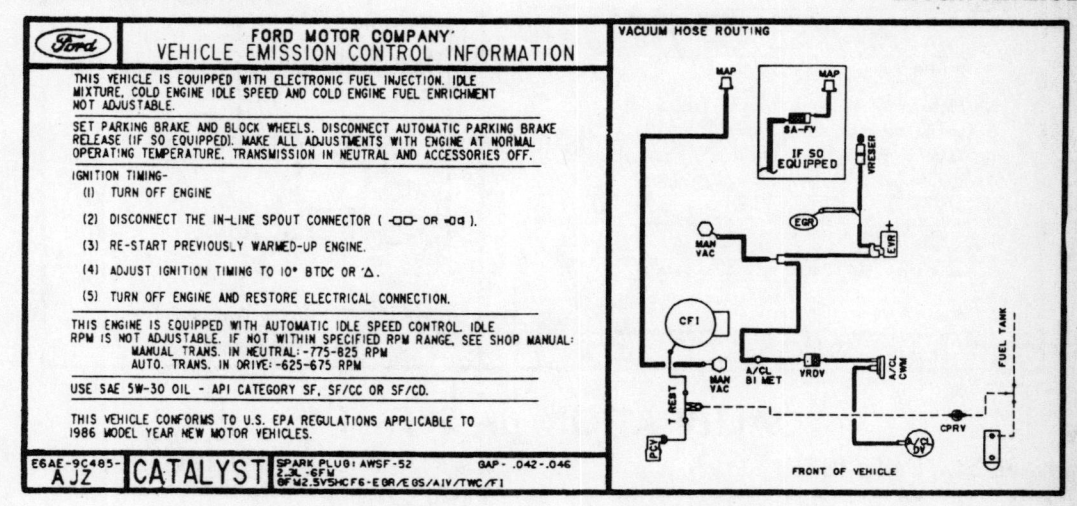

CALIBRATION: 6—25Q—R10
(Tempo/Topaz)

MODEL YEAR: 1986 **ENGINE: 2.3L**

```
FORD MOTOR COMPANY
VEHICLE EMISSION CONTROL INFORMATION

THIS VEHICLE IS EQUIPPED WITH ELECTRONIC FUEL INJECTION. IDLE
MIXTURE, COLD ENGINE IDLE SPEED AND COLD ENGINE FUEL ENRICHMENT
NOT ADJUSTABLE.
SET PARKING BRAKE AND BLOCK WHEELS. DISCONNECT AUTOMATIC PARKING BRAKE
RELEASE (IF SO EQUIPPED). MAKE ALL ADJUSTMENTS WITH ENGINE AT NORMAL
OPERATING TEMPERATURE, TRANSMISSION IN NEUTRAL AND ACCESSORIES OFF.
IGNITION TIMING-
  (1) TURN OFF ENGINE
  (2) DISCONNECT THE IN-LINE SPOUT CONNECTOR ( -⊂⊃- OR -◁◁ ).
  (3) RE-START PREVIOUSLY WARMED-UP ENGINE.
  (4) ADJUST IGNITION TIMING TO 10° BTDC OR △.
  (5) TURN OFF ENGINE AND RESTORE ELECTRICAL CONNECTION.
THIS ENGINE IS EQUIPPED WITH AUTOMATIC IDLE SPEED CONTROL. IDLE
RPM IS NOT ADJUSTABLE. IF NOT WITHIN SPECIFIED RPM RANGE, SEE SHOP MANUAL:
       MANUAL TRANS. IN NEUTRAL: -775-825 RPM
       AUTO. TRANS. IN DRIVE: -625-675 RPM
USE SAE 5W-30 OIL - API CATEGORY SF, SF/CC OR SF/CD.
THIS VEHICLE CONFORMS TO U.S. EPA AND CALIFORNIA REGULATIONS
APPLICABLE TO 1986 MODEL YEAR NEW MOTOR VEHICLES INTRODUCED
INTO COMMERCE SOLELY FOR SALE IN CALIFORNIA.

E6AE-9C485-  CATALYST   SPARK PLUG: AWSF-52      GAP- .042-.046
   AJY                  2.3L-6FM
                        6FM2.5V5HCH8-EGR/EOS/AIV/TWC/FI
```

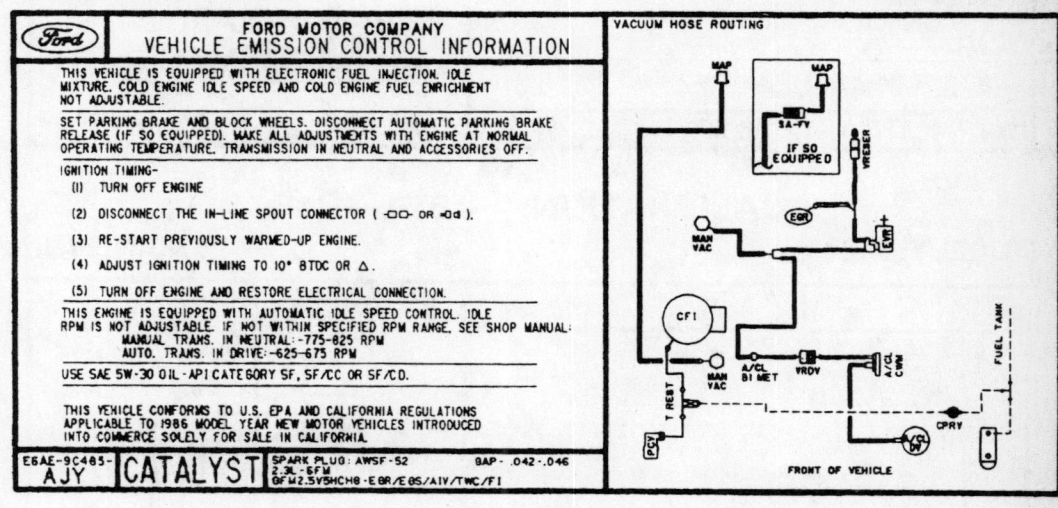

EMISSION CONTROLS

CALIBRATION: 6—26E—R00

MODEL YEAR: 1986　　　　　　　　　　　　　　　　**ENGINE: 2.3L**

FORD MOTOR COMPANY
VEHICLE EMISSION CONTROL INFORMATION

THIS VEHICLE IS EQUIPPED WITH ELECTRONIC FUEL INJECTION. IDLE MIXTURE, COLD ENGINE IDLE SPEED AND COLD ENGINE FUEL ENRICHMENT NOT ADJUSTABLE.

SET PARKING BRAKE AND BLOCK WHEELS. DISCONNECT AUTOMATIC PARKING BRAKE RELEASE (IF SO EQUIPPED). MAKE ALL ADJUSTMENTS WITH ENGINE AT NORMAL OPERATING TEMPERATURE, TRANSMISSION IN NEUTRAL AND ACCESSORIES OFF.

IGNITION TIMING-
(1) TURN OFF ENGINE
(2) DISCONNECT THE IN-LINE SPOUT CONNECTOR (-◻◻- OR -◁◁-).
(3) RE-START PREVIOUSLY WARMED-UP ENGINE.
(4) ADJUST IGNITION TIMING TO 10° BTDC OR △.
(5) TURN OFF ENGINE AND RESTORE ELECTRICAL CONNECTION.

THIS ENGINE IS EQUIPPED WITH AUTOMATIC IDLE SPEED CONTROL. IDLE RPM IS NOT ADJUSTABLE. IF NOT WITHIN SPECIFIED RPM RANGE, SEE SHOP MANUAL:
　　MANUAL TRANS. IN NEUTRAL:-775-825 RPM
　　AUTO. TRANS. IN DRIVE: -625-675 RPM

USE SAE 5W-30 OIL - API CATEGORY SF, SF/CC OR SF/CD.

THIS VEHICLE CONFORMS TO U.S. EPA REGULATIONS APPLICABLE TO 1986 MODEL YEAR NEW MOTOR VEHICLES.

E6AE-9C485-AJZ　CATALYST　SPARK PLUG: AWSF-52　GAP- .042-.046
2.3L-6FM
6FM2.5V5HCF6-EGR/EGS/AIV/TWC/FI

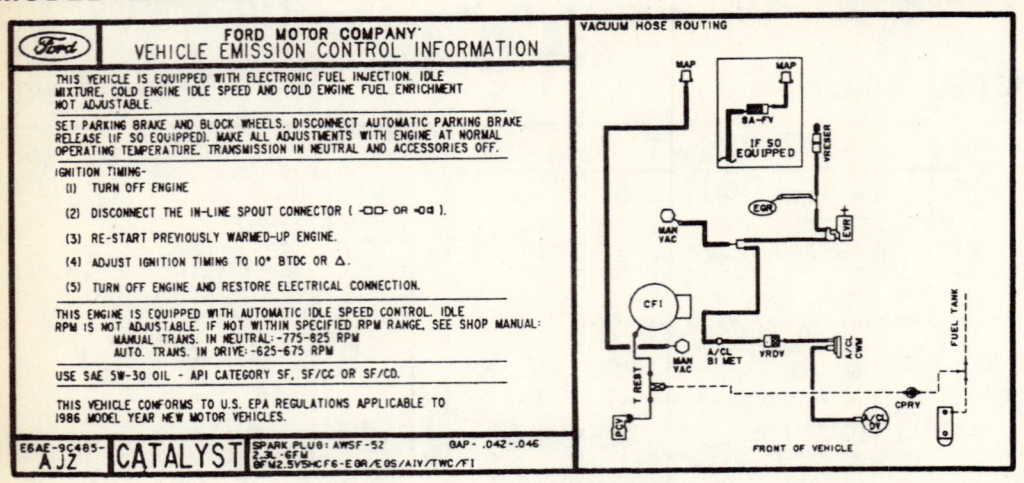

CALIBRATION: 6—26E—R10

MODEL YEAR: 1986　　　　　　　　　　　　　　　　**ENGINE: 2.3L**

FORD MOTOR COMPANY
VEHICLE EMISSION CONTROL INFORMATION

THIS VEHICLE IS EQUIPPED WITH ELECTRONIC FUEL INJECTION. IDLE MIXTURE, COLD ENGINE IDLE SPEED AND COLD ENGINE FUEL ENRICHMENT NOT ADJUSTABLE.

SET PARKING BRAKE AND BLOCK WHEELS. DISCONNECT AUTOMATIC PARKING BRAKE RELEASE (IF SO EQUIPPED). MAKE ALL ADJUSTMENTS WITH ENGINE AT NORMAL OPERATING TEMPERATURE, TRANSMISSION IN NEUTRAL AND ACCESSORIES OFF.

IGNITION TIMING-
(1) TURN OFF ENGINE
(2) DISCONNECT THE IN-LINE SPOUT CONNECTOR (-◻◻- OR -◁◁-).
(3) RE-START PREVIOUSLY WARMED-UP ENGINE.
(4) ADJUST IGNITION TIMING TO 10° BTDC OR △.
(5) TURN OFF ENGINE AND RESTORE ELECTRICAL CONNECTION.

THIS ENGINE IS EQUIPPED WITH AUTOMATIC IDLE SPEED CONTROL. IDLE RPM IS NOT ADJUSTABLE. IF NOT WITHIN SPECIFIED RPM RANGE, SEE SHOP MANUAL:
　　MANUAL TRANS. IN NEUTRAL:-775-825 RPM
　　AUTO. TRANS. IN DRIVE: -665-715 RPM

USE SAE 5W-30 OIL - API CATEGORY SF, SF/CC OR SF/CD.

THIS VEHICLE CONFORMS TO U.S. EPA REGULATIONS APPLICABLE TO 1986 MODEL YEAR NEW MOTOR VEHICLES.

E6AE-9C485-ANM　CATALYST　SPARK PLUG: AWSF-52　GAP- .042-.046
2.3L-6FM
6FM2.5V5HCF6-EGR/EGS/AIV/TWC/FI

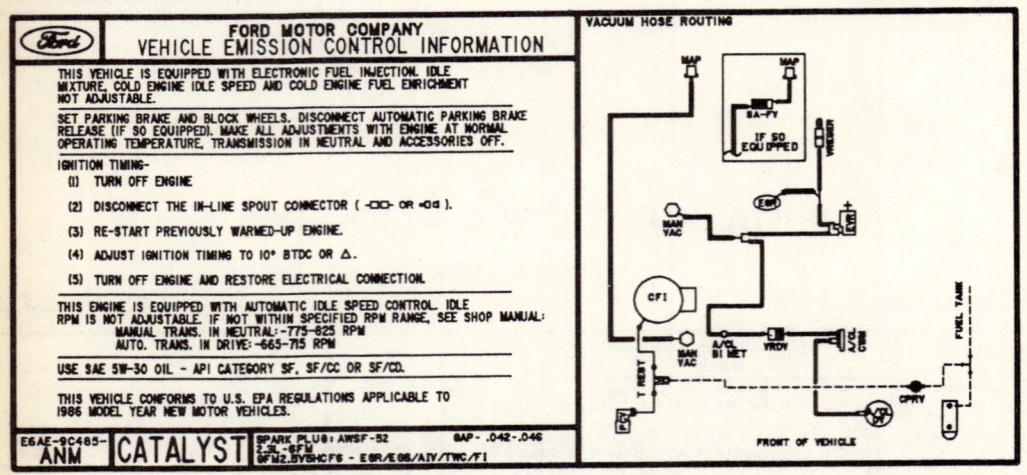

CALIBRATION: 7—07A—R10

MODEL YEAR: 1987　　　　　　　　　　　　　　　　**ENGINE: 1.9L**

FORD MOTOR COMPANY
IMPORTANT VEHICLE INFORMATION

THIS VEHICLE IS EQUIPPED WITH ELECTRONIC FUEL INJECTION. IDLE MIXTURE, COLD ENGINE IDLE SPEED AND COLD ENGINE FUEL ENRICHMENT NOT ADJUSTABLE.

SET PARKING BRAKE AND BLOCK WHEELS. MAKE ALL ADJUSTMENTS WITH ENGINE AT NORMAL OPERATING TEMPERATURE, TRANSMISSION IN NEUTRAL AND ACCESSORIES OFF.

IGNITION TIMING- ELECTRONICALLY ADJUSTED AT THE FACTORY- ADJUSTMENT REQUIRED ONLY IF DISTRIBUTOR HAS BEEN DISTURBED.
(1) TURN OFF ENGINE.
(2) DISCONNECT THE IN-LINE SPOUT CONNECTOR.(-◻◻- OR -◁◁-)
(3) RE-START PREVIOUSLY WARMED-UP ENGINE.
(4) ADJUST IGNITION TIMING TO 10° BTDC.
(5) TURN OFF ENGINE AND RESTORE ELECTRICAL CONNECTION.

THIS ENGINE IS EQUIPPED WITH AUTOMATIC IDLE SPEED CONTROL. IDLE RPM IS NOT ADJUSTABLE. IF NOT WITHIN SPECIFIED RPM RANGE, SEE SHOP MANUAL:
　　MANUAL TRANS. IN NEUTRAL: - 760-840 RPM
　　AUTO. TRANS. IN DRIVE: - 760-840 RPM

THIS VEHICLE CONFORMS TO U.S. EPA REGULATIONS APPLICABLE TO 1987 MODEL YEAR NEW MOTOR VEHICLES.

E7AE-9C485-CCT　CATALYST　SPARK PLUG: AGSF-34C　GAP- .042-.046
1.9L - 7FM
HFM1.9V5FFF1 - EGS/EGR/TWC/FI

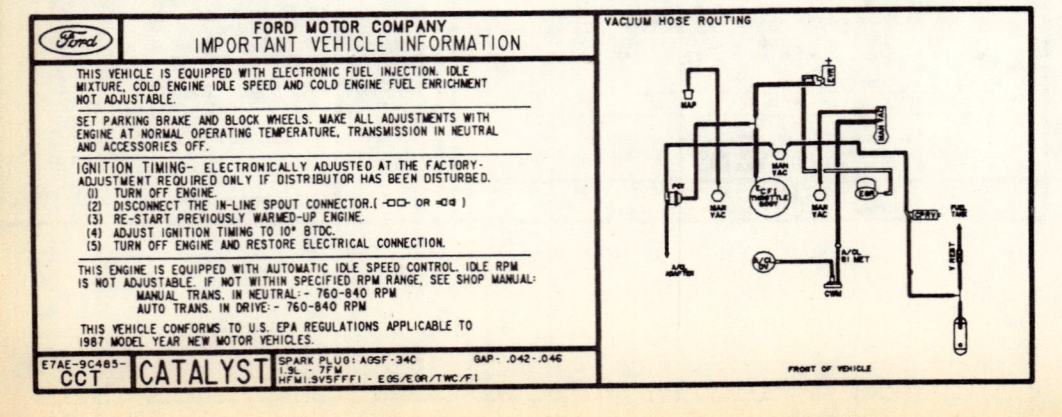

EMISSION CONTROLS 297

CALIBRATION: 6—26R—R11

MODEL YEAR: 1986 **ENGINE: 2.3L**

```
FORD MOTOR COMPANY
VEHICLE EMISSION CONTROL INFORMATION

THIS VEHICLE IS EQUIPPED WITH ELECTRONIC FUEL INJECTION. IDLE
MIXTURE, COLD ENGINE IDLE SPEED AND COLD ENGINE FUEL ENRICHMENT
NOT ADJUSTABLE.
SET PARKING BRAKE AND BLOCK WHEELS. DISCONNECT AUTOMATIC PARKING BRAKE
RELEASE (IF SO EQUIPPED). MAKE ALL ADJUSTMENTS WITH ENGINE AT NORMAL
OPERATING TEMPERATURE, TRANSMISSION IN NEUTRAL AND ACCESSORIES OFF.

IGNITION TIMING-
  (1) TURN OFF ENGINE
  (2) DISCONNECT THE IN-LINE SPOUT CONNECTOR ( -□□- OR -◁◁- ).
  (3) RE-START PREVIOUSLY WARMED-UP ENGINE.
  (4) ADJUST IGNITION TIMING TO 10° BTDC OR △.
  (5) TURN OFF ENGINE AND RESTORE ELECTRICAL CONNECTION.

THIS ENGINE IS EQUIPPED WITH AUTOMATIC IDLE SPEED CONTROL. IDLE
RPM IS NOT ADJUSTABLE. IF NOT WITHIN SPECIFIED RPM RANGE, SEE SHOP MANUAL:
        MANUAL TRANS. IN NEUTRAL:-775-825 RPM
        AUTO. TRANS. IN DRIVE: -665-715 RPM
USE SAE 5W-30 OIL-API CATEGORY SF, SF/CC OR SF/CD.

THIS VEHICLE CONFORMS TO U.S. EPA AND CALIFORNIA REGULATIONS
APPLICABLE TO 1986 MODEL YEAR NEW MOTOR VEHICLES INTRODUCED
INTO COMMERCE SOLELY FOR SALE IN CALIFORNIA.

E6AE-9C485-ANR   CATALYST   SPARK PLUG: AWSF-52   GAP .042-.046
                            2.3L -6FM
                            0FM2.5V5HCH0 -EGR/EGS/AIV/TWC/FI
```

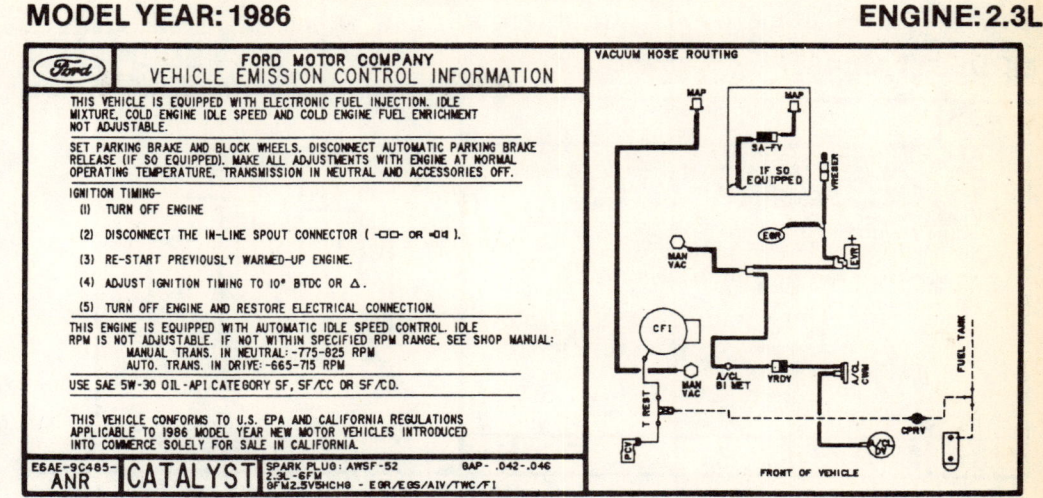

CALIBRATION: 7—07A—R00

MODEL YEAR: 1987 **ENGINE: 1.9L**

```
FORD MOTOR COMPANY
IMPORTANT VEHICLE INFORMATION

THIS VEHICLE IS EQUIPPED WITH ELECTRONIC FUEL INJECTION. IDLE
MIXTURE, COLD ENGINE IDLE SPEED AND COLD ENGINE FUEL ENRICHMENT
NOT ADJUSTABLE.
SET PARKING BRAKE AND BLOCK WHEELS. MAKE ALL ADJUSTMENTS WITH
ENGINE AT NORMAL OPERATING TEMPERATURE, TRANSMISSION IN NEUTRAL
AND ACCESSORIES OFF.
IGNITION TIMING- ELECTRONICALLY ADJUSTED AT THE FACTORY-
ADJUSTMENT REQUIRED ONLY IF DISTRIBUTOR HAS BEEN DISTURBED.
  (1) TURN OFF ENGINE.
  (2) DISCONNECT THE IN-LINE SPOUT CONNECTOR.( -□□- OR -◁◁- )
  (3) RE-START PREVIOUSLY WARMED-UP ENGINE.
  (4) ADJUST IGNITION TIMING TO 10° BTDC.
  (5) TURN OFF ENGINE AND RESTORE ELECTRICAL CONNECTION.
THIS ENGINE IS EQUIPPED WITH AUTOMATIC IDLE SPEED CONTROL. IDLE RPM
IS NOT ADJUSTABLE. IF NOT WITHIN SPECIFIED RPM RANGE, SEE SHOP MANUAL:
        MANUAL TRANS. IN NEUTRAL:- 760-840 RPM
        AUTO TRANS. IN DRIVE:- 760-840 RPM
THIS VEHICLE CONFORMS TO U.S. EPA REGULATIONS APPLICABLE TO
1987 MODEL YEAR NEW MOTOR VEHICLES.

E7AE-9C485-CCT   CATALYST   SPARK PLUG: AGSF-34C   GAP .042-.046
                            1.9L - 7FM
                            HFM1.9V5FFFI -EGS/EGR/TWC/FI
```

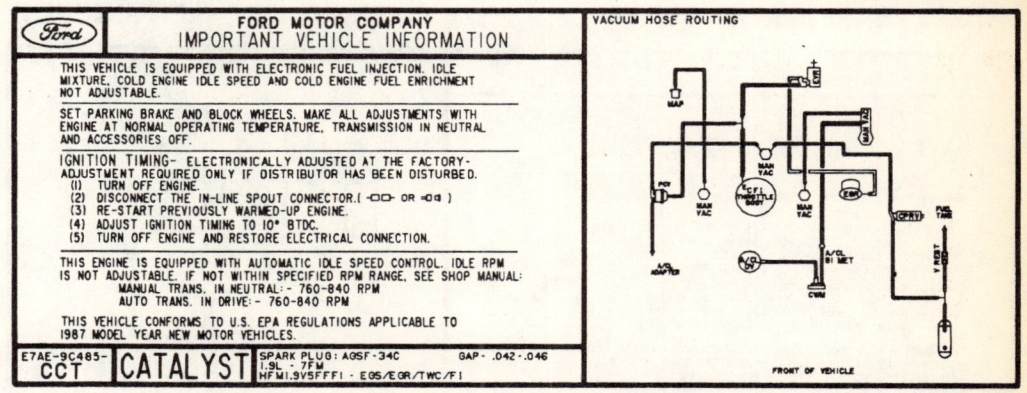

CALIBRATION: 6—26R—R10

MODEL YEAR: 1986 **ENGINE: 2.3L**

```
FORD MOTOR COMPANY
VEHICLE EMISSION CONTROL INFORMATION

THIS VEHICLE IS EQUIPPED WITH ELECTRONIC FUEL INJECTION. IDLE
MIXTURE, COLD ENGINE IDLE SPEED AND COLD ENGINE FUEL ENRICHMENT
NOT ADJUSTABLE.
SET PARKING BRAKE AND BLOCK WHEELS. DISCONNECT AUTOMATIC PARKING BRAKE
RELEASE (IF SO EQUIPPED). MAKE ALL ADJUSTMENTS WITH ENGINE AT NORMAL
OPERATING TEMPERATURE, TRANSMISSION IN NEUTRAL AND ACCESSORIES OFF.

IGNITION TIMING-
  (1) TURN OFF ENGINE
  (2) DISCONNECT THE IN-LINE SPOUT CONNECTOR ( -□□- OR -◁◁- ).
  (3) RE-START PREVIOUSLY WARMED-UP ENGINE.
  (4) ADJUST IGNITION TIMING TO 10° BTDC OR △.
  (5) TURN OFF ENGINE AND RESTORE ELECTRICAL CONNECTION.

THIS ENGINE IS EQUIPPED WITH AUTOMATIC IDLE SPEED CONTROL. IDLE
RPM IS NOT ADJUSTABLE. IF NOT WITHIN SPECIFIED RPM RANGE, SEE SHOP MANUAL:
        MANUAL TRANS. IN NEUTRAL:-775-825 RPM
        AUTO. TRANS. IN DRIVE:-625-675 RPM
USE SAE 5W-30 OIL-API CATEGORY SF, SF/CC OR SF/CD.

THIS VEHICLE CONFORMS TO U.S. EPA AND CALIFORNIA REGULATIONS
APPLICABLE TO 1986 MODEL YEAR NEW MOTOR VEHICLES INTRODUCED
INTO COMMERCE SOLELY FOR SALE IN CALIFORNIA.

E6AE-9C485-AJY   CATALYST   SPARK PLUG: AWSF-52   GAP .042-.046
                            2.3L -6FM
                            0FM2.5V5HCH0 -EGR/EGS/AIV/TWC/FI
```

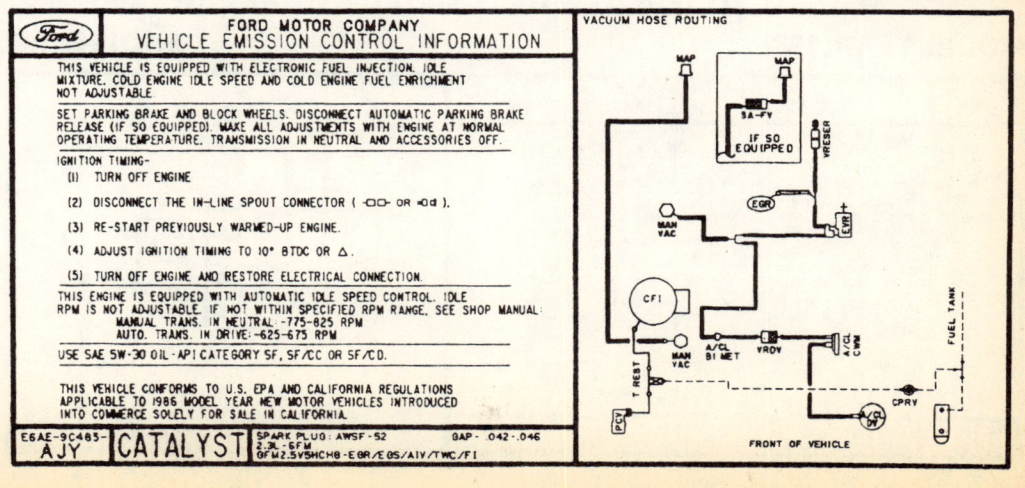

EMISSION CONTROLS

CALIBRATION: 7—07A—R00
(California)

MODEL YEAR: 1987 **ENGINE: 1.9L**

FORD MOTOR COMPANY — IMPORTANT VEHICLE INFORMATION

THIS VEHICLE IS EQUIPPED WITH ELECTRONIC FUEL INJECTION. IDLE MIXTURE, COLD ENGINE IDLE SPEED AND COLD ENGINE FUEL ENRICHMENT ARE NOT ADJUSTABLE.

SET PARKING BRAKE AND BLOCK WHEELS. MAKE ALL ADJUSTMENTS WITH ENGINE AT NORMAL OPERATING TEMPERATURE, TRANSMISSION IN NEUTRAL AND ACCESSORIES OFF.

IGNITION TIMING-ELECTRONICALLY ADJUSTED AT THE FACTORY-ADJUSTMENT REQUIRED ONLY IF DISTRIBUTOR HAS BEEN DISTURBED.
1. TURN OFF ENGINE
2. DISCONNECT THE IN-LINE SPOUT CONNECTOR.(-◻◻- OR ◻◻)
3. RE-START PREVIOUSLY WARMED-UP ENGINE.
4. ADJUST IGNITION TIMING TO 10° BTDC.
5. TURN OFF ENGINE AND RESTORE ELECTRICAL CONNECTION.

THIS ENGINE IS EQUIPPED WITH AUTOMATIC IDLE SPEED CONTROL. IDLE RPM IS NOT ADJUSTABLE. IF NOT WITHIN SPECIFIED RPM RANGE, SEE SHOP MANUAL:
  MANUAL TRANS. IN NEUTRAL: - 760-840 RPM
  AUTO. TRANS. IN DRIVE: - 760-840 RPM

THIS VEHICLE CONFORMS TO U.S. EPA AND CALIFORNIA REGULATIONS APPLICABLE TO 1987 MODEL YEAR NEW MOTOR VEHICLES INTRODUCED INTO COMMERCE SOLELY FOR SALE IN CALIFORNIA.

E7AE-9C485-CCU CATALYST SPARK PLUG: AGSF-34C GAP: .042-.046
1.9L - 7FM HFM1.9V5FFC9 - EGR/EGS/TWC/FI

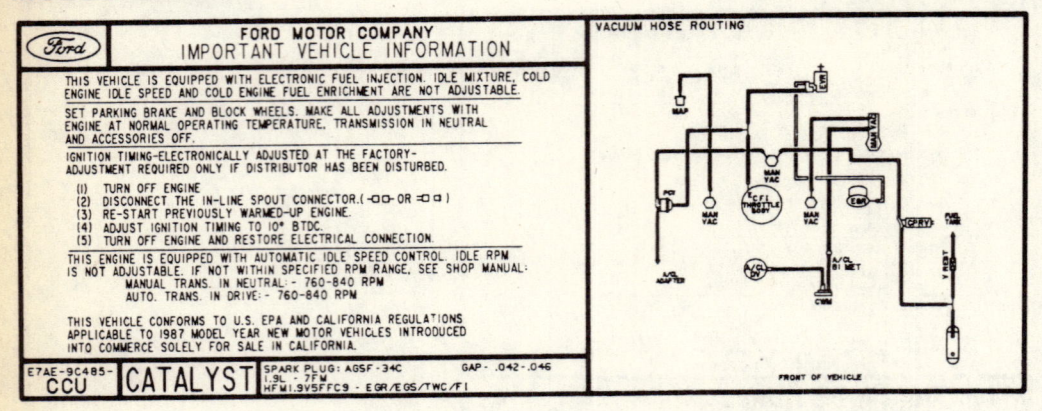

CALIBRATION: 7—07A—R10
(California)

MODEL YEAR: 1987 **ENGINE: 1.9L**

FORD MOTOR COMPANY — IMPORTANT VEHICLE INFORMATION

THIS VEHICLE IS EQUIPPED WITH ELECTRONIC FUEL INJECTION. IDLE MIXTURE, COLD ENGINE IDLE SPEED AND COLD ENGINE FUEL ENRICHMENT ARE NOT ADJUSTABLE.

SET PARKING BRAKE AND BLOCK WHEELS. MAKE ALL ADJUSTMENTS WITH ENGINE AT NORMAL OPERATING TEMPERATURE, TRANSMISSION IN NEUTRAL AND ACCESSORIES OFF.

IGNITION TIMING-ELECTRONICALLY ADJUSTED AT THE FACTORY-ADJUSTMENT REQUIRED ONLY IF DISTRIBUTOR HAS BEEN DISTURBED.
1. TURN OFF ENGINE
2. DISCONNECT THE IN-LINE SPOUT CONNECTOR.(-◻◻- OR ◻◻)
3. RE-START PREVIOUSLY WARMED-UP ENGINE.
4. ADJUST IGNITION TIMING TO 10° BTDC.
5. TURN OFF ENGINE AND RESTORE ELECTRICAL CONNECTION.

THIS ENGINE IS EQUIPPED WITH AUTOMATIC IDLE SPEED CONTROL. IDLE RPM IS NOT ADJUSTABLE. IF NOT WITHIN SPECIFIED RPM RANGE, SEE SHOP MANUAL:
  MANUAL TRANS. IN NEUTRAL: - 760-840 RPM
  AUTO. TRANS. IN DRIVE: - 760-840 RPM

THIS VEHICLE CONFORMS TO U.S. EPA AND CALIFORNIA REGULATIONS APPLICABLE TO 1987 MODEL YEAR NEW MOTOR VEHICLES INTRODUCED INTO COMMERCE SOLELY FOR SALE IN CALIFORNIA.

E7AE-9C485-CCU CATALYST SPARK PLUG: AGSF-34C GAP: .042-.046
1.9L - 7FM HFM1.9V5FFC9 - EGR/EGS/TWC/FI

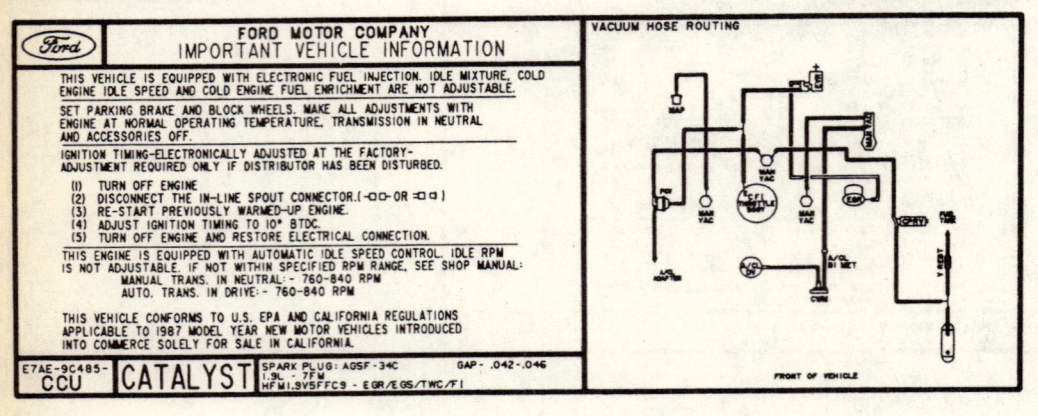

CALIBRATION: 7—07F—R00

MODEL YEAR: 1987 **ENGINE: 1.9L**

FORD MOTOR COMPANY — IMPORTANT VEHICLE INFORMATION

THIS VEHICLE IS EQUIPPED WITH ELECTRONIC FUEL INJECTION. IDLE MIXTURE, COLD ENGINE IDLE SPEED AND COLD ENGINE FUEL ENRICHMENT NOT ADJUSTABLE.

SET PARKING BRAKE AND BLOCK WHEELS. MAKE ALL ADJUSTMENTS WITH ENGINE AT NORMAL OPERATING TEMPERATURE, TRANSMISSION IN NEUTRAL AND ACCESSORIES OFF.

IGNITION TIMING- ELECTRONICALLY ADJUSTED AT THE FACTORY-ADJUSTMENT REQUIRED ONLY IF DISTRIBUTOR HAS BEEN DISTURBED.
1. TURN OFF ENGINE.
2. DISCONNECT THE IN-LINE SPOUT CONNECTOR. (-◻◻- OR ◻◻)
3. RE-START PREVIOUSLY WARMED-UP ENGINE.
4. ADJUST IGNITION TIMING TO 10° BTDC.
5. TURN OFF ENGINE AND RESTORE ELECTRICAL CONNECTION.

THIS ENGINE IS EQUIPPED WITH AUTOMATIC IDLE SPEED CONTROL. IDLE RPM IS NOT ADJUSTABLE. IF NOT WITHIN SPECIFIED RPM RANGE, SEE SHOP MANUAL:
  MANUAL TRANS. IN NEUTRAL: - 760-840 RPM

THIS VEHICLE CONFORMS TO U.S. EPA REGULATIONS APPLICABLE TO 1987 MODEL YEAR NEW MOTOR VEHICLES. COMPLIANCE DEMONSTRATED AND DESIGNED FOR PRINCIPAL USE BELOW 4000 FEET. THIS VEHICLE IS EXEMPT FROM MEETING EMISSIONS STANDARDS ABOVE 4000 FEET BECAUSE OF POSSIBLY UNSUITABLE PERFORMANCE, AND THE EMISSIONS PERFORMANCE WARRANTY DOES NOT APPLY ABOVE 4000 FEET.

E7AE-9C485-CDG CATALYST SPARK PLUG: AGSF-34C GAP: .042-.046
1.9L - 7FM HFM1.9V5FFI1 - EGS/EGR/TWC/FI

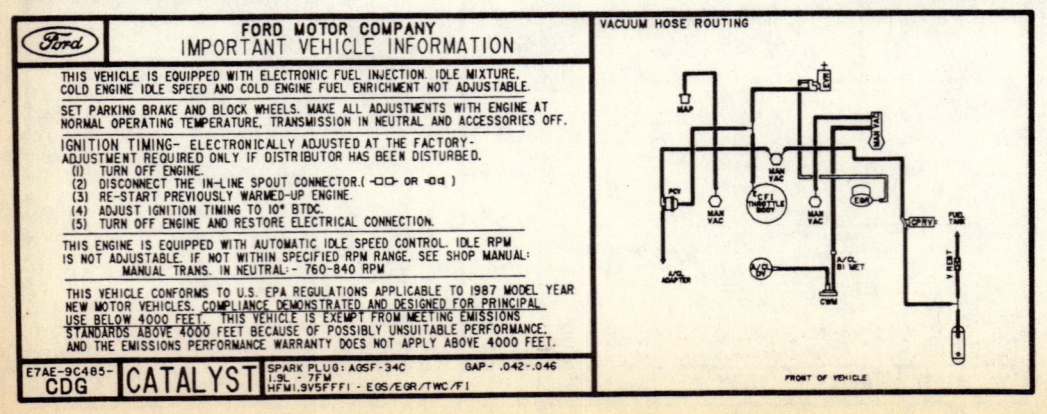

EMISSION CONTROLS 299

CALIBRATION: 7—07K—R00

MODEL YEAR: 1987   **ENGINE: 1.9L**

FORD MOTOR COMPANY — IMPORTANT VEHICLE INFORMATION

THIS VEHICLE IS EQUIPPED WITH ELECTRONIC FUEL INJECTION. IDLE MIXTURE, COLD ENGINE IDLE SPEED AND COLD ENGINE FUEL ENRICHMENT NOT ADJUSTABLE.

SET PARKING BRAKE AND BLOCK WHEELS. MAKE ALL ADJUSTMENTS WITH ENGINE AT NORMAL OPERATING TEMPERATURE, TRANSMISSION IN NEUTRAL AND ACCESSORIES OFF.

IGNITION TIMING- ELECTRONICALLY ADJUSTED AT THE FACTORY- ADJUSTMENT REQUIRED ONLY IF DISTRIBUTOR HAS BEEN DISTURBED.
(1) TURN OFF ENGINE.
(2) DISCONNECT THE IN-LINE SPOUT CONNECTOR.
(3) RE-START PREVIOUSLY WARMED-UP ENGINE.
(4) ADJUST IGNITION TIMING TO 10° BTDC.
(5) TURN OFF ENGINE AND RESTORE ELECTRICAL CONNECTION.

THIS ENGINE IS EQUIPPED WITH AUTOMATIC IDLE SPEED CONTROL. IDLE RPM IS NOT ADJUSTABLE. IF NOT WITHIN SPECIFIED RPM RANGE, SEE SHOP MANUAL:
    MANUAL TRANS. IN NEUTRAL: - 760-840 RPM
    AUTO TRANS. IN DRIVE: - 760-840 RPM

THIS VEHICLE CONFORMS TO U.S. EPA REGULATIONS APPLICABLE TO 1987 MODEL YEAR NEW MOTOR VEHICLES.

E7AE-9C485-CCT   CATALYST   SPARK PLUG: AGSF-34C   GAP: .042-.046
1.9L - 7FM   HFMI.9V5FFFI - EGS/EGR/TWC/FI

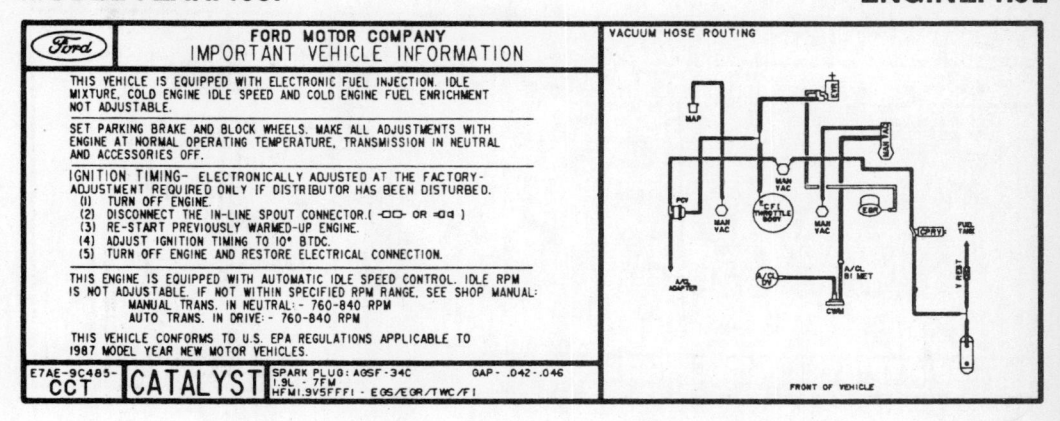

CALIBRATION: 7—07K—R10

MODEL YEAR: 1987   **ENGINE: 1.9L**

FORD MOTOR COMPANY — IMPORTANT VEHICLE INFORMATION

THIS VEHICLE IS EQUIPPED WITH ELECTRONIC FUEL INJECTION. IDLE MIXTURE, COLD ENGINE IDLE SPEED AND COLD ENGINE FUEL ENRICHMENT NOT ADJUSTABLE.

SET PARKING BRAKE AND BLOCK WHEELS. MAKE ALL ADJUSTMENTS WITH ENGINE AT NORMAL OPERATING TEMPERATURE, TRANSMISSION IN NEUTRAL AND ACCESSORIES OFF.

IGNITION TIMING- ELECTRONICALLY ADJUSTED AT THE FACTORY- ADJUSTMENT REQUIRED ONLY IF DISTRIBUTOR HAS BEEN DISTURBED.
(1) TURN OFF ENGINE.
(2) DISCONNECT THE IN-LINE SPOUT CONNECTOR.
(3) RE-START PREVIOUSLY WARMED-UP ENGINE.
(4) ADJUST IGNITION TIMING TO 10° BTDC.
(5) TURN OFF ENGINE AND RESTORE ELECTRICAL CONNECTION.

THIS ENGINE IS EQUIPPED WITH AUTOMATIC IDLE SPEED CONTROL. IDLE RPM IS NOT ADJUSTABLE. IF NOT WITHIN SPECIFIED RPM RANGE, SEE SHOP MANUAL:
    MANUAL TRANS. IN NEUTRAL: - 760-840 RPM
    AUTO TRANS. IN DRIVE: - 760-840 RPM

THIS VEHICLE CONFORMS TO U.S. EPA REGULATIONS APPLICABLE TO 1987 MODEL YEAR NEW MOTOR VEHICLES.

E7AE-9C485-CCT   CATALYST   SPARK PLUG: AGSF-34C   GAP: .042-.046
1.9L - 7FM   HFMI.9V5FFFI - EGS/EGR/TWC/FI

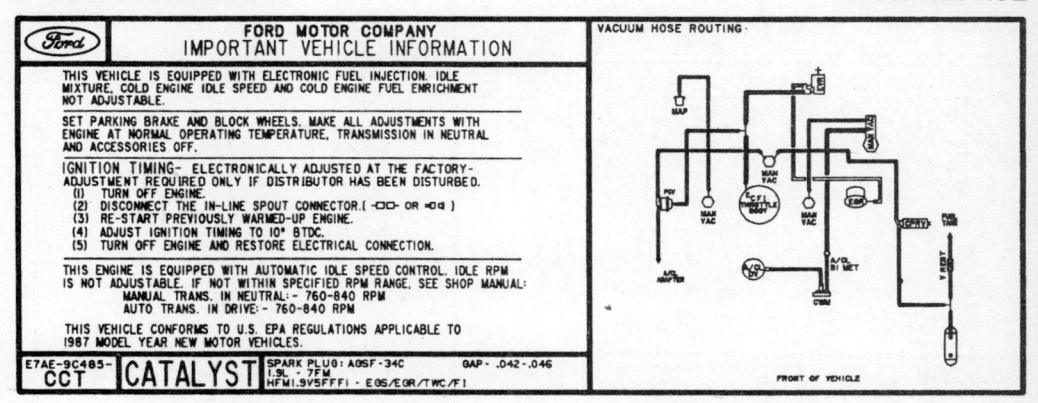

MODEL YEAR: 1987   **ENGINE: 1.9L**

FORD MOTOR COMPANY — IMPORTANT VEHICLE INFORMATION

THIS VEHICLE IS EQUIPPED WITH ELECTRONIC FUEL INJECTION. IDLE MIXTURE, COLD ENGINE IDLE SPEED AND COLD ENGINE FUEL ENRICHMENT ARE NOT ADJUSTABLE.

SET PARKING BRAKE AND BLOCK WHEELS. MAKE ALL ADJUSTMENTS WITH ENGINE AT NORMAL OPERATING TEMPERATURE, TRANSMISSION IN NEUTRAL AND ACCESSORIES OFF.

IGNITION TIMING-ELECTRONICALLY ADJUSTED AT THE FACTORY- ADJUSTMENT REQUIRED ONLY IF DISTRIBUTOR HAS BEEN DISTURBED.
(1) TURN OFF ENGINE
(2) DISCONNECT THE IN-LINE SPOUT CONNECTOR.
(3) RE-START PREVIOUSLY WARMED-UP ENGINE.
(4) ADJUST IGNITION TIMING TO 10° BTDC.
(5) TURN OFF ENGINE AND RESTORE ELECTRICAL CONNECTION.

THIS ENGINE IS EQUIPPED WITH AUTOMATIC IDLE SPEED CONTROL. IDLE RPM IS NOT ADJUSTABLE. IF NOT WITHIN SPECIFIED RPM RANGE, SEE SHOP MANUAL:
    MANUAL TRANS. IN NEUTRAL: - 760-840 RPM
    AUTO. TRANS. IN DRIVE: - 760-840 RPM

THIS VEHICLE CONFORMS TO U.S. EPA AND CALIFORNIA REGULATIONS APPLICABLE TO 1987 MODEL YEAR NEW MOTOR VEHICLES INTRODUCED INTO COMMERCE SOLELY FOR SALE IN CALIFORNIA.

E7AE-9C485-CCU   CATALYST   SPARK PLUG: AGSF-34C   GAP: .042-.046
1.9L - 7FM   HFMI.9V5FFC9 - EGR/EGS/TWC/FI

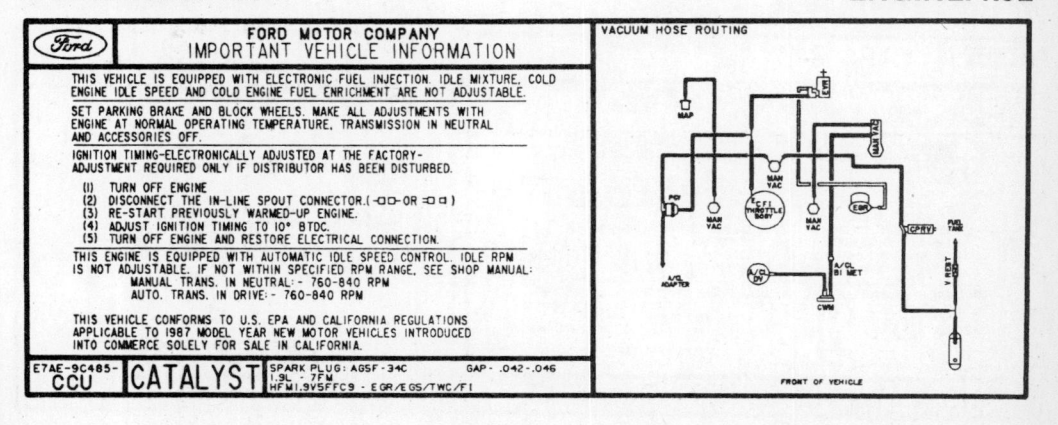

EMISSION CONTROLS

CALIBRATION: 7—07S—R00

MODEL YEAR: 1987   **ENGINE: 1.9L**

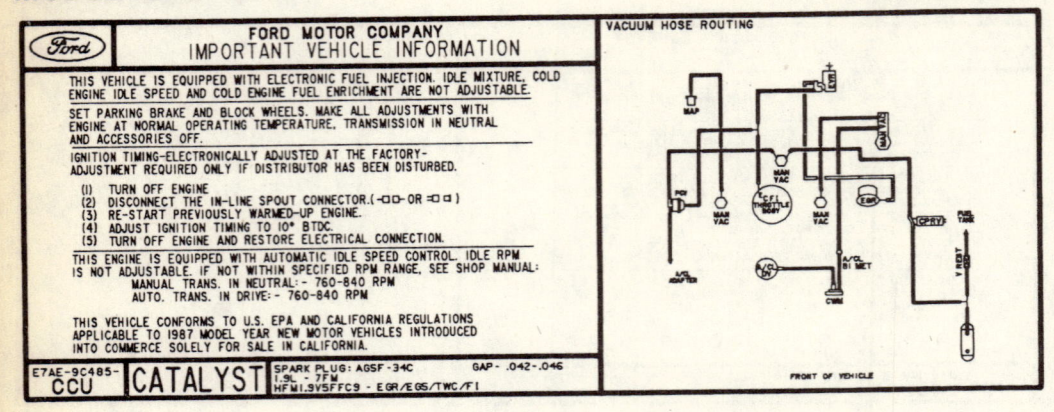

CALIBRATION: 7—07K—R10
(California)

MODEL YEAR: 1987   **ENGINE: 1.9L**

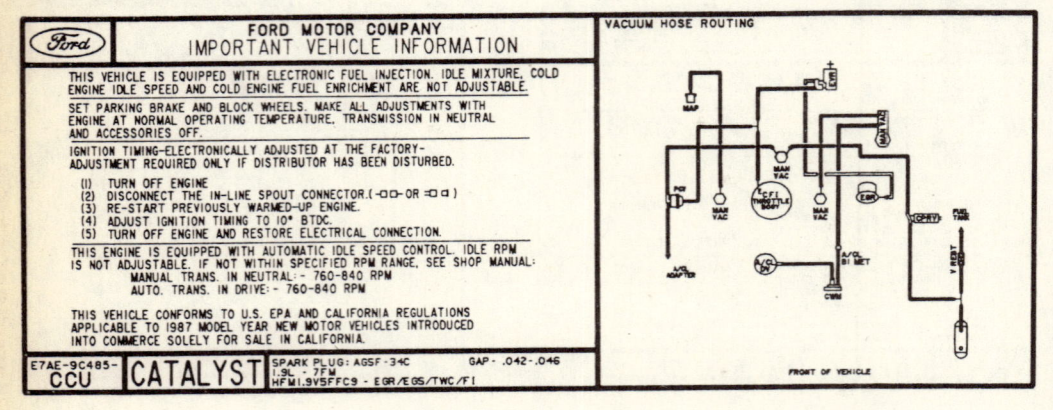

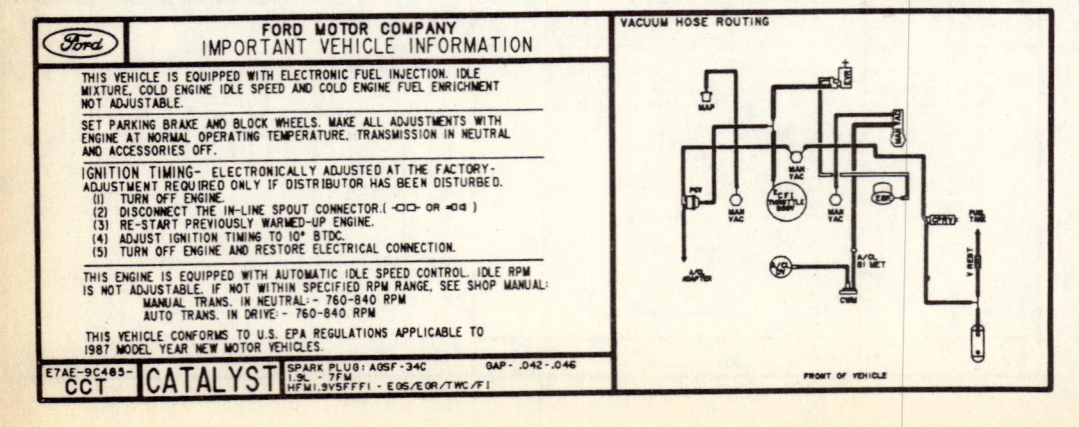

CALIBRATION: 7—08A—R00

MODEL YEAR: 1987   **ENGINE: 1.9L**

EMISSION CONTROLS 301

CALIBRATION: 7—08A—R00
(California)

MODEL YEAR: 1987 **ENGINE: 1.9L**

```
FORD MOTOR COMPANY
IMPORTANT VEHICLE INFORMATION

THIS VEHICLE IS EQUIPPED WITH ELECTRONIC FUEL INJECTION. IDLE MIXTURE, COLD
ENGINE IDLE SPEED AND COLD ENGINE FUEL ENRICHMENT ARE NOT ADJUSTABLE.
SET PARKING BRAKE AND BLOCK WHEELS. MAKE ALL ADJUSTMENTS WITH
ENGINE AT NORMAL OPERATING TEMPERATURE, TRANSMISSION IN NEUTRAL
AND ACCESSORIES OFF.
IGNITION TIMING-ELECTRONICALLY ADJUSTED AT THE FACTORY-
ADJUSTMENT REQUIRED ONLY IF DISTRIBUTOR HAS BEEN DISTURBED.
  (1) TURN OFF ENGINE
  (2) DISCONNECT THE IN-LINE SPOUT CONNECTOR.(-OO- OR =O=)
  (3) RE-START PREVIOUSLY WARMED-UP ENGINE.
  (4) ADJUST IGNITION TIMING TO 10° BTDC.
  (5) TURN OFF ENGINE AND RESTORE ELECTRICAL CONNECTION.
THIS ENGINE IS EQUIPPED WITH AUTOMATIC IDLE SPEED CONTROL. IDLE RPM
IS NOT ADJUSTABLE. IF NOT WITHIN SPECIFIED RPM RANGE, SEE SHOP MANUAL:
     MANUAL TRANS. IN NEUTRAL:- 760-840 RPM
     AUTO. TRANS. IN DRIVE:- 760-840 RPM
THIS VEHICLE CONFORMS TO U.S. EPA AND CALIFORNIA REGULATIONS
APPLICABLE TO 1987 MODEL YEAR NEW MOTOR VEHICLES INTRODUCED
INTO COMMERCE SOLELY FOR SALE IN CALIFORNIA.

E7AE-9C485- CCU   CATALYST   SPARK PLUG: AGSF-34C   GAP- .042-.046
                             1.9L - 7FM
                             HFM1.9V5FFC9 - EGR/EGS/TWC/FI
```

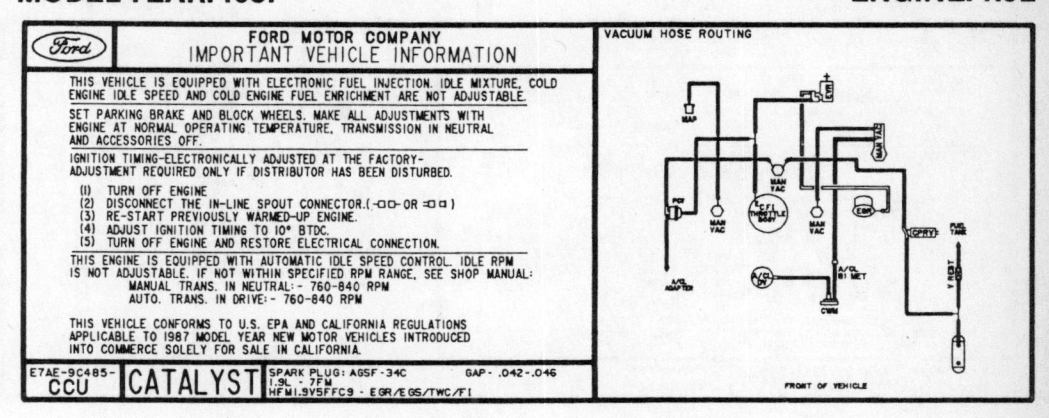

CALIBRATION: 7—08A—R10

MODEL YEAR: 1987 **ENGINE: 1.9L**

```
FORD MOTOR COMPANY
IMPORTANT VEHICLE INFORMATION

THIS VEHICLE IS EQUIPPED WITH ELECTRONIC FUEL INJECTION. IDLE
MIXTURE, COLD ENGINE IDLE SPEED AND COLD ENGINE FUEL ENRICHMENT
NOT ADJUSTABLE.
SET PARKING BRAKE AND BLOCK WHEELS. MAKE ALL ADJUSTMENTS WITH
ENGINE AT NORMAL OPERATING TEMPERATURE, TRANSMISSION IN NEUTRAL
AND ACCESSORIES OFF.
IGNITION TIMING- ELECTRONICALLY ADJUSTED AT THE FACTORY-
ADJUSTMENT REQUIRED ONLY IF DISTRIBUTOR HAS BEEN DISTURBED.
  (1) TURN OFF ENGINE.
  (2) DISCONNECT THE IN-LINE SPOUT CONNECTOR.( -OO- OR =O= )
  (3) RE-START PREVIOUSLY WARMED-UP ENGINE.
  (4) ADJUST IGNITION TIMING TO 10° BTDC.
  (5) TURN OFF ENGINE AND RESTORE ELECTRICAL CONNECTION.
THIS ENGINE IS EQUIPPED WITH AUTOMATIC IDLE SPEED CONTROL. IDLE RPM
IS NOT ADJUSTABLE. IF NOT WITHIN SPECIFIED RPM RANGE, SEE SHOP MANUAL:
     MANUAL TRANS. IN NEUTRAL:- 760-840 RPM
     AUTO. TRANS. IN DRIVE:- 760-840 RPM
THIS VEHICLE CONFORMS TO U.S. EPA REGULATIONS APPLICABLE TO
1987 MODEL YEAR NEW MOTOR VEHICLES.

E7AE-9C485- CCT   CATALYST   SPARK PLUG: AGSF-34C   GAP- .042-.046
                             1.9L - 7FM
                             HFM1.9V5FFF1 - EGS/EGR/TWC/FI
```

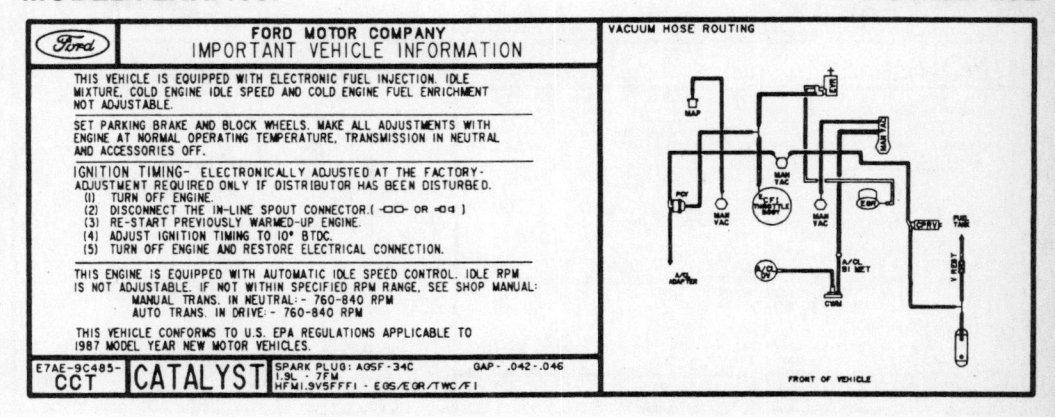

CALIBRATION: 7—37B—R00

MODEL YEAR: 1987 **ENGINE: 2.0L DIESEL**

```
FORD MOTOR COMPANY
IMPORTANT VEHICLE INFORMATION

SET PARKING BRAKE AND BLOCK WHEELS. MAKE ALL ADJUSTMENTS WITH
ENGINE AT NORMAL OPERATING TEMPERATURE. ACCESSORIES AND
HEADLIGHTS OFF UNLESS OTHERWISE INDICATED.
MAKE ALL ADJUSTMENTS WITH TRANSMISSION IN NEUTRAL.
FAST IDLE ADJUSTMENT: ATTACH SLAVE VACUUM HOSES TO
BOTH NIPPLES OF THE DOUBLE DIAPHRAM CSD (COLD START
DEVICE). APPLY VACUUM (20" IN. HG. MIN.), ADJUST FAST
IDLE TO 1450-1550 RPM BY TURNING FAST IDLE ADJUSTING ROD.
CURB IDLE ADJUSTMENT: ADJUST TO 725-775 RPM BY
TURNING THE CURB IDLE ADJUSTING SCREW.
IF EQUIPPED WITH AIR CONDITIONING, TURN A/C ON
WHILE THE COMPRESSOR IS RUNNING ADJUST TO 725-775
RPM BY TURNING THE A/C IDLE ADJUSTING SCREW.
INJECTION PUMP TIMING : 1 MM PLUNGER LIFT AT TOP DEAD
CENTER (ENGINE STATIC)
(FUEL INJECTION PUMP TIMING IS PRE-SET AT THE FACTORY.
ADJUSTMENT NOT REQUIRED DURING TUNE-UP).
INTAKE VALVE CLEARANCE : COLD - 0.25 MM (0.010 IN.)
EXHAUST VALVE CLEARANCE : COLD - 0.35 MM (0.014 IN.)
THIS VEHICLE CONFORMS TO U.S. EPA AND CALIFORNIA REGULATIONS
APPLICABLE TO 1997 MODEL YEAR NEW MOTOR VEHICLES.

E7AE-9C485- CBG   NON-CATALYST   2.0L - HFM2.0D6JBB4
```

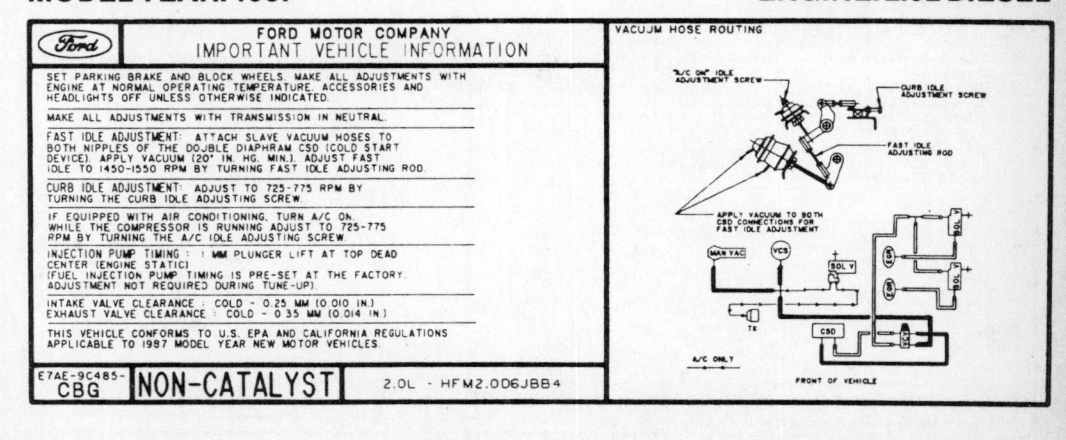

EMISSION CONTROLS

CALIBRATION: 7—08A—R10
(California)

MODEL YEAR: 1987 **ENGINE: 1.9L**

FORD MOTOR COMPANY — IMPORTANT VEHICLE INFORMATION

THIS VEHICLE IS EQUIPPED WITH ELECTRONIC FUEL INJECTION. IDLE MIXTURE, COLD ENGINE IDLE SPEED AND COLD ENGINE FUEL ENRICHMENT ARE NOT ADJUSTABLE.

SET PARKING BRAKE AND BLOCK WHEELS. MAKE ALL ADJUSTMENTS WITH ENGINE AT NORMAL OPERATING TEMPERATURE, TRANSMISSION IN NEUTRAL AND ACCESSORIES OFF.

IGNITION TIMING-ELECTRONICALLY ADJUSTED AT THE FACTORY-ADJUSTMENT REQUIRED ONLY IF DISTRIBUTOR HAS BEEN DISTURBED.
  (1) TURN OFF ENGINE
  (2) DISCONNECT THE IN-LINE SPOUT CONNECTOR.
  (3) RE-START PREVIOUSLY WARMED-UP ENGINE.
  (4) ADJUST IGNITION TIMING TO 10° BTDC.
  (5) TURN OFF ENGINE AND RESTORE ELECTRICAL CONNECTION.

THIS ENGINE IS EQUIPPED WITH AUTOMATIC IDLE SPEED CONTROL. IDLE RPM IS NOT ADJUSTABLE. IF NOT WITHIN SPECIFIED RPM RANGE, SEE SHOP MANUAL:
  MANUAL TRANS. IN NEUTRAL:- 760-840 RPM
  AUTO. TRANS. IN DRIVE:- 760-840 RPM

THIS VEHICLE CONFORMS TO U.S. EPA AND CALIFORNIA REGULATIONS APPLICABLE TO 1987 MODEL YEAR NEW MOTOR VEHICLES INTRODUCED INTO COMMERCE SOLELY FOR SALE IN CALIFORNIA.

E7AE-9C485-CCU CATALYST SPARK PLUG: AGSF-34C GAP: .042-.046
1.9L - 7FM
HFM1.9V5FFC9 - EGR/EGS/TWC/FI

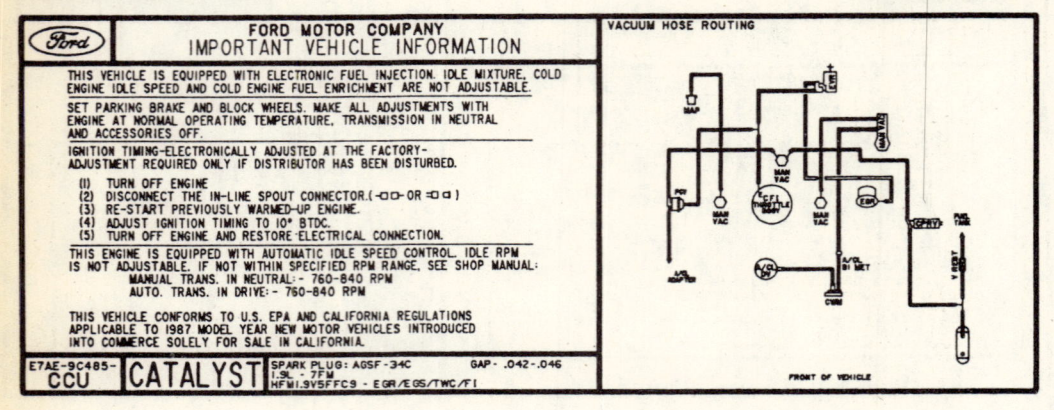

CALIBRATION: 7—05A—R10

MODEL YEAR: 1987 **ENGINE: 2.3L**

FORD MOTOR COMPANY — VEHICLE EMISSION CONTROL INFORMATION

THIS VEHICLE IS EQUIPPED WITH ELECTRONIC FUEL INJECTION. IDLE MIXTURE, COLD ENGINE IDLE SPEED AND COLD ENGINE FUEL ENRICHMENT ARE NOT ADJUSTABLE.

SET PARKING BRAKE AND BLOCK WHEELS. MAKE ALL ADJUSTMENTS WITH ENGINE AT NORMAL OPERATING TEMPERATURE, TRANSMISSION IN NEUTRAL AND ACCESSORIES OFF.

IGNITION TIMING-
  (1) TURN OFF ENGINE
  (2) DISCONNECT THE IN-LINE SPOUT CONNECTOR.
  (3) RE-START PREVIOUSLY WARMED-UP ENGINE.
  (4) ADJUST IGNITION TIMING TO 10° BTDC.
  (5) TURN OFF ENGINE AND RESTORE ELECTRICAL CONNECTION.

THIS ENGINE IS EQUIPPED WITH AUTOMATIC IDLE SPEED CONTROL. IDLE RPM IS NOT ADJUSTABLE. IF NOT WITHIN SPECIFIED RPM RANGE, SEE SHOP MANUAL:
  MANUAL TRANS. IN NEUTRAL:- 690-750 RPM
  AUTO. TRANS. IN DRIVE:- 690-750 RPM

THIS VEHICLE CONFORMS TO U.S. EPA AND CALIFORNIA REGULATIONS APPLICABLE TO 1987 MODEL YEAR NEW MOTOR VEHICLES.

E7AE-9C485-CBE CATALYST SPARK PLUG: AWSF-44C GAP: .042-.046
2.3L - 7HM
HFM2.3V5FF07 - EGR/EGS/TWC/FI

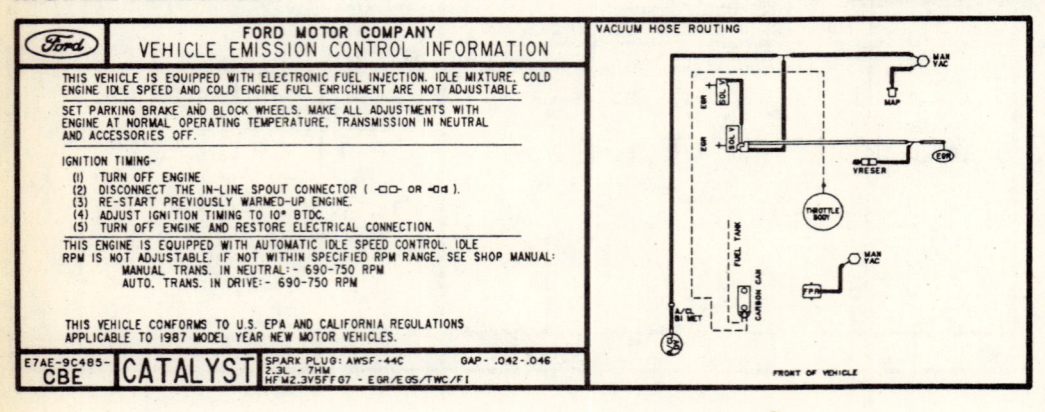

CALIBRATION: 7—05A—R11

MODEL YEAR: 1987 **ENGINE: 2.3L**

FORD MOTOR COMPANY — VEHICLE EMISSION CONTROL INFORMATION

THIS VEHICLE IS EQUIPPED WITH ELECTRONIC FUEL INJECTION. IDLE MIXTURE, COLD ENGINE IDLE SPEED AND COLD ENGINE FUEL ENRICHMENT ARE NOT ADJUSTABLE.

SET PARKING BRAKE AND BLOCK WHEELS. MAKE ALL ADJUSTMENTS WITH ENGINE AT NORMAL OPERATING TEMPERATURE, TRANSMISSION IN NEUTRAL AND ACCESSORIES OFF.

IGNITION TIMING-
  (1) TURN OFF ENGINE
  (2) DISCONNECT THE IN-LINE SPOUT CONNECTOR.
  (3) RE-START PREVIOUSLY WARMED-UP ENGINE.
  (4) ADJUST IGNITION TIMING TO 10° BTDC.
  (5) TURN OFF ENGINE AND RESTORE ELECTRICAL CONNECTION.

THIS ENGINE IS EQUIPPED WITH AUTOMATIC IDLE SPEED CONTROL. IDLE RPM IS NOT ADJUSTABLE. IF NOT WITHIN SPECIFIED RPM RANGE, SEE SHOP MANUAL:
  MANUAL TRANS. IN NEUTRAL:- 690-750 RPM
  AUTO. TRANS. IN DRIVE:- 690-750 RPM

THIS VEHICLE CONFORMS TO U.S. EPA AND CALIFORNIA REGULATIONS APPLICABLE TO 1987 MODEL YEAR NEW MOTOR VEHICLES.

E7AE-9C485-CBE CATALYST SPARK PLUG: AWSF-44C GAP: .042-.046
2.3L - 7HM
HFM2.3V5FF07 - EGR/EGS/TWC/FI

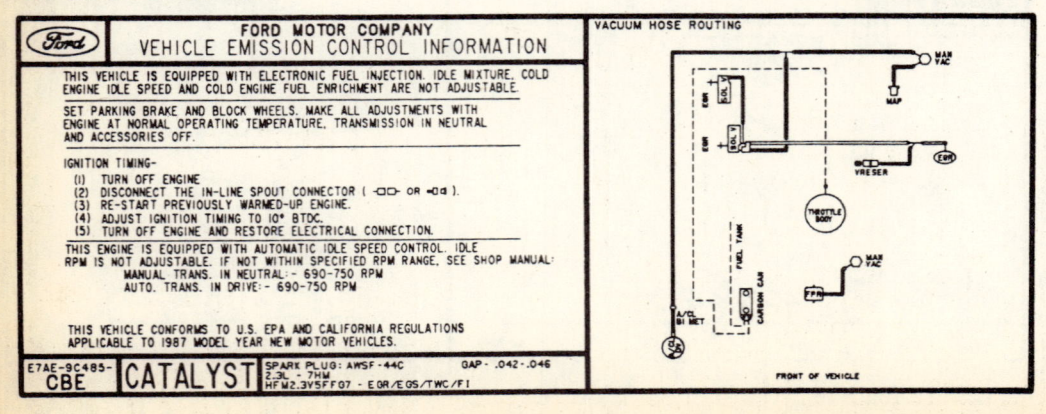

EMISSION CONTROLS

CALIBRATION: 7—06A—R00

MODEL YEAR: 1987 **ENGINE: 2.3L**

FORD MOTOR COMPANY — VEHICLE EMISSION CONTROL INFORMATION

THIS VEHICLE IS EQUIPPED WITH ELECTRONIC FUEL INJECTION. IDLE MIXTURE, COLD ENGINE IDLE SPEED AND COLD ENGINE FUEL ENRICHMENT ARE NOT ADJUSTABLE.

SET PARKING BRAKE AND BLOCK WHEELS. MAKE ALL ADJUSTMENTS WITH ENGINE AT NORMAL OPERATING TEMPERATURE, TRANSMISSION IN NEUTRAL AND ACCESSORIES OFF.

IGNITION TIMING-
(1) TURN OFF ENGINE
(2) DISCONNECT THE IN-LINE SPOUT CONNECTOR (-◻◻- OR -◁◁-).
(3) RE-START PREVIOUSLY WARMED-UP ENGINE.
(4) ADJUST IGNITION TIMING TO 10° BTDC.
(5) TURN OFF ENGINE AND RESTORE ELECTRICAL CONNECTION.

THIS ENGINE IS EQUIPPED WITH AUTOMATIC IDLE SPEED CONTROL. IDLE RPM IS NOT ADJUSTABLE. IF NOT WITHIN SPECIFIED RPM RANGE, SEE SHOP MANUAL:
    MANUAL TRANS. IN NEUTRAL:- 690-750 RPM
    AUTO. TRANS. IN DRIVE:- 690-750 RPM

THIS VEHICLE CONFORMS TO U.S. EPA AND CALIFORNIA REGULATIONS APPLICABLE TO 1987 MODEL YEAR NEW MOTOR VEHICLES.

E7AE-9C485-CBE   CATALYST   SPARK PLUG: AWSF-44C   GAP-.042-.046
2.3L - 7HM   HFM2.3V5FFG7 - EGR/EGS/TWC/FI

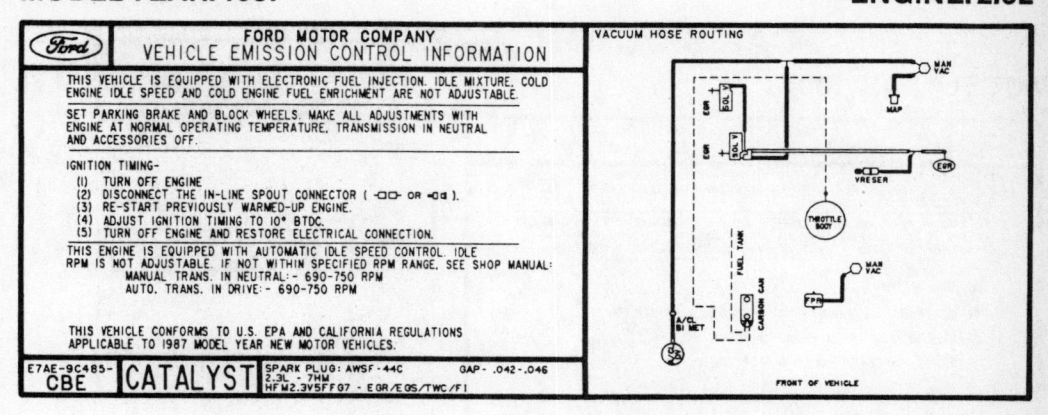

CALIBRATION: 7—06A—R10

MODEL YEAR: 1987 **ENGINE: 2.3L**

FORD MOTOR COMPANY — VEHICLE EMISSION CONTROL INFORMATION

THIS VEHICLE IS EQUIPPED WITH ELECTRONIC FUEL INJECTION. IDLE MIXTURE, COLD ENGINE IDLE SPEED AND COLD ENGINE FUEL ENRICHMENT ARE NOT ADJUSTABLE.

SET PARKING BRAKE AND BLOCK WHEELS. MAKE ALL ADJUSTMENTS WITH ENGINE AT NORMAL OPERATING TEMPERATURE, TRANSMISSION IN NEUTRAL AND ACCESSORIES OFF.

IGNITION TIMING-
(1) TURN OFF ENGINE
(2) DISCONNECT THE IN-LINE SPOUT CONNECTOR (-◻◻- OR -◁◁-).
(3) RE-START PREVIOUSLY WARMED-UP ENGINE.
(4) ADJUST IGNITION TIMING TO 10° BTDC.
(5) TURN OFF ENGINE AND RESTORE ELECTRICAL CONNECTION.

THIS ENGINE IS EQUIPPED WITH AUTOMATIC IDLE SPEED CONTROL. IDLE RPM IS NOT ADJUSTABLE. IF NOT WITHIN SPECIFIED RPM RANGE, SEE SHOP MANUAL:
    MANUAL TRANS. IN NEUTRAL:- 690-750 RPM
    AUTO. TRANS. IN DRIVE:- 690-750 RPM

THIS VEHICLE CONFORMS TO U.S. EPA AND CALIFORNIA REGULATIONS APPLICABLE TO 1987 MODEL YEAR NEW MOTOR VEHICLES.

E7AE-9C485-CBE   CATALYST   SPARK PLUG: AWSF-44C   GAP-.042-.046
2.3L - 7HM   HFM2.3V5FFG7 - EGR/EGS/TWC/FI

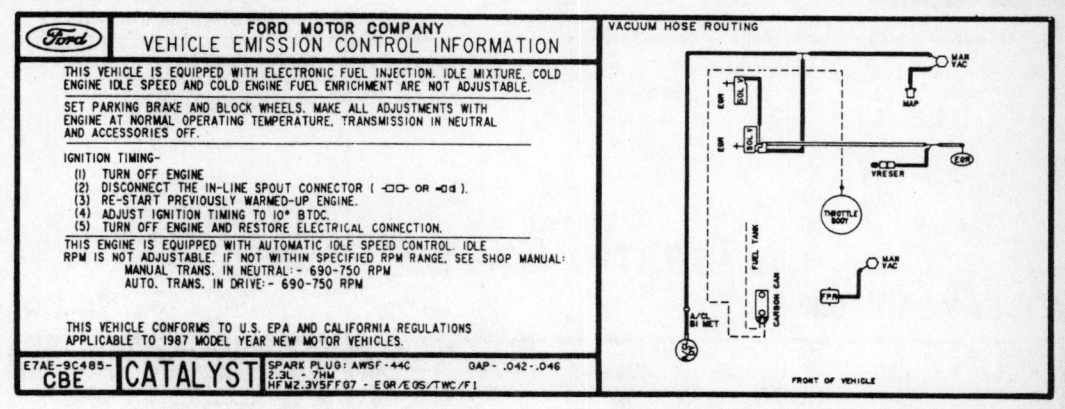

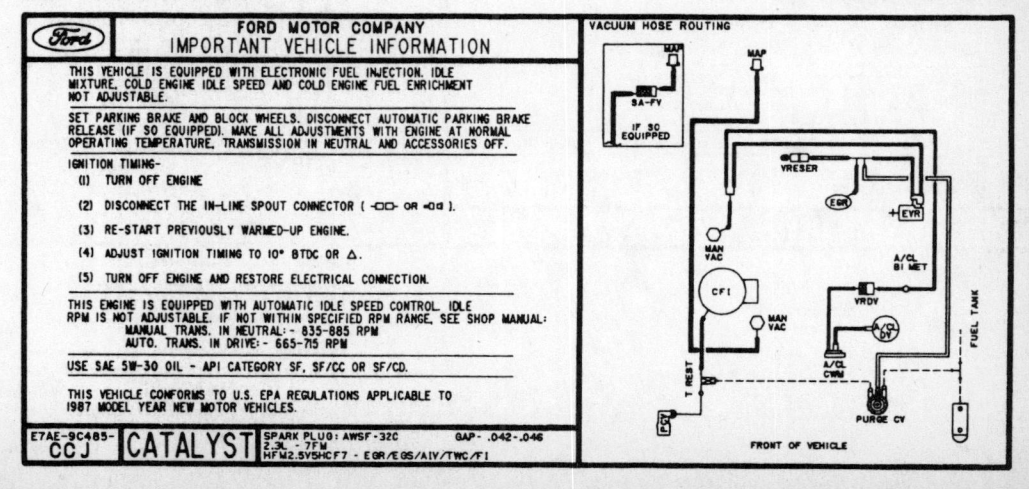

CALIBRATION: 7—25C—R00

MODEL YEAR: 1987 **ENGINE: 2.3L**

FORD MOTOR COMPANY — IMPORTANT VEHICLE INFORMATION

THIS VEHICLE IS EQUIPPED WITH ELECTRONIC FUEL INJECTION. IDLE MIXTURE, COLD ENGINE IDLE SPEED AND COLD ENGINE FUEL ENRICHMENT NOT ADJUSTABLE.

SET PARKING BRAKE AND BLOCK WHEELS. DISCONNECT AUTOMATIC PARKING BRAKE RELEASE (IF SO EQUIPPED). MAKE ALL ADJUSTMENTS WITH ENGINE AT NORMAL OPERATING TEMPERATURE, TRANSMISSION IN NEUTRAL AND ACCESSORIES OFF.

IGNITION TIMING-
(1) TURN OFF ENGINE
(2) DISCONNECT THE IN-LINE SPOUT CONNECTOR (-◻◻- OR -◁◁-).
(3) RE-START PREVIOUSLY WARMED-UP ENGINE.
(4) ADJUST IGNITION TIMING TO 10° BTDC OR △.
(5) TURN OFF ENGINE AND RESTORE ELECTRICAL CONNECTION.

THIS ENGINE IS EQUIPPED WITH AUTOMATIC IDLE SPEED CONTROL. IDLE RPM IS NOT ADJUSTABLE. IF NOT WITHIN SPECIFIED RPM RANGE, SEE SHOP MANUAL:
    MANUAL TRANS. IN NEUTRAL:- 835-885 RPM
    AUTO. TRANS. IN DRIVE:- 665-715 RPM

USE SAE 5W-30 OIL - API CATEGORY SF, SF/CC OR SF/CD.

THIS VEHICLE CONFORMS TO U.S. EPA REGULATIONS APPLICABLE TO 1987 MODEL YEAR NEW MOTOR VEHICLES.

E7AE-9C485-CCJ   CATALYST   SPARK PLUG: AWSF-32C   GAP-.042-.046
2.3L - 7HM   HFM2.5Y5HCF7 - EGR/EGS/AIV/TWC/FI

304   **EMISSION CONTROLS**

CALIBRATION: 7—25C—R10

MODEL YEAR: 1987   **ENGINE: 2.3L**

FORD MOTOR COMPANY — IMPORTANT VEHICLE INFORMATION

THIS VEHICLE IS EQUIPPED WITH ELECTRONIC FUEL INJECTION. IDLE MIXTURE, COLD ENGINE IDLE SPEED AND COLD ENGINE FUEL ENRICHMENT NOT ADJUSTABLE.

SET PARKING BRAKE AND BLOCK WHEELS. DISCONNECT AUTOMATIC PARKING BRAKE RELEASE (IF SO EQUIPPED). MAKE ALL ADJUSTMENTS WITH ENGINE AT NORMAL OPERATING TEMPERATURE, TRANSMISSION IN NEUTRAL AND ACCESSORIES OFF.

IGNITION TIMING-
(1) TURN OFF ENGINE
(2) DISCONNECT THE IN-LINE SPOUT CONNECTOR (-◯◯- OR -◁▷-).
(3) RE-START PREVIOUSLY WARMED-UP ENGINE.
(4) ADJUST IGNITION TIMING TO 10° BTDC OR △.
(5) TURN OFF ENGINE AND RESTORE ELECTRICAL CONNECTION.

THIS ENGINE IS EQUIPPED WITH AUTOMATIC IDLE SPEED CONTROL. IDLE RPM IS NOT ADJUSTABLE. IF NOT WITHIN SPECIFIED RPM RANGE, SEE SHOP MANUAL:
     MANUAL TRANS. IN NEUTRAL: - 835-885 RPM
     AUTO. TRANS. IN DRIVE: - 665-715 RPM

USE SAE 5W-30 OIL - API CATEGORY SF, SF/CC OR SF/CD.

THIS VEHICLE CONFORMS TO U.S. EPA REGULATIONS APPLICABLE TO 1987 MODEL YEAR NEW MOTOR VEHICLES.

E7AE-9C485-CCJ   CATALYST   SPARK PLUG: AWSF-32C   GAP: .042-.046
2.3L - 7FM
HFM2.5V5HCF7 - EGR/EGS/AIV/TWC/FI

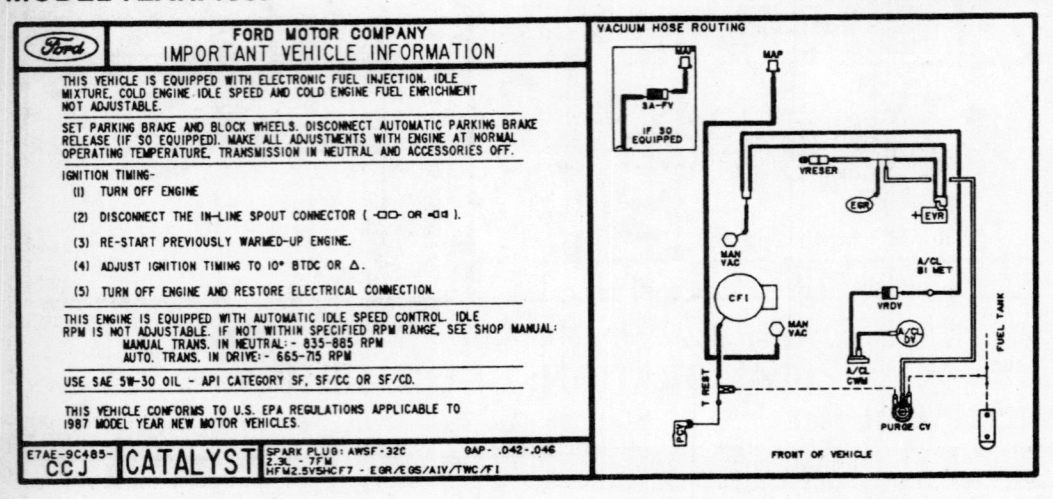

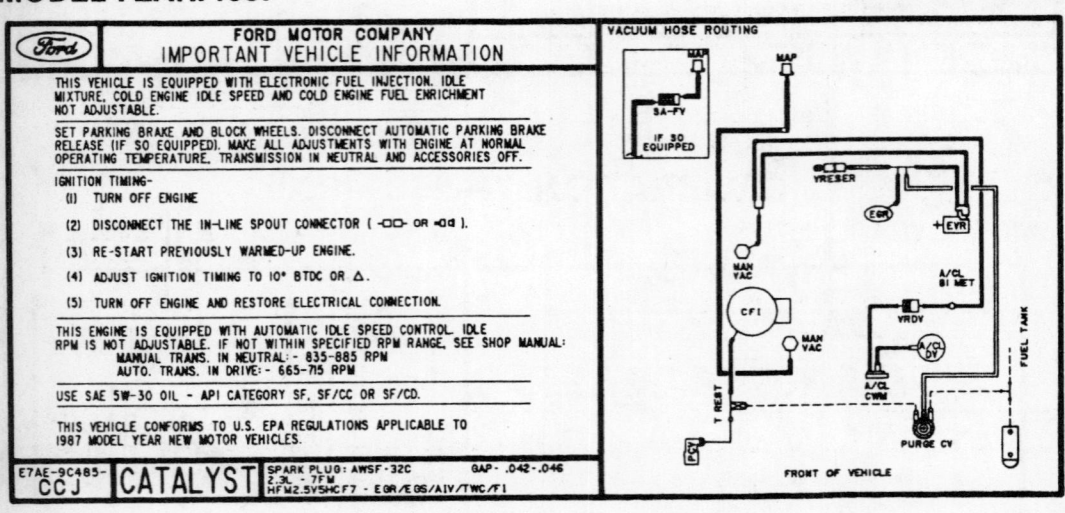

CALIBRATION: 7—25F—R00

MODEL YEAR: 1987   **ENGINE: 2.3L**

FORD MOTOR COMPANY — IMPORTANT VEHICLE INFORMATION

THIS VEHICLE IS EQUIPPED WITH ELECTRONIC FUEL INJECTION. IDLE MIXTURE, COLD ENGINE IDLE SPEED AND COLD ENGINE FUEL ENRICHMENT NOT ADJUSTABLE.

SET PARKING BRAKE AND BLOCK WHEELS. DISCONNECT AUTOMATIC PARKING BRAKE RELEASE (IF SO EQUIPPED). MAKE ALL ADJUSTMENTS WITH ENGINE AT NORMAL OPERATING TEMPERATURE, TRANSMISSION IN NEUTRAL AND ACCESSORIES OFF.

IGNITION TIMING-
(1) TURN OFF ENGINE
(2) DISCONNECT THE IN-LINE SPOUT CONNECTOR (-◯◯- OR -◁▷-).
(3) RE-START PREVIOUSLY WARMED-UP ENGINE.
(4) ADJUST IGNITION TIMING TO 10° BTDC OR △.
(5) TURN OFF ENGINE AND RESTORE ELECTRICAL CONNECTION.

THIS ENGINE IS EQUIPPED WITH AUTOMATIC IDLE SPEED CONTROL. IDLE RPM IS NOT ADJUSTABLE. IF NOT WITHIN SPECIFIED RPM RANGE, SEE SHOP MANUAL:
     MANUAL TRANS. IN NEUTRAL: - 835-885 RPM
     AUTO. TRANS. IN DRIVE: - 665-715 RPM

USE SAE 5W-30 OIL - API CATEGORY SF, SF/CC OR SF/CD.

THIS VEHICLE CONFORMS TO U.S. EPA REGULATIONS APPLICABLE TO 1987 MODEL YEAR NEW MOTOR VEHICLES.

E7AE-9C485-CCJ   CATALYST   SPARK PLUG: AWSF-32C   GAP: .042-.046
2.3L - 7FM
HFM2.5V5HCF7 - EGR/EGS/AIV/TWC/FI

EMISSION CONTROLS 305

CALIBRATION: 7—25F—R10

MODEL YEAR: 1987   **ENGINE: 2.3L**

FORD MOTOR COMPANY — IMPORTANT VEHICLE INFORMATION

THIS VEHICLE IS EQUIPPED WITH ELECTRONIC FUEL INJECTION. IDLE MIXTURE, COLD ENGINE IDLE SPEED AND COLD ENGINE FUEL ENRICHMENT NOT ADJUSTABLE.

SET PARKING BRAKE AND BLOCK WHEELS. DISCONNECT AUTOMATIC PARKING BRAKE RELEASE (IF SO EQUIPPED). MAKE ALL ADJUSTMENTS WITH ENGINE AT NORMAL OPERATING TEMPERATURE, TRANSMISSION IN NEUTRAL AND ACCESSORIES OFF.

IGNITION TIMING—
(1) TURN OFF ENGINE
(2) DISCONNECT THE IN-LINE SPOUT CONNECTOR (-⊂⊃- OR -◁▷-).
(3) RE-START PREVIOUSLY WARMED-UP ENGINE.
(4) ADJUST IGNITION TIMING TO 10° BTDC OR △.
(5) TURN OFF ENGINE AND RESTORE ELECTRICAL CONNECTION.

THIS ENGINE IS EQUIPPED WITH AUTOMATIC IDLE SPEED CONTROL. IDLE RPM IS NOT ADJUSTABLE. IF NOT WITHIN SPECIFIED RPM RANGE, SEE SHOP MANUAL:
    MANUAL TRANS. IN NEUTRAL - 835-885 RPM
    AUTO. TRANS. IN DRIVE - 665-715 RPM

USE SAE 5W-30 OIL - API CATEGORY SF, SF/CC OR SF/CD.

THIS VEHICLE CONFORMS TO U.S. EPA REGULATIONS APPLICABLE TO 1987 MODEL YEAR NEW MOTOR VEHICLES.

E7AE-9C485-CDS   CATALYST   SPARK PLUG: AWSF-52   GAP- .042-.046
2.3L - 7FM
HFM2.5V5HCF7 - EGR/EGS/AIV/TWC/FI

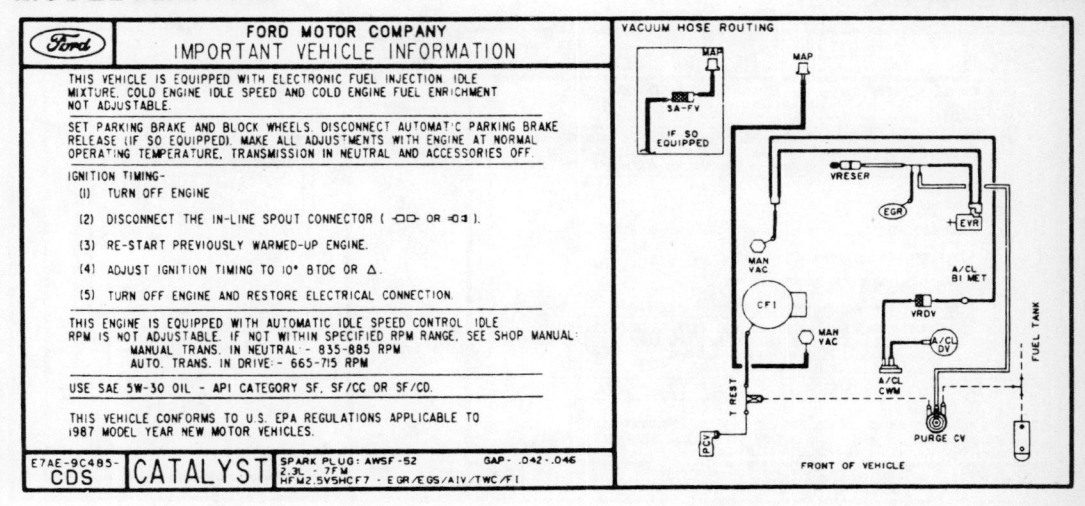

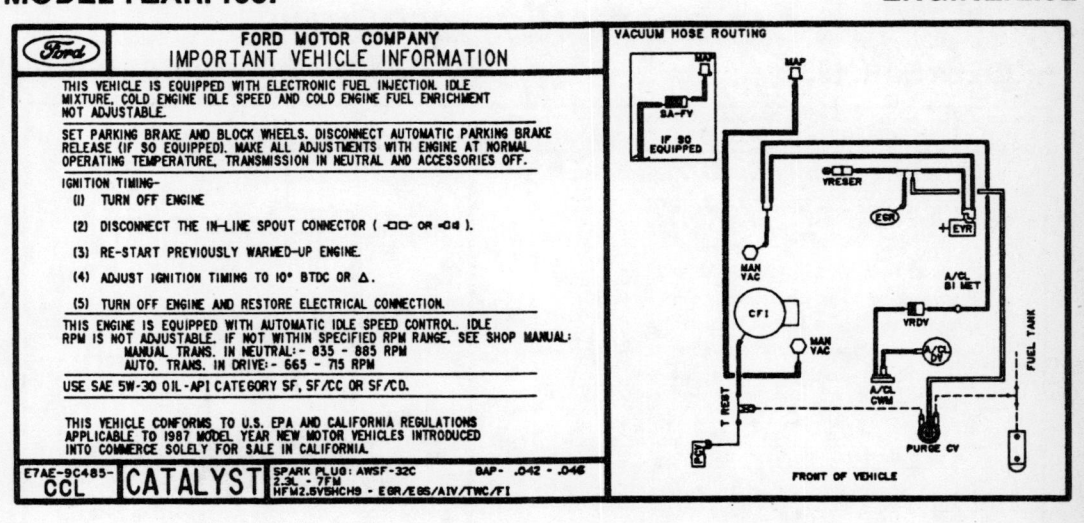

CALIBRATION: 7—25P—R00

MODEL YEAR: 1987   **ENGINE: 2.3L**

FORD MOTOR COMPANY — IMPORTANT VEHICLE INFORMATION

THIS VEHICLE IS EQUIPPED WITH ELECTRONIC FUEL INJECTION. IDLE MIXTURE, COLD ENGINE IDLE SPEED AND COLD ENGINE FUEL ENRICHMENT NOT ADJUSTABLE.

SET PARKING BRAKE AND BLOCK WHEELS. DISCONNECT AUTOMATIC PARKING BRAKE RELEASE (IF SO EQUIPPED). MAKE ALL ADJUSTMENTS WITH ENGINE AT NORMAL OPERATING TEMPERATURE, TRANSMISSION IN NEUTRAL AND ACCESSORIES OFF.

IGNITION TIMING—
(1) TURN OFF ENGINE
(2) DISCONNECT THE IN-LINE SPOUT CONNECTOR (-⊂⊃- OR -◁▷-).
(3) RE-START PREVIOUSLY WARMED-UP ENGINE.
(4) ADJUST IGNITION TIMING TO 10° BTDC OR △.
(5) TURN OFF ENGINE AND RESTORE ELECTRICAL CONNECTION.

THIS ENGINE IS EQUIPPED WITH AUTOMATIC IDLE SPEED CONTROL. IDLE RPM IS NOT ADJUSTABLE. IF NOT WITHIN SPECIFIED RPM RANGE, SEE SHOP MANUAL:
    MANUAL TRANS. IN NEUTRAL: - 835 - 885 RPM
    AUTO. TRANS. IN DRIVE: - 665 - 715 RPM

USE SAE 5W-30 OIL - API CATEGORY SF, SF/CC OR SF/CD.

THIS VEHICLE CONFORMS TO U.S. EPA AND CALIFORNIA REGULATIONS APPLICABLE TO 1987 MODEL YEAR NEW MOTOR VEHICLES INTRODUCED INTO COMMERCE SOLELY FOR SALE IN CALIFORNIA.

E7AE-9C485-CCL   CATALYST   SPARK PLUG: AWSF-32C   GAP- .042-.046
2.3L - 7FM
HFM2.5V5HCH9 - EGR/EGS/AIV/TWC/FI

EMISSION CONTROLS

CALIBRATION: 7—25P—R10

MODEL YEAR: 1987 **ENGINE: 2.3L**

FORD MOTOR COMPANY — IMPORTANT VEHICLE INFORMATION

THIS VEHICLE IS EQUIPPED WITH ELECTRONIC FUEL INJECTION. IDLE MIXTURE, COLD ENGINE IDLE SPEED AND COLD ENGINE FUEL ENRICHMENT NOT ADJUSTABLE.

SET PARKING BRAKE AND BLOCK WHEELS. DISCONNECT AUTOMATIC PARKING BRAKE RELEASE (IF SO EQUIPPED). MAKE ALL ADJUSTMENTS WITH ENGINE AT NORMAL OPERATING TEMPERATURE, TRANSMISSION IN NEUTRAL AND ACCESSORIES OFF.

IGNITION TIMING-
(1) TURN OFF ENGINE
(2) DISCONNECT THE IN-LINE SPOUT CONNECTOR (-⊂⊃- OR -⊂◁).
(3) RE-START PREVIOUSLY WARMED-UP ENGINE.
(4) ADJUST IGNITION TIMING TO 10° BTDC OR △.
(5) TURN OFF ENGINE AND RESTORE ELECTRICAL CONNECTION.

THIS ENGINE IS EQUIPPED WITH AUTOMATIC IDLE SPEED CONTROL. IDLE RPM IS NOT ADJUSTABLE. IF NOT WITHIN SPECIFIED RPM RANGE, SEE SHOP MANUAL:
  MANUAL TRANS. IN NEUTRAL: - 835 - 885 RPM
  AUTO. TRANS. IN DRIVE: - 665 - 715 RPM

USE SAE 5W-30 OIL - API CATEGORY SF, SF/CC OR SF/CD.

THIS VEHICLE CONFORMS TO U.S. EPA AND CALIFORNIA REGULATIONS APPLICABLE TO 1987 MODEL YEAR NEW MOTOR VEHICLES INTRODUCED IN COMMERCE SOLELY FOR SALE IN CALIFORNIA.

E7AE-9C485-CCL CATALYST SPARK PLUG: AWSF-32C GAP: .042 - .046 2.3L - 7FM HFM2.5V5HCH9 - EGR/EGS/AIV/TWC/FI

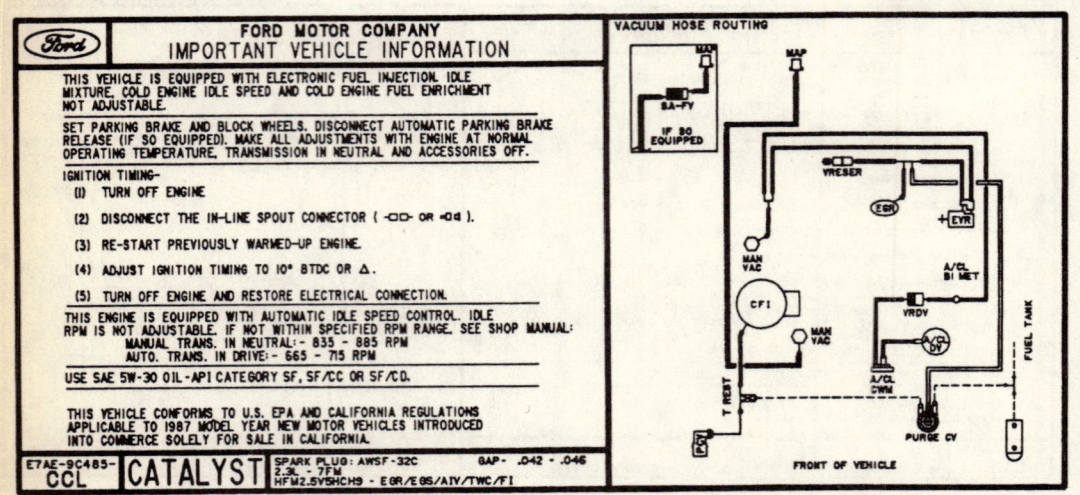

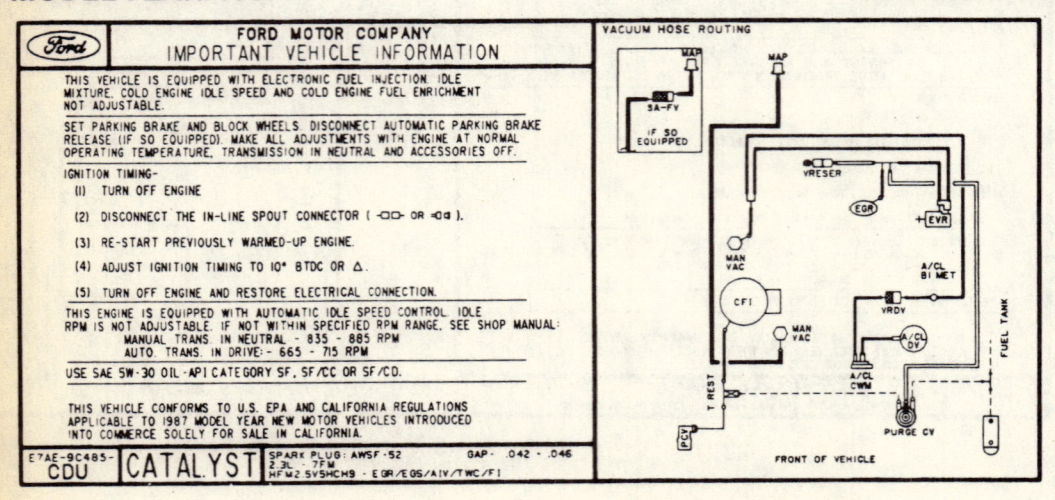

CALIBRATION: 7—25Q—R00

MODEL YEAR: 1987 **ENGINE: 2.3L**

FORD MOTOR COMPANY — IMPORTANT VEHICLE INFORMATION

THIS VEHICLE IS EQUIPPED WITH ELECTRONIC FUEL INJECTION. IDLE MIXTURE, COLD ENGINE IDLE SPEED AND COLD ENGINE FUEL ENRICHMENT NOT ADJUSTABLE.

SET PARKING BRAKE AND BLOCK WHEELS. DISCONNECT AUTOMATIC PARKING BRAKE RELEASE (IF SO EQUIPPED). MAKE ALL ADJUSTMENTS WITH ENGINE AT NORMAL OPERATING TEMPERATURE, TRANSMISSION IN NEUTRAL AND ACCESSORIES OFF.

IGNITION TIMING-
(1) TURN OFF ENGINE
(2) DISCONNECT THE IN-LINE SPOUT CONNECTOR (-⊂⊃- OR -⊂◁).
(3) RE-START PREVIOUSLY WARMED-UP ENGINE.
(4) ADJUST IGNITION TIMING TO 10° BTDC OR △.
(5) TURN OFF ENGINE AND RESTORE ELECTRICAL CONNECTION.

THIS ENGINE IS EQUIPPED WITH AUTOMATIC IDLE SPEED CONTROL. IDLE RPM IS NOT ADJUSTABLE. IF NOT WITHIN SPECIFIED RPM RANGE, SEE SHOP MANUAL:
  MANUAL TRANS. IN NEUTRAL - 835 - 885 RPM
  AUTO. TRANS. IN DRIVE: - 665 - 715 RPM

USE SAE 5W-30 OIL - API CATEGORY SF, SF/CC OR SF/CD.

THIS VEHICLE CONFORMS TO U.S. EPA AND CALIFORNIA REGULATIONS APPLICABLE TO 1987 MODEL YEAR NEW MOTOR VEHICLES INTRODUCED INTO COMMERCE SOLELY FOR SALE IN CALIFORNIA.

E7AE-9C485-CDU CATALYST SPARK PLUG: AWSF-52 GAP: .042 - .046 2.3L - 7FM HFM2.5V5HCH9 - EGR/EGS/AIV/TWC/FI

EMISSION CONTROLS

CALIBRATION: 7—25Q—R00
(California)

MODEL YEAR: 1987 **ENGINE: 2.3L**

FORD MOTOR COMPANY — IMPORTANT VEHICLE INFORMATION

THIS VEHICLE IS EQUIPPED WITH ELECTRONIC FUEL INJECTION. IDLE MIXTURE, COLD ENGINE IDLE SPEED AND COLD ENGINE FUEL ENRICHMENT NOT ADJUSTABLE.

SET PARKING BRAKE AND BLOCK WHEELS. DISCONNECT AUTOMATIC PARKING BRAKE RELEASE (IF SO EQUIPPED). MAKE ALL ADJUSTMENTS WITH ENGINE AT NORMAL OPERATING TEMPERATURE, TRANSMISSION IN NEUTRAL AND ACCESSORIES OFF.

IGNITION TIMING-
(1) TURN OFF ENGINE
(2) DISCONNECT THE IN-LINE SPOUT CONNECTOR (-◯◯- OR -◯◁).
(3) RE-START PREVIOUSLY WARMED-UP ENGINE.
(4) ADJUST IGNITION TIMING TO 10° BTDC OR △.
(5) TURN OFF ENGINE AND RESTORE ELECTRICAL CONNECTION.

THIS ENGINE IS EQUIPPED WITH AUTOMATIC IDLE SPEED CONTROL. IDLE RPM IS NOT ADJUSTABLE. IF NOT WITHIN SPECIFIED RPM RANGE, SEE SHOP MANUAL:
  MANUAL TRANS. IN NEUTRAL - 835 - 885 RPM
  AUTO. TRANS. IN DRIVE - 665 - 715 RPM

USE SAE 5W-30 OIL - API CATEGORY SF, SF/CC OR SF/CD.

THIS VEHICLE CONFORMS TO U.S. EPA AND CALIFORNIA REGULATIONS APPLICABLE TO 1987 MODEL YEAR NEW MOTOR VEHICLES INTRODUCED INTO COMMERCE SOLELY FOR SALE IN CALIFORNIA.

E7AE-9C485- **CCL** **CATALYST** SPARK PLUG: AWSF-32C GAP- .042 - .046
2.3L - 7FM
HFM2.5V5HCH9 - EGR/EOS/AIV/TWC/FI

VACUUM HOSE ROUTING

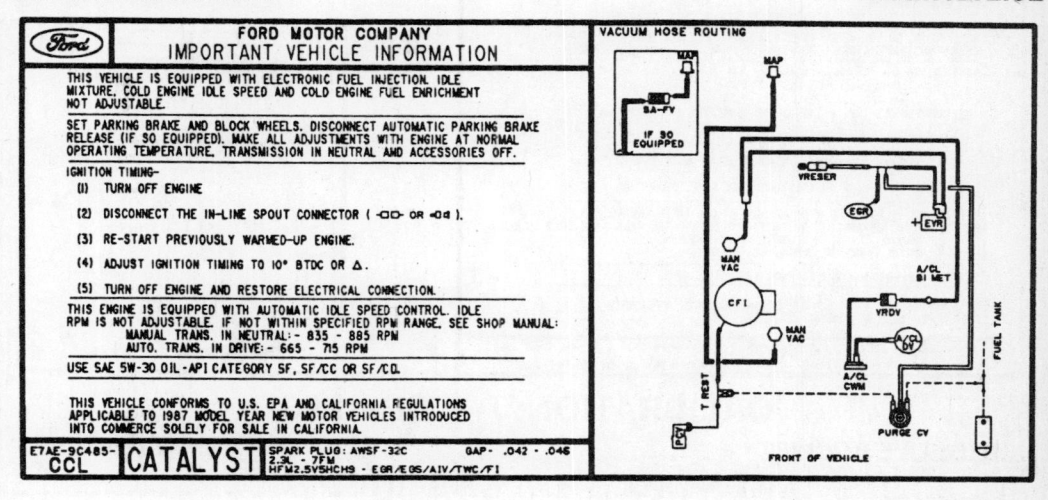

CALIBRATION: 7—25Q—R10

MODEL YEAR: 1987 **ENGINE: 2.3L**

FORD MOTOR COMPANY — IMPORTANT VEHICLE INFORMATION

THIS VEHICLE IS EQUIPPED WITH ELECTRONIC FUEL INJECTION. IDLE MIXTURE, COLD ENGINE IDLE SPEED AND COLD ENGINE FUEL ENRICHMENT NOT ADJUSTABLE.

SET PARKING BRAKE AND BLOCK WHEELS. DISCONNECT AUTOMATIC PARKING BRAKE RELEASE (IF SO EQUIPPED). MAKE ALL ADJUSTMENTS WITH ENGINE AT NORMAL OPERATING TEMPERATURE, TRANSMISSION IN NEUTRAL AND ACCESSORIES OFF.

IGNITION TIMING-
(1) TURN OFF ENGINE
(2) DISCONNECT THE IN-LINE SPOUT CONNECTOR (-◯◯- OR -◯◁).
(3) RE-START PREVIOUSLY WARMED-UP ENGINE.
(4) ADJUST IGNITION TIMING TO 10° BTDC OR △.
(5) TURN OFF ENGINE AND RESTORE ELECTRICAL CONNECTION.

THIS ENGINE IS EQUIPPED WITH AUTOMATIC IDLE SPEED CONTROL. IDLE RPM IS NOT ADJUSTABLE. IF NOT WITHIN SPECIFIED RPM RANGE, SEE SHOP MANUAL:
  MANUAL TRANS. IN NEUTRAL - 835 - 885 RPM
  AUTO. TRANS. IN DRIVE - 665 - 715 RPM

USE SAE 5W-30 OIL - API CATEGORY SF, SF/CC OR SF/CD.

THIS VEHICLE CONFORMS TO U.S. EPA AND CALIFORNIA REGULATIONS APPLICABLE TO 1987 MODEL YEAR NEW MOTOR VEHICLES INTRODUCED INTO COMMERCE SOLELY FOR SALE IN CALIFORNIA.

E7AE-9C485- **CDU** **CATALYST** SPARK PLUG: AWSF-52 GAP- .042 - .046
2.3L - 7FM
HFM2.5V5HCH9 - EGR/EOS/AIV/TWC/FI

VACUUM HOSE ROUTING

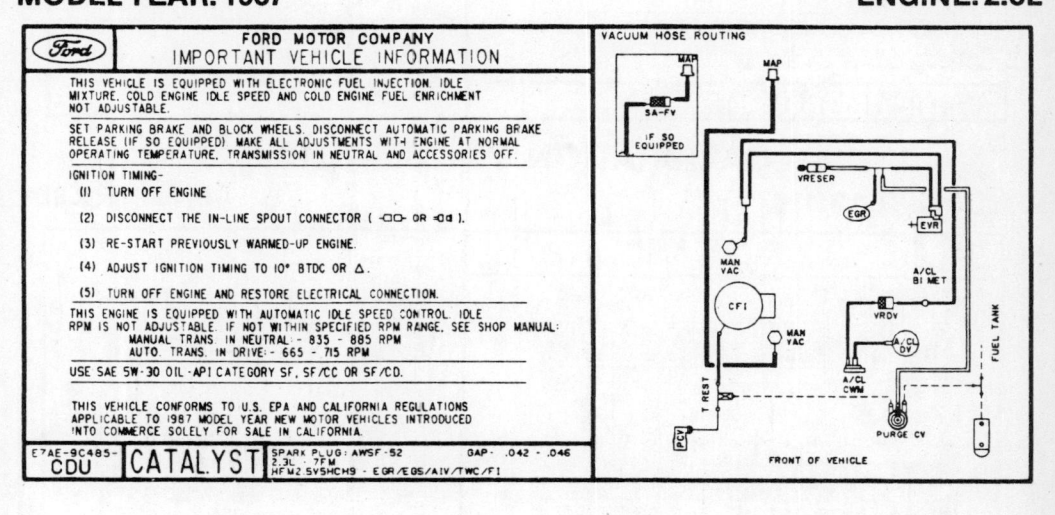

EMISSION CONTROLS

CALIBRATION: 7—26D—R00

MODEL YEAR: 1987 **ENGINE: 2.3L**

```
FORD MOTOR COMPANY
IMPORTANT VEHICLE INFORMATION

THIS VEHICLE IS EQUIPPED WITH ELECTRONIC FUEL INJECTION. IDLE
MIXTURE, COLD ENGINE IDLE SPEED AND COLD ENGINE FUEL ENRICHMENT
NOT ADJUSTABLE.

SET PARKING BRAKE AND BLOCK WHEELS. DISCONNECT AUTOMATIC PARKING BRAKE
RELEASE (IF SO EQUIPPED). MAKE ALL ADJUSTMENTS WITH ENGINE AT NORMAL
OPERATING TEMPERATURE, TRANSMISSION IN NEUTRAL AND ACCESSORIES OFF.

IGNITION TIMING-
  (1) TURN OFF ENGINE
  (2) DISCONNECT THE IN-LINE SPOUT CONNECTOR ( -CD- OR -Cd ).
  (3) RE-START PREVIOUSLY WARMED-UP ENGINE.
  (4) ADJUST IGNITION TIMING TO 10° BTDC OR Δ.
  (5) TURN OFF ENGINE AND RESTORE ELECTRICAL CONNECTION.

THIS ENGINE IS EQUIPPED WITH AUTOMATIC IDLE SPEED CONTROL. IDLE
RPM IS NOT ADJUSTABLE. IF NOT WITHIN SPECIFIED RPM RANGE, SEE SHOP MANUAL:
         MANUAL TRANS. IN NEUTRAL:- 835-885 RPM
         AUTO. TRANS. IN DRIVE - 665-715 RPM

USE SAE 5W-30 OIL - API CATEGORY SF, SF/CC OR SF/CD.

THIS VEHICLE CONFORMS TO U.S. EPA REGULATIONS APPLICABLE TO
1987 MODEL YEAR NEW MOTOR VEHICLES.

E7AE-9C485-  CATALYST   SPARK PLUG: AWSF-32C    GAP- .042-.046
    CCJ                 2.3L - 7FM
                        HFM2.5V5HCF7 - EGR/EGS/AIV/TWC/FI
```

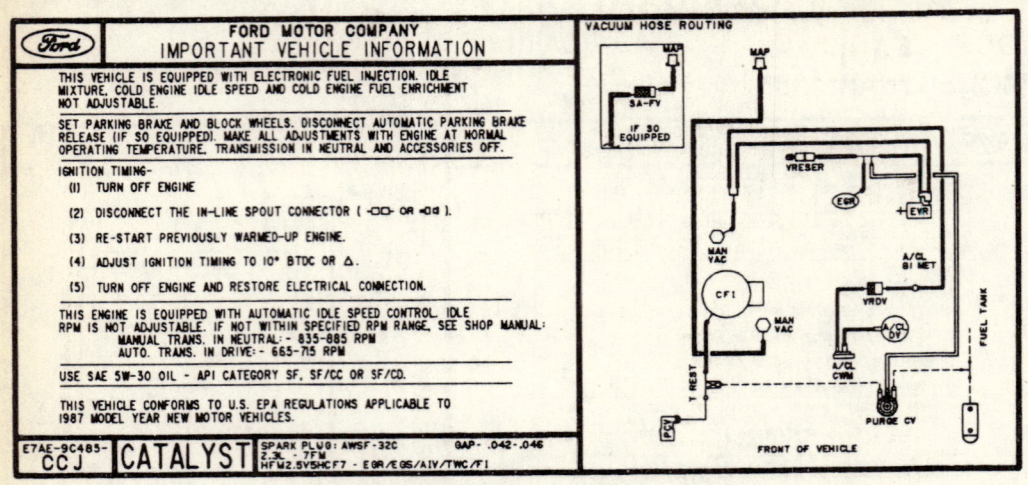

CALIBRATION: 7—26E—R00

MODEL YEAR: 1987 **ENGINE: 2.3L**

```
FORD MOTOR COMPANY
IMPORTANT VEHICLE INFORMATION

THIS VEHICLE IS EQUIPPED WITH ELECTRONIC FUEL INJECTION. IDLE
MIXTURE, COLD ENGINE IDLE SPEED AND COLD ENGINE FUEL ENRICHMENT
NOT ADJUSTABLE.

SET PARKING BRAKE AND BLOCK WHEELS. DISCONNECT AUTOMATIC PARKING BRAKE
RELEASE (IF SO EQUIPPED). MAKE ALL ADJUSTMENTS WITH ENGINE AT NORMAL
OPERATING TEMPERATURE, TRANSMISSION IN NEUTRAL AND ACCESSORIES OFF.

IGNITION TIMING-
  (1) TURN OFF ENGINE
  (2) DISCONNECT THE IN-LINE SPOUT CONNECTOR ( -CD- OR -Cd ).
  (3) RE-START PREVIOUSLY WARMED-UP ENGINE.
  (4) ADJUST IGNITION TIMING TO 10° BTDC OR Δ.
  (5) TURN OFF ENGINE AND RESTORE ELECTRICAL CONNECTION.

THIS ENGINE IS EQUIPPED WITH AUTOMATIC IDLE SPEED CONTROL. IDLE
RPM IS NOT ADJUSTABLE. IF NOT WITHIN SPECIFIED RPM RANGE, SEE SHOP MANUAL:
         MANUAL TRANS. IN NEUTRAL:- 835-885 RPM
         AUTO. TRANS. IN DRIVE - 665-715 RPM

USE SAE 5W-30 OIL - API CATEGORY SF, SF/CC OR SF/CD.

THIS VEHICLE CONFORMS TO U.S. EPA REGULATIONS APPLICABLE TO
1987 MODEL YEAR NEW MOTOR VEHICLES.

E7AE-9C485-  CATALYST   SPARK PLUG: AWSF-52     GAP- .042-.046
    CDS                 2.3L - 7FM
                        HFM2.5V5HCF7 - EGR/EGS/AIV/TWC/FI
```

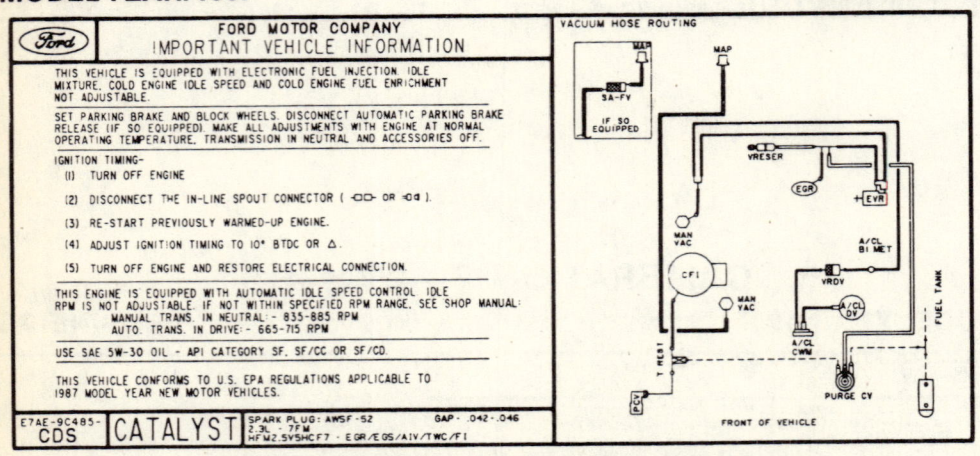

CALIBRATION: 7—26E—R10

MODEL YEAR: 1987 **ENGINE: 2.3L**

```
FORD MOTOR COMPANY
IMPORTANT VEHICLE INFORMATION

THIS VEHICLE IS EQUIPPED WITH ELECTRONIC FUEL INJECTION. IDLE
MIXTURE, COLD ENGINE IDLE SPEED AND COLD ENGINE FUEL ENRICHMENT
NOT ADJUSTABLE.

SET PARKING BRAKE AND BLOCK WHEELS. DISCONNECT AUTOMATIC PARKING BRAKE
RELEASE (IF SO EQUIPPED). MAKE ALL ADJUSTMENTS WITH ENGINE AT NORMAL
OPERATING TEMPERATURE, TRANSMISSION IN NEUTRAL AND ACCESSORIES OFF.

IGNITION TIMING-
  (1) TURN OFF ENGINE
  (2) DISCONNECT THE IN-LINE SPOUT CONNECTOR ( -CD- OR -Cd ).
  (3) RE-START PREVIOUSLY WARMED-UP ENGINE.
  (4) ADJUST IGNITION TIMING TO 10° BTDC OR Δ.
  (5) TURN OFF ENGINE AND RESTORE ELECTRICAL CONNECTION.

THIS ENGINE IS EQUIPPED WITH AUTOMATIC IDLE SPEED CONTROL. IDLE
RPM IS NOT ADJUSTABLE. IF NOT WITHIN SPECIFIED RPM RANGE, SEE SHOP MANUAL:
         MANUAL TRANS. IN NEUTRAL - 835-885 RPM
         AUTO. TRANS. IN DRIVE - 665-715 RPM

USE SAE 5W-30 OIL - API CATEGORY SF, SF/CC OR SF/CD.

THIS VEHICLE CONFORMS TO U.S. EPA REGULATIONS APPLICABLE TO
1987 MODEL YEAR NEW MOTOR VEHICLES.

E7AE-9C485-  CATALYST   SPARK PLUG: AWSF-52     GAP- .042-.046
    CDS                 2.3L - 7FM
                        HFM2.5V5HCF7 - EGR/EGS/AIV/TWC/FI
```

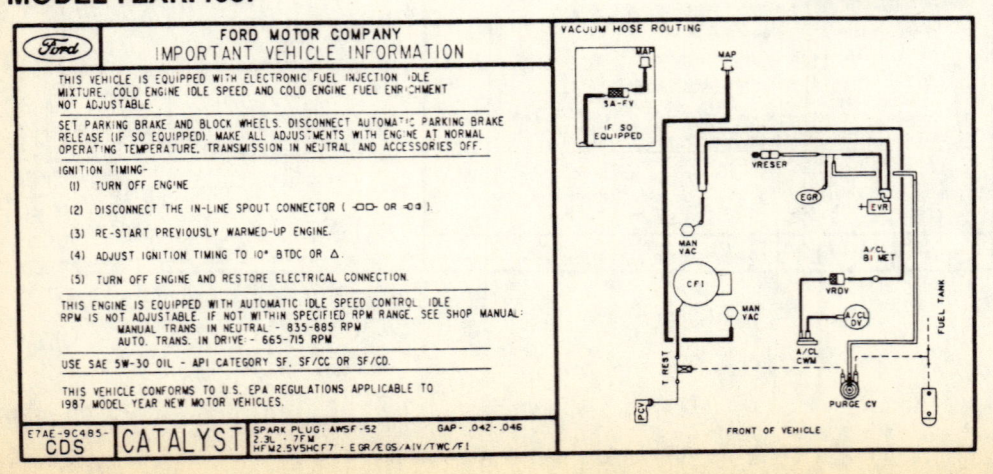

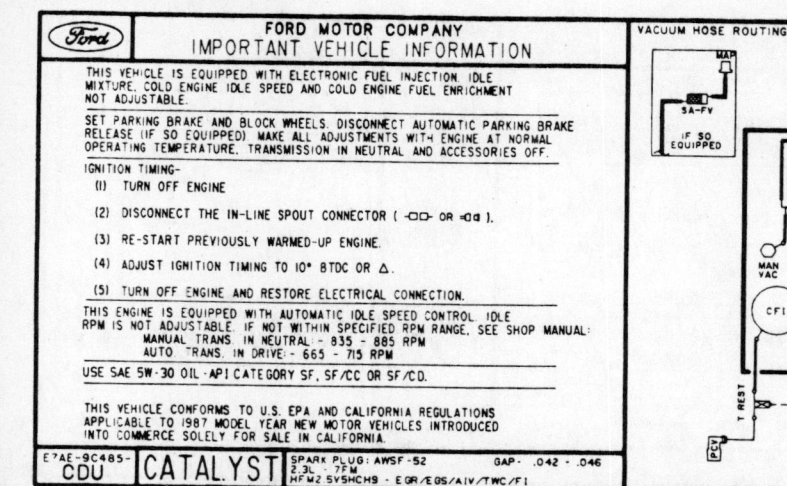

EMISSION CONTROLS

CALIBRATION: 7—26R—R00

MODEL YEAR: 1987 **ENGINE: 2.3L**

FORD MOTOR COMPANY — IMPORTANT VEHICLE INFORMATION

THIS VEHICLE IS EQUIPPED WITH ELECTRONIC FUEL INJECTION. IDLE MIXTURE, COLD ENGINE IDLE SPEED AND COLD ENGINE FUEL ENRICHMENT NOT ADJUSTABLE.

SET PARKING BRAKE AND BLOCK WHEELS. DISCONNECT AUTOMATIC PARKING BRAKE RELEASE (IF SO EQUIPPED). MAKE ALL ADJUSTMENTS WITH ENGINE AT NORMAL OPERATING TEMPERATURE, TRANSMISSION IN NEUTRAL AND ACCESSORIES OFF.

IGNITION TIMING—
(1) TURN OFF ENGINE
(2) DISCONNECT THE IN-LINE SPOUT CONNECTOR (-⊂⊃- OR -◁◁-).
(3) RE-START PREVIOUSLY WARMED-UP ENGINE.
(4) ADJUST IGNITION TIMING TO 10° BTDC OR △.
(5) TURN OFF ENGINE AND RESTORE ELECTRICAL CONNECTION.

THIS ENGINE IS EQUIPPED WITH AUTOMATIC IDLE SPEED CONTROL. IDLE RPM IS NOT ADJUSTABLE. IF NOT WITHIN SPECIFIED RPM RANGE, SEE SHOP MANUAL:
  MANUAL TRANS. IN NEUTRAL: - 835 - 885 RPM
  AUTO. TRANS. IN DRIVE: - 665 - 715 RPM

USE SAE 5W-30 OIL - API CATEGORY SF, SF/CC OR SF/CD.

THIS VEHICLE CONFORMS TO U.S. EPA AND CALIFORNIA REGULATIONS APPLICABLE TO 1987 MODEL YEAR NEW MOTOR VEHICLES INTRODUCED INTO COMMERCE SOLELY FOR SALE IN CALIFORNIA.

E7AE-9C485-CDU CATALYST SPARK PLUG: AWSF-52 GAP: .042 - .046
2.3L - 7FM
HFM2.5V5HCH9 - EGR/EGS/AIV/TWC/FI

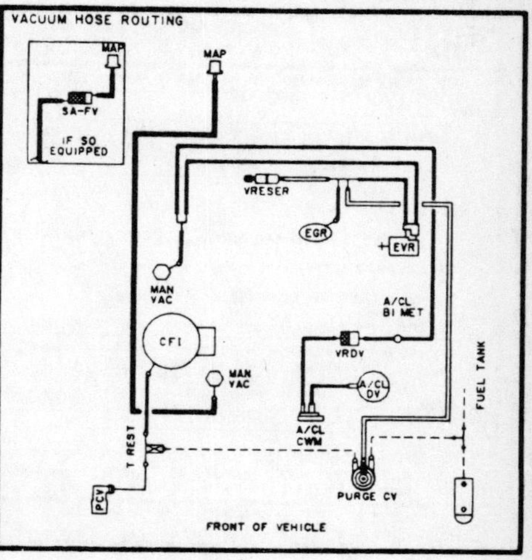

CALIBRATION: 7—26R—R00
(California)

MODEL YEAR: 1987 **ENGINE: 2.3L**

FORD MOTOR COMPANY — IMPORTANT VEHICLE INFORMATION

THIS VEHICLE IS EQUIPPED WITH ELECTRONIC FUEL INJECTION. IDLE MIXTURE, COLD ENGINE IDLE SPEED AND COLD ENGINE FUEL ENRICHMENT NOT ADJUSTABLE.

SET PARKING BRAKE AND BLOCK WHEELS. DISCONNECT AUTOMATIC PARKING BRAKE RELEASE (IF SO EQUIPPED). MAKE ALL ADJUSTMENTS WITH ENGINE AT NORMAL OPERATING TEMPERATURE, TRANSMISSION IN NEUTRAL AND ACCESSORIES OFF.

IGNITION TIMING—
(1) TURN OFF ENGINE
(2) DISCONNECT THE IN-LINE SPOUT CONNECTOR (-⊂⊃- OR -◁◁-).
(3) RE-START PREVIOUSLY WARMED-UP ENGINE.
(4) ADJUST IGNITION TIMING TO 10° BTDC OR △.
(5) TURN OFF ENGINE AND RESTORE ELECTRICAL CONNECTION.

THIS ENGINE IS EQUIPPED WITH AUTOMATIC IDLE SPEED CONTROL. IDLE RPM IS NOT ADJUSTABLE. IF NOT WITHIN SPECIFIED RPM RANGE, SEE SHOP MANUAL:
  MANUAL TRANS. IN NEUTRAL: - 835 - 885 RPM
  AUTO. TRANS. IN DRIVE: - 665 - 715 RPM

USE SAE 5W-30 OIL - API CATEGORY SF, SF/CC OR SF/CD.

THIS VEHICLE CONFORMS TO U.S. EPA AND CALIFORNIA REGULATIONS APPLICABLE TO 1987 MODEL YEAR NEW MOTOR VEHICLES INTRODUCED INTO COMMERCE SOLELY FOR SALE IN CALIFORNIA.

E7AE-9C485-CCL CATALYST SPARK PLUG: AWSF-32C GAP: .042 - .046
2.3 - 7FM
HFM2.5V5HCH9 - EGR/EGS/AIV/TWC/FI

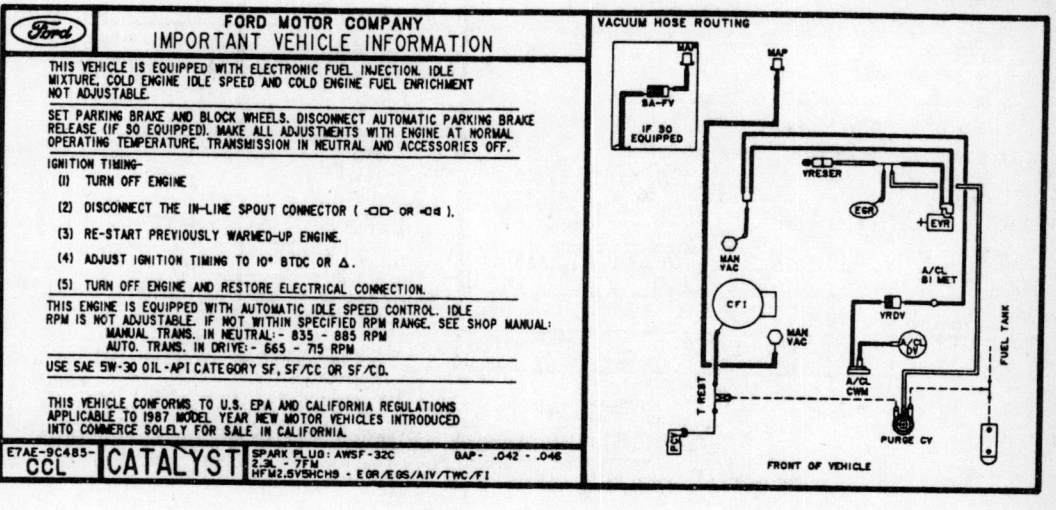

EMISSION CONTROLS

CALIBRATION: 7—26R—R10

MODEL YEAR: 1987 **ENGINE: 2.3L**

FORD MOTOR COMPANY
IMPORTANT VEHICLE INFORMATION

THIS VEHICLE IS EQUIPPED WITH ELECTRONIC FUEL INJECTION. IDLE MIXTURE, COLD ENGINE IDLE SPEED AND COLD ENGINE FUEL ENRICHMENT NOT ADJUSTABLE.

SET PARKING BRAKE AND BLOCK WHEELS. DISCONNECT AUTOMATIC PARKING BRAKE RELEASE (IF SO EQUIPPED). MAKE ALL ADJUSTMENTS WITH ENGINE AT NORMAL OPERATING TEMPERATURE, TRANSMISSION IN NEUTRAL AND ACCESSORIES OFF.

IGNITION TIMING-
(1) TURN OFF ENGINE
(2) DISCONNECT THE IN-LINE SPOUT CONNECTOR (-◻◻- OR -◁◁-).
(3) RE-START PREVIOUSLY WARMED-UP ENGINE.
(4) ADJUST IGNITION TIMING TO 10° BTDC OR Δ.
(5) TURN OFF ENGINE AND RESTORE ELECTRICAL CONNECTION.

THIS ENGINE IS EQUIPPED WITH AUTOMATIC IDLE SPEED CONTROL. IDLE RPM IS NOT ADJUSTABLE. IF NOT WITHIN SPECIFIED RPM RANGE, SEE SHOP MANUAL:
    MANUAL TRANS. IN NEUTRAL:- 835 - 885 RPM
    AUTO. TRANS. IN DRIVE:- 665 - 715 RPM

USE SAE 5W-30 OIL- API CATEGORY SF, SF/CC OR SF/CD.

THIS VEHICLE CONFORMS TO U.S. EPA AND CALIFORNIA REGULATIONS APPLICABLE TO 1987 MODEL YEAR NEW MOTOR VEHICLES INTRODUCED INTO COMMERCE SOLELY FOR SALE IN CALIFORNIA.

E7AE-9C485-CDU | CATALYST | SPARK PLUG: AWSF-52 GAP- .042-.046
2.3L - 7FM
HFM2.5V5HCH9 - EGR/EGS/AIV/TWC/FI

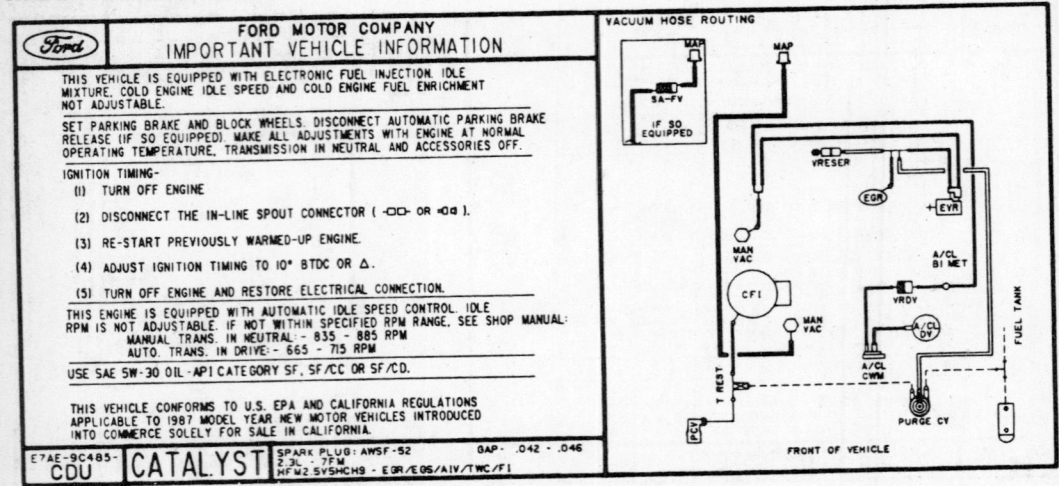

CALIBRATION: 7—26T—R00

MODEL YEAR: 1987 **ENGINE: 2.3L**

FORD MOTOR COMPANY
IMPORTANT VEHICLE INFORMATION

THIS VEHICLE IS EQUIPPED WITH ELECTRONIC FUEL INJECTION. IDLE MIXTURE, COLD ENGINE IDLE SPEED AND COLD ENGINE FUEL ENRICHMENT NOT ADJUSTABLE.

SET PARKING BRAKE AND BLOCK WHEELS. DISCONNECT AUTOMATIC PARKING BRAKE RELEASE (IF SO EQUIPPED). MAKE ALL ADJUSTMENTS WITH ENGINE AT NORMAL OPERATING TEMPERATURE, TRANSMISSION IN NEUTRAL AND ACCESSORIES OFF.

IGNITION TIMING-
(1) TURN OFF ENGINE
(2) DISCONNECT THE IN-LINE SPOUT CONNECTOR (-◻◻- OR -◁◁-).
(3) RE-START PREVIOUSLY WARMED-UP ENGINE.
(4) ADJUST IGNITION TIMING TO 10° BTDC OR Δ.
(5) TURN OFF ENGINE AND RESTORE ELECTRICAL CONNECTION.

THIS ENGINE IS EQUIPPED WITH AUTOMATIC IDLE SPEED CONTROL. IDLE RPM IS NOT ADJUSTABLE. IF NOT WITHIN SPECIFIED RPM RANGE, SEE SHOP MANUAL:
    MANUAL TRANS. IN NEUTRAL:- 835 - 885 RPM
    AUTO. TRANS. IN DRIVE:- 665 - 715 RPM

USE SAE 5W-30 OIL- API CATEGORY SF, SF/CC OR SF/CD.

THIS VEHICLE CONFORMS TO U.S. EPA AND CALIFORNIA REGULATIONS APPLICABLE TO 1987 MODEL YEAR NEW MOTOR VEHICLES INTRODUCED INTO COMMERCE SOLELY FOR SALE IN CALIFORNIA.

E7AE-9C485-CCL | CATALYST | SPARK PLUG: AWSF-32C GAP- .042-.046
2.3L - 7FM
HFM2.5V5HCH9 - EGR/EGS/AIV/TWC/FI

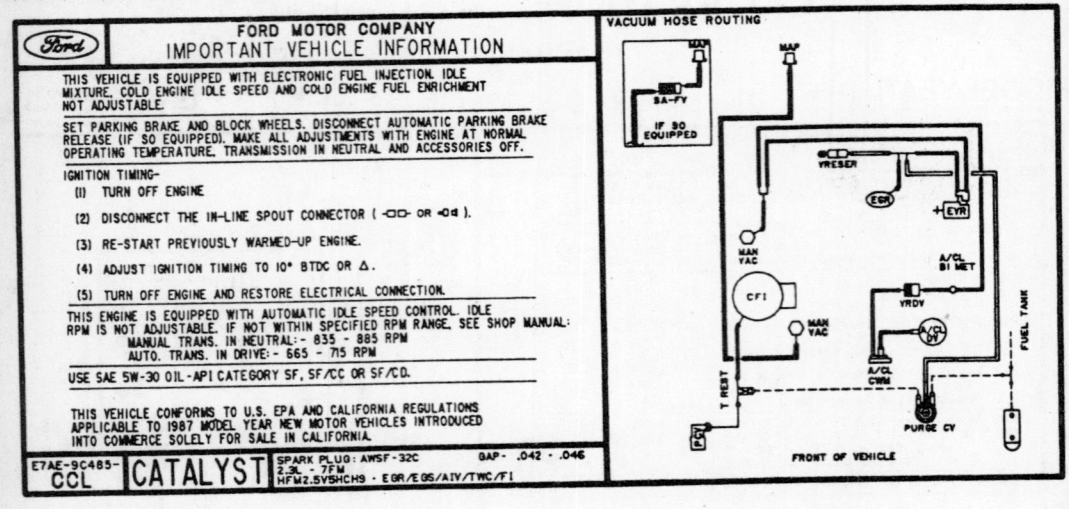

EMISSION CONTROLS 311

CALIBRATION: 7—19B—R00

MODEL YEAR: 1987 **ENGINE: 2.5L**

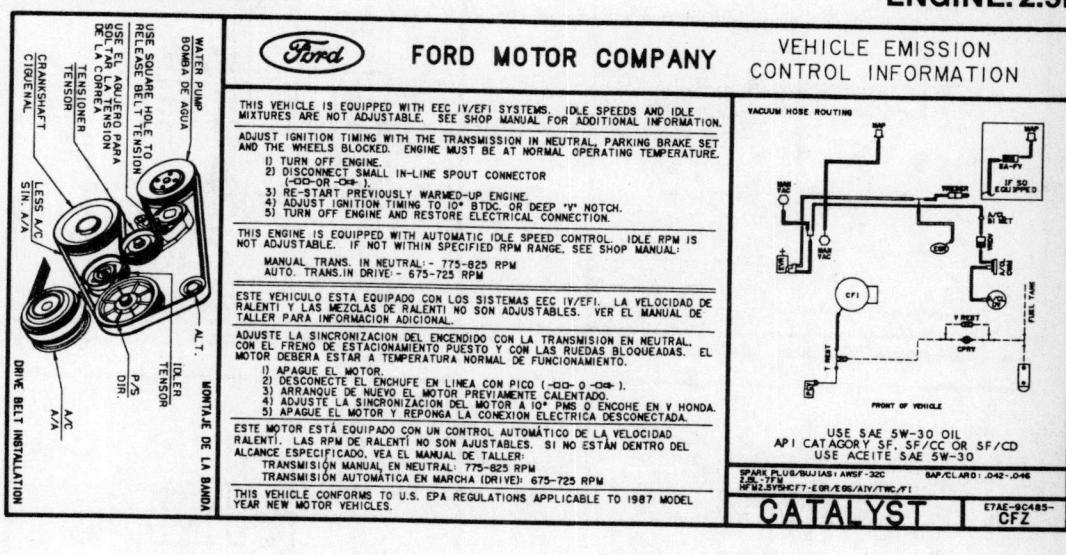

ENGINE: 1.9L

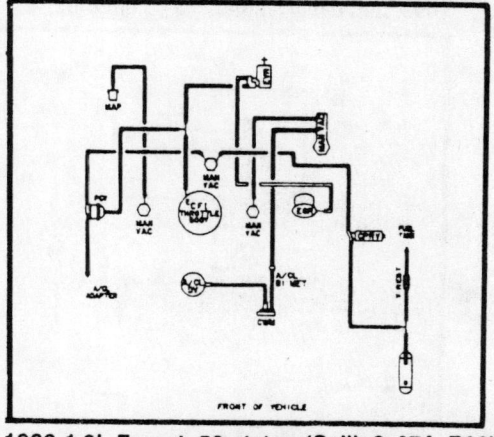

1988 1.9L Escort, 50 states (Calib.8–07A–R00)

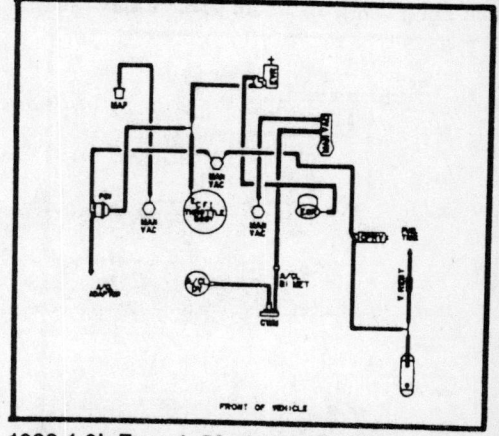

1988 1.9L Escort, 50 states (Calib.8–07A–R11)

312 EMISSION CONTROLS

ENGINE: 1.9L

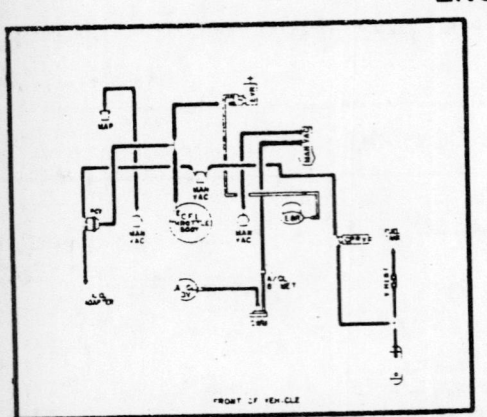

1988 1.9L Escort, 50 states (Calib.8–07F–R00)

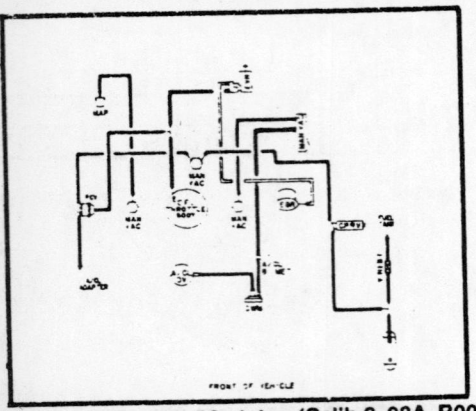

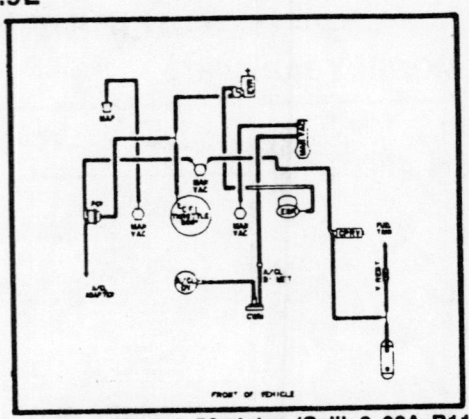

1988 1.9L Escort, 50 states (Calib.8–08A–R11)

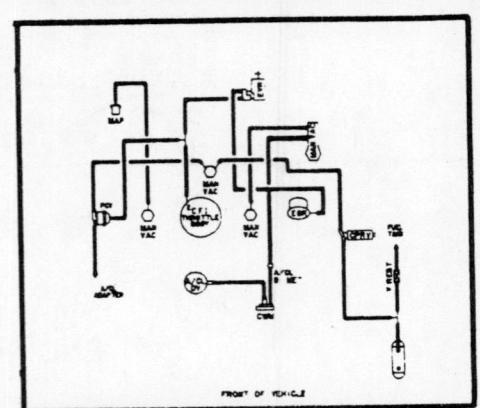

1988 1.9L Escort, 50 states (Calib.8–08A–R00)

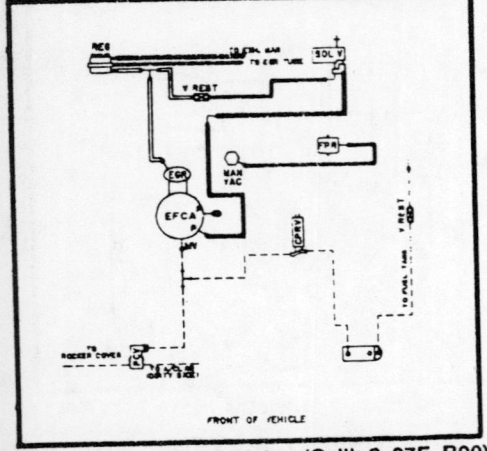

1988 1.9L Escort, 50 states (Calib.8–07F–R11)

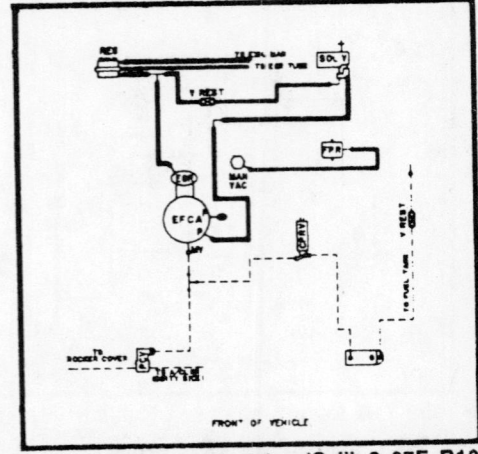

1988 1.9L Escort, 50 states (Calib.8–07E–R00)

1988 1.9L Escort, 50 states (Calib.8–07E–R10)

EMISSION CONTROLS

ENGINE: 2.3L

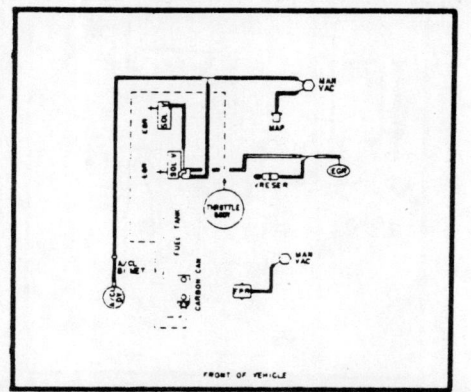

1988 2.3L Mustang, 50 States (Calib.7–05A–R11)

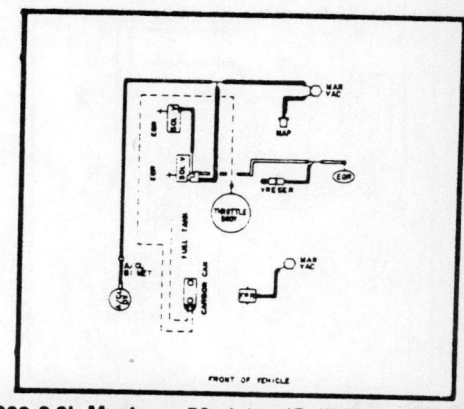

1988 2.3L Mustang, 50 states (Calib.8–05A–R10)

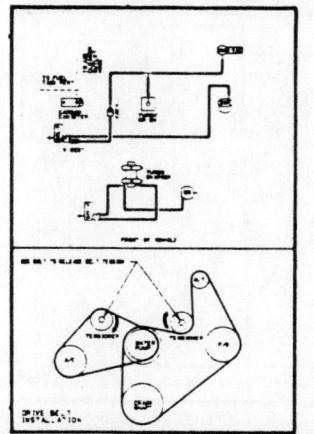

1988 2.3L Thunderbird, 50 states (Calib.705E–R10)

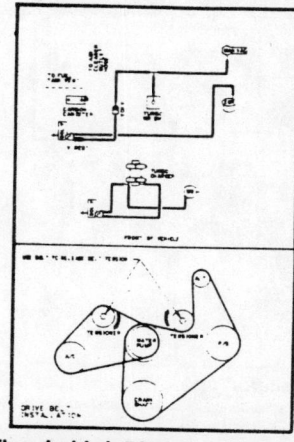

1988 2.3L Thunderbird, 50 states (Calib.7–06E–R11)

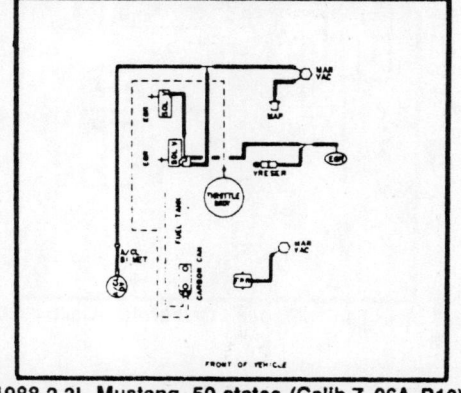

1988 2.3L Mustang, 50 states (Calib.7–06A–R10)

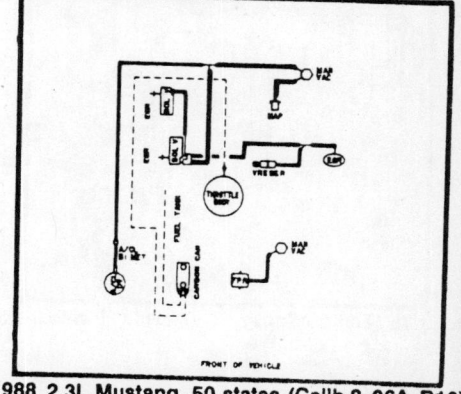

1988 2.3L Mustang, 50 states (Calib.8–06A–R10)

EMISSION CONTROLS

ENGINE: 2.3L

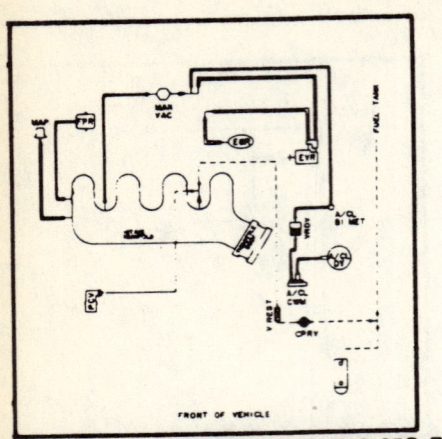

1988 2.3L Tempo/Topaz, 50 states (Calib.8-25C-R00)

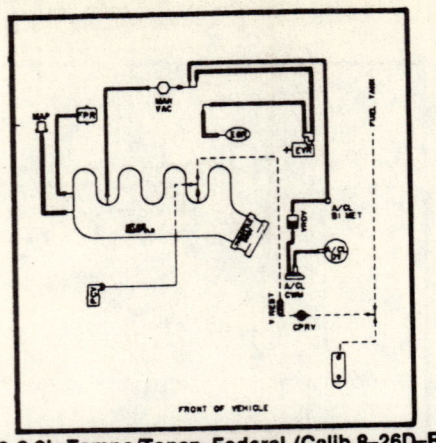

1988 2.3L Tempo/Topaz, Federal (Calib.8-26D-R10)

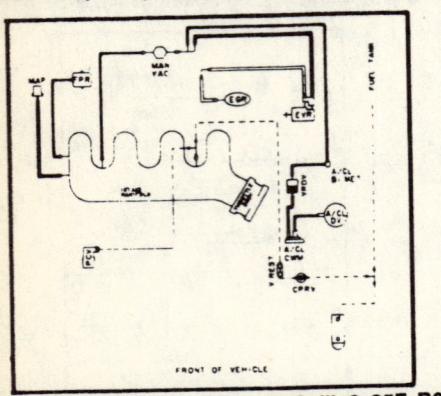

1988 2.3L Tempo/Topaz, Federal (Calib.8-25F-R00)

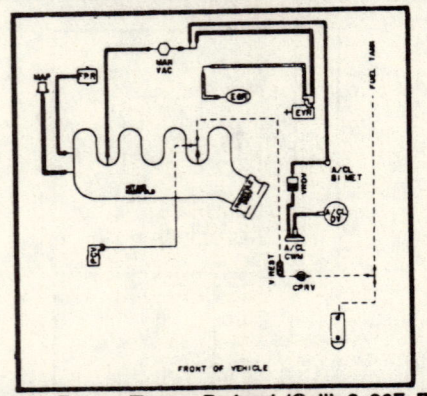

1988 2.3L Tempo/Topaz, Federal (Calib.8-26E-R00)

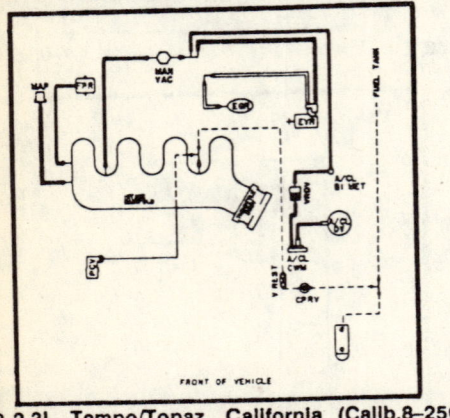

1988 2.3L Tempo/Topaz, California (Calib.8-25Q-R00)

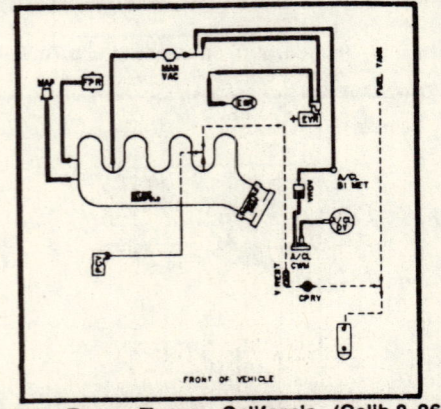

1988 2.3L Tempo/Topaz, California (Calib.8-26R-R00)

EMISSION CONTROLS 315

FORD MOTOR COMPANY
VEHICLE EMISSION CONTROL INFORMATION

THIS VEHICLE IS EQUIPPED WITH ELECTRONIC FUEL INJECTION. IDLE MIXTURE, COLD ENGINE IDLE SPEED AND COLD ENGINE FUEL ENRICHMENT ARE NOT ADJUSTABLE.

SET PARKING BRAKE AND BLOCK WHEELS. MAKE ALL ADJUSTMENTS WITH ENGINE AT NORMAL OPERATING TEMPERATURE, TRANSMISSION IN NEUTRAL AND ACCESSORIES OFF.

IGNITION TIMING -
1) TURN OFF ENGINE.
2) DISCONNECT THE IN-LINE SPOUT CONNECTOR (◁◁).
3) RE-START PREVIOUSLY WARMED-UP ENGINE.
4) ADJUST IGNITION TIMING TO 10° BTDC.
5) TURN OFF ENGINE AND RESTORE ELECTRICAL CONNECTION.

THROTTLE PLATE ADJUSTMENT -
1) ELECTRICALLY DISCONNECT THROTTLE AIR BYPASS VALVE.
2) RUN ENGINE AT 2000 RPM FOR 60 SECONDS MINIMUM.
3) RETURN TO IDLE AND TURN THROTTLE PLATE ADJUSTING SCREW UNTIL IDLE SPEED IS 930 RPM WITH THE FAN OFF. 1850 RPM FOR VEHICLE WITH LESS THAN 100 MILES. ADJUSTMENT MUST BE MADE WITHIN 120 SECONDS OF RETURN TO IDLE. TURN OFF ENGINE, RESTART AND REPEAT STEP 2 AND 3 IF 120 SECONDS ARE EXCEEDED.
4) RESTORE ELECTRICAL CONNECTION.
5) RESULTANT IDLE SPEED IS 1000 ± 100 RPM.

USE SAE 5W-30 OIL-API CATEGORY SG, SG/CC OR SG/CD.

THIS VEHICLE CONFORMS TO U.S. EPA AND CALIFORNIA REGULATIONS APPLICABLE TO 1989 MODEL YEAR NEW MOTOR VEHICLES.

E9AE-9C485-   CATALYST   SPARK PLUG: AGSF-24C   GAP: .042-.046
1.9L-9HW
KFM1.9V5HMK4 - EOR/EOS/AIV/TWC/FI

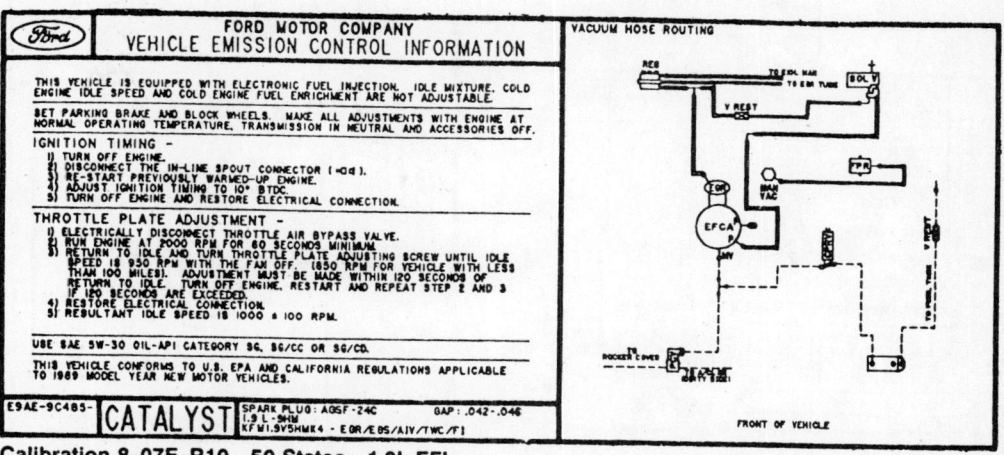

Calibration 8-07E-R10   50 States   1.9L EFI

FORD MOTOR COMPANY
VEHICLE EMISSION CONTROL INFORMATION

THIS VEHICLE IS EQUIPPED WITH ELECTRONIC FUEL INJECTION. IDLE MIXTURE, COLD ENGINE IDLE SPEED AND COLD ENGINE FUEL ENRICHMENT NOT ADJUSTABLE.

SET PARKING BRAKE AND BLOCK WHEELS. MAKE ALL ADJUSTMENTS WITH ENGINE AT NORMAL OPERATING TEMPERATURE, TRANSMISSION IN NEUTRAL AND ACCESSORIES OFF.

IGNITION TIMING - ELECTRONICALLY ADJUSTED AT THE FACTORY. ADJUSTMENT REQUIRED ONLY IF DISTRIBUTOR HAS BEEN DISTURBED.
(1) TURN OFF ENGINE.
(2) DISCONNECT THE IN-LINE SPOUT CONNECTOR (◁◁).
(3) RE-START PREVIOUSLY WARMED-UP ENGINE.
(4) ADJUST IGNITION TIMING TO 10° BTDC.
(5) TURN OFF ENGINE AND RESTORE ELECTRICAL CONNECTION.

THIS ENGINE IS EQUIPPED WITH AUTOMATIC IDLE SPEED CONTROL. IDLE RPM IS NOT ADJUSTABLE. IF NOT WITHIN SPECIFIED RPM RANGE, SEE SHOP MANUAL:
MANUAL TRANS. IN NEUTRAL: 760-840 RPM

USE SAE 5W-30 OIL - API CATEGORY SG, SG/CC OR SG/CD.

THIS VEHICLE CONFORMS TO U.S. EPA REGULATIONS APPLICABLE TO 1989 MODEL YEAR NEW MOTOR VEHICLES. COMPLIANCE DEMONSTRATED AND DESIGNED FOR PRINCIPAL USE BELOW 4000 FEET. THIS VEHICLE IS EXEMPT FROM MEETING EMISSIONS STANDARDS ABOVE 4000 FEET BECAUSE OF POSSIBLY UNSUITABLE PERFORMANCE, AND THE EMISSIONS PERFORMANCE WARRANTY DOES NOT APPLY ABOVE 4000 FEET.

E9AE-9C485-   CATALYST   SPARK PLUG: AGSF-34C   GAP: .042-.046
1.9L-9FM
KFM1.9V5FFF6 - EOS/EGR/TWC/FI

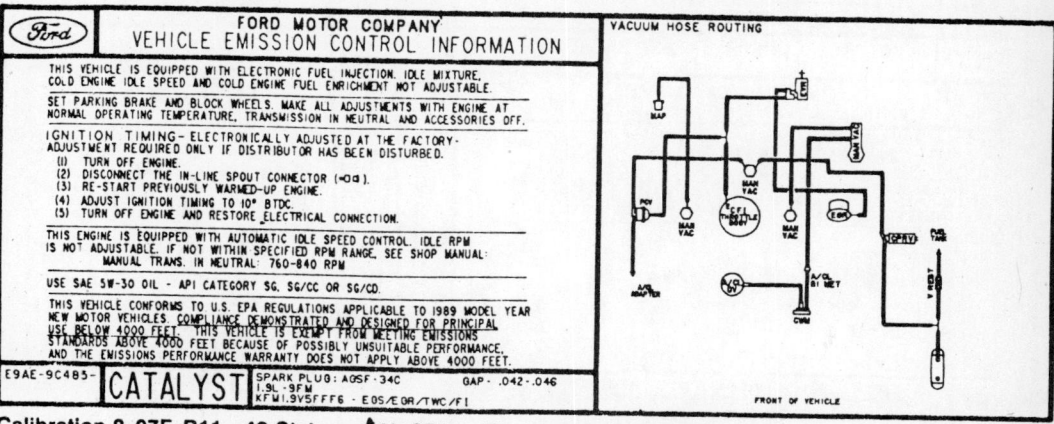

Calibration 8-07F-R11   49 States   1.9L CFI   For use under 4,000 ft. only

---

FORD MOTOR COMPANY
VEHICLE EMISSION CONTROL INFORMATION

THIS VEHICLE IS EQUIPPED WITH ELECTRONIC FUEL INJECTION. IDLE MIXTURE, COLD ENGINE IDLE SPEED AND COLD ENGINE FUEL ENRICHMENT NOT ADJUSTABLE.

SET PARKING BRAKE AND BLOCK WHEELS. MAKE ALL ADJUSTMENTS WITH ENGINE AT NORMAL OPERATING TEMPERATURE, TRANSMISSION IN NEUTRAL AND ACCESSORIES OFF.

IGNITION TIMING - ELECTRONICALLY ADJUSTED AT THE FACTORY. ADJUSTMENT REQUIRED ONLY IF DISTRIBUTOR HAS BEEN DISTURBED.
(1) TURN OFF ENGINE.
(2) DISCONNECT THE IN-LINE SPOUT CONNECTOR (◁◁).
(3) RE-START PREVIOUSLY WARMED-UP ENGINE.
(4) ADJUST IGNITION TIMING TO 10° BTDC.
(5) TURN OFF ENGINE AND RESTORE ELECTRICAL CONNECTION.

THIS ENGINE IS EQUIPPED WITH AUTOMATIC IDLE SPEED CONTROL. IDLE RPM IS NOT ADJUSTABLE. IF NOT WITHIN SPECIFIED RPM RANGE, SEE SHOP MANUAL:
MANUAL TRANS. IN NEUTRAL: 760-840 RPM
AUTO TRANS. IN DRIVE: 760-840 RPM

USE SAE 5W-30 OIL - API CATEGORY SG, SG/CC OR SG/CD.

THIS VEHICLE CONFORMS TO U.S. EPA REGULATIONS APPLICABLE TO 1989 MODEL YEAR NEW MOTOR VEHICLES.

E9AE-9C485-   CATALYST   SPARK PLUG: AGSF-34C   GAP: .042-.046
1.9L-9FM
KFM1.9V5FFF6 - EOS/EGR/TWC/FI

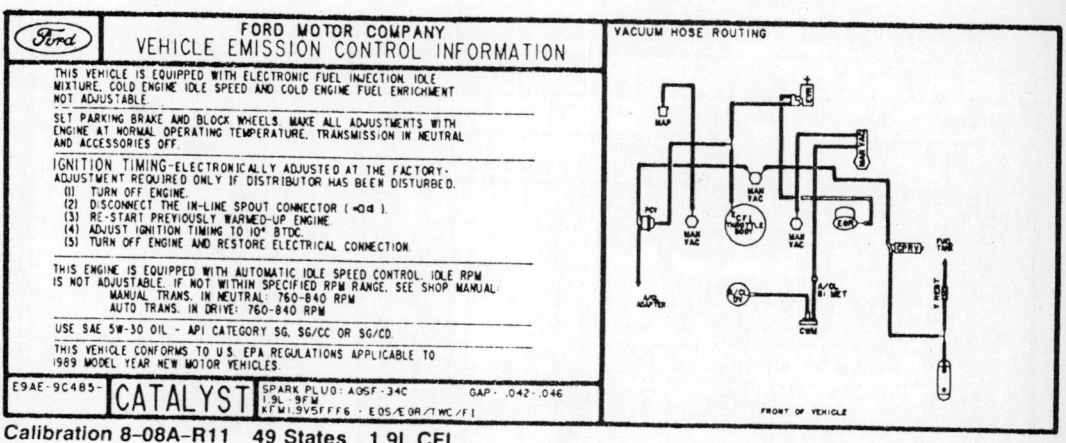

Calibration 8-08A-R11   49 States   1.9L CFI

EMISSION CONTROLS

FORD MOTOR COMPANY — VEHICLE EMISSION CONTROL INFORMATION

THIS VEHICLE IS EQUIPPED WITH ELECTRONIC FUEL INJECTION. IDLE MIXTURE, COLD ENGINE IDLE SPEED AND COLD ENGINE FUEL ENRICHMENT NOT ADJUSTABLE.

SET PARKING BRAKE AND BLOCK WHEELS. DISCONNECT AUTOMATIC PARKING BRAKE RELEASE (IF SO EQUIPPED). MAKE ALL ADJUSTMENTS WITH ENGINE AT NORMAL OPERATING TEMPERATURE, TRANSMISSION IN NEUTRAL AND ACCESSORIES OFF.

IGNITION TIMING-
(1) TURN OFF ENGINE
(2) DISCONNECT THE IN-LINE SPOUT CONNECTOR (◁◁).
(3) RE-START PREVIOUSLY WARMED-UP ENGINE.
(4) ADJUST IGNITION TIMING TO 15° BTDC OR D.
(5) TURN OFF ENGINE AND RESTORE ELECTRICAL CONNECTION.

THIS ENGINE IS EQUIPPED WITH AUTOMATIC IDLE SPEED CONTROL. IDLE RPM IS NOT ADJUSTABLE. IF NOT WITHIN SPECIFIED RPM RANGE, SEE SHOP MANUAL.
    MANUAL TRANS. IN NEUTRAL: 820-880 RPM
    AUTO. TRANS. IN DRIVE: 690-750 RPM

USE SAE 5W-30 OIL - API CATEGORY SG, SG/CC OR SG/CD.

THIS VEHICLE CONFORMS TO U.S. EPA REGULATIONS APPLICABLE TO 1989 MODEL YEAR NEW MOTOR VEHICLES.

E9AE-9C485-   CATALYST   SPARK PLUG: AWSF-42C   GAP: .052-.056
2.3L-9HM
KFW2.3V5HEF4 - EOS/EGR/AIV/FI/TWC

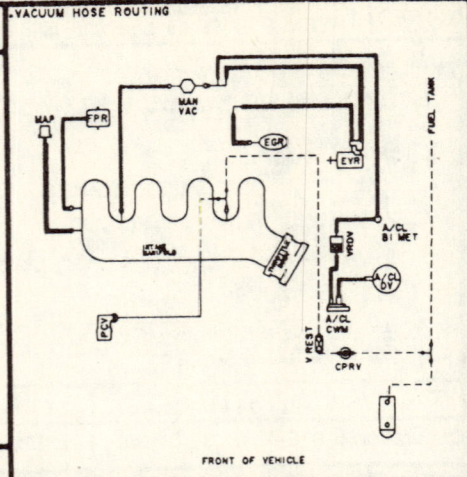

Calibration 8-26E-R00   49 States   2.3L HSC/EFI

FORD MOTOR COMPANY — VEHICLE EMISSION CONTROL INFORMATION

THIS VEHICLE IS EQUIPPED WITH ELECTRONIC FUEL INJECTION. IDLE MIXTURE, COLD ENGINE IDLE SPEED AND COLD ENGINE FUEL ENRICHMENT NOT ADJUSTABLE.

SET PARKING BRAKE AND BLOCK WHEELS. DISCONNECT AUTOMATIC PARKING BRAKE RELEASE (IF SO EQUIPPED). MAKE ALL ADJUSTMENTS WITH ENGINE AT NORMAL OPERATING TEMPERATURE, TRANSMISSION IN NEUTRAL AND ACCESSORIES OFF.

IGNITION TIMING-
(1) TURN OFF ENGINE
(2) DISCONNECT THE IN-LINE SPOUT CONNECTOR (◁◁).
(3) RE-START PREVIOUSLY WARMED-UP ENGINE.
(4) ADJUST IGNITION TIMING TO 15° BTDC OR D.
(5) TURN OFF ENGINE AND RESTORE ELECTRICAL CONNECTION.

THIS ENGINE IS EQUIPPED WITH AUTOMATIC IDLE SPEED CONTROL. IDLE RPM IS NOT ADJUSTABLE. IF NOT WITHIN SPECIFIED RPM RANGE, SEE SHOP MANUAL.
    MANUAL TRANS. IN NEUTRAL: 820-880 RPM
    AUTO. TRANS. IN DRIVE: 690-750 RPM

USE SAE 5W-30 OIL - API CATEGORY SG, SG/CC OR SG/CD.

THIS VEHICLE CONFORMS TO U.S. EPA REGULATIONS APPLICABLE TO 1989 MODEL YEAR NEW MOTOR VEHICLES.

E9AE-9C485-   CATALYST   SPARK PLUG: AWSF-42C   GAP: .052-.056
2.3L-9HM
KFW2.3V5HEF4 - EOS/EGR/AIV/FI/TWC

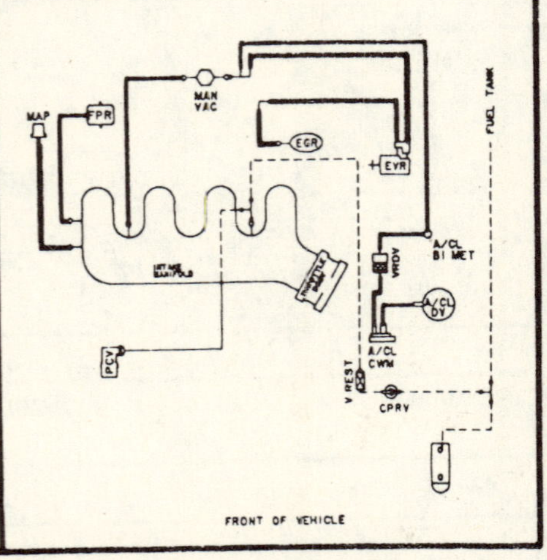

Calibration 8-25F-R00   49 States   2.3L HSC/EFI

FORD MOTOR COMPANY — VEHICLE EMISSION CONTROL INFORMATION

THIS VEHICLE IS EQUIPPED WITH ELECTRONIC FUEL INJECTION. IDLE MIXTURE, COLD ENGINE IDLE SPEED AND COLD ENGINE FUEL ENRICHMENT NOT ADJUSTABLE.

SET PARKING BRAKE AND BLOCK WHEELS. MAKE ALL ADJUSTMENTS WITH ENGINE AT NORMAL OPERATING TEMPERATURE, TRANSMISSION IN NEUTRAL AND ACCESSORIES OFF.

IGNITION TIMING- ELECTRONICALLY ADJUSTED AT THE FACTORY- ADJUSTMENT REQUIRED ONLY IF DISTRIBUTOR HAS BEEN DISTURBED.
(1) TURN OFF ENGINE.
(2) DISCONNECT THE IN-LINE SPOUT CONNECTOR (◁◁).
(3) RE-START PREVIOUSLY WARMED-UP ENGINE.
(4) ADJUST IGNITION TIMING TO 10° BTDC.
(5) TURN OFF ENGINE AND RESTORE ELECTRICAL CONNECTION.

THIS ENGINE IS EQUIPPED WITH AUTOMATIC IDLE SPEED CONTROL. IDLE RPM IS NOT ADJUSTABLE. IF NOT WITHIN SPECIFIED RPM RANGE, SEE SHOP MANUAL.
    MANUAL TRANS. IN NEUTRAL: 760-840 RPM
    AUTO. TRANS. IN DRIVE: 760-840 RPM

USE SAE 5W-30 OIL - API CATEGORY SG, SG/CC OR SG/CD.

THIS VEHICLE CONFORMS TO U.S. EPA REGULATIONS APPLICABLE TO 1989 MODEL YEAR NEW MOTOR VEHICLES.

E9AE-9C485-   CATALYST   SPARK PLUG: AGSF-34C   GAP: .042-.046
1.9L-9FM
KFW1.9V5FFF6 - EOS/EGR/TWC/FI

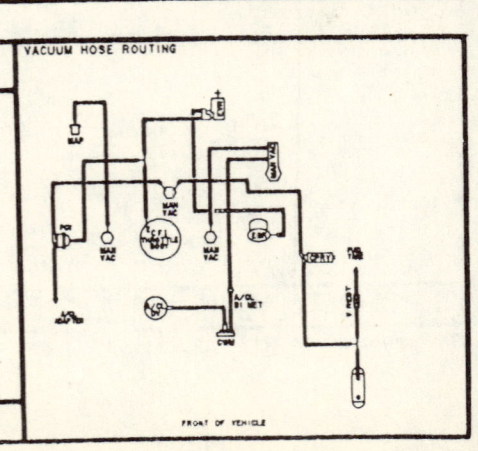

Calibration 8-07A-R11   49 States   1.9L CFI

EMISSION CONTROLS 317

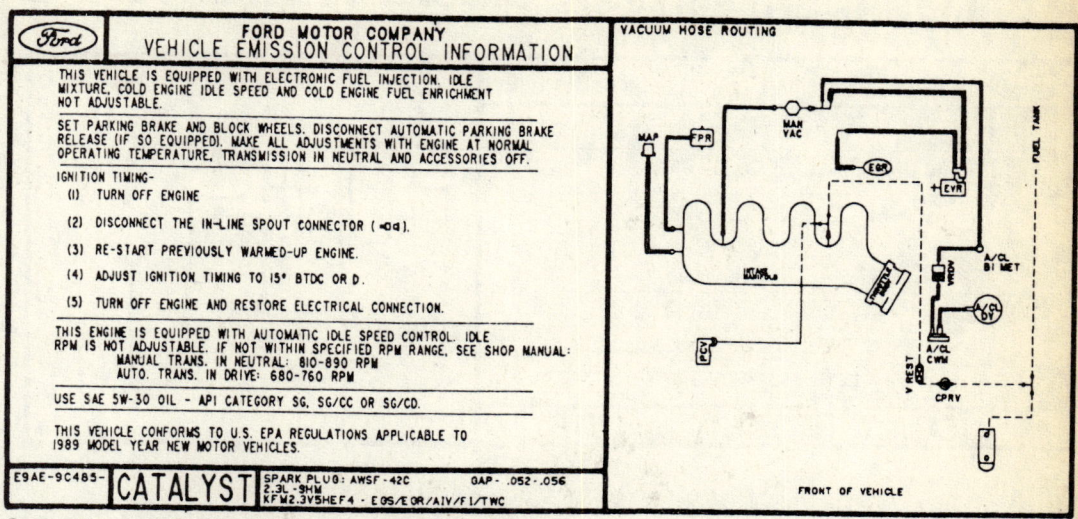

Calibration 8-25C-R00   49 States   2.3L HSC/EFI/HO

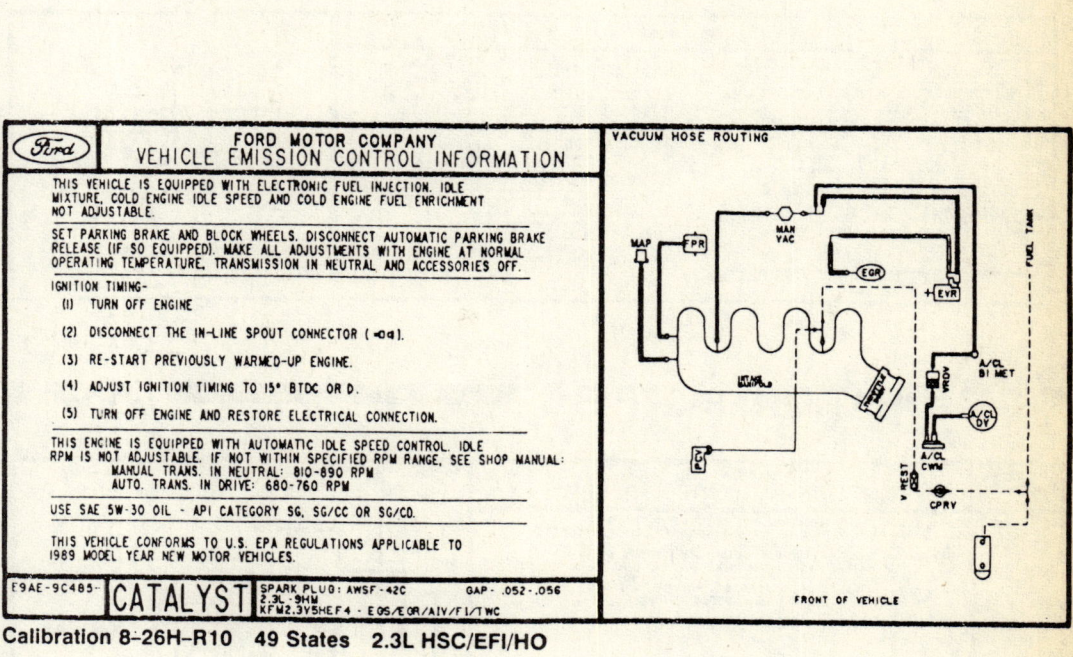

Calibration 8-26H-R10   49 States   2.3L HSC/EFI/HO

EMISSION CONTROLS

■ CALIBRATION: 8-07A-R11   1.9L CFI ■

FORD MOTOR COMPANY — VEHICLE EMISSION CONTROL INFORMATION

THIS VEHICLE IS EQUIPPED WITH ELECTRONIC FUEL INJECTION. IDLE MIXTURE, COLD ENGINE IDLE SPEED AND COLD ENGINE FUEL ENRICHMENT ARE NOT ADJUSTABLE.

SET PARKING BRAKE AND BLOCK WHEELS. MAKE ALL ADJUSTMENTS WITH ENGINE AT NORMAL OPERATING TEMPERATURE, TRANSMISSION IN NEUTRAL AND ACCESSORIES OFF.

IGNITION TIMING — ELECTRONICALLY ADJUSTED AT THE FACTORY — ADJUSTMENT REQUIRED ONLY IF DISTRIBUTOR HAS BEEN DISTURBED.
(1) TURN OFF ENGINE.
(2) DISCONNECT THE IN-LINE SPOUT CONNECTOR (⊐◁d).
(3) RE-START PREVIOUSLY WARMED-UP ENGINE.
(4) ADJUST IGNITION TIMING TO 10° BTDC.
(5) TURN OFF ENGINE AND RESTORE ELECTRICAL CONNECTION.

THIS ENGINE IS EQUIPPED WITH AUTOMATIC IDLE SPEED CONTROL. IDLE RPM IS NOT ADJUSTABLE. IF NOT WITHIN SPECIFIED RPM RANGE, SEE SHOP MANUAL:
   MANUAL TRANS. IN NEUTRAL: 760-840 RPM
   AUTO TRANS. IN DRIVE: 760-840 RPM

USE SAE 5W-30 OIL API SERVICE SG — ENERGY CONSERVING II.

THIS VEHICLE CONFORMS TO U.S. EPA REGULATIONS APPLICABLE TO 1990 MODEL YEAR NEW MOTOR VEHICLES.

CATALYST   SPARK PLUG: AGSF-34C   GAP: .042-.046
            1.9L-9FM
            LFM1.9V5FFD5 — TWC/HO2S/EGR/TBI

VACUUM HOSE ROUTING — FRONT OF VEHICLE

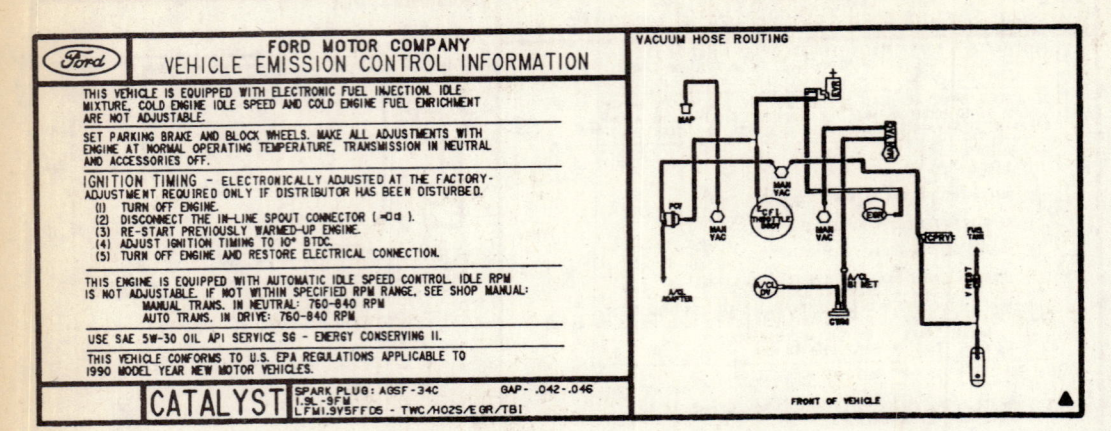

■ CALIBRATION: 8-07A-R11   1.9L CFI ■

VEHICLE EMISSION CONTROL INFORMATION — FORD MOTOR COMPANY — CONTRÔLE DES ÉMISSIONS DU VÉHICULE

THIS VEHICLE IS EQUIPPED WITH ELECTRONIC FUEL INJECTION. IDLE MIXTURE, COLD ENGINE IDLE SPEED AND COLD ENGINE FUEL ENRICHMENT ARE NOT ADJUSTABLE.

SET PARKING BRAKE AND BLOCK WHEELS. MAKE ALL ADJUSTMENTS WITH ENGINE AT NORMAL OPERATING TEMPERATURE, TRANSMISSION IN NEUTRAL, ACCESSORIES AND HEADLAMPS OFF.

IGNITION TIMING — ELECTRONICALLY ADJUSTED AT THE FACTORY — ADJUSTMENT REQUIRED ONLY IF DISTRIBUTOR HAS BEEN DISTURBED.
(1) TURN OFF ENGINE.
(2) DISCONNECT THE IN-LINE SPOUT CONNECTOR (⊐◁d).
(3) RE-START PREVIOUSLY WARMED-UP ENGINE.
(4) ADJUST IGNITION TIMING 10° BTDC.
(5) TURN OFF ENGINE AND RESTORE ELECTRICAL CONNECTION.

THIS ENGINE IS EQUIPPED WITH AUTOMATIC IDLE SPEED CONTROL. IDLE RPM IS NOT ADJUSTABLE. IF NOT WITHIN SPECIFIED RPM RANGE, SEE SHOP MANUAL:
   MANUAL TRANS. IN NEUTRAL: 760-840 RPM
   AUTO TRANS. IN DRIVE: 760-840 RPM

USE SAE 5W-30 OIL API SERVICE SG — ENERGY CONSERVING II.

CE VÉHICULE EST À INJECTION ÉLECTRONIQUE. LE MÉLANGE DE RALENTI, LE RÉGIME DE RALENTI MOTEUR FROID ET LE DISPOSITIF D'ENRICHISSEMENT À FROID NE SONT PAS RÉGLABLES.

SERRER LE FREIN DE STATIONNEMENT, BLOQUER LES ROUES. EFFECTUER TOUT RÉGLAGE SUR MOTEUR NORMALEMENT CHAUD, B.V. AU POINT MORT, CONTACT DES ACCESSOIRES ET DES PHARES COUPÉ.

CALAGE DE L'ALLUMAGE — RÉGLÉ ÉLECTRONIQUEMENT À L'USINE — NE CORRIGER QUE SI L'ALLUMEUR A ÉTÉ DÉPLACÉ.
(1) ARRÊTER LE MOTEUR.
(2) DÉBRANCHER LE CONNECTEUR (⊐◁d) INTERCALÉ DANS LE CIRCUIT DE DÉCLENCHEMENT DE L'ÉTINCELLE.
(3) REDÉMARRER LE MOTEUR PRÉALABLEMENT RÉCHAUFFÉ.
(4) CALER L'ALLUMAGE À 10° AVANT PMH.
(5) ARRÊTER LE MOTEUR ET REBRANCHER LE CONNECTEUR.

CE MOTEUR EST À COMMANDE DE RALENTI AUTOMATIQUE. LE RÉGIME DE RALENTI N'EST PAS RÉGLABLE. S'IL N'EST PAS DANS LES LIMITES PRESCRITES, CONSULTER LE MANUEL DE RÉPARATION.
   B.V.M. AU POINT MORT: 760-840 TR/MIN
   B.V.A. EN POSITION "D": 760-840 TR/MIN

HUILE PRÉCONISÉE: SAE 5W-30, CLASSE API
"SG" — "ÉCONOMIE D'ÉNERGIE II"

CATALYST/CATALYSEUR   1.9 L   SPARK PLUG / BOUGIES: AGSF-34C   GAP / ÉLECTRODES: .042-.046

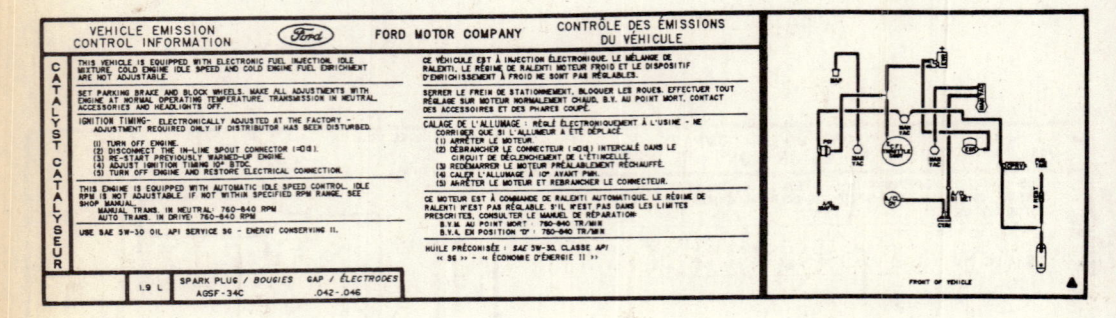

■ CALIBRATION: 8-07F-R11   1.9L CFI ■

FORD MOTOR COMPANY — VEHICLE EMISSION CONTROL INFORMATION

THIS VEHICLE IS EQUIPPED WITH ELECTRONIC FUEL INJECTION. IDLE MIXTURE, COLD ENGINE IDLE SPEED AND COLD ENGINE FUEL ENRICHMENT ARE NOT ADJUSTABLE.

SET PARKING BRAKE AND BLOCK WHEELS. MAKE ALL ADJUSTMENTS WITH ENGINE AT NORMAL OPERATING TEMPERATURE, TRANSMISSION IN NEUTRAL AND ACCESSORIES OFF.

IGNITION TIMING — ELECTRONICALLY ADJUSTED AT THE FACTORY — ADJUSTMENT REQUIRED ONLY IF DISTRIBUTOR HAS BEEN DISTURBED.
(1) TURN OFF ENGINE.
(2) DISCONNECT THE IN-LINE SPOUT CONNECTOR (⊐◁d).
(3) RE-START PREVIOUSLY WARMED-UP ENGINE.
(4) ADJUST IGNITION TIMING TO 10° BTDC.
(5) TURN OFF ENGINE AND RESTORE ELECTRICAL CONNECTION.

THIS ENGINE IS EQUIPPED WITH AUTOMATIC IDLE SPEED CONTROL. IDLE RPM IS NOT ADJUSTABLE. IF NOT WITHIN SPECIFIED RPM RANGE, SEE SHOP MANUAL:
   MANUAL TRANS. IN NEUTRAL: 760-840 RPM

USE SAE 5W-30 OIL API SERVICE SG — ENERGY CONSERVING II.

THIS VEHICLE CONFORMS TO U.S. EPA REGULATIONS APPLICABLE TO 1990 MODEL YEAR NEW MOTOR VEHICLES. COMPLIANCE DEMONSTRATED AND DESIGNED FOR PRINCIPAL USE BELOW 4000 FEET. THIS VEHICLE IS EXEMPT FROM MEETING EMISSIONS STANDARDS ABOVE 4000 FEET BECAUSE OF POSSIBLY UNSUITABLE PERFORMANCE, AND THE EMISSIONS PERFORMANCE WARRANTY DOES NOT APPLY ABOVE 4000 FEET.

CATALYST   SPARK PLUG: AGSF-34C   GAP: .042-.046
            1.9L-9FM
            LFM1.9V5FFD5 — TWC/HO2S/EGR/TBI

VACUUM HOSE ROUTING — FRONT OF VEHICLE

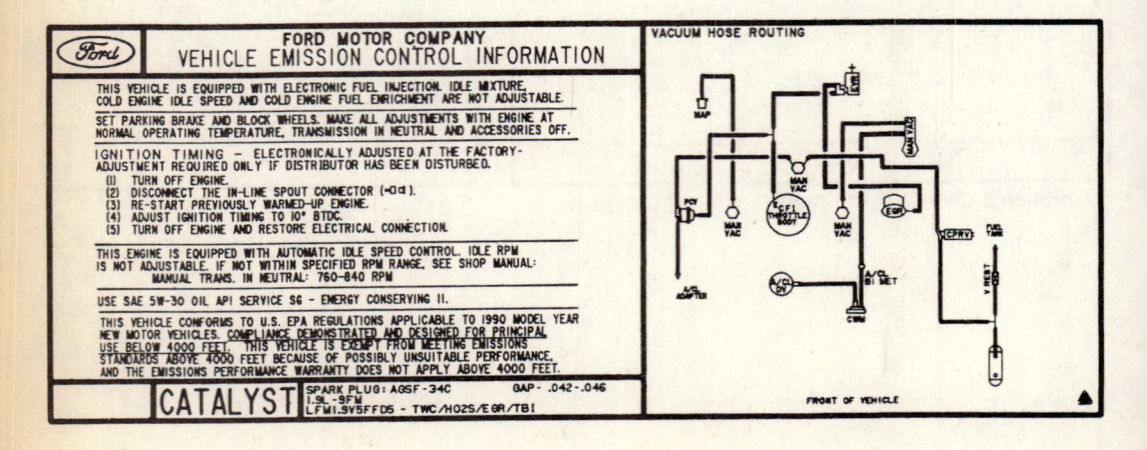

EMISSION CONTROLS

CALIBRATION: 8-07F-R11 — 1.9L CFI

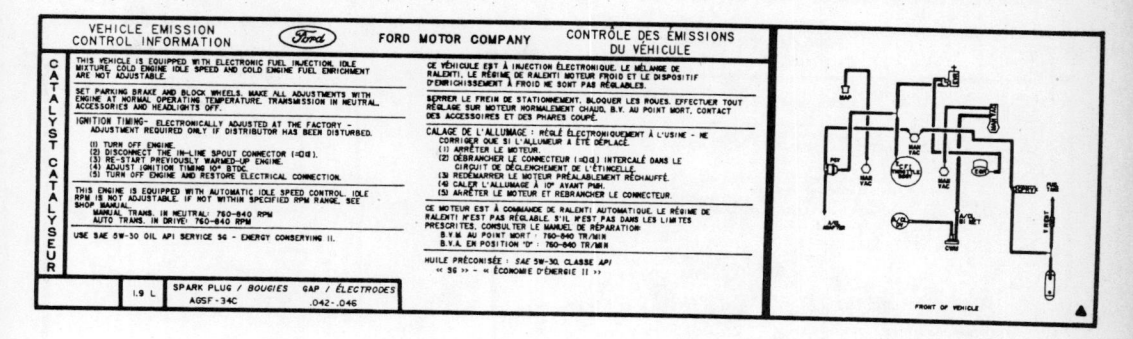

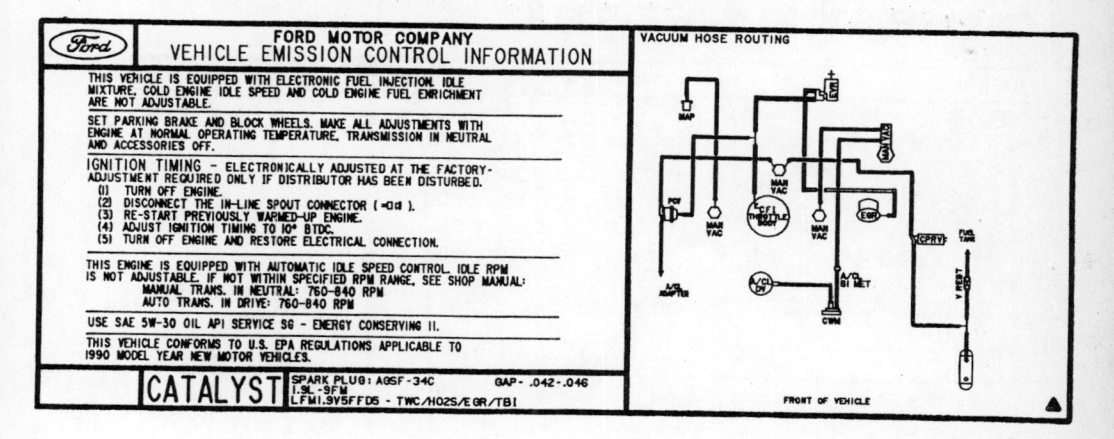

CALIBRATION: 8-08A-R11 — 1.9L CFI

CALIBRATION: 8-08A-R11 — 1.9L CFI

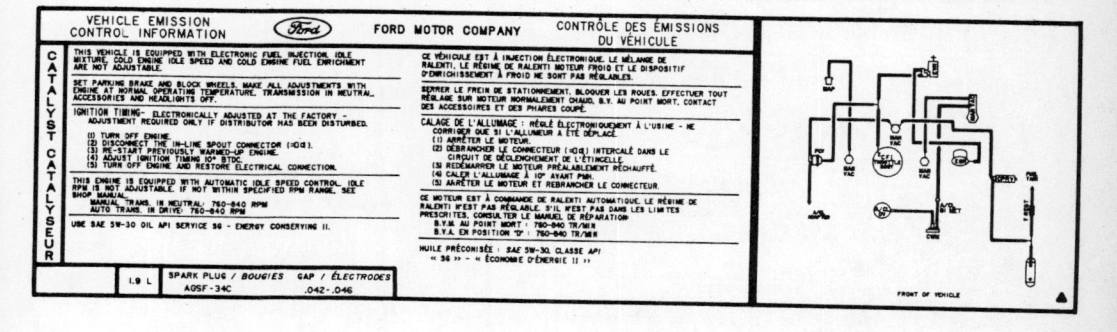

EMISSION CONTROLS

CALIBRATION: 9-07E-R10 — 1.9L EFI

FORD MOTOR COMPANY
VEHICLE EMISSION CONTROL INFORMATION

THIS VEHICLE IS EQUIPPED WITH ELECTRONIC FUEL INJECTION. IDLE MIXTURE, COLD ENGINE IDLE SPEED AND COLD ENGINE FUEL ENRICHMENT ARE NOT ADJUSTABLE.

CHECK TIMING WITH THE TRANSMISSION IN NUETRAL, PARKING BRAKE SET AND THE WHEELS BLOCKED. ENGINE MUST BE AT NORMAL OPERATING TEMPERATURE.
1) TURN OFF ENGINE.
2) DISCONNECT SMALL IN-LINE SPOUT CONNECTOR (-◁◁-).
3) RE-START PREVIOUSLY WARMED-UP ENGINE.
4) IGNITION TIMING IS 10° BTDC. IF NOT SEE SHOP MANUAL.
5) TURN OFF ENGINE AND RESTORE ELECTRICAL CONNECTION.

THROTTLE PLATE ADJUSTMENT
1) ELECTRICALLY DISCONNECT THROTTLE AIR BYPASS VALVE.
2) RUN ENGINE AT 2000 RPM FOR 60 SECONDS MINIMUM.
3) RETURN TO IDLE AND TURN THROTTLE PLATE ADJUSTING SCREW UNTIL IDLE SPEED IS 950 RPM WITH THE FAN OFF. (850 RPM FOR VEHICLE WITH LESS THAN 100 MILES). ADJUSTMENT MUST BE MADE WITHIN 120 SECONDS OF RETURN TO IDLE. TURN OFF ENGINE, RESTART AND REPEAT STEP 2 AND 3 IF 120 SECONDS ARE EXCEEDED.
4) RESTORE ELECTRICAL CONNECTION.
5) RESULTANT IDLE SPEED IS 1000 ± 100 RPM.

USE SAE 5W-30 OIL API SERVICE SG - ENERGY CONSERVING II.

THIS VEHICLE CONFORMS TO U.S. EPA REGULATIONS APPLICABLE TO 1990 MODEL YEAR NEW MOTOR VEHICLES.

CATALYST
SPARK PLUG: AGSF-24C   GAP: .052-.056
1.9L -9HM
LFM1.9V5HMF9 - TWC-OC/PAIR/HO2S/EGR/MPI

VACUUM HOSE ROUTING
FRONT OF VEHICLE

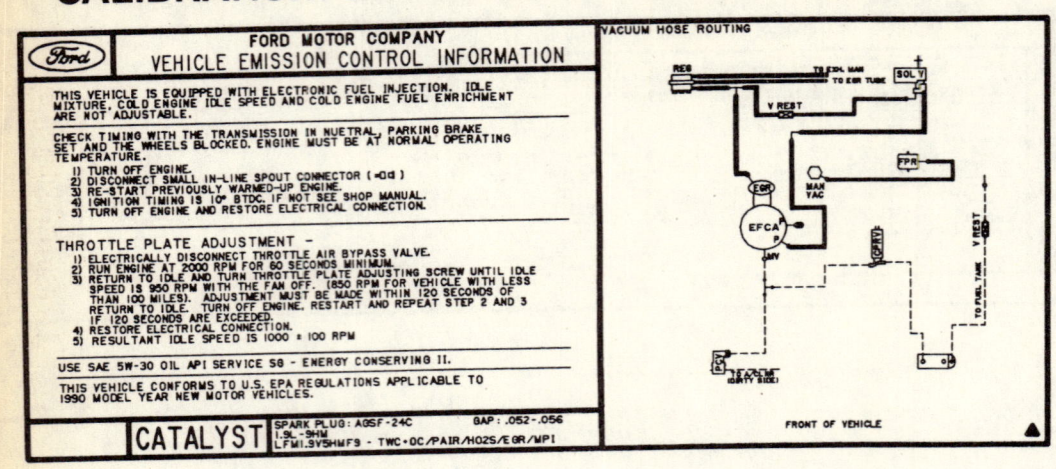

CALIBRATION: 9-07E-R10 — 1.9L EFI

FORD MOTOR COMPANY
VEHICLE EMISSION CONTROL INFORMATION / CONTRÔLE DES ÉMISSIONS DU VÉHICULE

CATALYST / CATALYSEUR

THIS VEHICLE IS EQUIPPED WITH ELECTRONIC FUEL INJECTION. IDLE MIXTURE, COLD ENGINE IDLE SPEED AND COLD ENGINE FUEL ENRICHMENT ARE NOT ADJUSTABLE.

CHECK TIMING WITH THE TRANSMISSION IN NEUTRAL, PARKING BRAKE SET AND THE WHEELS BLOCKED. ENGINE MUST BE AT NORMAL OPERATING TEMPERATURE.
(1) TURN OFF ENGINE.
(2) DISCONNECT SMALL. IN-LINE SPOUT CONNECTOR (-◁◁-) LOCATED ABOVE THE POWER STEERING PUMP.
(3) RE-START PREVIOUSLY WARMED-UP ENGINE.
(4) IGNITION TIMING IS 10° BTDC, IF NOT SEE SHOP MANUAL.
(5) TURN OFF ENGINE AND RESTORE ELECTRICAL CONNECTION.

THROTTLE PLATE ADJUSTMENT - TRANSMISSION IN "N".
(1) ELECTRICALLY DISCONNECT THROTTLE AIR BYPASS VALVE.
(2) RUN ENGINE AT 2000 RPM FOR 60 SECONDS MINIMUM.
(3) RETURN TO IDLE AND TURN THROTTLE PLATE ADJUSTING SCREW UNTIL IDLE SPEED IS 950 RPM WITH THE FAN OFF. (850 RPM FOR VEHICLE WITH LESS THAN 100 MILES). ADJUSTMENT MUST BE MADE WITHIN 120 SECONDS OF RETURN TO IDLE. TURN OFF ENGINE, RESTART AND REPEAT STEP 2 AND 3 IF 120 SECONDS ARE EXCEEDED.
(4) RESTORE ELECTRICAL CONNECTION.
(5) RESULTANT IDLE SPEED IS 1000 ± 100 RPM.

USE SAE 5W-30 OIL API SERVICE SG - ENERGY CONSERVING II.

CE VÉHICULE EST À INJECTION ÉLECTRONIQUE. LE MÉLANGE DE RALENTI, LE RÉGIME DE RALENTI MOTEUR FROID ET LE DISPOSITIF D'ENRICHISSEMENT À FROID NE SONT PAS RÉGLABLES.

POUR VÉRIFIER LE CALAGE DE L'ALLUMAGE, PLACER LE LEVIER DE VITESSE AU POINT MORT, SERRER LE FREIN DE STATIONNEMENT ET BLOQUER LES ROUES. LE MOTEUR DOIT ÊTRE NORMALEMENT CHAUD.
(1) ARRÊTER LE MOTEUR.
(2) DÉBRANCHER LE PETIT CONNECTEUR (-◁◁-) INTERCALÉ DANS LE CIRCUIT DE DÉCLENCHEMENT DE L'ÉTINCELLE, AU-DESSUS DE LA POMPE D'ASSISTANCE DE DIRECTION.
(3) REDÉMARRER LE MOTEUR PRÉALABLEMENT RÉCHAUFFÉ.
(4) L'ALLUMAGE DOIT ÊTRE CALÉ À 10° AVANT PMH. SINON, VOIR LE MANUEL DE RÉPARATION.
(5) ARRÊTER LE MOTEUR ET REBRANCHER LE CONNECTEUR.

RÉGLAGE DU PAPILLON - B.V. AU POINT MORT.
(1) DÉBRANCHER L'ÉLECTROVALVE D'AIR ADDITIONNEL.
(2) LAISSER TOURNER LE MOTEUR À 2000 TR/MIN PENDANT 60 S AU MOINS.
(3) RAMENER LE MOTEUR AU RALENTI ET, VENTILATEUR À L'ARRÊT, TOURNER LA VIS DE RÉGLAGE DU PAPILLON JUSQU'À CE QUE LE RÉGIME ATTEIGNE 950 TR/MIN (850 TR/MIN SI LE VÉHICULE A ROULÉ MOINS DE 160 KM). CE RÉGLAGE DOIT SE FAIRE DANS LES 120 SECONDES QUI SUIVENT LE RETOUR AU RALENTI. ARRÊTER LE MOTEUR, REDÉMARRER ET RÉPÉTER LES ÉTAPES 2 ET 3 SI LE DÉLAI DE 120 S EST DÉPASSÉ.
(4) REBRANCHER LE CIRCUIT ÉLECTRIQUE.
(5) LE RALENTI OBTENU EST DE 1000 ± 100 TR/MIN.

HUILE PRÉCONISÉE : SAE 5W-30, CLASSE API « SG » - ÉCONOMIE D'ÉNERGIE II.

1.9L   SPARK PLUG / BOUGIES: AGSF-24C   GAP / ÉLECTRODES: .052-.056

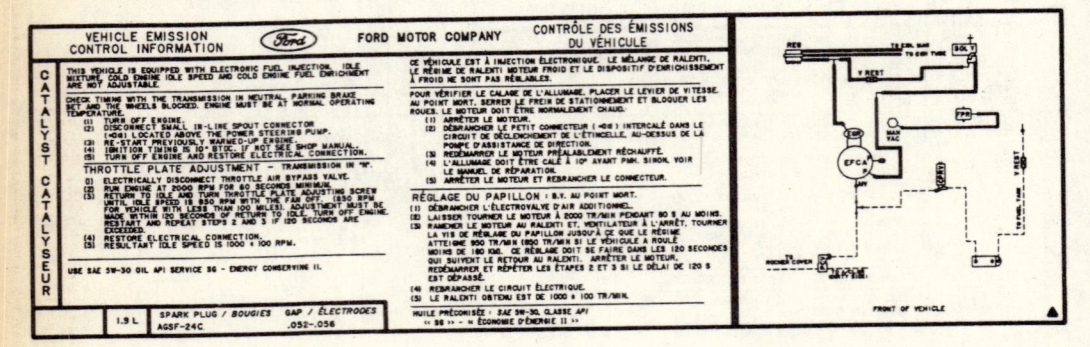

VACUUM HOSE ROUTING
FRONT OF VEHICLE

CALIBRATION: 9-07R-R11 — 1.9L EFI

FORD MOTOR COMPANY
VEHICLE EMISSION CONTROL INFORMATION

THIS VEHICLE IS EQUIPPED WITH ELECTRONIC FUEL INJECTION. IDLE MIXTURE, COLD ENGINE IDLE SPEED AND COLD ENGINE FUEL ENRICHMENT ARE NOT ADJUSTABLE.

CHECK TIMING WITH THE TRANSMISSION IN NUETRAL, PARKING BRAKE SET AND THE WHEELS BLOCKED. ENGINE MUST BE AT NORMAL OPERATING TEMPERATURE.
1) TURN OFF ENGINE.
2) DISCONNECT SMALL IN-LINE SPOUT CONNECTOR (-◁◁-).
3) RE-START PREVIOUSLY WARMED-UP ENGINE.
4) IGNITION TIMING IS 10° BTDC. IF NOT SEE SHOP MANUAL.
5) TURN OFF ENGINE AND RESTORE ELECTRICAL CONNECTION.

THROTTLE PLATE ADJUSTMENT
1) ELECTRICALLY DISCONNECT THROTTLE AIR BYPASS VALVE.
2) RUN ENGINE AT 2000 RPM FOR 60 SECONDS MINIMUM.
3) RETURN TO IDLE AND TURN THROTTLE PLATE ADJUSTING SCREW UNTIL IDLE SPEED IS 950 RPM WITH THE FAN OFF. (850 RPM FOR VEHICLE WITH LESS THAN 100 MILES). ADJUSTMENT MUST BE MADE WITHIN 120 SECONDS OF RETURN TO IDLE. TURN OFF ENGINE, RESTART AND REPEAT STEP 2 AND 3 IF 120 SECONDS ARE EXCEEDED.
4) RESTORE ELECTRICAL CONNECTION.
5) RESULTANT IDLE SPEED IS 1000 ± 100 RPM.

USE SAE 5W-30 OIL API SERVICE SG - ENERGY CONSERVING II.

THIS VEHICLE CONFORMS TO U.S. EPA AND CALIFORNIA REGULATIONS APPLICABLE TO 1990 MODEL YEAR NEW MOTOR VEHICLES INTRODUCED INTO COMMERCE SOLELY FOR SALE IN CALIFORNIA. OBD EXEMPT.

CATALYST
SPARK PLUG: AGSF-24C   GAP: .052-.056
1.9L -9HM
LFM1.9V5HMC6 - TWC-OC/PAIR/HO2S/EGR/MPI

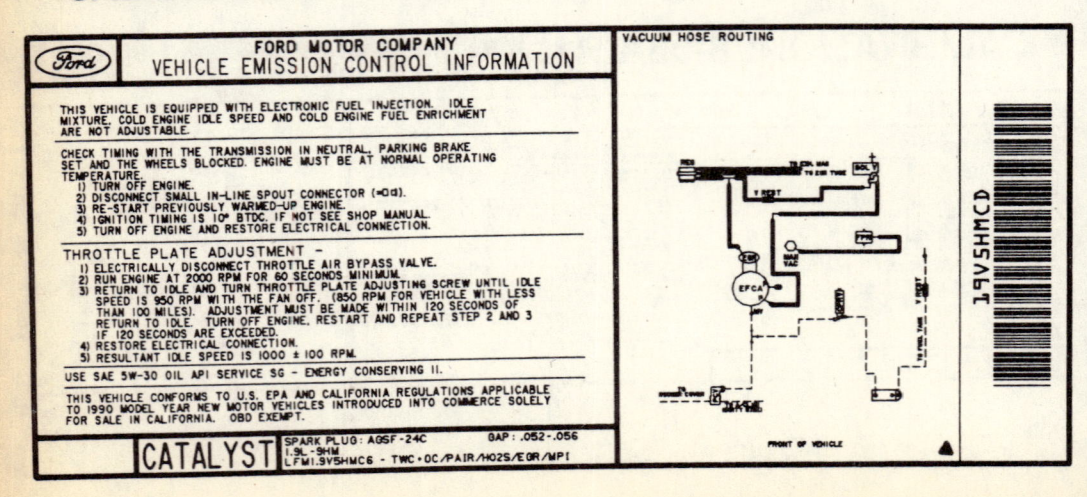

VACUUM HOSE ROUTING
FRONT OF VEHICLE
19V5HMCD

EMISSION CONTROLS 321

CALIBRATION: 0-06S-R00 — 2.3L OHC-EFI

FORD MOTOR COMPANY
VEHICLE EMISSION CONTROL INFORMATION

THIS VEHICLE IS EQUIPPED WITH ELECTRONIC FUEL INJECTION. IDLE MIXTURE, COLD ENGINE IDLE SPEED AND COLD ENGINE FUEL ENRICHMENT ARE NOT ADJUSTABLE.

SET PARKING BRAKE AND BLOCK WHEELS. MAKE ALL ADJUSTMENTS WITH ENGINE AT NORMAL OPERATING TEMPERATURE, TRANSMISSION IN NEUTRAL AND ACCESSORIES OFF.

IGNITION TIMING-
(1) TURN OFF ENGINE
(2) DISCONNECT THE IN-LINE SPOUT CONNECTOR (→◁).
(3) RE-START PREVIOUSLY WARMED-UP ENGINE.
(4) ADJUST IGNITION TIMING TO 10° BTDC.
(5) TURN OFF ENGINE AND RESTORE ELECTRICAL CONNECTION.

THIS ENGINE IS EQUIPPED WITH AUTOMATIC IDLE SPEED CONTROL. IDLE RPM IS NOT ADJUSTABLE. IF NOT WITHIN SPECIFIED RPM RANGE, SEE SHOP MANUAL:
  MAN. TRANS. IN NEUTRAL: 830-890 RPM
  AUTO. TRANS. IN DRIVE: 790-850 RPM

USE SAE 5W-30 OIL API SERVICE SG - ENERGY CONSERVING II.

THIS VEHICLE CONFORMS TO U.S. EPA AND CALIFORNIA REGULATIONS APPLICABLE TO 1990 MODEL YEAR NEW MOTOR VEHICLES INTRODUCED INTO COMMERCE SOLELY FOR SALE IN CALIFORNIA. OBD EXEMPT.

CATALYST SPARK PLUG: AWSF-44C   GAP - .042-.046
2.3L -9HM
LFM2.3V5FYC2 - TWC/HO2S/EGR/MPI

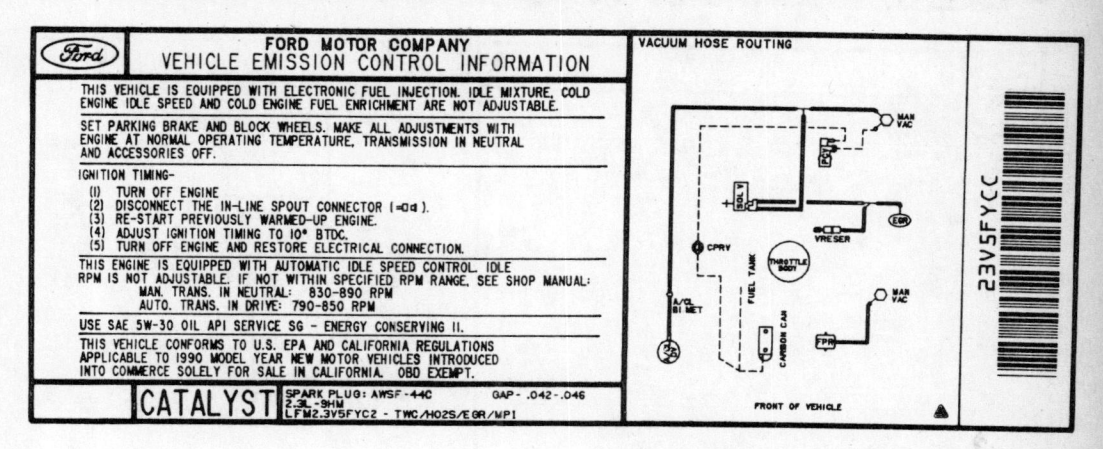

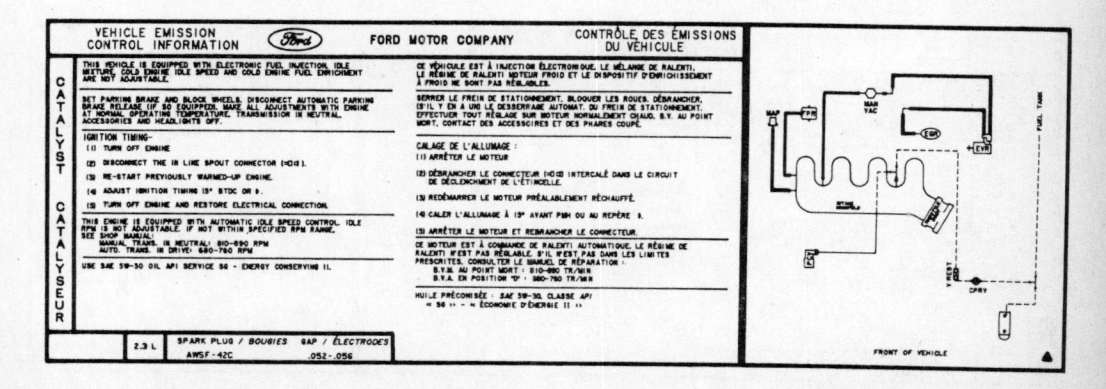

CALIBRATION: 0-25P-R00 — 2.3L HSC-EFI-HO

FORD MOTOR COMPANY
VEHICLE EMISSION CONTROL INFORMATION

THIS VEHICLE IS EQUIPPED WITH ELECTRONIC FUEL INJECTION. IDLE MIXTURE, COLD ENGINE IDLE SPEED AND COLD ENGINE FUEL ENRICHMENT ARE NOT ADJUSTABLE.

SET PARKING BRAKE AND BLOCK WHEELS. DISCONNECT AUTOMATIC PARKING BRAKE RELEASE (IF SO EQUIPPED). MAKE ALL ADJUSTMENTS WITH ENGINE AT NORMAL OPERATING TEMPERATURE, TRANSMISSION IN NEUTRAL AND ACCESSORIES OFF.

IGNITION TIMING-
(1) TURN OFF ENGINE
(2) DISCONNECT THE IN-LINE SPOUT CONNECTOR (→◁).
(3) RE-START PREVIOUSLY WARMED-UP ENGINE.
(4) ADJUST IGNITION TIMING TO 15° BTDC OR D.
(5) TURN OFF ENGINE AND RESTORE ELECTRICAL CONNECTION.

THIS ENGINE IS EQUIPPED WITH AUTOMATIC IDLE SPEED CONTROL. IDLE RPM IS NOT ADJUSTABLE. IF NOT WITHIN SPECIFIED RPM RANGE, SEE SHOP MANUAL:
  MANUAL TRANS. IN NEUTRAL: 810-890 RPM
  AUTO. TRANS. IN DRIVE: 690-750 RPM

USE SAE 5W-30 OIL API SERVICE SG - ENERGY CONSERVING II.

THIS VEHICLE CONFORMS TO U.S. EPA AND CALIFORNIA REGULATIONS APPLICABLE TO 1990 MODEL YEAR NEW MOTOR VEHICLES INTRODUCED INTO COMMERCE SOLELY FOR SALE IN CALIFORNIA. OBD EXEMPT.

CATALYST SPARK PLUG: AWSF-42C   GAP - .052-.056
2.3L -9HM
LFM2.3V5FXC0 - TWC/PAIR/HO2S/EGR/MPI

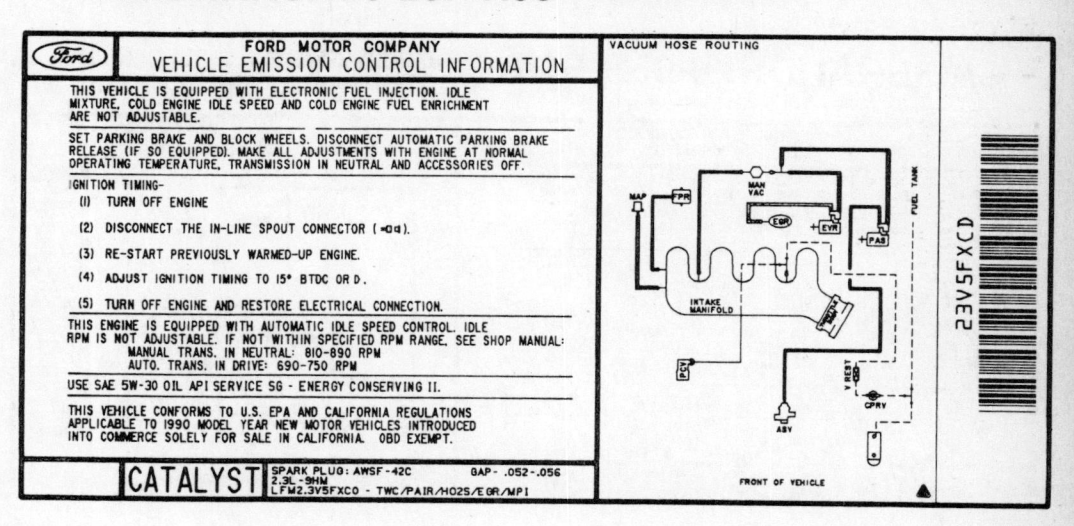

CALIBRATION: 9-26D-R10 — 2.3L HSC-EFI-HO

VEHICLE EMISSION CONTROL INFORMATION — **FORD MOTOR COMPANY** — **CONTRÔLE DES ÉMISSIONS DU VÉHICULE**

CATALYST / CATALYSEUR

THIS VEHICLE IS EQUIPPED WITH ELECTRONIC FUEL INJECTION. IDLE MIXTURE, COLD ENGINE IDLE SPEED AND COLD ENGINE FUEL ENRICHMENT ARE NOT ADJUSTABLE.

SET PARKING BRAKE AND BLOCK WHEELS. DISCONNECT AUTOMATIC PARKING BRAKE RELEASE (IF SO EQUIPPED). MAKE ALL ADJUSTMENTS WITH ENGINE AT NORMAL OPERATING TEMPERATURE, TRANSMISSION IN NEUTRAL, ACCESSORIES AND HEADLIGHTS OFF.

IGNITION TIMING-
(1) TURN OFF ENGINE
(2) DISCONNECT THE IN-LINE SPOUT CONNECTOR (→◁).
(3) RE-START PREVIOUSLY WARMED-UP ENGINE.
(4) ADJUST IGNITION TIMING 15° BTDC OR D.
(5) TURN OFF ENGINE AND RESTORE ELECTRICAL CONNECTION.

THIS ENGINE IS EQUIPPED WITH AUTOMATIC IDLE SPEED CONTROL. IDLE RPM IS NOT ADJUSTABLE. IF NOT WITHIN SPECIFIED RPM RANGE, SEE SHOP MANUAL:
  MANUAL TRANS. IN NEUTRAL: 810-890 RPM
  AUTO. TRANS. IN DRIVE: 690-750 RPM

USE SAE 5W-30 OIL API SERVICE SG - ENERGY CONSERVING II.

CE VÉHICULE EST À INJECTION ÉLECTRONIQUE. LE MÉLANGE DE RALENTI, LE RÉGIME DE RALENTI MOTEUR FROID ET LE DISPOSITIF D'ENRICHISSEMENT À FROID NE SONT PAS RÉGLABLES.

SERRER LE FREIN DE STATIONNEMENT, BLOQUER LES ROUES. DÉBRANCHER (S'IL Y EN A UN) LE DESSERRAGE AUTOMAT. DU FREIN DE STATIONNEMENT. EFFECTUER TOUT RÉGLAGE SUR MOTEUR NORMALEMENT CHAUD, B.V. AU POINT MORT, CONTACT DES ACCESSOIRES ET DES PHARES COUPÉ.

CALAGE DE L'ALLUMAGE:
(1) ARRÊTER LE MOTEUR
(2) DÉBRANCHER LE CONNECTEUR (→◁) INTERCALÉ DANS LE CIRCUIT DE DÉCLENCHEMENT DE L'ÉTINCELLE.
(3) REDÉMARRER LE MOTEUR PRÉALABLEMENT RÉCHAUFFÉ.
(4) CALER L'ALLUMAGE À 15° AVANT PMH OU AU REPÈRE D.
(5) ARRÊTER LE MOTEUR ET REBRANCHER LE CONNECTEUR.

CE MOTEUR EST À COMMANDE DE RALENTI AUTOMATIQUE. LE RÉGIME DE RALENTI N'EST PAS RÉGLABLE. S'IL N'EST PAS DANS LES LIMITES PRESCRITES, CONSULTER LE MANUEL DE RÉPARATION :
  B.V.M. AU POINT MORT : 810-890 TR/MIN
  B.V.A. EN POSITION "D" : 690-750 TR/MIN

HUILE PRÉCONISÉE : SAE 5W-30, CLASSE API « SG » - ÉCONOMIE D'ÉNERGIE II »

2.3L SPARK PLUG / BOUGIES GAP / ÉLECTRODES
AWSF-42C   .052-.056

EMISSION CONTROLS

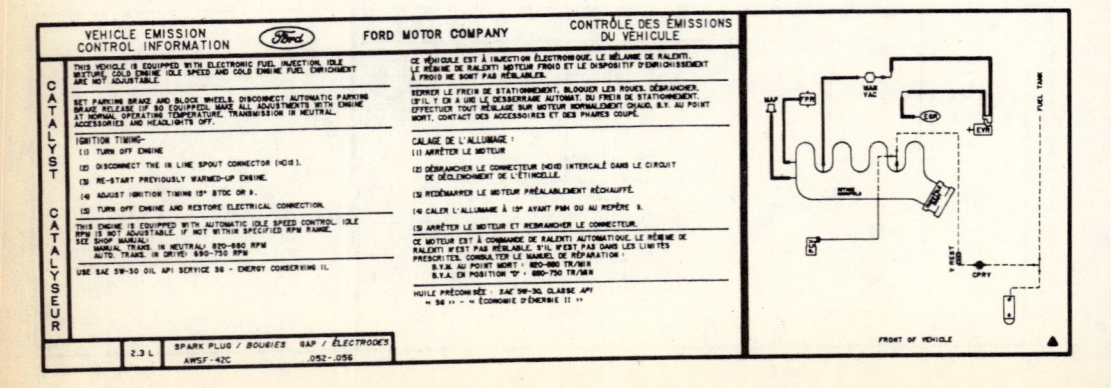

■ CALIBRATION: 0-25Q-R00 — 2.3L HSC-EFI

FORD MOTOR COMPANY — VEHICLE EMISSION CONTROL INFORMATION

THIS VEHICLE IS EQUIPPED WITH ELECTRONIC FUEL INJECTION. IDLE MIXTURE, COLD ENGINE IDLE SPEED AND COLD ENGINE FUEL ENRICHMENT ARE NOT ADJUSTABLE.

SET PARKING BRAKE AND BLOCK WHEELS. DISCONNECT AUTOMATIC PARKING BRAKE RELEASE (IF SO EQUIPPED). MAKE ALL ADJUSTMENTS WITH ENGINE AT NORMAL OPERATING TEMPERATURE, TRANSMISSION IN NEUTRAL AND ACCESSORIES OFF.

IGNITION TIMING-
(1) TURN OFF ENGINE
(2) DISCONNECT THE IN-LINE SPOUT CONNECTOR (-☐☐-).
(3) RE-START PREVIOUSLY WARMED-UP ENGINE.
(4) ADJUST IGNITION TIMING TO 15° BTDC OR D.
(5) TURN OFF ENGINE AND RESTORE ELECTRICAL CONNECTION.

THIS ENGINE IS EQUIPPED WITH AUTOMATIC IDLE SPEED CONTROL. IDLE RPM IS NOT ADJUSTABLE. IF NOT WITHIN SPECIFIED RPM RANGE, SEE SHOP MANUAL:
MANUAL TRANS. IN NEUTRAL: 820-880 RPM
AUTO. TRANS. IN DRIVE: 690-750 RPM

USE SAE 5W-30 OIL API SERVICE SG - ENERGY CONSERVING II.

THIS VEHICLE CONFORMS TO U.S. EPA AND CALIFORNIA REGULATIONS APPLICABLE TO 1990 MODEL YEAR NEW MOTOR VEHICLES INTRODUCED INTO COMMERCE SOLELY FOR SALE IN CALIFORNIA. OBD EXEMPT.

CATALYST — SPARK PLUG: AWSF-42C   GAP: .052-.056
2.3L-9HM
LFM2.3V5FXC0 - TWC/PAIR/HO2S/EGR/MPI

VACUUM HOSE ROUTING — 23V5FXCD

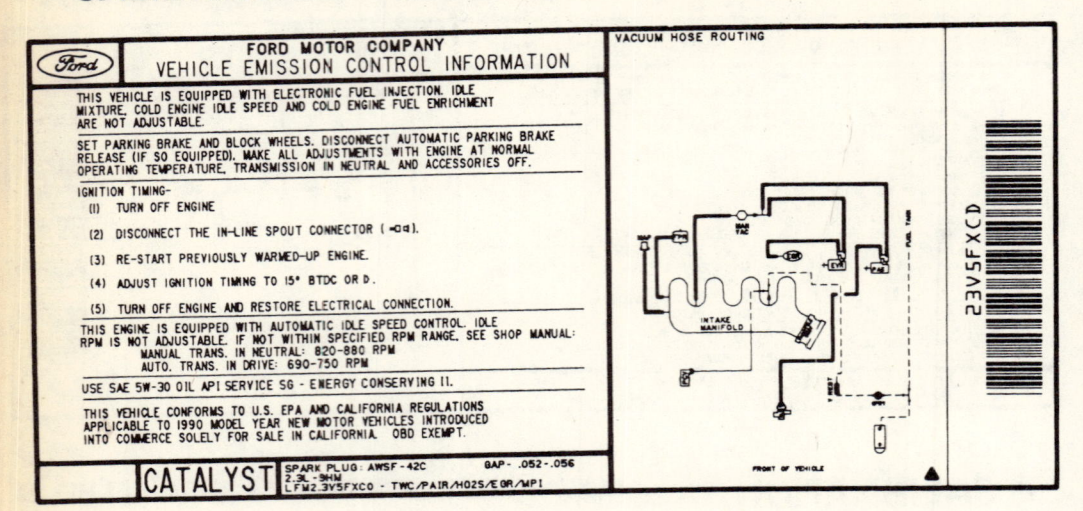

■ CALIBRATION: 0-05S-R00 — 2.3L OHC-EFI

FORD MOTOR COMPANY — VEHICLE EMISSION CONTROL INFORMATION

THIS VEHICLE IS EQUIPPED WITH ELECTRONIC FUEL INJECTION. IDLE MIXTURE, COLD ENGINE IDLE SPEED AND COLD ENGINE FUEL ENRICHMENT ARE NOT ADJUSTABLE.

SET PARKING BRAKE AND BLOCK WHEELS. MAKE ALL ADJUSTMENTS WITH ENGINE AT NORMAL OPERATING TEMPERATURE, TRANSMISSION IN NEUTRAL AND ACCESSORIES OFF.

IGNITION TIMING-
(1) TURN OFF ENGINE
(2) DISCONNECT THE IN-LINE SPOUT CONNECTOR (-☐☐-).
(3) RE-START PREVIOUSLY WARMED-UP ENGINE.
(4) ADJUST IGNITION TIMING TO 10° BTDC.
(5) TURN OFF ENGINE AND RESTORE ELECTRICAL CONNECTION.

THIS ENGINE IS EQUIPPED WITH AUTOMATIC IDLE SPEED CONTROL. IDLE RPM IS NOT ADJUSTABLE. IF NOT WITHIN SPECIFIED RPM RANGE, SEE SHOP MANUAL:
MAN. TRANS. IN NEUTRAL: 830-890 RPM
AUTO. TRANS. IN DRIVE: 790-850 RPM

USE SAE 5W-30 OIL API SERVICE SG - ENERGY CONSERVING II.

THIS VEHICLE CONFORMS TO U.S. EPA AND CALIFORNIA REGULATIONS APPLICABLE TO 1990 MODEL YEAR NEW MOTOR VEHICLES INTRODUCED INTO COMMERCE SOLELY FOR SALE IN CALIFORNIA. OBD EXEMPT.

CATALYST — SPARK PLUG: AWSF-44C   GAP: .042-.046
2.3L-9HM
LFM2.3V5FYC2 - TWC/HO2S/EGR/MPI

VACUUM HOSE ROUTING — 23V5FYCC

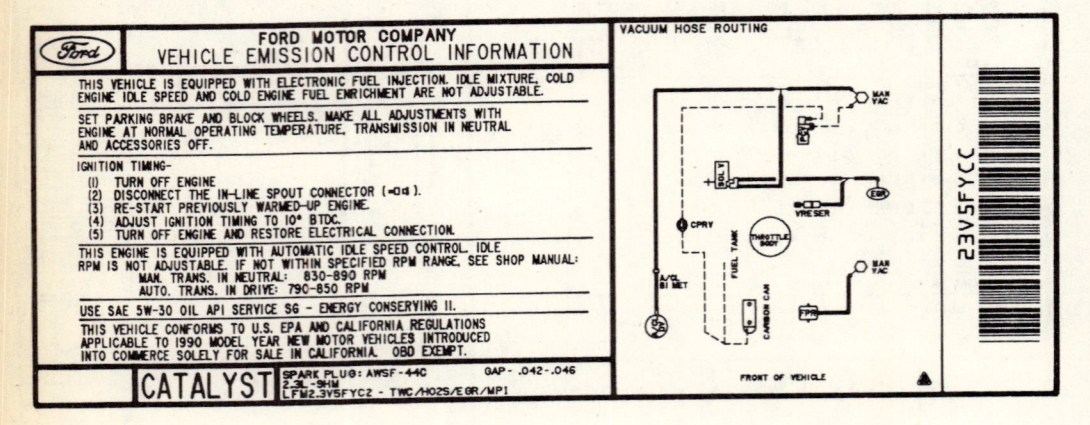

■ CALIBRATION: 9-26E-R10 — 2.3L HSC-EFI

VEHICLE EMISSION CONTROL INFORMATION — FORD MOTOR COMPANY — CONTRÔLE DES ÉMISSIONS DU VÉHICULE

CATALYST / CATALYSEUR

THIS VEHICLE IS EQUIPPED WITH ELECTRONIC FUEL INJECTION. IDLE MIXTURE IS NOT ADJUSTABLE.

SET PARKING BRAKE AND BLOCK WHEELS. DISCONNECT AUTOMATIC PARKING BRAKE RELEASE (IF SO EQUIPPED). MAKE ALL ADJUSTMENTS WITH ENGINE AT NORMAL OPERATING TEMPERATURE, TRANSMISSION IN NEUTRAL, ACCESSORIES AND HEADLIGHTS OFF.

IGNITION TIMING-
(1) TURN OFF ENGINE
(2) DISCONNECT THE IN LINE SPOUT CONNECTOR (-☐☐-).
(3) RE-START PREVIOUSLY WARMED-UP ENGINE.
(4) ADJUST IGNITION TIMING 15° BTDC OR D.
(5) TURN OFF ENGINE AND RESTORE ELECTRICAL CONNECTION.

THIS ENGINE IS EQUIPPED WITH AUTOMATIC IDLE SPEED CONTROL. IDLE RPM IS NOT ADJUSTABLE. IF NOT WITHIN SPECIFIED RPM RANGE, SEE SHOP MANUAL:
MANUAL TRANS. IN NEUTRAL: 820-880 RPM
AUTO. TRANS. IN DRIVE: 690-750 RPM

USE SAE 5W-30 OIL API SERVICE SG - ENERGY CONSERVING II.

CE VÉHICULE EST À INJECTION ÉLECTRONIQUE. LE MÉLANGE DE RALENTI, LE RÉGIME DE RALENTI MOTEUR FROID ET LE DISPOSITIF D'ENRICHISSEMENT À FROID NE SONT PAS RÉGLABLES.

SERRER LE FREIN DE STATIONNEMENT, BLOQUER LES ROUES. DÉBRANCHER LE DISPOSITIF DE DESSERRAGE AUTOMAT. DU FREIN DE STATIONNEMENT (S'IL Y EN A UN) LE DESSERRAGE AUTOM. DU FREIN DE STATIONNEMENT. EFFECTUER TOUT RÉGLAGE À 13° AVANT PMH OU NORMALEMENT CHAUD, B.V. AU POINT MORT, CONTACT DES ACCESSOIRES ET DES PHARES COUPÉ.

CALAGE DE L'ALLUMAGE :
(1) ARRÊTER LE MOTEUR
(2) DÉBRANCHER LE CONNECTEUR INDIQ INTERCALÉ DANS LE CIRCUIT DE DÉCLENCHEMENT DE L'ÉTINCELLE.
(3) REDÉMARRER LE MOTEUR PRÉALABLEMENT RÉCHAUFFÉ.
(4) CALER L'ALLUMAGE À 13° AVANT PMH OU AU REPÈRE D.
(5) ARRÊTER LE MOTEUR ET REBRANCHER LE CONNECTEUR.

B.V.M. AU POINT MORT: 820-880 TR/MIN
B.V.A. EN POSITION "D": 690-750 TR/MIN

HUILE PRÉCONISÉE : SAE 5W-30, CLASSE API
"SG" - - "ÉCONOMIE D'ÉNERGIE II"

2.3L — SPARK PLUG / BOUGIES   GAP / ÉLECTRODES
AWSF-42C   .052-.056

EMISSION CONTROLS

CALIBRATION: 0-26T-R00 — 2.3L HSC-EFI-HO

FORD MOTOR COMPANY
VEHICLE EMISSION CONTROL INFORMATION

THIS VEHICLE IS EQUIPPED WITH ELECTRONIC FUEL INJECTION. IDLE MIXTURE, COLD ENGINE IDLE SPEED AND COLD ENGINE FUEL ENRICHMENT ARE NOT ADJUSTABLE.

SET PARKING BRAKE AND BLOCK WHEELS. DISCONNECT AUTOMATIC PARKING BRAKE RELEASE (IF SO EQUIPPED). MAKE ALL ADJUSTMENTS WITH ENGINE AT NORMAL OPERATING TEMPERATURE, TRANSMISSION IN NEUTRAL AND ACCESSORIES OFF.

IGNITION TIMING-
(1) TURN OFF ENGINE
(2) DISCONNECT THE IN-LINE SPOUT CONNECTOR (⊲⊳).
(3) RE-START PREVIOUSLY WARMED-UP ENGINE.
(4) ADJUST IGNITION TIMING TO 15° BTDC OR D.
(5) TURN OFF ENGINE AND RESTORE ELECTRICAL CONNECTION.

THIS ENGINE IS EQUIPPED WITH AUTOMATIC IDLE SPEED CONTROL. IDLE RPM IS NOT ADJUSTABLE. IF NOT WITHIN SPECIFIED RPM RANGE, SEE SHOP MANUAL:
  MANUAL TRANS. IN NEUTRAL: 810-890 RPM
  AUTO. TRANS. IN DRIVE: 690-750 RPM

USE SAE 5W-30 OIL API SERVICE SG - ENERGY CONSERVING II.

THIS VEHICLE CONFORMS TO U.S. EPA AND CALIFORNIA REGULATIONS APPLICABLE TO 1990 MODEL YEAR NEW MOTOR VEHICLES INTRODUCED INTO COMMERCE SOLELY FOR SALE IN CALIFORNIA. OBD EXEMPT.

CATALYST SPARK PLUG: AWSF-42C GAP: .052-.056
2.3L-9HM
LFM2.3V5FXC0 - TWC/PAIR/HO2S/EGR/MPI

VACUUM HOSE ROUTING — 23V5FXC0

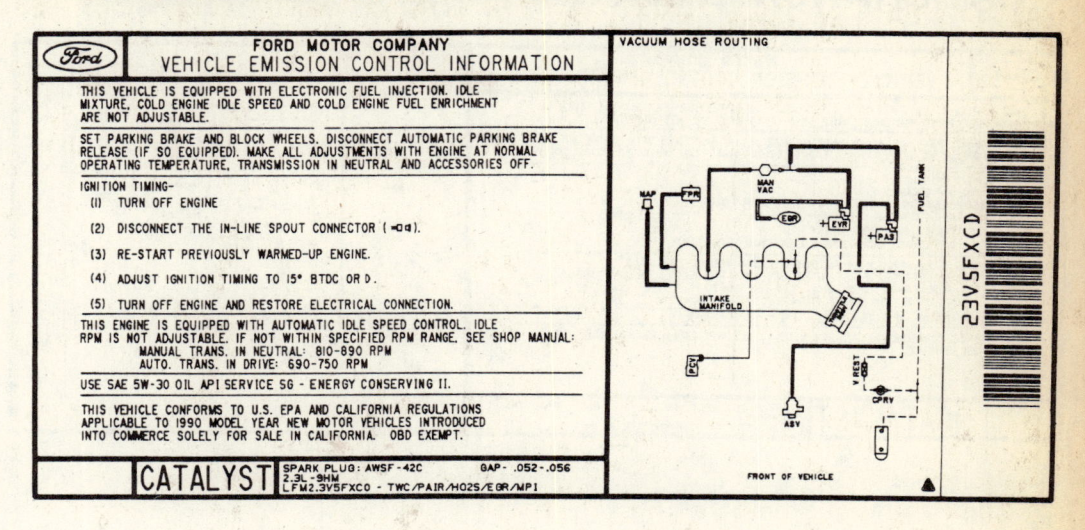

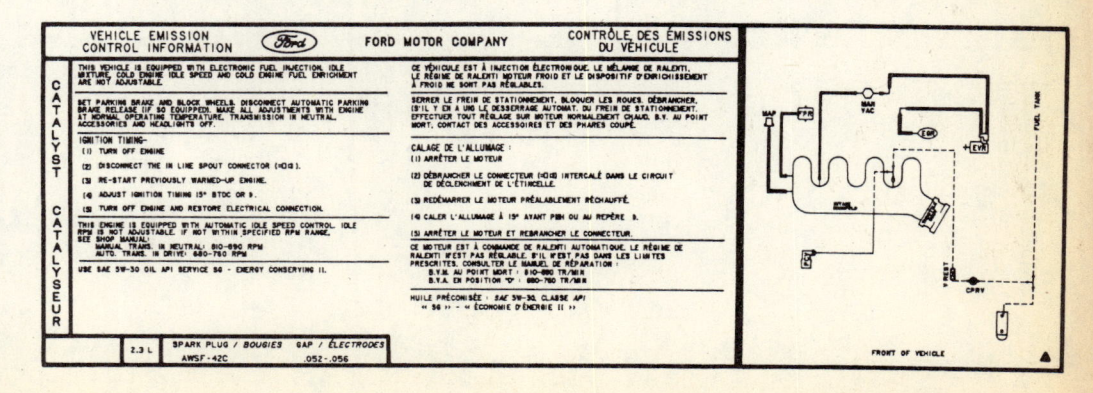

CALIBRATION: 8-06A-R10 — 2.3L OHC-EFI

FORD MOTOR COMPANY
VEHICLE EMISSION CONTROL INFORMATION

THIS VEHICLE IS EQUIPPED WITH ELECTRONIC FUEL INJECTION. IDLE MIXTURE, COLD ENGINE IDLE SPEED AND COLD ENGINE FUEL ENRICHMENT ARE NOT ADJUSTABLE.

SET PARKING BRAKE AND BLOCK WHEELS. MAKE ALL ADJUSTMENTS WITH ENGINE AT NORMAL OPERATING TEMPERATURE, TRANSMISSION IN NEUTRAL AND ACCESSORIES OFF.

IGNITION TIMING-
(1) TURN OFF ENGINE.
(2) DISCONNECT THE IN-LINE SPOUT CONNECTOR (⊲⊳).
(3) RE-START PREVIOUSLY WARMED-UP ENGINE.
(4) ADJUST IGNITION TIMING TO 10° BTDC.
(5) TURN OFF ENGINE AND RESTORE ELECTRICAL CONNECTION.

THIS ENGINE IS EQUIPPED WITH AUTOMATIC IDLE SPEED CONTROL. IDLE RPM IS NOT ADJUSTABLE. IF NOT WITHIN SPECIFIED RPM RANGE, SEE SHOP MANUAL:
  MANUAL TRANS. IN NEUTRAL: 770-830 RPM
  AUTO. TRANS. IN DRIVE: 770-830 RPM

USE SAE 5W-30 OIL API SERVICE SG - ENERGY CONSERVING II.

THIS VEHICLE CONFORMS TO U.S. EPA REGULATIONS APPLICABLE TO 1990 MODEL YEAR NEW MOTOR VEHICLES.

CATALYST SPARK PLUG: AWSF-44C GAP: .042-.046
2.3L-9HM
LFM2.3V5EYF5 - TWC/HO2S/EGR/MPI

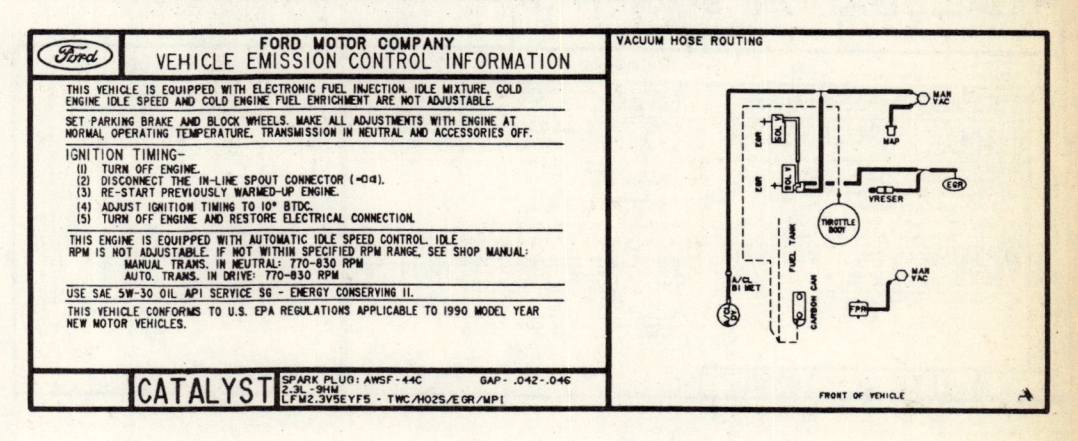

CALIBRATION: 9-25C-R10 — 2.3L HSC-EFI-HO

VEHICLE EMISSION CONTROL INFORMATION — **FORD MOTOR COMPANY** — **CONTRÔLE DES ÉMISSIONS DU VÉHICULE**

THIS VEHICLE IS EQUIPPED WITH ELECTRONIC FUEL INJECTION. IDLE MIXTURE, COLD ENGINE IDLE SPEED AND COLD ENGINE FUEL ENRICHMENT ARE NOT ADJUSTABLE.

SET PARKING BRAKE AND BLOCK WHEELS. DISCONNECT AUTOMATIC PARKING BRAKE RELEASE (IF SO EQUIPPED). MAKE ALL ADJUSTMENTS WITH ENGINE AT NORMAL OPERATING TEMPERATURE, TRANSMISSION IN NEUTRAL, ACCESSORIES OFF AND HEADLIGHTS OFF.

IGNITION TIMING-
(1) TURN OFF ENGINE
(2) DISCONNECT THE IN LINE SPOUT CONNECTOR (⊲⊳).
(3) RE-START PREVIOUSLY WARMED-UP ENGINE.
(4) ADJUST IGNITION TIMING 15° BTDC OR D.
(5) TURN OFF ENGINE AND RESTORE ELECTRICAL CONNECTION.

THIS ENGINE IS EQUIPPED WITH AUTOMATIC IDLE SPEED CONTROL. IDLE RPM IS NOT ADJUSTABLE. IF NOT WITHIN SPECIFIED RPM RANGE, SEE SHOP MANUAL.
  MANUAL TRANS. IN NEUTRAL: 810-890 RPM
  AUTO. TRANS. IN DRIVE: 680-750 RPM

USE SAE 5W-30 OIL API SERVICE SG - ENERGY CONSERVING II.

CE VÉHICULE EST À INJECTION ÉLECTRONIQUE. LE MÉLANGE DE RALENTI, LE RÉGIME DE RALENTI MOTEUR FROID ET LE DISPOSITIF D'ENRICHISSEMENT À FROID NE SONT PAS RÉGLABLES.

SERRER LE FREIN DE STATIONNEMENT. BLOQUER LES ROUES. DÉBRANCHER (S'IL Y EN A UN) LE DESSERRAGE AUTOMAT. DU FREIN DE STATIONNEMENT. EFFECTUER TOUT RÉGLAGE SUR MOTEUR NORMALEMENT CHAUD, B.V. AU POINT MORT, CONTACT DES ACCESSOIRES ET DES PHARES COUPÉ.

CALAGE DE L'ALLUMAGE :
(1) ARRÊTER LE MOTEUR
(2) DÉBRANCHER LE CONNECTEUR (HORS) INTERCALÉ DANS LE CIRCUIT DE DÉCLENCHEMENT DE L'ÉTINCELLE.
(3) REDÉMARRER LE MOTEUR PRÉALABLEMENT RÉCHAUFFÉ.
(4) CALER L'ALLUMAGE À 15° AVANT PMH OU AU REPÈRE D.
(5) ARRÊTER LE MOTEUR ET REBRANCHER LE CONNECTEUR.

CE MOTEUR EST À COMMANDE DE RALENTI AUTOMATIQUE. LE RÉGIME DE RALENTI N'EST PAS RÉGLABLE. S'IL N'EST PAS DANS LES LIMITES PRESCRITES, CONSULTER LE MANUEL DE RÉPARATION :
  B.V.M. AU POINT MORT : 810-890 TR/MIN
  B.V.A. EN POSITION "D" : 680-750 TR/MIN

HUILE PRÉCONISÉE : SAE 5W-30, CLASSE API
"SG" - "ÉCONOMIE D'ÉNERGIE II"

2.3L SPARK PLUG / BOUGIES   GAP / ÉLECTRODES
      AWSF-42C   .052-.056

324 EMISSION CONTROLS

■ CALIBRATION: 8-05A-R10   2.3L OHC-EFI

FORD MOTOR COMPANY
VEHICLE EMISSION CONTROL INFORMATION

THIS VEHICLE IS EQUIPPED WITH ELECTRONIC FUEL INJECTION. IDLE MIXTURE, COLD ENGINE IDLE SPEED AND COLD ENGINE FUEL ENRICHMENT ARE NOT ADJUSTABLE.

SET PARKING BRAKE AND BLOCK WHEELS. MAKE ALL ADJUSTMENTS WITH ENGINE AT NORMAL OPERATING TEMPERATURE, TRANSMISSION IN NEUTRAL AND ACCESSORIES OFF.

IGNITION TIMING-
(1) TURN OFF ENGINE.
(2) DISCONNECT THE IN-LINE SPOUT CONNECTOR (-◁◁-).
(3) RE-START PREVIOUSLY WARMED-UP ENGINE.
(4) ADJUST IGNITION TIMING TO 10° BTDC.
(5) TURN OFF ENGINE AND RESTORE ELECTRICAL CONNECTION.

THIS ENGINE IS EQUIPPED WITH AUTOMATIC IDLE SPEED CONTROL. IDLE RPM IS NOT ADJUSTABLE. IF NOT WITHIN SPECIFIED RPM RANGE, SEE SHOP MANUAL:
MANUAL TRANS. IN NEUTRAL: 770-830 RPM
AUTO. TRANS. IN DRIVE: 770-830 RPM

USE SAE 5W-30 OIL API SERVICE SG - ENERGY CONSERVING II.

THIS VEHICLE CONFORMS TO U.S. EPA REGULATIONS APPLICABLE TO 1990 MODEL YEAR NEW MOTOR VEHICLES.

CATALYST   SPARK PLUG: AWSF-44C   GAP - .042-.046
2.3L -9HM
LFM2.3V5EYF5 - TWC/HO2S/EGR/MPI

VACUUM HOSE ROUTING

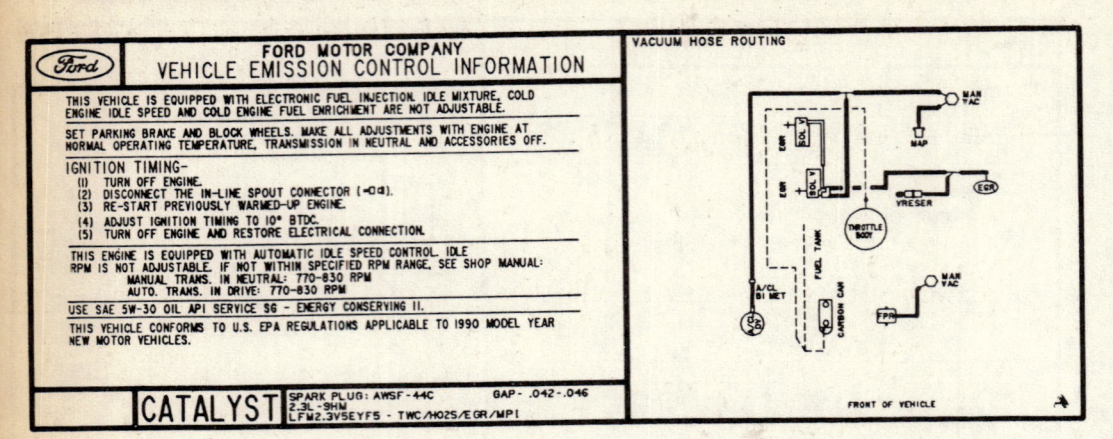

■ CALIBRATION: 9-25F-R10   2.3L HSC-EFI

VEHICLE EMISSION CONTROL INFORMATION — FORD MOTOR COMPANY — CONTRÔLE DES ÉMISSIONS DU VÉHICULE

CATALYST / CATALYSEUR

THIS VEHICLE IS EQUIPPED WITH ELECTRONIC FUEL INJECTION. IDLE MIXTURE, COLD ENGINE IDLE SPEED AND COLD ENGINE FUEL ENRICHMENT ARE NOT ADJUSTABLE.

SET PARKING BRAKE AND BLOCK WHEELS. DISCONNECT AUTOMATIC PARKING BRAKE RELEASE (IF SO EQUIPPED). MAKE ALL ADJUSTMENTS WITH ENGINE AT NORMAL OPERATING TEMPERATURE, TRANSMISSION IN NEUTRAL, ACCESSORIES AND HEADLIGHTS OFF.

IGNITION TIMING-
(1) TURN OFF ENGINE
(2) DISCONNECT THE IN LINE SPOUT CONNECTOR (-◁◁-).
(3) RE-START PREVIOUSLY WARMED-UP ENGINE.
(4) ADJUST IGNITION TIMING 15° BTDC OR P.
(5) TURN OFF ENGINE AND RESTORE ELECTRICAL CONNECTION.

THIS ENGINE IS EQUIPPED WITH AUTOMATIC IDLE SPEED CONTROL. IDLE RPM IS NOT ADJUSTABLE. IF NOT WITHIN SPECIFIED RPM RANGE, SEE SHOP MANUAL:
MANUAL TRANS. IN NEUTRAL: 620-680 RPM
AUTO. TRANS. IN DRIVE: 690-750 RPM

USE SAE 5W-30 OIL API SERVICE SG - ENERGY CONSERVING II.

CE VÉHICULE EST À INJECTION ÉLECTRONIQUE. LE MÉLANGE DE RALENTI, LE RÉGIME DE RALENTI MOTEUR FROID ET LE DISPOSITIF D'ENRICHISSEMENT À FROID NE SONT PAS RÉGLABLES.

SERRER LE FREIN DE STATIONNEMENT, BLOQUER LES ROUES. DÉBRANCHER, S'IL Y EN A UNE LE DESSERRAGE AUTOMAT. DU FREIN DE STATIONNEMENT. EFFECTUER TOUT RÉGLAGE SUR MOTEUR NORMALEMENT CHAUD, B.V. AU POINT MORT, CONTACT DES ACCESSOIRES ET DES PHARES COUPÉ.

CALAGE DE L'ALLUMAGE :
(1) ARRÊTER LE MOTEUR
(2) DÉBRANCHER LE CONNECTEUR (-◁◁-) INTERCALÉ DANS LE CIRCUIT DE DÉCLENCHEMENT DE L'ÉTINCELLE.
(3) REDÉMARRER LE MOTEUR PRÉALABLEMENT RÉCHAUFFÉ.
(4) CALER L'ALLUMAGE À 15° AVANT PMH OU AU REPÈRE P.
(5) ARRÊTER LE MOTEUR ET REBRANCHER LE CONNECTEUR.

CE MOTEUR EST À COMMANDE DE RALENTI AUTOMATIQUE. LE RÉGIME DE RALENTI N'EST PAS RÉGLABLE. S'IL N'EST PAS DANS LES LIMITES PRESCRITES, CONSULTER LE MANUEL DE RÉPARATION :
B.V.M. AU POINT MORT : 620-680 TR/MIN
B.V.A. EN POSITION "D" : 690-750 TR/MIN

HUILE PRÉCONISÉE : SAE 5W-30, CLASSE API
" SG " -- " ÉCONOMISE D'ÉNERGIE II ".

2.3 L   SPARK PLUG / BOUGIES   GAP / ÉLECTRODES
AWSF-42C   .052-.056

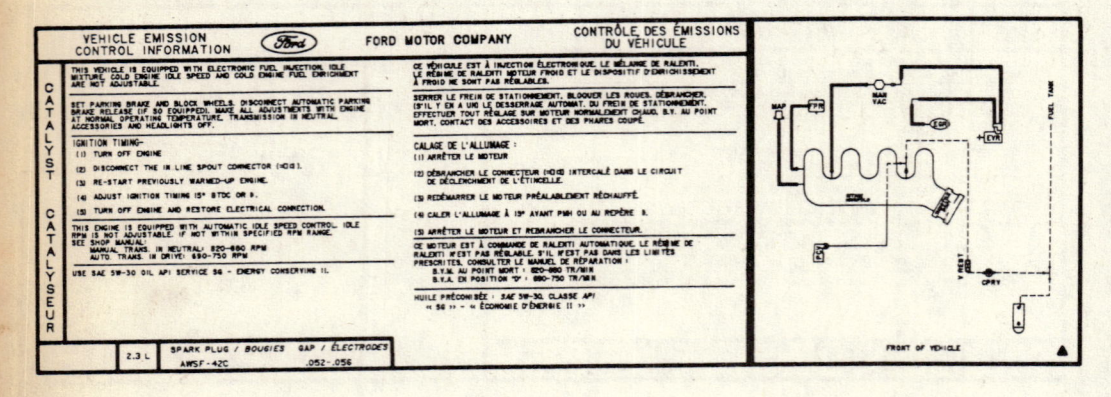

EMISSION CONTROLS 325

■ CALIBRATION: 0-26R-R00 ■   2.3L HSC-EFI ■

FORD MOTOR COMPANY
VEHICLE EMISSION CONTROL INFORMATION

THIS VEHICLE IS EQUIPPED WITH ELECTRONIC FUEL INJECTION. IDLE MIXTURE, COLD ENGINE IDLE SPEED AND COLD ENGINE FUEL ENRICHMENT ARE NOT ADJUSTABLE.

SET PARKING BRAKE AND BLOCK WHEELS. DISCONNECT AUTOMATIC PARKING BRAKE RELEASE (IF SO EQUIPPED). MAKE ALL ADJUSTMENTS WITH ENGINE AT NORMAL OPERATING TEMPERATURE, TRANSMISSION IN NEUTRAL AND ACCESSORIES OFF.

IGNITION TIMING-
(1) TURN OFF ENGINE
(2) DISCONNECT THE IN-LINE SPOUT CONNECTOR (◁◁).
(3) RE-START PREVIOUSLY WARMED-UP ENGINE.
(4) ADJUST IGNITION TIMING TO 15° BTDC OR D.
(5) TURN OFF ENGINE AND RESTORE ELECTRICAL CONNECTION.

THIS ENGINE IS EQUIPPED WITH AUTOMATIC IDLE SPEED CONTROL. IDLE RPM IS NOT ADJUSTABLE. IF NOT WITHIN SPECIFIED RPM RANGE, SEE SHOP MANUAL:
  MANUAL TRANS. IN NEUTRAL: 820-880 RPM
  AUTO. TRANS. IN DRIVE: 690-750 RPM

USE SAE 5W-30 OIL API SERVICE SG - ENERGY CONSERVING II.

THIS VEHICLE CONFORMS TO U.S. EPA AND CALIFORNIA REGULATIONS APPLICABLE TO 1990 MODEL YEAR NEW MOTOR VEHICLES INTRODUCED INTO COMMERCE SOLELY FOR SALE IN CALIFORNIA. OBD EXEMPT.

CATALYST SPARK PLUG: AWSF-42C   GAP- .052-.056
2.3L -9HM
LFM2.3V5FXC0 - TWC/PAIR/HO2S/EGR/MPI

VACUUM HOSE ROUTING — FRONT OF VEHICLE

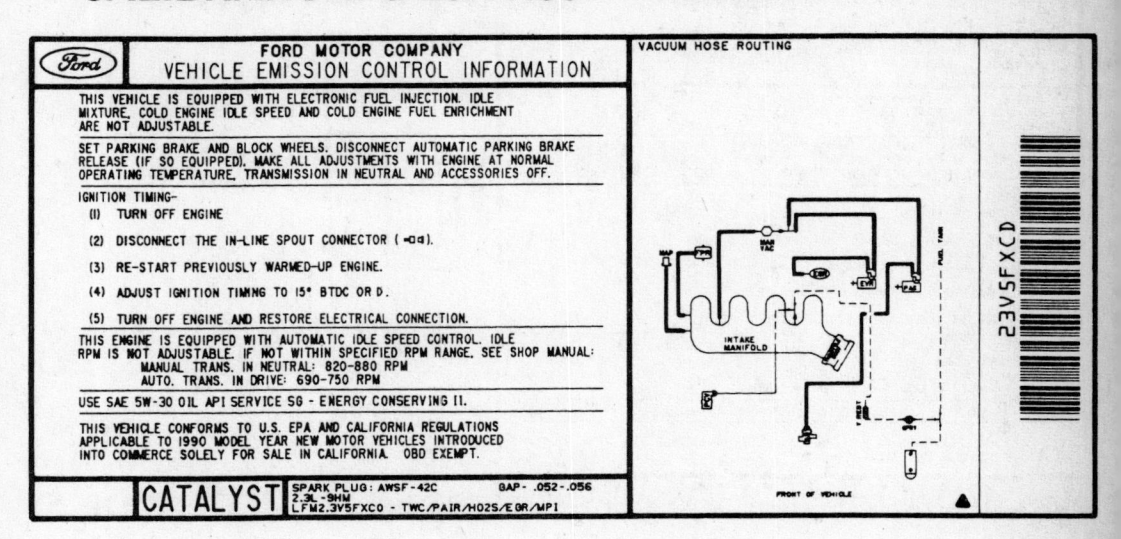

■ CALIBRATION: 9-25C-R10 ■   2.3L HSC-EFI-HO ■

FORD MOTOR COMPANY
VEHICLE EMISSION CONTROL INFORMATION

THIS VEHICLE IS EQUIPPED WITH ELECTRONIC FUEL INJECTION. IDLE MIXTURE, COLD ENGINE IDLE SPEED AND COLD ENGINE FUEL ENRICHMENT ARE NOT ADJUSTABLE.

SET PARKING BRAKE AND BLOCK WHEELS. DISCONNECT AUTOMATIC PARKING BRAKE RELEASE (IF SO EQUIPPED). MAKE ALL ADJUSTMENTS WITH ENGINE AT NORMAL OPERATING TEMPERATURE, TRANSMISSION IN NEUTRAL AND ACCESSORIES OFF.

IGNITION TIMING-
(1) TURN OFF ENGINE
(2) DISCONNECT THE IN-LINE SPOUT CONNECTOR (◁◁).
(3) RE-START PREVIOUSLY WARMED-UP ENGINE.
(4) ADJUST IGNITION TIMING TO 15° BTDC OR D.
(5) TURN OFF ENGINE AND RESTORE ELECTRICAL CONNECTION.

THIS ENGINE IS EQUIPPED WITH AUTOMATIC IDLE SPEED CONTROL. IDLE RPM IS NOT ADJUSTABLE. IF NOT WITHIN SPECIFIED RPM RANGE, SEE SHOP MANUAL:
  MANUAL TRANS. IN NEUTRAL: 810-890 RPM
  AUTO. TRANS. IN DRIVE: 680-760 RPM

USE SAE 5W-30 OIL API SERVICE SG - ENERGY CONSERVING II.

THIS VEHICLE CONFORMS TO U.S. EPA REGULATIONS APPLICABLE TO 1990 MODEL YEAR NEW MOTOR VEHICLES.

CATALYST SPARK PLUG: AWSF-42C   GAP- .052-.056
2.3L -9HM
LFM2.3V5HXF9 - TWC+OC/PAIR/HO2S/EGR/MPI

VACUUM HOSE ROUTING — FRONT OF VEHICLE

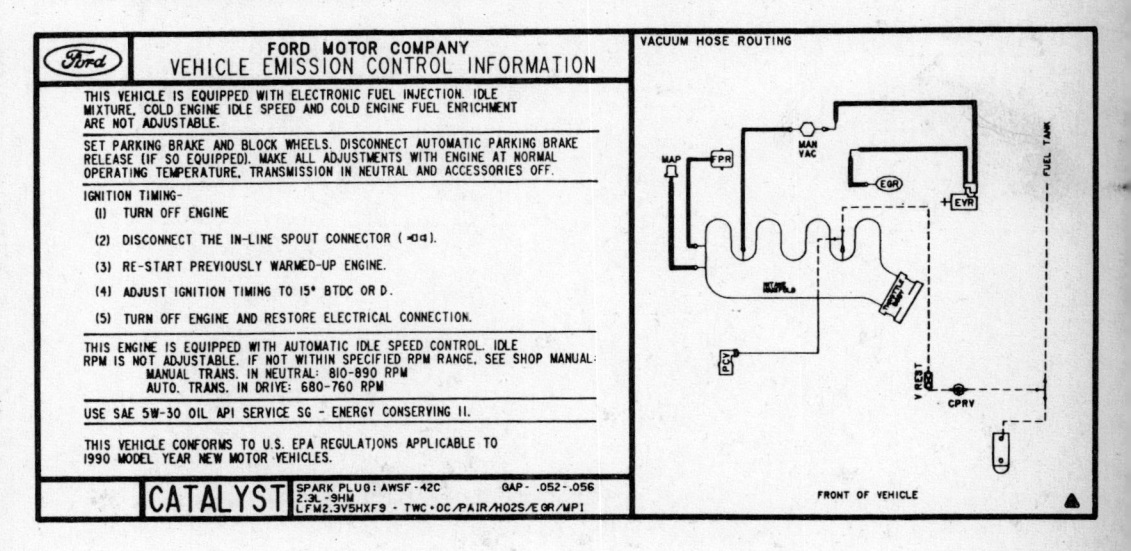

EMISSION CONTROLS

■ CALIBRATION: 9-26D-R10   2.3L HSC-EFI-HO ■

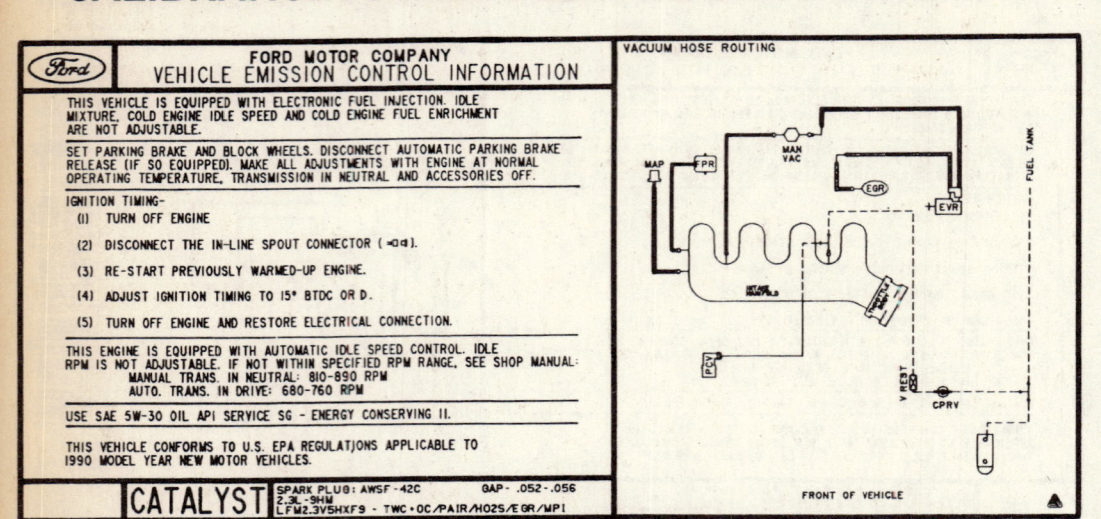

FORD MOTOR COMPANY
VEHICLE EMISSION CONTROL INFORMATION

THIS VEHICLE IS EQUIPPED WITH ELECTRONIC FUEL INJECTION. IDLE MIXTURE, COLD ENGINE IDLE SPEED AND COLD ENGINE FUEL ENRICHMENT ARE NOT ADJUSTABLE.

SET PARKING BRAKE AND BLOCK WHEELS. DISCONNECT AUTOMATIC PARKING BRAKE RELEASE (IF SO EQUIPPED). MAKE ALL ADJUSTMENTS WITH ENGINE AT NORMAL OPERATING TEMPERATURE, TRANSMISSION IN NEUTRAL AND ACCESSORIES OFF.

IGNITION TIMING-
(1) TURN OFF ENGINE
(2) DISCONNECT THE IN-LINE SPOUT CONNECTOR (=◁◁).
(3) RE-START PREVIOUSLY WARMED-UP ENGINE.
(4) ADJUST IGNITION TIMING TO 15° BTDC OR D.
(5) TURN OFF ENGINE AND RESTORE ELECTRICAL CONNECTION.

THIS ENGINE IS EQUIPPED WITH AUTOMATIC IDLE SPEED CONTROL. IDLE RPM IS NOT ADJUSTABLE. IF NOT WITHIN SPECIFIED RPM RANGE, SEE SHOP MANUAL.
  MANUAL TRANS. IN NEUTRAL: 810-890 RPM
  AUTO. TRANS. IN DRIVE: 680-760 RPM

USE SAE 5W-30 OIL API SERVICE SG - ENERGY CONSERVING II.

THIS VEHICLE CONFORMS TO U.S. EPA REGULATIONS APPLICABLE TO 1990 MODEL YEAR NEW MOTOR VEHICLES.

CATALYST   SPARK PLUG: AWSF-42C   GAP- .052-.056
2.3L -9HM
LFM2.3V5HXF9 - TWC•OC/PAIR/HO2S/EGR/MPI

VACUUM HOSE ROUTING
FRONT OF VEHICLE

Fuel System 5

CARBURETOR FUEL SYSTEM

Your car uses, depending on year and model, a staged two barrel unit (the second barrel is opened under heavy throttle situations), or a single barrel carburetor. Carburetors may be of the feedback or non-feedback type.

The staged carburetor usually has five basic metering systems. They are: the choke system, idle system, main metering system, acceleration system and the power enrichment system.

The choke system is used for cold starting. It incorporates a bimetal spring and an electric heater for faster cold weather starts and improved driveability during warm-up.

The idle system is a separate and adjustable system for the correct air/fuel mixture at both idle and low speed operation.

The main metering system provides the necessary air/fuel mixture for normal driving speeds. A main metering system is provided for both primary and secondary stages of operation.

The accelerating system is operated from the primary stage throttle linkage. The system provides fuel to the primary stage during acceleration. Fuel is provided by a diaphragm pump located on the carburetor.

The power enrichment system consists of a vacuum operated power valve and airflow regulated pullover system for the secondary carburetor barrel. The system is used in conjunction with the main metering system to provide acceptable performance during mid and heavy acceleration.

Mechanical Fuel Pump

The mechanical fuel pump provides fuel for the engine from the gas tank. The lever arm is actuated by a pushrod driven by an eccentric on the camshaft. The pump lever arm actuates the internal diaphragm and provides fuel on demand of the carburetor when the engine is running.

REMOVAL AND INSTALLATION

1. Disconnect the negative battery cable.
2. Loosen the threaded fuel line connection(s) a small amount. Do not remove lines at this time.
3. Loosen mounting bolts approximately 2 turns. Apply force with hand to loosen fuel pump if gasket is stuck. Rotate the engine until the fuel pump cam lobe is near its low position. The tension on the fuel pump will be greatly reduced at the low cam position.
4. Disconnect the fuel pump inlet and outlet lines.
5. Remove the fuel pump attaching bolts and remove the pump and gasket. Discard the old gasket and replace with new.
6. Measure the fuel pump pushrod length. It should be 2.34 in. (61.7mm) minimum. Replace if worn or out of specification.

To install:

7. Remove all fuel pump gasket material from the engine and the fuel pump if installing the original pump.
8. Install the attaching bolts into the fuel pump and install a new gasket. Position the fuel pump to the mounting pad. Tighten the attaching bolts alternately and evenly and tighten to 11–19 ft. lbs. (15–25 Nm).
9. Install fuel lines to fuel pump. Start the threaded fitting by hand to avoid cross threading. Tighten outlet nut to 15–18 ft. lbs. (20–24 Nm).
10. Start engine and inspect for fuel leaks.
11. Stop engine and check all fuel pump fuel line connections for fuel leaks by running a finger under the connections. Check for oil leaks at the fuel pump mounting gasket.

FUSL SYSTEM

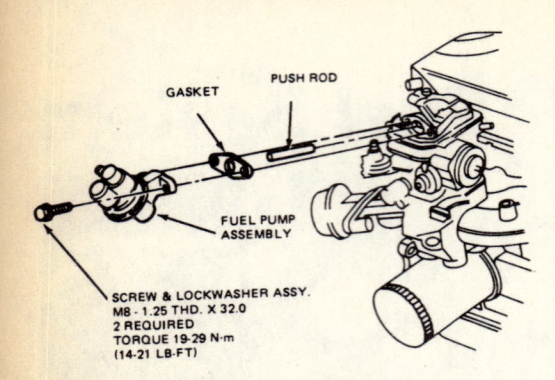

Typical fuel pump pushrod installation

PRESSURE TESTING

The fuel pump can fail in two ways: it can fail to provide a sufficient volume of gasoline under the proper pressure to the carburetor, or it can develop an internal or external leak. An external leak will be evident; not so with an internal leak. A quick check for an internal leak is to remove the oil dipstick and examine the oil on it. A fuel pump with an internal leak will leak fuel into the oil pan. If the oil on the dipstick is very thin and smells of gas, a defective fuel pump could be the cause.

To check the volume of gasoline from the fuel pump, disconnect the fuel pump line at the fuel filter. Connect a suitable rubber hose and clamp it to the fuel line. Insert it into a quart container. Start the engine. The fuel pump should provide one pint of gasoline in thirty seconds.

1. Connect a suitable pressure gauge, 0–15 psi (0–103 kPa), to fuel filter end of fuel line. No tee is required.
2. Start engine and read pressure after 10 seconds. Pressure should read 4.5–6.5 psi with fuel return line closed at fuel filter. Replace fuel pump if pressure is above or below specification.
3. Disconnect fuel pump and connect fuel line to fuel filter. Use a backup wrench on the filter and tighten fuel line to 15–18 ft. lbs. (20–24 Nm).

Motorcraft 740/5740 Carburetor

ADJUSTMENTS

Fast Idle Cam

1. Set the fast idle screw on the kickdown step of the cam against the shoulder of the top step.
2. Manually close the primary choke plate, and measure the distance between the downstream side of the choke plate and the air horn wall.
3. Adjust the right fork of the choke bi-metal shaft, which engages the fast idle cam, by bending the fork up and down to obtain the required clearance.

Fast Idle

1. Place the transmission in neutral or park.
2. Bring the engine to normal operating temperature.
3. Disconnect and plug the vacuum hose at the EGR and purge valves.
4. Identify the vacuum source to the air bypass section of the air supply control valve. If a vacuum hose is connected to the carburetor, disconnect the hose and plug the hose at the air supply control valve.
5. Place the fast idle adjustment on the second step of the fast idle cam. Run the engine until the cooling fan comes on.
6. While the cooling fan is on, check the fast idle rpm. If adjustment is necessary, loosen the locknut and adjust to specification on underhood decal.
7. Remove all plugs and reconnect hoses to their original position.

Dashpot

With the throttle set at the curb idle position, fully depress the dashpot stem and measure the distance between the stem and the throttle lever. Adjust by loosening the locknut and turning the dashpot.

Choke Plate Pulldown

NOTE: *The following procedure requires the removal of the carburetor and also the choke cap which is retained by two rivets.*

1. Remove the carburetor from the engine.
2. Remove the choke cap as follows:
   a. Check the rivets to determine if mandrel is well below the rivet head. If mandrel is within the rivet head thickness, drive it down or out with a $\frac{1}{16}$ in. (1.5mm) diameter tip punch.
   b. With a $\frac{1}{8}$ in. (3mm) diameter drill, drill into the rivet head until the rivet head comes loose from the rivet body. Use light pressure on the drill bit or the rivet will just spin in the hole.
   c. After drilling off the rivet head, drive the remaining rivet out of the hole with a $\frac{1}{8}$ in. (3mm) diameter punch.
   d. Repeat Steps a through c to remove the remaining rivet.
3. Set the fast idle adjusting screw on the high step of the fast idle cam by temporarily opening the throttle lever and rotating the choke bimetal shaft lever counterclockwise until the choke plates are in the fully closed position.

FUEL SYSTEM 329

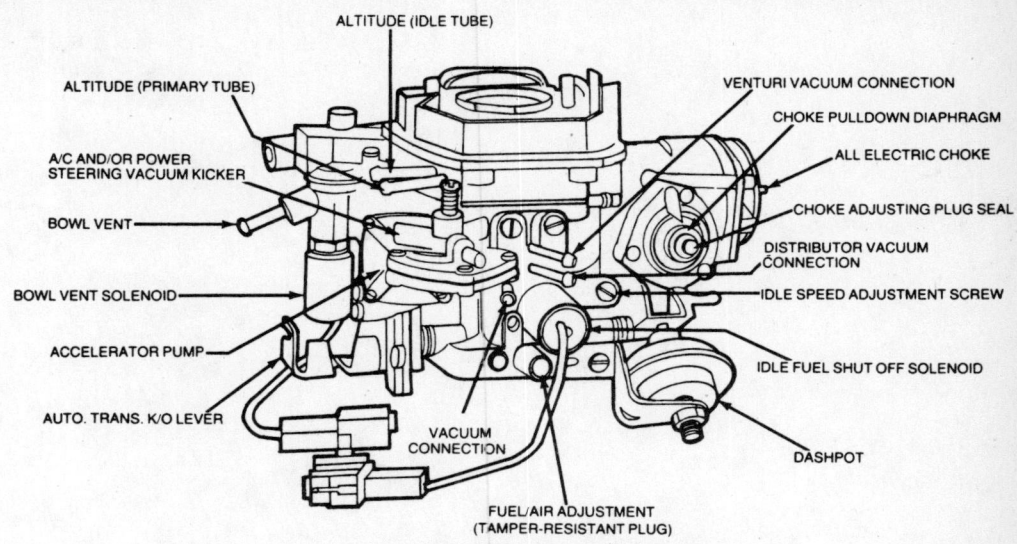

Motorcraft 740/5740 carburetor

4. With an external vacuum source, set to 17 in.Hg. Vacuum should be applied to the vacuum channel adjacent to the primary bore on the base of the carburetor.

NOTE: *The modulator spring should not be depressed.*

5. Measure the clearance between the downstream side of the choke plate and the air horn wall.

6. If an adjustment is necessary, turn the vacuum diaphragm adjusting screw in or out as required.

Float Level

1. Hold the air horn upside down, at about a 45° angle with the air horn gasket in position.
2. Use the gauge (supplied with the rebuilding kit) and measure the clearance between the float toe and air horn casting.
3. Adjust, if necessary, by removing the float and bending the adjusting tang. Use care when handling the float.

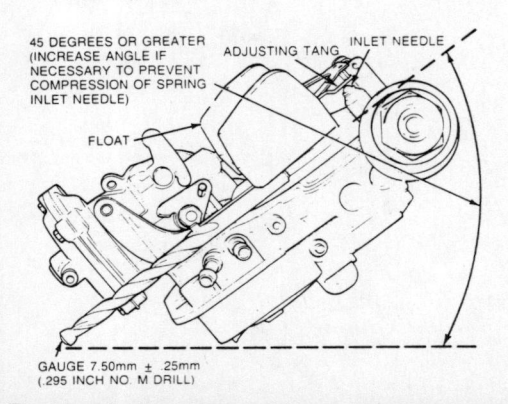

Float level adjustment — Motorcraft 740/5740 carburetor

Float Drop

Hold the air horn in its normal installed position. Measure the clearance from the gasket to the bottom of the float. Adjust, if necessary, by removing the float and bending the float drop adjusting tab.

Holley 1949/6149 Feedback Carburetor

ADJUSTMENTS

Float Level

1. Remove the carburetor air horn.
2. With the air horn assembly removed, place a finger over float hinge pin retainer, and invert the main body. Catch the accelerator pump check ball and weight.
3. Using a straight edge, check the position of the floats. The correct dry float setting is

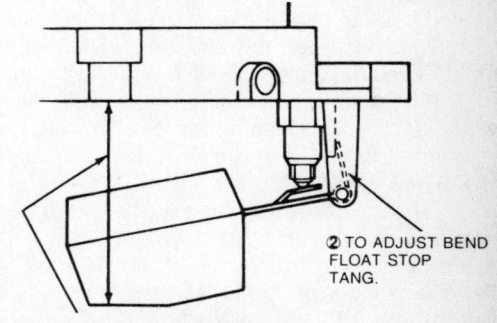

Float drip adjustment — Motorcraft 740/5740 carburetor

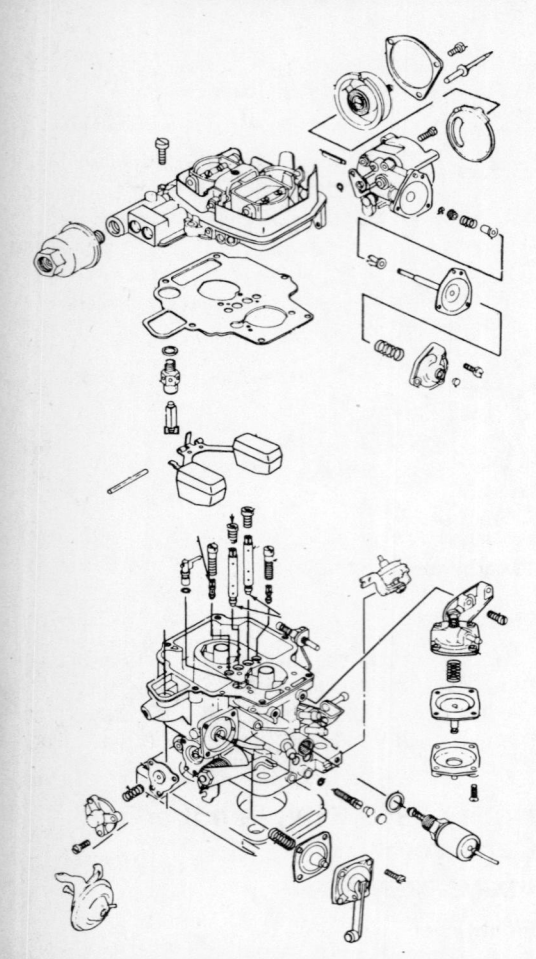

330 FUEL SYSTEM

Exploded view of Motorcraft model 740 carburetor

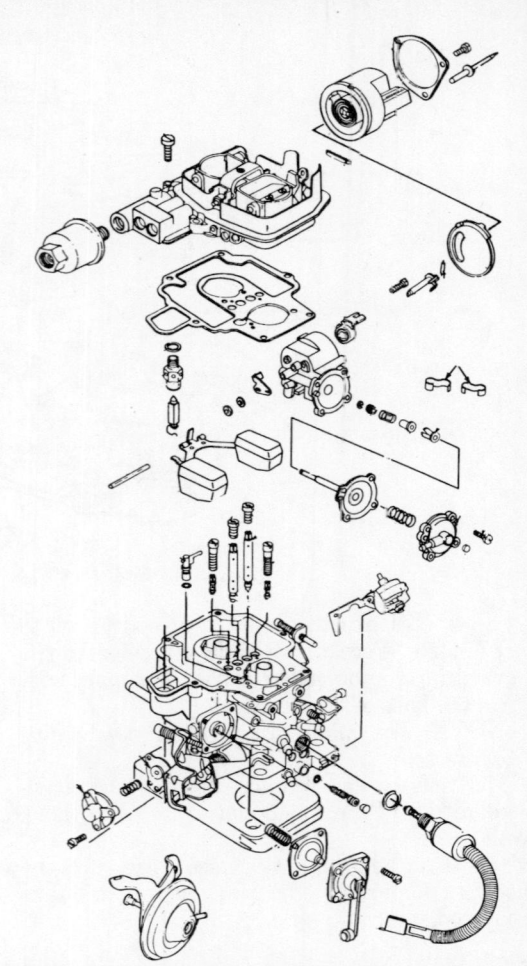

Exploded view of Motorcraft model 5740 carburetor

that both pontoons at the extreme outboard edge be flush with the surface of the main body casting (without gasket). If adjustment is required, bend the float tabs to raise or lower the float level.

4. Once adjustment is correct, turn main body right side up, and check the float alignment. The float should move freely throughout its range without contacting the fuel bowl walls. If the float pontoons are misaligned, straighten by bending the float arms. Recheck the float level adjustment.

5. During assembly, insert the check ball first and then the weight.

Feedback Controlled Main System Diaphragm Adjustment Model 6149 Carburetor Only

1. Remove the main system feedback diaphragm adjustment screw lead sealing disc from the air horn screw boss, by drilling a 2.38mm diameter hole through the disc. Then, insert a small punch to pry the disc out.

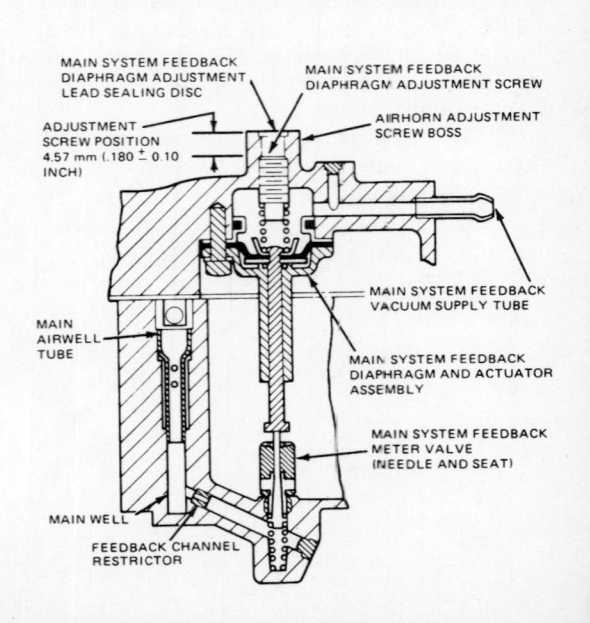

Diaphragm adjustment — 6149 carburetor

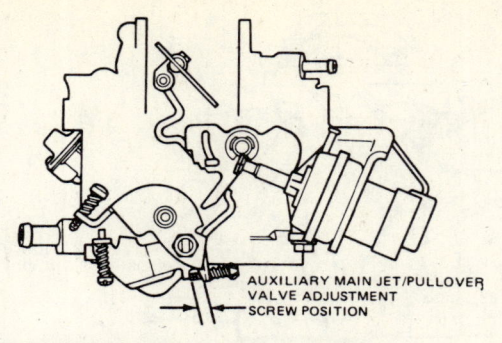

FUEL SYSTEM 331

Timing adjustment — 6149 carburetor

2. Turn the main system feedback adjustment screw as required to position the top of the screw 4.57mm ± 0.25mm below the top of the air horn adjustment screw boss.

NOTE: *For carburetors stamped with as **S** on the top of the air horn adjustment screw boss, adjust screw position to 6.35mm ± 0.25mm.*

3. Install a new lead sealing disc and stake with a 1/4 in. (6mm) flat ended punch. 4. Apply an external vacuum source (hand vacuum pump — 10 in.Hg max.) and check for leaks. The diaphragm should hold vacuum.

Auxiliary Main Jet/Pullover Valve — Timing Adjustment

The length of the auxiliary main jet/pullover valve adjustment screw which protrudes through the back side (side opposite the adjustment screw head) of the throttle pickup lever must be 8.76mm ± 0.25mm. To adjust, turn the screw in or out as required.

Mechanical Fuel Bowl Vent Adjustment Lever Clearance

OFF VEHICLE ADJUSTMENT

NOTE: *There are two methods for adjusting lever clearance.*

1. Secure the choke plate in the wide open position.
2. Set the throttle at the TSP Off position.
3. Turn the TSP Off idle adjustment screw counterclockwise until the throttle plate is closed in the throttle bore.
4. Fuel bowl vent clearance, Dimension **A**, should be 3.05mm ± 0.25mm.
5. If out of specification, bend the bowl vent actuator lever at the adjustment point to obtain the required clearance.

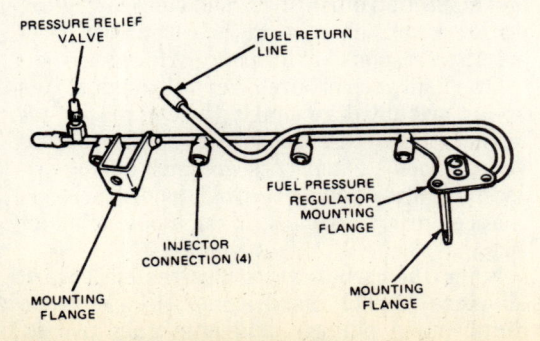

CAUTION: *Do not bend fuel bowl vent arm and/or adjacent portion of the actuator lever.*

NOTE: *TSP Off rpm must be set after carburetor installation.*

ON VEHICLE ADJUSTMENT

NOTE: *This adjustment must be performed after curb idle speed has been set to specification.*

1. Secure the choke plate in the wide open position.
2. Turn ignition key to the ON position to activate the TSP (engine not running). Open throttle so that the TSP plunger extends.
3. Verify that the throttle is in the idle set position (contacting the TSP plunger). Measure the clearance of the fuel bowl vent arm to the bowl vent actuating lever.
4. Fuel bowl vent clearance, Dimension **A**, should be 0.76mm.

NOTE: *There is a difference in the on-vehicle and off-vehicle specification.*

5. If out of specification, bend the bowl vent actuator lever at the adjustment point to obtain the required clearance.

CAUTION: *Do not bend fuel bowl vent arm and/or adjacent portion of the actuating lever!*

Accelerator Pump Stroke Adjustment

1. Check the length of the accelerator pump operating link from its inside edge at the accelerator pump operating rod to its inside edge at the throttle lever hole. The dimension should be 54.61 ± 0.25mm.
2. Adjust to proper length by bending loop in operating link.

Wide Open Throttle Air Conditioning Cut-Off Switch Adjustment — Model 1949 Carburetor Only

The WOT A/C cutoff switch is a normally closed switch (allowing current to flow at any throttle position other than wide open throttle).

1. Disconnect the wiring harness at the switch connector.
2. Connect a 12 volt DC power supply and test lamp. With the throttle at curb idle, TSP Off idle or fast idle position, the test light must be On. If the test lamp does not light, replace the switch assembly.
3. Rotate the throttle to the wide open posi-

Vent adjustment — 6149 carburetor

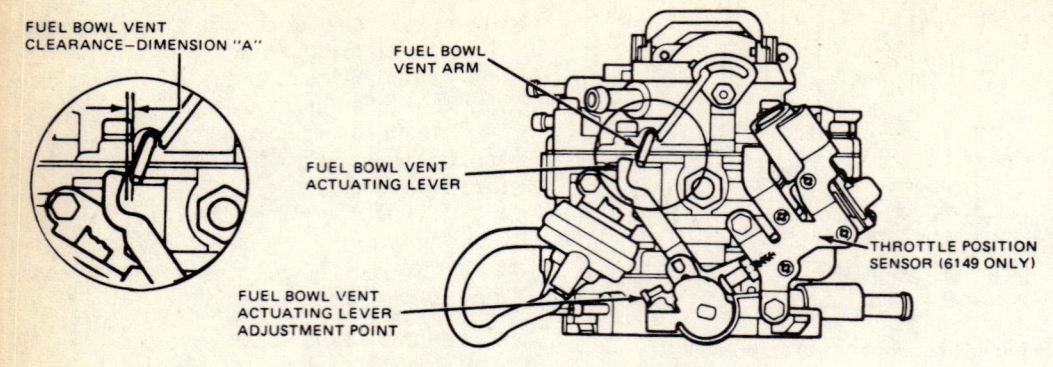

332 FUEL SYSTEM

Lever clearance adjustment — 6149 carburetor

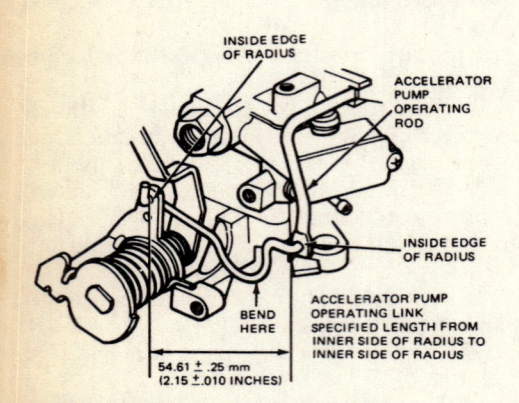

Accelerator pump stroke adjustment 6149 carburetor

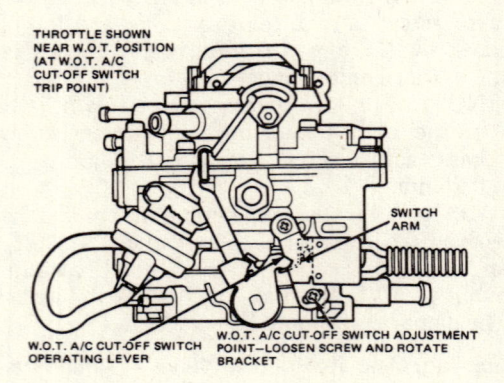

WOT/AC cut-off switch adjustment 6149 carburetor

tion. The test lamp must go Off, indicating an open circuit.

4. If the lamp remains On, insert a 4.19mm drill or gauge between the throttle lever WOT stop and the WOT stop boss on the carburetor main body casting. Hold the throttle open as far as possible against the gauge. Loosen the two switch mounting screws sufficiently to allow the switch to pivot. Rotate the switch assembly so the test lamp just goes out with the throttle held in the above referenced position. If the lamp does not go Off within the allowable adjustment rotation, replace the switch. If the light goes out, tighten the two switch bracket-to-carburetor screws to 45 inch lbs. and remove drill or gauge and repeat Step 3.

OVERHAUL NOTES

NOTE: *All major and minor repair kits contain detailed instructions and illustrations. Refer to them for complete rebuilding instructions.*

To prevent damage to the throttle plates, make a stand using four bolts, eight flat washers and eight nuts. Place a washer and nut on the bolt, install through the carburetor base and secure with a nut.

Generally, when a carburetor requires major service, rebuilt one is purchased on an exchange basis, or a kit may be bought for overhauling the carburetor.

The kit contains the necessary parts (see below) and some form of instructions for carburetor rebuilding. The instructions may vary between a simple exploded view and detailed step-by-step rebuilding instructions. Unless you are familiar with carburetor overhaul, the latter should be used.

There are some general overhaul procedures which should always be observed: Efficient carburetion depends greatly on careful cleaning and inspection during overhaul since dirt, gum, water, or varnish in or on the carburetor parts are often responsible for poor performance.

Overhaul you carburetor in a clean, dust free area. Carefully disassembly the carburetor, referring often to the exploded views. Keep all similar and look a like parts segregated during disassembly and cleaning to avoid accidental interchange during assembly. Make a note of all jet sizes.

When the carburetor is disassembled, wash all parts (except diaphragms, electric choke units. pump plunger, and any other plastic, leather, fiber, or rubber parts) in clean carbure-

FUEL SYSTEM 333

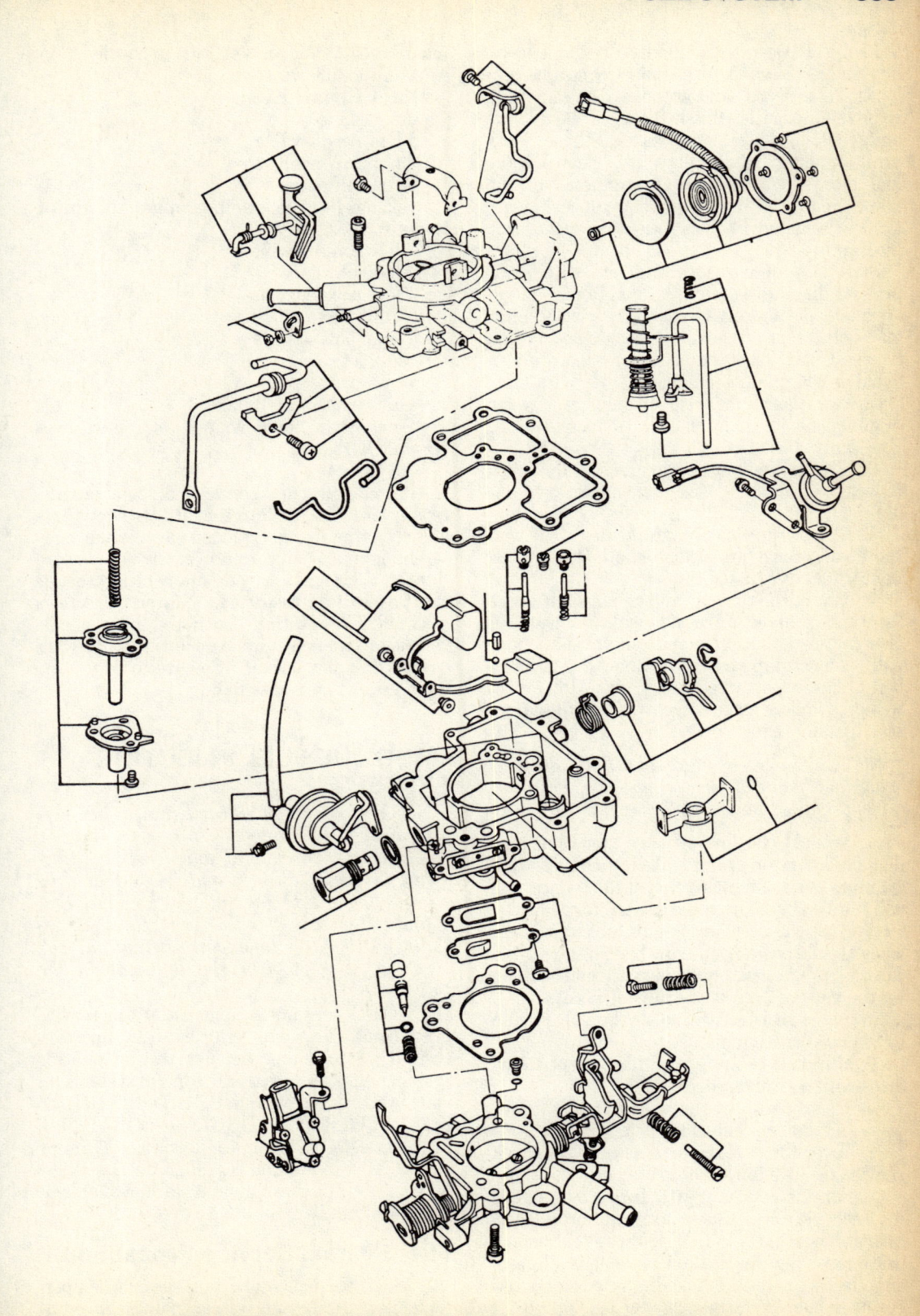

Exploded view of a 1949-C non-feedback & 6149 feedback carburetors

FUEL SYSTEM

tor solvent. Do not leave parts in the solvent any longer than is necessary to sufficiently loosen the deposits. Excessive cleaning may remove the special finish from the float bowl and choke valve bodies, leaving these parts unfit for service. Rinse all parts in clean solvent and blow them dry with compressed air or allow them to air dry. Wipe clean all cork, plastic, leather, and fiber parts with a clean, lint free cloth.

Blow out all passages and jets with compressed air and be sure that there are no restrictions or blockages. Never use wire or similar tools to clean jets, fuel passages, or air bleeds. Clean all jets and valves separately to avoid accidental interchange.

Check all parts for wear or damage. If wear or damage is found, replace the defective parts. Especially check the following:

1. Check the float needle and seat for wear. If wear is found, replace the complete assembly.

2. Check the float hinge pin for wear and the float(s) for dents or distortion. Replace the float if fuel has leaked into it.

3. Check the throttle and choke shaft bores for wear or an out-of-round condition. Damage or wear to the throttle arm, shaft, shaft bore will often require replacement of the throttle body. These parts require a close tolerance; wear may allow air leakage, which could affect starting and idling.

NOTE: *Throttle shafts and bushings are usually not included in overhaul kits. They can be purchased separately.*

4. Inspect the idle mixture adjusting needles for burrs or grooves. Any such condition requires replacement of the needle, since you will not be able to obtain a satisfactory idle.

5. Test the accelerator pump check valves. They should pass air one way but not the other. Test for proper seating by blowing and sucking on the valve. Replace the valve if necessary. If the valve is satisfactory, wash the valve again to remove breath moisture.

6. Check the bowl cover for warped surfaces with a straightedge.

7. Closely inspect the valves and seats for wear and damage, replacing as necessary.

8. After the carburetor is assembled, check the choke valve for freedom of operation.

Carburetor overhaul kits are recommended for each overhaul. These kits contain all gaskets and new parts to replace those that deteriorate most rapidly. Failure to replace all parts supplied with the kit (especially gaskets) can result in poor performance later.

Some carburetor manufacturers supply overhaul kits of three basic types: minor repair, major repair, and gasket kits. Basically, they contain the following:

Minor Repair Kits:
- All gaskets
- Float needle valve
- Volume control screw
- All diaphragms
- Spring for the pump diaphragm

Major Repair Kits:
- All jets and gaskets
- All diaphragms
- Float needle valve
- Volume control screw
- Pump ball valve
- Main jet carrier
- Float
- Other necessary items
- Some cover holddown screws and washers

Gasket Kits:
- All gaskets

After cleaning and checking all components, reassemble the carburetor, using new parts and referring to the exploded view. When reassembling, make sure that all screw and jets are tight in their seats, buy do not over tighten, as the tips will be distorted. Tighten all screws gradually, in rotation. Do not tighten needle valves into their seat; uneven jetting will result. Always use new gaskets. Be sure to adjust the float level when reassembling.

GASOLINE FUEL INJECTION SYSTEM

NOTE: *It is recommended that before performing this or any other procedure on your vehicle, you check with your local manufactures representative to make sure that if by doing these tests there may be a chance that you will violate your warranty, thus rendering you helpless to submit a claim on your vehicle if a problem should occur in the future.*

This book contains simple testing and service procedures for your vehicles fuel injection system. More comprehensive testing on this system and other electronic control systems on your Ford can be found in CHILTON'S GUIDE TO ELECTRONIC ENGINE CONTROLS, book part No. 7535 for 1978–85, No. 7768 for the 1984–88 years and No. 8024 for the 1988–90 years. All of these manuals are available at your local retailer.

Fuel System Service Precautions

Safety is the most important factor when performing not only fuel system maintenance but any type of maintenance. Failure to conduct maintenance and repairs in a safe manner may result in serious personal injury or death. Maintenance and testing of the vehicle's fuel system components can be accomplished safely and effectively by adhering to the following rules and guidelines.

- To avoid the possibility of fire and personal injury, always disconnect the negative battery cable unless the repair or test procedure requires that battery voltage be applied.
- Always relieve the fuel system pressure prior to disconnecting any fuel system component (injector, fuel rail, pressure regulator, etc.), fitting or fuel line connection. Exercise extreme caution whenever relieving fuel system pressure to avoid exposing skin, face and eyes to fuel spray. Please be advised that fuel under pressure may penetrate the skin or any part of the body that it contacts.
- Always place a shop towel or cloth around the fitting or connection prior to loosening to absorb any excess fuel due to spillage. Ensure that all fuel spillage (should it occur) is quickly removed from engine surfaces. Ensure that all fuel soaked cloths or towels are deposited into a suitable waste container.
- Always keep a dry chemical (Class B) fire extinguisher near the work area.
- Do not allow fuel spray or fuel vapors to come into contact with a spark or open flame.
- Always use a backup wrench when loosing and tightening fuel line connection fittings. This will prevent unnecessary stress and torsion to fuel line piping. Always follow the proper torque specifications.
- Always replace worn fuel fitting O-rings with new. Do not substitute fuel hose or equivalent, where fuel pipe is installed.

Relieving Fuel System Pressure

The pressure in the fuel system must be released before attempting to remove the fuel pump.

1. Disconnect the negative battery cable.
2. A special valve is incorporated in the fuel rail assembly for the purpose of relieving the pressure in the fuel system.
3. Remove the air cleaner.
4. Attach pressure gauge tool No. T80L-9974-A or equivalent, to the fuel pressure valve on the fuel rail assembly and release the pressure from the system.

Push Connect Fittings

Push connect fittings are designed with two different retaining clips. The fittings used with $5/16$ in. (8mm) diameter tubing use a hairpin clip. The fittings used with $1/4$ in. (6mm) and $1/2$ in. (12.7mm) diameter tubing use a "duck bill" clip. Each type of fitting requires different procedures for service.

Push connect fitting disassembly must be accomplished prior to fuel component removal (filter, pump, etc.) except for the fuel tank, where removal is necessary for access to the push connects.

REMOVAL AND INSTALLATION

$5/16$ in. Fittings (Hairpin Clip)

1. Inspect internal portion of fitting for dirt accumulation. If more than a light coating of dust is present, clean the fitting before disassembly.
2. Remove hairpin type clip from fitting. This is done (using hands only) by spreading the two clip legs about $1/8$ in. (3mm) each to disengage the body and pushing the legs into the fitting. Complete removal is accomplished by lightly pulling from the triangular end of the clip and working it clear of the tube and fitting.

NOTE: *Do not use any tools.*

3. Grasp the fitting and hose assembly and pull in an axial direction to remove the fitting from the steel tube. Adhesion between sealing surfaces may occur. A slight twist of the fitting may be required to break this adhesion and permit effortless removal.
4. When fitting is removed from the tube end, inspect clip to ensure it has not been damaged. If damaged, replace the clip. If undamaged, immediately reinstall clip, insert clip into any two adjacent openings with the triangular portion pointing away from the fitting opening. Install clip to fully engage the body (legs of hairpin clip locked on outside of body). Piloting with an index finger is necessary.
5. Before installing fitting on the tube, wipe tube end with a clean cloth. Inspect the inside of the fitting to ensure it is free of dirt and/or obstructions.
6. To reinstall the fitting onto the tube, align the fitting and tube axially and push the fitting onto the tube end. When the fitting is engaged, a definite click will be heard. Pull on fitting to ensure it is fully engaged.

$1/2$ in. and $1/4$ in. Fittings (Duck Bill Clip)

The fitting consists of a body, spacers, O-rings and a duck bill retaining clip. The clip maintains the fitting to steel tube juncture. When disassembly is required for service, one of the two following methods are to be followed:

$1/4$ in. FITTINGS

To disengage the tube from the fitting, align the slot on push connect disassembly Tool T82L-9500-AH or equivalent with either tab on the clip (90° from slots on side of fitting) and

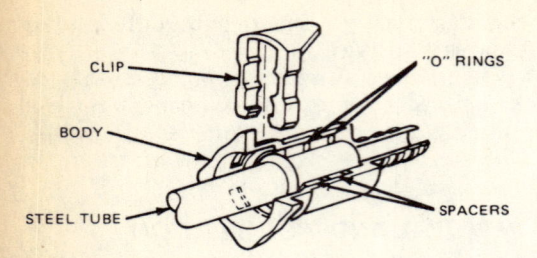

336 FUEL SYSTEM

Push connect fittings with hairpin clip

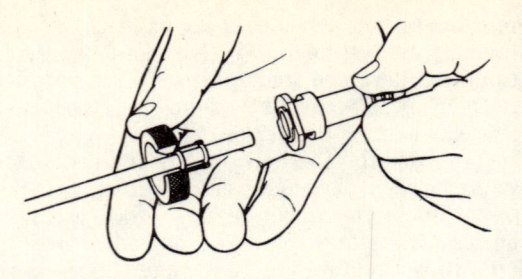

Pulling off push connect fitting

insert the tool. This disengages the duck bill from the tube. Holding the tool and the tube with one hand, pull fitting away from the tube.

NOTE: *Only moderate effort is required if the tube has been properly disengaged. Use hands only. After disassembly, inspect and clean the tube sealing surface. Also inspect the inside of the fitting for damage to the retaining clip. If the retaining clip appears to be damaged, replace it. Some fuel tubes have a secondary bead which aligns with the outer surface of the clip. These beads can make tool insertion difficult. If there is extreme difficulty, use the disassembly method following.*

½ in. FITTING AND ALTERNATE METHOD FOR ¼ in. FITTING

This method of disassembly disengages the retaining clip from the fitting body.

Use a pair of narrow pliers, (6 in. [153mm] locking pliers are ideal). The pliers must have a jaw width of 0.2 in. (5mm) or less.

Align the jaws of the pliers with the openings in the side of the fitting case and compress the portion of the retaining clip that engages the fitting case. This disengages the retaining clip from the case (often one side of the clip will disengage before the other. It is necessary to disengage the clip from both openings). Pull the fitting off the tube.

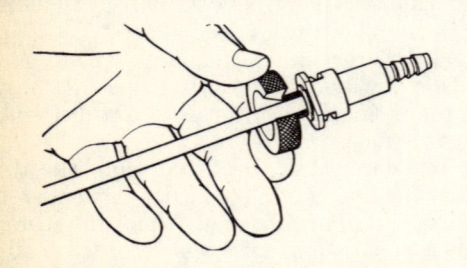

NOTE: *Only moderate effort is required if the retaining clip has been properly disengaged. Use hands only.*

The retaining clip will remain on the tube. Disengage the clip from the tube bead and remove. Replace the retaining clip if it appears to be damaged.

NOTE: *Slight ovality of the ring of the clip will usually occur. If there are no visible cracks and the ring will pinch back to its circular configuration, it is not damaged. If there is any doubt, replace the clip.*

Install the clip into the body by inserting one of the retaining clip serrated edges on the duck bill portion into one of the window openings. Push on the other side until the clip snaps into place. Slide fuel line back into the clip.

Electric Fuel Pump

1.6 & 1.9L fuel injected models are equipped with an externally mounted electric fuel pump. The pump is located at the right rear, under the car, near the fuel tank. The pump is controlled by the EEC system, via a pump relay, which provides power to the pump under various operating conditions.

REMOVAL AND INSTALLATION

Externally Mounted Fuel Pump

NOTE: *Fuel pressure must be relieved before servicing the fuel system. A valve is provided on the fuel rail assembly for this purpose. Remove the air cleaner and attach a special pressure gauge tool (Rotunda T80L9974A or equivalent) to the valve and relieve the pressure.*

1. Raise and support the rear of the car on jackstands.
2. Remove the pump mounting assembly by loosening the upper mounting bolt until the

Removing push connect with tool

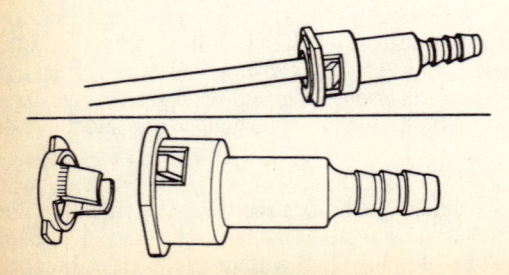

Push connect fittings with duck bill clip

FUEL SYSTEM

pump can be lowered. Remove the parking brake cable from mounting clip to provide necessary working room.

3. Disconnect the electrical connector and disconnect the fuel pump outlet fitting.

4. Disconnect the fuel pump inlet line from the pump. Either drain the tank or raise the end of the line above the tank level to prevent draining.

To install:

5. Install the fuel pump in the reverse order of removal.

6. Install the pressure gauge on the fuel rail. Turn the ignition ON for 2 seconds. Turn the switch OFF. Repeat procedure several times, until the pressure gauge shows 35 psi. Remove the gauge. Start the engine and check for leaks.

In-Tank Fuel Pump

CAUTION: *Extreme caution should be taken when removing the fuel tank from the vehicle! Ensure that all removal procedures are conducted in a well ventilated area! Have a sufficient amount of absorbent material in the vicinity of the work area to quickly contain fuel spillages should they occur. Never store waste fuel in an open container as it presents a serious fire hazard!*

NOTE: *The fuel pump is mounted on the fuel sender assembly in the tank.*

1. Depressurize the fuel system by disconnecting the electrical connector at the inertia switch. Crank the engine for a minimum of 15 seconds to reduce the fuel pressure in the lines or remove the air cleaner and attach pressure gauge tool T80L–9974–A or equivalent, to the fuel pressure valve on the fuel rail assembly and release the pressure from the system.

2. Disconnect the negative battery cable and remove the fuel from the fuel tank by pumping it out through the filler neck. Clean up any fuel spillage immediately.

3. Raise and support the vehicle safely and remove the fuel filler tube (neck). On all wheel drive vehicles, remove the exhaust system and rear axle assembly.

4. Support the fuel tank and remove the fuel tank straps, lower the fuel tank enough to be able to remove the fuel lines, electrical connectors and vent lines from the tank.

5. Remove the fuel tank from under the vehicle and place it on a suitable work bench. Remove any dirt around the fuel pump attaching flange.

6. Turn the fuel pump locking ring counterclockwise and remove the lock ring.

7. Remove the fuel pump from the fuel tank and discard the flange gasket.

8. On all wheel drive vehicles, partially raise the sender unit and disconnect the jet pump line and resistor electrical connector. Remove the fuel pump and bracket assembly with seal gasket. Remove the seal gasket and replace with new. Remove the jet pump assembly.

To install:

9. Clean fuel pump mounting flange and fuel tank mounting surface and seal ring groove.

10. Lightly coat the new seal ring gasket with a suitable lubricant compound part No. C1AZ–19590–B or equivalent, to hold the gasket in place during installation.

11. All-wheel drive vehicles only: install jet pump assembly and retaining screw.

12. Install fuel pump and sender. Ensure that nylon filter is not damaged and that locating keys are in key ways and seal ring remains in place.

13. All-wheel drive vehicles only: connect jet pump line and electrical connector to resistor. Ensure locating key ways and seal ring remain in place.

14. Hold assembly in place and install locking ring finger-tight. Ensure that all locking tabs are under tank lock ring tabs.

15. Secure unit with locking ring by rotating ring clockwise using fuel sender wrench tool D84P–9275–A or equivalent, until ring stops against stops.

16. Remove tank from bench to vehicle and support tank while connecting fuel lines, vent line and electrical connectors to appropriate places.

17. Install tank in vehicle and secure with retaining straps.

18. All-wheel drive vehicles only: install rear axle assembly and exhaust system.

19. Lower vehicle and install fuel in tank. Check for leaks.

20. Connect negative battery cable.

21. Check fuel pressure.

22. Remove the pressure gauge, start the engine and recheck for fuel leaks. Correct all fuel leaks immediately.

CHILTON TIPS

1989 Escort

1989 Escorts with the 1.9L EFI HO engine built between 4/3/89 and 5/5/89 have been known to exhibit a whining noise from the electrical fuel pump. This whining noise has been caused by the spring in the outlet check valve. The noise may be a constant or fluctuating low pitched whine.

The solution to this problem is to install a new design fuel pump that has a revised outlet check valve spring. The new, revised fuel pump

FUEL SYSTEM

is part No. E9FZ-9H307-A and is available at your local authorized dealer.

1990 Tempo and Topaz

The 1990 2.3L engine in the Tempo and Topaz is equipped with new deposit-resistant type service tips. These new injector tips are resistant to the formation of the deposits at the fuel metering area. These new tips are tan in body color (not connector color) and do not require cleaning. The new fuel injectors with the deposit resistant tips are labeled with part No. FO3Z-9F593-A and are available at your local authorized dealer.

PRESSURE TESTS

The diagnostic pressure valve (Schrader type) is located at the top of the Fuel charging main body on CFI systems, or on the fuel rail on multi-port systems. This valve provides a convenient point for service personnel to monitor fuel pressure, bleed down the system pressure prior to maintenance, and to bleed out air which may become trapped in the system during filter replacement. A pressure gauge with an adapter is required to perform pressure tests.

If the pressure tap is not installed or an adapter is not available, use a T-fitting to install the pressure gauge between the fuel filter line and the throttle body fuel inlet or fuel rail.

System Pressure Test

Testing fuel pressure requires the use of a special pressure gauge (T80L-9974-A or equivalent) that attaches to the diagnostic pressure tap fitting. Depressurize the fuel system before disconnecting any lines.

1. Disconnect fuel return line at throttle body (in-tank high pressure pump) or at fuel rail (inline high pressure and in-tank low pressure pumps) and connect the hose to a 1 quart calibrated container. Connect pressure gauge.

2. Disconnect the electrical connector to the fuel pump. The connector is located ahead of fuel tank (in-tank high pressure pump) or just forward of pump outlet (inline high pressure pump). Connect auxiliary wiring harness to connector of fuel pump. Energize the pump for 10 seconds by applying 12 volts to the auxiliary harness connector, allowing the fuel to drain into the calibrated container. Note the fuel volume and pressure gauge reading.

3. Correct fuel pressure for high pressure fuel systems should be 35-45 psi (241-310 kPa). Fuel volume should be 10 ounces in 10 seconds (minimum) and fuel pressure should maintain minimum 30 psi (206 kPa) immediately after pump cut-off. 2.3L HSC engines with a single CFI injector use a low pressure fuel system that maintains fuel pressure at 14.5 psi (100 kPa).

If pressure condition is met, but fuel flow is not, check for blocked filter(s) and fuel supply lines. After correcting problem, repeat test procedure. If fuel flow is still inadequate, replace high pressure pump. If flow specification is met but pressure is not, check for worn or damaged pressure regulator valve on throttle body. If both pressure and fuel flow specifications are met, but pressure drops excessively after de-energization, check for leaking injector valve(s) and/or pressure regulator valve. If injector valves and pressure regulator valve are okay, replace high pressure pump. If no pressure or flow is seen in fuel system, check for blocked filters and fuel lines. If no trouble is found, replace inline fuel pump, in-tank fuel pump and the fuel filter inside the tank.

Fuel Injector Pressure Test

HIGH PRESSURE CFI FUEL SYSTEM ONLY

1. Connect pressure gauge T80L-9974-A, or equivalent, to fuel pressure test fitting. Disconnect coil connector from coil. Disconnect electrical lead from one injector and pressurize fuel system. Disable fuel pump by disconnecting inertia switch or fuel pump relay and observe pressure gauge reading.

2. Crank engine for 2 seconds. Turn ignition OFF and wait 5 seconds, then observe pressure drop. If pressure drop is 2-16 psi (14-110 kPa), the injector is operating properly. Reconnect injector, activate fuel pump, then repeat the procedure for other injector.

3. If pressure drop is less than 2 psi (14 kPa) or more than 16 psi (110 kPa), switch electrical connectors on injectors and repeat test. If pressure drop is still incorrect, replace disconnected injector with one of the same color code, then reconnect both injectors properly and repeat test.

4. Disconnect and plug vacuum hose to EGR valve. Start and run the engine at 2000 rpm. Disconnect left injector electrical connector. Note rpm after engine stabilizes (around 1200 rpm). Reconnect injector and allow engine to return to high idle.

5. Perform same procedure for right injector. Note difference between rpm readings of left and right injectors. If difference is 100 rpm or less, check the oxygen sensor. If difference is more than 100 rpm, replace both injectors.

Fuel Pump Circuit Test

HIGH PRESSURE IN-TANK PUMP

Disconnect electrical connector just forward of the fuel tank. Connect voltmeter to body wiring harness connector. Turn key ON while

FUEL SYSTEM

watching voltmeter. Voltage should rise to battery voltage, then return to zero after about 1 second. Momentarily turn key to START position. Voltage should rise to about 8 volts while cranking. If voltage is not as specified, check electrical system.

HIGH PRESSURE INLINE AND LOW PRESSURE IN-TANK PUMPS

Disconnect electrical connector at fuel pumps. Connect voltmeter to body wiring harness connector. Turn key ON while watching voltmeter. Voltage should rise to battery voltage, then return to zero after about 1 second. If voltage is not as specified, check inertia switch and electrical system. Connect ohmmeter to inline pump wiring harness connector. If no continuity is present, check continuity directly at inline pump terminals. If no continuity at inline pump terminals, replace inline pump. If continuity is present, service or replace wiring harness.

Connect ohmmeter across body wiring harness connector. If continuity is present (about 5 ohms), low pressure pump circuit is okay. If no continuity is present, remove fuel tank and check for continuity at in-tank pump flange terminals on top of tank. If continuity is absent at in-tank pump flange terminals, replace assembly. If continuity is present at in-tank pump but not in harness connector, service or replace wiring harness to in-tank pump.

NOTE: *A safety inertia switch is installed to shut off the electric fuel pump in case of collision. The switch is located on the left hand side of the car, behind the rear most seat side trim panel, or inside the rear quarter shock tower access door. If the pump shuts off, or if the vehicle has been hit and will not start, check for leaks first, then reset the switch. The switch is reset by pushing down on the button provided.*

ELECTRONIC FUEL INJECTION

The Electronic Fuel Injection System (EFI) is a multi-point, pulse time, mass air flow fuel injection system. Fuel is metered into the air intake stream in accordance with engine demand through four injectors mounted on a tuned intake manifold. An onboard (EEC) computer receives input from various sensors to compute the required fuel flow rate necessary to maintain the necessary air/fuel ratio throughout the entire engine operational range.

The EFI system can be separated into four categories: Fuel Delivery, Air Induction, Sensors, and the Electronic Control Circuit.

NOTE: *A brief testing section is included at the end of the Chapter 4. Special tools and skills are required. If the tools or knowledge is not on hand, have the system serviced by a factory authorized technician.*

Fuel Injectors

The four fuel injector nozzles are electro-mechanical devices which both meter and atomize fuel delivered to the engine. The injectors are mounted in the lower intake manifold and are positioned so that their tips are directing fuel just ahead of the engine intake valves. The injector bodies consist of a solenoid actuated pintle and needle valve assembly. An electrical control signal from the Electronic Engine Control unit activates the injector solenoid causing the pintle to move inward off the seat, allowing fuel to flow. Since the injector flow orifice if fixed and the fuel pressure drop across the injector tip is constant, fuel flow to the engine is regulated by how long the solenoid is energized. Atomization is obtained by contouring the pintle at the point where the fuel separates.

Fuel Pressure Regulator

The fuel pressure regulator is attached to the fuel supply manifold assembly downstream of the fuel injectors. It regulates the fuel pressure supplied to the injectors. The regulator is a diaphragm operated relief valve in which one side of the diaphragm senses fuel pressure and the other side is subjected to intake manifold pressure. The nominal fuel pressure is established by a spring preload applied to the diaphragm. Balancing one side of the diaphragm with manifold pressure maintains a constant fuel pressure drop across the injectors. Fuel, in excess of that used by the varies depending on the volume of air flowing through the sensor. The temperature sensor in the air vane meter measures the incoming air temperature. These two inputs, air volume and temperature, are used by the Electronic Control Assembly to compute the mass air flow. This value is then used to compute the fuel flow necessary for the optimum air/fuel ration which is fed to the injectors.

Air Throttle Body Assembly

The throttle body assembly controls air flow to the engine through a sing butterfly type valve. The throttle position is controlled by conventional cable/cam throttle linkage. The body is a single piece die casting made of aluminum. It has a single bore with an air bypass channel around the throttle plate. This bypass channel controls both cold and warm engine idle airflow

FUEL SYSTEM

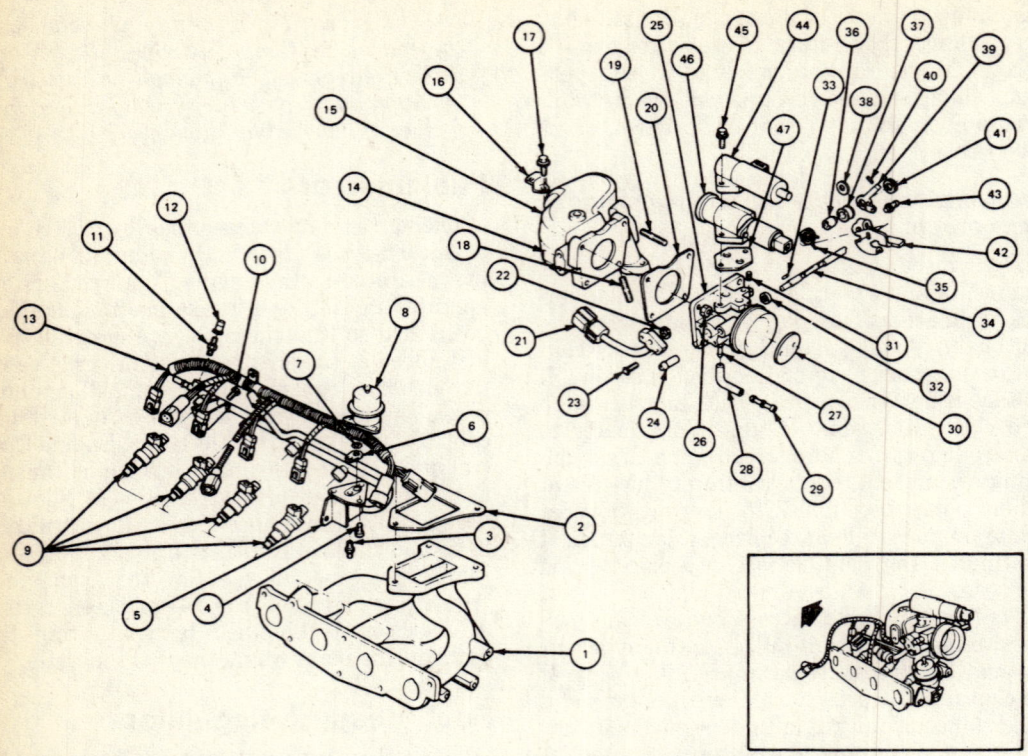

1. Manifold—intake lower
2. Gasket—intake manifold upper
3. Connector—¼ flareless x ⅛ external pipe
4. Screw—M5 x .8 x 10 socket head
5. Manifold assembly—fuel injection fuel supply
6. Gasket—fuel pressure regulator
7. Seal—⁵⁄₁₆ x .070 "O" ring
8. Regulator assembly—fuel pressure
9. Injector assembly—fuel
10. Bolt—M8 x 1.25 x 20 hex flange head
11. Valve assembly—fuel pressure relief
12. Cap—fuel pressure relief
13. Wiring harness—fuel charging
14. Decal—carburetor identification
15. Manifold—intake upper
16. Retainer—wiring harness
17. Bolt—M8 x 1.25 x 30 hex flange head
18. Stud—M6 x 1.0 x 1.0 x 40
19. Stud—M8 x 1.25 x 1.25 x 47.5
20. Gasket—air intake charge to intake manifold
21. Potentiometer—throttle position
22. Bushing—carburetor throttle shaft
23. Screw and washer assembly M4 x 22
24. Tube—emission inlet
25. Body—air intake charge throttle
26. Nut—M8 x 1.25
27. Tube
28. Hose—vacuum
29. Connector
30. Plate—air intake charge throttle
31. Screw—M4 x .7 x 8
32. Seal—throttle control shaft
33. Pin—spring coiled ¹⁄₁₆ x .42
34. Shaft
35. Spring—throttle return
36. Bushing—accelerator pump overtravel spring
37. Bearing—throttle control linkage
38. Spacer—throttle control torsion spring (MTX only)
39. Lever—carburetor transmission linkage
40. Screw—M5 x .8 x 16.25 slot head
41. Spacer—carburetor throttle shaft
42. Lever—carburetor throttle
43. Ball—carburetor throttle lever
44. Valve assembly—throttle air bypass (alt)
45. Bolt—M6 x 1.0 x 20 hex flange head
46. Valve assembly—throttle air bypass
47. Gasket—air bypass valve

EFI components

control as regulated by an air bypass valve assembly mounted directly to the throttle body.

The valve assembly is an electro-mechanical device controlled by the EEC computer. It incorporates a linear actuator which positions a variable area metering valve.

Other features of the air throttle body assembly include:

1. An adjustment screw to set the throttle plate to a minimum idle airflow position.
2. A preset stop to locate the WOT position.
3. A throttle body mounted throttle position sensor.
4. A PCV fresh air source located upstream of the throttle plate.
5. Individual ported vacuum taps (as required) for PCV and EVAP control signals.

FUEL SYSTEM 341

EXHAUST GAS OXYGEN (EGO) SENSOR

ENGINE COOLANT TEMPERATURE (ECT) SENSOR

A/C CLUTCH COMPRESSOR

THROTTLE POSITION SENSOR (TPS)

MAP SENSOR

PROFILE IGNITION PICK-UP (PIP)

EGR POSITION SENSOR

INPUTS ECA OUTPUTS

FEEDBACK CONTROL SOLENOID

SELF-TEST CONNECTOR

THICK FILM IGNITION (TFI)

UPSHIFT LIGHT (MTX)

THROTTLE KICKER SOLENOID (TKS)

A/C AND COOLING FAN CONTROLLER MODULE

EGR VALVE

TAB AND TAD

CANP

EEC-IV system inputs

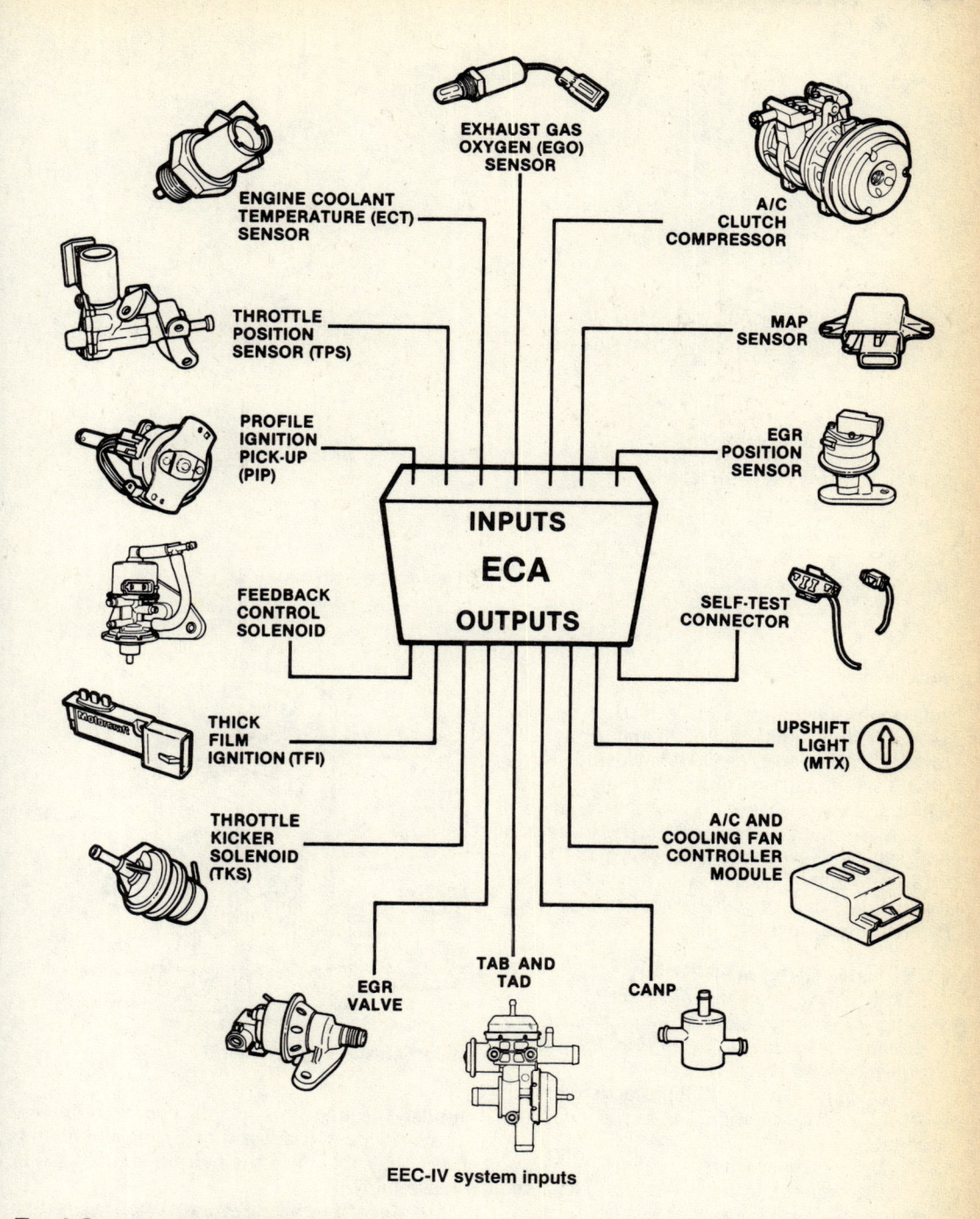

Fuel Supply Manifold Assembly

The fuel supply manifold assembly is the component that delivers high pressure fuel from the vehicle fuel supply line to the four fuel injectors. The assembly consists of a single preformed tube or stamping with four injector connectors, a mounting flange for the fuel pressure regulator, a pressure relief valve for diagnostic testing or field service fuel system pressure bleed down and mounting attachments which locate the fuel manifold assembly and provide fuel injector retention.

Air Intake Manifold

The air intake manifold is a two piece (upper and lower intake manifold) aluminum casting. Runner lengths are tuned to optimize engine torque and power output. The manifold pro-

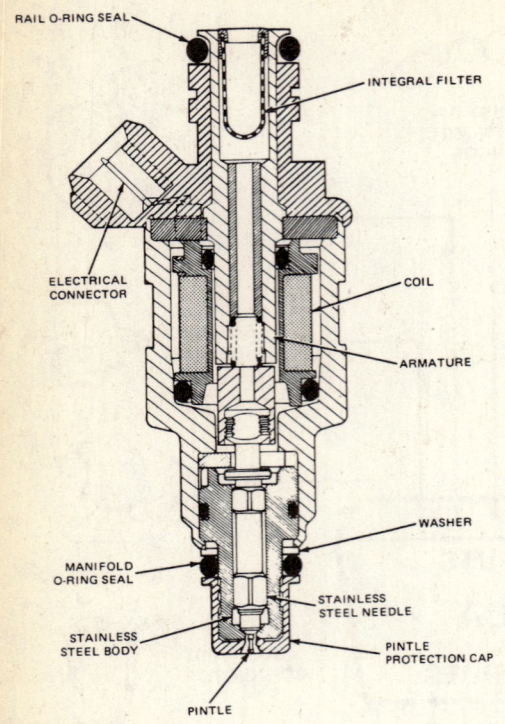

342 FUEL SYSTEM

Fuel injector

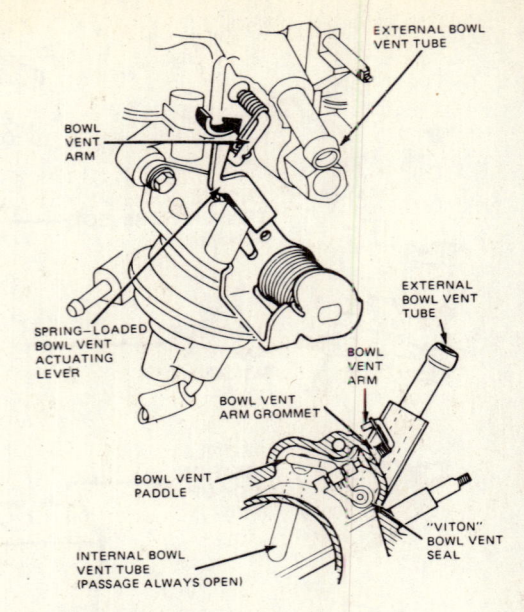

vides mounting flanges for the air throttle body assembly, fuel supply manifold and accelerator control bracket and the EGR valve and supply tube. Vacuum taps are provided to support various engine accessories. Pockets for the fuel injectors are machined to prevent both air and fuel leakage. The pockets, in which the injectors are mounted, are placed to direct the injector fuel spray immediately in front of each engine intake valve.

Fuel Charging Assembly

NOTE: *If the sub-assemblies are to be serviced and or removed with the fuel charging assembly mounted to the engine, the following steps must be taken:*

1. Open hood and install protective covers.
2. Make sure that ignition key is in Off position.
3. Drain coolant from radiator.
4. Disconnect the negative battery lead and secure it out of the way.
5. Remove fuel cap to relieve fuel tank pressure.
6. Release pressure from the fuel system at the fuel pressure relief valve on the fuel injection manifold assembly. Use tool T80L-9974-A or equivalent. To gain access to the fuel pressure relief valve, the valve cap must first be removed.
7. Disconnect the push connect fuel supply line. Using a small bladed screwdriver inserted under the hairpin clip tab, pop the clip free from the push connect tube fitting and disconnect the tube. Save the hairpin clip for use in reassembly.
8. Identify and disconnect the fuel return lines and vacuum connections.

NOTE: *Care must be taken to avoid combustion from fuel spillage.*

9. Disconnect the injector wiring harness by disconnecting the ECT sensor in the heater supply tube under lower intake manifold and the electronic engine control harness.
10. Disconnect air bypass connector from EEC harness.

Fuel supply manifold — EFI

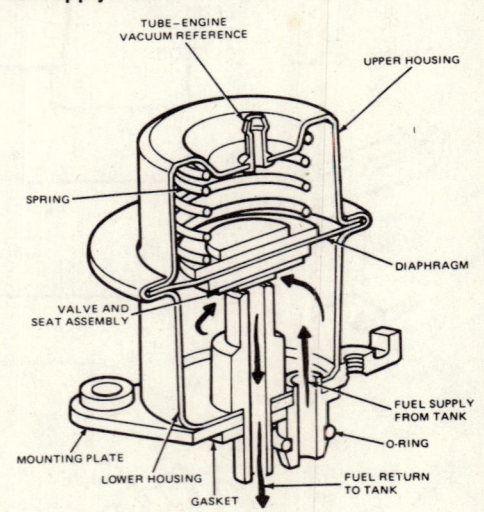

Fuel pressure regulator — EFI

NOTE: *Not all assemblies may be serviceable while on the engine. In some cases, removal of the fuel charging assembly may facilitate service of the various sub-assemblies. To remove the entire fuel charging assembly, the following procedure should be followed:*

REMOVAL AND INSTALLATION

EFI and MPI Engines

1. Remove the engine air cleaner outlet tube between the vane air meter and air throttle body by loosening two clamps.
2. Disconnect and remove the accelerator and speed control cables (if so equipped) from the accelerator mounting bracket and throttle lever.
3. Disconnect the top manifold vacuum fitting connections by disconnecting:
    a. Rear vacuum line to the dash panel vacuum tree.
    b. Front vacuum line to the air cleaner and fuel pressure regulator.
4. Disconnect the PCV system by disconnecting the hoses from:
    a. Two large forward facing connectors on the throttle body and intake manifold.
    b. Throttle body port hose at the straight plastic connector.
    c. Canister purge line at the straight plastic connector.
    d. PCV hose at rocker cover.
    e. Unbolt PCV separator support bracket from cylinder head and remove PCV system.
5. Disconnect the EGR vacuum line at the EGR valve.
6. Disconnect the EGR tube from the upper intake manifold by removing the two flange nuts.
7. Withdraw the dipstick and remove the dipstick tube by removing the tube bracket mounting nut and working the tube out of the block hole.
8. Remove the fuel return line.
9. Remove six manifold mounting nuts.
10. Remove the manifold with wiring harness and gasket.
11. Clean and inspect the mounting faces of the fuel charging manifold assembly and the cylinder head. Both surfaces must be clean and flat.
12. Clean and oil manifold stud threads.

To Install:

13. Install a new gasket.
14. Install manifold assembly to head and secure with top middle nut (tighten nut finger tight only at this time).
15. Install fuel return line to the fitting in the fuel supply manifold. Install two manifold mounting nuts, finger tight.
16. Install dipstick in block and secure with bracket nut finger tight.
17. Install remaining three manifold mounting nuts and tighten all six nuts to 12–15 ft. lbs. observing specified tightening sequence.
18. Install EGR tube with two oil coated flange nuts tightened to 6–8.5 ft. lbs.
19. Reinstall PCV system.
    a. Mount separator bracket to head.
    b. Install hose on rocker cover, tighten clamps.
    c. Connect vacuum line to canister purge.
    d. Connect vacuum line to throttle body port.
    e. Connect large PCV vacuum line to throttle body.
    f. Connect large PCV vacuum line to upper manifold.
20. Connect manifold vacuum connections:
    a. Rear connection to vacuum tree.
    b. Front connection to fuel pressure regulator and air cleaner.
21. Connect accelerator and speed control cables (if so equipped).
22. Install air supply tube and tighten clamps to 25 inch lbs.
23. Connect the wiring harness at:
    a. ECT sensor in heater supply tube.
    b. Electronic Engine Control harness.
24. Connect the fuel supply hose from the fuel filter to the fuel rail.
25. Connect the fuel return line.
26. Connect negative battery cable.
27. Install engine coolant using prescribed fill procedure.
28. Start engine and allow to run at idle until engine temperature is stabilized. Check for coolant leaks.
29. If necessary, reset idle speed.

REMOVAL AND INSTALLATION OF SUB-ASSEMBLIES

NOTE: *To prevent damage to fuel charging assembly, the unit should be placed on a work bench during disassembly and assembly procedures. The following is a step-by-step sequence of operations for servicing the assemblies of the fuel charging manifold. Some components may be serviced without a complete disassembly of the fuel charging manifold.*
To replace individual components, follow only the applicable steps.

These procedures are based on the fuel charging manifold having been removed from the vehicle.

Upper Intake Manifold

1. Disconnect the engine air cleaner outlet tube from the air intake throttle body.

FUEL SYSTEM

2. Unplug the throttle position sensor from the wiring harness.
3. Unplug the air bypass valve connector.
4. Remove three upper manifold retaining bolts.
5. Remove upper manifold assembly and set it aside.
6. Remove and discard the gasket from the lower manifold assembly.

NOTE: *If scraping is necessary, be careful not to damage the gasket surfaces of the upper and lower manifold assemblies, or allow material to drop into lower manifold.*

7. Ensure that the gasket surfaces of the upper and lower intake manifolds are clean.

To Install:

8. Place a new service gasket on the lower manifold assembly and mount the upper intake manifold to the lower, securing it with three retaining bolts. Tighten bolts to 15–22 ft. lbs.
9. Ensure the wiring harness is properly installed.
10. Connect electrical connectors to air bypass valve and throttle position sensor and the vacuum hose to the fuel pressure regulator.
11. Connect the engine air cleaner outlet tube to the throttle body intake securing it with a hose clamp. Tighten to 15–25 inch lbs.

Air Intake Throttle Body

1. Remove four throttle body nuts. Ensure that the throttle position sensor connector and air bypass valve connector have been disconnected from the harness. Disconnect air cleaner outlet tube.
2. Identify and disconnect vacuum hoses.
3. Remove throttle bracket.
4. Carefully separate the throttle body from the upper intake manifold.
5. Remove and discard the gasket between the throttle body and the upper intake manifold.

NOTE: *If scraping is necessary, be careful not to damage the gasket surfaces of the throttle body and upper manifold assemblies, or allow material to drop into manifold.*

6. Ensure that both throttle body and upper intake manifold gasket surfaces are clean.

To Install:

7. Install the upper/throttle body gasket on the four studs of the upper intake manifold.
8. Secure the throttle bracket and secure with two nuts. Tighten to 12–15 ft. lbs.
9. Install throttle bracket and secure with two nuts. Tighten to 12–15 ft. lbs.
10. Connect the air bypass valve and throttle position sensor electrical connectors and appropriate vacuum lines.
11. If the fuel charging assembly is still mounted to the engine, connect the engine air cleaner outlet tube to the throttle body intake securing it with a hose clamp. Tighten the clamp to 15–25 inch lbs.

Air Bypass Valve Assembly

1. Disconnect the air bypass valve assembly connector from the wiring harness.
2. Remove the two air bypass valve retaining screws.
3. Remove the air bypass valve and gasket.

NOTE: *If scraping is necessary, be careful not to damage the air bypass valve or throttle body gasket surfaces, or drop material into throttle body.*

4. Ensure that both the throttle body and air bypass valve gasket surfaces are clean.

To Install:

5. Install gasket on throttle body surface and mount the air bypass valve assembly securing it with two retaining screws. Tighten to 71–102 inch lbs.
6. Connect the electrical connector for the air bypass valve.

Throttle Position Sensor

1. Disconnect the throttle position sensor from the wiring harness.
2. Remove two throttle position sensor retaining screws.
3. Remove the throttle position sensor.
4. Install the throttle position sensor. Make sure that the rotary tangs on the sensor are in the proper alignment and the wires are pointing down.
5. Secure the sensor to the throttle body assembly with two retaining screws. Tighten to 11–16 inch lbs.

NOTE: *This throttle position sensor is not adjustable.*

6. Connect the electrical connector to the harness.

CHILTON TIPS

1983-89 All Models

All throttle position sensor (TPS) mounting screws have a Pozidrive head. The Pozidrive head looks a lot like a Phillips screw head. However the use of a Phillips head screwdriver to remove a Pozidrive screw will normally result in a rounded or damaged screw head. Many technicians think it is an overtorqued of frozen screw. An adhesive was also used as a thread sealant starting with the 1988 model year. This adhesive requires still more effort to loosen and remove the screw.

To prevent a rounded or damaged screw heads when servicing the TPS mounting

FUEL SYSTEM

screws, it is advisable to always use a Pozidrive screwdriver with this procedure.

Pressure Relief Valve

1. If the fuel charging assembly is mounted to the engine, remove fuel tank cap then release pressure from the system at the pressure relief valve on the fuel injection manifold using Tool T80L–9974–A or equivalent. Note the cap on the relief valve must be removed.
2. Using an open end wrench or suitable deep well socket, remove pressure relief valve for fuel injection manifold.
3. Install pressure relief valve and cap. Tighten valve to 48–84 inch lbs. and the cap to 4–6 inch lbs.

Fuel Injector Manifold Assembly

1. Remove fuel tank cap and release pressure from the fuel system at the fuel pressure relief valve using Tool T80L–9974–A.
2. Disconnect the fuel supply and fuel return lines.
3. Disconnect the wiring harness from the injectors.
4. Disconnect vacuum line from fuel pressure regulator valve.
5. Remove two fuel injector manifolds retaining bolts.
6. Carefully disengage manifold from the fuel injectors and remove manifold.
7. Make sure the injector caps are clean and free of contamination.

To Install:

8. Place fuel injector manifold over the four injectors making sure the injectors are well seated in the fuel manifold assembly.
9. Secure the fuel manifold assembly to the charging assembly using two retaining bolts.
10. Connect fuel supply and return lines.
11. Connect fuel injector wiring harness.
12. Connect vacuum line to fuel pressure regulator.

Fuel Pressure Regulator

1. Be sure that the assembly is depressurized by removing fuel tank cap and releasing pressure from the fuel system at the pressure relief valve on the fuel injection manifold using Tool T80L–9974–A or equivalent.
2. Remove the vacuum line at the pressure regulator.
3. Remove three Allen retaining screws from regulator housing.
4. Remove pressure regulator assembly, gasket and O-ring. Discard gasket and inspect O-ring for signs of cracks or deterioration.

NOTE: *If scraping is necessary, be careful not to damage the fuel pressure regulator or fuel supply line gasket surfaces.*

5. Lubricate fuel pressure regulator O-ring with light oil ESF–M6C2–A or equivalent.
6. Make sure gasket surfaces of fuel pressure regulator and fuel injection manifold are clean.
7. Install O-ring and new gasket on regulator.
8. Install the fuel pressure regulator on the injector manifold. Tighten the three retaining screws to 27–40 inch lbs.

Fuel Injector

1. Remove fuel tank cap and release pressure from the fuel system at the fuel pressure relief valve using Tool T80L–9974–A or equivalent.
2. Disconnect fuel supply and return lines.
3. Remove vacuum line from fuel pressure regulator.
4. Disconnect the fuel injector wiring harness.
5. Remove fuel injector manifold assembly.
6. Carefully remove connectors from individual injector(s) as required.
7. Grasping the injector's body, pull up while gently rocking the injector from side-to-side.

To Install:

8. Inspect the injector O-rings (two per injector) for signs of deterioration. Replace as required.
9. Inspect the injector plastic cover (covering the injector pintle) and washer for signs of deterioration. Replace as required. If hat is missing, look for it in intake manifold.
10. Lubricate new O-rings and install two on each injector (use a light grade oil ESF–M6C2–A or equivalent).
11. Install the injector(s). Use a light, twisting, pushing motion to install the injector(s).
12. Carefully seat the fuel injector manifold assembly on the four injectors and secure the manifold with two attaching bolts. Tighten to 15–22 ft. lbs.
13. Connect the vacuum line to the fuel pressure regulator.
14. Connect fuel injector wiring harness.
15. Connect fuel supply and fuel return lines. Tighten fuel return line to 15–18 ft. lbs.
16. Check entire assembly for proper alignment and seating.

Fuel Injector Wiring Harness

NOTE: *Be sure the ignition if Off and the fuel system is depressurized.*

1. Disconnect the electrical connectors from the four fuel injectors.
2. Disconnect the connectors from the main wiring harness and the throttle position sensor.
3. Remove wiring assembly.

FUEL SYSTEM

4. Position wiring harness alongside the fuel injectors.
5. Snap the electrical connectors into position on the four injectors.
6. Connect the throttle position sensor, ECT sensor and main harness connectors.
7. Verify that all electrical connectors are firmly seated.

Vane Air Meter

1. Loosen the hose clamp which secures engine air cleaner outlet hose to the vane air meter assembly and position outlet hose out of the way.
2. Remove air intake and air outlet tube from the air cleaner.
3. Disengage four spring clamps and remove air cleaner front cover and air cleaner filter panel.
4. Remove four screws and washers from the flange of the air cleaner where it is attached to the vane air meter assembly. Pull the air cleaner base away from the vane air meter and remove the air cleaner gasket. If the gasket shoes signs of deterioration, replace it.

NOTE: *If scraping is necessary, be careful not to damage the air cleaner outlet and vane air meter gasket surfaces.*

5. Remove the electrical connector from the vane air meter assembly.
6. Remove the two screw and washer assemblies which secure the vane air meter assembly to the vane air meter bracket and remove the vane air meter assembly.

To Install:
7. Clean mounting surfaces of air cleaner outlet flange and the vane air meter housing.
8. Place four retaining screws through the four holes in the air cleaner outlet flange and place a new gasket over the screws.
9. Mount the vane air meter assembly to the vane air meter bracket using two screw and washer assemblies. Note that these screws are not the physical size and care must be taken to ensure that the proper screw is in the proper hole. Tighten screws to 6–9 ft. lbs.
10. Secure the air cleaner outlet to the vane air meter with the four screws mentioned in Step 2. Tighten to 6–9 ft. lbs. Make sure the gasket is properly sealed and aligned.
11. Secure the engine air cleaner outlet tube to the vane air meter assembly with the hose clamp. Tighten to 15–25 inch lbs.
12. Install the engine air cleaner cover and snap spring clips into position.
13. Secure the air intake duct to air cleaner.
14. Connect all hoses to air cleaner.

Fuel Charging Assembly

REMOVAL AND INSTALLATION

CFI System

1. Remove the air cleaner.
2. Release pressure from the fuel system at the diagnostic valve on the fuel charging assembly by carefully depressing the pin and discharging fuel into the throttle body.
3. Disconnect the throttle cable and transmission throttle valve lever.
4. Disconnect fuel, vacuum and electrical connections.

NOTE: *Either the multi or single ten pin connectors may be used on the system. To disconnect electrical ten pin connectors, push in or squeeze on the right side lower locking tab while pulling up on the connection. Multi connectors disconnect by pulling apart. The ISC connector tab must be moved out while pulling apart.*

5. Remove fuel charging assembly retaining nuts, then, remove fuel charging assembly.
6. Remove mounting gasket from intake manifold. Always use a new gasket for installation.

To Install:
7. Clean gasket mounting surfaces of spacer and fuel charging assembly.
8. Place spacer between two new gaskets and place spacer and gaskets on the intake manifold. Position the charging assembly on the spacer and gasket.
9. Secure fuel charging assembly with attaching nuts. Tighten to 10 ft. lbs. (14 Nm). To prevent leakage, distortion or damage to the fuel charging assembly body flange, snug the nuts; then, alternately tighten each nut in a criss-cross pattern. Tighten to specifications.
10. Connect the fuel line, electrical connectors, throttle cable and all emission lines.
11. Start the engine, check for leaks. Adjust engine idle speed if necessary. Refer to the Engine/Emission Control Decal for idle speed specifications.

DISASSEMBLY

To prevent damage to the throttle plates, the fuel charging assembly should be placed on a work stand during disassembly and assembly procedures. If a proper stand is not available, use four bolts, $2^1/_2$ inches long, as legs. Install nuts on the bolts above and below the throttle body. The following is a step-by-step sequence of operations for completely overhauling the fuel charging assembly. Most components may be serviced without a complete disassembly of the fuel charging assembly. To replace individ-

FUEL SYSTEM 347

ual components follow only the applicable steps.

NOTE: *Use a separate container for the component parts of each sub-assembly to insure proper assembly. The automatic transmission throttle valve lever must be adjusted whenever the fuel charging assembly is removed for service or replacement.*

1. Remove the air cleaner stud. The air cleaner stud must be removed to separate the upper body from the throttle body.
2. Turn the fuel charging assembly over and remove four screws from the bottom of the throttle body.
3. Separate throttle body from main body. Set throttle body aside.
4. Carefully remove and discard gasket. Note if scraping is necessary, be careful not damage gasket surfaces of main and throttle screws.
5. Remove three pressure regulator retaining screws.
6. Remove pressure regulator. Inspect condition of gasket and O-ring.
7. Disconnect electrical connectors at each injector. Pull the connectors outward.

NOTE: *Pull the connector and the wire. Tape to identify the connectors. They must be installed on same injector as removed.*

8. Loosen, DO NOT REMOVE, wiring harness retaining screw with multi connector; with single 10-pin connector loosen the two retaining screws.
9. Push in on tabs on harness to remove from upper body.
10. Remove fuel injector retainer screw.
11. Remove the injector retainer.
12. One at a time, pull injectors out of upper body. Identify each injector as "choke" or "throttle" side.

NOTE: *Each injector has a small O-ring at its top. If the O-ring does not come out with the injector, carefully pick the O-ring out of the cavity in the throttle body.*

13. Remove fuel diagnostic valve assembly.
14. Note the position of index mark on choke cap housing.
15. Remove three retaining ring screws.
16. Remove choke cap retaining ring, choke cap, and gasket, if so equipped.
17. Remove thermostat lever screw, and lever, if so equipped.
18. Remove fast idle cam assembly, is so equipped.
19. Remove fast idle control rod positioner, if so equipped.
20. Hold control diaphragm cover tightly in position, while removing two retaining screws, if so equipped.
21. Carefully, remove cover, spring, and pull-down control diaphragm, if so equipped.
22. Remove fast idle retaining nut, if so equipped.
23. Remove fast idle cam adjuster lever, fast idle lever, spring and E-clip, if so equipped.
24. Remove throttle position sensor connector bracket retaining screw.
25. Remove throttle position sensor retaining screws and slide throttle position sensor off the throttle shaft.
26. If CFI assembly is equipped with a throttle positioner, remove the throttle positioner retaining screw, and remove the throttle positioner. If the CFI assembly is equipped with an ISC DC Motor, remove the motor.

ASSEMBLY

1. Install fuel pressure diagnostic valve and cap. Tighten valve to 48–84 inch lbs. (5–9 Nm). Tighten cap to 5–10 inch lbs. (0.6–2 Nm).
2. Lubricate new O-rings and install on each injector (use a light grade oil).
3. Identify injectors and install them in their appropriate locations (choke or throttle side). Use a light twisting, pushing motion to install the injectors.
4. With injectors installed, install injector retainer into position.
5. Install injector retainer screw, and tighten to 36–60 inch lbs. (4–7 Nm).
6. Install injector wiring harness in upper body. Snap harness into position.
7. Tighten injector wiring harness retaining screws, (two screws if equipped with a single 10-pin connector), to 8–10 inch lbs. (1 Nm).
8. Snap electrical connectors into position on injectors.
9. Lubricate new fuel pressure regulator O-ring with light oil. Install O-ring and new gasket on regulator.
10. Install pressure regulator in upper body. Tighten retaining screws to 27–40 inch lbs. (3–4 Nm).
11. Depending upon CFI assembly, install either the throttle positioner, or the ISC DC Motor.
12. Hold throttle position sensor so wire faces up.
13. Slide throttle position sensor on throttle shaft.
14. Rotate throttle position sensor clockwise until aligned with screw holes on throttle body. Install retaining screws and tighten to 11–16 inch lbs. (1–2 Nm).
15. Install throttle position wiring harness bracket retaining screw. Tighten screw to 18–22 inch lbs. (2–3 Nm).
16. Install E-clip, fast idle lever and spring,

FUEL SYSTEM

fast idle adjustment lever and fast idle retaining nut, if so equipped.

17. Tighten fast idle retaining nut to 16–20 inch lbs. (1–2 Nm), if so equipped.

18. Install pull down control diaphragm, control modulator spring and cover, is so equipped. Hold cover in position and install two retaining screws, and tighten to 13–19 inch lbs. (1–2 Nm).

19. Install fast idle control rod positions, if so equipped.

20. Install fast idle cam, if so equipped.

21. Install thermostat lever and retaining screws, if so equipped. Tighten to 13–19 inch lbs. (1–2 Nm).

22. Install choke cap gasket, choke cap, and retaining ring, if so equipped.

NOTE: *Be sure the choke cap bimetal spring is properly inserted between the fingers of the thermostat lever and choke cap index mark is properly aligned.*

23. Install choke cap retaining screws, tighten to 13–18 inch lbs. (1–2 Nm).

24. Install fuel charging gasket on upper body. Be sure gasket is positioned over bosses. Place throttle body in position on upper body.

25. Install four upper body to throttle body retaining screws. Tighten to specifications.

26. Install air cleaner stud. Tighten stud to 70–95 inch lbs. (8–11 Nm).

TESTING

NOTE: *Testing the EEC-IV system requires special equipment and an expert knowledge of the system. Troubleshooting and servicing should be performed by qualified personnel only.*

DIESEL FUEL SYSTEM

Injection Nozzles

REMOVAL AND INSTALLATION

1. Disconnect and remove injection lines from injection pump and nozzles. Cap all lines and fittings using Protective Cap Set T84P-9395-A or equivalent.

2. Remove nuts attaching the fuel return line to the nozzles, and remove return line and seals.

3. Remove nozzles using a 27mm deep well socket.

4. Remove nozzles gaskets and washers from nozzle seat, using O-ring Pick Tool T71P-19703-C or equivalent.

5. Clean the outside of the nozzle assemblies using Nozzle Cleaning Kit, Rotunda model 14-0301 or equivalent, and a suitable solvent. Dry thoroughly.

To Install:

6. Position new sealing gaskets in the nozzle seats.

NOTE: *Install gasket with red painted surface facing up.*

7. Position new copper washers in the nozzles bores.

8. Install nozzles and tighten to 44–51 ft. lbs.

9. Position fuel return line on the nozzles, using new seals.

10. Install fuel return line retaining nuts and tighten to 10 ft. lbs.

11. Install fuel lines on the injection pump and nozzles. Tighten capnuts to 18–22 ft. lbs.

12. Air bleed fuel system.

13. Run engine and check for fuel leaks.

NOTE: *Other servicing of the diesel fuel system requires special tool and equipment. Servicing should be done by a mechanic experienced with diesels.*

Fuel Cutoff Solenoid

REMOVAL AND INSTALLATION

1. Disconnect battery ground cable from the battery, located in the luggage compartment.

2. Remove connector from the fuel cutoff solenoid.

3. Remove the cutoff solenoid and discard the O-ring.

4. Install fuel cutoff solenoid using a new O-ring. Tighten to 30–33 ft. lbs.

5. Connect electrical connector.

6. Connect battery ground cable.

7. Run engine and check for fuel leaks.

Fuel Injector

REMOVAL AND INSTALLATION

1. Disconnect the negative battery cable.

2. Disconnect and remove the injection lines from the injection pump and nozzles. Cap all lines and fitting to prevent dirt contamination.

3. Remove the nuts attaching the fuel return line to the nozzles and remove the return line and seals.

4. Remove the injector nozzles using a 27mm socket. Remove the nozzle gaskets and washers from the nozzle seats using an O-ring pick tool.

To install:

5. Clean the outside of the nozzles with safety solvent and dry them thoroughly.

6. Position new sealing gaskets and heat shields in nozzle seats with the blue painted gasket surface facing up.

7. Position new copper gaskets in the noz-

CHILTON'S
FUEL ECONOMY & TUNE-UP TIPS

Tune-up • Spark Plug Diagnosis • Emission Controls
Fuel System • Cooling System • Tires and Wheels
General Maintenance

55 WAYS TO IMPROVE FUEL ECONOMY

CHILTON'S FUEL ECONOMY & TUNE-UP TIPS

Fuel economy is important to everyone, no matter what kind of vehicle you drive. The maintenance-minded motorist can save both money and fuel using these tips and the periodic maintenance and tune-up procedures in this Repair and Tune-Up Guide.

There are more than 130,000,000 cars and trucks registered for private use in the United States. Each travels an average of 10-12,000 miles per year, and, and in total they consume close to 70 billion gallons of fuel each year. This represents nearly 2/3 of the oil imported by the United States each year. The Federal government's goal is to reduce consumption 10% by 1985. A variety of methods are either already in use or under serious consideration, and they all affect you driving and the cars you will drive. In addition to "down-sizing", the auto industry is using or investigating the use of electronic fuel delivery, electronic engine controls and alternative engines for use in smaller and lighter vehicles, among other alternatives to meet the federally mandated Corporate Average Fuel Economy (CAFE) of 27.5 mpg by 1985. The government, for its part, is considering rationing, mandatory driving curtailments and tax increases on motor vehicle fuel in an effort to reduce consumption. The government's goal of a 10% reduction could be realized — and further government regulation avoided — if every private vehicle could use just 1 less gallon of fuel per week.

How Much Can You Save?

Tests have proven that almost anyone can make at least a 10% reduction in fuel consumption through regular maintenance and tune-ups. When a major manufacturer of spark plugs sur-

TUNE-UP

1. Check the cylinder compression to be sure the engine will really benefit from a tune-up and that it is capable of producing good fuel economy. A tune-up will be wasted on an engine in poor mechanical condition.

2. Replace spark plugs regularly. New spark plugs alone can increase fuel economy 3%.

3. Be sure the spark plugs are the correct type (heat range) for your vehicle. See the Tune-Up Specifications.

Heat range refers to the spark plug's ability to conduct heat away from the firing end. It must conduct the heat away in an even pattern to avoid becoming a source of pre-ignition, yet it must also operate hot enough to burn off conductive deposits that could cause misfiring.

The heat range is usually indicated by a number on the spark plug, part of the manufacturer's designation for each individual spark plug. The numbers in bold-face indicate the heat range in each manufacturer's identification system.

Manufacturer	Typical Designation
AC	R **45** TS
Bosch (old)	WA **145** T30
Bosch (new)	HR **8** Y
Champion	RBL **15** Y
Fram/Autolite	**4**15
Mopar	P-**62** PR
Motorcraft	BRF-**4**2
NGK	BP **5** ES-15
Nippondenso	W **16** EP
Prestolite	14GR **5** 2A

Periodically, check the spark plugs to be sure they are firing efficiently. They are excellent indicators of the internal condition of your engine.

On AC, Bosch (new), Champion, Fram/Autolite, Mopar, Motorcraft and Prestolite, a higher number indicates a hotter plug. On Bosch (old), NGK and Nippondenso, a higher number indicates a colder plug.

4. Make sure the spark plugs are properly gapped. See the Tune-Up Specifications in this book.

5. Be sure the spark plugs are firing efficiently. The illustrations on the next 2 pages show you how to "read" the firing end of the spark plug.

6. Check the ignition timing and set it to specifications. Tests show that almost all cars have incorrect ignition timing by more than 2°.

veyed over 6,000 cars nationwide, they found that a tune-up, on cars that needed one, increased fuel economy over 11%. Replacing worn plugs alone, accounted for a 3% increase. The same test also revealed that 8 out of every 10 vehicles will have some maintenance deficiency that will directly affect fuel economy, emissions or performance. Most of this mileage-robbing neglect could be prevented with regular maintenance.

Modern engines require that all of the functioning systems operate properly for maximum efficiency. A malfunction anywhere wastes fuel. You can keep your vehicle running as efficiently and economically as possible, by being aware of your vehicle's operating and performance characteristics. If your vehicle suddenly develops performance or fuel economy problems it could be due to one or more of the following:

PROBLEM	POSSIBLE CAUSE
Engine Idles Rough	Ignition timing, idle mixture, vacuum leak or something amiss in the emission control system.
Hesitates on Acceleration	Dirty carburetor or fuel filter, improper accelerator pump setting, ignition timing or fouled spark plugs.
Starts Hard or Fails to Start	Worn spark plugs, improperly set automatic choke, ice (or water) in fuel system.
Stalls Frequently	Automatic choke improperly adjusted and possible dirty air filter or fuel filter.
Performs Sluggishly	Worn spark plugs, dirty fuel or air filter, ignition timing or automatic choke out of adjustment.

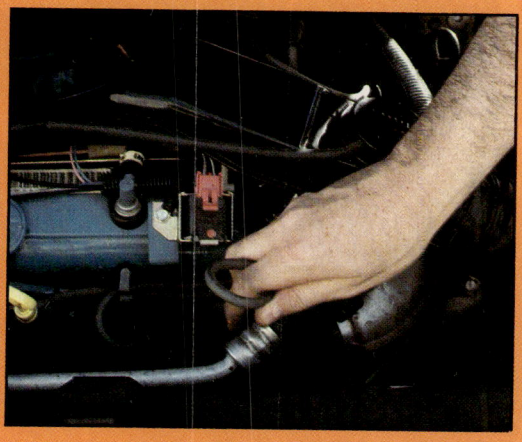

Check spark plug wires on conventional point type ignition for cracks by bending them in a loop around your finger.

Be sure that spark plug wires leading to adjacent cylinders do not run too close together. (Photo courtesy Champion Spark Plug Co.)

7. If your vehicle does not have electronic ignition, check the points, rotor and cap as specified.

8. Check the spark plug wires (used with conventional point-type ignitions) for cracks and burned or broken insulation by bending them in a loop around your finger. Cracked wires decrease fuel efficiency by failing to deliver full voltage to the spark plugs. One misfiring spark plug can cost you as much as 2 mpg.

9. Check the routing of the plug wires. Misfiring can be the result of spark plug leads to adjacent cylinders running parallel to each other and too close together. One wire tends to pick up voltage from the other causing it to fire "out of time".

10. Check all electrical and ignition circuits for voltage drop and resistance.

11. Check the distributor mechanical and/or vacuum advance mechanisms for proper functioning. The vacuum advance can be checked by twisting the distributor plate in the opposite direction of rotation. It should spring back when released.

12. Check and adjust the valve clearance on engines with mechanical lifters. The clearance should be slightly loose rather than too tight.

SPARK PLUG DIAGNOSIS

Normal

APPEARANCE: This plug is typical of one operating normally. The insulator nose varies from a light tan to grayish color with slight electrode wear. The presence of slight deposits is normal on used plugs and will have no adverse effect on engine performance. The spark plug heat range is correct for the engine and the engine is running normally.
CAUSE: Properly running engine.
RECOMMENDATION: Before reinstalling this plug, the electrodes should be cleaned and filed square. Set the gap to specifications. If the plug has been in service for more than 10-12,000 miles, the entire set should probably be replaced with a fresh set of the same heat range.

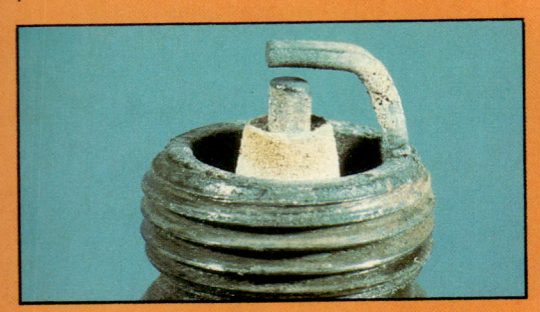

Oil Deposits

APPEARANCE: The firing end of the plug is covered with a wet, oily coating.
CAUSE: The problem is poor oil control. On high mileage engines, oil is leaking past the rings or valve guides into the combustion chamber. A common cause is also a plugged PCV valve, and a ruptured fuel pump diaphragm can also cause this condition. Oil fouled plugs such as these are often found in new or recently overhauled engines, before normal oil control is achieved, and can be cleaned and reinstalled.
RECOMMENDATION: A hotter spark plug may temporarily relieve the problem, but the engine is probably in need of work.

Incorrect Heat Range

APPEARANCE: The effects of high temperature on a spark plug are indicated by clean white, often blistered insulator. This can also be accompanied by excessive wear of the electrode, and the absence of deposits.
CAUSE: Check for the correct spark plug heat range. A plug which is too hot for the engine can result in overheating. A car operated mostly at high speeds can require a colder plug. Also check ignition timing, cooling system level, fuel mixture and leaking intake manifold.
RECOMMENDATION: If all ignition and engine adjustments are known to be correct, and no other malfunction exists, install spark plugs one heat range colder.

Carbon Deposits

APPEARANCE: Carbon fouling is easily identified by the presence of dry, soft, black, sooty deposits.
CAUSE: Changing the heat range can often lead to carbon fouling, as can prolonged slow, stop-and-start driving. If the heat range is correct, carbon fouling can be attributed to a rich fuel mixture, sticking choke, clogged air cleaner, worn breaker points, retarded timing or low compression. If only one or two plugs are carbon fouled, check for corroded or cracked wires on the affected plugs. Also look for cracks in the distributor cap between the towers of affected cylinders.
RECOMMENDATION: After the problem is corrected, these plugs can be cleaned and reinstalled if not worn severely.

Photos Courtesy Fram Corporation

MMT Fouled

APPEARANCE: Spark plugs fouled by MMT (Methycyclopentadienyl Maganese Tricarbonyl) have reddish, rusty appearance on the insulator and side electrode.

CAUSE: MMT is an anti-knock additive in gasoline used to replace lead. During the combustion process, the MMT leaves a reddish deposit on the insulator and side electrode.

RECOMMENDATION: No engine malfunction is indicated and the deposits will not affect plug performance any more than lead deposits (see Ash Deposits). MMT fouled plugs can be cleaned, regapped and reinstalled.

High Speed Glazing

APPEARANCE: Glazing appears as shiny coating on the plug, either yellow or tan in color.

CAUSE: During hard, fast acceleration, plug temperatures rise suddenly. Deposits from normal combustion have no chance to fluff-off; instead, they melt on the insulator forming an electrically conductive coating which causes misfiring.

RECOMMENDATION: Glazed plugs are not easily cleaned. They should be replaced with a fresh set of plugs of the correct heat range. If the condition recurs, using plugs with a heat range one step colder may cure the problem.

Ash (Lead) Deposits

APPEARANCE: Ash deposits are characterized by light brown or white colored deposits crusted on the side or center electrodes. In some cases it may give the plug a rusty appearance.

CAUSE: Ash deposits are normally derived from oil or fuel additives burned during normal combustion. Normally they are harmless, though excessive amounts can cause misfiring. If deposits are excessive in short mileage, the valve guides may be worn.

RECOMMENDATION: Ash-fouled plugs can be cleaned, gapped and reinstalled.

Detonation

APPEARANCE: Detonation is usually characterized by a broken plug insulator.

CAUSE: A portion of the fuel charge will begin to burn spontaneously, from the increased heat following ignition. The explosion that results applies extreme pressure to engine components, frequently damaging spark plugs and pistons.

Detonation can result by over-advanced ignition timing, inferior gasoline (low octane) lean air/fuel mixture, poor carburetion, engine lugging or an increase in compression ratio due to combustion chamber deposits or engine modification.

RECOMMENDATION: Replace the plugs after correcting the problem.

Photos Courtesy Champion Spark Plug Co.

EMISSION CONTROLS

13. Be aware of the general condition of the emission control system. It contributes to reduced pollution and should be serviced regularly to maintain efficient engine operation.

14. Check all vacuum lines for dried, cracked or brittle conditions. Something as simple as a leaking vacuum hose can cause poor performance and loss of economy.

15. Avoid tampering with the emission control system. Attempting to improve fuel econ-

FUEL SYSTEM

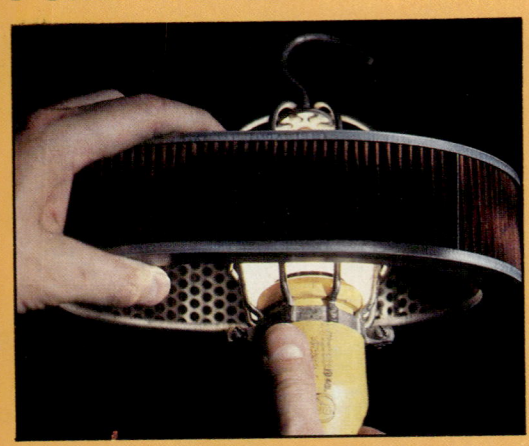

Check the air filter with a light behind it. If you can see light through the filter it can be reused.

Extremely clogged filters should be discarded and replaced with a new one.

18. Replace the air filter regularly. A dirty air filter richens the air/fuel mixture and can increase fuel consumption as much as 10%. Tests show that ⅓ of all vehicles have air filters in need of replacement.

19. Replace the fuel filter at least as often as recommended.

20. Set the idle speed and carburetor mixture to specifications.

21. Check the automatic choke. A sticking or malfunctioning choke wastes gas.

22. During the summer months, adjust the automatic choke for a leaner mixture which will produce faster engine warm-ups.

COOLING SYSTEM

29. Be sure all accessory drive belts are in good condition. Check for cracks or wear.

30. Adjust all accessory drive belts to proper tension.

31. Check all hoses for swollen areas, worn spots, or loose clamps.

32. Check coolant level in the radiator or expansion tank.

33. Be sure the thermostat is operating properly. A stuck thermostat delays engine warm-up and a cold engine uses nearly twice as much fuel as a warm engine.

34. Drain and replace the engine coolant at least as often as recommended. Rust and scale

TIRES & WHEELS

38. Check the tire pressure often with a pencil type gauge. Tests by a major tire manufacturer show that 90% of all vehicles have at least 1 tire improperly inflated. Better mileage can be achieved by over-inflating tires, but never exceed the maximum inflation pressure on the side of the tire.

39. If possible, install radial tires. Radial tires deliver as much as ½ mpg more than bias belted tires.

40. Avoid installing super-wide tires. They only create extra rolling resistance and decrease fuel mileage. Stick to the manufacturer's recommendations.

41. Have the wheels properly balanced.

omy by tampering with emission controls is more likely to worsen fuel economy than improve it. Emission control changes on modern engines are not readily reversible.

16. Clean (or replace) the EGR valve and lines as recommended.

17. Be sure that all vacuum lines and hoses are reconnected properly after working under the hood. An unconnected or misrouted vacuum line can wreak havoc with engine performance.

---

23. Check for fuel leaks at the carburetor, fuel pump, fuel lines and fuel tank. Be sure all lines and connections are tight.

24. Periodically check the tightness of the carburetor and intake manifold attaching nuts and bolts. These are a common place for vacuum leaks to occur.

25. Clean the carburetor periodically and lubricate the linkage.

26. The condition of the tailpipe can be an excellent indicator of proper engine combustion. After a long drive at highway speeds, the inside of the tailpipe should be a light grey in color. Black or soot on the insides indicates an overly rich mixture.

27. Check the fuel pump pressure. The fuel pump may be supplying more fuel than the engine needs.

28. Use the proper grade of gasoline for your engine. Don't try to compensate for knocking or "pinging" by advancing the ignition timing. This practice will only increase plug temperature and the chances of detonation or pre-ignition with relatively little performance gain.

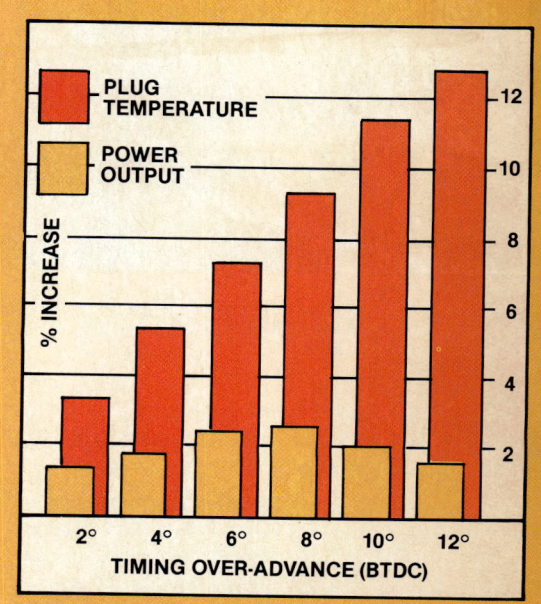

Increasing ignition timing past the specified setting results in a drastic increase in spark plug temperature with increased chance of detonation or preignition. Performance increase is considerably less. (Photo courtesy Champion Spark Plug Co.)

---

that form in the engine should be flushed out to allow the engine to operate at peak efficiency.

35. Clean the radiator of debris that can decrease cooling efficiency.

36. Install a flex-type or electric cooling fan, if you don't have a clutch type fan. Flex fans use curved plastic blades to push more air at low speeds when more cooling is needed; at high speeds the blades flatten out for less resistance. Electric fans only run when the engine temperature reaches a predetermined level.

37. Check the radiator cap for a worn or cracked gasket. If the cap does not seal properly, the cooling system will not function properly.

---

42. Be sure the front end is correctly aligned. A misaligned front end actually has wheels going in differed directions. The increased drag can reduce fuel economy by .3 mpg.

43. Correctly adjust the wheel bearings. Wheel bearings that are adjusted too tight increase rolling resistance.

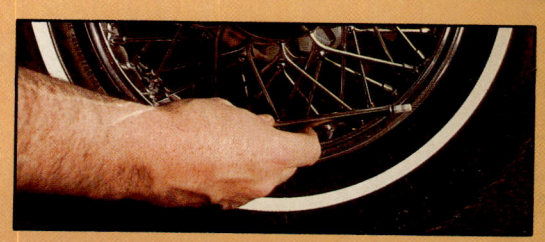

Check tire pressures regularly with a reliable pocket type gauge. Be sure to check the pressure on a cold tire.

GENERAL MAINTENANCE

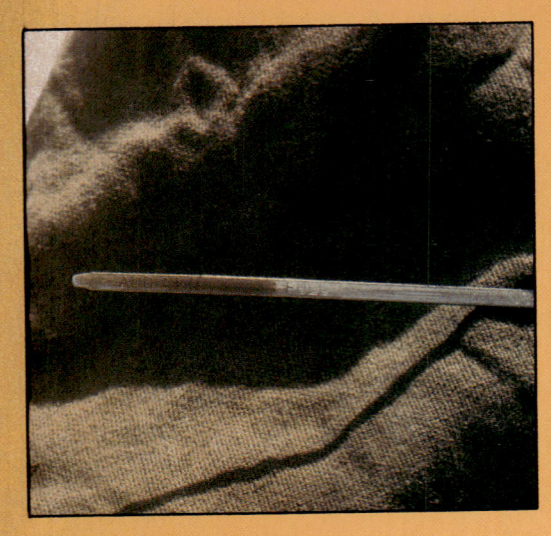

Check the fluid levels (particularly engine oil) on a regular basis. Be sure to check the oil for grit, water or other contamination.

A vacuum gauge is another excellent indicator of internal engine condition and can also be installed in the dash as a mileage indicator.

44. Periodically check the fluid levels in the engine, power steering pump, master cylinder, automatic transmission and drive axle.

45. Change the oil at the recommended interval and change the filter at every oil change. Dirty oil is thick and causes extra friction between moving parts, cutting efficiency and increasing wear. A worn engine requires more frequent tune-ups and gets progressively worse fuel economy. In general, use the lightest viscosity oil for the driving conditions you will encounter.

46. Use the recommended viscosity fluids in the transmission and axle.

47. Be sure the battery is fully charged for fast starts. A slow starting engine wastes fuel.

48. Be sure battery terminals are clean and tight.

49. Check the battery electrolyte level and add distilled water if necessary.

50. Check the exhaust system for crushed pipes, blockages and leaks.

51. Adjust the brakes. Dragging brakes or brakes that are not releasing create increased drag on the engine.

52. Install a vacuum gauge or miles-per-gallon gauge. These gauges visually indicate engine vacuum in the intake manifold. High vacuum = good mileage and low vacuum = poorer mileage. The gauge can also be an excellent indicator of internal engine conditions.

53. Be sure the clutch is properly adjusted. A slipping clutch wastes fuel.

54. Check and periodically lubricate the heat control valve in the exhaust manifold. A sticking or inoperative valve prevents engine warm-up and wastes gas.

55. Keep accurate records to check fuel economy over a period of time. A sudden drop in fuel economy may signal a need for tune-up or other maintenance.

© 1980 Chilton Book Company, Radnor, PA 19089

zles bores. Install the nozzles and tighten to 44–51 ft. lbs. (60–70 Nm).

8. Position the fuel return line on the nozzles using new seals. Install the retaining nuts and tighten to 10 ft. lbs. (14 Nm).

9. Install the fuel lines on the injection pump and nozzles. Tighten to 18–22 ft. lbs. (25–29 Nm).

10. Air bleed the fuel system. Run the engine and check for fuel leaks.

Injection Pump

REMOVAL AND INSTALLATION

1. Disconnect battery ground cable from the battery. located in the luggage compartment.

2. Disconnect air inlet duct from the air cleaner and intake manifold. Install protective cap in intake manifold.

NOTE: *Cap is part of Protective Cap Set, T84P–9395–A.*

3. Remove rear timing belt cover and flywheel timing mark cover.

4. Remove rear timing belt.

5. Disconnect throttle cable and speed control cable, if so equipped.

6. Disconnect vacuum hoses at the altitude compensator and cold start diaphragm.

7. Disconnect fuel cutoff solenoid connector.

8. Disconnect fuel supply and fuel return hoses at injection pump.

9. Remove injection lines at the injection pump and nozzles. Cap all lines and fittings using Protective Cap Set T84P–9395–A or equivalent.

10. Rotate injection pump sprocket until timing marks are aligned. Install two M8 × 1.25 bolts in holes to hold the injection pump sprocket. Remove sprocket retaining nut.

11. Remove injection pump sprocket using Gear Puller T77F–4220–B1 and Adapter D80L–625–4 or equivalent, using two M8 × 1.25 bolts installed in the threaded holes in the sprocket.

12. Remove bolt attaching the injection pump to the pump front bracket.

13. Remove two nuts attaching the injection pump to the pump rear bracket and remove the pump.

To install:

14. Install injection pump in position on the pump bracket.

15. Install two nuts attaching the pump to the rear bracket and tighten to 23–34 ft. lbs.

16. Install bolt attaching the pump to the front bracket and tighten to 12–16 ft. lbs.

17. Install injection pump sprocket. Hold the sprocket in place using the procedure described in Step 10, Removal. Install the sprocket retaining nut and tighten to 51–58 ft. lbs.

18. Remove protective caps and install the fuel lines at the injection pump and nozzles. Tighten the fuel line capnuts to 18–22 ft. lbs.

19. Connect fuel supply and fuel return hoses at the injection pump.

20. Connect fuel cutoff solenoid connector.

21. Connect vacuum lines to the cold start diaphragm and altitude compensator.

22. Connect throttle cable and speed control cable, if so equipped.

23. Install and adjust the rear timing belt.

24. Remove protective cap and install the air inlet duct to the intake manifold and air cleaner.

25. Connect battery ground cable to battery.

26. Air bleed fuel system as outlined.

27. Check and adjust the injection pump timing.

28. Run engine and check for fuel leaks.

29. Check and adjust engine idle.

Injection Timing

ADJUSTMENT

NOTE: *Engine coolant temperature must be above 80°C (176°F) before the injection timing can be checked and/or adjusted.*

1. Disconnect the battery ground cable from the battery located in luggage compartment.

2. Remove the injection pump distributor head plug bolt and sealing washer.

3. Install Static Timing Gauge Adapter, Rotunda 14–0303 or equivalent with Metric Dial Indicator, so that indicator pointer is in contact with injection pump plunger.

4. Remove timing mark cover from transmission housing. Align timing mark (TDC) with pointer on the rear engine cover plate.

5. Rotate the crankshaft pulley slowly, counterclockwise until the dial indicator pointer stops moving (approximately 30–50° BTDC).

6. Adjust dial indicator to Zero.

NOTE: *Confirm that dial indicator pointer does not move from zero by slightly rotating crankshaft left and right.*

7. Turn crankshaft clockwise until crankshaft timing mark aligns with indicator pin. Dial indicator should read 0.04 ± 0.0008 in. (± 0.02mm). If reading is not within specification, adjust as follows:

a. Loosen injection pump attaching bolt and nuts.

b. Rotate the injection pump toward the engine to advance timing and away from the engine to retard timing.

c. Rotate the injection pump until the

350 FUEL SYSTEM

dial indicator reads 0.04 ± 0.0008 in. (1 ± 0.02mm).

   d. Tighten the injection pump attaching nuts and bolt to 13–20 ft. lbs.

   e. Repeat Steps 5–7 to check that timing is adjusted correctly.

8. Remove the dial indicator and adapter and install the injection pump distributor head plug and tighten to 10–14 ft. lbs.

9. Connect the battery ground cable to the battery.

10. Run the engine, check and adjust idle rpm, if necessary. Check for fuel leaks.

Glow Plugs

The diesel start/glow plug control circuit applies power to the glow plugs which heat the combustion chambers, so that the cold diesel engine can be started.

GLOW PLUG CONTROL

The solid state diesel control module is mounted under the left hand side of the instrument panel. It controls glow plug pre-glow time, after-glow time and the operation of the wait-to-start indicator.

When the ignition switch is placed in the RUN position, the wait indicator lamp lights and the pre-glow No. 1 relay and the after-glow No. 2 relay go into operation. Voltage from the ignition switch is applied through pin 6 of the control module and then to the relays through pins 2 and 3. The contacts of the pre-glow relay close and the power is applied from fusible link S (located at the left hand side of the engine above the starter) to operate the glow plugs. The plugs will now start to heat up.

With power applied to the glow plugs, voltage is return through circuit 472 yellow wire with a black tracer to the control module at pin No. 11. After 3 seconds the wait-to-start indicator goes out and stays out. The glow plugs are now warm enough for the engine to be started. After 3 more seconds the pre-glow relay opens. Power is now applied through the after-glow relay and the dropping resistor (located in the air intake at the engine manifold) to keep the glow plugs operating at a reduced voltage.

   NOTE: *The after-glow and the pre-glow relays are located at the top center area of the dash panel, which could be either underneath the instrument panel or the center of the firewall.*

DIESEL START

Power is applied through heavy gauge wires to the starter relay located on the left hand front fender apron, then to the starter solenoid. When the wait-to-start indicator goes out, the ignition switch can be turned to the START position. Power is applied to the starter relay. The relay applies power to the solenoid coil, which in turn closes the contacts to apply battery power to the starter motor.

Even after the wait-to-start indicator goes out, the glow plugs must be kept hot because the combustion chambers may not be hot enough to keep the engine running smoothly. To compensate for this, the after-glow relay continues power to the glow plugs until one of the following conditions occurs:

1. The vehicle moves.
2. The coolant temperature rises above 86°F (30°C).
3. The glow plug voltage goes above 5.7 volts.

Vehicle movement is defined as a clutch switch closed (not depressed) and the neutral switch closed (transmission in any position except neutral). This means pin 10 of the diesel control module is grounded.

The coolant temperature is measured by the thermoswitch. Whenever the coolant temperature is above 86°F (30°C), the thermo switch is opened and there is no voltage on pin No. 8. This will prevent the entire glow plug circuit from operating because the engine is hot enough to start and run without the glow plugs working.

If the voltage on the glow plugs is over 5.7 volts, they may overheat and burn out. Therefore, if over 5.7 volts is detected at pin 11 (with the pre-glow relay off), then the after-glow relay is shut off.

When the ignition is in the START position, 12 volts is put on pin No. 7 of the module. This causes the pre-glow relay to cycle on and off to keep the glow plugs hot. The pre-glow relay will cycle only during cranking.

Power from fusible link B (which is connected to the starter relay) is applied to the fuel solenoid with the ignition switch in the START or RUN position. The fuel solenoid opens the fuel line to permit the engine to run. When the ignition switch is in the OFF position, the solenoid cuts off fuel flow and stops the engine.

DIAGNOSIS AND TESTING

REMOVAL AND INSTALLATION

1. Disconnect battery ground cable from the battery, located in the luggage compartment.
2. Disconnect glow plug harness from the glow plugs.
3. Using a 12mm deep well socket, remove the glow plugs.
4. Install glow plugs, using a 12mm deep well socket. Tighten the glow plugs to 11–15 ft. lbs.

FUEL SYSTEM

Wait-To-Start Lamp
(Refer to Quick Start Control System Schematic)

TEST STEP	RESULT	▶	ACTION TO TAKE
E0 WAIT LAMP • Turn ignition to RUN. Wait lamp should stay on for 3 seconds, then go out.	(OK)	▶	GO to Glow Plug Control System in this Section.
	Lamp does not light	▶	GO to E1.
	Lamp lights, but does not go out	▶	REPLACE glow plug control module and REPEAT test Step E0.
E1 WAIT LAMP BULB • Connect a jumper wire between glow plug control module connector terminal No. 1 and ground. **NOTE: Located under LH side of Instrument panel.** • Turn ignition to RUN.	Wait lamp lights	▶	GO to E2.
	Wait lamp does not light	▶	REPLACE wait lamp bulb or SERVICE or REPLACE wait lamp wiring as necessary. REPEAT Test Step E0.
E2 TERMINAL 6 (POWER CIRCUIT) • Connect a 12V test lamp to connector terminal No. 6 and ground. • Turn ignition to RUN.	Test lamp lights	▶	REPLACE glow plug control module. REPEAT Test Step E0.
	Test lamp does not light	▶	SERVICE and/or REPLACE ignition switch and/or wiring as necessary. REPEAT Test Step E0.

Glow Plug Diagnostic troubletree chart

FUEL SYSTEM

Glow Plug Control System
(Refer to Quick Start Control System Schematic)

TEST STEP	RESULT	ACTION TO TAKE
F0 CHECK VOLTAGE TO EACH GLOW PLUG • Place transmission gear selector in NEUTRAL. **NOTE:** If engine coolant temperature is above 30°C (86°F), jumper connections at coolant thermoswitch. • Turn ignition switch to RUN. • Using a voltmeter, check voltage at each glow plug lead. Minimum of 11 volts at each lead for 6 seconds, then drops to 4.2 to 5.3 volts.	Voltage OK	REMOVE jumper from coolant thermoswitch. GO to F13.
	No voltage	GO to F1.
	No voltage at 3 or less glow plugs	REPLACE glow plug harness. REPEAT Test Step F0.
	Voltage is OK for 6 seconds, then drops to zero	GO to F6.
	Voltage is OK for 6 seconds, then remains at a minimum of 11V	REPLACE glow plug control module.
F1 ENGINE HARNESS TO GLOW PLUG HARNESS • Disconnect glow plug harness from engine harness and glow plugs. • Connect a self-powered test lamp between glow plug harness connector and each glow plug terminal.	Test lamp lights	RECONNECT glow plug harness. GO to F2.
	Test lamp does not light	SERVICE or REPLACE glow plug harness. REPEAT Test Step F0.
F2 TERMINAL 6 (POWER CIRCUIT) • Connect a 12 volt test lamp between glow plug control module terminal No. 6 and ground. • Turn ignition switch to RUN.	Test lamp lights	GO to F3.
	Test lamp does not light	SERVICE and/or REPLACE ignition switch and/or wiring as necessary. REPEAT Test Step F0.

Glow Plug Diagnostic troubletree chart

Glow Plug Control System

TEST STEP	RESULT	ACTION TO TAKE
F3 TERMINAL 2 (NO. 1 GLOW PLUG RELAY SIGNAL) • Connect a 12 volt test lamp between glow plug control module terminal No. 2 (signal) and ground. • Turn ignition switch to RUN.	Test lamp lights for 6 seconds Test lamp does not light	GO to F4. REPLACE quick start control unit. REPEAT Test Step F3.
F4 NO. 1 GLOW PLUG RELAY WIRING • Connect a 12 volt test lamp between No. 1 glow plug relay signal terminal and ground. • Turn ignition to RUN.	Test lamp lights for 6 seconds Test lamp does not light	GO to F5. SERVICE or REPLACE wiring between quick start control unit terminal 2 and No. 1 glow plug relay. REPEAT Test Step F4.
F5 NO. 1 GLOW PLUG RELAY • Connect a voltmeter between No. 1 glow plug relay output terminal (to glow plugs) and ground. • Turn ignition switch to RUN.	11 volts or more for 6 seconds Less than 11 volts	GO to F12. REPLACE No. 1 glow plug relay. REPEAT Test Step F5.
F6 TERMINAL NO. 3 (NO. 2 GLOW PLUG RELAY SIGNAL) • Connect a 12 volt test lamp between glow plug control module terminal No. 3 (signal) and ground. • Turn ignition switch to RUN.	Test lamp lights Test lamp does not light	GO to F8. GO to F7.

Glow Plug Diagnostic troubletree chart

Glow Plug Control System

TEST STEP	RESULT	ACTION TO TAKE
F7 CLUTCH SWITCH/NEUTRAL SWITCH • Using a self-powered test lamp, check the functioning of clutch and neutral switch in both open and closed positions. • With transmission in gear and clutch pedal released, both switches should be open. • With transmission in Neutral and clutch pedal depressed, both switches should be closed.	OK ▶ not OK ▶	GO to **F8**. REPLACE malfunctioning clutch or neutral switch. REPEAT Test Step **F7**.
F8 NO. 2 GLOW PLUG RELAY WIRING • Connect a 12 volt test lamp between No. 2 glow plug relay signal terminal and ground. • Place transmission gear selector in Neutral. • Turn ignition switch to RUN.	Test lamp lights ▶ Test lamp does not light ▶	GO to **F9**. SERVICE or REPLACE wiring between glow plug control module terminal No. 3 and No. 2 glow plug relay. REPEAT Test Step **F8**.
F9 NO. 2 GLOW PLUG RELAY • Connect a 12 volt test lamp between No. 2 glow plug relay output terminal (to glow plugs) and ground. • Turn ignition to RUN.	Test lamp lights ▶ Test lamp does not light ▶	GO to **F10**. REPLACE No. 2 glow plug relay. REPEAT Test Step **F9**.
F10 DROPPING RESISTOR WIRING • Disconnect dropping resistor from wiring harness. • Connect a 12 volt test lamp between the dropping resistor input terminal on wiring harness and ground. • Turn ignition to RUN.	Test lamp lights ▶ Test lamp does not light ▶	GO to **F11**. SERVICE or REPLACE wiring between No. 2 glow plug relay and dropping resistor. REPEAT Test Step **F10**.

Glow Plug Diagnostic troubletree chart

Glow Plug Control System

TEST STEP	RESULT		ACTION TO TAKE
F11 DROPPING RESISTOR • Connect an ohmmeter to the connector terminals on the resistor. • Set multiply by knob to X1. • Ohmmeter should indicate less than 1 ohm.	(OK) ▶ (OK̸) ▶		RECONNECT dropping resistor to wiring harness. GO to **F12**. REPLACE dropping resistor. REPEAT Test Step **F11**.
F12 GLOW PLUG HARNESS • Connect a 12 volt test lamp between any glow plug terminal and ground. • Turn ignition to RUN.	Test lamp lights ▶ Test lamp does not light ▶		GO to **F0**. SERVICE or REPLACE wiring from No. 1 glow plug relay to glow plug harness. REPEAT Test Step **F12**.
F13 GLOW PLUGS • Disconnect leads from each glow plug. • Connect one lead of ohmmeter to glow plug terminal and one lead to a good ground. • Set ohmmeter multiply by knob to X1. • Test each glow plug.	Meter indicates less than one ohm ▶ Meter indicates one ohm or more ▶		Problem is not in glow plug system. REPLACE glow plug. REPEAT Test Step **F13**.

Glow Plug Diagnostic troubletree chart

356 FUEL SYSTEM

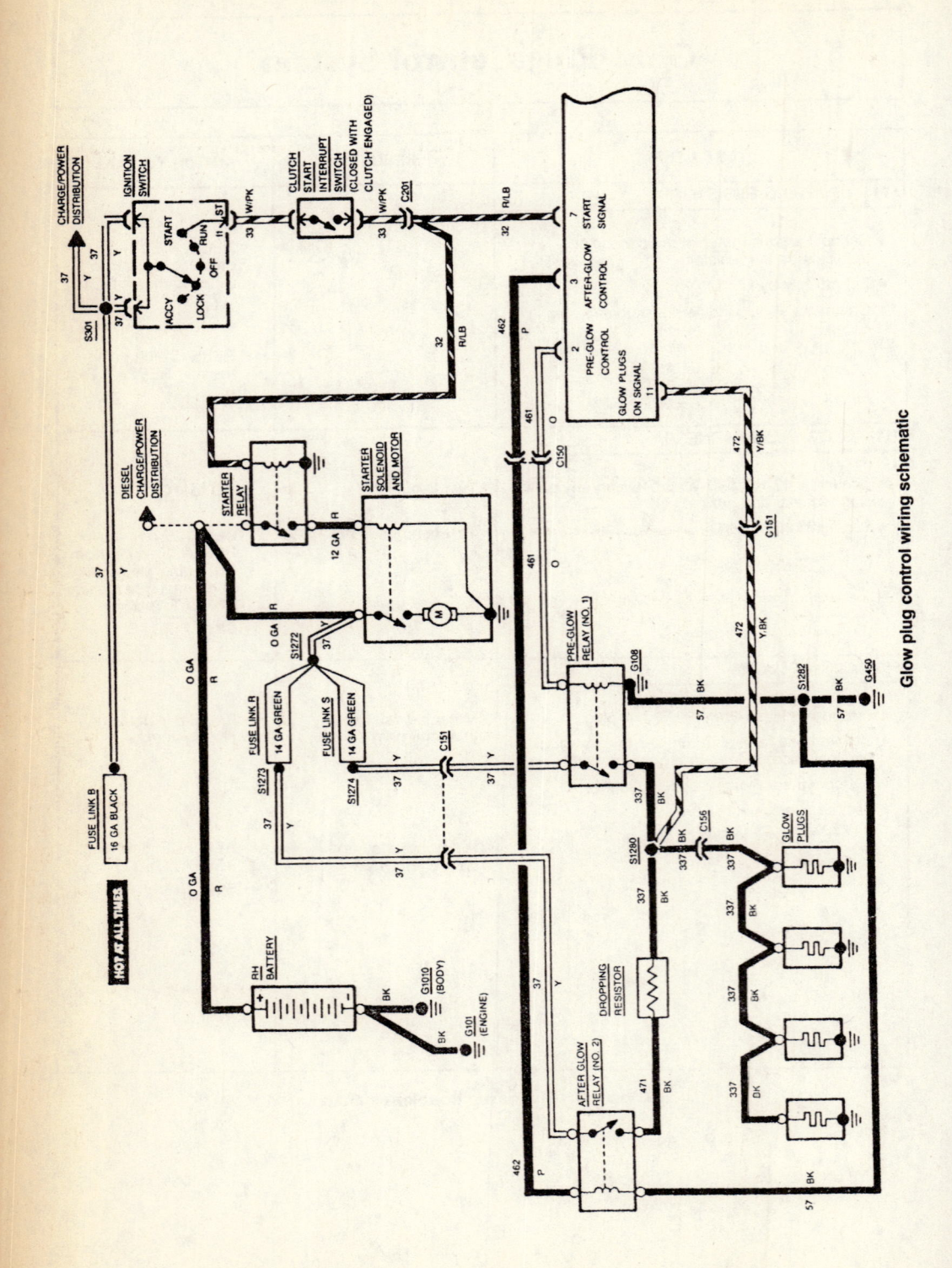

FUEL SYSTEM 357

Glow plug control wiring schematic (cont.)

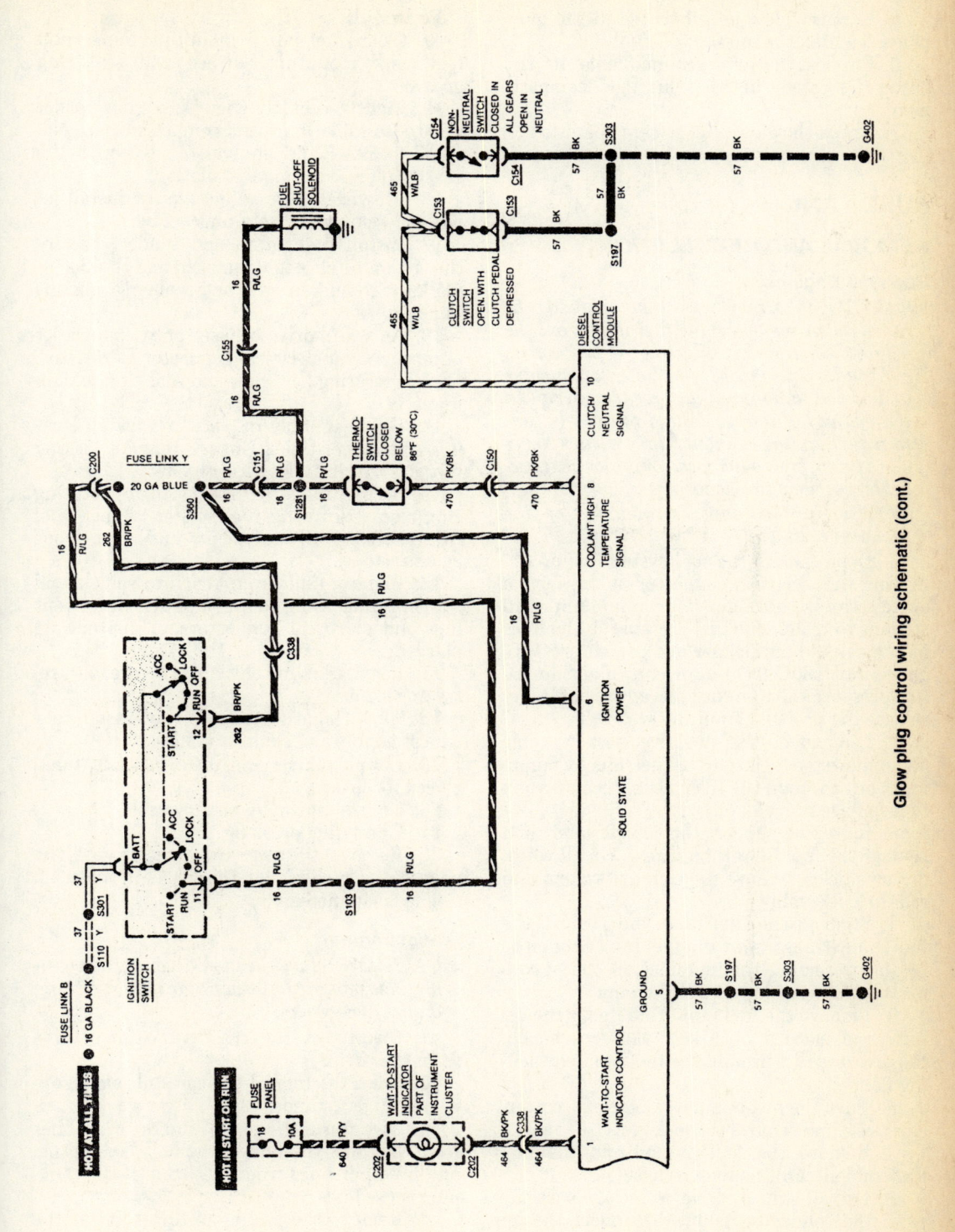

FUEL SYSTEM

5. Connect glow plug harness to the glow plugs. Tighten the nuts to 5–7 ft. lbs.
6. Connect battery ground cable to the battery located in the luggage compartment.
7. Check the glow plug system operation.

FUEL TANK

REMOVAL AND INSTALLATION

Gasoline Engines

CAUTION: *Extreme caution should be taken when removing the fuel tank from the vehicle. Ensure that all removal procedures are conducted in a well ventilated area. Have a sufficient amount of absorbent material in the vicinity of the work area to quickly contain fuel spillages should they occur. Never store waste fuel in an open container as it presents a serious fire hazard.*

NOTE: *The fuel pump is mounted on the fuel sender assembly in the tank.*

1. Depressurize the fuel system by disconnecting the electrical connector at the inertia switch. Crank the engine for a minimum of 15 seconds to reduce the fuel pressure in the lines or remove the air cleaner and attach pressure gauge tool T80L–9974–A or equivalent, to the fuel pressure valve on the fuel rail assembly and release the pressure from the system.
2. Disconnect the negative battery cable and remove the fuel from the fuel tank by pumping it out through the filler neck. Clean up any fuel spillage immediately.
3. Raise and support the vehicle safely and remove the fuel filler tube (neck). On all wheel drive vehicles, remove the exhaust system and rear axle assembly.
4. Support the fuel tank and remove the fuel tank straps, lower the fuel tank enough to be able to remove the fuel lines, electrical connectors and vent lines from the tank.
5. Remove the fuel tank from under the vehicle and place it on a suitable work bench. Remove any dirt around the fuel pump attaching flange.
6. Turn the fuel pump locking ring counterclockwise and remove the lock ring.
7. Remove the fuel pump from the fuel tank and discard the flange gasket.
8. On all wheel drive vehicles, partially raise the sender unit and disconnect the jet pump line and resistor electrical connector. Remove the fuel pump and bracket assembly with seal gasket. Remove the seal gasket and replace with new. Remove the jet pump assembly.

To install:

9. Clean fuel pump mounting flange and fuel tank mounting surface and seal ring groove.
10. Lightly coat the new seal ring gasket with a suitable lubricant compound part No. C1AZ–19590–B or equivalent, to hold the gasket in place during installation.
11. All-wheel drive vehicles only: install jet pump assembly and retaining screw.
12. Install fuel pump and sender. Ensure that nylon filter is not damaged and that locating keys are in key ways and seal ring remains in place.
13. All-wheel drive vehicles only: connect jet pump line and electrical connector to resistor. Ensure locating key ways and seal ring remain in place.
14. Hold assembly in place and install locking ring finger-tight. Ensure that all locking tabs are under tank lock ring tabs.
15. Secure unit with locking ring by rotating ring clockwise using fuel sender wrench tool D84P–9275–A or equivalent, until ring stops against stops.
16. Remove tank from bench to vehicle and support tank while connecting fuel lines, vent line and electrical connectors to appropriate places.
17. Install tank in vehicle and secure with retaining straps.
18. All-wheel drive vehicles only: install rear axle assembly and exhaust system.
19. Lower vehicle and install fuel in tank. Check for leaks.
20. Connect negative battery cable.
21. Check fuel pressure.
22. Remove the pressure gauge, start the engine and recheck for fuel leaks. Correct all fuel leaks immediately.

Diesel Engine

CAUTION: *Have the tank as empty as possible. No smoking or open flame while working on the fuel system.*

1. Disconnect the negative battery cable from the battery.
2. Raise the rear of the car and safely support it on jackstands.
3. Disconnect the gas fill and breather lines from the tank. Disconnect the fuel feed, return and breather lines from the front of the tank, plug these lines.
4. Remove the two mounting bolts at the top rear of the tank while supporting the tank on a piece of wood and a floor jack. Lower and remove the gas tank.
5. Installation is the reverse order of removal.

Troubleshooting Basic Fuel System Problems

Problem	Cause	Solution
Engine cranks, but won't start (or is hard to start) when cold	• Empty fuel tank • Incorrect starting procedure • Defective fuel pump • No fuel in carburetor • Clogged fuel filter • Engine flooded • Defective choke	• Check for fuel in tank • Follow correct procedure • Check pump output • Check for fuel in the carburetor • Replace fuel filter • Wait 15 minutes; try again • Check choke plate
Engine cranks, but is hard to start (or does not start) when hot— (presence of fuel is assumed)	• Defective choke	• Check choke plate
Rough idle or engine runs rough	• Dirt or moisture in fuel • Clogged air filter • Faulty fuel pump	• Replace fuel filter • Replace air filter • Check fuel pump output
Engine stalls or hesitates on acceleration	• Dirt or moisture in the fuel • Dirty carburetor • Defective fuel pump • Incorrect float level, defective accelerator pump	• Replace fuel filter • Clean the carburetor • Check fuel pump output • Check carburetor
Poor gas mileage	• Clogged air filter • Dirty carburetor • Defective choke, faulty carburetor adjustment	• Replace air filter • Clean carburetor • Check carburetor
Engine is flooded (won't start accompanied by smell of raw fuel)	• Improperly adjusted choke or carburetor	• Wait 15 minutes and try again, without pumping gas pedal • If it won't start, check carburetor

Chassis Electrical 6

UNDERSTANDING AND TROUBLESHOOTING ELECTRICAL SYSTEMS

At the rate which both import and domestic manufacturers are incorporating electronic control systems into their production lines, it won't be long before every new vehicle is equipped with one or more on-board computer. These electronic components (with no moving parts) should theoretically last the life of the vehicle, provided nothing external happens to damage the circuits or memory chips.

While it is true that electronic components should never wear out, in the real world malfunctions do occur. It is also true that any computer-based system is extremely sensitive to electrical voltages and cannot tolerate careless or haphazard testing or service procedures. An inexperienced individual can literally do major damage looking for a minor problem by using the wrong kind of test equipment or connecting test leads or connectors with the ignition switch **ON**. When selecting test equipment, make sure the manufacturers instructions state that the tester is compatible with whatever type of electronic control system is being serviced. Read all instructions carefully and double check all test points before installing probes or making any test connections.

The following section outlines basic diagnosis techniques for dealing with computerized automotive control systems. Along with a general explanation of the various types of test equipment available to aid in servicing modern electronic automotive systems, basic repair techniques for wiring harnesses and connectors is given. Read the basic information before attempting any repairs or testing on any computerized system, to provide the background of information necessary to avoid the most common and obvious mistakes that can cost both time and money. Although the replacement and testing procedures are simple in themselves, the systems are not, and unless one has a thorough understanding of all components and their function within a particular computerized control system, the logical test sequence these systems demand cannot be followed. Minor malfunctions can make a big difference, so it is important to know how each component affects the operation of the overall electronic system to find the ultimate cause of a problem without replacing good components unnecessarily. It is not enough to use the correct test equipment; the test equipment must be used correctly.

Safety Precautions

CAUTION: *Whenever working on or around any computer based microprocessor control system, always observe these general precautions to prevent the possibility of personal injury or damage to electronic components.*

• Never install or remove battery cables with the key ON or the engine running. Jumper cables should be connected with the key OFF to avoid power surges that can damage electronic control units. Engines equipped with computer controlled systems should avoid both giving and getting jump starts due to the possibility of serious damage to components from arcing in the engine compartment when connections are made with the ignition ON.

• Always remove the battery cables before charging the battery. Never use a high output charger on an installed battery or attempt to use any type of "hot shot" (24 volt) starting aid.

• Exercise care when inserting test probes into connectors to insure good connections without damaging the connector or spreading the pins. Always probe connectors from the rear (wire) side, NOT the pin side, to avoid acciden-

tal shorting of terminals during test procedures.
- Never remove or attach wiring harness connectors with the ignition switch ON, especially to an electronic control unit.
- Do not drop any components during service procedures and never apply 12 volts directly to any component (like a solenoid or relay) unless instructed specifically to do so. Some component electrical windings are designed to safely handle only 4 or 5 volts and can be destroyed in seconds if 12 volts are applied directly to the connector.
- Remove the electronic control unit if the vehicle is to be placed in an environment where temperatures exceed approximately 176°F (80°C), such as a paint spray booth or when arc or gas welding near the control unit location in the car.

ORGANIZED TROUBLESHOOTING

When diagnosing a specific problem, organized troubleshooting is a must. The complexity of a modern automobile demands that you approach any problem in a logical, organized manner. There are certain troubleshooting techniques that are standard:

1. Establish when the problem occurs. Does the problem appear only under certain conditions? Were there any noises, odors, or other unusual symptoms?
2. Isolate the problem area. To do this, make some simple tests and observations; then eliminate the systems that are working properly. Check for obvious problems such as broken wires, dirty connections or split or disconnected vacuum hoses. Always check the obvious before assuming something complicated is the cause.
3. Test for problems systematically to determine the cause once the problem area is isolated. Are all the components functioning properly? Is there power going to electrical switches and motors? Is there vacuum at vacuum switches and/or actuators? Is there a mechanical problem such as bent linkage or loose mounting screws? Doing careful, systematic checks will often turn up most causes on the first inspection without wasting time checking components that have little or no relationship to the problem.
4. Test all repairs after the work is done to make sure that the problem is fixed. Some causes can be traced to more than one component, so a careful verification of repair work is important to pick up additional malfunctions that may cause a problem to reappear or a different problem to arise. A blown fuse, for example, is a simple problem that may require more than another fuse to repair. If you don't look for a problem that caused a fuse to blow, for example, a shorted wire may go undetected.

Experience has shown that most problems tend to be the result of a fairly simple and obvious cause, such as loose or corroded connectors or air leaks in the intake system; making careful inspection of components during testing essential to quick and accurate troubleshooting. Special, hand held computerized testers designed specifically for diagnosing the system are available from a variety of aftermarket sources, as well as from the vehicle manufacturer, but care should be taken that any test equipment being used is designed to diagnose that particular computer controlled system accurately without damaging the control unit (ECM) or components being tested.

NOTE: *Pinpointing the exact cause of trouble in an electrical system can sometimes only be accomplished by the use of special test equipment. The following describes commonly used test equipment and explains how to put it to best use in diagnosis. In addition to the information covered below, the manufacturer's instructions booklet provided with the tester should be read and clearly understood before attempting any test procedures.*

TEST EQUIPMENT

Jumper Wires

Jumper wires are simple, yet extremely valuable, pieces of test equipment. Jumper wires are merely wires that are used to bypass sections of a circuit. The simplest type of jumper wire is merely a length of multi-strand wire with an alligator clip at each end. Jumper wires are usually fabricated from lengths of standard automotive wire and whatever type of connector (alligator clip, spade connector or pin connector) that is required for the particular vehicle being tested. The well equipped tool box will have several different styles of jumper wires in several different lengths. Some jumper wires are made with three or more terminals coming from a common splice for special purpose testing. In cramped, hard-to-reach areas it is advisable to have insulated boots over the jumper wire terminals in order to prevent accidental grounding, sparks, and possible fire, especially when testing fuel system components.

Jumper wires are used primarily to locate open electrical circuits, on either the ground (−) side of the circuit or on the hot (+) side. If an electrical component fails to operate, connect the jumper wire between the component and a good ground. If the component operates only with the jumper installed, the ground circuit is open. If the ground circuit is good, but the component does not operate, the circuit between the power feed and component is open. You can sometimes connect the jumper wire directly from the battery to the hot terminal of the component, but first make sure the component uses 12 volts in operation. Some electrical components, such as fuel injectors, are designed to operate on about 4 volts and running 12 volts directly to the injector terminals can burn out the wiring. By inserting an in-line fuse holder between a set of test leads, a fused jumper wire can be used for bypassing open circuits. Use a 5 amp fuse to provide protection against voltage spikes. When in doubt, use a voltmeter to check the voltage input to the component and measure how much voltage is being applied normally. By moving the jumper wire successively back from the lamp toward the power source, you can isolate the area of the circuit where the open is located. When the component stops functioning, or the power is cut off, the open is in the segment of wire between the jumper and the point previously tested.

CAUTION: *Never use jumpers made from wire that is of lighter gauge than used in the circuit under test. If the jumper wire is of too small gauge, it may overheat and possibly melt. Never use jumpers to bypass high resistance loads in a circuit. Bypassing resistances, in effect, creates a short circuit which may, in turn, cause damage and fire. Never use a jumper for anything other than temporary bypassing of components in a circuit.*

12 Volt Test Light

The 12 volt test light is used to check circuits and components while electrical current is flowing through them. It is used for voltage and ground tests. Twelve volt test lights come in different styles but all have three main parts; a ground clip, a probe, and a light. The most commonly used 12 volt test lights have pick-type probes. To use a 12 volt test light, connect the ground clip to a good ground and probe wherever necessary with the pick. The pick should be sharp so that it can penetrate wire insulation to make contact with the wire, without making a large hole in the insulation. The wrap-around light is handy in hard to reach areas or where it is difficult to support a wire to push a probe pick into it. To use the wrap around light, hook the wire to probed with the hook and pull the trigger. A small pick will be forced through the wire insulation into the wire core.

CAUTION: *Do not use a test light to probe electronic ignition spark plug or coil wires. Never use a pick-type test light to probe wiring on computer controlled systems unless specifically instructed to do so. Any wire insulation that is pierced by the test light probe should be taped and sealed with silicone after testing.*

Like the jumper wire, the 12 volt test light is used to isolate opens in circuits. But, whereas the jumper wire is used to bypass the open to operate the load, the 12 volt test light is used to locate the presence of voltage in a circuit. If the test light glows, you know that there is power up to that point; if the 12 volt test light does not glow when its probe is inserted into the wire or connector, you know that there is an open circuit (no power). Move the test light in successive steps back toward the power source until the light in the handle does glow. When it does glow, the open is between the probe and point previously probed.

NOTE: *The test light does not detect that 12 volts (or any particular amount of voltage) is present; it only detects that some voltage is present. It is advisable before using the test light to touch its terminals across the battery posts to make sure the light is operating properly.*

Self-Powered Test Light

The self-powered test light usually contains a 1.5 volt penlight battery. One type of self-powered test light is similar in design to the 12 volt test light. This type has both the battery and the light in the handle and pick-type probe tip. The second type has the light toward the open tip, so that the light illuminates the contact point. The self-powered test light is dual purpose piece of test equipment. It can be used to test for either open or short circuits when power is isolated from the circuit (continuity test). A powered test light should not be used on any computer controlled system or component unless specifically instructed to do so. Many engine sensors can be destroyed by even this small amount of voltage applied directly to the terminals.

Open Circuit Testing

To use the self-powered test light to check for open circuits, first isolate the circuit from the vehicle's 12 volt power source by disconnecting the battery or wiring harness connector. Connect the test light ground clip to a good ground and probe sections of the circuit sequentially with the test light. (start from either end of the circuit). If the light is out, the open is between the probe and the circuit ground. If the light is on, the open is between the probe and end of the circuit toward the power source.

Short Circuit Testing

By isolating the circuit both from power and from ground, and using a self-powered test light, you can check for shorts to ground in the circuit. Isolate the circuit from power and ground. Connect the test light ground clip to a good ground and probe any easy-to-reach test point in the circuit. If the light comes on, there is a short somewhere in the circuit. To isolate the short, probe a test point at either end of the isolated circuit (the light should be on). Leave the test light probe connected and open connectors, switches, remove parts, etc., sequentially, until the light goes out. When the light goes out, the short is between the last circuit component opened and the previous circuit opened.

NOTE: *The 1.5 volt battery in the test light does not provide much current. A weak battery may not provide enough power to illuminate the test light even when a complete circuit is made (especially if there are high resistances in the circuit). Always make sure that the test battery is strong. To check the battery, briefly touch the ground clip to the probe; if the light glows brightly the battery is strong enough for testing. Never use a self-powered test light to perform checks for opens or shorts when power is applied to the electrical system under test. The 12 volt vehicle power will quickly burn out the 1.5 volt light bulb in the test light.*

Voltmeter

A voltmeter is used to measure voltage at any point in a circuit, or to measure the voltage drop across any part of a circuit. It can also be used to check continuity in a wire or circuit by indicating current flow from one end to the other. Voltmeters usually have various scales on the meter dial and a selector switch to allow the selection of different voltages. The voltmeter has a positive and a negative lead. To avoid damage to the meter, always connect the negative lead to the negative (–) side of circuit (to ground or nearest the ground side of the circuit) and connect the positive lead to the positive (+) side of the circuit (to the power source or the nearest power source). Note that the negative voltmeter lead will always be black and that the positive voltmeter will always be some color other than black (usually red). Depending on how the voltmeter is connected into the circuit, it has several uses.

A voltmeter can be connected either in parallel or in series with a circuit and it has a very high resistance to current flow. When connected in parallel, only a small amount of current will flow through the voltmeter current path; the rest will flow through the normal circuit current path and the circuit will work normally. When the voltmeter is connected in series with a circuit, only a small amount of current can flow through the circuit. The circuit will not work properly, but the voltmeter reading will show if the circuit is complete or not.

Available Voltage Measurement

Set the voltmeter selector switch to the 20V position and connect the meter negative lead to the negative post of the battery. Connect the positive meter lead to the positive post of the battery and turn the ignition switch ON to provide a load. Read the voltage on the meter or digital display. A well charged battery should register over 12 volts. If the meter reads below 11.5 volts, the battery power may be insufficient to operate the electrical system properly. This test determines voltage available from the battery and should be the first step in any electrical trouble diagnosis procedure. Many electrical problems, especially on computer controlled systems, can be caused by a low state of charge in the battery. Excessive corrosion at the battery cable terminals can cause a poor contact that will prevent proper charging and full battery current flow.

Normal battery voltage is 12 volts when fully charged. When the battery is supplying current to one or more circuits it is said to be "under load". When everything is off the electrical system is under a "no-load" condition. A fully charged battery may show about 12.5 volts at no load; will drop to 12 volts under medium load; and will drop even lower under heavy load. If the battery is partially discharged the voltage decrease under heavy load may be excessive, even though the battery shows 12 volts or more at no load. When allowed to discharge further, the battery's available voltage under load will decrease more severely. For this reason, it is important that the battery be fully charged during all testing procedures to avoid errors in diagnosis and incorrect test results.

Voltage Drop

When current flows through a resistance, the voltage beyond the resistance is reduced (the larger the current, the greater the reduction in voltage). When no current is flowing, there is no voltage drop because there is no current flow. All points in the circuit which are connected to the power source are at the same voltage as the power source. The total voltage drop always equals the total source voltage. In a long circuit with many connectors, a series of small, unwanted voltage drops due to corrosion at the connectors can add up to a total loss of voltage which impairs the operation of the normal loads in the circuit.

INDIRECT COMPUTATION OF VOLTAGE DROPS

1. Set the voltmeter selector switch to the 20 volt position.

2. Connect the meter negative lead to a good ground.

3. Probe all resistances in the circuit with the positive meter lead.

4. Operate the circuit in all modes and observe the voltage readings.

DIRECT MEASUREMENT OF VOLTAGE DROPS

1. Set the voltmeter switch to the 20 volt position.

2. Connect the voltmeter negative lead to the ground side of the resistance load to be measured.

3. Connect the positive lead to the positive side of the resistance or load to be measured.

4. Read the voltage drop directly on the 20 volt scale.

Too high a voltage indicates too high a resistance. If, for example, a blower motor runs too slowly, you can determine if there is too high a resistance in the resistor pack. By taking voltage drop readings in all parts of the circuit, you can isolate the problem. Too low a voltage drop indicates too low a resistance. If, for example, a blower motor runs too fast in the MED and/or LOW position, the problem can be isolated in the resistor pack by taking voltage drop readings in all parts of the circuit to locate a possibly shorted resistor. The maximum allowable voltage drop under load is critical, especially if there is more than one high resistance problem in a circuit because all voltage drops are cumulative. A small drop is normal due to the resistance of the conductors.

HIGH RESISTANCE TESTING

1. Set the voltmeter selector switch to the 4 volt position.

2. Connect the voltmeter positive lead to the positive post of the battery.

3. Turn on the headlights and heater blower to provide a load.

4. Probe various points in the circuit with the negative voltmeter lead.

5. Read the voltage drop on the 4 volt scale. Some average maximum allowable voltage drops are:

FUSE PANEL: 7 volts
IGNITION SWITCH: 5 volts
HEADLIGHT SWITCH: 7 volts
IGNITION COIL (+): 5 volts
ANY OTHER LOAD: 1.3 volts

NOTE: *Voltage drops are all measured while a load is operating; without current flow, there will be no voltage drop.*

Ohmmeter

The ohmmeter is designed to read resistance in ohms (Ω) in a circuit or component. Although there are several different styles of ohmmeters, all will usually have a selector switch which permits the measurement of different ranges of resistance (usually the selector switch allows the multiplication of the meter reading by 10, 100, 1,000, and 10,000). A calibration knob allows the meter to be set at zero for accurate measurement. Since all ohmmeters are powered by an internal battery (usually 9 volts), the ohmmeter can be used as a self-powered test light. When the ohmmeter is connected, current from the ohmmeter flows through the circuit or component being tested. Since the ohmmeter's internal resistance and voltage are known values, the amount of current flow through the meter depends on the resistance of the circuit or component being tested.

The ohmmeter can be used to perform continuity test for opens or shorts (either by observation of the meter needle or as a self-powered test light), and to read actual resistance in a circuit. It should be noted that the ohmmeter is used to check the resistance of a component or wire while there is no voltage applied to the circuit. Current flow from an outside voltage source (such as the vehicle battery) can damage the ohmmeter, so the circuit or component should be isolated from the vehicle electrical system before any testing is done. Since the ohmmeter uses its own voltage source, either lead can be connected to any test point.

NOTE: *When checking diodes or other solid state components, the ohmmeter leads can only be connected one way in order to measure current flow in a single direction. Make sure the positive (+) and negative (−) terminal connections are as described in the test procedures to verify the one-way diode operation.*

In using the meter for making continuity checks, do not be concerned with the actual resistance readings. Zero resistance, or any resistance readings, indicate continuity in the circuit. Infinite resistance indicates an open in the circuit. A high resistance reading where there should be none indicates a problem in the circuit. Checks for short circuits are made in the same manner as checks for open circuits except that the circuit must be isolated from both power and normal ground. Infinite resistance indicates no continuity to ground, while zero resistance indicates a dead short to ground.

RESISTANCE MEASUREMENT

The batteries in an ohmmeter will weaken with age and temperature, so the ohmmeter must be calibrated or "zeroed" before taking measurements. To zero the meter, place the selector switch in its lowest range and touch the two ohmmeter leads together. Turn the calibration knob until the meter needle is exactly on zero.

NOTE: *All analog (needle) type ohmmeters must be zeroed before use, but some digital ohmmeter models are automatically calibrated when the switch is turned on. Self-calibrating digital ohmmeters do not have an adjusting knob, but its a good idea to check for a zero readout before use by touching the leads together. All computer controlled systems require the use of a digital ohmmeter with at least 10MΩ(megohms) impedance for testing. Before any test procedures are attempted, make sure the ohmmeter used is compatible with the electrical system or damage to the on-board computer could result.*

To measure resistance, first isolate the circuit from the vehicle power source by disconnecting the battery cables or the harness connector. Make sure the key is OFF when disconnecting any components or the battery. Where necessary, also isolate at least one side of the circuit to be checked to avoid reading parallel resistances. Parallel circuit resistances will always give a lower reading than the actual resistance of either of the branches. When measuring the resistance of parallel circuits, the total resistance will always be lower than the smallest resistance in the circuit. Connect the meter leads to both sides of the circuit (wire or component) and read the actual measured ohms on the meter scale. Make sure the selector switch is set to the proper ohm scale for the circuit being tested to avoid misreading the ohmmeter test value.

WARNING: *Never use an ohmmeter with power applied to the circuit. Like the self-powered test light, the ohmmeter is designed to operate on its own power supply. The normal 12 volt automotive electrical system current could damage the meter!*

Ammeters

An ammeter measures the amount of current flowing through a circuit in units called amperes or amps. Amperes are units of electron flow which indicate how fast the electrons are flowing through the circuit. Since Ohms Law dictates that current flow in a circuit is equal to the circuit voltage divided by the total circuit resistance, increasing voltage also increases the current level (amps). Likewise, any decrease in resistance will increase the amount of amps in a circuit. At normal operating voltage, most circuits have a characteristic amount of amperes, called "current draw" which can be measured using an ammeter. By referring to a specified current draw rating, measuring the amperes, and comparing the two values, one can determine what is happening within the circuit to aid in diagnosis. An open circuit, for example, will not allow any current to flow so the ammeter reading will be zero. More current flows through a heavily loaded circuit or when the charging system is operating.

An ammeter is always connected in series with the circuit being tested. All of the current that normally flows through the circuit must also flow through the ammeter; if there is any other path for the current to follow, the ammeter reading will not be accurate. The ammeter itself has very little resistance to current flow and therefore will not affect the circuit, but it will measure current draw only when the circuit is closed and electricity is flowing. Excessive current draw can blow fuses and drain the battery, while a reduced current draw can cause motors to run slowly, lights to dim and other components to not operate properly. The ammeter can help diagnose these conditions by locating the cause of the high or low reading.

Multimeters

Different combinations of test meters can be built into a single unit designed for specific tests. Some of the more common combination test devices are known as Volt/Amp testers, Tach/Dwell meters, or Digital Multimeters. The Volt/Amp tester is used for charging system, starting system or battery tests and consists of a voltmeter, an ammeter and a variable resistance carbon pile. The voltmeter will usually have at least two ranges for use with 6, 12 and 24 volt systems. The ammeter also has more than one range for testing various levels of battery loads and starter current draw and the carbon pile can be adjusted to offer different amounts of resistance. The Volt/Amp tester has heavy leads to carry large amounts of current and many later models have an inductive ammeter pickup that clamps around the wire to simplify test connections. On some models, the ammeter also has a zero-center scale to allow testing of charging and starting systems without switching leads or polarity. A digital multimeter is a voltmeter, ammeter and ohmmeter combined in an instrument which gives a digital readout. These are often used when testing solid state circuits because of their high input impedance (usually 10 megohms or more).

The tach/dwell meter combines a tachometer and a dwell (cam angle) meter and is a specialized kind of voltmeter. The tachometer scale is marked to show engine speed in rpm and the dwell scale is marked to show degrees of distributor shaft rotation. In most electronic ignition systems, dwell is determined by the control unit, but the dwell meter can also be used to check the duty cycle (operation) of some electronic engine control systems. Some tach/dwell meters are powered by an internal battery, while others take their power from the car battery in use. The battery powered testers usually require calibration much like an ohmmeter before testing.

Special Test Equipment

A variety of diagnostic tools are available to help troubleshoot and repair computerized engine control systems. The most sophisticated of these devices are the console type engine analyzers that usually occupy a garage service bay, but there are several types of aftermarket electronic testers available that will allow quick circuit tests of the engine control system by plugging directly into a special connector located in the engine compartment or under the dashboard. Several tool and equipment manufacturers offer simple, hand held testers that measure various circuit voltage levels on command to check all system components for proper operation. Although these testers usually cost about $300–500, consider that the average computer control unit (or ECM) can cost just as much and the money saved by not replacing perfectly good sensors or components in an attempt to correct a problem could justify the purchase price of a special diagnostic tester the first time it's used.

These computerized testers can allow quick and easy test measurements while the engine is operating or while the car is being driven. In addition, the on-board computer memory can be read to access any stored trouble codes; in effect allowing the computer to tell you where it hurts and aid trouble diagnosis by pinpointing exactly which circuit or component is malfunctioning. In the same manner, repairs can be tested to make sure the problem has been corrected. The biggest advantage these special testers have is their relatively easy hookups that minimize or eliminate the chances of making the wrong connections and getting false voltage readings or damaging the computer accidentally.

NOTE: *It should be remembered that these testers check voltage levels in circuits; they don't detect mechanical problems or failed components if the circuit voltage falls within the preprogrammed limits stored in the tester PROM unit. Also, most of the hand held testers are designed to work only on one or two systems made by a specific manufacturer.*

A variety of aftermarket testers are available to help diagnose different computerized control systems. Owatonna Tool Company (OTC), for example, markets a device called the OTC Monitor which plugs directly into the assembly line diagnostic link (ALDL). The OTC tester makes diagnosis a simple matter of pressing the correct buttons and, by changing the internal PROM or inserting a different diagnosis cartridge, it will work on any model from full size to subcompact, over a wide range of years. An adapter is supplied with the tester to allow connection to all types of ALDL links, regardless of the number of pin terminals used. By inserting an updated PROM into the OTC tester, it can be easily updated to diagnose any new modifications of computerized control systems.

Wiring Harnesses

The average automobile contains about $1/2$ mile of wiring, with hundreds of individual connections. To protect the many wires from damage and to keep them from becoming a confusing tangle, they are organized into bundles, enclosed in plastic or taped together and called wire harnesses. Different wiring harnesses serve different parts of the vehicle. Individual wires are color coded to help trace them through a harness where sections are hidden from view.

A loose or corroded connection or a replacement wire that is too small for the circuit will add extra resistance and an additional voltage drop to the circuit. A ten percent voltage drop can result in slow or erratic motor operation, for example, even though the circuit is complete. Automotive wiring or circuit conductors can be in any one of three forms:

1. Single strand wire
2. Multi-strand wire
3. Printed circuitry

Single strand wire has a solid metal core and is usually used inside such components as alternators, motors, relays and other devices. Multi-strand wire has a core made of many small strands of wire twisted together into a single conductor. Most of the wiring in an automotive electrical system is made up of multi-strand wire, either as a single conductor or grouped together in a harness. All wiring is color coded on the insulator, either as a solid color or as a colored wire with an identification stripe. A printed circuit is a thin film of copper or other conductor that is printed on an insulator backing. Occasionally, a printed circuit is sandwiched between two sheets of plastic for more protection and flexibility. A complete printed circuit, consisting of conductors, insulating material and connectors for lamps or other components is called a printed circuit board. Printed circuitry is used in place of individual wires or harnesses in places where space is limited, such as behind instrument panels.

Wire Gauge

Since computer controlled automotive electrical systems are very sensitive to changes in resistance, the selection of properly sized wires is critical when systems are repaired. The wire gauge number is an expression of the cross section area of the conductor. The most common system for expressing wire size is the American Wire Gauge (AWG) system.

Wire cross section area is measured in circular mils. A mil is $1/1000$ in. (0.001 in.); a circular mil is the area of a circle one mil in diameter. For example, a conductor 1/4 in. in diameter is 0.250 in. or 250 mils. The circular mil cross section area of the wire is 250 squared (250^2) or 62,500 circular mils. Imported car models usually use metric wire gauge designations, which is simply the cross section area of the conductor in square millimeters (mm^2).

Gauge numbers are assigned to conductors of various cross section areas. As gauge number increases, area decreases and the conductor becomes smaller. A 5 gauge conductor is smaller than a 1 gauge conductor and a 10 gauge is smaller than a 5 gauge. As the cross section area of a conductor decreases, resistance increases and so does the gauge number. A conductor with a higher gauge number will carry less current than a conductor with a lower gauge number.

NOTE: *Gauge wire size refers to the size of the conductor, not the size of the complete wire. It is possible to have two wires of the same gauge with different diameters because one may have thicker insulation than the other.*

12 volt automotive electrical systems generally use 10, 12, 14, 16 and 18 gauge wire. Main power distribution circuits and larger accessories usually use 10 and 12 gauge wire. Battery cables are usually 4 or 6 gauge, although 1 and 2 gauge wires are occasionally used. Wire length must also be considered when making repairs to a circuit. As conductor length increases, so does resistance. An 18 gauge wire, for example, can carry a 10 amp load for 10 feet without excessive voltage drop; however if a 15 foot wire is required for the same 10 amp load, it must be a 16 gauge wire.

An electrical schematic shows the electrical current paths when a circuit is operating properly. It is essential to understand how a circuit works before trying to figure out why it does not. Schematics break the entire electrical system down into individual circuits and show only one particular circuit. In a schematic, no attempt is made to represent wiring and components as they physically appear on the vehicle; switches and other components are shown as simply as possible. Face views of harness connectors show the cavity or terminal locations in all multi-pin connectors to help locate test points.

If you need to backprobe a connector while it is on the component, the order of the terminals must be mentally reversed. The wire color code can help in this situation, as well as a keyway, lock tab or other reference mark.

NOTE: *Wiring diagrams are not included in this book. As trucks have become more complex and available with longer option lists, wiring diagrams have grown in size and complexity. It has become almost impossible to provide a readable reproduction of a wiring diagram in a book this size. Information on ordering wiring diagrams from the vehicle manufacturer can be found in the owner's manual.*

WIRING REPAIR

Soldering is a quick, efficient method of joining metals permanently. Everyone who has the occasion to make wiring repairs should know how to solder. Electrical connections that are soldered are far less likely to come apart and will conduct electricity much better than connections that are only "pig-tailed" together. The most popular (and preferred) method of soldering is with an electrical soldering gun. Soldering irons are available in many sizes and wattage ratings. Irons with higher wattage ratings deliver higher temperatures and recover lost heat faster. A small soldering iron rated for no more than 50 watts is recommended, especially on electrical systems where excess heat can damage the components being soldered.

There are three ingredients necessary for successful soldering; proper flux, good solder and sufficient heat. A soldering flux is necessary to clean the metal of tarnish, prepare it for soldering and to enable the solder to spread into tiny crevices. When soldering, always use a resin flux or resin core solder which is non-corrosive and will not attract moisture once the job is finished. Other types of flux (acid core) will leave a residue that will attract moisture and cause the wires to corrode. Tin is a unique metal with a low melting point. In a molten state, it dissolves and alloys easily with many metals. Solder is made by mixing tin with lead. The most common proportions are 40/60, 50/50 and 60/40, with the percentage of tin listed first. Low priced solders usually contain less tin, making them very difficult for a beginner to use because more heat is required to melt the solder. A common solder is 40/60 which is well suited for all-around general use, but 60/40 melts easier, has more tin for a better joint and is preferred for electrical work.

CHASSIS ELECTRICAL

Soldering Techniques

Successful soldering requires that the metals to be joined be heated to a temperature that will melt the solder, usually 360–460°F (182–238°C). Contrary to popular belief, the purpose of the soldering iron is not to melt the solder itself, but to heat the parts being soldered to a temperature high enough to melt the solder when it is touched to the work. Melting flux-cored solder on the soldering iron will usually destroy the effectiveness of the flux.

> NOTE: *Soldering tips are made of copper for good heat conductivity, but must be "tinned" regularly for quick transference of heat to the project and to prevent the solder from sticking to the iron. To "tin" the iron, simply heat it and touch the flux-cored solder to the tip; the solder will flow over the hot tip. Wipe the excess off with a clean rag, but be careful as the iron will be hot.*

After some use, the tip may become pitted. If so, simply dress the tip smooth with a smooth file and "tin" the tip again. An old saying holds that "metals well cleaned are half soldered." Flux-cored solder will remove oxides but rust, bits of insulation and oil or grease must be removed with a wire brush or emery cloth. For maximum strength in soldered parts, the joint must start off clean and tight. Weak joints will result in gaps too wide for the solder to bridge.

If a separate soldering flux is used, it should be brushed or swabbed on only those areas that are to be soldered. Most solders contain a core of flux and separate fluxing is unnecessary. Hold the work to be soldered firmly. It is best to solder on a wooden board, because a metal vise will only rob the piece to be soldered of heat and make it difficult to melt the solder. Hold the soldering tip with the broadest face against the work to be soldered. Apply solder under the tip close to the work, using enough solder to give a heavy film between the iron and the piece being soldered, while moving slowly and making sure the solder melts properly. Keep the work level or the solder will run to the lowest part and favor the thicker parts, because these require more heat to melt the solder. If the soldering tip overheats (the solder coating on the face of the tip burns up), it should be retinned. Once the soldering is completed, let the soldered joint stand until cool. Tape and seal all soldered wire splices after the repair has cooled.

Wire Harness and Connectors

The on-board computer (ECM) wire harness electrically connects the control unit to the various solenoids, switches and sensors used by the control system. Most connectors in the engine compartment or otherwise exposed to the elements are protected against moisture and dirt which could create oxidation and deposits on the terminals. This protection is important because of the very low voltage and current levels used by the computer and sensors. All connectors have a lock which secures the male and female terminals together, with a secondary lock holding the seal and terminal into the connector. Both terminal locks must be released when disconnecting ECM connectors.

These special connectors are weather-proof and all repairs require the use of a special terminal and the tool required to service it. This tool is used to remove the pin and sleeve terminals. If removal is attempted with an ordinary pick, there is a good chance that the terminal will be bent or deformed. Unlike standard blade type terminals, these terminals cannot be straightened once they are bent. Make certain that the connectors are properly seated and all of the sealing rings in place when connecting leads. On some models, a hinge-type flap provides a backup or secondary locking feature for the terminals. Most secondary locks are used to improve the connector reliability by retaining the terminals if the small terminal lock tangs are not positioned properly.

Molded-on connectors require complete replacement of the connection. This means splicing a new connector assembly into the harness. All splices in on-board computer systems should be soldered to insure proper contact. Use care when probing the connections or replacing terminals in them as it is possible to short between opposite terminals. If this happens to the wrong terminal pair, it is possible to damage certain components. Always use jumper wires between connectors for circuit checking and never probe through weather-proof seals.

Open circuits are often difficult to locate by sight because corrosion or terminal misalignment are hidden by the connectors. Merely wiggling a connector on a sensor or in the wiring harness may correct the open circuit condition. This should always be considered when an open circuit or a failed sensor is indicated. Intermittent problems may also be caused by oxidized or loose connections. When using a circuit tester for diagnosis, always probe connections from the wire side. Be careful not to damage sealed connectors with test probes.

All wiring harnesses should be replaced with identical parts, using the same gauge wire and connectors. When signal wires are spliced into a harness, use wire with high temperature insulation only. With the low voltage and current levels found in the system, it is important that the best possible connection at all wire splices be made by soldering the splices together. It is seldom necessary to replace a complete harness. If replacement is necessary, pay close attention to insure proper harness routing. Secure the harness with suitable plastic wire clamps to prevent vibrations from causing the harness to wear in spots or contact any hot components.

NOTE: *Weatherproof connectors cannot be replaced with standard connectors. Instructions are provided with replacement connector and terminal packages. Some wire harnesses have mounting indicators (usually pieces of colored tape) to mark where the harness is to be secured.*

In making wiring repairs, it's important that you always replace damaged wires with wires that are the same gauge as the wire being replaced. The heavier the wire, the smaller the gauge number. Wires are color-coded to aid in identification and whenever possible the same color coded wire should be used for replacement. A wire stripping and crimping tool is necessary to install solderless terminal connectors. Test all crimps by pulling on the wires; it should not be possible to pull the wires out of a good crimp.

Wires which are open, exposed or otherwise damaged are repaired by simple splicing. Where possible, if the wiring harness is accessible and the damaged place in the wire can be located, it is best to open the harness and check for all possible damage. In an inaccessible harness, the wire must be bypassed with a new insert, usually taped to the outside of the old harness.

When replacing fusible links, be sure to use fusible link wire, NOT ordinary automotive wire. Make sure the fusible segment is of the same gauge and construction as the one being replaced and double the stripped end when crimping the terminal connector for a good contact. The melted (open) fusible link segment of the wiring harness should be cut off as close to the harness as possible, then a new segment spliced in as described. In the case of a damaged fusible link that feeds two harness wires, the harness connections should be replaced with two fusible link wires so that each circuit will have its own separate protection.

NOTE: *Most of the problems caused in the wiring harness are due to bad ground connections. Always check all vehicle ground connections for corrosion or looseness before performing any power feed checks to eliminate the chance of a bad ground affecting the circuit.*

Repairing Hard Shell Connectors

Unlike molded connectors, the terminal contacts in hard shell connectors can be replaced. Weatherproof hard-shell connectors with the leads molded into the shell have non-replaceable terminal ends. Replacement usually involves the use of a special terminal removal tool that depress the locking tangs (barbs) on the connector terminal and allow the connector to be removed from the rear of the shell. The connector shell should be replaced if it shows any evidence of burning, melting, cracks, or breaks. Replace individual terminals that are burnt, corroded, distorted or loose.

NOTE: *The insulation crimp must be tight to prevent the insulation from sliding back on the wire when the wire is pulled. The insulation must be visibly compressed under the crimp tabs, and the ends of the crimp should be turned in for a firm grip on the insulation.*

The wire crimp must be made with all wire strands inside the crimp. The terminal must be fully compressed on the wire strands with the ends of the crimp tabs turned in to make a firm grip on the wire. Check all connections with an ohmmeter to insure a good contact. There should be no measurable resistance between the wire and the terminal when connected.

Mechanical Test Equipment

Vacuum Gauge

Most gauges are graduated in inches of mercury (in.Hg), although a device called a manometer reads vacuum in inches of water (in. H_2O). The normal vacuum reading usually varies between 18 and 22 in.Hg at sea level. To test engine vacuum, the vacuum gauge must be connected to a source of manifold vacuum. Many engines have a plug in the intake manifold which can be removed and replaced with an adapter fitting. Connect the vacuum gauge to the fitting with a suitable rubber hose or, if no manifold plug is available, connect the vacuum gauge to any device using manifold vacuum, such as EGR valves, etc. The vacuum gauge can be used to determine if enough vacuum is reaching a component to allow its actuation.

Hand Vacuum Pump

Small, hand-held vacuum pumps come in a variety of designs. Most have a built-in vacuum gauge and allow the component to be tested without removing it from the vehicle. Operate the pump lever or plunger to apply the correct amount of vacuum required for the test specified in the diagnosis routines. The level of vacuum in inches of Mercury (in.Hg) is indicated on the pump gauge. For some testing, an additional vacuum gauge may be necessary.

Intake manifold vacuum is used to operate various systems and devices on late model vehi-

CHASSIS ELECTRICAL

cles. To correctly diagnose and solve problems in vacuum control systems, a vacuum source is necessary for testing. In some cases, vacuum can be taken from the intake manifold when the engine is running, but vacuum is normally provided by a hand vacuum pump. These hand vacuum pumps have a built-in vacuum gauge that allow testing while the device is still attached to the component. For some tests, an additional vacuum gauge may be necessary.

HEATER AND AIR CONDITIONER

Refer to Chapter 1 for discharging, recharging and Freon handling of the air conditioning system.

Heater Blower Motor

REMOVAL AND INSTALLATION

Without Air Conditioning

1. Disconnect the negative battery cable.
2. On Escort and Lynx, remove the air inlet duct assembly. On Tempo and Topaz, remove the right ventilator assembly.
3. Remove the hub clamp spring from the blower wheel hub. Pull the blower wheel from the blower motor shaft.
4. Remove the blower motor flange attaching screws located inside the blower housing.
5. Pull the blower motor out from the blower housing (heater case) and disconnect the blower motor wires from the motor.

To install:

6. Connect the wires to the blower motor and position the motor in the blower housing.
7. Install the blower motor attaching screws.
8. Position the blower wheel on the motor shaft and install the hub clamp spring.
9. Install the air inlet duct assembly and the right ventilator assembly.
10. Connect negative battery cable.
11. Check the system for proper operation.

With Air Conditioning

1. Disconnect the negative battery cable.
2. Remove the glove compartment door and glove compartment.
3. Disconnect the blower motor wires from the blower motor resistor.
4. Loosen the instrument panel at the lower right hand side prior to removing the motor through the glove compartment opening.
5. Remove the blower motor and mounting plate from the evaporator case.

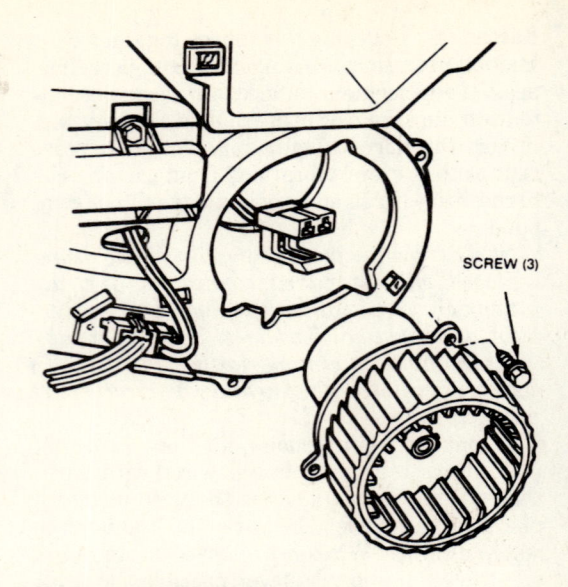

Blower motor and wheel removal

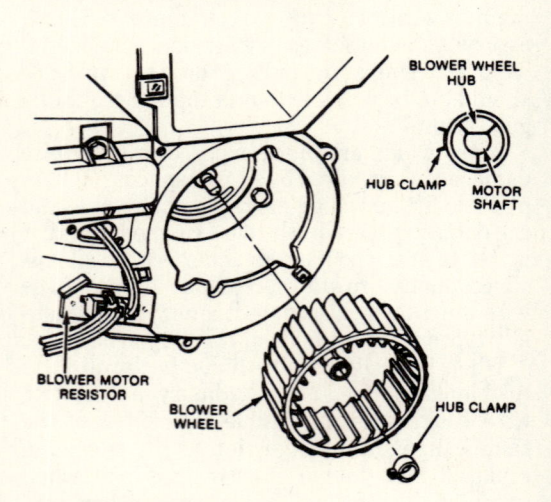

Blower wheel removal

6. Rotate the motor until the mounting plate flat clears the edge of the glove compartment opening and remove the motor.
7. Remove the hub clamp spring from the blower wheel hub. Then, remove the blower wheel from the motor shaft.
8. Complete the installation of the blower motor by reversing the removal procedure.

Heater Core

REMOVAL AND INSTALLATION

Vehicles may be equipped with either a brass or aluminum heater core. All replacement cores are copper/brass. It is important to positively identify the type of core being used because aluminum cores use different heater core-to-heater case seals than the copper/brass cores. Having the proper seal is necessary for proper sealing and heating system performance.

Identification can be made by looking at one of the core tubes after one of the hoses is disconnected. An aluminum core will have a colored tube. A brass core will have a brass colored tube.

If the vehicle is equipped with a copper/brass core, the old core seal may be used for the replacement core, providing that it is not damaged.

If the vehicle is equipped with an aluminum core, a new seal will be required for the replacement core.

1981–85 Models

NOTE: *In some cases removal of the instrument panel may be necessary.*

WITHOUT AIR CONDITIONING

1. Disconnect the negative battery cable.
2. Drain the coolant.

CAUTION: *When draining the coolant, keep in mind that cats and dogs are attracted by the ethylene glycol antifreeze, and are quite likely to drink any that is left in an uncovered container or in puddles on the ground. This will prove fatal in sufficient quantity. Always drain the coolant into a sealable container. Coolant should be reused unless it is contaminated or several years old.*

3. Disconnect the heater hoses from the core tubes at the firewall, inside the engine compartment. Plug the core tubes to prevent coolant spillage when the core is removed.
4. Open the glove compartment. Remove the glove compartment. Remove the glove compartment liner.
5. Remove the core access plate screws and remove the access plate.
6. Working under the hood, remove the two nuts attaching the heater assembly case to the dash panel.
7. Remove the core through the glove compartment opening.
8. Install the core through the glove compartment opening.
9. Working under the hood, install the two nuts attaching the heater assembly case to the dash panel.
10. Install the core access plate screws and install the access plate.
11. Install the glove compartment. Install the glove compartment liner.
12. Reconnect the heater hoses to the core tubes at the firewall, inside the engine compartment.
13. Refill the cooling system with coolant.
14. Reconnect the negative battery cable.

WITH AIR CONDITIONING

1. Disconnect the negative battery cable and drain the cooling system.

CAUTION: *When draining the coolant, keep in mind that cats and dogs are attracted by the ethylene glycol antifreeze, and are quite likely to drink any that is left in an uncovered container or in puddles on the ground. This will prove fatal in sufficient quantity. Always drain the coolant into a sealable container. Coolant should be reused unless it is contaminated or several years old.*

2. Disconnect the heater hoses from the heater core.
3. Working inside the vehicle, remove the floor duct from the plenum (2 screws).
4. Remove the four screws attaching the heater core cover to the plenum, remove the cover and remove the heater core.
5. To install: Install the heater core and install the cover. Install the four screws attaching the heater core cover to the plenum.
6. Working inside the vehicle, Install the floor duct to the plenum (2 screws).
7. Reconnect the heater hoses to the heater core.
8. Reconnect the negative battery cable and refill the cooling system.

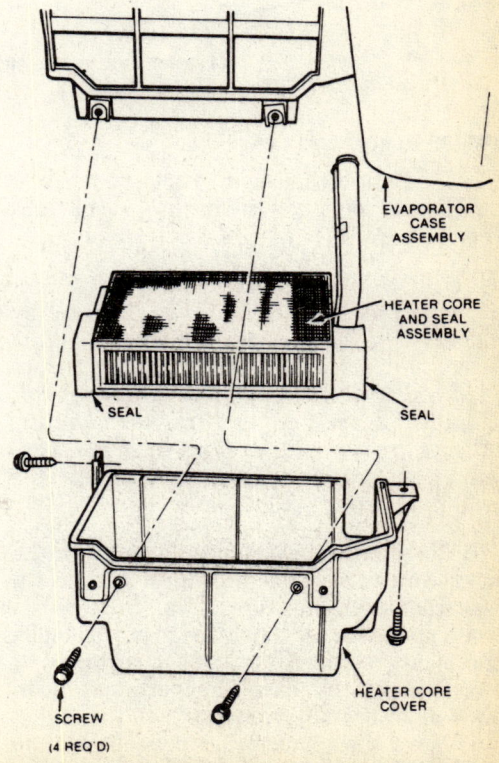

Heater core removal; with air conditioning

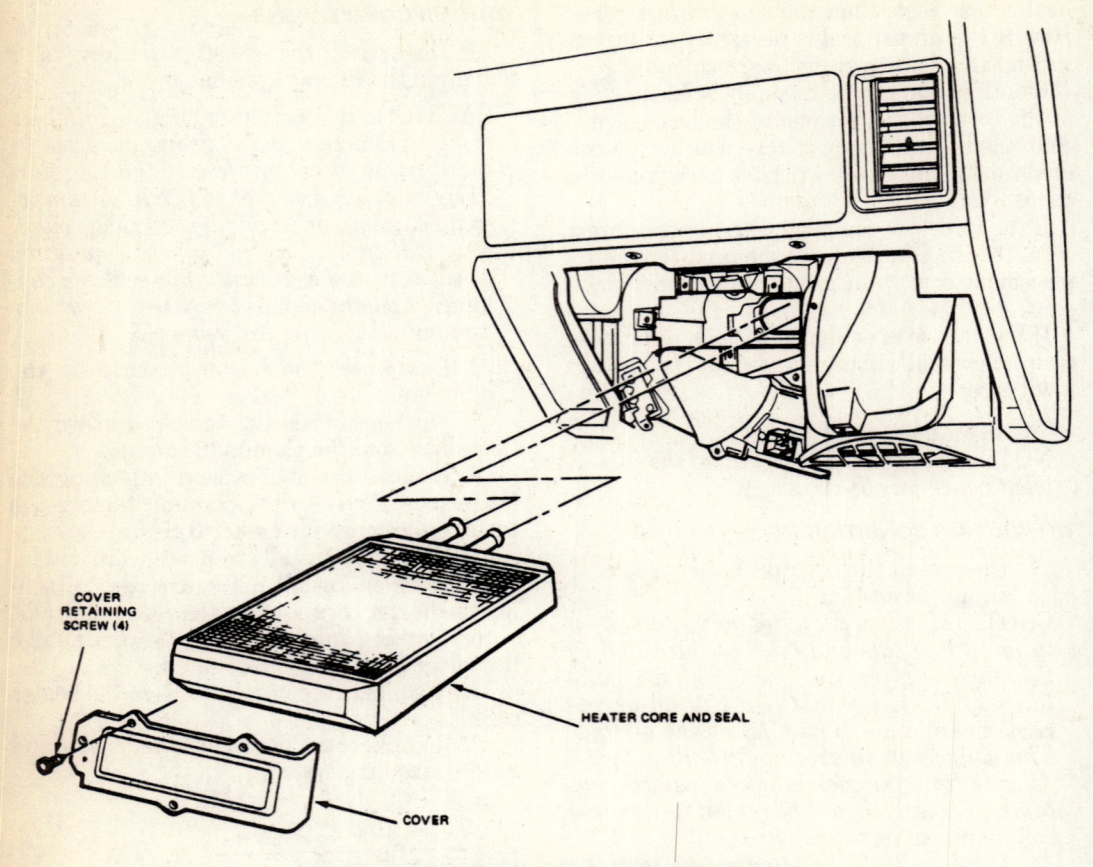

372 CHASSIS ELECTRICAL

Heater core removal; without air conditioning

1986–90 Escort and Lynx

1. Disconnect the negative battery cable.
2. Drain cooling system into clean container.

CAUTION: *When draining the coolant, keep in mind that cats and dogs are attracted by the ethylene glycol antifreeze, and are quite likely to drink any that is left in an uncovered container or in puddles on the ground. This will prove fatal in sufficient quantity. Always drain the coolant into a sealable container. Coolant should be reused unless it is contaminated or several years old.*

3. Loosen the heater hose clamps at the heater core tubes and disconnect the heater hoses from the heater core tubes.
4. Cap the heater core tubes to prevent spilling coolant into the passenger compartment.
5. Remove the glove compartment door, liner and lower reinforcement.
6. Move the temperature control lever to the **WARM** position.
7. Remove 4 screws attaching the heater core cover to the heater assembly and remove the cover.
8. Working in the engine compartment, loosen the 2 nuts attaching the heater case assembly to the dash panel.
9. Push the heater core tubes toward the passenger compartment to loosen the heater core from the heater case assembly.
10. Pull the heater core from the heater case assembly and remove the heater core through the glove compartment opening.

To install:

11. Position the heater core in the core opening in the case assembly with the heater core tubes on the top side of the end tank.
12. Slide the heater core into the opening of the heater case assembly.
13. Position the heater core a cover to the heater case assembly. Install the 4 attaching screws. Tighten the cover attaching screws securely.
14. Tighten the 2 nuts attaching the heater case assembly to the dash panel.
15. Connect the heater hoses to the heater core tubes. Tighten the hose clamps.

16. Fill the cooling system to the proper level with the correct mixture of coolant and water.

17. Install the glove compartment door, liner and hinge bar.

18. Connect negative battery cable.

19. Start engine and check for coolant leaks. Allow engine to come to normal operating temperature. Recheck for coolant leaks.

1986–90 Tempo and Topaz

1. Disconnect the negative battery cable.
2. Drain the cooling system.

CAUTION: *When draining the coolant, keep in mind that cats and dogs are attracted by the ethylene glycol antifreeze, and are quite likely to drink any that is left in an uncovered container or in puddles on the ground. This will prove fatal in sufficient quantity. Always drain the coolant into a sealable container. Coolant should be reused unless it is contaminated or several years old.*

3. Disconnect the heater hoses from the heater core.
4. From inside the vehicle, remove the 2 screws retaining floor duct to the plenum. Remove one screw retaining floor duct to instrument panel. Remove floor duct.

NOTE: *Most vehicles are equipped with a removable heater core cover to provide access for servicing.*

5. Remove the 4 screws attaching the heater core cover to the heater case assembly.
6. Remove the heater core and cover from the plenum.
7. Complete the installation of the heater core by reversing the removal procedure. Check the system for proper operation.

Control Assembly

REMOVAL AND INSTALLATION

Escort/EXP and Lynx

1. Move the Max A/C-Norm selector lever to the **MAX A/C** position.
2. Disconnect the air inlet cable housing and retainer from the air conditioning case bracket using the proper tool. Disconnect the cable from the inlet door cam.
3. Move the temperature control lever to the **COOL** position and disconnect the temperature control cable housing and retainer from the air conditioning case bracket using the proper tool. Disconnect the cable self-adjusting clip from the crank arm.

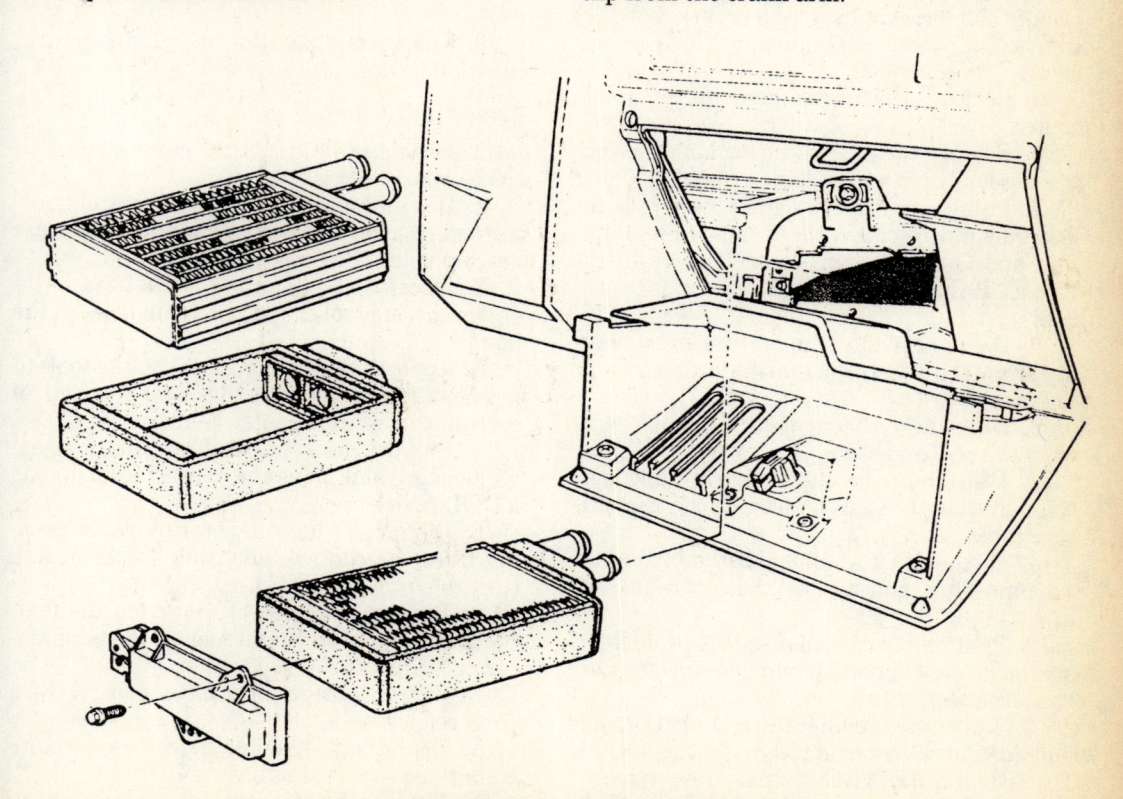

Heater core removal — 1986–90 Escort/Lynx

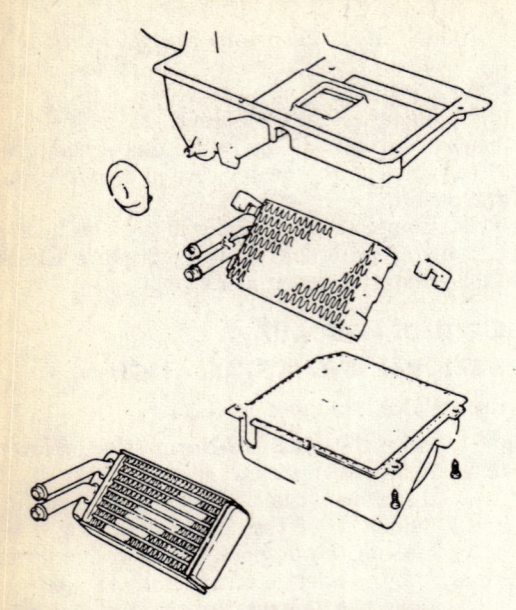

CHASSIS ELECTRICAL

Heater core removal — 1986–90 Tempo/Topaz

4. Move the function selector lever to the **PANEL** position and disconnect the function cable housing and retainer from the air conditioning case bracket using the proper tool. Disconnect the cable self-adjusting clip from the cam pin.
5. Remove the instrument panel finish center.
6. Remove the 4 screws attaching the control assembly to the instrument panel.
7. Pull the control assembly out from the instrument panel. Move the Temperature, Function and Outside/Recirc control levers to **COOL**, **PANEL** and **RECIRC** positions respectively.
8. Disconnect the temperature cable housing from the control mounting bracket using the proper tool.
9. Disconnect the temperature cable wire from the control lever.
10. Disconnect the outside/recirc cable from the control in the same manner as the temperature cable.
11. Disconnect the control assembly electrical connectors and remove the control assembly.
12. Position the control assembly near the instrument panel opening and connect the electrical connectors.
13. Move the Temperature, Function and Outside/Recirc control levers to the **COOL**, **PANEL** and **RECIRC** positions respectively.
14. Connect the function cable wire and then the cable housing to the control assembly.
15. Connect the outside recirc and then the temperature cable to the control assembly.
16. Position the control assembly onto the instrument panel and install the attaching screws.
17. Install the instrument panel finish center.
18. Move the Max A/C-Norm selector lever to the **MAX A/C** position.
19. Place the cable end loop over the pin on the air door cam and position the wire under the tab on the cam. Slide the cable housing end retainer into the plenum cable bracket to secure the cable to the evaporator.
20. Move the temperature selector lever to the **COOL** position.
21. Connect the temperature control cable self-adjusting clip to the temperature door crank arm. Slide the cable housing end retainer into the evaporator end case bracket and engage the tabs.
22. Move the function selector lever to the **PANEL** position.
23. Connect the function cable self-adjusting clip to the cam pin on the side of the plenum.
24. Slide the cable housing end retainer into the plenum cable bracket and engage the tabs.
25. Move the function selector lever to the **DEFROST** (full right) position to adjust the cable.
26. Check the operation of all the control function levers.

Tempo and Topaz

1. Move the temperature control lever to the **COOL** position.
2. Disconnect the temperature control housing end retainer from the air conditioning case bracket using the proper tool.
3. Insert the ends of two $1/8$ in. (3mm) diameter prying tools into the 3.5mm holes in the bezel.
4. Apply a light inboard force on the tools to depress the spring clips and release the control assembly from the register housing.
5. Pull the control assembly from the register housing and move the control lever to the **COOL** position.
6. Disconnect the temperature cable housing from the control mounting bracket using the proper tool.
7. Remove the twist off cap from the temperature control lever and remove the temperature control cable.
8. Remove the temperature control wire from the lever.
9. Disconnect the electrical connectors from the control assembly.
10. Detach the vacuum harness (2 spring nuts) and remove the control assembly from the instrument panel.
11. Position the control assembly near the in-

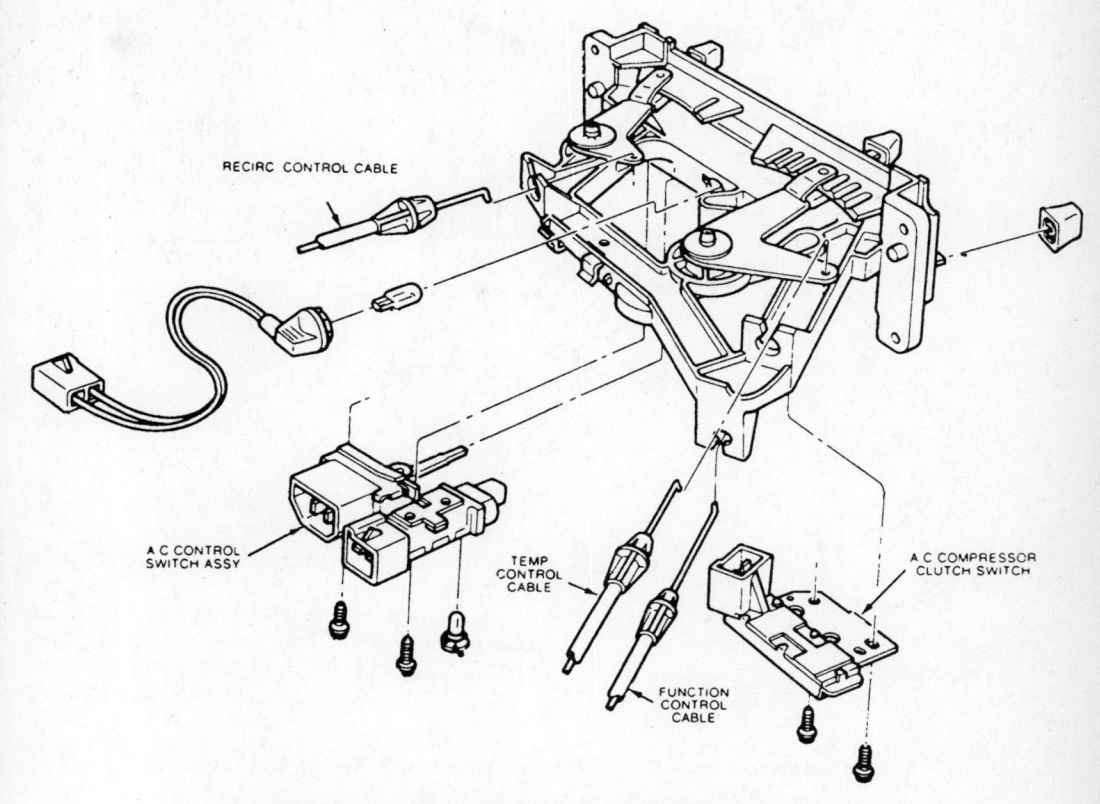

Exploded view of the A/C heater control assembly — Escort

strument panel opening and connect the vacuum harness with the spring nuts and connect the electrical connectors.

12. Move the temperature control lever to the **COOL** position.
13. Connect the temperature control cable to the control assembly.
14. Position the control assembly onto the register housing.
15. Align the control bracket metal locking tabs with the metal slide track in the instrument panel.
16. Slide the control assembly down the metal track until the spring clips snap and lock the control assembly into the register housing.
17. Move the temperature control lever to the **COOL** position.
18. Connect the temperature control cable self-adjusting clip to the temperature door crank arm.
19. Slide the cable housing end retainer into the plenum cable bracket and engage the tabs.
20. Move the function selector lever to the **WARM** position and adjust the cable.
21. Check the operation of all the control function levers.

TEMPERATURE CONTROL CABLE

Cable Preset and Self-Adjustment

BEFORE INSTALLATION

1. Insert the blade of a small pocket knife of equivalent into the wire and loop (crank arm end) of the function or temperature control cable.
2. Hold the self-adjusting cable attaching clip with a suitable tool and slide it down the shaft (away from the end loop) approximately 1 in. (25mm).
3. Install the cable assembly and move the temperature control lever to the top of the slot (temperature cable to warm and function to defrost) to position the self adjusting clip. Check for proper control operation.

AFTER INSTALLATION

1. Move the control lever(s) temperature to the **COOL** position and function to the **OFF** position.
2. Hold the crank arm firmly in position, insert the blade of a small pocket knife or equivalent into the wire loop and pull the cable wire end through the self-adjusting clip until there

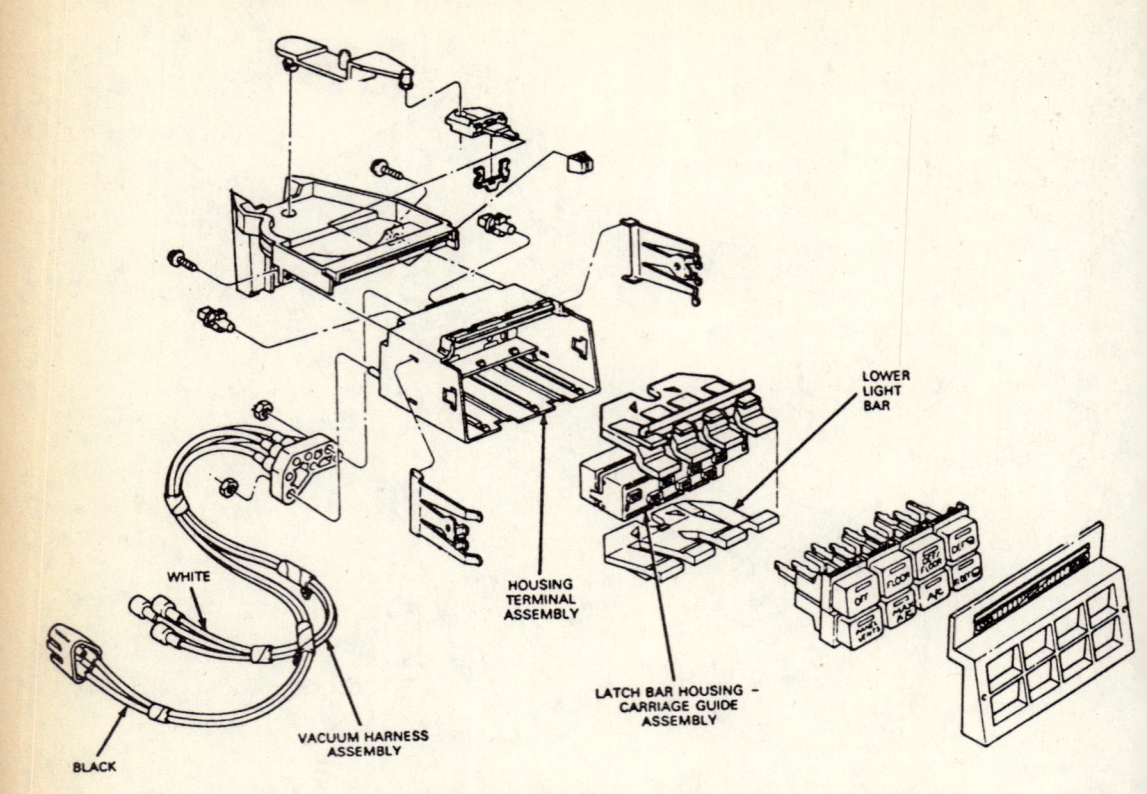

Exploded view of the A/C heater control assembly — Tempo and Topaz

is a space about 1 in. (50mm) between the clip and the wire end loop.

3. Force the control lever(s) to the top of the slot (temperature cable to the warm position and function to the defrost) to position the self-adjusting clip and check for proper control operation.

CHILTON TIPS

1989-90 Tempo and Topaz

The temperature control lever may not hold its set position and may require excessive effort to move when the blower motor fan control switch is set for high speed operation. This occurs because the temperature door does not have an assist spring. To install a temperature door assist spring, use the following procedure.

1. Reach up behind the instrument panel. Locate the temperature control cable where it attaches to the temperature blend door control arm.
2. Slide the cable spring clip and cable as an assembly off the end of the door control arm.
3. Install the temperature door assist spring (part #F03Z-19760-A).
4. After the assist spring is properly seated slide the spring clip - with the cable attached, onto the door control arm.

5. Adjust the cable as required. Make sure that the door travels the full distance between the maximum heat and maximum cool.

Evaporator Case

REMOVAL AND INSTALLATION

Escort/EXP, Lynx and Tempo/Topaz

1. Disconnect the negative battery cable.
2. Drain the radiator.

CAUTION: *When draining the coolant, keep in mind that cats and dogs are attracted by the ethylene glycol antifreeze, and are quite likely to drink any that is left in an uncovered container or in puddles on the ground. This will prove fatal in sufficient quantity. Always drain the coolant into a sealable container. Coolant should be reused unless it is contaminated or several years old.*

3. Discharge the air conditioning system.
4. Disconnect the heater hoses from the heater core. Plug the heater core tubes or blow any coolant from the heater core with low pressure air.
5. Disconnect the liquid line and the accumulator/drier inlet tube from the evaporator core at the dash panel. Cap the refrigerant lines

CHASSIS ELECTRICAL

and evaporator core to prevent the entrance of dirt and moisture.

6. Remove the instrument panel and lay on front seat.
7. Disconnect the wire harness connector from the blower motor resistor.
8. Remove 1 screw attaching the bottom of the evaporator case to the dash panel.
9. Remove the instrument panel brace from the cowl top panel.
10. Remove 2 nuts attaching the evaporator case to the dash panel in the engine compartment.
11. Loosen the sound insulation from the cowl top panel in the area around the air inlet opening.
12. Remove the 2 screws attaching the support bracket and the brace to the cowl top panels.
13. Position the evaporator case onto the dash and cowl top panels at the air inlet opening.
14. Attach the support panel and brace to the top cowl panel.
15. In the engine compartment, attach the evaporator case to dash panel.

NOTE: *Inspect the evaporator drain tube for a good seal. Make sure the drain tube is through the opening and is not obstructed.*

16. Position the sound insulation around the air inlet duct on the cowl top panel.
17. Install the instrument panel.
18. Attach the bottom of the evaporator to the dash panel.
19. Connect the heater core hoses.

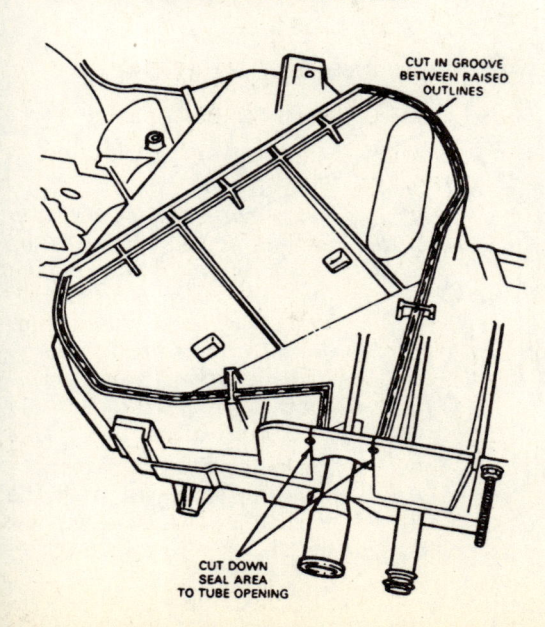

Outlines for cutting the evaporator case

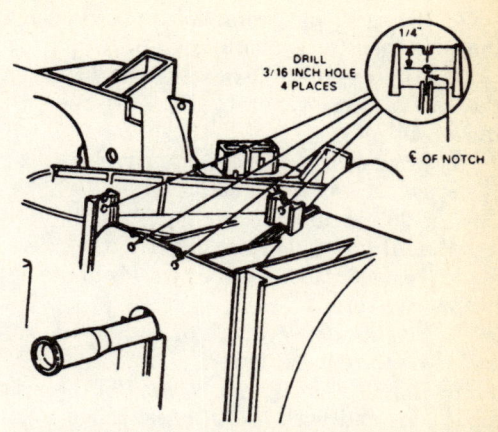

Locations for drilling holes in the evaporator case

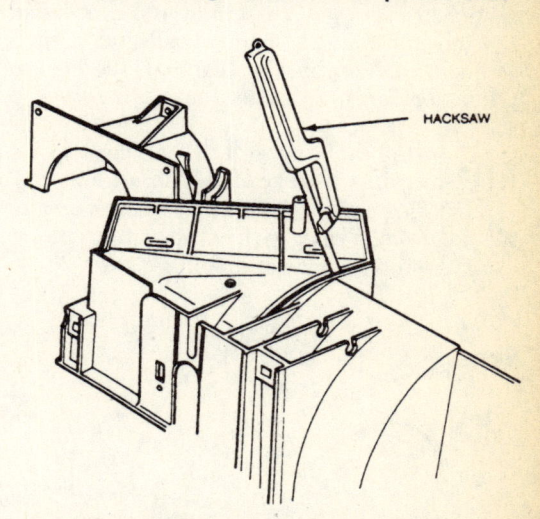

Cutting the outlines on the evaporator case with a suitable saw

20. Lubricate new liquid and suction line O-rings with clean refrigerant oil and connect lines to the evaporator core.
21. Fill the radiator.
22. Connect the battery ground cable.
23. Leak test, evacuate and charge the air conditioning system.
24. Check the system for proper operation.

Evaporator Core

NOTE: *Whenever the evaporator core is removed, the suction accumulator drier must also be replaced.*

REMOVAL AND INSTALLATION
Escort/EXP and Lynx

1. Remove the evaporator case as outlined.
2. Remove the air inlet duct from the evaporator case.
3. Remove the foam seal from the evaporator core tubes.

CHASSIS ELECTRICAL

4. Drill a 3/16 in. (5mm) hole in both upright tabs on top of the evaporator case.

5. Using a hot knife or small saw blade, cut the top of the evaporator case between the raised outlines.

6. Unscrew the blower motor resistor from the evaporator case.

7. Fold the cut out cover back from the opening and lift the evaporator core from the case.

8. Transfer the 2 foam core seals to the new evaporator core.

9. Position the evaporator core in the case and close the cut-out cover.

10. Install a spring nut on each of the 2 upright tabs and with the 2 holes drilled in the front flange. Be sure the hole in the spring nut is aligned with the 3/16 in. (5mm) holes drilled in the tab and flange. Then, install and tighten screw in each spring nut (through the hole in the tab or flange) to secure the cut-out cover in the closed position.

11. Install caulking cord to seal the evaporator case against leakage along the cut line.

12. Using new caulking (rope sealer), assemble the air inlet duct to the evaporator case.

13. Install the blower motor resistor.

14. Install the foam seal over the evaporator core and heater core tubes.

15. Install the evaporator case assembly.

Tempo and Topaz

NOTE: *Before the evaporator is replaced, it should be leak tested, to prevent the possibility of replacing a good core.*

1. Remove the evaporator case.
2. Unscrew the inlet duct from the evaporator.
3. Remove the evaporator-to-core seals from the evaporator tubes.
4. Using a small saw blade or hot knife, cut the entire top from the case using the outline.
5. Remove the cover from the base and lift the evaporator core from the case.
6. Remove any rough edges from the case that may have been caused by the sawing or cutting.
7. Install a new core into the case.
8. Install the 2 evaporator-to-cowl seals on the evaporator tubes.
9. Install the new cover following the instructions in the core kit.
10. Install the evaporator case.

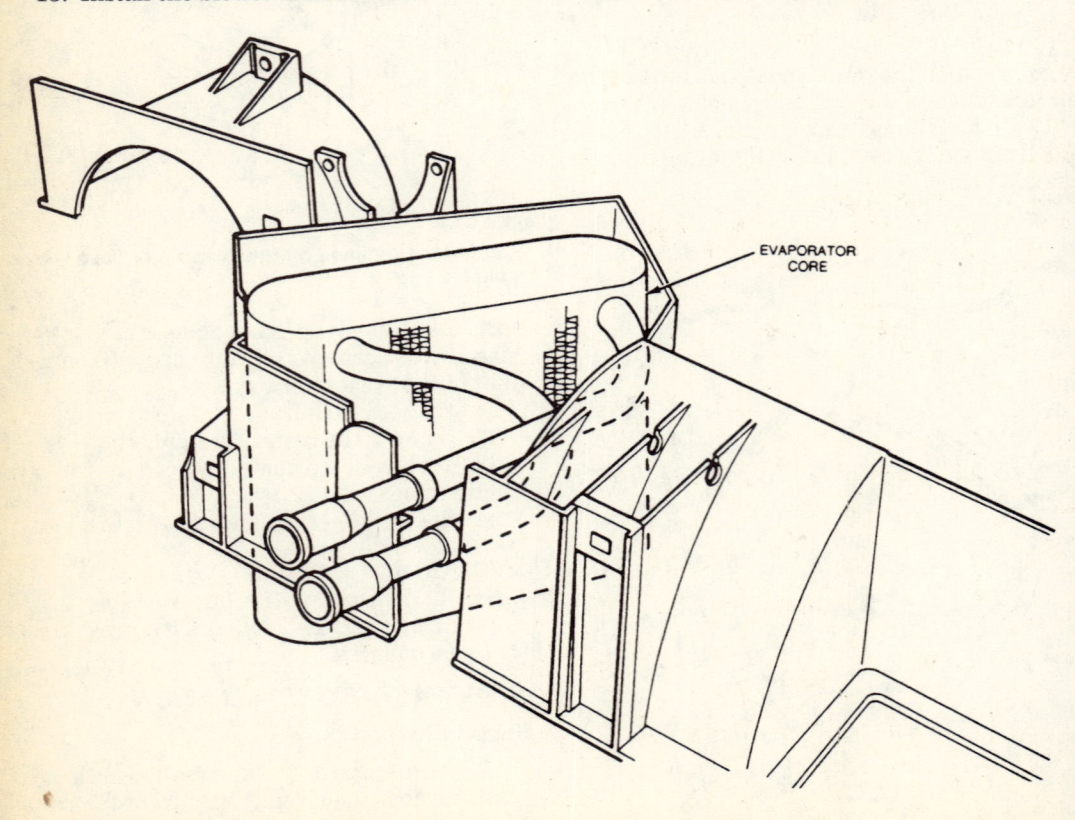

Removing the evaporator core assembly

CHASSIS ELECTRICAL

Accumulator/Drier

REMOVAL AND INSTALLATION

Escort/EXP, Lynx and Tempo/Topaz

1. Discharge the air conditioning system.
2. Remove the air pump, if equipped.
3. Disconnect the suction hose.
4. Disconnect the accumulator/drier inlet tube from the evaporator core outlet.
5. Disconnect the wiring harness connector from the pressure switch on top of the accumulator/drier.
6. Unscrew and remove the 2 strap clamps and remove the accumulator drier.
7. Position the mounting straps onto the accumulator/drier and temporarily hold them in place with tape or caulk.
8. Connect the drier inlet tube to the evaporator core outlet using a new O-ring lubricated with refrigerant oil.
9. Position the 2 mounting straps onto the mounting bracket and install the 2 screws.
10. Use a new special O-ring (part of Kit E35Y-19D690-A or equivalent) coated with refrigerant oil and connect the suction hose to the accumulator/drier at the spring lock coupling (2.3L engine).
11. Install the air pump, if equipped.
12. Leak test, evacuate and charge the system.
13. Check the system for proper operation.

Switch and Sensor Replacement

BLOWER SWITCH REMOVAL AND INSTALLATION

Escort/EXP and Lynx

1. Pull the blower switch knob from the blower switch shaft.
2. Remove the instrument cluster opening finish panel.
3. Unscrew the control assembly from the instrument panel.
4. Pull the control assembly from the instrument panel.
5. Disconnect the connectors from the blower switch and air conditioning push button switch.
6. Remove the attaching screw and remove the blower switch from the air conditioning pushbutton switch.
7. Position the blower and air conditioning push button switches and install the attaching screw.
8. Connect the switch connectors.
9. Install the control assembly onto the instrument panel.
10. Push the knob onto the switch and check for proper operation.

Tempo/Topaz

1. Insert the end of a small tool into the service slot in the blower switch bezel.
2. Apply slight upward pressure to the tool. This will depress the spring clips and release the blower switch from the instrument panel.
3. Pull the control assembly from the instrument panel.
4. Disconnect the harness connectors and remove the blower switch.
5. Connect the switch harness connectors.
6. Position the blower switch onto the instrument panel.
7. Push the blower switch into the instrument panel until the spring snaps in.
8. Check the blower for proper operation.

Clutch Cycling Pressure Switch

REMOVAL AND INSTALLATION

NOTE: *Discharge of the air conditioning system is not required to replace the switch.*

1. Disconnect the wire harness connector from the pressure switch.
2. Unscrew the pressure switch from the suction accumulator/drier.
3. Lubricate the accumulator nipple O-ring with clean refrigerant oil.
4. Screw the pressure switch onto the accumulator nipple.

NOTE: *If the pressure threaded fitting is plastic, tighten the switch finger tight only.*

5. Connect the switch wire connector.
6. Operate the system and check for leaks and proper operation.

Cooling Fan Controller

REMOVAL AND INSTALLATION

The cooling fan controller on all vehicles is attached to the top cowl panel behind the glove box opening with a screw. The con troller can be serviced through the glove box opening.

1. Empty the contents from the glove compartment.
2. Push the side of the glove box liner inward and pull the liner from the opening. Allow the glove compartment and door to hang on its hinges.
3. Through the glove compartment opening, remove the controller attaching screw located on the cowl top panel and remove the controller.
4. Disconnect the electrical connector from the controller.
5. Connect the electrical connector to the controller.
6. Position the controller to the top cowl panel and engage the mounting tab in the hole and install the attaching screw.

CHASSIS ELECTRICAL

7. Install the glove box liner.

Blower Resistor

REMOVAL AND INSTALLATION

1. Empty the contents from the glove compartment.
2. Push the side of the glove box liner inward and pull the liner from the opening.
3. Disconnect the wire connector from the resistor assembly.
4. Remove the attaching screws and remove the resistor through the glove box opening.
5. Install the resistor with the 2 attaching screws.
6. Connect the wire harness connectors.
7. Check the operation of the blower at all speeds.

RADIO

ADJUSTMENTS

For best FM reception, adjust the antenna to 31 in. (787mm) in height. Fading or weak AM reception may be adjusted by means of the antenna trimmer control, located either on the right rear of front side of the radio chassis. See the owner's manual for position. To adjust the trimmer:

1. Extend the antenna to maximum height.
2. Tune the radio to a weak station around 1600 KC. Adjust the volume so that the sound is barely audible.
3. Adjust the trimmer to obtain maximum volume.

REMOVAL AND INSTALLATION

Escort/Lynx

1. Disconnect the negative battery cable.
NOTE: *Remove the air conditioning floor duct if so equipped.*
2. Remove the ash tray and bracket.
3. Pull the knobs from the shafts.
4. Working under the instrument panel, remove the support bracket nut from the radio chassis.
5. Remove the shaft nuts and washers.
6. Drop the radio down from behind the instrument panel. Disconnect the power lead, antenna, and speaker wires. Remove the radio.
7. Installation is the reverse.

Tempo and Topaz

THROUGH 1987

1. Disconnect the negative battery cable.
2. Remove center instrument trim panel.
3. Remove 4 screws retaining radio and mounting bracket to instrument panel.
4. Pull radio to front and raise back end of radio slightly so rear support bracket clears clip in instrument panel.
5. Disconnect wiring connectors and antenna cable.
6. Transfer mounting brackets to new radio, if necessary.
7. Complete installation of radio by reversing the removal procedure.

NOTE: *Amplifier for Premium Sound System, available on Tempo/Topaz (1987), is located on bottom of package shelf, accessible from luggage compartment.*

1988–91

1. Disconnect the negative battery cable.
2. Insert radio removal tool T87P-19061-A or equivalent, into radio face plate. Press in 1 in. (25mm) to release radio retaining clips. Pull radio from instrument panel using tool as handles.

NOTE: *Do not use excessive force when installing radio removal tools, as this will damage retaining clips, making radio removal difficult.*

3. Disconnect wiring connectors and antenna cable.
4. Transfer rear mounting bracket to new radio, if necessary.
5. Complete installation of radio by reversing the removal procedure.

WINDSHIELD WIPERS

Wiper Blade (Tridon® Type)

REPLACEMENT

1. Pull up on the spring lock and pull the blade assembly from the pin.
2. To install, push the blade assembly onto the pin, so that the spring lock engages the pin.

Wiper Element (Tridon®)

REPLACEMENT

1. Locate a $7/16$ in. (11mm) long notch approximately 1 in. (25mm) from the end of the plastic backing strip, which is part of the rubber blade element assembly.
2. With the wiper blade removed from the arm place the blade assembly on a firm surface with the notched end of the backing strip visible.
3. Push down on one end of the wiper assembly until the blade is tightly bowed than grasp the tip of the backing strip firmly, pulling and twisting at the same time. The backing

CHASSIS ELECTRICAL 381

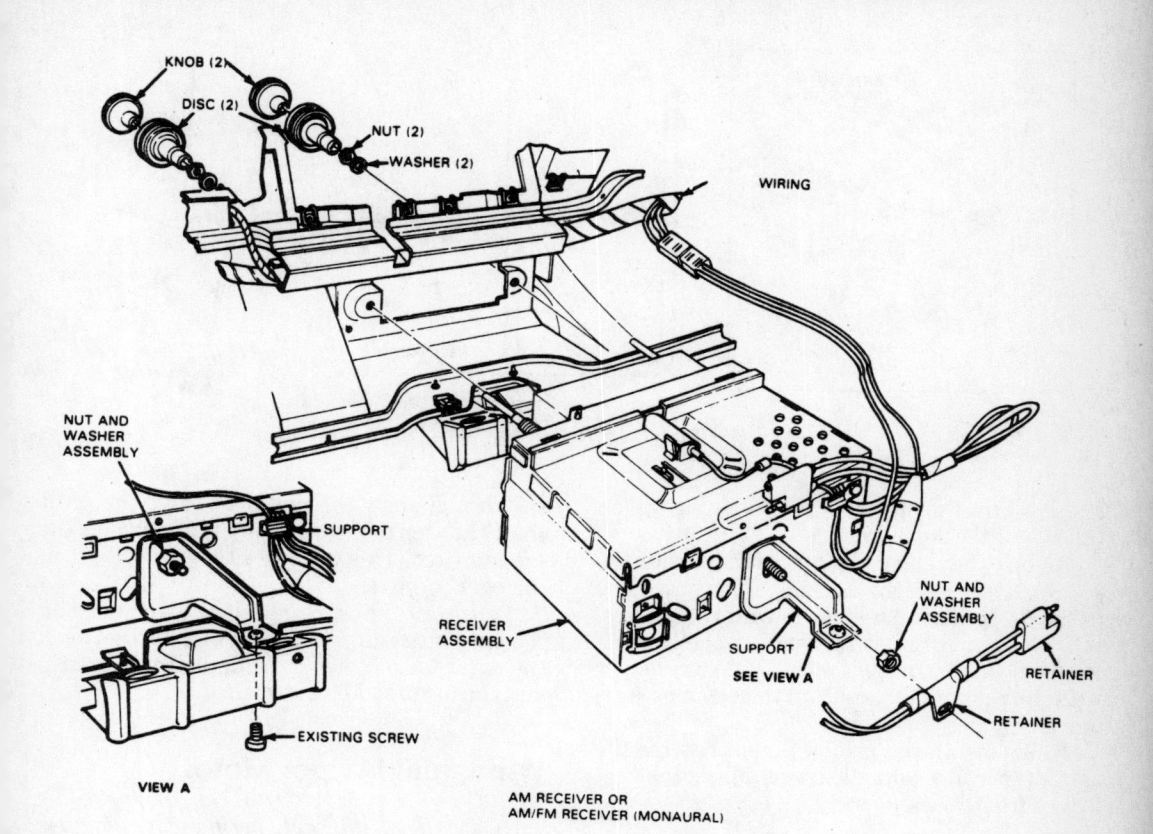

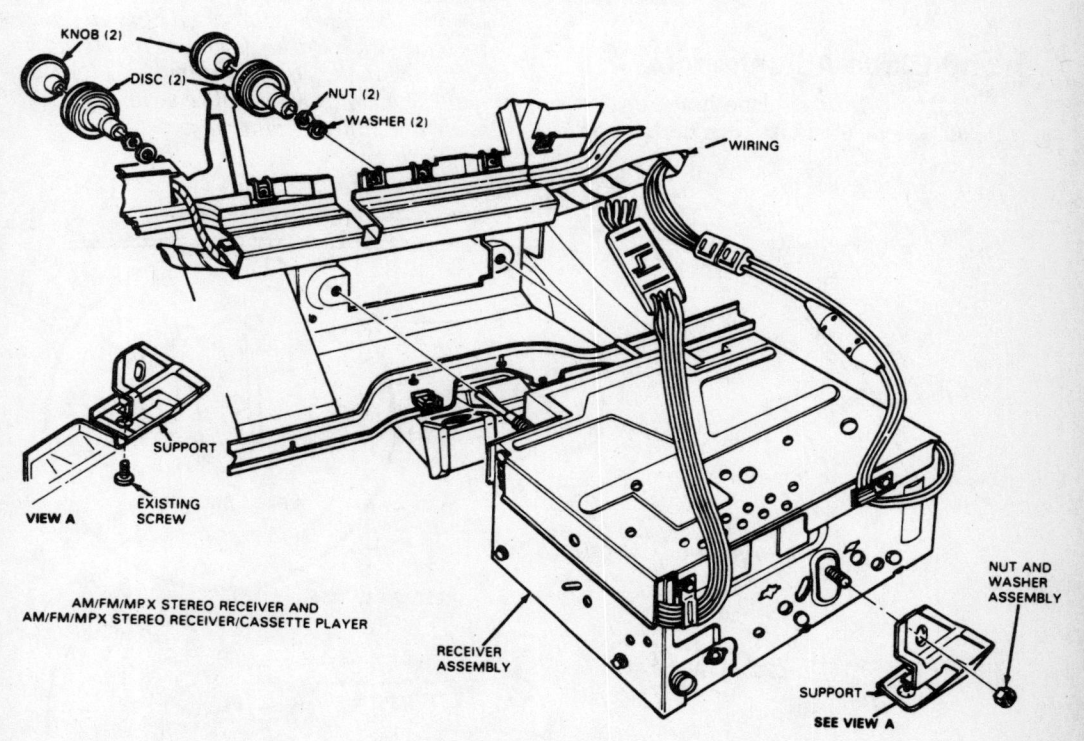

Radio installation

382   CHASSIS ELECTRICAL

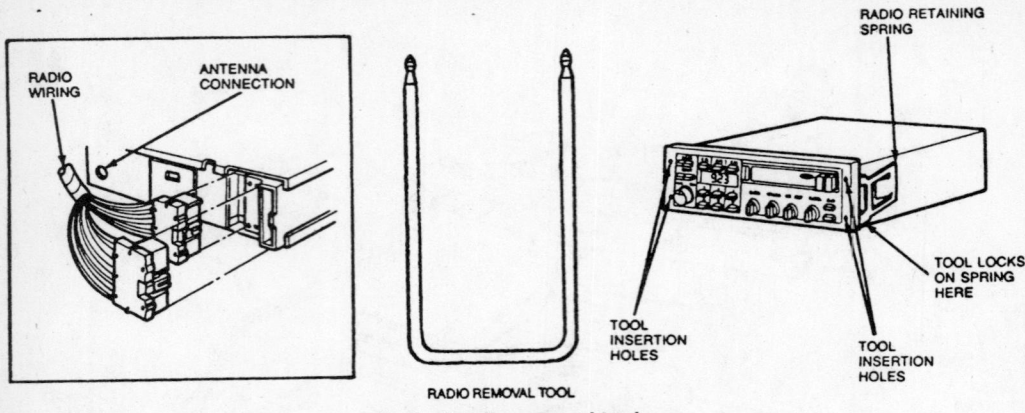

Typical radio removal tool

strip will then snap out of the retaining tab on the end of the wiper frame.

4. Lift the wiper blade assembly from the surface and slide the backing strip down the frame until the notch lines up with the next retaining tab then twist slightly and the backing strip will snap out. Follow this same procedure with the remaining tabs until the element is removed.

5. To install the blade element reverse the above procedure and make sure all six tabs are locked to the backing strip.

Arm and Blade Adjustment

1. With the arm and blade assemblies removed from the pivot shafts turn on the wiper switch and allow the motor to move the pivot shaft three or four cycles, and then turn off the wiper switch. This will place the pivot shafts in the park position.

2. Install the arm and blade assemblies on the pivot shafts to the correct distance between the windshield lower molding or weatherstrip and the blade saddle centerline.

Windshield Wiper Motor

NOTE: *The internal permanent magnets used in the wiper motor are a ceramic (glass-like) material. Care must be exercised in handling the motor to avoid damaging the magnets. The motor must not be struck or tapped with a hammer or other object.*

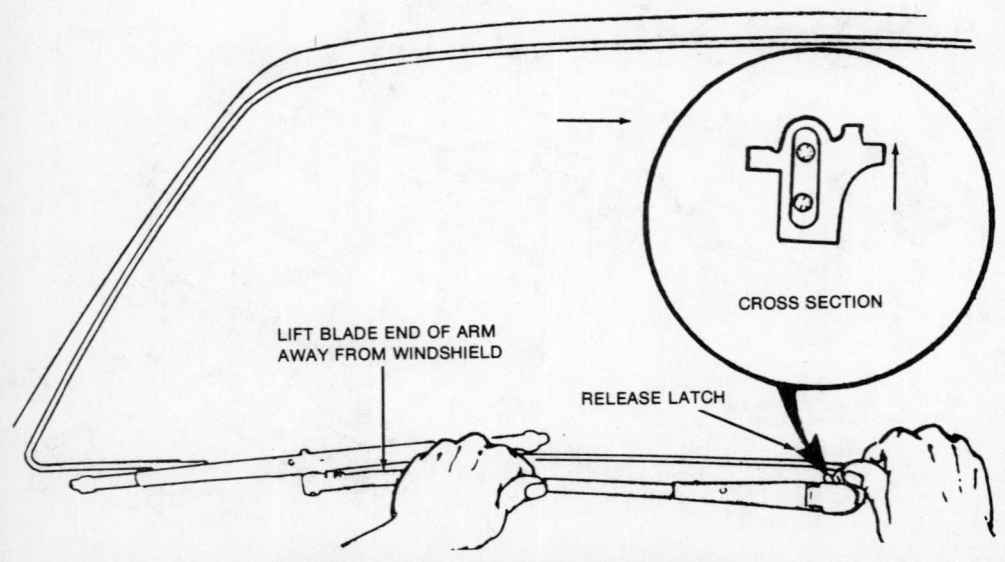

Removing the wiper arm and blade assembly

CHASSIS ELECTRICAL 383

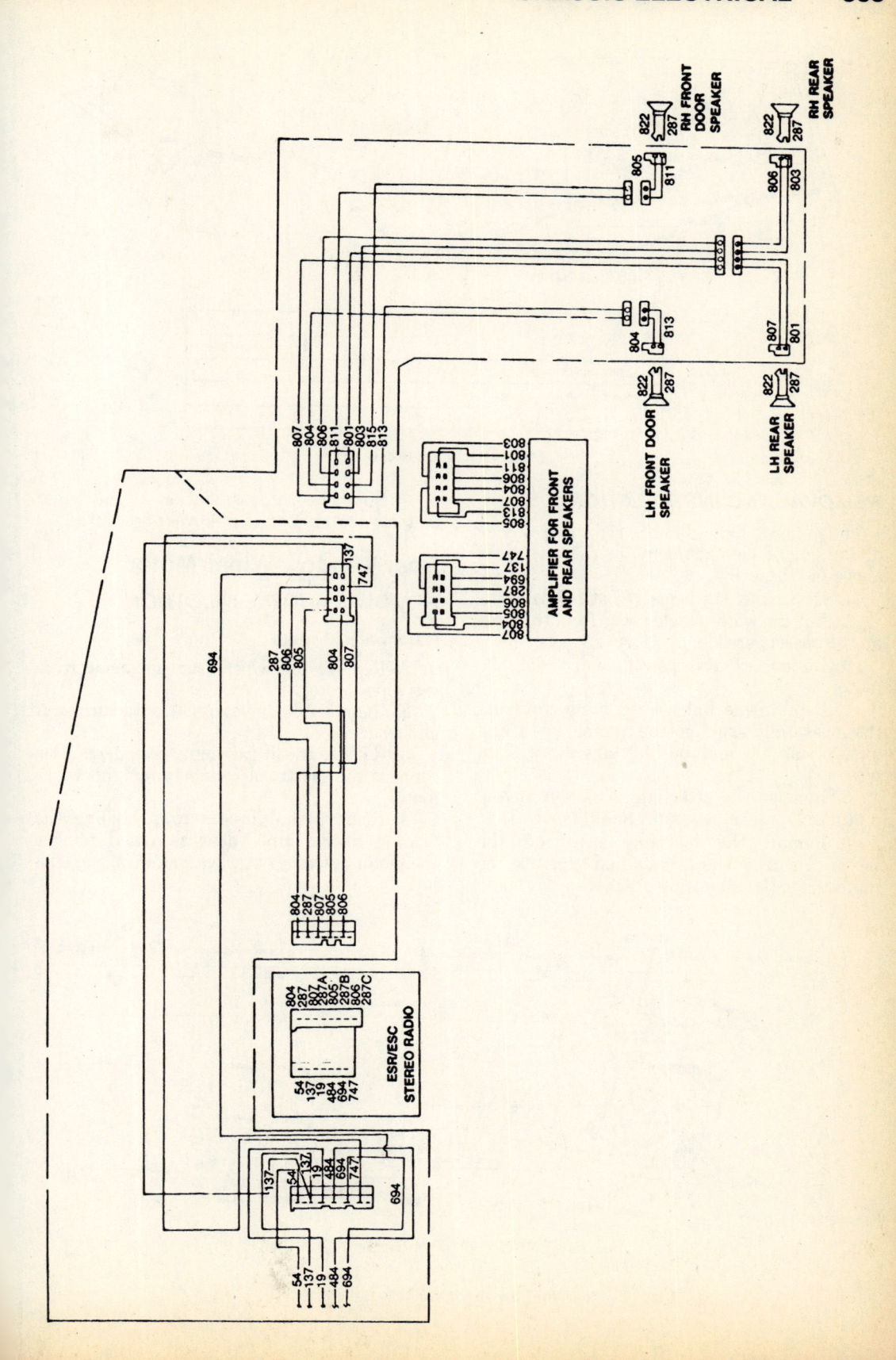

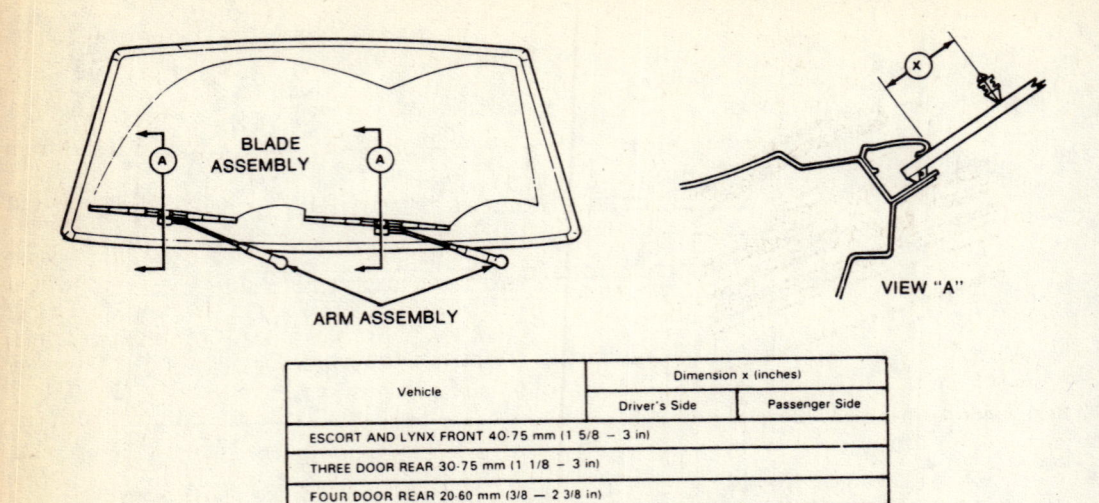

CHASSIS ELECTRICAL

Wiper arm adjustment

Vehicle	Dimension x (inches)	
	Driver's Side	Passenger Side
ESCORT AND LYNX FRONT 40-75 mm (1 5/8 – 3 in)		
THREE DOOR REAR 30-75 mm (1 1/8 – 3 in)		
FOUR DOOR REAR 20-60 mm (3/8 – 2 3/8 in)		

Wiper arm adjustment

REMOVAL AND INSTALLATION

The motor is located in the right rear corner of the engine compartment, in the cowl area above the firewall.

1. Disconnect the negative battery cable.
2. Lift the water shield cover from the cowl on the passenger side.
3. Disconnect the power lead from the motor.
4. Remove the linkage retaining clip from the operating arm on the motor by lifting locking tab up and pulling clip away from pin.
5. Remove the attaching screws from the motor and bracket assembly and remove.
6. Remove the operating arm from the motor. Unscrew the 3 bolts and separate the motor from the mounting bracket.
7. Complete the installation of the wiper motor by reversing the removal procedures.

Rear Window Wiper Motor

REMOVAL AND INSTALLATION

Hatchback Models

1. Remove the wiper arm and blade from the wiper motor.
2. Remove the pivot shaft attaching nut and spacers.
3. Remove the liftgate inner trim panel. Disconnect the electrical connector to the wiper motor.
4. Remove the three screws holding the bracket to the inner door skin and remove the motor assembly, bracket and linkage assembly.

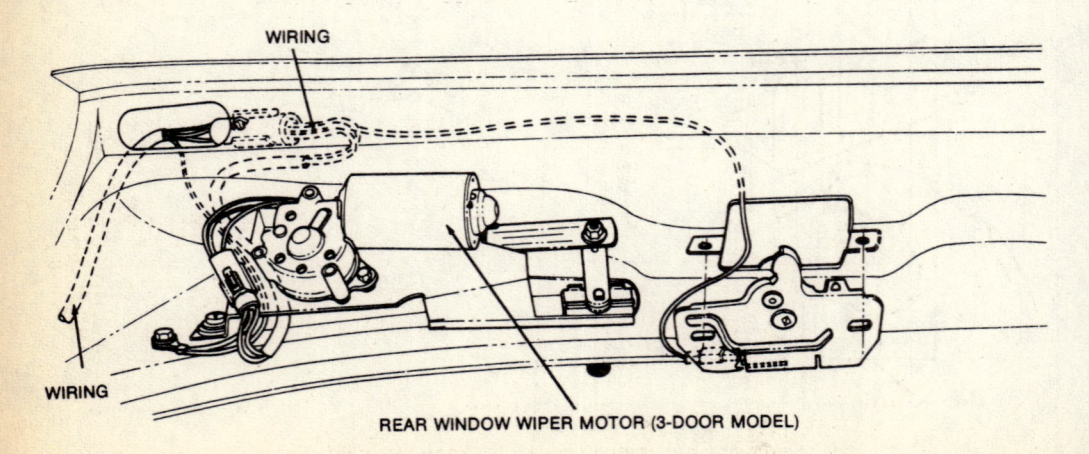

Rear Window wiper motor installation

CHASSIS ELECTRICAL 385

5. Installation is the reverse order of the removal procedure.

Station Wagon Models

1. Remove the wiper arm and blade from the wiper motor.
2. Remove the pivot shaft attaching nut and spacers.
3. Remove the screws attaching the license plate housing. Disconnect the license plate light and remove the housing. Remove the wiper motor and bracket assembly retaining screws, disconnect the electrical connector to the wiper motor and remove the motor.
4. Installation is the reverse order of the removal procedure.

Windshield Wiper Linkage

REMOVAL AND INSTALLATION

The wiper linkage is mounted below the cowl top panel and can be reached by raising the hood.

1. Remove the wiper arm and blade assembly from the pivot shaft. Pry the latch (on the arm) away from the shaft to unlock the arm from the pivot shaft.
2. Raise the hood and disconnect the negative battery cable.
3. Remove the clip and disconnect the linkage drive arm from the motor crank pin.
4. On Tempo/Topaz remove the screws re-

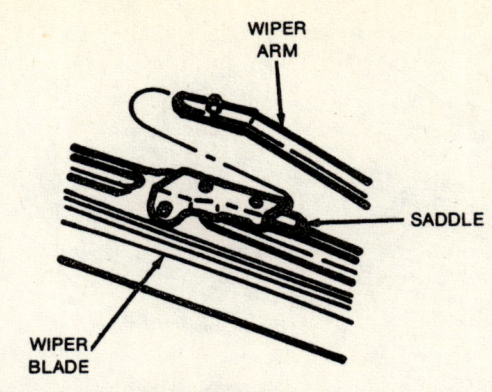

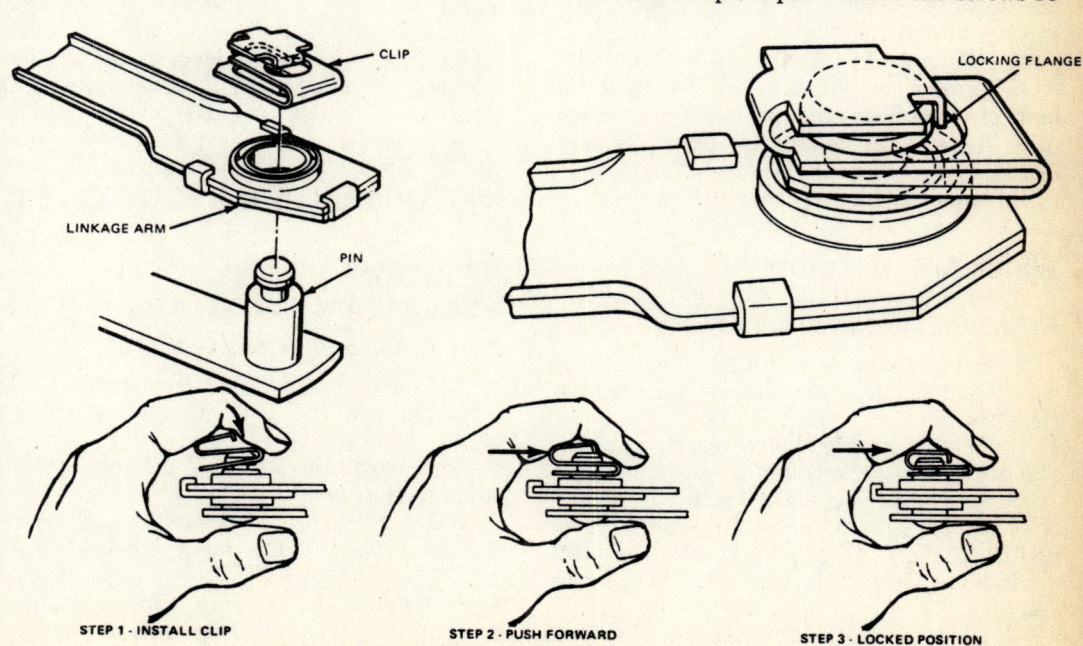

Rear window wiper blade removal

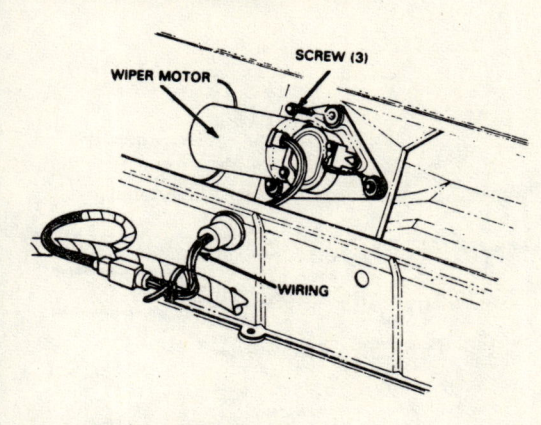

Wiper motor installation

Removing and installing wiper linkage retaining clips

CHASSIS ELECTRICAL

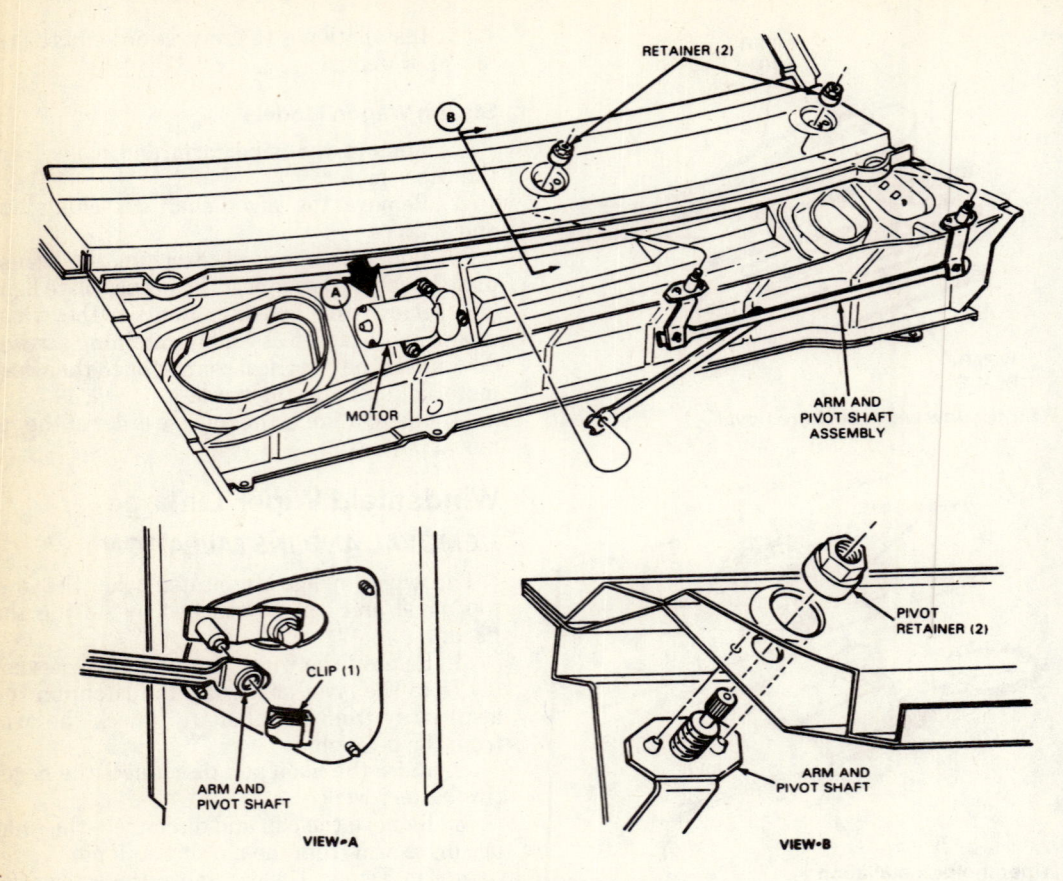

Wiper linkage

taining the pivot assemblies to the cowl.

6. On Escort/Lynx, EXP/LN-7 remove the large pivot retainer nuts from each pivot shaft.

7. Remove the linkage and pivot assembly from the cowl chamber.

8. Installation is the reverse of removal.

Wiper Arm Assembly

REMOVAL AND INSTALLATION

1. Raise the blade end of the arm off the windshield and move the slide latch away from the pivot shaft.

2. The wiper arm should not be unlocked and can now be pulled off of the pivot shaft.

3. To install, position the auxiliary arm (if so equipped) over the pivot pin, hold it down and push the main arm head over the pivot shaft. Make sure the pivot shaft is in the park position.

4. Hold the main arm head on the pivot shaft while raising the blade end of the wiper arm and push the slide latch into the lock under the pivot shaft. Lower the blade to the windshield.

NOTE: *If the blade does not touch the windshield, the slide latch is not completely in place.*

INSTRUMENTS AND SWITCHES

Instrument Cluster

REMOVAL AND INSTALLATION

1981–85 Escort/EXP and Lynx/LN7

1. Disconnect the negative battery terminal.
2. Remove the bottom steering column cover.
3. Remove the steering column opening cover reinforcement screws.

NOTE: *On cars equipped with speed control disconnect the wires from the amplified assembly.*

4. Remove the steering column retaining screws from the steering column support bracket and lower the column.
5. Remove the column trim shrouds.
6. Disconnect all electrical connections from the column.

CHASSIS ELECTRICAL

7. Remove the finish panel screws and the panel.
8. Remove the speedometer cable.
9. Remove the four cluster screws and remove the cluster.
10. Installation is the reverse of removal.

1986–90 Escort and Lynx

1. Disconnect the negative battery cable.
2. Remove 2 retaining screws at bottom of steering column opening and snap steering column cover out.
3. Remove 10 cluster opening finish panel retainer screws and remove finish panel.
4. Remove 2 upper and lower screws retaining cluster to instrument panel.
5. Reach under instrument panel and disconnect speedometer cable by pressing down on the flat surface of plastic connector (quick connect).
6. Pull cluster away from instrument panel. Disconnect cluster feed plug from its receptacle in printed circuit.
7. Complete installation of the instrument cluster by reversing the removal procedure.

1984–87 Tempo and Topaz

1. Disconnect the negative battery cable.
2. Remove the 2 retaining screws at the bottom of the steering column and snap the steering column cover out.
3. Remove the steering column trim shroud and the snap-in lower cluster finish panels.
4. Remove the 8 instrument cluster finish panel screws, radio knobs as required and remove the finish panel.
5. Remove the 2 upper and lower screws retaining the instrument cluster to the instrument panel.
6. Disconnect the speedometer cable by reaching under the instrument panel and pressing on the flat surface of the speedometer cable quick connector.
7. Pull the cluster away from the instrument panel and disconnect the electrical feed plug to the cluster from its receptacle in the printed circuit.
8. Complete the installation of the instrument cluster by reversing the removal procedure.

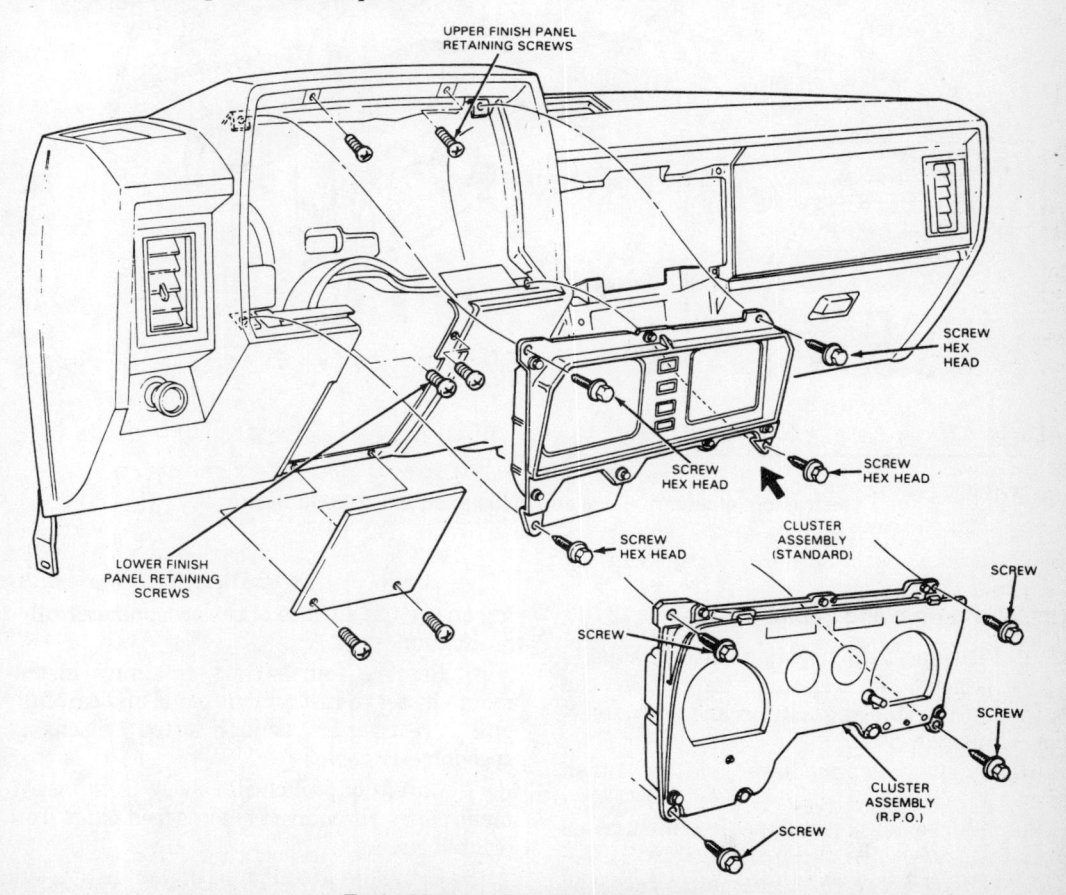

Typical instrument cluster installation

CHASSIS ELECTRICAL

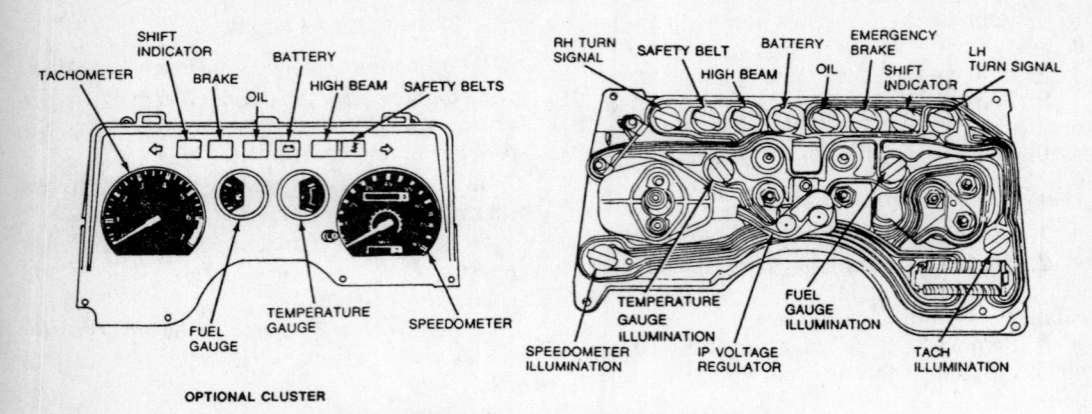

Optional instrument clusters for 1988–90 Escort

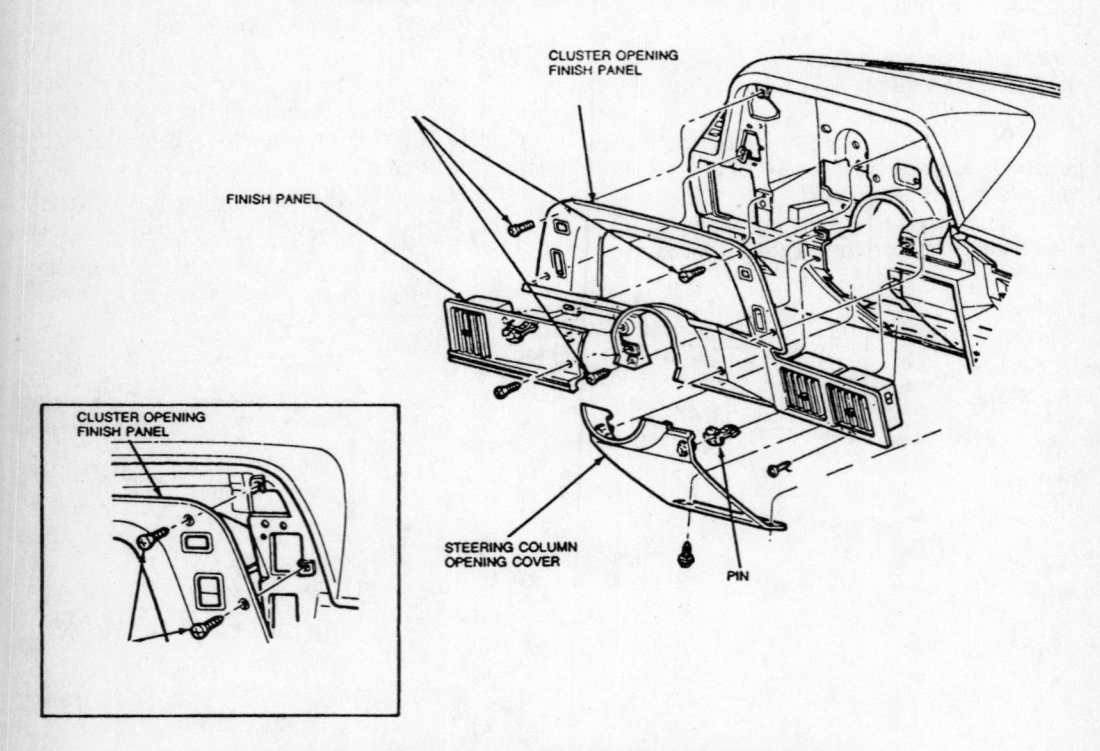

Instrument cluster removal and installation for 1988–90 Escort

1988–90 Tempo and Topaz

1. Disconnect the negative battery cable.
2. Remove two retaining screws at the bottom of the steering column and snap steering column cover out.
3. Remove snap-in lower cluster finish panels.
4. Remove four cluster opening finish panel retaining screws and pull panel forward.
5. Disconnect the speedometer cable by reaching under the instrument panel and pressing on the flat surface of the speedometer cable quick connector.
6. Remove four screws retaining instrument cluster to instrument panel and carefully pull rearward enough to disengage speedometer cable.
7. Carefully pull cluster away from instrument panel. Disconnect cluster feed plugs from printed circuit.
8. Complete installation of the instrument cluster by reversing the removal procedure.

CHASSIS ELECTRICAL   389

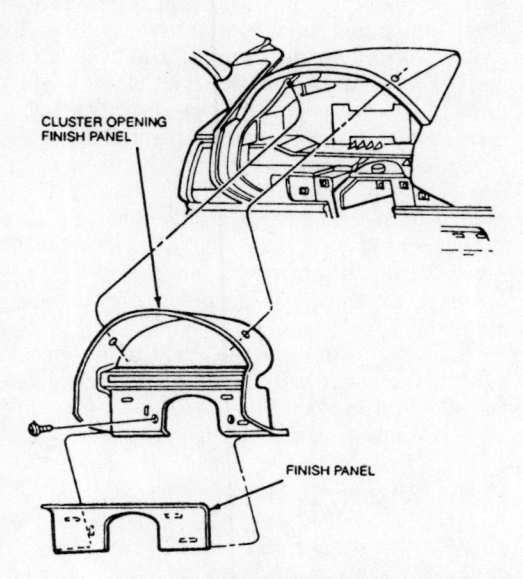

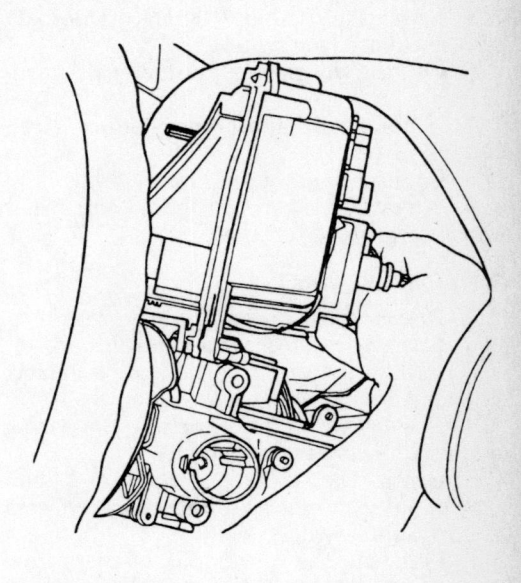

Instrument cluster removal and installation for 1988–90 Tempo and Topaz

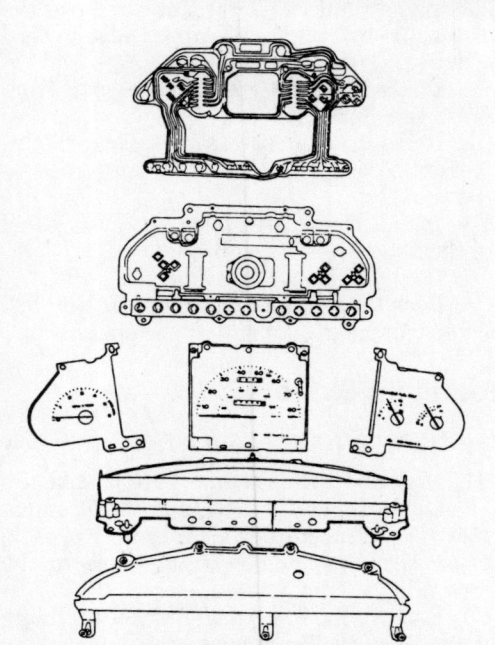

Exploded view of the instrument cluster assembly 1988–90 Tempo and Topaz

Wiper Switch

REMOVAL AND INSTALLATION

1981–83 Escort

NOTE: *The switch handle is an integral part of the switch and can not be removed separately. If there is any need for repairs to the wiper switch the multi-function switch must be replaced as a assembly.*

1. Disconnect the negative (ground) battery cable from the battery terminal.
2. Loosen the steering column attaching nuts enough to remove the upper trim shroud.
3. Remove the trim shrouds.
4. Disconnect the quick connect electrical connector.
5. Peel back the foam sight shield. Remove the two hex head screws holding the switch and remove the wash/wipe switch.

To install:

6. Position the switch on the column and install the two hex head screws. Replace the foam sight shield over the switch.
7. Connect the quick connect electrical connector.
8. Install the upper and lower trim shrouds.
9. Tighten the steering column attaching nuts to 17–25 ft. lbs. (23–33 Nm).
10. Connect the negative (ground) battery cable to the battery terminal.
11. Check the steering column for proper operation.

1984–90 Escort and Lynx

EXCEPT TILT STEERING WHEEL

1. Disconnect the negative battery cable.
2. Remove upper and lower trim shrouds.
3. Disconnect the quick connect electrical connector.
4. Peel back the foam sight shield. Remove the hex-head screws holding the switch and remove the wash/wiper switch.
5. Position the switch on the column and in-

CHASSIS ELECTRICAL

stall the hex-head screws. Replace the foam sight shield over the switch.

6. Connect the quick connect electrical connector.
7. Install the upper and lower trim shrouds.
8. Connect the negative battery cable.
9. Check the steering column and wiper switch for proper operation.

TILT STEERING WHEEL

1. Disconnect the negative battery cable.
2. Remove the steering column shroud.
3. Peel back the side shield and disconnect the switch wiring connector.
4. Remove the screw attaching the wiring retainer to the steering column.
5. Grasp the switch handle and pull straight out to disengage the wiper switch from the turn signal switch.
6. Complete the installation of the switch by reversing the removal procedure.

Tempo and Topaz

NOTE: *The standard and interval front wiper and washer systems on 1984–87 Tempo and Topaz vehicles feature an instrument panel-mounted manual switch for wiper and washer control. Tempo and Topaz models, 1988–90, use a rotary switch mounted on the side of the instrument panel.*

On Escort vehicles, the wiper/washer control switch is column-mounted for both tilt and non-tilt models. The switch handle is an integral part of the switch and cannot be removed separately.

DASH MOUNTED (FRONT)

1. Disconnect the negative battery cable.
2. Remove the instrument panel finish panel.
3. Remove the wiper switch housing retaining screws and remove the switch housing from the instrument panel.
4. Remove the wiper switch knob. Disconnect the electrical connectors from the switch assembly.
5. Remove the screws holding the wiper switch in the switch housing plate and remove the switch.
6. Complete the installation of the switch by reversing the removal procedure.

DASH MOUNTED ROTARY SWITCH (SIDE)

1. Disconnect the negative battery cable.
2. Insert a suitable prying tool into the small slots on top and bottom of the switch bezel.
3. Push down on the tool to work the top of the switch away from the instrument panel.
4. Work the bottom portion of the switch from the panel and completely remove the switch from the panel opening. Hold the switch and pull the wiring at the rear of the switch until the switch connector can be easily disconnected. Disconnect the connector and allow the wiring to hang from the switch mounting opening.
5. Connect the wiring connector to the new switch and route the wiring back into the mounting opening. Insert the switch into the opening so that the graphics are properly aligned.
6. Push on the switch until the bezel seats against the instrument panel and the clips lock the switch into place.
7. Connect negative battery cable.

Rear Wiper Switch

REMOVAL AND INSTALLATION

1. Remove the two or four cluster opening finish panel retaining screws and remove the finish panel by rocking the upper edge toward the driver.
2. Disconnect the wiring connector from the rear washer switch.
3. Remove the washer switch from the instrument panel.

To install:

4. Install the cluster opening finish panel and the two or four retaining screws.
5. Connect the wiring connector.
6. Push the rear washer switch into the cluster finish panel until it snaps into place.

Headlight Switch

REMOVAL AND INSTALLATION

1. Disconnect the negative battery cable.
2. On vehicles without air conditioning, remove the left hand side air vent control cable retaining screws and lower the cable to the floor.
3. Remove the fuse panel bracket retaining screws. Move the fuse panel assembly aside to gain access to the headlight switch.
4. Pull the headlight knob out to the **ON** position. Depress the headlight knob and shaft retainer button, which is located on the bottom of the headlight switch. Remove the knob and the shaft assembly from the switch.
5. Remove the headlight switch retaining bezel. Disconnect the multiple connector plug and remove the switch from the instrument panel.

To install:

6. Install the headlight switch into the instrument panel. Connect the multiple connec-

CHASSIS ELECTRICAL

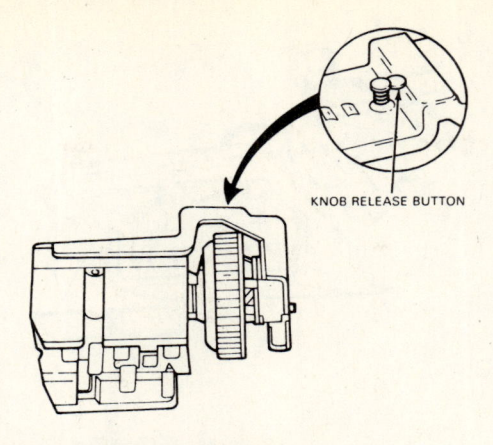

Headlight switch assembly

tor and install the headlight switch retaining bezel.

7. Install the knob and shaft assembly by inserting the shaft into the headlight switch gently pushing until the shaft is in the lock position.

8. Move the fuse panel back into position and install the fuse panel bracket with the two retaining screws.

9. On vehicles without air conditioning, install the left hand side air vent control cable and bracket. Install the negative battery cable and check the headlight switch for the proper operation.

Combination Switch

The combination switch assembly is a multi-function switch comprising turn signal, hazard, headlight dimmer and flash-to-pass functions. The switch lever on the left side of the steering column, above the wiper switch lever, controls the turn signal, headlight dimmer and flash-to-pass functions. The hazard function is controlled by the actuating knob on the bottom part of the steering column.

REMOVAL AND INSTALLATION

1. Disconnect the negative battery cable.
2. Remove the lower shroud.
3. Loosen the steering column attaching nuts enough to allow the removal of the upper trim shroud.
4. Remove the upper shroud.
5. Remove the turn signal switch lever by pulling the lever straight out from the switch. To make removal easier, work the outer end of the lever around with a slight rotary movement before pulling it out.
6. Peel back the foam sight shield from the turn signal switch.
7. Disconnect the turn signal switch electrical connectors.
8. Remove the self-tapping screws that attach the turn signal switch to the lock cylinder housing and disengage the switch from the housing.
9. Transfer the ground brush located in the turn signal switch canceling cam to the new switch assembly on vehicles equipped with speed control.

To install:

10. Align the turn signal switch mounting holes with the corresponding holes in the lock cylinder housing and install 2 self-tapping screws until tight.
11. Apply the foam sight shield to the turn signal switch.
12. Install the turn signal switch lever into the switch by aligning the key on the lever with the keyway in the switch and pushing the lever toward the switch to full engagement.
13. Install turn signal switch electrical connectors to full engagement.
14. Install the steering column trim shrouds.
15. Torque the steering column attaching nuts to 15–22 ft. lbs.
16. Connect the negative battery cable.
17. Check the steering column for proper operation.

Clock

REMOVAL AND INSTALLATION

1981–83 Models

1. Disconnect the negative battery cable.
2. Remove the 2 center radio speaker grill retaining screws and remove the grille.
3. Remove the 3 retaining screws attaching the clock to the instrument panel.
4. Remove the clock from the opening and disconnect the electrical connectors.
5. Installation is the reverse order of the removal procedure.

1984–85 Models

1. Disconnect the negative battery cable.
2. Remove the eight cluster opening finish panel screws. Remove the finish panel by rocking upper edge toward the driver.
3. Remove the 3 retaining screws attaching the clock to the instrument panel.
4. Remove the clock from the opening and disconnect the electrical connections.
5. Installation is the reverse order of the removal procedure.

1986–90 Models

NOTE: *On the Tempo and Topaz models, pry the clock module face out of the hole in the instrument panel with a spring hook in the slot at the bottom of the clock and discon-*

392 CHASSIS ELECTRICAL

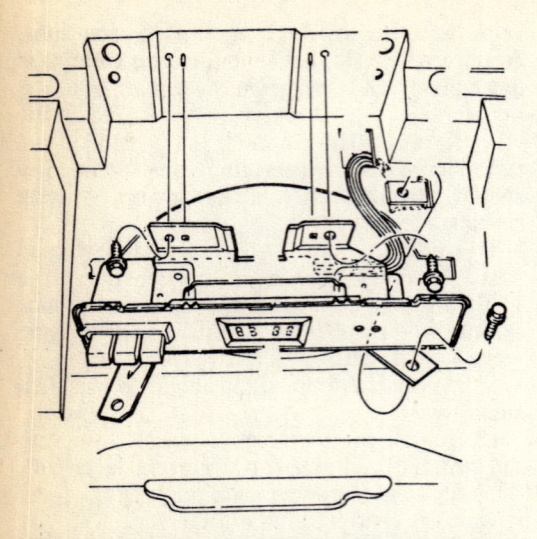

Digital clock removal and installation — 1981–85 models

nect the electrical connector. To install connect the electrical connector and snap the clock back into it hole.

1. Disconnect the negative battery cable.
2. Remove the lenses by inserting a suitable tool in one of the notches on the side of the lenses.
3. Remove the 2 screws one on the inside of each lens opening.
4. Remove the front screw while supporting the console.
5. Remove the console from roof. Slide the connector shield off of the electrical connector.

NOTE: *The shield is molded to fit securely over the connector. It may be necessary to lift a portion of the shield over the connector ribs before the shield will slide freely.*

6. Disconnect the electrical halves. Remove the 4 retaining screws attaching the clock to the console panel.
7. Remove the locators and remove the clock from the opening.

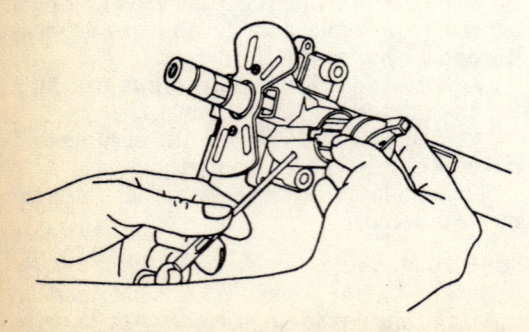

Typical ignition lock cylinder assembly removal and installation

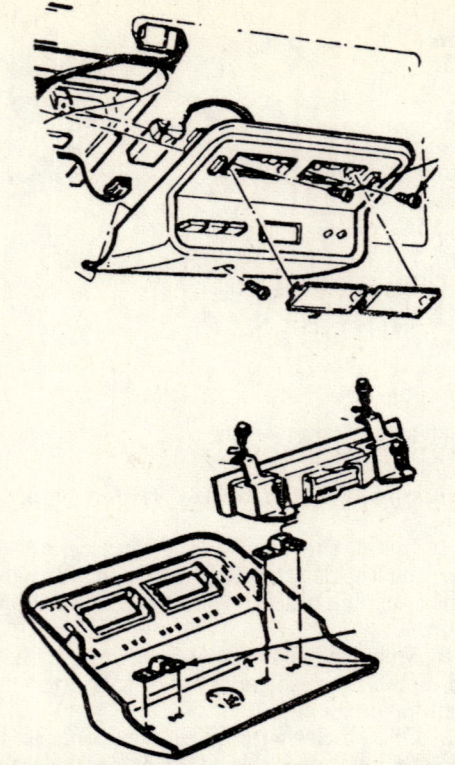

Digital clock removal and installation — 1986–90 models

8. Installation is the reverse order of the removal procedure.

Ignition Lock Cylinder

REMOVAL AND INSTALLATION

1. Disconnect the negative battery cable.
2. If equipped with a tilt steering column, remove the upper extension shroud by unsnapping the shroud from the retaining clip at the 9 o'clock position.
3. Remove the steering column lower shroud on Escort and Lynx. On Tempo and Topaz, remove the trim halves.
4. Disconnect the warning buzzer electrical connector. With the lock cylinder key, rotate the cylinder to the **RUN** position.
5. Take a $1/8$ in. (3mm) diameter pin or small wire punch and push on the cylinder retaining pin. The pin is visible through a hole in the mounting surrounding the key cylinder. Push on the pin and withdraw the lock cylinder from the housing.

To install:

6. Install the lock cylinder by turning it to the **RUN** position and depressing the retaining pin. Be sure the lock cylinder is fully seated and aligned in the interlocking washer before turning the key to the **OFF** position. This action

will permit the cylinder retaining pin to extend into the cylinder housing hole.

7. Rotate the lock cylinder, using the lock cylinder key, to ensure correct mechanical operation in all positions.

8. Install the electrical connector for the key warning buzzer.

9. Install the lower steering column shroud.

10. Connect the negative battery cable to battery terminal.

11. Check for proper start in **P** or **N**. Also, make certain that the start circuit cannot be actuated in the **D** and **R** positions and that the column is locked in the **LOCK** position.

Ignition Switch

REMOVAL AND INSTALLATION

1. Disconnect the negative battery cable.
2. Remove the steering column upper and lower trim shroud by removing the self-tapping screws. The steering column attaching nuts may have to be loosened enough to allow removal of the upper shroud.
3. Remove 2 bolts and nuts holding steering column assembly to steering column bracket assembly and lower steering column to the seat.
4. Remove steering column shrouds.
5. Disconnect electrical connector from ignition switch.
6. Rotate ignition lock cylinder to the **RUN** position.
7. Remove 2 screws attaching switch to the lock cylinder housing.
8. Disengage the ignition switch from the actuator pin.

To install:

9. Check to see that the actuator pin slot in ignition switch is in the **RUN** position.

NOTE: *A new switch assembly will be preset in the RUN position.*

10. Make certain that the ignition key lock cylinder is in approximately the **RUN** position. The **RUN** position is achieved by rotating the key lock cylinder approximately 90° from the **LOCK** position.

11. Install the ignition switch onto the actuator pin. It may be necessary to move the switch slightly back and fourth to align the switch mounting holes with the column lock housing threaded holes.

12. Install the new screws and tighten to 50–70 inch lbs. (5.6–7.9 Nm).

13. Connect electrical connector to ignition switch.

14. Connect negative battery cable.

15. Check the ignition switch for proper function including **START** and **ACC** positions. Also make certain that the steering column is locked when in the **LOCK** position.

16. Position the top half of the shroud on the steering column.

17. Install the 2 bolts and nuts attaching the steering column assembly to the steering column bracket assembly.

18. Position lower shroud to upper shroud and install 5 self-tapping screws.

Stoplight Switch

The mechanical stoplight switch assembly is installed on the pin of the brake pedal arm, so that it straddles the master cylinder pushrod.

REMOVAL AND INSTALLATION

1. Disconnect the negative battery cable.
2. Disconnect the wire harness at the connector from the switch.

NOTE: *The locking tab must be lifted before the connector can be removed.*

3. Remove the hairpin retainer and white nylon washer. Slide the stoplight switch and the pushrod away from the pedal. Remove the switch by sliding the switch up/down.

NOTE: *Since the switch side plate nearest the brake pedal is slotted, it is not necessary to remove the brake master cylinder pushrod black bushing and 1 white spacer washer nearest the pedal arm from the brake pedal pin.*

To install:

4. Position the switch so that the U-shaped side is nearest the pedal and directly over/under the pin. The black bushing must be in position in the push rod eyelet with the washer face on the side closest to the retaining pin.

5. Slide the switch up/down, trapping the master cylinder pushrod and black bushing between the switch side plates. Push the switch and pushrod assembly firmly towards the brake pedal arm. Assemble the outside white plastic washer to pin and install the hairpin retainer to trap the whole assembly.

NOTE: *Do not substitute other types of pin retainer. Replace only with production hairpin retainer.*

6. Connect the wire harness connector to the switch.
7. Connect negative battery cable.
8. Check the stoplight switch for proper operation. Stoplights should illuminate with less than 6 lbs. applied to the brake pedal at the pad.

NOTE: *The stoplight switch wire harness must have sufficient length to travel with the switch during full stroke at the pedal.*

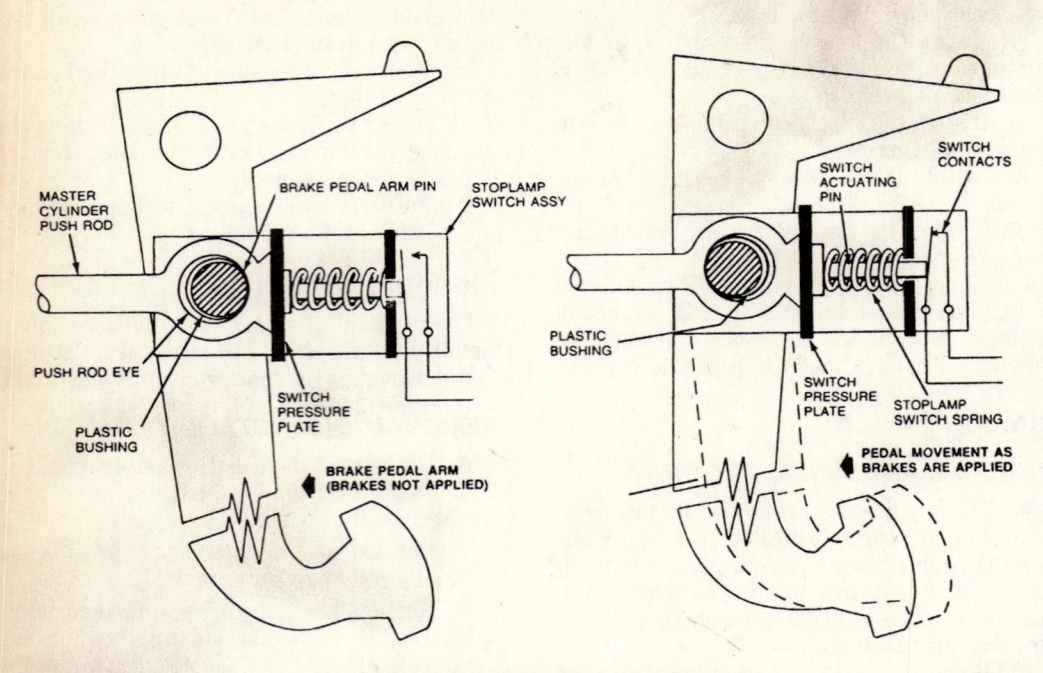

Typical mechanical stoplight switch

Neutral Safety Switch

ADJUSTMENT

The mounting location of the neutral safety switch does not provide for adjustment of the switch position when installed. If the engine will not start in **P** or **N** or if it will start in **R** or any of the **D** ranges, check the control linkage adjustment and/or replace with a known good switch.

REMOVAL AND INSTALLATION

1. Set parking brake.
2. Disconnect the battery negative cable.
3. Disconnect the wire connector from the neutral safety switch.
4. Remove the 2 retaining screws from the neutral start switch and remove the switch.

To install:

5. Place the switch on the manual shift shaft and loosely install the retaining bolts.
6. Use a No. 43 drill (0.089 in.) and insert it into the switch to set the contacts.
7. Tighten the retaining screws of the switch, remove the drill and complete the assembly by reversing the removal procedure.
8. Connect negative battery cable.
9. Check the ignition switch for proper starting in **P** or **N**. Also make certain that the start circuit cannot be actuated in the **D** or **R** position and that the column is locked in the **LOCK** position.

Speedometer Cable

REMOVAL AND INSTALLATION

1. Remove the instrument cluster.
2. Pull the speedometer cable from the casing. If the cable is broken, disconnect the casing from the transaxle and remove the broken piece from the transaxle end.
3. Lubricate the new cable with graphite lubricant. Feed the cable into the casing from the instrument panel end.
4. Attach the cable to the speedometer. Install the cluster.

Speedometer

REMOVAL AND INSTALLATION

1. Disconnect the negative battery cable.
2. Remove instrument cluster.
3. Remove 7 screws that retain the lens and mask to the back plate.
4. Remove the nuts retaining the fuel gauge assembly to the back plate. Remove the fuel gauge assembly and then remove the speedometer assembly.

To install:

5. Apply a small bead of silicone damping grease part number D7AZ–19A331–A or equivalent, in the drive hole of the speedometer head. Install speedometer head assembly into cluster.

NOTE: *The speedometer is calibrated at the time of manufacture. Excessive rough handling of the speedometer may disturb the calibration.*

6. Install retaining screws to retain the lens and mask to the back plate.
7. Install instrument cluster.
8. Connect battery ground and check operation of speedometer.

LIGHTING

Headlights

Two rectangular dual sealed beam headlamps are used on all models up to 1985$^1/_2$. A dash mounted switch controls them and the steering column dimmer switch controls the high and low beams.

All models 1985$^1/_2$ and later are equipped with flush mount headlights. On these models the bulb may be replaced without removing the lens and body assembly.

REMOVAL AND INSTALLATION

Sealed Beam Type — 1981–85$^1/_2$

1. Remove the headlamp door by removing the retaining screws. After the screws are removed, pull the door slightly forward (certain models have upper locking tabs which disengage by lifting out on the lower edge and pulling downward) and disconnect the parking light (if equipped). Remove the headlight door.
2. Remove the lamp retaining ring screws, pull the headlamp from the connector.
3. Installation is in the reverse order of removal.

Aerodynamic Type — 1985$^1/_2$ and later

CAUTION: *The replaceable Halogen headlamp bulb contains gas under pressure. The bulb may shatter if the glass envelope is scratched or the bulb is dropped. Handle the bulb carefully. Grasp the bulb ONLY by its plastic base. Avoid touching the glass envelope. Keep the bulb out of the reach of children.*

1. Check to see that the headlight switch is in the OFF position.
2. Raise the hood and locate the bulb installed in the rear of the headlight body.
3. Remove the electrical connector from the bulb by grasping the wires firmly and snapping the connector rearward.
4. Remove the bulb retaining ring by rotating it counterclockwise (when viewed from the rear) about $^1/_8$ of a turn, then slide the ring off the plastic base.

NOTE: *Keep the bulb retaining ring, it will be reused with the new bulb.*

5. Carefully remove the headlight bulb from its socket in the reflector by gently pulling it straight backward out of the socket. DO NOT rotate the bulb during removal.

To install:
6. With the flat side of the plastic base of the bulb facing upward, insert the glass envelope of the bulb into the socket. Turn the base slightly to the left or right, if necessary to align the grooves in the forward part of the plastic base with the corresponding locating tabs inside the socket. When the grooves are aligned, push the bulb firmly into the socket until the mounting flange on the base contacts the rear face of the socket.
7. Slip the bulb retaining ring over the rear of the plastic base against the mounting flange. Lock the ring into the socket by rotating the ring counterclockwise. A stop will be felt when the retaining ring is fully engaged.
8. Push the electrical connector into the rear of the plastic until it snaps and locks into position.
9. Turn the headlights on and check for proper operation.

Front Turn Signal and Parking Lights

REMOVAL AND INSTALLATION

Escort/Lynx

1981–85

1. Remove the screws that retain the headlamp door (bezel).
2. Pull the headlight door (bezel) forward and remove the parking light bulb socket from the light assembly.
3. To install, reverse the procedure.

1985$^1/_2$ AND LATER

1. Remove the 3 screws attaching the parking light to the headlight housing.
2. Hold the parking light with both hands and pull forward to release the hidden attachment.
3. From the side, remove the bulb socket and replace the bulb.
4. To install, reverse the procedure.

EXP/LN7

1. Remove the 2 parking light retaining screws and pull the light assembly forward.
2. Remove the bulb socket by twisting and remove the bulb.
3. To install, reverse the procedure.

396 CHASSIS ELECTRICAL

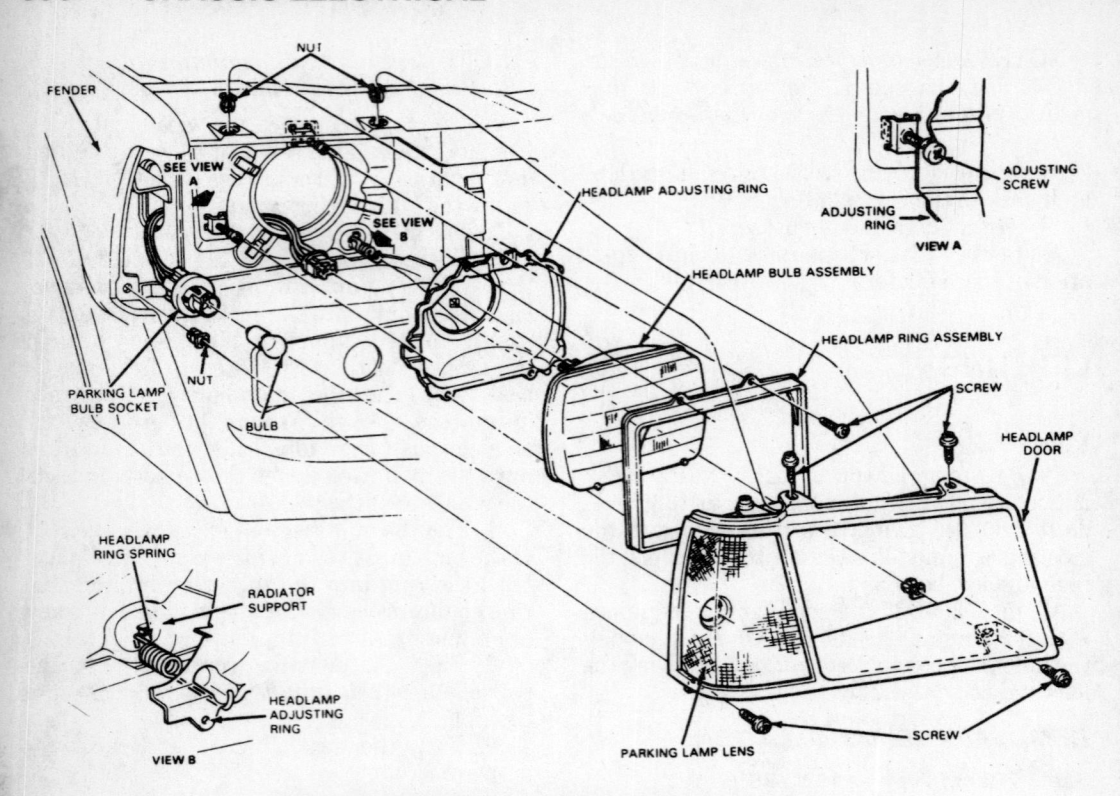

Headlight replacement — sealed beam type headlights

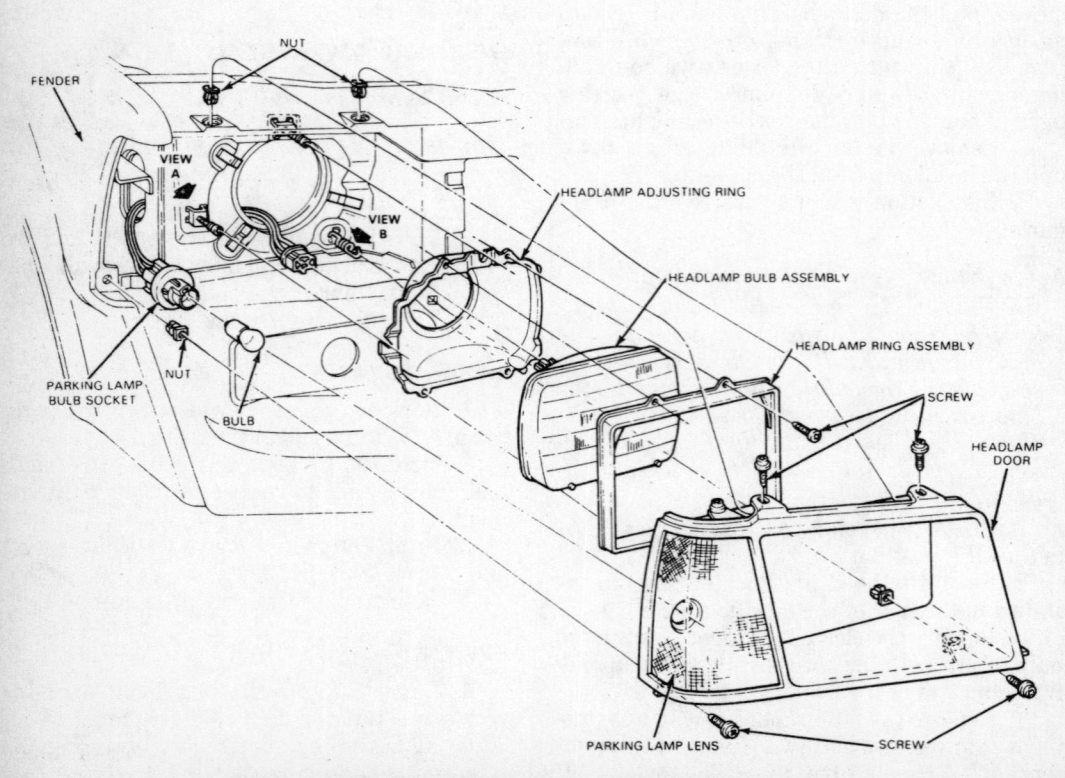

Front turn signal and parking light — 1981–85 Escort/Lynx

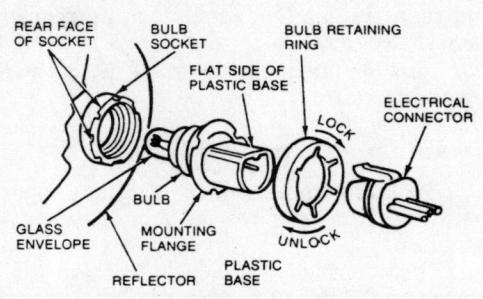

CHASSIS ELECTRICAL 397

Halogen bulb replacement — aerodynamic type headlights

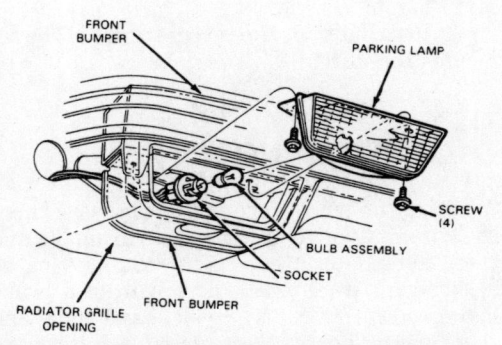

Front turn signal and parking light — EXP/LN7

Tempo/Topaz

1984–85

1. Remove the headlamp door.
2. Remove the 3 screws attaching the parking light and pull forward.
3. Remove the bulb socket by twisting and remove the bulb.
4. To install, reverse the procedure.

1986–91

1. Remove the 2 screws retaining the parking light to the grille opening panel.
2. Hold the parking light with both hands and pull forward to release the hidden attachment.
3. Remove the bulb socket by twisting and replace the bulb.
4. To install, reverse the procedure.

Rear Turn Signal, Brake and Parking Lights

REMOVAL AND INSTALLATION

All Models except Escort/Lynx 4-Door Liftgate

1. Bulbs can be serviced from the inside of the luggage compartment by removing the luggage compartment rear trim panel, if so equipped.
2. Remove the socket(s) from the lamp body and replace the bulb(s).

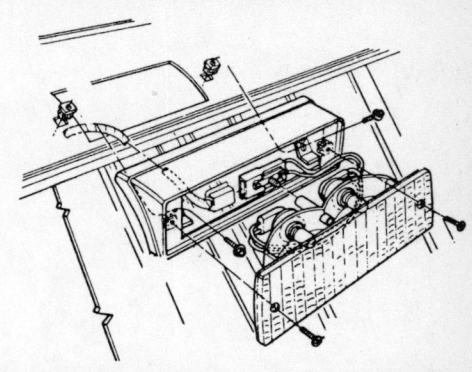

High mount stoplamp removal and installation Escort wagon models

3. Install the socket(s) in the lamp body and install the trim panel.

Escort/Lynx 4-Door Liftgate

1. The bulbs may be serviced by removing the 4 screws retaining the light assembly to the rear quarter opening.
2. Pull the light assembly out of the opening and remove the light socket to replace the bulb.
3. To install, reverse the procedure.

High Mount Stop Lamp

2-DOOR AND 4-DOOR ESCORT HATCHBACK

1. Remove the interior trim panel from the hatch.
2. Remove the socket and bulb from the lamp.
3. Remove the 2 nuts retaining the lamp assembly to the hatch.
4. Remove the lamp assembly from the vehicle.
5. Installation is the reverse order of the removal procedure.

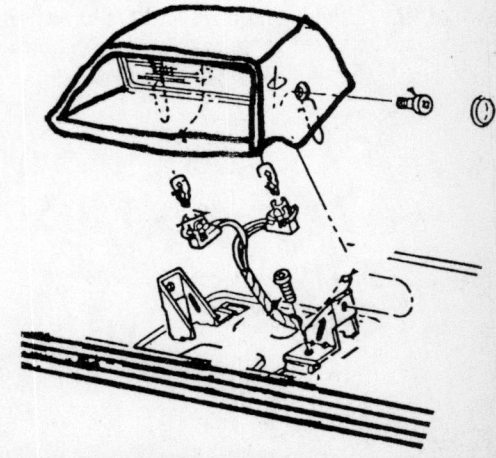

High mount stoplamp removal and installation Tempo and Topaz models

CHASSIS ELECTRICAL

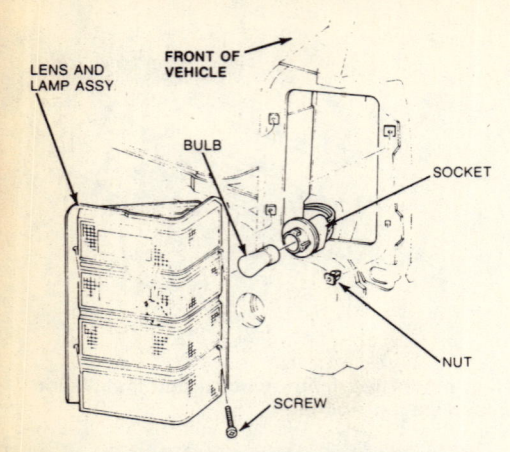

Rear turn signal and parking light — Escort/Lynx 4-door liftgate

ESCORT WAGON

1. Remove the 2 screws from the lens face.
2. With the lamp assembly detached from the bezel housing, disconnect the lamp wire assembly from the wiring harness.
3. The bezel housing can be removed if necessary, by removing the 2 screws which secure the bezel housing to the vehicle.
4. Installation is the reverse order of the removal procedure.

2-DOOR TEMPO AND TOPAZ

1. Locate the wire to hi-mount brake lamp under the package tray, from inside of the luggage compartment. Pull the wire loose from the plastic clip.
2. Remove the 2 beauty caps from the lamp cover.
3. Remove the 2 screws which can be accessed from the side of the lamp.
4. Pull the lamp assembly towards the front of the vehicle. The bulb sockets can then be removed by turning them counter clockwise

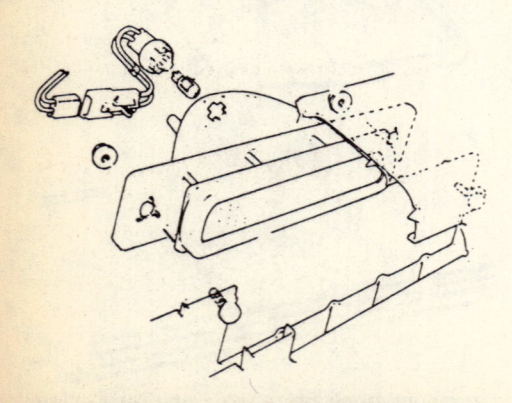

High mount stoplamp removal and installation 2 door and 4 door Escort hatchback models

and then the lamp assembly can be removed from the vehicle.

5. Installation is the reverse order of the removal procedure.

4-DOOR TEMPO AND TOPAZ

1. Working from inside the luggage compartment, twist and remove the 2 bulb socket assemblies.
2. From inside the vehicle, remove the 2 screws on the side of the lamp.
3. Slide the lamp assembly toward the front of the vehicle and lift up. Remove the lamp assembly from the vehicle.
4. Installation is the reverse order of the removal procedure.

TRAILER WIRING

Wiring the car for towing is fairly easy. There are a number of good wiring kits available and these should be used, rather than trying to design your own. All trailers will need brake lights and turn signals as well as tail lights and side marker lights. Most states require extra marker lights for overly wide trailers. Also, most states have recently required back-up lights for trailers, and most trailer manufacturers have been building trailers with back-up lights for several years.

Additionally, some Class I, most Class II and just about all Class III trailers will have electric brakes.

Add to this number an accessories wire, to operate trailer internal equipment or to charge the trailer's battery, and you can have as many as seven wires in the harness.

Determine the equipment on your trailer and buy the wiring kit necessary. The kit will contain all the wires needed, plus a plug adapter set which included the female plug, mounted on the bumper or hitch, and the male plug, wired into, or plugged into the trailer harness.

When installing the kit, follow the manufacturer's instructions. The color coding of the wires is standard throughout the industry.

One point to note: some domestic vehicles, and most imported vehicles, have separate turn signals. On most domestic vehicles, the brake lights and rear turn signals operate with the same bulb. For those vehicles with separate turn signals, you can purchase an isolation unit so that the brake lights won't blink whenever the turn signals are operated, or, you can go to your local electronics supply house and buy four diodes to wire in series with the brake and turn signal bulbs. Diodes will isolate the brake and turn signals. The choice is yours. The isolation units are simple and quick to install, but far more expensive than the diodes. The diodes, however, require more work to install properly, since they require the cutting of each bulb's wire and soldering in place of the diode.

One final point, the best kits are those with a spring loaded cover on the vehicle mounted socket. This cover prevents dirt and moisture from corroding the terminals. Never let the vehicle socket hang loosely; always mount it securely to the bumper or hitch.

CIRCUIT PROTECTION

Circuit breakers

Circuit breakers operate when a circuit overload exceeds its rated amperage. Once operated, they automatically reset after a certain period of time.

There are two kinds of circuit breaker, as previously mentioned, one type will reset itself. The second will not reset itself until the problem in the circuit has been repaired.

Circuit breakers are used to protect the various components of the electrical system, such as headlights and windshield wipers. The circuit breakers are located either in the control switch or mounted on or near the fuse panel.

LOCATIONS

Escort and Lynx

Headlights and High Beam Indicator —one 22 amp circuit breaker incorporated in the lighting switch.

Liftgate Wiper —one $4^1/_2$ amp circuit breaker located in the instrument panel to the left of the radio.

Windshield Wiper and Wiper Pump Circuit —one $8^1/_4$ amp circuit breaker located in the fuse block.

Tempo and Topaz

Headlights and High Beam Indicator —one 18 amp circuit breaker (22 amp in 1987 vehicles) incorporated in the lighting switch.

Front and Rear Marker, Side Parking, Rear and License Lamps —One 15 amp circuit breaker incorporated in the lighting switch.

Windshield Wiper and Rear Window Circuit —one $4^1/_2$ amp circuit breaker located in the windshield wiper switch.

Power Windows —there are two 20 amp circuit breakers located in the starter relay and the fuse block.

Power Seats and Power Door Locks —one 20 amp circuit breaker located in the fuse block.

Station Wagon Power Back Window (Tail light switch) —one 20 amp circuit breaker located in the fuse block.

Intermittent 2-Speed Windshield Wiper —one $8^1/_4$ amp circuit breaker located in the fuse block.

Door Cigar Lighter —one 20 or 30 amp circuit breaker located in the fuse block.

Liftgate Wiper —one $4^1/_2$ amp circuit breaker located in the instrument panel.

Turn Signal and Hazard Flasher

The turn signal flasher is located on the front side of the fuse panel.

The hazard warning flasher is located on the rear side of the fuse panel.

Fuse Panel

The fuse panel is located below and to the left of the steering column.

Fuses are a one-time circuit protection. If a circuit is overloaded or shorts, the fuse will blow thus protecting the circuit. A fuse will continue to blow until the circuit is repaired.

Fuse Link

The fuse link is a short length of special, Hypalon (high temperature) insulated wire, integral with the engine compartment wiring harness and should not be confused with standard wire. It is several wire gauges smaller than the circuit which it protects. Under no circumstances should a fuse link replacement repair be made using a length of standard wire cut from bulk stock or from another wiring harness.

Fusible links are used to prevent major wire harness damage in the event of a short circuit or an overload condition in the wiring circuits that are normally not fused, due to carrying high amperage loads or because of their locations within the wiring harness. Each fusible link is of a fixed value for a specific electrical load and should a fusible link fail, the cause of the failure must be determine and repaired prior to installing a new fusible link of the same value. Please be advised that the color coding of replacement fusible links may vary from the production color coding that is outlined in the text that follows.

Green 14 Gauge Wire —on Escort and Lynx equipped with diesel engine, there are 2 links (1 for Tempo and Topaz) located in the glow plug wiring to protect the glow plug control.

Black 16 Gauge Wire —on Escort and Lynx, there is 1 link located in the wiring for

400 CHASSIS ELECTRICAL

the rear window defogger. On Tempo and Topaz, there is 1 link located in the wiring for the anti-theft system.

Red 18 Gauge Wire —on Tempo and Topaz equipped with gasoline engines, there is 1 link used to protect the carburetor circuits. On the Escort and Lynx equipped with diesel engines, there is 1 link located in the heater fan wiring to protect the heater fan motor circuit.

Brown 18 Gauge Wire —on Tempo and Topaz, there is 1 link used to protect the rear window defogger and the fuel door release. On the Escort and Lynx, there is 1 link used to protect the heater fan motor circuit. There is 1 link used to protect the EEC module on Tempo, Topaz, Escort and Lynx with the 2.3L engine.

Blue 20 Gauge Wire —on Escort and Lynx with gasoline engines, there are 2 links in the wire between the starter relay and the EFE heater. On Tempo and Topaz there is link located in the wire between the ignition switch and the air conditioning-heater cooling fan. On Tempo and Topaz, there is 1 link located in the wire between the battery and the engine compartment light. On 1988–91 Escort, Tempo and Topaz, a fusible link is installed in the engine compartment near the starter relay and protects the passive restraint module circuit. On Escort, Lynx, Tempo and Topaz equipped with diesel engine, there is 1 link used to protect the vacuum pump circuit. On the Tempo and Topaz, there is 1 link used to protect the heater fan motor circuit.

NOTE: *Always disconnect the negative battery cable before servicing the high current fuses or serious personal injury may result.*

To repair any blown fuse link use the following procedure:

1. Determine which circuit is damaged, its location and the cause of the open fuse link. If the damaged fuse link is one of three fed by a common No. 10 or 12 gauge feed wire, determine the specific affected circuit.

2. Disconnect the negative battery cable.

3. Cut the damaged fuse link from the wiring harness and discard it. If the fuse link is one of three circuits fed by a single feed wire, cut it out of the harness at each splice end and discard it.

4. Identify and procure the proper fuse link and butt connectors for attaching the fuse link to the harness.

5. To repair any fuse link in a 3-link group with one feed:

   a. After cutting the open link out of the harness, cut each of the remaining undamaged fuse links close to the feed wire weld.

   b. Strip approximately $1/2$ in. (13mm) of insulation from the detached ends of the two good fuse links, Then insert two wire ends into one end of a butt connector and carefully push one stripped end of the replacement fuse link into the same end of the butt connector and crimp all three firmly together.

NOTE: *Care must be taken when fitting the three fuse links into the butt connector as the internal diameter is a snug fit for three wires. Make sure to use a proper crimping tool. Pliers, side cutter, etc. will not apply the proper crimp to retain the wires and withstand a pull test.*

   c. After crimping the butt connector to the three fuse links, cut the weld portion from the feed wire and strip approximately $1/2$ in. (13mm) of insulation from the cut end. Insert the stripped end into the open end of the butt connector and crimp very firmly.

   d. To attach the remaining end of the replacement fuse link, strip approximately $1/2$ in. (13mm) of insulation from the wire end of the circuit from which the blown fuse link was removed, and firmly crimp a butt connector or equivalent to the stripped wire. Then, insert the end of the replacement link into the other end of the butt connector and crimp firmly.

   e. Using rosin core solder with a consistency of 60 percent tin and 40 percent lead, solder the connectors and the wires at the repairs and insulate with electrical tape.

6. To replace any fuse link on a single circuit in a harness, cut out the damaged portion, strip approximately $1/2$ in. (13mm) of insulation from the two wire ends and attach the appropriate replacement fuse link to the stripped wire ends with two proper size butt connectors. Solder the connectors and wires and insulate with tape.

7. To repair any fuse link which has an eyelet terminal on one end such as the charging circuit, cut off the open fuse link behind the weld, strip approximately $1/2$ in. (13mm) of insulation from the cut end and attach the appropriate new eyelet fuse link to the cut stripped wire with an appropriate size butt connector. Solder the connectors and wires at the repair and insulate with tape.

8. Connect the negative battery cable to the battery and test the system for proper operation.

NOTE: *Do not mistake a resistor wire for a fuse link. The resistor wire is generally longer and has print stating, "Resistor-don't cut or splice".*

When attaching a single No. 16, 17, 18 or 20 gauge fuse link to a heavy gauge wire, always double the stripped wire end of the fuse link before inserting and crimping it into the butt connector for positive wire retention.

Various Relays

Escort and Lynx

Air Conditioning Fan Controller — located on the right side of the dash, behind the glove box.

Cold Start Module (Carbureted with automatic transaxle) — located at the left rear corner of the engine compartment.

Cooling Fan Relay — located on the left hand side of the instrument panel.

Electronic Control Assembly (ECA) — located at the front of the console.

Electronic Engine Control (EEC) Power Relay — located at the left hand side of the instrument panel.

EFE Heater Relay — mounted on the left hand side fender apron.

Fuel Pump Relay — located at the left

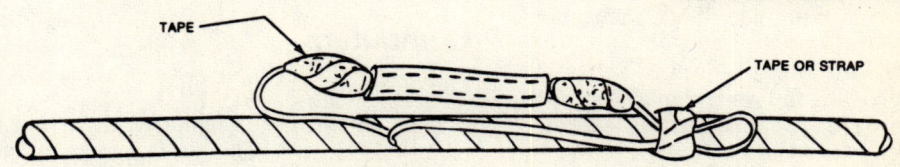

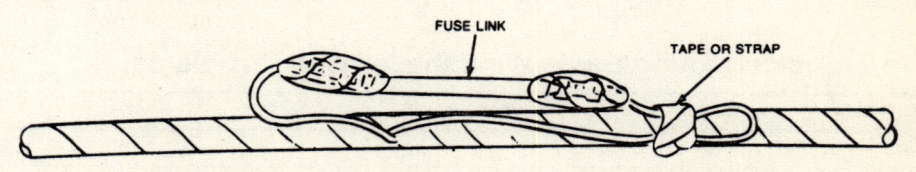

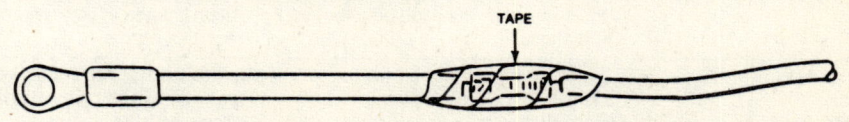

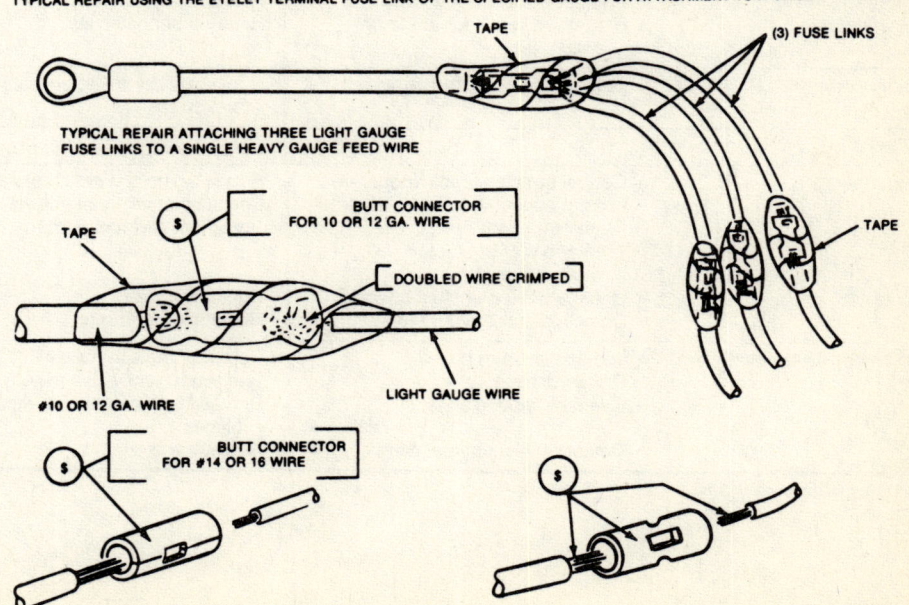

General fuse link repair procedures

CHASSIS ELECTRICAL

hand side of the instrument panel.
  Horn Relay —located behind the instrument panel on the left side of the radio.
  RPM Module —located behind the glove box.
  Starter Relay —located on the left hand side of the fender apron in front of the shock tower.

Tempo and Topaz

Cooling Fan Controller —located behind the left side of the instrument panel.
  Cooling Fan Controller Module —located behind the right side of the instrument panel.
  Cooling Fan Relay —located in the air conditioning cooling fan control module.
  Electronic Control Assembly —located under the left side of the instrument panel.
  Electronic Engine Control Power Relay —located behind the glove box on the right side of the instrument panel.
  Fuel Pump Relay —located behind the glove box.
  Horn Relay —located in the fuse block.
  Speed Sensor —located at the left rear side of the transaxle.
  Speed Control Servo —located on the left front shock tower.
  Speed Control Amplifier —located under the left side of the instrument panel.
  Starter Relay —located on the left front fender apron in front of the shock tower.

Computers

Location

The Electronic Engine Control (EEC) module is located behind left hand side of instrument panel.

Troubleshooting Basic Windshield Wiper Problems

Problem	Cause	Solution
Electric Wipers		
Wipers do not operate—Wiper motor heats up or hums	• Internal motor defect • Bent or damaged linkage • Arms improperly installed on linking pivots	• Replace motor • Repair or replace linkage • Position linkage in park and reinstall wiper arms
Wipers do not operate—No current to motor	• Fuse or circuit breaker blown • Loose, open or broken wiring • Defective switch • Defective or corroded terminals • No ground circuit for motor or switch	• Replace fuse or circuit breaker • Repair wiring and connections • Replace switch • Replace or clean terminals • Repair ground circuits
Wipers do not operate—Motor runs	• Linkage disconnected or broken	• Connect wiper linkage or replace broken linkage
Vacuum Wipers		
Wipers do not operate	• Control switch or cable inoperative • Loss of engine vacuum to wiper motor (broken hoses, low engine vacuum, defective vacuum/fuel pump) • Linkage broken or disconnected • Defective wiper motor	• Repair or replace switch or cable • Check vacuum lines, engine vacuum and fuel pump • Repair linkage • Replace wiper motor
Wipers stop on engine acceleration	• Leaking vacuum hoses • Dry windshield • Oversize wiper blades • Defective vacuum/fuel pump	• Repair or replace hoses • Wet windshield with washers • Replace with proper size wiper blades • Replace pump

Troubleshooting Basic Turn Signal and Flasher Problems

Most problems in the turn signals or flasher system can be reduced to defective flashers or bulbs, which are easily replaced. Occasionally, problems in the turn signals are traced to the switch in the steering column, which will require professional service.
F = Front   R = Rear   ● = Lights off   ○ = Lights on

Problem		Solution
Turn signals light, but do not flash		• Replace the flasher
No turn signals light on either side		• Check the fuse. Replace if defective. • Check the flasher by substitution • Check for open circuit, short circuit or poor ground
Both turn signals on one side don't work		• Check for bad bulbs • Check for bad ground in both housings
One turn signal light on one side doesn't work		• Check and/or replace bulb • Check for corrosion in socket. Clean contacts. • Check for poor ground at socket
Turn signal flashes too fast or too slow		• Check any bulb on the side flashing too fast. A heavy-duty bulb is probably installed in place of a regular bulb. • Check the bulb flashing too slow. A standard bulb was probably installed in place of a heavy-duty bulb. • Check for loose connections or corrosion at the bulb socket
Indicator lights don't work in either direction		• Check if the turn signals are working • Check the dash indicator lights • Check the flasher by substitution

One indicator light doesn't light		• On systems with 1 dash indicator: See if the lights work on the same side. Often the filaments have been reversed in systems combining stoplights with taillights and turn signals.
		   Check the flasher by substitution
		• On systems with 2 indicators: Check the bulbs on the same side
		   Check the indicator light bulb
		   Check the flasher by substitution

CHASSIS ELECTRICAL

Troubleshooting Basic Lighting Problems

Problem	Cause	Solution
Lights		
One or more lights don't work, but others do	• Defective bulb(s) • Blown fuse(s) • Dirty fuse clips or light sockets • Poor ground circuit	• Replace bulb(s) • Replace fuse(s) • Clean connections • Run ground wire from light socket housing to car frame
Lights burn out quickly	• Incorrect voltage regulator setting or defective regulator • Poor battery/alternator connections	• Replace voltage regulator • Check battery/alternator connections
Lights go dim	• Low/discharged battery • Alternator not charging • Corroded sockets or connections • Low voltage output	• Check battery • Check drive belt tension; repair or replace alternator • Clean bulb and socket contacts and connections • Replace voltage regulator
Lights flicker	• Loose connection • Poor ground • Circuit breaker operating (short circuit)	• Tighten all connections • Run ground wire from light housing to car frame • Check connections and look for bare wires
Lights "flare"—Some flare is normal on acceleration—if excessive, see "Lights Burn Out Quickly"	• High voltage setting	• Replace voltage regulator
Lights glare—approaching drivers are blinded	• Lights adjusted too high • Rear springs or shocks sagging • Rear tires soft	• Have headlights aimed • Check rear springs/shocks • Check/correct rear tire pressure
Turn Signals		
Turn signals don't work in either direction	• Blown fuse • Defective flasher • Loose connection	• Replace fuse • Replace flasher • Check/tighten all connections
Right (or left) turn signal only won't work	• Bulb burned out • Right (or left) indicator bulb burned out • Short circuit	• Replace bulb • Check/replace indicator bulb • Check/repair wiring
Flasher rate too slow or too fast	• Incorrect wattage bulb • Incorrect flasher	• Flasher bulb • Replace flasher (use a variable load flasher if you pull a trailer)
Indicator lights do not flash (burn steadily)	• Burned out bulb • Defective flasher	• Replace bulb • Replace flasher
Indicator lights do not light at all	• Burned out indicator bulb • Defective flasher	• Replace indicator bulb • Replace flasher

Troubleshooting Basic Dash Gauge Problems

Problem	Cause	Solution
Coolant Temperature Gauge		
Gauge reads erratically or not at all	• Loose or dirty connections • Defective sending unit • Defective gauge	• Clean/tighten connections • Bi-metal gauge: remove the wire from the sending unit. Ground the wire for an instant. If the gauge registers, replace the sending unit. • Magnetic gauge: disconnect the wire at the sending unit. With ignition ON gauge should register COLD. Ground the wire; gauge should register HOT.
Ammeter Gauge—Turn Headlights ON (do not start engine). Note reaction		
Ammeter shows charge Ammeter shows discharge Ammeter does not move	• Connections reversed on gauge • Ammeter is OK • Loose connections or faulty wiring • Defective gauge	• Reinstall connections • Nothing • Check/correct wiring • Replace gauge
Oil Pressure Gauge		
Gauge does not register or is inaccurate	• On mechanical gauge, Bourdon tube may be bent or kinked • Low oil pressure • Defective gauge • Defective wiring • Defective sending unit	• Check tube for kinks or bends preventing oil from reaching the gauge • Remove sending unit. Idle the engine briefly. If no oil flows from sending unit hole, problem is in engine. • Remove the wire from the sending unit and ground it for an instant with the ignition ON. A good gauge will go to the top of the scale. • Check the wiring to the gauge. If it's OK and the gauge doesn't register when grounded, replace the gauge. • If the wiring is OK and the gauge functions when grounded, replace the sending unit
All Gauges		
All gauges do not operate All gauges read low or erratically All gauges pegged	• Blown fuse • Defective instrument regulator • Defective or dirty instrument voltage regulator • Loss of ground between instrument voltage regulator and car • Defective instrument regulator	• Replace fuse • Replace instrument voltage regulator • Clean contacts or replace • Check ground • Replace regulator
Warning Lights		
Light(s) do not come on when ignition is ON, but engine is not started Light comes on with engine running	• Defective bulb • Defective wire • Defective sending unit • Problem in individual system • Defective sending unit	• Replace bulb • Check wire from light to sending unit • Disconnect the wire from the sending unit and ground it. Replace the sending unit if the light comes on with the ignition ON. • Check system • Check sending unit (see above)

CHASSIS ELECTRICAL

Troubleshooting the Heater

Problem	Cause	Solution
Blower motor will not turn at any speed	• Blown fuse • Loose connection • Defective ground • Faulty switch • Faulty motor • Faulty resistor	• Replace fuse • Inspect and tighten • Clean and tighten • Replace switch • Replace motor • Replace resistor
Blower motor turns at one speed only	• Faulty switch • Faulty resistor	• Replace switch • Replace resistor
Blower motor turns but does not circulate air	• Intake blocked • Fan not secured to the motor shaft	• Clean intake • Tighten security
Heater will not heat	• Coolant does not reach proper temperature • Heater core blocked internally • Heater core air-bound • Blend-air door not in proper position	• Check and replace thermostat if necessary • Flush or replace core if necessary • Purge air from core • Adjust cable
Heater will not defrost	• Control cable adjustment incorrect • Defroster hose damaged	• Adjust control cable • Replace defroster hose

Drive Train

7

TRANSAXLE

Your car uses a front wheel drive transmission called a transaxle. The transaxle may either be manual or automatic.

A 4- or 5-speed fully synchronized manual transaxle is available, depending on year and model. An internally gated shift mechanism and a single rail shift linkage eliminate the need for periodic shift linkage adjustments. The MT is designed to use Dexron®II automatic transmission fluid as a lubricant. Never use gear oil (GL) in the place of Dexron®II.

The automatic transaxle (AT) is a 3-speed unit. A unique feature is a patented split path torque converter. The engine torque in second and third gears is divided, so that part of the engine torque is transmitted hydrokinetically through the torque converter, and part if transmitted mechanically by direct connection of the engine and transaxle. In the third gear, 93% of the torque is transmitted mechanically, making the AT highly efficient. Torque splitting is accomplished through a splitter gear set. A conventional compound gear set is also used.

Only one band is used in the AT. No periodic adjustments are required. No fluid changes are ever necessary in normal service. In service fluid additions or severe condition fluid changes may be made with Dexron®II or Dexron®II Series D fluid.

NOTE: *Refer to Chapter 1 for the Transaxle Identification Code Chart.*

MANUAL TRANSAXLE

Application

The MTX 4- and 5-speed transaxles have been used since 1981 with the 5-speed coming out in the later years. The 4-speed manual transaxle is similar in construction to the 5-speed manual transaxle except for the deletion of a 5th gear driveshaft assembly and a 5th gear shift fork assembly. Although similar in appearance, the gear set of the 4-speed transaxle cannot interchange with those of the 5-speed transaxle.

Metric Fasteners

The metric fastener dimensions are very close to the dimensions of the familiar inch system fasteners, and for this reason, replacement fasteners must have the same measurement and strength as those removed.

CAUTION: *Do not attempt to interchange metric fasteners for inch system fasteners. Mismatched or incorrect fasteners can result in damage to the transaxle unit through malfunctions or breakage and possible personal injury.*

Capacities

The 4- and 5-speed transaxles use Dexron®II automatic transmission fluid. The capacity of the 4- and 5-speed transaxles is 6.1 pints or 2.9L. The correct fluid level is to the bottom of the filler hole.

Checking Fluid Level

The transaxle fluid level check must be made with the vehicle level and the engine must not be running. The fluid level can be checked by removing the fill plug. The correct fluid fill will be even with the bottom edge of the filler plug opening or within 1/4 inch (6mm) of this level. If fluid is low, added the specified fluid to correct level.

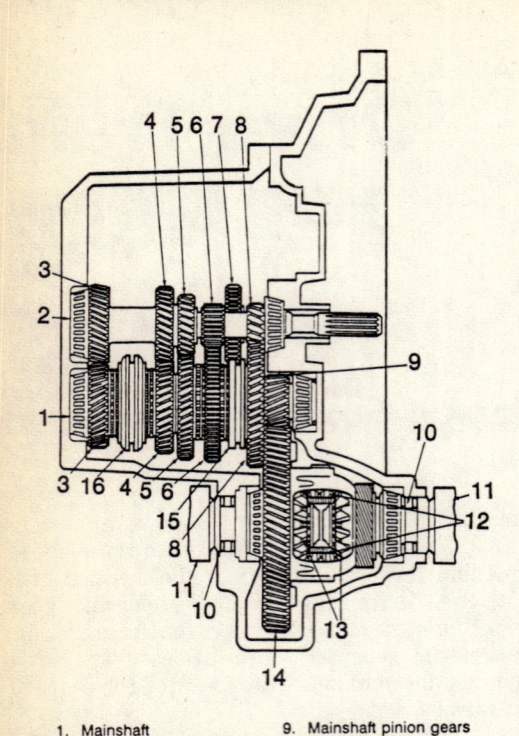

DRIVE TRAIN

Inside view of the 4-speed transaxle components

1. Mainshaft
2. Input cluster gear shaft
3. 4th speed gears
4. 3rd speed gears
5. 2nd speed gears
6. Reverse gears
7. Reverse idler gear
8. 1st speed gears
9. Mainshaft pinion gears
10. Differential oil seals
11. CV shafts
12. Differential pinion gears
13. Differential side gears
14. Final drive gear
15. 1st/2nd synchronizer
16. 3rd/4th synchronizer

Inside view of the 5-speed transaxle components

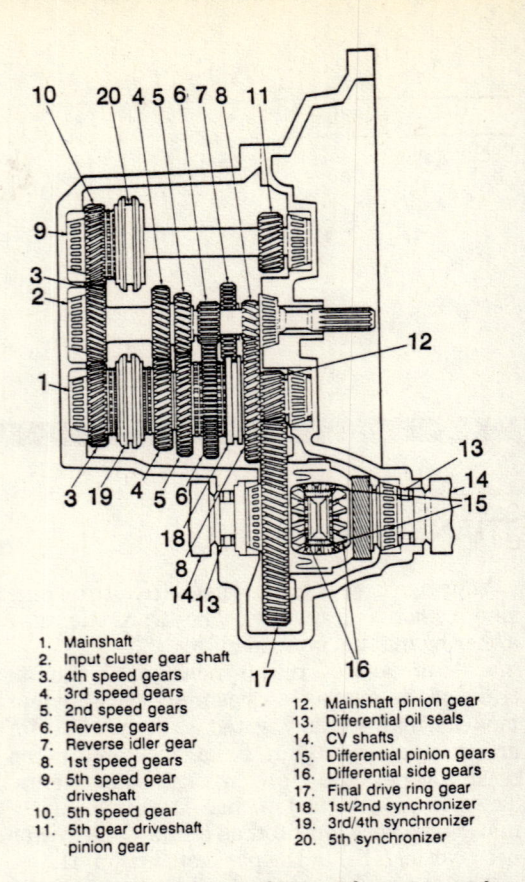

1. Mainshaft
2. Input cluster gear shaft
3. 4th speed gears
4. 3rd speed gears
5. 2nd speed gears
6. Reverse gears
7. Reverse idler gear
8. 1st speed gears
9. 5th speed gear driveshaft
10. 5th speed gear
11. 5th gear driveshaft pinion gear
12. Mainshaft pinion gear
13. Differential oil seals
14. CV shafts
15. Differential pinion gears
16. Differential side gears
17. Final drive ring gear
18. 1st/2nd synchronizer
19. 3rd/4th synchronizer
20. 5th synchronizer

Transaxle Modifications

MANUAL TRANSAXLE JUMPS OUT OF 2ND OR 4TH GEAR

Determine whether vehicle was manufactured between March 1, 1985 and February 3, 1986. If it was, make sure that the shift lever boot is seated in the top spring of the console.

1. If the transaxle is a 4-speed unit, inspect the paddle that operated the upshift light top gear switch. Bend the paddle so the switch can be depressed 4mm (0.16 in.).
2. Lift and safely support the engine just enough to relieve tension on the engine mounts. Then loosen the front and rear mounts and the rear shifter to body mounts.
3. Position the engine as far forward as the slots in the mounts allow. The mounts should then be tightened.
4. Remove the transaxle detent plunger retainer screw and install a differently designed transaxle detent plunger and spring assembly (part number E6FZ-7233-A). Coat the threads of the assembly with a sealant that contains Teflon. The assembly should be tightened to 66-96 inch lbs.
5. Check the transaxle fluid level and replenish the fluid, if necessary. If vehicle is equipped with the 2L diesel engine, the shift boot assembly should also be replaced with part number E6FZ-7277-B.

Power Flow

4-SPEED TRANSAXLE

From the clutch, engine torque is transferred to the mainshaft through the input cluster gear. Each gear on the input cluster is in constant mesh with a matching gear on the mainshaft. It is these matching gear sets which will provide the 4 forward gear ratios. The transaxle gear ratio is determined by the number of teeth on the input cluster gear and the number of teeth on the mainshaft gear.

Reverse is accomplished by sliding a spur gear into mesh with the input cluster shaft gear and the reverse idler gear. The reverse idler gear acts as an idler and reverses the direction of mainshaft rotation. In neutral, none of the gears on the mainshaft are locked to their shafts. Then, no torque from the engine to the input cluster gear shaft is transferred to the differential assembly and to the wheels through the halfshafts.

DRIVE TRAIN

CHILTON'S THREE C's TRANSAXLE DIAGNOSIS

Condition	Cause	Correction
Clicking noise in reverse gear	a) Damaged or rough gears b) Damaged linkage preventing complete gear travel	a) Replace damaged gears b) Check for damaged or misaligned shift linkage or other causes of shift linkage travel restrictions
Gear clash into reverse	a) Owner not familiar with manual transmission shift techniques b) Damaged linkage preventing complete gear travel	a) Instruct customer on non-synchronous reverse and clutch spin-time-lapse required before a shift into reverse b) Check for damaged or misaligned shift linkage or other causes of shift linkage bind
Gears clash when shifting from one forward gear to another	a) Improper clutch disengagement b) Clutch disc installed improperly with damper springs towards flywheel c) Worn or damaged shift forks, synchroteeth (usually high mileage phenomenon). Forward gears only	a) Check clutch system and adjustment b) Check clutch system c) Check for damage, and service or replace as required
Leaks	a) Excessive amount of lubricant in transaxle—wrong type b) Worn or damaged internal components c) Slight mist from vent	a) Check lube level and type. Fill to bottom of filler plug opening b) Remove transaxle clutch housing lower dust cover and inspect for lube inside housing. Inspect for leaks at the shift lever shaft seal, differential seals and input shift shaft seal. Service as required. c) Normal condition that does not require service. If dripping, check lubricant level
Locked in one gear—it cannot be shifted out of that gear	a) Damaged external shift mechanism b) Internal shift components worn or damaged c) Synchronizer damaged by burrs which prevent sliding action	a) Check external shift mechanism for damage. Service or replace as required b) Disconnect external shift mechanism and verify problem by trying to shift input shift rail. Remove transaxle. Inspect the problem gear, shift rails, and fork and synchronizer assemblies for wear or damage. Service or replace as required c) Replace synchronizer assembly
Noise in Neutral	a) Neutral rollover rattle	a) Normal condition exists

DRIVE TRAIN

CHILTON'S THREE C's TRANSAXLE DIAGNOSIS

Condition	Cause	Correction
Noisy in forward gears	a) Low lubricant level	a) Fill to bottom of filler plug opening with proper lubricant
	b) Contact between engine/transaxle and chassis	b) Check for contact or for broken engine motor mounts
	c) Transaxle to engine block bolts loose	c) Tighten to specification
	d) Worn or damaged input/output bearings. Worn or damaged gear teeth (usually high mileage phenomenon)	d) Remove transaxle. Inspect bearings and gear teeth for wear or damage. Replace parts as required.
	e) Gear rattle	e) Normal condition exists
Shifts hard	a) Improper clutch disengagement	a) Check clutch system and adjustment
	b) External shift mechanism binding	b) Check shift mechanism
	c) Clutch disc installed improperly with damper springs toward flywheel	c) Check clutch system
	d) Internal damage to synchronizers or shift mechanism	d) Check for damage to internal components
	e) Incorrect lubricant or sticking blocker ring	e) Verify that ATF type lube is present. Do not use gear lube or hypoid type lubricants
Walks out of gear	a) Damaged linkage preventing complete travel into gear	a) Check for damaged shift mechanism
	b) Floor shift stiff or improperly installed boot	b) Verify jumpout with boot removed, replace boot if necessary
	c) Floor shift interference between shift handle and console	c) Adjust console to eliminate interference
	d) Broken or loose engine mounts	d) Check for broken or loose engine mounts and service as required
	e) Loose shift mechanism stabilizer bar	e) Check stabilizer bar attaching bolt and torque to specification
	f) Worn or damaged internal components	f) Check shift forks, shift rails and shift rail detent system for wear or damage, synchronizer sliding sleeve and gear clutching teeth for wear or damage. Repair or replace as required
	g) Bent top gear locknut switch actuator	g) With shift lever in fourth gear, check actuator position with shift rod. Actuator should be positioned at a 90 degree angle to shift rod. Bend actuator to proper position, if required

5-SPEED TRANSAXLE

Engine torque is transferred from the clutch to the input cluster gear shaft. The 4 forward gears on the input cluster gear shaft are in constant mesh with a matching gear on the mainshaft. The 4th gear on the input cluster gear shaft is simultaneously meshed with the 5th speed gear on the 5th gear shaft. These meshed gearsets provide the 5 available forward gear ratios.

Both the mainshaft and the 5th gear shaft have a pinion gear, which is constantly engaged

DRIVE TRAIN 411

with the final drive ring gear of the differential assembly. If a single gear (1st through 4th) on the mainshaft is selected and that gear is locked to the shaft by its shift synchronizer, then the input cluster shaft gear will drive the mainshaft pinion gear; driving the differential final drive ring gear. If the 5th gear is selected, the input cluster shaft 4th gear will drive the 5th gear shaft pinion gear, driving the differential final drive ring gear. At this time, the mainshaft gears will rotate freely.

Reverse is accomplished by sliding a spur gear into mesh with the input cluster shaft gear and the reverse idler gear. The reverse idler gear acts as an idler and reverses the direction of mainshaft rotation.

Adjustments

SHIFT LINKAGE

The external gear shift mechanism consists of a gear shift lever, transaxle shift rod, stabilizer rod and shift housing. Adjustment of the external linkage is not necessary.

CLUTCH SWITCH

1. Remove panel above clutch pedal on the Tempo, Topaz vehicles.
2. Disengage the wiring connector by flexing the retaining tab on the switch and withdrawing the connector.
3. Using a test light, check to see that the switch is open with the clutch pedal up (engaged) and closed at approximately 1 in. (25mm) from the clutch pedal full down position (disengaged).
4. If the switch does not operate as outlined in Step 3, check to see if the self-adjusting clip is out of position on the rod. It should be near the end of the rod.
5. If the self-adjusting clip is out of position, remove and reposition the clip approximately 1 in. (25mm) from the end of the rod.
6. Reset the switch by pressing the clutch pedal to the floor. Repeat Step 3. If the switch is damaged or the clips do not remain in place replace the switch.

REMOVAL AND INSTALLATION

1. Disconnect the negative battery cable.
2. Remove panel above clutch pedal, if equipped.
3. Disconnect the switch wiring connector.
4. Remove clutch interlock attaching screw and hairpin clip and remove switch.

NOTE: *Always install the switch with the self-adjusting clip about 1 in. (25mm) from the end of the rod. The clutch pedal must be fully up (clutch engaged). Otherwise, the switch may be misadjusted.*

To install:

5. Insert eyelet end of rod over clutch pedal pin and secure with hairpin clip.
6. Swing switch around to line up hole in mounting boss with corresponding hole in bracket. Attach with screw.
7. Reset clutch interlock switch by pressing clutch pedal to floor.
8. Connect wiring connector.
9. Install the panel above the clutch, if equipped.
10. Connect negative battery cable.

Back-Up Light Switch

REMOVAL AND INSTALLATION

1. Disconnect the electrical connector from the back-up switch.
2. Place the transaxle in reverse.
3. Using a suitable wrench, remove the back-up light switch.
4. Installation is the reverse of the removal procedure. To prevent internal damage do not shift the transaxle until the switch has been installed.

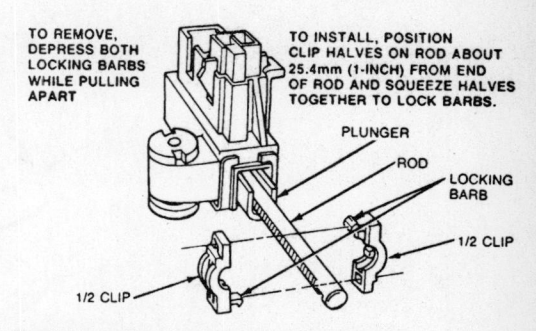

Typical starter/clutch interlock switch

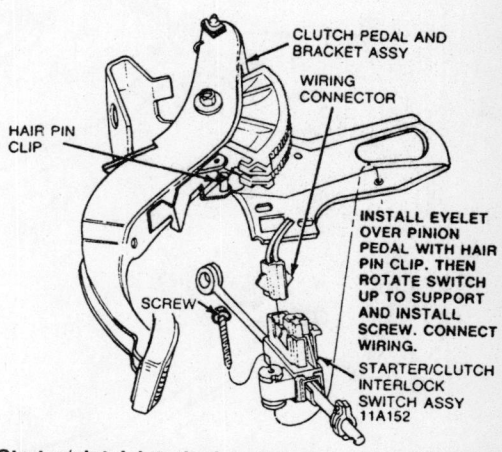

Starter/clutch interlock switch removal and installation

412 DRIVE TRAIN

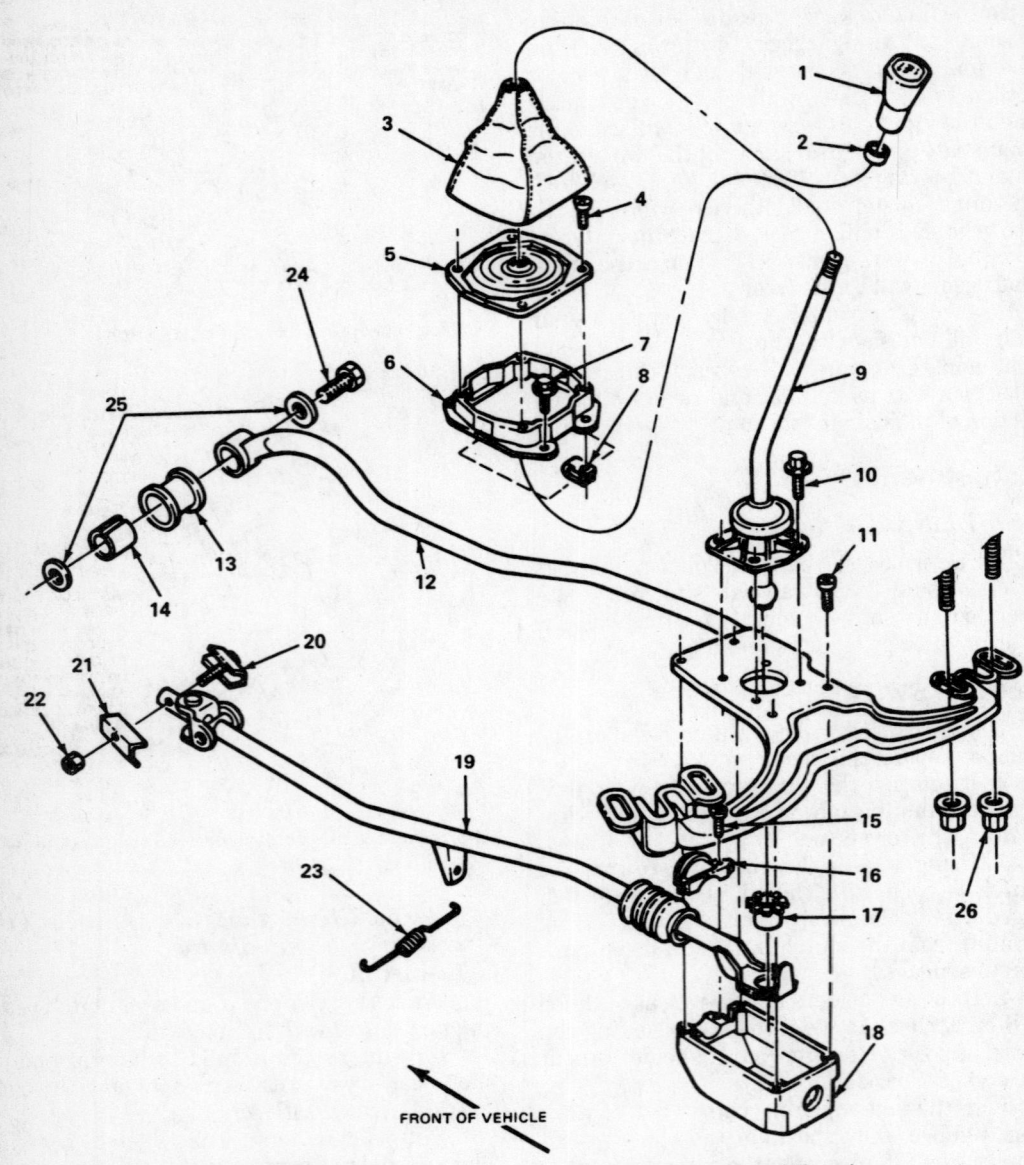

FRONT OF VEHICLE

1. Knob—gear shift lever
2. Nut—shift knob locking
3. Upper boot assembly—gear shift lever
4. Screw—tapping (4 required)
5. Lower boot assembly—gear shift lever
6. Boot retainer assembly—gear shift lever
7. Bolt—boot retainer (4 required)
8. Nut—spring (4 required)
9. Lever assembly—gearshift
10. Bolt—tapping (4 required)
11. Screw—tapping (4 required)
12. Support assembly (shift stabilizer bar)
13. Bushing—gear shift stabilizer bar
14. Sleeve—gear shift rod
15. Screw—tapping (2 required)
16. Cover—control selector
17. Bushing—anti tizz
18. Housing—control selector
19. Assembly—shift rod and clevis
20. Assembly—clamp
21. Clamp—gear shift lever (2 required)
22. Nut—clamp assembly
23. Retaining spring—gear shift tube
24. Bolt—stabilizer bar attaching
25. Washer—flat (2 required)
26. Assembly—nut/washer (4 required)

Components of a typical manual shift linkage

Bearing Cups and Preload Shims

REMOVAL AND INSTALLATION

The input cluster shaft, the mainshaft and the 5th gear driveshaft are supported at each end by tapered roller bearings. The cups, which support the bearings in the case, are located in the transaxle case and in the clutch housing. Shims, to preload the tapered roller bearings are located behind the bearing cups in the transaxle case only. It is important to keep the shim with its matching cup during the disassembly. It is equally important to label the bearing cups if they are removed from the case. After removal of the mainshaft bearing cups from the clutch housing, the funnels can be removed from the bearing cup bores. The funnels direct lubricant to a drilled hole in the center of the mainshaft. The lubricant flows through these shafts, where it lubricates the rotating gears.

A replacement bearing preload shim should be installed in place of the original shim when servicing any components listed in the Service Shim chart. Do not use more than 1 shim per shaft. If any parts are replaced other than the parts listed in the Service Shim chart, use the original shims.

1. Gently tap the bearing cup out of the transaxle case or the clutch housing, using a suitable tool.
2. Keep the bearing cup and shim in correct order.
3. Thoroughly clean the bearing cups, bores, shims and funnels.
4. Lightly grease the bearing cup lip.
5. Install bearing cup in the transaxle case

TRANSAXLE SERVICE SHIM—5 SPEED

Parts Replaced	Input Cluster Shaft	Main Shaft	5th Gear Shaft
1 Input Cluster Bearing	Yes	No	No
2 Input Cluster Bearings	Yes	No	No
1 Input Cluster Bearing 1 Mainshaft Bearing 1 5th Gear Shaft Bearing	Yes	Yes	Yes
2 Input Cluster Bearings 2 Mainshaft Bearings 2 5th Gear Shaft Bearings	Yes	Yes	Yes
1 Mainshaft Bearing	No	Yes	No
2 Mainshaft Bearings	No	Yes	No
1 5th Gear Shaft Bearing	No	No	Yes
2 5th Gear Shaft Bearings	No	No	Yes
Clutch Housing Assembly	Yes	Yes	Yes
Transaxle Case Assembly	Yes	Yes	Yes

NOTE: The shims must be installed only under the bearing cups at the transaxle case end of the three shafts.
NOTE: The use of a nominal thickness service shim eliminates the need for gauging bearing clearances prior to reassembly. While this method produces wider variations of bearing settings than are present in factory assembled units, the extreme possible settings have been tested and found to be acceptable.

TRANSAXLE SERVICE SHIM—4 SPEED

Parts Replaced	Input Cluster Shaft	Main Shaft	5th Gear Shaft
1 Input Cluster Bearing	Yes	No	No
2 Input Cluster Bearings	Yes	No	No
1 Input Cluster Bearing 1 Mainshaft Bearing	Yes	Yes	Yes
2 Input Cluster Bearings 2 Mainshaft Bearings	Yes	Yes	Yes
1 Mainshaft Bearing	No	Yes	No
2 Mainshaft Bearings	No	Yes	No
Clutch Housing Assembly	Yes	Yes	Yes
Transaxle Case Assembly	Yes	Yes	Yes

NOTE: The shims must be installed only under the bearing cups at the transaxle case end of the three shafts.
NOTE: The use of a nominal thickness service shim eliminates the need for gauging bearing clearances prior to reassembly. While this method produces wider variations of bearing settings than are present in factory assembled units, the extreme possible settings have been tested and found to be acceptable.

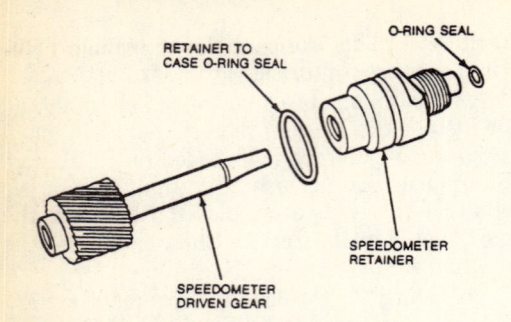

Speedometer gear assembly

or clutch housing. Tap bearing cup in with suitable tool until lip is flush with case or housing.

Speedometer Driven Gear
REMOVAL AND INSTALLATION

1. Using a 7mm socket or equivalent, remove the retaining screw from the speedometer driven gear retainer assembly.
2. Using a tool, carefully pry on the speedometer retainer to remove both the speedometer gear and retainer assembly from the clutch housing case bore. Be careful not to make contact with teeth on the speedometer gear.
3. Lightly grease the O-ring seal on the speedometer driven gear retainer.
4. Align the relief in the retainer with the attaching screw bore and using a tool, tap the assembly into its bore.
5. Tighten the retaining screw to 12–24 inch lbs.

Manual Transaxle
REMOVAL AND INSTALLATION
1981–85 Escort/Lynx/EXP

1. Disconnect the negative battery terminal.
2. Remove the two transaxle to engine top mounting bolts.
3. Remove the clutch cable from the clutch release lever, after wedging a wood block about 7 in. (178mm) long under the clutch pedal to hold it slightly beyond its normal position.
4. Raise the vehicle and support it on jackstands.
5. Remove the brake line routing clamps from the front wheels.
6. Remove the bolt that secures the lower control arm ball joint to the steering knuckle assembly, and pry the lower control arm away from the knuckle. When installing, a new nut and bolt must be used.
    NOTE: *The plastic shield installed behind the rotor contains a molded pocket for the lower control arm ball joint. When removing the control arm from the knuckle, bend the shield toward the rotor to provide clearance.*
7. Pry the right inboard CV-joint from the transaxle, then remove the CV-joint and halfshaft by pulling outward on the steering knuckle. Wire the CV-joint/halfshaft assembly in a level position to prevent it from expanding.
    NOTE: *When the CV-joint is pulled out of the transaxle fluid will leak out. Install shipping plugs T81P-1177-B or the equivalent to prevent the dislocation of the of the differential side gears.*
8. Repeat the procedures and remove the left hand CV-joint/halfshaft from the transaxle.
9. Remove the stabilizer bar.
10. Disconnect the speedometer cable and back-up light.
11. Remove the (3) nuts from the starter mounting studs which hold the engine roll restrictor bracket.
12. Remove the roll restrictor and the starter stud bolts.
13. Remove the stiffener brace.
14. Remove the shift mechanism crossover spring.
15. Remove the shift mechanism stabilizer bar.
16. Remove the shift mechanism.
17. Place a transmission jack under the transaxle.
18. Remove the rear transmission mounts.
19. Remove the front transmission mounts.
20. Lower the transaxle support jack until it clears the rear mount and support the engine with a jack, under the oil pan.
21. Remove the 4 remaining engine to transaxle bolts.
22. Remove the transaxle assembly. The case may have sharp edges. Wear protective gloves when handling the transaxle.
23. To install, install the transaxle and leave it on the transmission jack.
24. Install the four engine to transaxle bolts.
25. Install the front transmission mounts.
26. Install the rear transmission mounts.
27. Remove the transmission jack from under the transaxle.
28. Install the shift mechanism.
29. Install the shift mechanism stabilizer bar.
30. Install the shift mechanism crossover spring.
31. Install the stiffener brace.
32. Install the roll restrictor and the starter stud bolts.
33. Install the (3) nuts to the starter mounting studs which hold the engine roll restrictor bracket.
34. Reconnect the speedometer cable and back-up light.

35. Install the stabilizer bar.
36. Install the left and right CV-joint/halfshafts to the transaxle.

NOTE: *When installing the CV-joint/halfshaft assemblies into the transaxle, install new circlips on the inner stub shaft, carefully install the assemblies into the transaxle to prevent damaging the oil seals, and insure that both joints are fully seated in the transaxle by lightly prying outward to confirm they are seated. If the circlips are not seated, the joints will move out of the transaxle.*

37. Install the bolt that secures the lower control arm ball joint to the steering knuckle assembly. When installing, a new nut and bolt must be used.
38. Remove the brake line routing clamps from the front wheels.
39. Adjust the clutch. Lower the vehicle and remove the jackstands.
40. Install the two transaxle to engine top mounting bolts.
41. Reconnect the negative battery terminal.

1986–90 Escort/Lynx and All Tempo/Topaz Models

1. Disconnect the negative battery cable. Wedge a 7 in. (178mm) wooden block under the clutch pedal to hold the pedal up slightly beyond its normal position. Grasp the clutch cable, pull it forward and disconnect it from the clutch release shaft assembly. Remove the clutch casing from the rib on the top surface of the transaxle case.
2. Remove the upper 2 transaxle-to-engine bolts. Remove the air cleaner, if necessary, and the air management valve bracket-to-transaxle upper bolt, if equipped.
3. Raise and safely support the vehicle.
4. If equipped with a 5-speed, remove the front stabilizer bar-to-control arm nut and washer, on the driver's side and discard the nut. Remove both front stabilizer bar mounting brackets and discard the bolts.
5. Remove the lower control arm ball joint-to-steering knuckle nut/bolt and discard the nut/bolt; repeat this procedure on the opposite side.
6. Using a large pry bar, pry the lower control arm from the steering knuckle; repeat this procedure on the opposite side.

NOTE: *Be careful not to damage or cut the ball joint boot and do not contact the lower arm.*

7. Using a large pry bar, pry the left-side inboard CV-joint assembly from the transaxle.

NOTE: *Plug the seal opening to prevent lubricant leakage.*

8. Grasp the left-hand steering knuckle and swing it and the halfshaft outward from the transaxle; this will disconnect the inboard CV-joint from the transaxle.

NOTE: *If the CV-joint assembly cannot be pried from the transaxle, insert a differential rotator tool through the left-side and tap the joint out; the tool can be used from either side of transaxle.*

9. Using a wire, support the halfshaft in a near level position to prevent damage to the assembly during the remaining operations; repeat this procedure on the opposite side.
10. Disengage the locking tabs and remove the backup lamp switch connector from the transaxle backup lamp switch.
11. If equipped with a 5-speed, remove the starter studs-to-engine roll restrictor bracket nuts and the engine roll restrictor. Remove the starter stud bolts.
12. If equipped with a 4-speed, remove the starter bolts and the starter.
13. Remove the shift mechanism-to-shift shaft nut/bolt, the control selector indicator switch arm and the shift shaft.
14. Remove the shift mechanism stabilizer bar-to-transaxle bolt, control selector indicator switch and bracket assembly.
15. Using a crowsfoot wrench, remove the speedometer cable from the transaxle.
16. Remove both oil pan-to-clutch housing bolts.
17. Using a floor jack and a transaxle support, position it under the transaxle and secure the transaxle to it.
18. If equipped with a 5-speed, remove the both left-hand rear No. 4 insulator-to-body bracket nuts and the left-hand front No.1 insulator-to-body bracket bolts.
19. If equipped with a 4-speed, remove both rear mount-to-floor pan bolts, loosen the nut at the bottom of the front mount and remove the front mount-to-transaxle bolts.
20. Lower the floor jack, until the transaxle

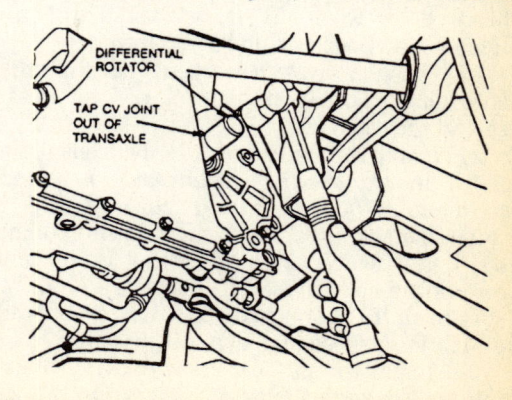

Removing the halfshaft from the transaxle using special tool

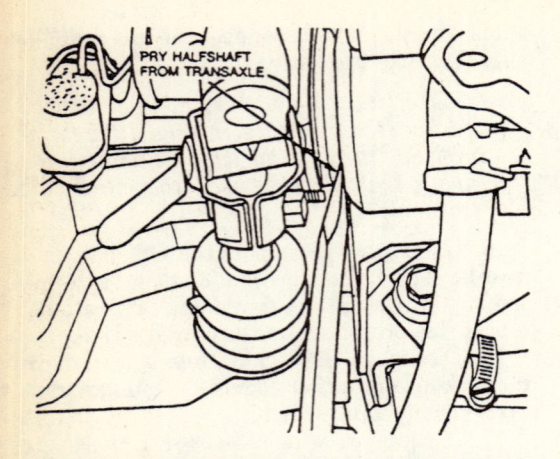

Removing the halfshaft from the transaxle using a suitable prybar

clears the rear insulator. Support the engine by placing wood under the oil pan.

21. Remove the engine-to-transaxle bolts and lower the transaxle from the vehicle.

NOTE: *One of the engine-to-transaxle bolts attaches the ground strap and wiring loom stand off bracket.*

To install:

22. Raise the transaxle into position and engage the input shaft with the clutch plate. Install the lower engine-to-transaxle bolts and torque to 28–31 ft. lbs. (38–42 Nm).

NOTE: *Never attempt to start the engine prior to installing the CV-joints or differential side gear for dislocation and/or damage may occur.*

23. Install the front mount-to-transaxle bolts and torque to 25–35 ft. lbs. (34–47 Nm); also, tighten the nut on the bottom of the front transaxle mount.

24. Install the air management valve-to-transaxle upper bolt, finger-tight and the bottom bracket bolt to 28–31 ft. lbs. (38–42 Nm).

25. Install both rear mount-to-floor pan brace bolts to 40–51 ft. lbs. (55–70 Nm). Remove the floor jack and adapter.

26. Using a crowsfoot wrench, install the speedometer cable; be careful not to cross-thread the cable nut.

27. Install the shifter stabilizer bar/control selector indicator switch-to-transaxle bolt and torque to 23–35 ft. lbs. (31–47 Nm).

28. Install the shift mechanism-to-shift shaft, the switch actuator bracket clamp and torque the bolt to 7–10 ft. lbs. (9–13 Nm); be sure to shift the transaxle into **4th** for 4-speed or **5th** for 5-speed and align the actuator.

29. Install the stiffener brace-to-clutch housing and torque the bolts to 15–21 ft. lbs. (21–28 Nm). Install the starter-to-engine and torque the bolts to 30–40 ft. lbs. (41–54 Nm).

30. Install the backup light switch connector to the transaxle switch.

31. Install the new circlip onto both inner joints of the halfshafts, insert the inner CV-joints into the transaxle and fully seat them; lightly, pry outward to confirm that the retaining rings are seated.

NOTE: *When installing the halfshafts, be careful not to tear the oil seals.*

32. Connect the lower ball joint to the steering knuckle, insert a new pinch bolt and torque the new nut to 37–44 ft. lbs.; be careful not to damage the boot.

33. Refill the transaxle and lower the vehicle.

34. Install the upper air management valve bracket-to-transaxle bolt and torque to 28–31 ft. lbs. (38–42 Nm).

35. Install the both upper transaxle-to-engine bolts and torque to 28–31 ft. lbs. (38–42 Nm).

36. Connect the clutch cable to the clutch release shaft assembly and remove the wooden block from under the clutch pedal. Connect the negative battery cable.

NOTE: *Prior to starting the engine, set the hand brake and pump the clutch pedal several times to ensure proper clutch adjustment.*

Transaxle Overhaul
BEFORE DISASSEMBLY

When servicing the unit, it is recommended that as each part is disassembled, it is cleaned in solvent and dried with compressed air. Disassembly and reassembly of this unit and its parts must be done on a clean work bench. Also, before installing bolts into aluminum parts, always dip the threads into clean transmission oil. Anti-seize compound can also be used to prevent bolts from galling the aluminum and seizing. Always use a torque wrench to keep from stripping the threads. Take care with the seals when installing them, especially the smaller O-rings. The slightest damage can cause leaks. Aluminum parts are very susceptible to damage so great care should be exercised when handling them. The internal snaprings should be expanded and the external snaprings compressed if they are to be reused. This will help insure proper seating when installed. Be sure to replace any O-ring, gasket, or seal that is removed.

TRANSAXLE DISASSEMBLY

1. Shift the transaxle into neutral using a drift in the input shaft hole. Pull or push the shaft into the center detent position.
2. Remove the 2 transaxle plugs T81P-

DRIVE TRAIN

1177–B or equivalent from the transaxle and drain the fluid.

NOTE: *Place the transaxle on a bench with the clutch housing facing down to facilitate draining and service.*

3. Remove the reverse idler shaft retaining bolt.
4. Remove the detent plunger retaining screw. Then using a magnet, remove the detent spring and the detent plunger.

NOTE: *Label these parts, as they appear similar to the input shift shaft plunger and spring contained in the clutch case.*

5. Remove the shift fork interlock sleeve retaining pin and fill plug.
6. Remove the clutch housing to transaxle case attaching bolts.
7. Tap the transaxle case with a plastic tipped hammer to break the seal between the case halves. Separate the halves.

NOTE: *Do not insert pry bars between case halves. Be careful not to drop out the tapered roller bearing cups or shims from the transaxle case housing.*

8. Remove the detent plunger retaining screw. Then, using a pencil magnet or equivalent, remove the detent spring and the detent plunger.
9. Remove the case magnet.
10. Using a small tool, remove the C-clip re-

1. 2nd speed gear
2. Synchronizer blocking ring
3. Synchronizer spring
4. 1st/2nd synchronizer assy.
5. Synchronizer hub 1st/2nd insert
6. Input shaft seal
7. Input shaft bearing
8. Input cluster shaft
9. Input shaft seal
10. Mainshaft funnel
11. Mainshaft
12. 1st speed gear
13. 2nd/3rd gear thrust washer retaining ring
14. 2nd/3rd gear thrust washer
15. 3rd speed gear
16. 4th speed gear
17. 3rd/4th fork
18. Fork selector arm
19. Fork interlock sleeve
20. 1st/2nd fork
21. Main shift shaft
22. Reverse idler shaft
23. Reverse idler gear
24. Reverse relay lever
25. Reverse relay lever pivot pin
26. Back-up lamp switch
27. Dowel
28. Shift lever shaft
29. Pinion shaft
30. Pinion thrust washer
31. Side gear
32. Side gear thrust washer
33. Shim
34. Differential bearing assembly
35. Finial drive output gear
36. Differential aasy.
37. Speedometer drive gear
38. Differential pinion gear
39. Input shift shaft selector plate arm
40. Case magnet
41. Input detent shift shaft spring
42. Input shift shaft detent plunger
43. Input shift shaft
44. Transaxle case
45. Main shift shaft detent plunger
46. Main shift shaft detent spring
47. Fork interlock sleeve retaining spring
48. Differential seal assembly
49. Shift shaft boot
50. Shift shaft oil seal
51. Differential oil seal
52. Speedometer driven gear
53. Gear retainer

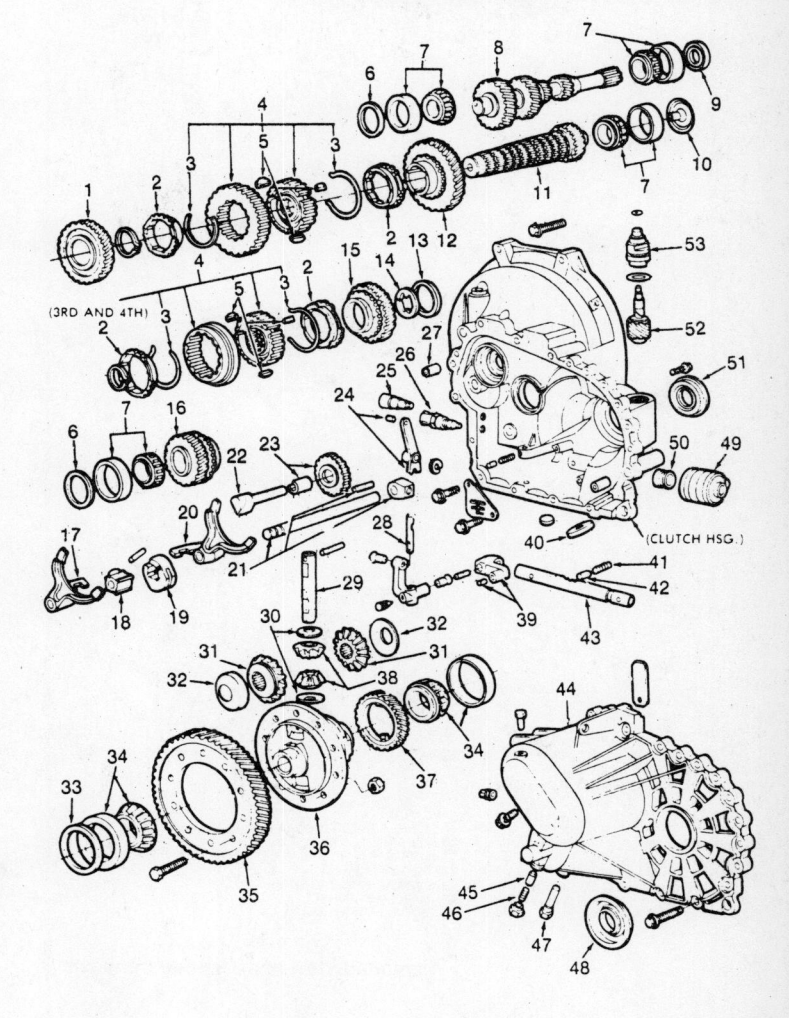

Exploded view of a 4-speed transaxle

418 DRIVE TRAIN

1. INPUT SHAFT SEAL ASSEMBLY
2. ROLLER BEARING CUP
3. INPUT SHAFT FRONT BEARING
4. INPUT CLUSTER SHAFT
5. INPUT SHAFT REAR BEARING
6. ROLLER BEARING CUP
7. BEARING PRELOAD SHIM
8. 5TH GEAR FUNNEL
9. ROLLER BEARING CUP
10. 5TH GEAR SHAFT—FRONT BEARING
11. 5TH GEAR DRIVESHAFT
12. SYNCHRONIZER INSERT RETAINER
13. SYNCHRONIZER RETAINING SPACER
14. SYNCHRONIZER SPRING
15. 5TH SYNCHRONIZER HUB
16. SYNCHRONIZER HUB 5TH INSERT
17. 5TH SYNCHRONIZER SLEEVE
18. SYNCHRONIZER SPRING
19. SYNCHRONIZER BLOCKING RING
20. 5TH SPEED GEAR
21. 5TH GEAR SHAFT-REAR BEARING
22. ROLLER BEARING CUP
23. BEARING PRELOAD SHIM
24. MAINSHAFT FUNNEL
25. ROLLER BEARING CUP
26. MAINSHAFT FRONT BEARING
27. MAIN SHAFT
28. 1ST SPEED GEAR
29. SYNCHRONIZER BLOCKING RING
30. SYNCHRONIZER SPRING
31. 1ST-2ND SYNCHRONIZER HUB
32. SYNCHRONIZER HUB 1ST-2ND INSERT
33. REVERSE SLIDING GEAR
34. SYNCHRONIZER SPRING
35. SYNCHRONIZER BLOCKING RING
36. 1ST-2ND SYNCHRONIZER RETAINING RING
37. 2ND SPEED GEAR
38. 2ND-3RD THRUST WASHER RETAINING RING
39. 2ND-3RD GEAR THRUST WASHER
40. 3RD SPEED GEAR
41. SYNCHRONIZER BLOCKING RING
42. SYNCHRONIZER SPRING
43. 3RD-4TH SYNCHRONIZER HUB
44. SYNCHRONIZER HUB 3RD-4TH INSERT
45. 3RD-4TH SYNCHRONIZER SLEEVE
46. SYNCHRONIZER SPRING
47. SYNCHRONIZER BLOCKING RING
48. 3RD-4TH SYNCHRONIZER RING
49. 4TH SPEED GEAR
50. MAINSHAFT REAR BEARING
51. ROLLER BEARING CUP
52. BEARING PRELOAD SHIM
53. CLUTCH HOUSING CASE
54. SWITCH ASSEMBLY BACK-UP LAMPS
55. REVERSE RELAY LEVER
56. REVERSE RELAY LEVER PIVOT PIN
57. EXTERNAL RETAINING RING
58. REVERSE RELAY LEVER PIN
59. SHIFT LEVER
60. 10.319mm BALL
61. 5TH/REVERSE INHIBITOR SPRING
62. 3RD/4TH SHIFT BIAS SPRING
63. SHIFT LEVER SHAFT
64. SHIFT LEVER PIN
65. SHIFT LEVER SHAFT SEAL
66. SHIFT GATE ATTACHING BOLTS
67. SHIFT GATE PLATE
68. SELECTOR ARM PIN
69. SHIFT GATE SELECTOR PIN
70. SHIFT GATE SELECTOR ARM
71. INPUT SHIFT SHAFT
72. SHIFT SHAFT DETENT PLUNGER
73. SHIFT SHAFT DETENT SPRING
74. ASSEMBLY–SHIFT SHAFT SEAL
75. SHIFT SHAFT BOOT
76. FORK CONTROL SHAFT BLOCK
77. REVERSE RELAY LEVER ACTUATING PIN
78. MAIN SHIFT FORK CONTROL SHAFT
79. 1ST/2ND FORK
80. FORK INTERLOCK SLEEVE
81. SPRING PIN
82. FORK SELECTOR ARM
83. 3RD/4TH FORK
84. 5TH SHIFT RELAY LEVER
85. REVERSE SHIFT RELAY LEVER PIN
86. 5TH RELAY LEVER PIVOT PIN
87. EXTERNAL RETAINING RING
88. 5TH FORK
89. 5TH FORK RETAINING PIN
90. 5TH FORK CONTROL SHAFT
91. REVERSE IDLER GEAR SHAFT
92. REVERSE IDLER GEAR BUSHING
93. REVERSE IDLER GEAR
94. CASE MAGNET
95. TRANSAXLE CASE
96. VENT ASSEMBLY
97. FILL PLUG
98. REVERSE SHAFT RETAINING BOLT
99. DETENT PLUNGER RETAINING SCREW
100. SHIFT SHAFT DETENT PLUNGER
101. SHIFT SHAFT DETENT SPRING
102. FORK INTERLOCK SLEEVE RETAINING PIN
103. TRANSAXLE CASE BOLT
104. SEAL ASSEMBLY (LH) DIFFERENTIAL
105. SHIM DIFFERENTIAL BEARING PRELOAD
106. DIFFERENTIAL BEARING CUP
107. DIFFERENTIAL BEARING ASSEMBLY
108. SIDE GEAR THRUST WASHER
109. SIDE GEAR
110. PINION GEAR
111. PINION GEAR THRUST WASHER
112. PINION GEAR SHAFT
113. PINION GEAR SHAFT RETAINING PIN
114. FINAL DRIVE GEAR
115. DIFFERENTIAL (LH) CASE
116. DIFFERENTIAL (RH) CASE
117. CASE AND DRIVE GEAR ATTACHING RIVET
118. SPEEDO DRIVE GEAR
119. 5.16mm × 1.6 O-RING SEAL
120. SPEEDO RETAINER
121. SPEEDO RETAINER-TO-CASE SEAL
122. SPEEDO DRIVEN GEAR
123. CASE-TO-CLUTCH HOUSING DOWEL
124. TRANSAXLE NEUTRAL SENSING SWITCH

Exploded view of a 5-speed transaxle

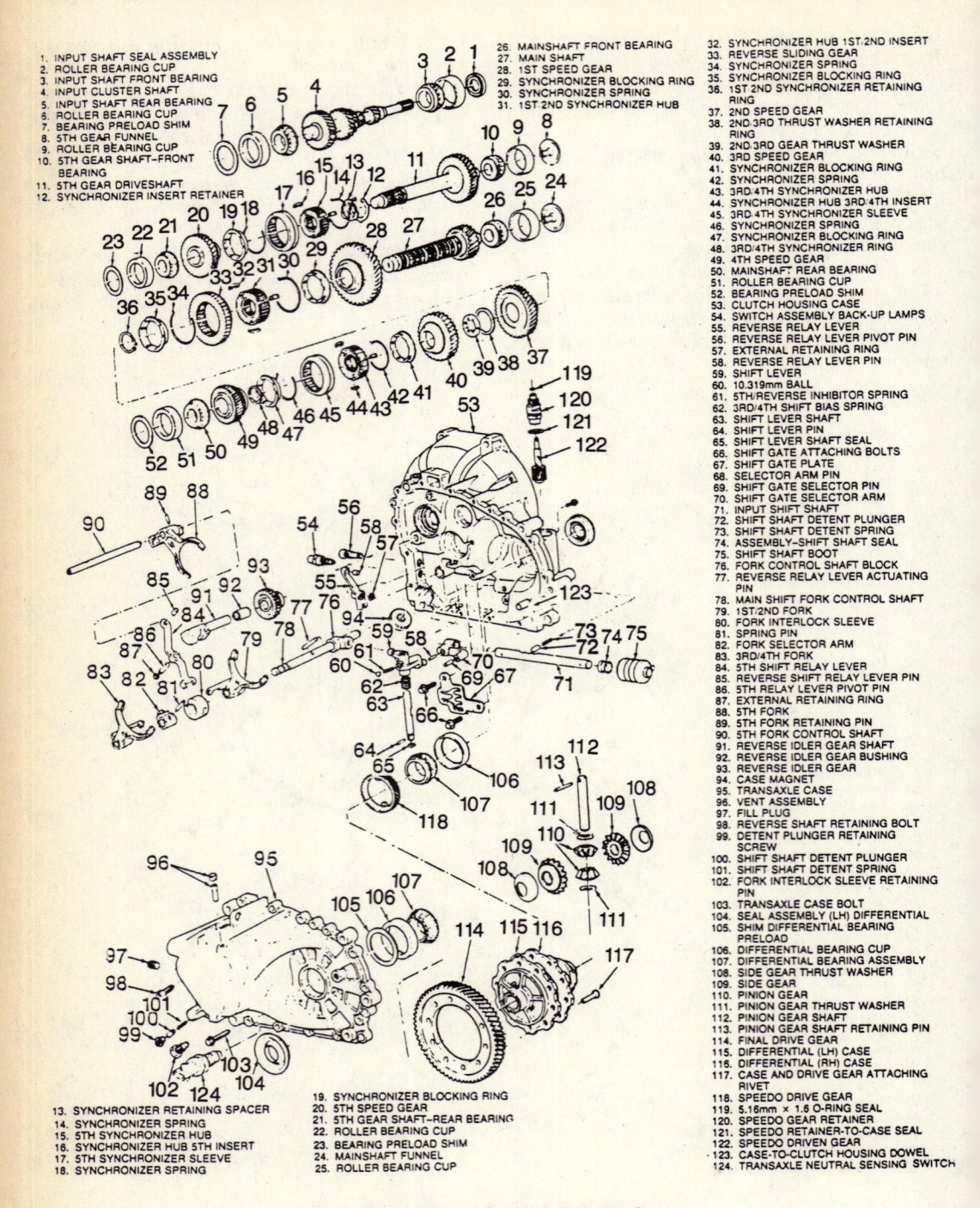

taining ring from the 5th relay lever pivot pin. Remove the 5th gear shift relay lever.

11. Lift the reverse idler shaft and reverse idler gear from the case.

12. Using a punch, drive the spring pin from the shift lever shaft.

13. Using a suitable tool, gently pry on the shift lever shaft so that the hole in the shaft is exposed. Be careful not to damage mainshaft gear teeth or pedestal when prying with tool.

NOTE: *On vehicles equipped with the 1.9L engine, remove 2 screws holding the shift lever cover to the shift lever and remove the inhibitor ball and spring*

14. Hold a shop towel over the hole in the lever to prevent the ball and the 5th/reverse inhibitor spring from shooting out and remove the shift lever shaft.

15. Remove the inhibitor ball and spring from the hole in the shift lever using a pencil magnet or equivalent. Remove the shift lever, 5th/reverse kickdown spring, and 3-4 bias spring.

16. Remove the mainshaft assembly, input cluster shaft assembly and the main shift control shaft assembly as a complete unit. Be careful not to drop bearings or gears.

17. On 4-speed transaxles, rotate shaft and remove the reverse actuator arm and shaft assembly from its bore in the case.

18. On 5-speed transaxles, remove the 5th gear shaft assembly and the 5th gear fork assembly from their bores in the case.

19. Lift the differential and final drive gear assembly from the clutch housing case.

20. Remove the 2 bolts retaining shift relay lever support bracket assembly.

MAINSHAFT

Disassembly

1. Remove the slip fit roller bearing on the 4th speed gear end of the shaft. Mark or tag the bearing for proper installation.

2. Remove the 4th speed gear and synchronizer blocker ring.

3. Remove the 3rd/4th synchronizer retaining ring. Slide the 3rd/4th gear synchronizer assembly, blocker ring and 3rd speed gear from the shaft.

4. Remove the 2nd/3rd thrust washer retaining ring and the 2 piece thrust washer.

5. Remove the 2nd speed gear and its blocker ring.

6. Remove the 1st/2nd synchronizer retaining ring. Slide the 1st/2nd synchronizer assembly, blocker ring and 1st speed gear off the shaft.

7. Remove the tapered roller bearing from the pinion end of the mainshaft using a socket

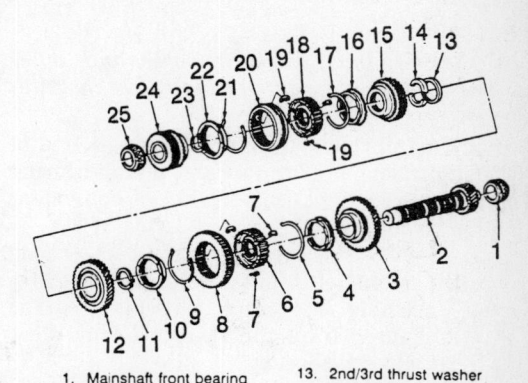

1. Mainshaft front bearing
2. Mainshaft
3. 1st speed gear
4. Synchro blocker ring
5. Synchronizer spring
6. 1st/2nd synchro hub
7. Synchro hub 1st/2nd insert
8. Reverse slinding gear
9. Synchronizer spring
10. Synchro blocker ring
11. 1st/2nd synchro retaining ring
12. 2nd speed gear
13. 2nd/3rd thrust washer retaining ring
14. 2nd/3rd gear thrust washer
15. 3rd speed gear
16. Synchro blocker ring
17. Synchronizer spring
18. 3rd/4th synchro hub
19. Synchro hub 3rd/4th insert
20. 3rd/4th synchro sleeve
21. Synchronizer spring
22. Synchro retaining ring
23. Retaining ring
24. 4th speed gear
25. Mainshaft rear bearing

Exploded view of the mainshaft assembly

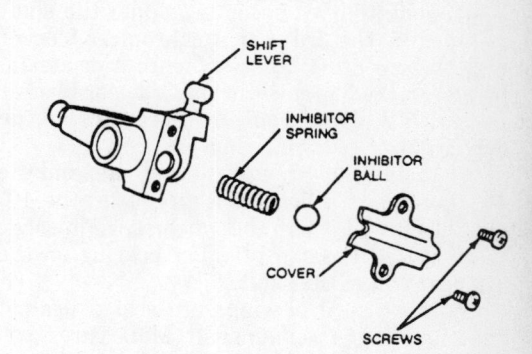

Shift lever assembly — 1.9L engine

or extension and pinion bearing cone remover tool D79L–4621–A or equivalent and an arbor press. Mark or tag bearing.

NOTE: *Bearing does not have to be removed to disassemble the mainshaft.*

Inspection

1. Inspect the tapered roller bearing for wear or damage.
2. Check the teeth, splines and journals of the mainshaft for damage.
3. Check all gears for chipped, broken or worn teeth.
4. Check synchronizer sleeves for free movement on their hubs.
5. Inspect the synchronizer blocking rings for wear marks.

Assembly

NOTE: *Lightly oil gear bores and other parts with the specified fluid before installation.*

1. Install the bearing on the pinion end of the shaft using a 27mm socket, pinion bearing cone remover tool D79L-4621-A or equivalent and an arbor press.
2. Slide the 1st speed gear and blocker ring onto the mainshaft. Slide the 1st/2nd synchronizer assembly into place, making sure the shift fork groove on the reverse sliding gear faces the 1st speed gear.
3. When installing the synchronizer, align the 3 grooves in the 1st gear blocker ring with the synchronizer inserts. This allows the synchronizer assembly to seat properly in the blocker ring. Install the synchronizer retaining ring.
4. Install the 2nd speed blocker ring and the 2nd speed gear. Align the 3 grooves in the 2nd gear blocker ring with the synchronizer inserts.
5. Install the thrust washer halves and retaining ring.
6. Slide the 3rd speed gear onto the shaft followed by the 3rd gear synchronizer blocker ring and the 3rd/4th gear synchronizer assembly. Align the 3 grooves in the 3rd gear blocker ring with the synchronizer inserts. Install the synchronizer retaining ring.
7. Install the 4th gear blocker ring and the 4th speed gear. Align the 3 grooves in the 4th gear blocker ring with the synchronizer inserts.
8. Install the slip fit roller bearing on the 4th gear end of the shaft.
9. Make sure bearings are seated against the shoulder of the mainshaft. Make sure bearings are placed on the proper end. Rotate each gear on the shaft to check for binding or roughness. Make sure that the synchronizer sleeves are in the neutral position.

INPUT CLUSTER SHAFT BEARING

Disassembly

1. Remove the bearing cone and roller assemblies using pinion bearing cone remover/installer D79L-4621-A or equivalent, and an arbor press.
2. Mark or tag bearings for proper installation.
3. Thoroughly clean the bearings and inspect their condition.

Inspection

1. Inspect the tapered roller bearing for wear or damage.
2. Check the teeth, splines and journals of the input shaft for damage.

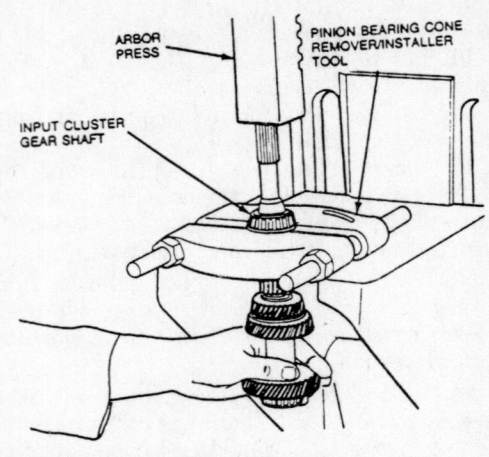

Removing the input cluster shaft bearing

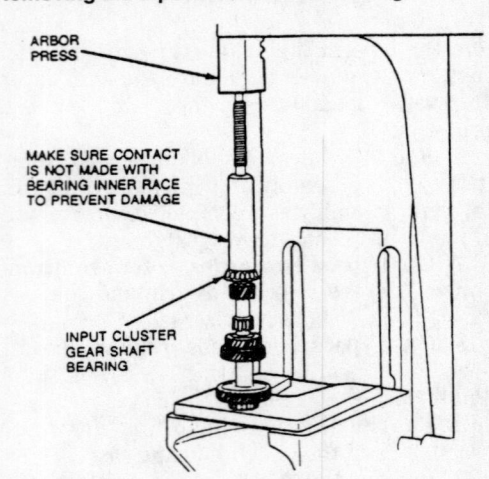

Installing the input cluster shaft bearing

3. Check all gears for chipped, broken or worn teeth.

Assembly

1. Lightly oil the bearings with the specified transmission fluid.
2. Using pinion bearing cone remover/installer D79L-4621-A or equivalent and an arbor press, install the bearing on the shaft.
3. Make sure the bearings are pressed on the proper end as marked during the disassembly.

SYNCHRONIZER

Disassembly

1. Note position of the index marks.
2. Remove the synchronizer springs with a small tool. Do not compress the springs more than is necessary.
3. Remove the 3 hub inserts.
4. Slide the hub and sleeve apart.

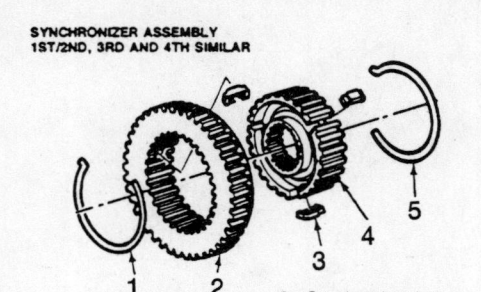

DRIVE TRAIN

SYNCHRONIZER ASSEMBLY
1ST/2ND, 3RD AND 4TH SIMILAR

1. Synchronizer spring
2. Synchronizer sleeve and gear
3. Synchronizer hub inserts
4. Synchronizer hub
5. Synchronizer spring

Exploded view of synchronizer assembly

Inspection

1. Check synchronizer sleeves for free movement on their hubs.
2. Check insert springs.
3. Inspect the synchronizer blocking rings for wear marks.

Assembly

1. Slide the sleeve over the hub. The shorter end of hub shoulder must face alignment mark on sleeve.
2. Place the 3 inserts into their slots. Place the tab on the synchronizer spring into the groove of one of the inserts and snap the spring into place.
3. Place the tab of the other spring into the same insert (on the other side of the synchronizer assembly) and rotate the spring in the opposite direction and snap into place.
4. When assembling synchronizers, notice that the sleeve and the hub have an extremely close fit and must be held square to prevent jamming. Do not force the sleeve onto the hub.

5TH GEAR SHAFT ASSEMBLY

Disassembly

1. Remove the slip fit bearing from the 5th gear end of the shaft and label it for correct installation.
2. Remove the 5th gear and blocking ring.
3. Remove the 5th gear synchronizer assembly.
4. Remove the press fit bearing from the pinion end of the shaft, using bearing remover/installer tool D79L-4621-A or equivalent bearing removal adapter.

Inspection

1. Inspect the tapered roller bearing for wear or damage.
2. Check all gears for chipped, broken or worn teeth.
3. Check synchronizer sleeves for free movement on their hubs.

4. Inspect the synchronizer blocking rings for wear marks.

Assembly

NOTE: *Lightly oil gear bores and other parts with the specified fluid before installation.*

1. Press the bearing onto the pinion gear end of the 5th gear shaft.
2. Install the 5th synchronizer assembly with the plastic insert retainer facing the pinion gear.
3. Install the 5th gear and blocking ring.
4. Install the slip fit bearing on the 5th gear end of the shaft.

CLUTCH HOUSING

Disassembly

1. Remove the 2 control selector plate attaching bolts and remove the plate from the case.
2. With the input shift shaft in the center detent position, using a drift, drive the spring pin through the selector plate arm assembly and through the input shift shaft into the recess in the clutch housing case.
3. Remove the shift shaft boot. Using a drift, rotate the input shift shaft 90 degrees, depressing the detent plunger from the shaft detent notches inside the housing and pull input shift shaft out. Remove the input shift selector plate arm assembly and the spring pin.
4. Using a pencil magnet or equivalent, remove the input shift shaft detent plunger and spring.
5. Using sector shaft seal tool T77F-7288-

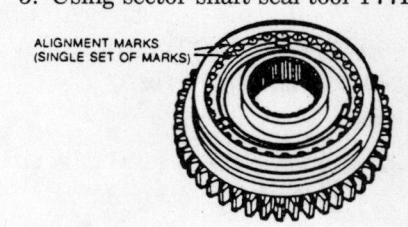

ALIGNMENT MARKS
(SINGLE SET OF MARKS)

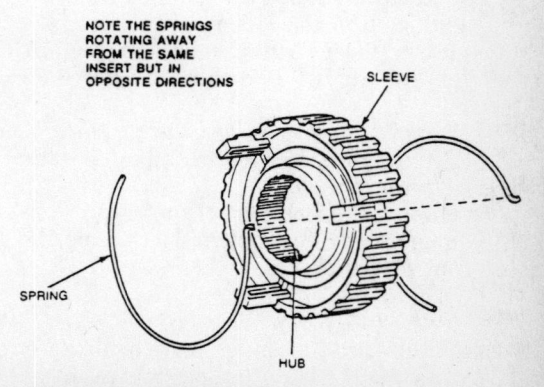

NOTE THE SPRINGS
ROTATING AWAY
FROM THE SAME
INSERT BUT IN
OPPOSITE DIRECTIONS

SLEEVE
SPRING
HUB

Synchronizer installation

DRIVE TRAIN

A or equivalent, remove the transaxle input shift shaft oil seal assembly.

Inspection

1. Inspect the clutch housing case for cracks, wear or damaged bearing bores.
2. Inspect for damaged threads in housing.
3. Inspect clutch housing case mating surfaces for small nicks or burrs that could cause misalignment of the 2 halves.

Assembly

NOTE: *Lightly oil all parts and bores with the specified fluid.*

1. Lubricate the seal lip of a new shift shaft oil seal. Using sector seal tool T77F-7288-A or equivalent, install a new input shift shaft oil seal assembly.
2. Install the input shift shaft detent spring and plunger in the clutch housing case.
3. Using a small drift, force the spring and plunger down into its bore while sliding the input shift shaft into its bore and over the plunger. Be careful not to cut the shift shaft oil seal when inserting the shaft.
4. Install the selector plate arm in its working position and slide the shaft through the selector plate arm. Align the hole in the selector plate arm with the hole in the shaft and install the spring pin. Install the input shift shaft boot.

NOTE: *Make sure the notches in the shift shaft face the detent plunger.*

5. Install the control selector plate. The pin in selector arm must ride in cutout of gate in the selector plate. Move input shift shaft through the selector plate positions to make sure everything works properly.

MAIN SHIFT CONTROL SHAFT

Disassembly

1. Rotate the 3rd/4th shift fork on the shaft until the notch in the fork is located over the interlock sleeve.
2. Rotate the 1st/2nd shift fork on the shaft until the notch in the fork is located over the selector arm finger. With the forks in position, slide the 3rd/4th fork and interlock sleeve off the shaft.
3. Remove the selector arm spring pin.
4. Remove the selector arm and the 1st/2nd shift fork from the shaft.
5. Remove the fork control spring pin.
6. Remove the fork control block from the shift control shaft.

Inspection

Check all components for wear or damage. Check the shift forks for proper alignment on the selector arm.

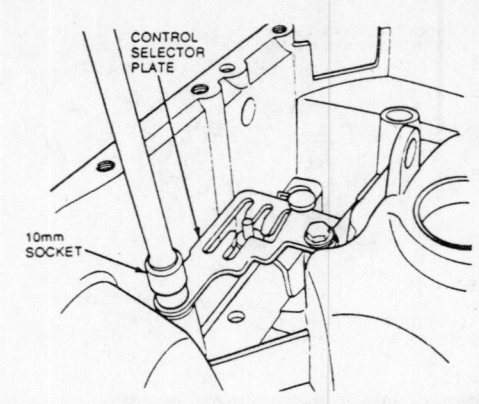

Pin in selector arm must ride in the cut out of the gate in the selector plate

Assembly

NOTE: *Lightly oil all parts with the specified fluid.*

1. Slide the fork control block onto the shift control shaft. Align the hole in the block with the hole in the shaft and install the fork control block spring pin.

NOTE: *With pin installed in control block, offset must point toward end of shaft. Also, check position of flat on shaft when installing control block.*

2. Install the 1st/2nd shift fork and the selector arm on the shaft. The 1st/2nd shift fork is thinner than the 3rd/4th shift fork.
3. Align the hole in the selector arm with the hole in the shaft and install the spring pin.
4. Position the slot in the 1st/2nd fork over the fork selector arm finger.
5. Position the slot in the 3rd/4th fork over the interlock sleeve.
6. Slide the 3rd/4th fork and interlock sleeve onto the main shift control shaft.
7. Align the slot in the interlock sleeve with

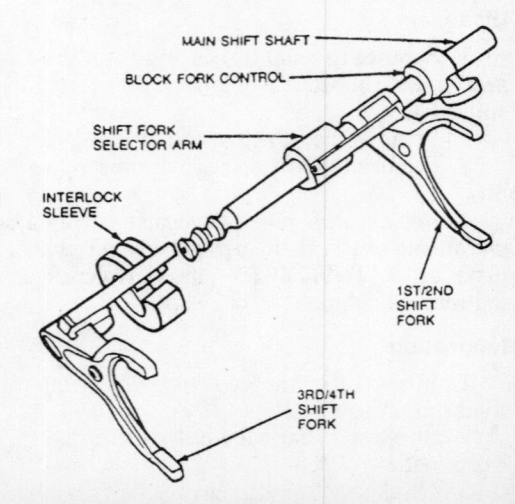

Main shaft control shaft assembly

DRIVE TRAIN

the splines on the fork selector arm and slide the sleeve and 3rd/4th fork into position. When assembled, the forks should be aligned.

5TH GEAR SHIFT CONTROL

Disassembly

1. Remove the spring pin.
2. Slide the fork from the shaft.

Assembly

1. Position the shaft with the hole on the left. Install the 5th gear shift fork so that the protruding arm is positioned toward the long end of the shaft.
2. Install the spring pin.

DIFFERENTIAL

Disassembly

1. Remove the left hand differential roller bearing using a suitable tool.
2. Remove the right hand differential bearing cup from the case and install over the right hand differential bearing.
3. With bearing cup in position, remove bearing from the speedometer side of the differential using suitable tool. Failure to use the bearing cup will result in damage to the bearing.
4. Remove the speedometer drive gear from the case.
5. Remove the differential side gears by rotating the gears toward the case window.
6. Remove the pinion shaft retaining pin.
7. Remove the pinion shaft, gears and thrust washer.
8. If final drive gear is to be replaced, drill out the rivets. To prevent distortion of the case, drill the preformed side of rivet only.

Inspection

Examine the pinion and side gears for scoring, excessive wear, nicks and chips. Worn, scored and damage gears cannot be serviced and must be replaced.

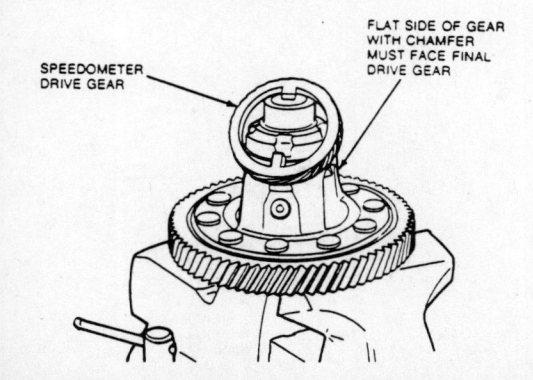

1. Differential roller bearings and cup
2. Final drive gear
3. Thrust washer
4. Side gears
5. Pinion gear shaft
6. Pinion shaft retaining pin
7. Pinion gears
8. Speedometer drive gear
9. Rivet
10. Final drive gear nut (for service replacement of gear only)
11. Differential case
12. Bolt (for service replacement of gear only)

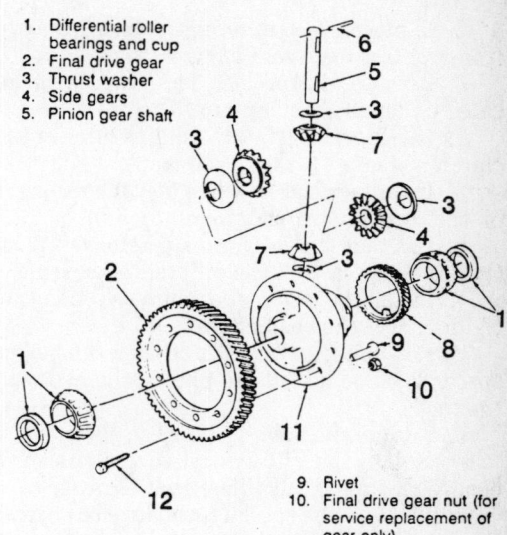

Exploded view of differential assembly

Assembly

1. Lubricate all components with the specified fluid before installation.
2. Install the pinion shaft, gears and thrust washer.
3. Install the pinion shaft retaining pin.
4. Install the differential side gears.
5. Install the speedometer drive gear. Install the drive gear with the bevel on the inside diameter facing the differential case.
6. Install the left and right differential roller bearings using a suitable tool.

DIFFERENTIAL BEARING PRELOAD

The differential preload is set at the factory and need not be checked or adjusted unless one of the following components are replaced.

   Transaxle case
   Differential case
   Differential bearings
   Clutch housing

1. Remove the differential seal from the transaxle case.

Installing the speedometer gear

DIFFERENTIAL SHIM SIZE

in. (mm)	in. (mm)	in. (mm)
0.012 (0.30)	0.026 (0.65)	0.039 (1.00)
0.014 (0.35)	0.028 (0.70)	0.041 (1.05)
0.016 (0.40)	0.030 (0.75)	0.043 (1.10)
0.018 (0.45)	0.032 (0.80)	0.045 (1.15)
0.020 (0.50)	0.033 (0.85)	0.047 (1.20)
0.022 (0.55)	0.035 (0.90)	0.049 (1.25)
0.024 (0.60)	0.037 (0.95)	

The shim is located behind the differential bearing cup in the transmission case.

DRIVE TRAIN

2. Remove the differential bearing cup from the transaxle case using a suitable tool.

3. Remove the preload shim which is located under the bearing cup.

4. If removed install the differential in the clutch housing.

5. Install special tool height gauge spacers on the clutch housing dowels.

6. Position the bearing cup removed from the transaxle case on the differential bearing.

7. Install the differential shim selection special tool over the bearing cup.

8. Position the transaxle case on the height spacer tool and install the 4 bolts supplied with the tool.

9. Torque the bolts to 17–21 ft. lbs.

10. Rotate the differential several times to ensure seating of the differential bearing.

11. Position the special tool gauge bar across the shim selection tool.

12. Using a feeler gauge, measure the gap between the gauge bar and the selector tool gauge surface.

NOTE: *This measurement can also be made using a depth micrometer.*

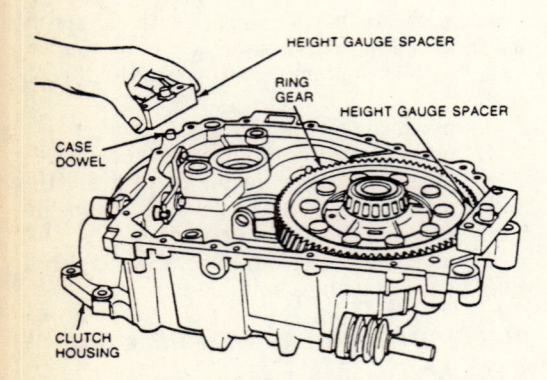

13. Obtain measurements from 3 positions around the tool and take the average of the readings.

14. Check the shim for the correct thickness, then install the shim in the transaxle case.

15. Apply a light film of the specified fluid to

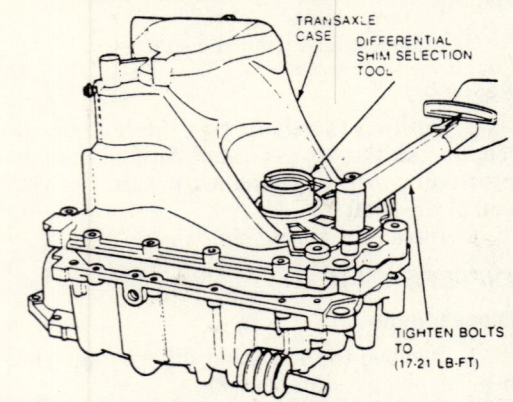

Step 3 — bearing preload positioning case on the height gauge

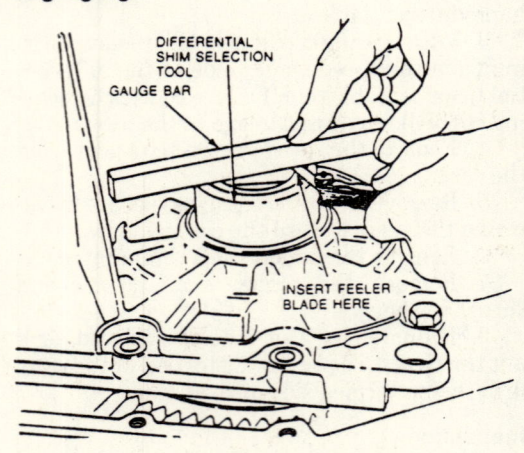

Step 1 — bearing preload installing height gauge spacers

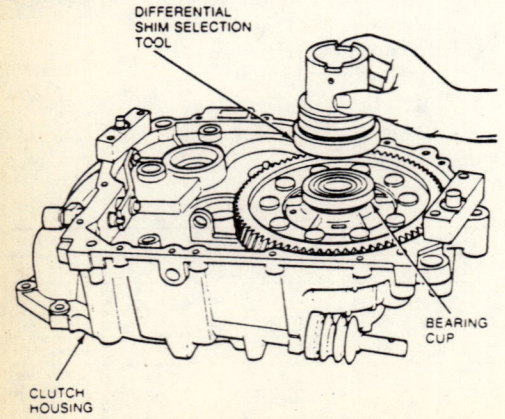

Step 2 — bearing preload installing differential shim selection tool

Step 4 — bearing preload measure gap

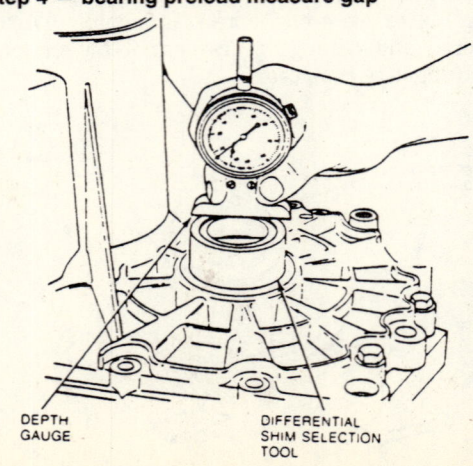

Using depth micrometer — bearing preload

the bearing bores in the transaxle case and the clutch housing.

16. Install the bearing cup in the transaxle case using a suitable tool.

17. Check that the cup is fully seated against the shim in the transaxle case and against the shoulder in the clutch housing.

18. Install the differential seal.

TRANSAXLE ASSEMBLY

NOTE: *Prior to installation, thoroughly clean all parts and inspect their condition. Lightly oil the bores with the specified fluid.*

1. Install the shift relay lever support bracket assembly to the case with 2 bolts. Tighten bolts to 6–9 ft. lbs.

2. Place the differential and the final drive gear assembly into the clutch housing case and align the differential gears.

3. If so equipped, install the 5th gear shaft assembly and the fork shaft assembly in the case. Be careful not to damage the 5th gear shaft oil funnel.

4. Position the main shift control shaft assembly so that the shift forks engage their respective slots in the synchronizer sleeves on the mainshaft assembly.

5. Bring the mainshaft assembly into mesh with the input cluster shaft assembly. Holding the 3 shafts (input cluster shaft, mainshaft and the main shift fork control shaft) in their respective working positions, lower them into their bores in the clutch housing case as a unit. Be careful not to damage the input shaft oil seal or mainshaft oil funnel.

NOTE: *While performing this operation, care should be taken to avoid any movement of the 3rd/4th synchronizer sleeve, which may result in an overtravel of the synchronizer sleeve to hub allowing inserts to pop out of position.*

6. Position the shift lever, 3–4 bias spring and 5th/reverse kickdown spring in their work-

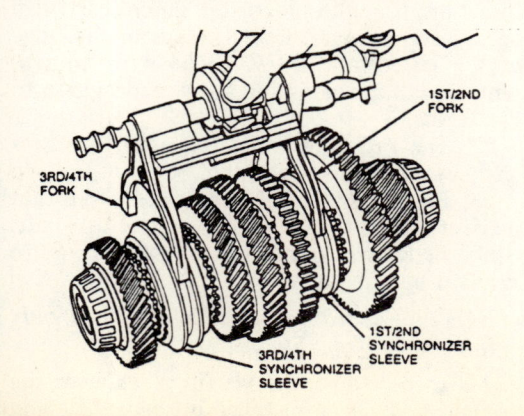

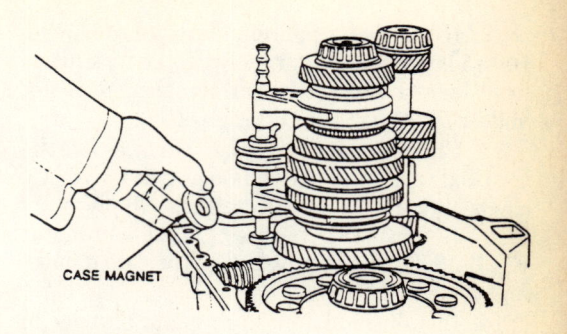

Installing the case magnet

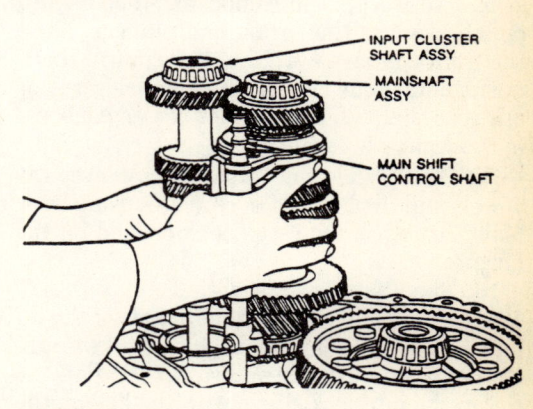

Installing the mainshaft assembly

Positioning the mainshaft

ing positions (with 1 shift lever ball located in the socket of the input shift gate selector plate arm assembly and the other in the socket of the main shift control shaft block). Install the spring and ball in the 5th/reverse inhibitor shift lever hole.

7. Slide the shift lever shaft (notch down) through the 3rd/4th bias spring and the shift lever. Then, using a small drift, depress the inhibitor ball and spring. Tap the shift shaft through the shift lever, the 5th/reverse gear kickdown spring and then tap into its bore in the clutch housing.

8. Align the shift shaft bore with the case bore and tap the spring pin in, slightly below the case mating surface.

9. Check that the selector pin is in the neutral gate of the control selector plate and the finger of the fork selector arm is partially engaged with the 1st/2nd fork and partially engaged with the 3rd/4th fork.

10. Position reverse idler gear to clutch housing while aligning reverse shift relay lever to the slot in the gear. Slide the reverse idler shaft through the gear and into its bore. Place the reverse idler gear groove in engagement with the reverse relay lever.

11. Install the magnet in its pocket in the clutch housing case.

DRIVE TRAIN

12. Install 5th gear relay lever onto the reverse idler shaft, aligning it with the fork interlock sleeve and reverse gear actuating arm slot and install the retaining ring C-clip.

13. Check that the gasket surfaces of the transaxle case and clutch housing are perfectly clean and free of burrs or nicks. Apply a $\frac{1}{16}$ inch (1.5mm) wide bead of gasket eliminator E1FZ-19562-A or equivalent to the clutch housing.

14. Install the detent spring and plunger in their bore in the case. Carefully lower the transaxle case over the clutch housing, then using a punch, depress the spring and plunger. Move the transaxle case until the shift control shaft, mainshaft, input cluster shaft and reverse or 5th gear shaft align with their respective bores in the transaxle case.

15. Gently slide the transaxle case over the dowels and flush onto the clutch housing case. Make sure that the case does not bind on the magnet.

16. Apply pipe sealant with Teflon® D8AZ-19554-A or equivalent to the threads of the interlock sleeve retaining pin, in a clockwise direction. Use a drift or equivalent to align the slot in the interlock sleeve with the hole in the

SPECIAL TOOLS

Tool Number	Description
T50T-100-A	Impact slide hammer
T81P-1177-A	Differential seal replacer
T81P-1177-B	Transaxle plugs
D83P-4026-A	Halfshaft remover
T81P-4026-A	Differential rotator
D79L-4621-A	Pinion bearing cone remover/installer
T77F-7050-B	Input shaft seal remover
T77F-7288-A	Sector shaft seal tool
T00L-4201-C	Dial indicator
T77F-1176-A	Draw bolt
T81P-1177-A	Differential seal replacer
T75T-1225-A	Stop differential bearing cup replacer
T57L-4220-A	Differential bearing cone remover
T77F-4220-B1	Differential bearing cone remover/installer
T81P-4220-A	Step plate differential bearing removal
T77F-4222-A	Differential bearing cup replacer
T77F-4222-B	Differential bearing cup remover
T80L-77003-A	Gauge bar
T83P-4220-CH	Bearing installer
T83P-4451-AH2	Height gauge spacer
T83P-4451-AH1	Shim selector tool
T81P-4451-B2	Height gauge spacer
014-00210	Hi-lift jack
014-00225	Manual transaxle adapter

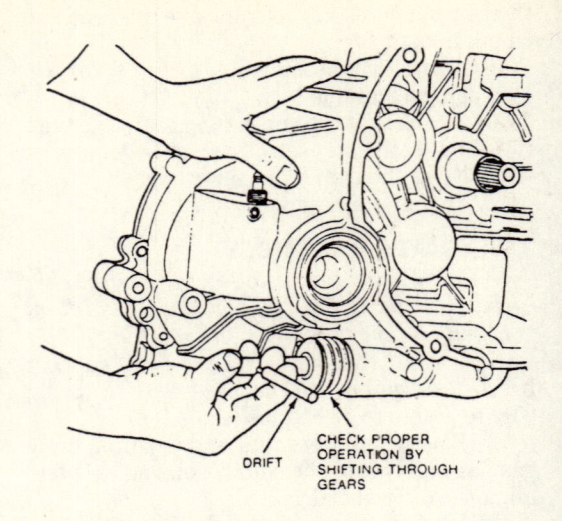

Check for proper operation — before vehicle installation

transaxle case and install the retaining pin. Tighten to 12–15 ft. lbs.

NOTE: *If the hole in the case does not align with the slot in the interlock sleeve, remove the case half and check for proper installation of the interlock sleeve.*

17. Install the transaxle case to clutch housing bolts. Tighten to 13–17 ft. lbs.

18. Use a drift to align the bore in the reverse idler shaft with the retaining screw hole in the transaxle case.

19. Install the reverse idler shaft retaining bolt. Tighten to 16–20 ft. lbs.

20. Apply pipe sealant with Teflon® D8AZ-19554-A or equivalent to the threads of the backup lamp switch in a clockwise direction and install. Tighten the switch to 12–15 ft. lbs.

21. Apply pipe sealant with Teflon® D8AZ-19554-A or equivalent to the treads of the detent plunger retaining screw, in a clockwise direction. If applicable, install detent cartridge spring and plunger. Coat threads of cartridge with pipe sealant D8AZ-19554-A or equivalent. Install the retaining screw and tighten to 6–8 ft. lbs.

22. Tap the differential seal into the transaxle case with a suitable tool.

23. Place the transaxle upright and position a drift through the hole in the input shift shaft. Shift the transaxle into and out of all gears to verify proper installation.

NOTE: *The transaxle will not shift directly into reverse from 5th gear.*

24. Install the transaxle fill plugs after the transaxle has been installed in the vehicle and fluid has been added.

DRIVE TRAIN

TORQUE SPECIFICATIONS

Component	ft. lbs.	Nm
ESCORT/LYNX/EXP		
Transaxle to engine bolts	25–35	34–47
Air manage valve bracket bolt to transaxle	28–31	38–42
Switch actuator bracket bolt	7–10	9–13
Control arm to steering knuckle	37–44	50–60
Rear mounting bolts	35–50	47–68
Transaxle mounting stud	38–41	52–56
Front mount bracket bolts	25–35	34–47
Stiffener brace bolts	28–38	38–51
Starter stud bolts	30–40	41–54
Roll restrictor nuts	25–30	34–40
Shift stabilizer bar to transaxle case	23–35	3–47
Speedometer	2.5–3.5	3.4–4.5
Transaxle case-to-clutch housing	13–18	18–24
Reverse idler shaft-to-case	15–20	21–27
Fork interlock sleeve pin	12–15	16–20
Detent plunger retainer screw	6–8	7.5–11
Backup lamp switch	12–15	16–20
Control selector plate	6–8	8–11
Speedo retaining	1.5–2	2–3
Reverse shift relay lever bracket	6–8	8–11
Filler plug	9–15	12–20
Clutch release fork to shaft	30–41	40–41
Shift lever cover screws	1.5–2.0	2–3
Final drive gear to differential case attaching bolts and nuts (service only)	55–70	75–95
Transmission oil fill plug	9–14	12–20

Component	ft. lbs.	Nm
TEMPO/TOPAZ		
Front stabilizer bar to control arm	107–125	145–169
Transaxle to engine bolts	25–35	34–47
Front stabilizer bar bracket bolts	47–55	64–74
Lower control arm ball joint to steering knuckle nut	37–44	50–60
Engine roll restrictor attaching nuts	14–20	19–27
Starter cable	70–130	7.9–14.7
Starter stud bolts	30–40	41–54
Shift mechanism to shift shaft	7–10	9–13
Shift mechanism stabilizer to transaxle bolt	23–35	31–47
Speedometer cable	30–40	3.4–4.5
Left hand rear no. 4 insulator to body bracket	35–50	47–68
Left hand front no. 1 insulator to body bracket	25–35	34–47
Oil pan to transaxle	28–38	38–51
Transaxle case-to-clutch housing	13–18	18–24
Reverse idler shaft-to-case	15–20	21–27
Fork interlock sleeve pin	12–15	16–20
Detent plunger retainer screw	6–8	7.5–11
Backup lamp switch	12–15	16–20
Control selector plate	6–8	8–11
Speedo retaining	1.5–2	2–3
Reverse shift relay lever bracket	6–8	8–11
Filler plug	9–15	12–20
Clutch release fork to shaft	30–41	40–41
Shift lever cover screws	1.5–2.0	2–3
Final drive gear to differential case attaching bolts and nuts (service only)	55–70	75–95
Transmission oil fill plug	9–14	12–20

DRIVE TRAIN

CHILTON TIPS
1987 Tempo and Topaz

The transmission cases for the PMA-AW ATX transaxles that are not stamped with a die number 56 will not assemble to the transfer case of the All Wheel Drive (AWD) vehicles. This is caused by the transfer gear bearing race interfering with the inside edge of the transmission case. The die number 56 is cast in the transmission case in 2 inch numerals on the outside surface of the top of the bell housing.

If service is required, do not use transmission cases stamped with a die number 56 on the 1987 All Wheel Drive vehicles with the ATX automatic transaxles. However, the ATX transmission cases with the die number 56 can be used to service two-wheel drive vehicles.

Halfshafts

The front wheel drive halfshafts are a one piece design. Constant velocity joint (CV) are used at each end. The left hand (driver's side) halfshaft is solid steel and is shorter than the right side halfshaft. The right hand (passenger's side) halfshaft is depending on year and model, constructed of tubular steel or solid construction. The automatic and manual transaxles use similar halfshafts.

The halfshafts can be replaced individually. The CV-joint or boots can be cleaned or replaced. Individual parts of the CV-joints are not available. The inboard and outboard joints differ in size. CV-joint parts are fitted and should never be mixed or substituted with a part from another joint.

Inspect the boots periodically for cuts or splits. If a cut or split is found, inspect the joint, repack it with grease and install a new boot.

REMOVAL AND INSTALLATION
1981–85 Models

NOTE: *Special tools are required for removing, installing and servicing halfshafts. They are listed by descriptive name (Ford part number). Front Hub Installer Adapter (T81P-1104-A), Wheel Bolt Adapters (T81P-1104-B or T83P-1104-BH), CV-Joint Separator (T81P-3514-A), Front Hub Installer/Remover (T81P-1104-C), Shipping Plug Tool (T81P-1177-B), Dust Deflector Installer CV-Joint (T83P-3425-AH), Differential Rotator (T81P-4026-A). It is necessary to have on hand new hub nuts and new lower control arm to steering knuckle attaching nuts and bolts. Once removed, these parts must not be reused. The torque holding ability is destroyed during removal.*

1. Loosen the front hub nut and the wheel lugs.

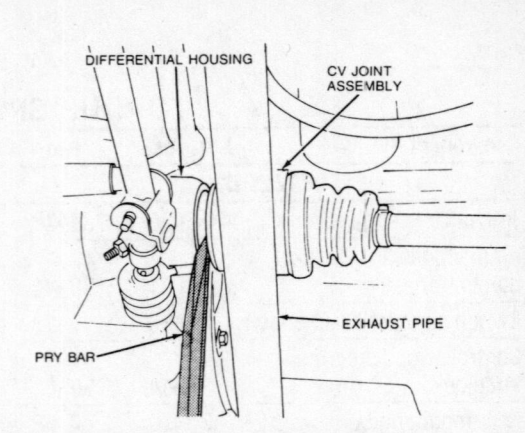

Separating the CV-joint from the differential with a prybar

2. Jack up the front of the car and safely support it on jackstands.
3. Remove the tire and wheel assembly. Remove and discard the front hub nut. Save the washers.

NOTE: *Halfshaft removal and installation are the same for Manual and Automatic transaxles EXCEPT: The configuration of the AT (automatic transaxle) differential case requires that the right hand halfshaft assembly be removed first. The differential service tool T81P-4026 (Differential Rotator) is then inserted to drive the left hand halfshaft from the transaxle. If only the left hand halfshaft is to be serviced, removed the right hand halfshaft from the transaxle side and support it with a length of wire. Drive the left hand halfshaft assembly from the transaxle.*

4. Remove the bolt that retains the brake hose to the strut.
5. Remove the nut and bolt securing the lower ball joint and separate the joint from the steering knuckle by inserting a pry bar between the stabilizer and frame and pulling downward. Take care not to damage the ball joint boot.

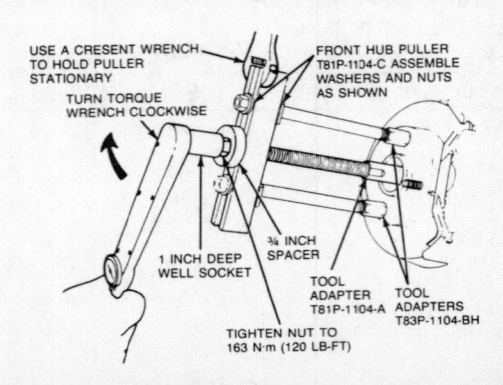

Installing the CV-joint shaft with the special tool

DRIVE TRAIN

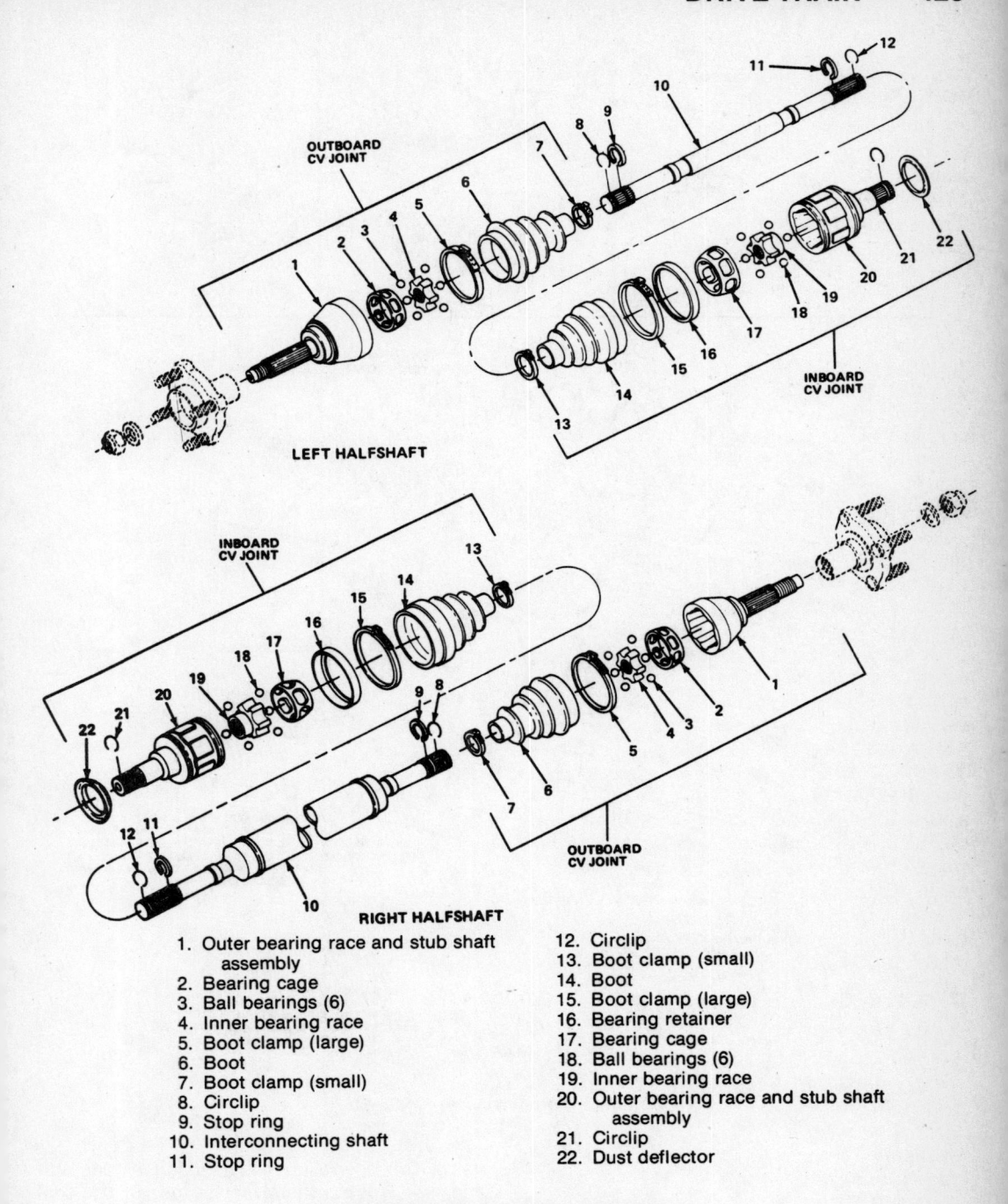

1. Outer bearing race and stub shaft assembly
2. Bearing cage
3. Ball bearings (6)
4. Inner bearing race
5. Boot clamp (large)
6. Boot
7. Boot clamp (small)
8. Circlip
9. Stop ring
10. Interconnecting shaft
11. Stop ring
12. Circlip
13. Boot clamp (small)
14. Boot
15. Boot clamp (large)
16. Bearing retainer
17. Bearing cage
18. Ball bearings (6)
19. Inner bearing race
20. Outer bearing race and stub shaft assembly
21. Circlip
22. Dust deflector

Halfshaft exploded view — 1981–85

NOTE: *The lower control arm ball joint fits into a pocket formed in a plastic disc rotor shield, on some models. The shield must be carefully bent back away from the ball joint while prying the ball joint out of the steering knuckle. Do not contact or pry on the lower control arm.*

6. Remove the halfshaft from the differential housing, using a pry bar. Position the pry bar between the case and the shaft and pry the joint away from the case. Do not damage the oil seal, the CV-joint boot or the CV-dust deflector. Install tool number T81P-1177-B (Shipping plug) to prevent fluid loss and differential side gear misalignment.

7. Support the end of the shaft with a piece of wire, suspending it from a chassis member.

8. Separate the shaft from the front hub

430 **DRIVE TRAIN**

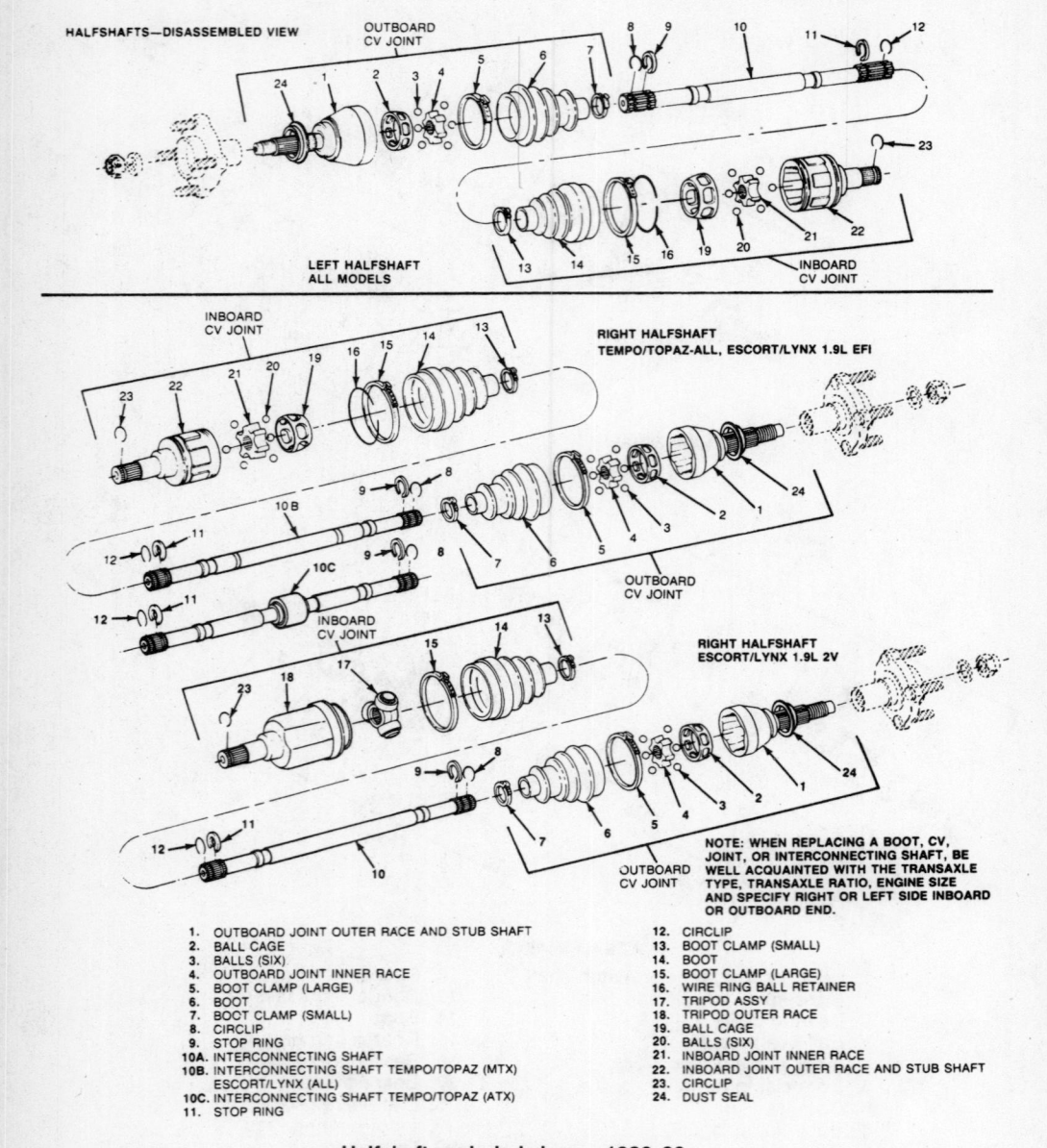

1. OUTBOARD JOINT OUTER RACE AND STUB SHAFT
2. BALL CAGE
3. BALLS (SIX)
4. OUTBOARD JOINT INNER RACE
5. BOOT CLAMP (LARGE)
6. BOOT
7. BOOT CLAMP (SMALL)
8. CIRCLIP
9. STOP RING
10A. INTERCONNECTING SHAFT
10B. INTERCONNECTING SHAFT TEMPO/TOPAZ (MTX) ESCORT/LYNX (ALL)
10C. INTERCONNECTING SHAFT TEMPO/TOPAZ (ATX)
11. STOP RING
12. CIRCLIP
13. BOOT CLAMP (SMALL)
14. BOOT
15. BOOT CLAMP (LARGE)
16. WIRE RING BALL RETAINER
17. TRIPOD ASSY
18. TRIPOD OUTER RACE
19. BALL CAGE
20. BALLS (SIX)
21. INBOARD JOINT INNER RACE
22. INBOARD JOINT OUTER RACE AND STUB SHAFT
23. CIRCLIP
24. DUST SEAL

Halfshaft exploded view — 1986–90

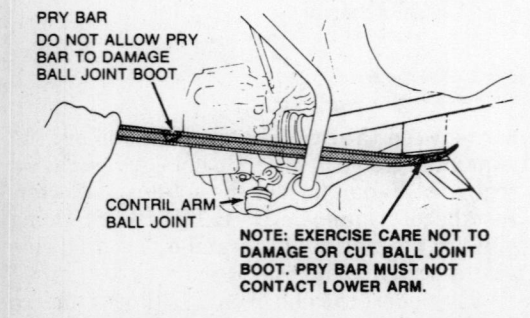

Separating the ball joint from the steering knuckle

using the special remover/installer tool and adapters. Instructions for the use of the tool may be found in Chapter 8 under the Front Wheel Bearing section.

NOTE: *Never use a hammer to force the shaft from the wheel hub. Damage to the internal parts of the CV-joint may occur.*

To install:

9. Install a new circlip on the inboard CV-joint stub shaft. Align the splines of the inboard CV-joint stub shaft with the splines in the differential. Push the CV-joint into the dif-

DRIVE TRAIN 431

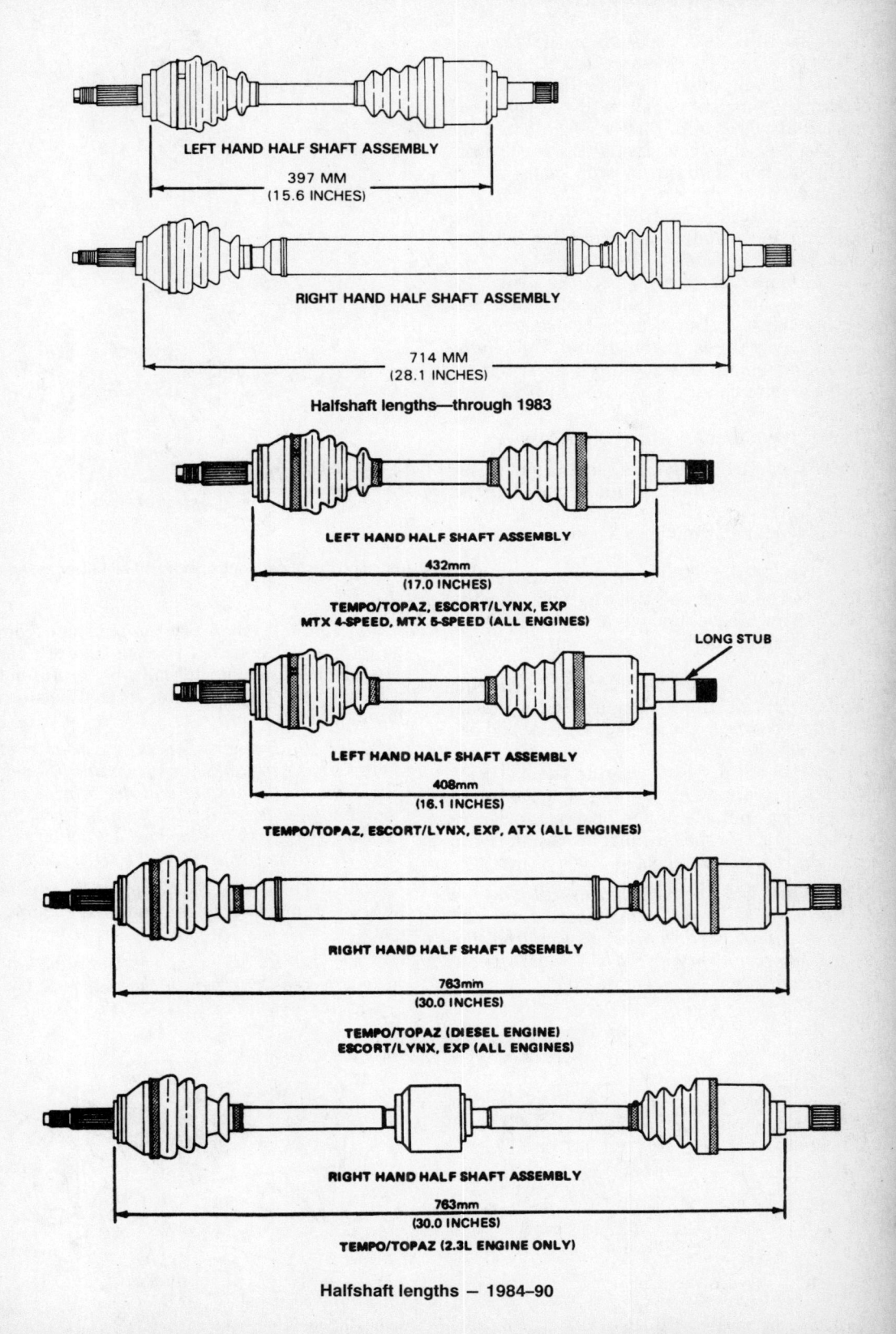

LEFT HAND HALF SHAFT ASSEMBLY
397 MM (15.6 INCHES)

RIGHT HAND HALF SHAFT ASSEMBLY
714 MM (28.1 INCHES)

Halfshaft lengths—through 1983

LEFT HAND HALF SHAFT ASSEMBLY
432mm (17.0 INCHES)
TEMPO/TOPAZ, ESCORT/LYNX, EXP
MTX 4-SPEED, MTX 5-SPEED (ALL ENGINES)

LONG STUB

LEFT HAND HALF SHAFT ASSEMBLY
408mm (16.1 INCHES)
TEMPO/TOPAZ, ESCORT/LYNX, EXP, ATX (ALL ENGINES)

RIGHT HAND HALF SHAFT ASSEMBLY
763mm (30.0 INCHES)
TEMPO/TOPAZ (DIESEL ENGINE)
ESCORT/LYNX, EXP (ALL ENGINES)

RIGHT HAND HALF SHAFT ASSEMBLY
763mm (30.0 INCHES)
TEMPO/TOPAZ (2.3L ENGINE ONLY)

Halfshaft lengths — 1984–90

DRIVE TRAIN

ferential until the circlip seats on the side gear. Some force may be necessary to seat.

10. Carefully align the splines of the outboard CV-joint stub shaft with the splines in the front wheel hub. Push the shaft into the hub as far as possible. Install the remover/installer tool and pull the CV-stub shaft through the hub.

11. Connect the control arm to the steering knuckle and install a new mounting bolt and nut. Torque to 37–44 ft. lbs.

12. Connect the brake line to the strut.

13. Install the front hub washer and new hub nut. Install the tire and wheel assembly.

14. Lower the car to the ground. Tighten the center hub nut to 180–200 ft. lbs. Stake the nut using a blunt chisel.

1986–90 Without All Wheel Drive (AWD)

1. Remove the cap from the hub and loosen the hub nut. Set the parking brake. The nut must be loosened without unstaking; the use of a chisel or similar tool may damage the spindle thread.

2. Raise and safely support the vehicle. Remove the wheel and tire assembly. Remove the hub nut/washer and discard the nut.

3. Remove the brake hose routing clip-to-strut bolt.

4. Remove the ball joint-to-steering knuckle nut. Using a hammer and a punch, drive the bolt from the steering knuckle and discard the bolt/nut.

5. Using a pry bar, separate the ball joint from the steering knuckle. Position the end of the pry bar outside of the bushing pocket to avoid damage to the bushing; be careful not to damage the ball joint boot.

NOTE: *The lower control arm ball joint fits into a pocket formed in the plastic disc brake rotor shield; bend the shield away from the ball joint while prying the ball joint from the steering knuckle.*

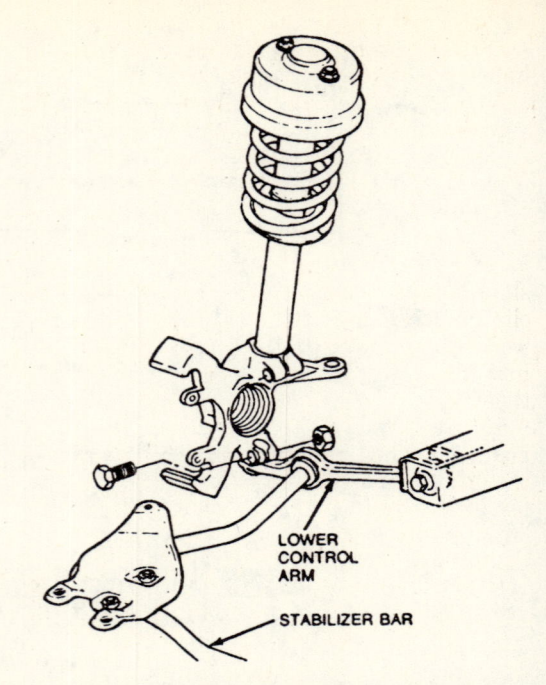

Installing the lower control arm and stabilizer assembly

6. Using a pry bar, pry the halfshaft from the differential housing. Position the pry bar between the case and the shaft; be careful not to damage the dust deflector located between the shaft and the case.

NOTE: *If extreme resistance is encountered when prying the halfshafts from the differential, remove the oil pan and use a large pry bar to dislodge the circlip from between the pinion shaft and the inboard CV-joint; this will free the halfshaft from the differential.*

7. Using a piece of wire, support the end of the shaft from a convenient underbody component.

NOTE: *Do not allow the shaft to hang unsupported, as damage to the outboard CV-joint may result.*

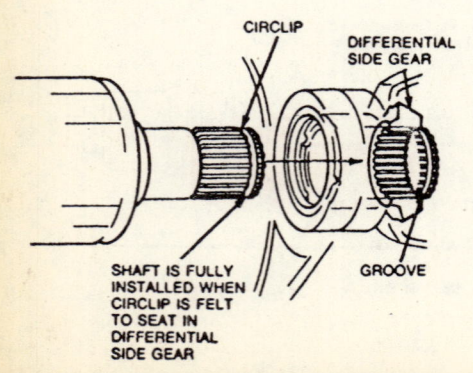

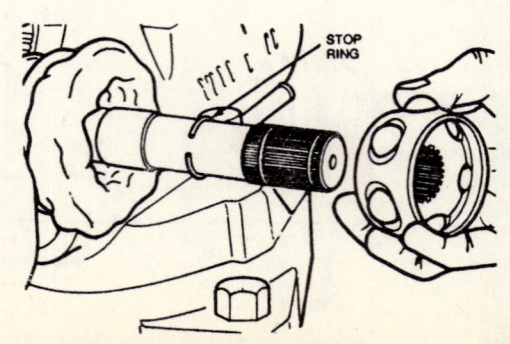

Installing the halfshaft into the differential side gear

Removing the inner race assembly

8. Using a front hub removal tool, press the halfshaft's outboard CV-joint from the hub.
NOTE: *Never use a hammer or separate the outboard CV-joint stub shaft from the hub. Damage to the CV-joint internal components may result.*

To install:
9. Install a new circlip onto the inboard CV-joint stub shaft; the outboard CV-joint stub shaft does not have a circlip. To install the circlip properly, start one end in the groove and work the circlip over the stub shaft end and into the groove; this will avoid over expanding the circlip.
10. Carefully, align the splines of the inboard CV-joint stub shaft with the splines in the differential. Push the CV-joint into the differential until the circlip is seated in the differential side gear. Use care to prevent damage to the differential oil seal.
NOTE: *A non-metallic mallet may be used to aid in seating the circlip into the differential side gear groove; if a mallet is necessary, tap only on the outboard CV-joint stub shaft.*
11. Carefully, align the outboard CV-joint stub shaft splines with the hub splines and push the shaft into the hub, as far as possible; use the front hub replacer tool to firmly press the halfshaft into the hub.
12. Connect the control arm-to-steering knuckle and torque the new nut/bolt to 40–54 ft. lbs. (54–74 Nm).
13. Position the brake hose routing clip on the suspension strut and torque the bolt to 8 ft. lbs. (11 Nm).
14. Install the hub nut washer and a new hub nut.
15. Install the wheel/tire assembly and torque the lug nuts to 80–105 ft. lbs. (108–144 Nm). Lower the vehicle and torque the hub nut to 180–200 ft. lbs. (244–271 Nm).
16. Refill the transaxle and road test.

With All Wheel Drive (AWD)
1. Raise and safely support the vehicle. Remove the rear suspension control arm bolt.
2. Remove the outboard U-joint retaining bolts and straps. Remove the inboard U-joint retaining bolts and straps.
3. Slide the shaft together; do not allow the splined shafts to contact with excessive force. Remove the halfshafts; do not drop the halfshafts as the impact may cause damage to the U-joint bearing cups.
4. Retain the bearing cups. Inspect the U-joint assemblies for wear or damage, replace the U-joint if necessary.

To install:
5. Install the halfshaft at the inboard U-joint; the inboard shaft has a larger diameter than the outboard shaft. Install the U-joint retaining caps and bolts and torque them to 15–17 ft. lbs. (21–23 Nm).
NOTE: *Be sure to lubricate the U-joint bolts with Loctite®.*
6. Install the halfshaft at the outboard U-joint. Install the U-joint retaining caps and bolts and torque them to 15–17 ft. lbs. (21–23 Nm).
7. Install the rear suspension control arm and torque the bolt to 60–86 ft. lbs. (82–116 Nm).

CV-Joint And Boot
OVERHAUL
NOTE: *When replacing a CV-boot, be aware of the transaxle type, transaxle ratio, engine size, CV-joint type, right hand or left side and inboard or outboard end.*

Inner Boot
NOTE: *There are two different types of inboard CV-joints (Double Offset Joint and Tripod-Type) requiring different removal procedures.*

DOUBLE OFFSET TYPE
1. Disconnect the negative battery cable.
2. Remove halfshaft assembly from vehicle. Place halfshaft in vise. Do not allow vice jaws to contact the boot or its clamp. The vise should be equipped with jaw caps to prevent damage to any machined surfaces.
3. Cut the large boot clamp using side cutters and peel away from the boot. After removing the clamp, roll boot back over shaft.
4. Remove wire ring ball retainer.
5. Remove outer race.
6. Pull inner race assembly out until it rests on the circlip. Using snapring pliers, spread stop ring and move it back on shaft.
7. Slide inner race assembly down the shaft to allow access to the circlip. Remove circlip.
8. Remove inner race assembly. Remove boot.
NOTE: *Circlips must not be reused. Replace with new circlips before assembly.*
9. When replacing damaged CV-boots, the grease should be checked for contamination. If the CV-joints were operating satisfactorily and the grease does not appear to be contaminated, add grease and replace the boot. If the lubricant appears contaminated, proceed with a complete CV-joint disassembly and inspection.
10. Remove balls by prying from cage.
NOTE: *Exercise care to prevent scratching or other damage to the inner race or cage.*
11. Rotate inner race to align lands with cage windows. Lift inner race out through the wider end of the cage.

434 DRIVE TRAIN

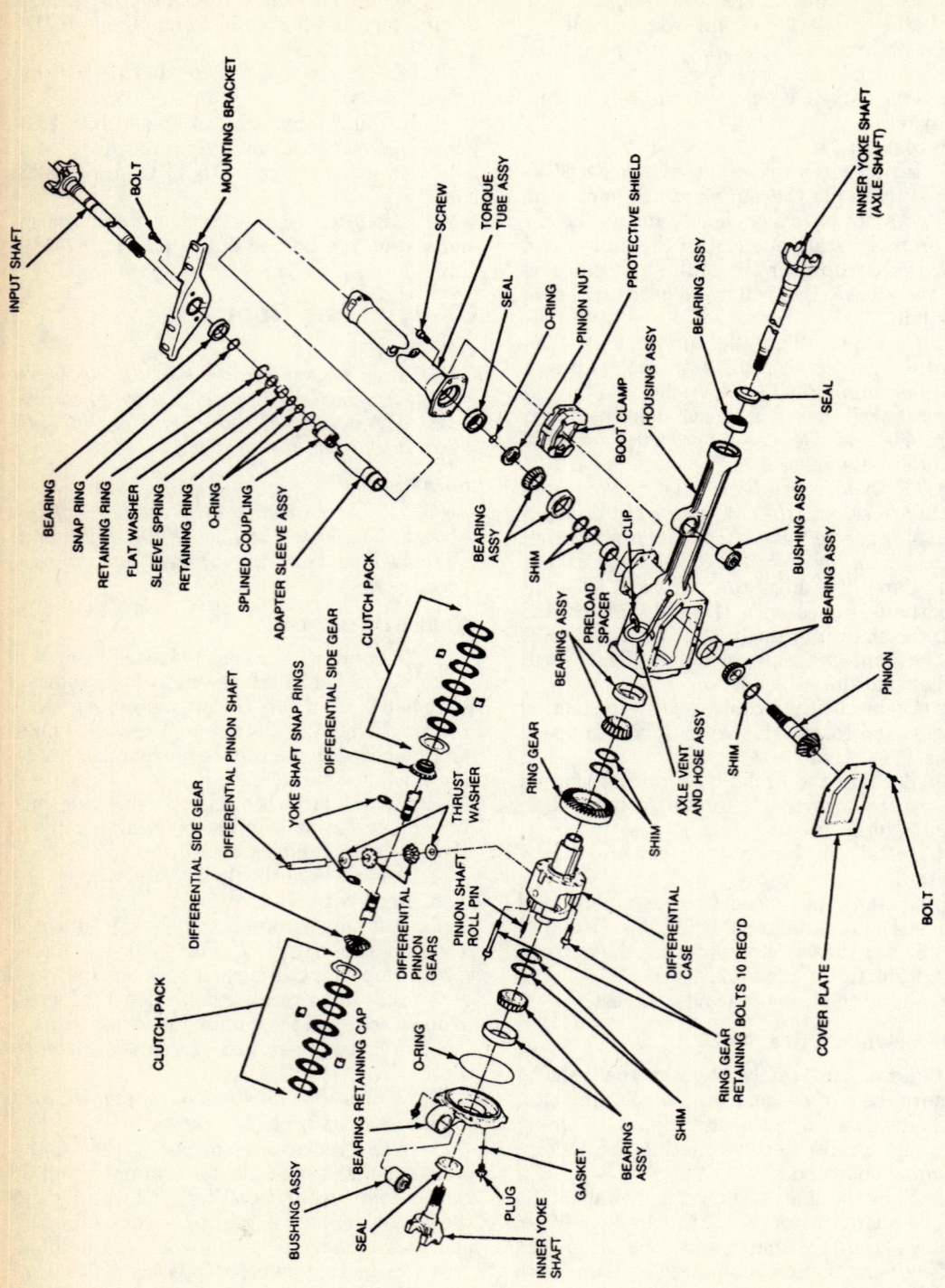

Exploded view of the all wheel drive assembly

DRIVE TRAIN 435

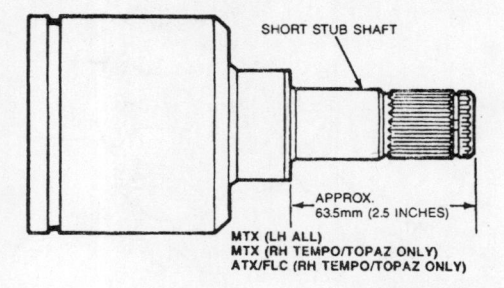

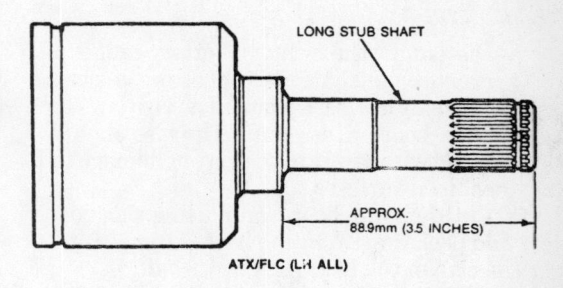

Typical double offset CV-joint

SHORT STUB SHAFT
APPROX. 63.5mm (2.5 INCHES)
MTX (LH ALL)
MTX (RH TEMPO/TOPAZ ONLY)
ATX/FLC (RH TEMPO/TOPAZ ONLY)

LONG STUB SHAFT
APPROX. 88.9mm (3.5 INCHES)
ATX/FLC (LH ALL)

To install:
12. Clean all parts (except boots) in a suitable solvent.
13. Inspect all CV-joint parts for excessive wear, looseness, pitting, rust and cracks.
NOTE: *CV-joint components are matched during assembly. If inspection reveals damage or wear the entire joint must be replaced as an assembly. Do not replace a joint merely because the parts appear polished. Shiny areas in ball races and on the cage spheres are normal.*
14. Install a new circlip, supplies with the service kit, in groove nearest end of shaft. Do not over-expand or twist circlip during installation.
15. Install inner race in the cage. The race is installed through the large end of the cage with the circlip counterbore facing the large end of the cage.
16. With the cage and inner race properly aligned, install the balls by pressing through the cage windows with the heel of the hand.
17. Assemble inner race and cage assembly in outer race.
18. Push the inner race and cage assembly by hand, into the outer race. Install with inner race chamfer facing out.
19. Install ball retainer into groove inside of outer race.
20. Install new CV-boot.
21. Tighten clamp securely but not to the point where the clamp bridge is cut or the boot is damaged.
22. Position stop ring and new circlip into grooves on shaft.
23. Fill CV-joint outer race with 3.2 oz. (90 grams) of grease, the spread 1.4 oz. (40 grams) of grease evenly inside boot for a total combined fill of 4.6 oz. (130 grams).
24. With boot peeled back, install CV-joint using soft tipped hammer. Ensure splines are aligned prior to installing CV-joint onto shaft.
25. Remove all excess grease from the CV-joint external surfaces.
26. Position boot over CV-joint. Before installing boot clamp, move CV-joint in or out, as necessary, to adjust to the proper length.
NOTE: *Insert a suitable tool between the boot and outer bearing race and allow the trapped air to escape from the boot. The air should be released from the boot only after adjusting to the proper dimensions.*
27. Ensure boot is seated in its groove and clamp in position.
28. Tighten clamp securely but not to the point where the clamp bridge is cut or the boot is damaged.
29. Install halfshaft assembly in vehicle.
30. Connect negative battery cable.

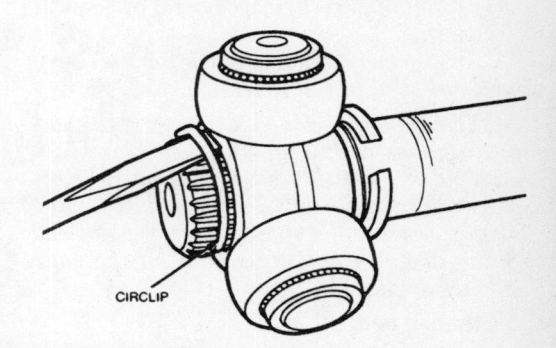

CIRCLIP

Removing the circlip from the shaft

Remove outer race.

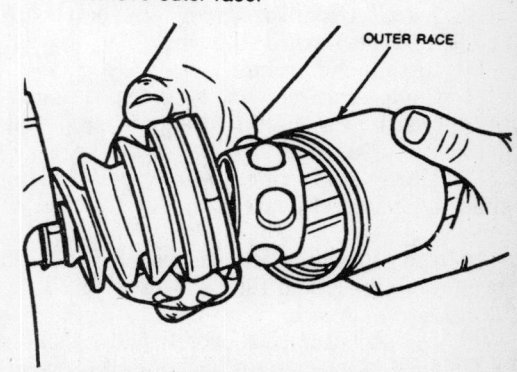

OUTER RACE

Removing the outer race assembly

436 DRIVE TRAIN

TRIPOD TYPE

1. Disconnect the negative battery cable.
2. Remove halfshaft assembly from vehicle. Place halfshaft in vice. Do not allow vise jaws to contact the boot or its clamp. The vise should be equipped with jaw caps to prevent damage to any machined surfaces.
3. Cut the large boot clamp using side cutters and peel away from the boot. After removing the clamp, roll boot back over shaft.
4. Bend retaining tabs back slightly to allow for tripod removal.
5. Separate outer race from tripod.
6. Move stop ring back on shaft using snapring pliers.
7. Move tripod assembly back on shaft to allow access to circlip.
8. Remove circlip from shaft.
9. Remove tripod assembly from shaft. Remove boot.
10. When replacing damaged CV-boots, the grease should be checked for contamination. If the CV-joints were operating satisfactorily and the grease does not appear to be contaminated, add grease and replace the boot. If the lubricant appears contaminated, proceed with a complete CV-joint disassembly and inspection.

To install:
11. Clean all parts (except boots) in a suitable solvent.
12. Inspect all CV-joint parts for excessive wear, looseness, pitting, rust and cracks.

NOTE: *CV-joint components are matched during assembly. If inspection reveals damage or wear the entire joint must be replaced as an assembly. Do not replace a joint merely because the parts appear polished. Shiny areas in ball races and on the cage spheres are normal.*

13. Install new CV-boot.
14. Tighten clamp securely but not to the point where the clamp bridge is cut or the boot is damaged.
15. Install tripod assembly on shaft with chamfered side toward stop ring.
16. Install new circlip.
17. Compress circlip and slide tripod assembly forward over circlip to expose stop ring groove.
18. Move stop ring into groove using snapring pliers. Ensure it is fully seated in groove.
19. Fill CV-joint outer race with 3.5 oz. (100 grams) of grease and fill CV-boot with 2.1 oz. (60 grams) of grease.
20. Install outer race over tripod assembly and bend 6 retaining tabs back into their original position.
21. Remove all excess grease from CV-joint

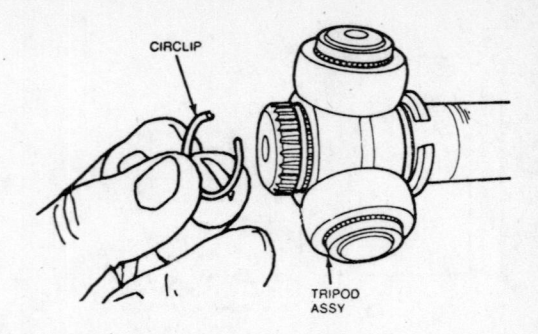

Installing a new circlip to the shaft

Removing the tripod assembly

external surfaces. Position boot over CV-joint. Move CV-joint in and out as necessary, to adjust to proper length.

NOTE: *Insert a suitable tool between the boot and outer bearing race and allow the trapped air to escape from the boot. The air should be released from the boot only after adjusting to the proper dimensions.*

22. Ensure boot is seated in its groove and clamp in position.
23. Tighten clamp securely but not to the point where the clamp bridge is cut or the boot is damaged.
24. Install a new circlip, supplied with service kit, in groove nearest end of shaft by starting one end in the groove and working clip over stub shaft end and into groove.
25. Install halfshaft assembly in vehicle.
26. Connect negative battery cable.

Outer Boot

1. Disconnect the negative battery cable.
2. Remove halfshaft assembly from vehicle.
3. Place halfshaft in vice. Do not allow vise jaws to contact the boot or its clamp. The vise should be equipped with jaw caps to prevent damage to any machined surfaces.
4. Cut the large boot clamp using side cutters and peel away from the boot. After removing the clamp, roll boot back over shaft.
5. Support the interconnecting shaft in a

DRIVE TRAIN 437

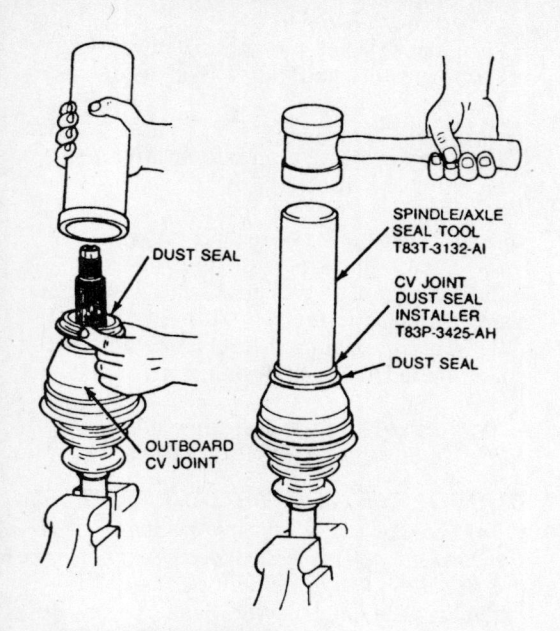

Installing a new dust shield

soft jaw vise and angle the CV-joint to expose inner bearing race.

6. Using a brass drift and hammer, give a sharp tap to the inner bearing race to dislodge the internal circlip and separate the CV-joint from the interconnecting shaft. Take care not to drop the CV-joint at separation.

7. Remove the boot.

8. When replacing damaged CV-boots, the grease should be checked for contamination. If the CV-joints were operating satisfactorily and the grease does not appear to be contaminated, add grease and replace the boot. If the lubricant appears contaminated, proceed with a complete CV-joint disassembly and inspection.

9. Remove circlip located near the end of the shaft. Discard the circlip. Use new clip supplied with boot replacement kit and CV-joint overhaul kit.

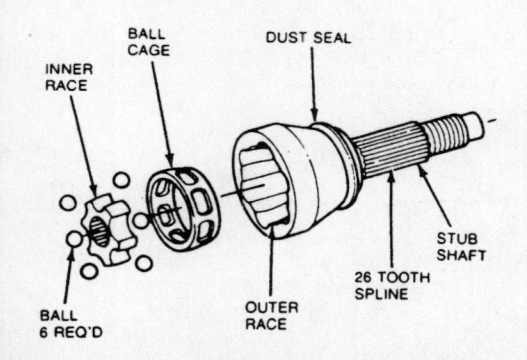

Exploded view of a typical outboard CV-joint and boot

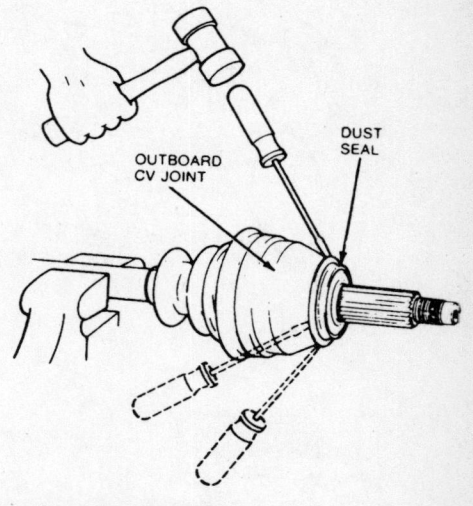

Removing the dust shield

10. Clamp CV-joint stub shaft in a vise with the outer face facing up. Care should be taken not to damage dust seal. The vise must be equipped with jaw caps to prevent damage to the shaft splines.

11. Press down on inner race until it tilts enough to allow removal of ball. A tight assembly can be tilted by tapping the inner race with wooden dowel and hammer. Do not hit the cage.

12. With cage sufficiently tilted, remove ball from cage. Remove all 6 balls in this manner.

13. Pivot cage and inner race assembly until it is straight up and down in outer race. Align cage windows with outer race lands while pivoting the bearing cage. With the cage pivoted and aligned, lift assembly from the outer race.

14. Rotate inner race up and out of the cage.

To install:

15. Clean all parts (except boots) in a suitable solvent.

16. Inspect all CV-joint parts for excessive wear, looseness, pitting, rust and cracks.

NOTE: *CV-joint components are matched during assembly. If inspection reveals damage or wear the entire joint must be replaced as an assembly. Do not replace a joint merely because the parts appear polished. Shiny areas in ball races and on the cage spheres are normal.*

17. Apply a light coating of grease on inner and outer ball races. Install the inner race in cage.

18. Install inner race and cage assembly in the outer race.

19. Install the assembly vertically and pivot 90 degrees into position.

20. Align cage and inner race with outer race. Tilt inner race and cage and install one of

DRIVE TRAIN

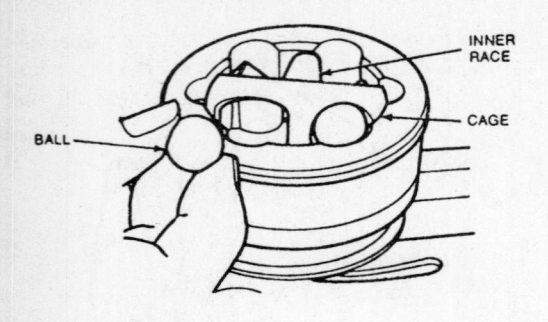

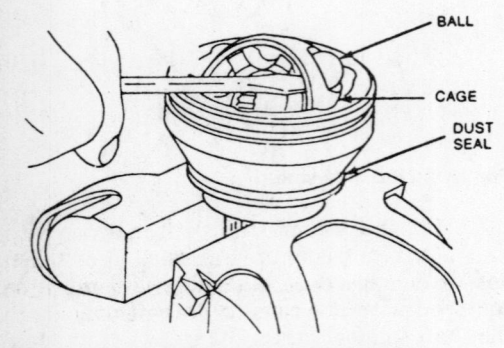

Removing the ball bearings from the cage

the 6 balls. Repeat this process until the remaining balls are installed.

21. Install new CV-joint boot.
22. Tighten clamp securely but not to the point where the clamp bridge is cut or the boot is damaged.
23. Install the stop ring, if removed.
24. Install a new circlip, supplied with the service kit, in groove nearest the end of the shaft.
25. Pack CV-joint with grease. Any grease remaining in tube should be spread evenly inside boot.
26. With the boot "peeled" back, position CV-joint on shaft and tap into position using a plastic tipped hammer.
27. Remove all excess grease from the CV-joint external surfaces.
28. Position boot over CV-joint.
29. Ensure boot is seated in its groove and clamp into position.
30. Tighten clamp securely but not to the point where the clamp bridge is cut or the boot is damaged.
31. Install halfshaft assembly in vehicle.
32. Connect negative battery cable.

DUST DEFLECTOR REPLACEMENT

NOTE: *The dust deflector should be replaced only if inspection determines it to be cracked, broken or deteriorated.*

Remove the old deflector. Soak the new dust deflector in a container of hot water and let it soak for five to ten minutes. Position the dust deflector over the sleeve with the ribbed side facing the CV-joint. Tap the deflector into position with the Dust Deflector Installer (T81P-3425-A) and a hammer.

CLUTCH

The transmission and clutch are employed to vary the relationship between engine speed and the speed of the wheels so that adequate engine power can be produced under all circumstances. The clutch allows engine torque to be

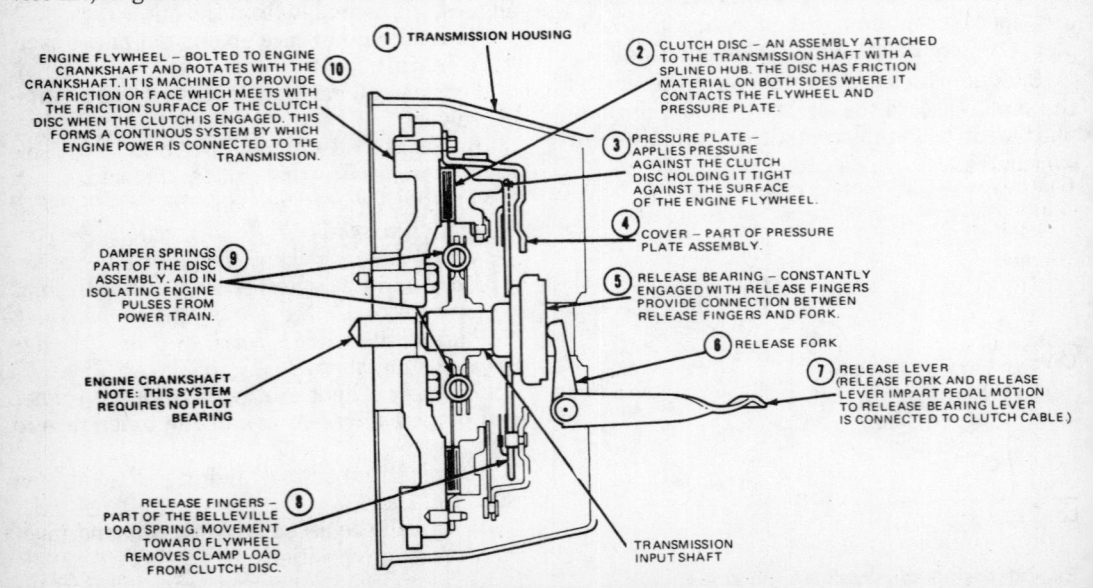

Operation of the clutch components

DRIVE TRAIN 439

applied to the transmission input shaft gradually, due to mechanical slippage. The car can, consequently, be started smoothly from a full stop.

The transmission changes the ratio between the rotating speeds of the engine and the wheels by the use of gears. The lower gears allow full engine power to be applied to the rear wheels during acceleration at low speeds.

The clutch driven plate is a thin disc, the center of which is splined to the transmission input shaft. Both sides of the disc are covered with a layer of material which is similar to brake lining and which is capable of allowing slippage without roughness or excessive noise.

The clutch cover is bolted to the engine flywheel and incorporates a diaphragm spring which provides the pressure to engage the clutch. The cover also houses the pressure plate. The driven disc is sandwiched between the pressure plate and the smooth surface of the flywheel when the clutch pedal is released, thus forcing it to turn at the same speed as the engine crankshaft.

The transmission contains a mainshaft which passes all the way through the transmission, from the clutch to the final drive gear in the transaxle. This shaft is separated at one

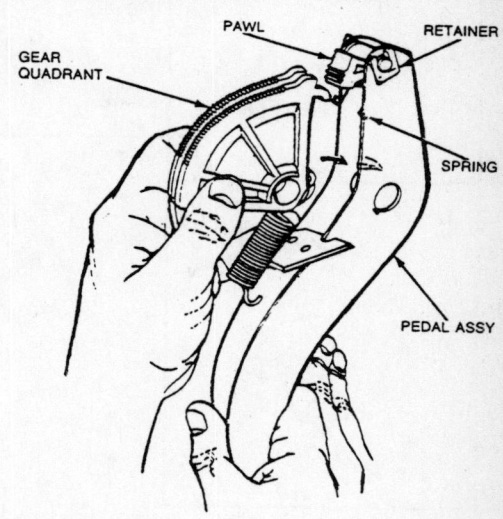

Assembling the gear quadrant tension spring to the gear quadrant of the clutch pedal assembly

Troubleshooting Basic Clutch Problems

Problem	Cause
Excessive clutch noise	Throwout bearing noises are more audible at the lower end of pedal travel. The usual causes are: • Riding the clutch • Too little pedal free-play • Lack of bearing lubrication A bad clutch shaft pilot bearing will make a high pitched squeal, when the clutch is disengaged and the transmission is in gear or within the first 2" of pedal travel. The bearing must be replaced. Noise from the clutch linkage is a clicking or snapping that can be heard or felt as the pedal is moved completely up or down. This usually requires lubrication. Transmitted engine noises are amplified by the clutch housing and heard in the passenger compartment. They are usually the result of insufficient pedal free-play and can be changed by manipulating the clutch pedal.
Clutch slips (the car does not move as it should when the clutch is engaged)	This is usually most noticeable when pulling away from a standing start. A severe test is to start the engine, apply the brakes, shift into high gear and SLOWLY release the clutch pedal. A healthy clutch will stall the engine. If it slips it may be due to: • A worn pressure plate or clutch plate • Oil soaked clutch plate • Insufficient pedal free-play
Clutch drags or fails to release	The clutch disc and some transmission gears spin briefly after clutch disengagement. Under normal conditions in average temperatures, 3 seconds is maximum spin-time. Failure to release properly can be caused by: • Too light transmission lubricant or low lubricant level • Improperly adjusted clutch linkage
Low clutch life	Low clutch life is usually a result of poor driving habits or heavy duty use. Riding the clutch, pulling heavy loads, holding the car on a grade with the clutch instead of the brakes and rapid clutch engagement all contribute to low clutch life.

DRIVE TRAIN

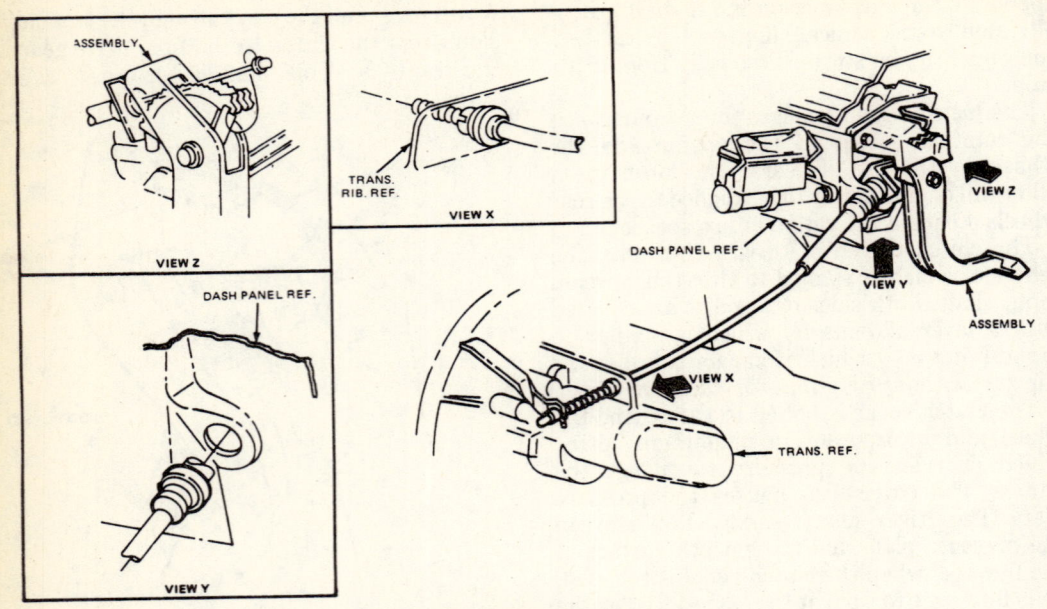

Clutch cable installing

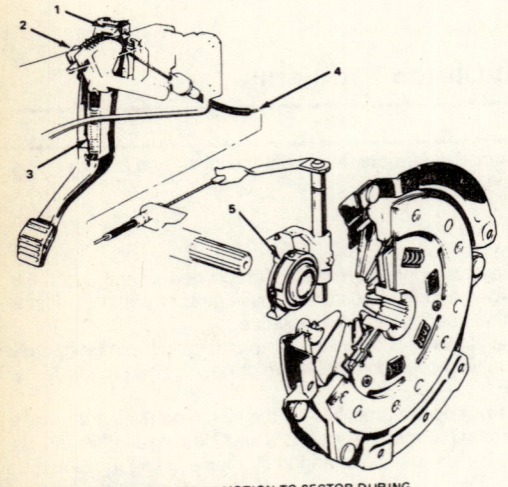

1 PAWL — IMPARTS PEDAL MOTION TO SECTOR DURING DOWNSTROKE. PAWL ENGAGES QUADRANT AT BEGINNING OF DOWNSTROKE.
2 QUADRANT — ACTUATES CABLE DURING PEDAL DOWN-STROKE FOLLOWING CABLE CORE AS CORE IS MOVED DURING DISC FACING WEAR.
3 ADJUSTER SPRING — KEEPS SECTOR IN FIRM CONTACT WITH CABLE. KEEPS RELEASE BEARING IN CONTACT WITH CLUTCH RELEASE FINGERS THROUGH CABLE LINKAGE WITH PEDAL IN UP POSITION.
4 CABLE
5 RELEASE BEARING

Identification of the clutch parts

point, so that front and rear portions can turn at different speeds.

Power is transmitted by a countershaft in the lower gears and reverse. The gears of the countershaft mesh with gears on the mainshaft, allowing power to be carried from one to the other. All the countershaft gears are integral with that shaft, while several of the mainshaft gears can either rotate independently of the shaft or be locked to it. Shifting from one gear to the next causes one of the gear to be freed from rotating with the shaft, and locks another to it. Gears are locked and unlocked by internal dog clutches which slide between the center of the gear and the shaft. The forward gears usually employ synchronizers: friction members which smoothly bring gear and shaft to the same speed before the toothed dog clutches are engaged. The clutch is operating properly if:

1. It will stall the engine when released with the vehicle held stationary.
2. The shift lever can be moved freely between first and reverse gears when the vehicle is stationary and the clutch disengaged.

CAUTION: *The clutch driven disc contains asbestos, which has been determined to be a cancer causing agent. Never clean the clutch surfaces with compressed air. Avoids inhaling any dust from the clutch surface. When cleaning the clutch surfaces, use a commercially available disc brake cleaning fluid.*

Adjustments

PEDAL HEIGHT AND CLUTCH FREE PLAY ADJUSTMENT

The pedal height and clutch free-play in the clutch is adjusted by a built in mechanism that allows the clutch controls to be self-adjusted during normal operation. The self-adjusting fea-

DRIVE TRAIN 441

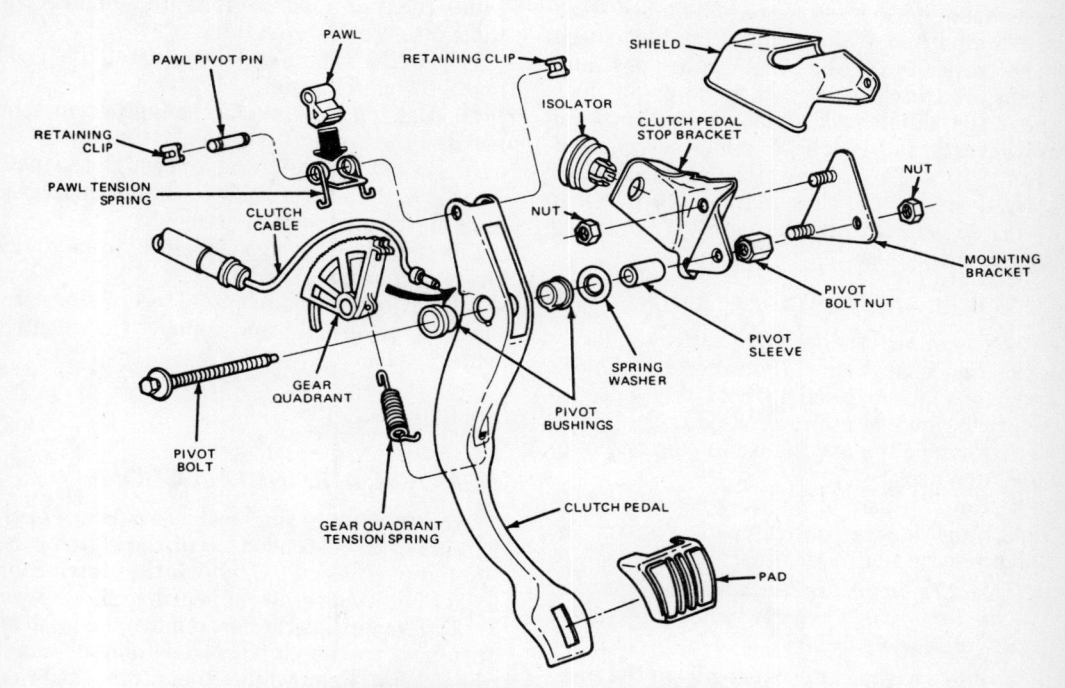

Self-adjusting clutch pedal components

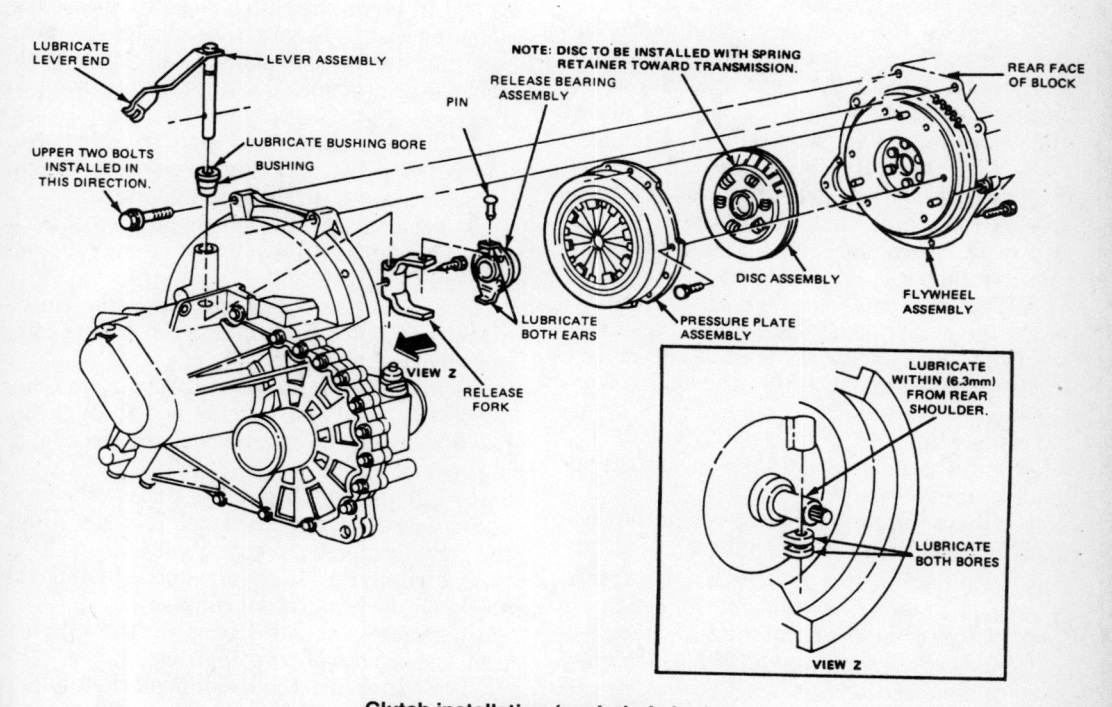

Clutch installation (exploded view)

442 DRIVE TRAIN

ture should be checked every 5000 miles. This is accomplished by insuring that the clutch pedal travels to the top of its upward position. Grasp the clutch pedal with hand or put foot under the clutch pedal, pull up on the pedal until it stops. Very little effort is required (about 10 lbs.). During the application of upward pressure, a click may be heard which means an adjustment was necessary and has been accomplished.

REMOVAL AND INSTALLATION

1. Disconnect the negative battery cable.
2. Wedge a 7 in. (178mm) wooden block under the clutch pedal to hold the pedal up slightly beyond its normal position.
3. Remove the air cleaner to gain access to the clutch cable.
4. Using a pair of pliers, grasp the clutch cable, pull it forward and disconnect it from the clutch release shaft assembly.

   NOTE: *Do not grasp the wire strand portion of the inner cable since it may cut the wires and cause cable failure.*

5. Remove the clutch casing from the insulator which is located on the rib on the top of the transaxle case.
6. On the Tempo or Topaz, remove the panel from above the clutch pedal pad.
7. Remove the rear screw and move the clutch shield away from the brake pedal support bracket. Loosen the front retaining screw, located near the toe board, rotate the shield aside and snug the screw to retain the shield.
8. With the clutch pedal raised to release the pawl, rotate the gear quadrant forward, unhook the clutch cable and allow the quadrant to swing rearward; do not allow the quadrant to snap back.
9. Pull the cable through the recess between the clutch pedal and the gear quadrant and from the insulator of the pedal assembly.
10. Remove the cable from the engine compartment.

To install:

11. Lift the clutch pedal to disengage the adjusting mechanism.
12. Insert the clutch cable through the dash panel and the dash panel grommet.

    NOTE: *Be sure the clutch cable is routed under the brake lines and not trapped at the spring tower by the brake lines. If equipped with power steering, rout the cable inboard of the power steering hose.*

13. Push the clutch cable through the insulator on the stop bracket and through the recess between the pedal and the gear quadrant.
14. Lift the clutch pedal to release the pawl, rotate the gear quadrant forward and hook the cable into the gear quadrant.
15. On the Tempo or Topaz, install the panel above the clutch pedal.
16. Using a piece of wire or tape, secure the pedal in the up-most position.
17. Insert the clutch cable through the insulator and connect the cable to the clutch release lever in the engine compartment.
18. Remove the wooden block from under the clutch pedal.
19. Depress the clutch pedal several times. Install the air cleaner and connect the negative battery cable.

Clutch Cable

REMOVAL AND INSTALLATION

1. From under the hood, use a pair of pliers and grasp the extended tip of the clutch cable (on top of transaxle). Unhook the clutch cable from the clutch throwout bearing release lever.
2. From inside the car, remove the fresh air duct next to the clutch pedal (non-air conditioned cars). Remove the shield from the brake pedal support bracket. On Tempo/Topaz models remove the panel above the clutch pedal.
3. Lift up on the clutch pedal to release the adjusting pawl. Rotate the adjustment gear quadrant forward. Unhook the clutch cable from the gear quadrant. Swing the quadrant to the rear.
4. Pull the clutch cable out from between the clutch pedal and the gear quadrant and from the isolator on the gear quadrant.
5. From under the hood, pull the clutch cable through the firewall and remove it from the car.
6. From under the hood, insert the clutch cable through the firewall into the drivers compartment.
7. Push the clutch cable through the isolator on the pedal stop bracket and through the recess between the clutch pedal and the adjusting gear quadrant.
8. Lift the clutch pedal to release the pawl and rotate the gear quadrant forward. Hook the clutch cable to the gear quadrant.
9. Install the fresh air duct. Install the shield on the brake pedal support.
10. Secure the clutch pedal in the up position. Use a piece of wire, tape, etc.
11. From under the hood, hook the cable to the clutch throwout bearing release lever.
12. Unfasten the clutch pedal and adjust the clutch by operating the clutch pedal several times. Pull up on the pedal to make sure it is reaching the maximum upward position.

Transmission Fluid Indications

The appearance and odor of the transmission fluid can give valuable clues to the overall condition of the transmission. Always note the appearance of the fluid when you check the fluid level or change the fluid. Rub a small amount of fluid between your fingers to feel for grit and smell the fluid on the dipstick.

If the fluid appears:	It indicates:
Clear and red colored	• Normal operation
Discolored (extremely dark red or brownish) or smells burned	• Band or clutch pack failure, usually caused by an overheated transmission. Hauling very heavy loads with insufficient power or failure to change the fluid, often result in overheating. Do not confuse this appearance with newer fluids that have a darker red color and a strong odor (though not a burned odor).
Foamy or aerated (light in color and full of bubbles)	• The level is too high (gear train is churning oil) • An internal air leak (air is mixing with the fluid). Have the transmission checked professionally.
Solid residue in the fluid	• Defective bands, clutch pack or bearings. Bits of band material or metal abrasives are clinging to the dipstick. Have the transmission checked professionally.
Varnish coating on the dipstick	• The transmission fluid is overheating

Driven Disc and Pressure Plate

REMOVAL AND INSTALLATION

1. Disconnect the negative battery cable. Raise and safely support the vehicle. Remove the transaxle.
2. Matchmark the pressure plate assembly and the flywheel so they can be assembled in the same position.
3. Loosen the pressure plate-to-flywheel bolts 1 turn at a time, in sequence, until spring tension is relieved to prevent pressure plate cover distortion.
4. Support the pressure plate and remove the bolts. Remove the pressure plate and clutch disc from the flywheel.
5. Inspect the flywheel, clutch disc, pressure plate, throwout bearing and the clutch fork for wear; replace parts, as required.

NOTE: *If the flywheel shows any signs of overheating (blue discoloration) or if it is badly grooved or scored, it should be refaced or replaced.*

To install:

6. Clean the pressure plate and flywheel surfaces thoroughly. Position the clutch disc and pressure plate into the installed position, aligning the matchmarks made previously; support them with a dummy shaft or clutch aligning tool.

NOTE: *The clutch disc must be assembled so that the flatter side is toward the flywheel.*

7. Install the pressure plate-to-flywheel bolts. Tighten them gradually in a criss-cross pattern to 12–24 ft. lbs. (17–32 Nm). Remove the alignment tool.
8. Lubricate the release bearing and install it in the fork.
9. To complete the installation, reverse the removal procedures. Lower the vehicle and connect the negative battery cable.

AUTOMATIC TRANSAXLE

Identification

The standard ATX automatic transaxle has been used on these vehicles since there conception the biggest change comes in 1990 when the Tempo/Topaz models switch over to the Fluid Lock-Up Torque Converter (FLC). This transmission change has caused a title change for the transaxle used in the Tempo/Topaz to ATX/FLC. With this FLC torque converter, the engine torque is transferred to the transaxle through the oil contained in the torque converter. The converter acts as an automatic clutch with the engine mechanically driving the impeller which, in turn drives the turbine hydraulically. The hydraulically driven turbine is the transaxle input member. It is the hydraulic connection between the impeller and the turbine where a certain amount of engine torque is lost to converter slip.

To minimize the converter inefficiency, the torque converter used in the ATX transaxle contains a splitter gear to provide a mechanical connection between the engine and the transaxle.

DRIVE TRAIN

The splitter gearset is very similar to a planetary gear set.

In first and reverse, the engine torque is 100 percent hydraulically transmitted. In second gear, the engine torque is split into 38 percent transmitted by the turbine (hydraulic) and 62 percent through the splitter gear set (mechanical). The torque converter slip is almost eliminated in third gear with 93 percent mechanical and only 7 percent hydraulic.

On the ATX/FLC transaxle the engine torque is 100 percent hydraulically transmitted in all gear ranges.

Fluid Pan and Filter

REMOVAL AND INSTALLATION

In normal service it should not be necessary nor is it required to drain and refill the AT fluid. However, under severe operation or dusty conditions the fluid should be changed every 20 months or 20,000 miles.

1. Raise the car and safely support it on jackstands.
2. Place a suitable drain pan underneath the transaxle oil pan. Loosen the oil pan mounting bolts and allow the fluid to drain until it reaches the level of the pan flange. Remove the attaching bolts, leaving one end attached so that the pan will tip and the rest of the fluid will drain.
3. Remove the oil pan. Thoroughly clean the pan. Remove the old gasket. Make sure that the gasket mounting surfaces are clean.
4. Remove the transmission filter screen retaining bolt. Remove the screen.
5. Install a new filter screen and O-ring. Place a new gasket on the pan and install the pan to the transmission.
6. Fill the transmission to the correct level. Remove the jackstands and lower the car to the ground.

TRANSAXLE FLUID CONDITION

Pull the transmission dipstick out. Observe the color and odor of the transmission fluid. The color should be red not brown or black. An

Troubleshooting Basic Automatic Transmission Problems

Problem	Cause	Solution
Fluid leakage	• Defective pan gasket	• Replace gasket or tighten pan bolts
	• Loose filler tube	• Tighten tube nut
	• Loose extension housing to transmission case	• Tighten bolts
	• Converter housing area leakage	• Have transmission checked professionally
Fluid flows out the oil filler tube	• High fluid level	• Check and correct fluid level
	• Breather vent clogged	• Open breather vent
	• Clogged oil filter or screen	• Replace filter or clean screen (change fluid also)
	• Internal fluid leakage	• Have transmission checked professionally
Transmission overheats (this is usually accompanied by a strong burned odor to the fluid)	• Low fluid level	• Check and correct fluid level
	• Fluid cooler lines clogged	• Drain and refill transmission. If this doesn't cure the problem, have cooler lines cleared or replaced.
	• Heavy pulling or hauling with insufficient cooling	• Install a transmission oil cooler
	• Faulty oil pump, internal slippage	• Have transmission checked professionally
Buzzing or whining noise	• Low fluid level	• Check and correct fluid level
	• Defective torque converter, scored gears	• Have transmission checked professionally
No forward or reverse gears or slippage in one or more gears	• Low fluid level	• Check and correct fluid level
	• Defective vacuum or linkage controls, internal clutch or band failure	• Have unit checked professionally
Delayed or erratic shift	• Low fluid level	• Check and correct fluid level
	• Broken vacuum lines	• Repair or replace lines
	• Internal malfunction	• Have transmission checked professionally

Lockup Torque Converter Service Diagnosis

Problem	Cause	Solution

No lockup	• Faulty oil pump
	• Sticking governor valve
	• Valve body malfunction
	  (a) Stuck switch valve
	  (b) Stuck lockup valve
	  (c) Stuck fail-safe valve
	• Failed locking clutch
	• Leaking turbine hub seal
	• Faulty input shaft or seal ring
		• Replace oil pump
		• Repair or replace as necessary
		• Repair or replace valve body or its internal components as necessary
		
		• Replace torque converter
		• Replace torque converter
		• Repair or replace as necessary

Will not unlock	• Sticking governor valve
	• Valve body malfunction
	  (a) Stuck switch valve
	  (b) Stuck lockup valve
	  (c) Stuck fail-safe valve
		• Repair or replace as necessary
		• Repair or replace valve body or its internal components as necessary

Stays locked up at too low a speed in direct	• Sticking governor valve
	• Valve body malfunction
	  (a) Stuck switch valve
	  (b) Stuck lockup valve
	  (c) Stuck fail-safe valve
		• Repair or replace as necessary
		• Repair or replace valve body or its internal components as necessary

Locks up or drags in low or second	• Faulty oil pump
	• Valve body malfunction
	  (a) Stuck switch valve
	  (b) Stuck fail-safe valve
		• Replace oil pump
		• Repair or replace valve body or its internal components as necessary

Sluggish or stalls in reverse	• Faulty oil pump
	• Plugged cooler, cooler lines or fittings
	• Valve body malfunction
	  (a) Stuck switch valve
	  (b) Faulty input shaft or seal ring
		• Replace oil pump as necessary
		• Flush or replace cooler and flush lines and fittings
		• Repair or replace valve body or its internal components as necessary

Loud chatter during lockup engagement (cold)	• Faulty torque converter • Failed locking clutch • Leaking turbine hub seal	• Replace torque converter • Replace torque converter • Replace torque converter
Vibration or shudder during lockup engagement	• Faulty oil pump • Valve body malfunction • Faulty torque converter • Engine needs tune-up	• Repair or replace oil pump as necessary • Repair or replace valve body or its internal components as necessary • Replace torque converter • Tune engine
Vibration after lockup engagement	• Faulty torque converter • Exhaust system strikes underbody • Engine needs tune-up • Throttle linkage misadjusted	• Replace torque converter • Align exhaust system • Tune engine • Adjust throttle linkage
Vibration when revved in neutral Overheating: oil blows out of dip stick tube or pump seal	• Torque converter out of balance • Plugged cooler, cooler lines or fittings • Stuck switch valve	• Replace torque converter • Flush or replace cooler and flush lines and fittings • Repair switch valve in valve body or replace valve body
Shudder after lockup engagement	• Faulty oil pump • Plugged cooler, cooler lines or fittings • Valve body malfunction • Faulty torque converter • Fail locking clutch • Exhaust system strikes underbody • Engine needs tune-up • Throttle linkage misadjusted	• Replace oil pump • Flush or replace cooler and flush lines and fittings • Repair or replace valve body or its internal components as necessary • Replace torque converter • Replace torque converter • Align exhaust system • Tune engine • Adjust throttle linkage

DRIVE TRAIN

odor can sometimes indicate an overheating condition, clutch disc or band failure.

Wipe the dipstick with a clean white rag. Examine the stain on the rag for specks of solids (metal or dirt) and for signs of contaminates (antifreeze, gum or varnish condition).

If examination shows evidence of metal specks or antifreeze contamination transaxle removal and inspection may be necessary.

TRANSAXLE MODIFICATIONS

Cooler Line Disconnect Tool Usage Push Connect Fittings

To service the transaxle cooler lines, tool T82L-9500-AH or equivalent, is required. The purpose of the tool is to spread the "duck bill" retainer to disengage the tube bead. The following steps are necessary for use of the tool:

To facilitate use of the tool, clean the road dirt from the fitting before inserting the tool into the fitting. Also, it is important to avoid any contamination of the fitting and transaxle, dirt in the fitting could cause an O-ring leak.

1. Slide the tool over the tube.
2. Align the opening of the tool with 1 of the 2 tabs on the fitting "duck bill" retainer.
3. Firmly insert tool into fitting until it seats against the tube bead (a definite click should be hard).
4. With a thumb held against the tool, firmly pull back on the tube until it disengages from the fitting.

> CAUTION: *Do not attempt to separate the cooler line from the fitting by prying with another tool. This will break the plastic insert in fitting and bend the cooler lines at the junction to the fitting.*

Before assembly of the lines in the fitting, visually inspect the plastic retainer in the fitting for a broken tab. If a tab is broken, the fitting must be replaced. Also visually inspect the cooler lines to make sure they are not bent at the junction of the fitting.

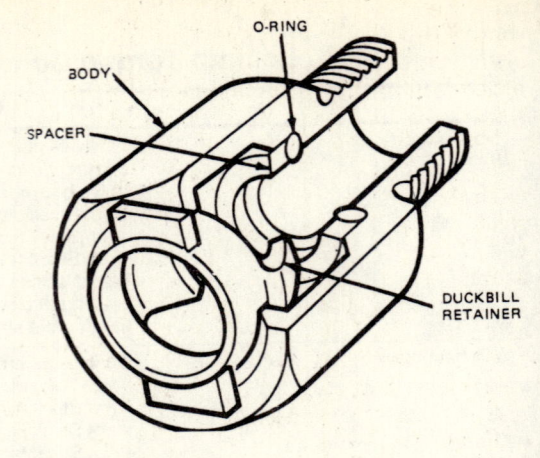

New type line fitting

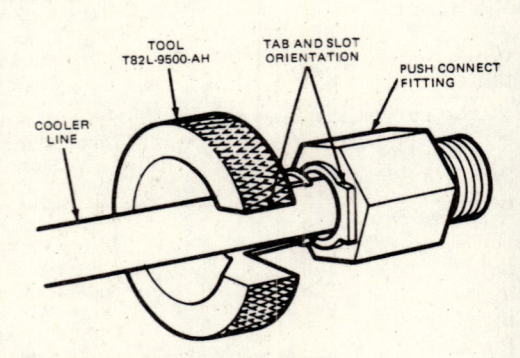

Use of cooler line disconnect tool

Tube assembly is accomplished by inserting the tube into the fitting until the retainer engages the tube head (a definite click should be heard). Pull back on the tube to ensure full engagement.

Sensitive Downshift and 3rd–2nd/2nd–3rd Shift Cycling On Light Throttle

On the 1984–85 Tempo/Topaz, concerns of 3-2 torque demand sensitivity and 3-2/2-3 shift hunting can be resolved by discarding the 3-2

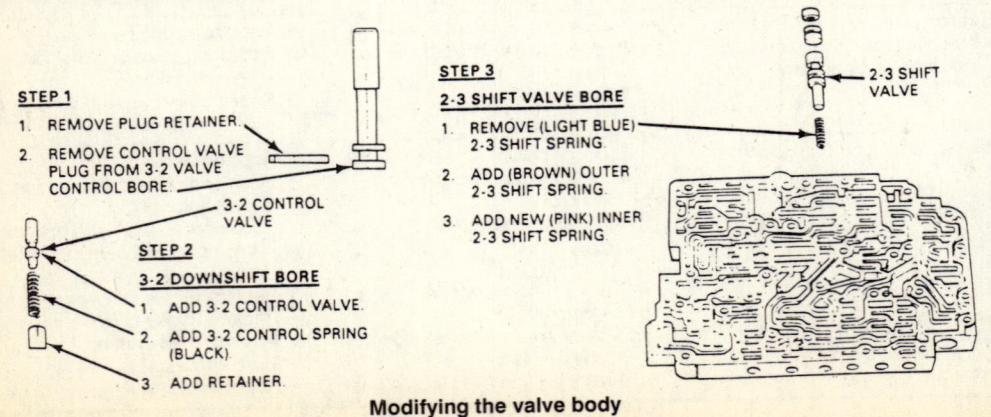

STEP 1
1. REMOVE PLUG RETAINER.
2. REMOVE CONTROL VALVE PLUG FROM 3-2 VALVE CONTROL BORE.

STEP 2
3-2 DOWNSHIFT BORE
1. ADD 3-2 CONTROL VALVE.
2. ADD 3-2 CONTROL SPRING (BLACK).
3. ADD RETAINER.

STEP 3
2-3 SHIFT VALVE BORE
1. REMOVE (LIGHT BLUE) 2-3 SHIFT SPRING.
2. ADD (BROWN) OUTER 2-3 SHIFT SPRING.
3. ADD NEW (PINK) INNER 2-3 SHIFT SPRING.

Modifying the valve body

DRIVE TRAIN

control valve spring and installing a check ball at the bottom of the bore. This repair is for vehicles with the following calibration codes:
- 4-26E-RO
- 4-26D-R18
- 4-26S-R13

To perform the repair the main control assembly must be removed and disassembled. Revised assembly of the 3rd-2nd control valve is as follows:

1. Remove main control assembly and disassemble.
2. Locate and remove the 3rd-2nd control valve components.
3. Discard the control valve spring (yellow or purple in color).
4. Install check ball (EOAZ-7E195-B) at bottom of bore.
5. Replace 3rd-2nd control valve with main control, do not install spring, and install retainer.
6. Assemble and install the main control assembly.

3rd-2nd/2nd-3rd Shift Cycling on Light Throttle

On the 1984-85 Tempo/Topaz, concerns of light throttle 2nd-3rd/3rd-2nd shift hunting at approximately 24 mph can be resolved by installing a new design governor spring. This repair is for vehicles with the following calibration codes:
- 4-26D-R18
- 4-26S-R13
- 4-26G-R11

To perform the repair, the governor assembly must be removed from the transaxle.

1. Remove the governor assembly.
2. Remove and discard the governor spring (pink in color) and replace with service spring (E43Z-7E467-A – brown in color).

NOTE: *Position 1 end of the governor spring onto the spring seat of the primary weight. Compress the spring and position the other end of the spring onto the spring seat of the secondary weight.*

3. Install the modified governor assembly into the transaxle.

Low Speed Shudder and Boom in 3rd Gear

On the 1986 Tempo/Topaz, a low speed shudder and boom while driving in 3rd gear may be caused by shift point variance in the 2-3 upshift and 3-2 downshift pattern. To correct this problem, install a new design main control service kit that revises the part throttle 2-3 upshift and 3-2 downshift pattern. Use the following procedure to perform the repair:

1. Obtain main control service kit (E6FZ-7A230-A).

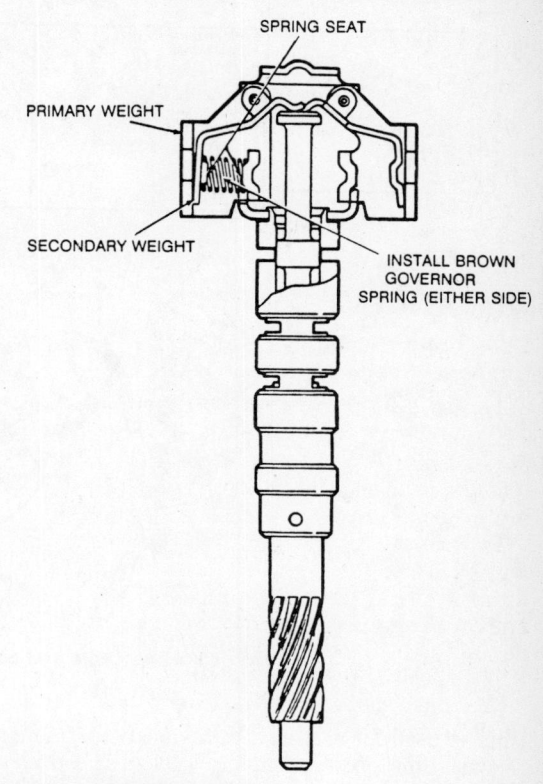

Governor modification

2. Replace the 3-2 control valve bore plug and retainer with a 3-2 downshift valve, spring and flat plate retainer.
3. Replace the 2-3 spring with the assembly from the repair kit.

Adjustments

THROTTLE VALVE CONTROL LINKAGE

The Throttle Valve (TV) Control Linkage System consists of a lever on the carburetor or throttle body of the injection unit, linkage shaft assembly, mounting bracket assembly, control rod assembly, a control lever on the transaxle and a lever return spring.

The coupling lever follows the movement of throttle lever and has an adjustment screw

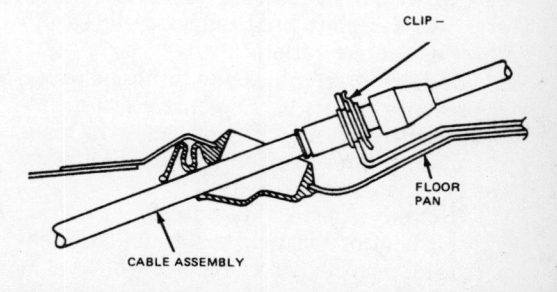

Shift cable (ATX) installation through the floor pan

448 DRIVE TRAIN

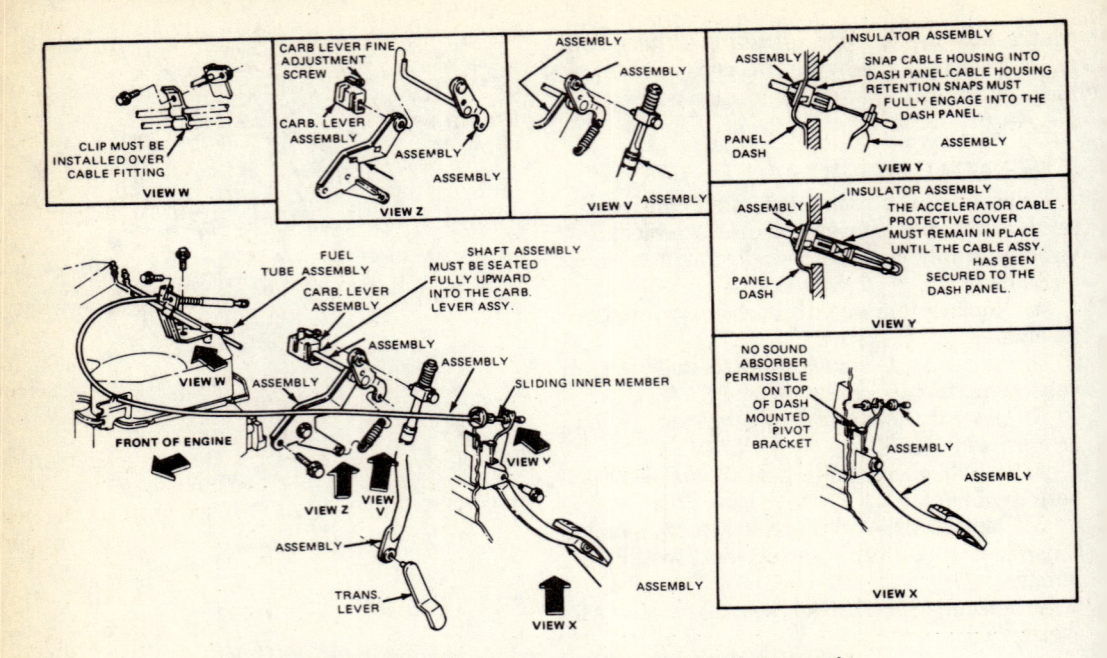

Throttle linkage cable and components; automatic transaxle

that is used for setting TV linkage adjustment when a line pressure gauge is used. If a pressure gauge is not available, a manual adjustment can be made.

A number of shift troubles can occur if the throttle valve linkage is not in adjustment. Some are:

1. **Symptom:** Excessively early and/or soft upshift with or without slip-bump feel. No forced downshift (kickdown) function at appropriate speeds.
   Cause: TV control linkage is set too short.
   Remedy: Adjust linkage.

2. **Symptom:** Extremely delayed or harsh upshifts and harsh idle engagement.
   Cause: TV control linkage is set too long.
   Remedy: Adjust linkage.

3. **Symptom:** Harsh idle engagement after the engine is warmed up. Shift clunk when throttle is backed off after full or heavy throttle acceleration. Harsh coasting downshifts (automatic 3–2, 2–1 shift in D range). Delayed upshift at light acceleration.
   Cause: Interference due to hoses, wires, etc. prevents return of TV control rod or TV linkage shaft. Excessive friction caused by binding grommets prevents the TV control linkage to return to its proper location.
   Remedy: Correct the interference area, check for bent or twisted rods, levers, or damaged grommets. Repair or replace whatever is necessary. Check and adjust linkage is necessary.

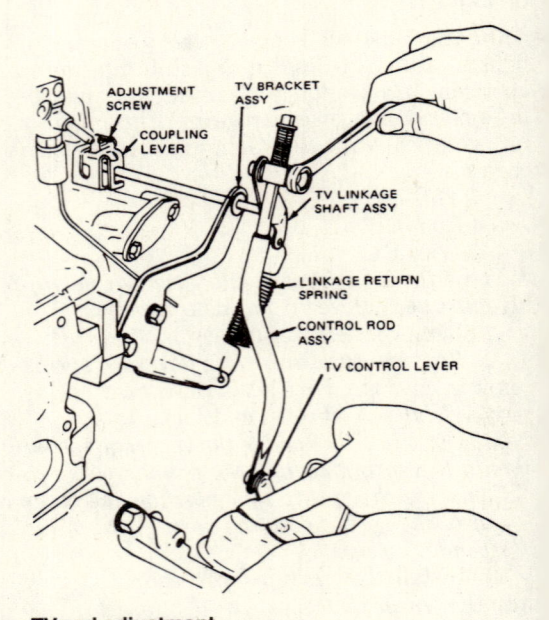

TV rod adjustment

4. **Symptom:** Erratic/delayed upshifts, possibly no kickdown, harsh engagement.
   Cause: Clamping bolt on trunion at the upper end of the TV control rod is loose.
   Remedy: Reset TV control linkage.

5. **Symptom:** No upshift and harsh engagements.
   Cause: TV control rod is disconnected or the linkage return spring is broken or disconnected.

Remedy: Reconnect TV control rod, check and replace the connecting grommet if necessary, reconnect or replace the TV return spring.

THROTTLE LINKAGE ADJUSTMENT

NOTE: *The TV linkage adjustment is set at the factory and is critical in establishing automatic transaxle upshift and downshift timing and feel. Any time the engine, transmission or throttle linkage components are removed, it is recommended that the TV linkage adjustment be reset after the component installation or replacement*

1981–85 Models

The TV control linkage is adjusted at the sliding trunion block.

1. Adjust the curb idle speed to specification as shown on the under hood decal.
2. After the curb idle speed has been set, shut off the engine. Make sure the choke is completely opened. Check the carburetor throttle lever to make sure it is against the hot engine curb idle stop.
3. Set the coupling lever adjustment screw at its approximate midrange. Make sure the TV linkage shaft assembly is fully seated upward into the coupling lever.

CAUTION: *If adjustment of the linkage is necessary, allow the EGR valve to cool so you won't get burned.*

4. To adjust, loosen the bolt on the sliding block on the TV control rod a minimum of one turn. Clean any dirt or corrosion from the control rod, free-up the trunion block so that it will slide freely on the control rod.
5. Rotate the transaxle TV control lever up using a finger and light force, to insure that the TV control lever is against its internal stop. With reducing the pressure on the control lever, tighten the bolt on the trunion block.
6. Check the carburetor throttle lever to be sure it is still against the hot idle stop. If not, repeat the adjustment steps.

1986–90 Except 1.9L Engine

1. Disconnect the negative battery cable.
2. Remove the splash shield from the cable retainer bracket.
3. Loosen the trunion bolt at the throttle valve rod.
4. Install a plastic clip to bottom the throttle valve rod; be sure the clip does not telescope.
5. Be sure the return spring is connected between the throttle valve rod and the retaining bracket to hold the transaxle throttle valve lever at it's idle position.
6. Make sure the throttle lever is resting on the throttle return control screw.

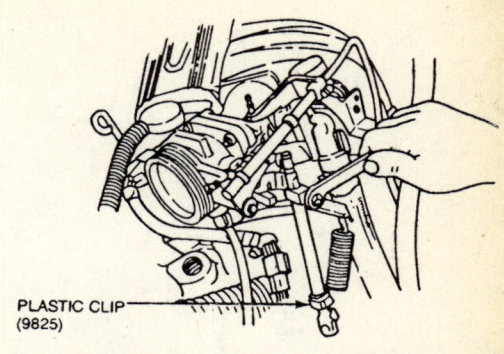

Making the TV (throttle linkage) linkage — Tempo and Topaz

7. Tighten the throttle valve rod trunion bolt and remove the plastic clip.
8. Install the splash shield. Connect the negative battery cable and check the vehicle's operation.

1.9L Engine

1. Disconnect the negative battery cable.
2. Set the parking brake and place the transaxle shift lever into **P**.
3. Loosen the sliding trunion block bolt, located on the throttle valve control rod assembly, a minimum of 1 turn.
4. Make sure the trunion block slides freely on the control rod.
5. Using a jumper wire, connect it between the STI connector and the signal return ground on the self-test connector.
6. Turn the ignition switch to the **RUN** position but do not start the engine. The Idle Speed Control (ISC) plunger should retract; wait until the plunger is fully retracted, about 10 seconds.
7. Turn the ignition switch **OFF** and remove the jumper wire.
8. Using light force, pull the throttle valve rod upward to ensure the control lever is against the internal stop.
9. Allow the trunion to slide on the rod to it's normal position.
10. Without relaxing the pressure on the throttle valve control lever, tighten the trunion block bolt.
11. Connect negative battery cable.

TRANSMISSION CONTROL LEVER ADJUSTMENT

1. Position the selector lever in Drive against the rear stop.
2. Raise the car and support it safely on jackstands. Loosen the manual lever to control lever nut.
3. Move the transmission lever to the Drive position, second detent from the rear most position. Tighten the attaching nut. Check the op-

450 DRIVE TRAIN

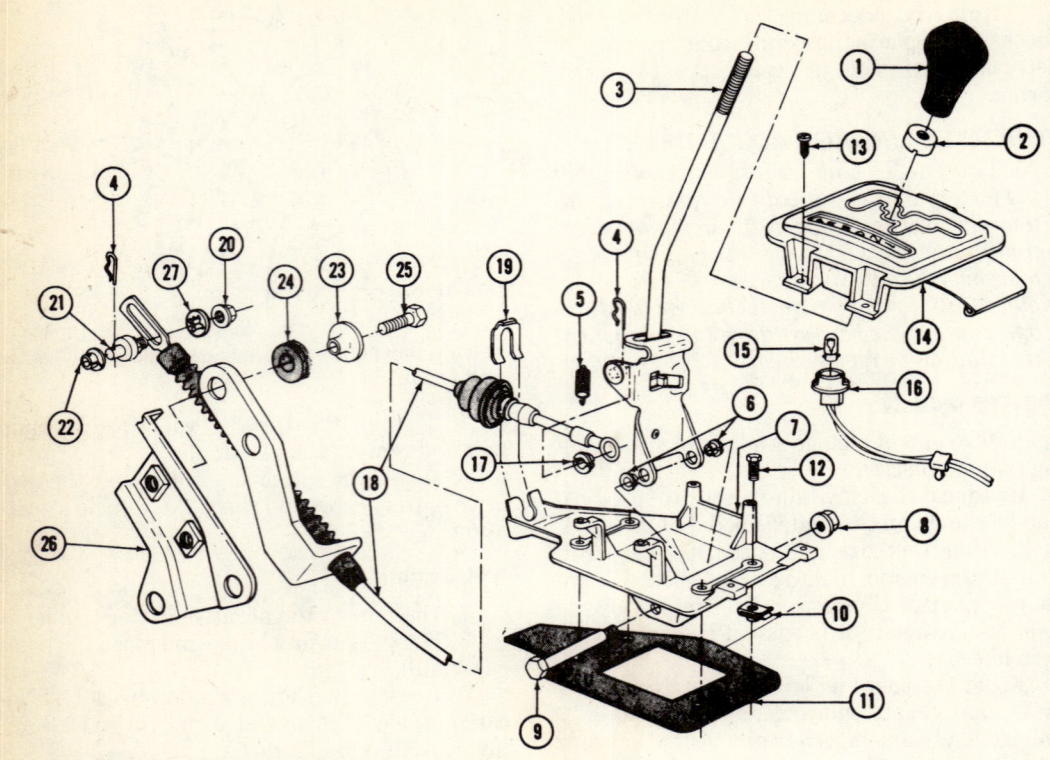

1. Knob assy., trans. gr. shift lever
2. Nut, trans. gr. shift lever ball lock
3. Lever & adaptor assy., trans. control selector
4. Pin, retaining
5. Spring, trans. park gear lockout rtn.
6. Bushing, trans. gear shift lever shaft
7. Housing, trans. control selector
8. Nut, M8-1.25 hex flg.
9. Bolt, M8 x 1.25 x 82.0 hex flg. pilot
10. Nut, M6-1.00 "U"
11. Seal, trans. control selector housing
12. Bolt, M6-1.00 x 25.0 hex flg. hd.
13. Screw, 4.2 x 13.0 hex wa. hd. tap.
14. Bezel assy., trans. control sel. dial
15. Bulb
16. Indicator bulb harness
17. Bushing, trans. gear shift lever cable
18. Cable & bracket assy.
19. Clip, hand brake cable spring lock
20. Nut & washer assy.
21. Stud, trans. gr. shift connecting rod adjusting
22. Bushing, trans. control shift rod clevis
23. Spacer, trans. control cable bracket
24. Insulator, trans. control cable bracket
25. Bolt, M10-1.5 x 20.0 hex flg. hd.
26. Retainer assy., trans. control cable bracket
27. Nut, 5/16-18 round push on

Shift lever components, automatic transaxle

eration of the transmission in each selector position. Readjust if necessary. Lower the car.

SHIFT LINKAGE ADJUSTMENT

1. Place the gear shift selector into **D**.

NOTE: *Be sure to hold the gear selector lever in the rearward position during linkage adjustment.*

2. Working at the transaxle, loosen the transaxle lever-to-control cable nut.
3. Move the transaxle lever to the **D** position or **2nd** detent from the rear.
4. Torque the adjusting nut to 10–15 ft. lbs. (14–20 Nm).
5. Make sure all gears engage correctly and the vehicle will only start in **P** or **D**.

SHIFT LEVER CABLE REMOVAL AND INSTALLATION

1. Remove the shift knob, locknut, console, bezel assembly, control cable clip and cable retaining pin.
2. Disengage the rubber grommet from the floor pan by pushing it into the engine compartment. Raise the car and safely support it on jackstands.
3. Remove the retaining nut and control cable assembly from the transmission lever. Remove the control cable bracket bolts. Pull the cable through the floor.
4. To install the cable, feed the round end through the floor board. Press the rubber grommet into its mounting hole.

DRIVE TRAIN

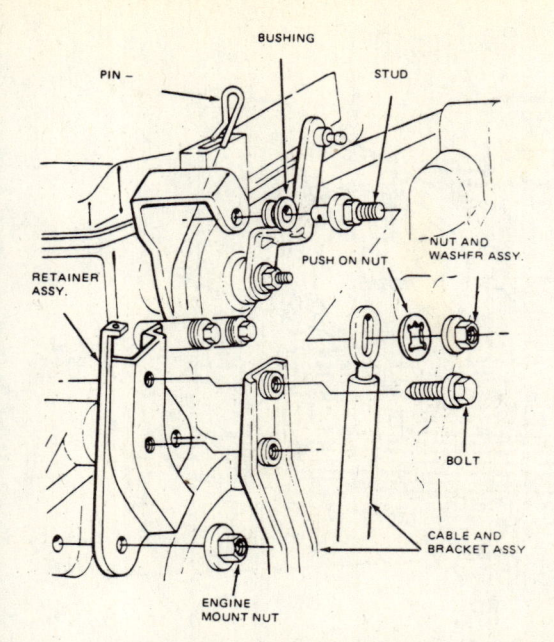

Exploded view of the installation of the shift cable and bracket

5. Position the control cable assembly in the selector lever housing and install the spring clip. Install the bushing and control cable assembly on the selector lever and housing assembly shaft and secure it with the retaining pin.

Install the bezel assembly, console, locknut and shift knob. Position the selector lever in the Drive position. The selector lever must be held in this position while attaching the other end of the control cable.

6. Position the control cable bracket on the retainer bracket and secure the tow mounting bolts.
7. Shift the control lever into the second detent from full rearward (Drive position).
8. Place the cable end on the transmission lever stud. Align the flats on the stud with the slot in the cable. Make sure the transmission selector lever has not moved from the second detent position and tighten the retaining nut.
9. Lower the car to the ground. Check the operation of the transmission selector in all positions. Make sure the neutral safety switch is operating properly. (The engine should start only in Park or Neutral position).

SELECTOR INDICATOR BULB REPLACEMENT

Remove the console and the four screws that mount the bezel. Lift the bezel assembly and disconnect the indicator bulb harness. Remove the indicator bulb. Install a new bulb and reverse the removal procedure.

Neutral Safety Switch

The mounting location of the neutral safety switch does not provide for adjustment of the switch position when installed. If the engine will not start in **P** or **N** or if it will start in **R** or any of the **D** ranges, check the control linkage adjustment and/or replace with a known good switch.

REMOVAL AND INSTALLATION

1. Set parking brake.
2. Disconnect the battery negative cable.
3. Disconnect the wire connector from the neutral safety switch.
4. Remove the 2 retaining screws from the neutral start switch and remove the switch.

To install:

5. Place the switch on the manual shift shaft and loosely install the retaining bolts.
6. Use a No. 43 drill (0.089 in.) and insert it into the switch to set the contacts.
7. Tighten the retaining screws of the switch, remove the drill and complete the assembly by reversing the removal procedure.
8. Connect negative battery cable.
9. Check the ignition switch for proper starting in **P** or **N**. Also make certain that the start circuit cannot be actuated in the **D** or **R** position and that the column is locked in the **LOCK** position.

TRANSAXLE REMOVAL AND INSTALLATION

1981–85 Escort/Lynx/EXP

1. Disconnect the negative battery cable from the battery.
2. From under the hood, remove the bolts that attach the air manage valve to the AT (automatic transaxle) valve body cover. Disconnect the wiring harness connector from the neutral safety switch.
3. Disconnect the throttle valve linkage and the manual control lever cable. Remove the two transaxle to engine upper attaching bolts. The bolts are located below and on either side of the distributor.
4. Loosen the front wheel lugs slightly. Jack up the front of the car and safely support it on jackstands. Remove the wheels.
5. Drain the transmission fluid. Disconnect the brake hoses from the strut brackets on both sides. Remove the pinch bolts that secure the lower control arms to the steering knuckles. Separate the ball joint from the steering knuckle. Remove the stabilizer bar attaching bracket. Remove the nuts that retain the stabilizer to the control arms. Remove the stabilizer bar. When removing the control arms from the steering knuckles, it will be necessary to bend

DRIVE TRAIN

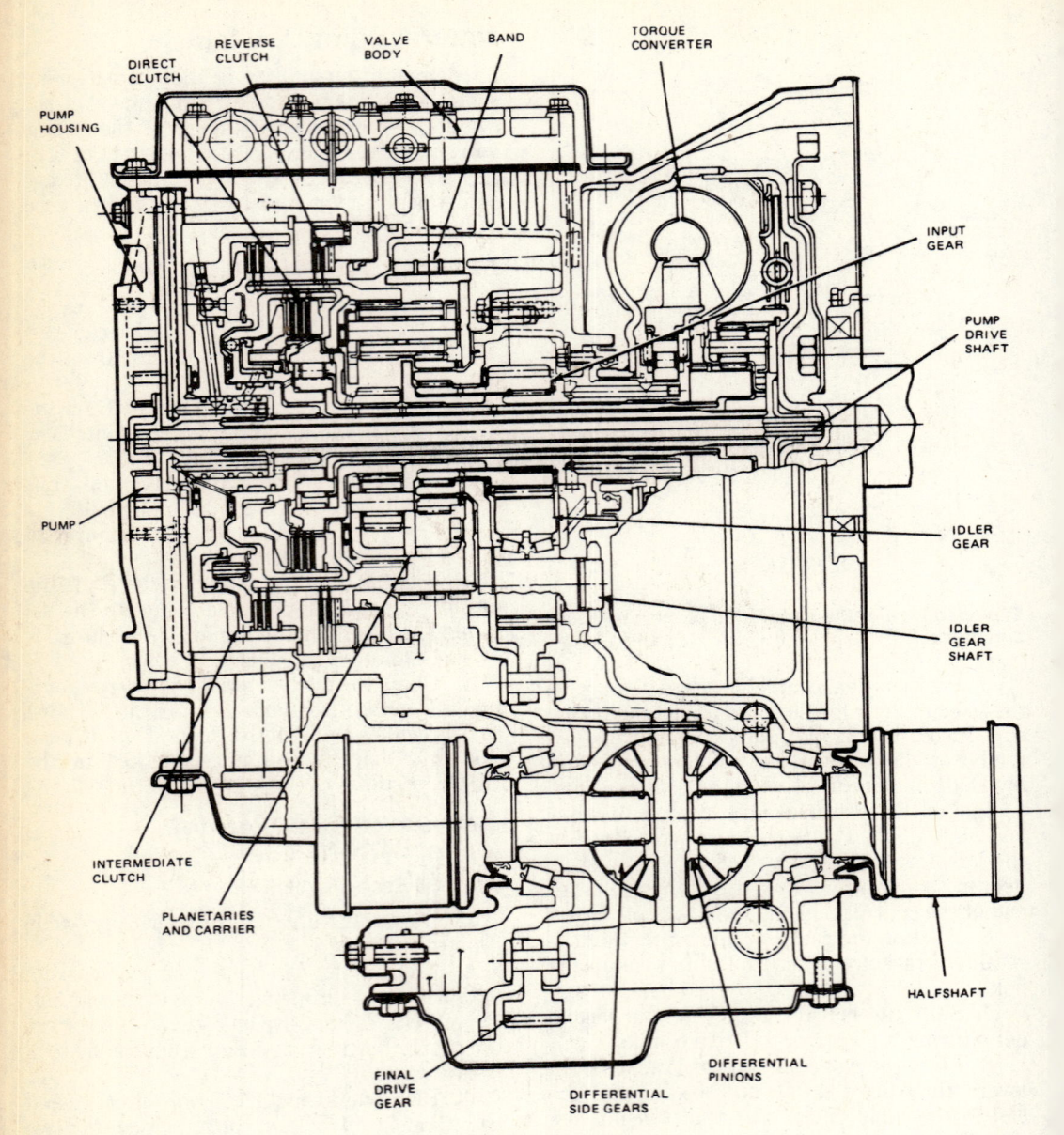

Automatic transaxle

the plastic shield slightly to gain ball joint clearance for removal.

6. Remove the tie rod ends from the steering knuckles. Use a special tie rod removing tool. Pry the right side halfshaft from the transaxle (see halfshaft removal section).

7. Remove the left side halfshaft from the transaxle. Support both right and left side halfshaft out of the way with wire.

8. Install sealing plugs or the equivalent into the transaxle halfshaft mounting holes.

9. Remove the starter support bracket. Disconnect the starter cable. Remove the starter mounting studs and the starter motor. Remove the transaxle support bracket.

10. Remove the lower cover from the transaxle. Turn the converter for access to the converter mounting nuts. Remove the nuts.

11. Remove the nuts that attach the left front insulator to the body bracket. Remove the bracket to body bolts and remove the bracket.

12. Remove the left rear insulator bracket attaching nut.

13. Disconnect the transmission cooler lines. Remove the bolts that attach the manual lever bracket to the transaxle case.

14. Position a floor jack with a wide saddle

DRIVE TRAIN 453

Installing the stabilizer bar assembly

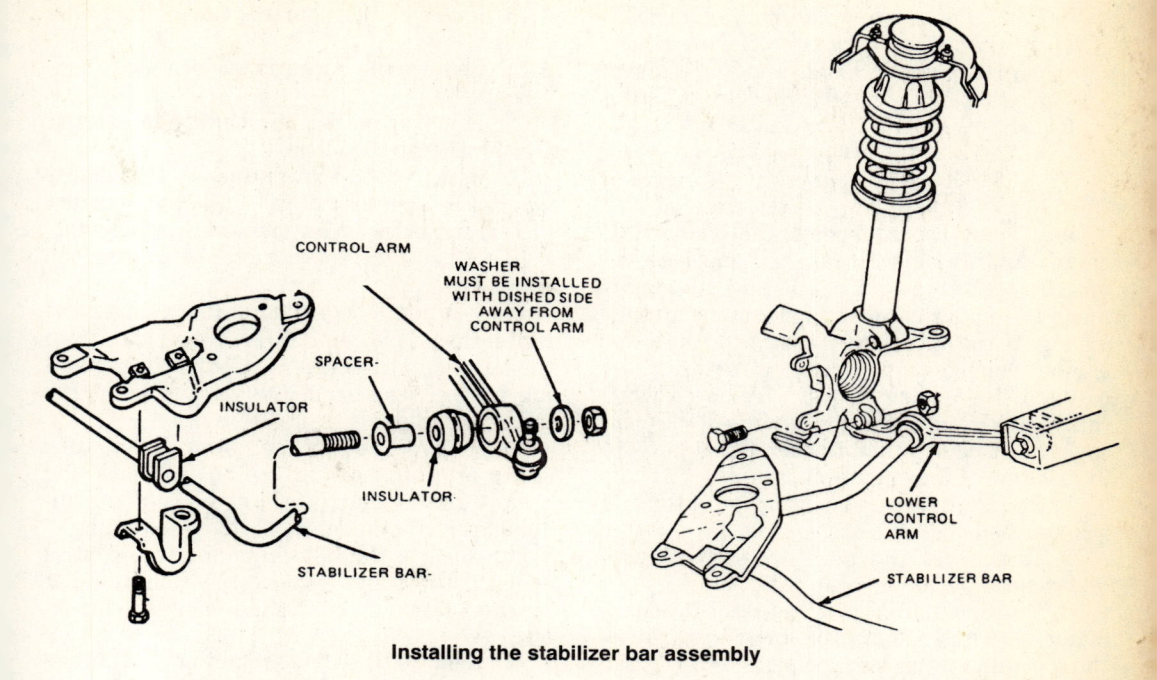

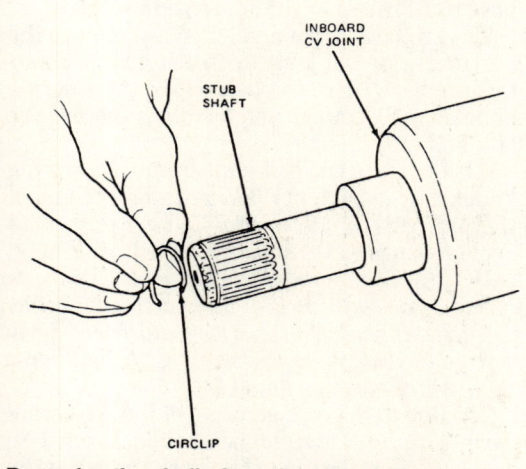

Removing the circlip from the stub shaft

under the transaxle and remove the four remaining transaxle to engine attaching bolts.

15. The torque converter mounting studs must be clear of the engine flywheel before the transaxle can be lowered from the car. Take a small pry bar and place it between the flywheel and the convertor. Carefully move the transaxle away from the engine. When the convertor mounting studs are clear lower the AT about 3 in. (76mm). Disconnect the speedometer cable from the AT. Lower the transaxle to the ground.

NOTE: *When moving the transaxle away from the engine watch the mount insulator. If it interferes with the transaxle before the* converter mounting studs clear the flywheel, remove the insulator.

16. Installation is in the reverse order of removal. Be sure to install new circlips on the halfshaft before reinstalling. Always use new pinch bolts when connecting the lower control arms to the steering knuckles.

To install:

16. Installation is the reverse order of the removal procedure. Be sure to pay strict attention to the following:

   a. Before installing the halfshaft into the transaxle, replace the circlip on the CV-joint stub shaft. Carefully work the clip over the end of the shaft, spreading it as little as possible.

   b. To install the halfshaft into the transaxle, carefully align the splines of the CV-joint with the splines in the differential.

   c. Exerting some force, push the CV-joint into the differential until the circlip is felt to seat the differential side gear. Be careful not to damage the differential oil seal.

NOTE: *A non-metallic, mallet may be used to aid in seating the circlip into the differential side gear groove. If a mallet is necessary, tap only on the outboard CV-joint stub shaft.*

   d. Attach the lower ball joint to the steering knuckle, taking care not to damage or cut the ball joint boot. Insert a new service pinch bolt and attach a new nut. Torque the nut to 37–44 ft. lbs. (50–60 Nm). Do not tighten the bolt.

DRIVE TRAIN

NOTE: *If the stabilizer bar required removal to perform another service procedure in conjunction with the transaxle removal, a disassembled view of the stabilizer bar mounting hardware is provided to aid in the its installation.*

1984–85 Tempo/Topaz

On Tempo/Topaz models the 2.3L HSC engine and automatic transaxle must be removed together as a unit. If any attempt is made to remove either component separately, damage to the automatic transaxle or the lower engine compartment metal structure may result. If the engine oil pan is removed while the transaxle and engine are separated, the transaxle must be attached to the engine prior to installation of the engine oil pan.

1. Mark the position of the hood and remove the hood from the vehicle.
2. Disconnect the negative battery cable and remove the air cleaner.
3. Position a drain pan under the lower radiator hose and remove the lower hose. Allow the coolant to drain into the pan.

CAUTION: *Do not drain the cooling system at this point if the coolant is at normal operation temperature. Personal injury can result, due to excessive heat of the coolant.*

4. Remove the upper radiator hose from the engine.
5. Disconnect the oil cooler lines at the rubber hoses below the radiator.
6. Remove the coil assembly from the cylinder head.
7. Disconnect the coolant fan electrical connector, remove the radiator shroud and cooling fan as an assembly. Remove the radiator.
8. If equipped with air conditioning, discharge the system and remove the pressure and suction lines from the air conditioning compressor.

CAUTION: *Refrigerant R-12 is contained in the air conditioning system under high pressure. Extreme care must be used when discharging the system, personal injury can result.*

9. Identify and disconnect all electrical and vacuum lines as necessary.
10. Disconnect the accelerator linkage, the fuel supply and return hoses on the engine and the Thermactor pump discharge hose at the pump. Disconnect T.V. linkage at transaxle.
11. If equipped with power steering, disconnect the pressure and return lines at the power steering pump. Remove the power steering lines bracket at the cylinder head.
12. Install an engine holding or support tool device to the engine lifting eye. Raise and safely support the vehicle.
13. Remove the starter cable from the starter.
14. Remove the hose from the catalytic converter.
15. Remove the bolt attaching the exhaust pipe bracket to the oil pan.
16. Remove the exhaust pipes to exhaust manifold retaining nuts. Pull the exhaust system from the rubber insulating grommets.
17. Remove the speedometer cable from the transaxle.
18. Position a coolant drain pan under the heater hoses and remove the heater hose from the water pump inlet tube. Remove the remaining heater hoses from the steel tube on the intake manifold.
19. Remove the water pump inlet tube clamp attaching bolt at the engine block and remove the 2 clamp attaching bolts at the underside of the oil pan. Remove the inlet tube.
20. Remove the bolts retaining the control arms to the body. Remove the stabilizer bar brackets retaining bolts and remove the brackets.
21. Remove the bolt retaining the brake hose routing clip to the suspension strut.
22. From the right and left sides, remove the nut from the ball joint to steering knuckle attaching bolt. Drive the bolt out of the steering knuckle with a punch and hammer. Discard the bolt and nut.
23. Separate the ball joint from the steering knuckle by using a pry bar. Position the end of the pry bar outside of the bushing pocket, to avoid damage to the bushing or ball joint boot.

NOTE: *The lower control arm ball joint fits into a pocket formed in the plastic disc brake shield. this shield must be bend back, away from the ball joint while prying the ball joint out of the steering knuckle.*

24. Due to the configuration of the ATX transaxle housing, the right side halfshaft must be removed first. Position the pry bar between the case and the shaft and pry outward.

NOTE: *Use extreme care to avoid damaging the differential oil seal or the CV-joint boot.*

25. Support the end of the shaft by suspending it from a convenient underbody component with a length of wire.

NOTE: *Do not allow the halfshaft to hang unsupported; damage to the outboard CV-joint may occur.*

26. Install driver tool T81P-4026-A or equivalent, in the right halfshaft bore of the transaxle and tap the left halfshaft from its circlip retaining groove in the differential side gear splines. Support the left halfshaft in the same manner as the right halfshaft. Install plugs in the left and right halfshaft bores.
27. Disconnect the manual shift cable clip

from the lever on the transaxle. Remove the manual shift linkage bracket bolts from the transaxle and remove the bracket.
28. Remove the left hand rear insulator mount bracket from the body bracket by removing the 2 retaining nuts.
29. Remove the left hand front insulator to transaxle mounting bolts.
30. Lower the vehicle and attach the lifting equipment to the existing lifting eyes on the engine. Remove the engine holding or support tool.

NOTE: *Do not allow the front wheels to touch the floor.*

31. Remove the right hand insulator intermediate bracket to engine bracket bolts, intermediate bracket to insulator attaching nuts and the nut on the bottom of the double ended stud which attaches the intermediate bracket to the engine bracket. Remove the bracket.
32. Carefully lower the engine/transaxle assembly to the floor. Raise the vehicle from over the assembly. Separate the engine from the transaxle and do the necessary repair work to the transaxle assembly.

To install:
33. Raise and safely support the vehicle.
34. Position the assembled engine/transaxle assembly directly under the engine compartment.
35. Slowly and carefully, lower the vehicle over the engine/transaxle assembly.

NOTE: *Do not allow the front wheels to touch the floor.*

36. With lifting equipment in place and attached to the lifting eyes on the engine, raise the engine/transaxle assembly up through the engine compartment and position it to be bolted.
37. Install the right hand insulator intermediate attaching nuts and intermediate bracket to the engine bracket bolts. Install the nut on the bottom of the double ended stud that attaches intermediate bracket to the engine bracket. Tighten to 75–100 ft. lbs. (100–135 Nm).
38. Install an engine support fixture to an engine lifting eye to support the engine/transaxle assembly. Remove the lifting equipment.
39. Raise the vehicle and position a lifting device under the engine. Raise the engine and transaxle assembly into its operating position.
40. Install the insulator to bracket nut and tighten to 75–100 ft. lbs. (100–135 Nm).
41. Tighten the left hand rear insulator bracket to body bracket nuts to 75–100 ft. lbs. (100–135 Nm).
42. Install the starter cable to the starter.
43. Install the lower radiator hose and install the remaining bracket and bolts. Tighten to specifications.
44. Install the manual shift linkage bracket bolts to the transaxle. Install the cable clip to the lever on the transaxle.
45. Connect the lower radiator hose to the radiator. Install the Thermactor pump discharge hose at the pump.
46. Install the speedometer cable to the transaxle.
47. Position the exhaust system up and into the insulating grommets, located at the rear of the vehicle.
48. Install the exhaust pipe to the exhaust manifold bolts and tighten to specifications.
49. Connect the gulp valve hose to the catalytic converter.
50. Position the stabilizer bar and the control arm assemblies in position and install the attaching bolts. Tighten all fasteners to specifications.
51. Install new circlips in the sub axle inboard spline grooves on both the left and right halfshafts. Carefully align the splines of the stub axle with the splines of the differential side gears and with some force, push the halfshafts into the differential unit until the circlips can be felt to seat in their grooves in the differential side gears.
52. Connect the control arm ball joint stud into its bore in the steering knuckle and install new bolts and nuts.
53. Tighten the new bolt and nut to 37–44 ft. lbs. (50–60 Nm).
54. Position the brake hose routing clip on the suspension components and install their remaining bolts.
55. Lower the vehicle and remove the engine support tool.
56. Connect the vacuum and electrical lines that were disconnected during the removal procedure.
57. Install the disconnected air conditioning components.
58. Connect the fuel supply and return lines to the engine and connect the accelerator cable.
59. Install the power steering pressure and return lines. Install the brackets.
60. Connect the T.V. linkage the transaxle.
61. Install the radiator shroud and the cooling fan assembly. Tighten the bolts to specifications.
62. Install the coil and connect the coolant fan electrical connector.
63. Install the upper radiator hose to the engine and connect the transaxle cooler lines to the rubber hoses under the radiator. Fill the radiator and engine with coolant.
64. Install the negative battery cable and the air cleaner assembly.

65. Install the hood in its original position.
66. Check all fluid levels and correct as required.
67. Start the engine and check for leakage.
68. Charge the air conditioning system and road test the vehicle as necessary.

1986–90 Escort/Lynx
All Tempo/Topaz Models

1. Disconnect the negative battery cable.

NOTE: *Due to automatic transaxle case configuration, the right-side halfshaft assembly must be removed first. The differential rotator tool or equivalent, is inserted into the transaxle to drive the left-side inboard CV-joint assembly from the transaxle.*

2. If necessary, remove the managed air valve-to-transaxle valve body cover bolts. Remove the air cleaner assembly, as required.
3. Disconnect the electrical harness connector from the neutral safety switch.
4. Disconnect the throttle valve linkage and the manual lever cable from their levers.

NOTE: *Failure to disconnect the linkage and allowing the transaxle to hang, will fracture the throttle valve cam shaft joint, which is located under the transaxle cover.*

5. To prevent contamination, cover the timing window in the converter housing. If equipped, remove the bolts retaining the Thermactor hoses.
6. If equipped, remove the ground strap, located above the upper engine mount, the coil and bracket assembly.
7. Remove both upper transaxle-to-upper engine bolts; the bolts are located below and on both ides of the distributor. Raise and safely support the vehicle. Remove the front wheels.
8. Remove the control arm-to-steering knuckle nut, at the ball joint.
9. Using a hammer and a punch, drive the bolt from the steering knuckle; repeat this step on the other side. Discard the nut and bolt.

NOTE: *Be careful not to damage or cut ball joint boot. The pry bar must not contact lower arm.*

10. Using a pry bar, disengage the control arm from the steering knuckle; repeat this step on the other side.

NOTE: *Do not hammer on the knuckle to remove the ball joints. The plastic shield installed behind the rotor contains a molded pocket into which the lower control arm ball joint fits. When disengaging the control arm from the knuckle, clearance for the ball joint can be provided by bending the shield back toward the rotor. Failure to provide clearance for the ball joint can result in damage to the shield.*

11. Remove the stabilizer bar bracket-to-frame rail bolts and discard the bolts; repeat this step on the other side.
12. Remove the stabilizer bar-to-control arm nut/washer and discard the nut; repeat this step on the other side.
13. Pull the stabilizer bar from of the control arms.
14. Remove the brake hose routing clip-to-suspension strut bracket bolt; repeat this step on the other side.
15. Remove the steering gear tie rod-to-steering knuckle nut and disengage the tie rod from the steering knuckle; repeat this step on the other side.
16. Using a halfshaft removal tool, pry the halfshaft from the right side of the transaxle and support the end of the shaft with a wire.

NOTE: *It is normal for some fluid to leak from the transaxle when the halfshaft is removed.*

17. Using a differential rotator tool or equivalent, drive the left-side halfshaft from the differential side gear.
18. Pull the halfshaft from the transaxle and support the end of the shaft with a wire.

NOTE: *Do not allow the shaft to hang unsupported, as damage to the outboard CV-joint may result.*

19. Install seal plugs into the differential seals.
20. Remove the starter support bracket and disconnect the starter cable. Remove the starter bolts and the starter. If equipped with a throttle body, remove the hose and bracket bolts on the starter and a bolt at the converter and disconnect the hoses.
21. Remove the transaxle support bracket and the dust cover from the torque converter housing.
22. Remove the torque converter-to-flywheel nuts by turning the crankshaft pulley bolt to bring the nuts into position.
23. Remove the left front insulator-to-body bracket nuts, the bracket-to-body bolts and the bracket. Remove the left rear insulator bracket nut.
24. Disconnect the transaxle cooler lines.
25. Remove the manual lever bracket-to-transaxle case bolts.
26. Support the engine. Position a transaxle jack under the transaxle and remove the remaining transaxle-to-engine bolts.
27. Make sure the torque converter studs will be clear the flywheel. Insert a pry bar between the flywheel and the converter, then, pry the transaxle and converter away from the engine. When the converter studs are clear of the flywheel, lower the transaxle about 2–3 in. (51–76mm).

28. Disconnect the speedometer cable and lower the transaxle.

NOTE: *When moving the transaxle away from the engine, watch the No. 1 insulator. If it contacts the body before the converter studs clear the flywheel, remove the insulator.*

To install:

29. Raise the transaxle and align it with the engine and flywheel. Install the No. 1 insulator, if it was removed. Torque the transaxle-to-engine bolts to 25–33 ft. lbs. (34–45 Nm) and the torque converter-to-flywheel bolts to 23–39 ft. lbs. (31–53 Nm).

30. Install the manual lever bracket-to-transaxle case bolts and connect the transaxle cooler lines.

31. Install the left front insulator-to-body bracket nuts and torque the nuts to 40–50 ft. lbs. (55–70 Nm). Install the bracket-to-body and torque the bolts to 55–70 ft. lbs. (75–90 Nm).

32. Install the transaxle support bracket and the dust cover to the torque converter housing.

33. If equipped with a throttle body, install the hose and bracket bolts on the starter and a bolt to the converter and connect the hoses. Install the starter and the support bracket; torque the bolts starter-to-engine bolts to 30–40 ft. lbs. (41–54 Nm). Connect the starter cable.

34. Remove the seal plugs from the differential seals and install the halfshaft by performing the following procedures:

 a. Prior to installing the halfshaft in the transaxle, install a new circlip onto the CV-joint stub.

 b. Install the halfshaft in the transaxle by carefully aligning the CV-joint splines with the differential side gears. Be sure to push the CV-joint into the differential until the circlip is felt to seat in the differential side gear. Use care to prevent damage to the differential oil seal.

 c. Attach the lower ball joint to the steering knuckle, taking care not to damage or cut the ball joint boot. Insert a new pinch bolt and a new nut. While holding the bolt with a 2nd wrench, torque the nut to 37–44 ft. lbs.

35. Engage the tie rod with the steering knuckle and torque the nut to 23–35 ft. lbs. (31–47 Nm).

36. Install the brake hose routing clip-to-suspension strut bracket and torque the bolt to 8 ft. lbs. (11 Nm).

37. Install the stabilizer bar to control arm and using a new nut, torque it to 98–125 ft. lbs. (133–169 Nm).

38. Install the stabilizer bar bracket-to-frame rail bolts and using new bolts, torque them to 60–70 ft. lbs. (81–95 Nm).

39. Install the wheels and lower the vehicle. Install the upper transaxle-to-engine bolts and torque to 25–33 ft. lbs. (34–45 Nm).

40. If equipped, install the ground strap, located above the upper engine mount, the coil and bracket assembly.

41. If equipped, install the bolts retaining the Thermactor hoses. Uncover the timing window in the converter housing.

42. Connect the throttle valve linkage and the manual lever cable to their levers.

43. Connect the electrical harness connector from the neutral safety switch.

44. Install the managed air valve-to-transaxle valve body cover bolts and the air cleaner assembly, as required.

45. Connect the negative battery cable and road test the vehicle.

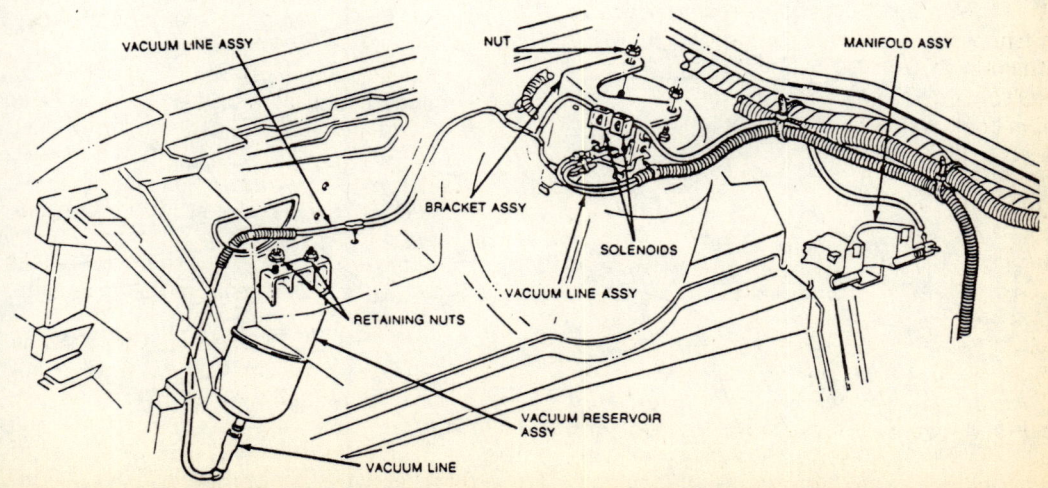

Location of the vacuum controls for the all wheel drive electronically control vacuum servo system

DRIVE TRAIN

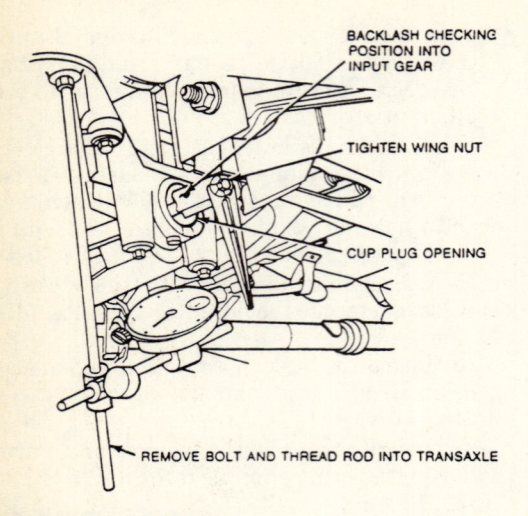

Checking the backlash

Halfshafts

For halfshaft removal and overhaul procedures, refer to the Halfshaft Procedures in this section

TRANSFER CASE

The transfer case is actuated by an electrically controlled vacuum servo system. When the all wheel drive switch is placed in the ON position, a relay activates the 4WD solenoid valve. The 4WD solenoid valves allows vacuum to be created in the left hand chamber of the vacuum servo. The vacuum moves the servo rod and sliding collar into engagement with the transfer case output gears, driveshaft and rear axle. When the 2WD switch is turned ON a relay activates the 2WD solenoid valve. Vacuum is created in the right hand chamber of the vacuum servo disengaging the transfer case, driveshaft and rear axle output gears. The transfer case lubrication is integral with the transaxle. The transaxle/transfer case assembly requires 8.3 quarts of Mercon automatic transmission fluid.

SELECT GASKET CHART

Measurement Obtained		Select Gasket Required
in.	mm	
.012–.020	0.30–0.50	7A191-H
.021–.024	0.51–0.62	7A191-G
.025–.030	0.63–0.76	7A191-F
.031–.035	0.77–0.90	7A191-E
.036–.042	0.91–1.06	7A191-D
.043–.048	1.07–1.21	7A191-C
.049–.054	1.22–1.38	7A191-B
.055–.064	1.39–1.62	7A191-A

REMOVAL AND INSTALLATION

1. Disconnect the negative battery cable.
2. Raise and safely support the vehicle.
3. Using a light hammer and a dull chisel, remove the cup plug from the transfer case and drain the oil.
4. Remove the vacuum line retaining bracket bolt.
5. Remove the driveshaft front retaining bolts and caps; disengage the front driveshaft from the drive yoke.
6. If the transfer case is to be disassembled, check the backlash through the cup plug open-

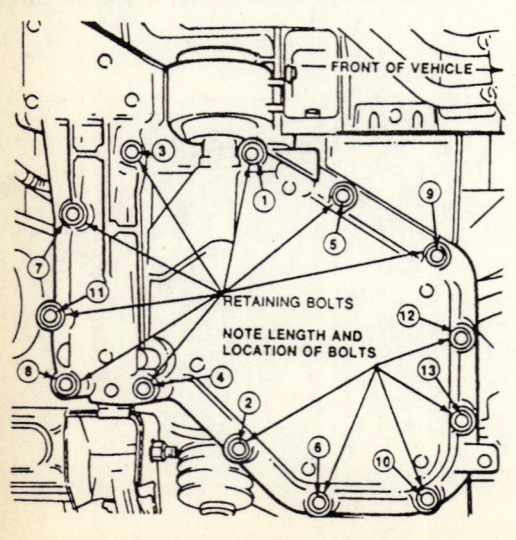

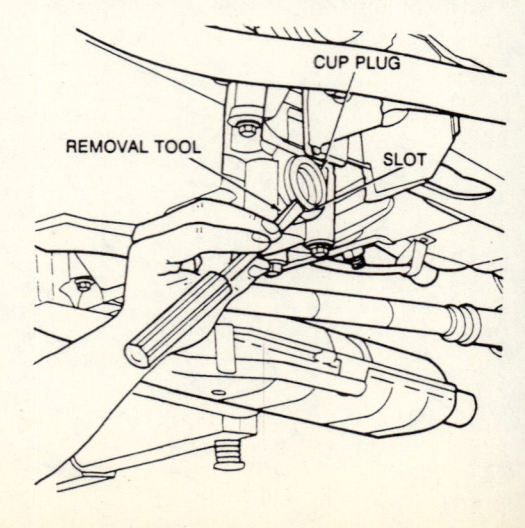

Transfer case bolt torque sequence

Removing the cap plug

CHILTON'S THREE C's TRANSFER CASE DIAGNOSIS
AWD—Vacuum Diagnosis

Condition	Cause	Correction
Insufficient vacuum	a) Damaged or clogged manifold fitting b) Damaged hoses c) Damaged or worn check valve	a) Service or replace fitting b) Service as required c) Replace/service
Reservoir not maintaining vacuum	a) Worn or damaged reservoir	a) Check for leak by installing a vacuum gauge at rubber tee (input to dual solenoids). Gauge should read (16–20 inches) 54–67 kPa vacuum
Dual solenoid assembly inoperative	a) Damaged or worn solenoid assembly	a) Check for vacuum at solenoids as outlined
No AWD engagement	a) Insufficient vacuum at vacuum servo b) Damaged or worn vacuum servo	a) Disconnect vacuum harness at single to double connector and install a vacuum gauge. With engine running and AWD switch in proper position, check for vacuum b) Place transaxle in neutral. Raise vehicle on a hoist and disconnect vacuum harness at single to double connector. Install a hand vacuum pump onto red tube connector and block off black connector. Apply (16–20 inches) 54–67 kPa vacuum at servo end of harness. While rotating front wheels, note that rear wheels also rotate. If rear wheels do not rotate, replace vacuum servo

CHILTON'S THREE C's TRANSFER CASE DIAGNOSIS
AWD—Electrical Diagnosis

Condition	Cause	Correction
AWD system inoperative	a) Blown fuse b) Connector at fuse panel disengaged	a) Replace fuse b) Install connector firmly into fuse panel
AWD switch indicator inoperative	a) Loose connection at switch b) Worn or damaged switch	a) Push connector firmly into switch b) Replace switch
AWD relay inoperative	a) Poor connection at relay b) Open or short in harness c) Worn or damaged relay	a) Check connection at relay b) Service or replace harness as necessary c) Replace relay
AWD dual solenoids inoperative	a) Open or short in harness	a) Service or replace harness

460 DRIVE TRAIN

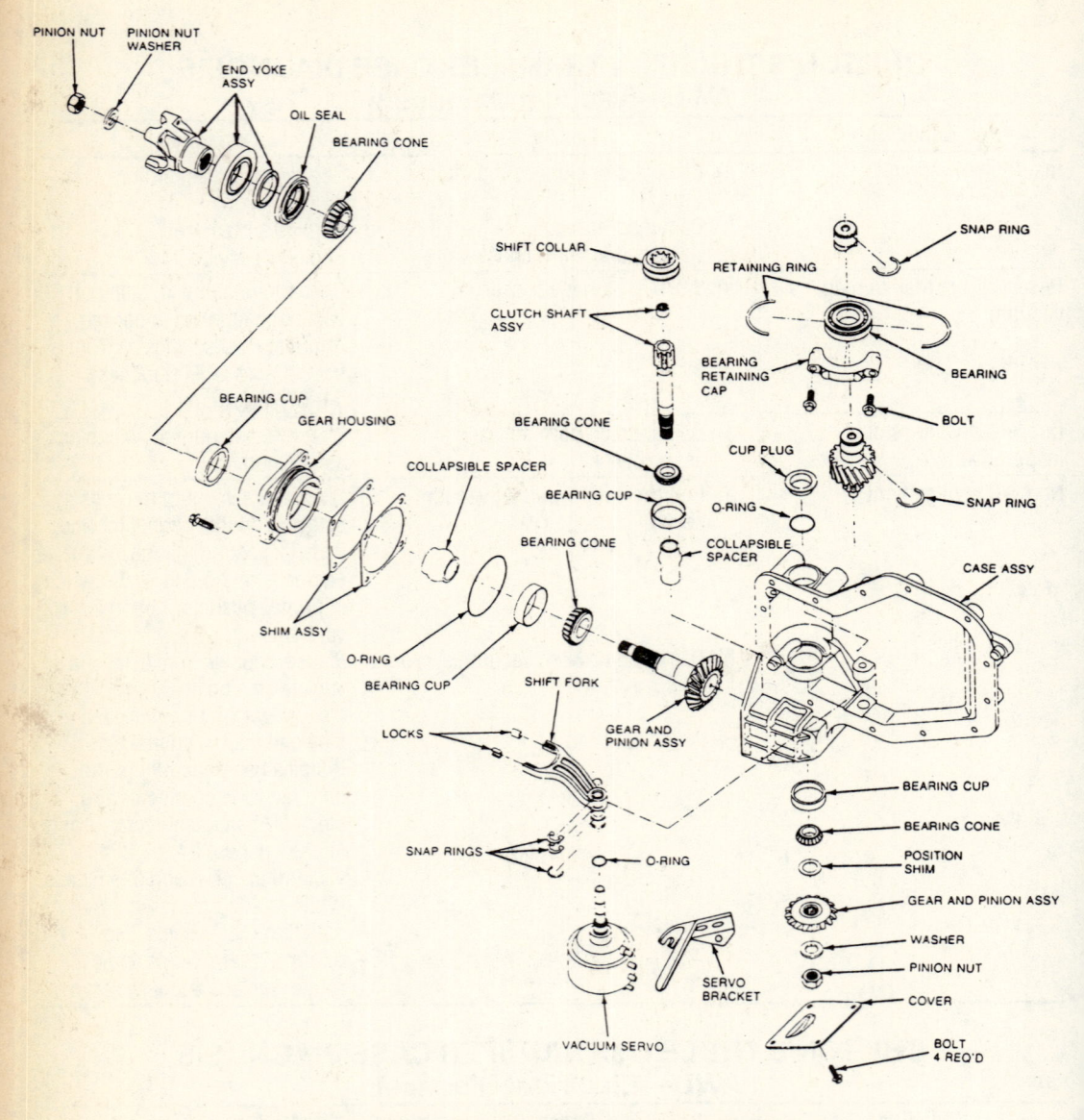

Exploded view of the disassembled transfer case assembly

ing before removal in order to reset to existing backlash at installation. The backlash should be 0.012–0.024 in. (0.3–0.6mm) on a 3 in. (76mm) radius.

7. Remove the vacuum motor shield bolts and the shield.
8. Remove the vacuum lines from the vacuum servo.
9. Remove the transfer case-to-transaxle bolts; note and record the length and locations of the bolts.
10. Remove the transfer case from the vehicle.

11. Position the transfer case to the transaxle.
12. Install the transfer case bolts in the proper positions and torque the bolts, in sequence, to 23–38 ft. lbs. (31–38 Nm) for 1987, 15–19 ft. lbs. (21–25 Nm) for 1988–89 or 12–15 ft. lbs. (16–20 Nm) for 1990–91.
13. Install the vacuum motor supply hose connector, vacuum motor shield and torque the bolts to 7–12 ft. lbs. (9–16 Nm).
14. Install the driveshaft-to-drive yoke, lubricate the bolts with Loctite® and torque the bolts to 15–17 ft. lbs. (21–23 Nm). Install the

DRIVE TRAIN

vacuum line retaining bracket and torque the bolt to 7–12 ft. lbs. (9–16 Nm).

15. Refill the transaxle and lower the vehicle. Road test the vehicle and check the performance of the transfer case.

Transfer Case Overhaul

CASE DISASSEMBLY

1. Drain the oil from the transfer case and remove it from the vehicle.
2. Remove the transfer case side cover bolts.
3. Clean the gasket material from the transfer case and cover.
4. Remove the housing retaining bolts and remove the gear housing assembly.
5. Remove the O-ring and shims. Wire the shim stacks together for reassembly.
6. Remove the snaprings from the vacuum servo shaft and shift fork. Be sure to wear eye protection when removing or installing snaprings.
7. Remove the shift motor assembly. Remove the shift fork and shift fork clips.
8. Remove the transfer case bearing cap retaining bolts and bearing cap.
9. Rotate the bearing and remove the 2 piece snapring from the bearing.
10. Using a thin prybar, remove the inner snapring which positions the input gear to the ball bearing. Slide the bearing toward the input gear and remove the outer snapring.
11. Remove the cup plug. Slide the input gear toward the ball bearing until the input gear and bearing can be lifted out of the transfer case.
12. Remove the ball bearing from the input gear.
13. Remove the shift collar from the clutch shaft.
14. Remove the pinion nut and washer from the clutch shaft. Use a breaker bar and holding tool T87P-7120-A or equivalent. Tap the

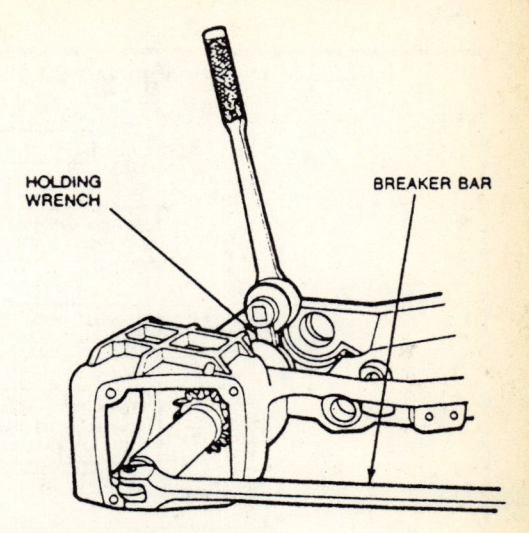

Removing the clutch shaft

clutch shaft from the transfer case, with a soft drift.

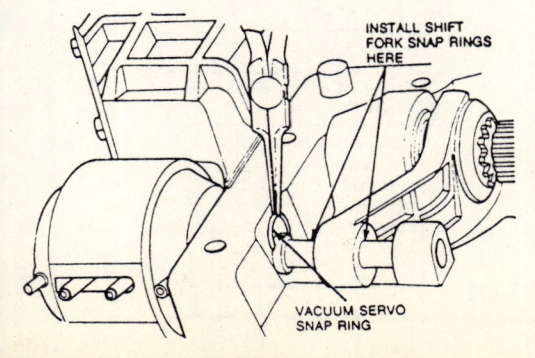

15. Remove the pinion gear, outer bearing and shims from the transfer case. Be sure to wire the shims together.
16. Remove and discard the clutch shaft collapsible spacer.
17. Mount the transfer case holding fixture T57L-500-B or equivalent.
18. Install the clutch shaft inner bearing cup removal tool T87P-7120-D. Remove the inner and outer bearing, using a suitable slide hammer into the cup remover.

Drive Gear

DISASSEMBLY

1. Place the gear housing subassembly in a soft jawed vise. Remove the pinion nut, yoke end and washer.
2. Tap in the drive gear with a soft faced hammer to remove from the gear housing. Remove and discard the collapsible spacer.
3. Remove the inner bearing cone from the drive gear, using a suitable press and a pinion bearing cone remover.
4. Mount the drive in a soft jawed vise. Remove the drive gear housing oil seal, using a roll head prybar.
5. Remove the inner and outer drive gear bearing cups, using a brass drift and hammer. Be sure to remove any burrs and wipe the bores clean.
6. Remove the gear housing from the vise. Install the new inner and outer drive bearing cups, using bearing cup replacer T87P-4616-A or equivalent.

To assemble:

7. Clean the drive gear in a suitable solvent.

Servo snapring location — Tempo/Topaz

462 DRIVE TRAIN

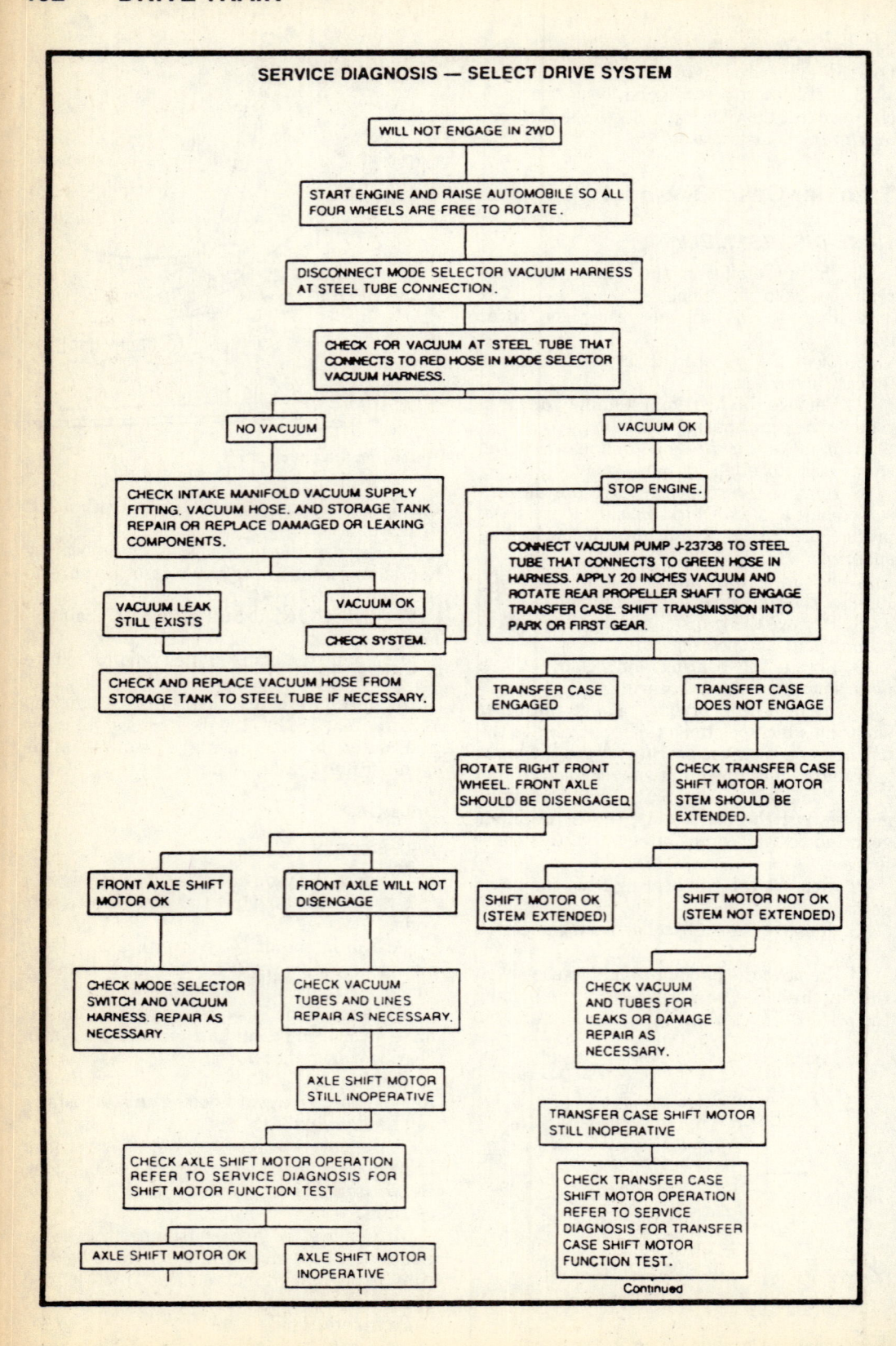

SERVICE DIAGNOSIS — SELECT DRIVE SYSTEM

WILL NOT ENGAGE IN 2WD

↓

START ENGINE AND RAISE AUTOMOBILE SO ALL FOUR WHEELS ARE FREE TO ROTATE.

↓

DISCONNECT MODE SELECTOR VACUUM HARNESS AT STEEL TUBE CONNECTION.

↓

CHECK FOR VACUUM AT STEEL TUBE THAT CONNECTS TO RED HOSE IN MODE SELECTOR VACUUM HARNESS.

├─ **NO VACUUM**
│   ↓
│   CHECK INTAKE MANIFOLD VACUUM SUPPLY FITTING, VACUUM HOSE, AND STORAGE TANK. REPAIR OR REPLACE DAMAGED OR LEAKING COMPONENTS.
│   ├─ VACUUM LEAK STILL EXISTS
│   │   ↓
│   │   CHECK AND REPLACE VACUUM HOSE FROM STORAGE TANK TO STEEL TUBE IF NECESSARY.
│   └─ VACUUM OK — CHECK SYSTEM.
│
└─ **VACUUM OK**
     ↓
     STOP ENGINE.
     ↓
     CONNECT VACUUM PUMP J-23738 TO STEEL TUBE THAT CONNECTS TO GREEN HOSE IN HARNESS. APPLY 20 INCHES VACUUM AND ROTATE REAR PROPELLER SHAFT TO ENGAGE TRANSFER CASE. SHIFT TRANSMISSION INTO PARK OR FIRST GEAR.
     ├─ **TRANSFER CASE ENGAGED**
     │   ↓
     │   ROTATE RIGHT FRONT WHEEL. FRONT AXLE SHOULD BE DISENGAGED.
     │   ├─ FRONT AXLE SHIFT MOTOR OK
     │   │   ↓
     │   │   CHECK MODE SELECTOR SWITCH AND VACUUM HARNESS. REPAIR AS NECESSARY.
     │   └─ FRONT AXLE WILL NOT DISENGAGE
     │   ↓
     │   CHECK VACUUM TUBES AND LINES REPAIR AS NECESSARY.
     │   ↓
     │   AXLE SHIFT MOTOR STILL INOPERATIVE
     │   ↓
     │   CHECK AXLE SHIFT MOTOR OPERATION REFER TO SERVICE DIAGNOSIS FOR SHIFT MOTOR FUNCTION TEST
     │   ├─ AXLE SHIFT MOTOR OK
     │   └─ AXLE SHIFT MOTOR INOPERATIVE
     │
     └─ **TRANSFER CASE DOES NOT ENGAGE**
          ↓
          CHECK TRANSFER CASE SHIFT MOTOR. MOTOR STEM SHOULD BE EXTENDED.
          ├─ SHIFT MOTOR OK (STEM EXTENDED)
          └─ SHIFT MOTOR NOT OK (STEM NOT EXTENDED)
               ↓
               CHECK VACUUM AND TUBES FOR LEAKS OR DAMAGE REPAIR AS NECESSARY.
               ↓
               TRANSFER CASE SHIFT MOTOR STILL INOPERATIVE
               ↓
               CHECK TRANSFER CASE SHIFT MOTOR OPERATION REFER TO SERVICE DIAGNOSIS FOR TRANSFER CASE SHIFT MOTOR FUNCTION TEST.

Continued

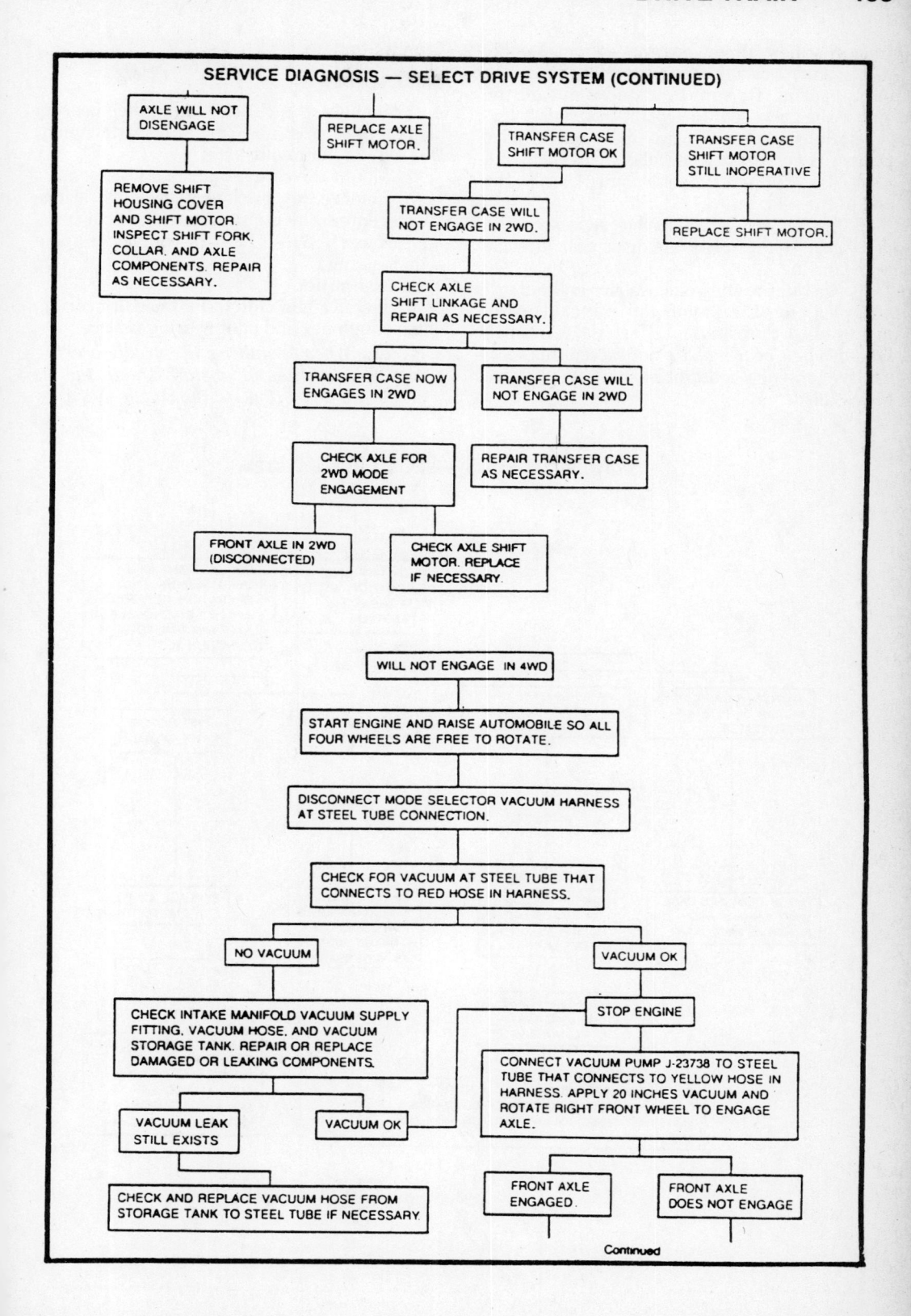

DRIVE TRAIN

SERVICE DIAGNOSIS — SELECT DRIVE SYSTEM (CONTINUED)

- AXLE WILL NOT DISENGAGE
  - REMOVE SHIFT HOUSING COVER AND SHIFT MOTOR. INSPECT SHIFT FORK, COLLAR, AND AXLE COMPONENTS. REPAIR AS NECESSARY.

- REPLACE AXLE SHIFT MOTOR.

- TRANSFER CASE SHIFT MOTOR OK
  - TRANSFER CASE WILL NOT ENGAGE IN 2WD.
  - CHECK AXLE SHIFT LINKAGE AND REPAIR AS NECESSARY.
    - TRANSFER CASE NOW ENGAGES IN 2WD
      - CHECK AXLE FOR 2WD MODE ENGAGEMENT
        - FRONT AXLE IN 2WD (DISCONNECTED)
        - CHECK AXLE SHIFT MOTOR. REPLACE IF NECESSARY.
    - TRANSFER CASE WILL NOT ENGAGE IN 2WD
      - REPAIR TRANSFER CASE AS NECESSARY.

- TRANSFER CASE SHIFT MOTOR STILL INOPERATIVE
  - REPLACE SHIFT MOTOR.

- WILL NOT ENGAGE IN 4WD
  - START ENGINE AND RAISE AUTOMOBILE SO ALL FOUR WHEELS ARE FREE TO ROTATE.
  - DISCONNECT MODE SELECTOR VACUUM HARNESS AT STEEL TUBE CONNECTION.
  - CHECK FOR VACUUM AT STEEL TUBE THAT CONNECTS TO RED HOSE IN HARNESS.
    - NO VACUUM
      - CHECK INTAKE MANIFOLD VACUUM SUPPLY FITTING, VACUUM HOSE, AND VACUUM STORAGE TANK. REPAIR OR REPLACE DAMAGED OR LEAKING COMPONENTS.
        - VACUUM LEAK STILL EXISTS
          - CHECK AND REPLACE VACUUM HOSE FROM STORAGE TANK TO STEEL TUBE IF NECESSARY
        - VACUUM OK
    - VACUUM OK
      - STOP ENGINE
      - CONNECT VACUUM PUMP J-23738 TO STEEL TUBE THAT CONNECTS TO YELLOW HOSE IN HARNESS. APPLY 20 INCHES VACUUM AND ROTATE RIGHT FRONT WHEEL TO ENGAGE AXLE.
        - FRONT AXLE ENGAGED.
        - FRONT AXLE DOES NOT ENGAGE

Continued

DRIVE TRAIN

Install a new inner bearing cone assembly using pinion bearing cone replacer T62F-4621- or equivalent. Be sure to install a nut on the end of the drive gear to protect the shaft.

8. Lubricate and install new outer drive bearing cone. Install a new oil seal, using install tool T87P-7065-B or equivalent. Grease the end of the seal.

9. Install a new collapsible spacer on the drive gear stem. Install the drive gear into the gear housing.

10. Install the end yoke, washer and nut.

11. Tighten the pinion nut in small increments until the rotation effort is 15–32 inch lbs. with new bearings. Do not exceed this specification or a new collapsible spacer will have to be installed.

Clutch Shaft

DISASSEMBLY

1. Remove the clutch shaft inner bearing using a press and a bearing puller attachment D84L-1123-A or equivalent.
2. Mount the clutch shaft in a vise.
3. Remove the clutch shaft needle bearings which centers the input gear, using pilot bearing replacer T87P-7120-C or equivalent and a slide hammer.

To assemble:

4. Install a new clutch shaft needle bearing, using a hammer and pilot bearing replacer.

NOTE: *When installing the needle bearing into the clutch shaft, install it with the tapered end down (toward the clutch shaft).*

SERVICE DIAGNOSIS — SELECT DRIVE SYSTEM

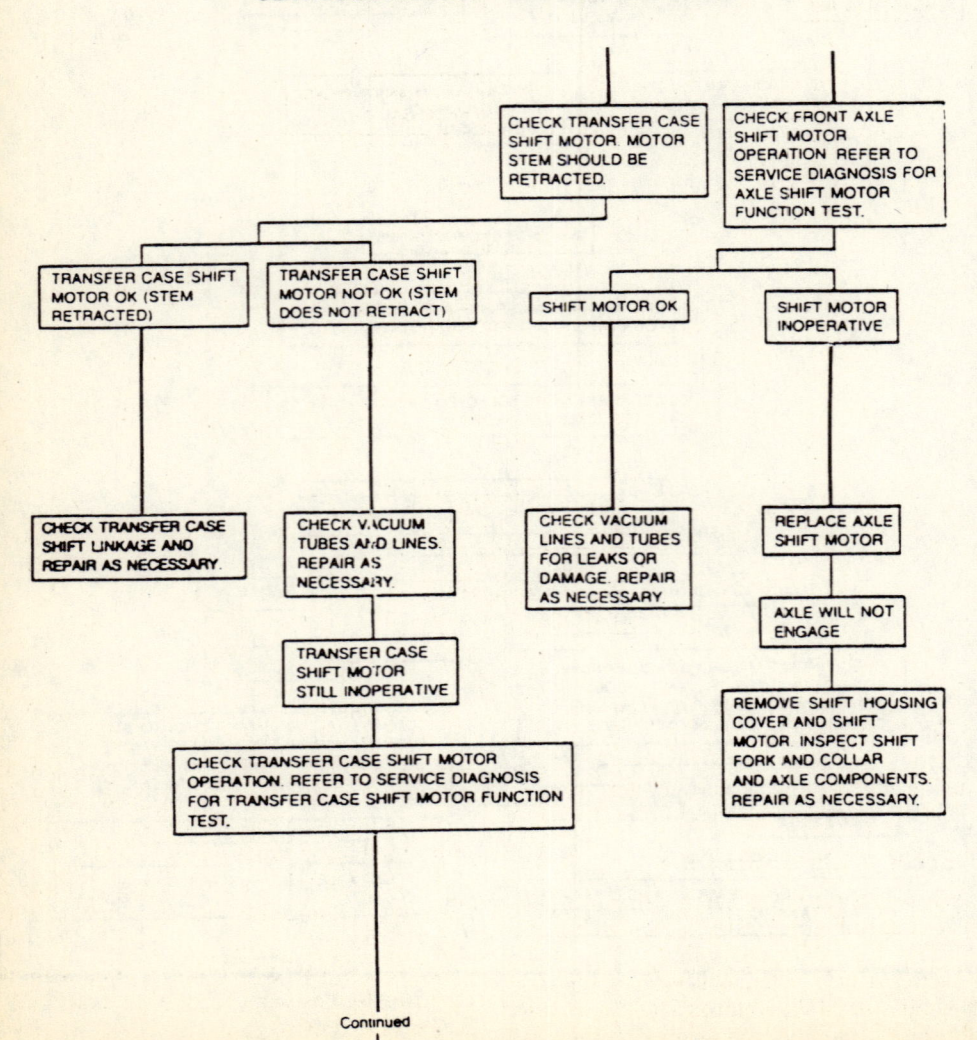

```
                          CHECK TRANSFER CASE        CHECK FRONT AXLE
                          SHIFT MOTOR. MOTOR         SHIFT MOTOR
                          STEM SHOULD BE             OPERATION. REFER TO
                          RETRACTED.                 SERVICE DIAGNOSIS FOR
                                                     AXLE SHIFT MOTOR
                                                     FUNCTION TEST.

   TRANSFER CASE SHIFT    TRANSFER CASE SHIFT
   MOTOR OK (STEM         MOTOR NOT OK (STEM         SHIFT MOTOR OK      SHIFT MOTOR
   RETRACTED)             DOES NOT RETRACT)                              INOPERATIVE

   CHECK TRANSFER CASE    CHECK VACUUM               CHECK VACUUM        REPLACE AXLE
   SHIFT LINKAGE AND      TUBES AND LINES.           LINES AND TUBES     SHIFT MOTOR
   REPAIR AS NECESSARY.   REPAIR AS                  FOR LEAKS OR
                          NECESSARY.                 DAMAGE. REPAIR
                                                     AS NECESSARY.
                                                                         AXLE WILL NOT
                                                                         ENGAGE

                          TRANSFER CASE                                  REMOVE SHIFT HOUSING
                          SHIFT MOTOR                                    COVER AND SHIFT
                          STILL INOPERATIVE                              MOTOR. INSPECT SHIFT
                                                                         FORK AND COLLAR
                          CHECK TRANSFER CASE SHIFT MOTOR                AND AXLE COMPONENTS.
                          OPERATION. REFER TO SERVICE DIAGNOSIS          REPAIR AS NECESSARY.
                          FOR TRANSFER CASE SHIFT MOTOR FUNCTION
                          TEST.
```

Continued

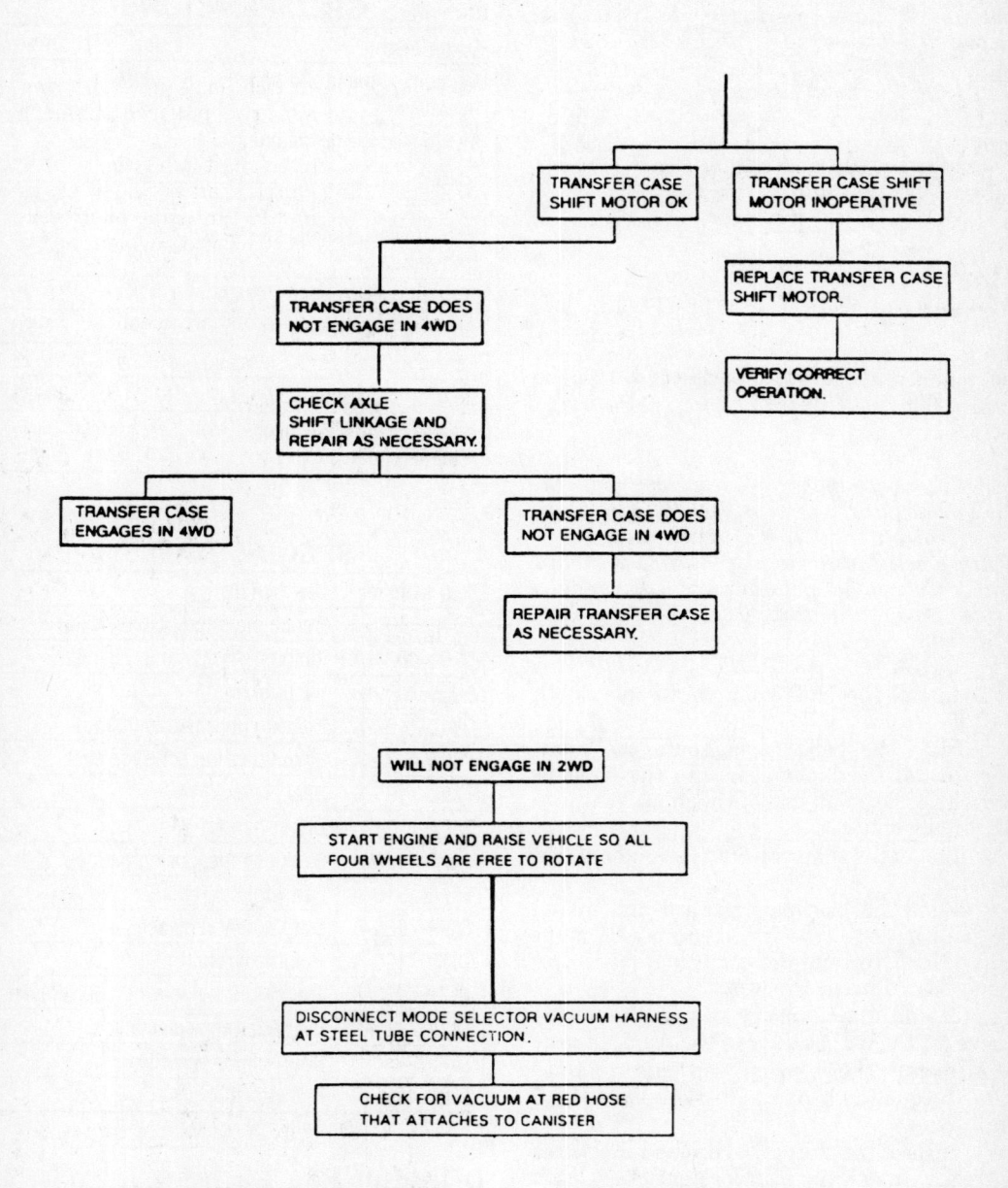

```
                            │
        ┌───────────────────┴───────────────────┐
   TRANSFER CASE                          TRANSFER CASE SHIFT
   SHIFT MOTOR OK                         MOTOR INOPERATIVE
        │                                       │
        │                                 REPLACE TRANSFER CASE
        │                                 SHIFT MOTOR.
   TRANSFER CASE DOES                           │
   NOT ENGAGE IN 4WD                      VERIFY CORRECT
        │                                 OPERATION.
   CHECK AXLE
   SHIFT LINKAGE AND
   REPAIR AS NECESSARY.
        │
   ┌────┴────┐
TRANSFER CASE   TRANSFER CASE DOES
ENGAGES IN 4WD  NOT ENGAGE IN 4WD
                     │
               REPAIR TRANSFER CASE
               AS NECESSARY.


            WILL NOT ENGAGE IN 2WD
                     │
            START ENGINE AND RAISE VEHICLE SO ALL
            FOUR WHEELS ARE FREE TO ROTATE
                     │
            DISCONNECT MODE SELECTOR VACUUM HARNESS
            AT STEEL TUBE CONNECTION.
                     │
            CHECK FOR VACUUM AT RED HOSE
            THAT ATTACHES TO CANISTER
```

5. Pack the bearing with grease to maintain proper needle position.

6. Install the clutch shaft inner bearing cone, using a press and bearing puller attachment D84L–1123–A or equivalent.

TRANSFER CASE ASSEMBLY

1. Wipe bearing bores clean. Install inner and outer bearing cups, using bearing cup replacer T87P–7120–B or equivalent.

2. Install a new collapsible spacer on the clutch shaft. Install the clutch shaft into the transfer case. Assemble the original shim and pinion gear.

3. Assemble the washer and pinion nut. Torque the nut using a breaker bar and holding wrench until rotational effort is 4.0–8.0 inch lbs. with new bearings. Do not exceed this specification or a new collapsible spacer will be required to obtain the proper preload.

4. Position shims and a new O-ring onto the gear housing. Be sure to lubricate the O-rings.

5. Install the gear housing subassembly to the transfer case and torque the bolts to 8–12 ft. lbs. (11–16 Nm).

6. Check the backlash between the drive

DRIVE TRAIN

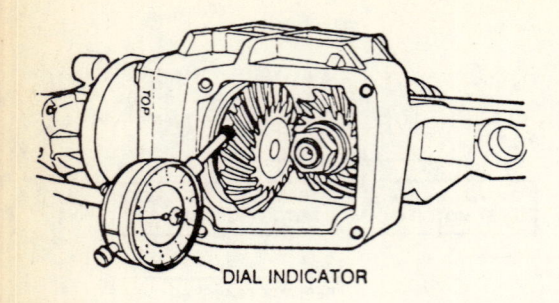

Checking the backlash

and pinion gear. Correct backlash should be 0.004–0.006 in. (0.10–0.15 mm).

NOTE: *Check the gear contact tooth pattern. If a gross pattern error is detected with backlash correct, adjust the drive pinion gear shim stack. Increasing the shim stack should move the contact pattern on the drive (pull) side of the gear toward toe of tooth.*

7. Install the shift collar onto the clutch shaft.
8. Slide the ball bearing onto the input gear. Install the input gear into the transfer case. Slide the small end of the input gear into the clutch shaft.
9. Install the snapring onto the outer end of the shaft.
10. Slide the bearing outboard and install the snapring onto the inner end of the input shaft. Make certain the snaprings are completely seated in the grooves.
11. Install the 2 piece snapring into the groove for the ball bearing in the transfer case.
12. Install the bearing cap and retainer bolts. Torque the bolts to 18–24 ft. lbs. (24–33 Nm).
13. Inspect the shift fork clips and replace as necessary. Install the shift fork onto the clutch collar.
14. Install a new O-ring onto the vacuum servo shaft. Lubricate O-ring with automatic transmission fluid.
15. Install the vacuum servo assembly into the transfer case. Install the snapring, making certain it is fully seated in the groove.
16. Install the shift fork snaprings.
17. Apply a bead of silicone rubber sealer on the cover surface. Install the transfer case side cover and torque the bolts to 7–12 ft. lbs. (9–16 Nm).
18. After checking the backlash, install the transfer case onto the transaxle.

SPECIFICATIONS

Description	ft. lbs.	Nm
Vacuum solenoids-to-shock tower	21–30	29–40
Vacuum reservoir retaining nuts	34–38 ①	3.8–4.3
Vacuum servo line bracket	7–12	9–16
Vacuum servo shield-to-transfer case	7–12	9–16
Transfer case retaining bolts	15–19	21–25
Driveshaft-to-drive yoke	15–17	21–23
Gear housing-to-transfer case	8–12	11–16
Bearing cap retaining bolts	18–24	24–33
Transfer case side cover retaining bolts	7–12	9–16

① Inch lbs.

SPECIAL TOOLS

Tool Number	Description
T57L-500-B	Bench mounted holding fixture
D79L-4621-A	Pinion bearing cone remover
D83L-7059-B	Vacuum pump
D84L-1123-A	Bearing puller attachment
T62F-4621-A	Pinion bearing cone replacer
T75L-1165-B	Seal plate
T80T-4000-W	Driver handle
T87P-4020-B	Backlash measuring gauge
T87P-4616-A	Bearing cup replacer
T87P-7065-B	Output seal replacer
T87P-7120-A	Holding wrench
T87P-7120-B	Transfer drive bearing cup replacer
T87P-7120-C	Pilot bearing replacer
T87P-7120-D	Bearing cup remover
T00L-4201-C	Dial indicator

DRIVELINE

Driveshaft and U-Joints

REMOVAL AND INSTALLATION

Tempo and Topaz With AWD

1. Raise the vehicle and support safely. Be sure to support the driveshaft using a suitable jack or hoist under the center bearing during removal and installation.
2. To maintain the driveshaft balance, mark the U-joints so they may be installed in their original position.
3. Remove the U-joint retaining bolts and

straps. Slide the driveshaft toward the rear of the vehicle to disengage it.

4. Remove the rear U-joint bolts and retaining the driveshaft, from the torque tube yoke flange.

5. Slide the driveshaft toward the front of the vehicle to disengage. Do not allow the splined shafts to contact with excessive force.

6. Remove the center bearing retaining bolts. Remove the driveshaft and retain the bearing cups with tape, if necessary.

7. Inspect the U-joint assemblies for wear and or damage, replace the U-joint, if necessary.

To install:

8. Install the driveshaft at the rear torque yoke flange. Ensure that the U-joint is in its original position.

9. Install the U-joint retaining bolts and caps. Torque them to 15–17 ft. lbs. (21–23 Nm). Position the front U-joint. Install the U-joint retaining caps and bolts. Torque them to 15–17 ft. lbs. (21–23 Nm).

10. Install the center bearing and retaining bolts. Torque to 23–30 ft. lbs. (31–41 Nm). Do not drop the assembled driveshafts as the impact may cause damage to the U-joint bearing cups.

NOTE: *Any time a U-joint retaining bolt is removed a suitable thread sealer should be applied to the retaining bolts prior to installation.*

Rear Wheel Spindle

REMOVAL AND INSTALLATION

1. Raise the rear of the car and safely support it on jackstands. Remove the tire and wheel assembly.

2. Disconnect the rear brake hose bracket from the strut mounting. Remove the rear brake drum, shoe assembly and brake backing plate. Refer to Chapter 8 for instructions on drum, shoe assembly and wheel cylinder removal. The backing plate is retained by four bolts, loosen and remove the bolts, and the backing plate.

3. Remove the tie rod to spindle retaining nut, washer and insulator. Remove the shock (strut) lower mounting nuts and bolts. Remove the nut and bolt retaining the lower control arm to the spindle. Remove the spindle.

4. Installation is in the reverse order of removal. Torque the mounting bolts and nuts.
Escort/Lynx/EXP/LN-7
Shock mount: 90–100 ft. lbs.
Control arm: 90–100 ft. lbs.
Tie rod: 65–75 ft. lbs. **Tempo/Topaz**
Spindle-to-Strut bolts: 70–96 ft. lbs.
Tie rod nut: 52–74 ft. lbs.

Control arm-to-Spindle nut: 60–86 ft. lbs.

Rear Axle Assembly

REMOVAL AND INSTALLATION

Tempo and Topaz With AWD

1. Raise the vehicle and support safely. Position a hoist or a suitable transaxle jack under the rear axle housing.

2. Remove the exhaust system.

3. Remove the rear U-joint bolts and straps retaining the driveshaft, from the torque tube yoke flange. Lower and support the driveshaft.

4. Remove the retaining bolts from the torque tube support bracket. Remove the axle retaining bolt from the left hand differential support bracket.

5. Remove the axle retaining bolt from the center differential support bracket.

6. Lower the axle assembly and remove the inboard U-joint retaining bolts and straps from each of the halfshaft. Remove and wire the halfshaft assemblies out of the way.

7. Lower the jack and remove the rear axle from the vehicle.

To install:

8. Position the rear axle assembly under the vehicle. Raise the rear axle far enough for the U-joint and halfshaft assemblies to be installed.

9. Position each inboard U-joint to the rear axle. Install the U-joint straps and retaining bolts. Using a T-30 Torx® bit, torque the bolts to 15–17 ft. lbs. (21–23 Nm) to each halfshaft.

10. Raise the rear axle into position and install the bolts attaching the differential housing to the left hand center differential support bracket. Torque to 70–80 ft. lbs. (95–108 Nm).

11. Position the torque tube and mounting bracket to the crossmember. Install the attaching bolts and torque to 28–35 ft. lbs. (38–47 Nm). Install the driveshaft and retaining bolts to the torque tube yoke flange. Using a T-30 Torx® bit, torque the bolts to 15–17 ft. lbs. (21–23 Nm).

NOTE: *Whenever a U-joint retaining bolt is removed, apply Loctite® or equivalent, to the bolt threads prior to installation.*

12. Install the exhaust system.

13. Check the lubricant level in the rear axle and add, if necessary. Lower the vehicle and road test to check the rear axle for proper operation.

Rear Axle Housing

REMOVAL AND INSTALLATION

1. Disconnect the negative battery cable.
2. Raise and safely support the vehicle.

DRIVE TRAIN

NOTE: *Anytime a U-joint retaining bolt is removed, Loctite® or equivalent, must be applied to the retaining bolts prior to installation.*

3. Position a hoist or jack under rear axle housing.
4. Remove muffler and exhaust system from catalytic converter back.
5. Remove rear U-joint retaining bolts and straps retaining driveshaft, from torque tube yoke flange. Remove driveshaft center bearing bolts. Disengage driveshaft from axle yoke and position driveshaft off to 1 side.
6. Remove 4 retaining bolts from torque tube support bracket. Remove damper.
7. Disconnect axle vent hose clip form body.
8. Remove axle retaining bolt from left hand differential support bracket.
9. Remove axle retaining bolt from center differential support bracket.
10. Lower axle assembly and remove inboard U-joint retaining bolts and straps from each halfshaft. Remove and wire halfshaft assemblies out of the way.
11. Remove rear axle assembly.

To install:

12. Position rear axle assembly under vehicle. Raise axle far enough for U-joint and halfshaft assemblies to be installed.
13. Position each inboard U-joint to rear axle. Install U-joint straps and retaining bolts. Using a T-30 Torx® bit, tighten bolts to 15–17 ft. lbs. (21–23 Nm).
14. Raise into position being careful not to trap or pinch axle vent hose. Install bolts attaching differential housing to left hand and center differential support bracket. Tighten to 70–80 ft. lbs. (95–108 Nm).
15. Attach axle vent hose clip to body.
16. Position torque tube and mounting bracket and damper to crossmember. Install 4 attaching bolts. Tighten to 28–35 ft. lbs. (38–47 Nm). Install driveshaft and retaining bolts to torque tube yoke flange. Using a T-30 Torx® bit, tighten to 15–17 ft. lbs. (21–23 Nm).
17. Install exhaust from catalytic converter back.
18. Check lubricant level in axle.
19. Lower vehicle.

Suspension and Steering

8

FRONT SUSPENSION

Your car is equipped with a MacPherson strut front suspension. The strut acts upon a cast steering knuckle, which pivots on a ball joint mounted on a forged lower control arm. A stabilizer bar, which also acts as a locating link, is standard equipment. To maintain good directional stability, negative scrub radius is designed into the suspension geometry. This means that an imaginary line extended from the strut intersects the ground outside the tire patch. Caster and camber are present and nonadjustable. The front suspension fittings are "lubed-for-life"; no grease fittings are provided.

The front suspension fasteners for the lower arm, tie rod and shock struts require only one wrench for loosening and tightening making them easier to work on.

The front strut is attached to a shear type upper mount to reduce engine, transaxle noise, vibration and harshness. The strut spring is contained between an offset lower spring seat fixed

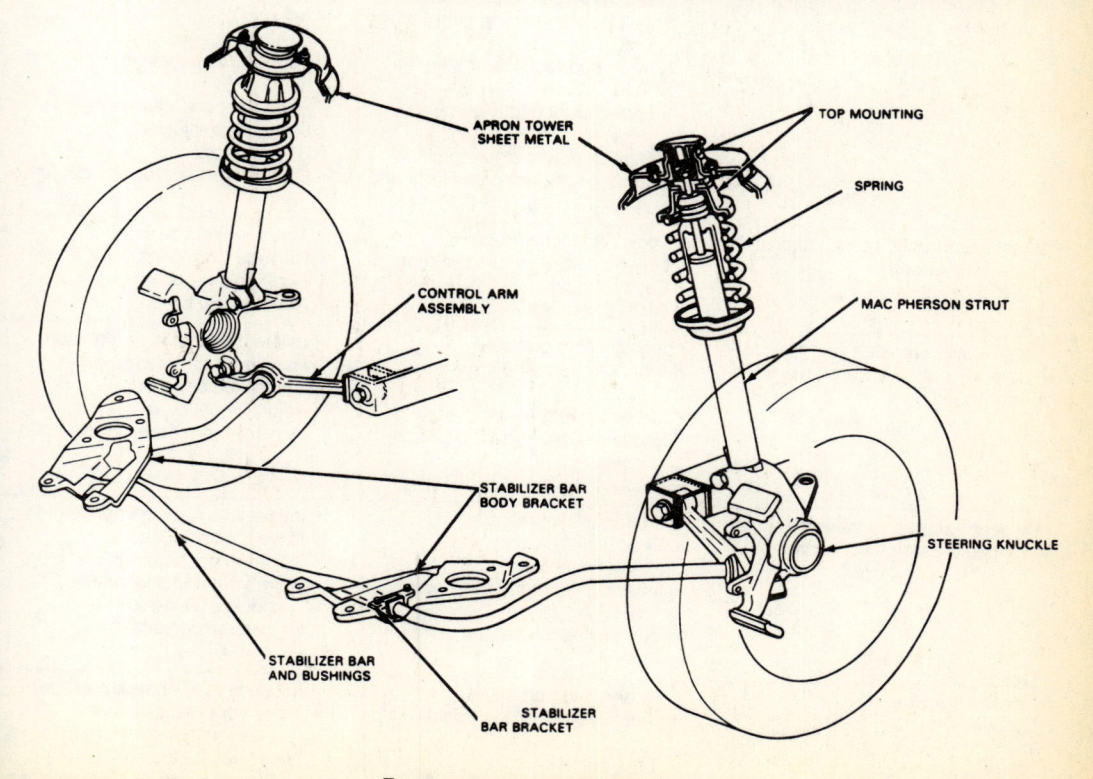

Front suspension components

SUSPENSION AND STEERING

Troubleshooting Basic Driveshaft and Rear Axle Problems

When abnormal vibrations or noises are detected in the driveshaft area, this chart can be used to help diagnose possible causes. Remember that other components such as wheels, tires, rear axle and suspension can also produce similar conditions.

BASIC DRIVESHAFT PROBLEMS

Problem	Cause	Solution
Shudder as car accelerates from stop or low speed	• Loose U-joint • Defective center bearing	• Replace U-joint • Replace center bearing
Loud clunk in driveshaft when shifting gears	• Worn U-joints	• Replace U-joints
Roughness or vibration at any speed	• Out-of-balance, bent or dented driveshaft • Worn U-joints • U-joint clamp bolts loose	• Balance or replace driveshaft • Replace U-joints • Tighten U-joint clamp bolts
Squeaking noise at low speeds	• Lack of U-joint lubrication	• Lubricate U-joint; if problem persists, replace U-joint
Knock or clicking noise	• U-joint or driveshaft hitting frame tunnel • Worn CV joint	• Correct overloaded condition • Replace CV joint

Troubleshooting Basic Steering and Suspension Problems

Problem	Cause	Solution
Hard steering (steering wheel is hard to turn)	• Low or uneven tire pressure • Loose power steering pump drive belt • Low or incorrect power steering fluid • Incorrect front end alignment • Defective power steering pump • Bent or poorly lubricated front end parts	• Inflate tires to correct pressure • Adjust belt • Add fluid as necessary • Have front end alignment checked/adjusted • Check pump • Lubricate and/or replace defective parts
Loose steering (too much play in the steering wheel)	• Loose wheel bearings • Loose or worn steering linkage • Faulty shocks • Worn ball joints	• Adjust wheel bearings • Replace worn parts • Replace shocks • Replace ball joints
Car veers or wanders (car pulls to one side with hands off the steering wheel)	• Incorrect tire pressure • Improper front end alignment • Loose wheel bearings • Loose or bent front end components • Faulty shocks	• Inflate tires to correct pressure • Have front end alignment checked/adjusted • Adjust wheel bearings • Replace worn components • Replace shocks
Wheel oscillation or vibration transmitted through steering wheel	• Improper tire pressures • Tires out of balance • Loose wheel bearings • Improper front end alignment • Worn or bent front end components	• Inflate tires to correct pressure • Have tires balanced • Adjust wheel bearings • Have front end alignment checked/adjusted • Replace worn parts
Uneven tire wear	• Incorrect tire pressure • Front end out of alignment • Tires out of balance	• Inflate tires to correct pressure • Have front end alignment checked/adjusted • Have tires balanced

SUSPENSION AND STEERING

to the strut body and a rotating upper seat attached to the upper mount. The offset spring seat reduces friction in the strut to improve ride and decrease wear. The hydraulic damping (shock) system for the front strut has twin tubes with a single acting piston attached to the rod.

Component Serviceability

The following components may be replaced individually or as components:
- Shock Absorber Struts (MacPherson)
- Strut Upper Mounts
- Coil Springs
- Ball Joints
- Lower Control Arm Bushing
- Forged Lower Control Arm
- Steering Knuckle
- Stabilizer Bar: The stabilizer bar is replaceable and contains the body mounting bushings. The stabilizer bar to lower arm insulator is replaceable as is the stabilizer bar to body bushing.

MacPherson Strut and Coil Spring
REMOVAL AND INSTALLATION

1981–85 Models

NOTE: *A coil spring compressor Ford Tool number T81P-5310-A for Escort/Lynx and EXP/LN-7 vehicles. DO NOT USE ON TEMPO/TOPAZ. Tempo/Topaz models require Rotunda 14-0259 or 86-0016 to compress the strut coil spring.*

1. Loosen the wheel lugs, raise the front of the car and safely support it on jackstands. Locate the jackstands under the frame jack pads, slightly behind the front wheels.
2. Remove the tire and wheel assembly.
3. Remove the brake line from the strut mounting bracket.
4. Place a floor jack or small hydraulic jack under the lower control arm. Raise the lower arm and strut as far as possible without raising the car.
5. Install the coil spring compressors. On Escort/Lynx/EXP/LN-7 models, place the top jaw of the compressors on the second coil from the top of the spring. Install the bottom jaw so that five coils will be gripped. Compress the spring evenly, from side to side, until there is about 1/8 in. (3mm) between any two spring coils. On Tempo/Topaz models, place the top jaw of the compressor on the fifth or sixth coil from the bottom. After the tool is installed, take a measurement from the bottom of the plate. Using the measurement as a reference, compress the spring a minimum of $3^{1}/_{2}$ in. (89mm). The coil spring must be compressed evenly. Always oil the compressor tool threads.
6. A pinch bolt retains the strut to the steering knuckle. Remove the pinch bolt.
7. Loosen, but do not remove, the two top mount to strut tower nuts. Lower the jack supporting the lower control arm.
8. Use a pry bar and slightly spread the pinch bolt joint (knuckle to strut connection).
9. Place a piece of 2 in. × 4 in. wood, $7^{1}/_{2}$ in. long (51mm × 102mm × 191mm), against the shoulder on the steering knuckle. Use a short pry bar between the wooden block and the lower spring seat to separate the strut from the knuckle.
10. Remove the two strut upper mounting nuts.
11. Remove the MacPherson strut, spring and top mount assembly from the car.
12. Place an 18mm deep socket that has an external hex drive top (Ford tool number D81P-18045-A1) over the strut shaft center nut. Insert a 6mm allen wrench into the shaft end. With the edge of the strut mount clamped in a vise, remove the top shaft mounting nut from the shaft while holding the allen wrench. Use vise grips, if necessary or a suitable extension to hold the allen wrench.

NOTE: *Make a wooden holding device the will clamp the strut barrel into the bench vise. (See illustration). Do not clamp directly onto the strut barrel, damage may occur.*

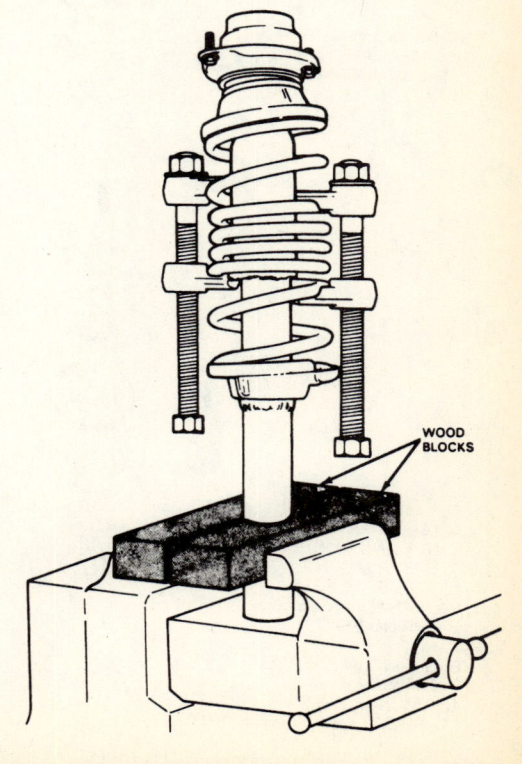

Mounting the strut in a bench vise

472 SUSPENSION AND STEERING

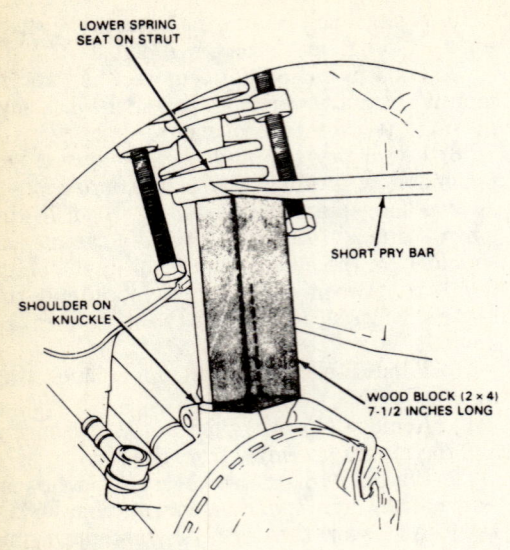

Block positioning

13. Clamp the strut into a bench vise. Remove the strut upper mount and the coil spring. If only the strut is to be serviced, do not remove the coil spring compressor from the spring.

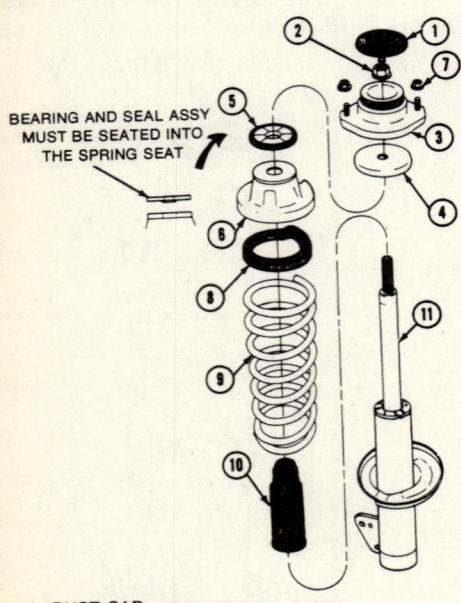

1. DUST CAP
2. NUT AND WASHER
3. UPPER MOUNT
4. THRUST PLAGE
5. BEARING AND SEAL
6. SPRING SEAT
7. NUT
8. SPRING INSULATOR
9. SPRING
10. JOUNCE BUMPER, FRONT
11. SHOCK ABSORBER STRUT

Typical strut upper mounting

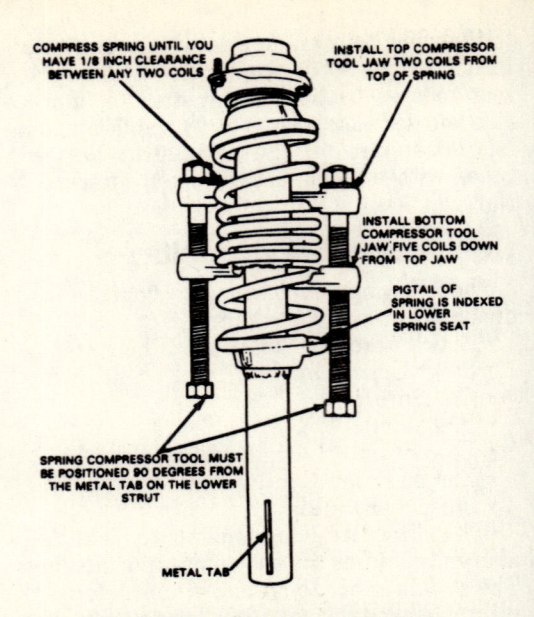

Typical coil spring compressor mounting

14. If the coil spring is to be replaced, remove the compressor from the old spring and install it on the new.

15. Mount the strut (if removed) in the vise using the wooden fixture. Position the coil spring in the lower spring seat. Be sure that the pigtail of the spring is indexed in the seat. That is, follows the groove in the seat and fits flush. Be sure that the spring compressors are positioned 90° from the metal tab on the lower part of the strut.

16. Use a new nut and assembly the top mount to the strut. Tighten the shaft nut to 48–62 ft. lbs.

17. Install the assembled strut, spring and upper mount into the car. If you have installed a new coil spring, be sure it has been compressed enough.

18. Position the two top mounting studs through the holes in the tower and install two new mounting nuts. Do not tighten the nuts completely.

19. Install the bottom of the strut fully into the steering knuckle pinch joint.

20. Install a new pinch bolt and tighten it to 68–81 ft. lbs. Tighten the tow upper mount nuts to 25–30 ft. lbs.

21. Remove the coil spring compressor. Make sure the spring is fitting properly between the upper and lower seats.

22. Install the brake line to the strut bracket. Install the front tire and wheel assembly. Lower the car and tighten the lugs.

SUSPENSION AND STEERING

1986–90 Models

NOTE: *All vehicles except Tempo with base suspension are equipped with gas pressurized shock absorbers which will extend unassisted. Do not apply heat or flame to the shock strut tube during removal.*

1. Loosen but do not remove, 2 top mount-to-shock tower nuts.
2. Raise and safely support the vehicle. Raise vehicle to a point where it is possible to reach the 2 top mount-to-shock tower nuts and the strut-to-knuckle pinch bolt.
3. Remove wheel and tire assembly.
4. Remove brake flex line-to-strut bolt.
5. Remove strut-to-knuckle pinch bolt.
6. Using a suitable tool, spread knuckle-to-strut pinch joint slightly.
7. Using a suitable bar, place top of bar under fender apron and pry down on knuckle until strut separates from knuckle.
8. Remove 2 top mount-to-shock tower nuts and remove strut from vehicle.
9. Install spring compressor in bench mount, install strut in compressor and compress spring.
10. Place deep 18mm socket on strut shaft nut. Insert an 8mm deep socket with $1/4$ in. drive socket with a suitable extension.

NOTE: *Do not attempt to remove shaft nut by turning shaft and holding nut. The nut must be turned and the shaft held to avoid possible damage to the shaft.*

11. Loosen spring compressor tool and remove top mount bracket assembly, bearing, insulator and spring.
12. Install replacement strut in spring compressor.

NOTE: *During reassembly of strut/spring assembly, be certain to follow correct sequence and proper positioning of bearing plate and seal assembly. If bearing and seal assembly are out of position, damage to the bearing will result.*

13. Install spring, insulator, bearing and top mount bracket assembly.
14. Install top shaft mounting nut while holding shaft with $1/4$ drive 8mm deep socket and extension. Tighten nut to 35–50 ft. lbs. (48–68 Nm).
15. Install strut assembly in vehicle. Install 2 top mount-to-shock tower nuts. Tighten to 25–30 ft. lbs. (37–41 Nm).
16. Slide strut mounting flange onto knuckle.
17. Install strut-to-knuckle pinch bolt. Tighten to 68–81 ft. lbs. (92–110 Nm).
18. Install brake flex line-to-strut bolt.
19. Install wheel and tire assembly.
20. Lower vehicle.
21. Check alignment.

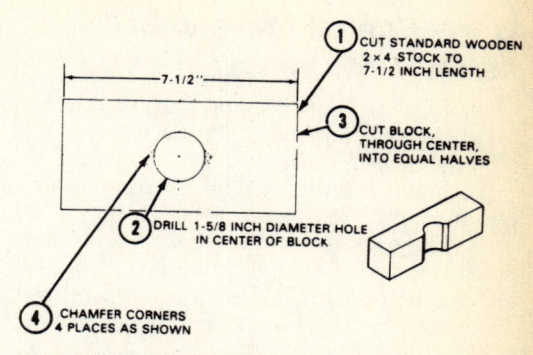

Strut holder construction

Lower Ball Joints

INSPECTION

1. Raise and safely support the vehicle so that wheels are in the full-down position.
2. Have an assistant grasp lower edge of the tire and move wheel and tire assembly in and out.
3. As wheel is being moved in and out, observe lower end of knuckle and lower control arm. Any movement indicates abnormal ball joint wear.
4. If any movement is observed, install new lower control arm assembly.

REMOVAL AND INSTALLATION

The lower ball joint is integral to the lower control assembly and cannot be serviced individually. Any movement of the lower ball joint detected as a result of inspection requires replacement of the lower control arm assembly.

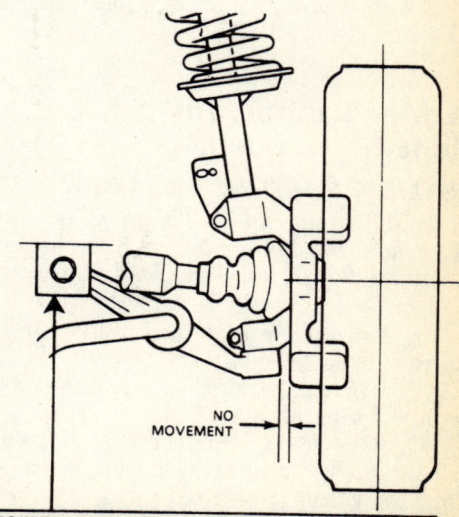

Checking the ball joint for excessive play

474 SUSPENSION AND STEERING

Lower Control Arm and Ball Joint
REMOVAL AND INSTALLATION

1. Raise and safely support the vehicle.
2. Remove nut from stabilizer bar end. Pull off large dished washer.
3. Remove lower control arm inner pivot nut and bolt.
4. Remove lower control arm ball joint pinch bolt. Using a suitable tool, slightly spread knuckle pinch joint and separate control arm from steering knuckle. A drift punch may be used to remove bolt.
5. Remove stabilizer bar spacer from the arm bushing.

NOTE: *Ensure steering column is in unlocked position. Do not use a hammer to separate ball joint from knuckle.*

To install:

6. Assemble lower control arm ball joint stud to the steering knuckle, ensuring that the ball stud groove is properly positioned.
7. Insert a new pinch bolt and nut. Tighten to 38–45 ft. lbs. (52–60 Nm).
8. Insert stabilizer bar spacer into arm bushing.
9. Clean stabilizer bar threads to remove dirt and contamination.
10. Position lower control arm onto stabilizer bar and position lower control arm to the inner underbody mounting. Install a new nut and bolt. On the 1981–85 models, torque them to 50–60 ft. lbs. The stabilizer mounting nut is tightened to 75–80 ft. lbs.
11. On the 1986–90 models, torque them to 48–55 ft. lbs. (65–74 Nm). Assemble stabilizer bar, dished washer and a new nut to stabilizer. Tighten nut to 98–115 ft. lbs. (132–156 Nm).
12. Lower vehicle.

Lower Control Arm Inner Pivot Bushing
REMOVAL AND INSTALLATION

NOTE: *A special C-Clamp type removal/installation tool is required. See note under Stabilizer Bar for the Ford part number of this tool.*

1. Raise the front of the car and safely support it on jackstands.
2. Remove the stabilizer bar to control arm nut and the dished washer.
3. Remove the inner control arm pivot nut and bolt. Pull the arm down from its mounting and away from the stabilizer bar.
4. Carefully cut away the retaining lip of the bushing. Use the special clamp type tool and remove the bushing.

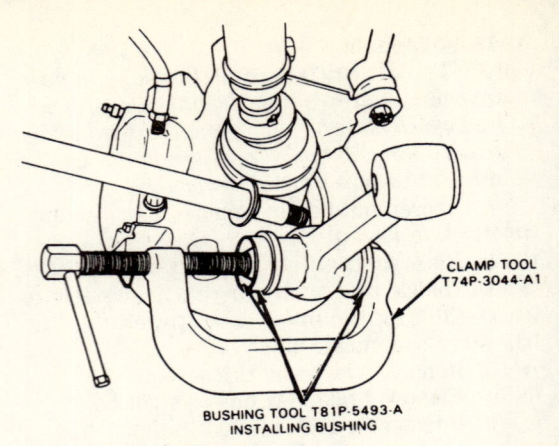

Using a C-clamp bushing tool

5. Saturate the new bushing with vegetable oil and install the bushing using the special tool.
6. Position the lower control arm over the stabilizer bar and install into the inner body mounting using a new bolt and nut. Tighten the inner nut and bolt to 44–53 ft. lbs. Tighten the stabilizer nut to 60–70 ft. lbs. Be sure to install the dished washer ahead of the nut.

Stabilizer Bar and/or Bushings
REMOVAL AND INSTALLATION

1981–98 Models

1. Raise the front of the car and safely support it on jackstands. The tire and wheel assembly may be removed for convenience.
2. Remove the stabilizer bar insulator mounting bracket bolts, end nuts and washers. Remove the bar assembly.
3. Carefully cut the center mounting insulators from the stabilizers.

NOTE: *A C-clamp type remover/installer tool is necessary to replace the control arm to stabilizer mounting bushings. The Ford part number of this tool is T81P-5493-A with T74P-3044-A1.*

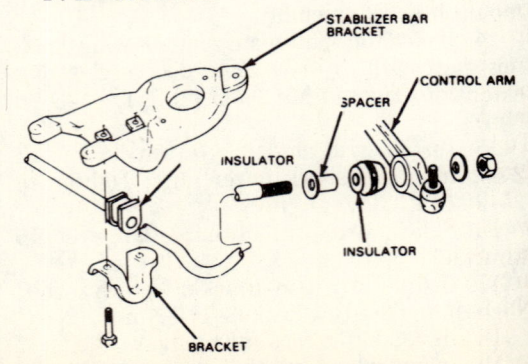

Stabilizer and related part mountings

SUSPENSION AND STEERING

4. Remove the control arm inner pivot nut and bolt. Pull the arm down from the inner mounting and away from the stabilizer bar (if still mounted on car).
5. Remove the old bar to control arm insulator bushing with the clamp type tool.
6. Use vegetable oil and saturate the new control arm bushing. Install the bushing with the clamp type tool. Coat the center stabilizer bar bushings with a suitable lubricant. Slide the bushings into place. Install the inner control arm mounting. Tighten to 60–75 ft. lbs.
7. Install the stabilizer bar using new insulator mounting bracket bolts. Tighten to 50–60 ft. lbs. Install new end nuts with the old dished washers. Tighten to 75–80 ft. lbs.
8. Install the wheel if removed. Lower the car.

1986–90 Models

1. Raise and safely support the vehicle.
2. Remove nut from stabilizer bar at each lower control arm and pull off large dished washer. Discard nuts.
3. Remove stabilizer bar insulator U-bracket bolts and U-brackets and remove stabilizer bar assembly. Discard bolts.

NOTE: *Stabilizer bar U-bracket insulators can be serviced without removing the stabilizer bar assembly.*

To install:
4. Slide new insulators onto the stabilizer bar and position them in the approximate location.
5. Clean stabilizer bar threads to remove dirt and contamination.
6. Install spacers into the control arm bushings from forward side of control arm so that washer end of spacer will seat against stabilizer bar machined shoulder and push mounting brackets over insulators.
7. Insert end of stabilizer bar into the lower control arms. Using new bolts, attach the stabilizer bar and the insulator U-brackets to the bracket assemblies. Hand start all 4 U-bracket bolts. Tighten all bolts halfway, then tighten bolts to 59–68 ft. lbs. (80–92 Nm) on Tempo/Topaz, 85–100 ft. lbs. (115–135 Nm) on Escort/Lynx.
8. Using new nuts and the original dished washers (dished side away from bushing), attach the stabilizer bar to the lower control arm. Tighten nuts to 98–115 ft. lbs. (132–156 Nm).
9. Lower vehicle.

Steering Knuckle
REMOVAL AND INSTALLATION

1. Loosen the wheel lugs, raise the front of the car and support safely on jackstands. Remove the tire and wheel assembly.
2. Remove the cotter pin from the tie rod end stud nut and remove the nut. Use a suitable removing tool and separate the tie rod end from the steering knuckle.
3. Remove the disc brake caliper, rotor and center hub as outlined in this section. Loosen, but do not remove the two top strut mounting nut.
4. Remove the lower control arm to steering knuckle pinch bolt, slightly spread the connection after the bolt has been removed.
5. Remove the strut to steering knuckle pinch bolt, slightly spread the connection after the bolt has been removed. Remove the driveaxle from the knuckle hub.
6. Remove the steering knuckle from the strut.
7. Remove the wheel bearings and rotor splash shield, as outlined in this section.

To install:
8. Install the rotor splash shield and wheel bearings, as outlined in this section.
9. Install the steering knuckle onto the strut. Install a new pinch bolt and tighten to specifications.
10. Install the center hub onto the stub driveshaft as outlined in this section.
11. Install the lower control arm to the knuckle. Make sure the ball joint groove is aligned so the pinch bolt can slide through. Install a new pinch bolt and tighten to specifications.
12. Install the rotor and disc brake caliper (see Chapter 9). Position the tie rod end into the steering knuckle, install a new nut and tighten to specifications. Align the cotter pin slot and install a new cotter pin.
13. Install the tire and wheel assembly. Lower the car and tighten the wheel lugs.

Front Wheel Hub, Knuckle and Bearings
REMOVAL, REPACKING AND INSTALLATION

1981–85 Models

NOTE: *The wheel hub and knuckle must be removed for bearing replacement or servicing. A special puller is required to remove and install the hub. (Ford Part Number T81P-1104-A, T81P-1104-C and adapters*

SUSPENSION AND STEERING

T81P-1104-B or T83P-1104-AH). *The adaptors screw over the lugs and attach to the puller, which uses a long screw attached to the end of the stub shaft to pull off or install the hub.*

1. Remove wheel cover and slightly loosen the lugs.
2. Remove the hub retaining nut and washer. The nut is crimped staked to the shaft. Use a socket and sufficient torque to overcome the locking force of the crimp.
3. Raise the front of the car and support safely with jackstands. Remove the tire and wheel assembly.
4. Remove the brake caliper and disc rotor. Refer to the proceeding sections in this chapter for the necessary procedures.
5. Disconnect the lower control arm and tie rod from the steering knuckle. Loosen tow top strut mounting nuts, but do not remove them. Install the hub remover/installer tool and remove the hub. If the outer bearing is seized on the hub remove it with a puller.
6. Remove the front suspension knuckle.
7. On models through 1983, after the front knuckle is removed, pull out the inner grease shield, the inner seal and bearing.
8. Remove the outer grease seal and bearing.
9. If you hope to reuse the bearings, clean them in a safe solvent. After cleaning the bearings and races, carefully inspect them for damage, pitting, heat coloring etc. If damage etc. has occurred, replace all components (bearings, cups and seals). Always replace the seals with new ones. Always use a new hub nut whenever the old one has been removed.
10. If new bearings are to be used, remove the inner and outer races from the knuckle. A three jawed puller on a slide hammer will do the job.
11. Clean the interior bore of the knuckle.
12. On 1984 and later models, remove the snapring that retains the bearing in the steering knuckle.
13. Position the knuckle, outboard side up under a hydraulic press with appropriate adapters in place, and press the bearing from the knuckle.
14. Clean the interior bore of the knuckle.

To install:

15. On models through 1983, install the new bearing cups using a suitable driver. Be sure the cups are fully seated in the knuckle bore.
16. Pack the wheel bearings with multi-purpose lubricant (Ford part number C1AZ-19590-B or the equivalent). If a bearing packer is not available, place a large portion of grease into the palm of your hand and slide the edge of the roller cage through the grease with your other hand. Work as much grease as you can between the bearing rollers.
17. Put a sufficient amount of grease between the bearing cups in the center of the knuckle. Apply a thin film of grease on the bearing cups.
18. Place the outer bearing and new grease seal into the knuckle. Place a thin film of grease on all three lips of the new outer seal.
19. Turn the knuckle over and install the inner bearing and seal. Once again, apply a thin film of grease to the three lips of the seal.
20. Install the inner grease shield. A small block of wood may be used to tap the seal into the knuckle bore.
21. Keep the knuckle in the vertical position or the inner bearing will fall out. Start the wheel hub into the outer knuckle bore and push the hub as far as possible through the outer and inner bearings by hand.

NOTE: *Prior to installing the hub, make sure it is clean and free from burrs. Use crocus cloth to polish the hub is necessary. It is important to use only hand pressure when installing the hub, make sure the hub is through both the outer and inner bearings.*

22. With the hub as fully seated as possible through the bearings, position the hub and knuckle to the front strut.
23. On 1984 and later models, position the knuckle. outboard side down on the appropriate adapter and press in the new bearing. Be sure the bearing is fully seated. Install a new retainer snapring.
24. Install the hub using tool T83T-1104-AH3 and press. Check that the hub rotates freely.
25. Lubricate the stub shaft splines with a thin film of SAE 20 motor oil. Use hand pressure only and insert the splines into the knuckle and hub as far as possible.

NOTE: *Do not allow the hub to back out of the bearings while installing the stub shaft, otherwise it will be necessary to start all over from Step 7.*

26. Complete the installation of the suspension parts.

To install:

27. Install the hub remover/installer tool and tighten the center adapter to 120 foot pounds, this ensures the hub is fully seated.
28. Remove the installer tool and install the hub washer and nut. Tighten the hub nut finger tight.
29. Install the disc rotor, caliper etc. in reverse order of removal. Refer to the proceeding sections of this chapter, if necessary, for procedures.
30. Install the tire and wheel assembly and snug the wheel lugs.

SUSPENSION AND STEERING

31. Lower the car to the ground, set the parking brake and block the wheels.
32. Tighten the wheel lugs to 80–105 ft. lbs.
33. Tighten the center hub nut to 180–200 ft. lbs. DO NOT USE A POWER WRENCH TO TIGHTEN THE HUB NUT!
34. Stake the hub nut using a rounded, dull chisel. DO NOT USE A SHARP CHISEL.

1986–90 Models

1. Remove wheel cover/hub cover from wheel and tire assembly and loosen wheel nuts.
2. Remove hub nut retainer and washer by applying sufficient torque to nut to break locking tab and remove hub nut retainer. The hub nut retainer must be discarded after removal.
3. Raise and safely support the vehicle. Remove wheel and tire assembly.
4. Remove brake caliper by loosening caliper locating pins and rotating caliper off rotor starting from lower end of caliper and lifting upward. Do not remove caliper pins from caliper assembly. Lift caliper off rotor and hang it free of rotor. Do not allow caliper assembly to hang from brake hose. Support caliper assembly with a length of wire.
5. Remove rotor from hub by pulling it off hub bolts. If rotor is difficult to remove from hub, strike rotor sharply between studs with a rubber or plastic hammer. If rotor will not pull off, apply rust penetrating fluid to inboard and outboard rotor hub mating surfaces. Install a 3 jaw puller and remove rotor by pulling on rotor outside diameter and pushing on hub center. If excessive force is required for removal, check rotor for lateral runout.
6. Later runout must be checked with nuts clamping hat section of rotor.
7. Remove rotor splash shield.
8. Disconnect lower control arm and tie rod from knuckle (leave strut attached).
9. Loosen the 2 strut top mount-to-apron nuts.
10. Install a suitable hub removal tool and remove hub/bearing/knuckle assembly by pushing out CV-joint outer shaft until it is free of assembly.
11. Support knuckle with a length of wire, remove strut bolt and slide hub/knuckle assembly off strut.
12. Carefully remove support wire and transfer hub/bearing assembly to bench.
13. Install a suitable front hub puller with jaws of puller on the knuckle bosses and remove hub.

NOTE: *Ensure the shaft protector is centered, clears the bearing inside diameter and rests on the end face of the hub journal.*

14. Remove snapring which retains bearing knuckle assembly and discard.
15. Using a hydraulic press, place a suitable front bearing spacer step side up on press plate and position knuckle on spacer with outboard side up. Install bearing removal tool on bearing inner race and press bearing out of knuckle.
16. Discard bearing.
17. Remove halfshaft.
18. Place halfshaft in vise. Remove bearing dust seal by uniformly tapping on outer edge with a light-duty hammer and screwdriver. Discard dust seal.

To install:
19. Place halfshaft in vise. Install a new dust seal using a suitable seal installer. Seal flange must face outboard.
20. Install halfshaft.
21. On bench, remove all foreign material from knuckle bearing bore and hub bearing journal to ensure correct seating of new bearing.

NOTE: *If hub bearing journal is scored or damaged, replace hub. Do not attempt to service. The front wheel bearings are of a cartridge design and are pregreased, sealed and require no scheduled maintenance. The bearings are preset and cannot be adjusted. If a bearing is disassembled for any reason, it must be replaced as a unit. No individual service seals, rollers or races are available.*

22. Place suitable bearing spacer step side down on hydraulic press plate and position knuckle on spacer with outboard side down. Position a new bearing in inboard side of knuckle. Install a suitable front bearing installer on bearing outer race face with undercut side facing bearing and press bearing into knuckle. Ensure that bearing seats completely against shoulder of knuckle bore.

NOTE: *Ensure proper positioning of bearing installer during installation to prevent bearing damage.*

23. Install a new snapring in knuckle groove using snapring pliers.
24. Place suitable front bearing spacer on arbor press plate and position hub on tool with lugs facing downward. Position knuckle assembly on hub barrel with outboard side down. Place a suitable front bearing remover on inner race of bearing and press down on tool until bearing is freely in knuckle after installation.
25. Suspend hub/knuckle/bearing assembly on vehicle with wire and attach strut loosely to knuckle. Lubricate CV-joint stub shaft splines with SAE 30 weight motor oil and insert shaft into hub splines as far as possible using hand pressure only. Check that spline are properly engaged.
26. Install suitable front hub installer and wheel bolt adapter to hub and stub shaft. Tighten hub installer tool to 120 ft. lbs. (162 Nm) to ensure that hub is fully seated.

SUSPENSION AND STEERING

27. Remove tool and install washer and new hub nut retainer. Tighten hub nut retainer finger-tight.
28. Complete installation of front suspension components.
29. Install disc brake rotor to hub assembly.
30. Install disc brake caliper over rotor.
31. Ensure outer brake shoe spring end is seated under upper arm of knuckle.
32. Install wheel and tire assembly, tightening wheel nuts finger-tight.
33. Lower vehicle and block wheels to prevent vehicle from rolling.
34. Tighten wheel nuts to 85–105 ft. lbs. (115–142 Nm).
35. Manually thread hub nut retainer assembly on constant velocity output shaft as far as possible using a 30mm or 1 1/8 in. socket, tighten retainer assembly to 180–200 ft. lbs. (245–270 Nm).

NOTE: *Do not use power or impact tools to tighten the hub nut. Do not move the vehicle before retainer is tightened.*

36. During tightening, an audible click sound will indicate proper ratchet function of the hub nut retainer. As the hub nut retainer tightens, ensure that one of the 3 locking tabs is in the slot of the CV-joint shaft. If the hub nut retainer is damaged, or more than 1 locking tab is broken, replace the hub nut retainer.
37. Install wheelcover or hub cover and lower vehicle completely to ground.
38. Remove wheel blocks.

Front End Alignment

CASTER AND CAMBER

Caster and camber angles on your car are preset at the factory and cannot be adjusted in the field. Improper caster and camber can be corrected only through replacement of worn or bent parts. The caster measurements must be made on the left hand side by turning the left hand wheel through the prescribed angle of sweep and on the right hand side by turning the right hand wheel through the prescribed angle of sweep. When using alignment equipment designed to measure caster on both the

Toe Adjustment

Model	Normal	Minimum	Maximum
Escort/Lynx EXP	0.10" Out	0.02" In	0.22" Out
Tempo/Topaz	1/8" Out	1/32" In	7/32" Out

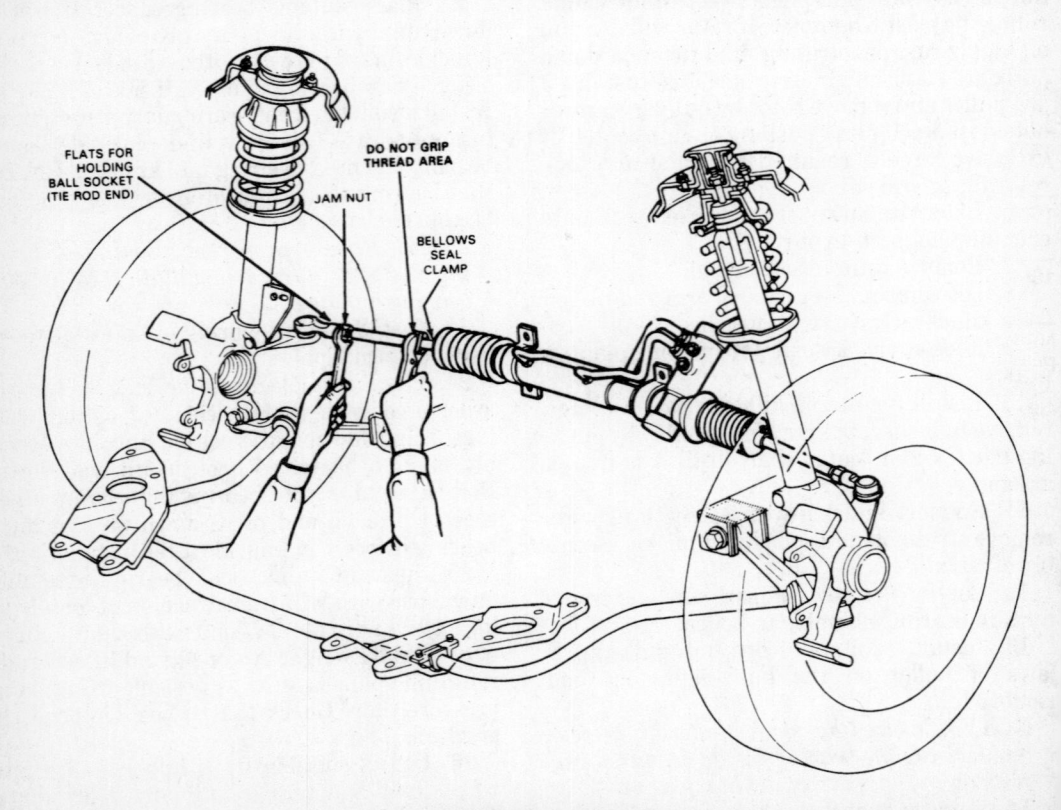

Adjusting front end toe

SUSPENSION AND STEERING

right hand and left hand side, turning only one wheel will result in a significant error in the caster angle for the opposite side.

TOE ADJUSTMENT

Toe is the difference in distance between the front and the rear of the front wheels.

1. On models equipped with power steering, move the steering wheel back and forth several times until the steering wheel is in the straight-ahead or centered position.

2. Turn the engine OFF and lock the steering wheel in place using a suitable steering wheel holder.

3. Loosen the slide off the small outer boot clamp so the boot will not twist during adjustment.

4. Loosen the locknuts on the outer tie rod ends.

5. Rotate both (right and left) tie rods in exactly equal amounts during adjustment. This will keep the steering wheel centered.

WHEEL ALIGNMENT

Years	Model	Caster Range (deg.)	Caster Preferred Setting (deg.)	Camber Range (deg.)	Camber Preferred Setting (deg.)	Toe-In (in.)	Steering Axis Inclination (deg.)
1981	Escort, Lynx	9/16P–2 1/16P	1 5/16P	②	③	7/32N–1/64P	④
1982	Escort, Lynx	9/16P–2 1/16P	1 5/16P	②	③	7/32N–1/64P	④
	EXP, LN7	9/16P–2 1/16P	1 5/16P	②	③	7/32N–1/64P	④
1983	Escort, Lynx	9/16P–2 1/16P	1 5/16P	②	③	7/32N–1/64P	④
	EXP, LN7	9/16P–2 1/16P	1 5/16P	②	③	7/32N–1/64P	④
1984	Escort, Lynx	5/8P–2 1/16P	1 2/3P	⑤	⑥	7/32N–1/64P	④
	EXP, LN7	5/8P–2 1/16P	1 2/3P	⑤	⑥	7/32N–1/64P	④
	Tempo, Topaz	9/16P–2 1/16P	1 5/16P	⑦	⑧	7/32N–1/64P	⑨
1985	Escort, EXP, Lynx	9/16P–2 1/16P	1 5/16P	⑤	⑥	7/32N–1/64P	④
	Tempo, Topaz	9/16P–2 1/16P	1 5/16P	⑦	⑧	7/32N–1/64P	⑨
1986	Escort, Lynx	1 11/16P–3 3/16P	2 7/16P	⑩	⑪	7/32N–1/64P	④
	Tempo, Topaz	1 11/16P–3 3/16P	2 7/16P	⑫	⑬	7/32N–1/64P	⑨
1987	Escort, Lynx	1 11/16P–3 3/16P	2 7/16P	⑩	⑪	7/32N–1/64P	④
	Tempo, Topaz	1 11/16P–3 3/16P	2 7/16P	⑫	⑬	7/32N–1/64P	⑨
1988	Escort	1 5/8P–3 1/8P	2 3/8P	⑭	⑮	1/4N–0	⑯
	Tempo, Topaz	1 11/16P–3 3/16P	2 7/16P	⑰	⑱⑲	⑳	㉑
1989–90	Escort	1 5/8P–3 1/8P	2 3/8P	⑭	⑮	1/4N–0	⑯
	Tempo, Topaz	1 11/16P–3 3/16P	2 7/16P	⑰	⑱⑲	⑳	㉑

N—Negative
P—Positive

① Caster measurements must be made on the left side by turning left wheel through the prescribed angle of sweep and on the right side by turning right wheel through prescribed angle of sweep for the equiment being used. When using alignment equipment designed to measure caster on both the right and left side, turning only one wheel will result in a significant error in caster angle for the opposite side.

② Left—1 13/32P–2 29/32P
   Right—31/32P–2 15/32P
③ Left—2 5/32P
   Right—1 23/32P
④ Left—1 4 21/32P
   Right—1 5 3/32P
⑤ Left—1 3/8P–2 7/8P
   Right—1 5/16P–2 7/16P
⑥ Left—2 1/8P
   Right—1 11/16P
⑦ Left—1 1/8P–2 5/8P
   Right—11/16P–2 3/16P

⑧ Left—1 7/8P
   Right—1 1/2P
⑨ Left—1 4 5/8P
   Right—1 5 1/8P
⑩ Left—5/8P–2 1/8P
   Right—3/16P–1 11/16P
⑪ Left—1 3/8P
   Right—15/16P
⑫ Left—13/32P–1 15/32P
   Right—1/32P–1 15/32P
⑬ Left—15/32P
   Right—23/32P

⑭ Left—3/8P–1 7/8P
   Right—0–1 1/8P
⑮ Left—1 1/8P
   Right—3/4P
⑯ Left—14 21/32
   Right—15 3/32
⑰ Front left—21/32P–2 5/32P
   Right—7/32P–1 23/32P
⑱ Front—1 13/32P
   Right—31/32P
⑲ Rear (FWD)—5/32N
   Rear (AWD)—11/32N
⑳ Front—1/4P–0
   Rear—3/16N–3/16P
㉑ Left—14 21/32
   Right—15 3/32

SUSPENSION AND STEERING

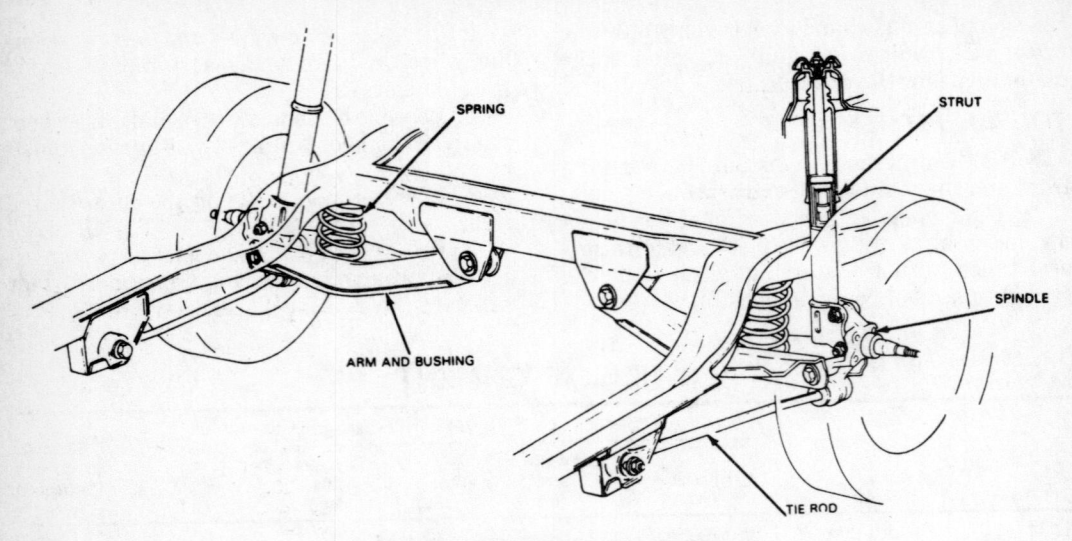

Rear suspension-Escort/Lynx/EXP

6. Tighten the locknuts when the adjustment has been made. Install and tighten the boot clamps.

FRONT SUSPENSION TIPS AND INSPECTION

- Maintain the correct tire pressures.
- Raise the front of the car and support on jackstands. Grasp the upper and lower edges of the tire. Apply up and downward movement to the tire and wheel. Check for looseness in the front ball joints. See previous ball joint inspection illustration. Inspect the various mounting bushings for wear. Tighten all loose nuts and bolts to specifications.
- Replace all worn parts found as soon as possible.
- Check the steering gear and assembly for looseness at its mountings. Check the tie rod ends for looseness.
- Check the shock absorbers. If any dampness from fluid leakage is observed, the shock should be replaced. Check the damping action of the shock by pushing up and down on each corner. If the damping effect is not uniform and smooth the shock should be suspect.

REAR SUSPENSION

Your car features a strut type independent rear suspension. Each side has a shock absorber (strut), lower control (transverse) arm, tie rod, forged spindle and a coil spring mounted between the lower control arm and the body crossmember side rail or on the strut itself.

The lower control (transverse) arm and the tie rod provide lateral and longitudinal control. The shock strut counters backing forces and provides the necessary suspension damping. The coil is mounted on the lower control arm and acts as a metal to metal jounce stop in case of heavy bottoming (going over bumps with weight in the back).

COMPONENT DESCRIPTION AND SERVICEABILITY

- **Rear Coil Spring:** Controls the suspension travel, provides ride height control and acts as a metal to metal jounce stop. The coil springs are replaceable, however the upper spring insulator must be replace at the same time.
- **Lower Control (Transverse) Arm:** Controls the side to side movement of each wheel and has the lower coil spring seat built in. The lower control arm is replaceable, however the control arm bushings are not. If the bushings are worn the control arm must be replaced.
- **Shock Absorber Strut:** Counters the braking forces and provides the necessary damping action to rear suspension travel caused by road conditions. The assembly is not repairable and must be replaced as a unit. The upper mounting may be serviced separately.
- **Tie Rod:** Controls the fore and aft wheel movement and holds the rear toe–in adjustment. The tie rod may be replaced as an assembly. Mounting bushings may be replaced separately, but new ones should be installed if the tie rod is replaced.
- **Wheel Spindle:** The one piece forged spindle attached to the lower arm, tie rod, shock strut and brake assembly. The rear wheel is mounted on the spindle. It may be replaced as a unit.

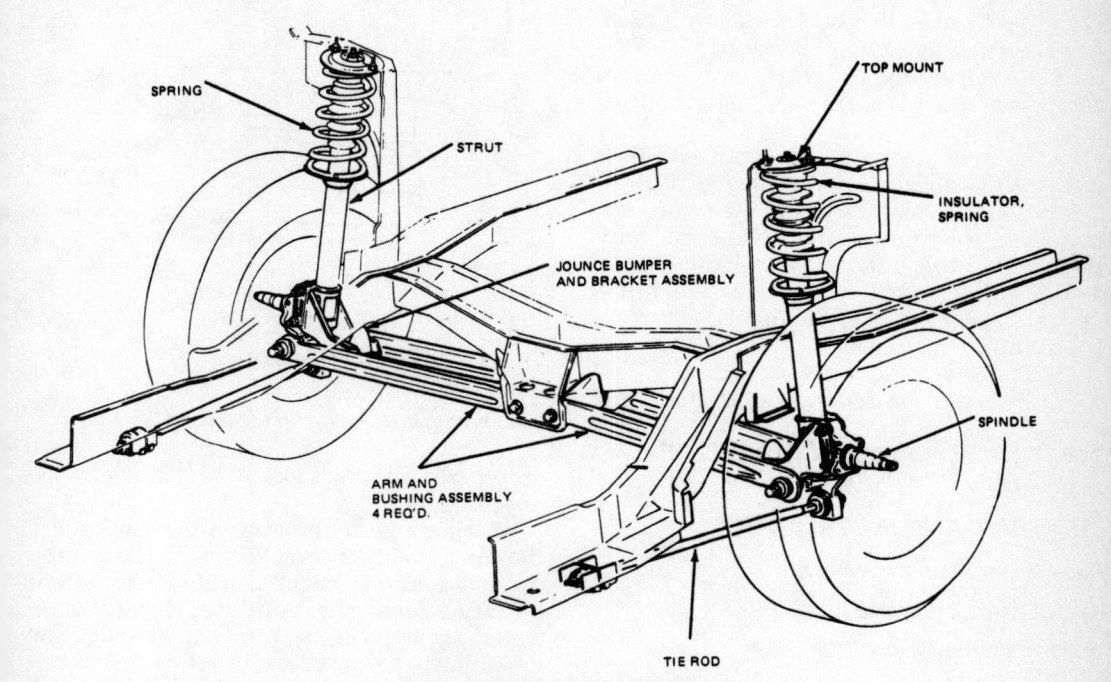

SUSPENSION AND STEERING

Tempo/Topaz, rear suspension

Rear Coil Spring

REMOVAL AND INSTALLATION

Escort/Lynx/EXP/LN-7

1. Jack up the rear of the car and safely support it on jackstands. The jackstand location should be on the frame pads slightly in front of the rear wheels.
2. Place a floor jack or small hydraulic jack under the rear control arm. Raise the control arm to its normal height with the jack, do not lift the car frame from the jackstands.

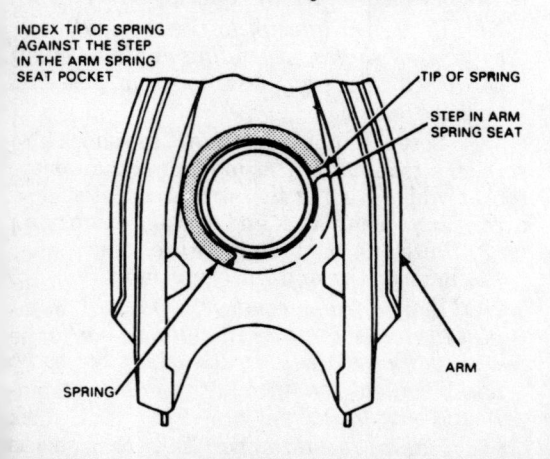

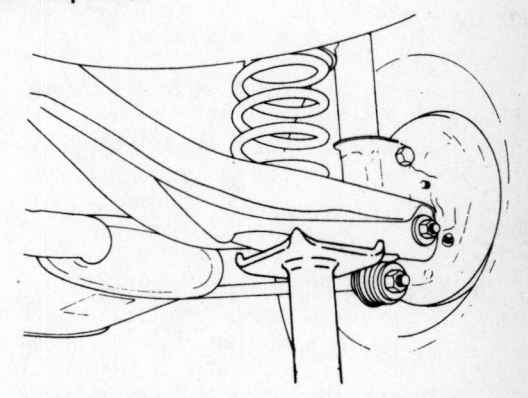

Supporting the rear suspension on Escort/Lynx/EXP

NOTE: *If a twin-post lift is used, vehicle must be supported on jackstands place under jack pads of the underbody forward of the tie rod bracket.*

3. Remove tire and wheel assembly.
4. Remove and discard nut, bolt and washers retaining lower control arm to spindle.
5. Slowly lower the jack under the control arm. The coil spring will relax as the control arm is lowered. Lower the control arm until the spring can be removed.

To install:

6. The spring insulator must be replaced when servicing spring.
7. Index the insulator on the spring and press insulator downward until it snaps into

Indexing the rear coil spring on the Escort/Lynx/EXP

SUSPENSION AND STEERING

place. Check again to ensure insulator is properly indexed against tip of the spring.

8. Install spring in control arm. Ensure spring is properly seated in control arm spring pocket.
9. Raise control arm and spring with floor jack. position spring in pocket on underbody.
10. Using a new bolt, nut and washers, attach control arm to spindle. Install bolt with the head toward front of the vehicle. On the 1981–85 models, tighten the nut and bolt to 90–100 ft. lbs. On the 1986–90 models, tighten to 70–96 ft. lbs. (95–130 Nm).
11. Install tire and wheel.
12. Remove floor jack and lower vehicle.

Rear Strut, Upper Mount, Coil Spring

REMOVAL AND INSTALLATION

Rear Shock Absorber Strut

REMOVAL AND INSTALLATION

1981–85 Escort/Lynx/EXP/LN-7

1. From inside the car, remove the rear compartment access panels (over the upper strut mount). On four door models remove the quarter trim panels.
2. Loosen, but do not remove the upper shock mounting nut.

NOTE: *A special 18mm deep socket is required, the socket should have a hex drive outer head so that it can be turned with an open-end wrench, as well as a ratchet. A 6mm Allen wrench is also required.*

To loosen the upper nut, place the socket over the nut, insert the Allen wrench through the center of the socket and into the upper strut rod. Hold the Allen wrench and loosen the nut by turning the socket with an open-end wrench. Use an extension to hold the Allen wrench, if necessary.

3. Jack up the rear of the car and support it safely on jackstands. Remove the rear tire and wheel assembly.
4. Remove the clip that holds the rear brake line to the shock. Locate the brake hose out of the way.
5. Loosen the two nuts and bolts that hold the shock to the wheel spindle. DO NOT REMOVE THEM at this time.
6. Remove the upper mounting nut, washer and rubber insulator.
7. Remove the two lower nuts and bolts and remove the shock strut assembly from the car.
8. Extend the shock to its maximum length. Install the new (upper mount) lower washer and insulator assembly. Lubricate the insulator with a tire lubricant. Position the

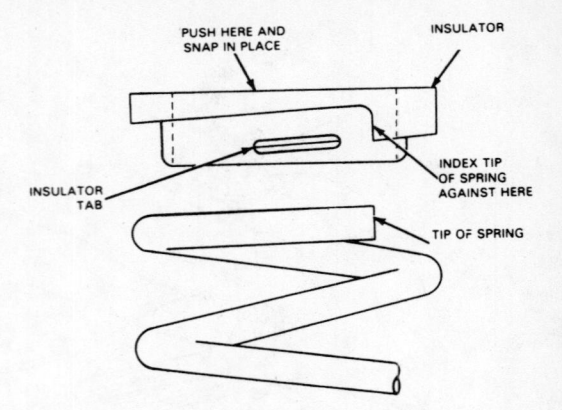

Rear spring installation on the Escort/Lynx/EXP

upper part of the shock shaft through the upper mount.

9. Slowly push upwards on the shock until the lower mounting holes align with the mounting holes in the spindle. Install new lower mounting bolts and nuts, buy do not completely tighten at this time. The heads of the mounting bolts must face the rear of the car.
10. Install the new top rubber insulator and washer. Tighten the mounting nuts to 60–70 ft. lbs.
11. Tighten the two lower mounting nuts and bolts to 90–100 ft. lbs.
12. Install the brake hose with the retaining clip. Put the tire and wheel assembly back on. Remove the jackstands and lower the car.
13. Reinstall the access or trim panels.

MacPherson Struts

REMOVAL AND INSTALLATION

1986–90 Escort and Lynx

1. Remove rear compartment access panels. On 4-door models, remove quarter trim panel.

NOTE: *Do not attempt to remove shaft nut by turning shaft and holding nut. Nut must be turned and shaft held to avoid possible damage to shaft.*

2. Loosen, but do not remove, top shock absorber attaching nut using an 18mm deep socket while holding the strut rod with a $^1/_4$ drive, 8mm deep socket and suitable extension.
3. Raise and safely support the vehicle.
4. Remove tire and wheel assembly.

NOTE: *If a frame contact lift is used, support the lower control arm with a floor jack. If a twin-post lift is used, support the body with floor jacks on lifting pads forward of the tie rod body bracket.*

5. Remove stabilizer bar link from shock bracket, if so equipped.
6. Remove clip retaining the brake line flex-

SUSPENSION AND STEERING

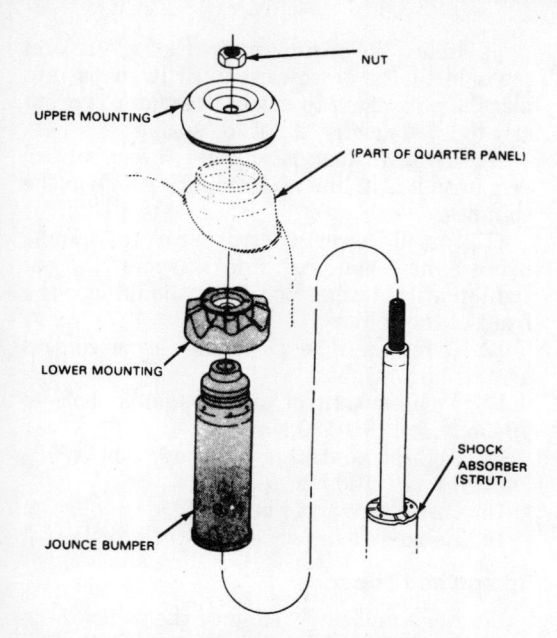

Rear strut mounting on the Escort/Lynx/EXP

ible hose to the rear shock absorber and move aside.

7. Loosen and discard 2 nuts and bolts retaining shock to the spindle. Do not remove bolts at this time.

8. Remove and discard top mounting nut, washer and rubber insulator.

9. Remove and discard 2 bottom mounting bolts and remove shock from the vehicle.

To install:

10. Extend shock absorber to its maximum length.

11. Install a new lower washer and insulator assembly, using tire lubricant to ease insertion into the quarter panel shock tower.

12. Position upper part of shock absorber shaft into shock tower opening in the body and push slowly on lower part of the shock until mounting holes are lined up with mounting holes in the spindle.

13. Install new lower mounting bolts and nuts. Do not tighten at this time.

NOTE: *The heads of both bolts must be to the rear of the vehicle.*

14. Place a new upper insulator and washer assembly and nut on the upper shock absorber shaft. Tighten nut to 35–55 ft. lbs. (48–75 Nm), using the 18mm deep socket and $1/4$ drive, 8mm deep socket with extension. Do not grip the shaft with pliers or vise grips.

15. Tighten 2 lower mounting bolts to 70–100 ft. lbs. (95–135 Nm).

16. Install stabilizer bar link to bracket on shock, if so equipped. Tighten bolts to 40–55 ft. lbs. (55–75 Nm).

17. Install brake line flex hose and retaining clip.

18. Install wheel and tire assembly.

19. Install quarter trim and access panels, if removed.

1984–85 Tempo/Topaz

1. Jack up the rear of the car and safely support it on jackstands. The jackstand location should be on the frame pads slightly in front of the rear wheels.

2. Open the trunk and loosen, but do not remove the two nuts retaining the upper strut mount to the body.

3. Remove the wheel and tire assembly. Raise the control arm slightly with a floor jack and support the arm on a jackstand. Do not jack the arm more than necessary. Just relieve the suspended position.

4. Remove the bolt that retains the brake hose to the strut. Position the hose out of the way of the strut removal.

5. Remove the jounce bumper retaining bolts and remove the bumper from the strut.

6. Disconnect the lower strut mounting from the spindle. Remove the two top mounting nuts. Remove the strut assembly from the car.

7. Refer to the Front Strut/Coil Spring service procedure proceeding this section for instructions on coil spring removal and replacement.

8. Install the strut assembly in the reverse order of removal. The lower mounting bolts are tightened to 70–96 ft. lbs. The upper to 25–30 ft. lbs. Tighten the upper mounting nuts after the car is resting on the ground.

1986–90 Tempo and Topaz

NOTE: *All Tempo and Topaz vehicles except Tempo with base suspension are equipped with gas-pressurized shock absorbers which will extend unassisted. Do not apply heat or flame to the shock strut during removal.*

1. Open luggage compartment and loosen but do not remove, 2 nuts retaining the upper strut mount to body.

2. Raise and safely support the vehicle.

3. Place a jack stand under the control arms to support the suspension.

4. Remove bolt attaching brake hose bracket to strut and move it aside.

5. Remove 2 bolts attaching shock strut to spindle.

6. Remove 2 upper mount-to-body nuts.

7. Remove strut from vehicle.

8. Place strut, spring and upper mount assembly in spring compressor.

CAUTION: *Attempting to remove the spring from the strut without first compressing the*

484 SUSPENSION AND STEERING

spring with a tool designed for that purpose could cause bodily injury.

NOTE: *Do not attempt to remove shaft nut by turning shaft and holding nut. Nut must be turned and shaft held to avoid possible fracture of shaft at base of hex.*

9. With the spring compressed, remove strut shaft-to-mount nut and then remove spring, strut and mount from compressor tool.

To install:

10. With spring compressed, install spring, spring insulator, top mount and upper washer on strut shaft.

11. Ensure spring is properly located in upper and lower spring seats. The dust shield must be within 10mm (0.39 in.) of the rod shoulder.

12. Tighten shaft nut to 35–50 ft. lbs. (48–68 Nm). Use 18mm deep socket to turn the nut and $1/4$ drive 8mm deep socket to hold shaft so it will not turn while tightening nut.

13. Insert 2 upper mount studs into strut tower and hand start 2 new nuts. Do not tighten at this time.

14. Position spindle into lower strut mount and install 2 new bolts. Tighten to 70–96 ft. lbs. (95–130 Nm).

15. Install brake flex-hose bracket on the strut.

16. Install wheel and tire.

17. Remove jack stand and lower vehicle to the ground.

18. Tighten 2 top mount-to-body nuts to 25–30 ft. lbs. (27–41 Nm).

Rear Control Arms

REMOVAL AND INSTALLATION

Escort and Lynx

1. Raise and safely support the vehicle.
2. Place floor jack under lower control arm. Raise lower control arm to curb position.

NOTE: *If a twin-post lift is used, vehicle must be supported on jackstands place under jack pads of the underbody forward of the tie rod bracket.*

3. Remove tire and wheel assembly.
4. Remove and discard nut, bolt and washers retaining lower control arm to spindle.
5. Slowly lower control arm with floor jack until spring can be removed.
6. Remove and discard bolt from the body end and remove control arm from vehicle.

To install:

7. Attach lower control arm-to-body bracket using a new bolt and nut. Head of the bolt should face the front of the vehicle. Do not tighten at this time.

8. The spring insulator must be replaced when servicing spring.

9. Index the insulator on the spring and press insulator downward until it snaps into place. Check again to ensure insulator is properly indexed against tip of the spring.

10. Using a floor jack, raise lower control arm until it is in line with mounting hole in the spindle.

11. Install lower control arm to spindle using a new bolt, nut and washers. Do not tighten at this time. Bolt head should face the front of the vehicle.

12. Using the floor jack, raise lower control arm to curb height.

13. Tighten control arm-to-spindle bolt to 70–96 ft. lbs. (95–130 Nm).

14. Tighten control arm-to-body bolt to 52–74 ft. lbs. (70–100 Nm).

15. Install tire and wheel.

16. Remove floor jack and lower vehicle.

Tempo and Topaz

1. Raise and safely support the vehicle.
2. Remove and discard arm-to-spindle bolt and nut.
3. Remove and discard center mounting bolt and nut.
4. Remove arm from vehicle.

To install:

NOTE: *When installing new control arms, the bushing with the 10mm (0.39 in.) hole is installed to the center of the vehicle and the bushing with the 12mm (0.48 in.) hole is installed to the spindle. The offset on the arm must face up on the right hand side of the vehicle and down on the left hand side of the vehicle. The flange edge of the arm stamping must also face the rear of the vehicle.*

5. Position arm at center of vehicle and insert new bolt and nut. Do not tighten at this time.

6. Move arm end up to spindle and insert new bolt, washer and nut. Ensure bolt engages both arms and spindle.

7. Tighten arm-to-body bolt to 30–40 ft. lbs. (40–54 Nm).

8. Tighten arm-to-spindle nut to 60–80 ft. lbs. (81–109 Nm).

9. Lower vehicle.

Tie Rod End

REMOVAL AND INSTALLATION

Escort/Lynx/EXP/LN-7

1. Jack up the rear of the car and safely support it on jackstands. Remove the tire and wheel assembly.

2. At the front mounting bracket of the tie rod, take a sharp tool and scribe a vertical mark at the mounting bolt head center. This is so the tie rod can be mounted in the same position.

SUSPENSION AND STEERING 485

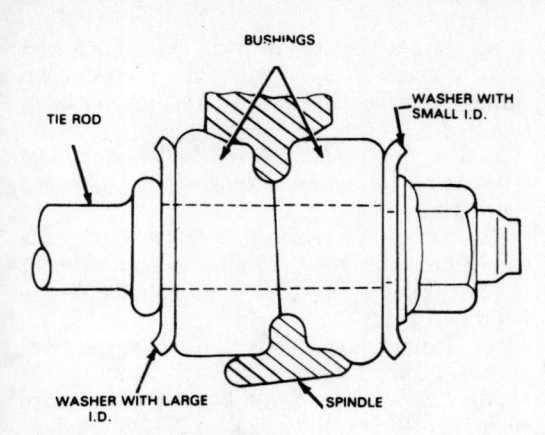

Typical tie rod installation

3. Remove the nut, washer and insulator that mount the rear of the tie rod to the wheel spindle.
4. Remove the front mounting nut and bolt that attach the tie rod to the front bracket. Remove the tie rod.

NOTE: *It may be necessary to separate the front body bracket slightly apart with a pry bar to remove the tie rod.*

5. Install new mounting bushings on the spindle end of the tie rod (reverse the removal order). Install the tie rod through the spindle and install the bushings, washer and nut. Tighten the nut to 65–75 ft. lbs.
6. Use a floor jack or a small hydraulic jack and slowly raise the rear control arm to its curb height.
7. Line up the new front mounting bolt with the mark you scribed on the mounting bracket. Install the bolt and nut (bolt head facing inward). Tighten the nut and bolt to 90–100 ft. lbs.

Tempo/Topaz

1. Raise and support the car on jackstands positioned ahead of the rear wheels on the body pads.
2. Loosen the two top strut mounting nuts, but do not remove them.
3. Position a jack under the rear suspension to relieve the suspended position.
4. Remove the wheel and tire assembly.
5. Remove the two mounting stud nuts.
6. Remove the nut that retains the tie rod to the rear spindle.
7. Remove the nut that retains the tie rod to the body.
8. Lower the rear suspension slightly until the upper strut mounting studs clear the body mounting holes.
9. Move the spindle rearward until the tie rod can be removed.

10. Install in the reverse order. The upper strut mounting nuts are tightened to 20–30 ft. lbs. The tie rod mounting nuts are tightened to 52–74 ft. lbs. The suspension should be at normal ride height before the tie rod mounting nuts are tightened.

Rear Wheel Spindle
REMOVAL AND INSTALLATION

1. Raise the rear of the car and safely support it on jackstands. Remove the tire and wheel assembly.
2. Disconnect the rear brake hose bracket from the strut mounting. Remove the rear brake drum, shoe assembly and brake backing plate. Refer to Chapter 9 for instructions on drum, shoe assembly and wheel cylinder removal. The backing plate is retained by four bolts, loosen and remove the bolts, and the backing plate.
3. Remove the tie rod to spindle retaining nut, washer and insulator. Remove the shock (strut) lower mounting nuts and bolts. Remove the nut and bolt retaining the lower control arm to the spindle. Remove the spindle.
4. Installation is in the reverse order of removal. Torque the mounting bolts and nuts.

Escort/Lynx/EXP/LN-7
- Shock mount: 90–100 ft. lbs.
- Control arm: 90–100 ft. lbs.
- Tie rod: 65–75 ft. lbs. **Tempo/Topaz**
- Spindle-to-Strut bolts: 70–96 ft. lbs.
- Tie rod nut: 52–74 ft. lbs.
- Control arm-to-Spindle nut: 60–86 ft. lbs.

Rear Wheel Bearings
ADJUSTMENT

Except Tempo and Topaz With AWD

1. Raise and safely support the vehicle.
2. Remove wheel cover or ornament and nut covers. Remove grease cap from hub.
3. Remove cotter pin and nut retainer. Discard cotter pin.
4. Back-off adjusting nut 1 full turn. Ensure nut turns freely on spindle threads. Correct any binding condition.
5. Tighten adjusting nut to 17–25 ft. lbs. (23–34 Nm) while rotating hub and drum assembly to seat bearings. Loosen adjusting nut $1/2$ turn and tighten adjusting nut to 24–28 inch lbs. (2.7–3.2 Nm) using inch lb. torque wrench.
6. Position adjusting nut retainer over adjusting nut so slots in nut retainer flange are in line with cotter pin hole in spline.
7. Install a new cotter pin and bend ends around retainer flange.
8. Check hub rotation. If hub rotates freely,

SUSPENSION AND STEERING

install grease cap. If not, check bearings for damage and replace as necessary.

9. Install wheel and tire assembly, wheel cover or ornaments, and nut covers as required.

10. Lower vehicle.

Tempo and Topaz With AWD

NOTE: *Bearings on 4WD vehicles are not adjustable.*

1. Raise the vehicle and support it safely.
2. Remove the wheel covers. Remove the grease cap from the hub being careful not to damage the cap.

NOTE: *Styled steel wheels and aluminum wheels require removal of the wheel assembly to remove the dust cover.*

3. Remove the cotter pin and nut retainer. Discard the cotter pin and replace with new.
4. Back-off the adjusting nut a full turn making certain that the nut rotates freely on the spindle thread. Correct any binding condition that may exist.
5. Tighten the adjusting nut to 17–25 ft. lbs. while rotating the hub and drum assembly to seat the bearings. Back-off the adjusting nut $1/2$ turn. Then retighten it to between 10–15 inch lbs.
6. Position the nut retainer on the nut and install the cotter pin so that the slots in the nut retainer flange are aligned with the cotter pin hole in the spindle.
7. Spread the ends of the cotter pin and bend then around the nut retainer.
8. Check the hub rotation. If the hub rotates freely, install the grease cap. If binding occurs, check the bearing for damage and replace as necessary.
9. Install the wheels and lower the vehicle.

REMOVAL AND INSTALLATION

Except Tempo and Topaz With AWD

1. Raise and safely support the vehicle.
2. Remove wheel cover or ornament and nut covers. Remove grease cap from hub.
3. Remove cotter pin and nut retainer. Discard cotter pin.
4. Pull hub and drum assembly off spindle being careful not to drop outer bearing assembly.
5. Remove outer bearing assembly.
6. Using seal remover, remove and discard grease seal. Remove inner bearing assembly from hub.
7. Wipe all lubricant from spindle and inside of hub. Cover spindle with a clean cloth and vacuum all loose dust and dirt from brake assembly. Carefully remove cloth to prevent dirt from falling on spindle.
8. Clean both bearing assemblies and cups using solvent. inspect bearing assemblies and cups for excessive wear, scratches, pits or other damage. Replace all worn or damaged parts as required.

NOTE: *Allow solvent to dry before repacking bearings. Do not spin-dry bearings with air pressure.*

9. If cups are replaced, remove them with wheel hub cup remover D80L–927–A and bearing cup puller T77F–1102–A or equivalent.

To install:

10. If inner or outer bearing cups were removed, install replacement cups using driver handle T80T–4000–W and bearing cup replacers T77F–1202–A and T73T–1217–A or equivalent. Support drum hub on wood block to prevent damage. Insure cups are properly seated in hub.

NOTE: *Do not use cone and roller assembly to install cup as this will cause damage to bearing cup and cone and roller assembly.*

11. Ensure all spindle and bearing surfaces are clean.
12. Using a bearing packer, pack bearing assemblies with a suitable wheel bearing grease.
13. Place inner bearing cone and roller assembly in inner cup. Apply light film of grease to lips of a new grease seal and install seal with rear hub seal replacer T81P–1249–A or equivalent. Ensure retainer flange is seated all around.
14. Apply light film of grease on spindle shaft bearing surfaces.
15. Install hub and drum assembly on spindle. Keep hub centered on spindle to prevent damage to grease seal and spindle threads.
16. Install outer bearing assembly and keyed flat washer on spindle. Install adjusting nut finger-tight. Adjust wheel bearings. Install a new cotter pin.
17. Install wheel and tire on drum.
18. Lower vehicle.

Tempo and Topaz With AWD

1. Raise and support the vehicle safely. Remove the tire and wheel assembly.
2. Remove the brake drum. Remove the parking brake cable from the brake backing plate.
3. Remove the brake line from the wheel cylinder. Remove the outboard U-joint retaining bolts. Remove the outboard end of the halfshaft from the wheel stub shaft yoke and wire it to the control arm.
4. Remove and discard the control arm to spindle bolt, washer and nut. Remove the tie rod nut, bushing and washer and discard the nut.
5. Remove and discard the 2 bolts retaining the spindle to the strut. Remove the spindle

SUSPENSION AND STEERING 487

from the vehicle. Mount the spindle and backing plate assembly in a suitable vise.

6. Remove the cotter pin and nut attaching the stub shaft yoke to the stub shaft. Discard the cotter pin.

7. Remove the spindle and backing plate assembly from the vise. Remove the stub shaft yoke using a 2 jaw puller and shaft protector.

8. Position the spindle and backing plate assembly into a vise and remove the wheel stub shaft.

9. Remove the snapring retaining the bearing. Remove the bolts retaining the spindle to the backing plate and remove the backing plate.

10. Remove the spindle from the vise and mount it into a suitable press. With the spindle side facing upward, carefully press out the bearing from the spindle, using a driver handle and bearing cup driver. Discard the bearing after removal.

To install:

11. Mount the spindle in a press, spindle side facing down. Position a new bearing in the outboard side of the spindle and carefully press in the new bearing using a driver handle and bearing installer.

12. Remove the spindle from the press and mount it in a vise. Install the snapring retaining the bearing. Position the backing plate to the spindle and install the retaining bolts.

13. Install the wheel stub shaft. Install the stub shaft yoke and attaching nut. Torque the nut to 120–150 ft. lbs. install a new cotter pin.

14. Remove the spindle and backing plate assembly from the vise. Position the spindle onto the tie rod and then into the strut lower bracket. Insert 2 new strut-to-spindle bolts. Do not tighten at this time.

15. Install the tie rod bushing washer and new nut. Install the new control arm to spindle bolt, washers and nut. Do not tighten them at this time.

16. Install a jack stand to support the suspension at the normal curb height before tightening the fasteners.

17. Torque the spindle to strut bolts to 70–96 ft. lbs. Torque the tie rod nut to 52–74 ft. lbs. Torque the control arm to spindle nut to 60–86 ft. lbs.

18. Position the outboard end of the halfshaft to the wheel stub shaft yoke. Install the retaining caps and bolts and torque them to 15–17 ft. lbs.

19. Install the brake line to wheel cylinder. Install the parking brake cable and brake drum. Install the wheel assembly, torque the lugs nuts to 80–105 ft. lbs.

20. Lower the vehicle and bleed the brake system. Check and adjust the toe, if necessary.

Rear Suspension Inspection

Check the rear suspension at regular intervals for the following:
- Rear shock struts for leakage. A slight seepage is all right, heavy leakage requires that the shock be replaced.
- Check shock operation. Push up and down on a rear corner, if the car bounces and feels spongy the shock might need replacement.
- Inspect the condition of the various mounting bushings. If they show signs of deterioration or looseness they must be replaced.
- Condition of the tire tread. If it shows unusual wear the caster, camber or toe could be out.

Rear End Alignment

Rear toe is adjustable but requires special equipment and procedures. If you suspect an alignment problem have it checked by a qualified repair shop. The alignment chart in this section is for factory setting reference.

ADJUSTMENT

Escort and Lynx

1. Loosen the locknut on the outer side of the tie rod and slide the tie rod toward the rear of the vehicle to increase the amount of toe-out.

2. Loosen the locknut on the inner side of the tie rod and slide the tie rod toward the front of the vehicle to increase the amount of toe-in.

3. After adjusting the toe, hold the tie rod flat with a wrench and tighten the tie rod lock nuts to 52–74 ft. lbs. (70–100Nm).

Tempo and Topaz

1. To adjust the toe of either wheel, loosen the bolt attaching the rear control arm to the body and rotate the alignment cam until the required alignment setting is obtained.

2. Torque the control arm attaching bolt to 30–40 ft. lbs. (40–54 Nm).

STEERING

Rack and pinion steering in either manual or power versions gives you car precise steering control. The manual rack and pinion gear is smaller and about seven and one half pounds lighten than that in any other Ford or Mercury small cars. The increased use of aluminum and the use of a one piece valve sleeve make this weight reduction possible.

Lightweight, sturdy bushings are used to mount the steering, these are long lasting and lend to quieter gear operation. The steering also features lifetime lubricated outer tie rod

488 SUSPENSION AND STEERING

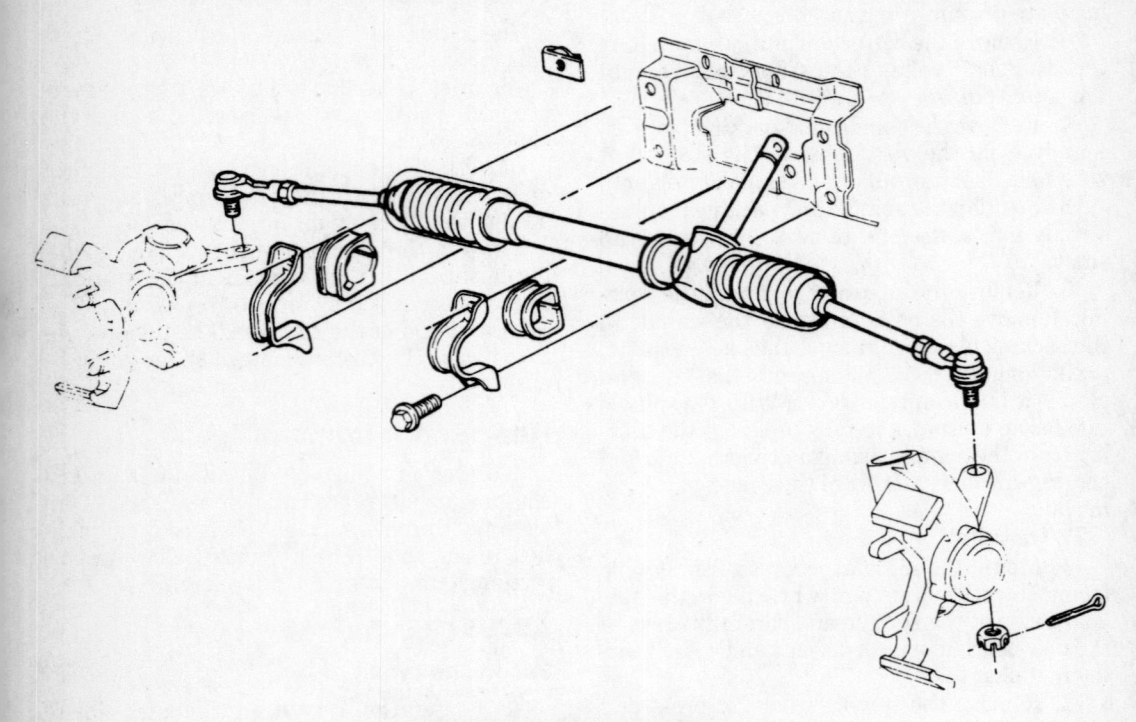

Manual rack and pinion steering

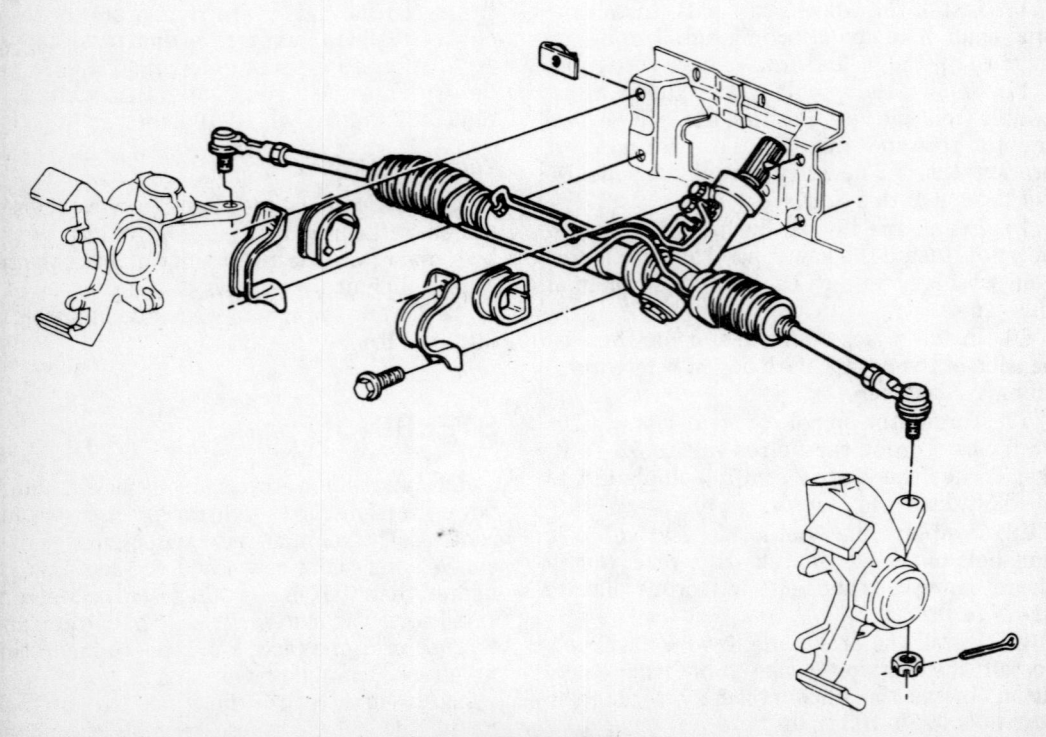

Power rack and pinion

SUSPENSION AND STEERING

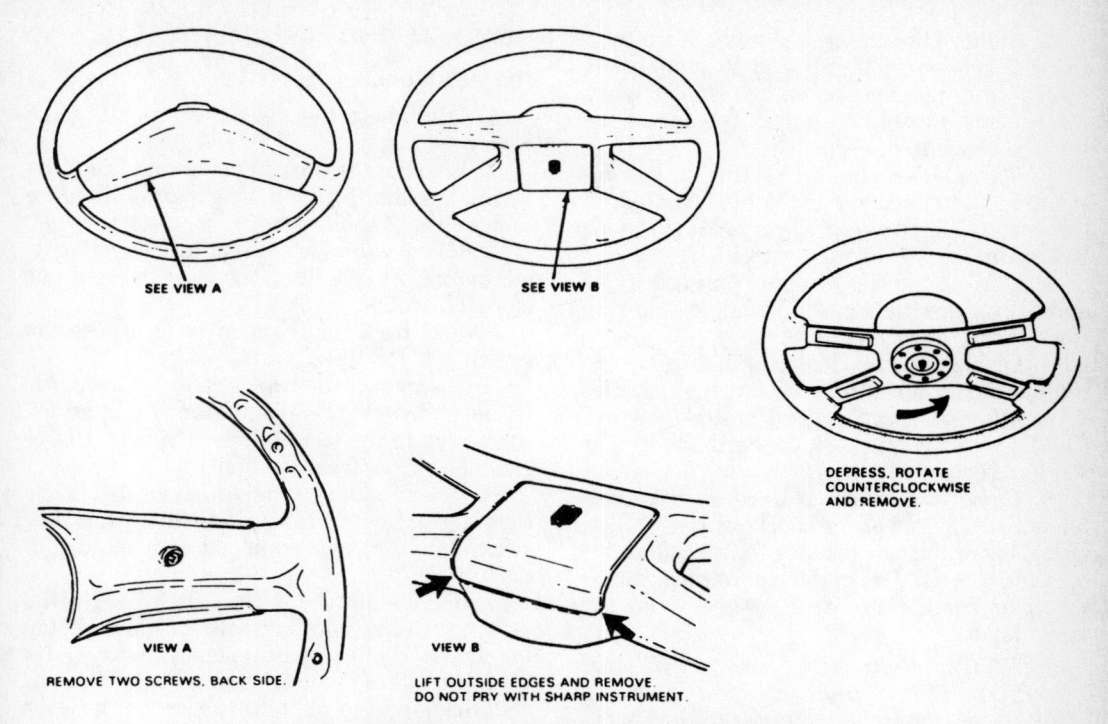

Typical wheel horn pad removal and installation

ends, eliminating the need for scheduled maintenance.

The power steering gear shares a common body mounting system with the manual gear. The power steering pump is of a smaller displacement than current pumps, it requires less power to operate and has streamlined inner porting to provide more efficient fluid flow characteristics.

The steering column geometry uses a double universal joint shaft system and separate column support brackets for improved energy absorbing capabilities.

Steering Wheel

REMOVAL AND INSTALLATION

1981–85 Models

1. Disconnect the negative (ground) battery cable from the battery.
2. Remove the steering wheel center hub cover (See illustration). Lift up on the outer edges, do not use a sharp tool or remove the screws from behind the steering wheel cross spoke. Loosen and remove the center mounting nut.
3. Remove the steering wheel with a crowsfoot steering wheel puller. DO NOT USE a knock-off type puller it will cause damage to the collapsible steering column.
4. To reinstall the steering wheel, align the marks on the steering shaft and steering wheel. Place the wheel onto the shaft. Install a new center mounting nut. Tighten the nut to 30–40 ft. lbs.
5. Install the center cover on the steering wheel. Connect the negative battery cable.

1986–90 Models

1. Disconnect the negative battery cable. Remove the steering wheel center horn pad cover by removing the retaining screws from the steering wheel assembly.

NOTE: *The emblem assembly is removed after the horn pad cover is removed, by pushing it out from the backside of the emblem.*

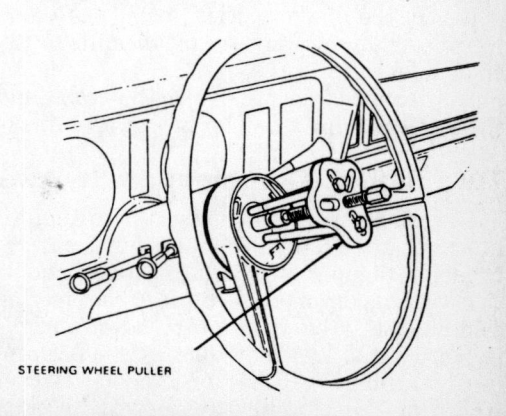

Removing the steering wheel

2. Remove the energy absorbing foam from the wheel assembly, if equipped. Remember the energy absorbing foam must be installed when the steering wheel is assembled. Disconnect the horn pad wiring connector.

3. On vehicles equipped with air bag restraint system, remove the 4 nuts located on the back of the steering wheel holding the air bag module to the steering wheel.

4. Lift the air bag module from the wheel and disconnect the air bag module to slip-ring clock spring connector.

5. On all vehicles, loosen and remove the center mounting nut and on the vehicles equipped with speed control system, remove the electrical connectors. Discard the center nut and replace with new.

6. Remove the steering wheel with a suitable puller. Do not use a knock-off type puller, because it will cause damage to the collapsible steering column. Grasp the rim of the steering wheel and pull the steering wheel from the upper shaft.

NOTE: *The multi-switch lever switch must be in the neutral position before installing the steering wheel or damage to the switch cam may result.*

7. Position the steering wheel on the end of the steering wheel shaft. Align the mark on the steering wheel with the mark on the shaft to assure the straight-ahead steering wheel position corresponds to the straight-ahead position of the front wheels.

8. Install a new service wheel locknut or bolt. Torque the nut to 50–60 ft. lbs. and the bolt to 23–33 ft. lbs. Connect all the electrical connectors on the vehicles equipped with speed control.

9. If equipped with air bag, connect the air bag module wire to slip ring connector and place the module on the steering wheel with the 4 attaching nuts, torque the nuts to 35–33 inch lbs.

10. On the other vehicles, install the steering wheel hub cover and torque the nuts to 13–20 inch lbs.

11. Reconnect the negative battery cable and check the steering wheel for proper operation.

Turn Signal (Combination Switch)

The combination switch assembly is a multi-function switch comprising turn signal, hazard, headlight dimmer and flash-to-pass functions. The switch lever on the left side of the steering column, above the wiper switch lever, controls the turn signal, headlight dimmer and flash-to-pass functions. The hazard function is controlled by the actuating knob on the bottom part of the steering column.

REMOVAL AND INSTALLATION

1981–85 Models

1. Disconnect the negative (ground) cable from the battery.
2. Remove the steering column shroud by taking out the five mounting screws. Remove both halves of the shroud.
3. Remove the switch lever by using a twisting motion while pulling the lever straight out from the switch.
4. Peel back the foam cover to expose the switch.
5. Disconnect the two electrical connectors. Remove the two self-tapping screws that attach the switch to the lock cylinder housing. Disengage the switch from the housing.
6. Transfer the ground brush located in the turn signal switch canceling cam to the new switch, if your car is equipped with speed control.
7. To install the new switch, align the switch with the holes in the lock cylinder housing. Install the two self-tapping screws.
8. Install the foam covering the switch. Install the handle by aligning the key on the lever with the keyway in the switch. Push the lever into the switch until it is fully engaged.
9. Reconnect the two electrical connectors. Install the upper and lower steering column shrouds.
10. Connect the negative battery cable. Test the switch operation.

1986–90 Models

1. Disconnect the negative battery cable.
2. Remove the lower shroud.
3. Loosen the steering column attaching nuts enough to allow the removal of the upper trim shroud.
4. Remove the upper shroud.
5. Remove the turn signal switch lever by pulling the lever straight out from the switch. To make removal easier, work the outer end of the lever around with a slight rotary movement before pulling it out.
6. Peel back the foam sight shield from the turn signal switch.
7. Disconnect the turn signal switch electrical connectors.
8. Remove the self-tapping screws that attach the turn signal switch to the lock cylinder housing and disengage the switch from the housing.
9. Transfer the ground brush located in the turn signal switch canceling cam to the new switch assembly on vehicles equipped with speed control.
10. Align the turn signal switch mounting holes with the corresponding holes in the lock

SUSPENSION AND STEERING 491

cylinder housing and install 2 self-tapping screws until tight.

11. Apply the foam sight shield to the turn signal switch.

12. Install the turn signal switch lever into the switch by aligning the key on the lever with the keyway in the switch and pushing the lever toward the switch to full engagement.

13. Install turn signal switch electrical connectors to full engagement.

14. Install the steering column trim shrouds.

15. Torque the steering column attaching nuts to 15–22 ft. lbs.

16. Connect the negative battery cable.

17. Check the steering column for proper operation.

Ignition Switch

REMOVAL AND INSTALLATION

1981–85 Models

1. Disconnect the negative (ground) battery cable from the battery.

2. Remove the upper and lower steering column shrouds by taking out the five retaining screws.

3. Disconnect the electrical harness at the ignition switch.

4. Remove the nuts and bolts retaining the steering column mounting brackets and lower the steering wheel and column to the front seat.

5. Use an 1/8 in. (3mm) drill bit and drill out the break-off head bolts mounting the ignition switch.

6. Take a small screw extractor (Easy Out) and remove the bolts.

7. Remove the ignition switch by disconnecting it from the actuator pin.

NOTE: *If reinstalling the old switch, it must be adjusted to the Lock or Run (depending on year and model) position. Slide the carrier of the switch to the required position and insert a $1/16$ in. (1.5mm) drill bit or pin through the switch housing into the carrier. This keeps the carrier from moving when the switch is connected to the actuator. It may be necessary to wiggle the carrier back and forth to line up the holes when installing the drill or pin. New switches come with a pin in place.*

8. When installing the ignition switch, rotate the key lock cylinder to the required position.

9. Install the ignition switch by connecting it to the actuator and loosely installing the two new mounting screws.

10. Move the switch up the steering column until it reaches the end of its elongated screw slots. Hold the switch in position, tighten the mounting screws until the heads bread off (special break-off bolts), or tighten to 15–25 ft. lbs. if non-break off head bolts are used.

11. Remove the pin or drill bit that is locking the actuator carrier in position.

12. Raise the steering column and secure the mounting brackets.

13. Connect the wiring harness to the ignition switch. Install the upper and lower steering column shrouds.

14. Connect the negative battery cable.

15. Check the ignition for operation. Make sure the car will start in Neutral and Park, if equipped with automatic transaxle, but be sure it will not start in Drive or reverse. Make sure the steering (wheel) locks when the key switch is in the LOCK position.

1986–90 Models

1. Disconnect the negative battery cable.

2. Remove the steering column upper and lower trim shroud by removing the self-tapping screws. The steering column attaching nuts may have to be loosened enough to allow removal of the upper shroud.

3. Remove 2 bolts and nuts holding steering column assembly to steering column bracket assembly and lower steering column to the seat.

4. Remove steering column shrouds.

5. Disconnect electrical connector from ignition switch.

6. Rotate ignition lock cylinder to the **RUN** position.

7. Remove 2 screws attaching switch to the lock cylinder housing.

8. Disengage the ignition switch from the actuator pin.

To install:

9. Check to see that the actuator pin slot in ignition switch is in the **RUN** position.

NOTE: *A new switch assembly will be pre-set in the RUN position.*

10. Make certain that the ignition key lock cylinder is in approximately the **RUN** position. The **RUN** position is achieved by rotating the

HOLD PRESSURE IN THIS DIRECTION WHILE TIGHTENING BREAK OFF HEAD BOLTS

PIN LOCKS SWITCH IN "LOCK" POSITION

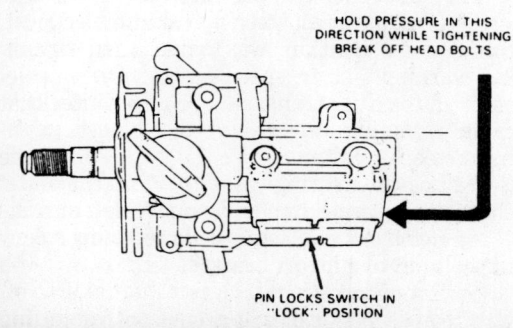

Typical ignition switch installation

SUSPENSION AND STEERING

key lock cylinder approximately 90° from the **LOCK** position.

11. Install the ignition switch onto the actuator pin. It may be necessary to move the switch slightly back and fourth to align the switch mounting holes with the column lock housing threaded holes.
12. Install the new screws and tighten to 50–70 inch lbs. (5.6–7.9 Nm).
13. Connect electrical connector to ignition switch.
14. Connect negative battery cable.
15. Check the ignition switch for proper function including **START** and **ACC** positions. Also make certain that the steering column is locked when in the **LOCK** position.
16. Position the top half of the shroud on the steering column.
17. Install the 2 bolts and nuts attaching the steering column assembly to the steering column bracket assembly.
18. Position lower shroud to upper shroud and install 5 self-tapping screws.

Ignition Lock Cylinder Assembly
REMOVAL AND INSTALLATION

1. Disconnect the negative battery cable.
2. If equipped with a tilt steering column, remove the upper extension shroud by unsnapping the shroud from the retaining clip at the 9 o'clock position.
3. Remove the steering column lower shroud on Escort and Lynx. On Tempo and Topaz, remove the trim halves.
4. Disconnect the warning buzzer electrical connector. With the lock cylinder key, rotate the cylinder to the **RUN** position.
5. Take a $1/8$ in. (3mm) diameter pin or small wire punch and push on the cylinder retaining pin. The pin is visible through a hole in the mounting surrounding the key cylinder. Push on the pin and withdraw the lock cylinder from the housing.

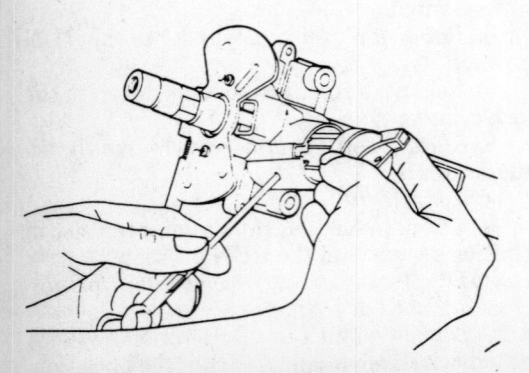

Ignition lock assembly replacement

To install:
6. Install the lock cylinder by turning it to the **RUN** position and depressing the retaining pin. Be sure the lock cylinder is fully seated and aligned in the interlocking washer before turning the key to the **OFF** position. This action will permit the cylinder retaining pin to extend into the cylinder housing hole.
7. Rotate the lock cylinder, using the lock cylinder key, to ensure correct mechanical operation in all positions.
8. Install the electrical connector for the key warning buzzer.
9. Install the lower steering column shroud.
10. Connect the negative battery cable to battery terminal.
11. Check for proper start in **P** or **N**. Also, make certain that the start circuit cannot be actuated in the **D** and **R** positions and that the column is locked in the **LOCK** position.

Steering Column
REMOVAL AND INSTALLATION

NOTE: *On air bag equipped vehicles, whenever the steering column is separated from the steering gear for any reason, the steering column must be locked to prevent the steering wheel from being rotated, which in turn will prevent damage to the air bag clock spring.*

1. Disconnect the negative battery cable.

NOTE: *Before disconnecting cable on air bag equipped vehicles, ensure wheels are in straight ahead position. Turn ignition switch to LOCK position and rotate steering wheel about 16° counterclockwise until locked into position.*

2. Remove steering column cover on lower portion of instrument panel (2 screws).
3. Remove speed control module, if so equipped (2 screws).
4. Remove lower steering column shroud (5 screws).
5. Loosen, but do not remove, 2 nuts and 2 bolts retaining steering column to support bracket and remove upper shroud.
6. Disconnect all steering column electrical connections: ignition, wash/wipe, turn signal, key warning buzzer, speed control. On console shift automatic transaxle, remove interlock cable retaining screw and disconnect cable from steering column.
7. Loosen steering column to intermediate shaft clamp connection and remove bolt or nut.
8. Remove 2 nuts and 2 bolts retaining steering column to support bracket.
9. Pry open steering column shaft in area of clamp on each side of bolt groove with steering column locked. Open enough to disengage

shafts with minimal effort. Do not use excessive force.

10. Inspect 2 steering column bracket clips for damage. If clips have been bent or excessively distorted, they must be replaced.

To install:

11. Engage lower steering shaft to intermediate shaft and hand start clamp bolt and nut.
12. Align 2 bolts on steering column support bracket assembly with outer tube mounting holes and hand start 2 nuts. Check for presence of 2 clips on outer bracket. The clips must be present to ensure adequate performance of vital parts and systems. Hand start 2 bolts through outer tube upper bracket and clip and into support bracket nuts. On console shift automatic transaxles, install interlock cable and retaining screw.
13. Connect all quick-connect electrical connections: turn signal, wash/wipe, key warning buzzer, ignition, speed control and air bag clock spring connector, if equipped.
14. Install upper shroud.
15. Tighten steering column mounting nuts and bolts to 15–25 ft. lbs. (20–34 Nm).
16. On air bag equipped vehicles, unlock steering column and cycle steering wheel 1 turn left and 1 turn right to align intermediate shaft into column shaft. Power steering vehicles must have engine running.
17. Tighten steering shaft clamp nut to 20–30 ft. lbs. (27–40 Nm).
18. Install lower trim shroud with 5 screws.
19. Install speed control module, if equipped, with 2 screws.
20. Install steering column cover on instrument panel with 2 screws.
21. Connect battery ground cable.
22. Check steering column for proper operation.

Steering Linkage

REMOVAL AND INSTALLATION

Tie Rod Ends

1. Remove and discard cotter pin and nut from worn tie rod end ball stud.
2. Disconnect tie rod end from spindle, using tie rod end remover tool 3290–D and adapter T81P–3504–W or equivalent.
3. Holding tie rod end with a wrench, loosen tie rod jam nut.
4. Grip tie rod hex flats with a pair of suitable locking pliers, and remove tie rod end assembly from tie rod. Note depth to which tie rod was located, using jam nut as a marker.

To install:

5. Clean tie rod threads. Apply a light coating of disc brake caliper slide grease D7AZ–19590–A or equivalent, to tie rod threads.

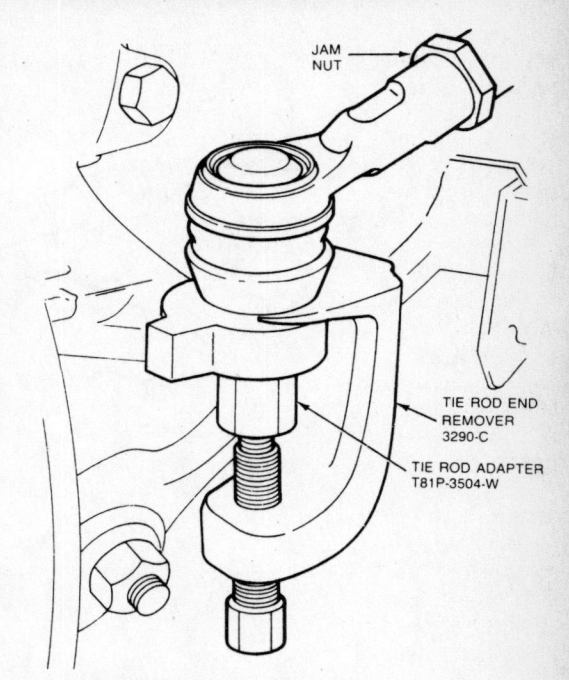

Tie rod end replacement

Thread new tie rod end on tie rod to same depth as removed tie rod end. Tighten jam nut.

6. Place tie rod end stud into steering spindle.
7. Install a new nut on tie rod end stud. Tighten nut to minimum specification, and continue tightening nut to align next castellation with cotter pin hole in stud. Install a new cotter pin.
8. Set toe to specification and tighten jam nuts to specification. Do not twist bellows.

Manual Rack and Pinion Steering

If your car is equipped with manual steering, it is of the rack and pinion type. The gear input shaft is connected to the steering shaft by a double U-joint. A pinion gear, machined on the input shaft, engages the rack. The rotation of the input shaft pinion causes the rack to move laterally. The rack has tow tie rods whose ends are connected to the front wheels. When the rack moves so do the front wheel knuckles. Toe adjustment is made by turning the outer tie rod ends in or out equally as required.

ADJUSTMENT

Tie Rod Articulation Effort

With outer tie rod end removed from steering knuckle, loop a piece of wire through the hole in the tie rod end stud. Insert hook of spring scale through wire loop. Effort to move the tie rod after initial breakaway should be 0.7–5.0 lb. (3.1–22.2 N).

494 SUSPENSION AND STEERING

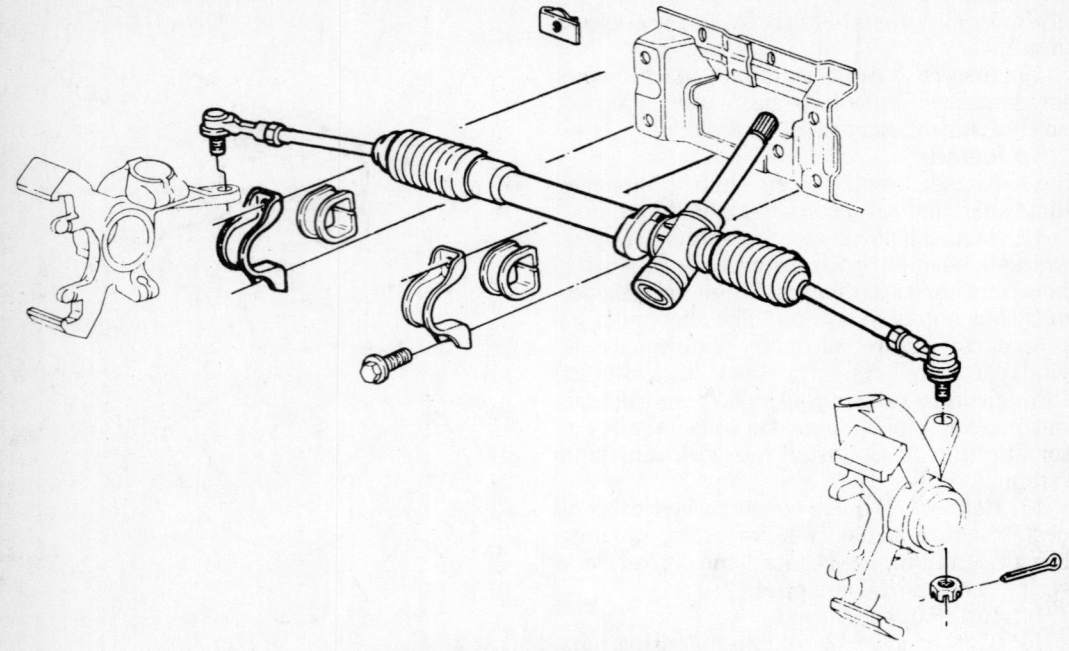

Manual steering gear replacement

NOTE: *Do not damage rod neck.*

2. Replace ball joint/tie rod assembly if effort falls outside this range. Save tie rod end for use on new tie rod assembly.

REMOVAL AND INSTALLATION

1981–85 Models

1. Disconnect the negative battery cable from the battery. Jack up the front of the car and support it safely on jackstands.
2. Turn the ignition switch to the **On/Run** position. Remove the lower access (kick) panel from below the steering wheel.
3. Remove the intermediate shaft bolts at the gear input shaft and at the steering column shaft.
4. Spread the slots of the clamp to loosen the intermediate shaft at both ends. The next steps must be performed before the intermediate shaft and gear input shaft can be separated.
5. Turn the steering wheel full left so the tie rod will clear the shift linkage. Separate the outer tie rod ends from the steering knuckle by using a tie rod end remover.
6. Remove the left tie rod end from the tie rod (wheel must be at full left position). Disconnect the speedometer cable from the transmission if the car is equipped with an automatic transaxle. Disconnect the secondary air tube at the check valve. Disconnect the exhaust pipe from the exhaust manifold and wire it out of the way to allow enough room to remove the steering gear.
7. Remove the exhaust hanger bracket from below the steering gear. Remove the steering gear mounting brackets and rubber mounting insulators.
8. Have someone help by holding the gear from the inside of the car. Separate the intermediate shaft from the input shaft.
9. Make sure the gear is still in the full left turn position. Rotate the gear forward and down to clear the input shaft through the opening. Move the gear to the right to clear the splash panel and other linkage that interferes with the removal. Lower the gear and remove from under the car.
10. Installation is in the reverse order of removal. Have the toe adjustment checked after installing a new rack and pinion assembly.

1986–90 Models

1. Disconnect the negative battery cable.
2. Turn the ignition key to the **RUN** position.
3. Remove the access trim panel from below the steering column.
4. Remove the intermediate shaft bolts at the rack and pinion input shaft and the steering column shaft.
5. Spread the slots enough to loosen the intermediate shaft at both ends. They cannot be separated at this time.
6. Raise the vehicle and support it safely. Separate the tie rod ends from the steering knuckles, using tool 3290–C or equivalent. Turn the steering wheel a full left turn so that

SUSPENSION AND STEERING

the tie rod will clear the shift linkage for removal.

7. Separate the tie rod ends from the steering knuckles. Turn the right wheel to the full left turn position.

8. Remove the left tie rod end from the left tie rod and disconnect the speedometer cable at the transaxle on automatic transaxles only.

9. Disconnect the secondary air tube at the check valve. Disconnect the exhaust system at the manifold and support the exhaust system to allow clearance for the gear removal.

NOTE: *Do not allow the exhaust system to hang by the rear support hangers. The system could fall to the floor.*

10. Remove the exhaust hanger bracket from below the steering gear.

11. Remove the gear mounting brackets and insulators. Keep separated as they are not interchangeable.

12. Separate the gear assembly from the intermediate shaft, with an assistant pulling upward on the shaft from the inside of the vehicle.

NOTE: *Care should be taken during steering gear removal and installation to prevent tearing or damaging the steering gear bellows.*

13. Rotate the gear forward and down to clear the input shaft through the dash panel opening.

14. With the gear in the full left turn position, move the gear through the right (passenger side) apron opening until the left tie rod clears the shift linkage and other parts so it may be lowered.

15. Lower the left side of the gear assembly and remove from the vehicle.

16. To install; rotate the input shaft to a full left turn stop. Position the right wheel to a full left turn.

17. Start the right side of the gear through the opening in the right apron. Move the gear in until the left tie rod clears all parts so that it may be raised up to the left apron opening.

18. Raise the gear and insert the left hand side through the apron opening. Rotate the gear so that the joint shaft enters the dash panel opening.

19. With an assistant guiding the intermediate shaft from the inside of the vehicle, insert the input shaft into the intermediate shaft coupling. Insert the intermediate shaft clamp bolts finger tight. Do not tighten at this time.

20. Install the gear mounting insulators and brackets in their proper places. Ensure the flat in the left mounting area is parallel to the dash panel. Tighten the bracket bolts in the sequence as described below:

 a. Tighten the left (driver's side) upper bolt halfway.
 b. Tighten the left hand lower bolt.
 c. Tighten the left hand upper bolt.
 d. Tighten the right hand bolts.
 e. Do not forget that the right hand and left hand insulators and brackets are not interchangeable side to side.

21. Attach the tie rod ends to the steering knuckles. Tighten the castellated nuts to minimum specifications, then tighten the nuts until the slot aligns with the cotter pin hole. Insert a new cotter pin.

22. Install the exhaust system. Install the speedometer cable, if removed.

23. Tighten the gear input shaft to intermediate shaft coupling clamp bolt first. Then, tighten the upper intermediate shaft clamp bolt.

24. Install the access panel below the steering column. Turn the ignition key to the **OFF** position.

25. Check and adjust the toe. Tighten the tie rod end jam nuts, check for twisted bellows.

Power Steering Rack

A rotary design control valve uses relative rotational motion of the input shaft and valve sleeve to direct fluid flow. When the steering wheel is turned, resistance of the wheels and the weight of the car cause a torsion bar to twist. The twisting causes the valve to move in the sleeve and aligns fluid passages for right/left and straight ahead position. The pressure forces on the valve and helps move the rack to assist in the turning effort. The piston is attached directly to the rack. The housing tube functions as the power cylinder. The hydraulic areas of the gear assembly are always filled with fluid. The mechanical gears are filled with grease making periodic lubrication unnecessary. The fluid and grease act as a cushion to absorb road shock.

ADJUSTMENT

Rack Yoke Plug Preload

NOTE: *This adjustment can be performed only with the gear out of the vehicle.*

1. Disconnect the negative battery cable.
2. Raise and safely support the vehicle.
3. Remove power rack assembly from vehicle.
4. Clean exterior of steering gear thoroughly.
5. Mount steering gear in a suitable rack housing holding fixture.

NOTE: *Do not mount gear in vice.*

6. Do not remove external pressure lines, unless they are leaking or damaged. If these

SUSPENSION AND STEERING

lines are removed, they must be replaced with new lines.

7. Drain power steering fluid by rotating input shaft lock-to-lock twice using input shaft torque adapter T81P–3504–R or equivalent. Position adapter and wrench on input shaft.

8. Loosen yoke plug locknut with yoke locknut wrench T81P–3504–G or equivalent.

9. Loosen yoke plug using yoke plug adapter T87P–3504–G or equivalent.

10. With rack at center of travel, tighten yoke plug to 44–50 inch lbs. (5.0–5.7 Nm). Clean threads of yoke plug prior to tightening to prevent a false reading.

11. install yoke plug adapter T87P–3504–G or equivalent. Mark the location of the 0 mark on housing. Back off the adjuster so the 48° mark lines up with 0 mark.

12. Place yoke locknut wrench T81P–3504–G or equivalent, on yoke plug locknut. While holding yoke plug, tighten locknut to 40–50 ft. lbs. (54–68 Nm). Do not allow yoke plug to move while tightening or preload will be affected. Check input shaft torque after tightening locknut.

13. If external pressure lines were removed, the Teflon® seal rings must be replaced. Clean out Teflon® seal shreds from housing ports prior to installation of new lines.

14. Install power rack assembly in vehicle.
15. Lower vehicle.
16. Connect negative battery cable.

REMOVAL AND INSTALLATION

1. Disconnect the negative battery cable.
2. Turn the ignition key to the **RUN** position.
3. Remove access panel from dash below the steering column.
4. Remove screws from steering column boot at the dash panel and slide boot up intermediate shaft.
5. Remove intermediate shaft bolt at gear input shaft and loosen the bolt at the steering column shaft joint.
6. With a suitable tool, spread the slots enough to loosen intermediates shaft at both ends. The intermediate shaft and gear input shaft cannot be separated at this time.
7. Remove the air cleaner.
8. On Escort and Lynx with air conditioning, wire the air conditioner liquid line above the dash panel opening. Doing so provides clearance for gear input shaft removal and installation.
9. Separate pressure and return lines at intermediate connections and drain fluid.
10. On Tempo and Topaz without diesel engine, remove the pressure switch.
11. Disconnect the exhaust secondary air tube at check valve. Raise the vehicle and support it safely. Disconnect exhaust system at exhaust manifold and remove exhaust system.

12. Separate tie rod ends from steering knuckles.

13. Remove left tie rod end from tie rod on manual transaxle vehicles. This will allow tie rod to clear the shift linkage.

NOTE: *Mark location of rod end prior to removal.*

14. Disconnect speedometer cable at transaxle on vehicles equipped with automatic transaxle. Remove the vehicle speed sensor.

15. Remove transaxle shift cable assembly at transaxle on vehicles equipped with automatic transaxle.

16. Turn steering wheel to full left turn stop for easier gear removal.

17. On Escort and Lynx, remove screws holding the heater water tube to shake brace below the oil pan.

18. On Escort and Lynx, remove nut from the lower of 2 bolts holding engine mount support bracket to transaxle housing. Tap bolt out as far as it will go.

19. Remove the gear mounting brackets and insulators.

20. Drape cloth towel over both apron opening edges to protect bellows during gear removal.

21. Separate gear from intermediate shaft by either pushing up on shaft with a bar from underneath the vehicle while pulling the gear down or with an assistant removing the shaft from inside the vehicle.

22. Rotate gear forward and down to clear the input shaft through the dash panel opening.

23. Make sure input shaft is in full left turn position. Move gear through the right (passenger) side apron opening until left tie rod clears left apron opening and other parts so it may be lowered. Guide the power steering hoses around the nearby components as the gear is being removed.

24. Lower the left hand side of the gear and remove the gear out of the vehicle. Use care not to tear the bellows.

To install:

25. Rotate the input shaft to a full left turn stop. Position the right road wheel to a full left turn.

26. Start the right side of the gear through the opening in the right apron. Move the gear in until the left tie rod clears all parts so that it may be raised up to the left apron opening.

27. Raise the gear and insert the left hand side through the apron opening. Move the power steering hoses into their proper position

SUSPENSION AND STEERING

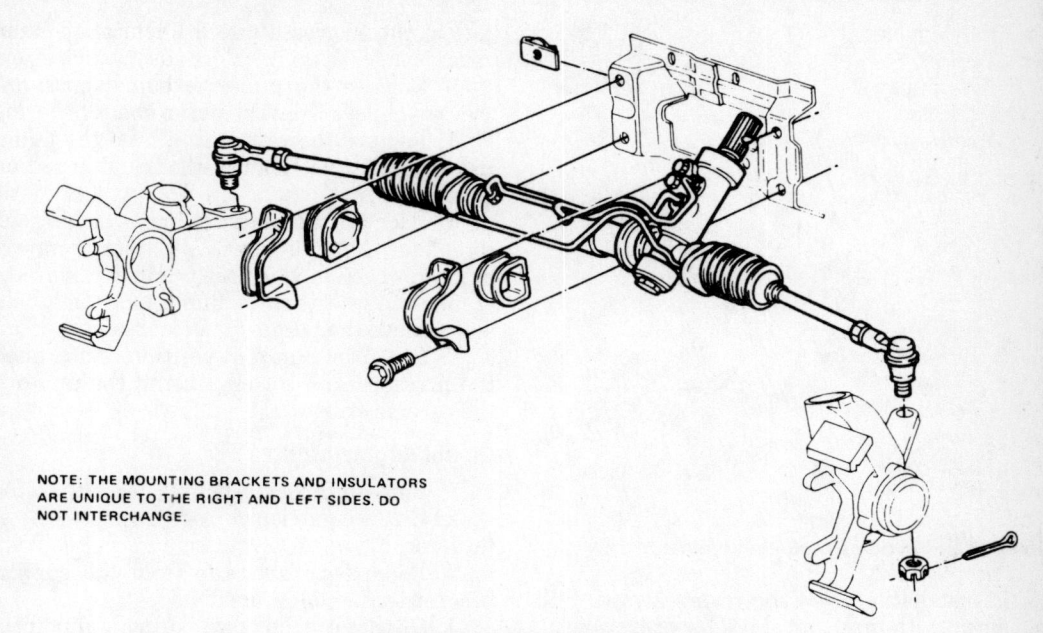

NOTE: THE MOUNTING BRACKETS AND INSULATORS ARE UNIQUE TO THE RIGHT AND LEFT SIDES. DO NOT INTERCHANGE.

Power steering gear replacement

at the same time. Rotate the gear so that the joint shaft enters the dash panel opening.

28. With an assistant guiding the intermediate shaft from the inside of the vehicle, insert the input shaft into the intermediate shaft coupling. Insert the intermediate shaft clamp bolts finger tight. Do not tighten at this time.

29. Install the gear mounting insulators and brackets in their proper places. Ensure the flat in the left mounting area is parallel to the dash panel. Tighten the bracket bolts in the sequence as described below:

    a. Tighten the left (driver's side) upper bolt halfway.
    b. Tighten the left hand lower bolts.
    c. Tighten the left hand upper bolts.
    d. Tighten the right hand bolts.
    e. Do not forget that the right hand and left hand insulators and brackets are not interchangeable side to side.

30. Attach the tie rod ends to the steering knuckles. Tighten the castellated nuts to minimum specification, then tighten the nuts until the slot aligns with the cotter pin hole. Insert a new cotter pin.

31. On the Escort and Lynx, install the engine mount nut.

32. On the Escort and Lynx, install the heater water tube to the shake brace.

33. Install the exhaust system. Install the speedometer cable, if removed. Install the vehicle speed sensor and the transaxle shift cable.

34. Connect the secondary air tube at the check valve. Connect the pressure and return lines at the steering gear. Install the pressure switch, if removed.

35. Tighten the gear input shaft to intermediate shaft coupling clamp bolt first. Then, tighten the upper intermediate shaft clamp bolt.

36. Install the access panel below the steering column. Turn the ignition key to the **OFF** position.

37. Fill the system. Check and adjust the toe. Tighten the tie rod end jam nuts, check for twisted bellows.

38. Connect negative battery cable.

Power Steering Pump

REMOVAL AND INSTALLATION

1981–85 Escort/Lynx/EXP/LN-7

1. Remove the air cleaner, air pump and belt. Remove the reservoir extension and plug the hole with a clean rag.

2. From under the car, loosen the pump adjusting bolt. Remove the pump to bracket mounting bolt and disconnect the fluid return line. Be prepared to catch any spilled fluid in a suitable container.

3. From above, loosen the adjusting bolt and remove the drive belt. Remove the two remaining mounting bolts. Remove the adjusting bolts.

4. Remove the pump by passing the pulley end through the adjusting bracket opening.

5. Remove the pressure hose from the pump.

SUSPENSION AND STEERING

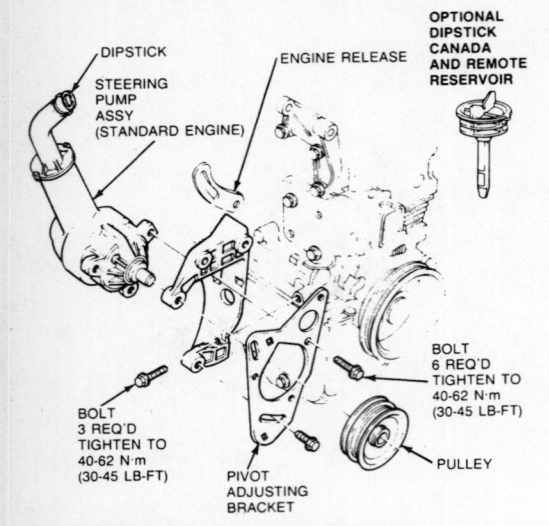

Power steering pump mounting-typical

6. Installation is in the reverse order. Fill the pump with fluid and check for proper operation.

1986–90 Escort and Lynx

1. Disconnect the negative battery cable. Remove the air cleaner, Thermactor air pump and belt. Remove the reservoir filler extension and cover the hole to prevent dirt from entering.
2. On vehicles equipped with EFI and remote reservoir, remove the reservoir supply hose at the pump, drain the fluid and plug or cap the opening at the pump to prevent entry of contaminants during removal.
3. From under the vehicle, loosen 1 pump adjusting bolt. Remove 1 pump to bracket mounting bolt and disconnect the fluid return line.
4. From above the vehicle, loosen 1 adjusting bolt and the pivot bolt. Remove the drive belt and the 2 remaining pump to bracket mounting bolts.
5. Remove the pump by passing the pulley through the adjusting bracket opening. Remove the pressure hose from the pump assembly.
6. Complete the installation of the pump assembly by reversing the removal procedure. Fill the pump with fluid and check the system for proper operation.

Tempo/Topaz

1. Loosen the alternator and remove the drive belt. Pivot the alternator to its most upright position.
2. Remove the radiator overflow bottle. Loosen and remove the power steering pump drive belt. Mark the pulley and pump drive hub with paint or grease pencil for location reference.
3. Remove the pulley retaining bolts and the two pulleys from the pump shaft.
4. Remove the return line from the pump. Be prepared to catch any spilled fluid in a suitable container.
5. Back off the pressure line attaching nut completely. The line will separate from the pump connection when the pump is removed.
6. Remove the three pump mounting bolts and remove the pump.
7. Place the pump in position and connect the pressure line loosely, Install the pump in the reverse order.

Diesel Engine Models

1. Remove the drive belts.
2. On air conditioned models, remove the alternator.
3. Remove both braces from the support bracket on air conditioned models.
4. Disconnect the power steering fluid lines and drain the fluid into a suitable container.
5. Remove the four bracket mounting bolts and remove the pump and bracket assembly.
6. The pulley must be remove before the pump can be separated from the mounting bracket. Tool T65P-3A733-C or equivalent is required to remove and install the drive pulley.
7. Install the pump and mounting bracket in the reverse order of removal.

SYSTEM BLEEDING

If air bubbles are present in the power steering fluid, bleed the system by performing the following:

1. Fill the reservoir to the proper level.
2. Operate the engine until the fluid reaches normal operating temperature (165–175°F).
3. Turn the steering wheel all the way to the left then all the way to the right several times. Do not hold the steering wheel in the far left or far right position stops.
4. Check the fluid level and recheck the fluid for the presence of trapped air. If apparent that air is still in the system, fabricate or obtain a vacuum tester and purge the system as follows:
    a. Remove the pump dipstick cap assembly.
    b. Check and fill the pump reservoir with fluid to the **COLD FULL** mark on the dipstick.
    c. Disconnect the ignition wire and raise the front of the vehicle and support safely.
    d. Crank the engine with the starter and check the fluid level. Do not turn the steering wheel at this time.

e. Fill the pump reservoir to the **COLD FULL** mark on the dipstick. Crank the engine with the starter while cycling the steering wheel lock-to-lock. Check the fluid level.

f. Tightly insert a suitable size rubber stopper and air evacuator pump into the reservoir fill neck. Connect the ignition coil wire.

g. With the engine idling, apply a 15 in.Hg vacuum to the reservoir for 3 minutes. As air is purged from the system, the vacuum will drop off. Maintain the vacuum on the system as required throughout the 3 minutes.

h. Remove the vacuum source. Fill the reservoir to the **COLD FULL** mark on the dipstick.

i. With the engine idling, re-apply 15 in.Hg vacuum source to the reservoir. Slowly cycle the steering wheel to lock-to-lock stops for approximately 5 minutes. Do not hold the steering wheel on the stops during cycling. Maintain the vacuum as required.

j. Release the vacuum and disconnect the vacuum source. Add fluid, as required.

k. Start the engine and cycle the wheel slowly and check for leaks at all connections.

l. Lower the front wheels.

5. In cases of severe aeration, repeat the procedure.

Troubleshooting the Ignition Switch

Problem	Cause	Solution
Ignition switch electrically inoperative	• Loose or defective switch connector • Feed wire open (fusible link) • Defective ignition switch	• Tighten or replace connector • Repair or replace • Replace ignition switch
Engine will not crank	• Ignition switch not adjusted properly	• Adjust switch
Ignition switch wil not actuate mechanically	• Defective ignition switch • Defective lock sector • Defective remote rod	• Replace switch • Replace lock sector • Replace remote rod
Ignition switch cannot be adjusted correctly	• Remote rod deformed	• Repair, straighten or replace

SUSPENSION AND STEERING

Troubleshooting the Steering Column

Problem	Cause	Solution
Will not lock	• Lockbolt spring broken or defective	• Replace lock bolt spring
High effort (required to turn ignition key and lock cylinder)	• Lock cylinder defective • Ignition switch defective • Rack preload spring broken or deformed • Burr on lock sector, lock rack, housing, support or remote rod coupling • Bent sector shaft • Defective lock rack • Remote rod bent, deformed • Ignition switch mounting bracket bent • Distorted coupling slot in lock rack (tilt column)	• Replace lock cylinder • Replace ignition switch • Replace preload spring • Remove burr • Replace shaft • Replace lock rack • Replace rod • Straighten or replace • Replace lock rack
Will stick in "start"	• Remote rod deformed • Ignition switch mounting bracket bent	• Straighten or replace • Straighten or replace
Key cannot be removed in "off-lock"	• Ignition switch is not adjusted correctly • Defective lock cylinder	• Adjust switch • Replace lock cylinder
Lock cylinder can be removed without depressing retainer	• Lock cylinder with defective retainer • Burr over retainer slot in housing cover or on cylinder retainer	• Replace lock cylinder • Remove burr
High effort on lock cylinder between "off" and "off-lock"	• Distorted lock rack • Burr on tang of shift gate (automatic column) • Gearshift linkage not adjusted	• Replace lock rack • Remove burr • Adjust linkage
Noise in column	• One click when in "off-lock" position and the steering wheel is moved (all except automatic column) • Coupling bolts not tightened • Lack of grease on bearings or bearing surfaces • Upper shaft bearing worn or broken • Lower shaft bearing worn or broken • Column not correctly aligned • Coupling pulled apart • Broken coupling lower joint • Steering shaft snap ring not seated • Shroud loose on shift bowl. Housing loose on jacket—will be noticed with ignition in "off-lock" and when torque is applied to steering wheel.	• Normal—lock bolt is seating • Tighten pinch bolts • Lubricate with chassis grease • Replace bearing assembly • Replace bearing. Check shaft and replace if scored. • Align column • Replace coupling • Repair or replace joint and align column • Replace ring. Check for proper seating in groove. • Position shroud over lugs on shift bowl. Tighten mounting screws.
High steering shaft effort	• Column misaligned • Defective upper or lower bearing • Tight steering shaft universal joint • Flash on I.D. of shift tube at plastic joint (tilt column only) • Upper or lower bearing seized	• Align column • Replace as required • Repair or replace • Replace shift tube • Replace bearings
Lash in mounted column assembly	• Column mounting bracket bolts loose • Broken weld nuts on column jacket • Column capsule bracket sheared	• Tighten bolts • Replace column jacket • Replace bracket assembly

Troubleshooting the Steering Column (cont.)

Problem	Cause	Solution
Lash in mounted column assembly (cont.)	• Column bracket to column jacket mounting bolts loose • Loose lock shoes in housing (tilt column only) • Loose pivot pins (tilt column only) • Loose lock shoe pin (tilt column only) • Loose support screws (tilt column only)	• Tighten to specified torque • Replace shoes • Replace pivot pins and support • Replace pin and housing • Tighten screws
Housing loose (tilt column only)	• Excessive clearance between holes in support or housing and pivot pin diameters • Housing support-screws loose	• Replace pivot pins and support • Tighten screws
Steering wheel loose—every other tilt position (tilt column only)	• Loose fit between lock shoe and lock shoe pivot pin	• Replace lock shoes and pivot pin
Steering column not locking in any tilt position (tilt column only)	• Lock shoe seized on pivot pin • Lock shoe grooves have burrs or are filled with foreign material • Lock shoe springs weak or broken	• Replace lock shoes and pin • Clean or replace lock shoes • Replace springs
Noise when tilting column (tilt column only)	• Upper tilt bumpers worn • Tilt spring rubbing in housing	• Replace tilt bumper • Lubricate with chassis grease
One click when in "off-lock" position and the steering wheel is moved	• Seating of lock bolt	• None. Click is normal characteristic sound produced by lock bolt as it seats.
High shift effort (automatic and tilt column only)	• Column not correctly aligned • Lower bearing not aligned correctly • Lack of grease on seal or lower bearing areas	• Align column • Assemble correctly • Lubricate with chassis grease
Improper transmission shifting—automatic and tilt column only	• Sheared shift tube joint • Improper transmission gearshift linkage adjustment • Loose lower shift lever	• Replace shift tube • Adjust linkage • Replace shift tube

SUSPENSION AND STEERING

Troubleshooting the Turn Signal Switch

Problem	Cause	Solution
Turn signal will not cancel	• Loose switch mounting screws • Switch or anchor bosses broken • Broken, missing or out of position detent, or cancelling spring	• Tighten screws • Replace switch • Reposition springs or replace switch as required
Turn signal difficult to operate	• Turn signal lever loose • Switch yoke broken or distorted • Loose or misplaced springs • Foreign parts and/or materials in switch • Switch mounted loosely	• Tighten mounting screws • Replace switch • Reposition springs or replace switch • Remove foreign parts and/or material • Tighten mounting screws
Turn signal will not indicate lane change	• Broken lane change pressure pad or spring hanger • Broken, missing or misplaced lane change spring • Jammed wires	• Replace switch • Replace or reposition as required • Loosen mounting screws, reposition wires and retighten screws
Turn signal will not stay in turn position	• Foreign material or loose parts impeding movement of switch yoke • Defective switch	• Remove material and/or parts • Replace switch
Hazard switch cannot be pulled out	• Foreign material between hazard support cancelling leg and yoke	• Remove foreign material. No foreign material impeding function of hazard switch—replace turn signal switch.
No turn signal lights	• Inoperative turn signal flasher • Defective or blown fuse • Loose chassis to column harness connector • Disconnect column to chassis connector. Connect new switch to chassis and operate switch by hand. If vehicle lights now operate normally, signal switch is inoperative • If vehicle lights do not operate, check chassis wiring for opens, grounds, etc.	• Replace turn signal flasher • Replace fuse • Connect securely • Replace signal switch • Repair chassis wiring as required
Instrument panel turn indicator lights on but not flashing	• Burned out or damaged front or rear turn signal bulb • If vehicle lights do not operate, check light sockets for high resistance connections, the chassis wiring for opens, grounds, etc. • Inoperative flasher • Loose chassis to column harness connection • Inoperative turn signal switch • To determine if turn signal switch is defective, substitute new switch into circuit and operate switch by hand. If the vehicle's lights operate normally, signal switch is inoperative.	• Replace bulb • Repair chassis wiring as required • Replace flasher • Connect securely • Replace turn signal switch • Replace turn signal switch
Stop light not on when turn indicated	• Loose column to chassis connection • Disconnect column to chassis connector. Connect new switch into system without removing old.	• Connect securely • Replace signal switch

SUSPENSION AND STEERING

Troubleshooting the Turn Signal Switch (cont.)

Problem	Cause	Solution
Stop light not on when turn indicated (cont.)	Operate switch by hand. If brake lights work with switch in the turn position, signal switch is defective.	
	• If brake lights do not work, check connector to stop light sockets for grounds, opens, etc.	• Repair connector to stop light circuits using service manual as guide
Turn indicator panel lights not flashing	• Burned out bulbs • High resistance to ground at bulb socket • Opens, ground in wiring harness from front turn signal bulb socket to indicator lights	• Replace bulbs • Replace socket • Locate and repair as required
Turn signal lights flash very slowly	• High resistance ground at light sockets • Incorrect capacity turn signal flasher or bulb • If flashing rate is still extremely slow, check chassis wiring harness from the connector to light sockets for high resistance • Loose chassis to column harness connection • Disconnect column to chassis connector. Connect new switch into system without removing old. Operate switch by hand. If flashing occurs at normal rate, the signal switch is defective.	• Repair high resistance grounds at light sockets • Replace turn signal flasher or bulb • Locate and repair as required • Connect securely • Replace turn signal switch
Hazard signal lights will not flash—turn signal functions normally	• Blow fuse • Inoperative hazard warning flasher • Loose chassis-to-column harness connection • Disconnect column to chassis connector. Connect new switch into system without removing old. Depress the hazard warning lights. If they now work normally, turn signal switch is defective. • If lights do not flash, check wiring harness "K" lead for open between hazard flasher and connector. If open, fuse block is defective	• Replace fuse • Replace hazard warning flasher in fuse panel • Conect securely • Replace turn signal switch • Repair or replace brown wire or connector as required

SUSPENSION AND STEERING

Troubleshooting the Manual Steering Gear

Problem	Cause	Solution
Hard or erratic steering	• Incorrect tire pressure	• Inflate tires to recommended pressures
	• Insufficient or incorrect lubrication	• Lubricate as required (refer to Maintenance Section)
	• Suspension, or steering linkage parts damaged or misaligned	• Repair or replace parts as necessary
	• Improper front wheel alignment	• Adjust incorrect wheel alignment angles
	• Incorrect steering gear adjustment	• Adjust steering gear
	• Sagging springs	• Replace springs
Play or looseness in steering	• Steering wheel loose	• Inspect shaft spines and repair as necessary. Tighten attaching nut and stake in place.
	• Steering linkage or attaching parts loose or worn	• Tighten, adjust, or replace faulty components
	• Pitman arm loose	• Inspect shaft splines and repair as necessary. Tighten attaching nut and stake in place
	• Steering gear attaching bolts loose	• Tighten bolts
	• Loose or worn wheel bearings	• Adjust or replace bearings
	• Steering gear adjustment incorrect or parts badly worn	• Adjust gear or replace defective parts
Wheel shimmy or tramp	• Improper tire pressure	• Inflate tires to recommended pressures
	• Wheels, tires, or brake rotors out-of-balance or out-of-round	• Inspect and replace or balance parts
	• Inoperative, worn, or loose shock absorbers or mounting parts	• Repair or replace shocks or mountings
	• Loose or worn steering or suspension parts	• Tighten or replace as necessary
	• Loose or worn wheel bearings	• Adjust or replace bearings
	• Incorrect steering gear adjustments	• Adjust steering gear
	• Incorrect front wheel alignment	• Correct front wheel alignment
Tire wear	• Improper tire pressure	• Inflate tires to recommended pressures
	• Failure to rotate tires	• Rotate tires
	• Brakes grabbing	• Adjust or repair brakes
	• Incorrect front wheel alignment	• Align incorrect angles
	• Broken or damaged steering and suspension parts	• Repair or replace defective parts
	• Wheel runout	• Replace faulty wheel
	• Excessive speed on turns	• Make driver aware of conditions
Vehicle leads to one side	• Improper tire pressures	• Inflate tires to recommended pressures
	• Front tires with uneven tread depth, wear pattern, or different cord design (i.e., one bias ply and one belted or radial tire on front wheels)	• Install tires of same cord construction and reasonably even tread depth, design, and wear pattern
	• Incorrect front wheel alignment	• Align incorrect angles
	• Brakes dragging	• Adjust or repair brakes
	• Pulling due to uneven tire construction	• Replace faulty tire

Troubleshooting the Power Steering Gear

Problem	Cause	Solution
Hissing noise in steering gear	There is some noise in all power steering systems. One of the most common is a hissing sound most evident at standstill parking. There is no relationship between this noise and performance of the steering. Hiss may be expected when steering wheel is at end of travel or when slowly turning at standstill.	Slight hiss is normal and in no way affects steering. Do not replace valve unless hiss is extremely objectionable. A replacement valve will also exhibit slight noise and is not always a cure. Investigate clearance around flexible coupling rivets. Be sure steering shaft and gear are aligned so flexible coupling rotates in a flat plane and is not distorted as shaft rotates. Any metal-to-metal contacts through flexible coupling will transmit valve hiss into passenger compartment through the steering column.
Rattle or chuckle noise in steering gear	• Gear loose on frame • Steering linkage looseness • Pressure hose touching other parts of car • Loose pitman shaft over center adjustment NOTE: A slight rattle may occur on turns because of increased clearance off the "high point." This is normal and clearance must not be reduced below specified limits to eliminate this slight rattle. • Loose pitman arm	• Check gear-to-frame mounting screws. Tighten screws to 88 N·m (65 foot pounds) torque. • Check linkage pivot points for wear. Replace if necessary. • Adjust hose position. Do not bend tubing by hand. • Adjust to specifications • Tighten pitman arm nut to specifications
Squawk noise in steering gear when turning or recovering from a turn	• Damper O-ring on valve spool cut	• Replace damper O-ring
Poor return of steering wheel to center	• Tires not properly inflated • Lack of lubrication in linkage and ball joints • Lower coupling flange rubbing against steering gear adjuster plug • Steering gear to column misalignment • Improper front wheel alignment • Steering linkage binding • Ball joints binding • Steering wheel rubbing against housing • Tight or frozen steering shaft bearings • Sticking or plugged valve spool • Steering gear adjustments over specifications • Kink in return hose	• Inflate to specified pressure • Lube linkage and ball joints • Loosen pinch bolt and assemble properly • Align steering column • Check and adjust as necessary • Replace pivots • Replace ball joints • Align housing • Replace bearings • Remove and clean or replace valve • Check adjustment with gear out of car. Adjust as required. • Replace hose
Car leads to one side or the other (keep in mind road condition and wind. Test car in both directions on flat road)	• Front end misaligned • Unbalanced steering gear valve NOTE: If this is cause, steering effort will be very light in direction of lead and normal or heavier in opposite direction	• Adjust to specifications • Replace valve

Troubleshooting the Power Steering Gear (cont.)

Problem	Cause	Solution
Momentary increase in effort when turning wheel fast to right or left	• Low oil level • Pump belt slipping • High internal leakage	• Add power steering fluid as required • Tighten or replace belt • Check pump pressure. (See pressure test)
Steering wheel surges or jerks when turning with engine running especially during parking	• Low oil level • Loose pump belt • Steering linkage hitting engine oil pan at full turn • Insufficient pump pressure • Pump flow control valve sticking	• Fill as required • Adjust tension to specification • Correct clearance • Check pump pressure. (See pressure test). Replace relief valve if defective. • Inspect for varnish or damage, replace if necessary
Excessive wheel kickback or loose steering	• Air in system • Steering gear loose on frame • Steering linkage joints worn enough to be loose • Worn poppet valve • Loose thrust bearing preload adjustment • Excessive overcenter lash	• Add oil to pump reservoir and bleed by operating steering. Check hose connectors for proper torque and adjust as required. • Tighten attaching screws to specified torque • Replace loose pivots • Replace poppet valve • Adjust to specification with gear out of vehicle • Adjust to specification with gear out of car
Hard steering or lack of assist	• Loose pump belt • Low oil level NOTE: Low oil level will also result in excessive pump noise • Steering gear to column misalignment • Lower coupling flange rubbing against steering gear adjuster plug • Tires not properly inflated	• Adjust belt tension to specification • Fill to proper level. If excessively low, check all lines and joints for evidence of external leakage. Tighten loose connectors. • Align steering column • Loosen pinch bolt and assemble properly • Inflate to recommended pressure
Foamy milky power steering fluid, low fluid level and possible low pressure	• Air in the fluid, and loss of fluid due to internal pump leakage causing overflow	• Check for leak and correct. Bleed system. Extremely cold temperatures will cause system aeriation should the oil level be low. If oil level is correct and pump still foams, remove pump from vehicle and separate reservoir from housing. Check welsh plug and housing for cracks. If plug is loose or housing is cracked, replace housing.
Low pressure due to steering pump	• Flow control valve stuck or inoperative • Pressure plate not flat against cam ring	• Remove burrs or dirt or replace. Flush system. • Correct
Low pressure due to steering gear	• Pressure loss in cylinder due to worn piston ring or badly worn housing bore • Leakage at valve rings, valve body-to-worm seal	• Remove gear from car for disassembly and inspection of ring and housing bore • Remove gear from car for disassembly and replace seals

Troubleshooting the Power Steering Pump

Problem	Cause	Solution
Chirp noise in steering pump	• Loose belt	• Adjust belt tension to specification
Belt squeal (particularly noticeable at full wheel travel and stand still parking)	• Loose belt	• Adjust belt tension to specification
Growl noise in steering pump	• Excessive back pressure in hoses or steering gear caused by restriction	• Locate restriction and correct. Replace part if necessary.
Growl noise in steering pump (particularly noticeable at stand still parking)	• Scored pressure plates, thrust plate or rotor • Extreme wear of cam ring	• Replace parts and flush system • Replace parts
Groan noise in steering pump	• Low oil level • Air in the oil. Poor pressure hose connection.	• Fill reservoir to proper level • Tighten connector to specified torque. Bleed system by operating steering from right to left—full turn.
Rattle noise in steering pump	• Vanes not installed properly • Vanes sticking in rotor slots	• Install properly • Free up by removing burrs, varnish, or dirt
Swish noise in steering pump	• Defective flow control valve	• Replace part
Whine noise in steering pump	• Pump shaft bearing scored	• Replace housing and shaft. Flush system.
Hard steering or lack of assist	• Loose pump belt • Low oil level in reservoir NOTE: Low oil level will also result in excessive pump noise • Steering gear to column misalignment • Lower coupling flange rubbing against steering gear adjuster plug • Tires not properly inflated	• Adjust belt tension to specification • Fill to proper level. If excessively low, check all lines and joints for evidence of external leakage. Tighten loose connectors. • Align steering column • Loosen pinch bolt and assemble properly • Inflate to recommended pressure
Foaming milky power steering fluid, low fluid level and possible low pressure	• Air in the fluid, and loss of fluid due to internal pump leakage causing overflow	• Check for leaks and correct. Bleed system. Extremely cold temperatures will cause system aeriation should the oil level be low. If oil level is correct and pump still foams, remove pump from vehicle and separate reservoir from body. Check welsh plug and body for cracks. If plug is loose or body is cracked, replace body.
Low pump pressure	• Flow control valve stuck or inoperative • Pressure plate not flat against cam ring	• Remove burrs or dirt or replace. Flush system. • Correct
Momentary increase in effort when turning wheel fast to right or left	• Low oil level in pump • Pump belt slipping • High internal leakage	• Add power steering fluid as required • Tighten or replace belt • Check pump pressure. (See pressure test)
Steering wheel surges or jerks when turning with engine running especially during parking	• Low oil level • Loose pump belt • Steering linkage hitting engine oil pan at full turn • Insufficient pump pressure	• Fill as required • Adjust tension to specification • Correct clearance • Check pump pressure. (See pressure test). Replace flow control valve if defective.

Troubleshooting the Power Steering Pump (cont.)

Problem	Cause	Solution
Steering wheel surges or jerks when turning with engine running especially during parking (cont.)	• Sticking flow control valve	• Inspect for varnish or damage, replace if necessary
Excessive wheel kickback or loose steering	• Air in system	• Add oil to pump reservoir and bleed by operating steering. Check hose connectors for proper torque and adjust as required.
Low pump pressure	• Extreme wear of cam ring • Scored pressure plate, thrust plate, or rotor • Vanes not installed properly • Vanes sticking in rotor slots • Cracked or broken thrust or pressure plate	• Replace parts. Flush system. • Replace parts. Flush system. • Install properly • Freeup by removing burrs, varnish, or dirt • Replace part

Brakes

BRAKE SYSTEM

Understanding the Brakes Hydraulic System

BASIC OPERATING PRINCIPLES

Hydraulic systems are used to actuate the brakes of all modern automobiles. The system transports the power required to force the frictional surfaces of the braking system together from the pedal to the individual brake units at each wheel. A hydraulic system is used for two reasons. First, fluid under pressure can be carried to all parts of an automobile by small hoses, some of which are flexible, without taking up a significant amount of room or posing routing problems. Second, a great mechanical advantage can be given to the brake pedal end of the system, and the foot pressure required to actuate the brakes can be reduced by making surface area of the master cylinder pistons smaller than that of any of the pistons in the wheel cylinders or calipers.

The master cylinder consists of a double reservoir and piston assembly as well as other springs, fittings etc. Double (dual) master cylinders are designed to separate two wheels from the others. Your car's braking system is separated diagonally. That is, the right front and left rear use one reservoir and the left front and right rear use the other.

Steel lines carry the brake fluid to a point on the car's frame near each wheel. A flexible hose usually carries the fluid to the disc caliper or wheel cylinder. The flexible line allows for suspension and steering movements.

The rear wheel cylinders contain two pistons each, one at either end, which push outward in opposite directions. The front disc brake calipers contain one piston each.

All pistons employ some type of seal, usually make of rubber, to minimize fluid leakage. A rubber dust boot seals the outer end of the cylinder against dust and dirt. The boot fits around the outer end of the piston on disc brake calipers, and around the brake actuating rod on wheel cylinders.

The hydraulic system operates as follows: When at rest, the entire system, from the piston(s) in the master cylinder to those in the wheel cylinders or calipers, is full of brake fluid. Upon application of the brake pedal, fluid trapped in front of the master cylinder piston(s) is forced through the lines to the wheel cylinders. Here, it forces the pistons outward, in the case of drum brakes, and inward toward the disc, in the case of disc brakes. The motion of the pistons is opposed by return springs mounted outside the cylinders in drum brakes, and by internal springs or spring seal, in disc brakes.

Upon release of the brake pedal, a spring located inside the master cylinder immediately return the master cylinder pistons to the normal position. The pistons contain check valves and the master cylinder has compensating ports drilled in it. These are uncovered as the pistons reach their normal position. The piston check valves allow fluid to flow toward the wheel cylinders or calipers as the pistons withdraw. Then, as the return springs force the brake pads or shoes into the released position, the excess fluid reservoir through the compensating ports. It is during the time the pedal is in the released position that any fluid that has leaked out of the system will be replaced from the reservoirs through the compensating ports.

The dual master cylinder has two pistons, located one behind the other. The primary piston is actuated directly by mechanical linkage from the brake pedal. The secondary piston is actuated by fluid trapped between the two pistons. If a leak develops in front of the secondary piston, it moves forward until it bottoms

BRAKES

Troubleshooting the Brake System

Problem	Cause	Solution
Low brake pedal (excessive pedal travel required for braking action.)	• Excessive clearance between rear linings and drums caused by inoperative automatic adjusters	• Make 10 to 15 alternate forward and reverse brake stops to adjust brakes. If brake pedal does not come up, repair or replace adjuster parts as necessary.
	• Worn rear brakelining	• Inspect and replace lining if worn beyond minimum thickness specification
	• Bent, distorted brakeshoes, front or rear	• Replace brakeshoes in axle sets
	• Air in hydraulic system	• Remove air from system. Refer to Brake Bleeding.
Low brake pedal (pedal may go to floor with steady pressure applied.)	• Fluid leak in hydraulic system	• Fill master cylinder to fill line; have helper apply brakes and check calipers, wheel cylinders, differential valve tubes, hoses and fittings for leaks. Repair or replace as necessary.
	• Air in hydraulic system	• Remove air from system. Refer to Brake Bleeding.
	• Incorrect or non-recommended brake fluid (fluid evaporates at below normal temp).	• Flush hydraulic system with clean brake fluid. Refill with correct-type fluid.
	• Master cylinder piston seals worn, or master cylinder bore is scored, worn or corroded	• Repair or replace master cylinder
Low brake pedal (pedal goes to floor on first application—o.k. on subsequent applications.)	• Disc brake pads sticking on abutment surfaces of anchor plate. Caused by a build-up of dirt, rust, or corrosion on abutment surfaces	• Clean abutment surfaces
Fading brake pedal (pedal height decreases with steady pressure applied.)	• Fluid leak in hydraulic system	• Fill master cylinder reservoirs to fill mark, have helper apply brakes, check calipers, wheel cylinders, differential valve, tubes, hoses, and fittings for fluid leaks. Repair or replace parts as necessary.
	• Master cylinder piston seals worn, or master cylinder bore is scored, worn or corroded	• Repair or replace master cylinder
Decreasing brake pedal travel (pedal travel required for braking action decreases and may be accompanied by a hard pedal.)	• Caliper or wheel cylinder pistons sticking or seized	• Repair or replace the calipers, or wheel cylinders
	• Master cylinder compensator ports blocked (preventing fluid return to reservoirs) or pistons sticking or seized in master cylinder bore	• Repair or replace the master cylinder
	• Power brake unit binding internally	• Test unit according to the following procedure: (a) Shift transmission into neutral and start engine (b) Increase engine speed to 1500 rpm, close throttle and fully depress brake pedal (c) Slow release brake pedal and stop engine (d) Have helper remove vacuum check valve and hose from power unit. Observe for backward movement of brake pedal. (e) If the pedal moves backward, the power unit has an internal bind—replace power unit

Troubleshooting the Brake System (cont.)

Problem	Cause	Solution
Spongy brake pedal (pedal has abnormally soft, springy, spongy feel when depressed.)	• Air in hydraulic system • Brakeshoes bent or distorted • Brakelining not yet seated with drums and rotors • Rear drum brakes not properly adjusted	• Remove air from system. Refer to Brake Bleeding. • Replace brakeshoes • Burnish brakes • Adjust brakes

Hard brake pedal (excessive pedal pressure required to stop vehicle. May be accompanied by brake fade.)	• Loose or leaking power brake unit vacuum hose
	• Incorrect or poor quality brakelining
	• Bent, broken, distorted brakeshoes
	• Calipers binding or dragging on mounting pins. Rear brakeshoes dragging on support plate.
	
	• Caliper, wheel cylinder, or master cylinder pistons sticking or seized
	• Power brake unit vacuum check valve malfunction
	
	• Power brake unit has internal bind
	
	• Master cylinder compensator ports (at bottom of reservoirs) blocked by dirt, scale, rust, or have small burrs (blocked ports prevent fluid return to reservoirs).
	• Brake hoses, tubes, fittings clogged or restricted
	• Brake fluid contaminated with improper fluids (motor oil, transmission fluid, causing rubber components to swell and stick in bores
	• Low engine vacuum
		• Tighten connections or replace leaking hose
		• Replace with lining in axle sets
		• Replace brakeshoes
		• Replace mounting pins and bushings. Clean rust or burrs from rear brake support plate ledges and lubricate ledges with molydisulfide grease.
		NOTE: If ledges are deeply grooved or scored, do not attempt to sand or grind them smooth—replace support plate.
		• Repair or replace parts as necessary
		• Test valve according to the following procedure:
		  (a) Start engine, increase engine speed to 1500 rpm, close throttle and immediately stop engine
		  (b) Wait at least 90 seconds then depress brake pedal
		  (c) If brakes are not vacuum assisted for 2 or more applications, check valve is faulty
		• Test unit according to the following procedure:
		  (a) With engine stopped, apply brakes several times to exhaust all vacuum in system
		  (b) Shift transmission into neutral, depress brake pedal and start engine
		  (c) If pedal height decreases with foot pressure and less pressure is required to hold pedal in applied position, power unit vacuum system is operating normally. Test power unit. If power unit exhibits a bind condition, replace the power unit.
		• Repair or replace master cylinder
		CAUTION: Do not attempt to clean blocked ports with wire, pencils, or similar implements. Use compressed air only.
		• Use compressed air to check or unclog parts. Replace any damaged parts.
		• Replace all rubber components, combination valve and hoses. Flush entire brake system with DOT 3 brake fluid or equivalent.
		• Adjust or repair engine

BRAKES

Troubleshooting the Brake System (cont.)

Problem	Cause	Solution
Grabbing brakes (severe reaction to brake pedal pressure.)	• Brakelining(s) contaminated by grease or brake fluid • Parking brake cables incorrectly adjusted or seized • Incorrect brakelining or lining loose on brakeshoes • Caliper anchor plate bolts loose • Rear brakeshoes binding on support plate ledges • Incorrect or missing power brake reaction disc • Rear brake support plates loose	• Determine and correct cause of contamination and replace brakeshoes in axle sets • Adjust cables. Replace seized cables. • Replace brakeshoes in axle sets • Tighten bolts • Clean and lubricate ledges. Replace support plate(s) if ledges are deeply grooved. Do not attempt to smooth ledges by grinding. • Install correct disc • Tighten mounting bolts
Dragging brakes (slow or incomplete release of brakes)	• Brake pedal binding at pivot • Power brake unit has internal bind • Parking brake cables incorrrectly adjusted or seized • Rear brakeshoe return springs weak or broken • Automatic adjusters malfunctioning • Caliper, wheel cylinder or master cylinder pistons sticking or seized • Master cylinder compensating ports blocked (fluid does not return to reservoirs).	• Loosen and lubricate • Inspect for internal bind. Replace unit if internal bind exists. • Adjust cables. Replace seized cables. • Replace return springs. Replace brakeshoe if necessary in axle sets. • Repair or replace adjuster parts as required • Repair or replace parts as necessary • Use compressed air to clear ports. Do not use wire, pencils, or similar objects to open blocked ports.
Vehicle moves to one side when brakes are applied	• Incorrect front tire pressure • Worn or damaged wheel bearings • Brakelining on one side contaminated • Brakeshoes on one side bent, distorted, or lining loose on shoe • Support plate bent or loose on one side • Brakelining not yet seated with drums or rotors • Caliper anchor plate loose on one side • Caliper piston sticking or seized • Brakelinings water soaked • Loose suspension component attaching or mounting bolts • Brake combination valve failure	• Inflate to recommended cold (reduced load) inflation pressure • Replace worn or damaged bearings • Determine and correct cause of contamination and replace brakelining in axle sets • Replace brakeshoes in axle sets • Tighten or replace support plate • Burnish brakelining • Tighten anchor plate bolts • Repair or replace caliper • Drive vehicle with brakes lightly applied to dry linings • Tighten suspension bolts. Replace worn suspension components. • Replace combination valve
Chatter or shudder when brakes are applied (pedal pulsation and roughness may also occur.)	• Brakeshoes distorted, bent, contaminated, or worn • Caliper anchor plate or support plate loose • Excessive thickness variation of rotor(s)	• Replace brakeshoes in axle sets • Tighten mounting bolts • Refinish or replace rotors in axle sets
Noisy brakes (squealing, clicking, scraping sound when brakes are applied.)	• Bent, broken, distorted brakeshoes • Excessive rust on outer edge of rotor braking surface	• Replace brakeshoes in axle sets • Remove rust

Troubleshooting the Brake System (cont.)

Problem	Cause	Solution
Noisy brakes (squealing, clicking, scraping sound when brakes are applied.) (cont.)	• Brakelining worn out—shoes contacting drum of rotor	• Replace brakeshoes and lining in axle sets. Refinish or replace drums or rotors.
	• Broken or loose holdown or return springs	• Replace parts as necessary
	• Rough or dry drum brake support plate ledges	• Lubricate support plate ledges
	• Cracked, grooved, or scored rotor(s) or drum(s)	• Replace rotor(s) or drum(s). Replace brakeshoes and lining in axle sets if necessary.
	• Incorrect brakelining and/or shoes (front or rear).	• Install specified shoe and lining assemblies
Pulsating brake pedal	• Out of round drums or excessive lateral runout in disc brake rotor(s)	• Refinish or replace drums, re-index rotors or replace

against the front of the master cylinder. The fluid trapped between the piston will operate one side of the diagonal system. If the other side of the system develops a leak, the primary piston will move forward until direct contact with the secondary piston takes place, and it will force the secondary piston to actuate the other side of the diagonal system. In either case the brake pedal drops closer to the floor board and less braking power is available.

The brake system uses a switch to warn the driver when only half of the brake system is operational. This switch is located in a valve body which is mounted on the firewall or the frame below the master cylinder. A hydraulic piston receives pressure from both circuits, each circuit's pressure being applied to one end of the piston. When the pressures are in balance, the piston remains stationary. When one circuit has a leak, however, the greater pressure in the circuit during application of the brakes will push the piston to one side, closing the switch and activating the brake warning light.

In disc brake system, this valve body contains a metering valve and, in some cases, a proportioning valve or valves, The metering valve keeps pressure from traveling to the disc brakes on the front wheels until the brake shoes on the rear wheels have contacted the drums, ensuring that the front brakes will never be used alone. The proportioning valve controls the pressure to the rear brakes to avoid rear wheel lock-up during very hard braking.

Warning lights may be tested by depressing the brake pedal and holding it while opening one of the wheel cylinder bleeder screws. If this does not cause the light to go on, substitute a new lamp, make continuity checks, and finally, replace the switch as necessary.

The hydraulic system may be checked for leaks by applying pressure to the pedal gradually and steadily. If the pedal sinks very slowly to the floor, the system has a leak. This is not to be confused with a springy or spongy feel due to the compression of air within the lines. If the system leaks, there will be a gradual change in the position of the pedal with a constant pressure.

Check for leaks along all lines and at wheel cylinders or calipers. If no external leaks are apparent, the problem is inside the master cylinder.

Disc Brakes

BASIC OPERATING PRINCIPLES

Instead of the traditional expanding brakes that press outward against a circular drum, disc brake systems utilize a disc (rotor) with brake pads positioned on either side of it. Braking effect is achieved in a manner similar to the way you would squeeze a spinning phonograph record between your fingers. The disc (rotor) is a casting with cooling fins between the two braking surfaces. This enables air to circulate between the braking surfaces making them less sensitive to heat buildup and more resistant to fade. Dirt and water do not affect braking action since contaminants are thrown off by the centrifugal action of the rotor or scraped off by the pads. Also, the equal clamping action of the two brake pads tends to ensure uniform, straight line stops. Disc brakes are inherently self-adjusting.

Your car uses a pin slider front wheel caliper. The brake pad on the inside of the brake rotor is moved in contact with the rotor by hydraulic pressure. The caliper, which is not held in a fixed position, moves slightly, bringing the outside brake pad into contact with the disc rotor.

BRAKES

Drum Brakes (Rear)

BASIC OPERATING PRINCIPLES

Drum brakes employ two brake shoes mounted on a stationary backing plate. These shoes are positioned inside a circular drum which rotates with the wheel assembly. The shoes are held in place by springs. This allows them to slide toward the drums (when they are applied) while keeping the linings and drums in alignment. The shoes are actuated by a wheel cylinder which is mounted at the top of the backing plate. When the brakes are applied, hydraulic pressure forces the wheel cylinder's actuating links outward. Since these links bear directly against the top of the brake shoes, the tops of the shoes are then forced against the inner side of the drum. This action forces the bottoms of the two shoes to contact the brake drum by rotating the entire assembly slightly (know as servo action). When pressure within the wheel cylinder is relaxed, return springs pull the shoes back away from the drum.

The rear drum brakes on your car are designed to self-adjust themselves during application. Motion causes both shoes to rotate very slightly with the drum, rocking an adjusting lever, thereby causing rotation of the adjusting screw or lever.

Power Brake Boosters

Power brakes operate just as standard brake systems except in the actuation of the master cylinder pistons. A vacuum diaphragm is located on the front of the master cylinder and assists the driver in applying the brakes, reducing both the effort and travel he must put into moving the brake pedal.

The vacuum diaphragm housing is connected to the intake manifold by a vacuum hose. A check valve is placed at the point where the hose enters the diaphragm housing, so that during periods of low manifold vacuum brake assist vacuum will not be lost.

Depressing the brake pedal closes off the vacuum sources and allows atmospheric pressure to enter on one side of the diaphragm. This causes the master cylinder pistons to move and apply the brakes. When the brake pedal is released, vacuum is applied to both sides of the diaphragm, and return springs return the diaphragm and master cylinder pistons to the released position. If the vacuum fails, the brake pedal rod will butt against the end of the master cylinder actuating rod, and direct mechanical application will occur as the pedal is depressed.

The hydraulic and mechanical problems that apply to conventional brake systems also apply to power brakes, and should be checked for if the tests below do not reveal the problem. **Test for a system vacuum leak as described below:**

1. Operate the engine at idle without touching the brake pedal for at least one minute.
2. Turn off the engine, and wait one minute.
3. Test for the presence of assist vacuum by depressing the brake pedal and releasing it several times. Light application will produce less and less pedal travel, if vacuum was present. If there is no vacuum, air is leaking into the system somewhere.

Test for system operation as follows:
1. Pump the brake pedal (with engine off) until the supply vacuum is entirely gone.
2. Put a light, steady pressure on the pedal.
3. Start the engine, and operate it at idle. If the system is operating, the brake pedal should fall toward the floor if constant pressure is maintained on the pedal.

Power brake systems may be tested for hydraulic leaks just as ordinary systems are tested.

Brake Adjustment

FRONT DISC BRAKES

Front disc brakes require no adjustment. Hydraulic pressure maintains the proper pad-to-disc contact at all times.

REAR DRUM BRAKES

The rear drum brakes, on your car, are self-adjusting. The only adjustment necessary should be an initial one after new brake shoes have been installed or some type of service work has been done on the rear brake system.

NOTE: *After any brake service, obtain a firm brake pedal before moving the car. Adjusted brakes must not drag. The wheel must turn freely. Be sure the parking brake cables are not too tightly adjusted. A special brake shoe gauge is necessary, if your car is equipped with 203mm (8 in.), for making an accurate adjustment after installing new brake shoes. The special gauge measures both the drum diameter and the brake shoe setting.*

Since no adjustment is necessary except when service work is done on the rear brakes, we will assume that the car is jacked up and safely supported by jackstands, and that the rear drums have been removed. (If not, refer to the appropriate sections of this chapter for the procedures necessary).

BRAKES

Cars Equipped with 178mm (7 in.) Brakes

Pivot the adjuster quadrant (see illustration) until the third or fourth notch from the outer end of the quadrant meshes with the knurled pin on the adjuster strut. Install the hub and drum.

Cars Equipped with 203mm (8 in.) Brakes

Measure and set the special brake gauge to the inside diameter of the brake drum. Lift the adjuster lever from the star wheel teeth. Turn the star wheel until the brake shoes are adjusted out to the shoe setting fingers of the brake gauge. Install the hub and drum.

NOTE: *Complete the adjustment by applying the brakes several times. After the brakes have been properly adjusted, check their operation by making several stops from varying forward speeds.*

Adjustment for Brake Drum Removal

If the brake drum will not come off for brake servicing, pry the rubber plug from the backing plate inspection hole and use the following procedure:

On 178mm (7 in.) brakes: Insert a thin blade screwdriver through the hole until it contacts the adjuster assembly pivot. Apply side pressure to the pivot point allowing the adjuster quadrant to ratchet and back off the brake adjustment.

On 203mm (8 in.) brakes: Remove the brake line to axle retention bracket. This will allow sufficient room for the use of a thin screwdriver and brake adjusting tool. Push the adjuster lever away from the adjuster wheel with the screwdriver and release adjustment with the brake tool.

Stoplight Switch

The mechanical stoplight switch assembly is installed on the pin of the brake pedal arm, so that it straddles the master cylinder pushrod.

REMOVAL AND INSTALLATION

1. Disconnect the negative battery cable.
2. Disconnect the wire harness at the connector from the switch.

NOTE: *The locking tab must be lifted before the connector can be removed.*

3. Remove the hairpin retainer and white nylon washer. Slide the stoplight switch and the pushrod away from the pedal. Remove the switch by sliding the switch up/down.

NOTE: *Since the switch side plate nearest the brake pedal is slotted, it is not necessary to remove the brake master cylinder pushrod black bushing and 1 white spacer washer nearest the pedal arm from the brake pedal pin.*

To install:

4. Position the switch so that the U-shaped side is nearest the pedal and directly over/under the pin. The black bushing must be in position in the push rod eyelet with the washer face on the side closest to the retaining pin.
5. Slide the switch up/down, trapping the master cylinder pushrod and black bushing between the switch side plates. Push the switch and pushrod assembly firmly towards the brake pedal arm. Assemble the outside white plastic washer to pin and install the hairpin retainer to trap the whole assembly.

NOTE: *Do not substitute other types of pin retainer. Replace only with production hairpin retainer.*

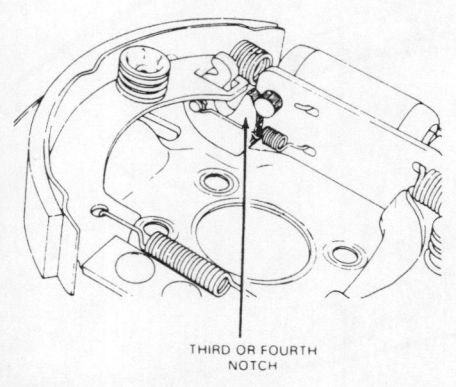

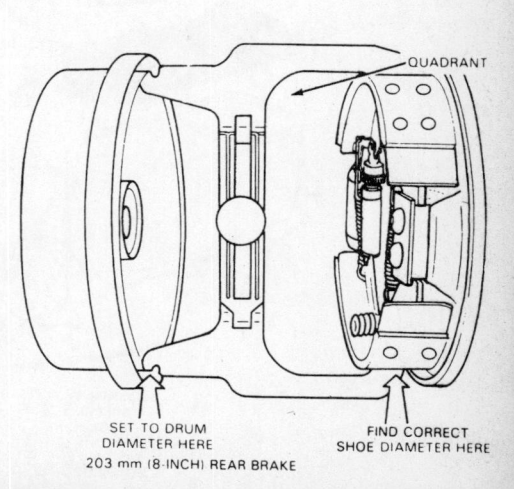

Rear brake shoe adjustment

BRAKES

6. Connect the wire harness connector to the switch.
7. Connect negative battery cable.
8. Check the stoplight switch for proper operation. Stoplights should illuminate with less than 6 lbs. applied to the brake pedal at the pad.

NOTE: *The stoplight switch wire harness must have sufficient length to travel with the switch during full stroke at the pedal.*

Master Cylinder

The fluid reservoir of the master cylinder has a large and small compartment. The larger serves the right front and left rear brakes, while the smaller serves the left front and right rear brakes.

Always be sure that the fluid level of the reservoirs is within 6mm (1/4 in.) of the top. Use only DOT 3 approved brake fluid.

REMOVAL AND INSTALLATION

Models without Power Brakes

1. Disconnect the negative (ground) battery cable from the battery.
2. From under the dash panel, disconnect the wires to the stoplight switch. Remove the spring clip that retains the stoplight switch and the master cylinder pushrod to the brake pedal.
3. Slide the stoplight switch off the brake pedal pin. Remove the switch.
4. From under the hood, loosen the two retaining nuts mounting the master cylinder to the firewall. Disconnect the brake lines from the master cylinder.
5. Slide the master cylinder pushrod, washers and bushings from the brake pedal pin.

NOTE: *Models with speed control have an adapter instead of a washer on the brake pedal mounting pin.*

6. Remove the cylinder mounting nuts. Lift the cylinder out and away from the firewall.

CAUTION: *Take care not to spill any brake fluid on the painted surfaces of your car. If you spill any on you car, flush off with water as soon as possible. Brake fluid will act like a paint remover.*

To install:

1. Insert the master cylinder pushrod through the opening in the firewall. Place the cylinder mounting flange over the studs on the firewall and loosely install the mounting nuts.
2. Coat the nylon pushrod mounting bushing with oil. Install the washer, pushrod and bushing on the brake pedal shaft. (Speed control models use a snap-on adapter instead of a washer).
3. Position the stoplight switch on the

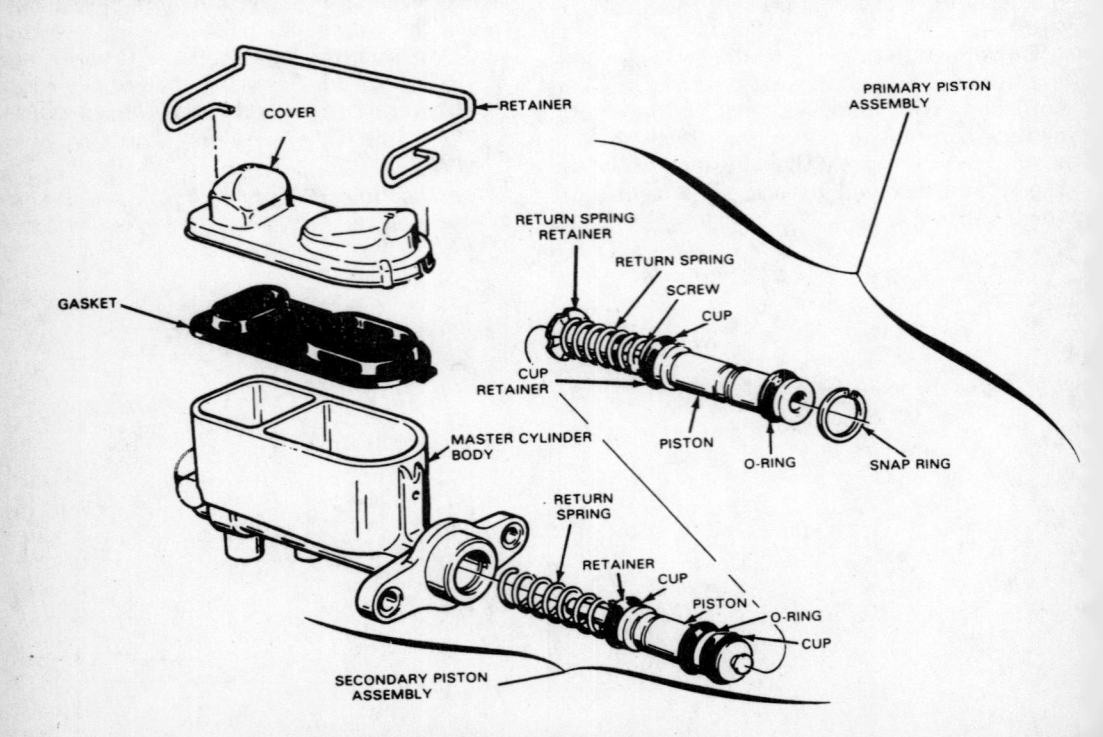

Exploded view of the master cylinder

brake pedal pin. Install the nylon bushing and washer and secure with the spring pin.

4. Connect the wires to the stoplight switch.

5. Connect the brake lines to the master cylinder, but do not tighten them completely.

6. Secure the cylinder mounting nuts. Fill the master cylinder to within 6mm (1/4 in.) of the top. Slowly pump the brake pedal to help evacuate the air in the master cylinder.

NOTE: *Cover the brake line connections (at the master cylinder) with a rag to prevent brake fluid spray.*

7. Tighten the brake lines at the master cylinder. Add brake fluid if necessary.

8. Connect the negative battery cable. Bleed the entire brake system. Centralize the pressure differential valve (refer to the following sections).

9. Check for hydraulic leaks. Road test the car.

Power Brake Models

1. Disconnect the brake lines from the master cylinder.

2. Remove the two nuts that mount the master cylinder to the brake booster.

3. Pull the master cylinder forward and away from the booster.

CAUTION: *Brake fluid acts like a paint remover. If you spill any on the finish of your car, flush it off with water.*

To install:

1. Slip the master cylinder base over the pushrod at the poser brake booster. Align the mounting flange and place over the mounting studs on the booster. Loosely secure with the two mounting nuts.

2. Connect the brake lines to the master cylinder. Tighten the mounting nuts. Tighten the brake lines.

3. Fill the master cylinder to within 6mm (1/4 in.) of the top. Bleed the brake system. Centralize the pressure differential valve (refer to the following sections). Check for system leaks. Road test the car.

MASTER CYLINDER OVERHAUL

Referring to the exploded view of the dual master cylinder components, disassemble the unit as follows: Clean the exterior of the cylinder and remove the filler cover and diaphragm. Any brake fluid remaining in the cylinder should be poured out and discarded. Remove the secondary piston stop bolt from the bottom of the cylinder and remove the bleed screw, if required. With the primary piston depressed, remove the snapring from its retaining groove at the rear of the cylinder bore. Withdraw the pushrod and the primary piston assembly from the bore.

Remove the secondary piston assembly. If the piston does not come out easily, apply air pressure carefully through the secondary outlet port to assist in piston removal.

NOTE: *Do not remove the outlet tube seats, outlet check valves and outlet check valve springs from the cylinder body unless they are damaged.*

All components should be cleaned in clean isopropyl alcohol or clean brake fluid and inspected for chipping, excessive wear and damage. Check to ensure that all recesses, openings and passageways are clear and free of foreign matter. Dirt and cleaning solvent may be removed by using compressed air. After cleaning, keep all parts on a clean surface. Inspect the cylinder bore for etching, pitting, scoring or

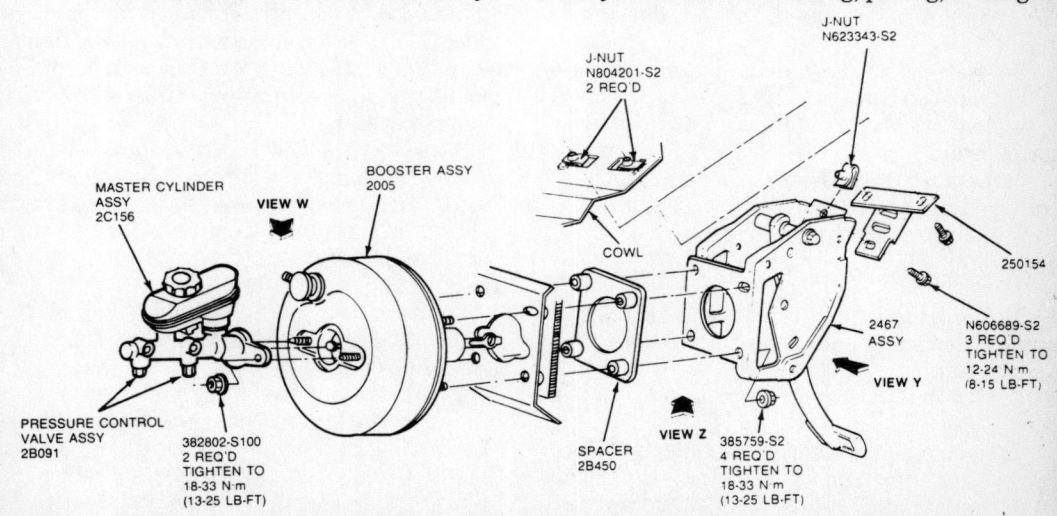

Power booster and master cylinder assembly

rusting. Since honing is not recommended for aluminum master cylinders, deep scratches or pitting will require master cylinder replacement.

During the assembly operation, be sure to use all parts supplied with the master cylinder repair kit. With the exception of the master cylinder body, submerge all parts in extra heavy duty brake fluid. Carefully insert the complete secondary piston and return spring assembly into the cylinder bore and install the primary piston assembly into the bore. With the primary piston depressed, install the snapring into its groove in the cylinder bore. Install the pushrod, boot and retainer (if equipped), then install the pushrod assembly into the primary piston. Be sure that the retainer is properly seated and is holding the pushrod securely. Position the inner end of the pushrod boot (if equipped) in the master cylinder body retaining groove. Install the secondary piston stop bolt and O-ring at the bottom of the master cylinder body. Install the bleed screw (if equipped) and position the gasket on the master cylinder filler cover. Be sure that the gasket is securely seated. Reinstall the master cylinder and fill the brake fluid. Install the cover and secure with the retainer. Bleed the brake system and road test the car.

Vacuum Booster

REMOVAL AND INSTALLATION

1981–85 Models

1. Working from inside the car, beneath the instrument panel, remove the booster pushrod from the brake pedal.
2. Disconnect the stop light switch wires and remove the switch from the brake pedal. Use care not to damage the switch during removal.
3. Raise the hood and remove the master cylinder from the booster.
4. Remove the manifold vacuum hose from the booster.
5. Remove the booster to firewall attaching bolts and remove the booster from the car.
6. Reverse above procedure to reinstall.

1986–90 Models

1. Disconnect the battery ground cable and remove the brake lines from the master cylinder.
2. Remove the retaining nuts and remove the master cylinder.
3. From under the instrument panel, remove the stoplight switch wiring connector from the switch. Remove the pushrod retainer and outer nylon washer from the brake pin, slide the stoplight switch along the brake pedal pin, far enough for the outer hole to clear the pin.
4. Remove the switch by sliding it upward. Remove the booster to dash panel retaining nuts. Slide the booster pushrod and pushrod bushing off the brake pedal pin.
5. Position the wire harness out of the way. Remove the transaxle shift cable and bracket.
6. Disconnect the manifold vacuum hose from the booster check valve and move the booster forward until the booster studs clear the dash panel and remove the booster.
7. Complete the installation of the power booster assembly by reversing the removal procedure. Bleed the brake system.

NOTE: *On vehicles equipped with speed control, the vacuum dump valve must be adjusted if the brake booster has been removed.*

8. To adjust the vacuum dump valve, complete the following:
   a. Firmly depress and hold the brake pedal.
   b. Push in the dump valve until the valve collar bottoms against the retaining clip.
   c. Place a (1.3–2.5mm) 0.050–0.10 in. shim between the white button of the valve and the pad on the brake pedal.
   d. Firmly pull the brake pedal rearward to its normal position, allowing the dump valve to ratchet backward in the retaining clip.

TESTING THE POWER BRAKE BOOSTER

The power brake booster depends on vacuum produced by the engine for proper operation.

If you suspect problems in the power brake system, check the following:

1. Inspect all hoses and hose connections. All unused vacuum connectors should be sealed. Hoses and connections should be tightly secured and in good condition. The hoses should be pliable with no holes or cracks and no collapsed areas.
2. Inspect the check valve which is located in line between the intake manifold and booster. Disconnect the hose on the intake manifold side of the valve. Attempt to blow through the valve. If air passes through the valve, it is defective and must be replaced.
3. Check the level of brake fluid in the master cylinder. If the level is low, check the system for fluid leaks.
4. Idle the engine briefly and then shut it off. Pump the brake pedal several times to exhaust all of the vacuum stored in the booster. Keep the brake pedal depressed and start the engine. The brake pedal should drop slightly, if vacuum is present after the engine is started less pressure should be necessary on the brake

BRAKES   519

pedal. If no drop, or action is felt the power brake booster should be suspect.

5. With the parking brake applied and the wheels blocked, start the engine and allow to idle in Neutral (Park if automatic). Disconnect the vacuum line to the check valve on the intake manifold side. If vacuum is felt, connect the hose and repeat Step 4. Once again, if no action is felt on the brake pedal, suspect the booster.

6. Operate the engine at a fast idle for about ten seconds, shut off the engine. Allow the car to sit for about ten minutes. Depress the brake pedal with moderate force (about 20 pounds). The pedal should feel about the same as when the engine was running. If the brake pedal feels hard (no power assist) suspect the power booster.

Brake Control Valve

REPLACEMENT

The brake control valve is located to the left and below the master cylinder and mounted to the shock (strut) tower by a removable bracket. Use the proper size flare wrench and disconnect the brake lines to the valve. Disconnect the warning switch wire. Remove the bolt(s) retaining the valve to the mount and remove the valve. Installation is in the reverse order of removal. Bleed the brake system after installing the new valve.

Pressure Differential Valve

If a loss of brake fluid occurs on either side of the diagonally split system when the brakes are applied, a piston mounted in the valve moves off center allowing the brakes on the non-leaking side of the split system to operate. When the piston moves off center a brake warning switch, located in the center of the valve body, will turn on a dash mounted warning light indicating brake problems.

After repairs are made on the brake system and the system bled, the warning switch will reset itself when you pump the brake pedal and the dash light will turn off.

Proportioning Valve

The dual proportioning valve, located between the rear brake system inlet and outlet port, controls the rear brake system hydraulic pressure. When the brakes are applied, the dual proportioning valve reduces pressure to the rear wheels and provides balanced braking.

TROUBLESHOOTING THE PROPORTIONING VALVE

If the rear brakes lock-up during light brake application or do not lock-up under heavy braking the problem could be with the dual proportioning valve.

1. Check tires and tire pressures.
2. Check the brake linings for thickness, and for contamination by fluid, grease etc.
3. Check the brake system hoses, steel lines, calipers and wheel cylinders for leaks.
4. If none of the proceeding checks have uncovered any problems, suspect the proportioning valve.

NOTE: *Take the car to a qualified service center and ask them to do a pressure test on the valve. If a pressure test is not possible, replace the control valve.*

Pressure Control Valves

These valves are housed in the master cylinder assembly. One valve controls each rear wheel brake cylinder. They are designed to

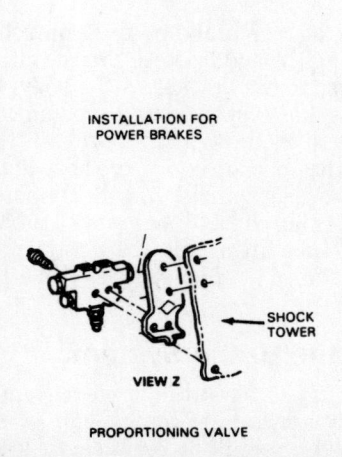

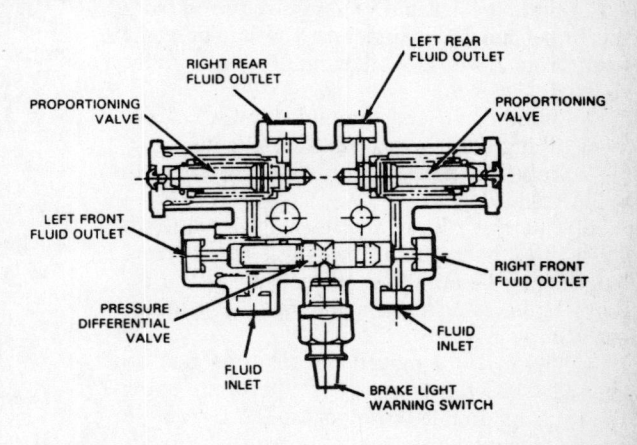

Combination brake valve

reduce the hydraulic pressure to the rear wheel brake cylinders when the pressure exceeds a preset value. The hydraulic pressure is limited in order to prevent rear wheel skidding during hard braking.

REMOVAL AND INSTALLATION

1. Disconnect and plug primary and secondary brake tubes from master cylinder, as necessary.
2. Loosen and remove pressure control valve from the master cylinder housing.

To install:

3. Install pressure control valve in master cylinder housing port and tighten to 10–18 ft. lbs. (13–24 Nm).
4. Install the brake tube and tighten to 10–18 ft. lbs. (13–24 Nm).
5. Fill and bleed hydraulic system as outlined.

Brake Tubing and Hoses

BRAKE TUBING

The hydraulic lines use a double wall steel tubing throughout the system with the exception of the flexible hoses at the front and rear wheel. When connecting a tube to a hose, tube connector, or brake cylinder, tighten the tube fitting nut to specifications.

All models utilize the brake tubes with ISO flares and metric tube nuts at the master cylinder. These brake tubes are installed from the brake master cylinder to the left and right front brake hoses. The fittings at the master cylinder are either M10 or M12 metric tube nuts, where as the fitting at the front brake hoses are $3/8$ in.–24 × $3/16$ in. tube nuts, used with a double flare.

If a brake tube replacement is required from the brake master cylinder to the left or right front brake hose, the following procedure must be used.

1. Obtain the recommended bulk $3/16$ in. steel tubing and correct standard $3/8$ in.–24 × $3/16$ in. tube nut. The M10 and M12 metric nuts will be reused.
2. Cut the tubing to the length required. Clean the burrs after cutting. The correct length may be obtained by measuring the removed tube using a string and adding $1/8$ in. for each flare.
3. Place the removed metric tube nut on the tube. ISO flare one ens of the tubing using the ISO and double flare tool kit D81L–2269–A or equivalent.
4. On the opposite end of the replacement tube, install a standard $3/8$ in.–24 × $3/16$ in. tube nut and double flare tube end.

NOTE: *Be sure to follow the flaring instructions included in the ISO and double flare tool kit D81L–2269–A or equivalent.*

5. Bend the replacement brake tube to match the removed tube using a suitable tube bender. When the replacement brake tube is installed, maintain adequate clearance to all moving or vibrating parts.

NOTE: *If a section of brake tubing becomes damaged, the entire section should be replaced with tubing of the same size, shape, length and material. Copper tubing should not be used in a hydraulic system. When bending the brake tubing to fit the body contours, be careful not to kink or crack the tubing.*

All brake tubing should be flared properly to provide a good leakproof connection. Clean the brake tubing by flushing it with clean brake fluid before installation. When connecting a tube to a hose, tube connector or brake cylinder, tighten the tube fitting nut to specifications with a suitable torque wrench.

Always bleed the applicable primary or secondary brake system after the hose or line replacement

BRAKE HOSE

A flexible brake hose should be replaced if it shows signs of softening, cracking or other damage. When installing a new front brake hose, 2 new sealing washers should be used.

Positioning of the front hose is controlled by a self indexing brass block. When attaching the block to the caliper, tighten the bolt to 30–40 ft. lbs. (41–54 Nm). Attach the intermediate bracket to the shock strut and tighten the screw. Engage the opposite end of the hose to the bracket on the body. Install the horseshoe type retaining clip and connect tube to hose with tube nut. Inspect the position of the installed hose for clearance to the other chassis components.

Positioning of rear brake hose is controlled by self indexing the end fittings. Engage either end of the hose to the bracket on the body. Install the horseshoe type retaining clip and connect the tube to the hose with the tube fitting nut. Engage the opposite end of the hose to the bracket on the rear spindle. Install the horseshoe type retaining clip and connect the tube to hose with the tube fitting nut. Inspect the position of the installed hose for contact with other chassis parts.

Bleeding the Brake System

It is necessary to bleed the brake system of air whenever a hydraulic component, of the system, has been rebuilt or replaced, or if the brakes feel spongy during application.

Your car has a diagonally split brake system. Each side of this system must be bled as an individual system. **Bleed the right rear brake, left front brake, left rear brake and right front brake. Always start with the longest line from the master cylinder first.**

CAUTION: *When bleeding the system(s) never allow the master cylinder to run completely out of brake fluid. Always use DOT 3 heavy duty brake fluid or the equivalent. Never reuse brake fluid that has been drained from the system or that has been allowed to stand in an opened container for an extended period of time. If your car is equipped with power brakes, remove the reserve vacuum stored in the booster by pumping the brake pedal several times before bleeding the brakes.*

1. Clean all of the dirt away from the master cylinder filler cap.
2. Raise and support the car on jackstands. Make sure your car is safely supported and it is raised evenly front and back.
3. Starting with the right rear wheel cylinder. Remove the dust cover from the bleeder screw. Place the proper size box wrench over the bleeder fitting and attach a piece of rubber tubing (about three feet long and snug fitting) over the end of the fitting.
4. Submerge the free end of the rubber tube into a container half filled with clean brake fluid.
5. Have a friend pump up the brake pedal and then push down to apply the brakes while you loosen the bleeder screw. When the pedal reaches the bottom of its travel close the bleeder fitting before your friend release the brake pedal.
6. Repeat Step 5 until air bubbles cease to appear in the container in which the tubing is submerged. Tighten the fitting, remove the rubber tubing and replace the dust cover.
7. Repeat Steps 3 through 6 to the left front wheel, then to the left rear and right front.

NOTE: *Refill the master cylinder after each wheel cylinder or caliper is bled. Be sure the master cylinder top gasket is mounted correctly and the brake fluid level is within 6mm ($1/4$ in.) of the top.*

8. After bleeding the brakes, pump the brake pedal several times, this ensures proper seating of the rear linings and the front caliper pistons.

FRONT DISC BRAKES

CAUTION: *Some brake pads contain asbestos, which has been determined to be a cancer causing agent. Never clean the brake surfaces with compressed air! Avoid inhaling any dust from any brake surface! When cleaning brake surfaces, use a commercially available brake cleaning fluid.*

Disc Brake Pads

INSPECTION

1. Loosen the front wheel lugs slightly, then raise the front of the car and safely support it on jackstands.
2. Remove the front wheel and tire assemblies.
3. The cut out in the top of the front brake caliper allows visual inspection of the disc brake pad. If the lining is worn to within 3mm ($1/8$ in.) of the metal disc shoe (check local inspection requirements) replace all four pads (both sides).
4. While you are inspecting the brake pads, visually inspect the caliper for hydraulic fluid leaks. If a leak is visible the caliper will have to be rebuilt or replaced.

PAD REMOVAL AND INSTALLATION

1. Remove master cylinder cap and check fluid level in reservoir. Remove brake fluid until reservoir is $1/2$ full. Discard removed fluid.
2. Raise and safely support the vehicle.
3. Remove wheel.
4. Back out the Torx® headed caliper locating pins. DO NOT REMOVE THEM ALL THE WAY! If removed, the pins are difficult to install and require new guide bushings.
5. Lift caliper assembly from integral knuckle and anchor plate and rotor using rotating motion. Do not pry directly against plastic piston or damage will occur.
6. Remove outer shoe and lining assembly.
7. Remove inner shoe and lining assembly.
8. Inspect both rotor braking surfaces. Minor scoring or buildup of lining material does not require machining or replacement of rotor. Hand-sand glaze from both rotor braking surfaces using garnet paper 100A (medium grit) or aluminum oxide 150–J (medium).
9. Suspend caliper inside fender housing with wire. Use care not to damage caliper or stretch brake hose.

To install:

10. Use a 102mm (4 in.) C-clamp and wood block 70mm × 25mm ($2 3/4$ in. × 1 in.) and approximately 19mm ($3/4$ in.) thick to seat caliper hydraulic piston in its bore.
11. Remove all rust buildup from inside of caliper legs where the outer shoe makes contact.
12. Install inner shoe and lining assembly in caliper piston(s). Do not bend shoe clips during installation in piston.

522 BRAKES

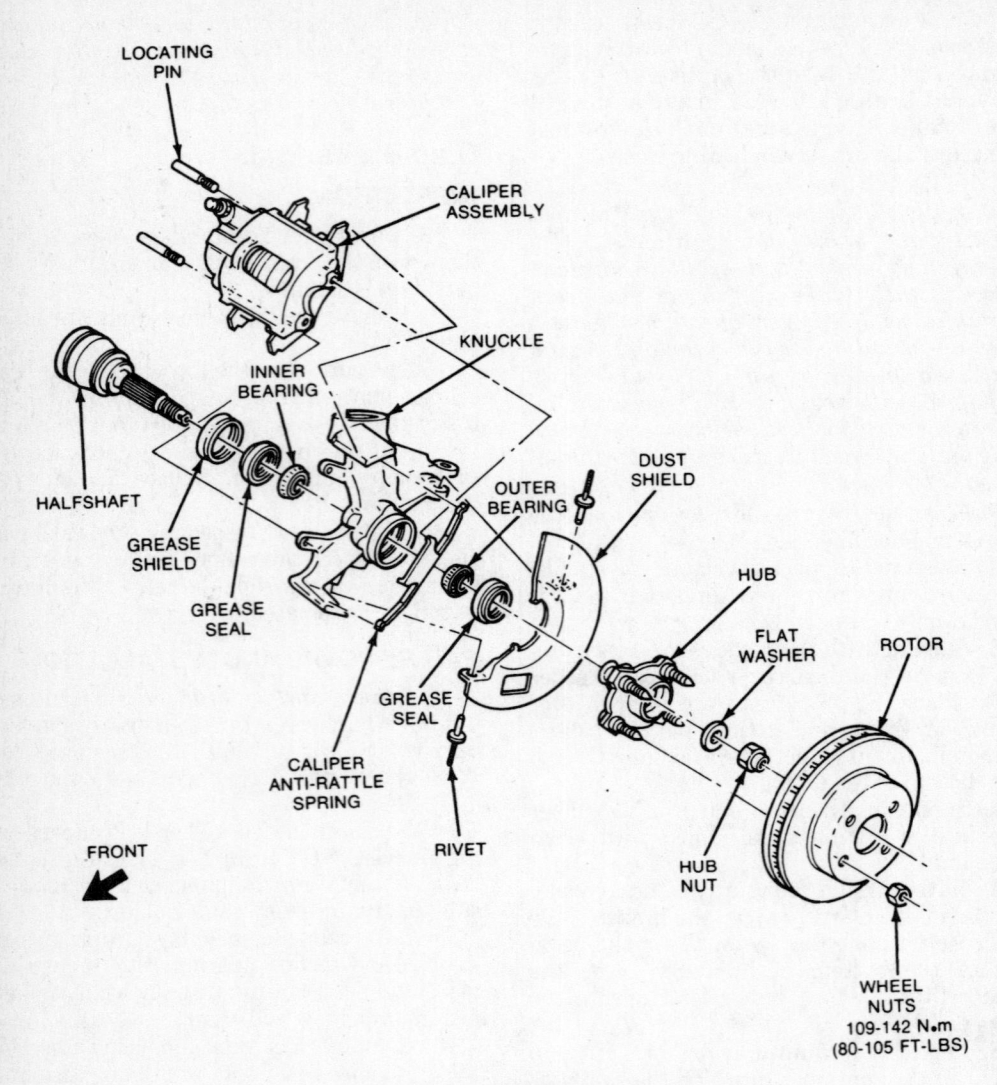

Disc brake components

13. Install correct outer shoe and lining assembly. Ensure clips are properly seated.
14. Install caliper over rotor.
15. Install wheel and tire assembly. Tighten wheel nuts to 80–105 ft. lbs. (109–142 Nm).
16. Pump brake pedal prior to moving vehicle to position brake linings.
17. Connect negative battery cable.
18. Road test vehicle.

Brake Caliper

REMOVAL AND INSTALLATION

1. Disconnect the negative battery cable.
2. Raise and safely support the vehicle.
3. Remove wheel and tire assembly from rotor mounting face.
4. Disconnect flexible brake hose from caliper. Remove hollow retaining bolt that connects hose fitting to caliper. Remove hose assembly from caliper and plug hose.
5. Remove caliper locating pins using Torx drive bit D79P-2100-T40 or equivalent.
6. Lift caliper off rotor and integral knuckle and anchor plate using rotating motion.

NOTE: *Do not pry directly against plastic piston or damage to piston will occur.*

To install:
7. Position caliper assembly above rotor with anti-rattle spring under upper arm of knuckle. Install caliper over rotor with rotating motion. Ensure inner shoe is properly positioned.

NOTE: *Ensure correct caliper assembly is installed on correct knuckle. The caliper bleed*

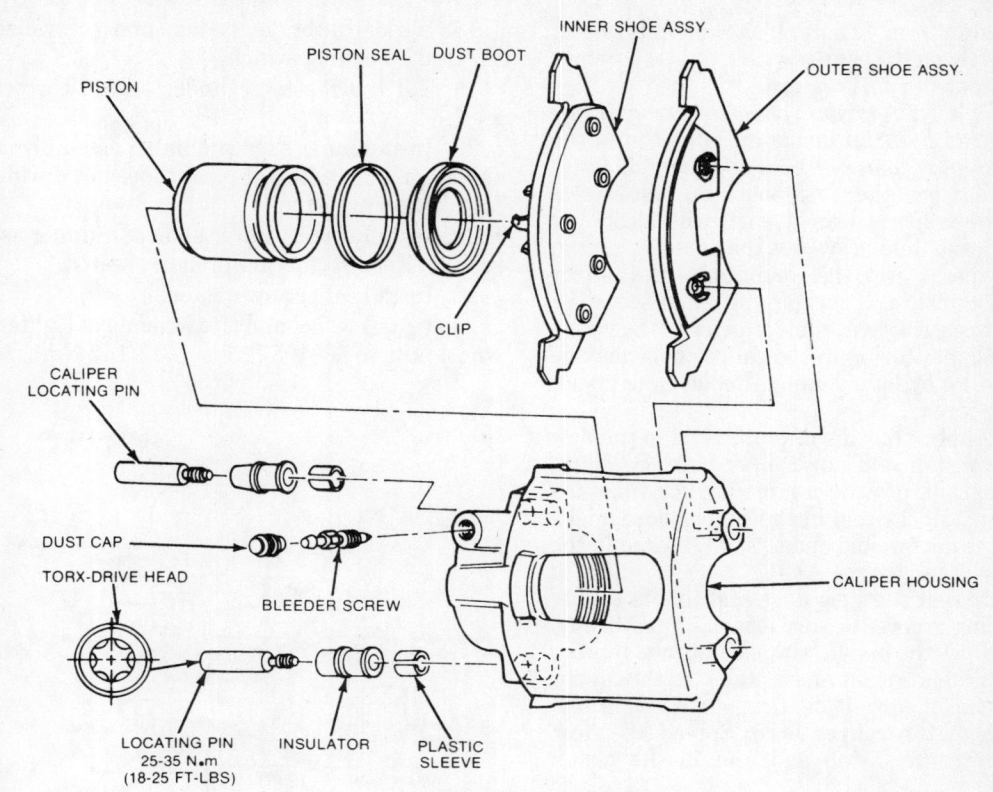

Caliper, exploded view

screw should be positioned on top of caliper when assembled on vehicle.

8. Lubricate locating pins and inside of insulators with silicone grease. Install locating pins through caliper insulators and into knuckle attaching holes. The caliper locating pins must be inserted and threads started by hand.

9. Using Torx drive bit D79P-2100-T40 or equivalent, tighten caliper locating pins to 18–25 ft. lbs. (24–34 Nm).

10. Remove plug and install brake hose on caliper with new gasket on each side of fitting outlet. Insert attaching bolt through washers and fittings. Tighten bolts to 30–40 ft. lbs. (40–54 Nm).

11. Bleed brake system. Always replace rubber bleed screw cap after bleeding.

12. Fill master cylinder as required.

13. Install wheel and tire assembly. Tighten wheel nuts to 80–105 ft. lbs. (109–142 Nm).

14. Connect negative battery cable.

15. Pump brake pedal prior to moving vehicle to position brake linings.

16. Road test vehicle.

OVERHAUL

1. Remove master cylinder cap and check fluid level in reservoir. Remove brake fluid until reservoir is $1/2$ full. Discard removed fluid.

2. Raise and safely support the vehicle.

3. Remove wheel.

4. Disconnect the hydraulic brake hose from the caliper. To disconnect the hose, loosen the tube fitting at the frame bracket. Remove the horseshoe clip from between the hose and bracket. Remove the hollow bolt fastening the hose to the caliper and remove the hose. Do not loosen the two gaskets used in mounting the brake hose to the caliper.

5. Back out the Torx® headed caliper locating pins. DO NOT REMOVE THEM ALL THE WAY! If removed, the pins are difficult to install and require new guide bushings.

6. Lift caliper assembly from integral knuckle and anchor plate and rotor using rotating motion. Do not pry directly against plastic piston or damage will occur.

7. Remove outer shoe and lining assembly.

8. Remove inner shoe and lining assembly.

9. The next step requires a controllable air source. If you have one fine, if not take the caliper(s) to your local gas station and ask them to do Step 5 for you.

10. Place a folded cloth, shop rag, etc. over the caliper piston. Apply air pressure through the brake line fitting hole with a rubber tipped air blow gun. The air pressure will force the cal-

524 BRAKES

iper piston from its bore. If the piston is seized, tap lightly on the caliper with a plastic hammer while applying air pressure.

CAUTION: *Apply air pressure slowly. Pressure can built up inside the caliper and the piston may come out with considerable force.*

11. Remove the dust boot and piston seal from the caliper. Clean all parts with alcohol or clean brake fluid. Blow out the passage ways in the caliper. Check the condition of the caliper bore and piston. If they are pitted or scored or show excessive wear, replacement will be necessary. Slight scoring in the caliper bore may be cleaned up by light honing. Replace the piston if it is scored.

12. Apply a coating of brake fluid to the new caliper piston seal and caliper bore. Some rebuilding kits provide a lubricant for this purpose. Install the seal in the caliper bore, make sure it is not twisted and is firmly seated in the groove.

13. Install the new dust seal in the caliper mounting groove, be sure it is mounted firmly.

14. Coat the piston with clean brake fluid or the special lubricant and install it in the caliper bore, make sure it is firmly seated in the bottom of the caliper bore. Spread the dust boot over the piston and seat in the piston groove.

15. Install the brake pads as outlined in the previous section.

16. Install the caliper over the rotor. Mount the caliper as described in the previous section.

17. Install the bake hose to the caliper. Be sure to use a new gasket on each side of the hose fitting. Position and install the upper end of the hose, remember to put the horseshoe clip in place, take care not to twist the hose.

18. Bleed the brake system and centralize the brake warning switch.

19. Fill the master cylinder to the correct level.

20. Install inner shoe and lining assembly in caliper piston(s). Do not bend shoe clips during installation in piston.

21. Install correct outer shoe and lining assembly. Ensure clips are properly seated.

22. Install caliper over rotor.

23. Install wheel and tire assembly. Tighten wheel nuts to 80–105 ft. lbs. (109–142 Nm).

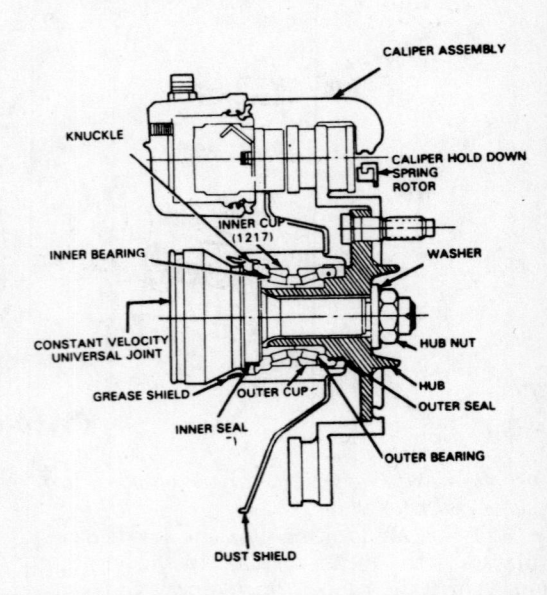

Cross section of the front wheel bearings — through 1982

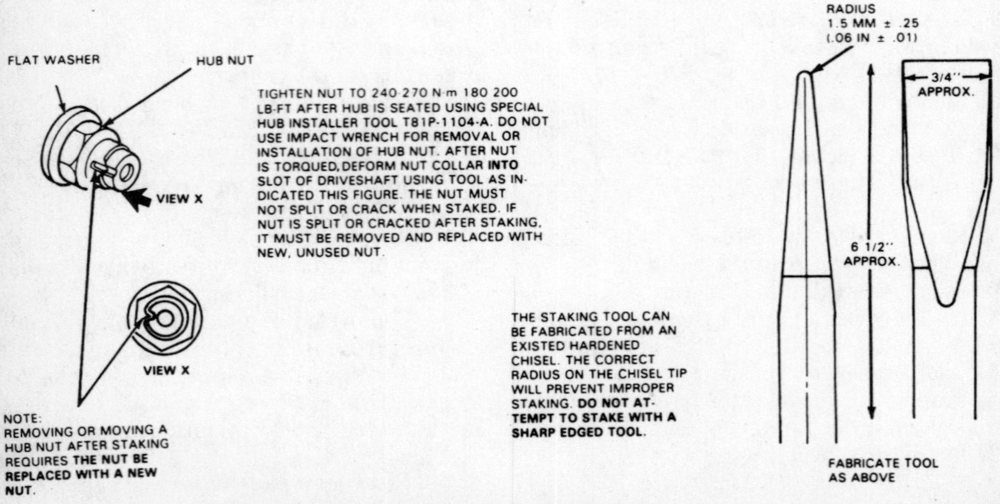

How to stake the front wheel retainer nut

BRAKES 525

Front Brake Disc (Rotor)

REMOVAL AND INSTALLATION

1. Disconnect the negative battery cable.
2. Raise and safely support the vehicle.
3. Remove wheel and tire assembly.
4. Remove caliper locating pins.
5. Lift caliper assembly from integral knuckle and anchor plate and rotor using rotating motion. Do not pry directly against plastic piston or damage will occur.
6. Position caliper out of the way and support it with a length of wire to avoid damaging caliper.
7. Remove rotor from hub assembly by pulling it off the hub studs.

To install:

8. If rotor is being replaced, remove protective coating from new rotor with carburetor degreaser. If original rotor is being installed, make sure rotor braking and mounting surfaces are clean.
9. Install rotor on hub assembly.
10. Install caliper assembly on rotor.

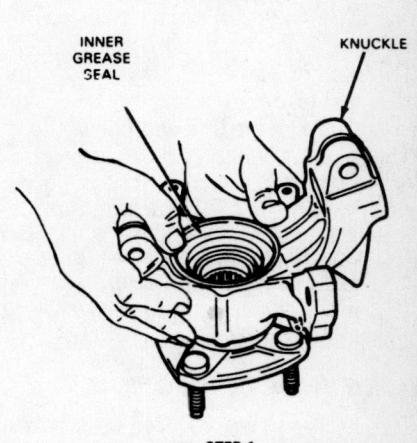

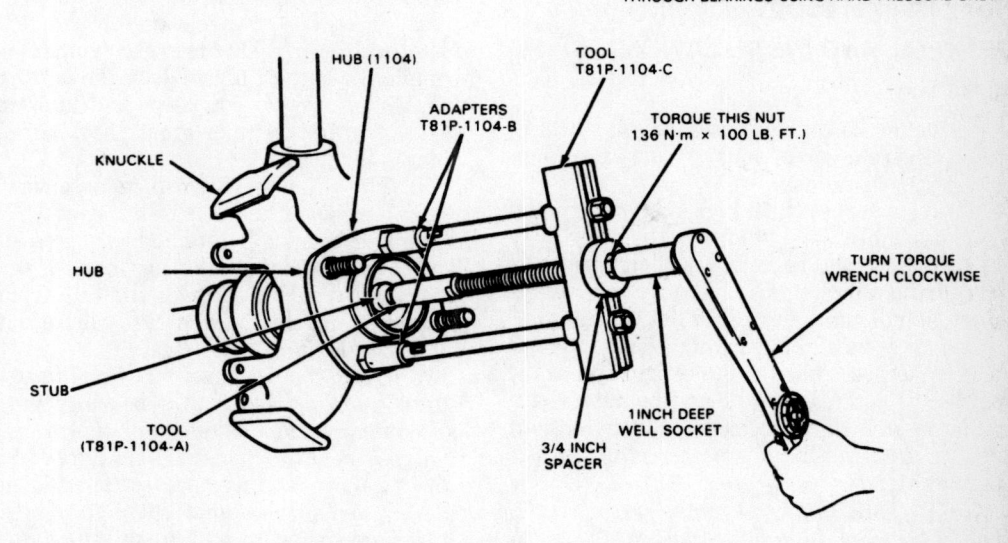

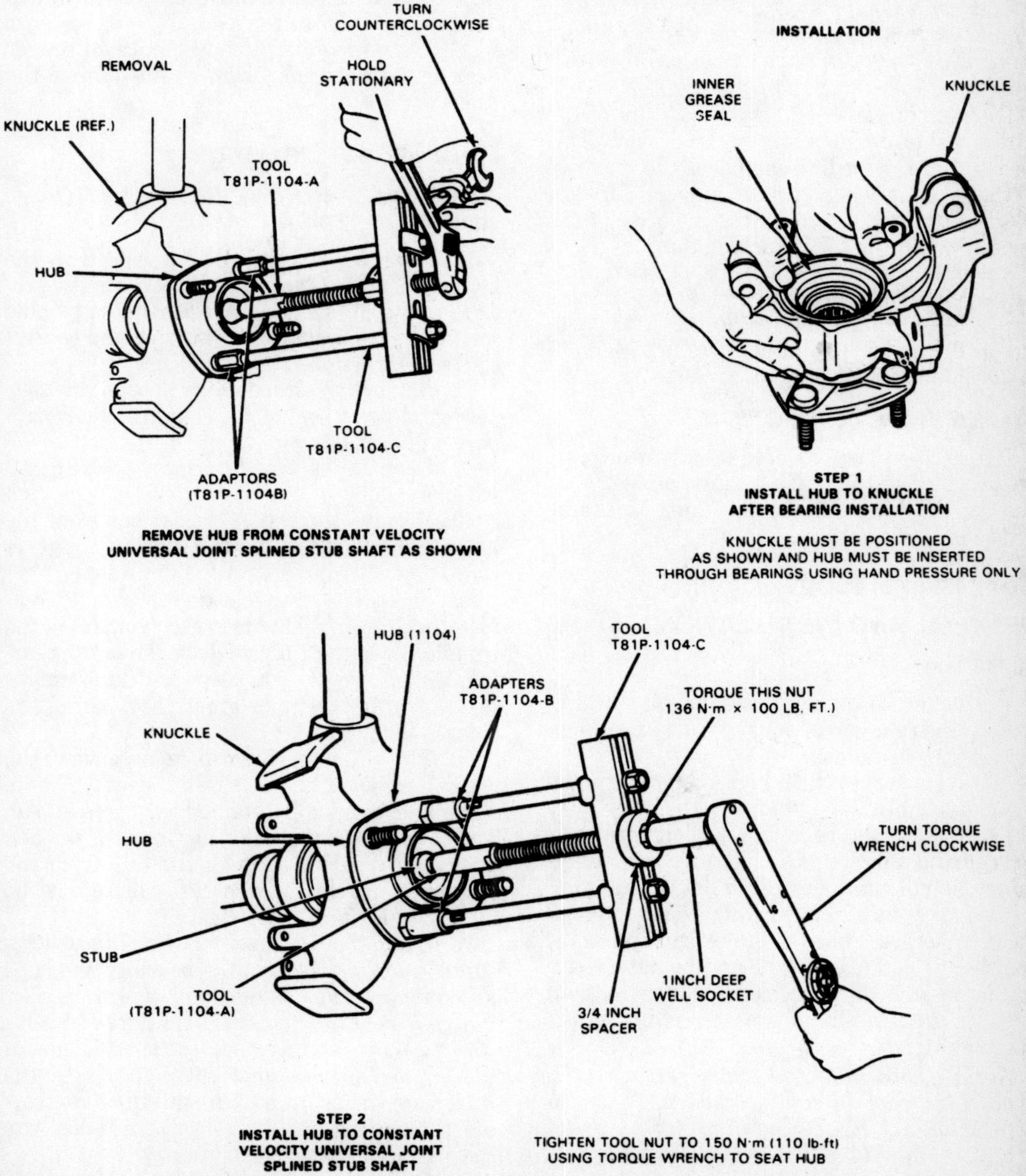

Using the front stub shaft remover/installer tool

526 BRAKES

11. Install wheel and tire assembly. Tighten wheel nuts to 80–105 ft. lbs. (109–142 Nm).
12. Pump brake pedal prior to moving vehicle to position brake linings.
13. Connect negative battery cable.
14. Road test vehicle.

REAR BRAKES

CAUTION: *Some brake pads contain asbestos, which has been determined to be a cancer causing agent. Never clean the brake surfaces with compressed air! Avoid inhaling any dust from any brake surface! When cleaning brake surfaces, use a commercially available brake cleaning fluid.*

The rear brakes used on your car are of the non-servo leading/trailing shoe design. This means that the leading shoe does the majority of the braking when the car is going forward and the trailing shoe does the majority of the braking when the car is backing up.

The brakes are self-adjusting. The only time any adjustment should be necessary is during servicing of brake shoe replacement. Depending on the model of your car, either 178mm (7 in.) or 203mm (8 in.) brakes are used.

BRAKE SHOE INSPECTION

Two access holes, covered by a rubber plug, are provided in the brake backing plate. By removing the plugs the brake lining thickness and condition can be inspected.

Rear Brake Drum

REMOVAL AND INSTALLATION

All Models

1. Remove the wheel cover, loosen the lugs, jack up the rear end of your car and safely support it on jackstands.
2. Remove the wheel lugs and the tire and wheel assembly.
3. Remove the center grease car from the brake drum hub. Remove the cotter pin, nut retainer, spindle nut, and keyed flat washer.
4. Make sure the parking brake is completely released. Slide the brake drum off of the spindle. Be careful not to drop the outer bearing. Make sure that you keep the drum straight and not drag the inner grease seal across the spindle threads.

NOTE: *If the hub and drum assembly will not slide off of the spindle, the brake shoe adjustment will have to be backed off.*

On 178mm (7 in.) brakes: Insert a thin blade screwdriver in to the inspection slot until it contacts the adjuster assembly pivot. Apply side pressure on the pivot point to allow the adjuster quadrant to ratchet and release the brake adjustment.

On 203mm (8 in.) brakes: Remove the brake line to axle bracket to gain enough room so a thin bladed screwdriver and brake adjusting tool may be inserted in the inspection slot. Push the adjusting lever away from the adjuster screw wheel. Back off the star wheel with the adjusting tool.

5. Inspect the brake drum for scoring, etc. Have the drum turned if necessary. Perform any necessary brake work. Pack the wheel bearings if required. Reinstall the brake drum in the reverse order of removal. Consult the next section on rear wheel bearing service for proper bearing adjustment when reinstalling the brake drum.

Rear Wheel Bearings

REMOVAL, PACKING, INSTALLATION AND ADJUSTMENT

The rear wheel bearings are located in the brake drum hub. The inner wheel bearing is protected by a grease seal. A washer and spindle nut retain the hub/drum assembly and control the bearing endplay.

1. Remove the wheel cover, loosen the lugs, jack up the rear end of your car and safely support it on jackstands.
2. Remove the wheel lugs and the tire and wheel assembly.
3. Remove the center grease car from the brake drum hub. Remove the cotter pin, nut retainer, spindle nut, and keyed flat washer.
4. Make sure the parking brake is completely released. Slide the brake drum off of the spindle. Be careful not to drop the outer bearing. Make sure that you keep the drum straight and not drag the inner grease seal across the spindle threads.
5. The outer bearing will be loose when the drum is removed and may be lifted out by hand. The inner bearing is retained by a grease seal. To remove the inner bearing, insert a wooden dowel or soft drift through the hub from the outer bearing side and carefully drive out the inner bearing and grease seal.
6. Clean the bearings, cups and hubs with a suitable solvent. Inspect the bearings and cups for damage or heat discoloring. Replace as a set if necessary. Always install a new grease seal.
7. If new bearings are to be used, use a three jawed slidehammer puller to remove the cups from the drum hub. Install the new bearing cups using a suitable driver. Make sure they are fully seated in the hub.
8. Pack the bearings with a multi-purpose grease. (See the front wheel bearing section for packing instructions).

9. Coat the cups with a thin film of grease. Install the inner bearing and grease seal.

10. Coat the bearing surfaces of the spindle with a thin film of grease. Slowly and carefully slide the drum and hub over the spindle and brake shoes. Install the outer bearing over the spindle and into the hub.

11. Install the keyed flat washer and adjusting nut on the spindle.

12. Tighten the adjusting nut to between 17–25 ft. lbs.

13. Back off the adjusting nut $1/2$ turn. Then retighten it to between 10–15 inch lbs.

14. Position the nut retainer on the nut and install the cotter pin. Do not tighten the nut to install the cotter pin.

15. Spread the ends of the cotter pin and bend then around the nut retainer. Install the center grease cap.

16. Install the tire and wheel assembly. Lower the car and tighten the wheel lugs.

Rear Brake Shoes Tips

After any brake service work, obtain a firm brake pedal before moving the car. Adjusted brakes must not put a drag on the wheel, the wheel must turn freely.

The rear brakes are self-adjusting and require adjustment only after new shoes have been installed or service work has been done which required the disassembly of the brake shoes.

When adjusting the rear brake shoes, make sure the parking brakes cables are not adjusted too tightly.

After the brakes have been installed and adjusted, check the operation of the brakes by making several stops from varying speeds. Readjust if necessary.

REMOVAL AND INSTALLATION

178mm (7 in.) Rear Brakes

1. Raise and safely support the vehicle.
2. Remove wheel and tire assembly. Remove hub and drum assembly.
3. Remove the holddown pins and springs by pushing down on and rotating the outer washer 90°. It may be necessary to hold the back of the pin (behind the backing plate) while pressing down and turning the washer.
4. After the holddown pins and spring have been removed from both brake shoes, remove both shoes and the adjuster assembly by lifting up and away from the bottom anchor plate and shoe guide. Take care not to damage the wheel cylinder boots when removing the shoes from the wheel cylinder.
5. Remove the parking brake cable from the brake lever to allow the removal of the shoes and adjuster assembly.
6. Remove the lower shoe to shoe spring by rotating the leading brake shoe to release the spring tension. Do not pry the spring from the shoe.
7. Remove the adjuster strut from the trailing shoe by pulling the strut away from the shoe and twisting it downward toward yourself until the spring tension is released. Remove the spring from the slot.
8. Remove the parking brake lever from the trailing shoe by disconnecting the horseshoe clip and spring washer and pulling the lever from the shoe.
9. If for any reason the adjuster assembly must be taken apart, do the following: pull the adjuster quadrant (U-shaped lever) away from the knurled pin on the adjuster strut by rotating the quadrant in either direction until the teeth are no longer engaged with the pin. Remove the spring and slide the quadrant out of the slot on the end of the adjuster strut. Do not put too much stress on the spring during disassembly.

To install:

10. Clean the brake backing (mounting) plate with a soft paint brush or vacuum cleaner.

CAUTION: *Never inhale the dust from the brake linings. Asbestos dust when inhaled can be injurious to your health. Use a vacuum cleaner. Do not blow off the dust with air pressure.*

11. Apply a thin film of high temperature grease at the points on the backing plate where the brake shoes make contact.

12. Apply a thin film of multi-purpose grease to the adjuster strut at the point between the quadrant and strut.

13. If the adjuster has been disassembled, install the quadrant mounting pin into the slot on the adjuster strut and install the adjuster spring.

14. Assemble the parking brake lever to the trailing shoe. Install the spring washer and a new horseshoe clip, squeeze the clip with pliers until the lever is secured on the shoe.

15. Install the adjuster strut attaching spring on to the trailing shoe. Attach the adjusting strut by fastening the spring in the slot and pivoting the strut into position. This will tension the spring. Make sure the end of the spring where the hook is parallel to the center line of the spring coils is hooked into the web of the brake shoe. The installed spring should be flat against the web and parallel to the adjuster strut.

16. Install the shoe to shoe spring with the longest hook attached to the trailing shoe.

528 BRAKES

178mm (7 in.) rear brakes

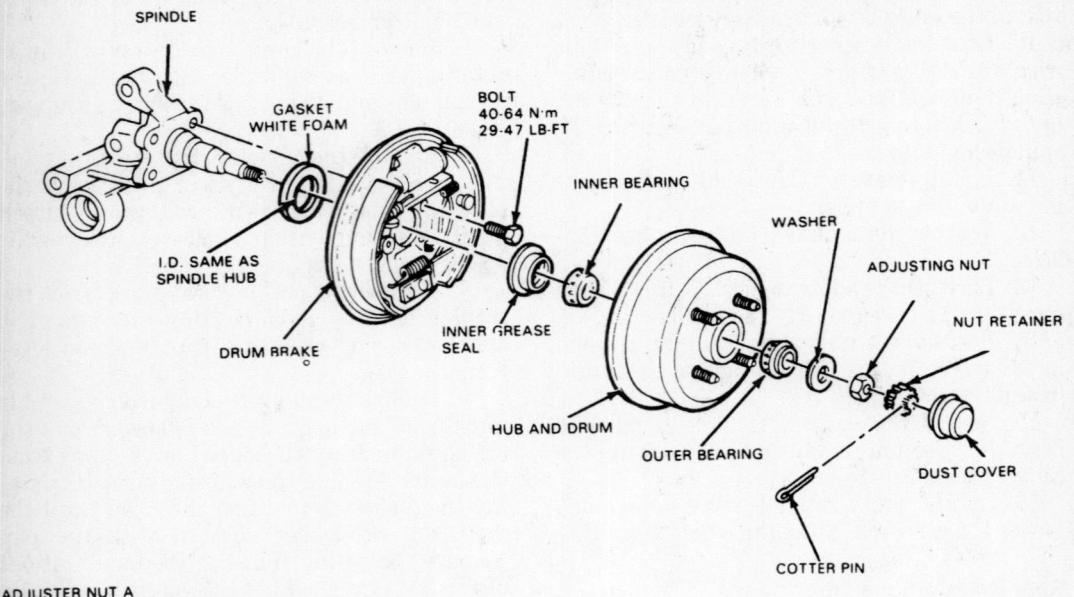

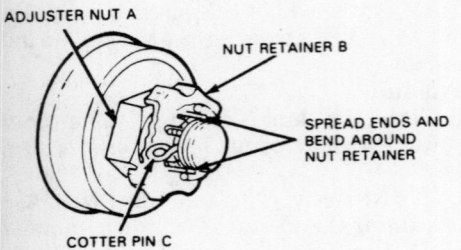

BEARING ADJUSTMENT: TIGHTEN ADJUSTING NUT "A" TO 23-34 N·m (17-25 LB-FT) WHILE ROTATING HUB AND DRUM ASSEMBLY. BACK OFF ADJUSTING NUT APPROXIMATELY 100 DEGREES. POSITION NUT RETAINER "B" OVER ADJUSTING NUT SO SLOTS ARE IN LINE WITH COTTER PIN HOLE WITHOUT ROTATING ADJUSTING NUT. INSTALL COTTER PIN.

NOTE: THE SPINDLE HAS A PREVAILING TORQUE FEATURE THAT PREVENTS ADJUSTING THE NUT BY HAND.

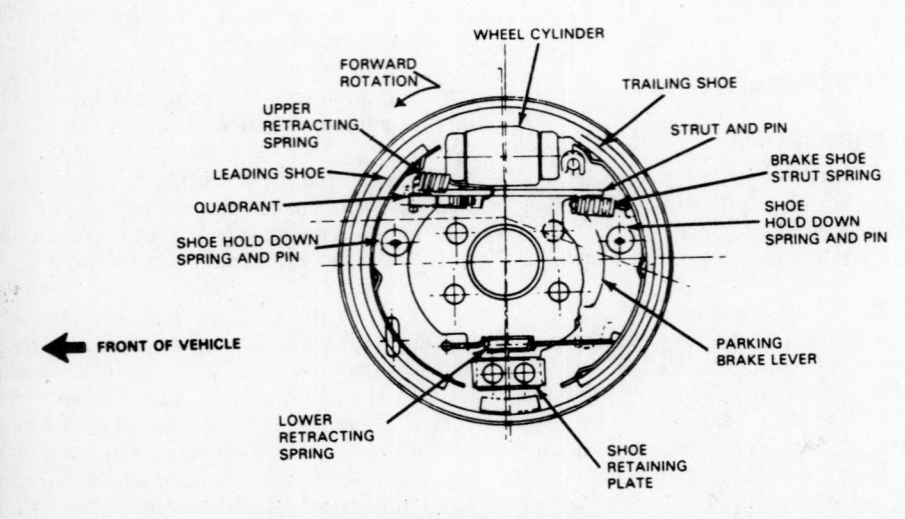

BRAKES 529

17. Install the leading shoe to adjuster strut spring by installing the spring to both parts and pivoting the leading shoe over the quadrant and into position, this will tension the spring.

18. Place the shoes and adjuster assembly onto the backing plate. Spread the shoes slightly and position them into the wheel cylinder piston inserts and anchor plate. Take care not to damage the wheel cylinder boots.

19. Attach the parking brake cable to the parking brake lever.

20. Install the holddown pins, springs, and washers.

21. Adjust the brakes as described in the proceeding brake adjustment section.

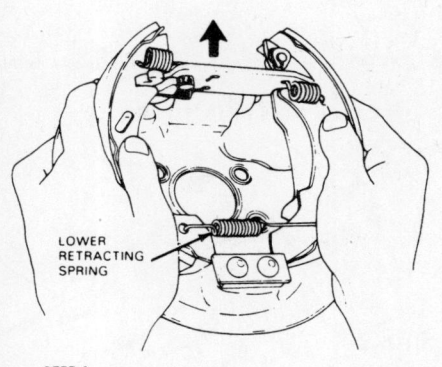

STEP 1

a. Remove holddown springs and pins.
b. Lift assembly off backing plate.
c. Disengage parking brake cable.
d. Remove lower retracting spring.

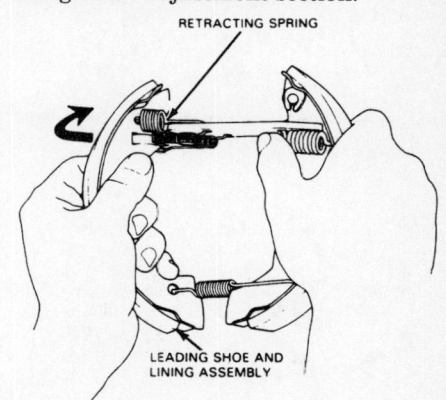

STEP 2

Remove leading shoe retracting spring by rotating shoe as shown to release spring tension. Do not pry spring off shoe.

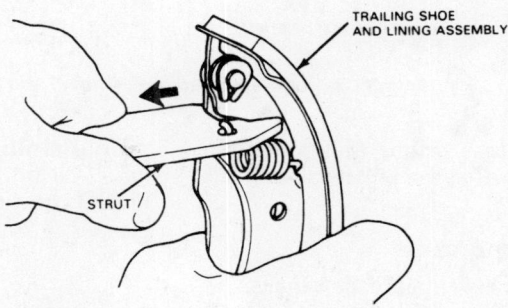

STEP 3a

Remove strut to trailing shoe and lining assembly by pulling strut away from shoe and...

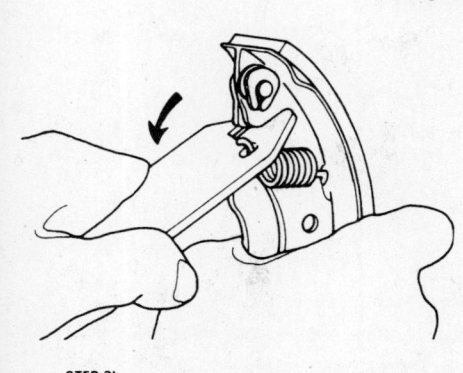

STEP 3b

...twisting strut downward

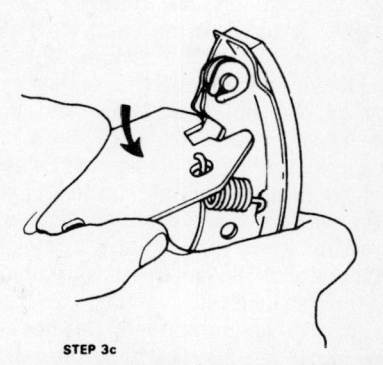

STEP 3c

...toward technician until spring tension is released. Remove spring from slots.

Removing the 178mm (7 in.) rear brake shoes

530 BRAKES

REMOVAL PROCEDURE

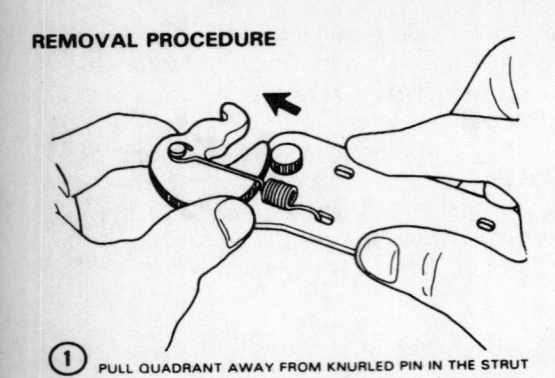

① PULL QUADRANT AWAY FROM KNURLED PIN IN THE STRUT

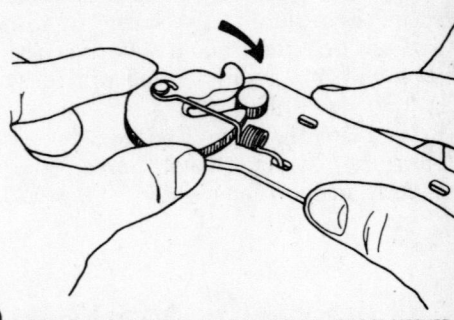

② ROTATE QUADRANT UNTIL TEETH ARE NO LONGER MESHED PIN.

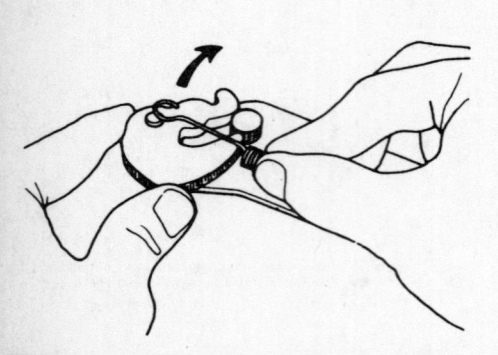

INSTALLATION PROCEDURE

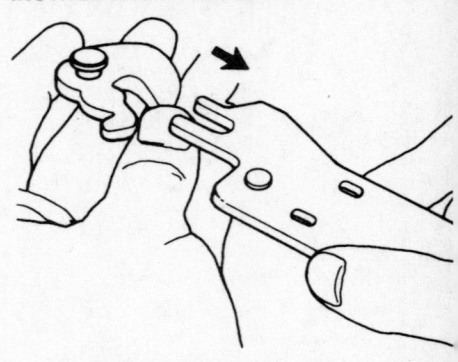

③ REMOVE THE SPRING AND SLIDE QUADRANT OUT OF STRUT — BE CAREFUL NOT TO OVERSTRESS SPRING.

INSTALL ADJUSTER QUADRANT PIN INTO SLOT IN STRUT. TU ASSEMBLY OVER AND INSTALL SPRING.

178mm (7 in.) brakes; quadrant removal and installation

22. Install the rear drums and adjust the bearings as described in the previous section.

203mm (8 in.) Rear Brakes

1. Raise and safely support the vehicle.
2. Remove wheel and tire assembly.
3. Remove hub and drum assembly.
4. Remove the holddown pins and springs by pushing down on and rotating the outer washer 90°. It may be necessary to hold the back of the pin (behind the backing plate) while pressing down and turning the washer.
5. After the holddown pins and springs have been removed, remove both shoes and the adjuster assembly by lifting up and away from the anchor plate and wheel cylinder. Take care not to damage the wheel cylinder boots or bend the adjusting lever.
6. Disconnect the parking brake cable from the parking brake lever.
7. Remove the lower shoe to shoe spring and the upper spring attaching the adjusting lever to the brake shoe. This will separate the brake shoes and disengage the adjuster.
8. Spread the horseshoe clip and remove the parking brake lever from the trailing shoe.

To install:
9. Clean the brake backing (mounting) plate with a soft paint brush or vacuum cleaner.

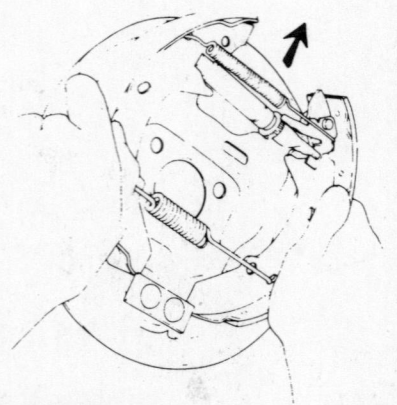

REMOVAL PROCEDURE
1. REMOVE BRAKE SHOE HOLDDOWN SPRINGS AND PINS
2. LIFT ASSEMBLY OFF THE BACKING PLATE.
3. REMOVE PARKING BRAKE CABLE FROM THE PARKING BRAKE.
4. REMOVE RETRACTING SPRINGS AND ADJUSTING LEVEL.

203mm (8 in.) brakes; removal

BRAKES 531

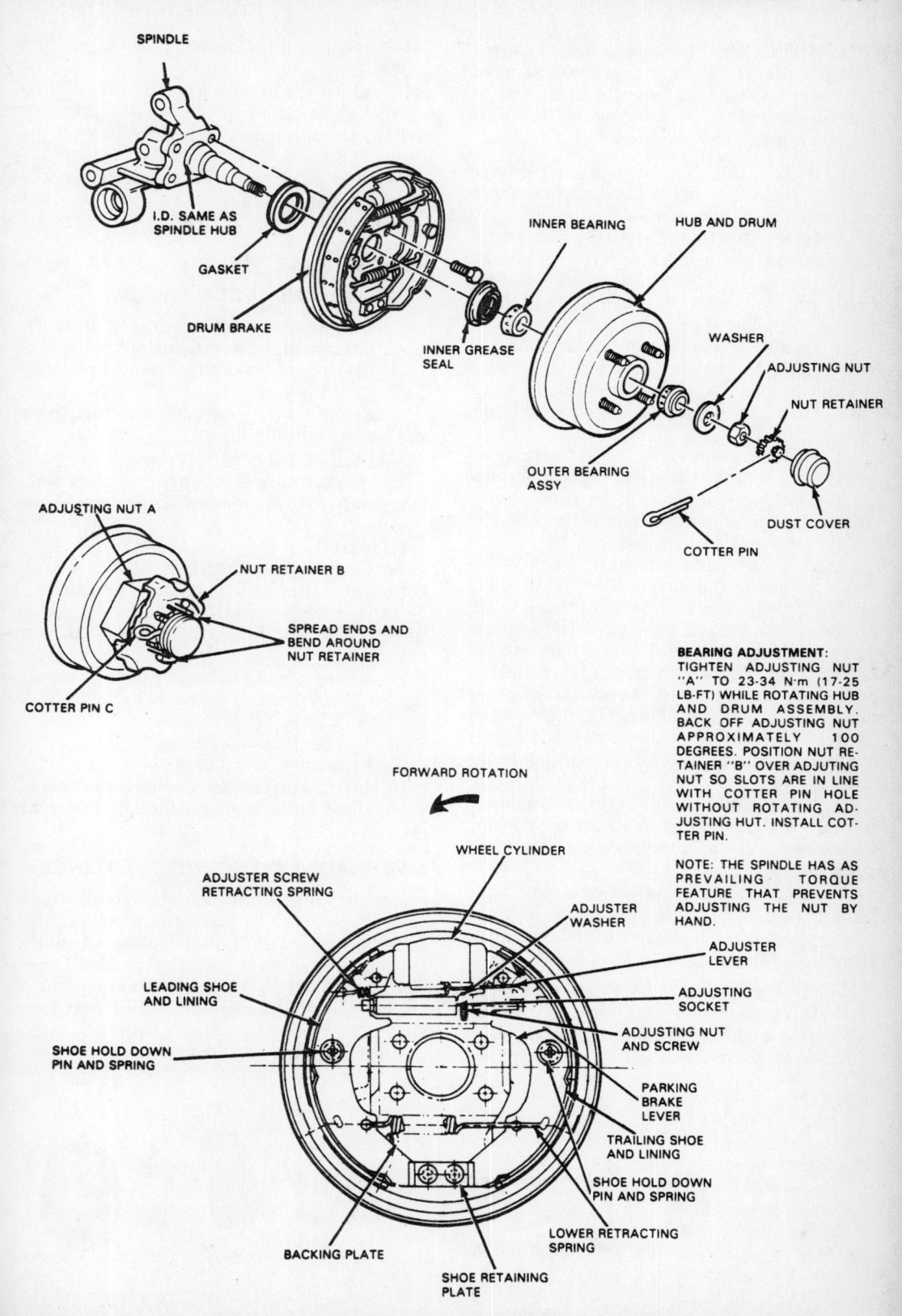

BEARING ADJUSTMENT: TIGHTEN ADJUSTING NUT "A" TO 23-34 N·m (17-25 LB-FT) WHILE ROTATING HUB AND DRUM ASSEMBLY. BACK OFF ADJUSTING NUT APPROXIMATELY 100 DEGREES. POSITION NUT RETAINER "B" OVER ADJUSTING NUT SO SLOTS ARE IN LINE WITH COTTER PIN HOLE WITHOUT ROTATING ADJUSTING NUT. INSTALL COTTER PIN.

NOTE: THE SPINDLE HAS AS PREVAILING TORQUE FEATURE THAT PREVENTS ADJUSTING THE NUT BY HAND.

203mm (8 in.) rear brakes

CAUTION: *Never inhale the dust from the brake linings! Asbestos dust when inhaled can be injurious to your health. Use a vacuum cleaner. Do not blow off the dust with air pressure.*

10. Apply a thin film of high temperature grease at the points on the backing plate where the brake shoes make contact.

11. Apply a thin film of multi-purpose grease to the threads of the adjuster screw and to the socket end of the adjuster. Turn the adjuster screw into the socket and then back off from bottom a number of threads.

12. Install the parking brake lever on the trailing shoe. Use a new horseshoe clip. Be sure to pull the spring washer in position. Connect the parking brake cable to the parking brake lever.

13. Attach the lower retracting spring between the two brake shoes and install the shoes on the backing plate. It will be necessary to spread the shoes apart to mount them on the anchor plate and wheel cylinder.

14. Install the adjuster screw assembly between the slot in the leading shoe and the slots in the trailing shoe and parking brake lever. Lengthen the screw if necessary. The adjuster socket blades are marked **L** for left side or **R** for right side and fit onto the trailing shoe and the parking brake lever (slots provided). The letter must face up toward the wheel cylinder when the blade is installed. This permits the deeper of the two slots to fit onto the parking brake lever.

15. Install the adjusting lever, also marked **L** or **R**, by sliding the groove over the parking brake lever pin slot and into a groove on the starwheel.

16. Attach the upper retracting spring to the leading shoe anchor hole. Use a pair of brake spring pliers, stretch the spring and attach the other end onto the adjuster lever notch.

NOTE: *If the adjuster lever does not contact the star wheel after installing the spring, make sure that the adjuster socket is installed correctly. (see Step 7).*

17. Install the hold down pins, spring and washers.

18. Adjust the brakes, using a brake adjusting tool as described in the brake adjustment section. Do not adjust with shoe drag on the drum. The wheel must turn freely.

19. Install the brake drum and adjust the wheel bearings.

20. Lower the car and road test.

Rear Wheel Cylinder

REMOVAL AND INSTALLATION

1. Remove wheel and hub/drum assemblies.
2. Remove brake shoe assembly.
3. Disconnect brake tube from wheel cylinder.
4. Remove wheel cylinder attaching bolts and remove wheel cylinder.

NOTE: *Use caution to prevent brake fluid from contacting brake linings and drum braking surface. Contaminated linings must be replaced.*

To install:

5. Ensure ends of hydraulic fittings are free of foreign matter before making connections.
6. Position wheel cylinder and foam seal on backing plate and finger-tighten brake tube to cylinder.
7. Secure cylinder to backing plate by installing attaching bolts. Tighten bolts to 8–10 ft. lbs. (10–14 Nm).
8. Tighten tube nut fitting.
9. Install and adjust brakes.
10. Install hub/drum and wheel assembly.
11. Bleed brake system before driving vehicle.

OVERHAULING THE WHEEL CYLINDER

Wheel cylinders need not be rebuilt unless they are leaking. To check the wheel cylinder for leakage, carefully pull the lower edge of the rubber end boot away from the cylinder. Excessive brake fluid in the boot or running out of the boot, when the edges are pulled away from the cylinder, denotes leakage. A certain (slight) amount of fluid in the boot is normal.

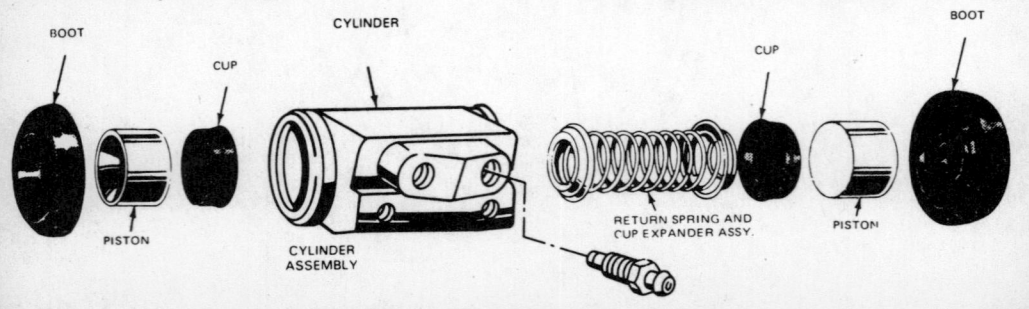

Exploded view of a rear wheel brake cylinder

BRAKES

1. It is not necessary to remove the cylinder from the brake backing (mounting) plate to rebuild the cylinder, however removal makes the job easier.

2. Disengage and remove the rubber boots from both ends of the wheel cylinder. The piston should come out with the boot. If not, remove the piston by applying finger pressure inward on one piston, the piston on the opposite end should come out. Take care not to splash brake fluid all over yourself when the piston pops from the cylinder.

3. Remove the rubber cups, center expander and spring from the wheel cylinder. Remove the bleeder screw from the back of the cylinder.

4. Discard all rubber boots and cups. Wash the pistons and cylinder in denatured alcohol or clean brake fluid.

5. Inspect the pistons for scratches, scoring or other visible damage. Inspect the cylinder bore for score marks or rust. The cylinder may be honed (with a brake cylinder hone) if necessary. Do not hone more than 0.076mm (0.003 in.) beyond original diameter. If the scoring or pitting is deeper, replace the cylinder.

6. After honing the cylinder, wash again with alcohol or clean brake fluid. Check the bleeder screw hole to make sure it is opened. Wipe the cylinder bore with a clean cloth. Install the bleeder screw.

7. Never reuse the old rubber parts. Always use all of the parts supplied in the rebuilding kit.

8. Apply a light coat of brake fluid, or the special lubricant if supplied with the rebuilding kit, on the pistons, rubber cups and cylinder bore.

9. Insert the spring and expander assembly into the cylinder bore. Put the cups, facing in, and the pistons into the cylinder. Install the boots and fit the outer lips into the retaining grooves on the outer edges of the wheel cylinder.

10. Install the wheel cylinder onto the backing plate. Be sure that the inlet port (where the brake hose connects) is toward the rear of the car. Install the brake shoes, drum and wheel assembly. Adjust and bleed the brake system. Road test the car.

PARKING BRAKE

The parking brake control is hand operated and mounted on the floor between the front seats. When the control lever is pulled up (from the floor) an attached cable applies the rear brakes.

Cable

REMOVAL AND INSTALLATION

1981–85 Models

1. Pull up slowly on the control lever and stop at the seventh notch position, count the clicks as you pull up on the handle. The adjusting nut is now accessible. Remove the adjusting nut. Completely release the control handle (push the release button and lower to the floor.

2. Raise the car and safely support on jackstands.

3. Disconnect the rear parking brake cables from the front equalizer and rod assembly.

4. If the front equalizer and rod assembly is to be replaced, drill out the rivets that hold the cable guide to the floor pan. Remove the equalizer and rod assembly from the parking brake control lever and withdraw it through the floor pan.

5. To install the front equalizer and rod assembly, feed the adjusting rod end of the assembly through the floor pan and into the parking control lever clevis. Attach the cable guide to the floor pan using new pop rivets. Borrow a pop rivet gun from a friend.

6. If the rear parking brake cable is to be replaced, first disconnect from the front equalizer and rod assembly. Remove the hairpin clip

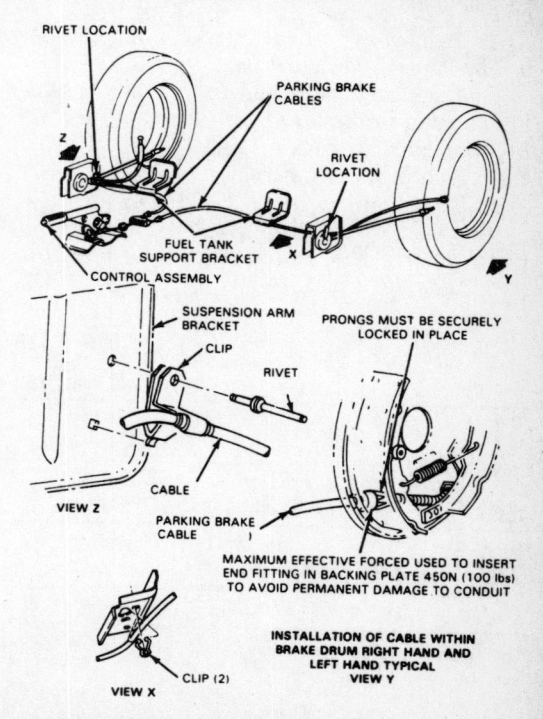

Parking brake cable installation

BRAKES

that holds the cable to the floor pan tunnel bracket.

7. Remove the wire retainer that hold the cable to the fuel tank mounting bracket. Remove the cable from the retaining clip.

8. Remove the rear tire and wheel assemblies and the brake drums.

9. Disconnect the parking brake cable from the trailing shoe parking brake levers. Depress the cable prongs that hold the cable in the backing plate hole. Remove the cable through the holes.

10. Installation is in the reverse order of removal.

11. Adjust the parking brake cable as per instructions in the next section.

1986–90 Models

1. Place control assembly in seventh notch position and loosen adjusting nut. Completely release control assembly.

2. Raise vehicle. Remove rear parking brake cable from equalizer.

3. Remove hairpin clip holding cable to floor pan tunnel bracket.

4. Remove wire retainer holding cable to fuel tank mounting bracket. Remove cable from wire retainer. Remove cable and clip from the fuel pump bracket (EFI only).

5. Remove screw holding cable retaining clip to rear side member. Remove cable from clip.

6. Remove wheel cover, wheel and tire assembly and rear brake drum.

7. Disengage cable end from brake assembly parking brake lever. Depress cable prongs holding cable to backing plate. Remove cable through hole in backing plate.

To install:

8. Insert cable through hole in backing plate. Attach cable end to rear brake assembly parking brake lever.

9. Insert conduit end fitting into backing plate. Ensure retention prongs are locked into place.

10. Insert cable into rear attaching clip and attach clip to rear side member with screw.

11. Route cable through bracket in floor pan tunnel and install hairpin retaining clip.

12. Install cable end into equalizer.

13. Insert cable into wire retainer and snap retainer into hole in fuel tank mounting bracket. On vehicles equipped with EFI, insert cable and install clip into fuel pump bracket.

14. Install rear drum, wheel and tire assembly and wheel cover.

15. Lower vehicle.

16. Adjust parking brake.

CABLE ADJUSTMENT

1. If a new cable has been installed, the parking brake lever control should be in the seventh notch and the adjusting nut run down to the approximate position it was removed from. Release the hand brake and pump the brake pedal several times. If you car has power brakes, start the engine and allow it to idle when pumping the brakes. Shut off the engine.

2. Apply the service brake approximately 3 times before adjusting the parking brake. On vehicles equipped with power brakes, the engine must be running.

3. Place the control lever in the twelfth notch, two notches before complete application. Tighten the adjusting nut until the rear brakes have a slight drag when the parking brake control lever is completely released. Repeat the parts of this step as necessary.

4. Reposition the control assembly in the 12th notch. Loosen the adjusting nut just enough to eliminate rear brake drag when the control assembly is fully released.

5. Lower the car and test the parking brake application.

BRAKE SPECIFICATIONS

(All specifications in inches)

Year	Model	Brake Disc Original Thickness	Brake Disc Minimum Thickness	Maximum Run-out	Brake Drum Orig. Inside Dia.	Brake Drum Maximum Machine O/S	Wheel Cyl. or Caliper Bore Front	Wheel Cyl. or Caliper Bore Rear
1981–86 w/7 in. rear brake	All	0.945	0.882	0.002	7.090	7.149	2.362	0.81
w/8 in. rear brake		0.945	0.882	0.002	8.000	8.060	2.362	0.811
1987–90 w/7 in. rear brake	All	0.945	0.882	0.003	7.090	7.149	2.362	0.81
w/8 in. rear brake		0.945	0.882	0.003	8.000	8.060	2.362	0.811

① Tempo/Topaz: 0.875 in.

Body 10

EXTERIOR

NOTE: *The electronic control modules, including the EEC processors (on board computer), may be damaged if the negative battery cable is not disconnected before any arc welding is done to the vehicle. This occurs because the arc welding process can produce high electrical currents in the body of the vehicle when the negative battery cable is left connected. Always disconnect the negative battery cable before using any electric welding equipment.*

Doors

REMOVAL

1. Remove the trim panel, watershield, and all usable outside moldings and clips (if the door is to be replaced).
2. Remove all usable window and door latch components from the door.
3. Support the door.
4. Remove the door hinge attaching bolts from the door and remove the door.
5. Disconnect any wiring harness connectors, if so equipped.

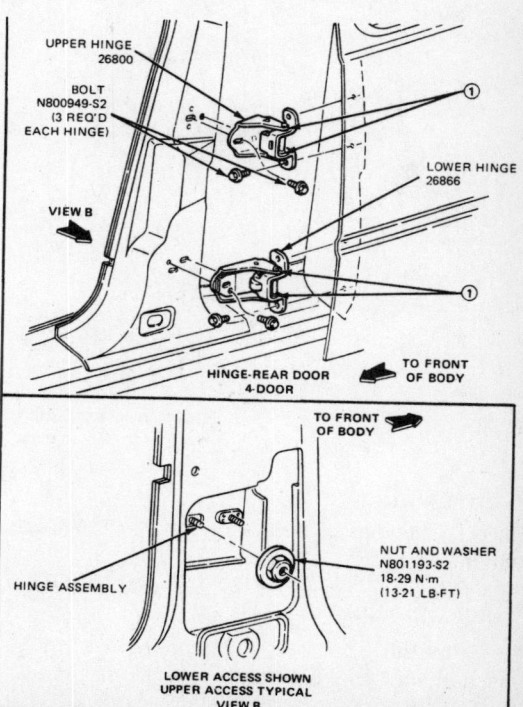

Parking brake cable installation

536 BODY

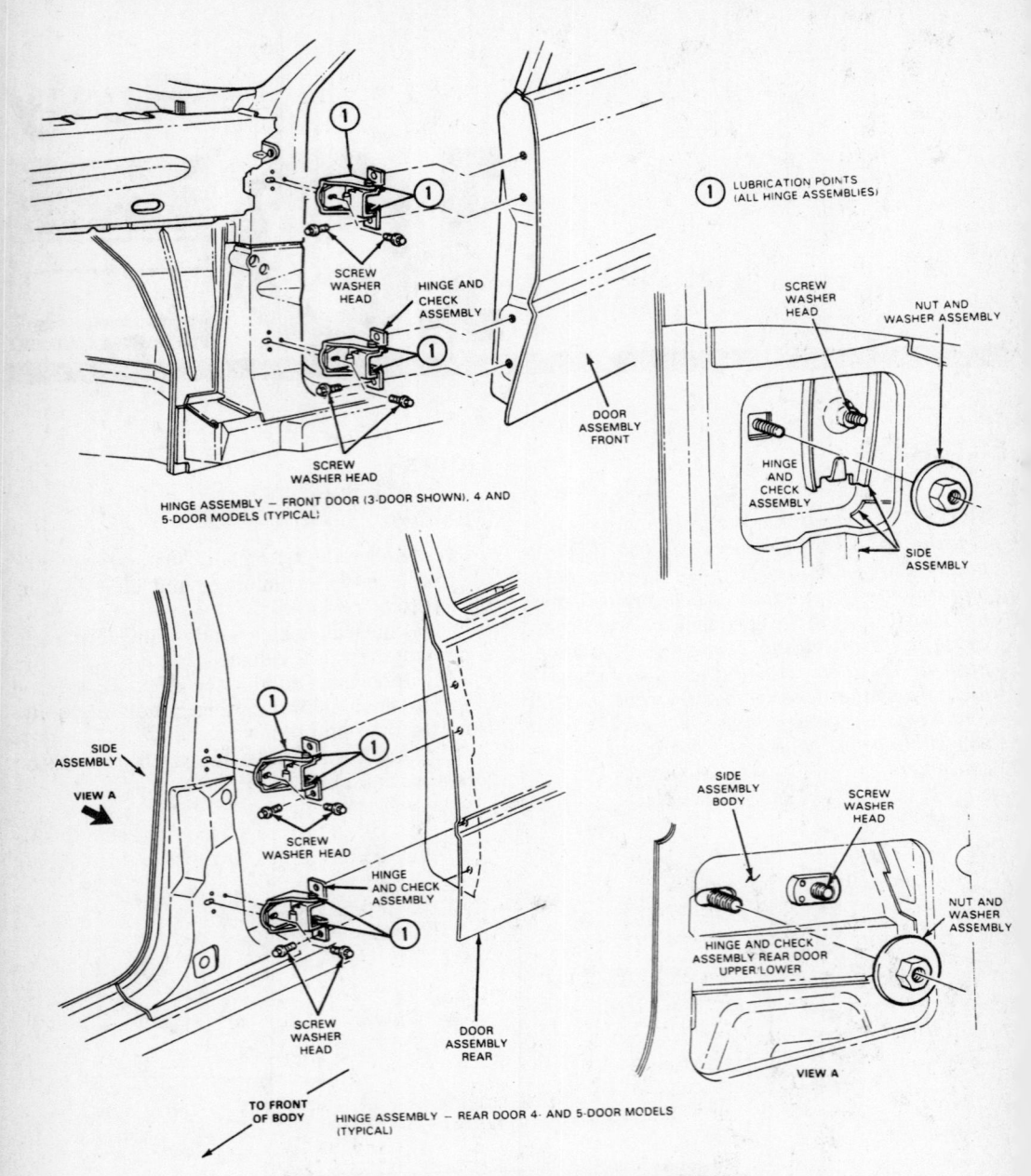

Door hinge assembly — Escort/Lynx, EXP/LN7

To install:

6. Drill holes, as necessary, for attaching outside molding.
7. Position the door hinges and partially tighten the bolts.
8. Install the latch mechanism, window mechanism, glass and glass weatherstripping. Adjust the window mechanism.
9. Install the exterior trim, watershield, and the interior trim.

ADJUSTMENTS

Door Alignment

The door hinges provide sufficient adjustment to correct most door misalignment conditions. The holes of the hinge and/or the hinge attaching points are enlarged or elongated to provide for hinge and door alignment.

NOTE: *DO NOT cover up a poor alignment with a latch striker adjustment.*

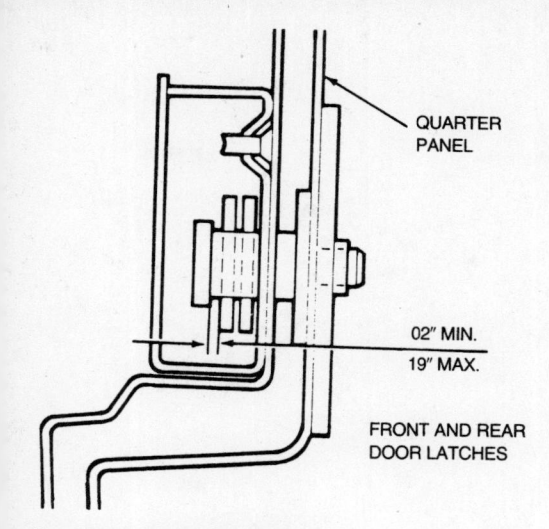

BODY 537

Door latch striker adjustment

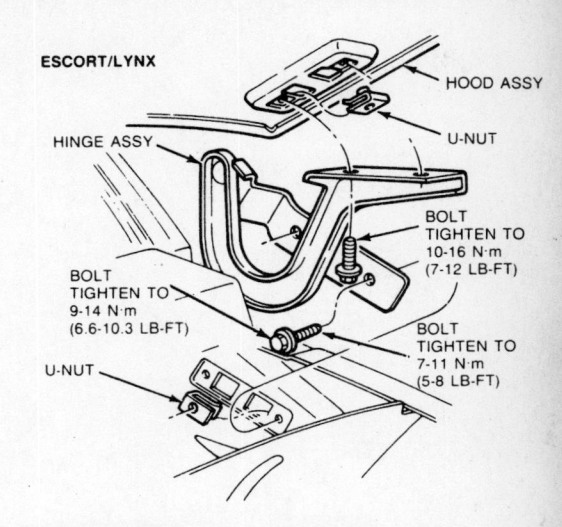

Hood hinge assembly — Escort/Lynx

SIDE DOOR ADJUSTMENT

1. Refer to the illustration to determine which hinge screws must be loosened to move the door in the desired direction.
2. Loosen the hinge screws just enough to permit movement of the door with a padded pry bar.
3. Move the door the distance estimated to be necessary for a correct fit. Tighten the hinge bolts and check the door fit to be sure there is no bind or interference with the adjacent panel.

DOOR LATCH STRIKER ADJUSTMENT

The door latch striker pin can be adjusted laterally and vertically as well as for and aft. The latch striker should not be adjusted to correct the door sag.

The latch striker should be shimmed to get the clearance shown in the illustration, between the striker and the latch. To check this clearance, clean the latch jaws and striker area. Apply a thin layer of dark grease to the striker. As the door is closed and opened, a measurable pattern will result on the latch striker.

NOTE: *Use a maximum of two shims under the striker.*

Hood

REMOVAL AND INSTALLATION

1. Open the hood and prop in the open position.
2. Cover the cowl area to prevent damage to the paint.
3. With the aid of a helper to hold the hood, remove the hinge bolts to the hood and remove the hood from the vehicle.
4. Installation is the reverse of removal.

Torque the hinge-to-hood bolts to 12–19 ft. lbs. Close the hood, check the alignment and adjust as necessary.

ALIGNMENT

The hood can be adjusted fore and aft and side to side by loosening the hood-to-hinge attaching bolts and reposition the hood. To raise or lower the hood, loosen the hinge hood on body attaching bolts and raise or lower the hinge as necessary.

The hood lock can be moved from side-to-side and up and down and laterally to obtain a snug

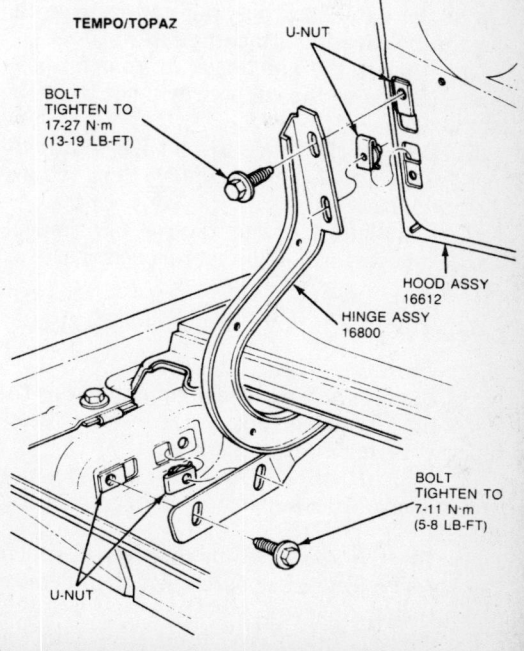

Hood hinge assembly — Tempo/Topaz

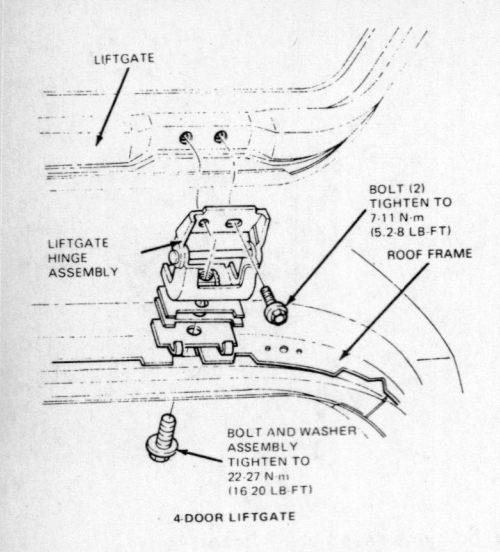

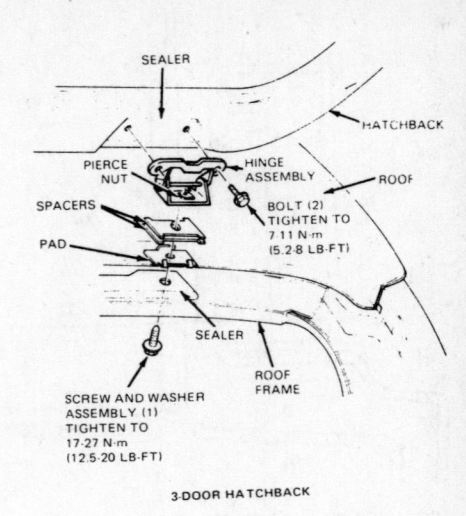

Hatchback and liftgate hinge assembly — Escort/Lynx, EXP/LN7

hood fit by loosening the lock attaching screws and moving as necessary.

Hatchback, Liftgate or Trunk Lid

REMOVAL AND INSTALLATION

Hatchback

1. Open the hatchback assembly.
2. Remove the weatherstripping along the top of the hatchback opening and remove the headlining covering attaching screw.
3. Support the hatchback in an open position and remove the support cylinder from the hatchback.
4. Remove the hinge to roof frame attaching screw and washer assembly, then remove the hatchback.
5. Installation is the reverse of removal. Check and perform alignment as necessary.

Liftgate

1. Open the liftgate assembly.
2. Remove the weatherstripping along the top of the liftgate opening and remove the headlining covering attaching screw.
3. Support the liftgate in an open position and remove the support cylinder from the liftgate.
4. Remove the hinge to roof frame attaching screw and washer assembly, then remove the liftgate.
5. Installation is the reverse of removal. Check and perform alignment as necessary.

HATCHBACK, LIFTGATE OR TRUNK LID ALIGNMENT

Hatchback Hinge

Escort/Lynx, EXP/LN-7 — 3-Door Hatchback

The hatchback can be adjusted fore-and-aft, and side-to-side by loosening the hinge to roof frame attaching screw at each hinge.

To adjust the hinge, pull down on the weatherstrip across the entire top edge of the hatchback opening. Carefully loosen and pull down the headlining to expose the access holes to the hinge screws. Adjust the hinge as necessary. Seal the hinge after adjustment with clear silicone sealer. Apply trim cement to the sheet metal flange, and install the headlining and smooth out any wrinkles. Install the weatherstrip.

The hatchback can be adjusted in and out by shimming the hinge at the header roof frame.

The hatchback should be adjusted for an even and parallel fit with the hatchback opening and shrouding panels.

Liftgate hinge

ESCORT/LYNX — 4-DOOR LIFTGATE

On the 4-door liftgate models the liftgate can be adjusted up and down and side to side by loosening the header roof frame attaching screw and washer assembly. The liftgate can be adjusted in and out by shimmering the hinge at the header roof frame.

The liftgate should be adjusted for an even parallel fit with the liftgate opening and surrounding panels.

To adjust a hinge, or hinges, remove th

weatherstrip and pull down the headliner to gain access to the hinge attachment(s). Adjust the hinge(s) as necessary. Seal the hinge after adjustment with clear silicone sealer. Apply trim cement to the sheet metal flange, and install the headlining and smooth out any wrinkles. Install the weatherstrip.

Trunk Lid

Tempo/Topaz

The trunk lid can be shifted fore and aft on all models and from side to side. The up and down adjustment is made by loosening the hinge to door attaching screws and raising or lowering the door.

The trunk lid should be adjusted for an even and parallel fit with the lid opening. The door should also be adjusted up and down for a flush fit with the surrounding panels. Care should be taken not to distort or mar the trunk lid or surrounding body panels.

Bumpers

REMOVAL AND INSTALLATION

Front Bumper

1981-85 MODELS

1. Remove all necessary trim molding and guards from the bumper in order to gain access to the bumper retaining bolts.
2. If the vehicle is equipped with the optional (long) bumper extension assemblies with attachments to the fender, remove the 2 screws through the tab on the inside surface of the extension assemblies.
3. Remove the isolator to reinforcement screws and retaining nut and remove the bumper assembly from the vehicle.

To install:

4. Transfer bumper guards, rub strip, extension assemblies, pads and license plate bracket and bumper mounting brackets to replacement bumper.

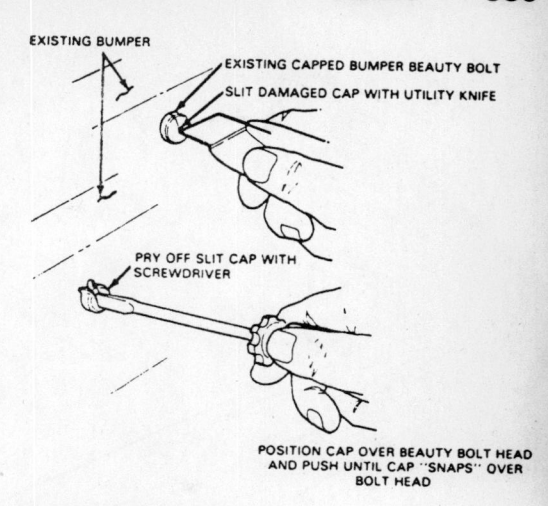

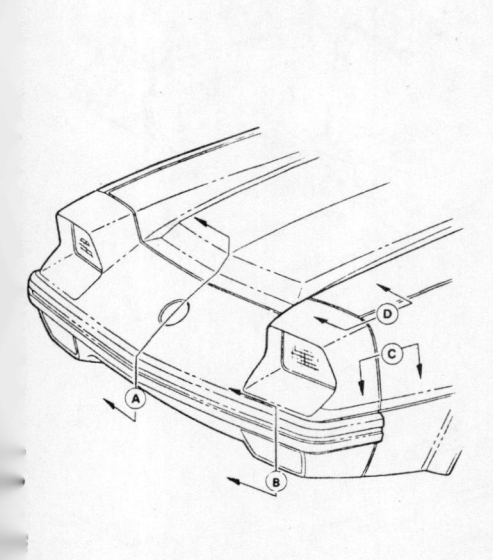

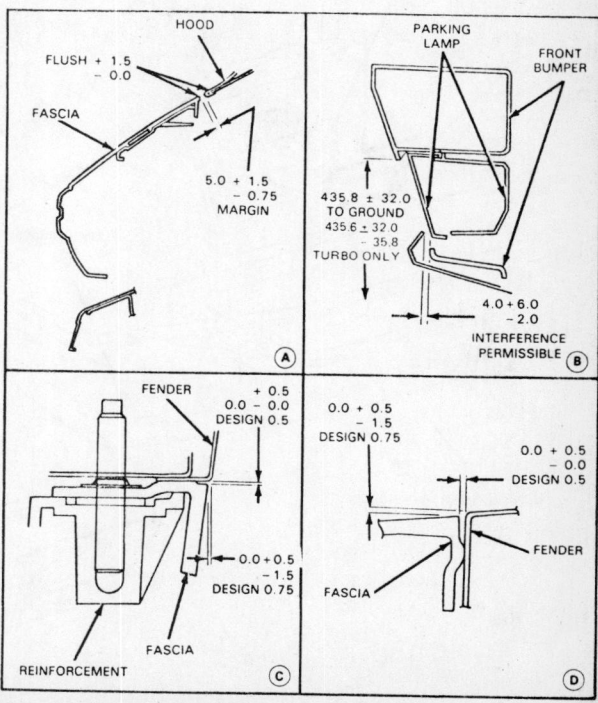

Bumper bolt cap removal

Bumper clearance specifications — EXP

540　BODY

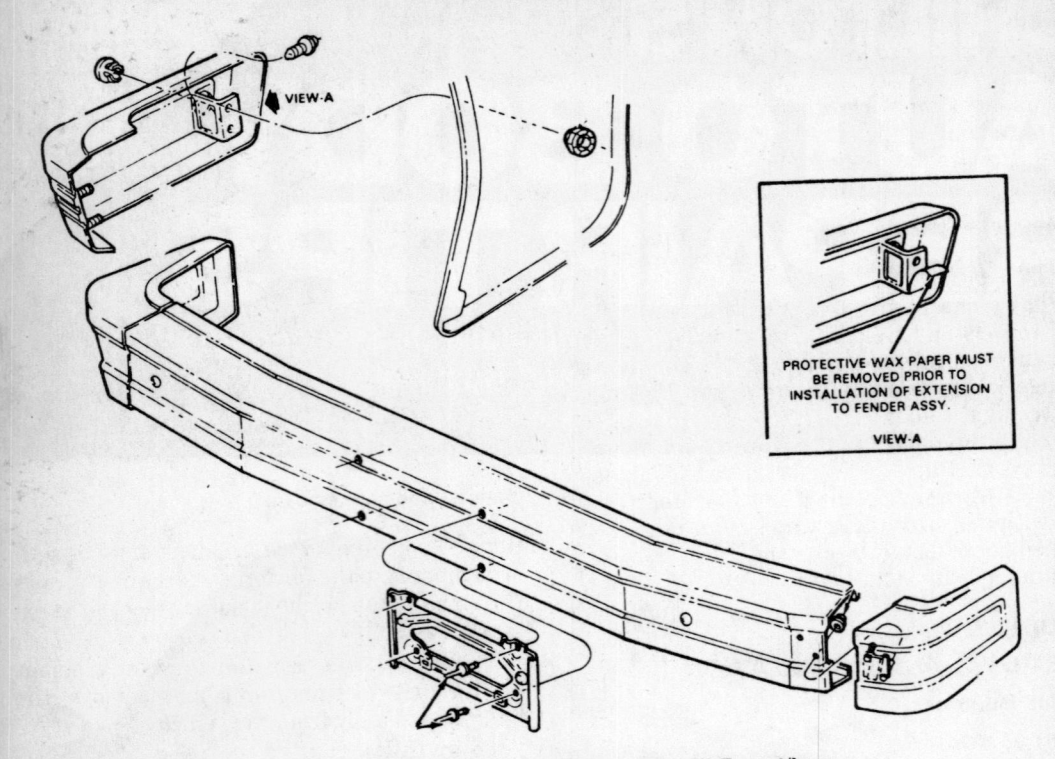

PROTECTIVE WAX PAPER MUST BE REMOVED PRIOR TO INSTALLATION OF EXTENSION TO FENDER ASSY.

VIEW-A

Typical front bumper assembly — 1981–85 Escort/Lynx

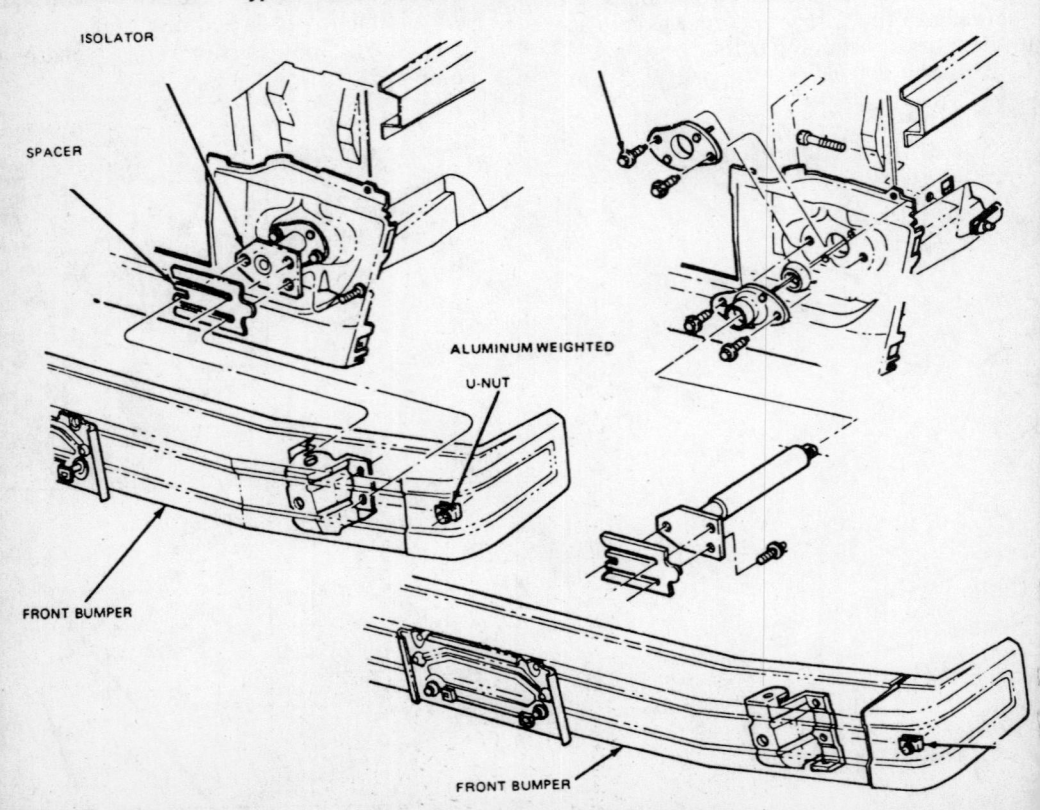

ISOLATOR

SPACER

ALUMINUM WEIGHTED

U-NUT

FRONT BUMPER

FRONT BUMPER

Tuned (weighted) aluminum front bumper

CHILTON'S
AUTO BODY REPAIR TIPS

**Tools and Materials • Step-by-Step Illustrated Procedures
How To Repair Dents, Scratches and Rust Holes
Spray Painting and Refinishing Tips**

EASY STEP-BY-STEP TIPS FROM PROS

With a little practice, basic body repair procedures can be mastered by any do-it-yourself mechanic. The step-by-step repairs shown here can be applied to almost any type of auto body repair.

TOOLS & MATERIALS

You may already have basic tools, such as hammers and electric drills. Other tools unique to body repair — body hammers, grinding attachments, sanding blocks, dent puller, half-round plastic file and plastic spreaders — are relatively inexpensive and can be obtained wherever auto parts or auto body repair parts are sold. Portable air compressors and paint spray guns can be purchased or rented.

Auto Body Repair Kits

The best and most often used products are available to the do-it-yourselfer in kit form, from major manufacturers of auto body repair products. The same manufacturers also merchandise the individual products for use by pros.

Kits are available to make a wide variety of repairs, including holes, dents and scratches and fiberglass, and offer the advantage of buying the materials you'll need for the job. There is little waste or chance of materials going bad from not being used. Many kits may also contain basic body-working tools such as body files, sanding blocks and spreaders. Check the contents of the kit before buying your tools.

BODY REPAIR TIPS

Safety

Many of the products associated with auto body repair and refinishing contain toxic chemicals. Read all labels before opening containers and store them in a safe place and manner.
- Wear eye protection (safety goggles) when using power tools or when performing any operation that involves the removal of any type of material.
- Wear lung protection (disposable mask or respirator) when grinding, sanding or painting.

Sanding

1 Sand off paint before using a dent puller. When using a non-adhesive sanding disc, cover the back of the disc with an overlapping layer or two of masking tape and trim the edges. The disc will last considerably longer.

2 Use the circular motion of the sanding disc to grind *into* the edge of the repair. Grinding or sanding away from the jagged edge will only tear the sand paper.

3 Use the palm of your hand flat on the panel to detect high and low spots. Do not use your fingertips. Slide your hand slowly back and forth.

WORKING WITH BODY FILLER

Mixing The Filler

1 Cleanliness and proper mixing and application are extremely important. Use a clean piece of plastic or glass or a disposable artist's palette to mix body filler.

1 Allow plenty of time and follow directions. No useful purpose will be served by adding more hardener to make it cure (set-up) faster. Less hardener means more curing time, but the mixture dries harder; more hardener means less curing time but a softer mixture.

2 Both the hardener and the filler should be thoroughly kneaded or stirred before mixing. Hardener should be a solid paste and dispense like thin toothpaste. Body filler should be smooth, and free of lumps or thick spots.

Getting the proper amount of hardener in the filler is the trickiest part of repairing the filler. Use the same amount of hardener in cold or warm weather. For contour filler (thick coats), a bead of hardener twice the diameter of the filler is about right. There's about a 5% margin on either side, but, if in doubt use less hardener.

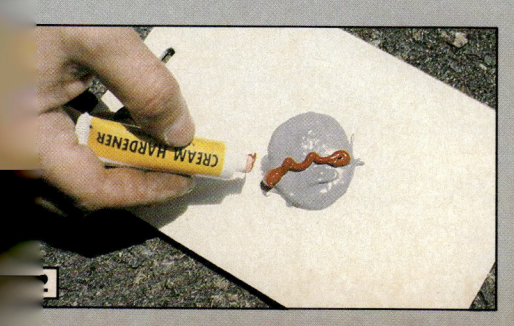

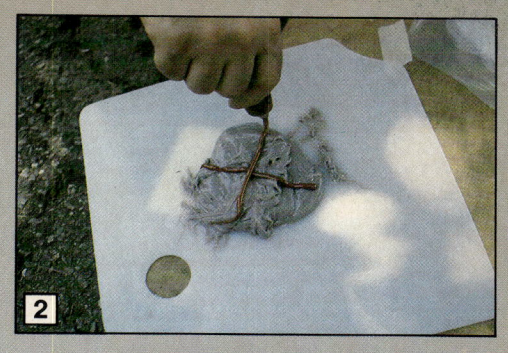

3 Mix the body filler and hardener by wiping across the mixing surface, picking the mixture up and wiping it again. Colder weather requires longer mixing times. Do not mix in a circular motion; this will trap air bubbles which will become holes in the cured filler.

Applying The Filler

1 For best results, filler should not be applied over 1/4" thick.

Apply the filler in several coats. Build it up to above the level of the repair surface so that it can be sanded or grated down.

The first coat of filler must be pressed on with a firm wiping motion.

Apply the filler in one direction only. Working the filler back and forth will either pull it off the metal or trap air bubbles.

REPAIRING DENTS

Before you start, take a few minutes to study the damaged area. Try to visualize the shape of the panel before it was damaged. If the damage is on the left fender, look at the right fender and use it as a guide. If there is access to the panel from behind, you can reshape it with a body hammer. If not, you'll have to use a dent puller. Go slowly and work the metal a little at a time. Get the panel as straight as possible before applying filler.

1 This dent is typical of one that can be pulled out or hammered out from behind. Remove the headlight cover, headlight assembly and turn signal housing.

2 Drill a series of holes ½ the size of the end of the dent puller along the stress line. Make some trial pulls and assess the results. If necessary, drill more holes and try again. Do not hurry.

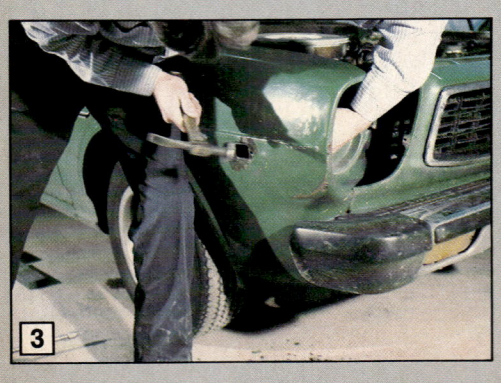

3 If possible, use a body hammer and block to shape the metal back to its original contours. Get the metal back as close to its original shape as possible. Don't depend on body filler to fill dents.

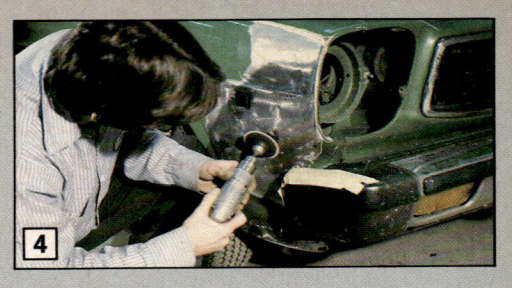

4 Using an 80-grit grinding disc on an electric drill, grind the paint from the surrounding area down to bare metal. Use a new grinding pad to prevent heat buildup that will warp metal.

5 The area should look like this when you're finished grinding. Knock the drill holes in and tape over small openings to keep plastic filler out.

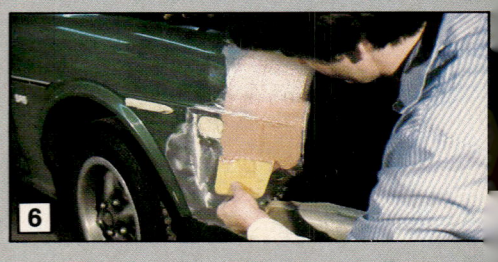

6 Mix the body filler (see Body Repair Tips). Spread the body filler evenly over the entire area (see Body Repair Tips). Be sure to cover the area completely.

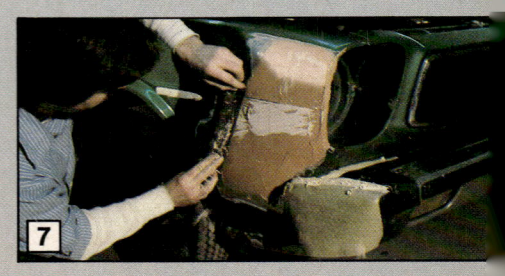

7 Let the body filler dry until the surface can just be scratched with your fingernail. Knock the high spots from the body filler with a body file ("Cheese grater"). Check frequently with the palm of your hand for high and low spots.

8 Check to be sure that trim pieces that will be installed later will fit exactly. Sand the area with 40-grit paper.

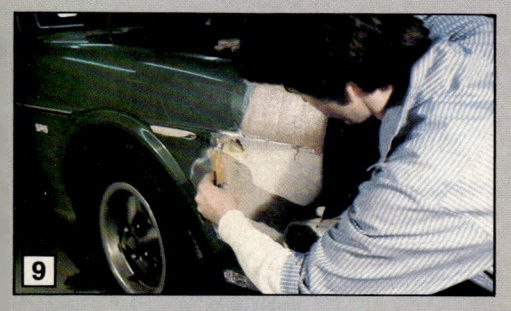

9 If you wind up with low spots, you may have to apply another layer of filler.

10 Knock the high spots off with 40-grit paper. When you are satisfied with the contours of the repair, apply a thin coat of filler to cover pin holes and scratches.

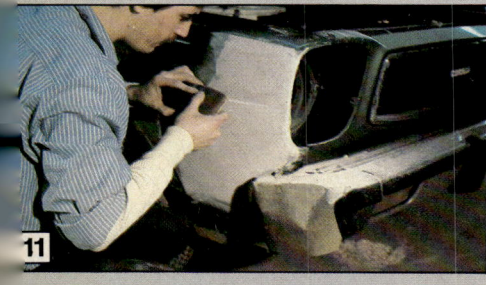

11 Block sand the area with 40-grit paper to a smooth finish. Pay particular attention to body lines and ridges that must be well-defined.

12 Sand the area with 400 paper and then finish with a scuff pad. The finished repair is ready for priming and painting (see Painting Tips).

Materials and photos courtesy of Ritt Jones Auto Body, Prospect Park, PA.

REPAIRING RUST HOLES

There are many ways to repair rust holes. The fiberglass cloth kit shown here is one of the most cost efficient for the owner because it provides a strong repair that resists cracking and moisture and is relatively easy to use. It can be used on large and small holes (with or without backing) and can be applied over contoured areas. Remember, however, that short of replacing an entire panel, no repair is a guarantee that the rust will not return.

1 Remove any trim that will be in the way. Clean away all loose debris. Cut away all the rusted metal. But be sure to leave enough metal to retain the contour or body shape.

2 Grind away all traces of rust with a 24-grit grinding disc. Be sure to grind back 3-4 inches from the edge of the hole down to bare metal and be sure all traces of paint, primer and rust are removed.

3 Block sand the area with 80 or 100 grit sandpaper to get a clear, shiny surface and feathered paint edge. Tap the edges of the hole inward with a ball peen hammer.

4 If you are going to use release film, cut a piece about 2-3" larger than the area you have sanded. Place the film over the repair and mark the sanded area on the film. Avoid any unnecessary wrinkling of the film.

5 Cut 2 pieces of fiberglass matte to match the shape of the repair. One piece should be about 1" smaller than the sanded area and the second piece should be 1" smaller than the first. Mix enough filler and hardener to saturate the fiberglass material (see Body Repair Tips).

6 Lay the release sheet on a flat surface and spread an even layer of filler, large enough to cover the repair. Lay the smaller piece of fiberglass cloth in the center of the sheet and spread another layer of filler over the fiberglass cloth. Repeat the operation for the larger piece of cloth.

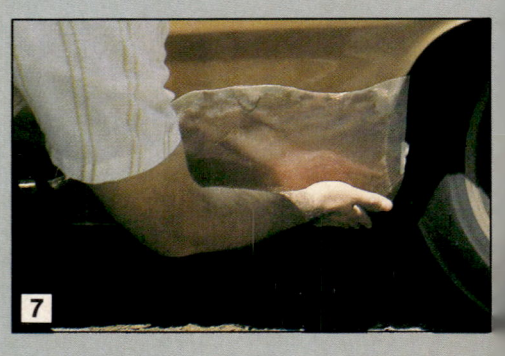

7 Place the repair material over the repair area, with the release film facing outward. Use a spreader and work from the center outward to smooth the material, following the body contours. Be sure to remove all air bubbles.

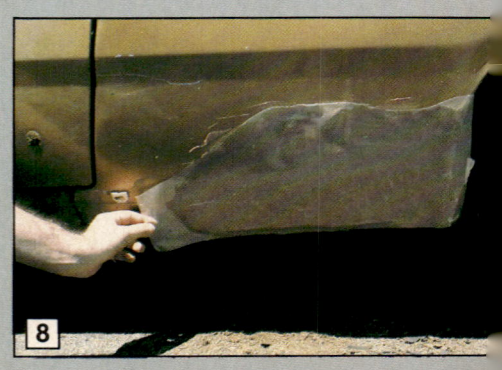

8 Wait until the repair has dried tack free and peel off the release sheet. The ideal working temperature is 60°-90° F. Cooler or warmer temperatures or high humidity may require additional curing time. Wait longer, if in doubt.

9 Sand and feather-edge the entire area. The initial sanding can be done with a sanding disc on an electric drill if care is used. Finish the sanding with a block sander. Low spots can be filled with body filler; this may require several applications.

10 When the filler can just be scratched with a fingernail, knock the high spots down with a body file and smooth the entire area with 80-grit. Feather the filled areas into the surrounding areas.

11 When the area is sanded smooth, mix some topcoat and hardener and apply it directly with a spreader. This will give a smooth finish and prevent the glass matte from showing through the paint.

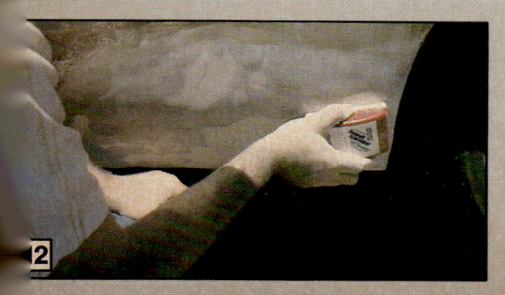

12 Block sand the topcoat smooth with finishing sandpaper (200 grit), and 400 grit. The repair is ready for masking, priming and painting (see Painting Tips).

Materials and photos courtesy Marson Corporation, Chelsea, Massachusetts

PAINTING TIPS

Preparation

1 SANDING — Use a 400 or 600 grit wet or dry sandpaper. Wet-sand the area with a 1/4 sheet of sandpaper soaked in clean water. Keep the paper wet while sanding. Sand the area until the repaired area tapers into the original finish.

2 CLEANING — Wash the area to be painted thoroughly with water and a clean rag. Rinse it thoroughly and wipe the surface dry until you're sure it's completely free of dirt, dust, fingerprints, wax, detergent or other foreign matter.

3 MASKING — Protect any areas you don't want to overspray by covering them with masking tape and newspaper. Be careful not get fingerprints on the area to be painted.

4 PRIMING — All exposed metal should be primed before painting. Primer protects the metal and provides an excellent surface for paint adhesion. When the primer is dry, wet-sand the area again with 600 grit wet-sandpaper. Clean the area again after sanding.

Painting Techniques

Paint applied from either a spray gun or a spray can (for small areas) will provide good results. Experiment on an old piece of metal to get the right combination before you begin painting.

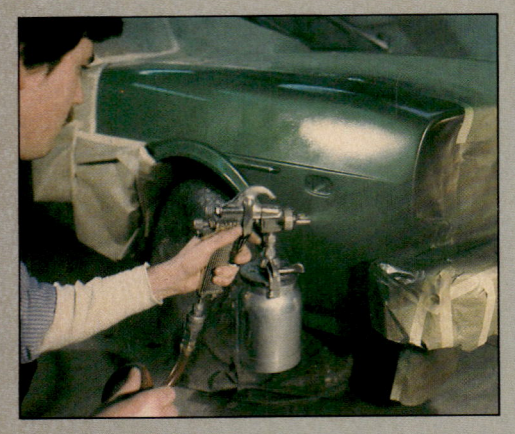

SPRAYING VISCOSITY (SPRAY GUN ONLY) — Paint should be thinned to spraying viscosity according to the directions on the can. Use only the recommended thinner or reducer and the same amount of reduction regardless of temperature.

AIR PRESSURE (SPRAY GUN ONLY) — This is extremely important. Be sure you are using the proper recommended pressure.

TEMPERATURE — The surface to be painted should be approximately the same temperature as the surrounding air. Applying warm paint to a cold surface, or vice versa, will completely upset the paint characteristics.

THICKNESS — Spray with smooth strokes. In general, the thicker the coat of paint, the longer the drying time. Apply several thin coats about 30 seconds apart. The paint should remain wet long enough to flow out and no longer; heavier coats will only produce sags or wrinkles. Spray a light (fog) coat, followed by heavier color coats.

DISTANCE — The ideal spraying distance is 8"-12" from the gun or can to the surface. Shorter distances will produce ripples, while greater distances will result in orange peel, dry film and poor color match and loss of material due to overspray.

OVERLAPPING — The gun or can should be kept at right angles to the surface at all times. Work to a wet edge at an even speed, using a 50% overlap and direct the center of the spray at the lower or nearest edge of the previous stroke.

RUBBING OUT (BLENDING) FRESH PAINT — Let the paint dry thoroughly. Runs or imperfections can be sanded out, primed and repainted.

Don't be in too big a hurry to remove the masking. This only produces paint ridges. When the finish has dried for at least a week, apply a small amount of fine grade rubbing compound with a clean, wet cloth. Use lots of water and blend the new paint with the surrounding area.

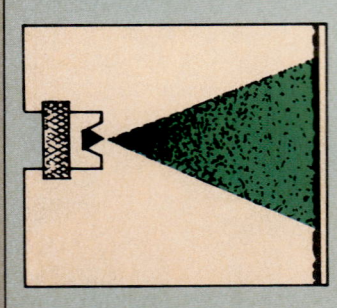

WRONG
Thin coat. Stroke too fast, not enough overlap, gun too far away.

CORRECT
Medium coat. Proper distance, good stroke, proper overlap.

WRONG
Heavy coat. Stroke too slow, too much overlap, gun too close.

BODY 541

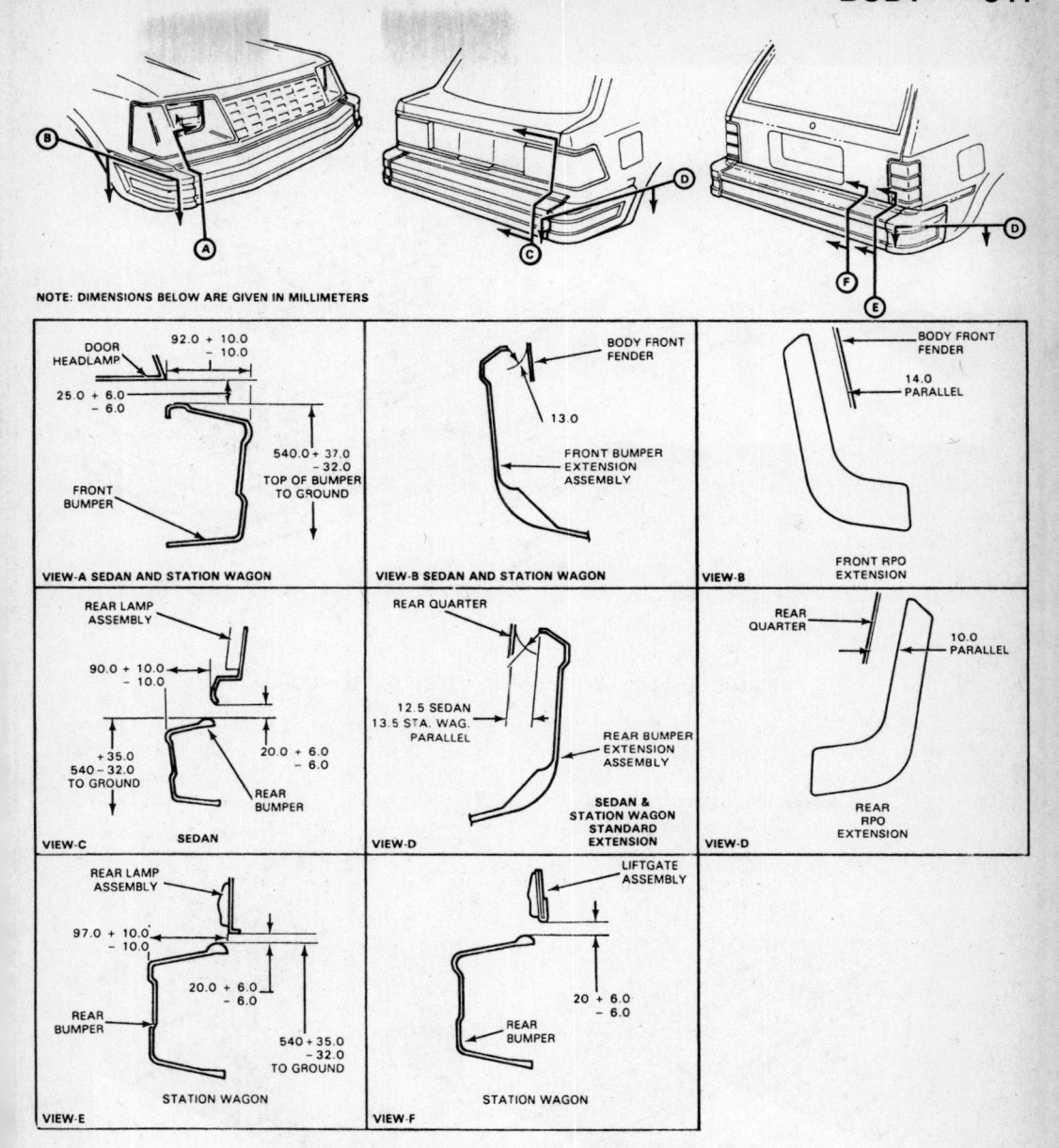

Bumper clearance specifications — 1981–85 Escort/Lynx

5. To install, position the bumper assembly to the isolators and install the attaching screws and retaining nuts, but do not tighten.

6. Adjust the bumper height so that the distance from the top edge to the ground meets the specifications given in the illustration.

7. Then, adjust the bumper to body clearance so that the vertical and horizontal body to bumper dimensions meet the specifications in the illustration provided. Torque the isolator to bumper bolts to 26-40 ft. lbs. (35-55 Nm).

8. On vehicle equipped with optional extension assemblies, secure the extension assembly to the fender with the retaining screws. New holes may have to be drilled through the tab in the extension housing.

1986-90 MODELS EXCEPT ESCORT GT

1. Remove all necessary trim molding and guards from the bumper in order to gain access to the bumper retaining bolts.

2. Support the bumper and remove the 6 bumper to isolator attaching bolts.

NOTE: *On the Tempo/Topaz models, the outboard ends of the bumper covers are attached to the fender panels by a single hidden slide attachment.*

542 BODY

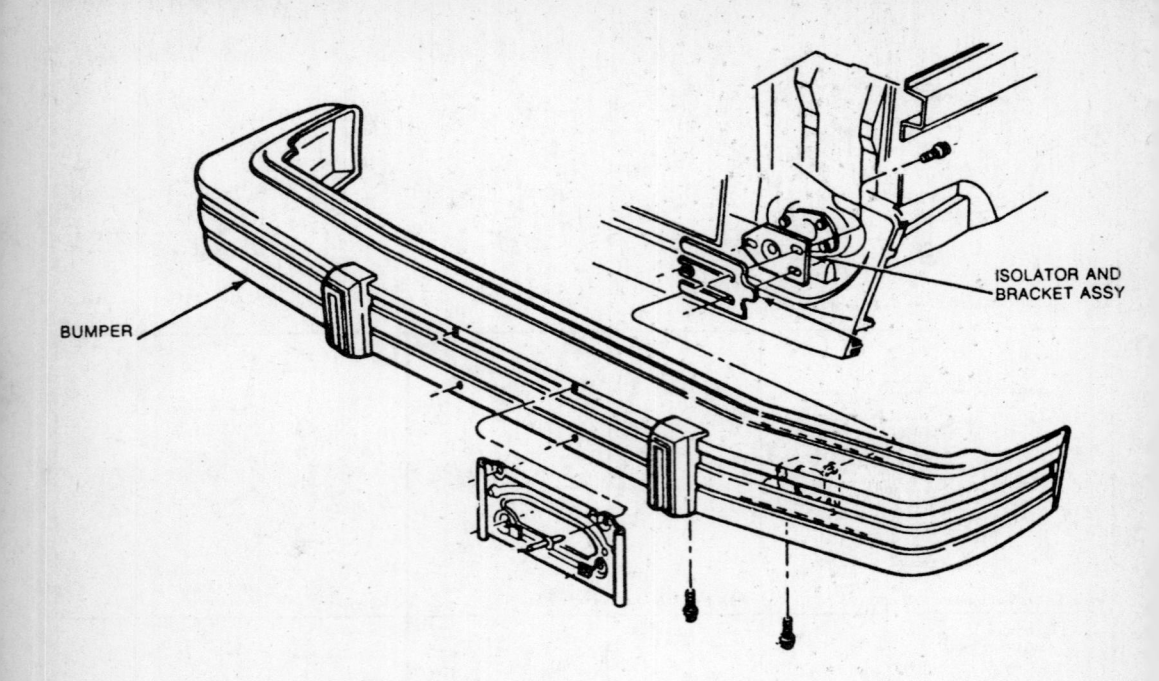

Plastic front bumper assembly — 1981-85 Escort/Lynx

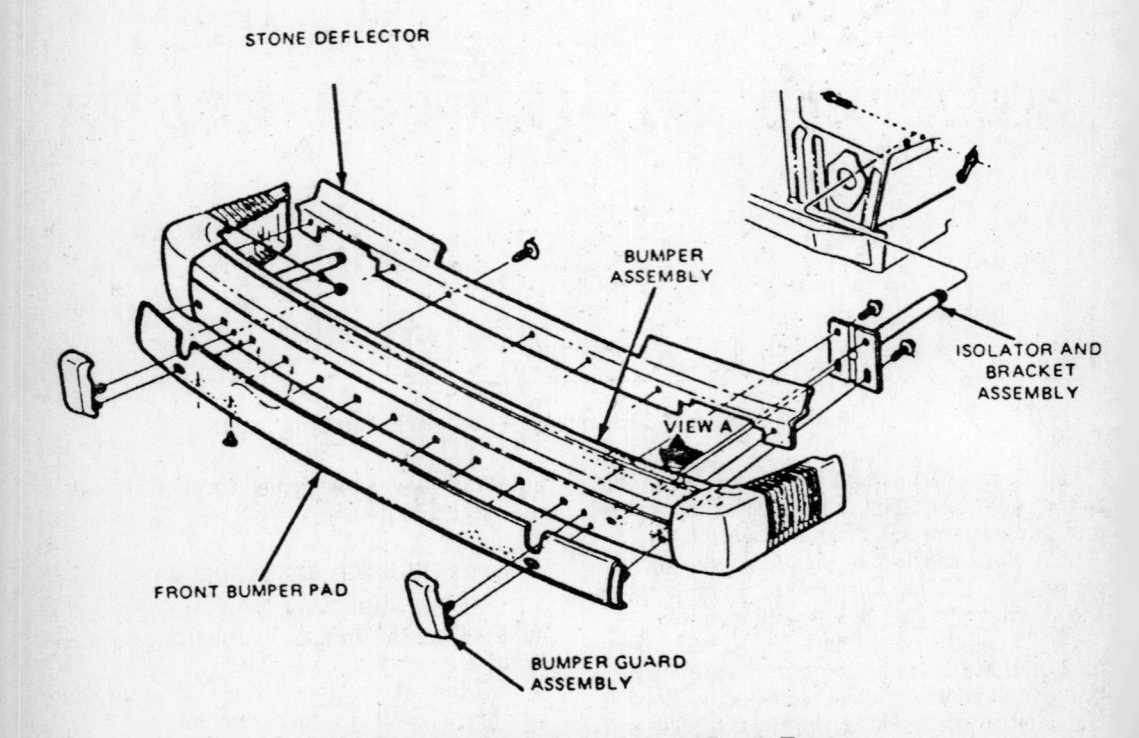

Front bumper installation — 1984-85 Tempo/Topaz

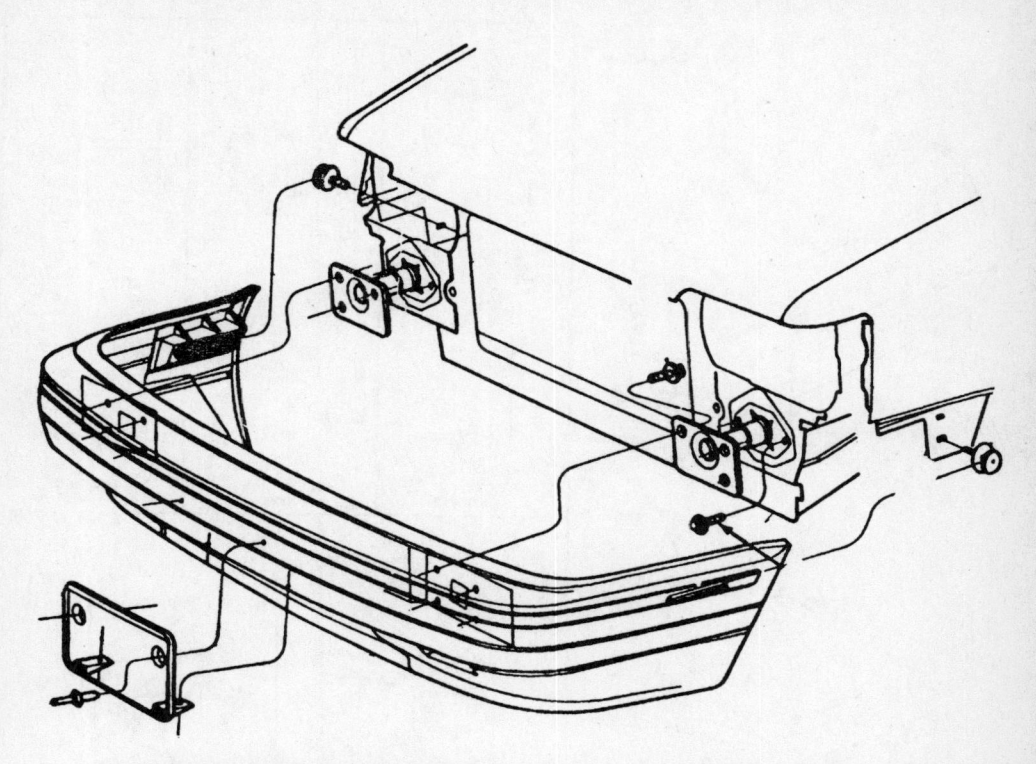

BODY 543

Standard front bumper removal and installation — 1986-90 Escort/Lynx

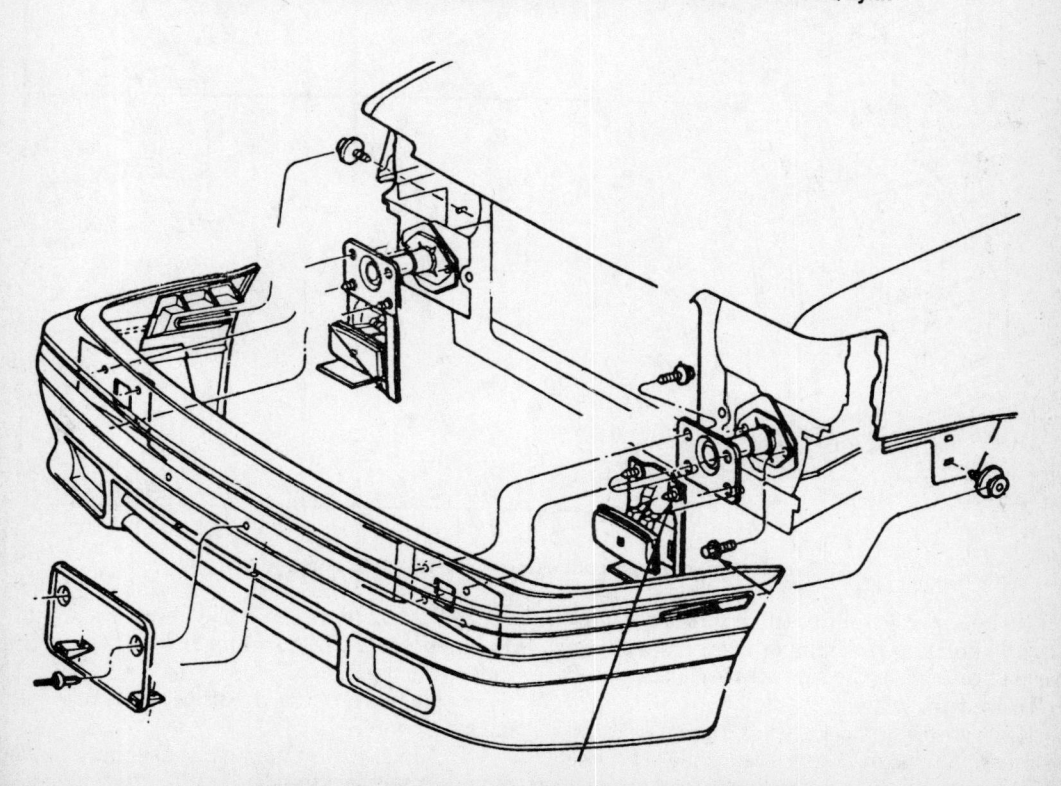

Front bumper removal and installation — Escort GT

544 BODY

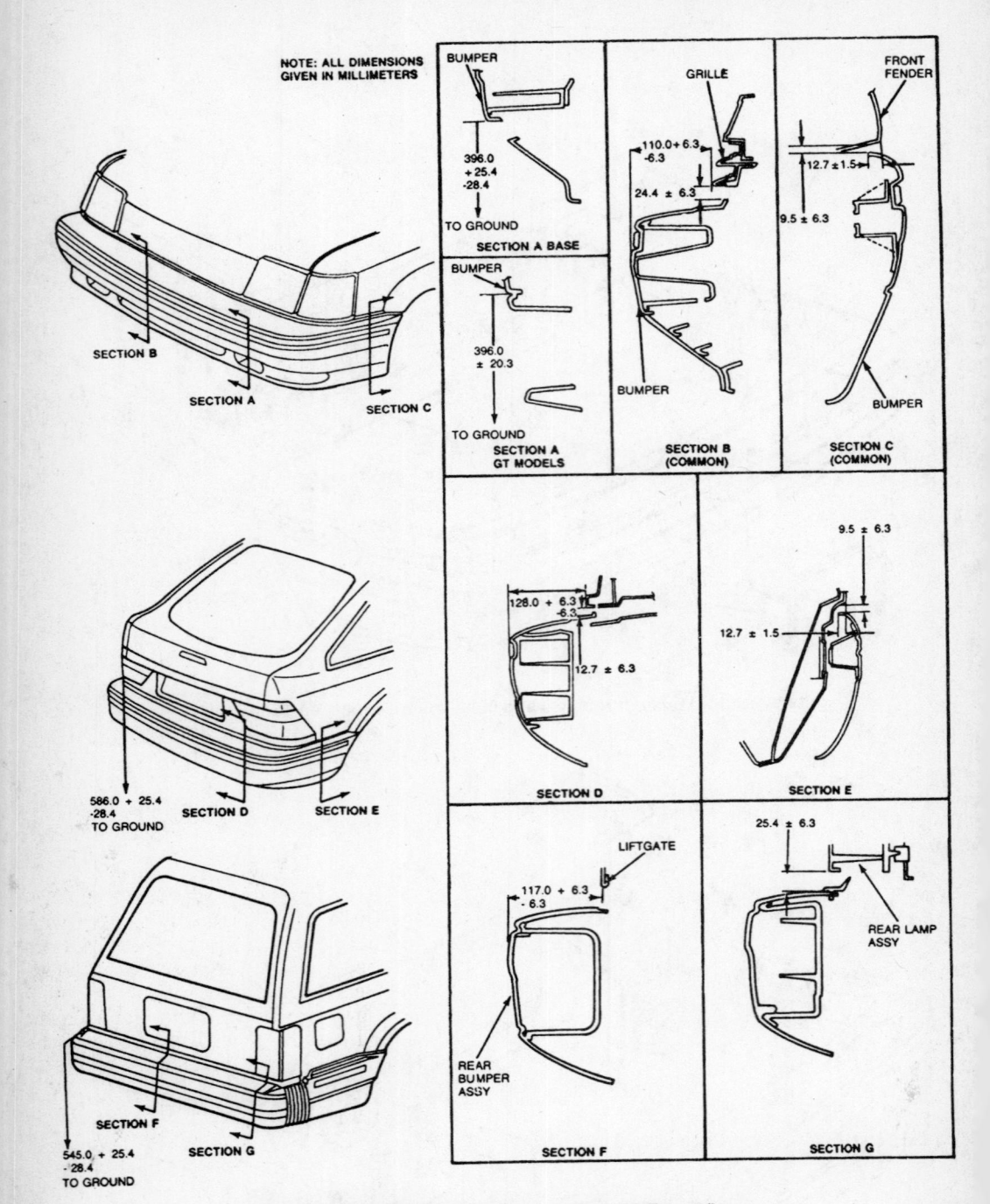

Bumper clearance specifications — 1986–90 Escort/Lynx

3. Lower the front of the bumper assembly slightly and pull the bumper away from the vehicle to disengage the side attachments.

To install:

4. Transfer bumper guards, rub strip, extension assemblies, pads and license plate bracket and bumper mounting brackets to replacement bumper.

5. To install, position the bumper assembly to the vehicle while sliding the ends over the side attachments.

6. Hand start the 6 bumper to isolator attaching bolts.

7. Adjust the bumper height so that the distance from the top edge to the ground meets the specifications given in the illustration.

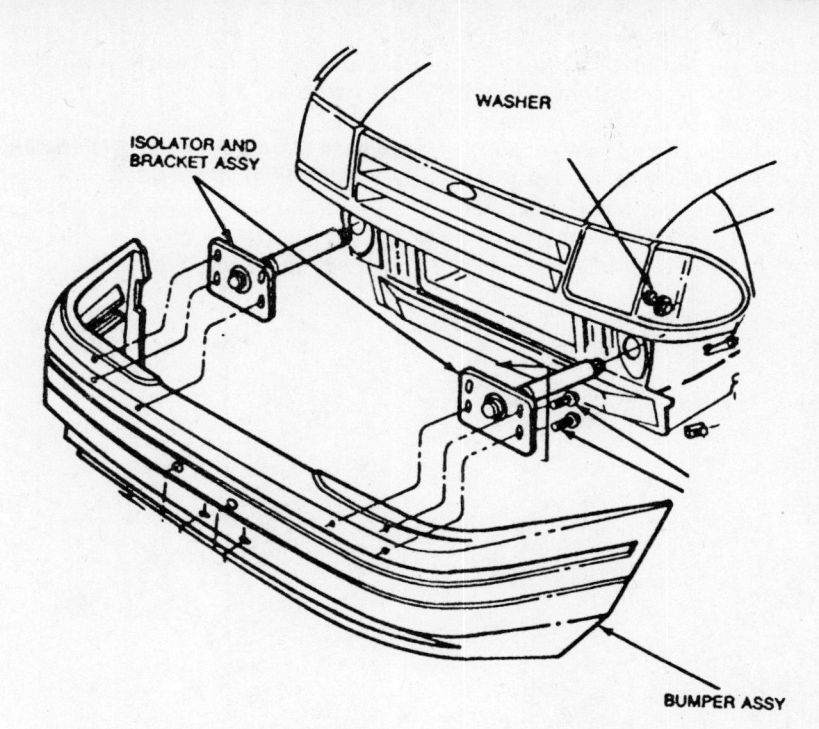

Front bumper installation — 1986–90 Tempo/Topaz

8. Then, adjust the bumper to body clearance so that the vertical and horizontal body to bumper dimensions meet the specifications in the illustration provided. Torque the isolator to bumper bolts to 17-25 ft. lbs. (22-33 Nm).

ESCORT GT

1. Support the fog lamp bracket assemblies. Remove the 4 (2 on each side) lower bumper to isolator attaching bolts. Remove the fog lamp and bracket assemblies.
2. Support the bumper and remove the 4 upper bumper to isolator attaching bolts.
3. Lower the front of the bumper assembly slightly and pull the bumper away from the vehicle to disengage the side attachments.

To install:

4. Transfer bumper guards, rub strip, extension assemblies, pads and license plate bracket and bumper mounting brackets to replacement bumper.
5. To install, position the bumper assembly to the vehicle while sliding the ends over the side attachments.
6. Hand start the 6 bumper to isolator attaching bolts.
7. Adjust the bumper height so that the distance from the top edge to the ground meets the specifications given in the illustration.
8. Then, adjust the bumper to body clearance so that the vertical and horizontal body to bumper dimensions meet the specifications in the illustration provided. Torque the isolator to bumper bolts to 17-25 ft. lbs.

Rear Bumper

1981-85 MODELS

1. Remove all necessary trim molding and guards from the bumper in order to gain access to the bumper retaining bolts.
2. If the vehicle is equipped with the optional (long) bumper extension assemblies with attachments to the fender, remove the 2 screws through the tab on the inside surface of the extension assemblies.
3. Remove the isolator to reinforcement screws and retaining nut and remove the bumper assembly from the vehicle.

NOTE: *Steel and aluminum bumpers have 4 screws and retaining nuts at each isolator, light weight aluminum bumpers have 3 screws and retaining nuts at each isolator.*

To install:

4. Transfer bumper guards, rub strip, extension assemblies, pads and license plate bracket and bumper mounting brackets to replacement bumper.
5. To install, position the bumper assembly to the isolators and install the attaching screws and retaining nuts, but do not tighten.
6. Adjust the bumper height so that the distance from the top edge to the ground meets the specifications given in the illustration.

546 BODY

7. Then, adjust the bumper to body clearance so that the vertical and horizontal body to bumper dimensions meet the specifications in the illustration provided. Torque the isolator to bumper bolts to 26-40 ft. lbs. (35-55 Nm).

8. On vehicle equipped with optional extension assemblies, secure the extension assembly to the fender with the retaining screws. New holes may have to be drilled through the tab in the extension housing.

1986-90 ALL MODELS EXCEPT ESCORT WAGON AND 1988-90 TEMPO/TOPAZ

1. Remove all necessary trim molding and guards from the bumper in order to gain access to the bumper retaining bolts.

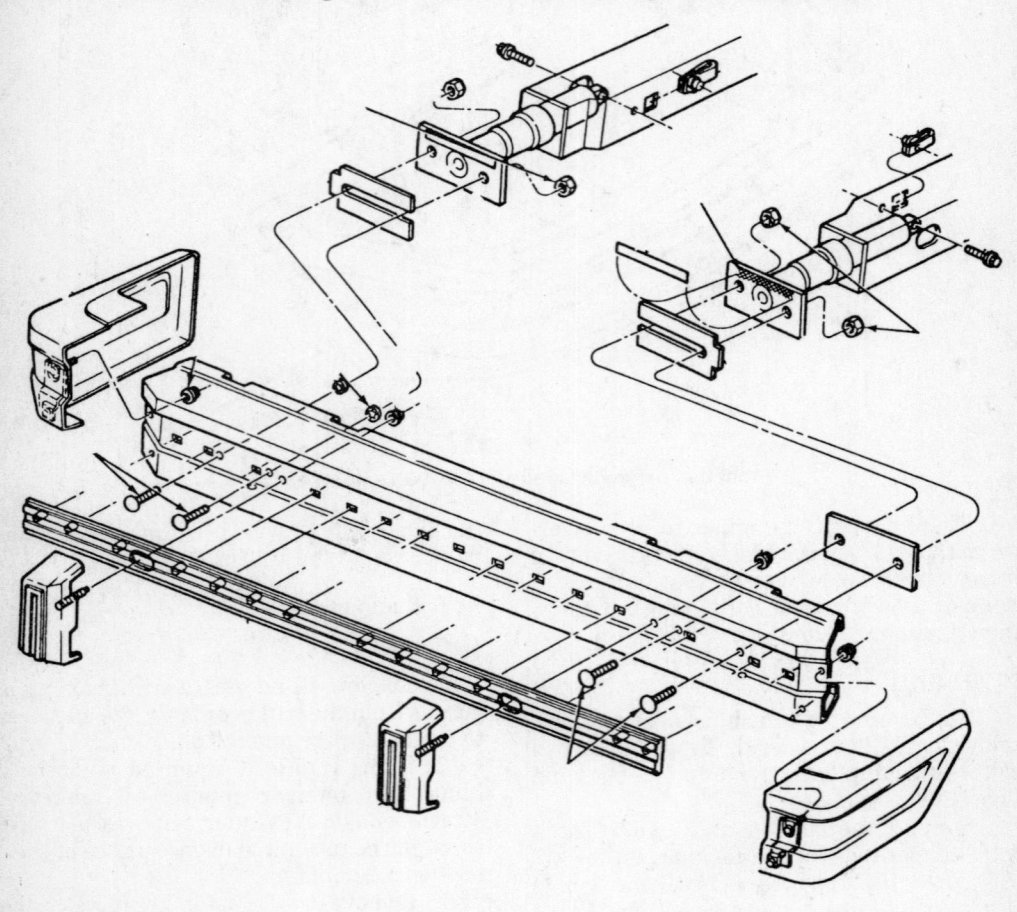

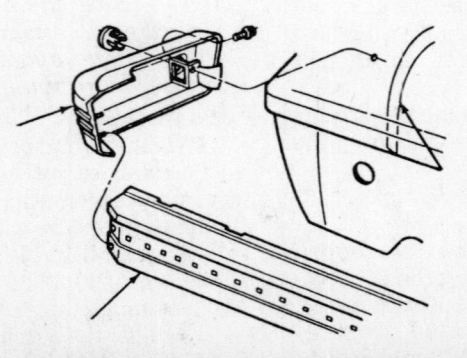

Rear bumper assembly — 1981–85 Escort/Lynx

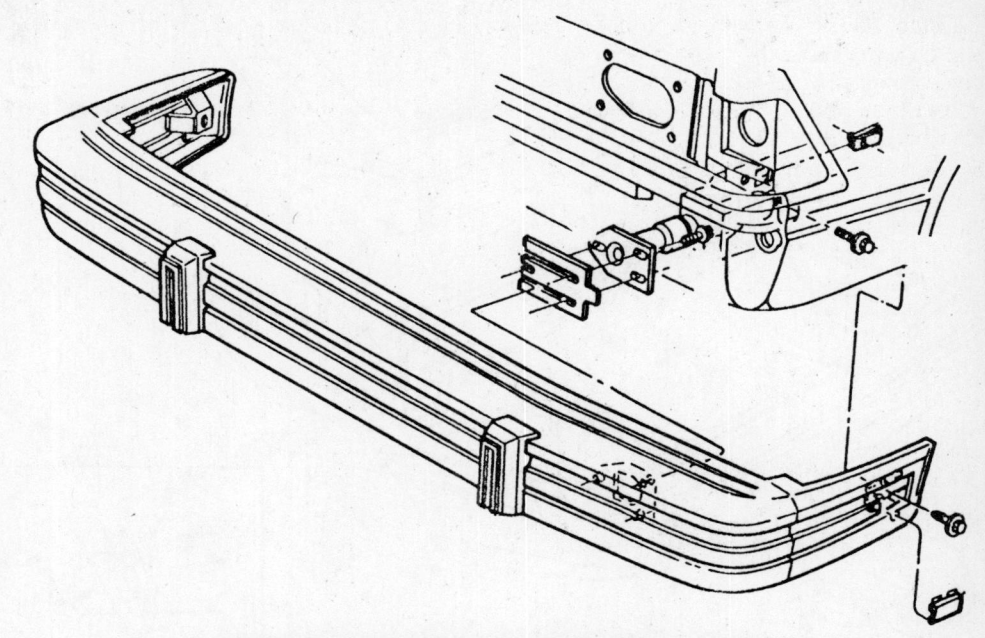

BODY 547

Plastic rear bumper assembly — 1981–85 Escort/Lynx

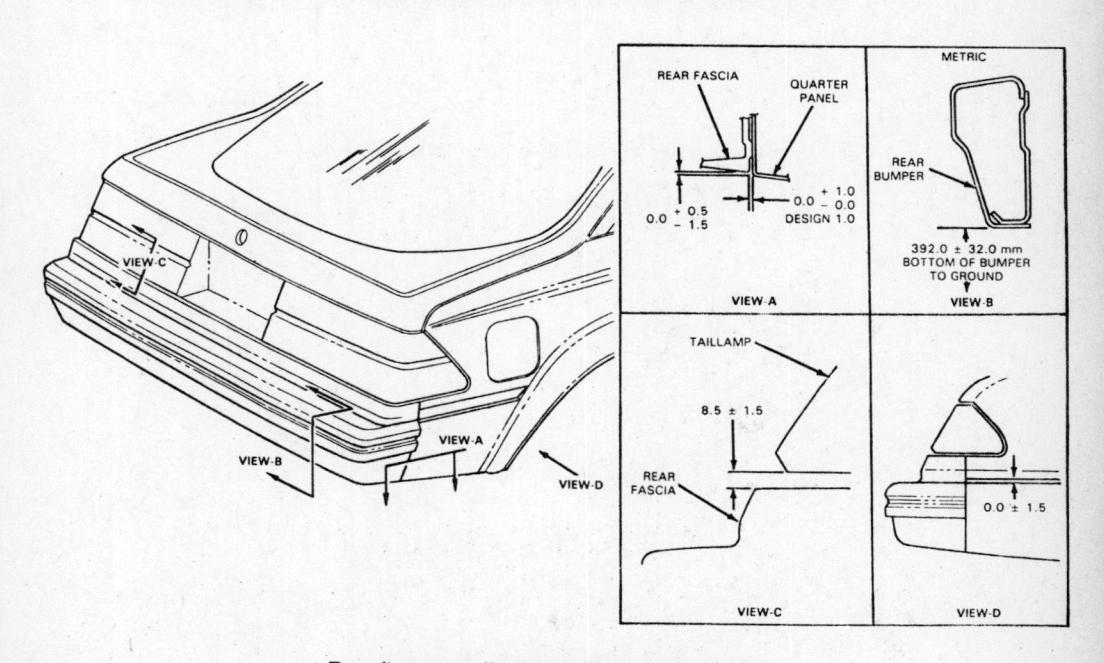

Rear bumper adjustment dimensions — EXP

2. Support the bumper and remove the 6 bumper to isolator attaching bolts.

3. Lower the front of the bumper assembly slightly and pull the bumper away from the vehicle to disengage the side attachments.

To install:

4. Transfer bumper guards, rub strip, extension assemblies, pads and license plate bracket and bumper mounting brackets to replacement bumper.

5. To install, position the bumper assembly to the vehicle while sliding the ends over the side attachments.

6. Hand start the 6 bumper to isolator attaching bolts.

7. Adjust the bumper height so that the dis-

548 BODY

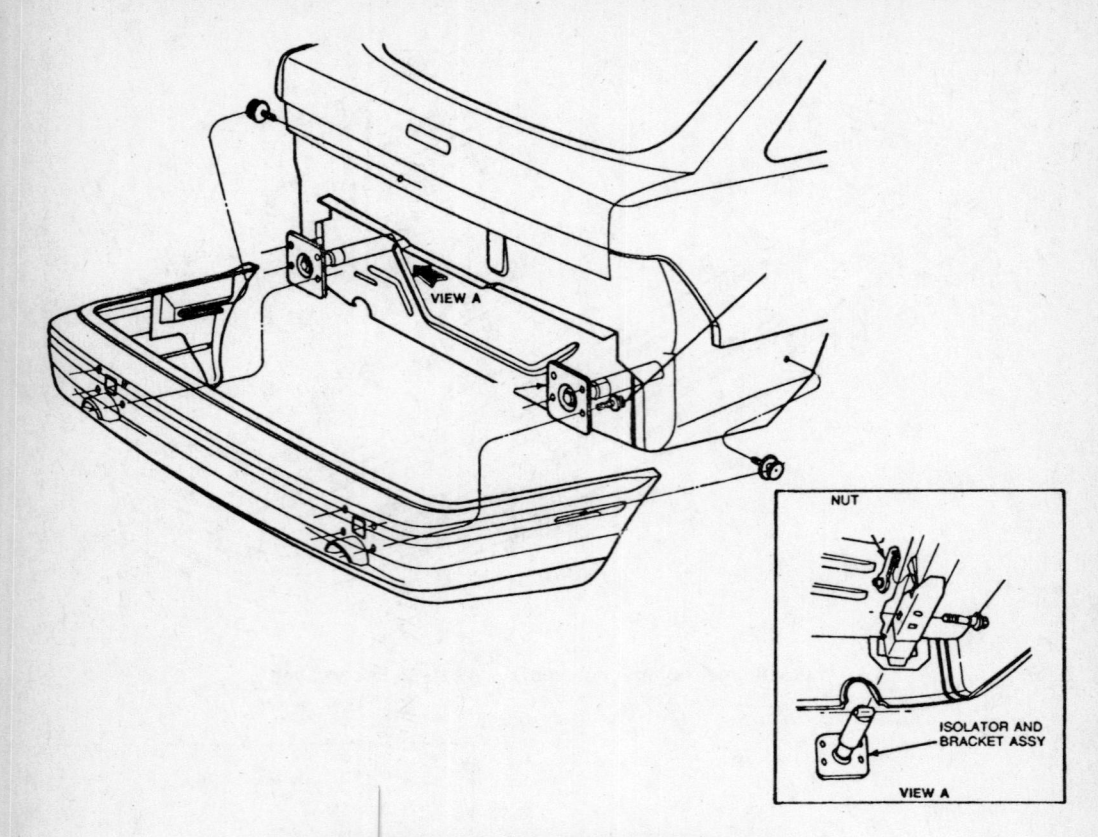

Rear bumper assembly — 1986–90 Escort/Lynx

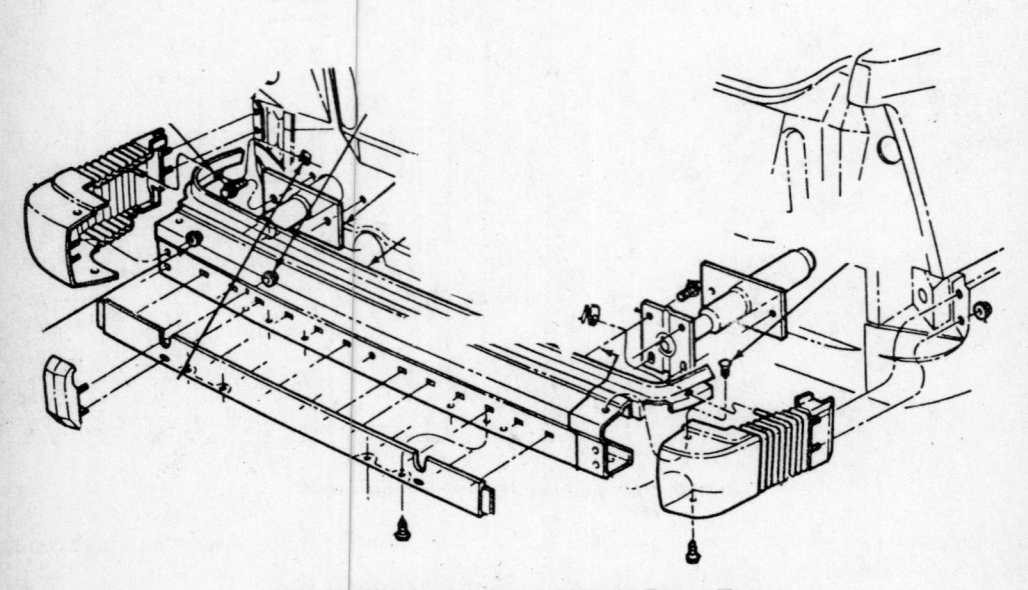

Rear bumper installation — 1984–85 Tempo/Topaz

BODY 549

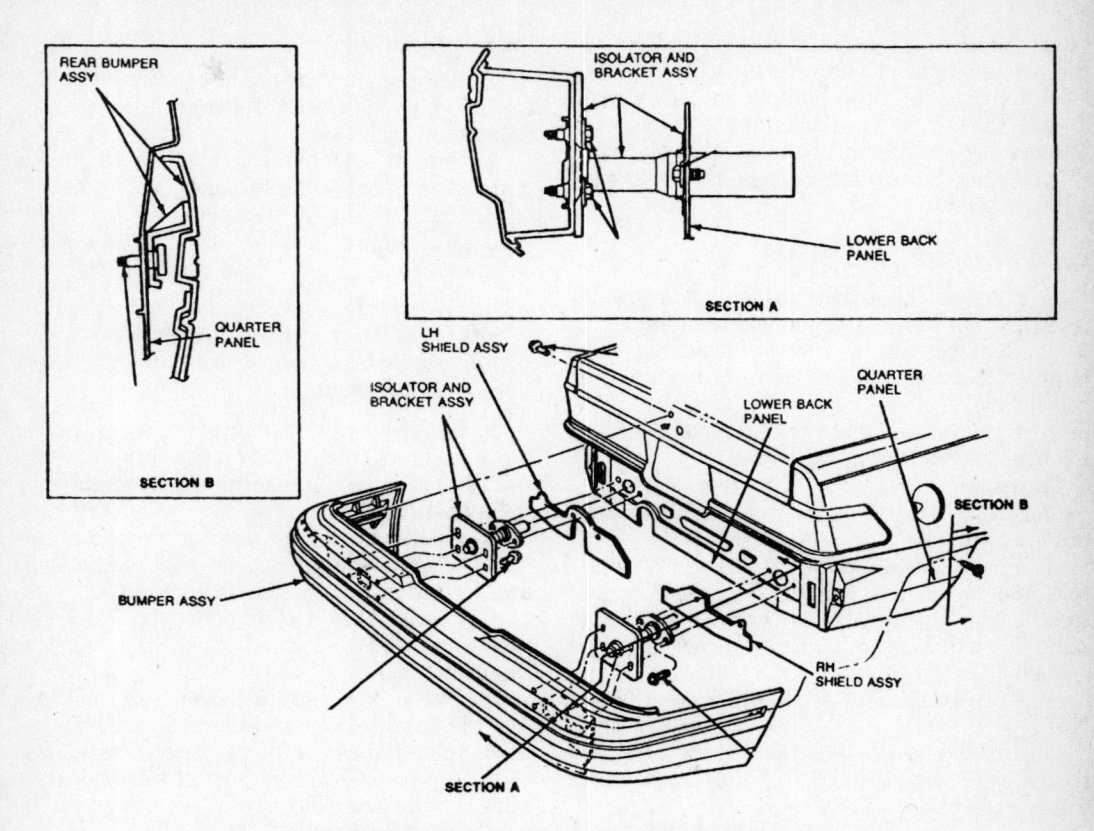

Rear bumper assembly — 1986-90 Tempo/Topaz 4-door

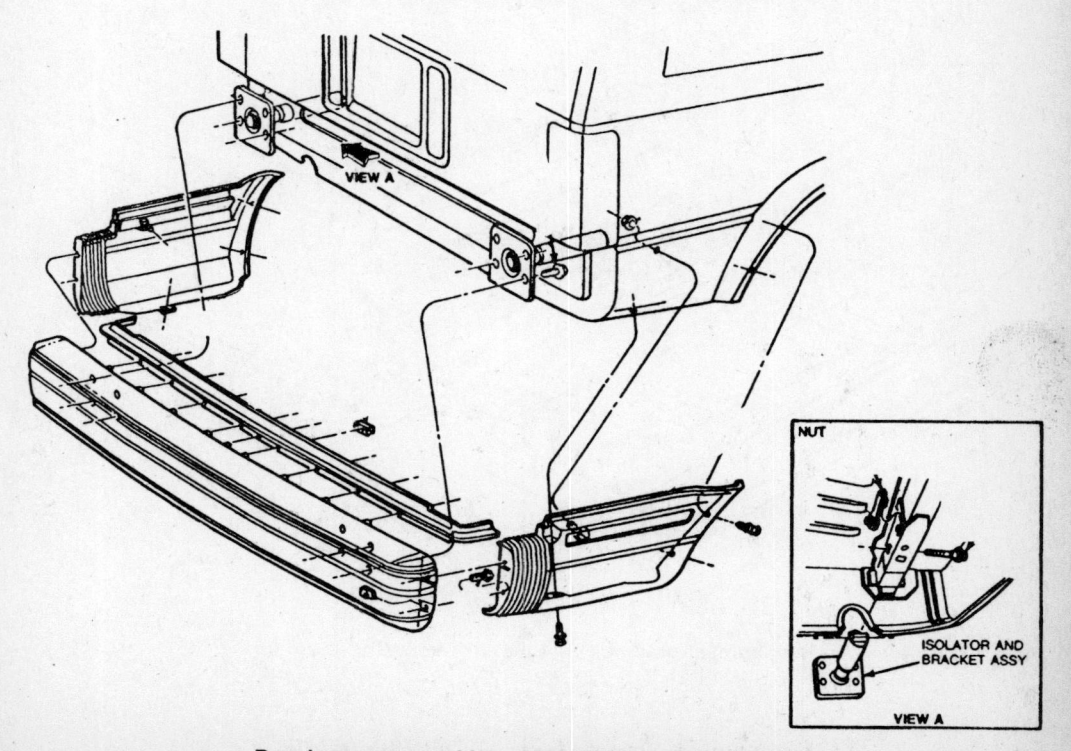

Rear bumper assembly — 1986-90 Escort/Lynx Wagon

tance from the top edge to the ground meets the specifications given in the illustration.

8. Then, adjust the bumper to body clearance so that the vertical and horizontal body to bumper dimensions meet the specifications in the illustration provided. Torque the isolator to bumper bolts to 17-25 ft. lbs. (22-33 Nm).

ESCORT WAGON

1. Remove the 4 bolts attaching the right hand and left hand extensions to the bumper.
2. Remove the 6 screws attaching the bumper isolators. Remove the bumper from the vehicle.
3. Remove the eight clips and stone deflector from the bumper.

To install:

4. Install the stone deflector and 8 clips onto the bumper.
5. Position the bumper assembly to isolators and install the attaching screws. Do not tighten them until all the screws have been hand started and the bumper is properly positioned.
6. Torque the screws to 17-25 ft. lbs. (22-34 Nm).
7. Install the 4 bolts attaching the bumper to the right hand and left hand extensions. Torque the bolts to 7-10 ft. lbs.

1988-90 Tempo/Topaz

1. Remove the rear bumper/cover assembly to quarter panel lower outboard (underside) retainers (one each side).
2. Remove the bumper/cover assembly to rear inside wheel well retainers (3 each side).
3. Remove the 4 bumper/cover to body (upper) retainers (located inside the luggage compartment).

NOTE: *On the 4 door models, the outboard ends of the bumper covers are attached to the quarter panels by a single hidden slide retainer attachment.*

4. Remove the rear bumper/cover to isolator and bracket assembly retainers (4 each side) and remove the rear bumper assembly.

To install:

5. Position the rear bumper properly. Install the rear bumper/cover to isolator and bracket assembly retainers (4 each side).
6. Install the 4 bumper/cover to body (upper) retainers (located inside the luggage compartment).
7. Install the bumper/cover assembly to rear inside wheel well retainers (3 each side).
8. Install the rear bumper/cover assembly to quarter panel lower outboard (underside) retainers (one each side).

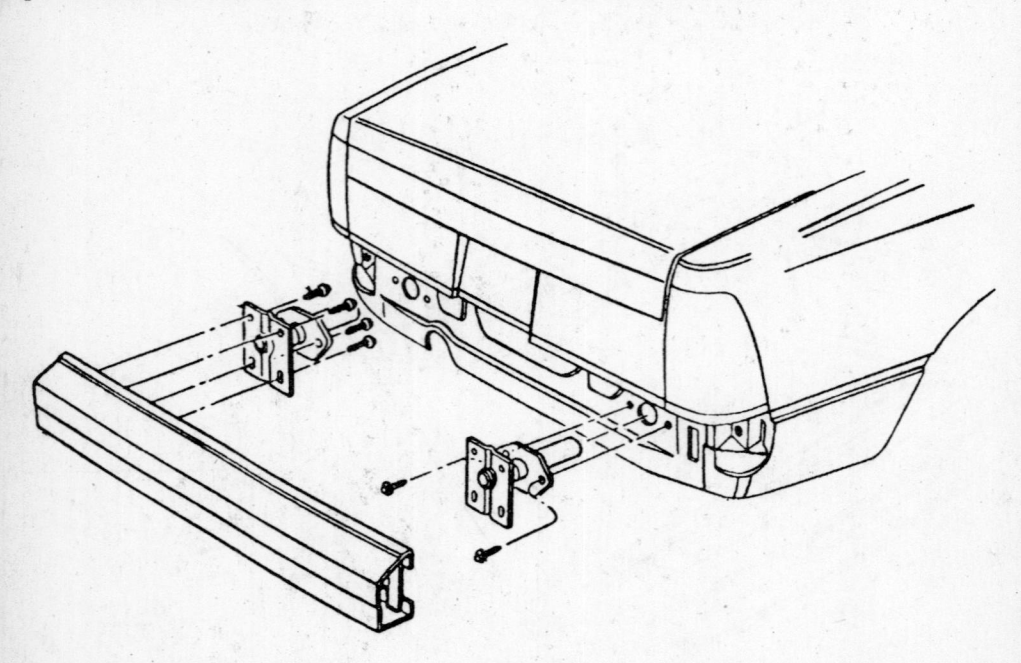

Rear bumper assembly — 1986–90 Tempo/Topaz 2-door

Radiator Grille

REMOVAL AND INSTALLATION

1981-85 MODELS

1. Remove the radiator grille attaching screws and remove the grille from the mounting brackets on the radiator support.

To install:

2. Position the grille to the vehicle and loosely install the grille attaching screws. The grille should rest on the locating tabs that extend from the headlamp doors.

3. Adjust the grille side to side so there is a uniform gap between the grille and the headlamp doors. Tighten the retaining bolts.

1986-90 Escort/Lynx

1. Push down on the top side of lower snap-in retainer at both sides of grille and pull the grille out at the bottom.

2. Push up on the bottom side of the upper snap-in retainer at both sides of the grille out at the top.

3. Put grille forward out of the grille opening panel.

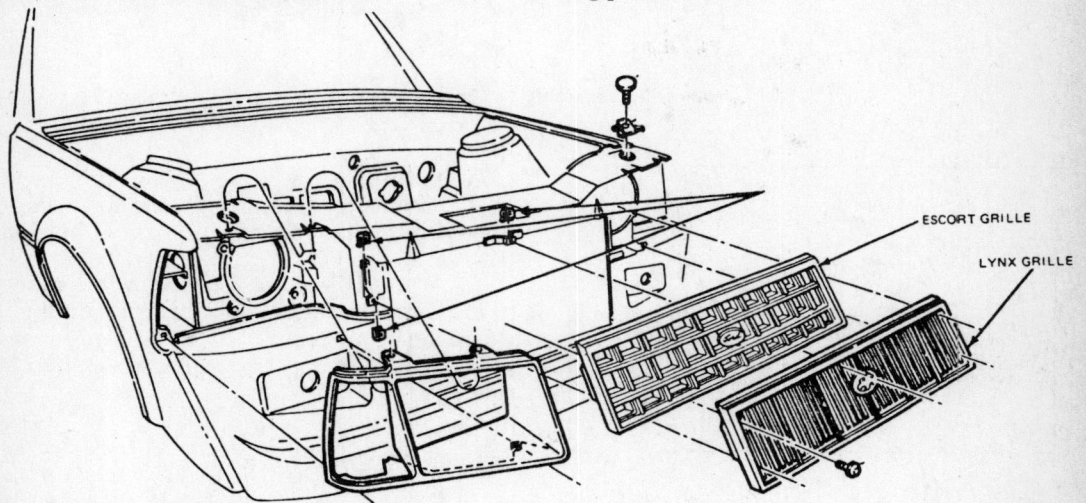

Front grille assembly — 1981–85 Escort/Lynx

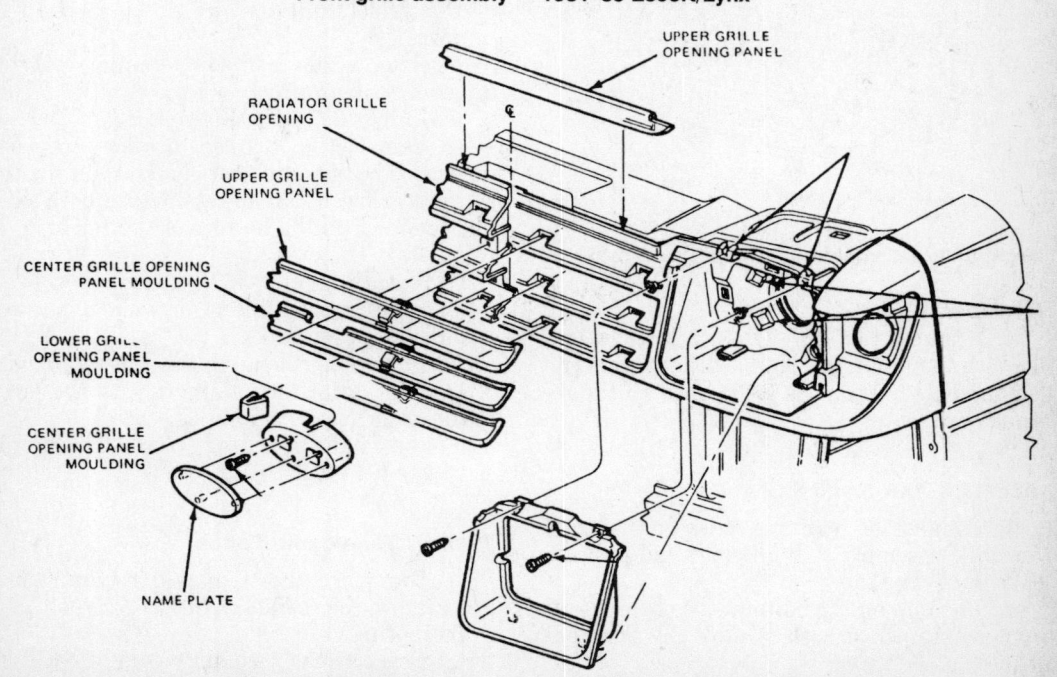

Front grille assembly — 1984–85 Tempo

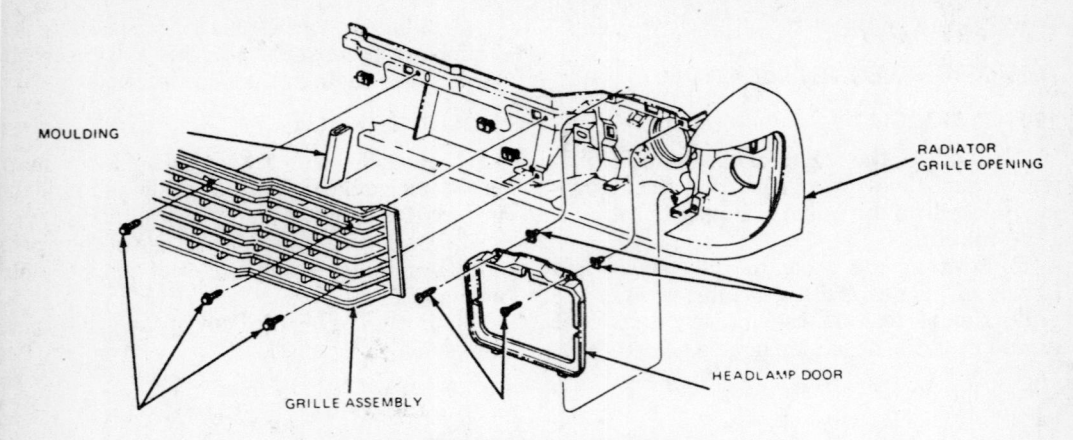

Front grille assembly — 1984–85 Topaz

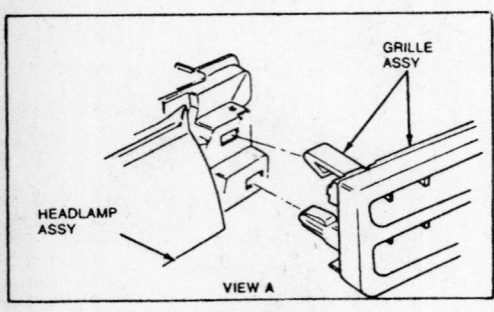

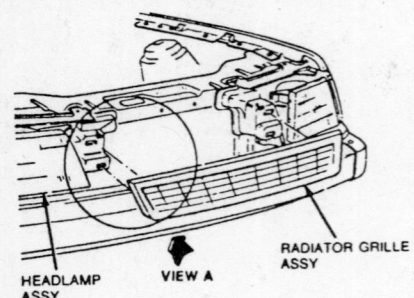

Front grille assembly — 1986–90 Escort/Lynx

To install:

4. Position the grille to the vehicle and align the snap-in retainers with appropriate slots and push in on the grille until all the retainers are seated.

1986-88 GT/XR-3 and EXP

1. Remove the retaining screw on the top of the grille assembly at both sides and pull the grille out at the top.
2. Push up on the bottom side of the upper snap-in retainer at both sides of the grille out at the top.
3. Put grille forward out of the grille opening panel.

To install:

4. Position the grille to align the lower snap-in retainers and upper tabs over the U-nuts at both sides.
5. Align the snap-in retainers with appropriate slots and push in on the grille until all the retainers are seated.
6. Install the upper retaining screw at both sides.

1989-90 ESCORT GT

1. Remove lower grille bar by pushing up on the 3 retaining tabs located on the back side of the grille. Pull the grille bar forward to remove.
2. Remove the 2 screws retaining grille at top ends to mounting brackets.
3. Pull grille forward to remove.
4. Remove the mounting brackets from the headlamp housing by pushing down on the top side of the lower snap-in retainers at both sides and push up on the bottom of the top snap-in retainers.

To install:

5. Position the grille to align the upper and lower snap-in retainers.
6. Push the grille in, to the seat retainers.
7. Align grille bar retainers with the holes in the grille and push in until seated.
8. Install the retaining screws. Torque the screws to 6-14 ft.lbs.

1986-87 Tempo and Topaz

1. Disengage the 8 snap-in retaining legs and remove the radiator grille.

To install:

2. Position the radiator opening cover to grille opening the panel and push to engage the cover retainers.

BODY 553

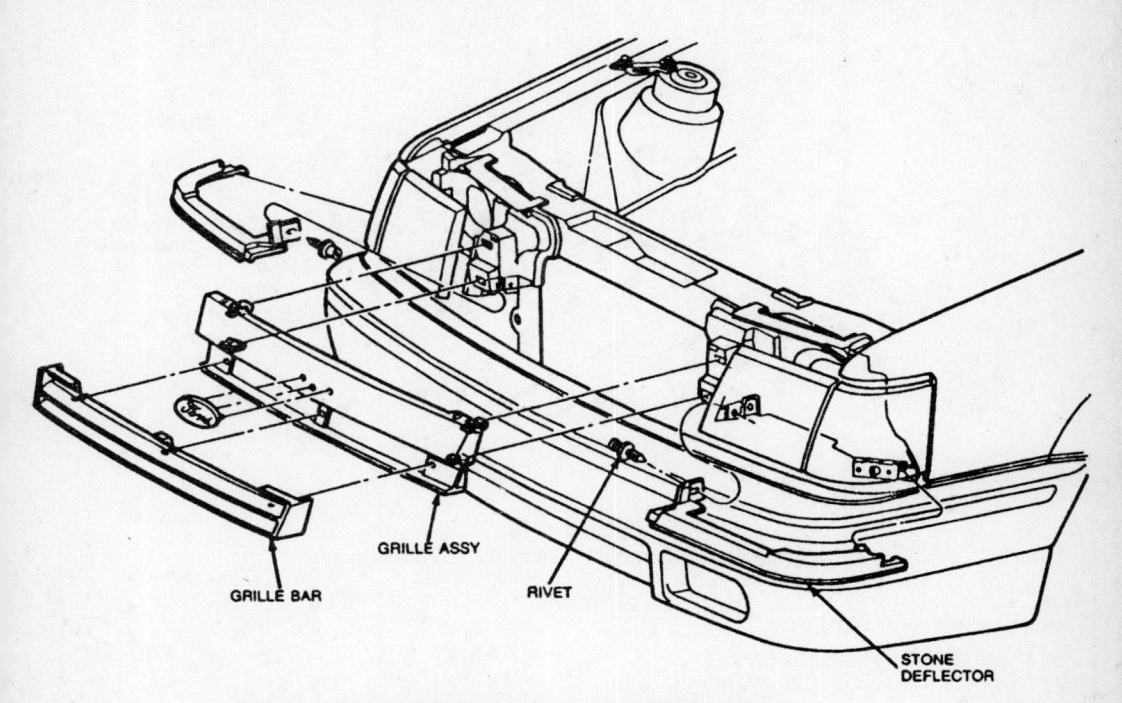

Front grille assembly — 1988-90 Escort GT

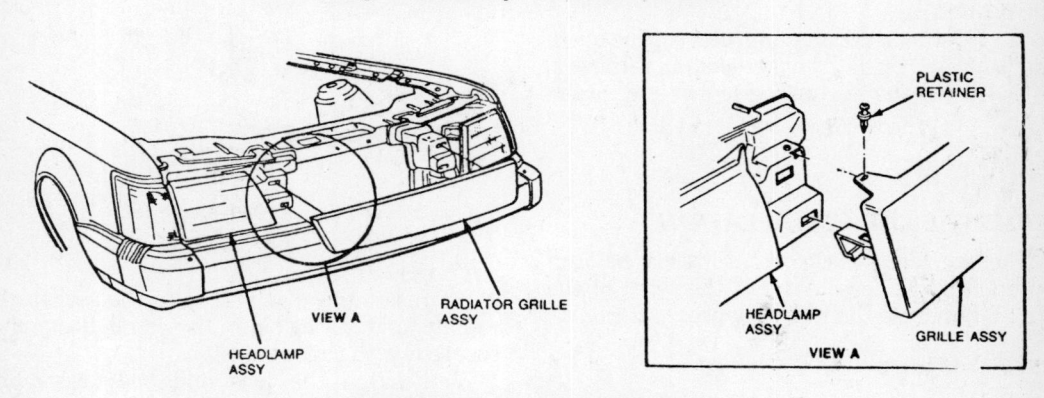

Front grille assembly — GT, XR3 and EXP

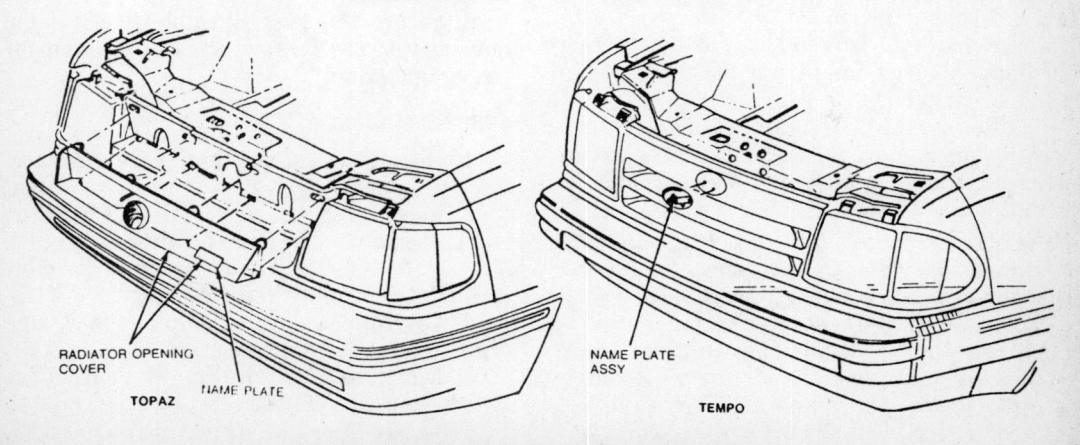

Front grille assembly — 1986-87 Tempo/Topaz

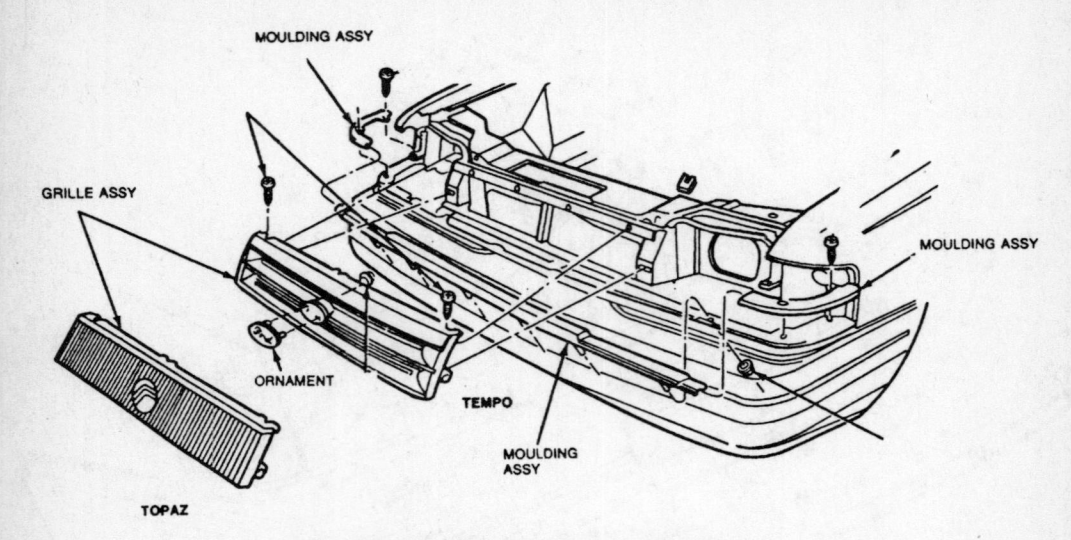

BODY

Front grille assembly — 1988–90 Tempo/Topaz

1988-90 Tempo and Topaz

1. Remove the 2 retaining screws.
2. Disengage the snap-in retainers by carefully pulling outward.

To install:

3. Position the radiator grille to grille opening panel and push to engage snap-in retainers.
4. Install the 2 retaining screws and torque them to 6-14 ft. lbs.

Fog Lights

REMOVAL AND INSTALLATION

The fog lamp assembly utilizes a halogen bulb and socket assembly. In the event of the bulb failure, use the following procedure:

1984-88 Models

1. Remove the 2 screws that retain the lens assembly to the lamp housing. Use caution to avoid dropping the lens.
2. Remove the lens and body assembly from the lamp housing and turn it to gain access to the rear lamp body.
3. Release the bulb socket retainer from the locking tab. Remove the bulb and socket assembly from the lamp body and pull the bulb directly out of the socket.

NOTE: *Do not touch the new bulb with bare hands. The stains will cause contamination of the quartz, which may result in early failure of the lamp. Do not remove the protective plastic sleeve until the lamp is inserted into the socket. Be sure the circuit is not energized. If the quartz was inadvertently handled, it should be cleaned with a clean cloth moistened with alcohol before installation.*

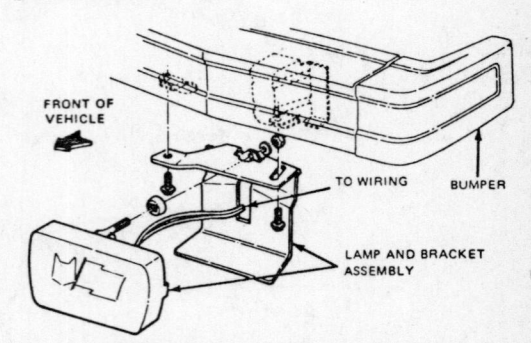

Fog lamp assembly — 1985–88 models

To install:

4. Insert the new bulb into the socket assembly and socket into the lamp body and secure it with the retainer.
5. Position the lens and body assembly right side up (as indicated on the lens) into the lamp housing.
6. Secure the lens assembly to the lamp housing with the 2 screws and test the lamp for proper operation.

1989-90 Models

1. Disconnect the fog lamp wiring connector.
2. Remove the 2 screws that retain the lamp assembly to the lamp mounting.
3. Pull the lamp and wiring assembly through the opening in the bumper.
4. Carefully peel back the rubber boot (covering the wires) from the socket.
5. Disconnect the wire connector from the bulb lead (inside of boot).
6. Rotate the bulb socket out of the lamp body to expose the bulb retainer.

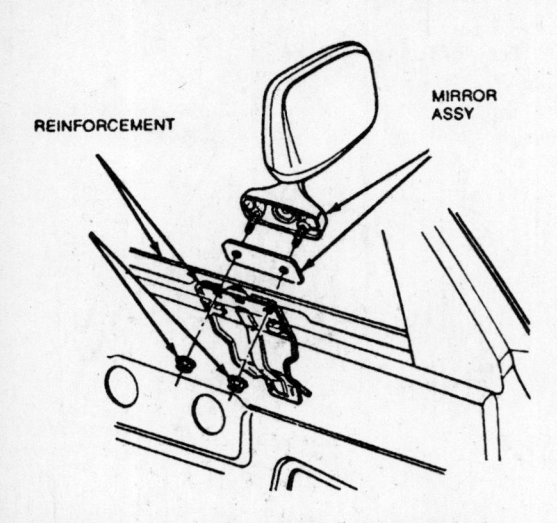

BODY 555

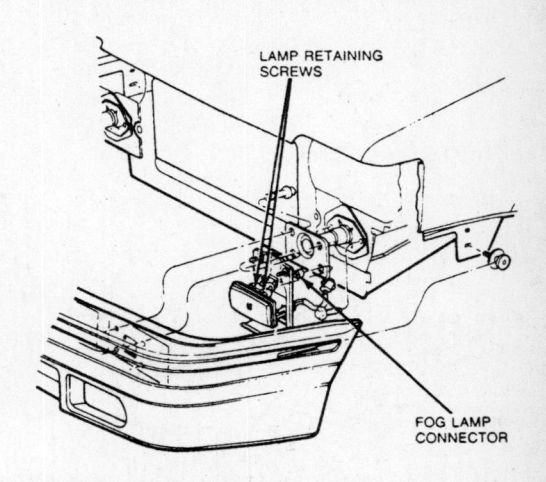

Fog lamp assembly — 1989–90 models

Typical manual mirror removal and installation

7. Squeeze the retainer wires and lift up. Carefully remove the bulb assembly from the lamp.
To install:
8. Install the bulb assembly into the lamp and install the retainer wires.
9. Rotate the bulb socket into the lamp body to cover the bulb retainer.
10. Reconnect the wire connector to the bulb lead (inside of boot).
11. Carefully push back the rubber boot (covering the wires) onto the socket.

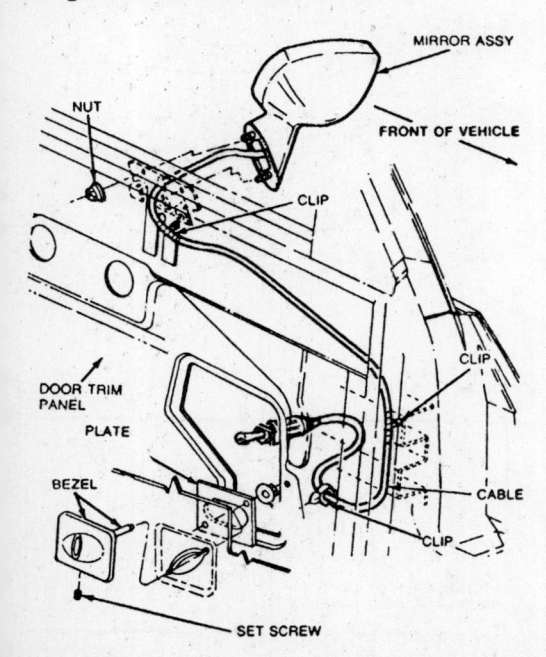

Typical remote control mirror removal and installation

12. Push the lamp and wiring assembly through the opening in the bumper.
13. Install the 2 screws that retain the lamp assembly to the lamp mounting.
14. Reconnect the fog lamp wiring connector.

Outside Mirrors

REMOVAL AND INSTALLATION

Standard Manual Mirrors

1. Remove the inside door trim panel from the door in which the mirror is to be taken from.
2. Remove the retaining nuts and washers from the mirror.
3. Lift the mirror up and out of the door and discard the gasket.
To install:
4. Install the mirror and gasket onto the door.
5. Install the nuts and washers and torque the nuts to 25-36 inch lbs.
6. Reinstall the door trim panel.

Remote Control Mirrors

1. Remove the set screw fastening the control lever end of the cable assembly to the control lever bezel on the door trim panel.
2. Remove the inside door trim panel and weather insulator from the door in which the mirror is to be taken from.
3. Disengage the cable from the routing clips and guides located inside the door.
4. Remove the mirror attaching nuts and washers. Remove the mirror and cable assembly from the door.
To install:
5. Place the remote cable into the hole and the door and position the mirror to the door.

556 **BODY**

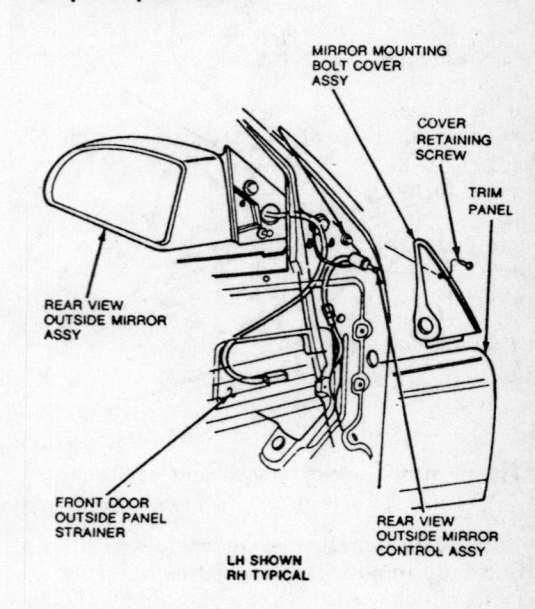

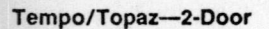

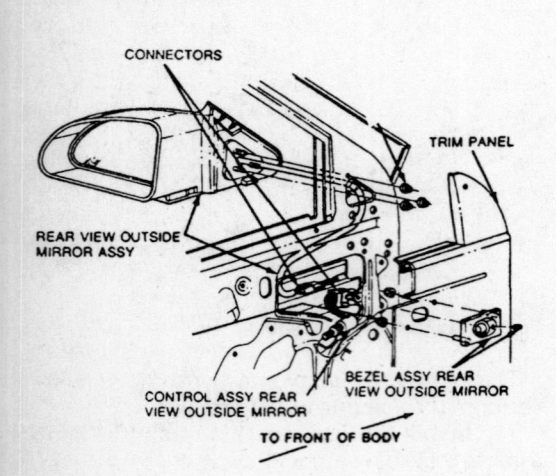

Typical power mirror removal and installation — Tempo/Topaz

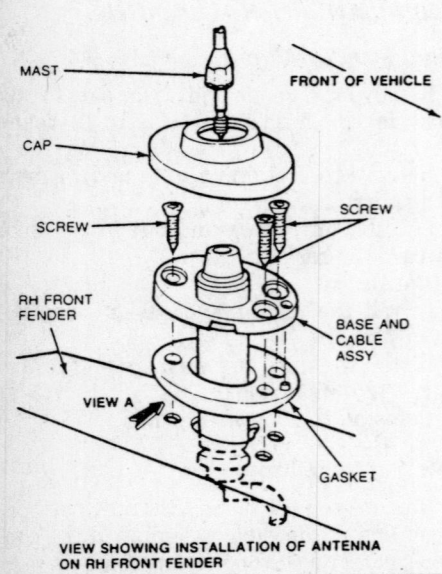

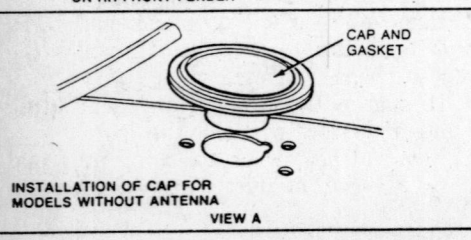

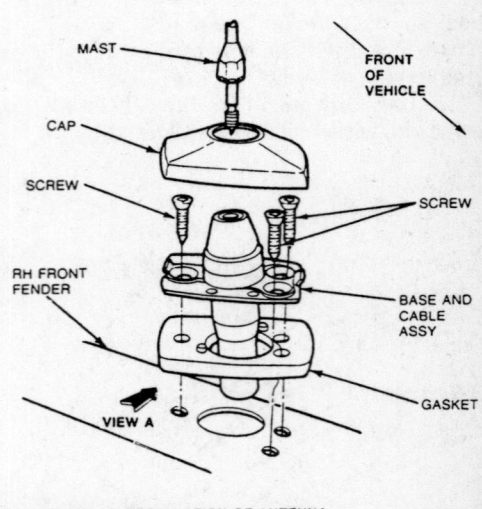

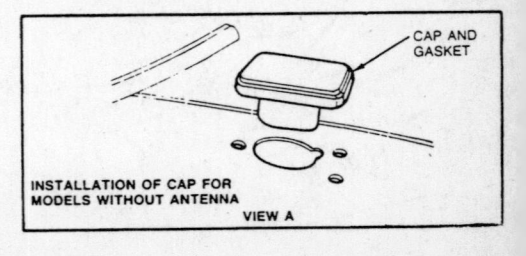

Typical antenna assembly removal and installation

Install the nuts and washers and torque them to 21-39 inch lbs.

6. Route the cable through the door into the cable guides and engage the cable into the locating clips.

7. Check the operation of the mirror and operate the mirror up and down to insure that the mirror cables do not interfere with the window mechanism.

8. Install the weather insulator and door trim panel.

9. Place the control lever bezel onto the door trim panel and install the set screw.

Power Mirrors

1. Disconnect the negative battery cable.
2. Remove the inside door trim panel and weather insulator from the door in which the mirror is to be taken from.
3. Disconnect the electrical connector from the mirror unit. Disengage the wire harness cable from the routing clips and guides located inside the door.
4. Remove the mirror attaching nuts and washers. Remove the mirror and wire assembly from the door.

To install:

5. Place the wire harness into the hole and the door and position the mirror to the door. Install the nuts and washers and torque them to 35-51 inch lbs.

6. Route the wire harness through the door into the harness guides and engage the wire harness connector into the mirror unit. Reconnect the negative battery cable.

7. Check the operation of the mirror and operate the mirror up and down to insure that the mirror wires do not interfere with the window mechanism.

8. Install the weather insulator and door trim panel.

Antenna

REMOVAL AND INSTALLATION

1. Disconnect the negative battery cable.
2. Remove the snap cap from the antenna, if so equipped.
3. Remove the base attaching screws.
4. Pull (do not pry) the antenna up through the fender.
5. Push in on the sides of the glove box door and place the door in the hinged downward position.
6. Disconnect the antenna lead from the rear of the radio and remove the antenna cable from the heater or air conditioning cable retaining clips.

NOTE: *On some models it may be necessary to remove the right hand side kick panel in order to gain access to some of the antenna cable retaining clips.*

7. Pull the antenna cable through the hole in the door hinge pillar and fender and remove the antenna assembly from the vehicle.

To install:

8. With the right front door open, put the gasket on the antenna and position the antenna base and wire harness assembly into the fender opening. Install the antenna base onto the fender using the retaining screws.

9. Install the antenna base cap and antenna mast assembly, if so equipped.

10. Pull the antenna lead through the door hinge pillar opening. Seat the grommet by pulling the antenna wiring harness cable through the hole from the inside of the vehicle.

11. Route the antenna cable behind the glove box, along the instrument panel and install the cable in the retaining clips from which they were removed.

12. Connect the antenna wiring connector into the back of the radio. Install the right hand kick panel, if removed.

13. Push in on the sides of the glove box door and place in the hinged upward position.

Windshield and Rear Window Glass

REMOVAL AND INSTALLATION

Ford cars use a Butyl/Urethane type sealed windshield and rear window which requires the use of special tools for removal and installation. It is advised that if the windshield needs replacement the vehicle be taken to a professional glass shop.

INTERIOR

Front Door Panels

REMOVAL AND INSTALLATION

Escort/Lynx, EXP/LN-7

1. Remove the window regulator handle retaining screw and handle.
2. Remove the door handle pull cup.
3. Remove the retaining screws from the armrest assembly. Remove the armrest. On vehicles with power door locks, disconnect the wiring connector.
4. Remove the trim panel retaining screws from the bottom of the map compartment, if so equipped.
5. Remove the retaining set screw from the remote control mirror bezel, if so equipped.
6. With a push pin tool, putty knife or simi-

558　BODY

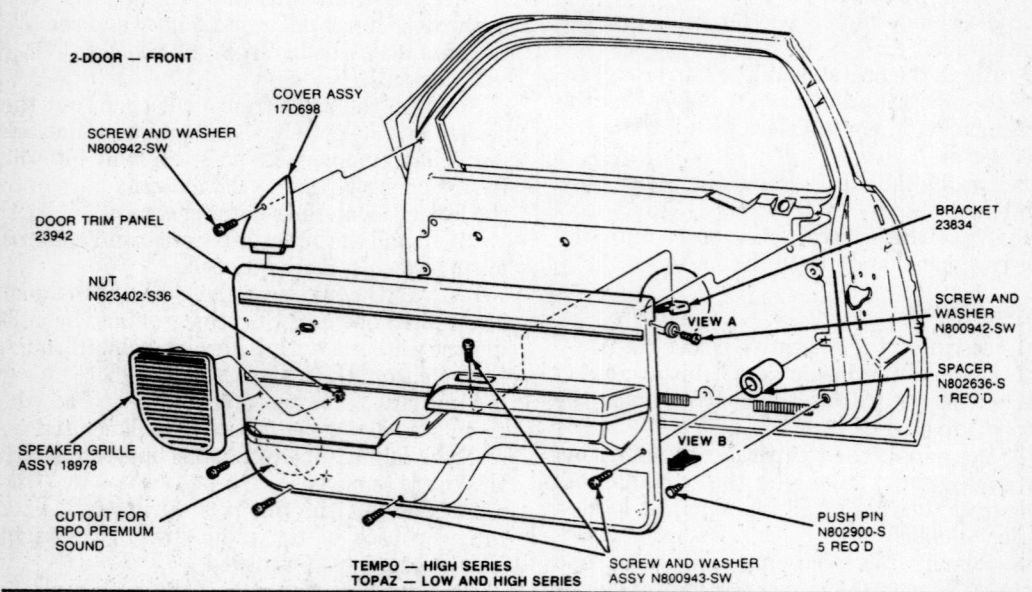

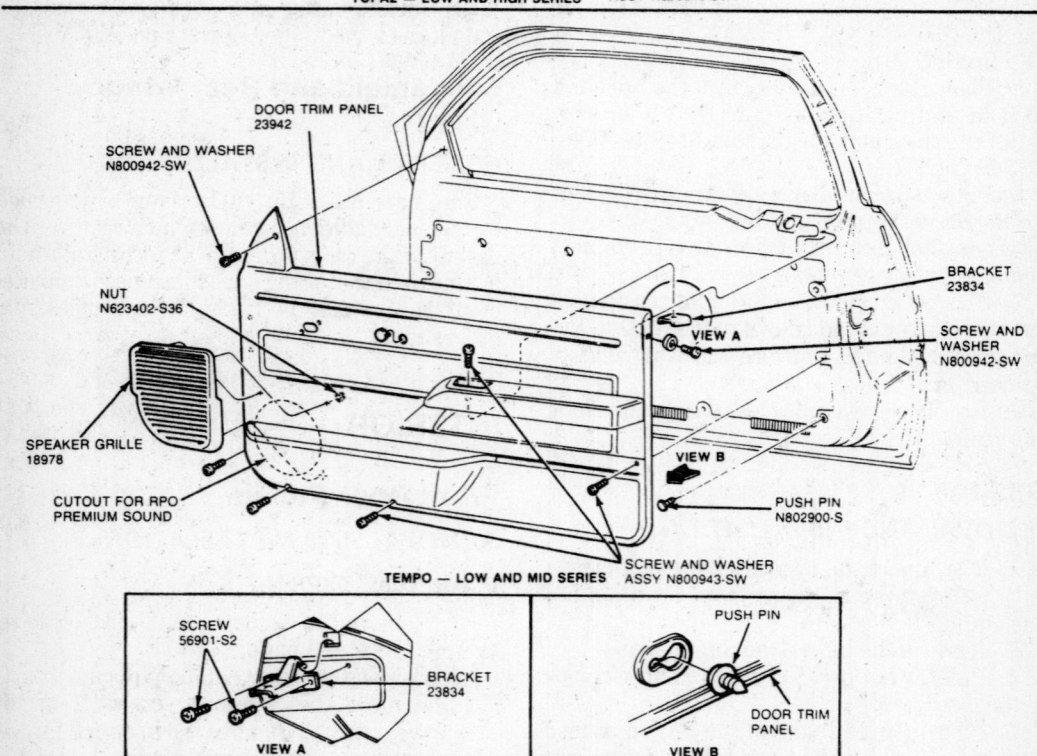

Tempo/Topaz door panel removal

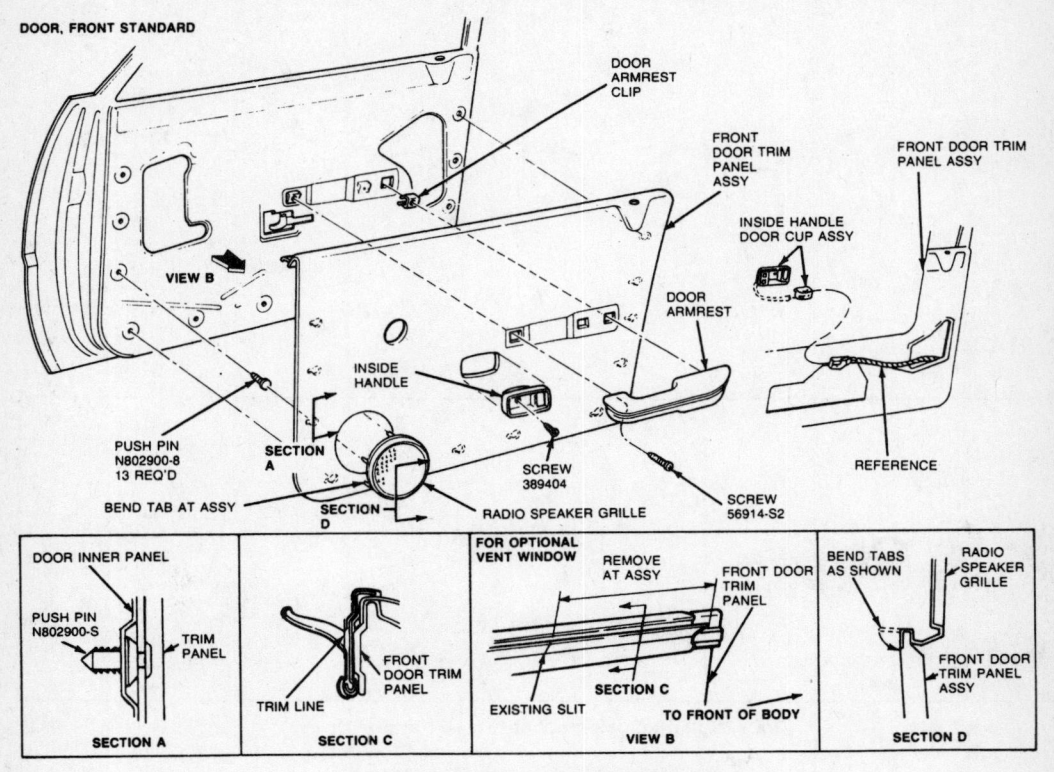

Escort/Lynx door panel removal

lar flat tool, pry the trim panel retaining push pins from the door interior panel.

NOTE: *Do not use the trim panel to pull the push pins from the door inner panel holes.*

7. If the trim panel is to be replaced, transfer the trim panel retaining push pins to the new panel assembly. Replace any bent, broken or missing push pins.

NOTE: *If the watershield has been removed, be sure to position it correctly before installing the trim panel.*

8. Be sure that the armrest retaining clips are properly positioned on the door inner panel. If they have been dislodged, they must be installed before installing the watershield.

9. Position the trim panel to the door inner panel. Route the remote control outside mirror cable through the bezel, if so equipped.

10. Position the trim panel to the door inner panel and locate the push pins in the countersunk holes. Firmly push the trim panel at the push pin locations to set each push pin.

11. Install the set screw from the remote control outside mirror bezel, if so equipped.

12. Install the trim panel retaining screws at the bottom of the map pocket, if so equipped.

13. On vehicles with power door locks, connect the wiring connector. Position the armrest to the trim panel and install the retaining screws.

14. Install the door handle pull cup.

15. Install the window regulator handle.

Tempo/Topaz

1. Remove the window regulator handle retaining screw and remove the handle.

2. Remove the retaining screw from the armrest recess and around the edge of the door panel.

3. Remove the retaining set screw from the remote control mirror bezel. Remove the bezel, if so equipped.

4. Remove the door handle pull cap, if so equipped.

5. With a push pin tool, putty knife or simi-

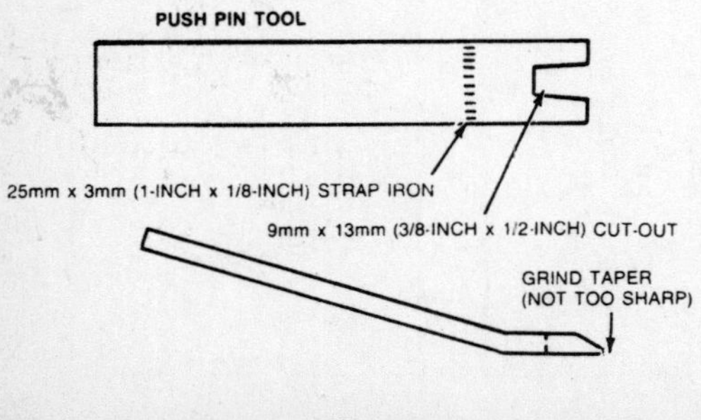

Push pin removal tool construction

560 BODY

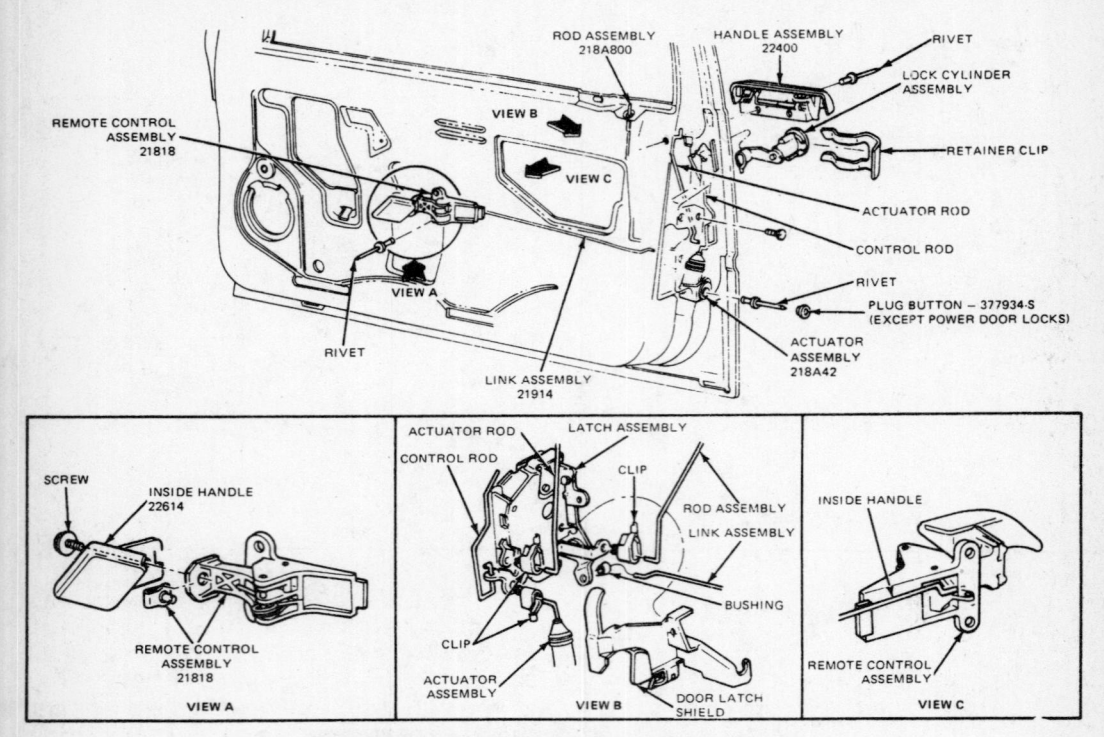

Door latch and lock mechanism — Tempo/Topaz

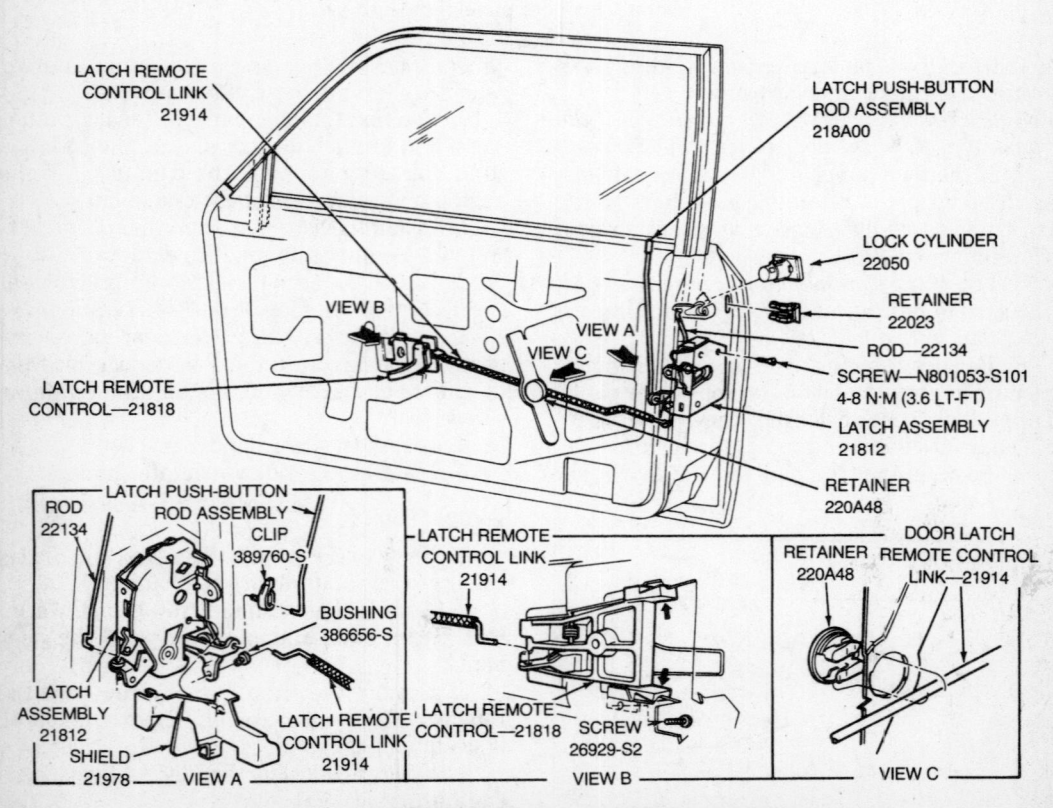

Door latch and lock mechanism — Escort/Lynx, EXP/LN7

BODY 561

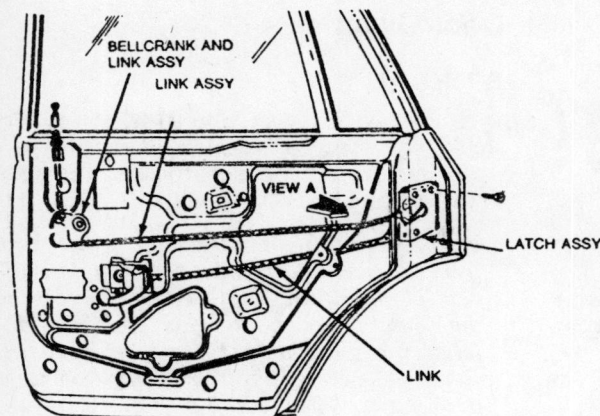

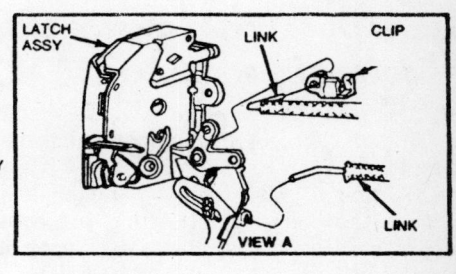

Typical door latch assembly — Escort/Lynx

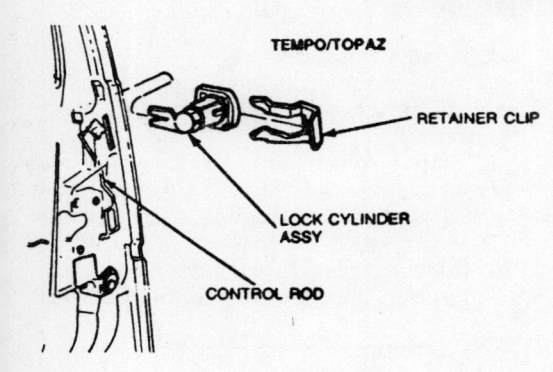

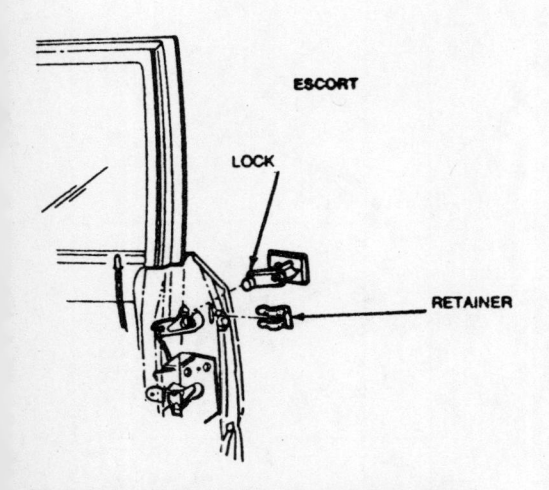

Door lock cylinder removal and installation

lar flat tool, pry the trim panel retaining push pins from the door interior panel.

NOTE: *Do not use the trim panel to pull the push pins from the door inner panel holes.*

6. If the trim panel is to be replaced, transfer the trim panel retaining push pins to the new panel assembly. Replace any bent, broken or missing push pins.

NOTE: *If the watershield has been removed, be sure to position it correctly before installing the trim panel.*

7. Be sure that the armrest retaining clips are properly positioned on the door inner panel. If they have been dislodged, they must be installed before installing the watershield.

8. Position the trim panel to the door inner panel. Route the remote control outside mirror cable through the bezel, if so equipped.

9. Position the trim panel to the door inner panel and locate the push pins in the countersunk holes. Firmly push the trim panel at the push pin locations to set each push pin.

10. Install the set screw from the remote control outside mirror bezel, if so equipped.

11. Install the trim panel retaining screws.

12. Install the door handle pull cup.

13. Install the window regulator handle.

Door Lock Cylinder

REMOVAL AND INSTALLATION

NOTE: *When a lock cylinder must be replaced, replace both locks in the set to avoid carrying an extra key which fits only one lock.*

1. Remove the door trim panel and the watershield.
2. Remove the clip attaching the lock cylinder rod to the lock cylinder.
3. Pry the lock cylinder retainer out of the slot in the door.
4. Remove the lock cylinder from the door.
5. Work the cylinder lock assembly into the outer door panel.
6. Install the cylinder retainer into its slot and push the retainer onto the lock cylinder.
7. Install the lock cylinder rod with the clip onto the lock assembly.
8. Lock and unlock the door to check the lock cylinder operation.

BODY

9. Install the watershield and door trim panel.

Power Door Lock Actuator Motor

REMOVAL AND INSTALLATION

1. Disconnect the negative battery cable.
2. Remove the door trim panel and the watershield.
3. Using a $1/4$ in. (6mm) diameter drill bit, remove the pop rivet attaching the actuator motor to the door. Disconnect the wiring at the connector.
4. Disconnect the actuator motor link from the door latch and remove the motor.

To install:

5. Connect the actuator motor link to the door latch.
6. Connect the wiring at the connector.
7. Install the door lock actuator motor to the door with a pop rivet, using a suitable rivet gun.

NOTE: *Make sure that the actuator boot is not twisted during installation. The pop rivet must be installed with the bracket base tight to the inner panel.*

8. Install the door trim panel and water shield. Reconnect the negative battery cable.

Door Glass

REMOVAL

1. Remove the door trim panel and watershield.
2. Remove the 2 rivets attaching the glass to the run and bracket assembly.

NOTE: *Prior to the removing center pins from the rivet, it is recommended that a suitable block support be inserted between the door outer panel and the glass bracket to stabilize the glass during the rivet removal. Remove the center pin from each rivet with a drift punch. Then, using a $1/4$ in. (6mm) diameter drill carefully drill out the remainder of each rivet as damage to the plastic glass retainer and spacer could result.*

3. Remove the glass.
4. Remove the drillings and pins from the bottom of the door.

To install:

5. Snap the plastic retainer and spacer into the two glass retainer holes. Make certain that the metal washer in the retainer assembly is on the outboard side of the glass.
6. Insert the glass into the door.
7. Position the door glass to the door glass

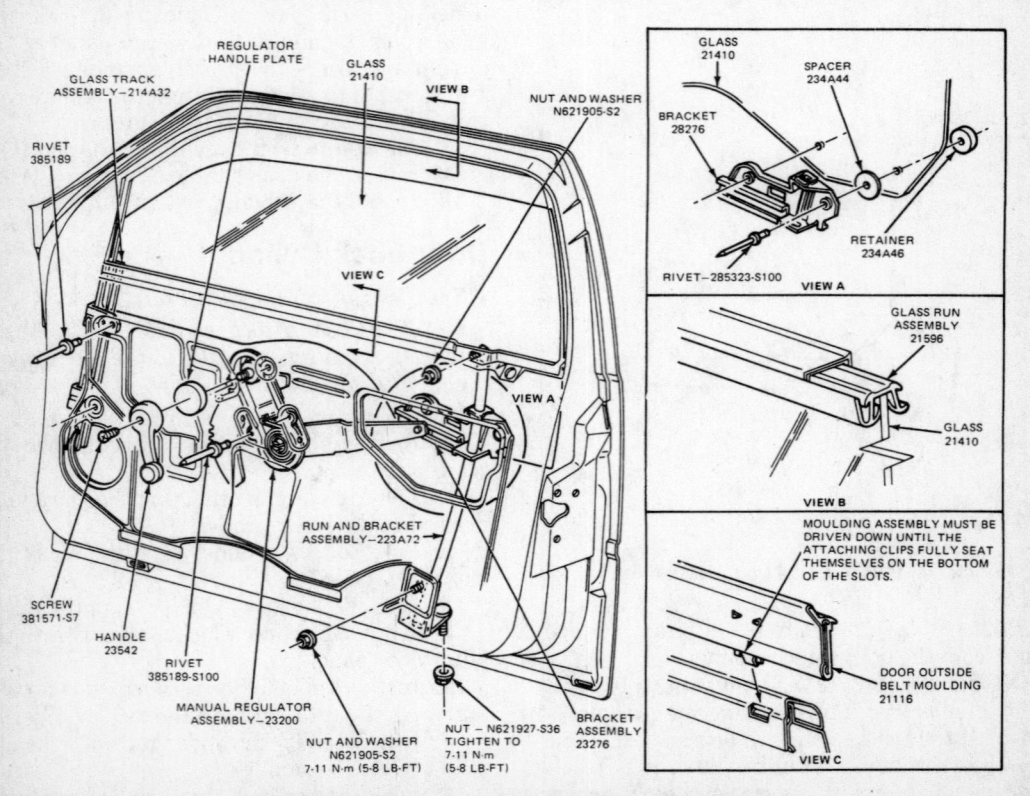

Tempo/Topaz door glass removal — others similar

BODY 563

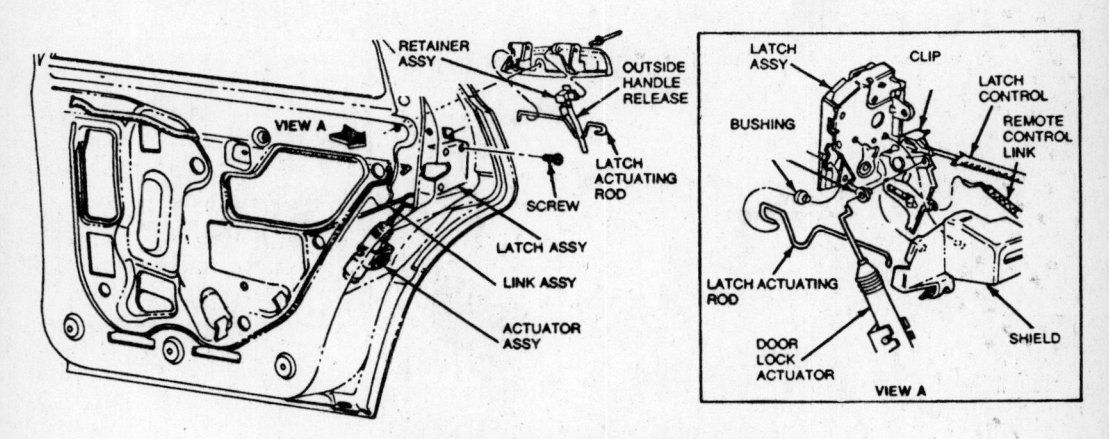

Typical rear door latch assembly — Tempo/Topaz

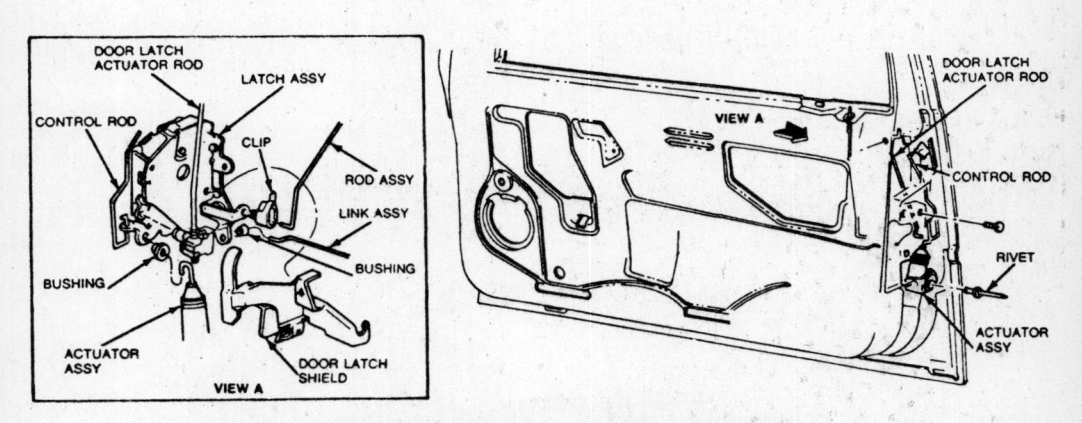

Power door lock actuator motor removal and installation

bracket and align the glass and glass bracket retaining holes

8. Install the retaining rivets.
9. Raise the glass to the full UP position.
10. Install the rear glass run retainer and rear glass run.
11. Check the operation of the window.
12. Install the trim panel and watershield.

Window Regulator

REMOVAL AND INSTALLATION

Front Windows

1. Remove the door trim panel and watershield.
2. Prop the glass if the full-up position.
3. Remove the 4 pop rivets attaching the reg-

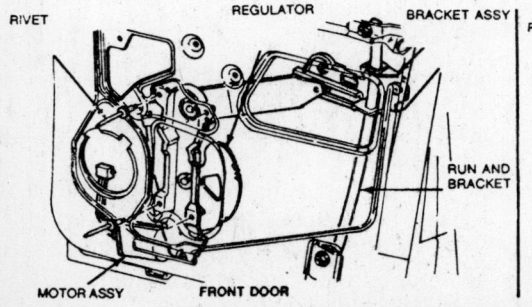

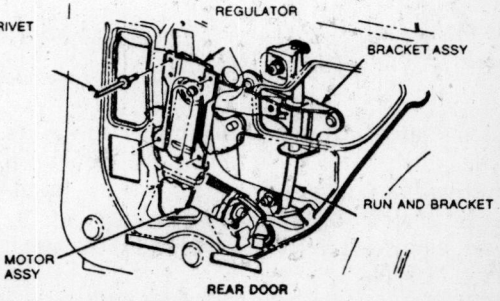

Typical front power window regulator assembly

564 BODY

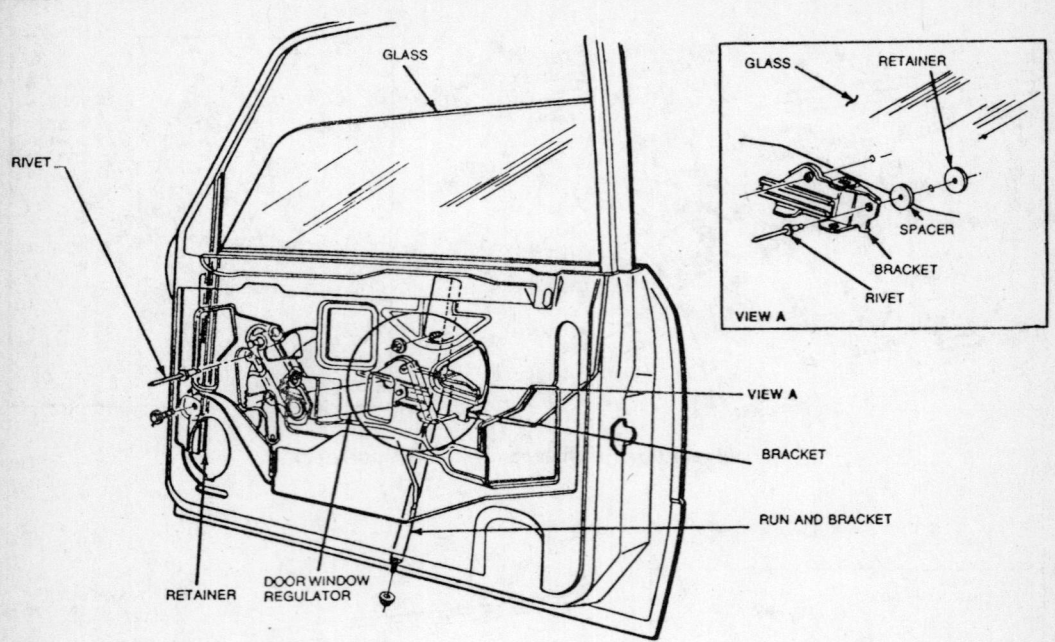

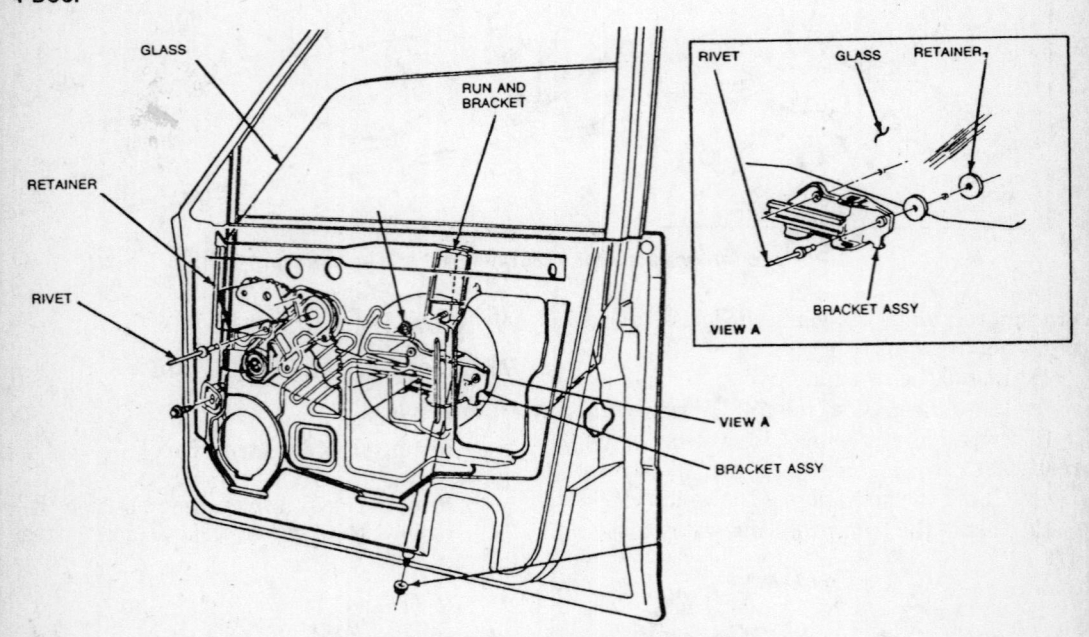

Typical front window regulator assemblies

ulator mounting plate assembly to the inner door panel. Remove the center pin from each rivet with a drift punch. Using a 1/4 in. (6mm) diameter drill, drill out the remainder of the rivet, using care not to enlarge the sheet metal retaining holes.

4. Remove the 2 nut and washer assemblies attaching the regulator tube to the inner panel and door sill.

5. On the Tempo/Topaz models, slide the tube up between the door belt and glass.

6. On the Escort/Lynx models, slide the run and bracket rearward at the bottom.

7. Remove the window regulator arm slide/

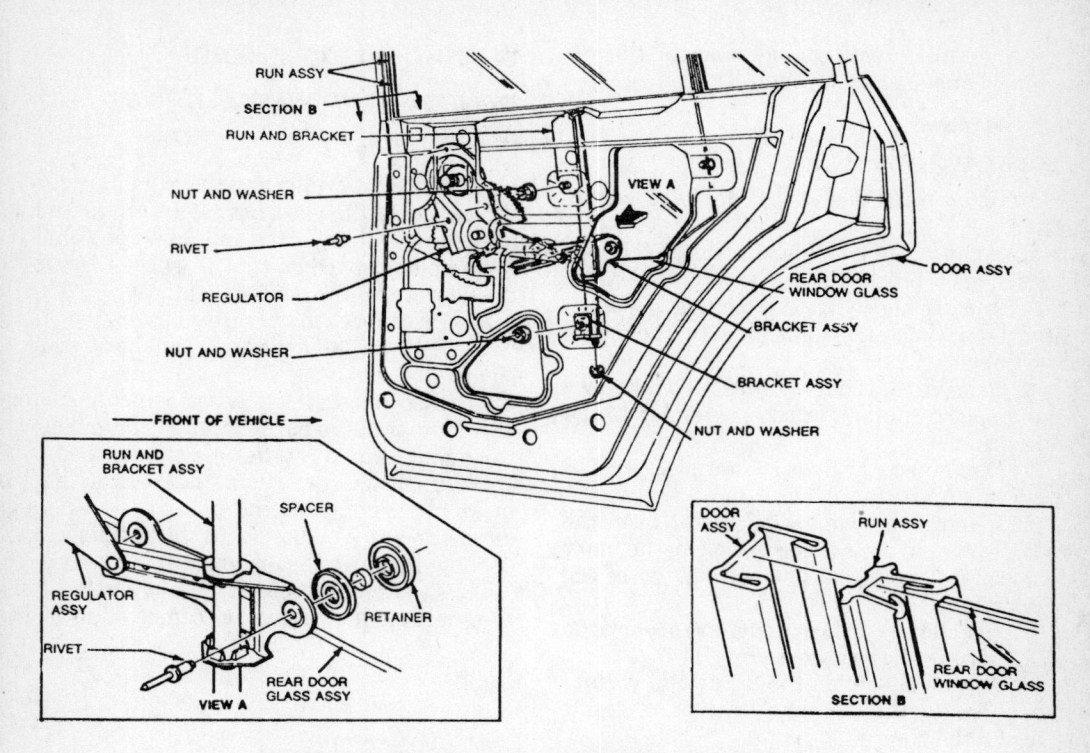

Typical rear window regulator assemblies — Escort/Lynx

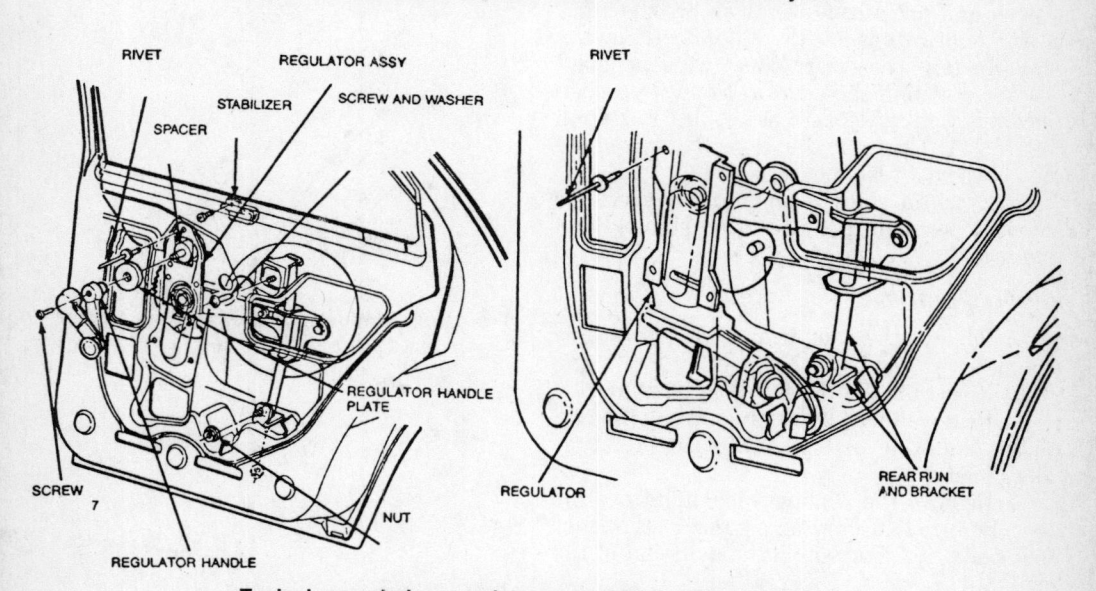

Typical rear window regulator assemblies — Tempo/Topaz

roller from the glass bracket C-channel and remove the regulator.

To install:

8. With glass in full position, install the window regulator through the access hole in the door and insert the slide roller into the glass bracket channel.

9. Slide the tube assembly (down for Tempo/Topaz vehicles, forward for Escort/Lynx vehicles) into position, loosely install the 2 nut and washer assemblies to the regulator tube guide.

10. Install the 4 rivets or 4, 1/4 in.-20 × 1/2 in. screws and washer assemblies and 2, 1/4 in.-20 nut/washer assemblies to secure the regulator handle mounting plate to door inner panel. Equivalent metric retainers may be used.

11. Tighten loosely assembled nut and washer assemblies from Step 9. 12. Cycle the

BODY

glass to ensure smooth operation. Install the watershield and door trim panel.

Rear Windows

ESCORT AND LYNX

1. Remove the door trim panel and watershield.
2. Remove the 2 rivets attaching the main glass-to-glass bracket.
3. Remove the 3 rivets attaching the regulator mounting plate assembly to the inner door panel.
4. Remove the 2 nut and washer assemblies retaining the run and bracket assembly to the inner panel.
5. Disconnect the door latch remote rods at the door latch.
6. Remove the window regulator from the door. Be sure to use the access hole in the inner door panel for removal and installation of the regulator.
7. Install the window regulator through the access hole in the rear door.
8. Loosely assemble the 2 nut and washer assemblies to the run and bracket assembly studs on the door inner panel.
9. Install 3 rivets or 3 equivalent screw, washer and nut assemblies to secure the regulator mounting plate to the inner door panel.
10. Install the rear door window glass bracket. Position the glass in the full up position and tighten loosely assembles nut from Step 8. 11. Connect the door latch remote rods at the door latch.
12. Cycle the glass up and down to check for smooth operation. Install the watershield and trim panel.

TEMPO AND TOPAZ

1. Remove the door trim panel and watershield.
2. Prop the glass if the full-up position.
3. Remove the pop rivets attaching the regulator mounting plate assembly to the inner door panel.
4. Remove the window regulator from the door. Be sure to use the access hole in the inner door panel for removal and installation of the regulator.

To install:

6. Install the window regulator through the access hole in the rear door and slide the arm roller into the glass bracket C-channel.
7. Install rivets or equivalent screw, washer and nut assemblies to secure the regulator mounting plate to the inner door panel.
8. Cycle the glass up and down to check for smooth operation. Install the watershield and trim panel.

Electric Window Motor

REMOVAL AND INSTALLATION

Front — 4-Door

1. Raise the window to the full up position, if possible. If the glass cannot be raised and is partially down or in the full down position, it must be supported so that it will not fall into the door well during motor removal.
2. Disconnect the negative battery cable.
3. Remove the door trim panel and watershield.
4. Disconnect the electric window motor wire from the wire harness connector and move the motor away from the area to be drilled.
5. Using a $3/4$ in. (19mm) hole saw with a $1/4$ in. (6mm) pilot, drill the hole at the existing dimple (point A) adjacent to the radio speaker opening. Remove the drillings.
6. At the upper motor mount screw head, the sheet metal interference can be removed by

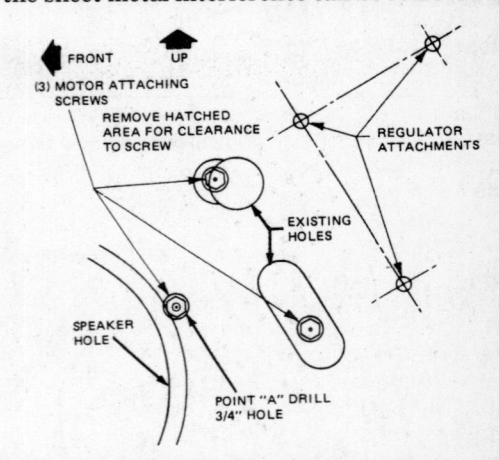

Front door window motor template — 4-door

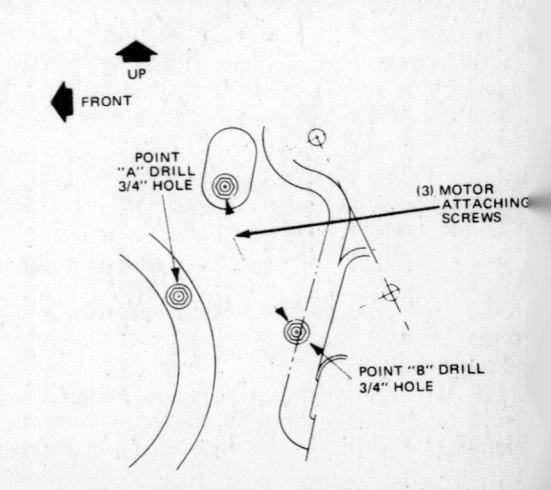

Front door window motor template — 2 door

grinding out the inner panel surface sufficiently to clear the screw head for easy removal. Remove the drillings.

NOTE: *Before the removal of the motor drive assembly, make certain that the regulator arm is in a fixed position to prevent counterbalance spring unwind.*

7. Remove the three window motor mounting screws and disengage the motor and drive assembly from the regulator quadrant gear.
8. Install the new motor and drive assembly. Tighten the three motor mounting screws to 50–85 inch lbs.
9. Connect window motor wiring harness leads.
10. Connect the negative battery cable.
11. Check the power window for proper operation.
12. Install the door trim panel and watershield. Check that all drain holes at the bottom of the doors are open to prevent water accumulation over the motor.

Rear — 4-Door

1. Raise the window to the full up position, if possible. If the glass cannot be raised and is partially down or in the full down position, it must be supported so that it will not fall into the door well during motor removal.
2. Disconnect the negative battery cable.
3. Remove the door trim panel and watershield.
4. Disconnect the electric window motor wire from the wire harness connector and move the motor away from the area to be drilled.
5. Using a ³/₄ in. (19mm) hole saw with a ¹/₄ in. (6mm) pilot, drill three holes in the door inner panel at the three existing dimples to gain access to the three motor and drive attaching screws. Remove the drillings.

NOTE: *Before the removal of the motor drive assembly, make certain that the regulator arm is in a fixed position to prevent counterbalance spring unwind.*

7. Remove the three window motor mounting screws and disengage the motor and drive assembly from the regulator quadrant gear.
8. Install the new motor and drive assembly. Tighten the three motor mounting screws to 50–85 inch lbs.
9. Connect window motor wiring harness leads.
10. Connect the negative battery cable.
11. Check the power window for proper operation.
12. Install the door trim panel and watershield. Check that all drain holes at the bottom of the doors are open to prevent water accumulation over the motor.

Front — 2-Door

1. Raise the window to the full up position, if possible. If the glass cannot be raised and is partially down or in the full down position, it must be supported so that it will not fall into the door well during motor removal.
2. Disconnect the negative battery cable.
3. Remove the door trim panel and watershield.
4. Disconnect the electric window motor wire from the wire harness connector and move the motor away from the area to be drilled.
5. Using a ³/₄ in. (19mm) hole saw with a ¹/₄ in. (6mm) pilot, drill the hole at point **A** and point **B** dimples. Remove the drillings.

NOTE: *Before the removal of the motor drive assembly, make certain that the regulator arm is in a fixed position to prevent counterbalance spring unwind.*

6. Remove the three window motor mounting screws and disengage the motor and drive assembly from the regulator quadrant gear.
7. Install the new motor and drive assembly. Tighten the three motor mounting screws to 50–85 inch lbs.
8. Connect window motor wiring harness leads.
9. Connect the negative battery cable.
10. Check the power window for proper operation.
11. Install the door trim panel and watershield. Check that all drain holes at the bottom of the doors are open to prevent water accumulation over the motor.

Inside Mirror

REMOVAL AND INSTALLATION

1. Loosen the mirror assembly-to-mounting bracket set screw.
2. Remove the mirror assembly by sliding upward and away from the mounting bracket.
3. Install it by attaching the mirror assembly to the mounting bracket and tighten the set screw to 10–20 inch lbs.

NOTE: *If the mirror bracket pad has to be removed from the windshield (or if it has fallen off), it will be necessary to use a suita-*

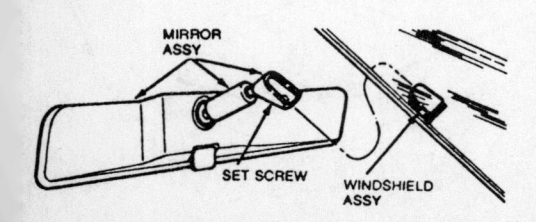

Typical rear view mirror removal and installation

568 BODY

ble heat gun to heat the vinyl pad until vinyl softens. Peel the vinyl off the windshield and discard. Install the new one as follows:

a. Make sure glass, bracket and adhesive kit (Rearview mirror adhesive D9AZ-19554-CA or equivalent) are at least at room temperature 65–75°F (18–24°C).

b. Locate and mark the mirror mounting bracket location on the outside surface of the windshield.

c. Thoroughly clean the bonding surfaces of the glass and bracket to remove old adhesive if reusing the old mirror bracket pad. Use a mild abrasive cleaner on the glass and fine sandpaper on the bracket to lightly roughen the surface. Wipe clean with a alcohol moistened cloth.

d. Crush the accelerator vial (part of the Rearview mirror adhesive kit D9AZ-19554-CA) and apply the accelerator to the bonding surface of the bracket and windshield. Let it dry for 3 minutes.

e. Apply 2 drops of adhesive (part of the Rearview mirror adhesive kit D9AZ-19554-CA) to the mounting surface of the bracket and windshield. Using a clean toothpick or a wooden match, quickly spread the adhesive evenly over the mounting surface of the bracket.

f. Quickly position the mounting bracket on the windshield. The 3/8 in. (9.5mm) circular depression in the bracket must be toward the inside of the passengers compartment. Press the bracket firmly against the windshield for one minute.

g. Allow the bond to set for five minutes. Remove any excess bonding material from the windshield with an alcohol dampened cloth.

Seats

REMOVAL AND INSTALLATION

Front Seats

MANUAL SEATS

The manual front seats are installed on a metal track that is retained to the floor board by studs with nut and washer assemblies or screws with a washer type head. Nuts and/or screws retaining the seat tracks are removed from inside and/or underneath the vehicle.

1. Remove the seat track plastic shield retaining pins, screws and/or nuts and washers from inside or underneath the vehicle. If the screws and/or nuts have to be removed from underneath the vehicle, be sure to raise the vehicle and support with the proper jack stands. Lift the seat and seat track assembly from the vehicle.

NOTE: *Be sure not to drop the seat and seat tracking assembly and do not sit on the seat if it is not secured in the vehicle because it may result in damaged components.*

2. Place the seat and seat track assemblies on a clean working area and disconnect the adjusting springs, assist spring and latch tie wire from the tracks.

3. Remove the seat track-to-seat cushion attaching screws and remove the seat cushion from the tracks.

NOTE: *To ease in the assist spring removal and installation, adjust the seat to the full forward position.*

4. If the seat tracks are being replaced, transfer the retracting springs and spacers (antisqueak) to the new track assembly.

5. Mount the seat tracks to the seat cushion.

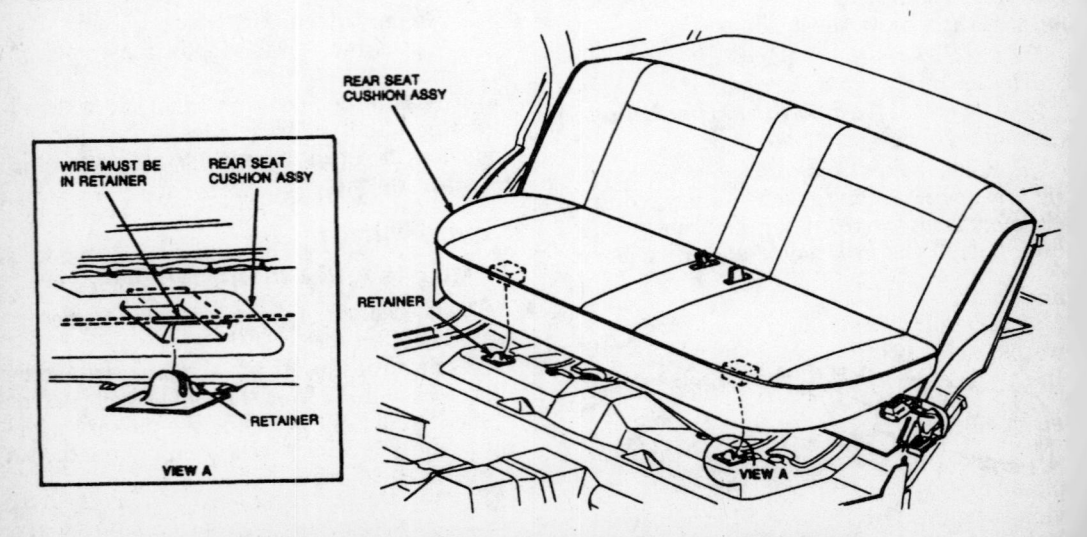

Typical conventional rear seat cushion removal and installation

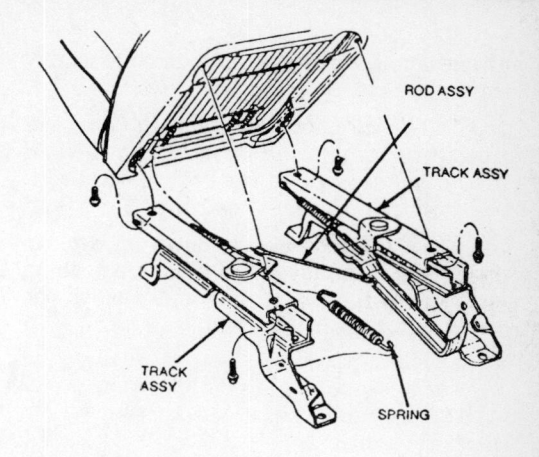

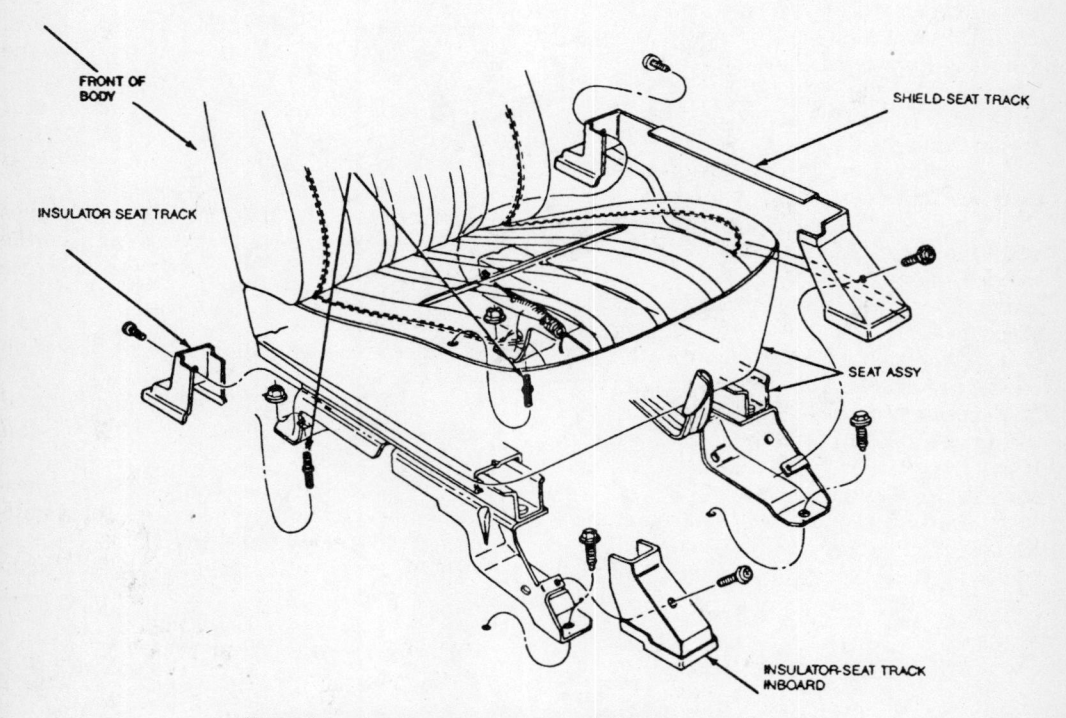

BODY 569

Typical front seat removal and installation — Tempo/Topaz

6. Install the seat-track-to-seat cushion retaining screws and tighten them to 9-18 ft. lbs. Install the tie wire to the track and install the assist springs.

7. Place the seat assembly into the vehicle and insure proper alignment.

8. Install the screws, studs and/or nuts and washer assemblies. Torque them to 9-18 ft. lbs. Install the plastic shield.

POWER SEATS

The driver's power seat uses a rack and pinion drive system. The 6-way power seat provides horizontal, vertical and tilt adjustments. It consists of a reversible 3 armature motor (tri-motor), a switch and housing assembly, vertical gear drives and horizontal rack and pinion drives.

1. Disconnect the negative battery cable.

2. Remove the heat shield (insulators) to expose the nuts and washers and/or bolts.

3. Remove the seat track screws and/or nuts and washers from inside or underneath the vehicle. If the screws and/or nuts have to be removed from underneath the vehicle, be sure to raise the vehicle and support with the proper jack stands.

4. Lift the seat up enough to disconnect the seat motor wires. Remove the 2 bolts attaching the safety belts to the floor and disconnect the

570　BODY

multiple connector. Remove the seat assembly from the vehicle.

NOTE: *Be sure not to drop the seat and seat tracking assembly and do not sit on the seat if it is not secured in the vehicle because it may result in damaged components.*

5. Place the seat upside down on a clean working area. Remove the 4 bolts attaching each track to the seat frame and remove the track assembly from each seat.

6. Mount the seat tracks to the seat cushion.

7. Install the 4 track-to-cushion attaching bolts. Measurements should be made between the track base channels.

8. Connect the seat control to the track assembly at the connectors.

9. Position the seat and track assembly in the vehicle.

Connect the seat motor wires at the connec-

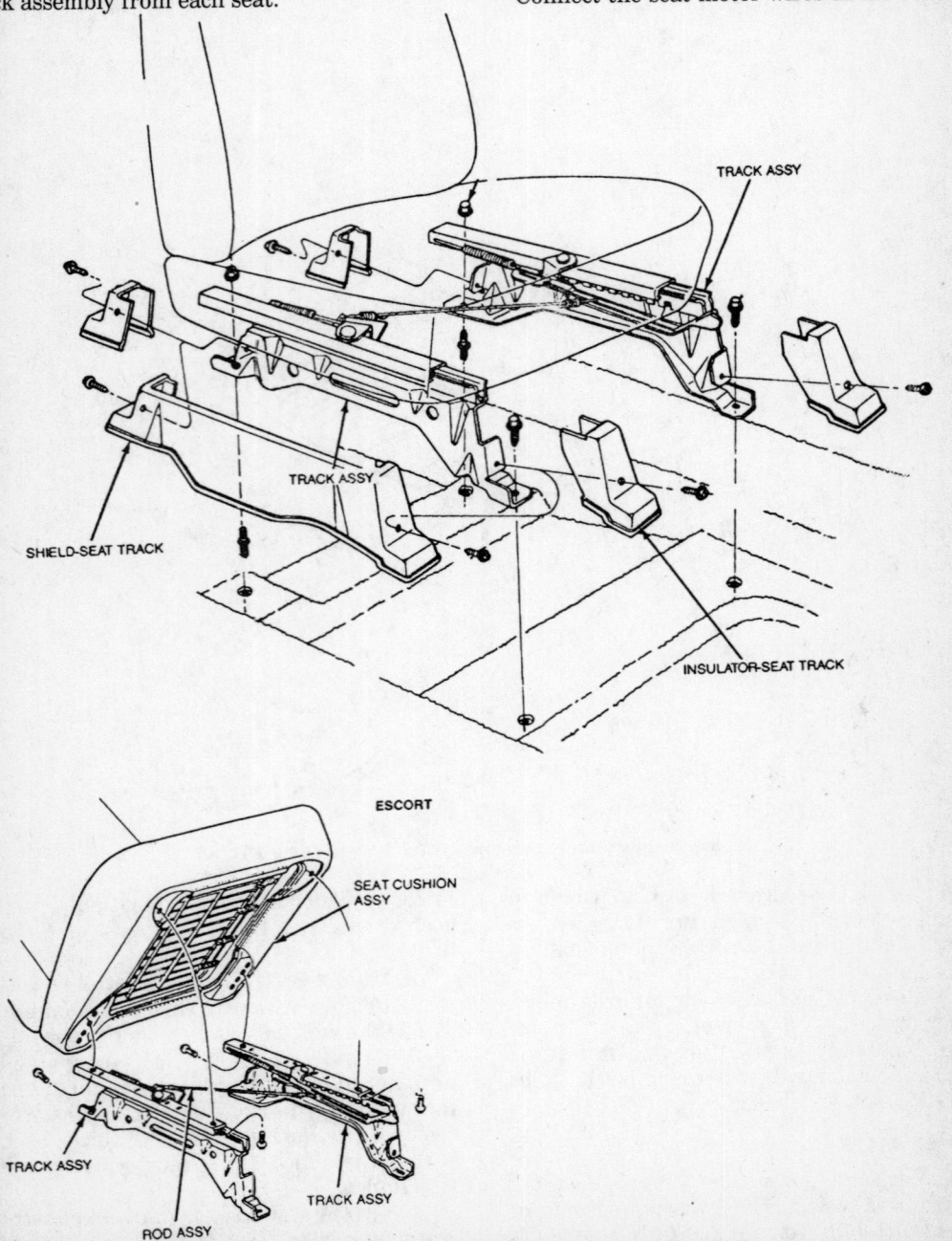

Typical front seat removal and installation — Escort/Lynx

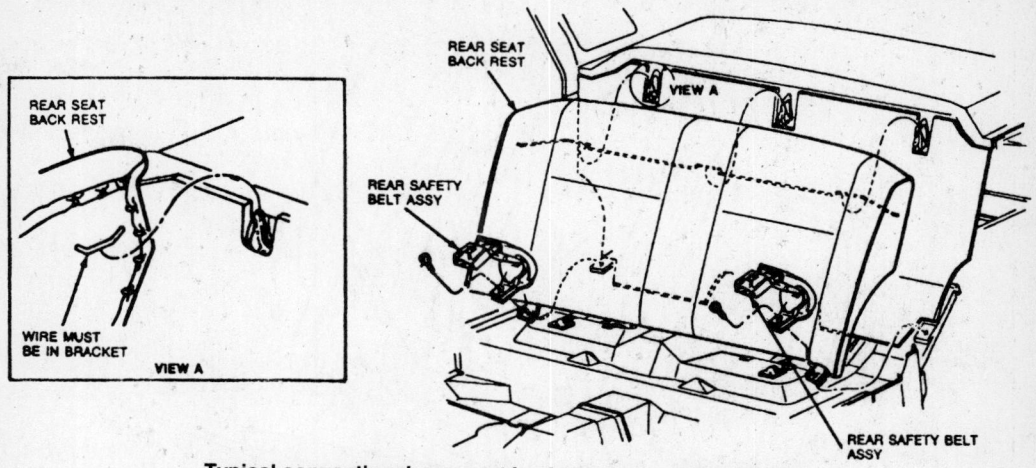

BODY 571

Typical conventional rear seat back removal and installation

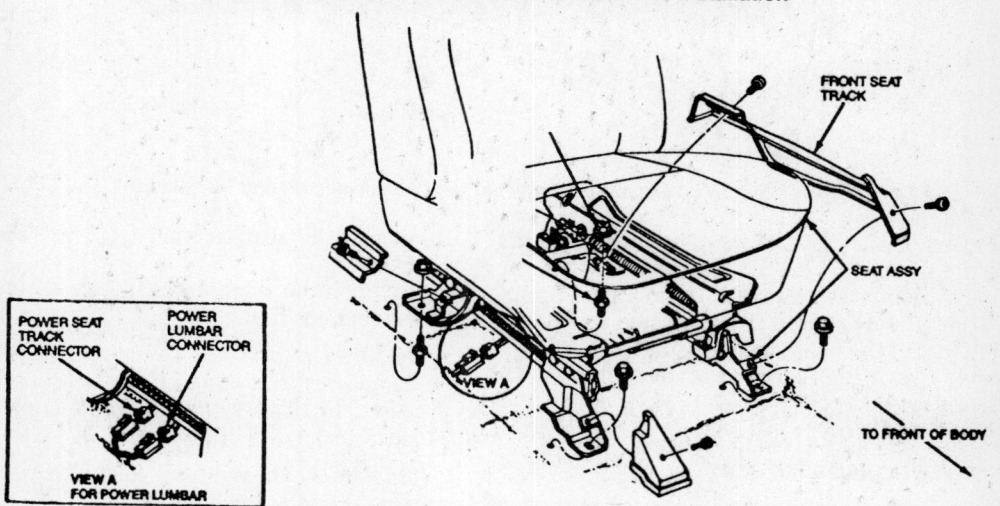

Typical power seat removal and installation

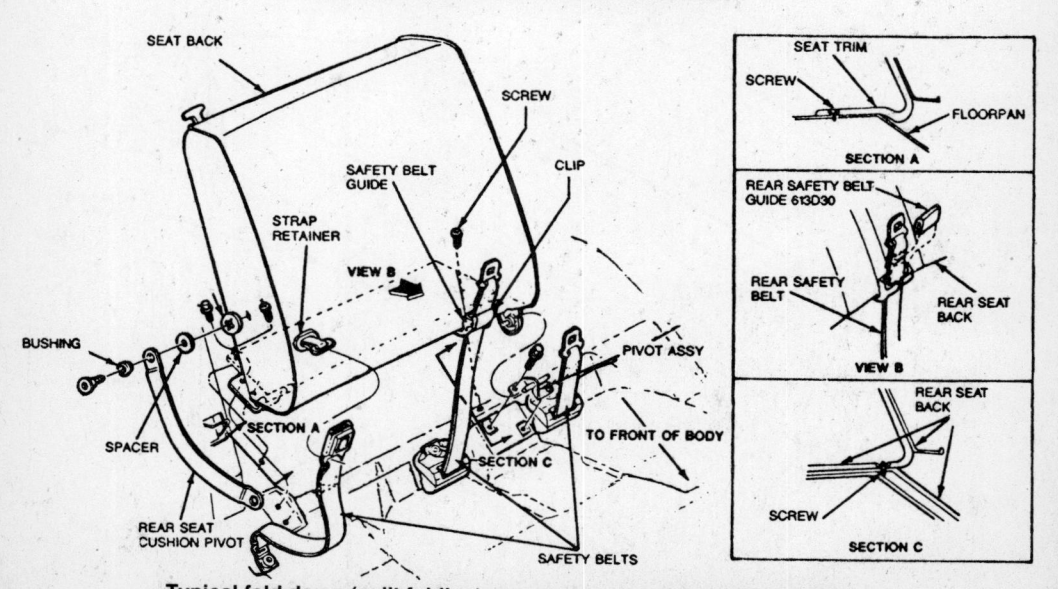

Typical fold down (split folding) rear seat back removal and installation

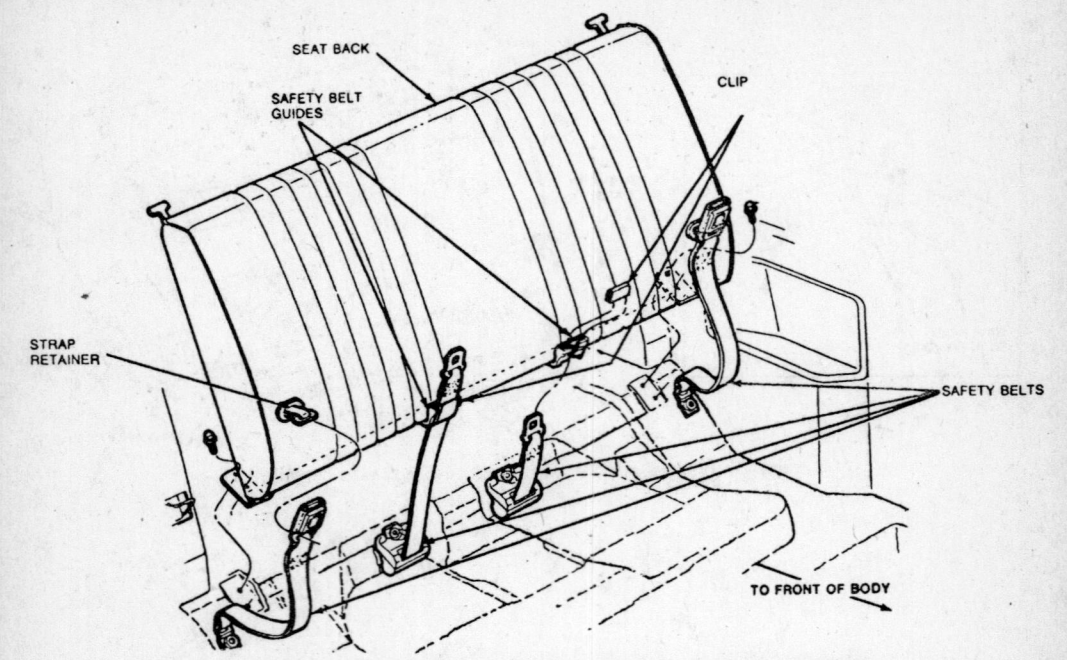

572 BODY

Typical fold down (full folding) rear seat back removal and installation

tor. Install the 2 bolts attaching the safety belts to the floor.

10. Install the seat track-to-floor pan retaining nuts and/or bolts. Torque them to 9-18 ft. lbs. Install the heat shield (insulators).

11. Check the operation of the seat.

Rear Seats

CONVENTIONAL REAR SEAT

1. Apply knee pressure to the lower portion of the rear seat cushion; then push rearward to disengage the seat cushion from the retainer brackets.

2. Push the safety belts through the bezels in the seat cushion.

NOTE: *The arm rest is an integral part of the quarter trim panel. Its removal is not required to remove the rear seat cushion or back.*

3. Remove the rear seat cushion, by first removing the safety belt assembly bolts.

4. Grasp the seat back assembly at the

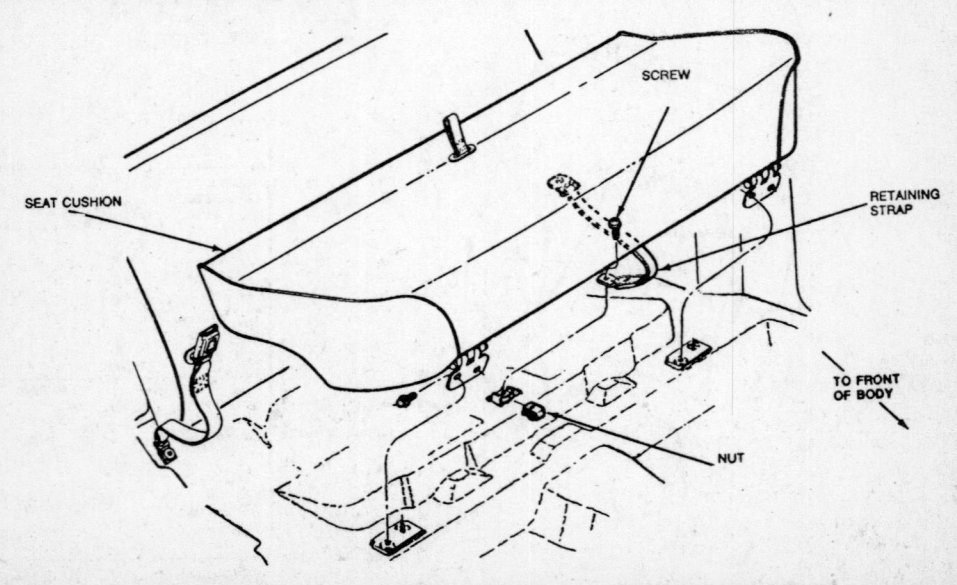

Typical fold down (full folding) rear cushion removal and installation

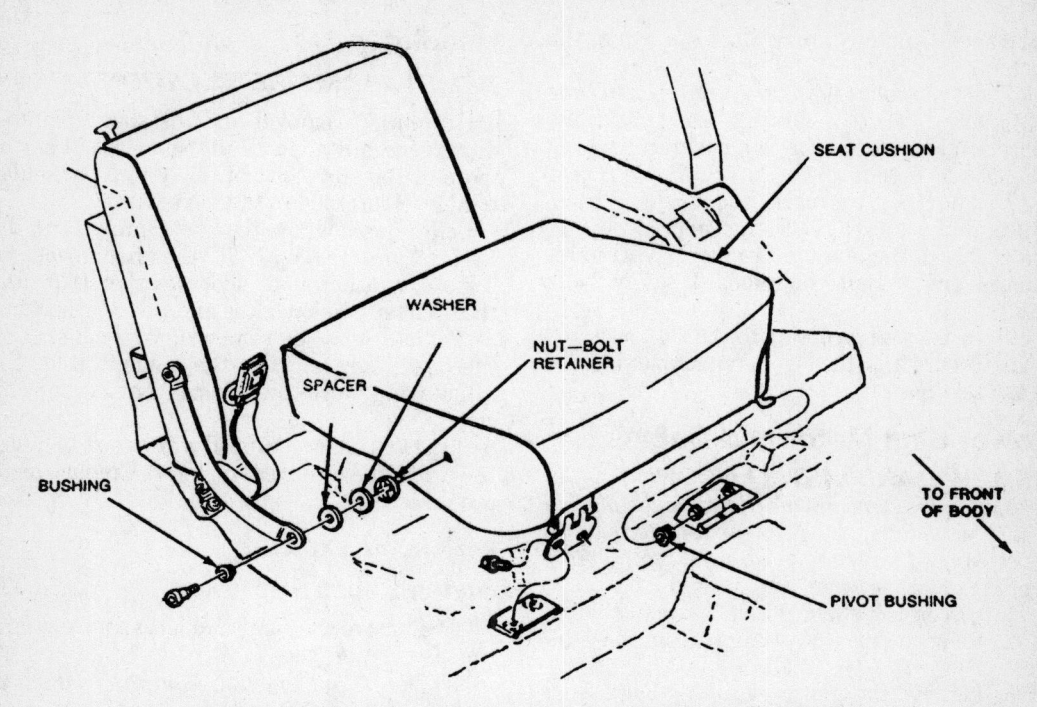

Typical fold down (split folding) rear cushion removal and installation

bottom and lift up to disengage the hanger wire from the retainer brackets.

To install:

5. Position the seat back in the vehicle so that hanger wire are engaged with the retaining brackets.
6. Install safety belt assemblies and tighten the bolts to 22-32 ft. lbs. Install the rear seat cushion as follows:

    a. Position the seat cushion assembly into the vehicle.
    b. Insert the safety belts through the cushions.
    c. Apply knee pressure to the lower portion of the seat cushion assembly and push rearward and down to lock the seat cushion into position.
    d. Pull the rear seat cushion forward to ensure it is secured into the floor retainer.

REAR FOLD DOWN SEATS

1. When removing the seat cushion portion of the rear split folding seat, remove the articulating arm mounting bolt, bushing, spacer and washer from the seat cushion. Fold the seat cushion forward.
2. On the full folding seat only, remove the retaining strap attaching screw.
3. Remove the hinge attaching screws.
4. Remove the seat cushion from the vehicle. On the split folding seat only, slide the seat cushion pivot pin out of the bushing and bracket.
5. To remove the seat back portion of the rear fold down seat, detach the luggage compartment cover from the seat back.
6. Remove the carpeting from the seat back.
7. Disengage the inboard safety belts from the guides and outboard safety belts from the strap retainers. Pull the strap retainers through the holes in the seat back from the rear.
8. Fold the seat back forward. Remove the 2 screws attaching each hinge to the floor.
9. Remove the seat back from the vehicle. For split folding seat only, slide the seat back off the pivot assembly to remove.

To install:

10. Install the seat back into the vehicle. For the spilt folding seats only, slide the seat back over the pivot assembly.
11. Install the hinge attaching screws and tighten to at this time.
12. Install the seat cushion in the vehicle. For split folding seats only, insert the seat cushion pivot pin into the bushing bracket.
13. Install the hinge attaching screws. Tighten the screws to 13-20 ft. lbs.
14. On the full folding seats only, install the retaining strap attaching screw. Fold the seat cushion back. Be sure that the seat cushion

574 BODY

latch is engaged by pulling up at the rear of the cushion.

15. On the split folding seats only, install the articulating arm mounting bolt, bushing, spacer and washer to the seat cushion. Tighten the bolt to 14-16 ft. lbs.

17. Fold the seat back and cushion back. Check that both seat back engage properly.

18. Install the outboard safety belt strap retainers and install the inboard safety belts guides.

19. Install the carpeting to the seat back.

20. Secure the luggage compartment cover to the seat back.

Power Seat Motor and Cables
REMOVAL AND INSTALLATION

NOTE: *It is recommended that when a cable is to be replaced, the power seat motor should be removed in order to ease the replacement of the defective cable.*

1. Disconnect the negative battery cable.
2. Remove the seat assembly from the vehicle.
3. Remove the motor retaining bolts from the seat mounting.
4. Disconnect the housings and the cables from the motor.
5. Remove the motor assembly from its mounting.
6. Installation is the reverse of removal.

Headliner
REMOVAL AND INSTALLATION

Headlining removal and installation procedures generally apply to all trim levels. If one or more of the steps do not apply to a particular trim level, proceed to the next step.

Before removing the headlining on the Escort/Lynx, EXP/LN-7, the hatchback or liftgate weatherstrip, door weatherstrip, and the quarter window glass and the weatherstrip assemblies must be removed. When installing the headlining, start at the hatchback, or the liftgate and move toward the front of the vehicle.

If the vehicle is equipped with assist handles, they must be removed during the replacement procedure.

Escort/Lynx, EXP/LN-7

3-DOOR, 2-DOOR HATCHBACK

1. Remove the right and left sun visors and the visor center clips.

NOTE: *If the vehicle is equipped with illuminated sun visors, disconnect the electrical leads.*

2. Remove the header garnish molding.
3. Remove the windshield side garnish moldings.
4. Remove the dome light.

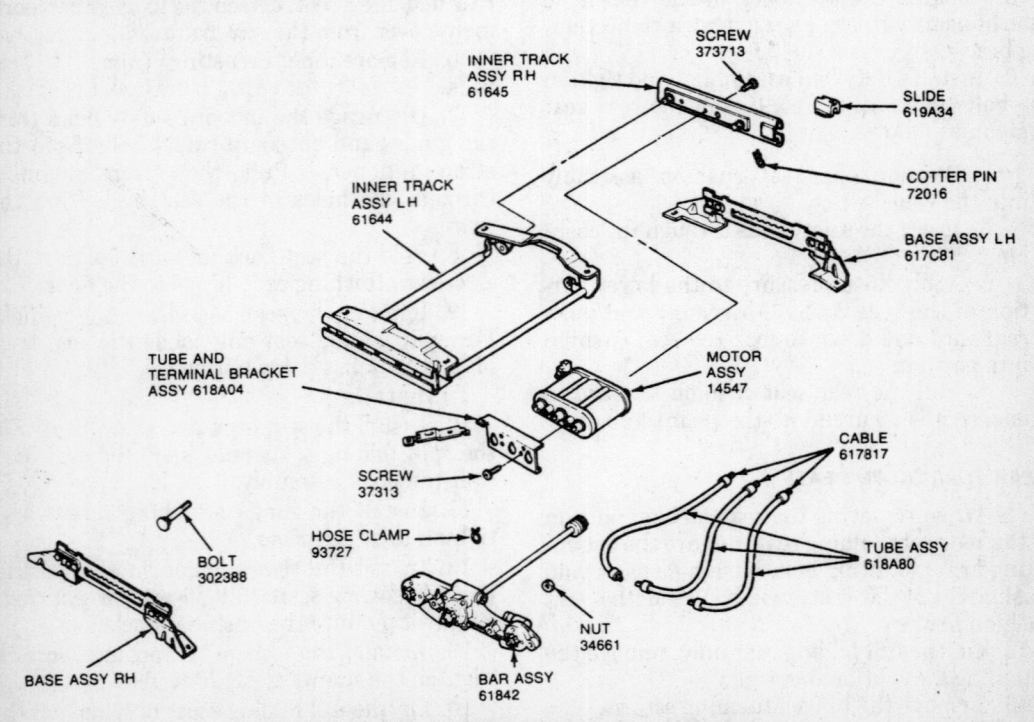

Power seat motor assembly — Tempo/Topaz

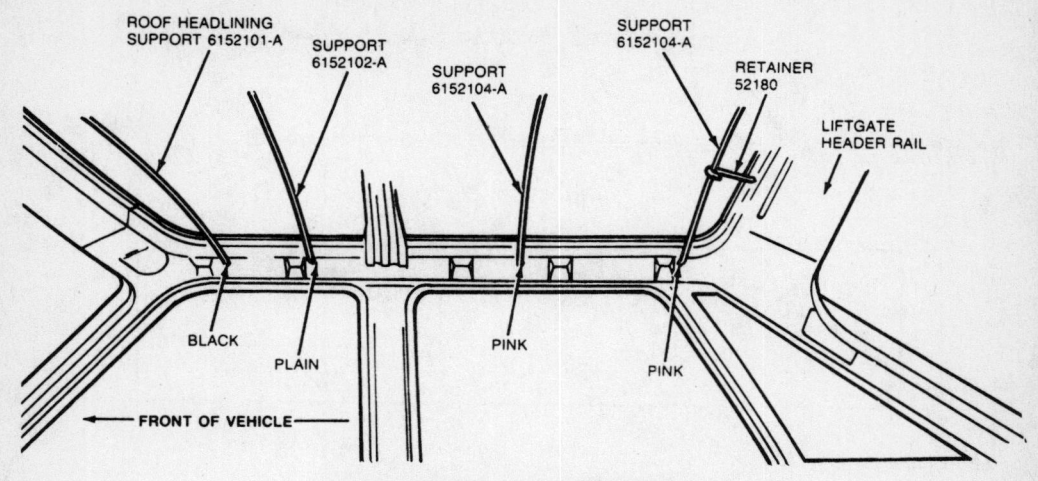

Headliner support rods — Escort/Lynx

5. Remove the roof rail assist handles and coat hooks.
6. Remove the roof rail weatherstrip assemblies.
7. Detach the liftgate gas cylinders at body opening.
8. Detach the ground wire for the heated rear window, if so equipped.
9. Remove the folding rear seat assembly including the luggage cover.
10. Remove the quarter window and weatherstrip assemblies.
11. Remove the headlining.

To install:

12. Unpackage the new headlining and lay it out on a flat surface. Mark and trim the new headlining using the old one as a pattern.
13. Trim the listings, pockets, on the new headlining to the approximate length of the old one. Remove the support rods from the old headlining and install them in the same relative rod positions of the new headliner. The roof headlining support rods are color coded at each end. When ordering new rods, be sure to note the color at each end of the rod.
14. Position the headliner in the vehicle, connect the bows.
15. Starting at the rear window area, apply trim cement and align the rear bow to the vertical position.
16. Working from the center to the outboard side, stretch and cement the headliner to the rear window opening flange.
17. Apply cement to the windshield opening flange, door opening weatherstrip flange, quarter glass and hatchback opening flanges. Align

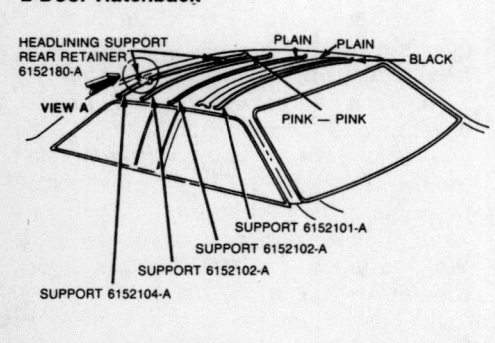

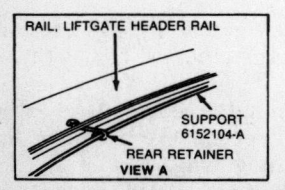

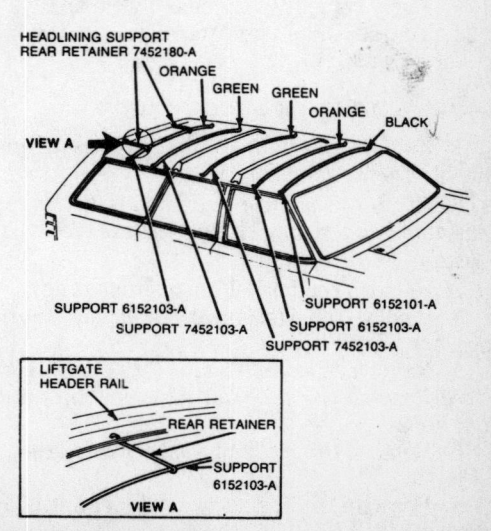

Headliner support rods — Escort/Lynx, EXP/LN7

576 BODY

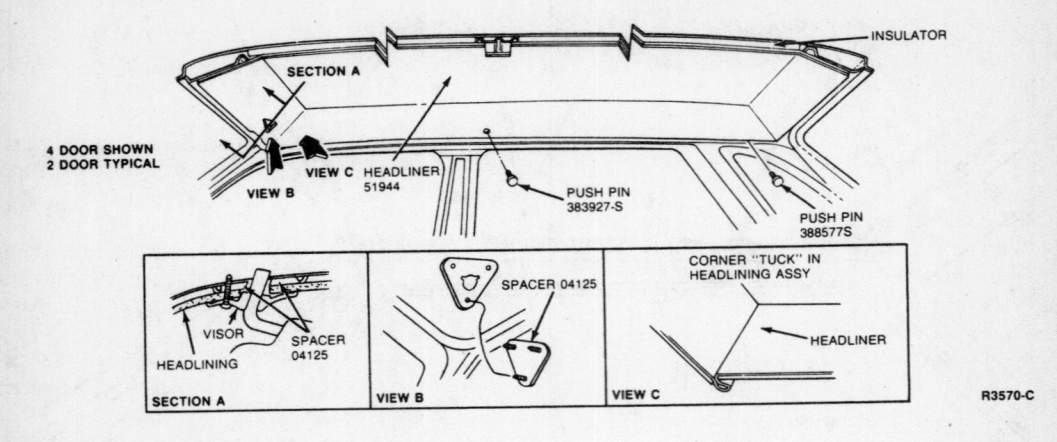

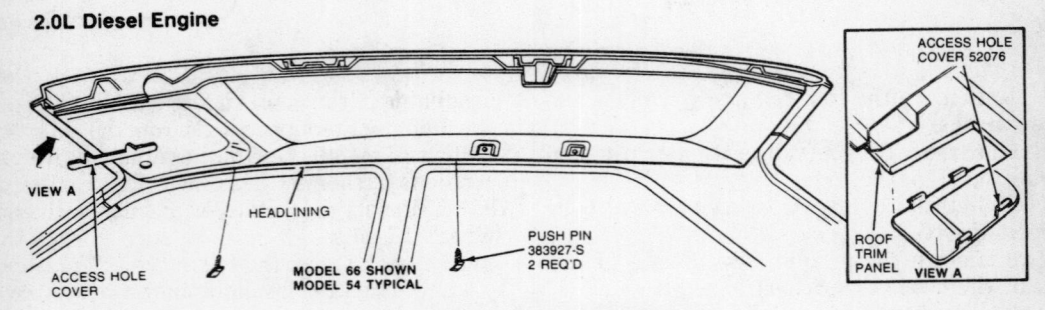

Tempo/Topaz headliner assembly

the bows and pull the headlining forward and cement into position at the windshield opening.

18. Working from the front to the rear, stretch and cement the headlining to the door(s), quarter window and hatchback opening.

19. Trim all excess material, leaving approximately 1/2 in. (13mm) to wrap into the pinch weld areas.

20. Apply cement to the pinch weld areas.

21. To install the trim items, reverse the removal procedures.

4-DOOR HATCHBACK 4-DOOR WAGON

1. Remove the right and left sun visors and the visor center clips.

   NOTE: *If the vehicle is equipped with illuminated sun visors, disconnect the electrical leads.*

2. Remove the header garnish molding.
3. Remove the windshield side garnish moldings.
4. Remove the dome light.
5. Remove the roof rail assist handles and coat hooks.
6. Remove the roof rail weatherstrip assemblies.
7. Detach the liftgate gas cylinders at body opening.
8. Remove the folding seat assembly.
9. Remove the luggage compartment cover.
10. Remove the center body pillar trim panels.
11. Remove the lower back trim panel.
12. Remove the quarter trim panels.
13. Remove the side window assemblies and seats.
14. Remove the headlining.

To install:

15. Unpackage the new headlining and lay it out on a flat surface. Mark and trim the new headlining using the old one as a pattern.

16. Trim the listings, pockets, on the new headlining to the approximate length of the old one. Remove the support rods from the old headlining and install them in the same relative rod positions of the new headliner. The roof headlining support rods are color coded at each end. When ordering new rods, be sure to note the color at each end of the rod.

17. Position the headliner in the vehicle, connect the bows.

18. Starting at the rear window area, apply trim cement and align the rear bow to the vertical position.

19. Working from the center to the outboard side, stretch and cement the headliner to the rear window opening flange.

20. Apply cement to the windshield opening flange, door opening weatherstrip flange, quar-

ter glass and hatchback opening flanges. Align the bows and pull the headlining forward and cement into position at the windshield opening.

21. Working from the front to the rear, stretch and cement the headlining to the door(s), quarter window and hatchback opening.

22. Trim all excess material, leaving approximately $1/2$ in. (13mm) to wrap into the pinch weld areas.

23. Apply cement to the pinch weld areas.

24. To install the trim items, reverse the removal procedures.

Tempo/Topaz

1. Remove the right and left sun visors and the center retaining clips.

NOTE: *If the vehicle is equipped with illuminated sun visors, disconnect the electrical leads.*

2. Remove the upper and side windshield moldings, rear window upper moldings and roof side rail moldings.

3. Remove the dome lamp assembly.

4. Remove the roof rail assist handles and coat hooks.

5. Shift the headlining all the way to one side allowing it to be removed and bend the opposite side flap inboard to remove.

NOTE: *On vehicles equipped with a sunroof, remove the headliner retainer before removing the headliner.*

6. Remove the headliner through the passenger door on the 2-door models and through either rear door on the 4-door models.

To install:

7. Pre-fold the replacement headliner along the score lines on the flat surface prior to installing it in the vehicle (side flaps should overlap the front and rear panels).

8. Install the headliner through the passenger door on the 2-door models and through either rear door on the 4-door models.

9. Position the headliner so the visors, dome light and roof rail assist handle holes line up properly.

10. Insert one side of the into place, then bend the opposite side flap into position.

11. Install the dome light.

12. Install the right and left sun visors and the center retaining clips.

13. Install the coat hooks and roof rail assist handles.

14. Install the upper and side windshield moldings and roof side rail moldings.

815. Install the headliner retainer on vehicles equipped with a sun roof.

How to Remove Stains from Fabric Interior

For best results, spots and stains should be removed as soon as possible. Never use gasoline, lacquer thinner, acetone, nail polish remover or bleach. Use a 3' x 3" piece of cheesecloth. Squeeze most of the liquid from the fabric and wipe the stained fabric from the outside of the stain toward the center with a lifting motion. Turn the cheesecloth as soon as one side becomes soiled. When using water to remove a stain, be sure to wash the entire section after the spot has been removed to avoid water stains. Encrusted spots can be broken up with a dull knife and vacuumed before removing the stain.

Type of Stain	How to Remove It
Surface spots	Brush the spots out with a small hand brush or use a commercial preparation such as K2R to lift the stain.
Mildew	Clean around the mildew with warm suds. Rinse in cold water and soak the mildew area in a solution of 1 part table salt and 2 parts water. Wash with upholstery cleaner.
Water stains	Water stains in fabric materials can be removed with a solution made from 1 cup of table salt dissolved in 1 quart of water. Vigorously scrub the solution into the stain and rinse with clear water. Water stains in nylon or other synthetic fabrics should be removed with a commercial type spot remover.
Chewing gum, tar, crayons, shoe polish (greasy stains)	Do not use a cleaner that will soften gum or tar. Harden the deposit with an ice cube and scrape away as much as possible with a dull knife. Moisten the remainder with cleaning fluid and scrub clean.
Ice cream, candy	Most candy has a sugar base and can be removed with a cloth wrung out in warm water. Oily candy, after cleaning with warm water, should be cleaned with upholstery cleaner. Rinse with warm water and clean the remainder with cleaning fluid.
Wine, alcohol, egg, milk, soft drink (non-greasy stains)	Do not use soap. Scrub the stain with a cloth wrung out in warm water. Remove the remainder with cleaning fluid.
Grease, oil, lipstick, butter and related stains	Use a spot remover to avoid leaving a ring. Work from the outisde of the stain to the center and dry with a clean cloth when the spot is gone.
Headliners (cloth)	Mix a solution of warm water and foam upholstery cleaner to give thick suds. Use only foam—liquid may streak or spot. Clean the entire headliner in one operation using a circular motion with a natural sponge.
Headliner (vinyl)	Use a vinyl cleaner with a sponge and wipe clean with a dry cloth.
Seats and door panels	Mix 1 pint upholstery cleaner in 1 gallon of water. Do not soak the fabric around the buttons.
Leather or vinyl fabric	Use a multi-purpose cleaner full strength and a stiff brush. Let stand 2 minutes and scrub thoroughly. Wipe with a clean, soft rag.
Nylon or synthetic fabrics	For normal stains, use the same procedures you would for washing cloth upholstery. If the fabric is extremely dirty, use a multi-purpose cleaner full strength with a stiff scrub brush. Scrub thoroughly in all directions and wipe with a cotton towel or soft rag.

Mechanic's Data

11

General Conversion Table

Multiply By	To Convert	To	
LENGTH			
2.54	Inches	Centimeters	.3937
25.4	Inches	Millimeters	.03937
30.48	Feet	Centimeters	.0328
.304	Feet	Meters	3.28
.914	Yards	Meters	1.094
1.609	Miles	Kilometers	.621
VOLUME			
.473	Pints	Liters	2.11
.946	Quarts	Liters	1.06
3.785	Gallons	Liters	.264
.164	Cubic inches	Liters	61.02
16.39	Cubic inches	Cubic cms.	.061
28.32	Cubic feet	Liters	.0353
MASS (Weight)			
28.35	Ounces	Grams	.035
.4536	Pounds	Kilograms	2.20
—	To obtain	From	Multiply by

Multiply By	To Convert	To	
AREA			
6.45	Square inches	Square cms.	.155
.836	Square yds.	Square meters	1.196
FORCE			
4.448	Pounds	Newtons	.225
.138	Ft. lbs.	Kilogram/meters	7.23
1.356	Ft. lbs.	Newton-meters	.737
.113	In. lbs.	Newton-meters	8.844
PRESSURE			
.068	Psi	Atmospheres	14.7
6.89	Psi	Kilopascals	.145
OTHER			
1.104	Horsepower (DIN)	Horsepower (SAE)	.9861
.746	Horsepower (SAE)	Kilowatts (KW)	1.34
1.609	Mph	Km/h	.621
.425	Mpg	Km/L	2.35
—	To obtain	From	Multiply by

Tap Drill Sizes

National Coarse or U.S.S.

Screw & Tap Size	Threads Per Inch	Use Drill Number
No. 5	40	39
No. 6	32	36
No. 8	32	29
No. 10	24	25
No. 12	24	17
1/4	20	8
5/16	18	F
3/8	16	5/16
7/16	14	U
1/2	13	27/64
9/16	12	31/64
5/8	11	17/32
3/4	10	21/32
7/8	9	49/64

National Coarse or U.S.S.

Screw & Tap Size	Threads Per Inch	Use Drill Number
1	8	7/8
1 1/8	7	63/64
1 1/4	7	1 7/64
1 1/2	6	1 11/32

National Fine or S.A.E.

Screw & Tap Size	Threads Per Inch	Use Drill Number
No. 5	44	37
No. 6	40	33
No. 8	36	29
No. 10	32	21

National Fine or S.A.E.

Screw & Tap Size	Threads Per Inch	Use Drill Number
No. 12	28	15
1/4	28	3
6/16	24	1
3/8	28	Q
7/16	20	W
1/2	20	29/64
9/16	18	33/64
5/8	18	37/64
3/4	16	11/16
7/8	14	13/16
1 1/8	12	1 3/64
1 1/4	12	1 11/64
1 1/2	12	1 27/64

Drill Sizes In Decimal Equivalents

Inch	Decimal	Wire	mm	Inch	Decimal	Wire	mm	Inch	Decimal	Wire & Letter	mm	Inch	Decimal	Letter	mm	Inch	Decimal	mm
1/64	.0156		.39		.0730	49			.1614		4.1		.2717		6.9		.4331	11.0
	.0157		.4		.0748		1.9		.1654		4.2		.2720	I		7/16	.4375	11.11
	.0160	78			.0760	48			.1660	19			.2756		7.0		.4528	11.5
	.0165		.42		.0768		1.95		.1673		4.25		.2770	J		29/64	.4531	11.51
	.0173		.44	5/64	.0781		1.98		.1693		4.3		.2795		7.1	15/32	.4688	11.90
	.0177		.45		.0785	47			.1695	18			.2810	K			.4724	12.0
	.0180	77			.0787		2.0	11/64	.1719		4.36	9/32	.2812		7.14	31/64	.4844	12.30
	.0181		.46		.0807		2.05		.1730	17			.2835		7.2		.4921	12.5
	.0189		.48		.0810	46			.1732		4.4		.2854		7.25	1/2	.5000	12.70
	.0197		.5		.0820	45			.1770	16			.2874		7.3		.5118	13.0
	.0200	76			.0827		2.1		.1772		4.5		.2900	L		33/64	.5156	13.09
	.0210	75			.0846		2.15		.1800	15			.2913		7.4	17/32	.5312	13.49
	.0217		.55		.0860	44			.1811		4.6		.2950	M			.5315	13.5
	.0225	74			.0866		2.2		.1820	14			.2953		7.5	35/64	.5469	13.89
	.0236		.6		.0886		2.25		.1850	13		19/64	.2969		7.54		.5512	14.0
	.0240	73			.0890	43			.1850		4.7		.2992		7.6	9/16	.5625	14.28
	.0250	72			.0906		2.3		.1870		4.75		.3020	N			.5709	14.5
	.0256		.65		.0925		2.35	3/16	.1875		4.76		.3031		7.7	37/64	.5781	14.68
	.0260	71			.0935	42			.1890		4.8		.3051		7.75		.5906	15.0
	.0276		.7	3/32	.0938		2.38		.1890	12			.3071		7.8	19/32	.5938	15.08
	.0280	70			.0945		2.4		.1910	11			.3110		7.9	39/64	.6094	15.47
	.0292	69			.0960	41			.1929		4.9	5/16	.3125		7.93		.6102	15.5
	.0295		.75		.0965		2.45		.1935	10			.3150		8.0	5/8	.6250	15.87
	.0310	68			.0980	40			.1960	9			.3160	O			.6299	16.0
1/32	.0312		.79		.0981		2.5		.1969		5.0		.3189		8.1	41/64	.6406	16.27
	.0315		.8		.0995	39			.1990	8			.3228		8.2		.6496	16.5
	.0320	67			.1015	38			.2008		5.1		.3230	P		21/32	.6562	16.66
	.0330	66			.1024		2.6		.2010	7			.3248		8.25		.6693	17.0
	.0335		.85		.1040	37		13/64	.2031		5.16		.3268		8.3	43/64	.6719	17.06
	.0350	65			.1063		2.7		.2040	6		21/64	.3281		8.33	11/16	.6875	17.46
	.0354		.9		.1065	36			.2047		5.2		.3307		8.4		.6890	17.5
	.0360	64			.1083		2.75		.2055	5			.3320	Q		45/64	.7031	17.85
	.0370	63		7/64	.1094		2.77		.2067		5.25		.3346		8.5		.7087	18.0
	.0374		.95		.1100	35			.2087		5.3		.3386		8.6	23/32	.7188	18.25
	.0380	62			.1102		2.8		.2090	4			.3390	R			.7283	18.5
	.0390	61			.1110	34			.2126		5.4		.3425		8.7	47/64	.7344	18.65
	.0394		1.0		.1130	33			.2130	3		11/32	.3438		8.73		.7480	19.0
	.0400	60			.1142		2.9		.2165		5.5		.3445		8.75	3/4	.7500	19.05
	.0410	59			.1160	32			.2188		5.55		.3465		8.8	49/64	.7656	19.44
	.0413		1.05		.1181		3.0	7/32	.2205		5.6		.3480	S			.7677	19.5
	.0420	58			.1200	31			.2210	2			.3504		8.9	25/32	.7812	19.84
	.0430	57			.1220		3.1		.2244		5.7		.3543		9.0		.7874	20.0
	.0433		1.1	1/8	.1250		3.17		.2264		5.75		.3580	T		51/64	.7969	20.24
	.0453		1.15		.1260		3.2		.2280	1			.3583		9.1		.8071	20.5
	.0465	56			.1280		3.25		.2283		5.8	23/64	.3594		9.12	13/16	.8125	20.63
3/64	.0469		1.19		.1285	30			.2323		5.9		.3622		9.2		.8268	21.0
	.0472		1.2		.1299		3.3		.2340	A			.3642		9.25	53/64	.8281	21.03
	.0492		1.25		.1339		3.4	15/64	.2344		5.95		.3661		9.3	27/32	.8438	21.43
	.0512		1.3		.1360	29			.2362		6.0		.3680	U			.8465	21.5
	.0520	55			.1378		3.5		.2380	B			.3701		9.4	55/64	.8594	21.82
	.0531		1.35		.1405	28			.2402		6.1		.3740		9.5		.8661	22.0
	.0550	54		9/64	.1406		3.57		.2420	C		3/8	.3750		9.52	7/8	.8750	22.22
	.0551		1.4		.1417		3.6		.2441		6.2		.3770	V			.8858	22.5
	.0571		1.45		.1440	27			.2460	D			.3780		9.6	57/64	.8906	22.62
	.0591		1.5		.1457		3.7		.2461		6.25		.3819		9.7		.9055	23.0
	.0595	53			.1470	26			.2480		6.3		.3839		9.75	29/32	.9062	23.01
	.0610		1.55		.1476		3.75	1/4	.2500	E	6.35		.3858		9.8	59/64	.9219	23.41
1/16	.0625		1.59		.1495	25			.2520		6.		.3860	W			.9252	23.5
	.0630		1.6		.1496		3.8		.2559		6.5		.3898		9.9	15/16	.9375	23.81
	.0635	52			.1520	24			.2570	F		25/64	.3906		9.92		.9449	24.0
	.0650		1.65		.1535		3.9		.2598		6.6		.3937		10.0	61/64	.9531	24.2
	.0669		1.7		.1540	23			.2610	G			.3970	X			.9646	24.5
	.0670	51		5/32	.1562		3.96		.2638		6.7		.4040	Y		31/32	.9688	24.6
	.0689		1.75		.1570	22		17/64	.2656		6.74	13/32	.4062		10.31		.9843	25.0
	.0700	50			.1575		4.0		.2657		6.75		.4130	Z		63/64	.9844	25.0
	.0709		1.8		.1590	21			.2660	H			.4134		10.5	1	1.0000	25.4
	.0728		1.85		.1610	20			.2677		6.8	27/64	.4219		10.71			

GLOSSARY 581

AIR/FUEL RATIO: The ratio of air to gasoline by weight in the fuel mixture drawn into the engine.

AIR INJECTION: One method of reducing harmful exhaust emissions by injecting air into each of the exhaust ports of an engine. The fresh air entering the hot exhaust manifold causes any remaining fuel to be burned before it can exit the tailpipe.

ALTERNATOR: A device used for converting mechanical energy into electrical energy.

AMMETER: An instrument, calibrated in amperes, used to measure the flow of an electrical current in a circuit. Ammeters are always connected in series with the circuit being tested.

AMPERE: The rate of flow of electrical current present when one volt of electrical pressure is applied against one ohm of electrical resistance.

ANALOG COMPUTER: Any microprocessor that uses similar (analogous) electrical signals to make its calculations.

ARMATURE: A laminated, soft iron core wrapped by a wire that converts electrical energy to mechanical energy as in a motor or relay. When rotated in a magnetic field, it changes mechanical energy into electrical energy as in a generator.

ATMOSPHERIC PRESSURE: The pressure on the Earth's surface caused by the weight of the air in the atmosphere. At sea level, this pressure is 14.7 psi at 32°F (101 kPa at 0°C).

ATOMIZATION: The breaking down of a liquid into a fine mist that can be suspended in air.

AXIAL PLAY: Movement parallel to a shaft or bearing bore.

BACKFIRE: The sudden combustion of gases in the intake or exhaust system that results in a loud explosion.

BACKLASH: The clearance or play between two parts, such as meshed gears.

BACKPRESSURE: Restrictions in the exhaust system that slow the exit of exhaust gases from the combustion chamber.

BAKELITE: A heat resistant, plastic insulator material commonly used in printed circuit boards and transistorized components.

BALL BEARING: A bearing made up of hardened inner and outer races between which hardened steel balls roll.

BALLAST RESISTOR: A resistor in the primary ignition circuit that lowers voltage after the engine is started to reduce wear on ignition components.

BEARING: A friction reducing, supportive device usually located between a stationary part and a moving part.

BIMETAL TEMPERATURE SENSOR: Any sensor or switch made of two dissimilar types of metal that bend when heated or cooled due to the different expansion rates of the alloys. These types of sensors usually function as an on/off switch.

BLOWBY: Combustion gases, composed of water vapor and unburned fuel, that leak past the piston rings into the crankcase during normal engine operation. These gases are removed by the PCV system to prevent the buildup of harmful acids in the crankcase.

BRAKE PAD: A brake shoe and lining assembly used with disc brakes.

BRAKE SHOE: The backing for the brake lining. The term is, however, usually applied to the assembly of the brake backing and lining.

BUSHING: A liner, usually removable, for a bearing; an anti-friction liner used in place of a bearing.

BYPASS: System used to bypass ballast resistor during engine cranking to increase voltage supplied to the coil.

CALIPER: A hydraulically activated device in a disc brake system, which is mounted straddling the brake rotor (disc). The caliper contains at least one piston and two brake pads. Hydraulic pressure on the piston(s) forces the pads against the rotor.

CAMSHAFT: A shaft in the engine on which are the lobes (cams) which operate the valves.

The camshaft is driven by the crankshaft, via a belt, chain or gears, at one half the crankshaft speed.

CAPACITOR: A device which stores an electrical charge.

CARBON MONOXIDE (CO): A colorless, odorless gas given off as a normal byproduct of combustion. It is poisonous and extremely dangerous in confined areas, building up slowly to toxic levels without warning if adequate ventilation is not available.

CARBURETOR: A device, usually mounted on the intake manifold of an engine, which mixes the air and fuel in the proper proportion to allow even combustion.

CATALYTIC CONVERTER: A device installed in the exhaust system, like a muffler, that converts harmful byproducts of combustion into carbon dioxide and water vapor by means of a heat-producing chemical reaction.

CENTRIFUGAL ADVANCE: A mechanical method of advancing the spark timing by using fly weights in the distributor that react to centrifugal force generated by the distributor shaft rotation.

CHECK VALVE: Any one-way valve installed to permit the flow of air, fuel or vacuum in one direction only.

CHOKE: A device, usually a movable valve, placed in the intake path of a carburetor to restrict the flow of air.

CIRCUIT: Any unbroken path through which an electrical current can flow. Also used to describe fuel flow in some instances.

CIRCUIT BREAKER: A switch which protects an electrical circuit from overload by opening the circuit when the current flow exceeds a predetermined level. Some circuit breakers must be reset manually, while most reset automatically

COIL (IGNITION): A transformer in the ignition circuit which steps up the voltage provided to the spark plugs.

COMBINATION MANIFOLD: An assembly which includes both the intake and exhaust manifolds in one casting.

COMBINATION VALVE: A device used in some fuel systems that routes fuel vapors to a charcoal storage canister instead of venting them into the atmosphere. The valve relieves fuel tank pressure and allows fresh air into the tank as the fuel level drops to prevent a vapor lock situation.

COMPRESSION RATIO: The comparison of the total volume of the cylinder and combustion chamber with the piston at BDC and the piston at TDC.

CONDENSER: 1. An electrical device which acts to store an electrical charge, preventing voltage surges.
2. A radiator-like device in the air conditioning system in which refrigerant gas condenses into a liquid, giving off heat.

CONDUCTOR: Any material through which an electrical current can be transmitted easily.

CONTINUITY: Continuous or complete circuit. Can be checked with an ohmmeter.

COUNTERSHAFT: An intermediate shaft which is rotated by a mainshaft and transmits, in turn, that rotation to a working part.

CRANKCASE: The lower part of an engine in which the crankshaft and related parts operate.

CRANKSHAFT: The main driving shaft of an engine which receives reciprocating motion from the pistons and converts it to rotary motion.

CYLINDER: In an engine, the round hole in the engine block in which the piston(s) ride.

CYLINDER BLOCK: The main structural member of an engine in which is found the cylinders, crankshaft and other principal parts.

CYLINDER HEAD: The detachable portion of the engine, fastened, usually, to the top of the cylinder block, containing all or most of the combustion chambers. On overhead valve engines, it contains the valves and their operating parts. On overhead cam engines, it contains the camshaft as well.

DEAD CENTER: The extreme top or bottom of the piston stroke.

DETONATION: An unwanted explosion of the air/fuel mixture in the combustion chamber caused by excess heat and compression, advanced timing, or an overly lean mixture. Also referred to as "ping".

DIAPHRAGM: A thin, flexible wall separating two cavities, such as in a vacuum advance unit.

DIESELING: A condition in which hot spots in the combustion chamber cause the engine to run on after the key is turned off.

DIFFERENTIAL: A geared assembly which allows the transmission of motion between drive axles, giving one axle the ability to turn faster than the other.

DIODE: An electrical device that will allow current to flow in one direction only.

DISC BRAKE: A hydraulic braking assembly consisting of a brake disc, or rotor, mounted on an axle, and a caliper assembly containing, usually two brake pads which are activated by hydraulic pressure. The pads are forced against the sides of the disc, creating friction which slows the vehicle.

DISTRIBUTOR: A mechanically driven device on an engine which is responsible for electrically firing the spark plug at a predetermined point of the piston stroke.

DOWEL PIN: A pin, inserted in mating holes in two different parts allowing those parts to maintain a fixed relationship.

DRUM BRAKE: A braking system which consists of two brake shoes and one or two wheel cylinders, mounted on a fixed backing plate, and a brake drum, mounted on an axle, which revolves around the assembly. Hydraulic action applied to the wheel cylinders forces the shoes outward against the drum, creating friction, slowing the vehicle.

DWELL: The rate, measured in degrees of shaft rotation, at which an electrical circuit cycles on and off.

ELECTRONIC CONTROL UNIT (ECU): Ignition module, amplifier or igniter. See Module for definition.

ELECTRONIC IGNITION: A system in which the timing and firing of the spark plugs is controlled by an electronic control unit, usually called a module. These systems have no points or condenser.

ENDPLAY: The measured amount of axial movement in a shaft.

ENGINE: A device that converts heat into mechanical energy.

EXHAUST MANIFOLD: A set of cast passages or pipes which conduct exhaust gases from the engine.

FEELER GAUGE: A blade, usually metal, of precisely predetermined thickness, used to measure the clearance between two parts. These blades usually are available in sets of assorted thicknesses.

F-HEAD: An engine configuration in which the intake valves are in the cylinder head, while the camshaft and exhaust valves are located in the cylinder block. The camshaft operates the intake valves via lifters and pushrods, while it operates the exhaust valves directly.

FIRING ORDER: The order in which combustion occurs in the cylinders of an engine. Also the order in which spark is distributed to the plugs by the distributor.

FLATHEAD: An engine configuration in which the camshaft and all the valves are located in the cylinder block.

FLOODING: The presence of too much fuel in the intake manifold and combustion chamber which prevents the air/fuel mixture from firing, thereby causing a no-start situation.

FLYWHEEL: A disc shaped part bolted to the rear end of the crankshaft. Around the outer perimeter is affixed the ring gear. The starter drive engages the ring gear, turning the flywheel, which rotates the crankshaft, imparting the initial starting motion to the engine.

FOOT POUND (ft.lb. or sometimes, ft. lbs.): The amount of energy or work needed to raise an item weighing one pound, a distance of one foot.

FUSE: A protective device in a circuit which prevents circuit overload by breaking the circuit when a specific amperage is present. The device is constructed around a strip or wire of a lower amperage rating than the circuit it is designed to protect. When an amperage higher than that stamped on the fuse is present in the circuit, the strip or wire melts, opening the circuit.

GEAR RATIO: The ratio between the number of teeth on meshing gears.

584 GLOSSARY

GENERATOR: A device which converts mechanical energy into electrical energy.

HEAT RANGE: The measure of a spark plug's ability to dissipate heat from its firing end. The higher the heat range, the hotter the plug fires. **HUB:** The center part of a wheel or gear.

HYDROCARBON (HC): Any chemical compound made up of hydrogen and carbon. A major pollutant formed by the engine as a byproduct of combustion.

HYDROMETER: An instrument used to measure the specific gravity of a solution.

INCH POUND (in.lb. or sometimes, in. lbs.): One twelfth of a foot pound.

INDUCTION: A means of transferring electrical energy in the form of a magnetic field. Principle used in the ignition coil to increase voltage.

INJECTION PUMP: A device, usually mechanically operated, which meters and delivers fuel under pressure to the fuel injector.

INJECTOR: A device which receives metered fuel under relatively low pressure and is activated to inject the fuel into the engine under relatively high pressure at a predetermined time.

INPUT SHAFT: The shaft to which torque is applied, usually carrying the driving gear or gears.

INTAKE MANIFOLD: A casting of passages or pipes used to conduct air or a fuel/air mixture to the cylinders.

JOURNAL: The bearing surface within which a shaft operates.

KEY: A small block usually fitted in a notch between a shaft and a hub to prevent slippage of the two parts.

MANIFOLD: A casting of passages or set of pipes which connect the cylinders to an inlet or outlet source.

MANIFOLD VACUUM: Low pressure in an engine intake manifold formed just below the throttle plates. Manifold vacuum is highest at idle and drops under acceleration.

MASTER CYLINDER: The primary fluid pressurizing device in a hydraulic system. In automotive use, it is found in brake and hydraulic clutch systems and is pedal activated, either directly or, in a power brake system, through the power booster.

MODULE: Electronic control unit, amplifier or igniter of solid state or integrated design which controls the current flow in the ignition primary circuit based on input from the pickup coil. When the module opens the primary circuit, the high secondary voltage is induced in the coil.

NEEDLE BEARING: A bearing which consists of a number (usually a large number) of long, thin rollers.

OHM:(Ω) The unit used to measure the resistance of conductor to electrical flow. One ohm is the amount of resistance that limits current flow to one ampere in a circuit with one volt of pressure.

OHMMETER: An instrument used for measuring the resistance, in ohms, in an electrical circuit.

OUTPUT SHAFT: The shaft which transmits torque from a device, such as a transmission.

OVERDRIVE: A gear assembly which produces more shaft revolutions than that transmitted to it.

OVERHEAD CAMSHAFT (OHC): An engine configuration in which the camshaft is mounted on top of the cylinder head and operates the valves either directly or by means of rocker arms.

OVERHEAD VALVE (OHV): An engine configuration in which all of the valves are located in the cylinder head and the camshaft is located in the cylinder block. The camshaft operates the valves via lifters and pushrods.

OXIDES OF NITROGEN (NOx): Chemical compounds of nitrogen produced as a byproduct of combustion. They combine with hydrocarbons to produce smog.

OXYGEN SENSOR: Used with the feedback system to sense the presence of oxygen in the exhaust gas and signal the computer which can reference the voltage signal to an air/fuel ratio.

PINION: The smaller of two meshing gears.

GLOSSARY

PISTON RING: An open ended ring which fits into a groove on the outer diameter of the piston. Its chief function is to form a seal between the piston and cylinder wall. Most automotive pistons have three rings: two for compression sealing; one for oil sealing.

PRELOAD: A predetermined load placed on a bearing during assembly or by adjustment.

PRIMARY CIRCUIT: Is the low voltage side of the ignition system which consists of the ignition switch, ballast resistor or resistance wire, bypass, coil, electronic control unit and pick-up coil as well as the connecting wires and harnesses.

PRESS FIT: The mating of two parts under pressure, due to the inner diameter of one being smaller than the outer diameter of the other, or vice versa; an interference fit.

RACE: The surface on the inner or outer ring of a bearing on which the balls, needles or rollers move.

REGULATOR: A device which maintains the amperage and/or voltage levels of a circuit at predetermined values.

RELAY: A switch which automatically opens and/or closes a circuit.

RESISTANCE: The opposition to the flow of current through a circuit or electrical device, and is measured in ohms. Resistance is equal to the voltage divided by the amperage.

RESISTOR: A device, usually made of wire, which offers a preset amount of resistance in an electrical circuit.

RING GEAR: The name given to a ring-shaped gear attached to a differential case, or affixed to a flywheel or as part a planetary gear set.

ROLLER BEARING: A bearing made up of hardened inner and outer races between which hardened steel rollers move.

ROTOR: 1. The disc-shaped part of a disc brake assembly, upon which the brake pads bear; also called, brake disc.
2. The device mounted atop the distributor shaft, which passes current to the distributor cap tower contacts.

SECONDARY CIRCUIT: The high voltage side of the ignition system, usually above 20,000 volts. The secondary includes the ignition coil, coil wire, distributor cap and rotor, spark plug wires and spark plugs.

SENDING UNIT: A mechanical, electrical, hydraulic or electromagnetic device which transmits information to a gauge.

SENSOR: Any device designed to measure engine operating conditions or ambient pressures and temperatures. Usually electronic in nature and designed to send a voltage signal to an on-board computer, some sensors may operate as a simple on/off switch or they may provide a variable voltage signal (like a potentiometer) as conditions or measured parameters change.

SHIM: Spacers of precise, predetermined thickness used between parts to establish a proper working relationship.

SLAVE CYLINDER: In automotive use, a device in the hydraulic clutch system which is activated by hydraulic force, disengaging the clutch.

SOLENOID: A coil used to produce a magnetic field, the effect of which is to produce work.

SPARK PLUG: A device screwed into the combustion chamber of a spark ignition engine. The basic construction is a conductive core inside of a ceramic insulator, mounted in an outer conductive base. An electrical charge from the spark plug wire travels along the conductive core and jumps a preset air gap to a grounding point or points at the end of the conductive base. The resultant spark ignites the fuel/air mixture in the combustion chamber.

SPLINES: Ridges machined or cast onto the outer diameter of a shaft or inner diameter of a bore to enable parts to mate without rotation.

TACHOMETER: A device used to measure the rotary speed of an engine, shaft, gear, etc., usually in rotations per minute.

THERMOSTAT: A valve, located in the cooling system of an engine, which is closed when cold and opens gradually in response to engine heating, controlling the temperature of the coolant and rate of coolant flow.

TOP DEAD CENTER (TDC): The point at which the piston reaches the top of its travel on the compression stroke.

GLOSSARY

TORQUE: The twisting force applied to an object.

TORQUE CONVERTER: A turbine used to transmit power from a driving member to a driven member via hydraulic action, providing changes in drive ratio and torque. In automotive use, it links the driveplate at the rear of the engine to the automatic transmission.

TRANSDUCER: A device used to change a force into an electrical signal.

TRANSISTOR: A semi-conductor component which can be actuated by a small voltage to perform an electrical switching function.

TUNE-UP: A regular maintenance function, usually associated with the replacement and adjustment of parts and components in the electrical and fuel systems of a vehicle for the purpose of attaining optimum performance.

TURBOCHARGER: An exhaust driven pump which compresses intake air and forces it into the combustion chambers at higher than atmospheric pressures. The increased air pressure allows more fuel to be burned and results in increased horsepower being produced.

VACUUM ADVANCE: A device which advances the ignition timing in response to increased engine vacuum.

VACUUM GAUGE: An instrument used to measure the presence of vacuum in a chamber.

VALVE: A device which control the pressure, direction of flow or rate of flow of a liquid or gas.

VALVE CLEARANCE: The measured gap between the end of the valve stem and the rocker arm, cam lobe or follower that activates the valve.

VISCOSITY: The rating of a liquid's internal resistance to flow.

VOLTMETER: An instrument used for measuring electrical force in units called volts. Voltmeters are always connected parallel with the circuit being tested.

WHEEL CYLINDER: Found in the automotive drum brake assembly, it is a device, actuated by hydraulic pressure, which, through internal pistons, pushes the brake shoes outward against the drums.

ABBREVIATION AND SYMBOLS

A: Ampere
AC: Alternating current
A/C: Air conditioning
A–h: Amper hour
AT: Automatic transmission
ATDC: After top dead center
μA: Microampere
bbl: Barrel
BDC: Bottom dead center
bhp: Brake horsepower
BTDC: Before top dead center
BTU: British thermal unit
C: Celsius (Centigrade)
CCA: Cold cranking amps
cd: Candela
cm^2: Square centimeter
cm^3, cc: Cubic centimeter
CO: Carbon monoxide
CO_2: Carbon dioxide
cu.in., in^3: Cubic inch
CV: Constant velocity
Cyl.: Cylinder
DC: Direct current
ECM: Electronic control module
EFE: Early fuel evaporation
EFI: Electronic fuel injection
EGR: Exhaust gas recirculation
Exh.: Exhaust
F: Farenheit

F: Farad
pF: Picofarad
μF: Microfarad
FI: Fuel injection
ft.lb., ft. lb., ft. lbs.: foot pound(s)
gal: Gallon
g: Gram
HC: Hydrocarbon
HEI: High energy ignition
HO: High output
hp: Horsepower
Hyd: Hydraulic
Hz: Hertz
ID: Inside diameter
in.lb; in. lbs.; in. lbs.: inch pound(s)
Int: Intake
K: Kelvin
kg: Kilogram
kHz: Kilohertz
km: Kilometer
km/h: Kilometers per hour
kΩ: Kilohm
kPa: Kilopascal
kV: Kilovolt
kW: Kilowatt
l: Liter
l/s: Liters per second
m: Meter
mA: Milliampere

ABBREVIATIONS AND SYMBOLS

mg: Milligram
mHz: Megahertz
mm: Millimeter
mm^2: Square millimeter
m^3: Cubic meter
MΩ: Megohm
m/s: Meters per second
MT: Manual transmission
mV: Millivolt
μm: Micrometer
N: Newton
N–m: Newton meter
NOx: Nitrous oxide
OD: Outside diameter
OHC: Over head camshaft
OHV: Over head valve
Ω: Ohm
PCV: Positive crankcase ventilation

psi: Pounds per square inch
pts: Pints
qts: Quarts
rpm: Rotations per minute
rps: Rotations per second
R–12: refrigerant gas (Freon)
SAE: Society of Automotive Engineers
SO$_2$: Sulfur dioxide
T: Ton
t: Megagram
TBI: Throttle Body Injection
TPS: Throttle Position Sensor
V: 1. Volt; 2. Venturi
μV: Microvolt
W: Watt
∞: Infinity
<: Less than
>: Greater than

INDEX

A

Air cleaner 5
Air conditioning
  Accumulator/drier 379
  Blower 370
  Compressor 131
  Condenser 135
  Control panel 373
  Evaporator 376, 377
  Gauge sets 30
  Preventive maintenance 29
  Safety precautions 29
  Switch and sensor 379
  Troubleshooting 32
Air pump 199
Alternator
  Alternator precautions 93
  Removal and installation 94
  Troubleshooting 184
Alignment, wheel
  Camber 478
  Caster 478
  Toe 479
Antenna 557
Antifreeze 41
Automatic transaxle
  Adjustments 447
  Application chart 443
  Back-up light switch 451
  Filter change 444
  Fluid change 41
  Linkage adjustments 450
  Neutral safety switch 451
  Removal and installation 451
  Troubleshooting 444

B

Back-up light switch
  Automatic transmission 451
  Manual transmission 411
Ball joints 473
Battery
  Fluid level and maintenance 18
  Jump starting 50
  Removal and installation 95
Belts 20
Boot (CV Joint)
  Replacement 433
Brakes
  Adjustments 514
  Bleeding 520
  Brake light switch 393, 515
  Disc brakes (Front)
    Caliper 522
    Operating principles 513
    Pads 521

    Rotor (Disc) 525
  Drum brakes (Rear)
    Adjustment 514
    Drum 526
    Shoes 527
    Wheel cylinder 532
  Fluid level 44
  Hoses and lines 520
  Master cylinder 516
  Operation 509
  Parking brake
    Adjustment 534
    Removal and installation 533
  Power booster
    Operating principals 514
    Removal and installation 518
  Proportioning valve 519
  Specifications 534
  Troubleshooting 510
Bumpers 539

C

Calipers
  Overhaul 523
  Removal and installation 522
Camber 478
Camshaft and bearings 167
Capacities Chart 52
Carburetor
  Adjustments 328, 329
  Overhaul 332
  Removal and Installation 328, 329
Caster 478
Catalytic converter 179
Charging system 88
Chassis electrical system
  Circuit protection 399
  Heater and air conditioning 370
  Instrument panel 386
  Troubleshooting 360
  Windshield wipers 380
Circuit breakers 399
Circuit protection 399
Clutch
  Adjustment 440
  Cable 442
  Operation 438
  Removal and installation 443
  Troubleshooting 439
Coil (ignition) 61
Combination switch 391, 490
Compression testing 109
Compressor 131
Condenser 135
Connecting rods and bearings
  Service 171
  Specifications 104

INDEX

Constant velocity (CV) joints   433
Control arm   474
Cooling system   41
Crankcase ventilation valve   17, 189
Crankshaft
   Service   174
   Specifications   104
Cylinder head   142
Cylinders   172

D

Diesel fuel system   348
Disc brakes   521
Distributor   91
Door glass   562
Door locks   561
Doors
   Glass   562
   Hinges   557
   Locks   561
   Removal and installation   535
   Striker plate   536
Door trim panel   557
Driveshaft   466
Drive Train   466
Drum brakes   526

E

EGR valve   194
Electric cooling fan   138
Electrical
   Chassis
     Battery   18, 95
     Circuit breakers   399
     Fuses   399
     Fusible links   95
     Heater and air conditioning   370
     Jump starting   50
     Spark plug wires   56
   Engine
     Alternator   93
     Coil   61
     Distributor   91
     Electronic engine controls   205
     Ignition module   67
     Starter   95
Electronic engine controls   205
Electronic Ignition   58
Emission controls
   Air pump   199
   Applications   189
   Catalytic Converter   179
   Evaporative canister   190
   Exhaust Gas Recirculation (EGR) system   194

PCV valve   189
Thermostatically controlled air cleaner   193
Vacuum Throttle Modulating (VTM) system   192
Engine
   Application chart   6
   Camshaft   167
   Compression testing   109
   Connecting rods and bearings   171
   Crankshaft   174
   Cylinder head   142
   Cylinders   172
   Electronic controls   205
   Exhaust manifold   128
   Fluids and lubricants   39
   Flywheel   176
   Front (timing) cover   159, 160
   Front seal   159, 163
   Identification   6
   Intake manifold   124
   Lifters   151
   Main bearings   175
   Mounts   119
   Oil pan   153
   Oil pump   156
   Overhaul   107
   Pistons   171
   Rear main seal   173
   Removal and installation   110
   Rocker arms   121
   Spark plug wires   56
   Specifications   101
   Thermostat   123
   Timing belt   159, 160, 165, 166
   Timing chain and gears   164, 165
   Turbocharging   130
   Valve guides   153
   Valve lifters   151
   Valves   149
   Valve seats   153
   Valve springs   153
   Valve stem oil seals   153
   Water pump   136
Evaporative canister   190
Evaporator   376, 377
Exhaust Manifold   128
Exhaust system   177

F

Fan   138
Filters
   Air   5
   Crankcase   17
   Fuel   13
   Oil   39
Firing orders   57

Flashers 399
Fluids and lubricants
  Automatic transmission 41
  Battery 18
  Coolant 41
  Engine oil 39
  Fuel 38
  Manual transmission 40
  Master cylinder 44
  Power steering pump 45
  Transfer case 41
  Windshield washer 45
Flywheel and ring gear 176
Fog lights 554
Front bumper 539
Front brakes 521
Front hubs 475
Front suspension
  Ball joints 473
  Description 469
  Knuckles 475
  Lower control arm 474
  Springs 471
  Stabilizer bar 474
  Struts 471
  Wheel alignment 478
Front wheel bearings 475
Fuel injection
  Fittings 335
  Fuel charging assembly 342, 346
  Fuel pressure regulator 339
  Fuel pump 336
  Injectors 339
  Operation 334
  Relieving fuel system pressure 335
  Throttle body 339
Fuel filter 13
Fuel pump
  Electric 336
  Mechanical 327
Fuel system
  Carbureted 327
  Diesel 348
  Gasoline Fuel injection 334
Fuel tank 358
Fuses and circuit breakers 399
Fusible links 95

G

Gearshift handle
Gearshift linkage
  Adjustment
    Automatic 450
    Manual 411
Glow plugs 350
Grille 551

H

Halfshaft 428
Hazard flasher 399
Headlights 395
Headliner 574
Heater
  Blower 370
  Control cable 375
  Control panel 373
  Core 370
Hood 537
Hoses
  Brake 520
  Coolant 26
  Fuel 16
How to Use This Book 1

I

Identification
  Engine 4
  Model 4
  Serial number 4
  Transfer case 5
  Transmission 5
  Vehicle 4
Idle speed and mixture adjustment 74
Ignition
  Coil 61
  Electronic 59
  Lock cylinder 392, 492
  Module 67
  Switch 393, 491
  Timing 69
Injectors, fuel 339, 349
Instrument cluster 386
Instrument panel
  Cluster 386
  Radio 380
  Speedometer cable 394
Intake manifold 124

J

Jacking points 51
Jump starting 50

K

Knuckles 475

L

Lighting
  Fog driving lights 554
  Headlights 395
  Signal and marker lights 395, 397
Liftgate 538
Lower ball joint 473
Lubrication
  Automatic transmission 41
  Engine 39
  Manual transmission 40
  Transfer case 41

M

MacPherson struts 471, 482
Main bearings 175
Manifolds
  Intake 124
  Exhaust 128
Manual steering gear
  Adjustments 493
  Removal and installation 494
Manual transmission
  Application 407
  Fluid level 40
  Linkage adjustment 411
  Operation 408
  Overhaul 416
  Removal and installation 414
  Troubleshooting 409
Marker lights 395, 397
Master cylinder 516
Mirrors 555, 567
Model identification 4
Module (ignition) 67
Muffler 179
Multi-function switch 391, 490

N

Neutral safety switch 394, 451

O

Oil and fuel recommendations 38
Oil and filter change (engine) 39
Oil level check
  Engine 39
  Transfer case 41
  Transmission 41
Oil pan 153
Oil pump 156

P

Parking brake 533
Pistons 171
PCV valve 17
Power brake booster 518
Power seat motor 574
Power steering gear
  Adjustments 495
  Removal and installation 496
Power steering pump
  Fluid level 45
  Removal and installation 497
Power windows 566
Pushing 47

R

Radiator 133
Radio 380
Rear brakes 526
Rear bumper 539
Rear main oil seal 173
Rear suspension
  Control arms 484
  Springs 481, 482
  Struts 482
  Tie rod ends 484
  Wheel alignment 487
Rear wheel bearings 485
Regulator
  Removal and installation 95
  Testing and adjustment 94
Rocker arms or shaft 121
Rotor (Brake disc) 525
Routine maintenance 5

S

Safety notice 2
Seats 568
Serial number location 4
Spark plugs 54
Spark plug wires 56
Specifications Charts
  Brakes 534
  Camshaft 106
  Capacities 52
  Crankshaft and connecting rod 104
  General engine 101
  Piston and ring 105
  Starter 96
  Torque 102
  Tune-up 55
  Valves 103
  Wheel alignment 478, 479

INDEX

Speedometer 394
Speedometer cable 394
Spindles 467, 485
Springs 471, 481, 482
Stabilizer bar 474
Stain removal 578
Starter
   Drive replacement 98
   Overhaul 97
   Removal and installation 95
   Specifications 96
Steering column 492
Steering gear
   Manual 493
   Power 495
Steering knuckles 475
Steering linkage 493
Steering wheel 489
Stripped threads 108
Switches
   Back-up light 411, 451
   Headlight 390
   Ignition switch 393, 491
   Multi-function switch 391
   Rear window wiper 390
   Windshield wiper 389

T

Tailpipe 179
Thermostat 123
Throttle body 339
Tie rod ends 484, 493
Timing (ignition) 69
Timing belt 159
Timing chain and gears 164, 165
Timing gear cover 160
Tires
   Description 35
   Inflation 35
   Rotation 35
   Troubleshooting 37
   Wear problems 36
Toe-in 479
Towing 47
Trailer towing 45
Transfer Case
   Fluid level 41
   Overhaul 461
   Removal and installation 458
   Troubleshooting 459
Trouble codes 217
Troubleshooting Charts
   Air conditioning 32
   Automatic transmission 444
   Brakes 510

Charging system 184
Clutch 439
Cooling system 185
Drive belts 187
Driveshaft 470
Emission control
   systems 191, 195, 203, 205
Engine mechanical 182
Engine performance 85
Fuel system 359
Gauges 4-5
Heater 406
Ignition switch 499
Ignition system 61, 64
Lights 404
Lockup torque converter 405
Manual steering gear 504
Manual transmission 409
Power steering gear 505
Power steering pump 506
Starting system 186
Steering and suspension 470
Steering column 500
Tires 37
Transfer case 459
Transmission fluid indications 443
Turn signals and flashers 403
Turn signal switch 502
Wheels 37
Windshield wipers 402
Trunk lid 538
Tune-up
   Idle speed 74
   Ignition timing 69
   Spark plugs and wires 54
   Specifications 55
Turbocharger 130
Turn signal flasher 399
Turn signal switch 490

U

U-joints 466

V

Vacuum diagrams 217
Valve guides 153
Valve lash adjustment 72
Valve seats 153
Valve service 149
Valve specifications 103
Valve springs 153
Vehicle identification 4

W

Water pump   136
Wheel alignment   478, 487
Wheel bearings
  Front wheel   475
  Rear wheel   485
Wheel cylinders   532
Wheels   35
Window glass   563
Window regulator   563
Windshield   557
Windshield wipers
  Arm   386
  Blade   33
  Linkage   385
  Motor   382
  Rear window wiper   384
  Rear window wiper switch   390
  Windshield wiper switch   389
Wiring
  Spark plug   56
  Trailer   398

CHILTON'S REPAIR MANUAL MODEL INDEX
Car and truck model names are listed in alphabetical and numerical order

Part No.	Model	Repair Manual Title	Part No.	Model	Repair Manual Title
6980	Accord	Honda 1973-88	6739	Cherokee 1974-83	Jeep Wagoneer, Commando, Cherokee, Truck 1957-86
7747	Aerostar	Ford Aerostar 1986-90	7939	Cherokee 1984-89	Jeep Wagoneer, Comanche, Cherokee 1984-89
7165	Alliance	Renault 1975-85			
7199	AMX	AMC 1975-86	6840	Chevelle	Chevrolet Mid-Size 1964-88
7163	Aries	Chrysler Front Wheel Drive 1981-88	6836	Chevette	Chevette/T-1000 1976-88
7041	Arrow	Champ/Arrow/Sapporo 1978-83	6841	Chevy II	Chevy II/Nova 1962-79
7032	Arrow Pick-Ups	D-50/Arrow Pick-Up 1979-81	7309	Ciera	Celebrity, Century, Ciera, 6000 1982-88
6637	Aspen	Aspen/Volare 1976-80			
6935	Astre	GM Subcompact 1971-80	7059	Cimarron	Cavalier, Skyhawk, Cimarron, 2000 1982-88
7750	Astro	Chevrolet Astro/GMC Safari 1985-90			
6934	A100, 200, 300	Dodge/Plymouth Vans 1967-88	7049	Citation	GM X-Body 1980-85
5807	Barracuda	Barracuda/Challenger 1965-72	6980	Civic	Honda 1973-88
6844	Bavaria	BMW 1970-88	6817	CJ-2A, 3A, 3B, 5, 6, 7	Jeep 1945-87
5796	Beetle	Volkswagen 1949-71	8034	CJ-5, 6, 7	Jeep 1971-90
6837	Beetle	Volkswagen 1970-81	6842	Colony Park	Ford/Mercury/Lincoln 1968-88
7135	Bel Air	Chevrolet 1968-88	7037	Colt	Colt/Challenger/Vista/Conquest 1971-88
5821	Belvedere	Roadrunner/Satellite/Belvedere/GTX 1968-73			
7849	Beretta	Chevrolet Corsica and Beretta 1988	6634	Comet	Maverick/Comet 1971-77
7317	Berlinetta	Camaro 1982-88	7939	Comanche	Jeep Wagoneer, Comanche, Cherokee 1984-89
7135	Biscayne	Chevrolet 1968-88			
6931	Blazer	Blazer/Jimmy 1969-82	6739	Commando	Jeep Wagoneer, Commando, Cherokee, Truck 1957-86
7383	Blazer	Chevy S-10 Blazer/GMC S-15 Jimmy 1982-87			
7027	Bobcat	Pinto/Bobcat 1971-80	6842	Commuter	Ford/Mercury/Lincoln 1968-88
7308	Bonneville	Buick/Olds/Pontiac 1975-87	7199	Concord	AMC 1975-86
6982	BRAT	Subaru 1970-88	7037	Conquest	Colt/Challenger/Vista/Conquest 1971-88
7042	Brava	Fiat 1969-81			
7140	Bronco	Ford Bronco 1966-86	6696	Continental 1982-85	Ford/Mercury/Lincoln Mid-Size 1971-85
7829	Bronco	Ford Pick-Ups and Bronco 1987-88			
7408	Bronco II	Ford Ranger/Bronco II 1983-88	7814	Continental 1982-87	Thunderbird, Cougar, Continental 1980-87
7135	Brookwood	Chevrolet 1968-88			
6326	Brougham 1975-75	Valiant/Duster 1968-76	7830	Continental 1988-89	Taurus/Sable/Continental 1986-89
6934	B100, 150, 200, 250, 300, 350	Dodge/Plymouth Vans 1967-88	7583	Cordia	Mitsubishi 1983-89
			5795	Corolla 1968-70	Toyota 1966-70
7197	B210	Datsun 1200/210/Nissan Sentra 1973-88	7036	Corolla	Toyota Corolla/Carina/Tercel/Starlet 1970-87
7659	B1600, 1800, 2000, 2200, 2600	Mazda Trucks 1971-89	5795	Corona	Toyota 1966-70
6840	Caballero	Chevrolet Mid-Size 1964-88	7004	Corona	Toyota Corona/Crown/Cressida/Mk.II/Van 1970-87
7657	Calais	Calais, Grand Am, Skylark, Somerset 1985-86	6962	Corrado	VW Front Wheel Drive 1974-90
6735	Camaro	Camaro 1967-81	7849	Corsica	Chevrolet Corsica and Beretta 1988
7317	Camaro	Camaro 1982-88	6576	Corvette	Corvette 1953-62
7740	Camry	Toyota Camry 1983-88	6843	Corvette	Corvette 1963-86
6695	Capri, Capri II	Capri 1970-77	6542	Cougar	Mustang/Cougar 1965-73
6963	Capri	Mustang/Capri/Merkur 1979-88	6696	Cougar	Ford/Mercury/Lincoln Mid-Size 1971-85
7135	Caprice	Chevrolet 1968-88			
7482	Caravan	Dodge Caravan/Plymouth Voyager 1984-89	7814	Cougar	Thunderbird, Cougar, Continental 1980-87
7163	Caravelle	Chrysler Front Wheel Drive 1981-88	6842	Country Sedan	Ford/Mercury/Lincoln 1968-88
7036	Carina	Toyota Corolla/Carina/Tercel/Starlet 1970-87	6842	Country Squire	Ford/Mercury/Lincoln 1968-88
			6983	Courier	Ford Courier 1972-82
7308	Catalina	Buick/Olds/Pontiac 1975-90	7004	Cressida	Toyota Corona/Crown/Cressida/Mk.II/Van 1970-87
7059	Cavalier	Cavalier, Skyhawk, Cimarron, 2000 1982-88	5795	Crown	Toyota 1966-70
7309	Celebrity	Celebrity, Century, Ciera, 6000 1982-88	7004	Crown	Toyota Corona/Crown/Cressida/Mk.II/Van 1970-87
7043	Celica	Toyota Celica/Supra 1971-87	6842	Crown Victoria	Ford/Mercury/Lincoln 1968-88
8058	Celica	Toyota Celica/Supra 1986-90	6980	CRX	Honda 1973-88
7309	Century FWD	Celebrity, Century, Ciera, 6000 1982-88	6842	Custom	Ford/Mercury/Lincoln 1968-88
			6326	Custom	Valiant/Duster 1968-76
7307	Century RWD	Century/Regal 1975-87	6842	Custom 500	Ford/Mercury/Lincoln 1968-88
5807	Challenger 1965-72	Barracuda/Challenger 1965-72	7950	Cutlass FWD	Lumina/Grand Prix/Cutlass/Regal 1988-90
7037	Challenger 1977-83	Colt/Challenger/Vista/Conquest 1971-88	6933	Cutlass RWD	Cutlass 1970-87
7041	Champ	Champ/Arrow/Sapporo 1978-83	7309	Cutlass Ciera	Celebrity, Century, Ciera, 6000 1982-88
6486	Charger	Dodge Charger 1967-70			
6845	Charger 2.2	Omni/Horizon/Rampage 1978-88	6936	C-10, 20, 30	Chevrolet/GMC Pick-Ups & Suburban 1970-87

Chilton's Repair Manuals are available at your local retailer or by mailing a check or money order for **$15.95** per book plus **$3.50** for 1st book and **$.50** for each additional book to cover postage and handling to:

**Chilton Book Company
Dept. DM
Radnor, PA 19089**

NOTE: When ordering be sure to include your name & address, book part No. & title.

CHILTON'S REPAIR MANUAL MODEL INDEX
Car and truck model names are listed in alphabetical and numerical order

Part No.	Model	Repair Manual Title
6817	4×4-63	Jeep 1981-87
6817	4-73	Jeep 1981-87
6817	4×4-73	Jeep 1981-87
6817	4-75	Jeep 1981-87
7035	4Runner	Toyota Trucks 1970-88
6982	4wd Wagon	Subaru 1970-88
6982	4wd Coupe	Subaru 1970-88
6933	4-4-2 1970-80	Cutlass 1970-87
6817	6-63	Jeep 1981-87
6809	6.9	Mercedes-Benz 1974-84
7308	88	Buick/Olds/Pontiac 1975-90
7308	98	Buick/Olds/Pontiac 1975-90
7587	98 Regency	GM C-Body 1985
5902	100LS, 100GL	Audi 1970-73
6529	122, 122S	Volvo 1956-69
7042	124	Fiat 1969-81
7042	128	Fiat 1969-81
7042	131	Fiat 1969-81
6529	142	Volvo 1956-69
7040	142	Volvo 1970-88
6529	144	Volvo 1956-69
7040	144	Volvo 1970-88
6529	145	Volvo 1956-69
7040	145	Volvo 1970-88
6529	164	Volvo 1956-69
7040	164	Volvo 1970-88
6065	190C	Mercedes-Benz 1959-70
6809	190D	Mercedes-Benz 1974-84
6065	190DC	Mercedes-Benz 1959-70
6809	190E	Mercedes-Benz 1974-84
6065	200, 200D	Mercedes-Benz 1959-70
7170	200SX	Nissan 200SX, 240SX, 510, 610, 710, 810, Maxima 1973-88
7197	210	Datsun 1200, 210, Nissan Sentra 1971-88
6065	220B, 220D, 220Sb, 220SEb	Mercedes-Benz 1959-70
5907	220/8 1968-73	Mercedes-Benz 1968-73
6809	230 1974-78	Mercedes-Benz 1974-84
6065	230S, 230SL	Mercedes-Benz 1959-70
5907	230/8	Mercedes-Benz 1968-73
6809	240D	Mercedes-Benz 1974-84
7170	240SX	Nissan 200SX, 240SX, 510, 610, 710, 810, Maxima 1973-88
6932	240Z	Datsun Z & ZX 1970-87
7040	242, 244, 245	Volvo 1970-88
5907	250C	Mercedes-Benz 1968-73
6065	250S, 250SE, 250SL	Mercedes-Benz 1959-70
5907	250/8	Mercedes-Benz 1968-73
6932	260Z	Datsun Z & ZX 1970-87
7040	262, 264, 265	Volvo 1970-88
5907	280	Mercedes-Benz 1968-73
6809	280	Mercedes-Benz 1974-84
5907	280C	Mercedes-Benz 1968-73
6809	280C, 280CE, 280E	Mercedes-Benz 1974-84
6065	280S, 280SE	Mercedes-Benz 1959-70
5907	280SE, 280S/8, 280SE/8	Mercedes-Benz 1968-73
6809	280SEL, 280SEL/8, 280SL	Mercedes-Benz 1974-84
6932	280Z, 280ZX	Datsun Z & ZX 1970-87
6065	300CD, 300D, 300SD, 300SE	Mercedes-Benz 1959-70
5907	300SEL 3.5, 300SEL 4.5	Mercedes-Benz 1968-73
5907	300SEL 6.3, 300SEL/8	Mercedes-Benz 1968-73
6809	300TD	Mercedes-Benz 1974-84
6932	300ZX	Datsun Z & ZX 1970-87
5982	304	Peugeot 1970-74
5790	310	Datsun 1961-72
7196	310	Datsun/Nissan F-10, 310, Stanza, Pulsar 1977-88
5790	311	Datsun 1961-72
6844	318i, 320i	BMW 1970-88
6981	323	Mazda 1978-89
6844	325E, 325ES, 325i, 325iS, 325iX	BMW 1970-88
6809	380SEC, 380SEL, 380SL, 380SLC	Mercedes-Benz 1974-84
5907	350SL	Mercedes-Benz 1968-73
7163	400	Chrysler Front Wheel Drive 1981-88
5790	410	Datsun 1961-72
5790	411	Datsun 1961-72
7081	411, 412	Volkswagen 1970-81
6809	450SE, 450SEL, 450 SEL 6.9	Mercedes-Benz 1974-84
6809	450SL, 450SLC	Mercedes-Benz 1974-84
5907	450SLC	Mercedes-Benz 1968-73
6809	500SEC, 500SEL	Mercedes-Benz 1974-84
5982	504	Peugeot 1970-74
5790	510	Datsun 1961-72
7170	510	Nissan 200SX, 240SX, 510, 610, 710, 810, Maxima 1973-88
6816	520	Datsun/Nissan Pick-Ups and Pathfinder 1970-89
6844	524TD	BMW 1970-88
6844	525i	BMW 1970-88
6844	528e	BMW 1970-88
6844	528i	BMW 1970-88
6844	530i	BMW 1970-88
6844	533i	BMW 1970-88
6844	535i, 535iS	BMW 1970-88
6980	600	Honda 1973-88
7163	600	Chrysler Front Wheel Drive 1981-88
7170	610	Nissan 200SX, 240SX, 510, 610, 710, 810, Maxima 1973-88
6816	620	Datsun/Nissan Pick-Ups and Pathfinder 1970-89
6981	626	Mazda 1978-89
6844	630 CSi	BMW 1970-88
6844	633 CSi	BMW 1970-88
6844	635CSi	BMW 1970-88
7170	710	Nissan 200SX, 240SX, 510, 610, 710, 810, Maxima 1973-88
6816	720	Datsun/Nissan Pick-Ups and Pathfinder 1970-89
6844	733i	BMW 1970-88
6844	735i	BMW 1970-88
7040	760, 760GLE	Volvo 1970-88
7040	780	Volvo 1970-88
6981	808	Mazda 1978-89
7170	810	Nissan 200SX, 240SX, 510, 610, 710, 810, Maxima 1973-88
7042	850	Fiat 1969-81
7572	900, 900 Turbo	SAAB 900 1976-85
7048	924	Porsche 924/928 1976-81
7048	928	Porsche 924/928 1976-81
6981	929	Mazda 1978-89
6836	1000	Chevette/1000 1976-88
6780	1100	MG 1961-81
5790	1200	Datsun 1961-72
7197	1200	Datsun 1200, 210, Nissan Sentra 1973-88
6982	1400GL, 1400DL, 1400GF	Subaru 1970-88
5790	1500	Datsun 1961-72

Chilton's Repair Manuals are available at your local retailer or by mailing a check or money order for **$15.95** per book plus **$3.50** for 1st book and **$.50** for each additional book to cover postage and handling to:

Chilton Book Company
Dept. DM
Radnor, PA 19089

NOTE: When ordering be sure to include your name & address, book part No. & title.

CHILTON'S REPAIR MANUAL MODEL INDEX
Car and truck model names are listed in alphabetical and numerical order

Part No.	Model	Repair Manual Title	Part No.	Model	Repair Manual Title
7675	Skylark	Calais, Grand Am, Skylark, Somerset 1985-86	7040	Turbo	Volvo 1970-88
7657	Somerset	Calais, Grand Am, Skylark, Somerset 1985-86	5796	Type 1 Sedan 1949-71	Volkswagen 1949-71
7042	Spider 2000	Fiat 1969-81	6837	Type 1 Sedan 1970-80	Volkswagen 1970-81
7199	Spirit	AMC 1975-86	5796	Type 1 Karmann Ghia 1960-71	Volkswagen 1949-71
6552	Sport Fury	Plymouth 1968-76	6837	Type 1 Karmann Ghia 1970-74	Volkswagen 1970-81
7165	Sport Wagon	Renault 1975-85	5796	Type 1 Convertible 1964-71	Volkswagen 1949-71
5796	Squareback	Volkswagen 1949-71	6837	Type 1 Convertible 1970-80	Volkswagen 1970-81
6837	Squareback	Volkswagen 1970-81	5796	Type 1 Super Beetle 1971	Volkswagen 1949-71
7196	Stanza	Datsun/Nissan F-10, 310, Stanza, Pulsar 1976-88	6837	Type 1 Super Beetle 1971-75	Volkswagen 1970-81
6935	Starfire	GM Subcompact 1971-80	5796	Type 2 Bus 1953-71	Volkswagen 1949-71
7583	Starion	Mitsubishi 1983-89	6837	Type 2 Bus 1970-80	Volkswagen 1970-81
7036	Starlet	Toyota Corolla/Carina/Tercel/Starlet 1970-87	5796	Type 2 Kombi 1954-71	Volkswagen 1949-71
7059	STE	Cavalier, Skyhawk, Cimarron, 2000 1982-88	6837	Type 2 Kombi 1970-73	Volkswagen 1970-81
5795	Stout	Toyota 1966-70	6837	Type 2 Vanagon 1981	Volkswagen 1970-81
7042	Strada	Fiat 1969-81	5796	Type 3 Fastback & Squareback 1961-71	Volkswagen 1949-71
6552	Suburban	Plymouth 1968-76	7081	Type 3 Fastback & Squareback 1970-73	Volkswagen 1970-70
6936	Suburban	Chevy/GMC Pick-Ups & Suburban 1970-87	5796	Type 4 411 1971	Volkswagen 1949-71
8055	Suburban	Chevy/GMC Pick-Ups & Suburban 1988-90	6837	Type 4 411 1971-72	Volkswagen 1970-81
6935	Sunbird	GM Subcompact 1971-80	5796	Type 4 412 1971	Volkswagen 1949-71
7059	Sunbird	Cavalier, Skyhawk, Cimarron, 2000, 1982-88	6845	Turismo	Omni/Horizon/Rampage 1978-88
7163	Sundance	Chrysler Front Wheel Drive 1981-88	5905	T-37	Tempest/GTO/LeMans 1968-73
7043	Supra	Toyota Celica/Supra 1971-87	6836	T-1000	Chevette/T-1000 1976-88
8058	Supra	Toyota Celica/Supra 1986-90	6935	Vega	GM Subcompact 1971-80
6837	Super Beetle	Volkswagen 1970-81	7346	Ventura	Pontiac Mid-Size 1974-83
7199	SX-4	AMC 1975-86	6696	Versailles	Ford/Mercury/Lincoln Mid-Size 1971-85
7383	S-10 Blazer	Chevy S-10 Blazer/GMC S-15 Jimmy 1982-87	6552	VIP	Plymouth 1968-76
7310	S-10 Pick-Up	Chevy S-10/GMC S-15 Pick-Ups 1982-87	7037	Vista	Colt/Challenger/Vista/Conquest 1971-88
7383	S-15 Jimmy	Chevy S-10 Blazer/GMC S-15 Jimmy 1982-87	6933	Vista Cruiser	Cutlass 1970-87
7310	S-15 Pick-Up	Chevy S-10/GMC S-15 Pick-Ups 1982-87	6637	Volare	Aspen/Volare 1976-80
7830	Taurus	Taurus/Sable/Continental 1986-89	7482	Voyager	Dodge Caravan/Plymouth Voyager 1984-88
6845	TC-3	Omni/Horizon/Rampage 1978-88	6326	V-100	Valiant/Duster 1968-76
5905	Tempest	Tempest/GTO/LeMans 1968-73	6739	Wagoneer 1962-83	Jeep Wagoneer, Commando, Cherokee, Truck 1957-86
7055	Tempo	Ford/Mercury Front Wheel Drive 1981-87	7939	Wagoneer 1984-89	Jeep Wagoneer, Comanche, Cherokee 1984-89
7036	Tercel	Toyota Corolla/Carina/Tercel/Starlet 1970-87	8034	Wrangler	Jeep 1971-90
7081	Thing	Volkswagen 1970-81	7459	W100, 150, 200, 250, 300, 350	Dodge/Plymouth Trucks 1967-88
6696	Thunderbird	Ford/Mercury/Lincoln Mid-Size 1971-85	7459	WM300	Dodge/Plymouth Trucks 1967-88
7814	Thunderbird	Thunderbird, Cougar, Continental 1980-87	6842	XL	Ford/Mercury/Lincoln 1968-88
7055	Topaz	Ford/Mercury Front Wheel Drive 1981-87	6963	XR4Ti	Mustang/Capri/Merkur 1979-88
6320	Torino	Fairlane/Torino 1962-75	6696	XR-7	Ford/Mercury/Lincoln Mid-Size 1971-85
6696	Torino	Ford/Mercury/Lincoln Mid-Size 1971-85	6982	XT Coupe	Subaru 1970-88
7163	Town & Country	Chrysler Front Wheel Drive 1981-88	7042	X1/9	Fiat 1969-81
6842	Town Car	Ford/Mercury/Lincoln 1968-88	6965	Zephyr	Fairmont/Zephyr 1978-83
7135	Townsman	Chevrolet 1968-88	7059	Z-24	Cavalier, Skyhawk, Cimarron, 2000 1982-88
5795	Toyota Pickups	Toyota 1966-70	6735	Z-28	Camaro 1967-81
7035	Toyota Pickups	Toyota Trucks 1970-88	7318	Z-28	Camaro 1982-88
7004	Toyota Van	Toyota Corona/Crown/Cressida/Mk.II/Van 1970-87	6845	024	Omni/Horizon/Rampage 1978-88
7459	Trail Duster	Dodge/Plymouth Trucks 1967-88	6844	3.0S, 3.0Si, 3.0CS	BMW 1970-88
7046	Trans Am	Firebird 1967-81	6817	4-63	Jeep 1981-87
7345	Trans Am	Firebird 1982-90			
7583	Tredia	Mitsubishi 1983-89			

Chilton's Repair Manuals are available at your local retailer or by mailing a check or money order for **$15.95** per book plus **$3.50** for 1st book and **$.50** for each additional book to cover postage and handling to:

Chilton Book Company
Dept. DM
Radnor, PA 19089

NOTE: When ordering be sure to include your name & address, book part No. & title.

CHILTON'S REPAIR MANUAL MODEL INDEX
Car and truck model names are listed in alphabetical and numerical order

Part No.	Model	Repair Manual Title	Part No.	Model	Repair Manual Title
5905	LeMans	Tempest/GTO/LeMans 1968-73	5790	Patrol	Datsun 1961-72
7346	LeMans	Pontiac Mid-Size 1974-83	6934	PB100, 150, 200, 250, 300, 350	Dodge/Plymouth Vans 1967-88
7308	LeSabre	Buick/Olds/Pontiac 1975-87	5982	Peugeot	Peugeot 1970-74
6842	Lincoln	Ford/Mercury/Lincoln 1968-88	7049	Phoenix	GM X-Body 1980-85
7055	LN-7	Ford/Mercury Front Wheel Drive 1981-87	7027	Pinto	Pinto/Bobcat 1971-80
6842	LTD	Ford/Mercury/Lincoln 1968-88	6554	Polara	Dodge 1968-77
6696	LTD II	Ford/Mercury/Lincoln Mid-Size 1971-85	7583	Precis	Mitsubishi 1983-89
7950	Lumina	Lumina/Grand Prix/Cutlass/Regal 1988-90	6980	Prelude	Honda 1973-88
6815	LUV	Chevrolet LUV 1972-81	7658	Prizm	Chevrolet Nova/GEO Prizm 1985-89
6575	Luxus	Opel 1971-75	8012	Probe	Ford Probe 1989
7055	Lynx	Ford/Mercury Front Wheel Drive 1981-87	7660	Pulsar	Datsun/Nissan F-10, 310, Stanza, Pulsar 1976-88
6844	L6	BMW 1970-88	6529	PV-444	Volvo 1956-69
6844	L7	BMW 1970-88	6529	PV-544	Volvo 1956-69
6542	Mach I	Mustang/Cougar 1965-73	6529	P-1800	Volvo 1956-69
6812	Mach I Ghia	Mustang II 1974-78	7593	Quantum	VW Front Wheel Drive 1974-87
6840	Malibu	Chevrolet Mid-Size 1964-88	7593	Rabbit	VW Front Wheel Drive 1974-87
6575	Manta	Opel 1971-75	7593	Rabbit Pickup	VW Front Wheel Drive 1974-87
6696	Mark IV, V, VI, VII	Ford/Mercury/Lincoln Mid-Size 1971-85	6575	Rallye	Opel 1971-75
7814	Mark VII	Thunderbird, Cougar, Continental 1980-87	7459	Ramcharger	Dodge/Plymouth Trucks 1967-88
6842	Marquis	Ford/Mercury/Lincoln 1968-88	6845	Rampage	Omni/Horizon/Rampage 1978-88
6696	Marquis	Ford/Mercury/Lincoln Mid-Size 1971-85	6320	Ranchero	Fairlane/Torino 1962-70
7199	Matador	AMC 1975-86	6696	Ranchero	Ford/Mercury/Lincoln Mid-Size 1971-85
6634	Maverick	Maverick/Comet 1970-77	6842	Ranch Wagon	Ford/Mercury/Lincoln 1968-88
6817	Maverick	Jeep 1945-87	7338	Ranger Pickup	Ford Ranger/Bronco II 1983-88
7170	Maxima	Nissan 200SX, 240SX, 510, 610, 710, 810, Maxima 1973-88	7307	Regal RWD	Century/Regal 1975-87
6842	Mercury	Ford/Mercury/Lincoln 1968-88	7950	Regal FWD 1988-90	Lumina/Grand Prix/Cutlass/Regal 1988-90
6963	Merkur	Mustang/Capri/Merkur 1979-88	7163	Reliant	Chrysler Front Wheel Drive 1981-88
6780	MGB, MGB-GT, MGC-GT	MG 1961-81	5821	Roadrunner	Roadrunner/Satellite/Belvedere/GTX 1968-73
6780	Midget	MG 1961-81	7659	Rotary Pick-Up	Mazda Trucks 1971-89
7583	Mighty Max	Mitsubishi 1983-89	6981	RX-7	Mazda 1978-89
7583	Mirage	Mitsubishi 1983-89	7165	R-12, 15, 17, 18, 18i	Renault 1975-85
5795	Mk.II 1969-70	Toyota 1966-70	7830	Sable	Taurus/Sable/Continental 1986-89
7004	Mk.II 1970-76	Toyota Corona/Crown/Cressida/Mk.II/Van 1970-87	7750	Safari	Chevrolet Astro/GMC Safari 1985-90
6554	Monaco	Dodge 1968-77	7041	Sapporo	Champ/Arrow/Sapporo 1978-83
6937	Monarch	Granada/Monarch 1975-82	5821	Satellite	Roadrunner/Satellite/Belvedere/GTX 1968-73
6840	Monte Carlo	Chevrolet Mid-Size 1964-88	6326	Scamp	Valiant/Duster 1968-76
6696	Montego	Ford/Mercury/Lincoln Mid-Size 1971-85	6845	Scamp	Omni/Horizon/Rampage 1978-88
6842	Monterey	Ford/Mercury/Lincoln 1968-88	6962	Scirocco	VW Front Wheel Drive 1974-90
7583	Montero	Mitsubishi 1983-89	6936	Scottsdale	Chevrolet/GMC Pick-Ups & Suburban 1970-87
6935	Monza 1975-80	GM Subcompact 1971-80	8055	Scottsdale	Chevrolet/GMC Pick-Ups & Suburban 1988-90
6981	MPV	Mazda 1978-89	5912	Scout	International Scout 1967-73
6542	Mustang	Mustang/Cougar 1965-73	8034	Scrambler	Jeep 1971-90
6963	Mustang	Mustang/Capri/Merkur 1979-88	7197	Sentra	Datsun 1200, 210, Nissan Sentra 1973-88
6812	Mustang II	Mustang II 1974-78	7462	Seville	Cadillac 1967-89
6981	MX6	Mazda 1978-89	7163	Shadow	Chrysler Front Wheel Drive 1981-88
6844	M3, M6	BMW 1970-88	6936	Siera	Chevrolet/GMC Pick-Ups & Suburban 1970-87
7163	New Yorker	Chrysler Front Wheel Drive 1981-88	8055	Siera	Chevrolet/GMC Pick-Ups & Suburban 1988-90
6841	Nova	Chevy II/Nova 1962-79	7583	Sigma	Mitsubishi 1983-89
7658	Nova	Chevrolet Nova/GEO Prizm 1985-89	6326	Signet	Valiant/Duster 1968-76
7049	Omega	GM X-Body 1980-85	6936	Silverado	Chevrolet/GMC Pick-Ups & Suburban 1970-87
6845	Omni	Omni/Horizon/Rampage 1978-88	8055	Silverado	Chevrolet/GMC Pick-Ups & Suburban 1988-90
6575	Opel	Opel 1971-75	6935	Skyhawk	GM Subcompact 1971-80
7199	Pacer	AMC 1975-86	7059	Skyhawk	Cavalier, Skyhawk, Cimarron, 2000 1982-88
7587	Park Avenue	GM C-Body 1985	7049	Skylark	GM X-Body 1980-85
6842	Park Lane	Ford/Mercury/Lincoln 1968-88			
6962	Passat	VW Front Wheel Drive 1974-90			
6816	Pathfinder	Datsun/Nissan Pick-Ups and Pathfinder 1970-89			

Chilton's Repair Manuals are available at your local retailer or by mailing a check or money order for **$15.95** per book plus **$3.50** for 1st book and **$.50** for each additional book to cover postage and handling to:

**Chilton Book Company
Dept. DM
Radnor, PA 19089**

NOTE: When ordering be sure to include your name & address, book part No. & title.

CHILTON'S REPAIR MANUAL MODEL INDEX
Car and truck model names are listed in alphabetical and numerical order

Part No.	Model	Repair Manual Title
8055	C-15, 25, 35	Chevrolet/GMC Pick-Ups & Suburban 1988-90
6324	Dart	Dart/Demon 1968-76
6962	Dasher	VW Front Wheel Drive 1974-90
5790	Datsun Pickups	Datsun 1961-72
6816	Datsun Pickups	Datsun Pick-Ups and Pathfinder 1970-89
7163	Daytona	Chrysler Front Wheel Drive 1981-88
6486	Daytona Charger	Dodge Charger 1967-70
6324	Demon	Dart/Demon 1968-76
7462	deVille	Cadillac 1967-89
7587	deVille	GM C-Body 1985
6817	DJ-3B	Jeep 1945-87
7040	DL	Volvo 1970-88
6326	Duster	Valiant/Duster 1968-76
7032	D-50	D-50/Arrow Pick-Ups 1979-81
7459	D100, 150, 200, 250, 300, 350	Dodge/Plymouth Trucks 1967-88
7199	Eagle	AMC 1975-86
7163	E-Class	Chrysler Front Wheel Drive 1981-88
6840	El Camino	Chevrolet Mid-Size 1964-88
7462	Eldorado	Cadillac 1967-89
7308	Electra	Buick/Olds/Pontiac 1975-90
7587	Electra	GM C-Body 1985
6696	Elite	Ford/Mercury/Lincoln Mid-Size 1971-85
7165	Encore	Renault 1975-85
7055	Escort	Ford/Mercury Front Wheel Drive 1981-87
7059	Eurosport	Cavalier, Skyhawk, Cimarron, 2000 1982-88
7760	Excel	Hyundai 1986-90
7163	Executive Sedan	Chrysler Front Wheel Drive 1981-88
7055	EXP	Ford/Mercury Front Wheel Drive 1981-87
6849	E-100, 150, 200, 250, 300, 350	Ford Vans 1961-88
6320	Fairlane	Fairlane/Torino 1962-75
6965	Fairmont	Fairmont/Zephyr 1978-83
6796	Fastback	Volkswagen 1949-71
6837	Fastback	Volkswagen 1970-81
6739	FC-150, 170	Jeep Wagoneer, Commando, Cherokee, Truck 1957-86
6982	FF-1	Subaru 1970-88
6571	Fiero	Pontiac Fiero 1984-88
6846	Fiesta	Fiesta 1978-80
6996	Firebird	Firebird 1967-81
6345	Firebird	Firebird 1982-90
7059	Firenza	Cavalier, Skyhawk, Cimarron, 2000 1982-88
7462	Fleetwood	Cadillac 1967-89
7587	Fleetwood	GM C-Body 1985
6829	F-Super Duty	Ford Pick-Ups and Bronco 1987-88
7165	Fuego	Renault 1975-85
6552	Fury	Plymouth 1968-76
6196	F-10	Datsun/Nissan F-10, 310, Stanza, Pulsar 1976-88
6933	F-85	Cutlass 1970-87
6913	F-100, 150, 200, 250, 300, 350	Ford Pick-Ups 1965-86
6829	F-150, 250, 350	Ford Pick-Ups and Bronco 1987-88
7583	Galant	Mitsubishi 1983-89
6842	Galaxie	Ford/Mercury/Lincoln 1968-88
7040	GL	Volvo 1970-88
6739	Gladiator	Jeep Wagoneer, Commando, Cherokee, Truck 1962-86
7081	GLC	Mazda 1978-89
7040	GLE	Volvo 1970-88
7040	GLT	Volvo 1970-88
7593	Golf	VW Front Wheel Drive 1974-90
7165	Gordini	Renault 1975-85
6937	Granada	Granada/Monarch 1975-82
6552	Gran Coupe	Plymouth 1968-76
6552	Gran Fury	Plymouth 1968-76
6842	Gran Marquis	Ford/Mercury/Lincoln 1968-88
6552	Gran Sedan	Plymouth 1968-76
6696	Gran Torino 1972-76	Ford/Mercury/Lincoln Mid-Size 1971-85
7346	Grand Am	Pontiac Mid-Size 1974-83
7657	Grand Am	Calais, Grand Am, Skylark, Somerset 1985-86
7346	Grand LeMans	Pontiac Mid-Size 1974-83
7346	Grand Prix	Pontiac Mid-Size 1974-83
7950	Grand Prix FWD	Lumina/Grand Prix/Cutlass/Regal 1988-90
7308	Grand Safari	Buick/Olds/Pontiac 1975-87
7308	Grand Ville	Buick/Olds/Pontiac 1975-87
6739	Grand Wagoneer	Jeep Wagoneer, Commando, Cherokee, Truck 1957-86
7199	Gremlin	AMC 1975-86
6575	GT	Opel 1971-75
7593	GTI	VW Front Wheel Drive 1974-90
5905	GTO 1968-73	Tempest/GTO/LeMans 1968-73
7346	GTO 1974	Pontiac Mid-Size 1974-83
5821	GTX	Roadrunner/Satellite/Belvedere/GTX 1968-73
5910	GT6	Triumph 1969-73
6542	G.T.350, 500	Mustang/Cougar 1965-73
6930	G-10, 20, 30	Chevy/GMC Vans 1967-86
6930	G-1500, 2500, 3500	Chevy/GMC Vans 1967-86
8040	G-10, 20, 30	Chevy/GMC Vans 1987-90
8040	G-1500, 2500, 3500	Chevy/GMC Vans 1987-90
5795	Hi-Lux	Toyota 1966-70
6845	Horizon	Omni/Horizon/Rampage 1978-88
7199	Hornet	AMC 1975-86
7135	Impala	Chevrolet 1968-88
7317	IROC-Z	Camaro 1982-88
6739	Jeepster	Jeep Wagoneer, Commando, Cherokee, Truck 1957-86
7593	Jetta	VW Front Wheel Drive 1974-90
6931	Jimmy	Blazer/Jimmy 1969-82
7383	Jimmy	Chevy S-10 Blazer/GMC S-15 Jimmy 1982-87
6739	J-10, 20	Jeep Wagoneer, Commando, Cherokee, Truck 1957-86
6739	J-100, 200, 300	Jeep Wagoneer, Commando, Cherokee, Truck 1957-86
6575	Kadett	Opel 1971-75
7199	Kammback	AMC 1975-86
5796	Karmann Ghia	Volkswagen 1949-71
6837	Karmann Ghia	Volkswagen 1970-81
7135	Kingswood	Chevrolet 1968-88
6931	K-5	Blazer/Jimmy 1969-82
6936	K-10, 20, 30	Chevy/GMC Pick-Ups & Suburban 1970-87
6936	K-1500, 2500, 3500	Chevy/GMC Pick-Ups & Suburban 1970-87
8055	K-10, 20, 30	Chevy/GMC Pick-Ups & Suburban 1988-90
8055	K-1500, 2500, 3500	Chevy/GMC Pick-Ups & Suburban 1988-90
6840	Laguna	Chevrolet Mid-Size 1964-88
7041	Lancer	Champ/Arrow/Sapporo 1977-83
5795	Land Cruiser	Toyota 1966-70
7035	Land Cruiser	Toyota Trucks 1970-88
7163	Laser	Chrysler Front Wheel Drive 1981-88
7163	LeBaron	Chrysler Front Wheel Drive 1981-88
7165	LeCar	Renault 1975-85

Chilton's Repair Manuals are available at your local retailer or by mailing a check or money order for **$15.95** per book plus **$3.50** for 1st book and **$.50** for each additional book to cover postage and handling to:

**Chilton Book Company
Dept. DM
Radnor, PA 19089**

NOTE: When ordering be sure to include your name & address, book part No. & title.

CHILTON'S REPAIR MANUAL MODEL INDEX
Car and truck model names are listed in alphabetical and numerical order

Part No.	Model	Repair Manual Title	Part No.	Model	Repair Manual Title
6844	1500	DMW 1970-88	6844	2000	BMW 1970-88
6936	1500	Chevy/GMC Pick-Ups & Suburban 1970-87	6844	2002, 2002Ti, 2002Tii	BMW 1970-88
8055	1500	Chevy/GMC Pick-Ups & Suburban 1988-90	6936	2500	Chevy/GMC Pick-Ups & Suburban 1970-87
6844	1600	BMW 1970-88	8055	2500	Chevy/GMC Pick-Ups & Suburban 1988-90
5790	1600	Datsun 1961-72	6844	2500	BMW 1970-88
6982	1600DL, 1600GL, 1600GLF	Subaru 1970-88	6844	2800	BMW 1970-88
6844	1600-2	BMW 1970-88	6936	3500	Chevy/GMC Pick-Ups & Suburban 1970-87
6844	1800	BMW 1970-88	8055	3500	Chevy/GMC Pick-Ups & Suburban 1988-90
6982	1800DL, 1800GL, 1800GLF	Subaru 1970-88	7028	4000	Audi 4000/5000 1978-81
6529	1800, 1800S	Volvo 1956-69	7028	5000	Audi 4000/5000 1978-81
7040	1800E, 1800ES	Volvo 1970-88	7309	6000	Celebrity, Century, Ciera, 6000 1982-88
5790	2000	Datsun 1961-72			
7059	2000	Cavalier, Skyhawk, Cimarron, 2000 1982-88			

Chilton's Repair Manuals are available at your local retailer or by mailing a check or money order for **$15.9** per book plus **$3.50** for 1st book and **$.50** for each additional book to cover postage and handling to:

Chilton Book Company
Dept. DM
Radnor, PA 19089

NOTE: When ordering be sure to include your name & address, book part No. & title.